NATURAL RESOURCES LAW

By

Jan G. Laitos
John A. Carver, Jr. Professor of Law
University of Denver Sturm College of Law

Sandra B. Zellmer
Professor of Law
University of Nebraska College of Law

Mary C. Wood
Professor of Law and Dean's Distinguished Faculty Fellow
University of Oregon School of Law

Daniel H. Cole
R. Bruce Townsend Professor of Law
Indiana University School of Law, Indianapolis

AMERICAN CASEBOOK SERIES®

THOMSON
™
WEST

Mat #40104492

ISBN–13: 978–0–314–14406–5
ISBN–10: 0–314–14406–4

 TEXT IS PRINTED ON 10% POST CONSUMER RECYCLED PAPER

*To Vicki, who taught me what matters in life; to Mom and
Dad, who showed me that I should appreciate life;
and to Erik, who completes my life.*

JGL

To Jessie Zellmer, the wind beneath my wings.

SBZ

*To Virginia Tooze Wood and to the memory
of Erskine Biddle Wood.*

MCW

To my parents, with love.

DHC

*

Preface

This is a casebook on "natural resources law." The law of natural resources is not the same as environmental law or federal public land law. To be sure, natural resources (and their use and development) are regulated by environmental laws, and natural resources include public lands. And like pollution, natural resources do not adhere to political boundaries—they are found on federal, state, tribal, and private lands (and, indeed, they sometimes consist of the lands themselves), and they are managed and regulated by every level of government. But natural resources are also subject to special statutes and legal regimes that are quite different than those governing air and water pollution and toxic and hazardous wastes.

The natural resources that are the subject of this casebook include commodity resources, such as private land, public rangeland, timber, and minerals, as well as non-commodity resources, such as wildlife, wetlands, marine resources, preservation lands, and recreation lands and waters. All of these resources constitute the very fabric of the American landscape, and each has played a significant role in the history and development of this country. You can easily visualize the nation's spectacular mountains and valleys, rivers and lakes, eagles and elk, wheat fields and grasslands, and forests full of trees, scenic vistas, and recreational trails. Perhaps more difficult to visualize, but no less important, are our gold veins, oil reserves, coal deposits, and groundwater reservoirs.

Natural resources law is the study of how legal institutions have attempted to resolve and manage the conflicts that emerge with the competing demands for natural resources. Conservation and preservation values compete with consumption and extraction desires. The law of natural resources referees these conflicts by weighing the interests of economic growth, ecology, historical expectations, political expediency, and geographic reality. It is a body of law based in large part on statutes and administrative rules, with an underlay of common law doctrine (particularly property law) and constitutional mandates (*e.g.*, federalism and the takings clause). This casebook analyzes the conflicts and legal responses that inevitably follow when natural resources are discovered, used, depleted, and fought over—in court, before agencies, and in the halls of the legislature.

As this book goes to press in the spring of 2006, the importance of sustainable policies on natural resources management is illustrated vividly by Hurricane Katrina, which hit the Gulf Coast on August 29, 2005. In the aftermath of this event—quite likely the most devastating natural disaster in our nation's history—the entire region is suffering from the lack of clean water, food, medical assistance, and shelter. Have we been fiddling (metaphorically) while Rome burned? For years, scientists had warned that the issue was not *if* but *when* a hurricane of this magnitude would hit New Orleans and the surrounding area. *See* Joel K. Bourne, Jr., *Gone with the Water*, Nat'l Geog., Oct. 2004 (predicting that the bayou "is in big trouble—with dire consequences for residents"). Did short-sighted land use policies and a disregard for natural ecological processes cause the hurricane? No, but these factors surely exacerbated the resulting damage. *See* Daniel Zwerdling, *Nature's Revenge: Louisiana's Vanishing Wetlands*, http://americanradioworks.publicradio. org/features/wetlands/ (Sept. 2002). The coastal marshes and islands that would otherwise serve as buffers against tropical storms have been lost, as channelization and a long network of levees along the Mississippi River cause essential sediments and nutrients to shoot out into the Gulf rather than settle into the delta. Meanwhile, engineering solutions (more levees) intended to protect New Orleans from the waters of Lake Pontchartrain failed. For years, ecologists and economists alike have called for more sustainable policies to protect and restore the delta, but the nation's priorities have been focused elsewhere. *See* Cornelia Dean and Andrew Revkin, *After Centuries of Controlling Land, Gulf Learns Who's the Boss*, New York Times, Aug. 30, 2005 ("what a terrible bargain the region made when it embraced . . . environmental degradation in exchange for economic gains"). As you embark on the study of natural resources law, try to envision appropriate national, regional and local responses to disasters like Hurricane Katrina.

Introduction

The natural resources discussed in this book range from special use lands like wilderness and rangeland, to commodity resources like minerals, agricultural products and timber, to ecological resources like forestland and wildlife. Because the array of natural resources is broad, and the laws affecting them so numerous, the law of natural resources has often been compartmentalized by subject matter. Management of federally owned resources is categorized as public land law. The law of hardrock minerals is known as mining law. Federal and state mechanisms for allocating water among competing users are studied as water law. Private legal arrangements between developers and owners of oil and gas are examined in oil and gas law. Protection of wildlife resources falls under the topic of wildlife law. Regulation of private activities upon the land is the subject of land use planning. Separate courses have been adopted in law schools on each of these topics.

For the student, teacher or practitioner wishing to have an overview of the integrated nature of all these subjects, however, what is needed is one book, and one course, that weaves these themes into one fabric. The purpose of this book is to provide, in one book, taught in one course, an integrated approach to the important topic of natural resources law.

When adopted in the standard three-credit survey course on natural resources law, this book, or more likely selected chapters within the book, should be useful both to schools which offer many natural resources courses and to schools which offer few. For schools which have the luxury of offering a broad selection of natural resources courses, students interested in concentrating on natural resources law may wish to enroll in a survey course, based on this book, to determine which specialty courses they may wish subsequently to select. By the same token, students in these schools who want to take just one general natural resources class may enroll in the survey course to acquire an overview of the field. Meanwhile, for schools that offer only one or two natural resources courses, a survey course, using this book, will expose students to the key natural resources topics.

The book is organized into four major parts. Professors and teachers adopting the book will decide which Parts, and chapters, to emphasize, summarize, or not include in their course. Part I lays out the predicates of natural resources law: the economics and ecological underpinnings of natural resources use; the management philosophies that guide resource decisions; the constitutional and administrative bases of natural resources management; and the chief environmental decisionmaking statute for resource use—NEPA. Part II sets out the differing ownership regimes that form the basis for natural resource use and regulation. Part III addresses the chief commodity resources—land, timber, minerals, and water. Finally, Part IV introduces the growing role of non-commodity natural resources—wildlife, preservation lands, and recreation resources.

This book—a "second generation" casebook—is quite different than the standard casebooks that have been used for decades by generations of law professors and students. It is a far cry from the usual book containing numerous cases, each followed by a series of pithy notes and unanswerable questions. First, this is intended to be a straightforward text which teaches students the basic physical characteristics of natural resources as well as ownership prerogatives and regulatory requirements. Both historic and cutting-edge conflicts and legal controversies that have arisen from competing resource demands are examined. The book depicts the processes and substantive priorities that emerge as these demands result in some kind of management decision, which in turn produces its own set of issues, conflicts, and cases reflected in court litigation.

Second, the book uses teaching techniques that convey, in a visual and thought-provoking fashion, discrete points of interest. Each chapter contains one or more of the following features, often set apart as a "box" within the text:

1. "Websources"—internet websites for further information

2. "In Practice"—practical tips in a specialized area of law

3. "In Focus"—mini-case studies and focused examples of the law's application to current topics and controversies

4. "Global Perspective"—an international dimension on select natural resource topics

5. "Exercises" or "Problems"—short exercises designed to integrate the material in the chapter in a problem-solving format

Third, the book contains maps, photographs, and other graphics, as well as newspaper articles and excerpts from scientific journals, both to lighten and enlighten the material and to provide context for the issue being discussed. This second generation feature is intended to take the instructor and student beyond the words of a case or regulation and directly into the land and resource at issue.

The authors have written extensively about the subjects addressed in this book, and we are grateful to be able to share our experiences in this intellectually rich and rewarding field. This book was a collaborative effort among the four of us, and a true labor of love. Each of us read each other's chapters, and made comments and suggestions which ultimately improved the quality and overall teachability of the book. Professor Zellmer edited the entire book when it was finished; the book reads with one distinct "voice" because of her efforts.

Acknowledgments

From Jan G. Laitos:

Professor Laitos wishes to thank and commend his co-authors. The book is the impressive work that it is because his co-authors always went that proverbial extra mile to ensure a quality and comprehensive product. He also wants to acknowledge and recognize the generous contributions made by the Rocky Mountain Mineral Law Foundation, especially its Grants Committee. The Foundation has been supportive of many of the books published in the field of natural resources law. Professor Laitos also wishes to thank the book's copy editor, Christine Ellison, along with the book's primary editor, Prof. Zellmer. Two of Professor Laitos' research assistants at the University of Denver Sturm College of Law have played important roles with respect to the chapters on Water Law, Wildlife Law, and Recreation and Preservation—Chessa Bieri and Lindsey Reimer. Many natural resources classes at the Sturm College of Law have labored through earlier drafts of this book, and their input and assistance is appreciated now. The Dean of the Sturm College of Law, Mary Ricketson, provided generous summer research grants, which gave Professor Laitos the time and reflection needed to work on this book. Finally, Professor Laitos wishes to remember and acknowledge the support early on provided by Doug Powell, former publisher of West Publishing. It is thanks to Doug's confidence in me, and the other co-authors, that we have all the considerable advantages of having our book published by West.

From Sandra B. Zellmer:

Professor Zellmer wishes to thank her co-authors and West editor Kathleen Vandergon for their dedication and patience throughout this project. She is thankful to the University of Nebraska College of Law and the University of Toledo College of Law for providing research funding for this project. Research assistants David Gecas, Nathan DeWald, and Kate Saunders provided invaluable assistance, as did Vida Eden, faculty assistant-extraordinaire. Last but far from least, she is eternally grateful to her husband, Randy Mercural, for his unflagging good humor and encouragement.

From Mary C. Wood:

I would like to thank my co-authors Jan Laitos, Sandi Zellmer, and Dan Cole. Working with them has been a true pleasure all along the way. My deep appreciation also goes to the following individuals at the University of Oregon School of Law: Dean Laird Kirkpatrick, Dean Margie

Paris and Debbie Thurman for administrative support of this project; Dianne Bass for manuscript assistance; and the following students who provided research assistance: Allison Bond, Jaimie Saylor, Rachel Bredfeldt, Jason Hartz, Kathryn Moore, Andrew Orahoske, Jonathan Manton, Sarah Peters, Brigid Turner, Nick Klingensmith, Matthew Yates, Jeremy Arling, and Barry Smith. I greatly appreciated the financial support of this project provided through the Alfred T. Goodwin Faculty Fellowship and the Love, Moore, Banks and Grebe Faculty Fellowship. Thanks also goes to Michael Anderson and Bryan Bird for helpful suggestions. Finally, I owe deepest gratitude to my husband, Joe Fox, and my boys Sage and Cameron, for their patient support of this project.

From Daniel H. Cole:

Professor Cole wishes to thank his co-authors: Jan Laitos for his brilliance, his inspiration, and his leadership; Sandi Zellmer for her strong support throughout the long gestation period of this project, and for putting more into it than anyone else; and Mary Wood for her thoughtful and innovative approach to casebook writing. He also wishes to thank his ever-able Assistant, Faith Long Knotts, and his loving and supportive family. Last but not least, he is grateful to the faculty and administration of the Indiana University School of Law at Indianapolis for providing Summer Faculty Fellowship funding for this project.

Professor John Martin Gillroy of Lehigh University authored certain preliminary draft chapters for this book. His unique inter-disciplinary perspective and full arguments for Professor Gillroy's distinctive philosophical-political approach to natural resource law can be found in both his upcoming Thomson/West book, tentatively entitled *Legal Foundations for the Analysis of Environmental/Natural Resource Law and Policy: A Primer in Legal Sources, Legal Paradigms and Legal Argument*, and in his most recent solo book, *Justice & Nature: Kantian Philosophy, Environmental Policy & The Law* (Georgetown University Press: 2000). The Thomson/West book, co-authored with Celia Campbell-Mohn and Breena Holland is expected to be published in early 2008 and will provide critical background for law students and undergraduates in the distinctive 'policy design' context of natural resource/environmental law. The Georgetown book provides a complete, non-theistic philosophical paradigm for ecosystem law that transcends resource markets and treats the moral integrity of humanity and the functional integrity of nature as critical interdependent variables in legal and policy decision-making.

Permissions

Chapter 1

Kenneth J. Arrow *et al.*, "Is there a role for benefit-cost analysis in environmental, health and safety regulation?," 272 *Science* 221–222 (12 April 1996). Excerpted with permission from Kenneth J. Arrow *et al.*, "Is there a role for benefit-cost analysis in environmental, health and safety regulation?," 272 *Science* 221–222 (12 April 1996). Copyright 1996 AAAS.

Daniel H. Cole and Peter Z. Grossman, *Principles of Law and Economics* (2005), pp. 46–47. Excerpted with permission of Pearson Education, Inc. Upper Saddle River, N.J.

Robert C. Ellickson, *Order Without Law: How Neighbors Settle Dispute* (1991), pp. 191–205. Reprinted by permission of the publisher from ORDER WITHOUT LAW: HOW NEIGHBORS SETTLE DISPUTES by Robert C. Ellickson, pp. 191–205, Cambridge, Mass: Harvard University Press. Copyright © 1991 by the President and Fellows of Harvard College.

Garrett Hardin, "The Tragedy of the Commons," 121 Science 1243 (1968), pp. 34–35. Excerpted with permission from Garrett Hardin, "The Tragedy of the Commons," 121 *Science* 1243 (1968). Copyright 1968 AAAS.

Elinor Ostrom, *Governing the Commons* (1990), pp. 18–21. Reprinted by permission of Cambridge University Press.

Chapter 2

Daniel H. Cole, *What is the Most Compelling Environmental Issue Facing the World On the Brink of the Twenty–First Century: Accounting for Sustainable Development*, 8 Fordham Envtl. Law J. 123, 126–27 (1996). Reprinted with permission of Danial H. Cole.

Holly Doremus, *The Purposes, Effects, and Future of the Endangered Species Act's Best Available Science Mandate*, 34 Envt. L. 397, 397, 399–401, 435–441 (2004). Reprinted with permission of Environmental Law and Holly Doremus.

Oliver A. Houck, *Tales from a Troubled Marriage: Science and Law in Environmental Policy*, 17 Tul. Envtl. L.J. 163, 164–174 (2003). Reprinted with permission of Tulane Environmental Law Journal.

Judy L. Meyer, *The Dance of Nature: New Concepts in Ecology*, 69 Chi.-Kent L. Rev. 875 (1994). Reprinted with permission of Chicago-Kent Law Review.

John Copeland Nagle, *Playing Noah*, 82 Minn. L.Rev. 1171, 1217–1229 (1998). Reprinted with permission of Minnesota Law Review and John Copeland Nagle.

Reed F. Noss, *Some Principles of Conservation Biology, as They Apply to Environmental Law,* 69 Chi.-Kent L. Rev. 893, 893–94, 896–899, 901–02, 908 (1994). Reprinted with permission of Chicago-Kent Law Review.

J.B. Ruhl, *Prescribing the Right Dose of Peer Review for the Endangered Species Act*, 83 Neb. L. Rev. 398, 402–407 (2004). Reprinted with permission of Nebraska Law Review.

Emily Yoffe, Silence of the Frogs, N.Y. Times Magazine 36–39, 64–66, 76, Dec. 13, 1992. Reprinted with permission of Emily Yoffe.

Sandra Zellmer, *A New Corps of Discovery for Missouri River Management,* 83 Neb. L. Rev. 305, 306–308 (2004). Reprinted with permission of Nebraska Law Review.

Chapter 3

Patrick Parenteau, *Citizen Suits Under The Endangered Species Act: Survival of the Fittest*, 10 Widener L. Rev. 321 (2004). Reprinted with permission of Widener Law Review.

Chapter 4

Methow Valley near Twisp, Washington, from the Methow Valley Citizens Council, http://www.okanogan1.com/mvcc/index.html (photo by George Wooten). Reprinted with permission.

Chapter 5

Maude Barlow and Tony Clarke, Who owns the Water? The Nation, Sept. 2, 2002. Reprinted with the permission of Maude Barlow and Tony Clarke.

Dale D. Goble, *The Property Clause—As If Biodiversity Mattered*, 75 U. Colo. L. Rev. 1195 (2004). Reprinted with permission of the University of Colorado Law Review and Dale D. Goble.

Erik Larson, Unrest in the West, Time Magazine, Oct. 23, 1995. Reprinted with permission of Time Magazine.

National Wilderness Institute, Map of Federal, State and Tribal Ownership in the United States, reprinted with permission.

Chapter 6

And see this ring right here, Jimmy? (release date 1/6/84). The Far Side ® by Gary Larson © 1983 FarWorks, Inc. All Rights Reserved. The FarSide ® and the Larson © signature are registered trademarks of FarWorks, Inc. Used with Permission.

Chapter 7

Mary Christina Wood, *The Tribal Property Right to Wildlife Capital (Part I)*, 37 Idaho L. Rev. 1 (2000). Reprinted with permission of Idaho Law Review and Mary Christina Wood.

Mary Christina Wood, *The Tribal Property Right to Wildlife Capital (Part II)*, 25 Vt. L. Rev. 355 (2001). © Vermont Law Review 2001. Reprinted with permission of Vermont Law Review and Mary Christina Wood.

Chapter 8

Harrison C. Dunning, *The Public Trust: A Fundamental Doctrine of American Property Law*, 19 Envtl. L. 515 (1989). Reprinted with permission of Environmental Law and Harrison Dunning.

Richard J. Lazarus, *Changing Conceptions of Property and Sovereignty in Natural Resources: Questioning the Public Trust Doctrine*, 71 Iowa L. Rev. 631, 650–55 (1986) (reprinted with permission).

Joseph L. Sax, *Liberating the Public Trust from its Historical Shackles*, 14 U.C. Davis L. Rev. 185 (1980). Reprinted with permission of Joseph L. Sax.

Joseph L. Sax, *The Public Trust Doctrine in Natural Resource Law: Effective Judicial Intervention*, 68 Mich. L. Rev. 471 (1970). Reprinted with permission of Joseph L. Sax and the Michigan Law Review.

Jon A. Souder and Sally K. Fairfax, State Trust Lands: History, Management, and Sustainable Use (University Press of Kansas, 1996). Reprinted with permission of Jon A. Souder, Sally K. Fairfax, and the University Press of Kansas.

State School Lands: Does the Federal Trust Mandate Prevent Preservation? By Alan Hager, published in Natural Resources & Environment, volume 12, No. 1, Summer 1997. Copyright 1997 by the American Bar Association. Reprinted with permission.

Charles F. Wilkinson, *The Headwaters of the Public Trust: Some of the Traditional Doctrine*, 19 Envtl. L. Rev. 425, 425–472 (1989). Reprinted with the permission of Environmental Law and Charles F. Wilkinson.

Sandi Zellmer, Photo of Mono Lake. Reprinted with permission of Sandi Zellmer.

Chapter 9

Craig Anthony Arnold, *Reconstitution of Property*, 26 Harvard Envtl. L. Rev. 281 (2002), © 2002 by the President and Fellows of Harvard College and the Harvard Environmental Law Review. Reprinted with permission.

Dana Beach, Create More Incentives for Easements, Open Space, at 13 (Summer, 2004). Reprinted with the permission of Dana Beach.

Federico Cheever, *Public Good and Private Magic in the Law of Land Trusts and Conservation Easements: A Happy Present and a Troubled*

Vicki Been, "Lucas v. the Green Machine: Using the Takings Clause to Promote More Efficient Regulation," *in Property Stories* 221–257 (G. Korngold & A. Morriss, eds., 2004). Reprinted with permission of Foundation Press.

Michael C. Blumm, "The Clinton Wetlands Plan: No Net Gain in Wetlands Protection," 9 *J.Land Use & Envtl. L.* 203, 226–28 (1994). Reprinted with permission of The Journal of Land Use & Environmental Law, © 1994.

Timothy Egan, "Owners of Malibu Mansions Cry, 'This Sand is My Sand'," New York Times, Aug. 25, 2002. Copyright © 2002 by The New York Times Co. Reprinted with permission.

Figure 2: Growth of the City of Baltimore, 1792–1992. Reprinted with permission of Dr. Timothy W. Foresman.

Figure 3: From Herbert Smith, *The Citizen's Guide to Zoning* (1983). Reprinted with permission from *The Citizen's Guide to Zoning*, copyright 1983 by the American Planning Association, Suite 1600, 122 South Michigan Ave., Chicago, IL 60603–6107.

Figure 4: Suburban Sprawl in New Jersey (photo). Alex S. MacLean/Landslides.

Figure 5: Monoculture (cartoon). Reprinted with permission of Kirk Anderson/Artizans.com.

David Malakoff, "Restored Wetlands Flunk Real-World Test," 280 *Science* 371–2 (Apr. 1988). Excerpted with permission from David Malakoff, "Restored Wetlands Flunk Real-World Test," 280 *Science* 371–2 (Apr. 1988). Copyright 1988 AAAS.

William B. Meyer, "Present Land Use and Land Cover in the USA," 1(1) *Consequences* (1995), pp. 24-33. Reprinted with permission of William B. Meyer.

Bob Ortega, "Urban Mecca: Portland, Ore., Shows Nation's City Planners How to Guide Growth," *Wall St. J.*, Dec. 26, 1995. Republished with permission of the Wall Street Journal from "Urban Mecca: Portland, Ore., Shows Nation's City Planners How to Guide Growth," Bob Ortega, Dec. 26, 1995, permission conveyed through Copyright Clearance Center, Inc.

Elisa Paster, "Preservation of Agricultural Lands Through Land Use Planning Tools and Techniques," 44 *Nat. Resources J.* 283–318 (2004). Reprinted with permission of the Natural Resources Journal.

J.B. Ruhl, "Farms, Their Environmental Harms, and Environmental Law," 27 *Ecol. L.Q.* 274–292 (2000). © 2000 by The Regents of the University of California. Reprinted from Ecology Law Quarterly, Vol. 27, No. 2, Pp. 274–292 by permission of the Regents of the University of California.

Samuel R. Staley, "The Sprawling of America," Policy Study No. 251, Reason Public Policy Institute (Feb. 1999). Reprinted with permission of Samuel R. Staley and the Reason Foundation.

Chapter 11

Forest Stewardship Council (FSC) Logo, 1996 Forest Stewardship Council A.C. Reprinted with permission.

Donald R. Leal, TURNING A PROFIT ON PUBLIC FORESTS, PERC Policy Series Issue PS–4 (September 1995). Adapted with permission from PERC Policy Series Issue PS–4 (September 1995).

Thomas N. Lippe and Kathy Bailey, *Regulation of Logging on Private Land in California under Governor Gray Davis*, 31 Golden Gate U. L. Rev. 351, 389–96 (2001). Reprinted with permission of Golden Gate University Law Review.

Scott Patterson, Jurassic Bark—Salvaging Ancient Logs Sunk In Lake Superior, Mother Earth News, Ogden Publications (Oct./Nov. 1998). Reprinted with permission, Copyright Clearance Center.

The Greenbelt Movement: Photo Gallery—Civic & Environmental Education. Photo reprinted with permission from the Greenbelt Photo Gallery Archives.

The Last Stand, by David Harris, from © *Rolling Stone* Magazine, Feb. 8, 1996. © Rolling Stone LLC 1996. All Rights Reserved. Reprinted with Permission.

The outdoors just calls to me (release date 5/3/84). The Far Side ® by Gary Larson © 1984 FarWorks, Inc. All Rights Reserved. The FarSide ® and the Larson © signature are registered trademarks of FarWorks, Inc. Used with Permission.

Virgin Growth Timber: A Piece of History For The Future, Timeless Timber. Reprinted with permission of Timeless Timber.

Chapter 12

Francis X. Clines, Judge Takes On the White House on Mountaintop Mining, New York Times, 18, May 19, 2002. Copyright © 2002 by The New York Times Co. Reprinted with permission.

Owen Oplin and A. Dan Tarlock, *Water that is Not Water*, 8 Land & Water L. Rev. 391 (1978). Reprinted with permission of the Wyoming Law Review.

Charles F. Wilkinson, *Crossing the Next Meridian* 68–9 (1992). From *Crossing the Next Meridian* by Charles F. Wilkinson. Copyright © 1992 by the author. Reproduced by permission of Island Press, Washington, D.C.

Chapter 13

Gary Ballesteros, *Great Lakes Water Exports and Diversions: Annex 2001 and the Looming Environmental Battle,* Environmental Law Institute.

Reprinted with the permission. Copyright © 2002 Environmental Law Institute, from the Environmental Law Reporter.

Bob Berwyn, *State to Ponder Flows of Recreational Water,* The Denver Post, November 17, 2003. Reprinted with permission of Bob Berwyn.

Michael Booth, *Future Murky for Sewage Water Residents Reluctant to Consider Reuse for Taps Drought Measure, but Recycling Common,* Denver Post, September 16, 2002. Reprinted with permission of The Denver Post.

Cement mill of the Los Angeles Aqueduct. Reprinted with permission of Joseph D. Lippincott Collection, Water Resources Center Archives—University of California, Berkeley.

Eric T. Freyfogle, *Water Rights and the Common Wealth,* Environmental Law, Lewis & Clark Law School. Reprinted with the permission of Environmental Law.

Casey S. Funk and Amy M. Cavanaugh, *1998 Basic Exchange,* Denver University Water Law Review. Approval is conditioned upon the placement of the proper legal citation to the original publication in the University of Denver Water Law Review in the form of 1 U.Denv.Water L.Rev. 206 (1998) on the cover page of each distributed copy.

Taiawagi Helton, *Indian Reserved Water Rights in the Dual-System State of Oklahoma,* Tulsa Law Review. Reprinted with permission of Tulsa Law Review.

Gregory J. Hobbs, *The Most Misunderstood Stick in the Bundle, Environmental Law.* Lewis & Clark Law School. Reprinted with the permission of Environmental Law.

V. Lane Jacobson, *Partial Forfeiture of a Water Right,* Idaho Law Review, University of Idaho College of Law. Reprinted with the permission of V. Lane Jacobson and Idaho Law Review.

J. Marshall Lawson, *Transboundary Groundwater Pollution: The Impact of Evolving Groundwater Use on Salt Water Intrusion of the Floridian Aquifer Along the South Carolina-Georgia Border,* Southeastern Environmental Law Journal, University of South Carolina School of Law. Reprinted with permission of the authors and Southeastern Environmental Law Journal.

Steve Lipsher, *Drought Prompts Water Board to Enforce Stream Rights, 800 Violations Noted in Unprecedented Action that Could Worsen Shortages,* The Denver Post, September 22, 2002. Reprinted with permission of The Denver Post.

Janet C. Neuman, *Beneficial Use, Waste, and Forfeiture: The Inefficient Search for Efficiency in Western Water Use, Environmental Law.* Lewis & Clark Law School. Reprinted with the permission of Environmental Law.

Kevin L. Patrick & Kelly E. Archer, *Comparison of State Groundwater Laws,* Tulsa Law Review. Reprinted with permission of Tulsa Law Review.

Chapter 14

Chapter 15

Robert Royen, *Line of Seismic Vibrator Trucks* (photo), The Denver Post, (no date).

Mike Stark, *Rebuilding a Road to Prosperity,* High Country News, October 8, 2001.

Theo Stein, *Off-Roading Limits Weighed for Forest,* Denver Post, July 8, 2004. Reprinted with permission of The Denver Post.

Robert Struckman, *Small Towns Court Upscale Tourists* (article and photo), High Country News, May 27, 2002. Reprinted with permission of Robert Struckman.

The Denver Post, *First Tracks* Thumper Truck Tracks (photo).

The Denver Post, (no author), Map of San Rafael Swell Region of Proposed Redrock Wilderness.

The Denver Post, (no author), *Super Sized* ORV Thumper Trucks, (photo).

*

Summary of Contents

PART I.   INTRODUCTION TO NATURAL RESOURCES LAW AND POLICY

PART II.   OWNERSHIP OF NATURAL RESOURCES

PART III.   LAND USE AND
COMMODITY RESOURCES

Table of Contents

PART I.   INTRODUCTION TO NATURAL RESOURCES LAW AND POLICY

PART II. OWNERSHIP OF NATURAL RESOURCES

PART III. LAND USE AND COMMODITY RESOURCES

PART IV. CONSERVATION, PRESERVATION, AND RECREATION RESOURCES

Page

Table of Cases

The principal cases are in bold type. Cases cited or discussed in the text are roman type. References are to pages. Cases cited in principal cases and within other quoted materials are not included.

NATURAL
RESOURCES LAW

*

Part I

INTRODUCTION TO NATURAL RESOURCES LAW AND POLICY

Part I of this book "sets the stage" for the study of natural resources law by examining the substantive and procedural underpinnings of this field. The nation's policies governing natural resources ownership, use, management, and preservation are strongly rooted in both economics and ecology. Chapters 1 and 2, written by Professors Daniel H. Cole and Sandra Zellmer respectively, introduce the reader to the basic concepts of these two disciplines, as relevant to the study of natural resources law, and provide context and a theoretical basis for the cases, statutes, and regulations covered in subsequent chapters. Chapters 3 and 4, written by Professor Zellmer, address, in turn, the jurisdictional and procedural framework for raising and resolving natural resources conflicts, as well as the bed-rock decisionmaking requirements and processes dictated by the National Environmental Policy Act (NEPA).

Chapter 1

ECONOMICS AND NATURAL RESOURCES LAW

I. INTRODUCTION

The natural resources base is finite, but growing populations place increasing demands on our limited resources, such as minerals, water, timber and fisheries. The purpose of this chapter is to describe how such limited resources are allocated, developed, and distributed in a free market system governed by the laws of supply and demand, or through legal and regulatory mechanisms.

This introductory section focuses on the common roots of both natural resources law and economics in the primary fact of scarcity and the consequent necessity of costly choice (*opportunity cost*). Section 2 then addresses the market system, which remains the primary method of allocating natural resources in the United States; Section 3 introduces the economic goal of efficiency. The market does not always attain efficiency, however, as noted in Section 4. Market failures give rise to government intervention to manage resource development and use. Such interventions, as discussed in Section 5, can take several forms, including public ownership, regulation, taxation, subsidization, and imposition of judicial liability. Cost-benefit analysis (CBA) as a means of assessing economic efficiency is explored in Section 6. However, government interventions create costs and benefits of their own, and government failures can be every bit as bad as market failures. In addition to government responses to market failures, there are also extra-governmental means of averting or resolving market failures, including social norms and common property regimes, as discussed in Section 7. However, those regimes also sometimes fail to allocate resources efficiently. Consequently, as Section 8 notes, institutional choice—the choice between market and governmental allocation of resource entitlements—becomes difficult, but necessary.

A. Scarcity: The First Premise of Law and Economics

Natural resources exhibit a wide array of characteristics. Wildlife and plants are alive, minerals are not. Water and oil are liquid, gold and timber are solid, geothermal steam is gaseous. Some natural resources such as bacteria are microscopically small; others, like the oceans, are immense. But all natural resources, whatever their different attributes, share at least two important traits in common: (1) they are by definition not produced (initially, at least) by humans, and (2) they are physically scarce. There is only so much water, oil, gas, or gold in the world (or the universe, so far as we know).

The physical scarcity of natural resources would not constitute a legal or economic problem, however, in the absence of human *demand* to use those resources. For some natural resources, human demand is highly limited or even nonexistent. Most diseases and many bacteria and viruses share this characteristic. They are demanded only in limited quantities by scientists and biotechnology companies interested in developing vaccines, antidotes, or exterminating agents. The ebola virus (a member of the Filoviridae family of RNA viruses which causes an often fatal hemorrhagic fever in humans and non-human primates), for example, is *physically scarce*, but it is not *economically scarce*, that is, scarce relative to the demand for it.

Most natural resources, including all of those addressed in the various chapters of this book, *are* positively valued (by humans), often for various uses (or non-uses) and for exchange. Some resources, such as coal, are valued primarily for their economic utility; they are commodity resources. Others, such as rivers and lakes are valued not just for their economic utility, but also for various non-economic uses, including as habitat for fish and wildlife. Still other natural resources, including endangered species such as the Red–Cockaded Woodpecker (depicted on pages 1187–188 of Chapter 14 on Wildlife Law) are valued not at all for their economic utility but for their very existence. Because all of these resources are *economically scarce*—scarce *relative to demand*—economics and law are relevant to their use (or non-use) and exchange.

> Consider the quintessential commodity resource: gold. Gold has been economically valued by diverse societies for thousands of years, regardless of differences in culture, systems of value, and political-economic structures. Yet it is easy to conceive a (mythical) world in which gold would have *zero* economic value and, so, zero price: It is the world in which gold is perfectly abundant. In this world, gold is everywhere, lying at everyone's feet. Anyone possessing less than enough gold can simply bend down and scoop up more. With gold perfectly plentiful, it holds no economic value, meaning no market would exist for it. No one would pay anyone else for gold, when it is there for the taking at virtually no cost.

DANIEL H. COLE AND PETER Z. GROSSMAN, PRINCIPLES OF LAW AND ECONOMICS 2 (2005).

Neither would society enact any legal rules governing the use or exchange of gold.

> What reason would there be to have laws establishing or protecting possessory rights in gold? Anyone who wanted gold (or more gold) could simply reach down and grab plenty. For that reason, no one would bother to take another's gold. And if someone *did* take another's gold, the 'victim' would not complain because an unlimited amount of gold would remain available at virtually zero cost.

Id. at 24.

In reality, gold *is* scarce both physically and economically. There is insufficient gold to meet all demand for gold at zero cost. And that is why law and economics are both relevant for the extraction, allocation, and use of gold. The extraction of gold is subject to various mining and environmental regulations, and the allocation of gold is determined both by the law of property and by economic markets.

B. The Inevitability of Costly Choice Under Scarcity

In the absence of scarcity, we could make choices without trade-offs; choosing one opportunity would not foreclose any other opportunity. We could have our cake and eat it too. We could maximize economic production without sacrificing resource preservation. The real world, however, is a place of ubiquitous scarcity where choice is costly, and trade-offs necessary. We cannot gratify every one of our individual (or social) wants at the same time. Making one choice forecloses others that we might have made instead. We cannot, at one time, extract a stand of old growth trees from the forest and still get aesthetic enjoyment from those same trees standing in the forest, or dedicate that same stand of trees in that forest for endangered species habitat. The choices we foreclose in making other choices constitute what economists call *opportunity costs*. We bear such opportunity costs whenever we make decisions about how to spend our assets, including time; those opportunity costs are borne in addition to the money prices we might pay for goods and services.

It is the combination of scarcity, choice, and cost that defines the field of economics. The English economist Lionel Robbins defined economics as " 'the science which studies human behavior as a relationship between ends and scarce means which have alternative uses.' " *Id.* at 1. In a similar vein, the American economist Paul Samuelson defines economics as ...

> the study of how people and society end up *choosing* * * * to employ *scarce* productive resources [labor, capital, natural resources] that could have alternative uses, to produce various commodities and distribute them for consumption, now or in the future, among various persons and groups in society. It analyzes the costs and benefits of improving patterns of resource allocation.

PAUL SAMUELSON, ECONOMICS 3 (10th ed. 1976).

C. Alternative Mechanisms for Allocating Scarce Resources

The fact of scarcity means that resources or, more accurately, entitlements to resources, must be rationed or *allocated* among alternative (or competing) uses and users. Two allocation mechanisms predominate for natural resources: (1) markets, which (in theory at least) allocate resources according to economic efficiency, based on buyers' willingness-to-pay and sellers' willingness-to-accept, as reflected in *prices*; and (2) governments, which allocate rights to resources according to various criteria including social justice (or equity), just desserts, lottery, political influence (cronyism), and (less frequently) economic efficiency.

II. THE MARKET SYSTEM OF RESOURCE ALLOCATION

Because the market is the primary method of allocating natural resources (as well as other goods and services) in the United States, it is important to understand how it operates. A market is comprised of two decisionmaking units: buyers and sellers. Buyers *demand* goods and services, which sellers *supply*. Both parties make their respective decisions about consumption and production based on a forward-looking assessment of costs and benefits, given their current circumstances and preferences. And they make their decisions at the *margin*. This means that they consider the costs and benefits of the *next unit* of consumption or production. An ice-cream lover who has just consumed five hot-fudge sundaes in less than an hour is unlikely to value the sixth hot-fudge sundae as highly as he valued the fifth or the first; the marginal benefits from eating the next hot-fudge sundae are likely to be significantly lower, at least for most consumers. Thus, the consumer is unlikely to be willing to pay as much for the sixth hot-fudge sundae as he paid for the fifth or the first. Producers similarly employ marginal analysis in determining how much of a good to produce and supply to the market.

A. Supply and Demand

1. The Law of Demand

The prices of goods and services in the market, and the quantities exchanged, are determined by supply and demand. The structure of supply and demand are revealed when buyers and sellers come into contact to exchange goods and services. Buyers comprise the demand sector of the economy; sellers constitute the supply side. Sellers seek to maximize the prices they get for the goods and services they sell, while buyers seek to minimize the prices they pay. Given the fact that buyers and sellers operate at cross-purposes, how are they able to reconcile their conflicting interests in markets?

An example from a theoretical natural resource market illustrates this process. Mary drives a gasoline-powered automobile to her kids' school, to work, to run errands, and occasionally on road trips. The amount of driving she does and the fuel she consumes are based on several factors including: the price of gasoline relative to the price of other goods and services that might fulfill alternative preferences: her budget constraint (how much she can afford to spend on *all* the goods and services she demands), her tastes or preferences for driving her kids to school as opposed to letting them take the bus, driving a more or less fuel-efficient car, and her expectations about the future, including future prices of gasoline and substitute goods, and her future budget constraint. All else being equal, the lower the price of gasoline, the more Mary will drive and the more fuel she will consume.

Figure 1–1 illustrates this point. If the price of one gallon of gas is $0.00, Mary will drive a lot, using 50 or more gallons for rides in the country. If the price per gallon is $1.00, Mary will buy 40 gallons for her driving needs. At a price of $2.00 per gallon, Mary will buy only 30 gallons per week, and reduce her driving if necessary. And so on, until the price reaches $5.00 per gallon, at which Mary will buy no gas at all and simply choose not to drive.

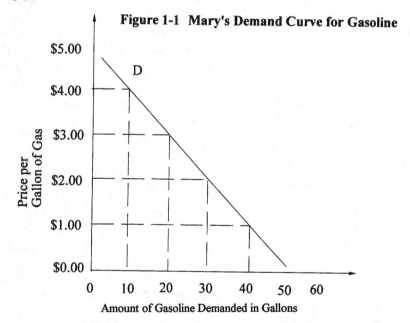

Figure 1-1 Mary's Demand Curve for Gasoline

Two crucial, but realistic, assumptions are implicit in Figure 1–1's illustration of Mary's weekly demand for gasoline. First, the slope of the demand curve–down and to the right–indicates that Mary responds rationally to price signals, buying more gasoline when the price goes down, and buying less when the price goes up. Second, Mary's response to price signals assumes that her overall goal is to maximize the total amount of welfare, utility, happiness, or satisfaction she derives from acting on her various preferences.

In Focus: The Rationality Assumption in Economics

Economists presume that individuals rationally seek to maximize, or at least satisfy, whatever preferences or goals they have. At a minimum (and sometimes at a maximum), this means individuals' *preferences are transitive*. This simply means that their preference orderings are internally consistent (at a given point in time). So, if Ben prefers steak to chicken, and prefers chicken to fish, Ben cannot prefer fish to steak. A stronger form of rationality found in neoclassical economic theory argues that people are able to fully maximize their preferences because they have complete information through market prices. That is, all prices reflect changes in market conditions, and these are instantly transferred to consumers and producers who then adjust their consumption and production accordingly.

The rationality assumption does not imply that individuals are necessarily greedy or selfish. Economics does not presume to dictate what anyone's preferences are or should be. A nun from the Missionaries of Charity (founded by Mother Teresa) is not economically irrational because she chooses to live in poverty and help the needy. Economists would merely expect that the nun would attempt to fulfill her preferences, including her preference to help the needy, to the utmost.

Research in Behavioral Economics has raised doubts about the abilities of individuals (and organizations) to act rationally in response to price signals and other incentives. In the 1950s, Herbert Simon noted that all individuals suffer from cognitive limitations that constrain our abilities to act rationally. We are only imperfectly or, in Simon's words, *boundedly* rational. *See* Herbert Simon, *Rationality as Process and a Product of Thought*, 68 AMER. ECON. REV. 1 (1978); Herbert Simon, *Rational Decision Making in Business Organizations*, 69 AMER. ECON. REV. 493 (1979). We are not the human calculators of conventional economic theory. Instead, we muddle through decisionmaking processes, using rules of thumb and other heuristic devices, often making mistakes. More recent research has shown that individual decisions may be based on the *way* choices are framed, rather than the choices themselves. For instance, medical patients who are told that 90 percent of individuals who undergo a certain surgical procedure survive are far more likely to agree to have that procedure than those who are told that 10 percent do not survive. Donald A. Redelmeier, Paul Rozin, and Daniel Kahneman, *Understanding Patients' Decisions*, 270 J.AMER. MED. ASSOC. 72 (1993).

So far, nothing in the Behavioral Economics literature has challenged the basic preference transitivity assumption of conventional economic theory. More generally, we should be cautious about implying too much from that literature about human rationality. After all, as Ronald Coase has pointed out, when "faced with a choice between $100 and $10, very few people will choose $10." Ronald H. Coase, *How Should Economists Choose?*, *reprinted in* RONALD H. COASE, ESSAYS ON ECONOMICS AND ECONOMISTS 25 (1994). Cass Sunstein suggests that "it is unproductive to see a *general* struggle between economic analysis of law and behavioral law and economics. The question is what kinds of assumptions produce good predictions about the effects of law, and this will vary with context. Sometimes the simple assumptions of conventional analysis work entirely well; sometimes it is necessary to introduce complications by, for example, saying a bit more about what is counted in the utility function (such as a desire to be treated fairly and willingness to punish those who act unfairly), or incorporating bounded rationality." Cass R. Sunstein, *Behavioral Law and Economics: A Progress Report*, 1 AMER. L. & ECON. REV. 115, 147 (1999).

The demand curve in Figure 1–1 provides only a snapshot in time of Mary's demand schedule for gasoline, given her preferences, budget constraint, and expectations for the future. If and when any of those variables change, so too might Mary's demand for gasoline. For instance, if Mary suddenly ceases to derive enjoyment from road trips, she will demand less (and possibly no) gasoline for that purpose. Or if Mary loses her job, the resulting reduction in her income (and tightening of her budget constraint) may lead her to drive less, even if she continues to derive the same level of satisfaction from driving, so as to conserve her resources for more pressing needs, such as housing and food. Driving less would, of course, reduce her demand for gasoline.

Finally, Mary's demand is not the only demand that matters in determining the market price of gasoline. Everyone who drives a car, truck or motorcycle contributes to the *market demand*, which is the sum of all individual demands. Assume, hypothetically, a gasoline market with just two buyers: our friend Mary and another driver named Jeff. We already know that Mary will buy 30 gallons of gas at a price of $2.00 per gallon. If Jeff is willing to buy 7 gallons at that same price, then the total market demand for gasoline at a price of $2.00 per gallon is 37 gallons. Just like an individual demand curve, a market demand curve slopes down and to the right; but in any market with more than one buyer, the quantity of market demand will exceed the quantity of any individual's demand at all prices.

2. *The Law of Supply*

The price of gasoline, or any other good, is determined not only by the market demand but also by the market supply. Like buyers, sellers are presumed to maximize their preferences. In the case of a commercial good such as gasoline, this usually means maximizing profits, defined as revenues over costs. Sellers will supply more of a good to the market when the price is high, and less when the price is low. If the price is too low, that is, below their average cost of production, the supply will fall to zero.

To continue our theoretical example from the gasoline market, the XYZ Oil Company is a large, integrated company which explores for and produces crude oil, refines it into gasoline, and transports it to stations it owns, which then sell the gasoline to consumers (demanders). Figure 1–2 illustrates how much gasoline XYZ will supply to the market at various prices. In contrast to the demand curve (D) from Figure 1–1, the supply curve (S) in Figure 1–2 slopes up and to the right, indicating that, XYZ will supply more gasoline to the market at higher prices than it will at lower prices. At a price of $5.00, XYZ will supply the market with 50,000 gallons of gasoline each week. At a lower price of $3.00 per gallon, XYZ will supply only 30,000 gallons per week. And as the price falls to $0.00, XYZ will provide no gasoline to the market.

Figure 1-2 XYZ Company's Supply Curve

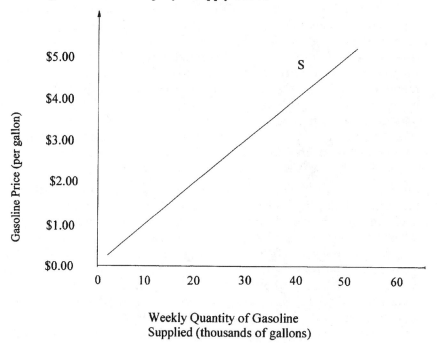

Figure 1–2 represents only the supply curve for a single supplier. A *market supply* curve would be the sum of XYZ's supply (at various prices) and those of all other suppliers of gasoline.

B. How Markets Function in Theory

1. *Market Equilibrium: Where Supply and Demand Meet*

In most natural resource markets, neither demanders nor suppliers alone set the price of goods and services.[a] Rather, it is the *combination* of market supply and market demand that determines prices. Consider Figure 1–3, which puts supply and demand curves together. In this figure, the *equilibrium price* of gasoline is determined where the supply curve (S) meets the demand curve (D) at point E. That point represents the price at which the quantity of gasoline demanded precisely equals the quantity supplied, leaving no unsatisfied demand and no residual supply. It is the *market clearing price*. In the case represented in Figure 1–3, that price is $2.00 per gallon. At that price, sellers will supply, and buyers will demand, precisely 40,000 gallons of gasoline. At this price, the total value of the gasoline market is maximized; at any other price, there would be either unsatisfied demand or residual supply, and the total value of the gasoline market would be lower.

Figure 1-3 Market Equilibrium

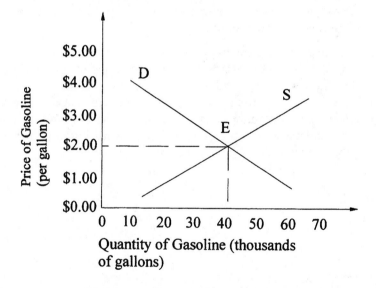

2. *Shifts in Supply, Demand, and Market Equilibria*

The equilibrium price is changeable and not always achieved. The quantities supplied and demanded tend to move almost continually, leading to changes in market prices. The demand and supply curves isolate the impacts of price changes on the quantity of a good demanded or supplied. A change in the quantity of a good demanded is indicated by a

a. The exceptions would be circumstances of: (a) monopoly, in which the monopoly producer or a cartel or producers might (or might not) be able to set prices, at least temporarily; and (b) monopsony, in which the lone buyer might be able to set prices, at least temporarily.

movement (upward or downward) along the demand curve (D). In Figure 1–4a, an increase in the price of gasoline (from P to P¹) results in a decrease in the quantity of gasoline demanded (from Q to Q¹).

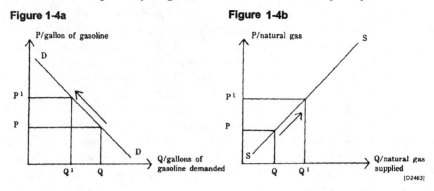

Figure 1-4a

Figure 1-4b

Similarly, a change in the quantity of a good supplied, due to a change in price of that good, is indicated by movement (upward or downward) along the supply curve. Figure 1–4b shows that an increase in the price of natural gas (from P to P¹) leads to an increase in supply (from Q to Q¹) of that resource to consumers, since the higher price creates an incentive to increase production.

As the price of a good increases, consumers faced with the same level of income (budget constraints) will economize on their use of that good. They may *shift* demand to less expensive *substitute goods*. For example, an increase in the price of oil after the Arab countries' embargo in 1973 decreased the quantity of oil demanded by consumers. (*See* Figure 1–5a). Consumers shifted their demand from home heating oil to natural gas or electricity, which are substitutes for oil.

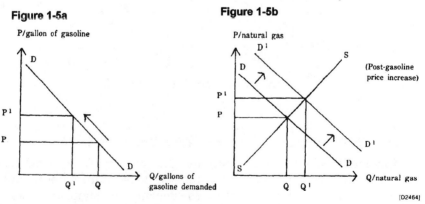

Figure 1-5a

Figure 1-5b

A consequence of this shift in demand was an increase in the demand for natural gas, represented in Figure 1–5b by a shift of the demand curve itself (from Q to Q¹), and an increase in its selling price (from P to P¹).

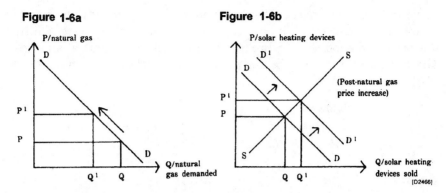

Figure 1-6a   **Figure 1-6b**

Recall that the equilibrium price and quantity for any market good is where the quantity demanded equals the quantity supplied. Factors causing the supply or demand curves to shift also shift the market's equilibrium price-quantity. One such factor, as already noted, is the change in the price of a related product. What other forces might change the market's equilibrium price?

A shift in demand (representing an increase or decrease in the quantity demanded *at all prices*) for a product can be triggered by changes in consumer income and tastes, population size, and expectations about future market conditions. The supply curve, on the other hand, shifts in response to changes in factors affecting production costs, such as changes in technology or input (e.g., labor) prices. For example, an invention that promotes the efficient recovery of oil from abandoned wells increases the oil supply, thereby shifting the oil market supply curve down and to the right (as in Figure 1–7). Increasing the quantity of oil supplied (from Q to Q^1) also lowers the price of oil (from P to P^1). Consequently, the equilibrium price falls from PQ to P^1Q^1. An even more dramatic shift in the supply curve of oil could occur if scientists perfected an economical method of producing energy from nuclear fusion.

Figure 1-7

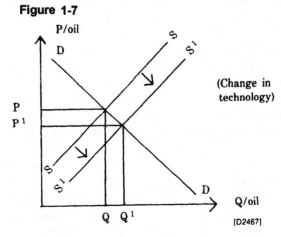

When supply increases as in the example above, the curve shifts down and to the right. But supply can also contract, in which case the curve shifts upward to the left. For example if government imposes a tax on oil production, this will necessarily raise production costs, shifting the curve to the left (from S to S¹), reflecting reduced supply at all prices. The tax alters the equilibrium price-quantity of gasoline from PQ to P¹Q¹.

Figure 1-8

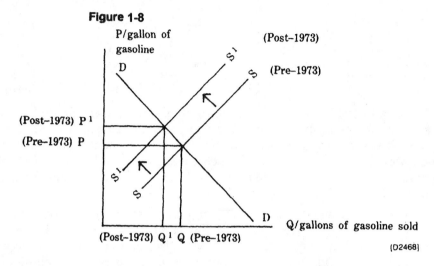

The preceding discussion illustrates how shifts in demand and supply curves change the equilibrium price-quantity. An increase in supply means the curve shifts down and prices fall; an increase in demand shifts the curve upward to the right and prices rise. But in analyzing the effects of these shifts, the degree to which the price and quantity change is important. Figures 1–9a and 1–9b (below) illustrate how the shift of the supply curve can have a greater or lesser effect on prices, depending on the responsiveness of demand, which is reflected in the slope or steepness of the demand curve. In both figures, the shift from S to S¹ is exactly the same; the only significant difference is in the slope of the demand curve. With a steeply sloped demand curve, as in Figure 1–9a, the shift in the supply curve has a relatively great effect on price, as reflected in the gap between P and P¹, but a relatively small effect on the quantity demanded, as reflected in the short move from Q to Q¹. In Figure 1–9b, by contrast, the same shift in the supply curve has a relatively small effect on price (a smaller gap between P and P¹) but a relatively pronounced effect on quantity demanded (a larger gap between Q and Q¹). The difference in the slopes of the D curves between Figures 1–9a and 1–9b realistically reflects the fact that demand and supply can be more or less responsive to changes in price, depending on various market factors, including, for example, the availability (or lack of availability) of substitute goods. The degree of responsiveness of demand and supply to changes in price is known as *price elasticity*.

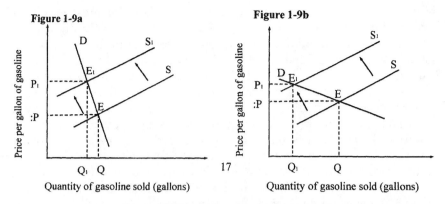

As Figure 1–10 (below) illustrates, if supply or demand is elastic, the percentage change in the quantity supplied or demanded will exceed the percentage change in price. If either is inelastic, the percentage change in the quantity supplied or demanded will be less than the percentage change in the price. Unitary elasticity of supply or demand means that the degree of change in the quantity supplied or demanded matches precisely the degree of change in price.

Figure 1–10

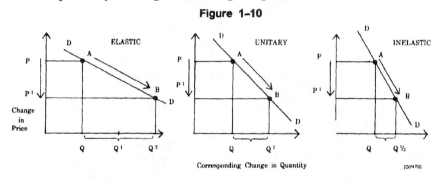

What determines the price elasticity of demand for a good or service? Demand inelasticity typifies a market in which a good or service is necessary and has no substitutes. Gasoline was once thought to have inelastic demand, since no substitute for it exists and some amount of it is viewed by most people as a necessity. The Houthakker–Taylor study conducted from 1929 to 1970 estimated the demand elasticity for gasoline as only .16, which means that a 10 percent increase in price would lead to only a 1.6% decrease in the quantity demanded. *See* R. Haveman and K. Knopf, The Market System: An Introduction to Microeconomics 153 (1978). However, with the onset of the Arab countries' oil embargo in 1973, which led to dramatic oil price increases, the public gradually learned to conserve, drive less, and buy smaller, more fuel-efficient cars. As a consequence, the long-run demand for gasoline proved to be more elastic than previously assumed.

Just as buyers respond to price changes by increasing or decreasing the quantity of demand (more or less depending on the relative elasticity of demand in a particular market), sellers respond to price changes by increasing or decreasing the quantity supplied. For most goods and services, supply is price elastic. If the price goes up, producers can add new equipment, more labor, and more resource inputs. But some goods, notably land, have a fixed supply, which is in some sense price inelastic. Nature may produce more land, for example through seismic and geologic processes, but the market cannot produce more land simply because someone is willing to pay for it. The market can, however, make some land available for different purposes as land prices change. For example, though land is fixed, an increase in the price of agricultural goods will lead land owners to make more of their property available for agricultural purposes. The same is more or less true of other fixed-stock natural resources, including minerals. The ultimate amount of gold in the world, for example, is fixed by nature, but if the price of gold rises substantially, that may make it cost-effective for mining companies to innovate new technologies that allow more gold than previously (when gold was priced lower) to be extracted at a profit.

3.   *Marginal Costs and Benefits of Production*

The supply curve is derived from the decisions individual firms make about production. As noted earlier, suppliers are willing to provide more gallons of gasoline at higher prices than at lower prices. See Figure 1–2. Why is this so? Because at higher prices, oil companies, for example, can afford the additional marginal costs of producing more gasoline for the market. Marginal production cost is a critical element in determining how much of a good will be supplied at a given market price. Production costs also determine the lowest price at which a firm can sell a certain unit of gasoline (or any other good) and stay in business.

In the market system, the goal of the business firm is to maximize profits. How are total costs calculated? When the XYZ Oil Company started in the industry, it incurred costs long before it produced and sold its first gallon of gasoline. Those costs included *fixed costs*, such as the costs of procuring drilling sites, exploratory surveys, the cost of drilling rigs and refining equipment, offices and office equipment, and pipelines or tankers for transporting the oil. The cost to the firm of the first gallon, and all subsequent gallons, of gasoline sold includes all of these fixed costs. But as more gallons are produced and sold, such costs are spread over a larger number of gallons produced, since fixed costs do not change as output rises. Thus, average total production costs may initially fall as the newly started oil company begins producing and selling gasoline.

In addition to fixed costs, XYZ will bear incremental or variable costs, including the costs of labor and resource inputs ("producer goods"). These costs are variable in that they vary with the level of production: at lower levels of production, fewer labor and resource inputs are required. But as output increases, so too do variable costs (for the vast majority of goods and services). The total cost of producing any level of output is the sum of total fixed costs and total variable costs.

The average variable cost (AVC) marks the lowest price a company can accept and still produce at least in the short run. If the price falls below AVC then a firm is better off stopping production even if it still must bear fixed costs. In the long run, average total costs (ATC) must at least equal market price. Otherwise firms would sell every unit at a loss.

While price is set in the competitive market through the intersection of supply and demand, the market supply curve itself is the horizontal sum of the marginal cost curves of all firms in the industry. The phrase "marginal cost" refers to the additional cost of producing the next unit of output. As noted above, if it takes $300 to produce 300 gallons of gasoline, the average price of producing a gallon is $1.00, but that does not necessarily mean the actual cost to XYZ of producing the 300th gallon was the same—$1.00—as the cost of producing the first gallon. The marginal cost of producing the 300th gallon may well have been higher. As variable costs increase, relative to fixed costs, as a percentage of total costs, marginal costs of production tend to rise. So, as pictured in Figure 1–11 (below), the marginal cost curve is U-shaped. The downward portion of the curve represents either technologically driven increasing returns to scale (that is where additional input leads to a greater percentage increase in output) or the spreading of fixed costs over increases in output; the rising portion reflects increasing variable costs, which eventually more than offset falling fixed costs per unit of output.

Figure 1–11

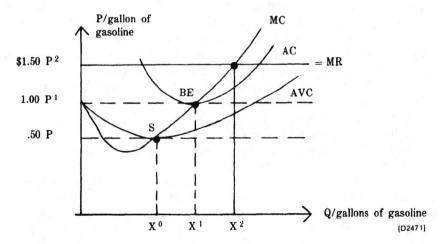

Figure 1–11 includes an average cost curve (AC), which is also U-shaped because its slope is determined by marginal production costs. If the cost of the last (marginal) increment of output is less than the average cost of all other increments of production, average costs will be falling. If and when marginal costs rise above average costs, the average cost curve will turn upward. When marginal cost is precisely equal to average cost (point BE in Figure 1–11), average cost is flat and at its

minimum. Thus, the average production cost curve is always bisected at its minimum point by the rising marginal cost curve.

Assume a normally competitive gasoline market, with an equilibrium price (where market supply and demand curves intersect) of $1.50 per gallon (at P^2 in Figure 1–11). How much gasoline would XYZ decide to supply to the market at that price, given its costs of production? As a rational seller, XYZ will only supply gasoline to the extent that it can profit from doing so. Because profit is the difference between total revenue and total costs, XYZ will increase its total profits so long as the additional (marginal) revenue from the last gallon it sells exceeds the marginal costs of producing that last gallon. The marginal revenue curve (MR) in Figure 1–11 is the line drawn at the current market price. (Indeed in perfectly competitive markets MR always equals price.) Marginal revenue is defined as the addition to total revenue created by the sale of one more unit of a good or service.

At any output level where the marginal revenue curve is above the marginal cost curve—all levels up to X^2, where marginal revenue (MR) equals marginal cost (MC), in Figure 1–11—XYZ realizes profit because total revenue exceeds total cost. Beyond that point, however, MC exceeds MR, so the next gallon of gasoline will cost more to produce than it is worth in the market, so that profits would fall. A profit maximizing firm, such as XYZ, would not produce that next gallon of gasoline it would produce only up to X^2, where MR = MC.

Of course, XYZ will not produce any gasoline at all if it does not expect to earn enough revenue to at least offset its fixed and variable costs of production. In Figure 1–11, the break-even level of output, where XYZ just recoups all of its long-run fixed and variable costs, is point BE. At this level of output, price equals both marginal cost and minimum average cost. At all points where price equals marginal cost, XYZ will be either maximizing its profits or, if market price drops below the BE point, minimizing losses (as some fixed costs will be recouped by continuing production). However, if the market price of gasoline falls below minimum average variable costs of production (point S in Figure 1–11), the firm will shut down completely to avoid incurring losses greater than the fixed costs it would incur if operations continued. Therefore, the firm's rising marginal cost curve above minimum average variable costs becomes the firm's supply curve. (Over the long run, the firm must recover both fixed and variable costs of production, break even, and remain competitive. It could not indefinitely supply gasoline at points on the supply curve below point BE.) A higher market price will encourage XYZ to explore for oil and supply more gasoline because the increased price pays for additional costs incurred as output is increased.

The concept of marginalism illustrated in Figure 1–11 applies to all economic activities relating to natural resources, including preservation. Figure 1–12 (below) applies the concept generally to environmental protection. Policies designed to protect the environment entail various costs and benefits. Typically, the first units of environmental protection confer significant social benefits at relatively low cost. But additional units of environmental protection may bring fewer marginal benefits and higher marginal cost. When the marginal costs of pollution control (or some other environmental protection measure) exceed the marginal benefits (above the point where MC crosses MB in Figure 1–12), additional units of environmental protection would create fewer marginal benefits and higher marginal cost. When the marginal costs of pollution control or resource preservation exceed the marginal benefits (above the point where MC crosses MB in Figure 1–12), additional units of environmental protection would cost more than they are worth. The (theoretically) optimum level of environmental protection is at the point where MC and MB meet. Of course, this presumes market participants can know and accurately assess all the various marginal costs and benefits associated with environmental protection. Information constraints on economic decisionmaking will be addressed later in this chapter, in the section in Market Failures.

Figure 1-12   Marginal Costs and Benefits of Environmental Protection

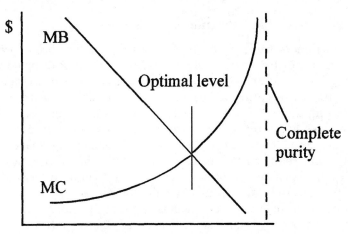

Quantity of Environmental Protection

III.   EFFICIENCY

By what criterion should market (or government) allocations of resources be judged? Why is the point where marginal benefits equal marginal costs (as described above in Figure 1–12) the theoretically "optimal" level of environmental protection? Economists use the standard of economic *efficiency*, which, in its simplest terms means to get the most out of available resources. The basic tenet of welfare economics is that resources should be utilized (or not utilized) so as to maximize the *net benefits* (that is, benefits over costs) for society as a whole. This is more easily said than done, however. Economists cannot tell society unambiguously what level of production and what allocation of resource entitlements will maximize social welfare because they cannot (1) know the preferences and preference-orderings of individual market participants before the occurrence of actual market transactions; and (2) aggregate the preferences of all individuals to determine the social welfare function. Economists can tell us, however, the total costs and benefits derived from various allocations of entitlements to scarce resources, given the expressed preferences of individuals in the market. They can explain the relative *efficiency* or *inefficiency* of a given allocation compared to some hypothetical alternative. Efficiency, thus, becomes the economists' proxy for social welfare. The more efficient is a given allocation, the greater the presumed welfare benefits for society. DANIEL H. COLE AND PETER Z. GROSSMAN, PRINCIPLES OF LAW AND ECONOMICS 10 (2005).

Two distinct notions of efficiency are relevant for the management of natural resources: (a) productive efficiency and (b) allocative efficiency. The first of these is concerned with minimizing the number of resource inputs required to produce a certain unit of output. The second is concerned with maximizing the social value of the allocation of entitlements to resources (including consumers goods and services) among various users and uses.

A. Productive Efficiency

Production is said to be efficient when the producer obtains the maximum output from the minimum number of inputs (including capital, labor, and natural resources). Thus, productive efficiency is concerned with conservation of resources or minimizing waste. By economizing on inputs per unit of output, producers maximize both the total value of production and their price-competitiveness in markets. At the same time, producers naturally assist in conserving scarce natural resources and reducing pollution (at least per unit of production). For example, the development of new, more efficient oil and gas furnaces in the 1980s required only about one-third of the energy to produce the same amount of heat as older models. EDWARD S. CASSEDY AND PETER Z. GROSSMAN, INTRODUCTION TO ENERGY: RESOURCES, TECHNOLOGY, AND SOCIETY 83 (1998). Because they required less energy, fewer resource inputs—coal, oil, and gas—were required to produce the same or greater levels of output (heat). And since fewer units of those polluting inputs were utilized per unit of production, less pollution was emitted per unit of production.

Improved Energy Efficiency in the U.S. Economy

Overall, thanks to greater dynamic efficiency in production, the US economy today consumes far fewer units of natural resources per unit of production than it did early in the twentieth century. According to the economist Mikhail Bernstam, the energy intensity of production in the United States fell by an average of one percent per year between 1929 and the late 1980s. This means that the economy used one percent *less* energy each year to achieve an equivalent amount of production. By 1990, the amount of energy required to produce one unit of gross domestic product in the US was 60 percent lower than it had been in 1930. MIKHAIL BERNSTAM, THE WEALTH OF NATIONS AND THE ENVIRONMENT 28–9 (1991). This does not necessarily mean that Americans today use less energy overall than we did in the early twentieth century. In absolute terms, we use more coal and electricity now, but we get a great deal more production out of each unit of coal and electricity we use. To illustrate, between 1973 and 1993 energy consumption in the US declined both per person (from 351 million BTUs to 326 million BTUs) and per dollar of GDP (from 22.73 thousand BTUs to 16.34 thousand BTUs). But *total* energy consumption in the United States increased (from 74.28 quadrillion *i.e.*, 10^{15} BTUs to 83.96 BTUs), primarily because of growth in the overall size of the US economy (of about 64 percent) and the US population (of approximately 20 percent). EDWARD S. CASSEDY AND PETER Z. GROSSMAN, INTRODUCTION TO ENERGY: RESOURCES, TECHNOLOGY, AND SOCIETY 74, Table 4.1 (1998).

For some natural resources, however, increasing factor productivity has led to a decline in the absolute amounts Americans consume each year. In the 1980s, for example, we used absolutely less oil and iron-ore than we used in the in the late 1920s, despite having a far larger population and a much bigger economy. MIKHAIL BERNSTAM, THE WEALTH OF NATIONS AND THE ENVIRONMENT 28 (1991). The combination of scarcity pricing for natural resource inputs and competitive markets creates a more or less constant incentive for producers to improve their productive efficiency.[b]

B. Allocative Efficiency

Economists are concerned not only with maximizing efficiency in production. They are also concerned with efficiency in the allocation and use of outputs in society. We want goods and services produced at the lowest possible cost, *and* we want those goods and services allocated to their "highest and best use" among all competing uses and users, so as to maximize their value to society.

Economists use various measures of allocative efficiency. The two most common are the Pareto criterion and Kaldor–Hicks (or "potential Pareto") criteria.

1. *Pareto Efficiency*

A transaction or resource allocation is said to be "Pareto efficient" (or "Pareto improving") if it makes at least one person better and makes no one else worse off. A situation in which no Pareto efficient (or improving) moves are possible—no one can be made better off without making

---

b. In the absence of scarcity pricing and competitive markets, the incentive to productive efficiency is lost, and economic growth will depend entirely on a constant or growing level of investment of resource inputs. *See, e.g.*, DANIEL H. COLE, INSTITUTING ENVIRONMENTAL PROTECTION: FROM RED TO GREEN IN POLAND 134–40 (1998). Even where scarcity pricing and competitive markets are present, factor productivity does not always increase, let alone at a constant rate.

at least one other person worse off—are said to be "Pareto optimal."[c] The Pareto criterion provides an unambiguous measure of welfare in that any transaction or resource allocation that meets its strict requirements is certain to leave society as a whole better off. However, its strict requirements are met in only a small fraction of actual transactions or resource allocations. In order to meet the Pareto criterion, the transaction or resource allocation must have the *voluntary and unanimous consent of all affected parties*; otherwise, we could not ensure that the transaction or allocation creates no losers. This rules out all non-consensual allocations, including all administrative, judicial, or governmental decisions that affect resource allocations. Even a government program that obviously generated huge *net* social benefits (social benefits minus social costs) could not be adjudged efficient according to the Pareto criteria either because it left at least one person worse off or because we simply could not be sure that the program had the voluntary and unanimous consent of all affected parties. The only transactions or allocations that meet the criteria are voluntary market transactions—gifts or contracts—with no negative *externalities*, defined as costs imposed on individuals or groups who are not parties to the gift or contract.[d] For this reason, the Pareto criterion has only limited application in measuring the efficiency of real-world transactions; and no application at all for judging non-market allocations of resources. In sum, the Pareto criterion is theoretically pure—capable of generating unambiguous results (which is useful for economic modeling)—but operationally deficient. *See, e.g.*, DANIEL H. COLE AND PETER Z. GROSSMAN, PRINCIPLES OF LAW AND ECONOMICS 10–11 (2005) and NICHOLAS MERCURO AND STEVEN G. MEDEMA, ECONOMICS AND THE LAW: FROM POSNER TO POST–MODERNISM Ch. 1 (1997)(discussing Pareto efficiency criterion and its limitations).

2. *Kaldor–Hicks ("Potential Pareto") Efficiency*

Because of the operational deficiencies of the strict Pareto criterion, economists had to come up with some other mechanism by which to adjudge the social welfare effects (i.e., efficiency) of the vast majority of all transactions and resource allocations that involve government policies and/or externalities. In the late 1930s, two economists working independently (but both at the London School of Economics), Nicholas Kaldor and John Hicks, came up with complementary efficiency criteria. According to Kaldor's formula, a transaction or resource allocation is efficient when it makes at least one person better off, and the gains exceed anyone else's losses, so that the gainers could, in theory, compensate the losers completely and still come out ahead. Nicholas Kaldor, *Welfare Propositions in Economics*, 49 ECON. J. 549 (Sept. 1939). According to John Hicks's formula, a transaction or resource allocation is effi-

---

c. This definition of efficiency is named for its founder, the Italian-born sociologist Vilfredo Pareto (1848–1923). *See* VILFREDO PARETO, MANUAL OF POLITICAL ECONOMY (1906).

d. Externalities are addressed in more detail in the next section of this chapter on market failures.

cient if those who might be made worse off as a result could not afford to bribe those who gain from the transaction or allocation into forgoing their gains, without suffering an even greater loss. J.R. Hicks, *The Foundations of Welfare Economics*, 49 ECON. J. 696 (Sept. 1939). The mirror image efficiency criteria of Kaldor and Hicks proved to be flawed, when applied individually; but when combined as the Kaldor–Hicks efficiency criteria they yielded robust (if not completely unambiguous) results. *See* Tibor Scitovsky, *A Note on Welfare Propositions in Economics*, 9 REV. ECON. STUD. 77 (Nov. 1941–42).

Two critical features distinguish Kaldor–Hicks efficiency from the Pareto criterion. First, Kaldor and Hicks do not presume that all transactions and resource allocations occur in completely voluntary and unanimous market transactions. This allows their criteria to apply to market transactions entailing negative externalities and to government allocations of resources, neither of which can be judged under the strict Pareto criterion. Second, Kaldor and Hicks require only theoretical, not actual, compensation of anyone who suffers a loss as the result of some transaction or allocation, to ensure a net gain to social welfare. Assume a certain allocation of resources affects just two parties, X and Y. The allocation yields benefits of +10 to X but imposes costs of –4 on Y (as Y subjectively values those costs). Under the Pareto criterion, we could only be certain of an actual improvement to social welfare if X compensates Y for Y's subjectively valued losses. Under the Kaldor–Hicks criteria, by contrast, we simply accept that some losses will occur; so long as X *could* (in theory) compensate Y and still come out ahead, we conclude that the allocation yields a net improvement to social welfare. This move to *theoretical* compensation allows economists to judge, within a margin of error, the efficiency of the vast majority of government (including judicial) allocations that create both winners and losers, but which do not provide compensation to the losers.

Unfortunately, in order to achieve greater applicability, the Kaldor–Hicks criteria sacrifice theoretical purity, i.e., certainty. Because losers are not actually compensated at their own subjective valuation of their losses, we cannot know for certain what price they would have demanded in order obtain their agreement to the transaction or resource allocation. That is to say, we cannot be certain of the measure of losses, which means that we cannot be absolutely certain that the transaction or allocation generates *net* social benefits.

In the absence of voluntary transactions in the market, where the preferences of all participants and their subjective valuations of their preferences are exhibited and supported by willingness to pay, economic valuations cannot be unambiguously derived and compared. In other words, because Kaldor–Hicks does not require those who benefit from some allocation or reallocation to compensation those who lose, it does not provide a market-determined price by which to evaluate the winners' utility and losers' disutility.

DANIEL H. COLE AND PETER Z. GROSSMAN, PRINCIPLES OF LAW AND ECONOMICS 12 (2005).

Because they are not completely supported by willingness to pay and willingness to accept, the economic valuations of Kaldor–Hicks analyses are subject to error and possible manipulation. In the absence of completely voluntary market transactions that would precisely determine values, analysts might make unintentional valuation errors; in some cases, they might be tempted to manipulate cost or benefit estimates to pre-determine a preferred outcome. Thus, the "potential Pareto" measure never yields unambiguous results.

As a consequence, some economists reject the Kaldor–Hicks criteria as a measure. But they offer nothing with which to replace it. As already noted, the Pareto criterion is disqualified by the very features that ensure its unambiguous results: the strict requirement of unanimous and voluntary consent of all affected parties to ensure that no one suffers any losses. Consequently, the combined Kaldor–Hicks efficiency criteria remain, despite their defects, dominant in the worlds of applied economics and policy analysis, where they are employed under the rubric of "Cost–Benefit Analysis" (CBA). We will discuss the technique of CBA in some detail in Section 5 of this chapter, which concerns government intervention to correct market failures.

IV. MARKET FAILURES

Economic theory predicts that markets will maximize allocative efficiency so long as the following assumptions hold: (1) the market includes many buyers and sellers, all of whom possess complete information about product quantities, qualities, and prices; (2) no buyer or seller has enough market power to set prices; (3) market participants respond rationally to price signals; (4) participants can enter and exit the market at will without cost; (5) all resources within the economy are owned and priced within the market according to the laws of supply and demand; (6) all costs and benefits fall within the market, so that there are no *externalities*; and (7) transacting in the market is costless. DANIEL H. COLE AND PETER Z. GROSSMAN, PRINCIPLES OF LAW AND ECONOMICS 13 (2005).

In real-world markets, assumption (7) never obtains, and the six other assumptions hold only occasionally and incompletely. Markets never function perfectly in accordance with theory. They are always characterized by some degree of *market failure*, which is defined as the inability to achieve and maintain maximal allocative efficiency. Markets fail for several reasons, including the absence of well-defined and enforceable property rights, the existence of negative externalities and public goods, transaction costs, and imperfect competition.

A. Lack of Property Rights

Markets will not function at all (let alone efficiently) if property rights are substantially uncertain. What rational buyer would pay a significant amount of money to a seller for some good, if the buyer could not be confident that the seller actually owned the good? Institutions to establish and protect legal title are a prerequisite to efficient market allocation.

Not only will the absence of property rights lead to allocative inefficiency, it will result in the over-exploitation of un-owned natural resources, as the biologist Garrett Hardin demonstrated in his famous 1968 article, "The Tragedy of the Commons."

"THE TRAGEDY OF THE COMMONS"
Garrett Hardin
121 Science 1243 (1968)

*   *   *

Picture a pasture open to all. It is to be expected that each herdsman will try to keep as many cattle as possible on the commons. Such an arrangement may work reasonably satisfactorily for centuries because tribal wars, poaching, and disease keep the numbers of both man and beast well below the carrying capacity of the land. Finally, however, comes the day of reckoning, that is, the day when the long-desired goal of social stability becomes a reality. At this point, the inherent logic of the commons remorselessly generates tragedy.

As a rational being, each herdsman seeks to maximize his gain. Explicitly or implicitly more or less consciously, he asks: "What is the utility *to me* of adding one more animal to my herd?" This utility has one negative and one positive component.

1) The positive component is a function of the increment of one animal. Since the herdsman receives all the proceeds from the sale of the additional animal, the positive utility is nearly +1.

2) The negative component is a function of the additional overgrazing, created by one more animal. Since, however, the effects of overgrazing are shared by all the herdsmen, the negative utility for any particular decisionmaking herdsman is only a fraction of –1.

Adding together the component partial utilities, the rational herdsman concludes that the only sensible course for him to pursue is to add another animal to his herd. And another; and another.... But this is the conclusion reached by each and every rational herdsman sharing a commons. Therein is the tragedy. Each man is locked into a system that compels him to increase his herd without limit—in a world that is limited. Ruin is the destination toward which all men rush, each pursuing his own best interest in a society that believes in the freedom of the commons. Freedom in a commons brings ruin to all....

What shall we do? We have several options. We might sell [the commons] off as private property. We might keep them as public property, but allocate the right to enter them. The allocation might be on the basis of wealth, by the use of an auction system. It might be on the basis of merit, as defined by some agreed-upon standards. It might be by lottery. Or it might be on a first-come, first-served basis, administered to long queues. These, I think, are all the reasonable possibilities. They are all objectionable. But we must choose—or acquiesce in the destruction of the commons....

What Hardin labels "The Tragedy of the Commons" is really a tragedy of "open-access" or non-ownership. His pasture is not a common-property resource, owned by one group of individuals to the exclusion of others. It is, rather, "a pasture open to all," such that no one has the right to exclude anyone else. That is the hallmark of non-property, rather than common property. However, Hardin's main point remains valid: in the absence of some ownership or regulatory control over access to and use of resources, rational self-interest will inexorably lead users to unsustainably exploit those resources. In the absence of some property system to allocate rights of access and use, markets will be unable to allocate the scarce resource among competing users, to the detriment of both economic efficiency and resource conservation. Part II of this casebook addresses the panoply of property regimes available to resolve open-access problems.

Notes and Questions

1. Can you think of other types of resources where the lack of ownership will lead to tragedy? Is privatization the answer? See Section V.A. below.

2. Hardin's theory of the "tragedy of the commons" has spawned a great deal of commentary, much of it critical. For a description of those criticisms, as well as an explanation of the important differences between "open access" (or non-property) and "common property," see, e.g. Daniel H. Cole, Pollution and Property: Comparing Ownership Institutions for Environmental Protection 8–13 (2002).

B. Externalities, Public Goods, and Congestible Goods

In the ideal market system, the effects of market transactions are confined to the market participants (buyers and sellers). In reality, however, externalities (or spillover effects) frequently occur. Externalities occur when some market activity harms or benefits third parties, who are not participants in that market activity, resulting in allocative inefficiencies. Just how externalities lead to allocative inefficiencies is more easily illustrated by example than explained. Consider a market for paper. The suppliers are paper mills and the demanders are wholesalers and retailers that sell various kinds of paper to newspaper, book, and magazine publishers, all kinds of business enterprises, schools and students, and others. In the process of producing paper, the paper mills

NEGATIVE EXTERNALITIES   [D2855]

emit both air and water pollution. That pollution constitutes a cost of production, but it is not a cost borne by the paper mills (in the absence of judicial liability or government regulation/taxation, which would internalize those costs to the mills). The pollution and its attendant costs are quite literally externalized to others downwind and downstream who happen to suffer harm as a result. For instance, the paper mills' effluents might destroy a downstream fishery and contaminate agricultural irrigation water. To the extent downstream fishers and farmers are harmed by those effluents, they are forced to bear some of the costs of paper production, even though they are not participants (suppliers or demanders) in the paper market. They involuntarily subsidize that market.

Figure 1–13a illustrates how the externalization of pollution costs from the paper market to downstream fishers and farmers leads to allocative inefficiency. The marginal private cost curve (MPC) for the paper mills does not include pollution as a cost of production. The marginal social cost curve (MSC) is the sum of the mills' private costs (MPC) plus the externalized pollution costs. The gap between the MPC and MSC curves represents the externalized pollution costs. The horizontal line (P) represents the current market price of paper, which is based on the mills' private (internalized) production costs (MPC). Note how much more paper the paper mills supply to the market at that price than they would supply to the market at a price based on total production costs (where the P line passes through the MSC curve), which are the sum of MPC plus externalized pollution costs; it is the difference between X1 and X.

Figure 1–13a   **Figure 1–13b**

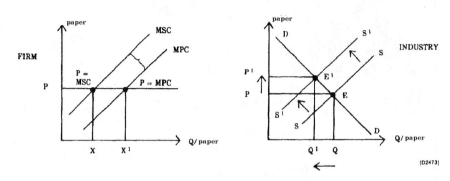

Not only do externalized pollution costs affect the quantity of paper supplied to the market, they also affect the quantity demanded, as Figure 1–13b illustrates. In that figure, the equilibrium price-quantity *appears* to be E, where the supply curve (S) meets the demand curve (D). At that point, the paper mills sell Q amount of paper at a price of P. However, S only reflects the mills' private or internalized costs of producing the paper; it does not include the pollution costs, which the mills externalized. *If* the mills were forced to internalize those pollution costs, they would figure into the mills' production costs, and would be reflected in an upward shift in the supply curve. Thus, S1 in Figure 1–13b reflects supply based on total or social costs of production, including the pollution costs. The upward shift reflects the fact that internalizing pollution costs would raise the costs to the paper mills of bringing paper to the market, and the mills would have to recoup that cost by obtaining a higher price at market. This would, of course, affect the buying decisions of paper demanders (assuming that the price-elasticity of demand for paper is fairly normal). All other things being equal, buyers will demand more paper at a lower price (P, reflecting only private production costs, *i.e.*, with pollution costs externalized) than at a higher price (P1, reflecting total or social production costs, including pollution costs). Thus, when the market price of a good is based on less than all production costs (*i.e.*, with some costs externalized), the quantity demanded is higher than it would be if all production costs were reflected in the price. When consumers are forced to pay the full price, reflecting all production costs, a reduction in the quantity demanded eventually forces producers to cut back on output. Some of the labor, capital, and natural resources that had been devoted to the production and supply of paper to the market will shift to the production and supply of other goods and services that society values more highly than the extra paper. In sum, the existence of production-cost externalities results in allocative inefficiencies by diverting resources from production of more highly valued goods and services to those goods and services that have artificially low market prices (and artificially high demand) because of the externalities.

Not all externalities are negative (costs); some are positive (benefits). If, for example, your next door neighbor plants a beautiful flower garden in her front yard, she may well create external benefits for you and other neighbors because you all may enjoy her garden without participating (as consumers) in the costs of production. In this case, the gardener could internalize the benefits by building a high wall around her garden and charging all the neighbors a small fee if they wanted to come in and enjoy the garden from the inside. In all likelihood, however, the cost of building and maintaining the wall would be greater than the value to the gardener of internalizing the positive externalities. That is to say, some externalities are probably not worth internalizing. Importantly, this can be as true for negative externalities as for positive ones.

It would be a serious mistake to presume that positive externalities pose less of a problem than negative ones for allocative efficiency. In the extreme, positive externalities are responsible for the problem of "public goods." In the economics literature, a public good is defined as a good possessing the following two attributes: (1) jointness of supply and (2) nonexcludability. "Jointness of supply" means that the supply is not reduced by consumption; one person's use of the good does not reduce the amount of the good available for others to use. "Nonexcludability" refers to the inability of owners or suppliers of the good to exclude non-payers from using the good. The provision of public goods creates positive externalities, which suppliers are unable (cost-effectively) to internalize. If they are unable to internalize enough of the benefits to cover the costs of providing the good or service to the market, they will not supply the good at all. Thus, economic theory predicts that markets will either undersupply public goods or not supply them at all, despite the fact that they are "goods" which *should* be supplied just because they are "goods," *i.e.*, they provide net social benefits.

The prototypical (if somewhat anachronistic) example of a public good is the lighthouse. Lighthouses were valuable in the days before radio, satellite and other navigation devices to keep ships from wrecking on rocky shoals as they navigated near coastal shorelines. By protecting ships and their cargos, lighthouses provided a valuable economic service. And yet private markets did not finance and build lighthouses,[e] because the service provided by lighthouses—light—was a public good: the amount of light produced by a lighthouse was not reduced by use—there

---

e. More accurately, private entrepreneurs *did* build lighthouses. *See* Ronald H. Coase, *The Lighthouse in Economics* 17 J.L. & Econ. 357 (1974). However, the lighthouses those entrepreneurs built were invariably supported by public subsidies. *See* David E. Van Zandt, *The Lessons of the Lighthouse: "Government" or "Private" Provision of Public Goods*, 22 J.Leg. Stud. 47 (1993).

was no limit to the number of ships, other than ocean congestion, that could benefit from its light—and the provider of the light could not limit the service only to ships willing to pay for the light. Once the light was "turned on," it was available for any and all ships in the area to use, whether they paid for it or not. Thus, private entrepreneurs could not rationally expect to recover from consumers the costs associated with providing the valuable light. Nevertheless, lighthouses were built, and many still exist around the world, but virtually all of them were supplied, or at least financed, by governments rather than markets.

Some natural resource amenities, such as clean air, can also be thought of as public goods, which markets will systematically under-supply.

> Imagine a socially conscious entrepreneur who sought to deal with air pollution problems private by building a plant that would supply clean air. The plant might be nothing more than a giant pollution filter, taking in dirty air and emitting clean air. It would, of course, cost something—presumably a good deal of money—to build and operate the plant. These costs might be worth bearing because the plant would be producing something of substantial economic value, namely clean air. The problem is, however, that the entrepreneur might not be able to capture enough of that economic value to compensate for the costs of providing the product. Every person within the locale of the entrepreneur's plant would benefit from having clean air to breathe…. The entrepreneur will not be able to charge everyone who uses the clean air the plant produces for the marginal value of their uses. First of all, the entrepreneur could not possibly identify everyone who benefits in a significant way from the air-filtering activity. Even if that were possible, the entrepreneur has no means of controlling who gets to use it, and thus, no way of internalizing the external benefits of this socially desirable activity. Knowing these factors, a rational entrepreneur would not build the clean air plant in the first place. For this reason, the production and protection of environmental amenities has largely been viewed throughout history as a function of governments rather than private markets.

Daniel H. Cole and Peter Z. Grossman, Principles of Law and Economics 316 (2005).

It is important to note that "public goods" are not immutably public. A good that has the characteristic of non-excludability today may, through technological innovations, become an excludable good tomorrow (or fifty years from now). Up to the middle of the nineteenth century, for example, rangelands in the Western United States had little market value because the costs of enclosing them were quite high. Consequently, the costs of privatizing and homesteading them were high. The invention of barbed wire in the 1870s greatly reduced the cost of enclosing lands, which facilitated settlement and privatization of public range-lands. Terry J. Anderson and Peter J. Hill, *The Evolution of Property*

Rights: A Study of the American West, 18 J.L. & ECON. 163 (1975). For more on the public rangelands and their settlement, *see* Chapter 5.

In addition to "public goods," externalities can also lead to problems for "congestible goods" (*see* Figure 1–14), which are goods capable of being shared at low marginal cost until a certain congestion point is reached, at which point joint consumption begins to produce substantial external costs. Yellowstone National Park is one example of a congestible good. When the Park was first created by Act of Congress in 1872, it could accommodate many users at low marginal cost; that is, the cost of providing park amenities to the thousandth user hardly exceeded, and may even have been lower (because of economies of scale) than the cost of providing park amenities to the first user. But when use reaches the congestion point, the slope of the marginal social cost curve suddenly deviates from the marginal private cost curve, becoming much steeper. At that point, individual users start to impose substantial external costs on one another. This same phenomenon occurs with oil and gas pipelines, where the marginal cost of additional use of a pipeline to transport oil and gas remains low until the capacity point is reached.

Figure 1-14   Congestible Goods

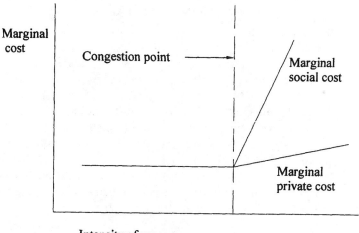

Intensity of use

C. Transaction Costs

Markets often fail to maximize allocative efficiency because of transaction costs. Transaction costs are distinct from production or opportunity costs. They include the costs of searching for market participants with whom to transact, discovering information about different goods and their various qualities and quantities, and negotiating, formalizing, monitoring, and enforcing contracts to buy or sell goods and services. Neoclassical economic theory assumed away these transaction costs, creating the mis-impression of "frictionless" markets. In the real world, of course, markets never function costlessly. It always costs something just to go to the store for a purchase or to discover information about products—for instance, how effective they are for a specific purpose the buyer has in mind—even where sellers don't affirmatively withhold information from the market. And in many circumstances, sellers and buyers each have an incentive to withhold information about the goods they exchange, in order to maintain valuable *information asymmetries*, which can advantage them in market transactions. A car dealer who sells the car with the worst auto safety record of all vehicles on the road has every reason *not* to share that information with a prospective buyer. Meanwhile, the buyer has every reason to withhold information about his poor credit record from the auto dealer.

Aside from basic information costs, negotiating market transactions, especially complex ones, can be expensive, as anyone knows who has ever hired an attorney to help negotiate and close a deal. Once a contract is signed, it costs something if one or both parties need to monitor performance and, if necessary, enforce the contract in court.

In some cases, the costs of transacting may be so high as to exceed the gains from trade, in which case an otherwise efficient market exchange will not be consummated. In other words, transaction costs can prevent markets from allocating resources to maximize social welfare.

D. Imperfect Competition

Markets may also fail to allocate goods and services efficiently due to a lack of competition within the market. In a market with only one supplier (monopoly), that supplier may be able to set prices above the efficient, competitive price-quantity equilibrium to maximize their profits. In a market with only one buyer (monopsony), that buyer may be able to set prices below that equilibrium. A monopolist, for example, will seek to set a price where the marginal revenue (MR in Figure 1–15) from the next unit sold equals the marginal cost (MC) of supplying that next unit for sale; that is, MR = MC. That is the point as which the monopolist's profits are maximized, but it is highly unlikely to be the point at which social welfare is maximized. It is rather more likely that there will be deadweight losses due to unexploited gains from trade.

PRINCIPLES OF LAW AND ECONOMICS 292 (2005)
Daniel H. Cole and Peter Z. Grossman

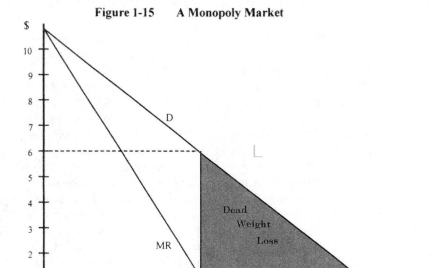

Figure 1-15   A Monopoly Market

Source: Daniel H. Cole and Peter Z. Grossman, *Principles of Law and Economics* 292, Figure 14-2 (2005).

* * * Suppose a monopolist—the sole car wash in a small town [with legal protection against entry by competitors]—knows the demand curve it faces. It can sell one car wash per day at $10. The additional revenue gained (the marginal revenue) is identical to the price and, so, at a point where demand equals one, marginal revenue and price are the same; and price and MR both intersect the demand curve at one unit. But consider what happens if the monopolist wants to sell two car washes. Going down the demand curve to two units, we see that the monopolist must lower the price, say to $9, and it must charge the same price for both washes. At that price, the total revenue would be $18, but the marginal revenue (the additional amount from the next unit) would be only $8, and so the MR curve at two car washes is $1 below the price paid by consumers [depicted on the demand curve in Figure 1–14]. The rational monopolist will choose that level of production where its marginal revenue equals the marginal cost. That is, the amount of output where the additional revenue gain is matched by the cost of production. By producing up to (but not beyond) that point, the monopolist maximizes profits. In the preceding case, let's say it costs the monopolist a constant $1 for every car wash. Then producing one wash yields $9 profit; two yields $16 (2 x $9 – $2); three, $21 (3 x $8 – $3); four, 24. Five, $25, but six, just $24 (6 x $5 = $30 – $1 x 6 = $24). These results illustrate *the basic rule* *of monopoly pricing:* choose the price and output where MR = MC. In this case, MR = $1 = MC at 5 units. Observe that at the profit-maximizing point the monopolist will produce five car washes, and the price it charges consumers will be $6 per wash.

The figure describing the monopoly market also shows the consequences of monopoly pricing for social welfare. In a competitive market, price is driven down toward marginal cost. Profitable markets that are open for entry and competition can be expected to attract new suppliers, who will increase supply relative to demand and thereby drive prices down toward the marginal costs of production. In the example, if the price were in fact equal to MC ($1) then more consumers could have purchased the product. But because the industry is a monopoly—the market is not open and competitive—they don't get the chance. The graph shows a triangle labeled "Dead Weight Loss." It represents the loss to social welfare of output that could have been, but was not, produced profitably. Resources that, in the absence of monopoly, would have been invested in this production went elsewhere; demand that could have been satisfied was not. Thus, monopoly generates market failures. Though the goods are sold in the market, the market does not efficiently allocate resources so as to achieve and maintain the proper level of production. Too little is produced, and it is sold at too high a price. Moreover, a monopolistic market of this kind is in equilibrium. It will not be made efficient by changes in demand. For a monopoly market to change, many would argue, some legal force must be exerted on it. * * *

It is somewhat misleading to refer to inefficiencies due to monopoly as "market failures" because historically most (and possibly all) monopolies, including so-called "natural monopolies" like electric utilities, were created by government regulations, that limited competition in those markets mainly by creating impassable barriers to entry. Thus, inefficiencies due to monopolies are more aptly described as "government failures," a category discussed later in this chapter. See THE END OF A NATURAL MONOPOLY: DEREGULATION AND COMPETITION IN THE ELECTRIC POWER INDUSTRY (P.Z. Grossman and Daniel H. Cole, eds., 2003) (discussing the theory of "natural monopoly" as applied to electric utilities). Nevertheless, it remains the case that markets are rarely, if ever, perfectly competitive, and to the extent they deviate from the perfect competition model of neoclassical economic theory, markets might fail to maximize allocative efficiency.

E. Equity Considerations

Economic efficiency concerns social welfare, but not the welfare of any particular individual or group. An economically efficient outcome is not necessarily a socially just or equitable outcome. Functionally, markets often fail to allocate goods and services according to some (or someone's) principles of justice. But these functional failures (if they are such) are not, technically speaking, "market failures." That phrase is an economic term of art, which refers exclusively to the inability of markets, under various conditions, to achieve allocative *efficiency*, *i.e.*, maximally efficient outcomes for society as a whole. This is not to say that goals other than efficiency are unimportant or not worth pursuing; it is only to say that economics, as a field of study, has nothing uniquely valuable to contribute to judgments about the justice of alternative distributions among the various individuals who together comprise society.

V. GOVERNMENT INTERVENTION TO CORRECT MARKET FAILURES

When the market fails to allocate resources efficiently, government intervention may or may not be economically desirable, depending on whether that intervention is likely to result in greater overall allocative efficiency. The administrative/regulatory machinery of government is costly, and once put into motion that machinery does not usually follow strict market rules of behavior. Few, if any, competitive checks exist to keep administrative/regulatory costs to a minimum; and government is always susceptible to political (*e.g.*, public choice) pressures that might hamper its efficiency.

If government intervention *is* appropriate to correct some market failure, the next question concerns the best (*i.e.*, most efficient) means of government response. The government has various options including common-law or statutory rules of liability, legislative prohibitions or restrictions, various types of regulations, taxation, government owner-ship, or some combination of these. Finally, intervention can occur at various or multiple levels of government, including local, state, regional, national, and international. The level and type of government interven-tion chosen will often depend on the type, cause, and specific circum-stances of any given market failure.

The sub-sections that follow address differential forms and levels of government intervention to deal with various *types* of market failures, including failures arising from: (A) the lack of property rights, (B) nega-tive externalities, (C) public goods, (D) transaction costs, and (E) imper-fect competition. Subsection F discusses government interventions designed *not* to improve economic efficiency but to achieve outcomes unrelated to economic goals, such as equity and social justice. Then, Section VI introduces the method of Cost–Benefit Analysis, by which government agencies can (1) assess the propriety of government inter-vention and (2) choose among different forms of intervention. Section VII adds an important caveat about government failure.

A. Lack of Property Rights

In "The Tragedy of the Commons," Garrett Hardin discusses two alternative mechanisms for avoiding the "tragedy": (1) the resource can be moved from open-access (non-property) to private ownership or (2) it can be subjected to government regulation of entry and use. Both of these solutions create property rights and duties (*i.e.*, rights and duties respecting things), where no rights and duties previously existed. *See* DANIEL H. COLE, POLLUTION AND PROPERTY: COMPARING OWNERSHIP INSTITUTIONS FOR ENVIRONMENTAL PROTECTION 7 (2002) (discussing government regulation as a mechanism for establishing property rights and duties). However, only one of these solutions actually resolves the problem that prevented the market from operating effectively in the first place. Government ownership and regulation displace the market as resource allocation mechanisms. With privatization—the establishment of private (individual or common) ownership—by contrast, the government initially allocates entitlements, and then permits the market to re-allocate those entitlements as necessary to maximize social welfare.

If private property rights could be completely specified and perfectly enforced at low cost, market failures presumably would not arise in the first place because: (a) by definition no public goods would exist–all resources and resource-amenities would be privately owned by virtue of the assumption of the low-cost specification of property rights and (b) all inefficient externalities would be internalized, by virtue of the assumption of perfect enforcement of property rights, including those rights owned by victims of externalities. The fact of the matter, however, is that privatization is *not* a solution for all sources of market failure simply because property rights are costly—sometimes too costly—to define and enforce. *See* Ronald H. Coase, *The Problem of Social Cost*, 3 J.L. & ECON. 1 (1960); YORAM BARZEL, ECONOMIC ANALYSIS OF PROPERTY RIGHTS 64 (1989). (Imagine the cost, for example, of privatizing the earth's atmosphere.) Such rights cannot be completely—specified and perfectly—enforced at any finite price. Consequently, externalities and public goods still present substantial threats to market performance, sometimes requiring alternative (if second-best) remedies. *But see, e.g.*, TERRY L. ANDERSON AND DONALD R. LEAL, FREE–MARKET ENVIRONMENTALISM (1991) (presenting a somewhat Utopian argument in favor of complete privatization as a solution to environmental and resource conservation problems).

B. Negative Externalities

When market failures result from negative externalities, governments have two options: they can act to internalize the externalities or do nothing (thereby leaving the externalities in place, along with the consequent market failure). From an economic point of view, the government should take no action to internalize an externality whenever the total social costs of internalization would exceed the total social benefits of internalization. It is clear that governments do not act to internalize all externalities and, although there is no necessary relation between the size and scope of an externality and the likelihood of government intervention, it seems more likely that government would intervene to internalize more significant, rather than less significant, externalities.

If the government chooses to act to internalize the externalities, it has three basic categories of actions to choose from: liability rules (enforced mainly in the judicial system), regulation, or taxes. Each of these categories includes two or more subcategories.

1. Common Law and Statutory Liability for Externalities

Common-law actions, such as nuisance and trespass, provide one means by which persons harmed by certain negative externalities, such as pollution costs, can internalize those costs to those who produced them through a judicial determination of liability and compensation for damages. Some statutes, such as the Comprehensive Environmental Response, Compensation, and Liability Act (CERCLA, *a.k.a.* the "Superfund" law) also impose liability on polluters.

Common-law remedies provide a minimal level of government intervention in the marketplace. The judicial machinery is set in motion by private market actors, seeking to protect their rights under established legal regimes. However, liability rules cannot effectively internalize all inefficient externalities. In the first place, they only effectively internalize externalities of those who suffer quantifiable harm, *and* are able to state a claim under the relevant common-law or statutory rule. For example, to sue in nuisance or trespass, the party must be able to claim a harm to property they own; non-owners—including mere visitors, renters as well homeless people—are not protected by those common-law remedies. Even property owners may have difficulty proving that the defendant actually caused the harm, and that the harm was "unreasonable." Causation is especially problematic if long distances or time lags exist between the production of the externality and the manifestation of harm. If a plaintiff cannot prove causation and unreasonable harm, her claim will fail, and the externality will not be internalized. In addition, the administrative costs associated with using the court system may be prohibitive in some cases, especially where the extent of the harm to any particular plaintiff is small but widely disseminated among many potential plaintiffs. There is also the problem of correctly estimating damages. If a court over- or under-estimates damages, it can internalize too many or too few costs, resulting either way in inefficiencies.

Despite their manifest disadvantages, common-law and statutory liability rules can create efficient incentives for producers to minimize externalities up to the point where the marginal cost of avoiding the next unit of externality equals the marginal benefit (measured by the reduction in expected liability, which is equal to the probability times the harm from some potential tort). The greater the probability and extent of liability, the more precaution producers presumably will take to minimize negative externalities in the first place (all other things being equal). The extensive liabilities imposed on Exxon for the 1989 Exxon–Valdez oil spill, for example, created an incentive for shipowners to take greater precautions to prevent oil spills, such as converting their fleets to double hulled tankers, which contain or minimize spills in the event of a wreck. Shipbuilders did in fact begin producing double hulled vessels, but because of the high costs of such vessels, demand was ultimately driven by United States' legislation (the Oil Pollution Act of 1990) and International Maritime Organization guidelines.

2. *Regulatory Responses to Market Failure*

Liability rules operate *after* the fact of harm to internalize negative externalities and create incentives to reduce future production of negative externalities. Another option is for government to control or internalize externalities *before* they occur by regulating their production. If the government decides to regulate either instead of, or in addition to, some liability regime, it has numerous regulatory methods to choose from, including design standards (technology-based standards), performance standards (emissions limitations or non-tradeable quotas), cap-and-trade schemes, product bans, information collection and disclosure rules, and environmental contracting.

Design standards require that regulated facilities be designed in such a way as to minimize harmful externalities. For example, an environmental regulation might require the installation of "scrubbers" on power-plant smokestacks to remove sulfur dioxide or other harmful pollutants from emissions. Economists dislike design standards because they constitute a "one-size-fits-all" solution, ignoring the fact that different plants, even within the same industry, have different cost-structures for minimizing external costs. It may, for example, cost one firm $10 million to comply with a certain design standard, while it costs another $100 million to comply with the same standard. The regulation consequently gives the first firm an unearned market advantage over the second, and society as a whole ends up paying more than is necessary to achieve a certain level of reduction in negative externalities.

Performance standards do not explicitly require regulated facilities to introduce any particular means of reducing negative externalities but merely establish targets—pollution-reduction goals or emissions quotas—that the plants must meet. A water pollution control regulation might, for example, require regulated facilities to reduce their effluent of a certain pollutant by, say, 50 percent by some deadline. Unlike the design standard, the performance standard does not dictate *how* the plants are to achieve that reduction. (However, in some cases the target itself will be based on the government's assessment of what can be achieved through the installation of certain technology, in which case the performance standard is really a design standard in disguise.) Economists generally prefer a (true) performance standard to a design standard, but still consider it relatively unwieldy and overly-expensive compared to other regulatory options because all regulated firms still must achieve the same level reduction in externalities, despite differential costs of reducing emissions.

Cap-and-trade schemes are similar to performance standards in that they establish emission reduction targets, but unlike performance standards they reduce compliance costs by authorizing firms to buy or sell units of their quotas; that is, firms are allowed to increase or decrease the size of their quotas through market trading. Assume that two producers, A and B, both produce pollution that creates significant external costs. Before regulation, A emits 100 tons per day (tpd) of pollution and B produces 50 tpd. The regulation establishes initial quota limits at 50 percent of pre-regulation emissions, so that A must reduce its emissions to 50 tpd and B must reduce its emissions to 25 tpd. So far, this is just a performance standard. Further assume that A is able to reduce its emissions at a constant rate of $100 per ton, while B can reduce its emissions at a constant rate of $1,000 per ton. Thus, under a non-tradeable quota (performance standard), it would cost A $5,000 to reduce its emissions from 100 tpd to the quota limit of 50 tpd, and B would have to pay $25,000 to reduce its emissions from 50 tpd to 25 tpd. The total costs of compliance with the performance standard would be $30,000 ($5,000 + $25,000). This is where the trade part of cap-and-trade comes into play. Because the regulation allows A and B to trade units of their emissions quotas in the market, they should be able to reduce total compliance costs. Source A should be willing to reduce its emissions beyond its quota limit, and sell unused units of emissions to source B, for some price above $100 per ton; and source B should be willing to buy emissions units from source A, instead of reducing its own emissions, at some price below $1000 per ton. In the absence of significant transaction costs, economists would predict that source A would end up reducing its emissions from 100 tpd to 25 tpd, at a total cost of $7,500; source B would not reduce its emissions at all, but instead would pay source A for 25 tpd to raise its quota to equal its pre-regulation emission rate. The amount source B would pay source A would be somewhere between $100 per ton and $1000 per ton. Let's assume that the sources agree upon a price of $500 per ton, so that source B would pay source A $12,500 to reduce emissions by an additional 25 tons per day. Those reductions would cost source A $2,500, leaving source A with a $10,000 profit on the transaction. Source B would benefit from the transaction as well because the transaction would raise its quota limit from 25 tpd up to 50 tpd, relieving source B of any emissions reduction requirements. As a consequence, source B saves $12,500 (the $25,000 it would have cost to reduce its own emissions less the $12,500 it paid for emissions reductions at source A). So, both sources are better off as a result of the trade (which otherwise they would not have undertaken), and society is better off as well. It realizes the same amount of total pollution (externality) reduction, but at much lower social cost—$10,000 with tradable quotas, as compared to $30,000 under a non-tradable quota system. Source A actually realizes a compliance *benefit* of $2,500 from the cap-and-trade program; its $7,500 in emissions reduction costs are more than offset by the $10,000 profit it earns from selling unused emissions credits to Source B, which has a compliance cost of $12,500. $12,500 – $2,500 = social compliance costs of $10,000.

Compliance-cost savings are the reason economists generally prefer cap-and-trade regulations to either performance or design standards.

However, cap-and-trade schemes are not invariably more efficient than other forms of regulation. *See* Daniel H. Cole and Peter Z. Grossman, *When is Command-and-Control Efficient? Institutions, Technology, and the Comparative Efficiency of Alternative Regulatory Regimes for Environmental Protection*, 1999 WISC. L.REV. 887; Daniel H. Cole and Peter Z. Grossman, *Toward a Total–Cost Approach to Environmental Instrument Choice*, in AN INTRODUCTION TO THE LAW AND ECONOMICS OF ENVIRONMENTAL POLICY: ISSUES IN INSTITUTIONAL DESIGN, 20 RES. L. & ECON. 223 (T. Swanson ed., 2002). Cap-and-trade schemes have been successfully used in the United States to reduce sulfur dioxide emissions from power plants at far lower cost than under traditional design or performance standards. *See, e.g.,* PAUL L. JOSKOW, A. DANNY ELLERMAN, JUAN–PABLO MONTERO, RICHARD SCHMALENSEE, AND ELIZABETH M. BAILEY, MARKETS FOR CLEAN AIR: THE U.S. ACID RAIN PROGRAM (2000). In addition, tradable quotas have been used successfully to conserve fisheries.

Until the early 1980s, most fisheries were either completely unmanaged or managed under command-and-control regulations that governed the size of vessels, types of nets, season length, and which areas are open to fishing. Such regulations fail to check the number of vessels or the level of fishing effort, and they encourage fishermen to work around equipment constraints. Under these regulations, a fisherman has no sense of ownership over the fish until they are caught. This creates a race to fish, and the historical record shows that the race will continue until fish stocks are depleted and the number and types of vessels in a fishery exceeds its viable capacity.

Individual transferable quota (ITQ) systems are a promising means to correct this market failure. They limit fishing operations by setting a total allowable catch (TAC), which is typically allocated in perpetuity to fishing participants based on historical catch. Because fishermen have access to a guaranteed share of the TAC, this approach significantly reduces incentives to engage in a race to fish. In addition, when transferability of the shares is permitted, the least efficient vessels will find it more profitable to sell their quotas rather than fish them. Over time, this should both reduce excess capacity and increase the efficiency of vessels operating in the fishery.

See, e.g., Richard G. Newell, James N. Sanchirico, and Suzi Kerr, Fishing Quota Markets, Resources for the Future Discussion Paper 02–20 (June 2002).

Prohibitions or Product Bans. One extreme method of eliminating the negative externalities from a certain production process is to shut down that process by banning the product from the market. This option entails sizeable social costs. By banning a useful product, the regulation is likely to generate deadweight losses due to unexploited gains from trade. Consequently, bans are seldom imposed. But there have been a few exceptional cases. For example, in 1972 the U.S. Environmental

Protection Agency (EPA) banned the domestic sale and use of the pesticide DDT (Dichloro-diphenyl-trichloroethane) because of a perceived threat to bird populations and aquatic ecosystems. In 1992, the EPA announced a four-year phase-out of all CFCs (chlorofluorocarbons)—chemicals widely used as propellants in aerosol spray cans, insulating agents, and refrigerants—after studies showed that CFCs were causing substantial damage to the stratospheric ozone layer, which protects the earth from the Sun's ultraviolet radiation. The EPA's ban was in accordance with international obligations under the 1987 Montreal Protocol on Substances that Deplete the Ozone Layer. Bans have also been used to protect natural resources from externalities. For example, a 1980 law expanding and consolidating the Arctic National Wildlife Refuge (ANWR) in Alaska (Alaska National Interest Lands Conservation Act, 16 U.S.C.A. § 3143) banned oil and gas development in the Refuge *except* with the express authorization of Congress. Despite more or less constant efforts to obtain congressional acquiescence to oil and gas development within ANWR, the ban has remained in place (as of the time this book went to press). One interesting point about all these bans is that their costs were fairly low. By the time DDT was banned in 1972, the US agricultural chemical industry was already producing useful, affordable, and safer substitutes; the same was true for the 1992–1996 phase-out of CFCs. As for ANWR, it is questionable whether any oil production would have taken place there had Congress lifted the ban on oil production in the 1980's or 1990's because of the high costs of extraction relative to the market price of oil. Even now, according to a 2001 study by the Congressional Research Service, any decline in the market price of oil due to production at ANWR is likely to be "modest and temporary." Bernard A. Gelb, ANWR Development: Economic Impacts, CRS Report for Congress, RS21030 CRS–5 (Update Dec. 3, 2001). Even if the social costs of banning DDT, CFCs, and oil development in ANWR were modest, product bans generally remain disfavored by economists.

Information collection and disclosure rules. Along with cap-and-trade schemes, economists generally prefer information collection and disclosure rules to other types of regulations mainly because they tend to have lower compliance costs and they are perceived to interfere less with market decisions. Information collection and disclosure rules can even enhance market efficiency. Information-based regulations are generally employed for two distinct purposes: (1) they provide information to regulators to ensure compliance with and enforcement of substantive regulations (design standards, performance standards, or cap-and-trade schemes); or (2) the publication of information itself can ameliorate market failures, especially to the extent that externalities arise from inefficient information asymmetries. The first purpose is served by the kind of reporting and record-keeping requirements that are found in virtually every environmental protection statute (or in subsidiary regulations). For example, § 517(b) of the Surface Mining Control and Reclamation Act (SMCRA, 30 U.S.C.A. § 1267(b)) requires regulated mining operations to:

(a) establish and maintain appropriate records, (b) make monthly reports to the regulatory authority, (c) install, use, and maintain any necessary monitoring equipment or methods, (d) evaluate results in accordance with such methods, at such locations, intervals, and in such a manner as a regulatory authority shall prescribe, and (e) provide such other information relative to surface coal mining and reclamation operations as the regulatory authority deems reasonable and necessary.

The regulated mining operations must also make "copies of any records, reports, inspection materials or information obtained under this subchapter ... immediately available to the public at central and sufficient locations in the county, multicounty, and State area of mining so that they are conveniently available to residents in the areas of mining." 30 U.S.C.A. § 1267(f). This last provision not only facilitates possible enforcement of SMCRA through citizen suits under § 520 (30 U.S.C.A. § 1270) of the Act.

In addition, the section requiring publication of monitoring and other information serves the second purpose of information-based regulation, which is to *inform the market* of a mine's noncompliance (*i.e.*, illegal activity). Studies indicate that consumers respond to negative publicity about companies in their buying decisions, which in turn affects prices and the profitability of firms subject to negative publicity. In the area of environmental protection, this phenomenon is referred to as "green consumerism." *See, e.g.*, Peter Menell, *Environmental Federalism: Structuring a Market–Oriented Federal Eco–Information Policy*, 54 MD. L.REV. 1435 (1995). Simply by providing information to the public about the externalities created by polluters, for example, the government is able to affect polluter behavior.

Green Consumerism

The causes and effects of "green consumerism" are not yet precisely known. *See* Tom Tietenberg, *Disclosure Strategies for Pollution Control*, 11 ENVTL. & RESOURCE ECON. 587, 599 (1998) ("The research to date is sufficiently sketchy and incomplete that it is not yet possible to draw firm conclusions about the efficient niche for disclosure strategies in the wider realm of environmental policy."). But there is some empirical evidence that disclosure requirements effect companies' market performance. For example, studies indicate that laws requiring public disclosure of pollution releases (pursuant, for example, to the US Toxic Release Inventory or TRI[f]), including releases of pollutants that are not subject to direct regulation, affect the stock prices of polluters, inducing them to reduce pollution releases. *See* David W. Case, *The Law and Economics of Environmental Information as Regulation*, 31 ELR 10773 (July 2001) (assessing various empirical and theoretical studies of the effects

---

f. The TRI was established in the Emergency Planning and Community Right-to-Know Act of 1986, 42 U.S.C.A. §§ 11021 to 11023. TRI data are freely available on the EPA's website: http://www.epa.gov/tri/tridata/index.htm.

of environmental information disclosure rules); Bradley Karkkainen, *Information as Environmental Regulation: TRI and Performance Benchmarking, Precursor to a New Paradigm*, 89 Geo. L.J. 257, 260 n. 7 (2001) (discussing economic studies finding a positive relation between disclosure requirements, stock prices, and subsequent emissions reductions); Werner Antweiler and Kathryn Harrison, *Toxic Release Inventories and Green Consumerism: Empirical Evidence from Canada*, 36 Can. J.Econ. 495 (2003); Shameek Konar and Mark A. Cohen, *Does the Market Value Environmental Performance?*, 83 Rev. Econ. & Stat. 281 (2001). Between 1986, when the TRI was established, and 1998 toxic releases declined by an estimated 44 percent. Tietenberg, *supra*, at 593 (1998). The Securities and Exchange Commission now requires all listed companies to report on their environmental liabilities. *See, e.g.*, Robert H. Feller, *Environmental Disclosure Under the Securities Laws*, 22 B.C. Envtl. Affairs L.Rev. 225 (1995).[g]

Environmental contracting. Governments sometimes enter into agreements with firms in which the firms agree to "voluntarily" reduce their emissions by a certain amount. In exchange, the government promises not to impose additional regulatory burdens on the firms for a certain period of time. Such agreements are quite common in several European countries, but less common in the United States. A few US programs, however, have relied on voluntary or contract-based pollution reductions. For example, the EPA's 33/50 program achieved a 33 percent reduction in releases of 17 toxic chemicals by 1992 (from a 1988 baseline), and 50 percent reduction by 1995 through "voluntary partnerships" with nearly 1,300 companies. *See* U.S. Environmental Protection Agency, Office of Pollution Prevention and Toxics, 33/50 Program: The Final Record, EPA 745–R–99–004 (March 1999). However, it is unclear to what extent the "voluntary" reductions may have been spurred by information disclosure requirements discussed earlier. Also, all such "voluntary" environmental contracts are negotiated in the shadow of potential regulation. It is unclear to what extent environmental contracting would occur without that looming threat to act as an inducement. Nevertheless, economists believe that voluntarily negotiated environmental contracts are likely to be substantially more efficient than coercive regulations.

3. *Tax–Based Responses to Market Failure*

Instead of directly regulating firm behavior to reduce or eliminate negative externalities, governments can simply impose a tax, which (if set correctly) should internalize negative externalities. Economists tend to prefer tax-based cost internalization to regulation-based cost-

---

g. However, a recent GAO report raises doubts about the effectiveness of current SEC rules, and promotes more detailed disclosure rules and enforcement of those rules. U.S. General Accounting Office, Report to Congressional Requesters, Environmental Disclosure: SEC Should Explore Ways to Improve Tracking and Transparency of Information, GAO–04–808 (July 2004).

internalization, although as a matter of economic theory there is no reason for such a preference. As Martin Weitzman explained in his seminal
article "Prices vs. Quantities":[h]

> When quantities are employed as planning instruments, the basic
> operating rules from the centre take the form of quotas, targets, or
> commands to produce a certain level of output. With prices as
> instruments, the rules specify either explicitly or implicitly that
> profits are to be maximized at the given parametric prices. Now a
> basic theme of resource allocation theory emphasizes the close con-
> nection between these two modes of control. No matter how one type
> of planning instrument is fixed, there is always a corresponding way
> to set the other which achieves the same result when implemented.
> From a strictly theoretical point of view there is really nothing to
> recommend one mode of control over the other. This notwithstand-
> ing, I think it is a fair generalization to say that the average econo-
> mist in the Western marginalist tradition has at least a vague pref-
> erence toward indirect control by prices, just as the typical non-
> economist leans toward the direct regulation of quantities.

Martin Weitzman, *Prices vs. Quantities*, 41 REV. ECON. STUD. 477, 477
(Oct. 1974).

Put simply, a chief effect for the firm of a regulation is to increase the
costs of production, which makes the regulation equivalent to a tax
assessed at a certain rate. This does not mean, however, that there is no
difference *in practice* between taxes and regulations, nor does it mean
that the choice is always made in accordance with economic principles.

Should a government decide to internalize externalities with a tax
it has many different types of taxes from which to choose, including
input taxes (such as a tax on the quantity of carbon in fuels), output
taxes (such as pollution emissions fees), excise taxes (such as gasoline
taxes), and deposit-refund schemes (*e.g.*, for reusable bottles). Whichever
kind of tax the government decides to use, the starting point is always
the same: set a tax rate per unit of input, output, value added, and so on,
or a schedule of tax rates (as with the graduated U.S. income tax).

If the tax is designed purely to internalize externalities, the tax rate
should be set to equal the value of externalized costs. That, however, is
more easily said than done. If the tax is set too low, externalities may
remain and the allocative inefficiency (market failure) may persist. If
the tax is set too high, all externalities will be internalized, but the tax
will result in deadweight losses from unrealized gains from trade. The
government can, of course, alter a tax rate that it discovers is set either
too low or too high. But if the rate of cost externalization is not constant,
then the government will only rarely and fleetingly attain the efficient
level of taxation.

h.   Although Weitzman's article is generally considered the *locus classicus* on this
issue, his analysis has recently been challenged. *See* Louis Kaplow and Steven Shavell, *On the Superiority of Corrective Taxes to
Quantity Regulation*, 4 AMER. L. & ECON.
REV. 1 (2002).

After the government sets the tax rate, it must then assess taxes based on monitoring of inputs, outputs, or quantities purchased. Some types of activities are more easily monitored than others. For example, it is fairly easy for the government to monitor income for purposes of income taxation because employees and employers both report on salaries and their interests are not aligned. It is in the interest of employees to understate their income so as to avoid paying taxes; but it is the interest of employers to overstate salary levels because the salaries they pay are deductible as business expenses. The IRS can use the employer's tax statement to ensure that an employee is declaring the right amount of taxable income, and it can use employees' tax returns to ensure that the employer is not overstating its employment-related expenses. Thus, monitoring for income taxes is fairly straightforward.

Monitoring for purposes of collecting pollution emission taxes, by contrast, is substantially more complicated. The government must either be able to monitor the amount of sulfur dioxide (or other air pollutant) leaving the smokestack of each tax-paying polluter, or it must rely on notoriously unreliable firm self-monitoring. Monitoring equipment is both expensive and fallible, but it is crucial for accurately assessing taxes. As with the setting of the tax rate, if tax assessments are too high, they could result in inefficient deadweight losses; if they are too low, they will fail to correct the market failure.

Deposit-refund schemes are refundable taxes. For example, the state might charge a 5 cent or 10 cent excise tax on the price of all bottled beverages. That tax is, however, refunded if the customer later returns the empty bottle for recycling or proper disposal. The deposit (tax) initially raises the cost to the consumer of purchasing the bottled beverage, and creates a positive incentive for returning the bottle. If the customer does not return the bottle, the tax remains as a price of improper disposal.

The effectiveness of taxes designed to internalize externalities varies greatly. The rates of most environmental taxes are not set anywhere close to social cost level, so that they cannot effectively internalize externalities. Even if they are, in theory, intended to internalize pollution externalities by some margin, input and output taxes often seem most important to governments as sources of revenue. *See* ORGANIZATION FOR ECONOMIC COOPERATION AND DEVELOPMENT, ENVIRONMENTAL TAXES IN OECD COUNTRIES (1995).

Notes and Questions

The effectiveness of environmental tax schemes arguably is enhanced by the so-called "double dividend." Ideally, taxes should contribute to improved environmental quality in two distinct ways. First, the taxes create incentives for polluters to reduce emissions. Second, they provide revenues that the government *may* use to fund further environmental improvements. Governments are more likely to take advantage of the potential double-dividend of environmental taxes *if* those taxes are "earmarked" for environmental protection projects, rather than placed in general revenue funds. *See, e.g.,* Lawrence H. Goulder, *Environmental Policy Making in a Second–Best Setting, in* ECO-NOMICS OF THE ENVIRONMENT: SELECTED READINGS 396 (R.N. Stavins ed., 2000).

C. Public Goods

Governments have three possible responses to market failures due to the existence of a public good: (1) do nothing and suffer the social costs associated with the absence of the good, (2) provide the good themselves, *e.g.,* by asserting public ownership and control, or (3) subsidize private provision (and ownership) of the good. The first option is preferable if the costs of providing the public good (including through subsidization of private activity) would exceed the benefits stemming from providing the good. But if the public good is sufficiently valuable that the benefits of providing it outweigh the costs, then option (2) or (3) is preferable.

Chapters 6 and 8, respectively federal and state ownership, illustrate how governments have asserted ownership over certain lands and other resources in order to provide public goods such as parklands, forest reserves, wilderness areas, and wild and scenic rivers. Government subsidization of the private provision of public goods is a rarer phenomenon. As noted earlier in this chapter, governments sometimes funded private construction and operation of lighthouses. More recently, state subsidies to private landowners for conserving forested areas constitute a similar type of public funding of privately provided public goods. Under California's Forest Stewardship Program, for example, the state will bear up to 75 percent of the cost to private landowners of conserving forested areas of at least 20 acres with at least 10 percent tree cover. *See* http://ceres.ca.gov/foreststeward/html/CFIP.html.

Assume the government wants to directly provide a public good such as a flood-control dam or park. How should it finance the project? Most public goods are financed from general tax revenues. This system works best when exclusion is impossible and government wishes to make the good available to everyone. This is the case, for example, with national defense. With respect to certain congestible goods, such as parks, from which exclusion is possible, government may supplement tax-based financing with user fees or other price mechanisms. Imposing a fee on those who use the park is more equitable than requiring taxpayers, most of whom will never use the park, to foot the entire bill. In addition, user fees (or other prices) provide valuable information about the level of demand for a public good. JOSEPH J. SENECA AND MICHAEL K. TAUSSIG, ENVI-RONMENTAL ECONOMICS 276–77 (1979).

D. Transaction Costs

Realistically, market failures due to the lack of property rights, externalities, and public goods could all be boiled down to problems of transaction (including information) costs. In the absence of such costs, private actors would be able to define property rights as needed, including in public goods, to avert or resolve all inefficient externalities.

When transaction costs impede the market from attaining optimal allocative efficiency, three issues must be addressed: (1) whether the government can reduce those transaction costs; (2) how; and (3) at what cost? The marginal principle, as always, applies: the government should only act to correct market failures resulting from transaction costs up to that point where the cost of the next marginal unit of government intervention would exceed the benefits derived from it.

Governments typically provide many services that reduce the costs of transacting, including, for example, defining property rights, instituting rules regarding the formation and enforcement of contracts, and establishing independent courts for resolving disputes. Each of these government services—which are themselves in the nature of public goods—reduce the costs of impersonal exchange (transacting), and thereby increase the volume of exchange, which enlarges the social product and improves social welfare. In addition, government can often reduce transaction costs by providing information, which may otherwise be difficult (*i.e.*, costly) for private actors to obtain. For example, agricultural extension services in just about every state provide valuable information to farmers and even home gardeners about soil conditions, what crops work best in which areas, etc.

E. Imperfect Competition

Imperfect competition, which sometimes occurs within natural resources industries, can lead to allocative inefficiency because too little of the resource will be produced and sold at too high a price (see Figure 1–15, above). Assuming the propriety of government intervention in imperfectly competitive markets, what might government do to correct problems of excessive profit (monopoly rents) and inadequate output?

The suitability of any particular government action depends upon the precise form of imperfect competition. One type of monopoly is a so-called "natural monopoly." A natural monopoly is said to exist where there are pervasive economies of scale such that average cost declines over the entire range of demand. In a case such as this, one firm that produces for the entire market can always under-price any other firms that produce for only a portion of the market, which inevitably creates a monopoly. Such conditions allegedly exist in the electric utility and transportation industries, and thus it has been argued that competition would not lead to economic efficiency because one firm could provide the service at lower average cost per unit of output than multiple, competing firms. *But see* THE END OF A NATURAL MONOPOLY: DEREGULATION AND COMPETITION IN THE ELECTRIC POWER INDUSTRY (P.Z. Grossman and D.H. Cole eds., 2003) (raising doubt whether such industries ever were in fact natural monopolies). Competition in natural monopoly industries would "wastefully" duplicate fixed expenses such as railroad tracks, gas pipelines, sewers, and telephone wires.

The role of government, in the case of a natural monopoly, is to prevent the monopolist from earning excess profits from consumers by controlling prices. This goal can be achieved with varying degrees of market intervention. Most commonly, intervention comes in one of two forms: either government asserts ownership and provides the service itself, or it merely establishes price controls (rates), and allows the monopoly to continue as a private-owned—but regulated—firm. In the later case, the government may establish a state commission to protect consumers from monopoly pricing by setting maximum rates for services. This is a difficult enterprise because if rates are set too high, consumers will suffer and complain. On the other hand, if rates are set too low, the regulated firm will not obtain a fair return on invested capital (normal profit), and the quality of service will suffer. Moreover, the state commission will come under intense public-choice pressures that may well politicize its rate-making process, leading to likely government failure.

Like natural monopolies, oligopolies (a market controlled by a small group of sellers) can lead to high prices, excessive profits, and restricted supply in natural resources markets, especially if firms collude on prices and output. Government intervention may not be justified when an oligopoly is characterized only by tacit collusion, such as price leadership (as when one airline in a certain market changes its prices, and all other airlines immediately adopt the same prices). The oligopoly may (indeed, is likely to) undo itself if one firm cheats by under-pricing its product to increase market share or by trying to differentiate its product. Also, government action requires proof of collusive agreement beyond similar prices. *See* George J. Stigler, The Organization of Industry (1968); Richard A. Posner, Economic Analysis of Law 309–311 (1998) (discussing oligopoly theories).

"Cartels" are oligopolies where collusion is overt. As with all oligopolies, market failures due to cartels are likely to be only temporary because cartel members have incentives to cheat, and cheating causes the cartel to fail. However, cartels are more likely to face government correction under the antitrust laws simply because they are overt. The Sherman Anti–Trust Act of 1890 (15 U.S.C.A. § 1) forbids "contracts" and combinations in "restraint of trade." The U.S. Justice Department enforces the Act in the courts. In 1911, this legislation was responsible for breaking up the famous Standard Oil trust into 34 separate companies. *See* How Cartels Endure and How They Fail (P.Z. Grossman ed., 2004) (cartel theory).

Cartels outside the United States, such as the OPEC cartel of oil producing countries, cannot be reached by U.S. antitrust laws. Thus, U.S. government action is limited to minimizing the effects such cartels may have on the domestic economy.[i] One short-term solution, which the government has undertaken, is to buy and store oil as a "strategic"

---

i. The following discussion is derived from Thomas H. Wonnacott and Ronald J. Wonnacott, An Introduction to Microeconomics 451–563 (1982).

reserve in the event of embargoes and price increases. Long term solutions would be directed toward limiting the ability of the cartel to effectively set prices by reducing the share of the market the cartel controls. Possible long-term solutions include increased energy conservation. Government can help to induce greater energy conservation by raising energy prices or granting tax incentives for conservation measures, such as installing insulation in buildings and driving smaller, fuel-efficient cars. Another long-term solution would be to increase domestic energy production. This option is emphasized by proponents of development in the Arctic National Wildlife Refuge (ANWR). Increasing production of domestic fossil fuels could only be a partial long-term solution, however, because US demand for energy resources far outstrips known domestic reserves of energy resources. Fossil fuel production could be supplemented by development of alternative energy sources, such as biomass ethanol fuels, hydroelectric power and nuclear fission.

Oligopolies also arise due to mergers and acquisitions. There are three kinds of mergers: (1) horizontal—combining previously competitive firms (Texaco with Getty Oil in 1984), (2) vertical—merging purchasing and supply operations within a single firm (Monsanto with Seminis Seed Company), and (3) conglomerate—combining firms in unrelated activities (DuPont's takeover of Conoco Oil in 1981). If no government action is taken to control or prohibit mergers, new firms may be foreclosed from entering the industry. Large firms can afford large capital expenditures, engage in pre-emptive exploration and control mineral leases to restrict entry into the industry. They may also delay efficient resource substitution or other technology improvements. Vertical mergers can force new firms to compete on more than one level or function. Mergers may, however, present a trade-off between competition and economic efficiency, especially in industries with significant economies of scale. In such industries, large firms can better afford research and development, and will likely have pricing advantages. Thus, mergers are not *per se* signals of market failure, even though they tend (at least at the outset) to reduce market competition.

The Clayton Act of 1914 (38 Stat. 730 (1914) (codified as amended in titles 15, 18, and 29 U.S.C.A.)) and the Celler–Kefauver Antimerger Act of 1950 (15 U.S.C.A. § 18) prohibit mergers through the acquisition of a competing firm's common stock or assets. The Federal Trade Commission can enforce the Clayton Act in court—just like the Justice Department under the Sherman Anti–Trust Act—as part of its role in dealing with "unfair methods of competition" (18 U.S.C.A. § 21). Remedies for collusive oligopolistic behavior include injunctions, divestiture, treble damages in private suits, and criminal sanctions.

F. Non–Efficiency–Related Government Interventions

The market system may efficiently allocate income and wealth from transactions involving natural resources, but society may deem the results inequitable. Equity, of course, involves judgments about the distribution of resources based not on efficiency but on fairness or social justice. Economic efficiency and equity do not always diverge, but when they do, government must decide how to trade-off these separate values. If and when the government is more concerned with equity (or social justice) than efficiency, it has any number of ways of intervening in markets to achieve its aims, including regulations, prohibitions, price controls, and taxes. As a rule, such measures will reduce allocative efficiency (if not overall social welfare) in order to accomplish other social goals. Economists have little to say about such measures, aside from recognizing their efficiency-reducing effects, precisely because they are undertaken for reasons having nothing to do with efficiency. *See* STEVEN SHAVELL AND LOUIS KAPLOW, FAIRNESS VERSUS WELFARE (2002)(arguing that equity should not be a separate goal from efficiency).

VI. COST–BENEFIT ANALYSIS

Given the wide range of options for government intervention to correct various types of market failures, when and how (and how much) should the government intervene? Efficiency dictates that the government should intervene only to that point where the marginal benefits of intervention equal the marginal costs. In other words, government should act to correct market failures only to the extent that its intervention might actually improve social welfare. How do we figure out exactly what that point is? Economists recommend the technique of Cost–Benefit Analysis (CBA),[j] which agencies have long utilized in their decisionmaking processes. In fact, Executive Order 12,886 requires CBA to be incorporated in certain types of federal regulatory decisions.

CBA is the method by which the Kaldor–Hicks efficiency criteria are applied to both private and public resource allocation decisions. More simply, it is the technique by which analysts determine whether or not the benefits of some private investment or public policy exceed the costs.

The technique of CBA is deceptively simple. It involves the following five steps:

1. Identify the investment/policy options (including the option of doing nothing);

2. List the foreseeable and significant impacts of the various investment/policy options;

3. Assess costs and benefits of the various impacts;

4. Calculate the net benefits or costs (total benefits minus total costs) of each option;

5. Choose the option with the greatest net benefits or the least net costs.

None of the first three of these steps (Steps 4 and 5 are purely

---

j. In recent years, some economists have begun referring to CBA as BCA (Benefit–Cost Analysis) in the apparent belief that the technique would garner broader public support if benefits were listed first.

mechanical) is as simple as it might appear. Starting in Step 1, there sometimes seem to be an almost unlimited number of policy options for dealing with a particular issue or problem. Consequently, policy analysts often have to draw more or less arbitrary lines between policy options that are included, and others that are excluded, from CBA. Where they draw that line can conceivably bias the outcome of the CBA.

Step 2 raises the obvious problem that "foreseeable and significant" impacts may be in the eye of the beholder. Do we consider only direct and immediate impacts? What about secondary, possibly even tertiary, impacts? Suppose a state agency is deciding where to locate a new road. This decision entails certain direct costs (e.g., for labor and machinery, lost alternative opportunities for using the land to be covered by the road, etc.) and benefits (reduced travel times between locations connected by the new road, reduced traffic congestion, etc.). In addition, once built, the road will have indirect and secondary effects, as its very existence spurs development of land alongside the road and particularly at major intersections. Are such indirect, secondary effects considered as part of an overall CBA of the road construction project? As with consideration of alternative policies, the consideration of policy impacts can be over- or under-inclusive, and thereby affect the outcome of the CBA.

Such problems are relatively minor, however, compared to those raised by Step 3, in which the various impacts are valued as either costs or benefits. Typically, markets establish values for only a fraction of the costs and benefits of policies affecting natural resources. And those market prices may not capture all of the relevant costs and benefits, some of which may be either externalized from the market or simply not valued in the market. Many costs and benefits of transactions, activities or policies concerning natural resources are not priced in markets at all. Consider, for example, the costs and benefits associated with the grounding of the *Exxon Valdez* oil tanker in Prince William Sound in Alaska in 1989. The tanker spilled 11 million gallons of crude oil into a previously pristine bay.

> The cost of the lost oil was well understood. Less well understood, and far more difficult to quantify, were the costs associated with environmental harm, including an estimated 250,000 dead sea birds, 2,800 dead sea otters, 300 dead harbor seals, 250 dead bald eagles, and as many as 22 dead killer whales.... No (legal) secondary markets exist in which bald eagles or killer whales are priced. Calculating the value of such environmental costs, in the absence of market prices, is among the great challenges of environmental protection. * * *

Because many of the environmental costs of economic activities are difficult to quantify, so too are the *benefits* of regulatory measures designed to reduce environmental harm. It is relatively straightforward to calculate the costs of environmental regulations; for the most part, those costs are borne by industry and are reflected in reduced production and higher costs of goods and services. The value of benefits of environmental regulations, however, tends to be far more nebulous. * * *

DANIEL H. COLE AND PETER Z. GROSSMAN, PRINCIPLES OF LAW AND ECONOMICS 318 (2005).

Environmental economists have responded to this problem of "missing markets" by developing several methods for deriving non-market prices for non-market goods, including unpriced natural resource amenities. The methods include contingent valuation, travel-cost valuation, and hedonic pricing. Each of these methods is utilized in CBAs, but none of them are perfect surrogates for market prices; they all suffer from deficiencies, which render the "prices" they derive ambiguous as measures of value.

A. Contingent Valuation

Researchers survey individuals to determine what those individuals *would* pay for a certain amenity or benefit (such as unpolluted water) or *would* accept or require in compensation to have a certain cost (such as water pollution or the destruction of a valued amenity) imposed on them. The problem with such an approach, from a valuation perspective, is that the individuals surveyed are not required to support their stated willingness-to-pay or willingness-to-accept with actual payments or acceptance of payments. Consequently, they may be inclined to overstate the amounts they would be willing to pay to gain some benefit or demand to accept a cost. Contingent valuation estimates are systematically skewed in favor of over-valuing non-market-priced goods.

B. Travel-cost Valuation

Researchers examined how much money individuals actually pay in support of their preferences for non-priced goods. For example, to assess the value of a national park, we can look at how much individuals actually spend on the park's amenities, including how much they spend to get there. This avoids the problems associated with contingent valuation, but likely under-values non-market-priced goods by assuming that only individuals who spend something traveling to, and staying in, a certain park value that park. There is no reason to believe, however, that individuals who do not pay to visit Denali National Park in Alaska assign a zero value to that Park. Travel-cost valuations are systematically skewed in favor of under-valuing non-market-priced goods.

C. Hedonic Pricing

Individuals' preferences for certain amenities, including non-market-priced environmental amenities, are revealed to a substantial (but incomplete) extent by decisions they make in the market. For example, people will pay a premium—some additional unit of money they would otherwise not pay—for a house located near a lake or public park. That premium can be used to measure their valuation of the lake or park. Likewise, their contributions to nature conservation organizations give some indication of individuals' valuations of protecting natural areas from development. As with travel-cost valuation, the hedonic method uses actual market transactions to estimate the values of non-market-priced goods. However, it is limited in application to natural resources that bear close relationships to goods or services that *are* priced in markets, such as housing. It is less useful where there are no surrogate market prices such as for certain endangered species of plants. In addition, surrogate market prices, when they are available, are not necessarily easy to measure. Differences in housing prices can be attributed to various factors; there is no way of specifying with certainty the premium that people are willing to pay to live near parks, lakes, or other natural amenities.

In Focus: Valuing Nature's Services

Which Costs More:
Preserving a Watershed or Building a New
Wastewater Treatment Plant?

Another way of placing economic value on non-commodity natural resources is functional. Those resources provide various beneficial functions that, in their absence, would have to be performed by human technologies. For example, wetlands provide a variety of services including natural flood control and water purification. When wetlands are destroyed by land development activities, those services are lost, and must be replaced by artificial mechanisms, such as flood control levees and water purification plants. Because those artificial technologies are priced (i.e., bought and sold) in markets, we can begin to get a sense of the value of wetlands by calculating the costs of their functional substitutes.

Efforts to assess the overall economic value of "nature's services" are in a nascent stage. *See* NATURE'S SERVICES: SOCIETAL DEPENDENCE ON NATURAL ECOSYSTEMS (Gretchen Daily ed., 1997)(representing an early effort). And there is substantial controversy over what to measure and how to measure it. There are, however, at least a few clear examples of how function-based valuations of natural resources can be usefully incorporated into CBAs.

Perhaps the clearest example comes from New York City, which after a careful CBA decided that the most cost-effective method of providing clean water for its residents was to purchase and protect watershed in the Catskill Mountains, instead of building a new sewage treatment plant. A combination of federal regulation and cost realities drove New York City to this program. Under the federal Safe Drinking Water Act [42 U.S.C.A. §§ 300f to 300j–26], municipal and other water suppliers must filter their water supplies unless they can demonstrate that they have taken other steps, including watershed protection measures, that protect their customers from harmful water contamination [42 U.S.C.A. § 300g–1(b)(7)(C)(i)]. Presented with a choice between building a filtration plant and preserving the watershed, New York City easily concluded that the latter was more cost effective. New York City estimated that a filtration plant would cost between $6 billion and $8 billion to build and another $300 million annually to operate. By contrast, watershed protection efforts, which would include not only the acquisition of critical watershed lands but also a variety of other programs designed to reduce contamination sources in the watershed, would cost only about $1.5 billion. James Salzman, Barton H. Thompson, Jr., Gretchen C. Daily, *Protecting Ecosystem Services: Science, Economics, and Law*, 20 STAN. ENVTL. L.J. 309, 315–16 (2001). In another example of function-based resource/ecosystem valuation, local governments near Boston concluded that the acquisition of 8,000 acres of wetlands capable of holding approximately 50,000 acre-feet of water would provide a higher level of flood control at less cost than the construction of a $100 million system of dams and levees. *See id*. at 320; THE TRUST FOR PUBLIC LAND, THE ECONOMIC BENEFITS OF PARKS AND OPEN SPACE: HOW LAND CONSERVATION HELPS COMMUNITIES GROW SMART AND PROTECT THE BOTTOM LINE 37 (1999), *available at* http://www.tpl.org/tier3_cdl.cfm?content_item_id=1145&folder_id=727. Function-based valuations of natural resource amenities should (in theory) have the virtue of relative accuracy, compared with contingent valuation, hedonic pricing, and other methods of valuing non-market environmental goods, because the valuations are based on functions that have market-based substitutes. However, function-based valuations are obviously limited to those natural resource amenities that provide useful functions for humans. Some resource amenities may be positively valued by humans even if they provide no function at all and those amenities would remain difficult to value in dollars, no matter how useful function-based valuations ultimately become.

For more on natural resource valuations based on production functions, *see, e.g.*, GRETCHEN C. DAILY AND KATHERINE ELLISON, THE NEW ECONOMY OF NATURE: THE QUEST TO MAKE CONSERVATION PROFITABLE (2002); Gretchen C. Daily *et al.*, *The Value of Nature and the Nature of Value*, 289 SCI. 395 (2003).

D. Discounting to Present Value

As if assigning values for non-market-priced goods were not difficult enough, those values must all be specified in terms of their present value (PV), which means that analysts must *discount* future costs and benefits of the activity or policy under consideration. Future costs and benefits must be discounted because they are worth less than present day costs and benefits. They are worth less because of the time-value of money and the opportunity cost of capital. If you take a dollar today and invest it at some positive rate of interest, it will be worth more than one dollar tomorrow, a year from today, or 10 years from today. At a compound interest rate of 10 percent, a dollar *today* is worth $1.10 one year from today, $1.21 in two years, and $2.59 in ten years.[k] Thus, a dollar today is worth more than a dollar in ten years. The discount rate is simply a reverse interest rate. Thus, if you are expecting a payment of $2.59 ten years from now, it is worth $1.00 today at a *discount rate* of 10 percent.[l]

The basic idea of discounting future costs and benefits to derive present value is not particularly controversial. Indeed, we all have and use discount rates in our own daily lives.

> Consider the decision of whether to buy a special long-life, energy-saving lightbulb or a normal, incandescent lightbulb. The retail price of the normal bulb is about $1.00; the "special" bulb is priced at $7.00. Two customers, both of whom are rational economic actors, are standing in the lightbulb aisle of the hardware store, deciding which bulb to purchase. Both are aware that the special bulb is expected to last 20 times longer than the normal bulb, and will consume less electricity over its lifetime. Over two or three years, the special bulb will "pay for itself" and, as a consequence, be less expensive than the normal bulb. It will also be responsible for less pollution because it uses less electricity than the normal bulb to produce the same amount of light. Neither of the customers has any reason to believe that the bulbs differ in quality. They have identical budget constraints, preference orderings, and neither has a cash flow problem. One of the customers decides to buy the special bulb; the other buys the normal bulb. This discrepancy in buying behavior is explained by a differential in the two customers' discount rates.

DANIEL H. COLE AND PETER Z. GROSSMAN, PRINCIPLES OF LAW AND ECONOMICS 325–26 (2005). Governments, likewise, employ *social* discount rates to determine the present value of public policies.

Although the basic idea of discounting is uncontroversial, the process of *choosing* an appropriate discount rate *is* controversial mainly for two reasons. First, there is no objectively correct (or incorrect) discount rate. In the case of the lightbulb buyers, neither customer's discount rate was right or wrong. Likewise, there is no objectively right or wrong *social* discount rate for estimating the present value of public policies. Indeed, in the policy analysis literature, "[t]hose looking for guidance on the choice of a discount rate could find justification for a rate at or near

---

k. The formula for calculating compound interest is $A=P(1+r)^n$, where P is the amount of the initial investment, A is the amount, including compound interest, after the nth period, and r is the interest rate per time period. Thus, $2.59=$1.00(1+.10)^{10}$.

l. The formula for discounting is $PV=FV/(1+r)^t$, where PV is present value, FV is future value, r is the discount rate, and t is the number of time periods. Thus, the PV on $2.59 received in 10 years is $PV=2.59/(1+.10)^{10}=$1.00$.

zero, as high as 20%, and any and all values in between." Paul R. Portney and John R. Weynant, *Introduction*, in DISCOUNTING AND INTERGENERATIONAL EQUITY 4 (P. Portney and J. Wyant eds., 1999). Second, and even more importantly, the choice of one discount rate rather than another can, by itself, determine the outcome of a CBA. The difference between a 1 percent discount rate and a 20 percent discount rate is immense, especially with respect to public or private investments with future cost and benefit streams extending far into the future.

Consider a hypothetical situation in which a certain investment has high up-front costs of $1 million (present value), but provides no benefits until the 20th year. In the 20th year (and only in that year) the investment provides a benefit of $2 million. To determine whether this investment is a good idea, we need to discount to present value that $2 million received in the 20th year. Using a discount rate of 3 percent, the present value of the $2 million would be $1,107,400, which would make the investment worthwhile (PV of benefits $1,107,400 v. PV of costs of $1,000,000). However, if we substituted a 4 percent discount rate, the PV of the $2,000,000 benefit in the 20th year would be only $912,800, which would make the investment unattractive (PV of benefits of $912,800 v. PV of costs of $1,000,000).

Professor Cass Sunstein laments that:

Usually statutes are silent on the question of appropriate discount rate. In fact, I have been unable to find *any* statute that specifies a discount rate for agencies to follow. On judicial review, the question will therefore involve a claim that the agency's choice is arbitrary. Here the national government shows strikingly (and inexplicably) variable practices.... [T]he Office of Management and Budget suggests a 7% discount rate, departing from a 10% rate in the 1980s. But agencies are not bound by OMB guidelines, and they have ranged from as low as 3% (Food and Drug Administration, Department of Housing and Urban Development) to as high as 10% (EPA). In fact, the same agency sometimes endorses different discount rates for no apparent reason—with EPA, for example, selecting a 3% rate for regulation of lead-based paint as compared to 7% for regulation of drinking water and 10% for regulation of emissions from locomotives. Here government practice seems extremely erratic.

Cass R. Sunstein, *Risk and Reason: Safety, Law and the Environment* 225 (Cambridge: Cambridge University Press 2002) (footnotes omitted).

The various subjective and contestable features of CBA—choosing what policy options to include (and exclude), determining foreseeable and significant impacts (costs and benefits), assessing the values of all those impacts, and discounting future costs and benefits to present value—render CBA an imperfect and contestable tool for judging policies. That is why most economists and policy analysts do not recommend the adoption of CBA as a "decision rule" to which would determine policy/investment choices. Instead, they recommend it as *one* tool for informing policy/investment choices.

IS THERE A ROLE FOR BENEFIT–COST ANALYSIS IN ENVIRONMENTAL, HEALTH, AND SAFETY REGULATION?

Kenneth J. Arrow, Maureen L. Cropper, George C. Eads, Robert W. Hahn, Lester B. Lave, Roger G. Noll, Paul R. Portney, Milton Russell, Richard Schmalensee, V. Kerry Smith, Robert N. Stavins

272 Science 221–222 (12 April 1996)

We suggest that benefit-cost analysis has a potentially important role to play in helping inform regulatory decision-making, although it should not be the sole basis for such decision-making. We offer the following eight principles on the appropriate use of benefit-cost analysis.

1) *Benefit-cost analysis is useful for comparing the favorable and unfavorable effects of policies.* Benefit-cost analysis can help decision-makers better understand the implications of decisions by identifying and, where appropriate, quantifying the favorable and unfavorable consequences of a proposed policy change, even when information on benefits and costs, is highly uncertain. * * *

2) *Decision-makers* should not be precluded from considering the economic costs and benefits of different policies in the development of regulations. * * * Removing statutory prohibitions on the balancing of benefits and costs can help promote more efficient and effective regulation. * * *

3) *Benefit-cost analysis should be required for all major regulatory decisions.* Although the precise definition of "major" requires judgment, this general requirement should be applied to all government agencies. The scale of the benefit-cost analysis should depend on both the stakes involved and the likelihood that the resulting information will affect the ultimate decision. For example, benefit-cost analyses of policies intended to retard or halt depletion of stratospheric ozone were worthwhile because of the large stakes involved and the potential for influencing public policy.

4) *Although agencies should be required to conduct benefit-cost analyses for major decisions and to explain why they have selected actions for which reliable evidence indicates that the expected benefits are significantly less than expected costs, those agencies should not be bound by strict benefit-cost tests.* Factors other than aggregate economic benefits and costs, such as equity within and across generations, may be important in some decisions.

5) *Benefits and costs of proposed policies should be quantified wherever possible. Best estimates should be presented along with a description of the uncertainties.* In most instances, it should be possible to describe the effects of proposed policy changes in quantitative terms; however,

not all impacts can be quantified, let alone given a monetary value. Therefore, care should be taken to assure that quantitative factors do not dominate important qualitative factors in decision-making. If an agency wishes to introduce a "margin of safety" into a decision, it should do so explicitly.

* * *

6) *The more external review that regulatory analyses receive, the better they are likely to be.* Historically, the U.S. Office of Management and Budget has played a key role in reviewing selected major regulations, particularly those aimed at protecting the environment, health, and safety. Peer review of economic analyses should be used for regulations with potentially large economic impacts. Retrospective assessments of selected regulatory impact analyses should be carried out periodically.

7) *A core set of economic assumptions should be used in calculating benefits and costs. Key variables include the social discount rate, the value of reducing risks of premature death and accidents, and the values associated with other improvements in health.* It is important to be able to compare results across analyses, and a common set of economic assumptions increases the feasibility of such comparisons ... [and] improve the quality of individual analyses. A single agency should estimate a set of default values for typical benefits and costs and should develop a standard format for presenting results.

* * *

8) *Although benefit-cost analysis should focus primarily on the overall relation between benefits and costs, a good analysis will also identify important distributional consequences.* Available data often permit reliable estimation of major policy impacts on important subgroups of the population. On the other hand, environmental, health, and safety regulations are neither effective nor efficient tools for achieving redistributional goals.

Conclusion. Benefit-cost analysis can play an important role in legislative and regulatory policy debates on protecting and improving health, safety, and the natural environment. Although formal benefit-cost analysis should not be viewed as either necessary or sufficient for designing sensible public policy, it can provide an exceptionally useful framework for consistently organizing disparate information, and in this way, it can greatly improve the process and, hence, the outcome of policy analysis. If properly done, benefit-cost analysis can be of great help to agencies participating in the development of environmental, health, and safety regulations, and it can likewise be useful in evaluating agency decision-making and in shaping statutes.

Notes and Questions

1. Not all scholars agree with the conclusions of the article excerpted above, *Is There A Role For Benefit–Cost Analysis In Environmental, Health, And Safety Regulation?* Indeed, some environmentalists and scholars criticize any and all efforts to assign dollar values to non-

commodity natural resource amenities. They claim that environmental values are simply "incommensurable" with dollars. *See* FRANK ACKERMAN AND LISA HEINZERLING, PRICELESS: ON KNOWING THE PRICE OF EVERYTHING AND THE VALUE OF NOTHING (2004). How can we place a dollar value, for example, on the sea birds and ocean mammals killed by the Exxon Valdez oil spill? Or the aesthetic qualities and peace and quiet that would be lost if we were to construct roads or allow commercial logging in wilderness areas? This incommensurability claim challenges the very notion of CBA. If environmental values cannot be expressed in economic terms, CBA cannot perform any useful function. Do you agree? As Daniel Cole and Peter Grossman have pointed out, excluding environmental values from CBA could be potentially ruinous for the conservation of natural resource amenities because, all too often in the past, difficulties in estimating their economic value has resulted in their being assigned a dollar value of $0. DANIEL H. COLE AND PETER Z. GROSSMAN, PRINCIPLES OF LAW AND ECONOMICS 327 (2005). Is it better to value such amenities imperfectly than not at all? According to Cole and Grossman, unless we are willing to assign such resources infinite value (the implication is that society would be willing to spend *all* of its assets and bear every opportunity cost, no matter how high, to protect that resource from harm), then CBA becomes not only possible, but inevitable. We might conduct a formal CBA or engage in a less formal weighing of options but various costs and benefits *will* be compared, if only very roughly, because no society is willing to bankrupt itself to protect some natural resource amenity. Still, the tricky problem remains of assigning (inevitably uncertain) valuations to non-market-priced goods.

2. The authors of *Is There A Role For Benefit–Cost Analysis* claim that "both economic efficiency and intergenerational equity require that benefits and costs experienced in future years be given less weight in decision-making than those experienced today." They argue that "[t]he rate at which future benefits and costs should be discounted to present values will generally not equal the rate of return on private investment. Thus, the discount rate should be based on how individuals trade off current for future consumption." *Id.* What are the advantages and disadvantages of this approach?

3. Do you agree with recommendation #8, above, which asserts that "environmental, health, and safety regulations are neither effective nor efficient tools for achieving redistributional goals"? Do you think that CBA can identify (and maybe even rectify) disproportionate effects on discrete population groups, such as minorities, in a more effective way than governmental regulation?

4. Love it or hate it, federal rulemaking initiatives typically incorporate CBA. In fact, cost-benefit analysis is required for any major agency rule that has an annual affect of $100 million or more. *See* Exec. Order No. 12,291, 46 Fed. Reg. 13,193 (Feb. 17, 1981); Exec. Order No. 12,886, 58 Fed. Reg. 51,735, 51,736 (Oct. 4, 1993). One illustrative example is the CBA for the Clinton Roadless Rule, issued by the Depart-

ment of Agriculture in 2001 to "protect the social and ecological values and characteristics of inventoried roadless areas from road construction and reconstruction and [from] certain timber harvest activities." Special Areas, Roadless Conservation, 66 Fed. Reg. 3244, 3245 (Jan. 12, 2001). The CBA for the Rule concluded that many of the benefits of roadless area conservation were "not quantifiable," but that, on balance, benefits would outweigh costs. *Id.* at 3267. It conceded that the Rule would result in some lost opportunity costs, including diminished revenues and jobs (for example, $36 million in lost annual timber income and $128 million in oil and gas income). As for benefits, the Rule was expected to generate tourism dollars, increase the value of adjacent properties, improve air and water quality, provide undisturbed habitat for resident and migratory species, and promote scenic values and exceptional opportunities for recreation. Passive use values (*e.g.,* existence values associated with preserving biological diversity in the forests) were estimated at around $280 million in annual benefits. Regulatory Impact Analysis for the Roadless Area Conservation Rule 18 (2001), available at http://roadless.fs.fed.us/documents/feis/specrep/xria_ spec_ rpt.pdf. Preserving roadless areas would also provide savings to the federal treasury by alleviating the backlog of construction needs elsewhere in the National Forest System. Nevertheless, the Rule was reexamined when the Bush Administration took office, and it was ultimately rescinded and replaced with a final rule that allows road construction. Special Areas; State Petitions for Inventoried Roadless Area Management, 70 Fed. Reg. 25654 (May 13, 2005). Do you think that the reversal in policy turned on an assessment of economic costs and benefits, or something else entirely? The Roadless Rule is discussed in detail in Chapter 6.II.G, *supra.*

VII. EXTRA–GOVERNMENTAL INSTITUTIONS FOR AVERTING OR REDUCING MARKET FAILURES (AND THEIR FAILURES)

The existence of market failure is not an automatic justification for some government "solution" because governments fail, too. Government failures and potential non-governmental solutions are described in the next two sub-sections.

A. Government Failure

As Ronald Coase remarked, "there is no reason to suppose that governmental regulation is called for simply because the problem is not well handled by the market or the firm." Ronald H. Coase, *The Problem of Social Cost*, 3 J.L. & Econ. 1, 18 (1960). If the government's corrective device (legislation, regulation, tax scheme or subsidy) would not improve efficiency, then it should not be undertaken, and the market failure should be allowed to persist. Government should only act to correct market failures (aside from reasons of equity or social justice), when the government's "solution" is likely to enhance allocative efficiency.

There are several reasons why government "solutions" to market failures may be as or more inefficient than the market failures they are designed to correct. In the first place, the nature of the procedural constraints on government and its natural inertia make it unable to respond quickly to market problems. These constraints may weaken or even undermine its intended effect. When government is able to respond in a timely fashion, it frequently lacks the information necessary to respond appropriately, and a wrong response may be difficult to correct. *See* Jan G. Laitos, *A Leap of Faith: Some Observation's On Law's Effect Upon the Earth's Natural Resources*, 25 Am. U.L. Rev. 131 (1975).

Both the legislative and executive branches of government are highly susceptible to narrowly-focused interest groups, which can exert pressure and influence disproportionate to their number. *See* Mancur Olson, The Logic of Collective Action: Public Goods and the Theory of Groups (1971). In addition, legislators and bureaucrats often seek to advance their own interests, rather than some conception of the public interest. The legislator wants to benefit constituents to gain re-election; and bureaucrats seek to maximize their budgets and administrative turf. *See, e.g.*, James M. Buchanan and Gordon Tullock, The Calculus of Consent: Logical Foundations of Constitutional Democracy (1962); Antony Downs, Inside Bureaucracy (1993).William Niskanen, Jr., Bureaucracy and Representative Government (1971). Government, unlike market participants, is subject to no competitive checks that force it to be cost-conscious.

In some administrations, regulators may be committed environmentalists who are skeptical of the market behavior of those they are charged with regulating. In other administrations, the regulators may come from the industries they are charged with regulating. Either way, regulatory proceedings might be biased. In addition, Congress may delegate over-broad authority to administrative agencies with little subsequent oversight.

Perhaps the most economically problematic aspect of government action is crisis-oriented decisionmaking. Controversial problems tend to be avoided until there is an obvious and pressing need for action. This is particularly problematic with regard to natural resources, which require long-range planning to avert depletion and destruction. In the final analysis, one's view of the justifiable level of government intervention in the marketplace will depend on one's view of government itself: is it a market-like mechanism that simply reacts to signals of its "buyers" or does it "forge a public interest"? Peter O. Steiner, *Public Expenditure Budgeting, in* The Economics of Public Finance 248–257 (A.S. Blinder, R.M. Solow, G.F. Break, P.O. Steiner, and D. Netzer eds., 1974).

B. Extra-Governmental Institutions

When market failures arise in natural resources markets, other mechanisms besides the government can assist in resolving them. Two of the most important extra-governmental mechanisms are social norms and common property regimes.

1. Social Norms

ORDER WITHOUT LAW: HOW NEIGHBORS SETTLE DISPUTES
Robert C. Ellickson
191–206 (1991)

Whaling Norms

The practices of high-seas whalers in the pre-steamship era powerfully illustrate how nonhierarchical groups can create welfare-maximizing substantive norms. Especially during the period from 1750 to 1870, whales were an extraordinarily valuable source of oil, bone, and other products. Whalers therefore had powerful incentives to develop rules for peaceably resolving rival claims to the ownership of a whale. In *Moby-Dick*, Herman Melville explains why these norms were needed:

It frequently happens that when several ships are cruising in company, a whale may be struck by one vessel, then escape, then be finally killed and capture by another vessel.... [Or], after a weary and perilous chase and capture of a whale, the body may get loose from the ship by reason of a violent storm; and drifting far away to leeward, be retaken by a second whaler, who, in a calm, snugly tows it alongside, without risk of life or line. Thus the most vexatious and violent disputes would often arise between fishermen, were there not some written, universal, undisputed law applicable to all cases. ... [T]he American fishermen have been their own legislators and lawyers in this matter.

Melville's last sentence might prompt the inference that whalers had some sort of hierarchical trade association that established rules governing the ownership of contested whales. There is no evidence, however, that this was so. Anglo–American whaling norms seem to have emerged spontaneously over time, not from decrees handed down by either organizational or governmental authorities. In fact whalers' norms not only did not mimic the law; they *created* law. In the dozen reported Anglo–American cases in which ownership of a whole whale carcass was contested, judges regarded themselves as bound to honor whalers' usages that had been proved at trial.

The Whaling Industry

At first blush it might be thought that high-sea whalers would have been too dispersed to constitute a close-knit social group. During the industry's peak in the nineteenth century, for example, whaling ships from ports in several nations were hunting their prey in remote seas of every ocean. The international whaling community was a tight one, however, primarily because whaling ships commonly encountered one another at sea, and because whalers' home and layover ports were few, intimate, and socially interlinked. The scant evidence available suggests that whalers' norms of capture were internationally binding. * * *

Evidence of the details of actual whaling norms is fragmentary. The best sources are the court reports in which evidence of usages was admitted, especially when the contesting whalers agreed on the usage and only disputed its application. Seamen's journals, literary works such as *Moby-Dick*, and historical accounts provide additional glimpses of the rules in use.

Whalers developed three basic norms, each of which was adapted to its particular context. As will be evident, each of the three norms was sensitive to the goal of avoiding deadweight losses; each not only rewarded the ship whose crew had sunk the first harpoon but also enabled others to harvest dead or wounded whales that had seemingly been abandoned by prior hunters. All three norms were also sensitive to the problem of transaction costs. In particular, norms that bestowed on a whaling ship an exclusive right to capture tended to be shaped so as to provide relatively clear starting and ending points for the time period of that entitlement.

The fast-fish, loose-fish rule. Prior to 1800, the British whalers operating in the Greenland fishery established the norm that a claimant owned a whale, dead or alive, so long as the whale was fast–that is, physically connected by line or other device to the claimant's boat or ship. This fast-fish rule was well suited to this fishery, because the prey hunted off Greenland was the right whale. Right whales, compared with the sperm whales that later became American whalers' preferred prey, are both slow swimmers and feeble antagonists.... The fast-fish norm entitled the harpooning boat to an exclusive claim of ownership superior to that of any subsequent harpooner. If the whale happened to break free, either dead or alive, it was then regarded as a "loose fish" and was again up for grabs. Although whalers might occasionally dispute whether a whale had indeed been fast, the fast-fish rule usually provided sharp beginning and ending points for a whaler's exclusive entitlement to capture and thus promised to limit the transaction costs involved in dispute resolution. * * * In sum, the fast-fish rule was a bright-line rule that created incentives for both first pursuers of live whales and final takers of lost dead whales.

The iron-holds-the-whale rule. In fisheries where the more vigorous sperm whales predominated, whalers tended to shift away from the fast-fish rule. The fast-fish rule's main competitor—the rule that "iron holds the whale"—also provided incentives for whalers to perform the hardest part of the hunt. Stated in its broadest form, this norm conferred an exclusive right to capture upon a whaler who had first affixed a harpoon, lance, or other whaling weapon to the body of the whale. The iron-holds-the-whale rule differed from the fast-fish rule in that the weapon did not have to be connected by line or other means to the claimant. The norm-makers had to create a termination point for the exclusive right to capture, however, because it would be foolish for a Moby Dick to belong to an Ahab who had sunk an ineffectual harpoon days or years before. Whalers therefore allowed an iron to hold the whale only during the time that the claimant remained in fresh pursuit of the iron-bearing animal. * * *

American whalers tended to adopt the iron-holds-the-whale rule whenever it was a utilitarian response to how and what they hunted....

The iron-holds-the-whale rule ... was a relatively bright-line way of rewarding whoever won the race to accomplish the major feet of sinking the first harpoon into a sperm whale. It also rewarded the persistent and skillful because it conferred its benefits only so long as fresh pursuit was maintained.

* * *

Because the iron-holds-the-whale usage required determinations of the freshness of the pursuit and sometimes of the reasonableness of the time period elapsed, it was inherently more ambiguous than the fast-fish norm was. By hypothesis, this is why the whalers who pursued right whales off Greenland preferred the fast-fish rule.... According to the hypothesis, whalers switched to iron holds the whale because the rule's advantages in reducing deadweight losses outweighed its transaction-cost disadvantages.

Rules that split ownership. In a few contexts whaling norms called for the value of the carcass to be split between the first harpooner and the ultimate seizer.... An example is the New England coastal tradition of splitting a beached or floating dead whale between its killer and the person who finally finds it. The best known of the U.S. judicial decisions on whales, *Ghen v. Rich*,[m] involved a dispute over the ownership of a dead finback whale beached in eastern Cape Cod. Because finback whales are exceptionally fast swimmers, whalers of the late nineteenth century slew them from afar with bomb-lances. A finback whale killed in this way immediately sank to the bottom and typically washed up on shore some days later. The plaintiff in *Ghen* had killed the finback whale with a bomb-lance. When the whale later washed up on the beach, a stranger found it and sold it to the defendant tryworks. The trial judge held a hearing that convinced him that there existed a usage on the far reaches of Cape Cod that entitled the bomb-lancer to have the carcass of the dead animal, provided in the usual case that the lancer pay a small amount (a "reasonable salvage") to the stranger who had found the carcass on the beach. As was typical in whaling litigation, the court deferred to this norm and held the tryworks liable for damages, reasoning: "Unless it is sustained, this branch of industry much necessarily cease, for no person would engage in it if the fruits of his labor could be appropriated by any chance finder.... That the rule works well in practice is shown by the extent of the industry which has grown up under it,

---

m. 8 F. 159 (D. Mass. 1881).

and the general acquiescence of a whole community interested to dispute it."[n]

The norm enforced in *Ghen* divided ownership of a beached finback whale roughly according to the opportunity costs of the labor that the whaler and the beach-finder had expended. It thus ingeniously enabled distant and unsupervised specialized laborers with complementary skills to coordinate with one another by implicit social contract. According to the hypothesis, the remote location and small population of the far reaches of Cape Cod provided social conditions conducive to the evolution of this utilitarian solution. Local fishermen who engaged in offshore whaling apparently were able to use their informal social networks to control beachcombers who were not formally connected to the whaling industry.

The choice between entitling the ultimate seizer to a preestablished fraction of the whale ... is a typical rule/standard conundrum. "Reasonableness" standards allow consideration of the exact relative contributions of the claimants. Compared with rules, however, standards are more likely to provoke disputes about proper application. The hypothesis supposes that norm-makers, seeing that rules better reduce transaction costs and that standards better reduce deadweight losses, develop workaday norms with an eye on minimizing *total* costs.

Whaling Norms and Whaling Law

The example of the high-seas whalers illustrates, contrary to the legal-centralist view, that informal social networks are capable of creating rules that establish property rights. Whalers had little use for law or litigation. * * * The lack of litigation over whale ownership * * * is remarkable for two reasons. First, it suggests that form more than a century American whalers were able to resolve their disputes without any guidance from American courts. Second, whalers succeeded in doing this during a time period in which all British decisions on whale ownership supported norms other than the iron-holds-the-whale rule that the Americans were increasingly adopting. * * *

Were Whalers' Norms Welfare Maximizing?

Ex post explanations are less persuasive than successful ex ante predictions. An analyst armed with the hypothesis of welfare-maximizing norms would be unlikely to succeed in predicting the precise substantive whaling norms that would develop in a particular fishery. Information about costs and benefits is inevitably fuzzy, both to the norm-makers themselves and to analysts. However, an analyst could confidently identify a large set of substantive norms that would *not* be observed, such as, in the whaling case, "possession decides," "the first boat in the water," or "a reasonable prospect of capture." The contest of the three basic norms that the whalers did develop tends to support the hypothesis; all three were consistently sensitive to both productive

n. *Id.* at 162.

incentives and transaction costs and were adapted in utilitarian fashion to conditions prevailing in different fisheries. * * *

Notes and Questions

1. Professor Ellickson goes on to note that the whalers' norms may not have been *maximally* efficient, and may even have been somewhat "short-sighted," encouraging overwhaling. Indeed, he notes, "the nineteenth-century whalers in fact depleted their fisheries so rapidly that they were steadily impelled to fish in ever more remote areas." He accepts that this point might illustrate a general shortcoming of informal, as opposed to formal, legal systems of social control: "The whaling saga is thus a reminder that norms that enrich one group's members may impoverish, to a greater extent, those outside the group." As seen in the next subsection, this same problem plagues virtually all common property regimes.

2. Professor Ellickson does *not* claim that social norms are always welfare improving. As Richard McAdams has written, "[s]ometimes norms are the cure; sometimes the disease." Richard H. McAdams, *The Origin, Development, and Regulation of Norms*, 96 MICH. L. REV. 338, 397 (1997). For example, norms of racial discrimination in the United States, which persist to this day, are almost certainly inefficient; they cause deadweight losses by preventing socially productive transactions. For other examples of arguably inefficient social norms, *see, e.g.*, JAN ELSTER, THE CEMENT OF SOCIETY: A STUDY OF SOCIAL ORDER 138–51 (1989). It may even be the case that norms do not usually evolve efficiently because of transaction costs, including information costs and strategic behavior. *See* Eric A. Posner, *Law, Economics, and Efficient Norms*, 144 U. PA. L. REV. 1697 (1996). In light of the fact that social norms can be either efficient or inefficient, the interesting and as yet unanswered question is how society might inculcate and, perhaps, replicate the former while eradicating the later. *But see id.* at 1728 (noting how law can create positive inducements to violate or change inefficient norms); Robert Cooter, *Normative Failure Theory of Law*, 82 CORNELL L.REV. 947, 977–8 (1997) (asserting that law can be used to destabilize discriminatory norms).

2. Common Property Regimes

The nineteenth-century whaling norms discussed by Professor Ellickson gave rise to a kind of common property regime (CPR), defined as a legal or quasi-legal system establishing collective ownership and control over a resource or collection of resources. Many CPRs have been established by the accretion over time of social norms of behavior and inter-action, which eventually become formalized into systems of local self-governance. And like social norms, the history of CPRs is a mixed bag of both success stories that conserve resources and achieve some level of allocative efficiency over long periods of time as well as failures.

GOVERNING THE COMMONS: THE EVOLUTION OF INSTITUTIONS FOR COLLECTIVE ACTION 18–21 (1990)
Elinor Ostrom

* * * The inshore fishery at Alanya (Turkey) ... is a relatively small operation. Many of the approximately 100 local fishers operate in two- or

three-person boats using various types of nets. Half of the fishers belong to a local producers' cooperative. * * * [T]he early 1970s were the "dark ages" for Alanya. The economic viability of the fishery was threatened by two factors: First, unrestrained use of the fishery had led to hostility and, at times, violent conflict among the users. Second, competition among the fishers for the better fishing spots had increased production costs, as well as the level of uncertainty regarding the harvest potential of any particular boat.

Early in the 1970s, members of the local cooperative began experimenting with an ingenious system for allotting fishing sites to local fishers. After more than a decade of trial-and-error efforts, the rules used by the Alanya inshore fishers are as follows:

- Each September, a list of eligible fishers is prepared, consisting of all licensed fishers in Alanya, regardless of co-op membership.

- Within the area normally used by Alanya fishers, all usable fishing locations are named and listed. These sites are spaced so that the nets set in one site will not block the fish that should be available at the adjacent sites.

- These named fishing locations and their assignments are in effect from September to May.

- In September, the eligible fishers draw lots and are assigned to the named fishing locations.

- From September to January, each day each fisher moves east to the next location. After January, the fishers move west. This gives the fishers equal opportunities at the stocks that migrate from east to west between September and January and reverse their migration through the area from January to May.

The system has the effect of spacing the fishers far enough apart on the fishing grounds that the production capabilities of each site are optimized. All fishing boats also have equal chances to fish at the best spots. Resources are not wasted searching for or fighting over a site. No signs of over-capitalization are apparent.

The list of fishing locations is endorsed by each fisher and deposited with the mayor and local gendarme once a year at the time of the lottery. The process of monitoring and enforcing the system is, however, accomplished by the fishers themselves as a by-product of the incentive created by the rotation system. On a day when a given fisher is assigned one of the most productive spots, that fisher will exercise that option with certainty (leaving aside last-minute breakdowns in equipment). All other fishers can expect that the assigned fisher will be at the spot bright and early. Consequently, an effort to cheat on the system by traveling to a good spot on a day when one is assigned to a poor spot has little chance of remaining undetected. Cheating on the system will be observed by the very fishers who have rights to be in the best spots and will be willing to defend their rights using physical means if necessary.

Their rights will be supported by everyone else in the system. The others will want to ensure that their own rights will not be usurped on the days when they are assigned good sites. The few infractions that have occurred have been handled easily by the fishers at the local coffeehouse.

Although this is not a private-property system, rights to use fishing sites and duties to respect these rights are well defined. And though it is not a centralized system, national legislation that has given such cooperatives jurisdiction over "local arrangements" has been used by the cooperative officials to legitimize their role in helping to devise a workable set of rules. That local officials accept the signed agreement each year also enhances legitimacy. The actual monitoring and enforcing of the rules, however, are left to the fishers.

Central-government officials could not have crafted such a set of rules without assigning a full-time staff to work (actually fish) in the area for an extended period. Fishing sites with various economic value are commonly associated with inshore fisheries, but they are almost impossible to map without extensive on-site experience. Mapping this set of fishing sites, such that one boat's fishing activities would not reduce the migration of fish to other locations, would have been a daunting challenge had it not been for the extensive time-and-place information provided by the fishers and their willingness to experiment for a decade with various maps and systems. Alanya provides an example of a self-governed common-property arrangement in which the rules have been devised and modified by the participants themselves and also are monitored and enforced by them. * * *

Notes and Questions

1.   The success story of the Alanya common-property fishery, recounted by Professor Ostrom, is offset by the failures of other common-property fisheries, including in Turkey. The fishery at Bodrum, for example, collapsed because the fishers failed to develop effective rules for limiting entry and use. See ELINOR OSTROM, GOVERNING THE COMMONS 144–6 (1990). Similarly, farmers and others who pump groundwaters in the Southwestern United States seem to have acted against their own collective interest in obstructing efforts to limit the rate of withdrawal of dwindling groundwater supplies. See Barton H. Thompson, *Tragically Difficult: The Obstacles to Governing the Commons*, 15 STAN. ENVTL. L.J. 241, 249–53 (2000). Thus, CPRs are not always an efficient method of averting or resolving market failures and collective action problems.

2.   Because CPRs seem to fail as often as they succeed, we need a theory to explain and, hopefully, predict success and failure. In this respect, our understanding of CPRs is more advanced than our understanding of social norms because Professor Ostrom has provided a workable theory of CPR success and failure. In GOVERNING THE COMMONS she offers seven "design principles" for efficient and effective CPRs:

(1) resource boundaries and the group of users with access to the resource are both clearly defined;

(2) resource-use rules are ecologically, economically, and institutionally appropriate to the circumstances;

(3) the users have a direct stake in making and changing the rules;

(4) the users themselves (or agents accountable to them) can monitor compliance with resource-use rules at fairly low cost;

(5) the users themselves (or agents accountable to them) enforce a graduated schedule of sanctions against rule violators, based on the seriousness of the offense;

(6) conflicts among users (and officials) over rules and enforcement can be resolved at fairly low cost;

(7) external government officials recognize and respect the CPR.

If all these design principles are met, Ostrom's theory would predict that a CPR would be robust. To the extent any one of them is missing, the prospects for success diminish accordingly.

3. The seven "design principles" for successful CPRs outlined in the previous note do not explain why the fishers (or other groups of resource users) would cooperate in the first place. This is the problem identified by Professor Thompson (in Note 1 above). In response, Professor Ostrom offers several conditions, which, if met, would predict successful cooperation among resource users to create a CPR. Among the most important are that (1) the size of the group is fairly small and stable; (2) most individuals within the group must share a perception that cooperation is in their rational self interest, and social norms of trust and reciprocity predominate within the group; and (3) CPR rules and rule changes affect individuals within the group similarly.

4. Are CPRs and social norms really just the same thing? They are similar in that both evolve from the resource users themselves and from poorly understood origins. But whereas social norms may arise from either intentional cultivation or unintentional habituation, CPRs tend to be purposefully instituted to resolve collective action problems relating to open-access or congestible goods. Such CPRs may be comprised, in large measure, of social norms. But CPRs are on a larger scale, and actually constitute a kind of property system, as opposed to a simple community norm of behavior.

5. Just like social norms, CPRs may be efficient for the users themselves but inefficient for society as a whole.

There is no reason to presume that a common property regime instituted to govern a fishery, for example, will preserve related, noncommodity amenities. While fish stocks are sustained, other marine resources may be degraded or even intentionally destroyed because they have no commodity or exchange value *to the users*. A common property regime designed to preserve a local tuna fishery, for example, may be considered a "success," as conventionally defined in the literature, even if it authorizes the use of nets that decimate local dolphin populations, so long as stable tuna populations are maintained. Similarly, a common property irrigation system will be deemed a "success," so long as it effectively and efficiently provides water for member farmers, even if their irrigation activities cause pesticide run-off that harms fish populations and downstream, nonmember farmers. The criterion for success is the long-term sustainable harvest of the commodity resource *for the users*, not the general preservation of environmental amenities. * * *

DANIEL H. COLE, POLLUTION AND PROPERTY: COMPARING OWNERSHIP INSTITUTIONS FOR ENVIRONMENTAL PROTECTION 128–9 (2002). Like markets and governments, then, CPRs and social norms efficiently allocate entitlements to resources in some, but not all, circumstances. Like other social institutions, they are prone to failure.

VIII. THE IMPORTANCE OF COMPARATIVE INSTITUTIONAL ANALYSIS

In 1964, Ronald Coase wrote that all of our methods of social organization are "more or less failures." Ronald H. Coase, *Discussion: The Regulated Industries*, 54 AMER. ECON. REV. 194 (1964). Markets do not always maximize allocative efficiency, nor do governments, even when they purport to be correcting market failures. And as we have just seen, social norms and CPRs may be occasionally able to avert or resolve market failures instead of government action, but they are not always first-best solutions either. The fact of the matter is we live in a second-best world, in which we will rarely, if ever, have a chance to achieve first-best outcomes.

In this second-best world, no single institutional solution to resource allocation and collective action problems is likely to work better than the available alternatives in all circumstances. For most circumstances, perhaps, the market allocates resources about as well as we reasonably can expect. Some cases of market failure, though, might be severe enough to make governmental (public property, regulatory or tax) or extra-governmental (social norm or CPR) "solutions" preferable, even with their own manifest inefficiencies. In any case ...

> we have to bear in mind that a change in the existing system which will lead to an improvement in some decisions may well lead to a worsening of others. Furthermore we have to take into account the costs involved in operating the various social arrangements (whether it be the working of a market or of a government department), as well as the costs involved in moving to a new system. In devising and choosing among social arrangements we should have regard for the total effect.

Ronald H. Coase, *The Problem of Social Cost*, 3 J.L. & ECON. 1, 44 (1960). To that end, we should choose that means of organizing social (including economics) activities that in the circumstances is least likely to fail, or is likely to fail the least.

Chapter 2

BIODIVERSITY AND THE SUSTAINABILITY OF ECOSYSTEMS

Chapter 1 (Economics) focused on the use of natural resources as commodities to sustain human life. Natural resources are also biological and physical components of interconnected ecological systems. United States law and policy began to take note of the ecological dimension of natural resources in the 1970's when modern environmental statutes, such as the Endangered Species Act (ESA), were passed. Ecological influences became more prevalent in the 1990's when federal land management agencies warmed to the notion of "ecosystem management" as a viable approach to resource use, allocation, and conservation. One facet of ecosystem management is a concept that has been common in international legal instruments for several decades: "sustainable development."

This chapter examines ecological systems and biological diversity (known as biodiversity), as well as ecosystem management and sustainable development strategies. It begins with basic ecological principles in Section I. Five specific ecological concepts relevant to the field of natural resources law are explored in Section II: (1) the dynamic nature of ecological systems and the now-discredited myth that intact natural systems find equilibrium; (2) the importance of landscape linkages; (3) the significance of indirect effects on natural systems; (4) the influence of environmental stress on populations; and (5) the impacts of organisms (including humans) on natural systems and vice versa.[a]

The drive toward sustainable development as a means of incorporating these five ecological principles into law to govern human activities is explored in Section III, while Section IV considers whether ecosystem management and "sound science" can help us attain sustainability. The chapter concludes with a quest for an ethical or philosophical basis to support a national commitment to sustainable development. Subsequent chapters of this casebook demonstrate the ways that current law addresses (or fails to address) ecological principles.

I. ECOLOGY, ECOSYSTEMS AND ECOSYSTEM INTEGRITY

Ecology and conservation biology provide the fundamental scientific underpinnings for natural resource managers and policy-makers. In turn, natural resources law and policy are influenced by biological and ecological principles, but economic influences tend to be more pervasive, as you saw in Chapter 1. In truth, "conservation problems are inherently transdisciplinary * * * [and] must involve not only biologists, but also geographers, sociologists, economists, philosophers, lawyers, political scientists, educators, artists, and other professionals." Reed F. Noss, *Some Principles of Conservation Biology, as They Apply to Environmental Law*, 69 CHI.-KENT L. REV. 893, 895 (1994). There are common threads between the fields of ecology and of economics:

> The words ecology and economics are interestingly derived from the same Greek root *oikos*, meaning the "household". While the latter deals primarily with understanding human behavior across society's institutions and purposeful choice, ecology is the science or study of all other living organisms, their relationships with other organisms and the environment. Although ecology and economics are largely separate disciplines, many of the processes and concepts within both are quite similar including resource use, material transformation, population growth, and competition. * * * Increasingly, both the fields of ecology and economics are expanding their realms of inquiry to include aspects of the other.

a. This list was developed by Judy L. Meyer, a Professor of Ecology, in *The Dance of Nature: New Concepts in Ecology*, 69 Chi.-Kent L. Rev. 875 (1994), and is derived from a longer list by Eugene Odum in *Great Ideas In Ecology for the 1990s*, 42 BioScience 542 (1992).

Jeffrey W. White and Kristian P. Preston, *Ecological Systems*, in ECOLOGY, LAW AND ECONOMICS 25 (2d ed. 1997) (ed. Nicholas Mercuro).

A. The Basics: Ecology, Conservation Biology and Ecosystems

Ecology is the study of the interaction of organisms with both their physical environment and other organisms within the environment. EDWARD O. WILSON, THE DIVERSITY OF LIFE 396 (1999). Ecology as a field and ecosystems as an organizing concept within that field are relatively new. Ecology became recognized as a discipline unto itself in the early twentieth century, but ecology majors and advanced degrees did not become widespread in universities until much later. Eugene P. Odum, *The Emergence of Ecology as a New Discipline*, 195 SCI. 1289–93 (1977).

In Practice: Vocabulary

Adaptive management—a tool for ensuring progress toward a measurable set of goals within a broader ecosystem management strategy; an iterative process of "learning by doing."

Biological diversity (biodiversity)—the variability among living organisms and the ecological complexes of which they are part, including diversity within species, between species and of ecosystems.

Ecosystem—a unit of physical and biological organization with recognizable boundaries formed by topography, geology, soils, vegetation, and/or watersheds.

Ecosystem management—consideration, adaptation and decision-making that reflects the health and integrity of interacting components of ecosystems and their inhabitants.

Ecosystem services—the role played by organisms and physical processes in creating a healthful and productive environment, such as air and water purification and pollination.

Indicator species—species that provide a first alert system against impending environmental threats; figuratively, the "canary in the coal mine." Examples include northern spotted owls, snail darters and frogs.

Keystone species—a species that affects the abundance and survival of many other species in its community, and whose removal or addition will result in a significant shift in the community's composition and even the physical structure of the ecosystem. Examples include sea otters, beavers and gray wolves.

Species—the basic unit of classification, consisting of a population or populations of closely related organisms. In sexually reproductive

---

organisms, species refers to populations that interbreed with one another in natural conditions.

Sustainable development—development that meets the needs of the present without compromising the well-being and sustainability of future generations.

Sources

Holly Doremus, *Adaptive Management, The Endangered Species Act, and the Institutional Challenges of "New Age" Environmental Protection*, 41 Washburn L.J. 50 (2001); Judy L. Meyer, *The Dance of Nature: New Concepts in Ecology*, 69 Chi.-Kent L. Rev. 875 (1994); Reed F. Noss, *Some Principles of Conservation Biology, as They Apply to Environmental Law*, 69 CHI.-KENT L. REV. 893, 895 (1994); EDWARD O. WILSON, THE DIVERSITY OF LIFE 391–407 (1999); WORLD COMMISSION ON ENVIRONMENT AND DEVELOPMENT, OUR COMMON FUTURE 43 (1987).

Conservation biology became a distinct discipline in the late 1970's, and gained widespread recognition when the Society for Conservation Biology was founded in the mid–1980's. This discipline is a subset of ecology that focuses on biodiversity, the physical processes that contribute to biodiversity, and the sustainability of biodiversity in the face of anthropogenic disturbances. WILSON, *supra*, at 394. According to conservation biologist Reed Noss, the field "can be traced to the increasing interest of ecologists, geneticists, and other 'basic' biological scientists in conservation problems and the dissatisfaction of these scientists with wildlife management, forestry, fisheries, and other traditional natural resource disciplines." *Id.* at 894. Noss readily admits:

> A distinguishing feature of conservation biology is that it is mission oriented. Underlying any mission is a set of values. Philosophers of science now recognize that no science is value free, despite all we were taught in school about the strict objectivity of the scientific method. Conservation biology is more value-laden than most sciences because it is not concerned with knowledge for its own sake but rather is directed toward particular goals. Maintaining biodiversity is an unquestioned goal of conservation biologists.

Id. at 895.

The term "ecosystem" was first coined in 1935 by British ecologist A.G. Tansley in *The Use and Abuse of Vegetational Concepts and Terms*, 16 ECOLOGY 284 (1935). An ecosystem consists of both living and nonliving elements; it is "a functional unit of physical and biological organization" with "recognizable boundaries [and] … some degree of internal homogeneity." Odum, *supra*, at 1289–93. An ecosystem can be as large as an ocean or even an entire planet, but land managers typically look at a more moderate scale—a watershed or a forest, for example—for management purposes.

E. Odum promoted the concept of ecosystems as an organizing principle when he published his seminal textbook, *Fundamentals of Ecology*, in 1953. *See* Inge Ropke, *The Early History of Modern Ecological Economics,* 50 Eco. Economics 293, 293–314 (2004). Odum's book became "a landmark for the establishment of ecology with a systems perspective." *Id.*

> Contrary to other textbooks, the book introduced the whole before the parts, starting with the ecosystem level and proceeding with the organisms that were parts of the system. Furthermore, the description of the ecosystems included both biotic and abiotic components, using energy as the common denominator that integrated biotic and physical components.

Id.

Conservationists generally agree that "ecosystem management" is desirable for maintaining biodiversity and ecological integrity. Noss, *supra,* at 894. Ecosystem management emphasizes the ecological health and integrity of interacting components of ecosystems, including their resiliency, stability, elasticity and persistence. *See* Benjamin D. Haskell, et al., *What Is Ecosystem Health and Why Should We Worry About It?, in* ECOSYSTEM HEALTH: NEW GOALS FOR ENVIRONMENTAL MANAGEMENT 3, 4 (Robert Costanza et al. eds., 1992).

An ecosystem-based approach can be justified on at least two grounds. First, natural ecosystems have intrinsic values, worthy of protection independent of human interests. For human societies, this theory invokes an ethical obligation to protect ecological systems. "To treasure an ecological community is to see it has a good of its own—and therefore a 'health' or 'integrity'—that we should protect even when to do so does not profit us." Mark Sagoff, *Has Nature a Good of Its Own?, in* ECOSYSTEM HEALTH, *supra,* at 67, 70. This does not necessarily mean that human needs are ignored, but it elevates natural communities so that they demand consideration on their own terms.

The second argument for ecosystem management emphasizes the importance of maintaining systems that provide valuable services to humans. Ecosystem services provided by intact, functional natural resources and ecological systems include:

Proliferation of game species and beneficial non-game species

Air purification

Surface and groundwater purification

Groundwater recharge

Flood control

Food supply (through soil fertility, pollination and other ecological functions)

Pharmaceuticals

Recreational benefits

Cultural and aesthetic qualities

See James Salzman, Barton H. Thompson, Jr. and Gretchen C. Daily, *Protecting Ecosystem Services: Science, Economics, and Law*, 20 Stan. Envtl. L.J. 309 (2001); SANDRA POSTEL AND BRIAN RICHTER, RIVERS FOR LIFE 6–8, 170 (2003).

Case Study 1: The Arctic National Wildlife Refuge

Whether oil and gas development should be allowed in the Arctic National Wildlife Refuge (ANWR) is one of the most controversial issues ever to arise on our federal lands. Located in the far northeast coast of Alaska, 200 miles north of the Arctic Circle, ANWR has stimulated the interest of both preservationists and oil companies. Congress has taken steps to protect the special qualities of ANWR's coastal plain since at least 1960. Although half of the 19 million acres that comprise ANWR have since been designated as a federal wilderness area and the balance is managed as a wildlife refuge, 1.5 million acres along the coast, known as the "section 1002 lands," continue to be studied for development potential.

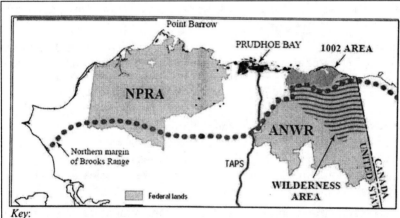

Key:
ANWR: The Arctic Wildlife Refuge
TAPS = Trans-Alaska Pipeline System
NPRA = National Petroleum Reserve - Alaska

Photo Credit: U.S. Geological Survey, Arctic National Wildlife Refuge, 1002 Area, Petroleum Assessment 1998, p.1, available at http://pubs.usgs.gov/fs/fs-0028-01/fs-0028-01.pdf.

According to federal law, one of the main purposes for the establishment of ANWR was to conserve populations of fish, wildlife, and natural habitats. Alaska National Interest Lands Conservation Act of 1980, Pub.L.No.96–487, Tit. III, 94 Stat. 2371, 2384 (1980). Oil and gas development is precluded until such time Congress decides to allow it.

The debate over the section 1002 lands has been raging for decades, and reemerges in the halls of Congress nearly every session. It involves a seemingly intractable policy conflict: should we extract oil from domestic reserves to reduce our reliance on foreign reserves and fuel our automobiles and other power needs, or should we keep this remarkable area as pristine as possible?

> Development of ANWR's oil has been approved repeatedly in the House as part of broad energy legislation, only to run into staunch opposition in the Senate from most Democrats and a handful of moderate Republicans. In 1995, an ANWR drilling provision made it into a budget measure—the same tactic now surfacing again—only to have the bill vetoed by President Clinton, an opponent to drilling. Bush strongly supports ANWR development. He argued for it in two election campaigns and made it a key part of the energy blueprint issued in 2001 by Vice President Cheney. But it is Alaska's congressional delegation's that has pushed hardest for opening the refuge as Prudhoe Bay oil production continues to dwindle.

H. Josef Hebert, *Senate Republicans Ready to Push Arctic Refuge Drilling Measure,* ENVIRONMENTAL NEWS NETWORK (Associated Press), http://www.enn.com, Mar. 2, 2005.

Numerous studies have been prepared on the extent of potential reserves underlying ANWR and the possible environmental consequences of development. According to U.S. Geological Survey estimates, there are around 10 billion barrels of recoverable oil. By comparison, the giant field at Prudhoe Bay, on the state-owned portion of the coastal plain west of ANWR, contained an estimated 11–13 billion barrels, much of which has been extracted since drilling began in the 1960's. At present, about half of our nation's oil supplies are from foreign sources, and the Bush Administration's National Energy Plan asserts that production from the Section 1002 lands "could equal 46 years of current oil imports from Iraq." National Energy Plan 5–9 (2001), *available at* www-.whitehouse.gov. But because this area has never been explored through actual drilling, estimates vary widely, and there may be far less oil underlying the Section 1002 lands. Opponents scoff at the government's optimistic appraisals, asserting that ANWR's oil would be exhausted within a few months of development.

Perspectives on the ecological attributes of ANWR vary at least as widely as the divergent opinions on potential oil reserves. Many have referred to the 1002 lands as an "American Serengeti," because of its pristine nature and diverse communities of plant and animal species. The Natural Resources Defense Council portrays it as a remarkable area that "pulse[s] with million-year-old ecological rhythms." NRDC, http://www.nrdc.org/ land/wilderness/arctic.asp. Others, however, view it as a mosquito-infested wasteland, good for nothing but oil and gas development.

Although there appear to be no endangered species that would be jeopardized by development in the area, ANWR provides essential habitat for musk ox, porcupine caribou, polar bears, migratory birds, fragile tundra plants and other rare and important species. Many of these species are protected by international treaties or bilateral agreements with

Canada. The porcupine caribou herd is an indigenous species of special concern. It relies on ANWR for breeding grounds, and in turn is relied upon by the Gwich'in, an Alaskan Native community, for physical and cultural sustenance. Yet development has been ongoing in nearby Prudhoe Bay for years, with the support of the Arctic Slope Regional Corporation, which represents the Inupiat Eskimos of Alaska.

Development appeared inevitable in the late 1980's—that is, until the wreck of the Exxon Valdez in 1989, which spilled nearly 200,000 tons of Prudhoe Bay crude in Prince William Sound. The push for drilling in ANWR was squelched for several years, while the country watched horrific news casts of oil-soaked otters, seals and sea birds. The Exxon–Valdez incident was a vivid reminder of the potentially catastrophic impacts of oil contamination from tanker accidents, as well as from leaks in the Trans–Alaska Pipeline and spills during transfer to tankers.

As is the case with many controversial environmental issues, it seems that both proponents and opponents can find some study or another to support any given point they wish to raise. The uncertainties inherent in development proposals for such a remote, untouched area, however, are extremely troubling, and the stakes are high. Oil companies claim that new technologies allow them to extract oil and gas with little environmental disruption, especially if seasonal restrictions are imposed to protect breeding and nesting activities. Yet given the controversy, "major companies have shown only modest interest. * * * ChevronTexaco, ConocoPhillips and BP, companies that have been prominent in Alaska North Slope oil development, have pulled out of Arctic Power, a pro-drilling lobbying group financed by the state of Alaska." Hebert, *supra*.

Would development in ANWR be consistent with an ecosystem based approach to resource management? Would it compromise important ecosystem services provided by ANWR? Do you think it can be accomplished in a sustainable fashion, consistent with biodiversity as well as long-term human needs? Should energy conservation be prioritized as a component of a national energy policy? Can geology, biology and other sciences give us the answers? Keep these questions in mind as you continue through the rest of this chapter. ANWR will be revisited in Section III, below, and in Chapter 6 of this book.

In Practice:
Ecological Resources for the Practitioner

There are dozens of high quality books and journals on ecology, conservation biology and sustainability. Here are a few that the authors have found useful:

Books

RICHARD PRIMACK, ESSENTIALS OF CONSERVATION BIOLOGY (2002)

FRANK GOLLEY, THE HISTORY OF THE ECOSYSTEM CONCEPT IN ECOLOGY (1996)

NATURE'S SERVICES: SOCIETAL DEPENDENCE ON NATURAL ECOSYSTEMS (GRETCHEN DAILY ED., 1997)

E.O WILSON, THE DIVERSITY OF LIFE (1992) (revised ed. 1999)

ECOSYSTEM HEALTH: NEW GOALS FOR ENVIRONMENTAL MANAGEMENT (ROBERT COSTANZA ET AL. EDS., 1992)

DANIEL BOTKIN, DISCORDANT HARMONIES: A NEW ECOLOGY FOR THE TWENTY–FIRST CENTURY (1990)

WORLD WATCH INSTITUTE, STATE OF THE WORLD (annual report on issues related to sustainable development). Information is available at http://www.worldwatch.org/.

Ecological Organizations and Journals

The Society for Conservation Biologists issues several publications pertinent to ecology and conservation biology. The Society's mission is "[t]o develop the scientific and technical means for the protection, maintenance, and restoration of life on Earth: species, ecosystems, and the processes that sustain them." http://www.conbio.org/SCB/Information/. To accomplish its goals, the Society promotes high quality research, disseminates scientific, technical, and management information, and supports collaboration between conservation biologists and other disciplines. Two key journals are:

- *Conservation in Practice,* a non-technical quarterly journal, useful for policymakers, land managers, researchers, and advocates interested in conservation matters. Editors use case-studies to provide a close-up look at successes and failures of conservation projects worldwide. Conservation in Practice, http://www.conbio.org/CIP/. Articles can be browsed by topic on the web: http://www.conbio.org/cip/browsearticles.cfm.

- *Conservation Biology*, first issued in 1987, "quickly became the most important journal dealing with the topic of biological diversity." Conservation Biology, http://www.conbio.org/SCB/Publications/ConsBio/. The journal publishes scientific papers on topics ranging from ecosystem management to genetics, as well as the human dimensions of conservation. *Id*.

The Ecological Society of America publishes research and journals useful to lawyers and policymakers. *See* ESA, www.esa.org.

- *Ecology* is its flagship journal, established in 1920. It publishes research on all aspects of ecology, "with particular emphasis on papers that develop new concepts in ecology, that test ecological theory, or that lead to an increased appreciation for the diversity of ecological phenomena." *Id*.

- *Frontiers in Ecology and the Environment* is international and interdisciplinary in scope. Although it is aimed at professional ecologists and scientists working in related disciplines, it is relevant to "all users of ecological science, including policy makers, resource managers, and educators." *Id.*

The American Institute of Biological Sciences (AIBS) "represents more than 80 professional societies and organizations with a combined membership exceeding 240,000 scientists and educators..." About AIBS, http://www.aibs.org/about-aibs.

- *BioScience*, a peer-reviewed, monthly journal edited for accessibility to researchers, educators, and students, includes articles "about the latest frontiers in biology." Recent issues have addressed ecological boundaries, protected areas, acid rain, and agricultural bioterrorism. Bioscience, http://www.aibs.org/bioscience/index.html.

B. The Law's Response to Ecological Imperatives

A concern for ecological integrity emerged as a theme in federal natural resources law in 1970 when the National Environmental Policy Act (NEPA) was enacted. 42 U.S.C. §§ 4321–4361. In NEPA, Congress declared "a national policy which will encourage productive and enjoyable harmony between man and his environment." *Id.* § 4321. As a matter of policy, NEPA strives "to promote efforts which prevent or eliminate damage to the environment and biosphere and stimulate the health and welfare of man ... [and] to enrich the understanding of the ecological systems and natural resources important to the Nation.... " *Id.* The statute's actual mandate, however, is wholly procedural. Federal agencies must prepare an environmental impact statement (EIS) for proposals for major federal action to study environmental effects and possible alternatives, but they are not required to select the most environmentally friendly alternative. Robertson v. Methow Valley Citizens Council, 490 U.S. 332, 109 S.Ct. 1835, 104 L.Ed.2d 351 (1989). *See* Chapter 4 on NEPA.

Ecosystem concerns were elevated in federal law in 1972 with the enactment of the Marine Mammal Protection Act (MMPA), 16 U.S.C. §§ 1361–1407, and again in 1973 with the enactment of the Endangered Species Act (ESA), 16 U.S.C. §§ 1531–1543. In the MMPA, Congress declared that marine mammals are resources of great aesthetic, recreational and economic significance, and that they should be protected to the greatest extent feasible commensurate with sound policies of resource management. The primary objective of the MMPA is "to maintain the health and stability of the marine ecosystem" and to sustain "optimum sustainable populations" (OSP) of marine mammals. 16 U.S.C. § 1361. OSP means "the number of animals which will result in the maximum productivity of the population or species, keeping in mind the optimum carrying capacity of the habitat and the health of the ecosystem of which they form a constituent element." *Id.* § 1362(9). To accomplish its goals, the MMPA prohibits the "take" of marine mammals, but provides little substantive protection for their habitat. *See id.* § 1372(a).

The ESA takes the theme of ecological protection a step further. It has been called " 'the most comprehensive legislation for the preservation of endangered species ever enacted by any nation.' " Babbitt v. Sweet Home Chapter of Communities for a Great Or., 515 U.S. 687, 698, 115 S.Ct. 2407, 2413, 132 L.Ed.2d 597, 611 (1995), *quoting* TVA v. Hill, 437 U.S. 153, 180, 98 S.Ct. 2279, 2294, 57 L.Ed.2d 117, 137 (1978). The ESA aims to "provide a means whereby the ecosystems upon which endangered species and threatened species depend may be conserved." 16 U.S.C. § 1531(b). Conservation includes "methods and procedures which are necessary to bring any endangered ... species ... to the point at which the measures provided.... are no longer necessary." *Id.* § 1531(3). The ESA requires that threatened and endangered species be listed solely on the basis of ecological data; economic consequences play no role in the listing decision. *Id.* § 1533(b). Listed species may not be put in jeopardy by any federal action, *id.* § 1536(b)–(c), and individual members of a listed species may not be taken by any person, *id.* § 1538(a). The ESA's prohibition against take includes habitat destruction that injures the species. *Sweet Home,* 515 U.S. at 708. *See* Chapter 15 on Wildlife.

Several of the public lands management statutes passed during the 1970's also refer to the importance of ecosystem integrity. (Public lands law is detailed in Chapter 6, below.) A key example is found in the National Forest Management Act of 1976 (NFMA), 16 U.S.C. §§ 1600–14, which governs our Nation's 190 million acres of federal forests. The lands within the National Forest System are administered pursuant to NFMA and its predecessors, the Forest Service Organic Act of 1897, 16 U.S.C. §§ 473–482, 551, and the Multiple–Use Sustained–Yield Act of 1960 (MUSYA), 16 U.S.C. §§ 528–531. The earliest federal land management statutes prioritized the sustained yield of commodities over all other considerations: "the achievement and maintenance in perpetuity of a high-level annual or regular periodic output of the various renewable resources of the national forests without impairment of the productivity of the land." 16 U.S.C. § 531(b). MUSYA added a multiple-use component to this edict, directing the management of National Forest System lands in a manner that supports watersheds, fish and wildlife, recreation, and wilderness, as well as timber and range resources. 16 U.S.C. § 528. NFMA strengthens protection for fish and wildlife by explicitly requiring regulations for the development of land and resource management plans that "provide for diversity of plant and animal communities based on the suitability and capability of the specific land area in order to meet overall multiple-use objectives.... " 16 U.S.C. § 1604(g)(3)(B). It also requires an interdisciplinary, science-based approach to planning and management "to achieve integrated consideration of physical, biological, economic and other sciences." 16 U.S.C. § 1604(b). The Forest Service is one of the leading agencies to incorporate science into its planning processes—albeit with the help of these congressional mandates to protect diversity and to utilize scientific findings. *See* 16 U.S.C. § 1604(g)(3)(C), (h) (2000); Charles F. Wilkinson, *The National Forest Management Act: The Twenty Years Behind, The Twenty Years Ahead*, 68 U. COLO. L. REV. 659, 673 (1997).

The diversity standard applies to timber harvest and all other activities that occur in the Forest System pursuant to the management plans. NFMA also requires the plans to "provide, where appropriate, to the degree practicable, for steps to be taken to preserve the diversity of tree species similar to that existing in the region controlled by the plan." 16 U.S.C. § 1604(g)(3)(B). In addition, the Act states that cutting may only occur where "soil, slope or other watershed conditions will not be irreversibly damaged." *Id.* § 1604(g)(3)(E). Harvesting must be conducted "in a manner consistent with protection of soil, watershed, fish, wildlife, recreation, and esthetic resources, and the regeneration of the timber resource." *Id.* § 1604(g)(3)(F)(v).

Congress extended the multiple-use concept to Bureau of Land Management (BLM) lands when it enacted the Federal Land Policy and Management Act of 1976 (FLPMA), 43 U.S.C. §§ 1701–1733 (2000). FLPMA unifies existing public land laws through comprehensive legislation governing a broad range of activities, and specifically governs the activities of the BLM. Like NFMA, this statute expresses a national policy that public lands be managed "on the basis of multiple use and sustained yield." 43 U.S.C. § 1701(a)(7). FLPMA has no parallel diversity provision, but it does declare, as a matter of policy, that the public lands should be managed in a manner that will protect ecological resources, *id.* § 1701(a)(8), and it directs the BLM to "give priority to the designation and protection of areas of critical environmental concern" (ACECs) in its planning processes. *Id.* § 1712(c)(3). ACECs are areas "where special management attention is required ... to protect and prevent irreparable damage to important historic, cultural, or scenic values, fish and wildlife resources or other natural systems or processes, or to protect life and safety from natural hazards." *Id.* § 1702(a).

Perhaps the strongest substantive expression of ecosystem integrity as a priority is found in the newest addition to the federal lands management statutes, the Wildlife Refuge Administration Improvement Act of 1997. The overarching mission of the system, which includes over 500 National Wildlife Refuges spanning nearly 100 million acres of land, "is to administer a national network of lands and waters for the conservation, management, and where appropriate, restoration of the fish, wildlife, and plant resources and their habitats within the United States for the benefit of present and future generations of Americans." 16 U.S.C. § 668dd(a)(2).

In administering the System, the U.S. Fish and Wildlife Service is required to—

(A) promote "the conservation of fish, wildlife, and plants, and their habitats";

(B) "ensure that the biological integrity, diversity, and environmental health of the System are maintained for the benefit of present and future generations of Americans";

(C) "contribute to the conservation of the ecosystems of the United States" * * *

16 U.S.C. § 668dd(a)(4). *See* Robert L. Fischman, *The National Wildlife Refuge System and the Hallmarks of Modern Organic Legislation,* 29 ECOLOGY L.Q. 457 (2002). Only those uses that are compatible with the purposes of the refuge system, as well as the individual enabling act for the particular refuge at issue, are allowed. 16 U.S.C. § 668dd(a)(3)(D).

The Wilderness Act, 16 U.S.C. §§ 1131–34, is also notable in terms of ecosystem protection. The United States and Canada are unique among nations worldwide for establishing and maintaining official wilderness areas. In fact, wilderness has been characterized as one of the "seven wonders" of U.S. environmental law. William H. Rodgers, Jr., *The Seven Statutory Wonders of U.S. Environmental Law: Origins and Morphology*, 27 LOY. L.A. L. REV. 1009, 1009–10 (1994). The Wilderness Act is the most preservation-oriented of the federal lands management statutes. At present, congressionally designated wilderness areas envelope 106 million acres of federal land in 44 states. ROSS W. GORTE, CONG. RESEARCH SERV., REPORT NO. RL31477, WILDERNESS: OVERVIEW AND STATISTICS 1 (2002). Although this sounds like a vast preservation system, wilderness areas constitute less than three percent of the land base in the contiguous 48 states. *Id.*

The Act declares that our nation's "increasing population, accompanied by expanding settlement and growing mechanization, [should] not occupy and modify all areas within the United States ... leaving no lands designated for preservation and protection in their natural condition ..." 16 U.S.C. § 1131(a). It defines wilderness as an "area where the earth and its community of life are untrammeled by man, where man himself is a visitor who does not remain." 16 U.S.C. § 1131(c). The Act, passed in 1964, does not explicitly mention ecological concerns, but by reserving "untrammeled" roadless lands from intensive forms of development, wilderness areas promote biodiversity and ecosystem integrity. Sandra Zellmer, *A Preservation Paradox: Political Prestidigitation and an Enduring Resource of Wildness,* 34 ENVTL. L. 1015 (2004).

Opponents of the Act argue that it places critical energy and timber resources off limits, resulting in non-optimal waste of those resources, but the facts don't bear this out. Most wilderness areas are remote, high elevation, aesthetically remarkable areas of "rock and ice," rather than wetlands, grasslands and other areas more readily accessible to development. This also means that many biologically productive but less visually spectacular areas are left out of the system. *Id.* at 1042.

Although Congress has recognized the importance of ecosystem integrity as a guiding principle, it has not necessarily made it a top priority in the implementation of our environmental and natural resources statutes. Other priorities, particularly economic ones, often take precedence, as you'll see in the following chapters. Even when ecosystem integrity is featured as a priority in any given statute, it is not always clear that Congress has given the federal agencies the proper tools to accomplish the task. This may be due, in part, to the inherent uncertainties in the field of ecology and particularly ecosystem management. Scientists are constantly making new discoveries about the implications and interactions of the innumerable variables that play a role in ecosystem function and integrity, so it's not surprising that few (if any) of our federal statutes address these variables—or scientific uncertainty, for that matter—in a comprehensive, logical way.

II. THE DYNAMIC, INTERRELATED NATURE OF NATURAL SYSTEMS

The Millennium Ecosystem Assessment of 2005, conducted by 1,300 experts from 95 countries, concluded that nearly "60 percent of the ecosystem services that support life on Earth—such as fresh water, fisheries, air and water regulation, and the regulation of regional climate, natural hazards and pests—are being degraded or used unsustainably." Millennium Ecosystem Assessment Synthesis Report, http://www.millenniumassessment.org/en/index.aspx (visited Apr. 13, 2005). It warns that the harmful consequences of ecological degradation could grow "significantly worse in the next 50 years." *Id.* Ecological mismanagement and degradation are problems that span political and social boundaries: "Any progress achieved in addressing the goals of poverty and hunger eradication, improved health, and environmental protection is unlikely to be sustained if most of the ecosystem services on which humanity relies continue to be degraded." *Id.*

The Millennium Assessment, which was launched by U.N. Secretary–General Kofi Annan in 2001, is an international program designed to meet the needs of decision makers and the public for scientific information on the consequences of ecosystem change. To understand the potential consequences of ecological processes and change, and to develop the capacity to respond and sustain ecosystems, a basic understanding of ecological systems is essential.

A. Ever–Changing Ecological Systems

1. The "Balance of Nature" Myth

A.G. Tansley, the ecologist credited with inventing the term "ecosystem," posited that "the organisms and the inorganic factors alike are [ecosystem] components ... in relatively stable dynamic equilibrium."

Meyer, *supra*, at 875–76 (citing A.G. Tansley, *The Use and Abuse of Vegetational Concepts and Terms*, 16 ECOLOGY 284, 306 (1935)). An entire generation of ecologists believed in the stability of natural systems.

THE DANCE OF NATURE: NEW CONCEPTS IN ECOLOGY

Judy L. Meyer

69 CHI.-KENT L. REV. 875 (1994)

These early ecological thinkers conceived of an ideal system that was stable, and they viewed nature as striving to achieve that ideal. In the field of plant ecology, individuals sought to identify the stable, self-perpetuating, climax community in an area and the well-defined stages leading to that climax [the terminal stage of ecological succession]. * * * Empirical data in several disciplines of ecology did not necessarily fit this classical paradigm. Natural communities were found to have multiple persistent states rather than a local climax, and there were multiple successional pathways—that is, several ways of getting there. Ecologists recognized that terrestrial and aquatic ecosystems in nature were frequently subjected to a wide range of disturbances including fires, windstorms, insect outbreaks, floods, and droughts. These disturbances alter succession and influence the distribution and abundance of species in the ecosystem. * * *

The contemporary paradigm recognizes that ecosystems are open and not necessarily in equilibrium. It recognizes disturbance to be a natural and necessary part of ecosystems. It recognizes that systems are influenced by and can, in fact, be controlled by events occurring in neighboring or even distant ecosystems. The focus of the contemporary paradigm is on process rather than endpoint—on the trajectory of change rather than on the final endpoint. It recognizes historical contingency: the state of the system today depends on what happened yesterday as well as decades ago. * * * Unfortunately, we have not yet developed and popularized an image to replace that of the "balance of nature." I suggest "the dance of nature" as an image that conveys a sense of change and movement in response to a myriad of influences, just as a modern dancer moves in response to a musical score. * * *

The classical view of nature is of a system striving for equilibrium, which implies that systems will maintain themselves in balance if they are protected from human disturbance. This view results in a very different conservation and management strategy than the strategy that would result from the non-equilibrium paradigm.

* * * [Daniel Botkin] offers examples of the consequences of managing according to the classical paradigm in a world of change * * * In 1955, the Hutcheson Memorial Forest was preserved as the last remaining old growth oak forest in central New Jersey. Because the forest was considered to be at climax and hence at equilibrium, no manipulation or

disturbance of the forest was to be permitted. As a consequence, the forest today looks quite different than it did in 1955: * * * there is little evidence of successful oak regeneration; sugar maple saplings are abundant * * *; gypsy moth defoliation and the presence of exotic species in the neighborhood led to invasion of the understory by light-loving imported herbs and shrubs. What went wrong? It is now clear that the dominant species in this forest, like many others, requires periodic fire disturbance for regeneration and suppression of competitors * * * Thus, the conservation strategy of fire suppression that was developed based on a classical equilibrium paradigm failed to protect what the designers of the preserve valued most. Rather than simply protecting the endpoint, we need to preserve the processes that generate the desired result. Disturbance—in this case fire—is an essential part of the process. Disturbance is also inevitable, and a recognition of this should inform our management strategy. * * *

Management plans that do not consider the consequences of these rare, inevitable, and potentially catastrophic events will not be successful in the longterm preservation of landscape fragments or species, particularly if the area being preserved or the species population size is small. * * * When a natural disturbance does occur, management based on the contemporary paradigm would allow the system to recover from the disturbance. Not only is disturbance necessary, but natural systems need to be allowed to reap the fruits of that disturbance. * * *

Non-equilibrium concepts also apply to the maintenance of biodiversity, including the conservation of endangered species. If we follow the non-equilibrium paradigm, rather than simply trying to preserve a single species (the endpoint), we need to preserve the ecosystem of which it is a part and the process that has given rise to that interacting set of species, so that the assemblage can continue to change in response to environmental change. Our recovery plans need to ensure adequate population sizes and sufficient genetic diversity to maintain the ability of the species and the community to evolve and change in response to environmental variation. Species are not static objects; they must be able to change in order to persist. Natural communities must also be able to change in order to persist. A landscape is composed of a mosaic of patches, each shifting in composition over time. With a large enough landscape, we can expect to reach some stable distribution of patches in different stages of change. Some landscapes may however be too small relative to the size of patches that natural disturbances create, and a stable distribution will not be reached. This is clearly an issue faced by managers of national parks and other natural areas in our modern fragmented landscape. * * *

Notes and Questions

1. The premier wildlife preservation statute in the United States, the Endangered Species Act of 1973 (ESA), does precisely what Meyer cautions against: it strives to protect single species rather than ecosystems. *See* 16

U.S.C. § 1533(a) (directing that species be listed as endangered or threatened). Should the statute be overhauled to better reflect current ecological
understanding?

2. The dynamic nature of ecosystems is perhaps best illustrated by
river systems. Meyer notes: "Disturbance is a determining feature of aquatic
ecosystems. When the disturbance regime of a river is altered—for example,
by construction of a dam or by altering the seasonality of flows—the system
changes." *Id.* at 878. Dams are obvious culprits, but more subtle activities
have resulted in significant change as well. "The trapping of beaver in the
18th and 19th centuries largely eliminated from the landscape an animal
that had been responsible for shaping river channels throughout North
America for millennia * * * channels are less braided, food webs are
altered, and retention of organic matter is greatly reduced." *Id.* at 879.
Dams, dredging, channel alteration and agricultural practices have all contributed to a dramatic loss of biodiversity on the nation's longest river, the
Missouri.

> Two hundred years ago, President Thomas Jefferson sent Meriwether
> Lewis and William Clark on an expedition along the Missouri River in
> hopes of discovering an all-water route to the Northwest. Although this
> dream was not fulfilled, the Corps of Discovery brought back "a treasure
> of scientific information." Its zoological and botanical discoveries, in par-
> ticular, were "beyond any value." Today, at the expedition's bicentennial,
> * * * controversy on the Missouri River [reigns due to] scarcity of key-
> stone species; diminishment of the natural flow regime; and a paucity of
> willingness to adapt as necessary to ensure the long-term viability of
> human and ecological communities. * * *

> [T]ensions have run high ever since the Corps of Discovery explored the
> River's furthest reaches in the early 1800's. The conflict between navi-
> gation and ecological protection in the Missouri River basin has given
> rise to a veritable "clash of the titans" * * * Upper basin states are pit-
> ted against lower basin states and both have had their run-ins with fed-
> eral agencies. * * * The most recent Missouri River litigation conflagra-
> tion has drawn in five states, two federal agencies, several Native
> American tribes and numerous private litigants over the largest dam
> and reservoir system on the longest river system in the nation. It impli-
> cates three federally protected species, as well as barge operators, ship-
> pers and recreational and commercial interests related to tourism and
> sport fisheries. * * * The result so far has been dozens of court orders
> from six different federal courts. * * *

Sandra Zellmer, *A New Corps of Discovery for Missouri River Management,*
83 Neb. L.Rev. 305, 306–308 (2004) (citations omitted).

Professor Zellmer concludes that a "failure to adapt outdated and ill-suited
human strategies in the face of long-term ecosystem needs" has been a primary cause of biodiversity losses and human conflicts on the River, and suggests, "[a] new way of thinking, supported by a complete legislative overhaul, is long overdue." *Id.* at 308, 310.

3. Wetlands provide another good example of Meyer's "dance of
nature" thesis. A functioning wetland consists of interconnected habitats

with different inundation frequencies; some patches may not be wet every year. Yet the mix of species present in the landscape requires diverse inundation frequencies. Wetlands are a dynamic landscape that require recognition of both local and regional variation for effective protection and mitigation. *Id.* at 881–82. The Clean Water Act, 33 U.S.C. § 1344, requires developers to obtain permits before draining wetlands, and they may be compelled to replace affected wetlands or utilize credits from a pre-existing wetlands bank to ensure that there is no "net loss" of wetland acres as a result of their development. In theory, replacement wetlands could maintain environmental conditions if the newly created or banked wetlands were of comparable quality. However, the law provides no assurance that the replacement wetlands are the functional equivalent of lost wetlands, or that they provide the same ecosystem values and services as those that are lost to development. Wetlands replacement plans have been generally unsuccessful because developers fail to follow through and because regulators are often unable or unwilling to provide continuous monitoring to ensure that developers are meeting their promises and that the new wetlands function as intended. National Research Council, Committee on Mitigating Wetland Losses, Board on Environmental Studies and Toxicology—Water Science and Technology Board, Compensating for Wetland Losses under the Clean Water Act (2001).

4. If natural systems are constantly changing, how are managers supposed to identify goals and articulate effective standards to ensure ecological integrity and sustainability? Even though we no longer follow the "Balance of Nature" theory, ecosystem stability gives us a viable end-goal. Management based on ecosystem stability focuses on predictable functions and outcomes over time. *See* Daniel B. Botkin, Discordant Harmonies: A New Ecology for the Twenty–First Century 190 (1990); Jim Chen, *Webs of Life: Biodiversity Conservation as a Species of Information Policy*, 89 Iowa L. Rev. 495, 549 (2004). "Land managers who seek to attain sustainability in the face of uncertainty might prioritize the protection of elements of the ecosystem that are slow-changing and that generate familiar or expected patterns of outcomes." Daniel A. Farber, *Building Bridges over Troubled Waters: Eco–Pragmatism and the Environmental Prospect*, 87 Minn. L. Rev. 851, 880–81 (2003). This idea is explored in the following sections of this chapter.

2. *Biodiversity and Ecosystem Integrity*

Historic efforts to conserve biodiversity focused almost exclusively on protecting individual species, without much thought given to the big picture–ecosystems–or, conversely, anything more discrete than species, such as population or genetic diversity. Not only that, early conservation efforts were aimed at economically valuable game species, rather than insects, amphibians or other important keystone or indicator species. It was not until the 1970's that conservation efforts in the United States began to evolve to encompass a broader array of biodiversity concerns.

The Convention on Biological Diversity provides a good working definition of the term "biodiversity":

[T]he variability among living organisms from all sources including, inter alia, terrestrial, marine and other aquatic ecosystems and the ecological complexes of which they are part; this includes diversity within species, between species and of ecosystems.

Convention on Biological Diversity, adopted by the UN Conference on Environment and Development, June 5, 1992, 31 I.L.M. 818, 823. Scientific classification systems for species and ecosystems are provided in the box below.

In Practice:

Classification Systems

Both the taxonomy of species and their place within ecosystems are important to the study and understanding of biodiversity.

Taxonomic Classification

Kingdom

Phylum

Class

Order

Family

Genus

Species

The kingdoms are broken down into five categories: Animal; Plant; Fungi; Protista (protozoans and other single-celled organisms); and Monera (bacteria and other single-celled organisms) kingdoms. A house cat, a member of the animal kingdom, is within the chordata phylum and the mammalia class. Its order is carnivore and its family is felidae. Its genus and species, respectively, comprise its Latin name: *Felis domestica.*

Ecologists also look at levels of biological organization to describe diversity.

Biological organization

Ecosystem

Community

Guild

Species

Population

Organism

Gene

> ***Source:***
>
> E.O. WILSON, THE DIVERSITY OF LIFE 152, 157 (1999 ed.).

If biodiversity is the goal, where do social and economic considerations fit in? Of course, human considerations will always play some role in crafting a set of conservation tools for preserving and managing natural resources–our decisionmakers are human, after all—but if the baseline is not a scientific one, we risk losing sight of the goal altogether.

In light of the "chaos theory" described by Meyer above, what scientific factors should we consider and prioritize? As the definition provided by the Convention on Biological Diversity indicates, biodiversity entails a range of factors, including the presence and viability of populations of endemic or rare species and their related biological communities within an ecosystem, and the geographic distribution of a rich variety of species. Sandra B. Zellmer and Scott A. Johnson, *Biodiversity in and Around McElligot's Pool*, 38 IDAHO L.Rev. 473, 486–87 (2002). Precise criteria have not yet been articulated in the law, but land managers could take an initial cue from the ESA, which requires the protection of both species' populations and their critical habitat. 16 U.S.C. § 1533(a).

> Species well distributed across their native range are less susceptible to extinction than species confined to small portions of their range. The idea here is that a widely distributed species will be unlikely to experience a catastrophe, disturbance, or other negative influence across its entire range at once. For instance, a severe drought may dry up the breeding ponds used by a species of salamander for several years in a row across two or three states. If that salamander occurs nowhere else, it may become extinct. However, if the salamander is distributed broadly, at least some areas within its range are likely to contain breeding ponds that do not dry out completely. From those refugia, the species can slowly recolonize areas where it had been eliminated. * * * Keeping species well distributed is therefore a sensible conservation goal and corresponds to the well-accepted "multiplicity" principle, where it is preferable to have many reserves rather than few.

Noss, *Principles of Conservation Biology, supra,* at 900.

As for habitat, essential features vary among ecosystem types. The physical features and functions of a forest ecosystem will be quite different than those of a desert, and both are distinct from marine or freshwater ecosystems. Good information about habitat quality, as well as species' population numbers and distribution, is an essential part of any biodiversity conservation effort. Although inventories have been prepared on much of our federal land, because physical conditions and species' populations change over time, keeping the existing inventories up to date is a resource-intensive challenge, to say the least. The challenge is far greater when it comes to private lands. "Information about biological resources on private lands is limited—different parties possess mere fragments of data, and have little to no incentive to centralize the data in any user friendly, readily accessible format." Zellmer & Johnson, *supra,* at 489. This leads us to our next topic—uncertainty.

3. Uncertainty

The old adage, "the more we know, the more we know we don't know," is certainly true when it comes to ecological issues.

> If environmental law has done anything in the epistemological sense, it has taught us how little we know about the physical world and, even more so, how little we know about how to improve the physical world through law. Alas, environmental law seems puny and confused compared to its intended beneficiary, and we have made many mistakes as it has developed.

J.B. Ruhl, *Prescribing the Right Dose of Peer Review for the Endangered Species Act*, 83 Neb. L. Rev. 398, 400 (2004).

Scientific uncertainty reigns in the field of natural resources and environmental law and policy. Uncertainty can make it difficult to recognize environmental problems and even more challenging, sometimes virtually impossible, to determine their cause. Uncertainty can make it equally difficult to reach consensus on the adoption of appropriate responses once a problem is identified. The following excerpt, *Silence of the Frogs,* depicts a modern-day horror story, and vividly illustrates the potential consequences of uncertainty.

California Red-legged Frog
Listed as Threatened in 1996
USFWS File Photo

SILENCE OF THE FROGS
Emily Yoffe
N.Y. Times Magazine 36–39, 64–66, 76, Dec. 13, 1992

In the early 70's, a bizarre, inexplicable illness was sabotaging the academic career of Cynthia Carey. Then a young biologist, she was writing a dissertation on the physiology of coldblooded animals. Her creature of choice was *Bufo boreas*, named for the ancient Greek god of the north wind, an extravagant tag for a warty, blotchy, four-inch toad. It is more commonly and appropriately known as the western toad, its range encompassing the mountains of western North America. Twice a week,

Carey went into the vast, pristine wilderness of Colorado to do her research. At times the toads were so plentiful she had to be careful when driving away not to crush them under her wheels. In 1973, two years into her work, the illness struck. When she went into the field, Carey started coming upon an alarming sight: dozens of dying toads, toads barely able to move because their legs were puffy and red. She took one back to a veterinarian, who told her the toads were dying from an opportunistic infection because their immune systems had collapsed. But why? * * *

* * * [I]n 1988, she read a scientific paper on how environmental disturbances suppress the immune systems of fish. "That's when all the lights went on," Carey says. She has since set out to discover what happened to *Bufo boreas*, now missing from at least 80 percent of its historic range.

Around that time the same light bulb was clicking on for herpetologists (scientists who study amphibians and reptiles) all over the world. * * * The subject * * * could be summed up in one ominous question: Where have all the frogs gone? * * *

In the United States, *Bufo boreas* is not the only amphibian disappearing from the West. Also in decline are the Yosemite toad, the mountain yellow-legged frog and the red-legged frog, which was likely the protagonist in Mark Twain's famous story "The Celebrated Jumping Frog of Calaveras County." These frogs are missing from sites where they have been abundant in naturalists' accounts going back 75 years. * * * In all, almost one-third of North America's 86 species of frogs and toads appear to be in trouble. * * *

PERHAPS THE NEED TO FIND overarching explanations is encoded in our genes. From the search for a unified field theory of physics, to deconstructing the big bang, to proving that it was a straying asteroid that wiped out the dinosaurs, we like definitive theories to explain the phenomena that create and govern life. What is killing the frogs? In many instances, the answer, as with much of the world's disappearing flora and fauna, is no mystery. Humans are destroying habitats with unprecedented frenzy. * * * There are other obvious human causes. For one thing, pesticides and herbicides that have been found safe for humans may be devastating to other animals at vulnerable points in their life cycles. * * * But nothing explains it all. "I wish there were a death star to explain it," says David B. Wake, ... director of the Museum of Vertebrate Zoology at the University of California. "I don't see a single toxin, a single virus. My theory is that it's general environmental degradation. That's the worst thing. Frogs are telling us about the environment's overall health. They are the medium and the message."

Most herpetologists recognize that the world will never rally around their cosmetically challenged creatures. Their only hope is to portray frogs as four-legged, bug-eating Cassandras, and pray the prophecy is heard. "Frogs are in essence a messenger," Wake says. "This is about biodiversity and disintegration, the destruction of our total environment." * * *

Herpetologists, with perhaps not the greatest objectivity, say frogs are the ideal creature to reflect the health of the environment. In their view, frogs are living environmental assayers, moving over their life cycles from water to land, from plant-eater to insect-eater, covered only by a permeable skin that offers little shield from the outside world. Over and over, these scientists say amphibians represent the global equivalent of the proverbial canary in the coal mine. * * *

There is a paradox in portraying frogs as delicate creatures experiencing a collective case of the evolutionary vapors. After all, in the 200 million years since frogs first surfaced on the earth, they have survived whatever killed the dinosaurs, whatever did in the woolly mammoths and other huge animals that wandered this continent.* * * It is precisely because frog species have been so historically hardy that scientists now find themselves so baffled—and alarmed. * * *

But a few herpetologists—a decided minority—are deeply troubled about the lack of long-term data. * * * Rutgers University biologist, Peter J. Morin, recalls: * * * We need more real data on populations to find out if they are increasing, "decreasing or just fluctuating." To be conclusive, such studies take 10 to 20 years. * * * [C]onclusions about a global frog crisis should not be generalized from existing evidence. "It remains an open question whether declines and disappearances of some frog species in isolated, pristine environments represent a natural fluctuation or some subtle effect of human activities that we don't understand," [Joseph Pechmann, who published a study of frog populations in South Carolina], says. "My money is on the natural fluctuations, but I can't prove that. Only further research will say for sure."

No herpetologist disputes the value of long-term studies. But many insist that to wait for the data to come in would be foolhardy. "These declines, in many cases, are so catastrophic and are occurring simultaneously in so many parts of the world that we cannot wait for monitoring studies before we express our concern," says James Vial of Oregon State University. * * *

Many researchers refuse to wait, and are now exploring the possible causes of the mysterious declines—those not clearly linked to habitat destruction. At the top of the list is an increase in ultraviolet radiation. Among the hardest-hit amphibians are those that live at high altitudes, or near-the-ozone-hole southerly latitudes, from the Rockies and Sierras to the Andes to Australia. * * * While there may be indications that those who wear sunblock will inherit the earth, right now it's difficult to prove that increased ultraviolet radiation is a major cause of the decline. The simple reason is that studies have yet to be done to show if UV radiation really is increasing, and there is little historical information. * * * "I can't believe how little we know," says Wake. * * *

The mystery of the frog decline challenges the distinction between what is local and what is global. Because we as a species are so successful, so pervasive, the consequences of our local actions now ripple across the globe. No pristine place can protect a species from hazardous levels of, say, UV radiation. What is happening to frogs calls into question our belief that we can preserve the natural world in small, unsullied pockets. "You cannot lock up nature," Wake says. "There's no Noah's ark big enough." * * *

Almost 20 years after she first wondered why all the western toads she saw were dying, [Cynthia] Carey * * * is trying to decipher the immune system of frogs. The sick toad she had autopsied many years ago died of a massive infection from the bacteria Aeromonas hydrophila, which is ubiquitous in fresh water. * * * A healthy frog should not succumb to massive Aeromonas hydrophila infection, just as a healthy human should be able to fight off the staph and strep infections that can be so devastating to AIDS patients. * * *

Departing from several of her colleagues who are looking to prove that a specific environmental factor kills frogs outright, Carey says she believes the problem is more complex. Her hypothesis is that a combination of several factors—be it ultraviolet radiation, acid snow or something yet unknown—creates a degree of sublethal stress sufficient to cause the cascading breakdown of the immune system.

With a $20,000 grant from the National Science Foundation, Carey is figuring out what a healthy toad's immune system looks like. Once she has this basic information, the next step will be to expose toads to acidified water, pesticides, ultraviolet light and rapid temperature change. The object is to try to find out which of these conditions, if any, will induce the collapse of toad immune systems. * * * In a way, Carey's research is as metaphorical as molecular. What if she does find that what's killing frogs is some mix of global environmental changes? Aren't they really, then, a disturbing sign about the health of the planet's immune system? "Frogs aren't the only thing disappearing," she says. "The more biological diversity we destroy, the less flexibility we have to create new food sources that can tolerate the environment we are creating." * * *

WHAT WOULD HAPPEN if frogs died out? * * * One consequence … may be a field day for insects; amphibians provide a far safer method for keeping insect populations in check than any chemical insecticide. Bangladesh, where native frogs have been nearly wiped out to appease the French appetite for their legs, appears to be reaping the consequences. "They now have increased numbers of mosquitoes and malaria," William Duellman says. And the indisputable importance of frogs to the food chain is not just a matter of what they eat, but who eats them; they are a major food source for many birds, fish, reptiles and mammals.

But herpetologists say that simply saving frogs is not the point. "We don't know how many species can be lost before the system ceases to function," says Richard L. Wyman, adjunct associate professor of biology at the State University of New York at Albany. "But eliminate enough species and sooner or later it will cease to function. In the past, life responded to change through evolution, and that process depends on genetic diversity. If everything's the same, evolution stops. It's as if we are killing evolution itself." * * *

* * * So far, six mass extinctions have reset the earth's evolutionary clock—like the one that happened at the end of the Cretaceous period that took the dinosaurs with it. And some scientists * * * insist we are in the midst of another cataclysm—the first to be caused by man.

* * *

Notes and Questions

1. Kermit the Frog notwithstanding, are Americans likely to get excited about the loss of a few frog species? There are lots of them—"about 3,800 known species of frogs and toads," Yoffe, *supra,* and they're not exactly cuddly, like pandas, or charismatic, like bald eagles. Yet ecologists and herpetologists agree that frogs are important "indicator" species, in large part because "[a]mphibians—the word comes from the Greek 'amphi' and 'bios' (living a double life)—are a bridge between the aquatic and the terrestrial, the link between fish and reptile." *Id.* As such, they experience environmental stress at various stages of their lifespan, both in rivers, streams and lakes as well as on land. This characteristic makes them important members of the ecological community, particularly in terms of providing a warning signal if something is wrong. But because they move between aquatic and terrestrial habitats, it is exceedingly difficult to isolate the cause of their demise.

2. If scientists agree that the well-being of frogs is essential to overall ecosystem integrity, how can they convey that message to the general public in a way that makes us take action or demand action from our government? If they can't provide clear, unequivocal answers to questions about normal population variation, much less about the cause of population crashes, is anyone likely to sit up and take notice? In the article below, Reed Noss explains the difficulty of translating scientific concerns into policy and action.

SOME PRINCIPLES OF CONSERVATION BIOLOGY, AS THEY APPLY TO ENVIRONMENTAL LAW
Reed F. Noss
69 CHI.-KENT L. REV. 893, 893–94, 896–899, 908 (1994)

Conservation is not as simple today as in the past. One hundred years ago it seemed that if we could just stop the plume hunters from shooting egrets to decorate ladies' hats, and if we could only save a few areas of spectacular scenery in national parks, we were doing well. Somewhat later it became apparent that we had to protect many kinds of habitats—wetlands, grasslands, deserts, forests of all kinds—to save wildlife. To that end, we established a series of reserves including national wildlife refuges, research natural areas, state nature preserves, and private sanctuaries managed by groups such as The Nature Conservancy and National Audubon Society. The tacit assumption was that these little enclaves of nature would persist forever in the stable "climax" condition in which we found them. * * *

Putting the burden of proof on those who would protect the environment is consistent with conventional practice in scientific research, where the statistical significance of a result corresponds to how low the chance is of committing a Type I error. A Type I error occurs when one rejects a true null hypothesis and claims an effect (say, of a real estate development or a timber sale) when none really exists. Conventional statistical analyses are designed to minimize the probability of Type I errors, but in so doing they increase the chance of committing a Type II error, failing to reject a false null hypothesis or claiming no effect when one actually exists. The scientific preference for committing Type II rather than Type I errors is congruent with the "innocent until proven guilty" standard in criminal law, as opposed to cases in torts. In criminal law, it is assumed that acquitting a guilty person is not as bad as convicting an innocent person. However, the innocent until proven guilty standard sometimes imposes unacceptable risks on society. Several scientists have pointed out that Type II errors are more dangerous than Type I errors in applied sciences such as medicine, environmental engineering, and conservation biology because they can result in irreversible damage, for example death of a patient due to side effects of a drug, death and sickness of many innocent people in the cases of Bhopal and Chernobyl, or extinction of species. * * * "Conservation biologists ... should be similarly concerned with false negatives." Barbara L. Taylor & Tim Gerrodette, The Uses of Statistical Power in Conservation Biology: The Vaquita and Northern Spotted Owl, 7 Conservation Biology 489, 490 (1993).

The philosophy underlying conservation biology and other applied sciences is one of prudence: in the face of uncertainty, applied scientists have an ethical obligation to risk erring on the side of preservation. Thus, anyone attempting to modify a natural environment and put biodiversity at risk is guilty until proven innocent. This shift in burden of proof is consistent with the precautionary principle, which is gaining increased support in many professions. * * *

The general principles of conservation biology emerge from an appreciation of the complexity of nature, and an understanding that we will never know precisely how nature works. Thus, we had better be as cautious and gentle as possible in our manipulations. * * * Humility demands that we prefer erring on the side of preservation to erring on the side of development. * * *

The less data or more uncertainty involved, the more conservative a conservation plan must be. * * * When information on species locations, population sizes and trends, interspecific interactions, responses to disturbance, and other factors is scarce or questionable, the best interim strategy is one that minimizes development and other human disturbance during the time needed to gather the necessary biological information. * * *

Notes and Questions

1. Noss demonstrates his point with an example involving an interim conservation plan for coastal sage scrub in an area of southern California facing acute development pressure. There was not enough data to create a long-term plan, so the interim plan capped habitat losses to five percent in the planning area while field inventories and additional research on habitat needs of species in the region were being conducted. The interim plan restricted habitat losses "to patches of low to moderate conservation value such as small sites lacking rare species and surrounded by development." *Id.* Why five percent? Who should determine whether an area possesses "low" versus "high" conservation value? How?

2. The problems posed by uncertainty are not just a matter of inherent scientific limitations. They stem from social and political factors as well. Humans typically deal with uncertainty through "denial and avoidance." Daniel A. Farber, *Building Bridges over Troubled Waters: Eco–Pragmatism and the Environmental Prospect*, 87 MINN. L. REV. 851, 882 (2003). According to geophysics professor Henry Pollack, an expert on global climate change, "To look neither far ahead nor far afield is elemental in a Darwinian sense." HENRY N. POLLACK, UNCERTAIN SCIENCE, UNCERTAIN WORLD 59 (2003) (*citing* E.O WILSON, THE FUTURE OF LIFE (2002)). Donning the "blinders" of uncertainty provides politicians with "a pretext for inaction and for refusing to invest in conservation initiatives or to limit resource consumption." Zellmer, *Preservation Paradox, supra*, at 1028.

> Danger lurks in misinterpretation of the new paradigm: if change is a part of nature, then can we view anthropogenic change as just part of the natural way? Absolutely not; the new paradigm is not a license for environmental abuse. Anthropogenic change differs from natural change in both quality and rate. It is more rapid and often of a type never before experienced by natural ecosystems (for example, exposure to man-made chemicals). Anthropogenic change is acceptable only if that change is within limits. The limits to change at a site are set by physiological capabilities of organisms present, evolutionary limits (only a certain number of species have evolved that are able to prosper under a given suite of environmental conditions), and historical limits (there is a group of species that has been able to reach the site). In the past, evolution of new species and their migration has kept pace with changes that have occurred in Earth's history. Natural systems were able to adapt to past changes because they had a long time and large spaces; but anthropogenic change is rapid, and space is limited. We can use natural rates of change to help set acceptable limits for anthropogenic change. One important role for ecological science is to determine natural rates of change—to understand intrinsic variation in ecological phenomena over long periods of time.

Meyer, *supra*, at 882–83.

Has Meyer convinced you that our scientists and decisionmakers will be able to surmount problems posed by scientific uncertainty in their efforts to manage complex ecosystems? In the face of uncertainty, should the burden of proof be placed on development proponents, whose projects would be considered "guilty" of environmental harm until proven innocent? Noss refers to the "precautionary principle" as a theory that justifies this result. The principle is one tenet of sustainable development, and it is explored in more detail in Section III of this chapter. The topic of uncertainty permeates the field of natural resources and environmental law, and it is raised again in subsequent parts of this chapter on sustainable development (Section III), and on the drive for "sound science" in environmental decisionmaking (Section IV.B).

B. Landscape Linkages

The concept of ecological linkages is a corollary to the concepts of disturbance and the interrelatedness of natural systems discussed above. Activities in one area of the landscape can have a significant influence on other areas. Meyer, *supra*, at 883–84.

SOME PRINCIPLES OF CONSERVATION BIOLOGY, AS THEY APPLY TO ENVIRONMENTAL LAW
Reed F. Noss
69 CHI.-KENT L. REV. 893, 901–902 (1994)

The principle of "bigness" is another of the universally accepted generalizations of conservation biology. All else being equal, large populations are less vulnerable than small populations to extinction. A larger block of suitable habitat will usually contain a larger population. In line with the preceding principle, large blocks of habitat are also less likely to experience a disturbance throughout their area. Thus, refugia and recolonization sources are more likely to occur in large blocks of habitat than in small blocks, thus enhancing population persistence.

Blocks of habitat close together are better than blocks far apart. Many organisms are capable of crossing narrow swaths of unsuitable habitat, such as a trail, a narrow road, or a vacant lot; far fewer are able to successfully traverse a six-lane highway or the City of Chicago. In the absence of impenetrable barriers, habitat blocks that are close together will experience more interchange of individuals of a target species than will blocks far apart. If enough interchange occurs between habitat blocks, they are functionally united into a larger population that is less vulnerable to extinction for any number of reasons.

Habitat in continuous blocks is better than fragmented habitat. This rule follows logically from the previous two but also brings in some new considerations. Fragmentation involves a reduction in size and an increase in isolation of habitats. The theory of island biogeography predicts that either of these processes will lead to lower species richness due to decreased immigration rates (in the case of isolation) and increased extinction rates (in the case of small size). Thus, a small island far from the mainland is predicted to have the lowest species richness. Looking at a single target species, as is now the fashion in fragmentation studies, a small and isolated habitat patch is expected to have a smaller population and less opportunity for demographic or genetic "rescue" from surrounding populations. In metapopulation theory, an unoccupied patch of suitable habitat isolated by fragmentation is less likely to be colonized or recolonized by the target species. If enough connections between suitable habitat patches are severed, the metapopulation as a whole is destabilized and less likely to persist.

But fragmentation involves more than population effects for single species. Effects at community, ecosystem, and landscape levels are also well documented. Briefly, problems at these higher levels include abiotic and biotic edge effects that reduce the area of secure interior habitat in small habitat patches and often lead to proliferation of weedy species; increased human trespass and disturbance of sensitive habitats and species; and disruption of natural disturbance regimes, hydrology, and other natural processes. The end result of fragmentation is often a landscape that has lost sensitive native species and is dominated by exotics and other weeds. * * *

Interconnected blocks of habitat are better than isolated blocks. Connectivity—the opposite of fragmentation—has become one of the best accepted principles of conservation planning. * * * [F]ew conservation biologists would disagree that habitats functionally connected by natural movements of organisms are less subject to extinctions than habitats artificially isolated by human activity. * * *

* * *

Professor Meyer uses both groundwater and migratory species to demonstrate the importance of landscape linkages.

[W]e know that in many landscapes, streams and groundwater are linked physically, chemically and biologically. Yet a legal scholar writes: "[t]he essential problem with groundwater law is fragmentation. In the past, lawmakers and courts have pretended that groundwater and surface water are not connected. They have failed to recognize that, while some groundwater is essentially isolated, most groundwater is really part of a stream." David H. Getches, *Controlling Groundwater Use and Quality: A Fragmented System*, 17 Nat. Res. Law 623 (1984). In some cases, a pipe that pumps water from a stream is subject to a different set of laws than a pipe that pumps water from the ground a few feet from the channel. This makes little ecological sense. What is needed is an approach that recognizes the connections between ecosystems—streams and groundwater—in the landscape.

A similar recognition of connections is also essential when dealing with populations of species. The openness of systems and the dependence of one system upon events in another is dramatically illustrated by migrating animals, be they Pacific salmon, butterflies, sea turtles, neotropical migrant songbirds, or California grey whales that breed and give birth in Mexico and feed in Alaska. * * *

Meyer, *supra*, at 883–84.

One physical feature in particular is a key culprit of habitat fragmentation: " 'no single feature of human-dominated landscapes is more threatening to biodiversity ... than roads.' " Zellmer, *Preservation Paradox, supra*, at 1023 (citing Reed F. Noss, *Wilderness Recovery: Thinking Big in Restoration Ecology*, in THE GREAT NEW WILDERNESS DEBATE 523 (J. BAIRD CALLICOTT & MICHAEL P. NELSON EDS. 1998)).

> Roads, both paved and unpaved, have significant adverse effects on wildlife, vegetation, and water, soil, and air quality. * * * Roads crisscross natural boundaries, altering preexisting patterns of movement and communication within and between ecosystems. The abundance and diversity of native species is diminished near roads, while opportunistic exotic species thrive in and near the clearings created by roads. Roads provide greater access for humans, contributing to direct death or injury to wildlife species from roadkill and hunting, as well as indirect effects due to noise, air and water pollution. * * * From jeep tracks to highways, roads are pervasive across the American landscape, even in remote areas managed by the federal government. * * *

Id. at 1023–24 (citing Kurt H. Riitters & James D. Wickham, *How Far to the Nearest Road?*, 1 FRONTIERS IN ECOLOGY & ENV'T 125, 125–128 (2003) (other citations omitted)).

The "footprint" of a road, or its "edge effect" on the surrounding environment, reaches far beyond the road corridor.

> Based on conservative estimates, over 20 percent of the total land base in the contiguous United States is affected by roads * * * although only one percent of the land is physically covered by roads. "[A] remarkably high proportion of the conterminous US is located within a short distance [1 kilometer] of the nearest road. Ecological impacts from roads may be the rule rather than the exception in many regions, and few places are likely to be immune from all road-mediated impacts."

Id. at 1024 (citing Riitters, *supra*, at 128).

Roadless areas, on the other hand, provide a variety of ecological benefits:

> 1) high quality soil, water and air;
>
> 2) diverse communities of plants and animals; and
>
> 3) blocks of contiguous habitat for species, especially large carnivores and omnivores, dependent on expansive, undisturbed areas of land.

Id. The Forest Service took the remarkable step of prohibiting road construction on 58 million acres—30 percent—of the National Forest lands in its Roadless Area Conservation Rule of 2001, characterized as the "most significant land conservation initiative in nearly a century." Wyoming v. United States Dep't of Agric., 277 F. Supp. 2d 1197, 1220 (D. Wyo. 2003) (citing Roadless Area Conservation Rule, 66 Fed. Reg. 3245 (Jan. 12, 2001)), vacated as moot, 414 F.3d 1207 (10th Cir.2005). But the pressure to build and maintain roads, even in the most remote areas, can be extreme. Cross-country transportation relies on an extensive network of roads, as do most extractive uses, such as timber harvest, mining, and grazing. Perhaps not surprisingly, the 2001 Rule was subsequently suspended and replaced by a Rule that effectively dismantles roadless area protection. *See Trouble in the Forests*, N.Y. Times, Jan. 1, 2005, at A12.

Our experiences with wetlands, roads and isolated islands indicate that our legal systems should recognize and respond to natural connections in the landscape by spanning physical and jurisdictional boundaries. At present, U.S. natural resources law does so only in the most rudimentary fashion, if at all, as you'll see in subsequent chapters of this book. One notable exception is found in environmental (pollution control) law. The federal Clean Water Act, 33 U.S.C. §§ 1251 *et seq.*, reflects Congress's concern for the overall integrity of our nation's water ways by protecting not only surface waters, like lakes and streams, but also adjacent marshes and other wetlands that are "inseparably bound up with the 'waters' of the United States." Solid Waste Agency of Northern Cook County v. U.S. Army Corps of Engineers, 531 U.S. 159, 167, 121 S.Ct. 675, 680, 148 L.Ed.2d 576, 584 (2001) (citing United States v. Riverside Bayview Homes, Inc., 474 U.S. 121, 134, 106 S.Ct. 455, 463, 88 L.Ed.2d 419, 431 (1985)). How might the Endangered Species Act and resource management statutes governing forestry, mining and grazing expand their coverage beyond single species and/or single resources to reflect landscape linkages?

C. Indirect Effects and Natural Systems

To recover for environmental harms at common law, an injured party must show causation. Typically this involves proof of a direct or foreseeable link between the defendant's action and the plaintiff's injury. The lawsuit depicted in Jonathan Harr's book, A CIVIL ACTION (1996), provides a vivid example of the limitations of the common law. There, residents of Woburn, Massachusetts were exposed to solvents and other contaminants in their drinking water. Many of them developed leukemia and other illnesses and death. They were largely unsuccessful in their lawsuit against industries in the area because they could not establish that they were exposed to specific contaminants from specific industries, or that those contaminants ultimately caused their illnesses. *See* Anderson v. W.R. Grace & Co., 628 F.Supp. 1219 (D. Mass. 1986).

Of course, indirect and unforeseeable effects can be just as detrimental to the environment and to human health over the long-run.

Ecologists have long observed the importance of direct effects in ecosystems: for example, the response of lakes to nutrient additions from municipal wastewater. Yet it is not just these direct, "bottom-up" effects that influence aquatic ecosystems. "Top-down" and indirect effects are often equally important; altering higher trophic levels affects lower trophic levels in a "trophic cascade." A simple description of a lake food web illustrates how this trophic cascade can be manipulated by lake managers. In a lake, algae are fed on by herbivorous zooplankton, which are fed on by planktivorous (plankton eating) fish like bluegill, which become food for piscivorous fish like bass. As bass numbers increase (for example, from stocking), bluegill numbers decrease, large herbivorous zooplankton ... increase and graze heavily on algae, which then decrease.

Meyer, *supra*, at 884.

How should resource managers respond when the indirect effects of management actions become apparent?

This trophic cascade can be used as a management tool; it is possible to reduce nuisance algae blooms by stocking a lake with piscivorous fish like walleye * * * It is important that regulators and managers recognize the multiplicity of control points in natural systems. Controlling nutrient inputs is important, but the structure of the food web will influence the effectiveness of that control measure.

Id. at 885.

The National Environmental Policy Act (NEPA) requires consideration of direct, indirect and cumulative effects of proposed federal actions on the environment. 42 U.S.C. § 4332(C). NEPA requires resource managers to anticipate both direct and indirect effects in an effort to ensure that they "look before they leap." NEPA, however, applies only to major federal actions, and it only imposes procedural obligations at that. *See* Chapter 4, *infra.* Should our lawmakers impose substantive requirements, as a matter of federal or state law, to force resource managers to both consider and avoid indirect effects of logging, fishing, hunting, mining, grazing and recreational activities? If so, how?

D. Populations and Environmental Stress

Monitoring and detecting human influence on the physical environment can be a daunting task. Ensuring that the use of natural resources is sustainable over time requires resource managers to consider "macro-level" landscape changes as well as more discrete "micro-level" changes. How can a land manager possibly keep track of all of the discrete yet interacting components of an ecosystem? Studying species' or populations' responses to environmental change can help fill in our knowledge gaps, mitigate ongoing impacts, and guide future management decisions. Managers might start by focusing on species most threatened by human activities. Also, monitoring the physical responses of species most sensitive to human disturbance—like frogs—can help managers "fine tune" their conservation approaches long before the more resilient members of the ecological community demonstrate a reaction. Another option is to focus attention on "hot spots":

> Biodiversity is not distributed randomly or uniformly across the landscape. In establishing protection priorities, focus on "hot spots." Hot spots are areas of concentrated conservation value, such as centers of endemism or areas of high species richness. Hot spots can be recognized at many spatial scales. For example, globally, the humid tropics stand out as hot spots of species richness, with the greatest diversity for most taxa in Central and South America. But within an area such as the Amazon Basin, biologists have identified hot spots of endemism. Some kinds of organisms, such as coniferous trees, are most diverse in North America. Looking more closely, the greatest diversity of conifers appears to be the seventeen species in the Russian Peak area of northern California. Every landscape has areas of concentrated biodiversity. Map overlays that display multiple conservation criteria can show the locations of these hot spots.

Noss, *Some Principles of Conservation Biology, supra*, at 905.

In another section of his article, Noss acknowledges that "hot spot" preservation may not be enough: "ecological phenomena operate across vast landscapes, and* * * areas set aside for their natural qualities are inevitably buffeted by exotic species invasions, uncontrolled human activities, disruptions of hydrology, and other cross-boundary effects." *Id.* at 893–94. Is it better to preserve hot spots that are rich in biodiversity through protective designations like wilderness areas or marine sanctuaries, or should we instead focus on populations of species, wherever they are found? What if the populations at issue are highly migratory? What if they are found only on private lands?

At least two federal statutes provide for a population-oriented focus. The ESA allows species to be listed not just as entire species, but also as subspecies or as a local or distinct population segment (DPS). 16 U.S.C. § 1532(16). Once a species, subspecies or DPS is listed, it is given the full protections of the Act. This approach is consistent with the "multiplicity" principle of conservation biology: it is better to have many population reserves rather than few. Noss, *supra*, at 900.

Along the same lines, the National Forest Management Act (NFMA) requires that land and resource management plans for the national forests provide for the diversity of plant and animal species. 16 U.S.C. § 1604(g)(3)(B)–(C). According to the 1982 Forest Service regulations, this means that forest plans must support viable populations of plant and animal communities, 36 C.F.R. § 219.19–.20, and thus must provide sufficient habitat to support a number of reproductive individuals. Utah Envtl. Cong. v. Bosworth, 285 F.Supp.2d 1257, 1267 (D. Utah 2003); *see* Seattle Audubon Soc'y v. Lyons, 871 F.Supp. 1291, 1317 (W.D. Wash. 1994), *aff'd*, 80 F.3d 1401 (9th Cir. 1996). The NFMA diversity provisions have been implicated in recent ecosystem management initiatives, and are discussed in more detail in Section IV.A, below, and Chapter 6, *infra*.

E.   The Physical Environment's Effect on Organisms and Vice Versa

If you were to view a picture of the earth's surface taken from Mars, you would get the sense that the physical and biological systems of our planet are highly interdependent. "We readily accept a determining role for physical factors (for example, climatic influences on vegetation), but we forget the extent to which physical factors are influenced by biological activity." Meyer, *supra*, at 885. Human and non-human organisms can affect the physical environment in significant ways. Of course, the converse is true as well—the effects of the environment on the activities and well-being of its inhabitants, both human and non-human, can be considerable.

A dramatic case-study of the effects of organisms on their physical environment is provided by studies of wolf reintroduction in the Greater Yellowstone Area. Gray wolves are indigenous to the Rocky Mountains, but they were extirpated from the area in the 1920's. The National Park Service and U.S. Fish and Wildlife Service reintroduced 30 adult wolves in 1995 and 1996 as part of the species' recovery plan required under the Endangered Species Act. The reintroduced wolves and their descendants are thriving and influencing a web of plants and animals (not to mention people) in at least three states. "The return of one of the region's top predators, now numbering up to 900, may be altering everything from elk behavior to tree growth to beaver populations." Warren Cornwall, *Ecological Changes Linked to Wolves*, Seattle Times, Jan. 12, 2005, B1. Can the return of just one species really be so significant?

ECOLOGICAL CHANGES LINKED TO WOLVES
Warren Cornwall
SEATTLE TIMES, Jan. 12, 2005, B1

Oregon State University forester Bill Ripple went to Yellowstone National Park in 1997 looking for an answer to the decline in aspen groves there. He emerged with a surprising answer: wolves.

A study of growth rings on the trees showed that the youngest dated to the 1920s, around the time when wolves were eradicated from the park. Ripple hypothesized that the disappearance of the predators emboldened elk, which then ate young, tasty trees with impunity. He and a colleague followed up with research that found similar age patterns in cottonwood trees, and evidence that willows have had a resurgence in recent years. "As soon as we get rid of wolves, plants stop flourishing. Soon after we bring wolves back, plants are flourishing again," Ripple said.

If true, it shows how wolves can influence a broad web of plants and animals. Beaver rely on willows for food and songbirds live in aspens and willows, so their populations might rebound. Animals that thrive around beaver dams could get a boost.   * * * The wolf's arrival also has coincided with a 50 percent drop in coyote populations. That could help red foxes, which are killed by coyotes. It also could increase populations of rodents eaten by coyotes, a potential boon for hawks that prey on mice. * * *

Humans impact their ecosystems, too, and sometimes the ecosystem responds in kind. The following article describes a startling example.

THE VANISHING
Malcolm Gladwell
THE NEW YORKER 70–73, Jan. 3, 2005

Book Review of JARED DIAMOND, COLLAPSE:
HOW SOCIETIES CHOOSE TO FAIL OR SUCCEED (2004)

A thousand years ago, a group of Vikings led by Erik the Red set sail from Norway for the vast Arctic landmass ... known as Greenland. It was largely uninhabitable—a forbidding expanse of snow and ice. But along the southwestern coast there were two deep fjords protected from the harsh winds ...., and as the Norse sailed upriver they saw grassy slopes flowering with buttercups, ... and thick forests of willow and birch and alder. * * * Norse colonies in Greenland were law-abiding, economically viable, fully integrated communities, numbering at their peak five thousand people. They lasted for four hundred and fifty years—and then they vanished. * * *

The problem with the settlements, [Jared] Diamond argues, was that the Norse ... treated it [Greenland] as if it were the verdant farmland of southern Norway. They cleared the land to create meadows for their cows, and to grow hay to feed their livestock through the long winter. They chopped down the forests for fuel.... To make houses warm enough for the winter, they built their homes out of six-foot thick slabs of turf, which meant that a typical home consumed about ten acres of grassland. But Greenland's ecosystem was too fragile to withstand that kind of pressure. Topsoil layers were shallow and lacking in soil constituents * * * Without adequate pastureland, the summer hay yields shrank; without adequate supplies of hay, keeping livestock through the long winter got harder. * * * The Norse needed to reduce their reliance on livestock—particularly cows, which consumed an enormous amount of agricultural resources. But cows were a sign of high status * * * They needed to copy the Inuit practice of burning seal blubber for heat and light in the winter, and to learn from the Inuit the difficult art of hunting ringed seals, which were the most reliably plentiful source of food available in the winter. But the Norse had contempt for the Inuit—they called them *skraelings, "wretches"* * * * In the end, the Norse starved to death.

* * *

Notes and Questions

1. Erik the Red and other Viking chiefs left Scandinavia in large part because they did not care to take orders and pay taxes to King Harald Finehair, who had been consolidating his power base in Norway around 870 A.D. They initially settled in Iceland, where their population blossomed to 150,000 by the year 1250. Erik the Red, a bloodthirsty and unscrupulous Viking, was eventually banished from Iceland by his fellow chiefs, so he set up a farmstead on the west coast of Greenland. Ironically, "[t]he incongruous name for this barren, frigid island dominated by a vast ice cap comes from the outcast's attempt to lure other settlers." Eugene Linden, *The Vikings: A Memorable Visit to America*, SMITHSONIAN 92, 98 (2004). Erik's son, Leif Erikson, led the first expedition to the New World, but the Vikings' presence in both Greenland and North America vanished long before Columbus's expedition in 1492. The primary force behind their demise may have been climate change. Although many of the expeditions and settlements occurred in the 11th century during a "Medieval Warming" period in the North Atlantic, the weather deteriorated in the 12th century with the Little Ice Age. *Id.* at 98. According to archeology professor Tom McGovern, the Greenland colony suffered eight harsh winters in a row, culminating in 1355 with one of the worst winters that century. *Id.*

2. Although Diamond does not explain how or why societies become "cultural determinists," he does identify five factors that contribute to societal longevity or collapse: environmental damage; climate change; friendly and accessible trade partners; hostile neighbors; cultural responses to the changing environment. David Rains Wallace, *Not How, But Why? Beyond Proximate Cause for Environmental Degradation*, 6 Conservation in Practice 1: 42, 43 (2005). The Maya, for example, chose societal collapse because their ruling class demanded that their natural resources be harvested and ultimately exhausted to ensure their prestige. The Easter Islanders chose to ignore critical (and seemingly obvious) differences between the island's physical environment and their own tropical homelands. *Id.* How do Diamond's five factors influence decisionmakers in modern societies? Are one or more of these factors most compelling in ensuring a societies' success or downfall?

3. Cultural norms are extremely powerful. To decisionmakers, "choosing environmental collapse can often seem more rational than choosing success because logical needs such as profit, group solidarity, and religious transcendence can motivate the choice." Wallace, *supra*, at 43. In COLLAPSE, Diamond observes that the Inuit survived while the Norse died out, even though the Norse had iron tools and other advantages. Yet the Norse couldn't (or wouldn't) adapt to Greenland's environment. Diamond's proof lies in the garbage dumps and archeological sites at the Western Settlement,

which yielded European-style crucifixes, furniture and dishes, but no fish bones. Although eating fish would have minimized the intensive ecological demands of the settlements, the Norse weren't nearly as concerned with their physical survival as they were about cultural survival. "Food taboos are one of the idiosyncrasies that define a community. Not eating fish served the same function as building lavish churches, and doggedly replicating the untenable agricultural practices of their land of origin." Gladwell, *supra*, at 73. Cultural collapse apparently occurred with lightening speed. When archeologists combed through the remains of the Settlements, they found the bones of newborn calves and dog bones scratched by knife marks: "the Norse, in that final winter, had given up on the future." *Id.* Why is it so difficult for even the most technologically sophisticated societies to adapt to the physical conditions of their surroundings?

4.   American cultural norms include confidence and great pride in the miracles of modern technology. But some of our technologies are responsible for severe environmental degradation. Can technology itself become a society's downfall? Over 140 nations have ratified the Kyoto Treaty on Climate Change, which went into effect in February 2005. Although the United States is the largest contributor of emissions responsible for global warming, it has not ratified the Treaty. Why not?

5.   Erik the Red's colony, the Mayans, and other ancient cultures are not the only examples of societal collapse attributable to environmental degradation. After examining the rise and fall of the Norse settlements in COLLAPSE, Diamond takes a look at a few modern case studies, including Rwanda. He concludes that genocide wasn't a preordained result of religious or even cultural differences. The Hutus turned on the Tutsi and on each other because the society was on the brink of ecological disaster. Farms had been carved out of steep hills, without any terracing; soil erosion smothered the streams; and the exhaustion of the soils and deforestation led to famine and desperation. "Rivers and streams and forests and soil ... are a tangible, finite thing, and societies collapse when they get so consumed with addressing the fine points of their history and culture and deeply held beliefs ... that they forget that the pastureland is shrinking and the forest cover is gone." Gladwell, *supra*, at 73. How can the world community help societies like the Rwandans avoid environmental and societal collapse? Is intervention appropriate, or can it be a form of oppression and even racism?

6.   Werner Heisenberg's Uncertainty Principle posits that the very act of observing something may distort the item or phenomenon being observed. *See* Lawrence H. Tribe, *The Curvature of Constitutional Space: What Lawyers Can Learn from Modern Physics,* 103 HARV. L. REV. 1, 17–18 (1989). In 1926, Heisenberg noted that the velocity and position of a particle could not be measured without shining light on it, but that the light's energy disrupts the particle's velocity, demonstrating the uncertainties of observation and measurement. He concluded that it is impossible to measure something with 100% accuracy because the very process of observation affects the result. *See* STEPHEN HAWKING, A BRIEF HISTORY OF TIME 56–57 (10th ed. 1996). Of course, the study of archeological sites is less likely to change the object of study to a great extent, at least not in the sense that the study of particles or living organisms and communities might. How can scientists minimize the effect of

the Uncertainty Principle in the study of, for example, wolves and their associates in an ecosystem?

III. SUSTAINABLE ECOSYSTEMS AND SUSTAINABLE DEVELOPMENT

Given the physical limitations of our environment and the political impetus for maintaining or expanding our economic well-being, can development of our natural resources occur in a fashion that is sustainable over time? And, if so, is sustainable development necessarily compatible with sustainable ecosystems?

Sustainable development is a persistent theme in international environmental law. The 1987 Brundtland Report, *Our Common Future,* defines sustainable development as "development that meets the needs of the present without compromising the ability of future generations to meet their own needs." WORLD COMMISSION ON ENVIRONMENT AND DEVELOPMENT, OUR COMMON FUTURE 43 (Oxford Press 1987). In other words, "[s]ustainability is a relationship between dynamic human economic systems and larger, dynamic, but normally slower-changing ecological systems * * * in which the effects of human activities remain within bounds so as not to destroy the health and integrity of self-organizing systems." Bryan G. Norton, *A New Paradigm for Environmental Management*, in ECOSYSTEM HEALTH, *supra,* at 25. A management philosophy based on sustainable development reorients the use and allocation of natural resources to ensure their availability for present and future generations. Sandra Zellmer, *A Preservation Paradox: Political Prestidigitation and an Enduring Resource of Wildness,* 34 ENVTL. L. 1015, 1038 (2004). Resource use and consumption occurs only in a time, place and manner that allow regeneration and continuity into the future. The concept of sustainable development also strives for both intergenerational equity and distributive justice in the access to essential resources among human communities, be they wealthy or impoverished. *Id.*

Societies that dedicate themselves to sustainable development find that it is an elusive goal, given "the inherent uncertainties about managing resources associated with complex and dynamic ecosystems with non-linear properties.... " Daniel A. Farber, *Building Bridges over Troubled Waters: Eco–Pragmatism and the Environmental Prospect,* 87 MINN. L. REV. 851, 858 (2003). The challenges posed by scientific uncertainty are described in detail above in Section II.A.3. Professor Daniel Cole grapples with the sustainable development concept in the following article.

WHAT IS THE MOST COMPELLING ENVIRONMENTAL ISSUE FACING THE WORLD ON THE BRINK OF THE TWENTY–FIRST CENTURY: ACCOUNTING FOR SUSTAINABLE DEVELOPMENT
Daniel H. Cole
8 FORDHAM ENVTL. LAW J. 123, 126–127 (1996)

The costs of environmental regulations are comparatively easy to estimate; they are mostly born by market participants (industry and consumers), and thus are commonly denominated in dollars. The benefits of environmental regulations, however, which include breathing cleaner air and water, are not easily converted into dollar signs. Consequently, cost-benefit analyses tend to be biased against regulatory policies aimed at pollution prevention and resource conservation. * * *

The task, then, ... is to devise workable criteria and methods for refining cost-benefit analysis (on the micro-level) and national income accounting (on the macro-level), to more accurately assess the real environmental costs of pollution and resource consumption and corresponding benefits from pollution prevention and resource conservation. However, this is more easily said than done. Economists have been working at it since at least the mid–1940s, when Sir John Hicks, a Nobel Prize-winning economist from Britain, showed that the most relevant indicator of economic welfare is not Gross National Product, but net income, defined as the amount a country can consume without depleting its capital stock. *See* J. R. Hicks, Value and Capital (2d ed. 1946). If "capital stock" is defined to include all natural resources used in or affected by production, then Hicks's definition of "income" could also serve to define the concept of "sustainable development."

However, to date economists have had little success designing workable adjustments to national income calculations. One early effort by James Tobin and William Nordhaus attempted to refine GNP by: (1) subtracting pollution costs, (2) excluding "regrettable necessities," such as police protection, national defense, and possibly some costs of environmental regulation, and (3) adding in the estimated value of certain nonmarket goods, such as household productive activities and leisure. * * * But, like more recent efforts to amend the system of national accounts, their proposal was plagued by a fundamental problem: they could not provide an "objective" (i.e., non-controversial) method for valuing nonmarket goods and bads. * * *

Notes and Questions

1. If society were to place more emphasis on quantifying the benefits of ecosystem services, see Section I.A, *supra,* would sustainable development policies necessarily follow?

2. One way of ensuring sustainable development is to incorporate the precautionary principle in all decisions where the direct, indirect, long-term

and cumulative effects of the decision are not certain. The precautionary principle "requires decision makers to proceed with caution (or not at all) in the face of uncertainty." Zellmer, *Preservation Paradox, supra,* at 1038. As Reed Noss argues in the article excerpted in Section II.A.3 of this chapter, this principle places the burden of proof on the development proponent, who must show that their proposed activity is benign over the long run or the activity may not proceed. Noss, *supra,* at pp 39–42. Other nations, including members of the European Union, have embraced a precautionary principle in their approach to genetically modified (GM) foods, by imposing a moratorium on imports of new GM products and by adopting strict labeling requirements for GM products that are used within their jurisdiction. *See* John S. Applegate, *The Prometheus Principle: Using the Precautionary Principle to Harmonize the Regulation of Genetically Modified Organisms,* 9 IND. J. GLOBAL LEGAL STUD. 207 (2001). The 1992 Rio Declaration adopts the principle in Article 15:

> Where there are threats of serious or irreversible damage, lack of full scientific certainty shall not be used as a reason for postponing cost-effective measures to prevent environmental degradation.

Rio Declaration of the United Nations Conference on Environment and Development (UNCED), 31 I.L.M. 874 (1992).

3.   Should the United States adopt a precautionary principle as a legally binding component of a comprehensive sustainable development statute? Instead, should it adopt the principle on a case-by-case basis or as part of a more discrete legal provision addressing, for example, GM foods, toxic chemical substances, endangered species, or other issues? How about global climate change? What are the advantages and disadvantages of applying the precautionary principle to resource management issues?

Case Study 2: The Arctic National Wildlife Refuge (ANWR)

The basic facts of the dispute about oil and gas development proposals in ANWR—a veritable witches' brew of opinions and assertions–are provided in Section I.A of this chapter. In 2003, the National Research Council reported that oil exploration in Prudhoe Bay and elsewhere in Alaska has resulted in a "steady accumulation of harmful environmental and social effects.... " National Research Council, Cumulative Environmental Effects of Oil and Gas Activities on Alaska's North Slope (2003), *available at* http://www.nap.edu. It noted that very few (less than 1 percent) of old drilling areas had been reclaimed, and that the effects of "unrestored landscapes could persist for centuries and accumulate." *Id.* According to the report, adverse effects will, in all likelihood, increase as exploration expands. Modern technologies, such as ice roads and other measures to protect the fragile tundra and minimize oil spills, can reduce the footprint and overall impact of development, but global warming trends may diminish the effectiveness of these measures.

The American public generally favors continued protection of ANWR. A 2004 survey found that 55 percent of all respondents opposed drilling in the area. NRDC, http://www.nrdc.org/land/wilderness/arctic.asp. Yet Americans are also concerned about the price of gas when they fill up their SUV's and mini-vans. In March 2005, in the face of soaring gasoline prices in the wake of the war in Iraq, the Senate voted 51–49 to attach a "rider" to a huge budget package, which would open the coastal plain to drilling. This particular bill failed, but congressional interest in ANWR continues. H. Josef Hebert, *Senate Votes to Open Oil Drilling in Refuge*, Lincoln J–Star, Mar. 16, 2005, A1.

Given what you've learned about biodiversity and sustainable development, do you think development in ANWR can be accomplished in a sustainable fashion? What measures should be required to prevent or diminish direct, indirect and cumulative effects of development? What additional information would you need if you were required to make a decision? Would you adopt a precautionary approach and preclude development until you get that information? Can science provide us with the answers, or does the ANWR debate really boil down to a dispute about values? Finally, if development proceeds, who should be in charge, and who should get royalties: the federal agencies that manage the area, the state of Alaska, Alaska Natives, or someone else entirely?

IV. A WORLD IN PERIL: ARE ECOSYSTEM MANAGEMENT AND SOUND SCIENCE THE ANSWER?

Two themes have become prevalent in the quest for sustainable development: ecosystem management and "sound science." If our scientists and decisionmakers can agree on normative standards to sustain ecosystem integrity, all we need, then, is more and better scientific data and analysis to get us there, right? Conservation biologist Reed Noss expresses skepticism: "Ecosystems are not only more complex than we think, but more complex than we *can* think." Noss, *Principles of Conservation Biology, supra,* at 898 (emphasis added). It's a daunting task, but ecosystem management has come into vogue, as has the drive for "sound science."

A. Ecosystem Management

Ecosystem management strives to maintain the health and integrity of interacting components of ecosystems and their inhabitants. It has gained such recognition that "[t]he logic behind ecosystem-based management is no longer being seriously questioned." Robert B. Keiter, *Beyond the Boundary Line: Constructing a Law of Ecosystem Management,* 65 U. Colo. L. Rev. 293, 333 (1994). In fact, "no politically aware person ... [would] openly oppos[e] the idea of ecosystem management, for that would be tantamount to proposing ecosystem *mismanagement*." J.B. Ruhl, *Ecosystem Management, the ESA, and the Seven Degrees of Relevance,* 14 Nat. Resources & Env't 156, 157 (2000) (emphasis added).

The federal land management agencies, led by the Forest Service, began an ongoing experiment with ecosystem management in the early 1990's in response to a series of lawsuits that had virtually shut down logging throughout the Pacific Northwest. Challenges to Forest Service and Bureau of Land Management (BLM) plans for timber lands were based on the agencies' organic acts as well as the ESA. *See* Seattle Audubon Soc'y v. Lyons, 871 F.Supp. 1291, 1317 (W.D. Wash. 1994), *aff'd*, 80 F.3d 1401 (9th Cir. 1996) (describing decades-long litigation history). To resolve the deficiencies identified in the lawsuits and respond to the needs of the northern spotted owl (*Strix occidentalis caurina*), a federally protected species, the agencies, with the backing of high-level officials in the Clinton Administration, crafted the Northwest Forest Plan in 1994. The Plan covers 19 million acres within 19 National Forests and three million acres within seven BLM districts. It is designed to protect the owl and dozens of species that rely on old-growth habitat throughout the owl's range. It set aside "Late Successional Reserves," in which commercial logging and other potentially destructive activities are restricted. *Seattle Audubon Society*, 871 F.Supp. at 1304. "The reserve areas * * * protect about eighty percent of the remaining [old growth] forest acres in the planning area * * * " *Id.* at 1305.

The court upheld the Plan in the face of challenges from both industry and environmental groups. According to *Seattle Audubon Society v. Lyons*, NFMA's provisions allow, and in some cases require, coordinated landscape-level planning to satisfy forest diversity needs. *Id.* at 1307, 1325. As described in Section I.B of this chapter, NFMA requires forest plans to utilize scientifically sound management, and, more specifically, to provide for the diversity of plant and animal species. 16 U.S.C. § 1604(C)(g)(3). According to the 1982 Forest Service regulations, this means that plans must support viable populations of species. *See* 36 C.F.R. § 219.19.[b] Section 219.19 required the Forest Service, through its land and resource management plans, to provide sufficient habitat "to support, at least, a minimum number of reproductive individuals." Utah Envtl. Cong. v. Bosworth, 285 F.Supp.2d 1257, 1267 (D. Utah 2003); *see also Seattle Audubon Soc'y*, 871 F.Supp. at 1317. In addition, habitat must be well distributed so that individuals can disperse and interact with each other in the planning area. *See Utah Envtl. Congress*, 285 F.Supp.2d at 1267; *Seattle Audubon Soc'y*, 871 F.Supp. at 1315.

The *Seattle Audubon Society* opinion also placed its stamp of approval on ecosystem management as applied to BLM lands: the Plan's designation and conservation of protected reserves were an appropriate "exercise of the Secretary's multiple-use planning responsibilities" under the Federal Land Policy and Management Act (FLPMA). *Id.* at 1314–15.

In spite of the accomplishments of the Northwest Forest Plan, the federal agencies have not achieved the sweeping results from their ecosystem management experience that many had hoped. The next attempt

---

b. The 1982 regulations were revised in 2000, National Forest System Land and Resource Management Planning, 65 Fed. Reg. 67,514 (Nov. 9, 2000), and again in 2005, 70 Fed. Reg. 1023 (Jan. 5, 2005), but the 1982 version is still applied to pre-existing plans and some plan revisions and amendments. *See* 36 C.F.R. 219.35(b) (2003). The regulations are covered in more detail in Chapter 6, *infra*. The new planning regulations may be less likely to promote biodiversity, as they do not explicitly reference viable populations. Why do you suppose the Forest Service would opt to walk away from the viability requirement, after it had been in place for over 20 years?

at large-scale ecosystem management, known as the Interior Columbia Basin Ecosystem Management Project (ICBEMP), cost a fortune and produced very little in terms of concrete results.

ECOSYSTEM MANAGEMENT IN THE NORTHWEST:
"IS EVERYBODY HAPPY?"

Rebecca W. Watson

14 NAT. RESOURCES & ENV'T 173, 175–176 (2000)

ICBEMP began with the national forests and BLM lands east of the Cascade Crest in Washington and Oregon ... [and] was expanded to include agency lands in much of Idaho, western Montana, and small portions of Nevada, Wyoming, and Utah * * * ICBEMP includes 72 million acres of federal land in an area of 144 million acres. * * *

Whereas the Northwest Forest Plan focused largely on one species, the spotted owl, and one land use, timber harvest, ICBEMP encompasses a diverse mixture of forest and range types that supports many species (e.g., salmon, bull trout, grizzly bears, lynx, eagles, wolves, sport fish, deer, elk); produces a wide array of goods and services (e.g., agriculture, electricity, mining, manufacturing, timber, grazing, recreation, navigation); and has varied requirements for development, restoration, and conservation. * * *

* * * [T]he ICBEMP planning process held more than 200 public meetings and received and analyzed an astounding 83,000 comments. Despite this Herculean effort to bring the public along in support of ICBEMP, by the time the DEIS comment process closed, in May 1998, support for ICBEMP had evaporated. Conservationists complained that ICBEMP ignored the science, failed to close enough roads, and was not proscriptive [sic] enough to protect rare species, their habitats, and watersheds. * * * The timber and mining industries argued that ICBEMP closed too many roads ... and that it relied on one-size-fits-all management standards instead of standards developed from demonstrated cause and effect ecosystem processes. * * *

Congress reacted by including ICBEMP termination language in House and Senate fiscal year 1999 appropriation bills. * * *

In 2003, the Bush Administration announced that instead of preparing a record of decision on ICBEMP, it would merely direct the agencies to incorporate any pertinent scientific findings developed during

ICBEMP into their land and resource management plans. DEPT. OF AGRI-
CULTURE ET AL., THE INTERIOR COLUMBIA BASIN STRATEGY 1 (2003). As a result,
none of ICBEMP's recommendations are binding, and management decisions will continue to be made at the local level.

As the ICBEMP experience indicates, although the ecosystem management initiative appeared to usher in a paradigm shift in agency agen-
das, "business as usual" still seems to rule the day. Environmental
groups and ecologists alike criticize the Forest Service for placing heavy
reliance on logging (or "thinning") to fix problems caused by logging, and
for failing to protect old-growth stands, roadless areas and riparian habitat. *See* Sierra Club, *Restoring America's Forests*, available at
http://www.sierraclub.org/forests/report02/restoration_ report.pdf. Meanwhile, officials within the Forest Service have publicly questioned the
efficacy of ecosystem management, and they readily admit that
entrenched interests have captured previous initiatives. All evidence
indicates that, in spite of the resources dedicated to the Northwest Forest Plan and ICBEMP, the mission of the agency as a whole remains
fundamentally unchanged. "[T]he agency's transition to ecosystem management is severely impeded by an organizational structure that, while
well-suited to the previous era of multiple-use management, is obsolete."
Winifred B. Kessler & Hal Salwasser, *Natural Resource Agencies: Trans-
forming From Within*, in A NEW CENTURY FOR NATURAL RESOURCES MANAGE-
MENT 184 (Richard Knight & Sarah Bates eds., 1995).

What about the Northwest Forest Plan itself? Surely, it provides a
shining ray of hope for ecosystem management and sustainable development. Well, then again, maybe not. According to Jim Lyons, who, as
former undersecretary of agriculture under President Clinton, helped
craft the plan, the Bush Administration has undermined the plan's "very
essence," which was "forest management based on science rather than
commercial imperatives." Glen Martin, *Bush Accord Could Revive Timber Wars Logging to Double on Federal Lands in the Northwest*, SAN
FRANCISCO CHRONICLE, April 12, 2004. Lyons criticized the administration's
decision to increase timber harvesting in the region covered by the plan,
stating, "[t]he changes are an attempt to set a new standard, one counter
to ecosystem management * * * They're going from survey and manage
[old-growth species] to don't ask, don't tell." *Id.*

Notes and Questions

1.   What, if any, hope for ecosystem integrity and sustainability can be
drawn from these experiences? Citizens' suits like the one brought by the
Seattle Audubon Society over logging in the Pacific Northwest have served
as an important catalyst, but having long-term management driven by litigation priorities is not ideal. Is ecosystem management doomed to the dust-
bin of misguided bureaucracy? Or might there be some basis for optimism?
Professor Charles Wilkinson observes,

   [T]he Forest Service is still timber-dominated, and that fact skews every
   decision to some degree, small or great. Yet timber determines less than

before. This is a more open and diverse, and a better, agency.... The new winds are blowing strong and will grow ever more hearty.

Charles F. Wilkinson, *The National Forest Management Act: The Twenty Years Behind, The Twenty Years Ahead*, 68 U. COLO. L. REV. 659, 673 (1997).

2. Ecologists and conservation biologists insist that ecosystem management must not be constrained by jurisdictional lines.

Ecosystem boundaries should be determined by reference to ecology, not politics. Ecosystems do not respect property and jurisdictional lines. Ecologists often say that the boundaries of all ecosystems—even the biosphere—are open, exchanging energy and materials with other systems. * * * The scale and boundaries of the ecosystem should correspond to the management problems at hand.

Noss, *Some Principles of Conservation Biology, supra*, at 905–06.

Can large-scale ecosystem initiatives on lands with multiple owners ever be successful, and, if so, how? It may be possible to determine the boundaries of an ecosystem from an ecological standpoint, but is it possible to manage them in a coordinated fashion across jurisdictional lines?

3. Absent a scientific baseline, ecosystem management can become "a policy choice masquerading as an inevitability." Bruce Pardy, *Changing Nature: The Myth of the Inevitability of Ecosystem Management*, 20 PACE ENVTL. L. REV. 675, 691 (2003) (citing DANIEL BOTKIN, DISCORDANT HARMONIES: A NEW ECOLOGY FOR THE TWENTY-FIRST CENTURY 193 (1990)). Ironically, identifying ecosystem management as the end goal may defeat ecosystem preservation. "The mandate of ecosystem management is to measure, control and change ecosystems to produce the most desirable environment in human terms ... a utilitarian approach in which human ends define what kind of 'nature' managers will choose to make." *Id.* at 675. *See* Oliver A. Houck, *On The Law of Biodiversity and Ecosystem Management*, MINN. L. REV. 869, 952–53 (1997) (cautioning that, absent clear and objective scientifically based criteria, ecosystem management becomes "whatever humans want it to be"). Whether "sound science" can provide the necessary baseline for ecosystem management is explored below.

B. "Sound Science"

Even if there were a nationwide commitment to ecosystem management, it is not entirely clear that we have the tools to implement it in an effective, sustainable way. Good decisionmaking depends on good science. The scientific method—formulating hypotheses and testing them to determine their accuracy in a fashion that enables replication and review by other scientists—is a critical component of good science and hence good decisionmaking. Many of us believe that "hard" science, like biology or ecology, is objective, in a way that law and political studies may not be. If so, reaching consensus on the appropriate strategies to ensure ecosystem integrity and sustainable development shouldn't be so difficult, right? Of course, scientific uncertainties will arise and there may be questions that science cannot yet answer, but decisionmakers should be able to at least identify those areas of uncertainty (with the help of scientists, of course) and dedicate resources toward collecting the necessary information and ultimately reaching a common goal. But "good science" is a loaded term.

> In theory, science is non-partisan. The Earth goes around the Sun, gravity is a constant, smoking causes cancer, whether you are a Republican, Democrat, conservative, or liberal. In practice, however, as Galileo and many others discovered, science is not always pure or certain, our knowledge is not always complete or correct, and politics sometimes trumps rationality. * * * Unfortunately, in recent years, the creation of deceptive science and false information has become a thriving industry * * *

Peter H. Gleick, *"Political" Science: The Rise of Junk Science and the Fall of Reason—An ENN Commentary*, Environmental News Network, http://www.enn.com/today.html?id=7110, Feb. 10, 2005.

How can this be? Scientists don't really "sell out" to the politicians, or manipulate their findings for political expediency, do they? Some scholars and decisionmakers claim that the influence of politics could be removed, or at least diminished, if our legislatures adopted "air tight" requirements for "sound science" in our environmental and natural resource laws. Requiring sound science, however, is no panacea.

> Lately, ... we hear much about science coming to the rescue of environmental law. The so-called "sound science" movement claims to be able to improve decisionmaking under environmental law—to make it more rational and objective by infusing the field with more and better practice of science. * * * The "sound science" movement, as its name suggests, advocates that environmental law decisions be based principally on scientific information and conclusions that have been derived through the rigorous, unbiased practice of science. Science is generally regarded as a formalized system for gathering and evaluating information about the world in which prescribed methods of observation, communication, informed criticism, and response must be carefully followed. If these steps work for science, so goes the argument, they should work for environmental law as well. * * * Of course, I am not about to argue against sound science, whatever it means, as it is a loaded term that almost begs a fight. Who is for unsound science? Not I—but I am for a sound approach to sound science. Maybe sound science is good for environmental law, but we all know that too much of a good thing can be bad. So, I ask, could sound science, depending on how it is dosed out to environmental law, be counterproductive?

J.B. Ruhl, *Prescribing the Right Dose of Peer Review for the Endangered Species Act*, 83 Neb. L. Rev. 398, 400–401 (2004).

Professor Ruhl isn't the only one who questions the "sound science" movement. As Professor Holly Doremus explains:

> In recent years, the use of scientific data in administrative decisions has become increasingly contentious. The Endangered Species Act,

because it repeatedly calls for consideration of the best available
scientific data and has been at the center of a number of fierce disputes, provides a useful case study of the role of science in environmental policy. * * * As a society, we hunger for objective, rule-based
decision making, especially when the decision pits human interests
against those of another species. We worry that decisions lacking a
firm, objective basis may be arbitrary, wholly "political," wholly
dependent upon the whims of the particular decision maker, or
made on the basis of improper motivations. We look to "science" to
provide the objectivity we crave. * * *

Science, however, is not as objective or neutral a basis for decisions
as we might hope. In recent years, the uncertainties and gaps in the
supposedly "scientific" decision making of the ESA have become
increasingly apparent, and increasingly the source of controversy
and contention. * * * Needless to say, ESA implementation is not
the only context in which these issues arise. While the Bush Administration was trumpeting the value of increased peer review to
improve the science of regulatory decisions, Congressman Henry
Waxman (D–Cal.) issued a report excoriating the Administration's
manipulation of science in a variety of contexts, including health,
agricultural, environmental and natural resources, and defense
policy. * * * While there is little evidence that federal regulatory
agencies are routinely or intentionally misusing science, those agencies are not always making the best use of science. They are not
addressing openly the limitations of science and their treatment of
uncertainty, they do not put enough emphasis on updating both science and the regulatory decisions that depend upon science, and
their procedures are not calculated to build credibility.* * *

Holly Doremus, *The Purposes, Effects, and Future of the Endangered
Species Act's Best Available Science Mandate*, 34 Envt. L. 397, 397, 399–
401 (2004).

Notes and Questions

1. Professor Doremus notes that "the ESA embodies an unusually
strong legislative commitment to science as a foundation for policy, and it
has been at the center of a series of very public controversies about the use
of science." *Id.* at 400. She concludes that the ESA "therefore offers an excellent case study of the use of science in environmental policy." *Id.* Can you
think of other statutes that provide good examples of the interplay between
science and environmental policy?

2. The interplay between law, policy and science is an important
dynamic, especially in environmental and natural resources law. Is science
likely to guide our decisionmakers to appropriate results, or can it instead
be used as an obstructionist tactic?

TALES FROM A TROUBLED MARRIAGE:
SCIENCE AND LAW IN ENVIRONMENTAL POLICY
Oliver A. Houck
17 TUL. ENVTL. L.J. 163, 164–174 (2003)

Back in the predawn of public environmental statutes, there were private remedies for environmental harms, in tort and nuisance * * * These remedies proved insufficient for at least two reasons. The first is that a civil law response to harm already done is small solace for someone who has lost her livelihood, or the health of her child. The second is illustrated by the real-life saga described in A Civil Action, involving the contamination of drinking water from, in all probability, industrial waste sites. Children died, others were rendered vegetables for life, and their parents suffered a grief that is impossible to describe. But their legal case failed, as many others did, over the requirements of proof and causation. Which chemical, of the many toxins in the waste sites, caused these strange infirmities and through exactly what exposure pathways? * * * Civil law failed because the science could not make the proof. * * *

Beginning in the 1960s, Congress surmounted these difficulties with new statutes, each based on environmental standards. The standards would operate by preventing rather than compensating for harm. They would, further, bypass the rigors of causation and proof: once a standard was set, one had only to see whether or not it was met. The question remained, however: who would set the standard? The answer seemed apparent. Scientists would, on the basis of scientific analysis. After all, it was scientists such as Rachel Carson ... who had sounded the alarm. * * * [But] [n]one of these ... [first generation environmental laws based on scientific risk assessment] worked well, and some, after enormous investment, failed utterly. We began to realize that science, although endlessly fascinating and constantly revelatory, is rarely dispositive. And in the world of environmental policy, that which is not dispositive is dead on arrival. The reason is political: environmental policy faces a degree of resistance unique in public law. No one who has to comply with environmental law likes it, and many hate it outright. * * *

* * * Facing these difficulties [of making a scientific determination of "unreasonable risk"], and with each of their decisions subject to legal challenges, the toxic programs of the air, water, pesticide, and related laws fell into a swoon. Mountains of paper spanning decades produced only a handful of standards, against a backlog of thousands of toxic substances. * * * For the opponents of these standards, there was always an unexplored factor. That is the essence of science. Meanwhile, global temperatures are rising. Parts of the Arctic ice shelf are breaking off into the sea.

* * * For these reasons, all approaches became necessary in cutting the Gordian knot: engineering, science, tort actions, and, more recently, economic and market incentives.* * * There is no longer one way, there are many; and science is no longer king. Science still, however, plays

lead roles. One is to sound the alarm, as it has done for decades and done recently regarding ozone thinning, climate change, and the loss of biological diversity. It is up to science as well to provide a rationale … [for expensive "best available technology" standards]. It also falls to science to identify substances that are so noxious (bioaccumulative toxins, for example) that they need to be phased out completely* * *

With such power and so much riding on the opinions of scientists, however, four notes of caution are in order.

The first is to beware the lure of a return to "scientific management." * * * What we need, goes the refrain, is "iterative," "impact-based," "localized" management focused on the scientifically determined needs of this river, that airshed, this manufacturing plant, or that community. It sounds as attractive and rational as it did forty years ago, but we have tried that for decades and failed. * * * [These programs] eat up heroic amounts of money, remain information-starved, feature shameless manipulation of the data, face crippling political pressure, and produce little abatement. On the natural resources side of the ledger, the most abused concept in public lands management is "multiple use" and the most obeyed is the no-jeopardy standard of the ESA. One is a Rorschach blot; the other is law.

The second caution is the lure of "good science." Every lawyer knows what "good science" is: the science that supports his or her case. All of the other science is bad. If you are opposed to something, be it the control of dioxins, global warming, or obesity, the science is never good enough. * * * When … scientists have said that the ozone layer was thinning, the planet warming, and the fishery disappearing, they were usually ahead of their time, vilified, and on target. * * *

The third caution is the lure of money, which works like the pull of the moon. One knows where lawyers are coming from; they speak for their clients. For whom does the scientist speak? Apparently truth and wisdom, but who pays for their work? Most academics in the sciences receive their salaries and technical support through grants and outside funding, nearly a third of it from industry. * * * In 1998, the New England Journal of Medicine published an article with the unremarkable but statistically documented conclusion that there was a "significant difference" between the opinions of scientists who received corporate funding and those who did not, on the very same issues. Hearing this, do we fall over with surprise? To put it crudely, money talks, and among scientists, the money is too often hidden. * * *

A final caution is the lure of the "safe" life, the apolitical life, free from the application of what scientists know to the issues around them. One must respect … the … need of the profession for the appearance, and fact, of objectivity. The question is, notwithstanding: given the pressure of environmental issues today and their dependence on science, can scientists afford to sit it out? As we speak, an increasing number of scientists are being pulled off of studies, sanctioned, and even dismissed for conclusions that contradict the ideology of their bosses. This question does not concern who pays for what conclusions. It concerns a duty to act and to defend your own.

*   *   *

Notes and Questions

1. Professor Houck's cautionary tale finds support in a flurry of news and journal articles about a government-sponsored scientific study that concluded that fish need no (or little) water to survive in the Klamath River Basin. *See, e.g.,* Robert F. Service, *"Combat Biology" on the Klamath: Biologists Charged with Protecting Endangered Species are Caught in a Battle over Water Rights*, 300 Sci. 36 (Apr. 4, 2003); Michael Grunwald, *Science Group Backs Farmers in Klamath Basin Water Battle*, Journal-Gazette, Feb. 4, 2002, at 10. The National Research Council (NRC) report "concluded that there was no scientific evidence that turning off the irrigation spigot would help two populations of endangered suckers in Upper Klamath Lake, or that increasing the flow of water in the Klamath River below the lake would benefit threatened coho salmon." Robert F. Service, *NRC backs Ecosystem-wide Changes to save Klamath Fish*, 302 Sci. 765 (Oct. 31, 2003). Politicians pointed to the report as proof that a previous Fish and Wildlife Service (FWS) decision to curtail irrigation to protect the fish was based on "junk science." *Id.* Of course, the NRC report is more nuanced than the headlines might lead you to believe. Although the NRC found no strong correlation between water levels and fish kills in the lake, it concluded:

> The basin's problems are legion. Algae blooms choke the lake every summer fed by nutrients from natural sources as well as runoff from farms and ranches. The blooms trigger conditions that strip the water of oxygen and suffocate the suckers. But changing farming and ranching practices upstream will have little immediate impact, because lake sediments are already saturated with nutrients * * * Instead, fisheries agencies should improve spawning and rearing habitat in hopes of bolstering the number of fry.

Id.

The problem was not that the FWS, in concluding that fish needed more water, had used unsound science. According to an FWS official, "the NRC's report 'didn't say the science proves we were wrong; they just said there wasn't enough science to prove us right.'" Marcilynn A. Burke, *Klamath Farmers and Cappuccino Cowboys: The Rhetoric of the Endangered Species Act and Why it (Still) Matters*, 14 Duke Envtl. L & Pol'y F. 441, 512 (2004).

2. The NRC, the research arm of the National Academy of Sciences, was also charged with reviewing FWS's conclusion that endangered species on the Missouri River would be jeopardized by "status quo" operations of upstream dams by the Corps of Engineers. It agreed with the FWS in this case, but the White House "is flexing its muscles to make the agencies fall in line" on the Missouri River. Burke, *supra*, at 511.

> It ordered the Fish and Wildlife Service and the Army Corps of Engineers to rethink their plans to release more water down the Missouri

River to save endangered fish and birds. * * * Though the National Academy of Science supported the release, President Bush supported the status quo during a campaign trip to Missouri * * * Later, according to a report by the Union of Concerned Scientists (UCS), the Bush Administration formed a new ["SWAT"] team to review the situation and make a quick judgment. Union of Concerned Scientists, *Scientific Integrity in Policymaking: An Investigation into the Bush Administration's Misuse of Science* 16 (2004), available at http://www.ucsusa.org/documents/RSI_final_fullreport.pdf. According to UCS, the new fifteen-member team * * * was led by co-leaders with little expertise on the Missouri River. Unlike the original report, the new team's report was not independently peer-reviewed. * * * As one commentator opined, when President Bush receives sound science, he says, "hear no science, see no science, delete all science." Derrick Z. Jackson, *Bush Doesn't Hear "Sound Science"*, Seattle Post-Intelligencer, Aug. 5, 2003, at B7.

Burke, *supra*, at 511–512.

3. The UCS describes itself as "an independent nonprofit alliance ... founded in 1969 by faculty members and students at the Massachusetts Institute of Technology who were concerned about the misuse of science and technology in society. * * * We augment rigorous scientific analysis with innovative thinking and committed citizen advocacy to build a cleaner, healthier environment and a safer world." About UCS, http://www.ucsusa.org/ucs/about/index.cfm. The UCS Report referenced above made broad-sweeping accusations:

> More than 60 influential scientists, including 20 Nobel laureates, issued a statement yesterday asserting that the Bush administration had systematically distorted scientific fact in the service of policy goals on the environment, health, biomedical research and nuclear weaponry at home and abroad. * * * The ... documents accuse the administration of repeatedly censoring and suppressing reports by its own scientists, stacking advisory committees with unqualified political appointees, disbanding government panels that provide unwanted advice and refusing to seek any independent scientific expertise in some cases. * * * Dr. John H. Marburger III, science adviser to President Bush ... said the report consisted of a largely disconnected list of events that did not make the case for a suppression of good scientific advice by the administration. * * * "In most cases," he added, "these are not profound actions that were taken as the result of a policy. They are individual actions that are part of the normal processes within the agencies."
> * * *

James Glanz, *Scientists Say Administration Distorts Facts*, N.Y. Times, Feb. 19, 2004, *at* A18.

Given the heated rhetoric over contentious issues like endangered species, how is a lay person supposed to discern sound science from snake oil?

THE PURPOSES, EFFECTS, AND FUTURE OF THE ENDANGERED SPECIES ACT'S BEST AVAILABLE SCIENCE MANDATE
Holly Doremus
34 Envtl. L. 397, 397, 399–401, 435–441 (2004)

Proposals for legislative reforms focused on the use of science under the ESA have been around since 1978, but they too are growing more common. In recent years a number of bills have proposed new thresholds for the use of scientific information, particularly favoring field data over other types of information and prescribing detailed requirements for review of the science used in regulatory decisions.

The scientific world itself is the latest battleground. Two general reviews of the scientific foundations of the ESA have been positive, but both focused on the Act's structure rather than its implementation. * * * The National Research Council (NRC)* * * regularly conducts studies of science-intensive policy decisions at the request of the federal government. * * * In recent years, the NRC has repeatedly been asked to review policy decisions either directly made under the authority of the ESA or closely related to endangered species protection. The NRC's preliminary report on the Klamath Basin created a furor when it concluded that biological opinions setting minimum lake levels to protect endangered suckers and minimum river flow levels to protect threatened salmon had no substantial scientific basis.

Perhaps the best available science mandate once provided political cover for the ESA, but the scientific basis for many ESA actions is in fact surprisingly thin. As that becomes increasingly apparent, the political usefulness of the mandate seems to be fading. * * *

There is little evidence that federal agencies are affirmatively misusing science in their implementation of the ESA. To the extent there is evidence of abuse or disregard of scientific data, it lies in the failure of the wildlife agencies to list controversial species without judicial prompting. The best available science mandate attempts to counter that tendency by limiting the extent to which the agencies can openly rely on political considerations, and judicial review ensures that the ultimate decision must have at least some scientific grounding. The mandate does not completely eliminate the role of politics, but it is difficult to imagine a practical change that would take politics completely out of the picture. That might not even be desirable because it would put inordinate political stress on the Act as a whole, perhaps for little gain. If a species lacks sufficient public support to overcome the political barriers to protection, its protection may offer society little of value.

* * * Many aspects of ESA decisions are dominated by science, but the existing data is limited and equivocal, leaving a great deal of uncertainty. Choices of how to interpret equivocal data and what to do in the face of uncertainty are not "scientific" as the public understands that term, although they are familiar to scientists and indeed are an unavoid-

able part of the scientific enterprise. Uncertainty is endemic in the ESA context. It can plague our understanding of (among other things): the historic conditions to which the species was exposed and the extent to which those conditions have been altered by human activity; population sizes and trends; life cycles, including the relationship between survival at particular stages and population status; threats to the species and, where there are multiple threats, their relative importance; and the effect of management actions on species.

In part, what to do about uncertainty is the question Professor J.B. Ruhl frames as a choice of "methodology." When faced with uncertain data, we must decide how much certainty to require—that is, what level of confidence we want to have in our decision—before altering the status quo. The question essentially is what burden of proof we want to impose on the wildlife agencies. * * *

At present, the ESA does not explicitly mandate any specific confidence level for any of the decisions it requires, but as interpreted by the courts it is not entirely indifferent on the methodology question. The wildlife agencies cannot require "conclusive evidence" (essentially the "Scientific Method") that a species is near extinction before listing it. That makes good sense, given that the Act's primary goal is to protect species from extinction. Because data about the status of dwindling species are often limited and difficult to obtain, requiring scientific certainty as a predicate for listing would surely undermine that goal. * * * Given the extraordinary levels of uncertainty surrounding most endangered species, the wildlife agencies must enjoy some discretion to take their best cautious guess at what conservation measures are required, or they would be paralyzed. That does not mean, however, that they must be given unreviewable authority to deal with uncertainty as they see fit. The wildlife agencies should be more transparent about the level of uncertainty in the information supporting their actions, how they have chosen to deal with that uncertainty and the basis for those choices, whether the uncertainty can be reduced, and if so what steps would be required to reduce it. An excellent model is the Council on Environmental Quality regulation for dealing with uncertainty in the context of compliance with the National Environmental Policy Act (NEPA).[c] That regulation requires agencies to acknowledge gaps and uncertainties in information and, if the missing information cannot reasonably be obtained, to include a statement explaining how it would be relevant to evaluation of the project's environmental impacts. * * * The agencies, in other words, must use their professional judgment to interpret incomplete information, but they must also be prepared to show that they have exercised that judgment according to relevant professional standards. * * *

c. The regulation, 40 C.F.R. 1502.22 (Incomplete or Unavailable Information), is discussed in the Chapter 4, *infra* (NEPA).

Notes and Questions

1.   Do you agree with the hypothesis that, "If a species lacks sufficient public support to overcome the political barriers to protection, its protection may offer society little of value"? Doremus, *supra,* at 436. How would you test and confirm this hypothesis?

2.   The arbitrary and capricious standard of review of the Administrative Procedure Act (APA), 5 U.S.C. § 706, requires courts to uphold agency decisions unless they ignore relevant facts or run completely contrary to the evidence. Should courts engage in more probing review of agencies' scientific findings and conclusions? More generally, what role should courts play in ensuring that agencies follow appropriate scientific methodology? These questions are particularly difficult when it comes to decisions that must be made on the frontiers (or beyond) of science. Professor Doremus suggests:

> If the agencies do not volunteer ... transparency, ... courts can and should force them to provide it. * * * The rationality of the agencies' choices cannot be understood without an explanation of potentially confounding uncertainties, and the agency cannot be made politically responsible for the manner in which it deals with uncertainty unless those dealings are publicly revealed.

Doremus, *supra,* at 441.

How can courts force agencies to provide transparency? Would a "gatekeeping" function, requiring courts to exclude questionable scientific evidence, work? *See* Daubert v. Merrell Dow Pharmaceuticals, Inc., 509 U.S. 579, 113 S.Ct. 2786, 125 L.Ed.2d 469 (1993) (holding that the Federal Rules of Evidence require the trial judge to ensure that expert testimony rests on a reliable foundation). Doremus thinks not.

> [B]ecause agencies have access to scientific and technical expertise in making their decisions, and because those decisions need not be made for all time on a short timeline, it would be inappropriate to apply *Daubert* to administrative decisions. * * * *Daubert* rests on the perceived need ... to keep irrelevant or misleading information from the jury. There is no such need in the context of legislative agency decision making. Not only does the agency have full access to expertise that a jury will often lack, but agencies, unlike juries, must explain their decisions. If evidence relied upon by an agency does not support its decision, the decision can (indeed, must) be reversed by a reviewing court. As a result, there is no need to prevent agencies from being exposed to evidence that might encourage them to make irrational or illegitimate decisions. * * *

Doremus, *supra,* at 416–417. Do you agree?

3.   Professor Doremus offers some observations about the implementation of science through law and policy:

> [There are] several steps that could improve the use of science. First, the agencies should more forthrightly acknowledge the limits of science, including both the extent to which their decisions require nonscientific elements and the uncertainties in the data they use to make those decisions. Second, they should do more to expand and update their knowl-

edge base, and to put new knowledge to use. Third, they should build public credibility and political acceptance of their decisions by ... making greater efforts to overcome their project-specific myopia.

Doremus, *supra*, at 437.

Industries and some scientists and scholars have argued that a fourth step—peer review—would be an appropriate mechanism for ensuring that governmental decisions are based on sound science. Would a requirement for scientific peer review and consensus before species could be protected or toxic chemicals restricted be beneficial in the quest for sustainable development and ecosystem integrity? The following article explores this issue.

PRESCRIBING THE RIGHT DOSE OF PEER REVIEW FOR THE ENDANGERED SPECIES ACT
J.B. Ruhl
83 NEB. L. REV. 398, 402–407 (2004)

Peer review is generally described as a scientifically rigorous review and critique of a study's methods, results, and findings that is conducted by others in the relevant field who have the requisite training and expertise, who have no pecuniary or other disqualifying bias with respect to the topic, and who are independent of the persons who performed the study. * * * Within science, peer review is widely considered "essential to the integrity of scientific and scholarly communication." For many scientists, indeed, peer review "does not merely reflect the scientific method, it is the scientific method." * * *

[I]f peer review is part of sound science, which it is, and sound science is part of environmental decisionmaking in many instances, which it is, ought not peer review be a part of environmental decisionmaking? But the answer is: not necessarily.

* * * Even when science does produce robust results, in many value-laden societal decisionmaking contexts scientific findings simply are not all that matter. In short, "decisionmaking is often driven by a variety of nonscientific, adversarial, and stakeholder dynamics. Thus, even though science helps inform choices, it is only one of many values and interests considered by each stakeholder."

* * * [There are] three conflicts that unrestrained doses of regulatory peer review pose for [environmental] decisionmaking * * * First, because its advocates regularly overstate what peer review will accomplish for environmental law decisionmaking, mandating peer review across the board raises unrealistic expectations of the quality of agency decisions and weakens the position of other important components of decisionmaking. Second, inflexibly mandating rigorous peer review adds substantial demands on agency resources, potentially draining resources from other decisionmaking components and, in many cases, impeding decisionmaking altogether. Finally, peer review is subject to abuse if it is implemented in ways that allow agencies to manipulate the process and

thereby rig outcomes so as to justify agency decisions that would not withstand legitimate peer scrutiny. Peer review, in other words, can be prescribed at overdose levels for the ESA, and environmental law generally, even though it is an essential component of sound science. * * * The optimal use of peer review in environmental law, I contend, is not all the way all of the time. * * *

Notes and Questions

1. What is the right "dose" of peer review when it comes to restoring and sustaining depleted fisheries or exhausted rangelands, or logging within old-growth habitat? Which decisions are most likely to benefit from the advantages that peer review can offer? If the potential costs of extending protection to, for example, an endangered species are high, would focused, rigorous peer review promote focused, rigorous decisionmaking? *See id.* at 430–431. According to Professor Oliver Houck, a healthy dose of skepticism may be in order.

> [W]e see today, in the name of "good science," a proposal for "peer review" of all science-based agency decisions. If the Environmental Protection Agency (EPA) proposes an environmentally protective action, it will likely be stalled for lack of consensus among "independent" peers. More studies will be commissioned, years will pass. Administrations will change. The opponents win. If, on the other hand, the EPA decides that TCE does not pose a significant risk to human health, or the Department of the Interior decides not to protect the Alabama beach mouse as an endangered species, there is no peer review, because no action is being proposed. What you have, then, is a knife that cuts only one way: against environmental protection. * * * Beware of being so used.

Houck, supra, at 173.

2. What role should scientists play when resource management decisions are challenged in court? Most of them are reluctant to play any role whatsoever.

> The probabilistic character of all natural phenomena and all statements about nature is not congruent with a legal system that demands certainty. The apparent inability of many people—including lawyers, judges, legislators, and journalists—to appreciate the inherent uncertainty in science is a primary reason why many scientists feel uncomfortable in the courtroom, testifying at congressional hearings, or being involved in public debates of any kind.

Noss, *Some Principles of Conservation Biology, supra*, at 907–908 (*citing* Botkin, *supra*, at 11–12).

Scientists sometimes accuse their colleagues who express concrete conclusions while acting as expert witnesses in contested cases of being "Lysenkoists" who distort scientific findings for economic or political gain. Trofim Lysenko, Stalin's scientist in charge of the Soviet biological sciences, "perpetuated grievous consequences on the Soviet economy and sciences" by suppressing classical genetics and ignoring Darwinian principles of evolution. *See* Bailey Kuklin, *Evolution, Politics and Law*, 38 Val. U. L. Rev. 1129, 1227

n. 339 (2004). Lysenko was also "instrumental in the censorship, disappearance, and imprisonment of numerous scientists" who espoused politically incorrect theories. David E. Adelman, *Scientific Activism and Restraint: The Interplay of Statistics, Judgment, and Procedure in Environmental law, 79* NOTRE DAME L.REV. 497, 534 n.156 (2004). Lysenkoism, which reigned in the Soviet Union from the mid–1930's to the 1960's, is "the classic example of politics undermining the integrity of science." *Id.*

How can lawyers and decisionmakers encourage scientists to take part in the legal and administrative processes, when their discipline discourages them from making concrete findings, much less recommendations, in the face of uncertainty? Finding the answer to this question will be crucial to any effort to formulate rational, sustainable objectives and standards for managing natural resources.

V. CONCLUDING THOUGHTS: BIODIVERSITY, MORALITY AND LAW

Creating a viable legal framework for sustainable development and biodiversity preservation through ecosystem management or other means requires an alternative philosophical foundation to dislodge or at least take its place beside classical economic drivers. Biodiversity cannot compete with economically driven management philosophies unless it expresses a distinct and persuasive core principle that takes hold of the public imagination and attains solid footing among decision-makers. Ethical, moral and perhaps even religious justifications can be employed to support biodiversity preservation. Indeed, Christian theology has had a palpable influence on resource management philosophies, as explained by Professor Nagle below.

PLAYING NOAH
John Copeland Nagle
82 MINN. L. REV. 1171, 1217–1229 (1998)

The tale of Noah and his ark resonates with young children and government officials alike * * * and it has played an unexpected role in the recent debate over the future of the ESA. * * * God instructed Noah to build an ark—a prototype houseboat—that he and his family could use to survive the impending flood. Additionally, God directed Noah "to bring into the ark two of all living creatures, male and female, to keep them alive with you. Two of every kind of bird, of every kind of animal and every kind of creature that moves along the ground will come to you to be kept alive." Genesis 6:19–20 (New Int'l). Noah obeyed God's command. The promised flood destroyed all living things on the earth except for the occupants of the ark. * * *

That story features prominently in the defenses of the ESA * * * God "did not specify that Noah should limit the ark to two charismatic species, two good for hunting, two species that might provide some cure down the road, and, two that draw crowds to the city zoo." Bruce Babbitt, *Between the Flood and the Rainbow: Our Covenant to Protect the*

Whole of Creation, 2 Animal L. 1, 5 (1996). * * * The resulting covenant between God and Noah "was made to protect the whole of creation, not for the exclusive use and disposition of mankind, but for the purposes of the Creator." * * *

* * * Noah's example allows for some uncertainty about whether he (and God) intended to protect all of the species that we recognize today, and the balance of the scriptural record indicates a more nuanced relationship between people and the world in which we live. The claim that Noah imposes a duty to protect all endangered species, however, remains sound. This is true regardless of the authority (if any) one attributes to Genesis because Noah also supports moral, nonreligious theories of species preservation. * * *

* * * Assume for a moment, therefore, that faithfulness to God includes a desire to follow Noah's example. That assumption * * * [has] been challenged as contrary to the balance of the scriptural teachings on the environment. * * * A related concern objects to the use of the story of Noah as a "proof text," plucking a biblical teaching out of context to support a point it was never intended to make. * * * To be sure, there is no biblical verse that commands "thou shalt preserve every species on earth," nor does species preservation figure prominently elsewhere in the scriptures. But to dismiss the story of Noah so readily ignores that God must have had a reason in commanding Noah to take every species onto the ark. * * * [T]o the extent that Noah was concerned about saving himself, not just the animals, it is possible that our fate is linked to the survival of the life around us, too. Maybe we are in the same boat as Noah after all.

Those seeking to avoid a duty to protect every endangered species are more likely to turn to other parts of the scriptures. Genesis records that God entrusted man with dominion over the earth, a notoriously difficult passage for environmentalists. See Genesis 1:26 * * * Genesis further directs man to "fill the earth and subdue it." Genesis 1:28. Former Interior Secretary Manuel Lujan cited the dominion command to justify actions that could result in the loss of a species. * * * The gist of such statements is that people are more important than animals. One possible corollary of that assertion is that the value of each species is measured by its value to humans. But such an effort to justify choices among species conflicts with other biblical texts that indicate that all parts of creation have value to God independent of their utilitarian value. * * *

There is a more basic problem, though, with such lines of argument. The dominion of which Genesis speaks should not be understood as a license for humans to do whatever they want to the world for whatever purpose they happen to have in mind. The word "dominion" is used elsewhere in the scriptures to refer to a peaceful rule designed to serve those living subject to it. * * * Dominion as kingship reflects the just, righteous rule that God expected of Israelite kings. Dominion as servanthood imitates the way in which God provides for creation and the kind of rule that Jesus described in the New Testament. Dominion as stewardship posits that God is the owner of creation who has asked us to serve as a trustee responsible for managing the earth on God's behalf.

Stewardship is the prevalent model. * * * This stewardship model is further supported by the instruction given by God to Adam in Genesis to tend the earth and to "keep" it. The stewards of creation, therefore, must treat the creation in a manner that reflects the value and purpose that God places on the creation. * * *

* * * Noah's example can be understood to establish a moral principle, not a uniquely religious one. * * * [B]iologist David Ehrenfeld affixes the label the "Noah Principle" to the claim that "[l]ong-standing existence in Nature is deemed to carry with it the unimpeachable right to continued existence." In particular, Noah provides "an excellent precedent" because "[n]ot a single species was excluded on the basis of low priority, and by all accounts not a single species was lost." All species, therefore, have a right to exist.

*   *   *

Notes and Questions

1.   Does the argument that we have a religious duty to protect biodiversity resonate with you? Are there other more compelling moral grounds that should be advanced in persuading policy makers and their constituents? Renowned ecologist Aldo Leopold drew upon ethics when he wrote, "A thing is right when it tends to preserve the integrity, stability, and beauty of the biotic community. It is wrong when it tends otherwise." ALDO LEOPOLD, A SAND COUNTY ALMANAC 262 (Ballantine 1991) (1949). *See* ERIC T. FREYFOGLE, BOUNDED PEOPLE, BOUNDLESS LANDS: ENVISIONING A NEW LAND ETHIC (1998). Leopold's experiences as a Forest Service employee in the Southwest during the 1910's, along with time spent on his own Wisconsin farm, "transformed him from a conventional resource-based thinker to a proponent of the idea that humans are on an ethical continuum with all animals and plants." Sarah Krakoff, *Mountains Without Handrails ... Wilderness Without Cellphones*, 27 HARV. ENVTL. L. REV. 417, 457 (2003). His "land ethic" views humans as members of a community larger than themselves. How does a land ethic square (if at all) with the moral obligations reflected in our criminal law system—those that we've been taught by our elders from day one—thou shalt not lie, cheat, steal or kill other *human beings*?

2.   Professor Nagle is well aware that critics believe the Noah Principle is "unethical and impracticable":

> It is unethical, because trying to save every species perfectly would force our society to destroy many or all of its other accomplishments, an act of self-immolation that the ecologically concerned cannot force on others, who may have different but equally worthy goals. And it is impracticable, because this perfect duty is impossible to fulfill, even if our society were willing to turn back three hundred years of its history.

Nagle, supra, at 1231–32 (citing CHARLES C. MANN & MARK L. PLUMMER, NOAH'S CHOICE: THE FUTURE OF ENDANGERED SPECIES 216 (1995)). Which argument is more persuasive, Nagle's or his detractors?

3.　Assuming that you agree that there is a religious and/or moral duty to preserve biodiversity, does that duty extend to biodiversity wherever it is found? Does such a duty extend to remote, sparsely populated areas that most of us will never visit, such as ANWR? What about private lands? America's view of property rights has been indelibly shaped by Sir William Blackstone, who described property ownership as "absolute dominion over the land, to the exclusion of all conflicting claims." Eric T. Freyfogle, *The Owning and Taking of Sensitive Lands*, 43 UCLA L. REV. 77, 99 (1995) *(citing* BLACKSTONE, COMMENTARIES 2). Is it possible to rectify a biodiversity duty with the Blackstonian notion of inviolate, sacrosanct property rights? Perhaps the question throws you a red herring: is the Blackstonian notion just that—a notion, but not a legal reality?

Chapter 3

CONSTITUTIONAL AND ADMINISTRATIVE THEMES IN NATURAL RESOURCES LAW

Federal, state and local governments, Native American tribes, and private landowners jealously safeguard their authorities over wildlife, water, land, minerals and other natural resources within their jurisdiction or ownership. This chapter provides a rough sketch of the basic sources of governmental authority for natural resource ownership, management and regulation. It also covers the basics of administrative law, jurisdiction, and judicial review. Subsequent chapters explore themes related to federal, state, tribal and private ownership and management in greater depth.

I.   WHO'S GOT THE POWER?

Sources of power vary depending on the entity and the type of resource in question. Ownership is, of course, a fundamental source of control of land and many other types of resources, and it is considered in detail in Part II of this book. The focus of this section is on constitutional and other federal and state powers to manage, preserve, and utilize natural resources.

A. Constitutional Authority Over Natural Resources and Public Lands

Federal power to manage natural resources and public lands flows from various provisions of the U.S. Constitution.

• The Commerce Clause, U.S. CONST. art. 1, § 8, cl. 3, provides federal authority over economic activities that have a substantial relation to interstate commerce. *See* Hodel v. Virginia Surface Min. and Reclamation Ass'n, Inc., 452 U.S. 264, 101 S.Ct. 2352, 69 L.Ed.2d 1 (1981) (upholding the Surface Mining Control and Reclamation Act).

• The Property Clause, art. IV, § 3, cl. 2, gives Congress "the Power to dispose of and make all needful Rules and Regulations respecting the Territory or other Property belonging to the United States." *See* Kleppe v. New Mexico, 426 U.S. 529, 96 S.Ct. 2285, 49 L.Ed.2d 34 (1976) (upholding the Wild Free-roaming Horses and Burros Act); United States v. Midwest Oil Co., 236 U.S. 459, 35 S.Ct. 309, 59 L.Ed. 673 (1915) (upholding President Taft's decision to withdraw federal lands from mining to preserve oil reserves).

• The Treaty Clause, U.S. CONST., art. II, § 2, provides the President with "the Power, by and with the Advice and Consent of the Senate, to make Treaties, provided two-thirds of the Senators present concur." *See* Missouri v. Holland, 252 U.S. 416, 40 S.Ct. 382, 64 L.Ed. 641 (1920) (upholding the Migratory Bird Treaty Act of 1918).

• The Spending Clause, U.S. CONST. art. I, § 8, provides authority by which Congress may urge states to adopt programs consistent with federal interests by attaching conditions to receipt of federal funds. New York v. United States, 505 U.S. 144, 112 S.Ct. 2408, 120 L.Ed.2d 120 (1992) (upholding, in part, the Low–Level Radioactive Waste Policy Act, which included various incentives for states to provide for disposal of waste generated within their borders).

• The Necessary and Proper Clause, U.S. CONST. art. I, § 8, cl. 18, provides authority "to make all laws which shall be necessary and proper for carrying into execution" other specifically enumerated powers. *See* McCulloch v. Maryland, 17 U.S. (4 Wheat.) 316, 324–25, 4 L.Ed. 579 (1819) (upholding constitutionality of national bank).

• The Supremacy Clause, U.S. CONST. art. IV, § 3, cl.2, preempts state laws that are incompatible with federal requirements imposed pursuant to the constitutional powers described above. *See* Douglas v. Seacoast Products, Inc., 431 U.S. 265, 97 S.Ct. 1740, 52 L.Ed.2d 304 (1977) (concluding that Congress has Commerce Clause power to grant federal fishing licenses for use in state waters, thereby preempting conflicting state laws); California Coastal Comm'n v. Granite Rock Co., 480 U.S. 572, 107 S.Ct. 1419, 94 L.Ed.2d 577 (1987) (finding that neither federal regulations nor federal land use statutes preempted the state coastal commission's imposition of an environmentally protective permit requirement on an unpatented mining claim in a national forest).

Many of the early federal land management statutes delegated broad-sweeping authority to the Forest Service and other agencies, while providing very few concrete parameters on the agency's discretion. This led to complaints that the agencies were allowed to exercise "legislative" powers, as opposed to merely executing the laws laid down by Congress, in violation of Article III separation of powers. U.S. Const. Art. III. Throughout the years, these "nondelegation" claims have been rejected at nearly every turn by the federal courts.

UNITED STATES v. PIERRE GRIMAUD

Supreme Court of the United States, 1911.
220 U.S. 506, 31 S.Ct. 480, 55 L.Ed. 563.

JUSTICE LAMAR:

By the act of March 3, 1891 (26 Stat. at L. 1103, chap. 561, U. S. Comp. Stat. 1901, p.1537), the President was authorized, from time to time, to set apart and reserve, in any state or territory, public lands, wholly or in part covered with timber or undergrowth, whether of commercial value or not, as public forest reservations. And by the act of June 4, 1897 (30 Stat. at L. 35, chap. 2, U. S. Comp. Stat. 1901, p. 1539), the purposes of these reservations were declared to be "to improve and protect the forest within the reservation, or for the purpose of securing favorable conditions of water flows, and to furnish a continuous supply of timber for the use and necessities of citizens of the United States." * * * It is also provided that nothing in the act should "be construed as prohibiting ... any person from entering upon such forest reservations for all proper and lawful purposes, ... provided that such persons comply with the rules and regulations covering such forest reservations." * * *

The original act provided that the management and regulation of these reserves should be by the Secretary of the Interior; but in 1905 that power was conferred upon the Secretary of Agriculture (33 Stat. at L. 628, chap. 288, U. S. Comp. Stat. Supp. 1909, p. 576), and by virtue of those various statutes he was authorized to "make provisions for the protection against destruction by fire and depredations upon the public forests and forest reservations ... ; and he may make such rules and regulations and establish such service as will insure the objects of such reservations; namely, to regulate their occupancy and use, and to preserve the forests thereon from destruction; and any violation of the provisions of this act or such rules and regulations shall be punished," as prescribed in Rev. Stat. 5388, U. S. Comp. Stat. 1901, p. 3649,—which, as amended, provides for a fine of not more than $500 and imprisonment for not more than twelve months, or both, at the discretion of the court. * * *

Under these acts, the Secretary of Agriculture, on June 12, 1906, promulgated and established certain rules for the purpose of regulating the use and occupancy of the public forest reservations and preserving

the forests thereon from destruction, and among those established was
the following:

> "Regulation 45. All persons must secure permits before grazing any
> stock in a forest reserve, except the few head in actual use by pros-
> pectors, campers, and travelers, and milch or work animals, not
> exceeding a total of six head, owned by bona fide settlers residing in
> or near a forest reserve, which are excepted and require no permit."

The defendants were charged with driving and grazing sheep on a
reserve, without a permit. The grand jury in the district court for the
southern district of California * * * indicted Pierre Grimaud and J. P.
Carajous, charging that on April 26, 1907, after the Sierra Forest
Reserve had been established, and after regulation 45 had been promulgated, "they did knowingly, wilfully, and unlawfully pasture and graze,
and cause and procure to be pastured and grazed, certain sheep ...
within the limits of and a part of said Sierra Forest Reserve, without
having theretofore or at any time secured or obtained a permit or any
permission for said pasturing or grazing of said sheep or any part of
them, as required by the said rules and regulations of the Secretary of
Agriculture," the said sheep not being within any of the excepted
classes.* * *

* * * [Defendants] demurred on the ground that the forest reserve
act of 1897 [30 Stat. at L. 35, chap. 2, U. S. Comp. Stat. 1901, p. 1540]
was unconstitutional, in so far as it delegated to the Secretary of Agriculture power to make rules and regulations, and made a violation
thereof a penal offense. * * *

Under these acts [of 1891 and 1897], * * * any use of the reservation for grazing or other lawful purpose was required to be subject to the
rules and regulations established by the Secretary of Agriculture. To
pasture sheep and cattle on the reservation, at will and without
restraint, might interfere seriously with the accomplishment of the purposes for which they were established. But a limited and regulated use
for pasturage might not be inconsistent with the object sought to be
attained by the statute. The determination of such questions, however,
was a matter of administrative detail. What might be harmless in one
forest might be harmful to another. What might be injurious at one stage
of timber growth, or at one season of the year, might not be so at another.

In the nature of things it was impracticable for Congress to provide
general regulations for these various and varying details of management. Each reservation had its peculiar and special features; and in
authorizing the Secretary of Agriculture to meet these local conditions,
Congress was merely conferring administrative functions upon an agent,
and not delegating to him legislative power. The authority actually given
was much less than what has been granted to municipalities by virtue
of which they make by-laws, ordinances, and regulations for the government of towns and cities. Such ordinances do not declare general rules
with reference to rights of persons and property, nor do they create or

regulate obligations and liabilities, nor declare what shall be crimes, nor fix penalties therefor.

By whatever name they are called, they refer to matters of local management and local police. Brodbine v. Revere, 182 Mass. 599, 66 N. E. 607. They are "not of a legislative character in the highest sense of the term; and as an owner may delegate to his principal agent the right to employ subordinates, giving to them a limited discretion, so it would seem that Congress might rightfully intrust to the local legislature [authorities] the determination of minor matters." Butte City Water Co. v. Baker, 196 U.S. 126.

It must be admitted that it is difficult to define the line which separates legislative power to make laws, from administrative authority to make regulations. This difficulty has often been recognized, and was referred to by Chief Justice Marshall in Wayman v. Southard, 10 Wheat. 42, 6 L.Ed. 262, where he was considering the authority of courts to make rules. He there said: "It will not be contended that Congress can delegate to the courts, or to any other tribunals, powers which are strictly and exclusively legislative. But Congress may certainly delegate to others powers which the legislature may rightfully exercise itself." What were these nonlegislative powers which Congress could exercise, but which might also be delegated to others, was not determined, for he said: "The line has not been exactly drawn which separates those important subjects which must be entirely regulated by the legislature itself, from those of less interest, in which a general provision may be made, and power given to those who are to act under such general provisions to fill up the details."

From the beginning of the government, various acts have been passed conferring upon executive officers power to make rules and regulations,—not for the government of their departments, but for administering the laws which did govern. None of these statutes could confer legislative power. But when Congress had legislated and indicated its will, it could give to those who were to act under such general provisions "power to fill up the details" by the establishment of administrative rules and regulations, the violation of which could be punished by fine or imprisonment fixed by Congress, or by penalties fixed by Congress, or measured by the injury done. * * *

That "Congress cannot delegate legislative power is a principle universally recognized as vital to the integrity and maintenance of the system of government ordained by the Constitution." Marshall Field & Co. v. Clark, 143 U. S. 692, 36 L. ed. 309, 12 Sup. Ct. Rep. 495. But the authority to make administrative rules is not a delegation of legislative power, nor are such rules raised from an administrative to a legislative character because the violation thereof is punished as a public offense.

It is true that there is no act of Congress which, in express terms, declares that it shall be unlawful to graze sheep on a forest reserve. But the statutes from which we have quoted declare that the privilege of using reserves for "all proper and lawful purposes" is subject to the proviso that the person so using them shall comply "with the rules and regulations covering said forest reservation." The same act makes it an offense to violate those regulations; that is, to use them otherwise than in accordance with the rules established by the Secretary. Thus the implied license under which the United States had suffered its public domain to be used as a pasture for sheep and cattle * * * was curtailed and qualified by Congress, to the extent that such privilege should not be exercised in contravention of the rules and regulations. * * * If, after the passage of the act and the promulgation of the rule, the defendants drove and grazed their sheep upon the reserve, in violation of the regulations, they were making an unlawful use of the government's property. * * *

The Secretary of Agriculture could not make rules and regulations for any and every purpose. * * * As to those here involved, they all relate to matters clearly indicated and authorized by Congress. The subjects as to which the Secretary can regulate are defined. * * * He is authorized "to regulate the occupancy and use and to preserve the forests from destruction." A violation of reasonable rules regulating the use and occupancy of the property is made a crime, not by the Secretary, but by Congress. The statute, not the Secretary, fixes the penalty.

The indictment charges, and the demurrer, admits that rule 45 was promulgated for the purpose of regulating the occupancy and use of the public forest reservation and preserving the forest. The Secretary did not exercise the legislative power of declaring the penalty or fixing the punishment for grazing sheep without a permit, but the punishment is imposed by the act itself. The offense is not against the Secretary, but, as the indictment properly concludes, "contrary to the laws of the United States and the peace and dignity thereof." * * *

Notes and Questions

1. The latest word from the Court on a non-delegation challenge to an environmental law was in Whitman v. American Trucking, 531 U.S. 457, 121 S.Ct. 903, 149 L.Ed.2d 1 (2001). The challengers alleged that the Clean Air Act violated the non-delegation doctrine by providing sweeping legislative authorities to the Environmental Protection Agency (EPA) to adopt National Ambient Air Quality Standards for certain "criteria" air pollutants, including ozone and particulate matter. The Court concluded that the delegation of authority to set standards at a level "requisite to protect public health" provided an "intelligible principle" to guide agency implementation of the Act and therefore avoided a non-delegation problem. *Id.* at 474–76.

2. In the modern, complex administrative world, is there still a need for a non-delegation doctrine? What is its purpose? For more detailed discussion of non-delegation and separation of powers concerns in the natural resources context, *see* Sandra Zellmer, *The Nondelegation Doctrine: Fledgling Phoenix or Ill-fated Albatross?*, 31 ELR 11,151 (2001); Sandra Zellmer, *The Devil, The Details, and the Dawn of the 21st Century Administrative State: Beyond the New Deal*, 32 ARIZ. ST. L.J. 941 (2000).

B. State Authority, Sagebrush Rebels and Federalism

States possess police powers to protect the public health and welfare, and this power extends to measures employed to "protect an important and traditional food source," such as game species, Conservation Force, Inc. v. Manning, 301 F.3d 985, 997 (9th Cir. 2002), as well as fruit trees, water resources, wetlands and coastal zones. *See* Miller v. Schoene, 276 U.S. 272, 48 S.Ct. 246, 72 L.Ed. 568 (1928) (upholding Virginia's decree to cut down red cedar trees because cedar rust was fatal to nearby apple orchards); Maine v. Taylor, 477 U.S. 131, 151, 106 S.Ct. 2440, 2454, 91 L.Ed.2d 110, 129 (1986) ("[Each state] retains broad regulatory authority to protect the health and safety of its citizens and the integrity of its natural resources" such as fisheries); Sporhase v. Nebraska, 458 U.S. 941, 954, 102 S.Ct. 3456, 3463, 73 L.Ed.2d 1254, 1265 (1982) (describing the state's interest in conserving ground water as "unquestionably legitimate and highly important"); Tahoe–Sierra Preservation Council, Inc. v. Tahoe Regional Planning Agency, 34 F.Supp.2d 1226, 1239 (D.Nev. 1999) (finding a legitimate state interest in controlling development on "high hazard" lands when development could damage the beauty and clarity of Lake Tahoe), *aff'd in part, rev'd in part,* 216 F.3d 764 (9th Cir. 2000), *aff'd,* 535 U.S. 302, 122 S.Ct. 1465, 152 L.Ed.2d 517 (2002).

States have also asserted an ownership interest in natural resources as a source of their authority. The Supreme Court has rejected this particular theory, at least as it relates to wildlife and migratory birds: "To put the claim of … [State authority] upon title is to lean upon a slender reed." Hughes v. Oklahoma, 441 U.S. 322, 332, 99 S.Ct. 1727, 1734, 60 L.Ed.2d 250, 259 (1979), citing Missouri v. Holland, 252 U.S. 416, 434, 40 S.Ct. 382, 64 L.Ed. 641 (1920). Even absent title, though, states have "ample allowance for preserving … the legitimate state concerns for conservation and protection of wild animals underlying the 19th-century legal fiction of state ownership." *Id.* at 335. State ownership interests are addressed in detail in Chapter 8, *infra.*

When states take regulatory action over natural resources pursuant to their police powers, they (like the federal government) sometimes bump up against constitutional constraints. For example, if state action affects private interests, states might find themselves constrained by the Equal Protection Clause, the Due Process Clause and the Takings Clause of the Fifth Amendment, just to name a few pertinent provisions. If state action conflicts with federal prerogatives, states might also find themselves constrained by the Supremacy Clause and the Dormant Commerce Clause. Constitutional constraints are explored in detail in subsequent chapters on wildlife resources, timber management, land use planning, and public and private ownership.

States occasionally raise federalism and related themes to avoid restrictions on their authority over land and resources within state boundaries, as illustrated by Nevada's opposition to the siting of a federal nuclear storage site at Yucca Mountain, detailed below.

NUCLEAR ENERGY INSTITUTE, INC. v. ENVIRONMENTAL PROTECTION AGENCY

United States Court of Appeals, District of Columbia Circuit, 2004.
373 F.3d 1251.

[*ed.* Nevada brought various challenges to federal decisions governing the creation of a nuclear waste repository at Yucca Mountain, Nevada.]

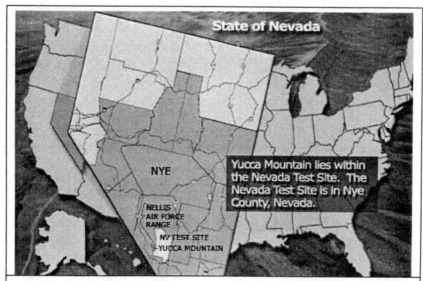

Office of Civilian Radioactive Waste Management, Yucca Mountain Project, Photo History of Yucca Mountain – Maps,
http://www.ocrwm.doe.gov/newsroom/photos/photos_maps.shtml

Having the capacity to outlast human civilization as we know it and the potential to devastate public health and the environment, nuclear waste has vexed scientists, Congress, and regulatory agencies for the last half-century. After rejecting disposal options ranging from burying nuclear waste in polar ice caps to rocketing it to the sun, the scientific consensus has settled on deep geologic burial as the safest way to isolate this toxic material in perpetuity. Following years of legislative wrangling and agency deliberation, the political consensus has now selected Yucca Mountain, Nevada as the nation's nuclear waste disposal site. * * *

Nevada asserts that the Constitution requires Congress, when it decides to use federal property in a manner that imposes a unique burden on a particular State, to choose the relevant site on the basis of facially neutral criteria that are applicable nationwide. * * * The so-called "equal treatment" claim Nevada asserts is not based upon any specific provision of the Constitution, but rather on principles of federalism ostensibly inherent in the Constitution as a whole. * * * [I]ts argument is based primarily on the Supreme Court's interpretation of the Tenth Amendment in South Carolina v. Baker, 485 U.S. 505 (1988). In *Baker,* the Court suggested "the possibility that some extraordinary defects in the national political process might render congressional regulation of state activities invalid under the Tenth Amendment." *Id.* at 512. Such a defect might arise, the Court indicated, where a State "was singled out in a way that left it politically isolated and powerless." *Id.* at 513. Nevada argues that this occurs when Congress legislates in violation of the asserted "equal treatment" principle: "A State can negotiate and politick with other States when the issue before Congress is what general standards to apply in deciding where to bury nuclear waste, because all States have an interest in fair, reasonable and workable rules, given that all are at risk of being stuck with an unpopular burden." Petitioners' Br. at 53. Where, by contrast, Congress is asked to give an up-or-down vote on a single preannounced site, "then the State where that site is located loses its natural allies in the national political process." *Id.* We find no basis in the Constitution for Nevada's proposed "equal treatment" requirement. * * *

[T]he Resolution does not infringe upon state interests of the kind protected by the Tenth Amendment. *Baker,* upon which Nevada bases its claim, construed the Tenth Amendment as broadly as possible to refer to "any implied constitutional limitation on Congress' authority to *regulate state activities,* whether grounded in the Tenth Amendment itself or in principles of federalism derived generally from the Constitution." 485 U.S. at 511 n. 5 (emphasis added). *Baker* then unequivocally states that "the possibility that some extraordinary defects in the national political process might render congressional regulation ... invalid under the Tenth Amendment" would be an issue only with respect to *"congressional regulation of state activities."* 485 U.S. at 512 (emphasis added). Congress's decision to designate Yucca Mountain for development as a repository does not in any way regulate Nevada's activities; it merely prescribes the use of a particular piece of *federal property.* Nor, of course, does the Resolution "commandeer" the state legislative process or state officials so as to violate the Tenth Amendment constraint on federal powers recognized in New York v. United States, 505 U.S. 144 (1992), and Printz v. United States, 521 U.S. 898 (1997). Congress's decision to use the Yucca site as a repository does preempt Nevada from adopting conflicting legislation or regulations. But this is merely the natural and constitutionally unobjectionable result of the Supremacy Clause. In short, while the designation of Yucca as a repository may impose a burden on Nevada, it does not infringe upon state sovereign interests of the limited type protected by the Tenth Amendment.

Moreover, the Tenth Amendment limitation adumbrated by the Court in *Baker* applies to defects in the *political process.* But the "equal treatment" claim asserted by Nevada plainly goes to the *substantive basis* of congressional legislation over federal property and does not involve the political *process* at all. The Court made clear in *Baker* that "nothing in ... the Tenth Amendment [broadly construed] authorizes courts to second-guess the substantive basis for congressional legislation. Where, as here, the national political *process* did not operate in a defective manner, the Tenth Amendment is not implicated." 485 U.S. at 513 (citation omitted). If anything, therefore, *Baker* appears positively to preclude us from subjecting congressional legislation to the so-called "equal treatment" requirement conjured up by Nevada.

* * * Nevada purports to find support for its "equal treatment" claim in the Guarantee Clause, the Port Preference Clause, the Uniformity Clause, the Bill of Attainder Clause, and the equal footing doctrine. Nevada does not assert that the Resolution violates any of these provisions or doctrines taken individually, and it is clear that any such claim would fail. Rather, Nevada contends that these provisions and doctrines express fundamental principles of state equality and a general constitutional preference for legislation based on neutral and generally applicable criteria. Nevada attempts to distill these principles and to synthesize from them a novel constitutional "equal treatment" requirement. But in so doing, Nevada effectively discards the text, the substantive context, and the jurisprudential history of each of the individual provisions or doctrines upon which it relies. The end product is an entirely new creation. It has no textual basis in the Constitution. And, perhaps not surprisingly, Nevada cites no juridical precedent or historical practice hinting at the existence of such a restraint on congressional authority over federal lands.

We are aware, of course, that the Supreme Court has recognized—in the context of its state sovereign immunity and "commandeering" decisions—constitutional limitations on congressional authority that are not solely or strictly based upon the text of the Constitution. * * * The Court's sovereign immunity decisions are premised on the conclusion that, "as the Constitution's structure, its history, and the authoritative interpretations by this Court make clear, the States' immunity from suit is a fundamental aspect of sovereignty which the States enjoyed before the ratification of the Constitution." *Alden v. Maine,* 527 U.S. 706, 713 (1999). This preexisting immunity was "confirmed ... as a constitutional principle" by the ratification of the Eleventh Amendment. * * * The Court's recognition of the anticommandeering principle similarly was rooted in the history and structure of the Constitution, *Printz,* 521 U.S. at 905–23, and, "most conclusively," in the Court's prior jurisprudence, *id.* at 925. Nevada's proposed "equal treatment" requirement has no such roots in Supreme Court precedent or the history of the Constitution. As for Nevada's contention that the requirement is inherent in the Constitution's structure, we have already shown that the Tenth Amendment does not protect the type of state interests implicated by this case. As the following discussion makes clear, the inferential leap from the remaining constitutional sources relied upon by Nevada to the proposed "equal treatment" requirement is too great to be plausible. * * *

The equal footing doctrine, upon which Nevada also relies, applies to the terms on which new states enter the Union. * * * Its principal application has been to guarantee that newly admitted States take title to the bed of all navigable waters in their territories, just as did the original thirteen States. But the Supreme Court has made clear that the doctrine "negatives any implied, special limitation of any of the paramount powers of the United States in favor of a State." United States v. Texas, 339 U.S. 707, 717 (1950). This includes, of course, Congress's exercise of its Property Clause powers. * * * The other purported constitutional bases of the "equal treatment" claim are even more tenuous.

* * *

Nearly 85 percent of the land in Nevada, and between 60–65 percent of the land in Alaska, Idaho and Utah, is under federal control. U.S. Bureau of Land Management, Public Land Statistics 1999, p.7 (Table 1–3). In contrast, in each of the states of Connecticut, Delaware, Iowa, Maine, New York and Rhode Island, less than one percent of the land is federally controlled. This discrepancy has been a persistent irritant to the western states, who feel the "heavy handed" federal presence puts them at a marked disadvantage. The equal footing doctrine, raised in the Yucca Mountain case above, frequently surfaces in these debates.

COURT PUTS DOWN REBELLION OVER
CONTROL OF FEDERAL LAND
Timothy Egan
N.Y. TIMES, Mar. 16, 1996, at 1

Dealing a major blow to dozens of counties that have passed ordinances asserting that the Federal Government does not in fact own the public lands that make up nearly half of the American West, a Federal judge in Nevada has ruled that such measures are illegal. The ruling* * * knocks out the legal basis for a number of county ordinances that have been used to disregard Federal law and, in some cases, intimidate Federal employees.

The ordinances are at the heart of a rural revolt sometimes referred to as Sagebrush Rebellion II. Nearly two years ago, Richard Carver, a commissioner in Nye County, Nev., took a bulldozer to a Forest Service road, declaring that the county's newly passed ordinance meant the Government no longer owned the property. * * *

The Justice Department, comparing the situation to a rebellion of Southern counties against Federal civil rights laws in the late 1960's, sued Nye County one year ago. * * *

* * * "[T]he United States owns and has the power and authority to manage and administer the unappropriated public lands and National Forest System lands within Nye County, Nev.," Judge George wrote. * * *

In the first Sagebrush Rebellion in 1979, the State of Nevada had asserted that it owned the Federal land within its borders. This time, the state refused to back Nye County. * * * In Nevada, Idaho, New Mexico and elsewhere, some ranchers have cited ordinances like Nye County's as a basis to refuse to pay grazing fees, or to run cattle on land that is considered environmentally sensitive. * * *

Top Federal officials took a conciliatory stance after the ruling * * * "Public lands are owned by all Americans, to be managed by the United States—that's the rule of law," said Attorney General Janet Reno. * * *

Notes and Questions

1. The Nye County case, United States v. Nye County, Nevada, 920 F.Supp. 1108 (D. Nev. 1996), was a "rallying cry" for some conservative groups, who provided funds and legal assistance for the county's defense. Ironically, Yucca mountain is situated within Nye County, which hosts numerous federal sites. *See* Erik Larson, *Unrest in the West,* Time, Oct. 23, 1995 (in Chapter 5.III.A., *infra*). What possible legal theory could the sagebrush rebels rely on for their argument that the federal government has no authority to own, much less regulate or restrict, federal lands within the county? Nye County Commissioner Richard Carver claimed that he was merely trying to enforce "the original intent of the Constitution." *Id.* Does the Property Clause or any other constitutional provision support Nye County's position? Does the County's theory appear to be so frivolous that Rule 11 sanctions should have been invoked? *See* Fed. R. Civ. P. 11.

2. Nye County relied in part on the equal footing doctrine in its defense of the case. *Nye County,* 920 F.Supp. at 1114. The court traced the roots and the parameters of the doctrine, and, just as in the Yucca Mountain case above, ultimately rejected the County's argument:

> The equal footing doctrine ensures that each state shares "those attributes essential to its equality in dignity and power with other states." * * * The Supreme Court has long recognized that certain types of property—specifically lands submerged by navigable or tidal waters—must pass to the states as a circumstance of sovereignty. Dominion over navigable waters and property in the soil under them are so identified with the sovereign power of government that a presumption against their separation from sovereignty must be indulged, in construing either grants by the sovereign of the lands to

be held in private ownership or transfer of sovereignty itself. For that reason, upon the admission of a state to the Union, the title of the United States to lands underlying navigable waters within the state passes to it, as incident to the transfer of local sovereignty, and is subject only to the paramount power of the United States to control such waters for purposes of navigation in interstate and foreign commerce. The question before this court, however, is not whether the lands submerged by navigable waters passed to the states pursuant to the equal footing doctrine, but whether the dry lands also passed to the states pursuant to the equal footing doctrine.

* * * [T]idal and navigable waters pass to the states because it understood that, under the English common law, the sovereign owned these lands as a public trust. This public trust doctrine was first developed in Martin v. Waddell's Lessee, 41 U.S. (16 Pet.) 367, 10 L.Ed. 997 (1842). Recognizing that the powers and attributes of sovereignty had vested in New Jersey, the court found that, "the people of New Jersey have exercised and enjoyed the rights of fishery for shell-fish and floating fish, as a common and undoubted right.... " Id. 41 U.S. (16 Pet.) at 417. * * *

The Court extended this holding to the new states in Pollard's Lessee v. Hagan, 44 U.S. (3 How.) 212 (1845). At issue in Pollard's Lessee was whether, subsequent to Alabama's admission, the federal government could transfer title to lands that had been submerged by navigable waters at the time of statehood. Citing Martin v. Waddell's Lessee ... the Court held that Alabama was also entitled to this attribute of sovereignty. Id., 44 U.S. (3 How.) at 229. * * * As in Martin v. Waddell's Lessee, the Court's conclusion arose from its interpretation of the public trust imposed on the sovereign, a trust requiring the sovereign to hold the navigable waters and submerged lands open for public access.

In sum, ... the attribute of sovereignty that is so identified with title to submerged lands ... is the public trust to these lands. Not only were these lands to be held for the common good, but title to these lands resided in the sovereign so that the sovereign could ensure that the people continued to hold and have access to the lands. In contrast, the court is unaware of any Supreme Court decision holding that the original thirteen states gained title to the dry lands as a public trust, that is, to hold in common for all people. Rather, states could and did pass ownership of the unappropriated dry lands to private individuals to the exclusion of the people in common. * * * [T]itle to lands that are not submerged under navigable-in-fact or tidal waters, including dry and fast lands, did not pass to the states upon admission. * * *

Id. at 1114–1116. Both the Nye County case and the equal footing doctrine are explored in detail in Chapter 5.III.A.

3. A few years after the Nye County case, High Country News reported: "Nevada Rebellion Ends with a Whimper." Jon Christensen, Nevada Rebellion Ends with a Whimper, Oct. 25, 1999. As recently as 2004, however, the same source reported that a federal proposal to designate criti-

cal habitat for the endangered bull trout in Elko County, Nevada, triggered a sagebrush rebel-like response. *See* Dan Wilcock, *Trout Wriggles Into a Sagebrush Rebellion*, HIGH COUNTRY NEWS, Oct. 11, 2004. It appears that, after all, there is "nothing new under the sun," Ecclesiastes 1:9.

II. JURISDICTION: GETTING THROUGH THE COURTHOUSE DOOR

Article III of the United States Constitution provides federal courts with power to adjudicate cases or controversies. U.S. CONST. art. III, § 2, cl.1. Some state constitutions include a similar provision governing judicial review in state courts. *See, e.g.,* OHIO CONST. art. IV. By limiting review to concrete cases brought by the appropriate parties at the appropriate time, the "case or controversy" proviso acts as a considerable check on the power of judges to make broad-sweeping public policy.

The landmark case of Sierra Club v. Morton, 405 U.S. 727, 740–741, 92 S.Ct. 1361, 1368–69, 31 L.Ed.2d 636, 646–47 (1972), was the Supreme Court's first recognition that an injury to "esthetic and environmental well-being" could constitute a legally cognizable injury-in-fact. Prior to this case, plaintiffs generally had to allege an economic or physical injury to get through the federal courthouse door.

> The trend of cases arising under the APA and other statutes authorizing judicial review of federal agency action has been toward recognizing that injuries other than economic harm are sufficient to bring a person within the meaning of the statutory language, and toward discarding the notion that an injury that is widely shared is ipso facto not an injury sufficient to provide the basis for judicial review. We noted this development with approval * * * in saying that the interest alleged to have been injured "may reflect 'aesthetic, conservational, and recreational' as well as economic values."

Id. at 738.

A. Parties: Constitutional Standing

The plaintiffs in the *Sierra Club* case sought a declaratory judgment that the construction of a proposed ski resort in a national game refuge and forest violated various federal laws. Although they had stated a cognizable injury, their claims were ultimately dismissed for lack of standing, as they had failed to allege that the organization or its members would be affected in any of their personal activities by the proposed project. The following case picks up on this theme.

MANUEL LUJAN, JR., SECRETARY OF THE INTERIOR v. DEFENDERS OF WILDLIFE, ET AL.

Supreme Court of the United States, 1992.
504 U.S. 555, 112 S.Ct. 2130, 119 L.Ed.2d 351.

JUSTICE SCALIA delivered the opinion of the Court* * *

This case involves a challenge to a rule promulgated by the Secretary of the Interior interpreting § 7 of the Endangered Species Act of

1973 (ESA), 87 Stat. 884, 892, as amended, 16 U.S.C. § 1536, in such fashion as to render it applicable only to actions within the United States or on the high seas. The preliminary issue, and the only one we reach, is whether respondents here, plaintiffs below, have standing to seek judicial review of the rule.

I

The ESA, 87 Stat. 884, as amended, 16 U.S.C. § 1531 et seq., seeks to protect species of animals against threats to their continuing existence caused by man. * * * The ESA instructs the Secretary of the Interior to promulgate by regulation a list of those species which are either endangered or threatened under enumerated criteria, and to define the critical habitat of these species. 16 U.S.C. §§ 1533, 1536. Section 7(a)(2) of the Act then provides, in pertinent part: "Each Federal agency shall, in consultation with and with the assistance of the Secretary [of the Interior], insure that any action authorized, funded, or carried out by such agency ... is not likely to jeopardize the continued existence of any endangered species or threatened species or result in the destruction or adverse modification of habitat of such species which is determined by the Secretary, after consultation as appropriate with affected States, to be critical." 16 U.S.C. § 1536(a)(2).

In 1978, the Fish and Wildlife Service (FWS) and the National Marine Fisheries Service (NMFS), on behalf of the Secretary of the Interior and the Secretary of Commerce respectively, promulgated a joint regulation stating that the obligations imposed by § 7(a)(2) extend to actions taken in foreign nations. 43 Fed.Reg. 874 (1978). The next year, however, the Interior Department began to reexamine its position. * * * A revised joint regulation, reinterpreting § 7(a)(2) to require consultation only for actions taken in the United States or on the high seas, was ... promulgated in 1986, 51 Fed.Reg. 19926; 50 CFR 402.01 (1991).

Shortly thereafter, respondents, organizations dedicated to wildlife conservation and other environmental causes, filed this action against the Secretary of the Interior, seeking a declaratory judgment that the new regulation is in error as to the geographic scope of § 7(a)(2) and an injunction requiring the Secretary to promulgate a new regulation restoring the initial interpretation.* * *

II

While the Constitution of the United States divides all power conferred upon the Federal Government into "legislative Powers," Art. I, § 1, "[t]he executive Power," Art. II, § 1, and "[t]he judicial Power," Art. III, § 1, it does not attempt to define those terms. To be sure, it limits the jurisdiction of federal courts to "Cases" and "Controversies," but an executive inquiry can bear the name "case" (the Hoffa case) and a legislative dispute can bear the name "controversy" (the Smoot–Hawley controversy). Obviously, then, the Constitution's central mechanism of separation of powers depends largely upon common understanding of what activities are appropriate to legislatures, to executives, and to courts. In The Federalist No. 48, Madison expressed the view that "[i]t is not infrequently a question of real nicety in legislative bodies whether the operation of a particular measure will, or will not, extend beyond the legislative sphere," whereas "the executive power [is] restrained within a narrower compass and ... more simple in its nature," and "the judiciary [is] described by landmarks still less uncertain." The Federalist No. 48, p. 256 (Carey and McClellan eds. 1990). One of those landmarks, setting apart the "Cases" and "Controversies" that are of the justiciable sort ... is the doctrine of standing. Though some of its elements express merely prudential considerations that are part of judicial self-government, the core component of standing is an essential and unchanging part of the case-or-controversy requirement of Article III. * * *

Over the years, our cases have established that the irreducible constitutional minimum of standing contains three elements. First, the plaintiff must have suffered an "injury in fact"—an invasion of a legally protected interest which is (a) concrete and particularized, ... and (b) "actual or imminent, not 'conjectural' or 'hypothetical,'" * * * Second, there must be a causal connection between the injury and the conduct complained of—the injury has to be "fairly ... trace[able] to the challenged action of the defendant, and not ... th[e] result [of] the independent action of some third party not before the court." Simon v. Eastern Ky. Welfare Rights Organization, 426 U.S. 26, 41–42, 96 S.Ct. 1917, 1926, 48 L.Ed.2d 450 (1976). Third, it must be "likely," as opposed to merely "speculative," that the injury will be "redressed by a favorable decision." Id., at 38, 43, 96 S.Ct., at 1924, 1926.

The party invoking federal jurisdiction bears the burden of establishing these elements. * * * Since they are not mere pleading requirements but rather an indispensable part of the plaintiff's case, each element must be supported in the same way as any other matter on which the plaintiff bears the burden of proof, i.e., with the manner and degree of evidence required at the successive stages of the litigation. See Lujan v. National Wildlife Federation, 497 U.S. 871, 883–889 (1990) * * * At the pleading stage, general factual allegations of injury resulting from the defendant's conduct may suffice, for on a motion to dismiss we "presum[e] that general allegations embrace those specific facts that are necessary to support the claim." *National Wildlife Federation, supra,* 497 U.S., at 889. In response to a summary judgment motion, however, the plaintiff can no longer rest on such "mere allegations," but must "set forth" by affidavit or other evidence "specific facts," Fed.Rule Civ.Proc. 56(e), which for purposes of the summary judgment motion will be taken to be true. And at the final stage, those facts (if controverted) must be "supported adequately by the evidence adduced at trial." * * *

When the suit is one challenging the legality of government action or inaction, the nature and extent of facts that must be averred (at the summary judgment stage) or proved (at the trial stage) in order to establish standing depends considerably upon whether the plaintiff is himself an object of the action (or forgone action) at issue. If he is, there is ordinarily little question that the action or inaction has caused him injury, and that a judgment preventing or requiring the action will redress it. When, however, as in this case, a plaintiff's asserted injury arises from the government's allegedly unlawful regulation (or lack of regulation) of someone else, much more is needed. In that circumstance, causation and redressability ordinarily hinge on the response of the regulated (or regulable) third party to the government action or inaction—and perhaps on the response of others as well. The existence of one or more of the essential elements of standing "depends on the unfettered choices made by independent actors not before the courts and whose exercise of broad and legitimate discretion the courts cannot presume either to control or to predict," * * * and it becomes the burden of the plaintiff to adduce facts showing that those choices have been or will be made in such manner as to produce causation and permit redressability of injury. * * * Thus, when the plaintiff is not himself the object of the government action or inaction he challenges, standing is not precluded, but it is ordinarily "substantially more difficult" to establish. * * *

III

We think the Court of Appeals failed to apply the foregoing principles in denying the Secretary's motion for summary judgment. Respondents had not made the requisite demonstration of (at least) injury and redressability.

A

Respondents' claim to injury is that the lack of consultation with respect to certain funded activities abroad "increas[es] the rate of extinction of endangered and threatened species." Complaint ¶ 5, App. 13. Of course, the desire to use or observe an animal species, even for purely esthetic purposes, is undeniably a cognizable interest for purpose of standing. See, e.g., [Sierra Club v. Morton, 405 U.S. 727, 734 (1972)]. "But the 'injury in fact' test requires more than an injury to a cognizable interest. It requires that the party seeking review be himself among the injured." Id., at 734–735. To survive the Secretary's summary judgment motion, respondents had to submit affidavits or other evidence showing, through specific facts, not only that listed species were in fact being threatened by funded activities abroad, but also that one or more of respondents' members would thereby be "directly" affected apart from their " 'special interest' in th[e] subject." Id., at 735, 739, 92 S.Ct., at 1366, 1368. * * *

With respect to this aspect of the case, the Court of Appeals focused on the affidavits of two Defenders' members—Joyce Kelly and Amy Skilbred. Ms. Kelly stated that she traveled to Egypt in 1986 and "observed the traditional habitat of the endangered Nile crocodile there and intend[s] to do so again, and hope[s] to observe the crocodile directly," and that she "will suffer harm in fact as the result of [the] American ... role ... in overseeing the rehabilitation of the Aswan High Dam on the

Nile ... and [in] develop[ing] ... Egypt's ... Master Water Plan." App. 101. Ms. Skilbred averred that she traveled to Sri Lanka in 1981 and "observed th[e] habitat" of "endangered species such as the Asian elephant and the leopard" at what is now the site of the Mahaweli project funded by the Agency for International Development (AID), although she "was unable to see any of the endangered species"; "this development project," she continued, "will seriously reduce endangered, threatened, and endemic species habitat including areas that I visited ... [, which] may severely shorten the future of these species"; that threat, she concluded, harmed her because she "intend[s] to return to Sri Lanka in the future and hope[s] to be more fortunate in spotting at least the endangered elephant and leopard." Id., at 145–146. When Ms. Skilbred was asked at a subsequent deposition if and when she had any plans to return to Sri Lanka, she reiterated that "I intend to go back to Sri Lanka," but confessed that she had no current plans: "I don't know [when]. There is a civil war going on right now. I don't know. Not next year, I will say. In the future." Id., at 318.

We shall assume for the sake of argument that these affidavits contain facts showing that certain agency-funded projects threaten listed species—though that is questionable. They plainly contain no facts, however, showing how damage to the species will produce "imminent" injury to Mses. Kelly and Skilbred. That the women "had visited" the areas of the projects before the projects commenced proves nothing. As we have said in a related context, " 'Past exposure to illegal conduct does not in itself show a present case or controversy regarding injunctive relief ... if unaccompanied by any continuing, present adverse effects.' " * * * And the affiants' profession of an "inten[t]" to return to the places they had visited before—where they will presumably, this time, be deprived of the opportunity to observe animals of the endangered species—is simply not enough. Such "some day" intentions—without any description of concrete plans, or indeed even any specification of when the some day will be—do not support a finding of the "actual or imminent" injury that our cases require.* * *[2]

2. The dissent acknowledges the settled requirement that the injury complained of be, if not actual, then at least imminent, but it contends that respondents could get past summary judgment because "a reasonable finder of fact could conclude ... that ... Kelly or Skilbred will soon return to the project sites." * * * This analysis suffers either from a factual or from a legal defect, depending on what the "soon" is supposed to mean. If "soon" refers to the standard mandated by our precedents—that the injury be "imminent," * * *—we are at a loss to see how, as a factual matter, the standard can be met by respondents' mere profession of an intent, some day, to return. But if, as we suspect, "soon" means nothing more than "in this lifetime," then the dissent has undertaken quite a departure from our precedents. Although "imminence" is concededly a somewhat elastic concept, it cannot be stretched beyond its purpose, which is to ensure that the alleged injury is not too speculative for Article III purposes—that the injury is "certainly impending," * * * It has been stretched beyond the breaking point when, as here, the plaintiff alleges only an injury at some indefinite future time, and the acts necessary to make the injury happen are at least partly within the plaintiff's own control. In such circumstances we have insisted that the injury proceed with a high degree of immediacy, so as to reduce the possibility of deciding a case in which no injury would have occurred at all. * * *

Our insistence upon these established requirements of standing does not mean that we would, as the dissent contends, "demand ... detailed descriptions" of damages, such as a "nightly schedule of attempted activities" from plaintiffs alleging loss of consortium.* * * That case and the others posited by the dissent all involve actual harm; the existence of standing is clear, though the precise extent of harm remains to be determined at trial. Where there is no actual harm, however, its imminence (though not its precise extent) must be established.

Besides relying upon the Kelly and Skilbred affidavits, respondents propose a series of novel standing theories. The first, inelegantly styled "ecosystem nexus," proposes that any person who uses any part of a "contiguous ecosystem" adversely affected by a funded activity has standing even if the activity is located a great distance away. This approach, as the Court of Appeals correctly observed, is inconsistent with our opinion in *National Wildlife Federation*, which held that a plaintiff claiming injury from environmental damage must use the area affected by the challenged activity and not an area roughly "in the vicinity" of it. 497 U.S., at 887–889, 110 S.Ct., at 3188–3189 * * * It makes no difference that the general-purpose section of the ESA states that the Act was intended in part "to provide a means whereby the ecosystems upon which endangered species and threatened species depend may be conserved," 16 U.S.C. § 1531(b). To say that the Act protects ecosystems is not to say that the Act creates (if it were possible) rights of action in persons who have not been injured in fact, that is, persons who use portions of an ecosystem not perceptibly affected by the unlawful action in question.

Respondents' other theories are called, alas, the "animal nexus" approach, whereby anyone who has an interest in studying or seeing the endangered animals anywhere on the globe has standing; and the "vocational nexus" approach, under which anyone with a professional interest in such animals can sue. Under these theories, anyone who goes to see Asian elephants in the Bronx Zoo, and anyone who is a keeper of Asian elephants in the Bronx Zoo, has standing to sue because the Director of the Agency for International Development (AID) did not consult with the Secretary regarding the AID-funded project in Sri Lanka. This is beyond all reason. Standing is not "an ingenious academic exercise in the conceivable," United States v. Students Challenging Regulatory Agency Procedures (SCRAP), 412 U.S. 669, 688, 93 S.Ct. 2405, 2416, 37 L.Ed.2d 254 (1973), but as we have said requires, at the summary judgment stage, a factual showing of perceptible harm. It is clear that the person who observes or works with a particular animal threatened by a federal decision is facing perceptible harm, since the very subject of his interest will no longer exist. It is even plausible—though it goes to the outermost limit of plausibility—to think that a person who observes or works with animals of a particular species in the very area of the world where that species is threatened by a federal decision is facing such harm, since some animals that might have been the subject of his interest will no

longer exist* * * It goes beyond the limit, however, and into pure speculation and fantasy, to say that anyone who observes or works with an
endangered species, anywhere in the world, is appreciably harmed by a
single project affecting some portion of that species with which he has no
more specific connection.[3]

Justice Stevens, by contrast, would allow standing on an apparent
"animal nexus" theory to all plaintiffs whose interest in the animals is
"genuine." Such plaintiffs, we are told, do not have to visit the animals
because the animals are analogous to family members. * * * We decline
to join Justice Stevens in this Linnaean leap. It is unclear to us what
constitutes a "genuine" interest; how it differs from a "nongenuine"
interest (which nonetheless prompted a plaintiff to file suit); and why
such an interest in animals should be different from such an interest in
anything else that is the subject of a lawsuit.

B

Besides failing to show injury, respondents failed to demonstrate redressability. Instead of attacking the separate decisions to fund particular
projects allegedly causing them harm, respondents chose to challenge a
more generalized level of Government action (rules regarding consultation), the invalidation of which would affect all overseas projects. This
programmatic approach has obvious practical advantages, but also obvious difficulties insofar as proof of causation or redressability is concerned. As we have said in another context, "suits challenging, not specifically identifiable Government violations of law, but the particular
programs agencies establish to carry out their legal obligations ... [are],
even when premised on allegations of several instances of violations of
law, ... rarely if ever appropriate for federal-court adjudication." *Allen*,
468 U.S., at 759–760, 104 S.Ct., at 3329.

The most obvious problem in the present case is redressability. Since
the agencies funding the projects were not parties to the case, the District Court could accord relief only against the Secretary: He could be
ordered to revise his regulation to require consultation for foreign
projects. But this would not remedy respondents' alleged injury unless
the funding agencies were bound by the Secretary's regulation, which is
very much an open question. Whereas in other contexts the ESA is quite

---

3. * * * Respondents had to adduce
facts ... on the basis of which it could reasonably be found that concrete injury to
their members was, as our cases require,
"certainly impending." The dissent may be
correct that the geographic remoteness of
those members (here in the United States)
from Sri Lanka and Aswan does not "necessarily "prevent such a finding—but it assuredly does so when no further facts have
been brought forward (and respondents
have produced none) showing that the
impact upon animals in those distant

places will in some fashion be reflected
here. The dissent's position to the contrary
reduces to the notion that distance never
prevents harm, a proposition we categorically reject. It cannot be that a person with
an interest in an animal automatically has
standing to enjoin federal threats to that
species of animal, anywhere in the world.
* * * Justice BLACKMUN's accusation
that a special rule is being crafted for "environmental claims," * * * is correct, but he
is the craftsman.

explicit as to the Secretary's controlling authority, see, e.g., 16 U.S.C. § 1533(a)(1) ("The Secretary shall" promulgate regulations determining endangered species); § 1535(d)(1) ("The Secretary is authorized to provide financial assistance to any State"), with respect to consultation the initiative, and hence arguably the initial responsibility for determining statutory necessity, lies with the agencies, see § 1536(a)(2) ("Each Federal agency shall, in consultation with and with the assistance of the Secretary, insure that any" funded action is not likely to jeopardize endangered or threatened species). When the Secretary promulgated the regulation at issue here, he thought it was binding on the agencies, see 51 Fed.Reg. 19928 (1986). The Solicitor General, however, has repudiated that position here, and the agencies themselves apparently deny the Secretary's authority. (During the period when the Secretary took the view that § 7(a)(2) did apply abroad, AID and FWS engaged in a running controversy over whether consultation was required with respect to the Mahaweli project, AID insisting that consultation applied only to domestic actions.)

Respondents assert that this legal uncertainty did not affect redressability (and hence standing) because the District Court itself could resolve the issue of the Secretary's authority as a necessary part of its standing inquiry. Assuming that it is appropriate to resolve an issue of law such as this in connection with a threshold standing inquiry, resolution by the District Court would not have remedied respondents' alleged injury anyway, because it would not have been binding upon the agencies. They were not parties to the suit, and there is no reason they should be obliged to honor an incidental legal determination the suit produced. * * * We do not know what would justify that confidence, particularly when the Justice Department (presumably after consultation with the agencies) has taken the position that the regulation is not binding. * * * The short of the matter is that redress of the only injury in fact respondents complain of requires action (termination of funding until consultation) by the individual funding agencies; and any relief the District Court could have provided in this suit against the Secretary was not likely to produce that action.

A further impediment to redressability is the fact that the agencies generally supply only a fraction of the funding for a foreign project. AID, for example, has provided less than 10% of the funding for the Mahaweli project. Respondents have produced nothing to indicate that the projects they have named will either be suspended, or do less harm to listed species, if that fraction is eliminated. * * *

IV

The Court of Appeals found that respondents had standing for an additional reason: because they had suffered a "procedural injury." The so-called "citizen-suit" provision of the ESA provides, in pertinent part, that "any person may commence a civil suit on his own behalf (A) to enjoin any person, including the United States and any other governmental instrumentality or agency ... who is alleged to be in violation of any provision of this chapter." 16 U.S.C. § 1540(g). The court held that, because § 7(a)(2) requires interagency consultation, the citizen-suit provision creates a "procedural righ[t]" to consultation in all "persons"—so that anyone can file suit in federal court to challenge the Secretary's (or presumably any other official's) failure to follow the assertedly correct consultative procedure, notwithstanding his or her inability to allege any discrete injury flowing from that failure. 911 F.2d, at 121–122. To understand the remarkable nature of this holding one must be clear about what it does not rest upon: This is not a case where plaintiffs are seeking to enforce a procedural requirement the disregard of which could impair a separate concrete interest of theirs (e.g., the procedural requirement for a hearing prior to denial of their license application, or the procedural requirement for an environmental impact statement before a federal facility is constructed next door to them).[7] Nor is it simply a case where concrete injury has been suffered by many persons, as in mass fraud or mass tort situations. Nor, finally, is it the unusual case in which Congress has created a concrete private interest in the outcome of a suit against a private party for the government's benefit, by providing a cash bounty for the victorious plaintiff. Rather, the court held that the injury-in-fact requirement had been satisfied by congressional conferral upon all persons of an abstract, self-contained, noninstrumental "right" to have the Executive observe the procedures required by law. We reject this view.[8]

We have consistently held that a plaintiff raising only a generally available grievance about government—claiming only harm to his and every citizen's interest in proper application of the Constitution and laws, and seeking relief that no more directly and tangibly benefits him than it does the public at large—does not state an Article III case or controversy. For example, in Fairchild v. Hughes, 258 U.S. 126, 129–130, 42 S.Ct. 274, 275, 66 L.Ed. 499 (1922), we dismissed a suit challenging the propriety of the process by which the Nineteenth Amendment was ratified. Justice Brandeis wrote for the Court:

> "[This is] not a case within the meaning of ... Article III.... Plaintiff
> has [asserted] only the right, possessed by every citizen, to require

---

7. There is this much truth to the assertion that "procedural rights" are special: The person who has been accorded a procedural right to protect his concrete interests can assert that right without meeting all the normal standards for redressability and immediacy. Thus, under our case law, one living adjacent to the site for proposed construction of a federally licensed dam has standing to challenge the licensing agency's failure to prepare an environmental impact statement, even though he cannot establish with any certainty that the statement will cause the license to be withheld or altered, and even though the dam will not be completed for

many years.* * * What respondents' "procedural rights" argument seeks, however, is quite different from this: standing for persons who have no concrete interests affected—persons who live (and propose to live) at the other end of the country from the dam.

8. The dissent's discussion of this aspect of the case ... distorts our opinion. We do not hold that an individual cannot enforce procedural rights; he assuredly can, so long as the procedures in question are designed to protect some threatened concrete interest of his that is the ultimate basis of his standing. * * *

that the Government be administered according to law and that the public moneys be not wasted. Obviously this general right does not entitle a private citizen to institute in the federal courts a suit...."

* * *

Whether the courts were to act on their own, or at the invitation of Congress, in ignoring the concrete injury requirement described in our cases, they would be discarding a principle fundamental to the separate and distinct constitutional role of the Third Branch—one of the essential elements that identifies those "Cases" and "Controversies" that are the business of the courts rather than of the political branches. "The province of the court," as Chief Justice Marshall said in Marbury v. Madison, 5 U.S. (1 Cranch) 137, 170, 2 L.Ed. 60 (1803), "is, solely, to decide on the rights of individuals." Vindicating the public interest (including the public interest in Government observance of the Constitution and laws) is the function of Congress and the Chief Executive. * * *

* * *

JUSTICE STEVENS, concurring in the judgment.

Because I am not persuaded that Congress intended the consultation requirement in § 7(a)(2) of the Endangered Species Act of 1973 (ESA), 16 U.S.C. § 1536(a)(2), to apply to activities in foreign countries, I concur in the judgment of reversal. I do not, however, agree with the Court's conclusion that respondents lack standing because the threatened injury to their interest in protecting the environment and studying endangered species is not "imminent." * * * In my opinion a person who has visited the critical habitat of an endangered species has a professional interest in preserving the species and its habitat, and intends to revisit them in the future has standing to challenge agency action that threatens their destruction. Congress has found that a wide variety of endangered species of fish, wildlife, and plants are of "aesthetic, ecological, educational, historical, recreational, and scientific value to the Nation and its people." 16 U.S.C. § 1531(a)(3). Given that finding, we have no license to demean the importance of the interest that particular individuals may have in observing any species or its habitat, whether those individuals are motivated by esthetic enjoyment, an interest in professional research, or an economic interest in preservation of the species.

* * *

JUSTICE BLACKMUN, with whom JUSTICE O'CONNOR joins, dissenting.

I part company with the Court in this case in two respects. First, I believe that respondents have raised genuine issues of fact—sufficient to survive summary judgment—both as to injury and as to redressability. Second, I question the Court's breadth of language in rejecting standing for "procedural" injuries. * * *

Were the Court to apply the proper standard for summary judgment, I believe it would conclude that the sworn affidavits and deposition testimony of Joyce Kelly and Amy Skilbred advance sufficient facts to create a genuine issue for trial concerning whether one or both would be imminently harmed by the Aswan and Mahaweli projects. In the first instance, as the Court itself concedes, the affidavits contained facts making it at least "questionable" (and therefore within the province of the factfinder) that certain agency-funded projects threaten listed species.* * * The only remaining issue, then, is whether Kelly and Skilbred have shown that they personally would suffer imminent harm. * * *

By requiring a "description of concrete plans" or "specification of when the some day [for a return visit] will be," ... the Court, in my view, demands what is likely an empty formality. No substantial barriers prevent Kelly or Skilbred from simply purchasing plane tickets to return to the Aswan and Mahaweli projects. This case differs from other cases in which the imminence of harm turned largely on the affirmative actions of third parties beyond a plaintiff's control.* * * To be sure, a plaintiff's unilateral control over his or her exposure to harm does not necessarily render the harm nonspeculative. Nevertheless, it suggests that a finder of fact would be far more likely to conclude the harm is actual or imminent, especially if given an opportunity to hear testimony and determine credibility.

I fear the Court's demand for detailed descriptions of future conduct will do little to weed out those who are genuinely harmed from those who are not. More likely, it will resurrect a code-pleading formalism in federal court summary judgment practice, as federal courts, newly doubting their jurisdiction, will demand more and more particularized showings of future harm. Just to survive summary judgment, for example, a property owner claiming a decline in the value of his property from governmental action might have to specify the exact date he intends to sell his property and show that there is a market for the property, lest it be surmised he might not sell again. * * * And a Federal Tort Claims Act plaintiff alleging loss of consortium should make sure to furnish this Court with a "description of concrete plans" for her nightly schedule of attempted activities. * * *

I have difficulty imagining this Court applying its rigid principles of geographic formalism anywhere outside the context of environmental claims. As I understand it, environmental plaintiffs are under no special constitutional standing disabilities. Like other plaintiffs, they need show only that the action they challenge has injured them, without necessarily showing they happened to be physically near the location of the alleged wrong. * * *

The Court concludes that any "procedural injury" suffered by respondents is insufficient to confer standing. It rejects the view that the "injury-in-fact requirement [is] satisfied by congressional conferral upon all persons of an abstract, self-contained, noninstrumental 'right' to have the Executive observe the procedures required by law." Ante, at 2143.

Whatever the Court might mean with that very broad language, it cannot be saying that "procedural injuries" as a class are necessarily insufficient for purposes of Article III standing. Most governmental conduct can be classified as "procedural." Many injuries caused by governmental conduct, therefore, are categorizable at some level of generality as "procedural" injuries. Yet, these injuries are not categorically beyond the pale of redress by the federal courts. * * *

* * * In Japan Whaling Assn. v. American Cetacean Society, 478 U.S. 221 (1986), the Court examined a statute requiring the Secretary of Commerce to certify to the President that foreign nations were not conducting fishing operations or trading which "diminis[h] the effectiveness" of an international whaling convention. Id., at 226. The Court expressly found standing to sue. * * *

The consultation requirement of § 7 of the Endangered Species Act is a similar, action-forcing statute. Consultation is designed as an integral check on federal agency action, ensuring that such action does not go forward without full consideration of its effects on listed species. * * * These action-forcing procedures are "designed to protect some threatened concrete interest," of persons who observe and work with endangered or threatened species. That is why I am mystified by the Court's unsupported conclusion that "[t]his is not a case where plaintiffs are seeking to enforce a procedural requirement the disregard of which could impair a separate concrete interest of theirs." * * *

It is to be hoped that over time the Court will acknowledge that some classes of procedural duties are so enmeshed with the prevention of a substantive, concrete harm that an individual plaintiff may be able to demonstrate a sufficient likelihood of injury just through the breach of that procedural duty. For example, in the context of the NEPA requirement of environmental-impact statements, this Court has acknowledged "it is now well settled that NEPA itself does not mandate particular results [and] simply prescribes the necessary process," but "these procedures are almost certain to affect the agency's substantive decision." Robertson v. Methow Valley Citizens Council, 490 U.S., at 350 * * * This acknowledgment of an inextricable link between procedural and substantive harm does not reflect improper appellate factfinding. It reflects nothing more than the proper deference owed to the judgment of a coordinate branch—Congress—that certain procedures are directly tied to protection against a substantive harm. * * *

In conclusion, I cannot join the Court on what amounts to a slash-and-burn expedition through the law of environmental standing. In my view, "[t]he very essence of civil liberty certainly consists in the right of every individual to claim the protection of the laws, whenever he receives an injury." Marbury v. Madison, 1 Cranch 137, 163, 2 L.Ed. 60 (1803). I dissent.

Notes and Questions

1. Are procedural injuries special? Should it be easier to establish standing to bring claims to redress procedural harm?

2. Blackmun's dissent, *supra*, points out that "environmental plaintiffs are under no special constitutional standing disabilities." Does the majority's opinion belie his assertion? Is it easier for developers and other economic interests to establish standing?

3. Can persons interested in the conservation of wildlife located in distant lands ever satisfy the *Defenders of Wildlife* standard? What if you can't buy a plane ticket? Would you have standing to challenge a project in South America that might adversely affect a species of migratory songbird that frequents your yard in the springtime? What if you were a wildlife biologist that had tagged a specific bird so that you could record its migratory path? Could Defenders of Wildlife establish standing to challenge a project in Sri Lanka by implementing an "adopt an elephant" project, where members donate money towards the conservation of an individual elephant in Sri Lanka, and receive photographs and periodic updates on that elephant's well-being?

4. In Friends of the Earth v. Laidlaw Environmental Services, Inc., 528 U.S. 167, 120 S.Ct. 693, 145 L.Ed.2d 610 (2000), environmental groups brought an action pursuant to the Clean Water Act (CWA) against the holder of a CWA permit, alleging a violation of the permit's mercury discharge limits and seeking declaratory and injunctive relief, civil penalties, costs, and attorney fees. The district court found numerous permit violations and imposed a penalty of $405,800, but it denied the request for declaratory and injunctive relief. The Supreme Court held that the group had standing to seek both injunctive relief and civil penalties and that the action was not rendered moot by the permit holder's compliance with permit limits or its shut down of the facility absent a showing that violations could not reasonably be expected to recur. The plaintiffs could not prove that the mercury discharges caused harm to the environment, but the Court stated:

> The relevant showing ... is not injury to the environment but injury to the plaintiff. To insist upon the former rather than the latter as part of the standing inquiry ... is to raise the standing hurdle higher than the necessary showing for success on the merits in an action alleging non-compliance with an NPDES permit. Focusing properly on injury to the plaintiff, the District Court found that FOE had demonstrated sufficient injury to establish standing. For example, FOE member Kenneth Lee Curtis averred in affidavits that he lived a half-mile from Laidlaw's facility; that he occasionally drove over the North Tyger River, and that it looked and smelled polluted; and that he would like to fish, camp, swim, and picnic in and near the river between 3 and 15 miles downstream from the facility, as he did when he was a teenager, but would not do so because he was concerned that the water was polluted by Laidlaw's discharges. Curtis reaffirmed these statements in extensive deposition testimony. For example, he testified that he would like to fish in the river at a specific spot he used as a boy, but that he would not do so now because of his concerns about Laidlaw's discharges. * * * These sworn statements ... adequately documented injury in fact. We have held that environmental plaintiffs adequately allege injury in fact when they aver that they use the affected area and are persons "for whom the aesthetic and recreational values of the area will be lessened" by the

challenged activity. Sierra Club v. Morton, 405 U.S. 727, 735 (1972).

Id. at 181–83.

5. Organizations like Friends of the Earth, Defenders of Wildlife, and trade associations and industry groups have standing to bring suit on behalf of their members when members would otherwise have standing to sue in their own right, the interests at stake are germane to the organization's purpose, and neither the claim asserted nor the relief requested requires the participation of individual members in the lawsuit. *Laidlaw,* 528 U.S. at 181; Hunt v. Washington State Apple Advertising Comm'n, 432 U.S. 333, 343, 97 S.Ct. 2434, 2441, 53 L.Ed.2d 383, 394 (1977). Is it possible to bring suit in the name of the species in question, *e.g., In re: Nile Crocodile?* If you are an attorney championing the cause of environmental protection in court, who is your client? Should involvement be limited to environmental interest groups, or could industrial representatives participate in the lawsuit in the name of the crocodile? *See Sierra Club v. Morton,* 405 U.S. at 741–42, 750 n.8 (Douglas, J., dissenting) (stating that inanimate natural objects should have standing; judges should consider appointment of a guardian to protect their interests) (*citing* Christopher D. Stone, *Should Trees Have Standing?— Toward Legal Rights for Natural Objects,* 45 S. Cal. L. Rev. 450 (1972)).

6. Although dams like the Aswan Dam provide relatively cheap and "clean" power, the adverse effects of large dam and reservoir projects on fisheries, riparian zones and wetlands, and other environmental features and processes are well documented. *See generally* World Commission on Dams, Dams and Development: A New Framework for Decision–Making 92–93, available at http://www.damsreport.org/report/contents.htm (last visited Apr. 12, 2005). There are less obvious, but equally troubling, impacts as well:

> One of the most serious charges against hydropower, though it applies to all dams, is its high social cost in terms of involuntary resettlement. * * * 30 million people have been ousted by dams. Most often, "oustees" are poor or indigenous people who often leave behind productive farms and ancestral homes. Opponents claim that, though these groups pay the social and environmental costs of dam construction, they don't receive the benefits—instead, those go to urban areas and industries. The Aswan High Dam ousted 100,000 people, according to the World Bank, and the planned Three Gorges Dam in China, a 600–foot-thick, mile-wide project so large it will be visible from outer space, will expel 1.3 million people from the area.

Stephanie Joyce, *Is it Worth a Dam?,* 105 Env'l Health Perspectives #10 (1997).

Would the application of consultation requirements under the ESA or other federal environmental assessment procedures be beneficial in avoiding the adverse environmental and social impacts of a project like the rehabilitation of the Aswan Dam? Are you concerned that the imposition of U.S. requirements might be paternalistic toward developing countries?

B. Parties: Zone of Interests

Once the plaintiffs have established constitutional standing, they aren't "home free" yet. Plaintiffs must also satisfy prudential considerations to proceed in federal court.

BRAD BENNETT, ET AL. v. MICHAEL SPEAR, ET AL.

Supreme Court of the United States, 1997.
520 U.S. 154, 117 S.Ct. 1154, 137 L.Ed.2d 281.

JUSTICE SCALIA delivered the opinion of the Court.

This is a challenge to a biological opinion issued by the Fish and Wildlife Service in accordance with the Endangered Species Act of 1973 (ESA), 87 Stat. 884, as amended, 16 U.S.C. § 1531 et seq., concerning the operation of the Klamath Irrigation Project by the Bureau of Reclamation, and the project's impact on two varieties of endangered fish. The question for decision is whether the petitioners, who have competing economic and other interests in Klamath Project water, have standing to seek judicial review of the biological opinion under the citizen-suit provision of the ESA, § 1540(g)(1), and the Administrative Procedure Act (APA) * * *

The ESA requires the Secretary of the Interior to promulgate regulations listing those species of animals that are "threatened" or "endangered" under specified criteria, and to designate their "critical habitat." 16 U.S.C. § 1533. The ESA further requires each federal agency to "insure that any action authorized, funded, or carried out by such agency ... is not likely to jeopardize the continued existence of any endangered species or threatened species or result in the destruction or adverse modification of habitat of such species which is determined by the Secretary ... to be critical." § 1536(a)(2). If an agency determines that action it proposes to take may adversely affect a listed species, it must engage in formal consultation with the Fish and Wildlife Service, * * * after which the Service must provide the agency with a written statement (the Biological Opinion) explaining how the proposed action will affect the species or its habitat, 16 U.S.C. § 1536(b)(3)(A). If the Service concludes that the proposed action will "jeopardize the continued existence of any [listed] species or threatened species or result in the destruction or adverse modification of [critical habitat]," § 1536(a)(2), the Biological Opinion must outline any "reasonable and prudent alternatives" that the Service believes will avoid that consequence, § 1536(b)(3)(A). * * *

The Klamath Project, one of the oldest federal reclamation schemes, is a series of lakes, rivers, dams, and irrigation canals in northern California and southern Oregon. The project was undertaken by the Secretary of the Interior pursuant to the Reclamation Act of 1902 * * * and is administered by the Bureau of Reclamation, which is under the Secretary's jurisdiction. In 1992, the Bureau notified the Service that operation of the project might affect the Lost River Sucker (*Deltistes luxatus*) and Shortnose Sucker (*Chasmistes brevirostris*), species of fish that were listed as endangered in 1988 * * * After formal consultation with the Bureau * * * the Service issued a Biological Opinion which concluded that the " 'long-term operation of the Klamath Project was likely to jeopardize the continued existence of the Lost River and shortnose suckers.' " * * * The Biological Opinion identified "reasonable and prudent alternatives" the Service believed would avoid jeopardy, which included the maintenance of minimum water levels on Clear Lake and Gerber reservoirs. The Bureau later notified the Service that it intended to operate the project in compliance with the Biological Opinion.

Petitioners, two Oregon irrigation districts that receive Klamath Project water and the operators of two ranches within those districts, filed the present action against the director and regional director of the Service and the Secretary of the Interior. Neither the Bureau nor any of its officials is named as defendant. The complaint asserts that ... "[t]here is no scientifically or commercially available evidence indicating that the populations of endangered suckers in Clear Lake and Gerber reservoirs have declined, are declining, or will decline as a result" of the Bureau's operation of the Klamath Project, id., at 37; that "[t]here is no commercially or scientifically available evidence indicating that the restrictions on lake levels imposed in the Biological Opinion will have any beneficial effect on the ... populations of suckers in Clear Lake and Gerber reservoirs," id., at 39; and that the Bureau nonetheless "will abide by the restrictions imposed by the Biological Opinion," id., at 32.

Petitioners' complaint * * * allege[s] that the Service's jeopardy determination with respect to Clear Lake and Gerber reservoirs, and the ensuing imposition of minimum water levels, violated § 7 of the ESA, 16 U.S.C. § 1536. * * * The complaint asserts that petitioners' use of the reservoirs and related waterways for "recreational, aesthetic and commercial purposes, as well as for their primary sources of irrigation water," will be "irreparably damaged" by the actions complained of, App. to Pet. for Cert. 34, and that the restrictions on water delivery "recommended" by the Biological Opinion "adversely affect plaintiffs by substantially reducing the quantity of available irrigation water," id., at 40. In essence, petitioners claim a competing interest in the water the Biological Opinion declares necessary for the preservation of the suckers.

The District Court dismissed the complaint for lack of jurisdiction. It concluded that petitioners did not have standing because their "recreational, aesthetic, and commercial interests ... do not fall within the zone of interests sought to be protected by ESA." id., at 28. The Court of Appeals for the Ninth Circuit affirmed. * * *

* * * In addition to the immutable requirements of Article III, "the federal judiciary has also adhered to a set of prudential principles that bear on the question of standing." * * * Like their constitutional counterparts, these "judicially self-imposed limits on the exercise of federal jurisdiction," Allen v. Wright, 468 U.S. 737, 751, 104 S.Ct. 3315, 3324, 82 L.Ed.2d 556 (1984), are "founded in concern about the proper—and prop-

erly limited—role of the courts in a democratic society," * * * but unlike their constitutional counterparts, they can be modified or abrogated by Congress * * * Numbered among these prudential requirements is the doctrine of particular concern in this case: that a plaintiff's grievance must arguably fall within the zone of interests protected or regulated by the statutory provision or constitutional guarantee invoked in the suit. * * *

We have made clear ... that the breadth of the zone of interests varies according to the provisions of law at issue. * * *

* * * The first question in the present case is whether the ESA's citizen-suit provision, [16 U.S.C. § 1540(g)] ... negates the zone-of-interests test (or, perhaps more accurately, expands the zone of interests). We think it does. The first operative portion of the provision says that "any person may commence a civil suit"—an authorization of remarkable breadth when compared with the language Congress ordinarily uses. Even in some other environmental statutes, Congress has used more restrictive formulations, such as "[any person] having an interest which is or may be adversely affected," 33 U.S.C. § 1365(g) (Clean Water Act); * * * or "any person having a valid legal interest which is or may be adversely affected ... whenever such action constitutes a case or controversy," 42 U.S.C. § 9124(a) (Ocean Thermal Energy Conversion Act). And in contexts other than the environment, Congress has often been even more restrictive. In statutes concerning unfair trade practices and other commercial matters, for example, it has authorized suit only by "[a]ny person injured in his business or property," 7 U.S.C. § 2305(c) * * * or only by "competitors, customers, or subsequent purchasers," § 298(b).

Our readiness to take the term "any person" at face value is greatly augmented by two interrelated considerations: that the overall subject matter of this legislation is the environment (a matter in which it is common to think all persons have an interest) and that the obvious purpose of the particular provision in question is to encourage enforcement by so-called "private attorneys general"—evidenced by its elimination of the usual amount-in-controversy and diversity-of-citizenship requirements, its provision for recovery of the costs of litigation (including even expert witness fees), and its reservation to the Government of a right of first refusal to pursue the action initially and a right to intervene later. * * *

It is true that the plaintiffs here are seeking to prevent application of environmental restrictions rather than to implement them. But the "any person" formulation applies to all the causes of action authorized by § 1540(g)—not only to actions against private violators of environmental restrictions, and not only to actions against the Secretary asserting underenforcement under § 1533, but also to actions against the Secretary asserting overenforcement under § 1533. ... [T]he citizen-suit provision does favor environmentalists in that it covers all private violations of the ESA but not all failures of the Secretary to meet his administrative responsibilities; but there is no textual basis for saying that its expansion of standing requirements applies to environmentalists alone. * * *

In the claims that we have found not to be covered by the ESA's citizen-suit provision, petitioners allege a violation of § 7 of the ESA, 16 U.S.C. § 1536, which requires, inter alia, that each agency "use the best scientific and commercial data available," § 1536(a)(2). Petitioners contend that the available scientific and commercial data show that the continued operation of the Klamath Project will not have a detrimental impact on the endangered suckers, that the imposition of minimum lake levels is not necessary to protect the fish, and that by issuing a Biological Opinion which makes unsubstantiated findings to the contrary the defendants have acted arbitrarily and in violation of § 1536(a)(2). The obvious purpose of the requirement that each agency "use the best scientific and commercial data available" is to ensure that the ESA not be implemented haphazardly, on the basis of speculation or surmise. While this no doubt serves to advance the ESA's overall goal of species preservation, we think it readily apparent that another objective (if not indeed the primary one) is to avoid needless economic dislocation produced by agency officials zealously but unintelligently pursuing their environmental objectives. That economic consequences are an explicit concern of the ESA is evidenced by § 1536(h), which provides exemption from § 1536(a)(2)'s no-jeopardy mandate where there are no reasonable and prudent alternatives to the agency action and the benefits of the agency action clearly outweigh the benefits of any alternatives. We believe the "best scientific and commercial data" provision is similarly intended, at least in part, to prevent uneconomic (because erroneous) jeopardy determinations. Petitioners' claim that they are victims of such a mistake is plainly within the zone of interests that the provision protects.

* * *

Notes and Questions

1. Does the *Bennett* case allow plaintiffs asserting economic interests to bring suit under any environmentally protective statute? In Nevada Land Action Ass'n v. U.S. Forest Service, 8 F.3d 713 (9th Cir. 1993), ranchers who held permits to graze livestock on national forest lands challenged the management plan for the National Forest as violating both the National Environmental Policy Act (NEPA) and the National Forest Management Act. The court found that the ranchers lacked standing to raise their claims under NEPA:

NLAA [Nevada Land Action Association] admits that the primary injury suffered by its members is economic, but contends that the [Forest Plan] also affects the "human environment" of the NLAA members and has therefore caused "lifestyle loss" as well as economic loss.... NLAA cannot invoke NEPA to prevent "lifestyle loss" when the lifestyle in question is damaging to the environment. Since NLAA's suit is "more likely to frustrate than to further" the objectives of NEPA, ... NLAA lacks standing to challenge the LRMP under NEPA.

Id. at 716 (citations omitted).

The court acknowledged that NEPA is unique.

NEPA was enacted in order "to promote efforts which will prevent or eliminate damage to the environment and biosphere and stimulate the health and welfare of man." 42 U.S.C.A. § 4321 (1988). The purpose of NEPA is to protect the environment, not ... economic interests.... Therefore, a plaintiff who asserts purely economic injuries does not have standing to challenge an agency action under NEPA.

Id.

2.   The *Nevada Land Action* case preceded *Bennett* by several years. Would the outcome of *Nevada Land Action* be different today?

3.   The requirements of the ESA are explored in detail in Chapter 14 (Wildlife). The saga of the Klamath Irrigation Project continues today, pitting farmers and irrigators against suckers and federal agencies, with Indian tribes weighing in as well. Attorney Paul Simmons, who represents irrigation interests in the Basin, offers the following description:

The words "Klamath Basin" implicate nearly every water law issue known to humankind. The basin lies in two states. There is irrigation use in both states, including a century-old federal reclamation project. There is water diverted in Oregon for use in California, and vice versa (in some areas a molecule of water may cross the border several times). * * * Four recognized tribes have strong interests in the basin water resources. A complex water rights adjudication is ongoing in the Oregon section of the basin. There are hydroelectric developments on the Klamath River in both states. There are listed threatened and endangered species whose demands for water are competing. Federal wildlife refuges also compete for available water supplies.

Paul S. Simmons, *Klamath Basin: Endangered Species Act and Other Water Management Issues*, SJ023 ALI-ABA 127, 129 (2003).

Professor Reed Benson provides more detail:

The Klamath River of Oregon and California is the third-largest river on the U.S. west coast, but many people had never heard of it until 2001, when a water crisis that had been quietly brewing for many years suddenly exploded into a national news story. An extreme drought left the Klamath Basin with a fraction of its normal water supply, and federal officials concluded that what little water was available was needed to ensure the survival of three fish species protected by the ESA. As a result, farmers who for decades had reliably received water from a federal irrigation project got little or none in 2001. The media stories of "farmers versus suckers" were oversimplified at best, but they helped turn the embattled Klamath Basin irrigator into a powerful new poster child for the cause of revising the Act. The controversy flared again in September 2002 when 33,000 salmon died in the lower Klamath River, allegedly because irrigation demands left too little water in the river to support salmon returns. * * * Court decisions on the Klamath in 2001 [Kandra v. United States, 145 F.Supp.2d 1192 (D.Or. 2001)] * * *, effectively forcing the Bureau of Reclamation to release more water for fish in a time of drought, triggered a mediagenic storm of political and ideological conflict. * * *

Reed D. Benson, *So Much Conflict, Yet So Much in Common: Considering the Similarities Between Western Water Law and the Endangered Species Act*, 44 NAT. RESOURCES J. 29, 30, 63 (2004).

The courts have not (yet) had the last word in the Basin, and the controversy continues to date. *See* Glen Martin, *Salmon Kill Linked to Level of Klamath River's Flow*, S.F. Chronicle, Nov. 19, 2003, at A4.

C. Timing: Final Agency Action and Exhaustion

Just as the parties must be the appropriate ones to bring a claim in federal court, the timing of an action must be appropriate as well. The APA authorizes review of "agency action made reviewable by statute" and "final agency action for which there is no other adequate remedy in court." 5 U.S.C. § 704. In *Bennett v. Spear, supra,* the United States asserted that the petitioners could not proceed under the APA because the Biological Opinion did not constitute "final agency action," as required by § 704. According to the government, "[w]hatever the practical likelihood that the [Bureau of Reclamation] would adopt the reasonable and prudent alternatives (including the higher lake levels) identified by the Service, the Bureau was not legally obligated to do so. Even if the Bureau decided to adopt the higher lake levels ... nothing in the biological opinion would constrain the [Bureau's] discretion as to how the available water should be allocated among potential users." *Id.* (citing Brief for Respondents). The Court was unmoved.

As a general matter, two conditions must be satisfied for agency action to be "final": First, the action must mark the "consummation" of the agency's decisionmaking process,—it must not be of a merely tentative or interlocutory nature. And second, the action must be one by which "rights or obligations have been determined," or from which "legal consequences will flow" * * * It is uncontested that the first requirement is met here; and the second is met because, as we have discussed above, the Biological Opinion and accompanying Incidental Take Statement alter the legal regime to which the action agency is subject, authorizing it to take the endangered species if (but only if) it complies with the prescribed conditions. In this crucial respect the present case is different from the cases upon which the Government relies, Franklin v. Massachusetts, 505 U.S. 788 (1992), and Dalton v. Specter, 511 U.S. 462 (1994). In the former case, the agency action in question was the Secretary of Commerce's presentation to the President of a report tabulating the results of the decennial census; our holding that this did not constitute "final agency action" was premised on the observation that the report carried "no direct consequences" and served "more like a tentative recommendation than a final and binding determination." 505 U.S., at 798. And in the latter case, the agency action in question was submission to the President of base closure recommendations by the Secretary of Defense and the Defense Base Closure and Realignment Commission; our holding that this was not "final agency action" followed from the fact that the recommendations were in no way binding on the President, who had absolute discretion to accept or reject them. 511 U.S., at 469–471. Unlike the reports in *Franklin* and *Dalton*, which were purely advisory and in no way affected the legal rights of the relevant actors, the Biological Opinion at issue here has direct and appreciable legal consequences.

Id. at 177–178.

Many of the federal natural resource agencies provide some form of administrative review of agency actions, although some are more formal than others. The BLM and the Forest Service are among the agencies with detailed requirements for internal appeals. An appeal of most BLM actions must be lodged with the Interior Board of Land Appeals (IBLA). IBLA review is available for "a specific action being proposed to implement some portion of a resource management plan or amendment." 43 C.F.R. § 1610.5–3(b). The BLM's decisions regarding the use and disposition of public lands and resources are reviewed by the IBLA, but the approval of BLM land use plans are protested to the BLM director. *Id.* § 1610.5–2. *See* Norton v. Southern Utah Wilderness Alliance, 542 U.S. 55, 124 S.Ct. 2373, 159 L.Ed.2d 137 (2004). Why should the appeal or protest of a plan go to the director instead of the IBLA? Are land use plans somehow different than decisions to allow, for example, mineral leasing or off-road vehicle use in a particular area of a BLM district? For discussion, see Chapter 6, *infra*.

With respect to the Forest Service, Congress has explicitly required exhaustion of remedies:

> Notwithstanding any other provision of law, a person shall exhaust all administrative appeal procedures established by the Secretary [of Agriculture] or required by law before the person may bring an action in a court of competent jurisdiction against—
>
> (1) the Secretary;
>
> (2) the Department; or
>
> (3) an agency, office, officer, or employee of the Department.

Department of Agriculture Reorganization Act of 1994, 7 U.S.C. § 6912. Forest Service regulations provide that, "Unless waived in a specific case, * * * any filing for Federal judicial review of a decision subject to review under this part [governing notice, comment, and appeal procedures for national forest system projects and activities] is premature and inappropriate unless the plaintiff has first sought to invoke and exhaust the procedures available under this part." 36 C.F.R. § 215.21.

If an agency has procedures in place that require interested parties to challenge the agency's actions through an administrative review process, the challengers generally have to utilize those processes before going to court. *See* William Funk, *Exhaustion of Administrative Remedies—New Dimensions Since Darby*, 18 PACE ENVTL. L. REV. 1 (2000).

> If a statute sets up an appeal procedure within the agency or the department, a party must adhere to that procedure before going to court. The deadlines for filing administrative appeals are usually jurisdictional; if the appeal is not filed within the time specified, it is barred. * * * Similarly, the courts may refuse to consider grounds omitted from an administrative appeal or issues raised by a party that failed to participate in rulemaking proceedings. The Eleventh Circuit refused to permit the defendant in a criminal prosecution under the Endangered Species Act to rely on evidence which it could have but failed to submit to the Interior Secretary in the rulemaking that resulted in species listing. * * * United States v. Guthrie, 50 F.3d 936, 943–44 (11th Cir. 1995). The court indicated that "collateral review of an agency regulation in a criminal proceeding should be narrow or nonexistent." *Id.* at 943. But in suits involving review under the APA, federal courts may not dismiss for failure to exhaust if neither the statute nor agency regulations specifically mandate exhaustion as a prerequisite to judicial review.

George Cameron Coggins and Robert L. Glicksman, Public Natural Resources Law § 8.20 (current through the Feb. 2005 update).

Plaintiffs have been able to get around the exhaustion requirement in limited circumstances. "[T]he exhaustion doctrine will not foreclose review when administrative remedies are inadequate, or pursuing them would be futile, or when the question is purely legal." *Id.* In Sierra Club v. Espy, 822 F.Supp. 356 (E.D. Tex. 1993), *rev'd on other grounds*, 18 F.3d 1202 (5th Cir. 1994), the court allowed the plaintiffs to pursue their claims in court in spite of a failure to exhaust administrative remedies because the Forest Service's excessive delays in processing their appeals amounted to an "absolute shut-down" of the administrative process. Likewise, in Idaho Watersheds Project v. Hahn, 307 F.3d 815 (9th Cir. 2002), the court allowed the plaintiff's challenge to grazing permits to continue despite the failure to seek a stay pending appeal, because a stay would not have rendered the challenged decisions inoperative.

D. Timing: Ripeness and Mootness

In addition to the requirements described above, Article III imposes certain timing requirements for any and all cases brought in federal court. To be considered a concrete "case or controversy," claims must not be too early (in other words, they must be ripe), and they must not be too late (they may not be moot).

OHIO FORESTRY ASSOCIATION, INC.
v. SIERRA CLUB ET AL.
Supreme Court of the United States, 1998.
523 U.S. 726, 118 S.Ct. 1665, 140 L.Ed.2d 921.

JUSTICE BREYER delivered the opinion of the Court.

The Sierra Club challenges the lawfulness of a federal land and resource management plan adopted by the United States Forest Service for Ohio's Wayne National Forest on the ground that the plan permits too much logging and too much clearcutting. We conclude that the controversy is not yet ripe for judicial review.

I

The National Forest Management Act of 1976 (NFMA) requires the Secretary of Agriculture to "develop, maintain, and, as appropriate, revise land and resource management plans for units of the National Forest System." 90 Stat. 2949, as renumbered and amended, 16 U.S.C. § 1604(a). * * * The National Forest Service, which manages the System, develops land and resource management plans pursuant to NFMA, and uses these forest plans to "guide all natural resource management activities," 36 CFR § 219.1(b) (1997), including use of the land for "outdoor recreation, range, timber, watershed, wildlife and fish, and wilderness." 16 U.S.C. § 1604(e)(1). * * *

This case focuses upon a plan that the Forest Service has developed for the Wayne National Forest located in southern Ohio. When the Service wrote the plan, the forest consisted of 178,000 federally owned acres (278 sq. mi.).... See Land and Resource Management Plan, Wayne National Forest, United States Department of Agriculture, Forest Service, Eastern Region (1987) * * * The Plan permits logging to take place on 126,000 (197 sq. mi.) of the federally owned acres. At the same time, it sets a ceiling on the total amount of wood that can be cut—a ceiling that amounts to about 75 million board feet over 10 years, and which, the Plan projects, would lead to logging on about 8,000 acres (12.5 sq. mi.) during that decade. According to the Plan, logging on about 5,000 (7.8 sq. mi.) of those 8,000 acres would involve clearcutting, or other forms of what the Forest Service calls "even-aged" tree harvesting. * * *

Although the Plan sets logging goals, selects the areas of the forest that are suited to timber production, 16 U.S.C. § 1604(k), and determines which "probable methods of timber harvest" are appropriate, § 1604(f)(2), it does not itself authorize the cutting of any trees. Before the Forest Service can permit the logging, it must: (a) propose a specific area in which logging will take place and the harvesting methods to be used * * *; (b) ensure that the project is consistent with the Plan * * *; (c) provide those affected by proposed logging notice and an opportunity to be heard * * *; (d) conduct an environmental analysis pursuant to the National Environmental Policy Act of 1969 (NEPA) * * * to evaluate the effects of the specific project and to contemplate alternatives

* * *; and (e) subsequently make a final decision to permit logging, which affected persons may challenge in an administrative appeals process and in court * * * Furthermore, the statute requires the Forest Service to "revise" the Plan "as appropriate." 16 U.S.C. § 1604(a). Despite the considerable legal distance between the adoption of the Plan and the moment when a tree is cut, the Plan's promulgation nonetheless makes logging more likely in that it is a logging precondition; in its absence logging could not take place. * * *

When the Forest Service first proposed its Plan, the Sierra Club and the Citizens Council on Conservation and Environmental Control each objected. In an effort to bring about the Plan's modification, they (collectively Sierra Club), pursued various administrative remedies. * * * The Sierra Club then brought this lawsuit in federal court, initially against the Chief of the Forest Service, the Secretary of Agriculture, the Regional Forester, and the Forest Supervisor. The Ohio Forestry Association, some of whose members harvest timber from the Wayne National Forest or process wood products obtained from the forest, later intervened as a defendant.

The Sierra Club's second amended complaint * * * allege[s] that erroneous analysis leads the Plan wrongly to favor logging and clearcutting. * * * The complaint then sets forth three claims for relief. The first claim for relief says that the "defendants in approving the plan for the Wayne [National Forest] and in directing or permitting below-cost timber sales accomplished by means of clearcutting" violated various laws including the NFMA, the NEPA, and the Administrative Procedure Act. The second claim says that the "defendants' actions in directing or permitting below-cost timber sales in the Wayne [National Forest] under the plan violate [their] duties as public trustees." The third claim says that, in selecting the amount of the forest suitable for timber production, the defendants followed regulations that failed properly to identify "economically unsuitable lands." * * * It adds that, because the Forest Service's regulations thereby permitted the Service to place "economically unsuitable lands" in the category of land where logging could take place, the regulations violated their authorizing statute, NFMA, 16 U.S.C. § 1600 et seq., and were "arbitrary, capricious, an abuse of discretion, and not in accordance with law," pursuant to the Administrative Procedure Act, 5 U.S.C. § 701 et seq. * * *

The District Court reviewed the Plan, decided that the Forest Service had acted lawfully in making the various determinations that the Sierra Club had challenged, and granted summary judgment for the Forest Service. * * * The Court of Appeals for the Sixth Circuit held that the dispute was justiciable, finding both that the Sierra Club had standing to bring suit, and that since the suit was "ripe for review," there was no need to wait "until a site-specific action occurs." Sierra Club v. Thomas, 105 F.3d 248, 250 (6th Cir.1997). The Court of Appeals disagreed with the District Court about the merits. It held that the Plan improperly favored clearcutting and therefore violated NFMA. * * *

II

* * * As this Court has previously pointed out, the ripeness requirement is designed

> "to prevent the courts, through avoidance of premature adjudication, from entangling themselves in abstract disagreements over administrative policies, and also to protect the agencies from judicial interference until an administrative decision has been formalized and its effects felt in a concrete way by the challenging parties."

Abbott Laboratories v. Gardner, 387 U.S. 136, 148–149, 87 S.Ct. 1507, 1515, 18 L.Ed.2d 681 (1967).

In deciding whether an agency's decision is, or is not, ripe for judicial review, the Court has examined both the "fitness of the issues for judicial decision" and the "hardship to the parties of withholding court consideration." Id., at 149, 87 S.Ct., at 1515. To do so in this case, we must consider: (1) whether delayed review would cause hardship to the plaintiffs; (2) whether judicial intervention would inappropriately interfere with further administrative action; and (3) whether the courts would benefit from further factual development of the issues presented. These considerations, taken together, foreclose review in the present case.

First, to "withhol[d] court consideration" at present will not cause the parties significant "hardship" as this Court has come to use that term. Ibid. For one thing, the provisions of the Plan that the Sierra Club challenges do not create adverse effects of a strictly legal kind, that is, effects of a sort that traditionally would have qualified as harm. * * * [T]hey do not command anyone to do anything or to refrain from doing anything; they do not grant, withhold, or modify any formal legal license, power, or authority; they do not subject anyone to any civil or criminal liability; they create no legal rights or obligations. Thus, for example, the Plan does not give anyone a legal right to cut trees, nor does it abolish anyone's legal authority to object to trees being cut.

Nor have we found that the Plan now inflicts significant practical harm upon the interests that the Sierra Club advances—an important consideration in light of this Court's modern ripeness cases. * * * As we have pointed out, before the Forest Service can permit logging, it must focus upon a particular site, propose a specific harvesting method, prepare an environmental review, permit the public an opportunity to be heard, and (if challenged) justify the proposal in court. The Sierra Club thus will have ample opportunity later to bring its legal challenge at a time when harm is more imminent and more certain. Any such later challenge might also include a challenge to the lawfulness of the present Plan if (but only if) the present Plan then matters, i.e., if the Plan plays a causal role with respect to the future, then-imminent, harm from logging. Hence we do not find a strong reason why the Sierra Club must bring its challenge now in order to get relief. * * * Nor has the Sierra Club pointed to any other way in which the Plan could now force it to modify its behavior in order to avoid future adverse consequences, as, for example, agency regulations can sometimes force immediate compliance through fear of future sanctions. * * *

The Sierra Club does say that it will be easier, and certainly cheaper, to mount one legal challenge against the Plan now, than to pursue many challenges to each site-specific logging decision to which the Plan might eventually lead. It does not explain, however, why one initial site-specific victory (if based on the Plan's unlawfulness) could not, through preclusion principles, effectively carry the day. * * * And, in any event, the Court has not considered this kind of litigation cost saving sufficient by itself to justify review in a case that would otherwise be unripe. The ripeness doctrine reflects a judgment that the disadvantages of a premature review that may prove too abstract or unnecessary ordinarily outweigh the additional costs of—even repetitive— postimplementation litigation. * * * ("The case-by-case approach ... is understandably frustrating to an organization such as respondent, which has as its objective across-the-board protection of our Nation's ... forests.... But this is the traditional, and remains the normal, mode of operation of the courts") * * *

Second, from the agency's perspective, immediate judicial review directed at the lawfulness of logging and clearcutting could hinder agency efforts to refine its policies: (a) through revision of the Plan, e.g., in response to an appropriate proposed site-specific action that is inconsistent with the Plan * * *, or (b) through application of the Plan in practice, e.g., in the form of site-specific proposals, which are subject to review by a court applying purely legal criteria. * * * And, here, the possibility that further consideration will actually occur before the Plan is implemented is not theoretical, but real. See, e.g., 60 Fed.Reg. 18886, 18901 (1995) (forest plans often not fully implemented), id., at 18905–18907 (discussing process for amending forest plans); 58 Fed.Reg. 19369, 19370–19371 (1993) (citing administrative appeals indicating that plans are merely programmatic in nature and that plan cannot foresee all effects on forest); Appeal Nos. 92–09–11–0008, 92–09–11–0009 (Lodging II) (successful Sierra Club administrative appeals against Wayne timber harvesting site-specific projects). Hearing the Sierra Club's challenge now could thus interfere with the system that Congress specified for the agency to reach forest logging decisions.

Third, from the courts' perspective, review of the Sierra Club's claims regarding logging and clearcutting now would require time-consuming judicial consideration of the details of an elaborate, technically based plan, which predicts consequences that may affect many different parcels of land in a variety of ways, and which effects themselves may change over time. That review would have to take place without benefit of the focus that a particular logging proposal could provide. Thus, for example, the court below in evaluating the Sierra Club's claims had to focus upon whether the Plan as a whole was "improperly skewed," rather than focus upon whether the decision to allow clearcutting on a particular site was improper, say, because the site was better suited to another use or logging there would cumulatively result in too many trees being cut. * * * And, of course, depending upon the agency's future actions to revise the Plan or modify the expected methods of implementation, review now may turn out to have been unnecessary. * * *

This type of review threatens the kind of "abstract disagreements over administrative policies," Abbott Laboratories, 387 U.S., at 148, 87 S.Ct., at 1515, that the ripeness doctrine seeks to avoid. In this case, for example, the Court of Appeals panel disagreed about whether or not the Forest Service suffered from a kind of general "bias" in favor of timber production and clearcutting. Review where the consequences had been "reduced to more manageable proportions," and where the "factual components [were] fleshed out, by some concrete action" might have led the panel majority either to demonstrate that bias and its consequences through record citation (which it did not do) or to abandon the claim. * * *

III

The Sierra Club makes one further important contrary argument. It says that the Plan will hurt it in many ways that we have not yet mentioned. Specifically, the Sierra Club says that the Plan will permit "many intrusive activities, such as opening trails to motorcycles or using heavy machinery," which "will go forward without any additional consideration of their impact on wilderness recreation." Brief for Respondents 34. At the same time, in areas designated for logging, "affirmative measures to promote undisturbed backcountry recreation, such as closing roads and building additional hiking trails," will not take place. Ibid. These are harms, says the Sierra Club, that will not take place at a distant future time. Rather, they will take place now.

This argument suffers from the legally fatal problem that it makes its first appearance here in this Court in the briefs on the merits. The Complaint, fairly read, does not include such claims. Instead, it focuses on the amount and method of timber harvesting. * * *

The matter is significant because the Government concedes that if the Sierra Club had previously raised these other kinds of harm, the ripeness analysis in this case with respect to those provisions of the Plan that produce the harm would be significantly different. The Government's brief in the Court of Appeals said:

> If, for example, a plan incorporated a final decision to close a specific area to off-road vehicles, the plan itself could result in imminent concrete injury to a party with an interest in the use of off-road vehicles in that area. * * *

And, at oral argument, the Solicitor General agreed that if the Sierra Club's claim was "that [the] plan was allowing motorcycles into a bird-watching area or something that like, that would be immediately justi ciable." * * * Thus, we believe these other claims that the Sierra Club now raises are not fairly presented here, and we cannot consider them.

* * *

Notes and Questions

1.   The Court observed that the Sierra Club had not "pointed to any other way in which the Plan could now force it to modify its behavior in order to avoid future adverse consequences." *Ohio Forestry Ass'n, supra.* Can any environmental group, seeking to assert its interest in environmental preservation, point to such behavior-modifying impact of an agency action allowing timber harvesting, oil and gas leasing, grazing, or other economic pursuits undertaken by third parties on federal lands?

2.   How can something like a forest plan be a "final agency action," where the record of decision has been finalized and signed, but not ripe? Can you think of other examples where this might occur?

3.   Is there any way plaintiffs can obtain review of a forest plan? What about the FEIS that accompanies the plan? The Court observed:

> [Forest plans] … are tools for agency planning and management. * * * [T]he Plan, which through standards guides future use of forests, [does not] resemble an environmental impact statement prepared pursuant to NEPA. That is because in this respect NEPA, unlike the NFMA, simply guarantees a particular procedure, not a particular result. Compare 16 U.S.C. § 1604(e) (requiring that forest plans provide for multiple coordinated use of forests, including timber and wilderness) with 42 U.S.C. § 4332 (requiring that agencies prepare environmental impact statements where major agency action would significantly affect the environment). Hence a person with standing who is injured by a failure to comply with the NEPA procedure may complain of that failure at the time the failure takes place, for the claim can never get riper.

Ohio Forestry Ass'n, 523 U.S. at 737.

4.   Mootness can be considered the "flip side" of ripeness, but courts tend to be more willing to dismiss claims for lack of ripeness than for mootness.

> One explanation for this apparent inconsistency is that the standing requirement is stricter to ensure that the plaintiff has the requisite personal stake at the outset of the litigation; then, once the requisite personal stake is established, a strong presumption attaches that the personal stake will continue throughout the litigation. Another, perhaps better, explanation is that the Court has been inconsistent in its approach to justiciability and needs to reassess the doctrinal exceptions and formulate a consistent justiciability jurisprudence that accurately reflects the Article III case or controversy requirement. Despite the inconsistencies in standing and mootness analysis, both doctrines share a constitutional core. Specifically, the parties must retain a personal stake throughout the litigation to assure an adversarial presentation of the case. * * * An [ ] example of the relaxed nature of the mootness exceptions is provided by comparing Roe v. Wade, 410 U.S. 113 (1973),

with Lujan v. Defenders of Wildlife, 504 U.S. 555 (1992). In *Roe*, the Court applied the "capable of repetition yet evading review" exception to mootness, under which a case will not be dismissed as moot despite the lack of continuing injury when the injury is "reasonably expected" to reoccur with regard to the same plaintiff but will again evade review by the Court. * * * In *Roe*, the plaintiff, a pregnant woman who sought a determination regarding the constitutionality of a state statute limiting her right to obtain an abortion, was no longer pregnant by the time the case reached the Supreme Court and did not have plans to again become pregnant. The Court noted that "[p]regnancy often comes more than once to the same woman," and on that basis, concluded that the case was not moot. *See id.* at 125. Compare this with *Lujan*, in which an environmental group was denied standing to challenge an administrative interpretation of a statute because the members of the group did not have concrete plans to visit the affected areas, as was required to satisfy the "actual or imminent injury" requirement, even though the members had professed an "intent" to visit the areas in the future.

Cynthia L. Fountaine, *Article III and the Adequate and Independent State Grounds Doctrine*, 48 Am. U.L. Rev. 1053, 1092–93 and n.274 (1999).

5. In Friends of the Earth v. Laidlaw Environmental Services, Inc., 528 U.S. 167, 120 S.Ct. 693, 145 L.Ed.2d 610 (2000), the Supreme Court held that an environmental group's action pursuant to the Clean Water Act against a permit holder for noncompliance with the permit's mercury discharge limits was not rendered moot by the defendant's compliance with permit limits or even by the subsequent shut down of the plant in question. The last recorded mercury violation occurred in January 1995, long after the complaint was filed but about two years before judgment was rendered by the district court. *Id.* at 178. The Court explained:

> [A] defendant claiming that its voluntary compliance moots a case bears the formidable burden of showing that it is absolutely clear the allegedly wrongful behavior could not reasonably be expected to recur. By contrast, in a lawsuit brought to force compliance, it is the plaintiff's burden to establish standing by demonstrating that, if unchecked by the litigation, the defendant's allegedly wrongful behavior will likely occur or continue, and that the "threatened injury [is] certainly impending." * * *

Id. at 191 (citations omitted). Are you convinced that the Friends' lawsuit should have been allowed to continue even when the allegedly noncompliant facility was shut down? After the suit was initiated, but before the district court rendered judgment, Laidlaw violated the mercury discharge limitation in its permit 13 times, and also committed 13 monitoring and 10 reporting violations. Does Laidlaw's spotty track record change your mind?

III. NOW WHAT? JUDICIAL REVIEW OF AGENCY ACTION

What happens once you've satisfied all of the jurisdictional and prudential requirements for bringing a lawsuit and you've made it through the courthouse door? Most challenges to agency's decisions are brought under Section 702 of the APA, which grants a right to sue to any person "suffering legal wrong because of agency action, or to any person adversely affected or aggrieved by agency action within the meaning of a relevant statute...." 5 U.S.C. § 702. Section 702 waives sovereign immunity for lawsuits so long as the plaintiffs "seek relief other than monetary damages" and all other requirements of the APA are met. *Id.* Judicial review is not allowed, however, where the relevant or controlling "statutes preclude judicial review" or where "agency action is committed to agency discretion by law." 5 U.S.C. § 701(a)(1), (2).

There are two primary themes that arise in APA cases: the scope of review and the standard of review.

A. Scope of Review: The Administrative Record

Unlike civil trials governed by the Rules of Evidence, the parties rarely get an opportunity to call witnesses or submit new documentary evidence in court when they challenge agency actions. The APA directs the court to "review the whole record or those parts of it cited by a party." 5 U.S.C. § 706. This means that "the focal point for judicial review should be the administrative record already in existence, not some new record made initially in the reviewing court." Camp v. Pitts, 411 U.S. 138, 142, 93 S.Ct. 1241, 1244, 36 L.Ed.2d 106 (1973).

Extra-record materials are allowed only if: (1) necessary to determine "whether the agency has considered all relevant factors and has explained its decision," Friends of the Payette v. Horseshoe Bend Hydroelectric Co., 988 F.2d 989, 997 (9th Cir.1993) (per curiam); (2) the agency relied on documents not in the record; (3) the materials are necessary to explain technical terms or complex subjects; or (4) plaintiffs can establish bad faith on the part of the agency. National Audubon Soc. v. U.S. Forest Serv., 46 F.3d 1437, 1447 n. 9 (9th Cir.1993). These exceptions are only applied "under extraordinary circumstances, and are not to be casually invoked unless the party seeking to depart from the record can make a strong showing that the specific extra-record material falls within one of the limited exceptions." Voyageurs Nat. Park Ass'n v. Norton, 381 F.3d 759, 766 (8th Cir. 2004).

In Practice:

   If you embark on a career in natural resources or environmental law, one of the most useful things you can do on behalf of your clients is to "make the record" whenever an agency's rulemaking or other decisionmaking process might affect their interests. Your first step is to review the Federal Register on a regular basis. It is the government's legal newspaper published every business day by the National Archives and Records Administration (NARA). The Federal Register reports on the daily business of the federal government: agency regulations; proposed rules and notices; and Executive orders and other Presidential documents. It is readily accessible on-line both through NARA, http://www.archives.gov/federal_ register/index.html, and most agencies' individual web pages.

Once you've determined that a rulemaking or other agency action of interest is proposed or occurring, you'll have a chance to submit comments on behalf of your client, or perhaps even participate through oral or written testimony in a public hearing. *See* 5 U.S.C. § 553(b)–(c) (specifying requirements for agencies' informal rulemaking processes). You can provide the agency with expert analyses and other materials during the public comment process. If you don't do this, you will likely be precluded from raising your evidence in court if your client wants to challenge the action when it is finalized by the agency. Fortunately, the agencies have made it more and more convenient to engage in the process through digital technologies.

For details, see Orly Lobel, *The Renew Deal: The Fall of Regulation and the Rise of Governance in Contemporary Legal Thought*, 89 MINN. L. REV. 342, 438–440 (2004).

B. Standard of Review

When an action is brought under the APA, § 706 provides the reviewing court with the applicable standards of review. "Informal" agency action, such as rulemaking and the issuance of environmental impact statements (EISs), is generally reviewed under the "arbitrary and capricious" standard of § 706. Section 706 provides:

* * * [T]he reviewing court shall decide all relevant questions of law, interpret constitutional and statutory provisions, and determine the meaning or applicability of the terms of an agency action. The reviewing court shall—

(1) compel agency action unlawfully withheld or unreasonably delayed; and

(2) hold unlawful and set aside agency action, findings, and conclusions found to be—

(A) arbitrary, capricious, an abuse of discretion, or otherwise not in accordance with law;

(B) contrary to constitutional right, power, privilege, or immunity;

(C) in excess of statutory jurisdiction, authority, or limitations, or short of statutory right;

(D) without observance of procedure required by law* * *

5 U.S.C. § 706.

1. *The Arbitrary and Capricious Standard of Review*

Courts will find an agency's decision arbitrary and capricious if the agency:

1) relied on factors that Congress did not intend it to consider;

2) failed to consider an important aspect of the problem;

3) offered an explanation for its decision that runs counter to the evidence in its administrative record; or

4) rendered a decision that is so implausible that it could not be ascribed to a mere difference in opinion or a battle of the experts.

Motor Vehicle Mfrs. Ass'n v. State Farm, 463 U.S. 29, 43, 103 S.Ct. 2856, 2867, 77 L.Ed.2d 443, 458 (1983). In *State Farm*, the Supreme Court held that the National Highway Traffic Safety Administration acted arbitrarily when it revoked a requirement that all new motor vehicles be equipped with passive restraints (seatbelts or airbags) to protect passengers in the event of a collision. It concluded that the agency had failed to present an adequate explanation for rescinding the passive restraint requirement, which it had adopted under a previous political administration:

> [W]e fully recognize that "regulatory agencies do not establish rules of conduct to last forever," * * * and that an agency must be given ample latitude to "adapt their rules and policies to the demands of changing circumstances." * * * [Yet] "[t]he agency has no basis at this time for changing its earlier conclusions ... that basic airbag technology is sound and has been sufficiently demonstrated to be effective in those vehicles in current use.... " * * * "An agency's view of what is in the public interest may change, either with or without a change in circumstances. But an agency changing its course must supply a reasoned analysis" * * * We ... conclude that the agency has failed to supply the requisite "reasoned analysis" in this case.

Id. at 42–43, 57.

The *State Farm* criteria can be applied in both "as applied" challenges and "facial" challenges to agency action. A challenge to an agency's decision to issue a permit, license, or lease, or to adopt an environmental impact statement, a land use plan or some other instrument governing a particular area or activity is generally considered an "as applied" challenge. In contrast, a challenge to the agency's regulations or broadly applicable, general directives is considered a "facial" challenge. The distinction between the two types of challenges is subtle, but it can be significant, as you'll see in the following cases. The first two cases involve "as applied" challenges to the National Park Service's decisions on snowmobiling in Yellowstone and Grand Teton National Parks. During the Clinton Administration, the NPS banned snowmobiles, but it changed its mind after the Bush Administration took office. Two different courts issued contradictory opinions, provided below. The third case in this series, *Mineral Policy Center v. Norton*, involves a facial challenge to federal regulations governing mining on the public lands.

THE FUND FOR ANIMALS v. NORTON

United States District Court, District of Columbia, 2003.
294 F.Supp.2d 92.

Plaintiffs the Fund for Animals ("Fund") and the Greater Yellowstone Coalition ("Yellowstone Coalition") challenge the National Park Service's ("Service" or "NPS") administrative decision, codified in a 2003 Supplemental Environmental Impact Statement ("SEIS") and Record of Decision ("2003 ROD"), to allow continued snowmobiling and trail grooming in Yellowstone National Park, Grand Teton National Park, and the John D. Rockefeller, Jr. Memorial Parkway (collectively "Yellowstone" or "Parks"). Plaintiffs allege that snowmobiling and trail grooming cause air and noise pollution, threaten wildlife and endangered species, and create health threats to visitors and park employees. Given these adverse effects, plaintiffs argue that NPS's decision to allow the continuation of these winter activities belies the evidence collected during the rule-making process, thus violating the Administrative Procedure Act's ("APA") prohibition against decision-making that is "arbitrary, capricious, an abuse of discretion, or otherwise not in accordance with law." 5 U.S.C. § 706(2)(A) (2003). * * *

The use of snowmobiles in the Parks was first permitted in 1963, and in 1968 park administrators, responding to growing concerns about the effects of snowmobiling on park resources, implemented the first official winter-use policy. In 1971, the NPS began grooming snow-covered roads to allow for safe passage by over-snow vehicles, and over the next three decades winter use, including snowmobile use, increased dramatically. Between 1983 and 1993, winter use doubled, increasing from 70,000 visitors per winter season to 140,000 visitors per season. * * * Today, over 180 miles of Park roads are groomed at least every other night, and historical use demonstrates that as many as 1700 snowmobiles enter the Parks on peak days. * * *

Inevitably, a conflict arose between the NPS's mandate to protect Park resources and the accommodation of visitors' desires to view the parks via snowmobiles during the winter season. Of particular concern were the effects of trail grooming and snowmobiling on the Parks' wildlife, especially bison. During the winter of 1996–1997, Park officials documented that large numbers of bison left the Parks, some traveling along the manmade groomed trails created to facilitate oversnow vehicle use. As a consequence of this migration, over 1000 bison had to be killed to prevent the spread of brucellosis to livestock in areas outside of the Parks.

* * * The Park Service Yellowstone Act, the federal statute governing the Agency's administration of Yellowstone Park, requires that the NPS preserve "from injury or spoilation" the "wonders" of the park and insure "their retention in their natural condition." 16 U.S.C. § 22 (2003). The Secretary is also required to "provide against the wanton destruction of the fish and game found within the park, and against their cap-

ture or destruction for the purposes of merchandise or profit." *Id.* The Organic Act, creating the National Park Service, defines the Service's purpose as "conserv[ing] the scenery and the natural and historic objects and the wildlife therein and ... provid[ing] for the enjoyment of the same in such manner and by such means as will leave them unimpaired for the enjoyment of future generations." 16 U.S.C. § 1 (2003). * * *

The Court is faced with the review of an agency decision that amounts to a 180 degree reversal from a decision on the same issue made by a previous administration. The 2001 Rule, explicitly citing the negative environmental impacts of snowmobiling on the resources and wildlife of the National Parks, mandated that snowmobiling be phased out in favor of snowcoaches. Three years later, at the exact time this phase-out was to be complete, the Court now reviews a newly promulgated rule which allows 950 snowmobiles to enter the Parks each day.

This dramatic change in course, in a relatively short period of time and conspicuously timed with the change in administrations, represents precisely the "reversal of the agency's views" that triggers an agency's responsibility to supply a reasoned explanation for the change. *State Farm,* 463 U.S. at 41, 103 S.Ct. 2856 * * * While the Snowcoach Rule was not a rule of long-standing, as it was immediately stayed by the incoming Bush Administration, the process leading to the phase-out decision was lengthy, complex, and complete: the Snowcoach Final Rule was promulgated after almost a decade of study, followed by a complete notice and comment rulemaking process, and was ultimately published in the Federal Register. Thus, because there is a "presumption that ... policies will be carried out best if the settled rule is adhered to," the NPS is charged with fully explaining the need for, and identifying the record evidence supporting, this change in course. *State Farm,* 463 U.S. at 41–43, 103 S.Ct. 2856 * * * Moreover, an explanation for this abrupt change, and the court's review of that change, must be made in view of the statutory mandate that governs the agency's actions. * * * NPS is bound by a conservation mandate, and that mandate trumps all other considerations. 2003 ROD at 18, A.R. 81,479 ("Congress has provided that when there is a conflict between conserving resources and value [in the Parks] and providing for enjoyment of them, *conservation is to be the primary concern.*") * * * Finally, with regard to snowmobile use in the National Parks, two Executive Orders, as well as NPS regulations, demand that if it is determined that snowmobile use has an adverse effect on the Park's resources, or disturbs wildlife, the snowmobile use must immediately cease. * * *

In 2000–01 the NPS faced the question of whether to permit snowmobile use in the National Parks, and concluded in the ROD that the elimination of snowmobiling in favor of snowcoach use was the "best way to comply with applicable legal requirements." Snowcoach Final Rule, 66 Fed.Reg. 7,260 (Jan. 22, 2001). The 2000 ROD explicitly acknowledged that "there are overall adverse impacts associated with snowmobile use in the parks," and that "snowmobile use at current levels adversely affects wildlife, air quality, and natural soundscapes and natural odors." 65 Fed.Reg. at 80,915. These impacts were deemed to rise to the level of "impairment" of the Parks' resources and values, thus violating the Organic Act. 65 Fed.Reg. at 80,916. Consequently, the 2000 ROD concluded that "elimination of these impacts is most easily and most effectively accomplished by eliminating snowmobile use." 65 Fed.Reg. at 80,915.

Less than three years later, while acknowledging that the 2001 Snowcoach Rule was based on a finding that existing snowmobile use "impaired park resources and values, thus violating the statutory mandate of the NPS," the NPS has decided to allow 950 snowmobiles to enter the Parks each day. * * * Defendants have continually explained that the decision to now allow snowmobiling is based on the availability of "cleaner, quieter snowmobiles," largely due to the transition from two-stroke snowmobiles to four-stroke snowmobiles and the implementation of Best Available Technology ("BAT") requirements. * * * However, the prospect of improved technology is not "new." The possibility of improved technology was explicitly considered in the 2000 ROD, and just as explicitly rejected as an inadequate solution for reducing the negative impacts of snowmobiling. Explaining the need for a complete phase-out of snowmobiles, the 2001 Snowcoach Rule states: "* * * *Cleaner, quieter snowmobiles would do little, if anything, to reduce the most serious impacts on wildlife.*" * * *

The gap between the decision made in 2001, and the decision made in 2003 is stark. In 2001, the rulemaking process culminated in a finding that snowmobiling so adversely impacted the wildlife and resources of the Parks that all snowmobile use must be halted. A scant three years later, the rulemaking process culminated in the conclusion that nearly one thousand snowmobiles will be allowed to enter the park each day. In 2001, the NPS selected the "environmentally preferred alternative." In 2003, the NPS rejected the environmentally preferred alternative, and instead chose an alternative whose "primary beneficiaries" are the "park visitors who ride snowmobiles in the parks and the businesses that serve them." 68 Fed.Reg. at 69,279. In light of its clear conservation mandate, and the previous conclusion that snowmobile use amounted to unlawful impairment, the Agency is under an obligation to explain this 180 degree reversal. NPS has not met this obligation.[11]

NPS's explanation that technological improvements and mitigation measures justify this change has, as noted above, proven weak at best. In "swerv[ing] from prior precedents" without a cogent, supported explanation, the agency has "crossed the line from the tolerably terse to the

---

11. Indeed, there is evidence in the Record that there *isn't* an explanation for this change, and that the SEIS was completely politically driven and result oriented. *See* NPS Meeting Agenda for June 3, A.R. 51,392 (defining the "internal objective" as "to determine under what terms and conditions snowmobiling will continue in the three parks," and the external objective as "whether to affirm the previous decision or to make a new one."); A.R. 51,416 (participant in NPS meeting noting that "Gale Norton wants to be able to come away saying some snowmobiles are allowed.").

intolerably mute." *Greater Boston Television Corp. v. F.C.C.*, 444 F.2d 841 (D.C.Cir.1970). An agency decision codifying such an unreasoned change is "quintessentially arbitrary and capricious," and thus cannot stand. Therefore, the Court remands the 2003 SEIS and ROD to the agency for further consideration not inconsistent with this opinion.

* * *

INTERNATIONAL SNOWMOBILE MANUFACTURERS ASSOCIATION v. NORTON
United States District Court, D.Wyoming, 2004.
340 F.Supp.2d 1249.

Plaintiff International Snowmobile Manufacturers Association ("ISMA") is an organization of snowmobile manufacturers established in 1995. * * *

* * * On December 11, 2003, the NPS issued its final rule allowing 950 snowmobiles a day in Yellowstone and a total of 1,140 snowmobiles a day in the Parks. The 2003 Final Rule required four stroke engines on eighty percent of the snowmobiles entering the Parks. Before the NPS completed the 2003 FEIS, the Fund for Animals and the Greater Yellowstone Coalition had filed two lawsuits challenging * * * the 2003 Final Rule in the United States District Court for the District of Columbia ("D.C. District Court"). * * * The D.C. District Court issued a Judgment and Memorandum Opinion on December 16, 2003, only four days after the publication of the 2003 Final Rule, vacating * * * the 2003 Final Rule. The D.C. District Court * * * ordered the 2001 Snowcoach Rule * * * to remain in effect until further order. * * *

* * * [T]he Court believes that 2001 Snowcoach Rule was improperly promulgated. The 2001 Snowcoach Rule was the product of a prejudged, political decision to ban snowmobiles from all the National Parks. * * * The 2001 Snowcoach Rule was rushed through the * * * [decisionmaking] process and all along the way, the public was left out * * *

The Court believes that the decision * * * was a radical departure from the policy used by the NPS in the park for almost forty years. It was a lot like banning all pickups in summer months would have been—a pretty radical move in our eyes. After reviewing the administrative record, it appears to this Court that the NPS did not consider the impacts of increased snowcoach use in the Parks, the effectiveness of snowcoach transportation in the Parks' interior, or the real economic impacts to the surrounding areas. * * * This failure to adequately explain the change bolsters this Court's opinion that the decision to ban snowmobiles from the Parks was a prejudged, political decision, and is therefore arbitrary. * * *

The Court does not believe that the Federal Defendants violated the Organic Act by allowing snowcoach only transportation in the Parks. The determination ... was a decision that was within the discretion of the NPS, even though for obvious reasons it was a wrong-headed decision, based on poor judgment. * * *

The Court FINDS that the NPS violated both NEPA and the APA in its rush to push through the politically predetermined ban on snowmobiles in the Parks.* * * In a case as important as this, where the agency action was driven by political haste, poor judgment, and only *pro forma* compliance with NEPA and the APA, it is the province of the Court to vacate the * * * 2001 Rule. * * *

Notes and Questions

1.   The National Park Service found itself facing two contradictory federal court opinions, one issued by the District of Wyoming and the other by the District of Columbia. Which opinion, the D.C. court's or the Wyoming court's, is most persuasive with respect to the APA? What about the NPS Organic Act? The Organic Act and the snowmobiling controversy are addressed in detail in Chapter 6 (Federal Ownership), *infra.*

2.   If the 2003 Rule gave the ISMA what it wanted (more snowmobile use in the Park), why weren't its claims moot? Should the Wyoming district court have dismissed the case?

3.   A "postscript" to the snowmobiling saga is provided in the following news article.

LAWSUITS SWARM AROUND YELLOWSTONE SNOWMOBILES
HIGH COUNTRY NEWS, Dec. 20, 2004, at 7

[A]fter seven years of lawsuits, * * * the National Park Service announced * * * it will continue to allow hundreds of snowmobiles per day into Yellowstone and Grand Teton national parks * * * The new rules will allow 720 snowmobiles into Yellowstone and 140 into Grand Teton each day—only slightly fewer than the number permitted in the late 1990s, when the Park Service originally decided to ban the polluting machines. The snowmobiles must be newer models that are quieter and cleaner-running than those in the past, and they must travel in guided caravans.

Just days after the announcement, the lawsuits began flying. * * * [T]he Wyoming Lodging and Restaurant Association filed one in federal court in Wyoming, saying its members want more traffic in the parks. The Greater Yellowstone Coalition filed a motion * * * in Washington, D.C., asking the Park Service to monitor the snowmobiles' impacts and reduce the numbers allowed if they exceed pollution thresholds. The Fund for Animals and the Bluewater Network filed a separate lawsuit in the same court, charging the Park Service still fails to address the impacts of trail grooming. * * * Meanwhile, to ensure that the parks stay open to snowmobiles this winter, Montana Sen. Conrad Burns, R, tacked a rider onto the omnibus spending bill * * * It prevents the Park Service from changing the rules until next year.

* * *

2. *"Facial" Challenges: Statutory Interpretation and Chevron Deference*

Courts are even more deferential when reviewing an agency's interpretation of an ambiguous statute under its administration, as the following case demonstrates.

MINERAL POLICY CENTER v. NORTON AND NATIONAL MINING ASSOCIATION

United States District Court, District of Columbia, 2003.

292 F.Supp.2d 30.

Plaintiffs, Mineral Policy Center, Great Basin Mine Watch, and Guardians of the Rural Environment, bring this action to challenge the revision of federal mining regulations promulgated by defendant, Bureau of Land Management ("BLM"), United States Department of the Interior ("Interior") * * * According to plaintiffs, the regulations, codified at 43 C.F.R. § 3809 (2003) ("2001 Regulations") "substantially weaken, and in many instances eliminate, BLM's authority to protect the public's lands, waters, cultural and religious sites, and other resources threatened by industrial mining operations in the West." Plaintiffs therefore contend that the regulations run counter to BLM's statutory duty, as set forth in its guiding statute, the Federal Land Policy and Management Act, 43 U.S.C. §§ 1701 et seq. (2000) ("FLPMA"), to "take any action necessary to prevent unnecessary or undue degradation of the [public] lands." 43 U.S.C. § 1732(b). Accordingly, plaintiffs ask this court to vacate and remand any portion of the 2001 Regulations not in accordance with federal law. * * *

A correct resolution of the issues presented by this case requires an understanding and analysis of the pertinent legislative scheme and must begin with the General Mining Law, 30 U.S.C. §§ 21 et seq. (2000) ("Mining Law"), a law that was enacted in 1872. The Mining Law provides: "All valuable mineral deposits in lands belonging to the United States, both surveyed and unsurveyed, are hereby declared to be free and open to exploration and purchase ... by citizens of the United States.... " 30 U.S.C. § 22. The Mining Law gives claimants the right to "a unique form of property." Best v. Humboldt Placer Mining Co., 371 U.S. 334, 335 (1963). It gives any citizen the right to enter onto federal public lands, stake a claim on these lands, and obtain the exclusive right to extract the minerals thereon—all without payment to the United States and without acquiring title to the land itself. * * *

Much changed in this nation in the 100 years following the Mining Law's 1872 enactment. Accordingly, in 1976, Congress enacted FLPMA to amend the Mining Law and reflect the nation's changed view toward land and minerals. FLPMA establishes standards for BLM to regulate hardrock[5] mining activities on the public lands. Such regulation is vital. BLM administers roughly one-fifth of the land mass of the United States[6] and, while the surface area of the land physically disturbed by active mining is comparatively small, the impact of such mining is not. * * * Mining activity emits vast quantities of toxic chemicals, including mercury, hydrogen, cyanide gas, arsenic, and heavy metals. The emission of such chemicals affects water quality, vegetation, wildlife, soil, air purity, and cultural resources. * * * The emissions are such that the hardrock/metal mining industry was recently ranked the nation's leading emitter of toxic pollution. * * *

FLPMA thus attempts to balance two vital—but often competing—interests. On one hand, FLPMA recognizes the "need for domestic sources of minerals, food, timber, and fiber from the public lands," 43 U.S.C. § 1701(a)(12), and, on the other hand, FLPMA attempts to mitigate the devastating environmental consequences of hardrock mining, to "protect the quality of scientific, scenic, historical, ecological, environmental, air, and atmospheric, water resource, and archeological values," id. § 1701(a)(8). * * *

The heart of FLPMA amends and supersedes the Mining Law to provide: "In managing the public lands the Secretary shall, by regulation or otherwise, take any action necessary to prevent unnecessary or undue degradation of the lands." 43 U.S.C. § 1732(b) * * *

After FLPMA was enacted in 1976, BLM commenced a rulemaking to implement it. BLM issued its proposed rules on December 6, 1976, and finalized them on November 26, 1980. * * * These rules, commonly known as the "1980 Regulations," established "procedures to prevent unnecessary or undue degradation of Federal lands which may result from operations authorized by the mining laws." 45 Fed.Reg. at 78,909–10 (Nov. 26, 1980). The 1980 Regulations defined "unnecessary or undue degradation," commonly referred to as "UUD," as being: (1) "surface disturbance greater than that which would normally result when an activity is being" conducted by "a prudent operator in usual, customary, and proficient operations"; (2) "failure to comply with applicable environmental protection statutes and regulations thereunder"; and (3) "[f]ailure to initiate and complete reasonable mitigation measures, including reclamation of disturbed areas or creation of a nuisance." Id. at 78,910. These rules, formerly codified at 43 C.F.R. § 3809.0–5(k) (1999), governed the mining industry for quite some time.

In the 1990s, however, Interior conducted a comprehensive review of the 1980 Regulations, and on January 6, 1997, commenced a rulemaking to amend them. * * * Interior finally amended the 1980 Regulations in 2000. The 2000 Regulations, which ... became effective in the final hours of the Clinton Administration, ... differed in fundamental ways

---

5. Hardrock minerals are minerals such as gold, silver, copper, and uranium. * * *

6. BLM is responsible for 260 million acres of land in the western states. Ninety percent of such lands are open to hardrock mining. * * *

from the previous 1980 Regulations. * * * Most importantly, the 2000 Regulations replaced the 1980 Regulations' UUD "prudent operator" standard with a new and more restrictive UUD standard, commonly referred to as the "substantial irreparable harm" or "SIH" standard. 65 Fed.Reg. at 70,115 (formerly codified at 43 C.F.R. § 3809.5(f) (2001)). * * *

The "substantial irreparable harm" standard is so named because in the 2000 Regulations, for the first time, BLM stated that it would deny a plan of operations, i.e., a mining permit,[10] if the plan failed to comply with performance standards or would result in "substantial irreparable harm" to a "significant" scientific, cultural, or environmental resource value of the public lands that could not be "effectively mitigated." * * * Thus, under the 2000 Regulations, BLM asserted its authority to deny a mining permit, simply because a potential site was unsuitable for mining because of, for instance, the area's environmental sensitivity or cultural importance. * * *

These 2000 Regulations were short lived, however. On March 23, 2001, after a change in the Administration, Interior published a Notice in the Federal Register stating its intention to amend the regulations once again. * * * In so doing, the Interior Solicitor issued a legal opinion examining FLPMA and concluding that the 2000 Regulation's SIH standard was ultra vires, a conclusion with which the Interior Secretary agreed. The 2001 Regulations, promulgated on October 30, 2001, thus abolished the 2000 Regulations' SIH standard. 66 Fed.Reg. at 54,837–38. What was left after the revision was a standard more akin to the "prudent operator" standard utilized by the 1980 Regulations. * * * The stated reason for the elimination of the SIH standard was that Interior determined that the standard's "implementation and enforcement ... would be difficult and potentially subjective, as well as expensive for both BLM and the industry," and that "other means" would "protect the resources covered by the SIH standard." *Id.* at 54,838, 54,846. Interior further determined that the SIH standard would precipitate a "10%– 30% decline overall in minerals production." 65 Fed.Reg. at 70,107.

The 2001 Regulations provide:

Unnecessary or undue degradation means conditions, activities, or practices that:

(1) Fail to comply with one or more of the following: the performance standards in § 3809.420, the terms and conditions of an approved plan of operations, operations described in a complete notice, and other Federal and state laws related to environmental protection and protection of cultural resources;

---

10. A "plan of operations" describes what activities the applicant proposes to conduct on public land. A plan of operations must be submitted to BLM for approval before certain mining operations may commence and must document all actions that the operator plans to take from exploration through reclamation. * * *

(2) Are not "reasonably incident" to prospecting, mining, or processing operations as defined in § 3715.0–5 of this chapter; [or]

(3) Fail to attain a stated level of protection or reclamation required by specific laws in areas such as the California Desert Conservation Area, Wild and Scenic Rivers, BLM-administered portions of the National Wilderness System, and BLM-administered National Monuments and National Conservation Areas. 43 C.F.R. § 3809.5.

*   *   *

* * * Challenges to agency rulemaking are reviewed under the Administrative Procedure Act ("APA"), which authorizes courts to set aside final agency actions, findings, and conclusions that are arbitrary and capricious, an abuse of discretion, or otherwise not in accordance with law. 5 U.S.C. § 706(2)(A) (2000). * * *

Chevron, U.S.A., Inc. v. Natural Resources Defense Council, Inc., 467 U.S. 837 (1984), provides the framework that governs judicial review of agency decisions. In *Chevron*, the Supreme Court set out the now-familiar two-step test for reviewing an agency's interpretation of a statute. First, the reviewing court must ask "whether Congress has directly spoken to the precise question at issue." *Chevron*, 467 U.S. at 842. If so, "that is the end of the matter; for the court, as well as the agency, must give effect to the unambiguously expressed intent of Congress." *Id*. If, however, the statute is silent or ambiguous with respect to the specific issue, the reviewing court must defer to the agency's construction of the statute, so long as it is reasonable. * * *

Chevron and its progeny make clear that "[w]hen a challenge to an agency construction of a statutory provision, fairly conceptualized, really centers on the wisdom of the agency's policy, rather than whether it is a reasonable choice within a gap left open by Congress, the challenge must fail." *Chevron*, 467 U.S. at 866. However, if a regulation unreasonably interprets a statute or is inconsistent with the statute under which it is promulgated, the regulation may not be sustained. * * *

In this case, plaintiffs challenge Interior's decision to rescind a validly-issued rule and replace it with the 2001 Regulations. Rescission of agency rules that previously met Congress's legislative mandate are judged by the rulemaking record. That is, " '[a]n agency's view of what is in the public interest may change, either with or without a change in circumstances. But an agency changing its course must supply a reasoned analysis.' " Motor Vehicle Mfrs. Ass'n of U.S., Inc. v. State Farm Mut. Auto. Ins. Co., 463 U.S. 29, 57 (1983) * * * Louisiana Pub. Serv. Comm'n v. FERC, 184 F.3d 892, 897 (D.C.Cir.1999) ("For the agency to reverse its position in the face of a precedent it has not persuasively distinguished is quintessentially arbitrary and capricious."). An agency must therefore "examine the relevant data and articulate a satisfactory explanation for its action including a 'rational connection between the facts found and the choice made.' " Motor Vehicle Mfrs. Ass'n, 463 U.S. at 43. * * *

In this case, moreover, plaintiffs mount a facial challenge to the 2001 Regulations. In so doing, according to Interior and NMA, plaintiffs assume an unusually "heavy burden" in prevailing on the merits. United States v. Salerno, 481 U.S. 739, 745, 107 S.Ct. 2095, 95 L.Ed.2d 697 (1987) * * * According to Interior and NMA, under the Supreme Court's standard set forth in *Salerno*, plaintiffs must show that " 'no set of circumstances exists under which the regulations would be valid.' " * * *

Plaintiffs, meanwhile, concede that they cannot clear *Salerno's* high threshold—but they challenge defendants' claim that they must. That is, plaintiffs maintain that this action, challenging the validity of an agency regulation, is not governed by the *Salerno* "no set of circumstances" test. * * *

The Supreme Court has never adopted a "no set of circumstances" test to assess the validity of a regulation challenged as facially incompatible with governing statutory law. Indeed, the Court in at least one case, Sullivan v. Zebley, 493 U.S. 521, 110 S.Ct. 885, 107 L.Ed.2d 967 (1990), upheld a facial challenge under normal *Chevron* standards, despite the existence of clearly valid applications of the regulation. * * *

Our own cases confirm that the normal *Chevron* test is not transformed into an even more lenient "no valid applications" test just because the attack is facial. We have on several occasions invalidated agency regulations challenged as facially inconsistent with governing statutes despite the presence of easily imaginable valid applications. * * *

[H]owever * * * confusion in this Circuit remains. * * * Indeed, the D.C. Circuit is not alone; other courts have also wrestled with the *Salerno* standard, with only limited success. *See, e.g.,* A Woman's Choice–East Side Women's Clinic v. Newman, 305 F.3d 684, 687 (7th Cir.2002) (providing that the Supreme Court's inconsistent utilization of the *Salerno* standard puts "courts of appeals in a pickle" and, as a result, declining to rely on *Salerno's* no-set-of-circumstances test) * * * Even the Supreme Court's application of *Salerno* has been spotty, at best. *See, e.g.,* Janklow v. Planned Parenthood Sioux Falls Clinic, 517 U.S. 1174, 1175–76, 116 S.Ct. 1582, 134 L.Ed.2d 679 (1996) (Stevens, J., mem. opinion denying cert.) (stating that "Salerno's rigid and unwise dictum has been properly ignored in subsequent cases" and listing examples of such cases). * * * Consequently, this court is left with little to guide it. * * * Thus, based upon the uneven application of the no-set-of-circumstances test, the confusion surrounding the doctrine, and this court's own view that *Chevron* is adequately deferential to the decisions of administrative agencies, the court declines to rely upon *Salerno* here. The court's decision is not outcome determinative, however, because, for reasons set forth more fully below, plaintiffs' primary challenge must fail, even when analyzed under the more traditional *Chevron* framework. * * *

* * * [P]laintiffs * * * argue that the 2001 Regulations fail to meet BLM's statutory mandate to "take any action necessary to prevent

unnecessary or undue degradation of the [public] lands." 43 U.S.C. § 1732(b). Plaintiffs argue that in promulgating the 2001 Regulations, BLM essentially abdicated its duty to prevent "undue degradation" and instead, revised its definition of "unnecessary or undue degradation" to limit its authority to prevent only operations that are "unnecessary" for mining. Plaintiffs maintain that by reading "undue degradation" as superfluous to the statute, defendants contravene the plain language of FLPMA, in violation of the APA.

* * * In response to plaintiffs' claims, * * * Interior maintains that, in this case, plaintiffs espouse mere policy preferences for less or no mining on the public lands, untethered to the requirements of FLPMA or the Mining Law. * * *

* * * The 2000 Regulations explicitly adopted the view that Congress had authorized the Secretary to prohibit mining activities found unduly degrading, although potentially lucrative. * * * This view was succinctly expressed in the preamble to the 2000 Regulations, which states:

> Congress did not define the term "unnecessary or undue degradation," but it is clear from the use of the conjunction "or" that the Secretary has the authority to prevent "degradation" that is necessary to mining, but undue or excessive. This includes the authority to disapprove plans of operations that would cause undue or excessive harm to the public lands.

65 Fed.Reg. 69,998 (Nov. 21, 2000).

Interior's interpretation of FLPMA's UUD standard potentially changed in 2001, however. Before the 2001 Regulations were promulgated, Interior's Solicitor, William G. Myers III, wrote an opinion in which he reviewed the meaning of the words "unnecessary" and "undue," as well as FLPMA's legislative history. Based on this analysis, Solicitor Myers determined that the terms "unnecessary" and "undue" were not two distinct statutory mandates, as the 2000 Regulations presumed, but were instead "two closely related subsets or equivalents." * * * Based on this interpretation of the UUD standard, Solicitor Myers determined that as long as a proposed mining activity is "necessary to mining," the BLM has no authority to prevent it. * * * Accordingly, Solicitor Myers provided that the 2000 Regulations' SIH standard could not be sustained; BLM could not disapprove of an otherwise allowable mining operation merely because such an operation would cause "substantial irreparable harm" to the public lands.* * *

Plaintiffs challenge the Solicitor's interpretation and argue that, based upon FLPMA's statutory language, it is clear that Congress intended to prevent "unnecessary degradation" as well as "undue degradation." * * *

Upon careful consideration, the court agrees with plaintiffs' view. The court finds that the Solicitor misconstrued the clear mandate of

FLPMA. FLPMA, by its plain terms, vests the Secretary of the Interior with the authority—and indeed the obligation—to disapprove of an otherwise permissible mining operation because the operation, though necessary for mining, would unduly harm or degrade the public land.

Three well-established canons of statutory construction compel the court's conclusion. First, it is well settled that the language of the statute should govern. As stated by the Supreme Court: "The starting point in interpreting a statute is its language, for 'if the intent of Congress is clear, that is the end of the matter.'" Good Samaritan Hosp. v. Shalala, 508 U.S. 402, 409 (1993) (quoting *Chevron*, 467 U.S. at 842) * * * The second rule is that when construing a statute, the court is "obliged to give effect, if possible, to every word Congress used." * * *

Third and finally, it is clearly established that "[i]n statutory construction the word 'or' is to be given its normal disjunctive meaning unless such a construction renders the provision in question repugnant to other provisions of the statute," * * * or "the context dictates otherwise," Reiter, 442 U.S. at 339, 99 S.Ct. 2326. See In re Espy, 80 F.3d 501, 505 (D.C.Cir.1996) ("[A] statute written in the disjunctive is generally construed as 'setting out separate and distinct alternatives.'") * * *

Applying these well-established canons to the matter at hand, FLPMA provides that the Secretary "shall by regulation or otherwise, take any action necessary to prevent unnecessary or undue degradation of the lands." 43 U.S.C. § 1732(b). Accordingly, in this case: (1) the disjunctive is used, (2) the disjunctive interpretation is neither "at odds" with the intention of the FLPMA's drafters ..., nor contrary to the statute's legislative history; and (3) the "or" separates two terms that have different meanings.[17] Consequently, the court finds that in enacting FLPMA, Congress's intent was clear: Interior is to prevent, not only unnecessary degradation, but also degradation that, while necessary to mining, is undue or excessive. * * *

With that resolved, the question now before this court is whether the 2001 Regulations effectuate that statutory requirement. * * * Plaintiffs contend that the 2001 Regulations ignore FLPMA's "undue" language and essentially limit BLM's authority to prevent only surface disturbance greater than necessary. Plaintiffs insist that "if an activity such as locating a waste dump on top of a Native American sacred site or dewatering an entire drinking water aquifer is 'necessary for mining,' and the mining company pledged to meet a few technical requirements, the BLM would be powerless to protect those resources." * * *

Interior, on the other hand, maintains that, despite the elimination of the 2000 Regulations' SIH standard, and the Solicitor's understanding that the terms "undue" and "unnecessary" "overlap in many ways," the 2001 Regulations nevertheless prevent UUD, as properly defined by this

---

17. "A reasonable interpretation of the word 'unnecessary' is that which is not necessary for mining. 'Undue' is that which is excessive, improper, immoderate, or unwarranted." Utah v. Andrus, 486 F.Supp. 995, 1005 n. 13 (D.Utah 1979).

court. * * * Specifically, Interior argues that it will protect the public lands from any UUD by exercising case-by-case discretion to protect the environment through the process of: (1) approving or rejecting individual mining plans of operations; * * * (4) linking performance standards to those set forth in existing laws and regulations. These existing laws and regulations include: the Endangered Species Act, 16 U.S.C. §§ 1531–1534 (2000); the Archeological Resources and Protection Act, 16 U.S.C. §§ 470aa–470mm (2000); the Clean Water Act, 33 U.S.C. §§ 1251–1387 (2000); [and] the Comprehensive Environmental Response, Control and Liability Act, 42 U.S.C. §§ 9601–9675 (2000) * * *

* * * The court finds ... that the terms "unnecessary" and "undue," which are not defined in the FLPMA, are themselves ambiguous. In tasking the Secretary to prevent "unnecessary or undue" degradation, Congress left two broad gaps for the Secretary to fill, which the Secretary has elected to fill through the exercise of her discretion, on a case-by-case basis. * * *

Because FLPMA is silent or ambiguous with respect to what specifically constitutes "unnecessary or undue degradation," and the means Interior should take to prevent it, the court * * * must determine, not whether the 2001 Regulations represent the best interpretation of the FLPMA, but whether they represent a reasonable one. *Chevron*, 467 U.S. at 843, 104 S.Ct. 2778. Here, upon careful consideration, the court finds that they do. Plaintiffs have neither demonstrated that the 2001 Regulations fail to prevent unnecessary or undue degradation of the public lands, in contravention of FLPMA, nor that Interior, in promulgating the 2001 Regulations, toiled under an erroneous view of its own authority. The 2001 Regulations are neither "procedurally defective" nor "arbitrary or capricious in substance," nor "manifestly contrary" to the FLPMA. United States v. Mead Corp., 533 U.S. 218, 227 (2001). Thus, the regulations must be accorded due deference. * * *

* * * [I]t is clear that mining operations often have significant—and sometimes devastating—environmental consequences. It is also clear that the 2001 Regulations, in many cases, prioritize the interests of miners, who seek to conduct these mining operations, over the interests of persons such as plaintiffs, who seek to conserve and protect the public lands. While such prioritization may well constitute unwise and unsustainable policy, * * * the court cannot find that the 2001 Regulations unreasonably implement the FLPMA, in violation of the Administrative Procedures Act, nor can the court conclude that the Secretary acted arbitrarily or capriciously in promulgating the 2001 Regulations, such that this court may intervene. Accordingly, * * * plaintiffs' facial challenge must fail. * * *

Notes and Questions

1. In 1995, Glamis Imperial Gold Corp. submitted a proposed plan of operations to the Bureau of Land Management (BLM) to construct and operate a huge gold mine on its unpatented mining claims on 1,570 acres in

California. *See infra* Chapter 6 (Public Lands); 12 (Hard Rock Mining). The company's proposal calls for the removal of 450 million tons of rock and ore from three pits nearly 900 feet deep, a heap leach facility (consisting of a pad and processing ponds), a recovery plant, an electric substation, and multiple waste piles up to 30 stories high. The Quechan Indian Tribe insisted that the project's effects on historic and cultural resources in the area would be devastating, while the U.S. EPA voiced concerns about damage to wetlands in the area and environmental groups pointed out the adverse impacts to rare desert tortoises. Given these concerns and the potential adverse effects, then-Secretary Babbitt issued a Record of Decision (ROD) in January 2001, in the waning days of the Clinton Administration, denying approval for the plan. If the current Secretary of the Interior were to change course and issue a new ROD in 2004, adopting the plan of operations as proposed by Glamis Corp., what if anything could opponents do to challenge that new ROD? Can opponents use the *Mineral Policy Center* case to their advantage, or does the opinion foreclose their challenge to the new ROD? Is *Fund for Animals v. Norton*, 294 F.Supp.2d 92 (D.D.C. 2003), *supra,* persuasive precedent?

2. As the D.C. court explained in *Mineral Policy Center*, "[w]hen a challenge to an agency construction of a statutory provision, fairly conceptualized, really centers on the wisdom of the agency's policy, rather than whether it is a reasonable choice within a gap left open by Congress, the challenge must fail." *Id.* (*citing Chevron*, 467 U.S. at 866). Does this mean that a court would apply the deferential *Chevron* standard to BLM's interpretation of the Occupational Safety and Health Act (OSHA) regarding workplace safety in BLM offices? Does *Chevron* apply to an Environmental Protection Agency (EPA) determination that Title VII of the Civil Rights Act, prohibiting discrimination in employment, does not apply to consultants that regularly contract with the agency? Do you think Congress intended to delegate decisionmaking authority over these matters to the BLM and the EPA, respectively?

3. If the National Park Service were to issue regulations prohibiting "indecent exposure" by park visitors, would the regulation be entitled to *Chevron* deference? Assume that a nudist society sues, challenging the constitutionality of such restrictions on expressive conduct in public areas. Does APA § 706 indicate that judges should review constitutional challenges under the arbitrary and capricious standard? *See* Naturist Soc., Inc. v. Fillyaw, 958 F.2d 1515 (11th Cir. 1992) (reviewing challenge to state park's dress code); Williams v. Kleppe, 539 F.2d 803 (1st Cir. 1976) (reviewing challenge to ban on nude sunbathing in Cape Cod National Seashore).

C. Review of Agency Delays or Failure to Act

The APA also authorizes challenges in limited circumstances where an agency has failed to take action. Section 706(1) states: "The reviewing court shall ... compel agency action unlawfully withheld or unreasonably delayed." The Supreme Court has construed this provision quite narrowly.

NORTON v. SOUTHERN UTAH WILDERNESS ALLIANCE
Supreme Court of the United States, 2004.
542 U.S. 55, 124 S.Ct. 2373, 159 L.Ed.2d 137.

JUSTICE SCALIA delivered the opinion for a unanimous court. * * *

I

Almost half the State of Utah, about 23 million acres, is federal land administered by the Bureau of Land Management (BLM), an agency within the Department of Interior. For nearly 30 years, BLM's management of public lands has been governed by the Federal Land Policy and Management Act of 1976 (FLPMA), 90 Stat. 2744, 43 U.S.C. § 1701 et seq., which "established a policy in favor of retaining public lands for multiple use management." * * * "Multiple use management" is a deceptively simple term that describes the enormously complicated task of striking a balance among the many competing uses to which land can be put, "including, but not limited to, recreation, range, timber, minerals, watershed, wildlife and fish, and [uses serving] natural scenic, scientific and historical values." 43 U.S.C. § 1702(c). * * * To these ends, FLPMA establishes a dual regime of inventory and planning. * * *

Of course not all uses are compatible. Congress made the judgment that some lands should be set aside as wilderness at the expense of commercial and recreational uses. A pre-FLPMA enactment, the Wilderness Act of 1964, 78 Stat. 890, provides that designated wilderness areas, subject to certain exceptions, "shall [have] no commercial enterprise and no permanent road," no motorized vehicles, and no manmade structures. 16 U.S.C. § 1133(c). * * *

Pursuant to § 1782, the Secretary of the Interior has identified so-called "wilderness study areas" (WSAs), roadless lands of 5,000 acres or more that possess "wilderness characteristics," as determined in the Secretary's land inventory. § 1782(a); see 16 U.S.C. § 1131(c). As the name suggests, WSAs (as well as certain wild lands identified prior to the passage of FLPMA) have been subjected to further examination and public comment in order to evaluate their suitability for designation as wilderness. In 1991, out of 3.3 million acres in Utah that had been identified for study, 2 million were recommended as suitable for wilderness designation. * * * This recommendation was forwarded to Congress, which has not yet acted upon it. Until Congress acts one way or the other, FLPMA provides that "the Secretary shall continue to manage such lands ... in a manner so as not to impair the suitability of such areas for preservation as wilderness." 43 U.S.C. § 1782(c). * * *

Aside from identification of WSAs, the main tool that BLM employs to balance wilderness protection against other uses is a land use plan—what BLM regulations call a "resource management plan." 43 CFR § 1601.0–5(k) (2003). Land use plans, adopted after notice and comment, are "designed to guide and control future management actions," § 1601.0–2. See 43 U.S.C. § 1712; 43 CFR § 1610.2 (2003). Generally, a land use plan describes, for a particular area, allowable uses, goals for future condition of the land, and specific next steps. § 1601.0–5(k). Under FLPMA, "[t]he Secretary shall manage the public lands ... in accordance with the land use plans ... when they are available." 43 U.S.C. § 1732(a).

Protection of wilderness has come into increasing conflict with another element of multiple use, recreational use of so-called off-road vehicles (ORVs), which include vehicles primarily designed for off-road use, such as lightweight, four-wheel "all-terrain vehicles," and vehicles capable of such use, such as sport utility vehicles. See 43 CFR § 8340.0–5(a) (2003). According to the United States Forest Service's most recent estimates, some 42 million Americans participate in off-road travel each year, more than double the number two decades ago. H. Cordell, Outdoor Recreation for 21st Century America 40 (2004). United States sales of all-terrain vehicles alone have roughly doubled in the past five years, reaching almost 900,000 in 2003. * * * The use of ORVs on federal land has negative environmental consequences, including soil disruption and compaction, harassment of animals, and annoyance of wilderness lovers. Thus, BLM faces a classic land use dilemma of sharply inconsistent uses, in a context of scarce resources and congressional silence with respect to wilderness designation.

In 1999, respondents Southern Utah Wilderness Alliance and other organizations (collectively SUWA) filed this action in the United States District Court for Utah against petitioners BLM, its Director, and the Secretary. In its second amended complaint, SUWA sought declaratory and injunctive relief for BLM's failure to act to protect public lands in Utah from damage caused by ORV use. SUWA made three claims that are relevant here: (1) that BLM had violated its nonimpairment obligation under § 1782(a) by allowing degradation in certain WSAs; (2) that BLM had failed to implement provisions in its land use plans relating to ORV use; (3) that BLM had failed to take a "hard look" at whether, pursuant to the National Environmental Policy Act of 1969 (NEPA), 83 Stat. 852, 42 U.S.C. § 4321 et seq., it should undertake supplemental environmental analyses for areas in which ORV use had increased. SUWA contended that it could sue to remedy these three failures to act pursuant to the APA's provision of a cause of action to "compel agency action unlawfully withheld or unreasonably delayed." 5 U.S.C. § 706(1).

The District Court entered a dismissal with respect to the three claims. * * * [T]he Tenth Circuit reversed. The majority acknowledged that under § 706(1), "federal courts may order agencies to act only where the agency fails to carry out a mandatory, nondiscretionary duty." It concluded, however, that BLM's nonimpairment obligation was just such a duty, and therefore BLM could be compelled to comply. * * *

II

All three claims at issue here involve assertions that BLM failed to take action with respect to ORV use that it was required to take. Failures to act are sometimes remediable under the APA, but not always. * * * The APA authorizes suit by "[a] person suffering legal wrong because of agency action, or adversely affected or aggrieved by agency action within the meaning of a relevant statute." 5 U.S.C. § 702. Where no other statute provides a private right of action, the "agency action" complained of must be "final agency action." § 704. "Agency action" is defined in § 551(13) to include "the whole or a part of an agency rule, order, license, sanction, relief, or the equivalent or denial thereof, or failure to act." * * * The APA provides relief for a failure to act in § 706(1): "The reviewing court shall ... compel agency action unlawfully withheld or unreasonably delayed."

Sections 702, 704, and 706(1) all insist upon an "agency action," either as the action complained of (in §§ 702 and 704) or as the action to be compelled (in § 706(1)). The definition of that term begins with a list of five categories of decisions made or outcomes implemented by an agency—"agency rule, order, license, sanction [or] relief." § 551(13). All of those categories involve circumscribed, discrete agency actions, as their definitions make clear: "an agency statement of ... future effect designed to implement, interpret, or prescribe law or policy" (rule); "a final disposition ... in a matter other than rule making" (order); a "permit ... or other form of permission" (license); a "prohibition ... or taking [of] other compulsory or restrictive action" (sanction); or a "grant of money, assistance, license, authority," etc., or "recognition of a claim, right, immunity," etc., or "taking of other action on the application or petition of, and beneficial to, a person" (relief). §§ 551(4), (6), (8), (10), (11).

The terms following those five categories of agency action are not defined in the APA: "or the equivalent or denial thereof, or failure to act." § 551(13). But an "equivalent ... thereof" must also be discrete (or it would not be equivalent), and a "denial thereof" must be the denial of a discrete listed action (and perhaps denial of a discrete equivalent).

The final term in the definition, "failure to act," is in our view properly understood as a failure to take an agency action—that is, a failure to take one of the agency actions (including their equivalents) earlier defined in § 551(13). Moreover, even without this equation of "act" with "agency action" the interpretive canon of ejusdem generis would attribute to the last item ("failure to act") the same characteristic of discreteness shared by all the preceding items. * * * A "failure to act" is not the same thing as a "denial." The latter is the agency's act of saying no to a request; the former is simply the omission of an action without formally rejecting a request—for example, the failure to promulgate a rule or take some decision by a statutory deadline. The important point is that a "failure to act" is properly understood to be limited, as are the other items in § 551(13), to a discrete action.

A second point central to the analysis of the present case is that the only agency action that can be compelled under the APA is action legally required. This limitation appears in § 706(1)'s authorization for courts to "compel agency action unlawfully withheld."[1] In this regard the APA carried forward the traditional practice prior to its passage, when judicial review was achieved through use of the so-called prerogative writs—principally writs of mandamus under the All Writs Act, now codified at 28 U.S.C. § 1651(a). The mandamus remedy was normally limited to enforcement of "a specific, unequivocal command," * * * the ordering of a " 'precise, definite act ... about which [an official] had no discretion whatever,' " * * * As described in the Attorney General's Manual ..., § 706(1) empowers a court only to compel an agency "to perform a ministerial or non-discretionary act," or "to take action upon a matter, without directing how it shall act." Attorney General's Manual on the Administrative Procedure Act 108 (1947). * * *

Thus, a claim under § 706(1) can proceed only where a plaintiff asserts that an agency failed to take a discrete agency action that it is required to take. These limitations rule out several kinds of challenges. The limitation to discrete agency action precludes the kind of broad programmatic attack we rejected in Lujan v. National Wildlife Federation, 497 U.S. 871 (1990). There we considered a challenge to BLM's land withdrawal review program, couched as unlawful agency "action" that the plaintiffs wished to have "set aside" under § 706(2). We concluded that the program was not an "agency action":

> "[R]espondent cannot seek wholesale improvement of this program by court decree, rather than in the offices of the Department or the halls of Congress, where programmatic improvements are normally made. Under the terms of the APA, respondent must direct its attack against some particular 'agency action' that causes it harm." * * *

The limitation to required agency action rules out judicial direction of even discrete agency action that is not demanded by law (which includes, of course, agency regulations that have the force of law). Thus, when an agency is compelled by law to act within a certain time period, but the manner of its action is left to the agency's discretion, a court can compel the agency to act, but has no power to specify what the action must be. For example, 47 U.S.C. § 251(d)(1), which required the Federal Communications Commission "to establish regulations to implement" interconnection requirements "[w]ithin 6 months" ... would have supported a judicial decree under the APA requiring the prompt issuance of regulations, but not a judicial decree setting forth the content of those regulations.

III

With these principles in mind, we turn to SUWA's first claim, that by permitting ORV use in certain WSAs, BLM violated its mandate to "continue to manage [WSAs] ... in a manner so as not to impair the suit-

---

1. Of course § 706(1) also authorizes courts to "compel agency action ... unreasonably delayed"—but a delay cannot be unreasonable with respect to action that is not required.

ability of such areas for preservation as wilderness," 43 U.S.C. § 1782(c). SUWA relies not only upon § 1782(c) but also upon a provision of BLM's Interim Management Policy for Lands Under Wilderness Review, which interprets the nonimpairment mandate to require BLM to manage WSAs so as to prevent them from being "degraded so far, compared with the area's values for other purposes, as to significantly constrain the Congress's prerogative to either designate [it] as wilderness or release it for other uses." App. 65. Section 1782(c) is mandatory as to the object to be achieved, but it leaves BLM a great deal of discretion in deciding how to achieve it. It assuredly does not mandate, with the clarity necessary to support judicial action under § 706(1), the total exclusion of ORV use.

SUWA argues that § 1782 does contain a categorical imperative, namely the command to comply with the nonimpairment mandate. It contends that a federal court could simply enter a general order compelling compliance with that mandate, without suggesting any particular manner of compliance. It relies ... upon language in a case cited by the [Attorney General's] Manual noting that "mandamus will lie ... even though the act required involves the exercise of judgment and discretion." Safeway Stores v. Brown, 138 F.2d 278, 280 (Emerg.Ct.App.1943). The action referred to ..., however, is discrete agency action.... General deficiencies in compliance, unlike the failure to issue a ruling that was discussed in *Safeway Stores*, lack the specificity requisite for agency action.

The principal purpose of the APA limitations we have discussed—and of the traditional limitations upon mandamus from which they were derived—is to protect agencies from undue judicial interference with their lawful discretion, and to avoid judicial entanglement in abstract policy disagreements which courts lack both expertise and information to resolve. If courts were empowered to enter general orders compelling compliance with broad statutory mandates, they would necessarily be empowered, as well, to determine whether compliance was achieved—which would mean that it would ultimately become the task of the supervising court, rather than the agency, to work out compliance with the broad statutory mandate, injecting the judge into day-to-day agency management. To take just a few examples from federal resources management, a plaintiff might allege that the Secretary had failed to "manage wild free-roaming horses and burros in a manner that is designed to achieve and maintain a thriving natural ecological balance," or to "manage the [New Orleans Jazz National] [H]istorical [P]ark in such a manner as will preserve and perpetuate knowledge and understanding of the history of jazz," * * * 16 U.S.C. §§ 1333(a), 410bbb–2(a)(1) * * * The prospect of pervasive oversight by federal courts over the manner and pace of agency compliance with such congressional directives is not contemplated by the APA.

SUWA's second claim is that BLM failed to comply with certain provisions in its land use plans, thus contravening the requirement that "[t]he Secretary shall manage the public lands ... in accordance with the land use plans ... when they are available." 43 U.S.C. § 1732(a); see also 43 CFR § 1610.5–3(a) (2003) ("All future resource management authorizations and actions ... and subsequent more detailed or specific planning, shall conform to the approved plan"). The relevant count in SUWA's second amended complaint alleged that BLM had violated a variety of commitments in its land use plans, but over the course of the litigation these have been reduced to two, one relating to the 1991 resource management plan for the San Rafael area, and the other to various aspects of the 1990 ORV implementation plan for the Henry Mountains area.

* * * There remains the claim, with respect to the Henry Mountains plan, that "in light of damage from ORVs in the Factory Butte area," a sub-area of Henry Mountains open to ORV use, "the [plan] obligated BLM to conduct an intensive ORV monitoring program." Brief for SUWA7. This claim is based upon the plan's statement that the Factory Butte area "will be monitored and closed if warranted." SUWA does not contest BLM's assertion in the court below that informal monitoring has taken place for some years, * * * but it demands continuing implementation of a monitoring program. By this it apparently means to insist upon adherence to the plan's general discussion of "Use Supervision and Monitoring" in designated areas, which ... provides that "[r]esource damage will be documented and recommendations made for corrective action," "monitoring in open areas will focus on determining damage which may necessitate a change in designation," and "emphasis on use supervision will be placed on [limited and closed areas]." * * * In light of the continuing action that existence of a "program" contemplates, and in light of BLM's contention that the program cannot be compelled under § 706(1), this claim cannot be considered moot.

The statutory directive that BLM manage "in accordance with" land use plans, and the regulatory requirement that authorizations and actions "conform to" those plans, prevent BLM from taking actions inconsistent with the provisions of a land use plan. Unless and until the plan is amended, such actions can be set aside as contrary to law pursuant to 5 U.S.C. § 706(2). The claim presently under discussion, however, would have us go further, and conclude that a statement in a plan that BLM "will" take this, that, or the other action, is a binding commitment that can be compelled under § 706(1). In our view it is not—at least absent clear indication of binding commitment in the terms of the plan.

FLPMA describes land use plans as tools by which "present and future use is projected." 43 U.S.C. § 1701(a)(2) (emphasis added). The implementing regulations make clear that land use plans are a preliminary step in the overall process of managing public lands—"designed to guide and control future management actions and the development of subsequent, more detailed and limited scope plans for resources and uses." 43 CFR § 1601.0–2 (2003). The statute and regulations confirm that a land use plan is not ordinarily the medium for affirmative deci-

sions that implement the agency's "project[ions]."[4] Title 43 U.S.C.
§ 1712(e) provides that "[t]he Secretary may issue management decisions to implement land use plans"—the decisions, that is, are distinct
from the plan itself. Picking up the same theme, the regulation defining
a land use plan declares that a plan "is not a final implementation decision on actions which require further specific plans, process steps, or
decisions under specific provisions of law and regulations." 43 CFR
§ 1601.0–5(k) (2003). The BLM's Land Use Planning Handbook specifies
that land use plans are normally not used to make site-specific implementation decisions. * * *

The San Rafael plan provides an apt illustration of the immense
scope of projected activity that a land use plan can embrace. Over 100
pages in length, it presents a comprehensive management framework for
1.5 million acres of BLM-administered land. Twenty categories of
resource management are separately discussed, including mineral
extraction, wilderness protection, livestock grazing, preservation of cultural resources, and recreation. The plan lays out an ambitious agenda
for the preparation of additional, more detailed plans and specific next
steps for implementation. Its introduction notes that "[a]n [ORV] implementation plan is scheduled to be prepared within 1 year following
approval of the [San Rafael plan]." * * * Quite unlike a specific statutory command requiring an agency to promulgate regulations by a certain date, a land use plan is generally a statement of priorities; it guides
and constrains actions, but does not (at least in the usual case) prescribe
them. It would be unreasonable to think that either Congress or the
agency intended otherwise, since land use plans nationwide would commit the agency to actions far in the future, for which funds have not yet
been appropriated. * * * A statement by BLM about what it plans to do,
at some point, provided it has the funds and there are not more pressing
priorities, cannot be plucked out of context and made a basis for suit
under § 706(1).

Of course, an action called for in a plan may be compelled when the
plan merely reiterates duties the agency is already obligated to perform,
or perhaps when language in the plan itself creates a commitment binding on the agency. But allowing general enforcement of plan terms would
lead to pervasive interference with BLM's own ordering of priorities. For
example, a judicial decree compelling immediate preparation of all of the
detailed plans called for in the San Rafael plan would divert BLM's
energies from other projects throughout the country that are in fact
more pressing. And while such a decree might please the environmental
plaintiffs in the present case, it would ultimately operate to the detriment of sound environmental management. Its predictable consequence
would be much vaguer plans from BLM in the future—making coordina-

---

4. The exceptions "are normally limited to those required by regulation, such as
designating [ORV] areas, roads, and trails
(see 43 CFR 8342)." U.S. Dept. of Interior,
BLM, Land Use Planning Handbook II–2
(2000). * * *

tion with other agencies more difficult, and depriving the public of important information concerning the agency's long-range intentions.

We therefore hold that the Henry Mountains plan's statements to the effect that BLM will conduct "use supervision and monitoring" in designated areas—like other "will do" projections of agency action set forth in land use plans—are not a legally binding commitment enforceable under § 706(1). That being so, we find it unnecessary to consider whether the action envisioned by the statements is sufficiently discrete to be amenable to compulsion under the APA.[5]

* * *

Notes and Questions

1. In the *SUWA* opinion, the Court distinguished discrete regulatory duties from the types of obligations expressed in the BLM's plans. Is a regulatory commitment different than a commitment expressed in an agency's plan, such that a failure to enforce the regulation might be subject to review under § 706(1)? The nature of BLM plans is explored in detail in Chapter 6.

2. The *SUWA* case poses a catch–22. On one hand, the Court's refusal to require agency action increases the potential for both private influence and public harm. It allows an interest group (off-road vehicle enthusiasts) to ride rough-shod over a clear statutory objective (wilderness preservation). On the other hand, allowing the plaintiff's challenge to proceed against the BLM could raise the potential for excessive intrusion on executive discretion. *See* Lisa Schultz Bressman, *Judicial Review of Agency Inaction: an Arbitrariness Approach*, 79 N.Y.U. L. Rev. 1657 (2004). The Court seemed to believe that such a result would have opened the door for courts and plaintiffs, not agencies and presidents, to manage broad regulatory programs. Arguably, the courts (or litigants) would be placed in a position to control the general content of administrative programs if SUWA's claims had been justiciable. Is an agency's failure to convert broad statutory mandates into particular requirements or prohibitions truly different from an agency's failure to enforce existing requirements or prohibitions?

3. In Heckler v. Chaney, 470 U.S. 821, 105 S.Ct. 1649, 84 L.Ed.2d 714 (1985), the Court expressed a presumption against judicial review of an agency's decision not to take an enforcement action. According to the Court, where the governing statute does not provide explicit standards for prosecution, the decision is committed to the agency's own judgment. *Id.* at 830. The reasons for such a "hands off" approach include:

a) courts lack the expertise to evaluate relevant enforcement factors, such as the agency's enforcement priorities, available resources, and the likelihood of a successful prosecution;

b) an agency's refusal to prosecute a violation of the law does not constitute coercive powers over individual liberty or property rights;

5. We express no view as to whether a court could, under § 706(1), enforce a duty to monitor ORV use imposed by a BLM regulation, see 43 CFR § 8342.3 (2003). That question is not before us.

c) a decision not to enforce a violation of the law provides no focal point for judicial review;

d) like decisions not to indict a violator, decisions not to pursue enforcement actions are within the special province of the Executive Branch.

Id. at 832. Should we accept a presumption against judicial review of claims like those asserted in *SUWA*? What are the dangers of such an approach? According to Justice Marshall,

> The *sine qua non* of the APA was to alter … judicial reluctance to constrain the exercise of discretionary administrative power—to rationalize and make fairer the exercise of such discretion * * * Discretion may well be necessary to carry out a variety of important administrative functions, but discretion can be a veil for laziness, corruption, incompetency, lack of will, or other motives, and for that reason, "the presence of discretion should not bar a court from considering a claim of illegal or arbitrary use of discretion."

Heckler, 470 U.S. at 848 (Marshall, J., concurring) (citation omitted).

4. Is the Court's treatment of SUWA's challenge to the BLM's plans consistent with its treatment of National Forest plans in *Ohio Forestry Assn. v. Sierra Club, supra*? Why didn't the Court simply dismiss SUWA's challenge for lack of ripeness?

5. Can environmental groups like SUWA avoid dismissal when they challenge the Environmental Protection Agency's failure to issue a Clean Air Act standard by the deadline specified in the statute? What about the Fish & Wildlife Service's failure to respond to a petition to list a species as endangered within statutorily imposed deadlines?

6. The *SUWA* case also involved a NEPA issue, which is addressed in Chapter 4.V.A, *infra*. *SUWA's* implications for public lands management and litigation are described in Chapter 6, *infra*.

IV. CITIZENS' SUITS

Although most federal actions related to the management of public lands and natural resources can be challenged in court using the APA, the Endangered Species Act and many pollution control statutes (*e.g.,* the Clean Water Act and the Clean Air Act) include explicit citizens' suit provisions that specify who, what, when and how challenges must be brought under those statutes.

The ESA's citizen suit provision is fairly typical:

[With certain exceptions,] any person may commence a civil suit on his own behalf—

(A) to enjoin any person, including the United States and any other governmental instrumentality or agency (to the extent permitted by the eleventh amendment to the Constitution), who is alleged to be in violation of any provision of this chapter or regulation issued under the authority thereof; or

(B) to compel the Secretary to apply ... the prohibitions ... of this title with respect to the taking of any resident endangered species or threatened species within any State; or

(C) against the Secretary where there is alleged a failure of the Secretary to perform any act or duty under section 1533 of this title which is not discretionary with the Secretary.

16 U.S.C. § 1540(g)(1). The following article highlights the key provisions.

CITIZEN SUITS UNDER THE ENDANGERED SPECIES ACT: SURVIVAL OF THE FITTEST
Patrick Parenteau
10 WIDENER L. REV. 321 (2004)

[A. Who Can Sue?]

* * * The ESA defines "person" as any

individual, corporation, partnership, trust, association, or any other private entity; or any officer, employee, agent, department, or instrumentality of the Federal Government, of any State, municipality, or political subdivision of a State, or of any foreign government; any State, municipality, or political subdivision of a State; or any other entity subject to the jurisdiction of the United States. Id. § 1532(13).

* * * The leading case interpreting the scope of the term "any person" is Bennett v. Spear, where Justice Scalia characterized this language as "an authorization of remarkable breadth." 520 U.S. 154, 164 (1997). In that case irrigators sought to challenge a U.S. Fish and Wildlife Service's biological opinion requiring reductions in water deliveries from Bureau of Reclamation's Klamath Basin Project in Oregon to avoid jeopardy to two species of protected fish. The Ninth Circuit held that economic interests were not within the "zone of interests" protected by the ESA. *Id.* at 160–61. The Supreme Court unanimously reversed, holding that, unlike other environmental statutes, such as NEPA, the ESA's zone of interests was all-encompassing. * * *

Does "person" include critters? * * * In Palila v. Hawaii Department of Land & Natural Resources, the Ninth Circuit observed, in dictum, that the palila "wings its way into federal court as a plaintiff in its own right." 852 F.2d 1106, 1107 (9th Cir. 1988). But note that defendants did not challenge the palila's standing. * * * In Hawaiian Crow (Alala) v. Lujan, 906 F.Supp. 549, 552 (D. Haw. 1991), the district court ruled that the crow did not have standing but granted the human plaintiffs standing to sue on its behalf. * * *

B. Who Can Be Sued?

"[A]ny person, including the United States and any other governmental instrumentality or agency (to the extent permitted by the eleventh amendment to the Constitution).... " may be sued. 16 U.S.C. § 1540 (g)(1)(A) (2000). * * * Does the 11th Amendment bar suit against a State official for prospective injunctive relief? * * * In Natural Resources Defense Council (NRDC) v. California Department of Transportation, 96 F.3d 420, 423–24 (9th Cir. 1996), the district court applied the Ex Parte Young doctrine to allow citizen suits against state officials under [the] CWA where only prospective relief, not damages, [were] sought.

C.   What Violations Can Be Enforced Under the Citizen Suit Provision?

1.   Category One: "[T]o enjoin any person, including the United States and any other governmental instrumentality or agency (to the extent permitted by the eleventh amendment to the Constitution), who is alleged to be in violation of any provision of this chapter or regulation issued under the authority thereof.... " 16 U.S.C. § 1540(g)(1)(A) (2000). This category covers a wide range of ESA requirements including:

1.1   duty of federal agencies to engage in "programmatic"consultation under section 7(a)(1) to identify authorities that can be used to "conserve" listed species;

1.2   duty to consult on individual "agency actions" that "may affect" listed species under section 7(a)(2); * * *

1.4   duty to "insure that [agency actions are] not likely to jeopardize the continued existence of any listed species or result [ ] in the destruction or adverse modification of [designated] critical habitat" under section 7(a)(2); * * * [and]

1.6   prohibition on "take" of listed species (i.e. actual injury or imminent threat) under section 9 * * *

However, in Bennett v. Spear, 520 U.S. 154, 117 S.Ct. 1154, 137 L.Ed.2d 281 (1997), the Court held that this category does not include allegations that Secretaries of Interior or Commerce acted illegally in performing one of their discretionary duties under the statute. Nevertheless, the Court held that such challenges may be brought under the APA. For example, parties may challenge biological opinions issued under section 7(b), ... on any of the grounds set forth in APA section 706.

2.   Category Two: "[T]o compel the Secretary to apply ... the prohibitions set forth in or authorized pursuant to section 1533(d) or 1538(a)(1)(B) of this title with respect to the taking of any resident endangered species or threatened species within any State.... " * * *

3.   Category Three: "[A]gainst the Secretary where there is alleged a failure of the Secretary to perform any act or duty under section 1533 of this title which is not discretionary with the Secretary." * * *

D.   When Can Suit Be Filed?

1.   For Category One:

No action may be commenced under subparagraph (1)(A) of this section—

(i) prior to sixty days after written notice of the violation has been given to the Secretary, and to any alleged violator of any such provision or regulation;

(ii) if the Secretary has commenced action to impose a penalty pursuant to subsection (a) of this section; or

(iii) if the United States has commenced and is diligently prosecuting a criminal action in a court of the United States or a State to redress a violation of any such provision or regulation.

16 U.S.C. § 1540(g)(2)(A) (2000).

2. For Category Two:

No action may be commenced under subparagraph (1)(B) of this section—

(i) prior to sixty days after written notice has been given to the Secretary setting forth the reasons why an emergency is thought to exist with respect to an endangered species or a threatened species in the State concerned; or

(ii) if the Secretary has commenced and is diligently prosecuting action under section 1535(g)(2)(B)(ii) of this title to determine whether any such emergency exists. *Id.* § 1540(g)(2)(B).

3. For Category Three:

No action may be commenced under subparagraph (1)(C) of this section prior to sixty days after written notice has been given to the Secretary; except that such action may be brought immediately after such notification in the case of an action under this section respecting an emergency posing a significant risk to the well-being of any species of fish or wildlife or plants.

Id. § 1540(g)(2)(C).

* * * In the seminal case of Hallstrom v. Tillamook County, 493 U.S. 20, 110 S.Ct. 304, 107 L.Ed.2d 237 (1989), the U.S. Supreme Court held that statutory "60–day [notice] requirements are mandatory conditions precedent," and the failure to comply required dismissal of the action. In her majority opinion, Justice O'Connor said that they need not determine whether the requirement to give notice was "jurisdictional in the strict sense of the term." Nevertheless, the net result is the same: failure to comply means that the court lacks subject matter jurisdiction. * * * Though *Hallstrom* dealt with the citizen suit provision under the Resource Conservation and Recovery Act (RCRA), its rationale has been applied to 60–day notice requirements under other citizen suits including the ESA. * * *

E. When Will Citizen Suits Be Barred?

1. Where the Secretary has "commenced [an] action to impose a penalty pursuant to subsection (a)"; or

2. Where the United States "has commenced and is diligently prosecuting a criminal action in a court of the United States or a State to redress a violation"; or

3. Where the Secretary has commenced an action under § 1535(g)(2)(B)(ii) to determine if an emergency exists.

16 U.S.C. § 1540(g)(2)(B)(ii). * * *

F.   What Relief is Available?

1. The district courts shall have jurisdiction, without regard to the amount in controversy or the citizenship of the parties, to enforce any such provision or regulation, or to order the Secretary to perform such act or duty, as the case may be. * * *

2. The injunctive relief provided by this subsection shall not restrict any right which any person (or class of persons) may have under any statute or common law to seek enforcement of any standard or limitation or to seek any other relief (including relief against the Secretary or a State agency). Id. § 1540(g)(5). * * *

* * *

Notes and Questions

1. Why are Congress and the courts so strict about forcing plaintiffs to provide notice to the defendants and federal enforcement agencies before bringing suit? Professor Parenteau explains,

> The purpose of the 60–day notice provision is to put the agencies on notice of a perceived violation of the statute and an intent to sue. When given notice, the agencies have an opportunity to review their actions and take corrective measures if warranted. The provision therefore provides an opportunity for settlement or other resolution of a dispute without litigation.* * * The notice also is designed to give the government, as the preferred enforcer, the opportunity to take enforcement action against third parties.

Id. at 328–29.

2. Failure to comply with the notice requirements of citizens' suit provisions can result in dismissal and "other unpleasant consequences, like Rule 11 sanctions against plaintiff's attorney." Parenteau, *supra*, at 331. In Maine Audubon Society v. Purslow, 907 F.2d 265, 266 (1st Cir. 1990), the plaintiff's attorney filed suit one day after sending the notice letter. The defendants moved to dismiss the case and sought sanctions. The district court obliged, and imposed a $250 penalty on both counsel for plaintiffs. On appeal, the First Circuit affirmed the sanction, stating:

> While we are not unsympathetic to appellants' position, we do not believe that they can shoulder their "heavy burden" [of overcoming the discretion afforded district courts under Rule 11]. * * * Our earlier decisions made it quite clear that * * * we were committed to "read [ ] the 60–day notice requirement in environmental statute citizen suit provisions strictly." The handwriting was on the wall.

See Parenteau, *supra*, at 331 (*citing Maine Audubon Society,* 907 F.2d at 268).

3. There are certain exceptions to the ESA notice requirement. Section 1540(g)(2)(C) provides that a lawsuit may be filed immediately upon service of the notice if the action being challenged " 'pos[e][s] a significant risk to the well-being of any [protected species].' " *Id.* There are few if any judicially crafted exceptions, but in Loggerhead Turtle v. County Council of Volusia County, 148 F.3d 1231, 1255 (11th Cir. 1998), plaintiffs were allowed to amend their complaint to add another species of endangered turtle because the failure to include that species in the original notice was deemed harmless error. Parenteau, *supra*, at 332–333.

4. With respect to injunctive relief, courts are not required to engage in their traditional role of equitable balancing for ESA violations: "Congress has spoken in the plainest of words, making it abundantly clear that the balance has been struck in favor of affording endangered species the highest of priorities.... " TVA v. Hill, 437 U.S. 153, 194, 98 S.Ct. 2279, 2302, 57 L.Ed.2d 117, 146 (1978). Accordingly, "courts have a duty to enjoin substantive violations of the ESA." Parenteau, *supra*, at 342. In *TVA v. Hill*, the Court enjoined the construction of a multi-million dollar dam, even though it was nearly completed by the time the Court heard the case. Why shouldn't economic harm be balanced with environmental considerations before an injunction under the ESA is issued? For detail, see Chapter 14, below.

5. Regardless of whether you represent clients who are considering bringing a citizens' suit against a violator or clients who need your services to defend a citizens' suit, you should consider the specific language of the statutory provision at issue carefully. In Gwaltney of Smithfield, Ltd. v. Chesapeake Bay Foundation, Inc., 484 U.S. 49, 108 S.Ct. 376, 98 L.Ed.2d 306 (1987), the Supreme Court held that plaintiffs attempting to sue under the Clean Water Act citizens' suit provision must allege ongoing violations of a continuous or intermittent character at the time of the complaint to survive dismissal of their lawsuit. Section 505 of the Clean Water Act states that citizen plaintiffs may any person "who is alleged to be in violation" of certain provisions of the Act. 33 U.S.C. § 1365(a)(1). The Court construed this language to mean that plaintiffs cannot bring suit to redress wholly past violations. Is this an appropriate result? Can you imagine a case where violations have ceased but the claims would not be deemed moot? *See* Friends of the Earth v. Laidlaw Env. Services, Inc., 528 U.S. 167, 120 S.Ct. 693, 145 L.Ed.2d 610 (2000), *supra* Section II.A. Compare the citizens' suit provision of the ESA, 16 U.S.C. § 1540(g)(1). Must ESA plaintiffs allege ongoing violations to maintain their citizens' suit?

6. Citizen plaintiffs face additional statutory and common law obstructions as they attempt to proceed against violators of environmental laws.

All of the major environmental statutes provide that citizens may not sue if the government is "diligently prosecuting" the violator for the same violations or conditions. As simple as the rule may seem in concept, it has posed vexing problems in practice. Does an action by a state preclude a citizen suit in the same way EPA action does? Must the government action be filed in a court of law? Or will an administrative proceeding suffice? What exactly constitutes diligence? What happens if the government institutes its own action and settles the matter after the citizen suit is filed? Are citizens in privity with the government or other environmental groups for purposes of res judicata or collateral estoppel? Will a consent decree in a citizen suit bar a subsequent suit by the government? * * *

One question is readily answered. The citizen suit provisions of the Clean Air Act, the Clean Water Act, RCRA, SMCRA and SDWA all expressly provide that actions instituted by states with authorized programs comparable to the federal programs will have the same preclusive effect as actions taken by the federal government. Settlements with municipal authorities such as publicly owned sewer treatment plants may not preclude a citizen suit, however.

Daniel J. Dunn, *Environmental Citizen Suits Against Natural Resource Companies*, 17 NAT. RESOURCES & ENVTL. 161, 197 (2003).

The fear of common law liability might also act as an impediment to the commencement of a citizens' suit. Defendants accused of environmental violations sometimes bring lawsuits and/or counterclaims against citizen plaintiffs for alleged libel, slander, interference with contract or prospective economic advantage, and even racketeering. This type of response is known as "strategic litigation against public participation" (SLAPP). *See* GEORGE W. PRING & PENELOPE CANAN, SLAPPS: GETTING SUED FOR SPEAKING OUT (1996) (highlighting the proliferation of SLAPP suits and their adverse effects on public participation); Robert R. Kuehn, *Shooting the Messenger: The Ethics of Attacks on Environmental Representation*, 29 HARV. ENVTL. L. REV. 417 (2002) (assessing ethical infractions of attorneys who use SLAPP suits to silence plaintiffs). Defendants who bring SLAPP lawsuits often seek injunctive relief and compensatory damages, and some have sought punitive damages as well. *See* Highland Enterprises, Inc. v. Barker, 133 Idaho 330, 986 P.2d 996 (1999) (affirming a jury award of $150,000 compensatory damages and $999,996 punitive damages against EarthFirst! activists) (discussed *infra*, Chapter 11 II.D, Timber Resources).

* * *

In Practice:

Choice of Federal or State Forum Can be Outcome–Determinative

In San Remo Hotel v. San Francisco, 125 S.Ct. 2491, 162 L.Ed.2d 315 (2005), hotel owners in San Francisco challenged a city ordinance requiring them to pay a $567,000 fee to convert residential rooms to tourist rooms. They initially sought mandamus in state court, but then filed suit in federal court asserting both facial and as-applied challenges to the ordinance under the Fifth Amendment Takings Clause. The federal district court granted summary judgment for the city. The Ninth Circuit affirmed its ruling that the as-applied claim was unripe, but abstained from ruling on the facial challenge under the *Pullman* doctrine, Railroad Comm'n of Tex. v.

Pullman Co., 312 U.S. 496, 61 S.Ct. 643, 85 L.Ed. 971 (1941), because the pending state case could moot the federal question.

Back in state court, the hotel owners attempted to reserve a right to go to federal court with their federal takings claims. After the California courts rejected their state takings claims, they returned to federal court. To avoid being barred by issue preclusion, the hotel owners asked the federal court to exempt their claims from the reach of the full faith and credit statute, 28 U.S.C. § 1738. They asserted that, unless the court disregarded § 1738, they would be forced to litigate their takings claims in state court without any possibility of obtaining federal review. The district court held that the facial attack was barred by issue preclusion, as § 1738 requires federal courts to give preclusive effect to state court judgments. Because the California courts had construed the state takings law coextensively with federal law, the federal claims were essentially the same as those resolved in the state courts. Both the Ninth Circuit and the Supreme Court affirmed the decision.

The Supreme Court refused to craft an exception to the full faith and credit statute in order to provide a federal forum for litigants with federal takings claims. It explained that courts are not free to ignore § 1738 just to guarantee plaintiffs their day in federal court. Although some lower courts had held that parties who are forced to litigate state-law takings claims in state court cannot be precluded from having their claims resolved by a federal court, the Supreme Court rejected this line of cases, stating that plaintiffs have no right to vindicate their federal claims in a federal forum. *San Remo Hotel*, 125 S.Ct. at 2505, citing Allen v. McCurry, 449 U.S. 90, 103–104, 101 S.Ct. 411, 66 L.Ed.2d 308 (1980). Moreover, exceptions to § 1738 can only be allowed if a statute contains an express or implied partial repeal. The Court noted, "Congress has not expressed any intent to exempt from the full faith and credit statute federal takings claims. Consequently, we apply our normal assumption that the weighty interests in finality and comity trump the interest in giving losing litigants access to an additional appellate tribunal." *San Remo Hotel*, 125 S.Ct. at 2505. Finally, because petitioners were never required in state court to ripen their claim that the ordinance was facially invalid for failure to advance a legitimate state interest, they could have raised their facial takings challenge directly in federal court.

The implications of this case extend beyond takings claims. Although the *San Remo Hotel* case involved the Takings Clause, the opinion seemingly extends to virtually any of the property-protective clauses in the U.S. Constitution (*e.g.,* the Contracts Clause or Due Process Clause). In effect, claims against state and local governments involving the Constitution must be litigated in state court first, and after all state court proceedings are over, there may be no opportunity to relitigate those claims in federal court. Owners of natural resources wishing to challenge allegedly heavy-handed government treatment of those resources under constitutional theories must find their remedy in state court. The Court explained that the *San Remo Hotel* plaintiffs could have asserted their claim for compensation under state law together with an alternative claim that the denial of compensation would violate federal law. *Id*. at 2506–07. In sum, it appears that many litigants will have only one bite out of the apple, and that apple is in state court. The Court remarked, "State courts are fully competent to adjudicate constitutional challenges to local land-use decisions. Indeed, state courts undoubtedly have more experience than federal courts do in resolving the complex factual, technical, and legal questions related to zoning and land-use regulations." *Id*. at 2507.

With all of the pitfalls described above, why would any group or attorney dare to bring a citizens suit? Most statutory provisions provide an enticement by allowing prevailing parties to recover their attorney fees and costs. *See, e.g.,* ESA, 16 U.S.C. § 1540(g)(4); Clean Water Act, 33 U.S.C. § 1365(d). What must a party do to "prevail"? What if the parties ultimately settle the case, and the defendants agree to change their ways? Circuit courts had allowed plaintiffs to receive attorneys' fees for activities that served as a "catalyst" for compliance.

[But in] * * * Buckhannon Board & Care Home, Inc. v. West Virginia Department of Health & Human Resources. 532 U.S. 598 (2001), the Supreme Court held that, under ... a "prevailing party" standard, a party must "secure a judgment on the merits or a court-ordered consent decree.... " The Court defined "prevailing party" as requiring a " 'material alteration of the legal relationship of the parties,' " bearing a "judicial imprimatur." * * *

In Loggerhead Turtle v. County Council of Volusia County, the Eleventh Circuit ... "agree[d] that *Buckhannon* does not invalidate use of the catalyst test as a basis for awarding attorney's fees under the ESA.... " 307 F.3d 1318, 1325 (11th Cir. 2002). * * * [U]nlike the situation presented in *Buckhannon*, there was a very real problem that " 'mischievous' " or "simply rational" defendants could "cripple the citizen suit provision of the [ESA]" by changing their conduct, after protracted litigation, just to avoid liability for fees. The court concluded: "[W]e hold as a matter of law that the Supreme Court's decision in Buckhannon does not prohibit use of the catalyst test as a basis for awarding attorney's fees and costs under the 'whenever ... appropriate' fee-shifting provision of the Endangered Species Act."

Parenteau, *supra*, at 344, 346, 347–48.

Why did Congress think a provision for attorney fees and costs was necessary to encourage citizens' suits, when the general American rule is that each litigant bears his or her own freight? Was Congress correct?

Citizens' suits provisions and various facets of APA review will be applied to specific factual situations related to natural resources management in the upcoming chapters.

Chapter 4

ENVIRONMENTAL DECISIONMAKING: NEPA

I. SETTING THE STAGE: NEPA'S BACKGROUND AND CONTEXT

The National Environmental Policy Act (NEPA) is the granddaddy of an extended family of federal environmental statutes enacted around 1970, which together became the cornerstone of a new environmental era. Judge Skelly Wright provided this early description of NEPA and its statutory cohorts:

> Several recently enacted environmental statutes attest to the commitment of the Government to control, at long last, the destructive engine of material "progress." * * * NEPA, first of all, makes environmental protection a part of the mandate of every federal agency and department. * * * It takes the major step of requiring all federal agencies to consider values of environmental preservation in their spheres of activity, and it prescribes certain procedural measures to ensure that those values are in fact fully respected.

Calvert Cliffs' Coordinating Committee, Inc. v. U. S. Atomic Energy Commission, 449 F.2d 1109, 1111–12 (D.C.Cir. 1971).

NEPA sets forth remarkably ambitious statutory goals. Among other things, Congress declared "the continuing policy of the Federal Government ... to use all practicable means and measures ... in a manner calculated to foster and promote the general welfare, to create and maintain conditions under which man and nature can exist in productive harmony, and fulfill the social, economic, and other requirements of present and future generations of Americans." 42 U.S.C.A. § 4331(a). Congress also hinted at an enduring public trust responsibility for safeguarding the nation's natural resources:

> In order to carry out the policy set forth in this chapter, it is the continuing responsibility of the Federal Government to use all practicable means, consistent with other essential considerations of national policy, to improve and coordinate Federal plans, functions, programs, and resources to the end that the Nation may:
>
> > (1) fulfill the responsibilities of each generation as trustee of the environment for succeeding generations....

Id. § 4331(b).

NEPA aims primarily at federal agencies, but its policies reach well beyond the federal government. In a provision that comes as close to an environmental right as anything in federal law, Congress "recognize[d] that each person should enjoy a healthful environment...." *Id.* § 4331(c). So far, so good, but the same provision goes on to state that "each person has a *responsibility* to contribute to the preservation and enhancement of the environment." *Id.* (emphasis added). Imagine if this were taken to its logical extreme, or even taken very seriously. According to World-watch Institute, "[i]f we are going to reverse biodiversity loss, dampen the effects of global warming, and eliminate the scourge of persistent poverty, we need to reinvent ourselves—as individuals, as societies, as corporations, and as governments." State of the World 2003, http://www.worldwatch.org/pubs/sow/2003/ (visited Aug. 6, 2003). Does NEPA require each of us to give up our sport-utility vehicles and take mass transit, and to eradicate domestic waste by composting or recycling every scrap of leftover food and paper, along with cans, plastics and glass? Beyond that, what might be required of us in terms of environmental *enhancement*? Compliance would be tough, to be sure, and just imagine the challenges of enforcement.

Take a moment to read 42 U.S.C.A. § 4331 in its entirety. Policies, of course, do not in and of themselves create "hard" law. They do, however, provide guidance in the interpretation of the mandatory provisions found in the next section, Section 4332. That section requires an environmental impact statement (EIS) on "every recommendation or report on proposals for legislation ... and other major federal actions significantly affecting the quality of the human environment." 42 U.S.C.A. § 4332(2)(c). Rather than establishing enforceable standards to effectuate a substantive right to a healthy environment, NEPA has revolutionized the way governmental agencies do business by disseminating pertinent information about their activities in a very public fashion, thereby throwing open the doors of bureaucratic decisionmaking to citizen involvement and judicial review—no small feat.

Due largely to the EIS requirement, NEPA has taken on a dual personality over the years. It has been characterized as "the Magna Carta of U.S. environmental law," as well as the "most admired" environmental statute worldwide. *See* Ray Clark, NEPA: THE RATIONAL APPROACH TO CHANGE, IN ENVIRONMENTAL POLICY AND NEPA: PAST, PRESENT AND FUTURE 15 (Ray Clark & Larry Canter eds., 1997); William H. Rogers, Jr., *The Most Creative Moments in the History of Environmental Law: "The Whats"*, 2000 U. Ill. L. Rev. 1, 31. No one can deny that NEPA has opened governmental decisions "to an unprecedented level of public scrutiny, with consequent political implications that decisionmakers ignore only at their peril." Bradley C. Karkkainen, *Toward a Smarter NEPA: Monitoring and Managing Governments Environmental Performance,* 102 COLUM. L. REV. 903, 907 (2002).

At the same time, critics attack NEPA both for going too far and for not going far enough. Perhaps the most frequently heard complaint is that the EIS requirement is a "paper tiger" that forces cumbersome,-

time-consuming, and expensive procedures while providing only minimal environmental benefits. *See id.* More specifically,

> it places extreme demands on agency resources, often generates little useful information, and produces a work product too late in the decisionmaking cycle to influence the agency's course of action. Agency managers therefore have strong incentives to avoid the NEPA-mandated environmental impact statement whenever possible, which proves to be most of the time. All these observed effects are traceable to the statute's misguided insistence on comprehensiveness and clairvoyance, and they are compounded by the ready availability of judicial review to force the agency to go back and do more if it fails to produce a sufficiently comprehensive study the first time around.

Id. at 907.

Other critics take a different tack. They agree that NEPA's informational requirements are environmentally beneficial, but argue that Congress should have seized the opportunity provided by the pro-environmental sentiment that prevailed at the time of NEPA's enactment and imposed rigorous substantive environmental standards.

Despite its shortcomings, perceived or actual, NEPA has become the "most widely emulated of the major U.S. environmental laws" domestically and around the world. *Id.* at 905. Proposals to "water down" the statute have surfaced over the years, but none have been acted upon. NEPA has proven its durability, and several of the more recently enacted "second-generation" environmental laws have picked up on NEPA's information-disseminating theme as their *raison d'etre,* including the Environmental Planning and Community Right to Know Act of 1986, 42 U.S.C.A. §§ 11001, *et seq.,* which requires corporations to provide detailed information about their use and releases of toxic substances.

II. ADMINISTRATION AND ENFORCEMENT

A. Process–Forcing, Not Action–Forcing

The primary thrust of NEPA is the requirement that agencies prepare an environmental impact statement (EIS) to accompany "every recommendation or report on proposals ... and other major federal actions significantly affecting the quality of the human environment." 42 U.S.C.A. § 4332(2)(c). Do not let the seemingly straightforward nature of this statement mislead you. NEPA has become the favorite tool of opponents of government projects to delay, reshape, or even dismantle those projects. It is estimated that at least 40 percent of all environmental litigation brought against the federal government has involved NEPA. *See* Council on Environmental Quality, The 1997 Annual Report of the Council on Environmental Quality, Appendix—"NEPA Statistical Tables," at 355 Tbl.1 (1997), available at http://ceq.eh.doe.gov/nepa/reports/1997/appendix.pdf. As a result, the sheer volume of each EIS has increased dramatically, as agencies attempt to "bulletproof" their analyses by making them longer and more detailed. Although early cases considered a 250 page EIS "sizeable" and of "impressive" bulk, *see* Chelsea Neighborhood Associations v. U.S. Postal Service, 516 F.2d 378, 387 (2d Cir. 1975), today it is not uncommon to see multi-volume EISs hundreds and even thousands of pages long.

There is no guarantee that an increase in length produces a better assessment, but courts seem more comfortable with longer EISs. One court noted that, "[w]hile quantity does not connote quality," a two-page assessment of alternatives "raises a red flag that there has not been an examination to the 'fullest extent possible.'" Appalachian Mountain Club v. Brinegar 394 F.Supp. 105, 118 (D.N.H. 1975). In Seattle Audubon Soc. v. Lyons, 871 F.Supp. 1291 (W.D.Wash. 1994), *aff'd*, 80 F.3d 1401 (9th Cir. 1996), the court took pains to describe the "voluminous administrative record" for the Northwest Forest Plan, explicitly noting both the number of pages of analysis on specific ecological issues and the total length of the decisional documents and appendices, which, by the way, weighed in at over 4,000 pages. *Id.* at 1308, 1322–24. Agency officials have begun to describe this phenomenon as leading to "analysis paralysis"—inaction or lengthy delays. *See* Statement of Forest Service Chief Dale Bosworth to the House Subcommittee on Forests and Forest Health, June 12, 2002, at http://www.usda.gov/agency/ocr/download/FS–Bosworth–6.12.02.pdf. The charges are not unwarranted. In Hughes River Watershed Conservancy v. Johnson, 165 F.3d 283 (4th Cir. 1999), for example, the court described the NEPA process for a dam construction project that generated multiple EISs and judicial opinions over the course of a 24 year-long decisionmaking process.

The regulations envision a more streamlined analysis, as shown in the box below.

---

40 C.F.R. § 1502.2 Implementation.

* * *

(a) Environmental impact statements shall be analytic rather than encyclopedic.

(b) Impacts shall be discussed in proportion to their significance. There shall be only brief discussion of other than significant issues. * * *

(c) Environmental impact statements shall be kept concise and shall be no longer than absolutely necessary to comply with NEPA and with these regulations. Length should vary first with potential environmental problems and then with project size. * * * *

40 C.F.R. § 1502.7 Page limits.

The text of final environmental impact statements ... shall normally be less than 150 pages and for proposals of unusual scope or complexity shall normally be less than 300 pages.

40 C.F.R. § 1502.8 Writing.

Environmental impact statements shall be written in plain language and may use appropriate graphics so that decisionmakers and the public can readily understand them.

NEPA requires agencies to "look before they leap" by taking a "hard look" at the environmental effects and alternatives to their proposals. This can be an onerous duty, but it is limited one in that it is wholly procedural. The Supreme Court has made it abundantly clear that NEPA mandates certain procedures, but does not force any particular substantive outcome. In other words, the statute does not compel an agency to adopt the most environmentally friendly plan of action, as the following case illustrates.

ROBERTSON v. METHOW VALLEY CITIZENS COUNCIL
Supreme Court of the United States, 1989.
490 U.S. 332, 109 S.Ct. 1835, 104 L.Ed.2d 351.

JUSTICE STEVENS delivered the opinion of the Court.

* * * This case arises out of the Forest Service's decision to issue a special use permit authorizing the development of a major destination Alpine ski resort at Sandy Butte in the North Cascade Mountains. Sandy Butte is a 6,000–foot mountain located in the Okanogan National Forest in Okanogan County, Washington. At present Sandy Butte, like the Methow Valley it overlooks, is an unspoiled, sparsely populated area that the District Court characterized as "pristine." * * *

In response to [Methow Recreation, Inc.'s] MRI's application [for a special use permit authorizing the development of a ski resort], the Forest Service, in cooperation with state and county officials, prepared an EIS known as the Early Winters Alpine Winter Sports Study (Early Winters Study or Study). * * * The Early Winters Study is a printed document containing almost 150 pages of text and 12 appendices. It evaluated five alternative levels of development of Sandy Butte that might be authorized, the lowest being a "no action" alternative and the highest being development of a 16–lift ski area able to accommodate 10,500 skiers at one time. The Study considered the effect of each level of development on water resources, soil, wildlife, air quality, vegetation, and visual quality, as well as land use and transportation in the Methow Valley, probable demographic shifts, the economic market for skiing and other summer and winter recreational activities in the Valley, and the energy requirements for the ski area and related developments. The Study's discussion of possible impacts was not limited to on-site effects, but also, as required by Council on Environmental Quality (CEQ) regulations, see 40 CFR § 1502.16(b) (1987), addressed "off-site impacts that each alternative might have on community facilities, socio-economic and other environmental conditions in the Upper Methow Valley." Early Winters Study 1. As to off-site effects, the Study explained that "due to the uncertainty of where other public and private lands may become developed," it is difficult to evaluate off-site impacts, id., at 76, and thus the document's analysis is necessarily "not site-specific," id., at 1. Finally, the Study outlined certain steps that might be taken to mitigate adverse effects, both on Sandy Butte and in the neighboring Methow Valley, but indicated that these proposed steps are merely conceptual and "will be made more specific as part of the design and implementation stages of the planning process." *Id.* at 14.

The effects of the proposed development on air quality and wildlife received particular attention in the Study. In the chapter on "Environmental Consequences," the first subject discussed is air quality. As is true of other subjects, the discussion included an analysis of cumulative impacts over several years resulting from actions on other lands as well as from the development of Sandy Butte itself. The Study concluded that although the construction, maintenance, and operation of the proposed ski area "will not have a measurable effect on existing or future air quality," the off-site development of private land under all five alternatives—including the "no action" alternative—"will have a significant effect on air quality during severe meteorological inversion periods." * * *

In its discussion of adverse effects on area wildlife, the EIS concluded that no endangered or threatened species would be affected by the proposed development and that the only impact on sensitive species was the probable loss of a pair of spotted owls and their progeny. *Id.*, at 75.[a] With regard to other wildlife, the Study considered the impact on 75 different indigenous species and predicted that within a decade after development vegetational change and increased human activity would lead to a decrease in population for 31 species, while causing an increase in population for another 24 species on Sandy Butte. Two species, the pine marten and nesting goshawk, would be eliminated altogether from the area of development.

In a comment in response to the draft EIS, the Washington Department of Game voiced a special concern about potential losses to the State's largest migratory deer herd, which uses the Methow Valley as a critical winter range and as its migration route.... The state agency ... explained that hunters had "harvested" 3,247 deer in the Methow Valley area [and] ... contributed over $6 million to the State's economy in 1981. Because the deer harvest is apparently proportional to the size of the herd, the state agency predicted that "Washington business can expect to lose over $3 million annually from reduced recreational opportunity." The Forest Service's own analysis of the impact on the deer herd was more modest. It first concluded that the actual operation of the ski hill would have only a "minor" direct impact on the herd, but then recognized that the off-site effect of the development "would noticeably reduce numbers of deer in the Methow [Valley] with any alternative." *Id.*, at 76. Although its estimate indicated a possible 15 percent decrease in the size of the herd, it summarized the State's contrary view in the text of the EIS, and stressed that off-site effects are difficult to estimate due to uncertainty concerning private development. * * *

a. The so-called "spotted owl wars," during which logging in the national forests in the Pacific Northwest was substantially curtailed by litigation over the northern spotted owl, were just getting started when this EIS was prepared. *See supra,* Chapter 6, Public Lands. The spotted owl was not listed under the Endangered Species Act until 1990.

As was true of its discussion of air quality, the EIS also described both on-site and off-site mitigation measures. Among possible on-site mitigation possibilities, the Study recommended locating runs, ski lifts, and roads so as to minimize interference with wildlife, restricting access to selected roads during fawning season, and further examination of the effect of the development on mule deer migration routes. Off-site options discussed in the Study included the use of zoning and tax incentives to limit development on deer winter range and migration routes, encouragement of conservation easements, and acquisition and management by local government of critical tracts of land. * * * As with the measures suggested for mitigating the off-site effects on air quality, the proposed options were primarily directed to steps that might be taken by state and local government. * * *

Ultimately, the Early Winters Study recommended the issuance of a permit for development at the second highest level considered—a 16–lift ski area able to accommodate 8,200 skiers at one time. On July 5, 1984, the Regional Forester decided to issue a special use permit as recommended by the Study.[10] In his decision, the Regional Forester found that no major adverse effects would result directly from the federal action, but that secondary effects could include a degradation of existing air quality and a reduction of mule deer winter range. *Id.*, at 67a. He therefore directed the supervisor of the Okanogan National Forest, both independently and in cooperation with local officials, to identify and implement certain mitigating measures.

Four organizations ... appealed the Regional Forester's decision to the Chief of the Forest Service. After a hearing, he affirmed the Regional Forester's decision. Stressing that the decision, which simply approved the general concept of issuing a 30–year special use permit for development of Sandy Butte, did not authorize construction of a particular ski area and, in fact, did not even act on MRI's specific permit application, he concluded that the EIS' discussion of mitigation was "adequate for this stage in the review process." * * *

Thereafter, respondents brought this action under the Administrative Procedure Act, 5 U. S. C. §§ 701–706, to obtain judicial review of the Forest Service's decision. Their principal claim was that the Early Winters Study did not satisfy the requirements of NEPA, 42 U. S. C. § 4332. * * *

Section 101 of NEPA declares a broad national commitment to protecting and promoting environmental quality. 83 Stat. 852, 42 U. S. C. § 4331. To ensure that this commitment is "infused into the ongoing programs and actions of the Federal Government, the act also estab-

---

10. His decision did not identify a particular developer, but rather simply authorized the taking of competitive bids. It was not until July 21, 1986, almost one month after the District Court affirmed the Forester's decision, that a special use permit was issued to MRI.

lishes some important 'action-forcing' procedures." 115 Cong. Rec. 40416 (remarks of Sen. Jackson). Section 102 thus, among other measures,

> directs that, to the fullest extent possible … all agencies of the Federal Government shall: (C) include in every recommendation or report on proposals for legislation and other major Federal actions significantly affecting the quality of the human environment, a detailed statement by the responsible official on:
>
> (i) the environmental impact of the proposed action,
>
> (ii) any adverse environmental effects which cannot be avoided should the proposal be implemented,
>
> (iii) alternatives to the proposed action,
>
> (iv) the relationship between local short-term uses of man's environment and the maintenance and enhancement of long-term productivity, and
>
> (v) any irreversible and irretrievable commitments of resources which would be involved in the proposed action should it be implemented.

83 Stat. 853, 42 U.S.C. § 4332.

The statutory requirement that a federal agency contemplating a major action prepare such an environmental impact statement serves NEPA's "action-forcing" purpose in two important respects. It ensures that the agency, in reaching its decision, will have available, and will carefully consider, detailed information concerning significant environmental impacts; it also guarantees that the relevant information will be made available to the larger audience that may also play a role in both the decisionmaking process and the implementation of that decision.

Simply by focusing the agency's attention on the environmental consequences of a proposed project, NEPA ensures that important effects will not be overlooked or underestimated only to be discovered after resources have been committed or the die otherwise cast. * * *

Publication of an EIS, both in draft and final form, also serves a larger informational role. It gives the public the assurance that the agency "has indeed considered environmental concerns in its decision-making process," and, perhaps more significantly, provides a springboard for public comment. Thus, in this case the final draft of the Early Winters Study reflects not only the work of the Forest Service itself, but also the critical views of the Washington State Department of Game, the Methow Valley Citizens Council, and Friends of the Earth, as well as many others, to whom copies of the draft Study were circulated.[13] More-

---

13. The CEQ regulations require that, after preparing a draft EIS, the agency request comments from other federal agencies, appropriate state and local agencies, affected Indian tribes, any relevant applicant, the public generally, and, in particular, interested or affected persons or organizations. 40 CFR § 1503.1 (1987). In preparing the final EIS, the agency must "discuss at appropriate points … any responsible opposing view which was not adequately discussed in the draft statement and [must] indicate the agency's response to the issue raised." § 1502.9. See also § 1503.4.

over, with respect to a development such as Sandy Butte, where the adverse effects on air quality and the mule deer herd are primarily attributable to predicted off-site development that will be subject to regulation by other governmental bodies, the EIS serves the function of offering those bodies adequate notice of the expected consequences and the opportunity to plan and implement corrective measures in a timely manner.

The sweeping policy goals announced in § 101 of NEPA are thus realized through a set of "action-forcing" procedures that require that agencies take a " 'hard look' at environmental consequences," ... and that provide for broad dissemination of relevant environmental information. Although these procedures are almost certain to affect the agency's substantive decision, it is now well settled that NEPA itself does not mandate particular results, but simply prescribes the necessary process. * * * If the adverse environmental effects of the proposed action are adequately identified and evaluated, the agency is not constrained by NEPA from deciding that other values outweigh the environmental costs. In this case, for example, it would not have violated NEPA if the Forest Service, after complying with the Act's procedural prerequisites, had decided that the benefits to be derived from downhill skiing at Sandy Butte justified the issuance of a special use permit, notwithstanding the loss of 15 percent, 50 percent, or even 100 percent of the mule deer herd. Other statutes may impose substantive environmental obligations on federal agencies, but NEPA merely prohibits uninformed— rather than unwise—agency action.

To be sure, one important ingredient of an EIS is the discussion of steps that can be taken to mitigate adverse environmental consequences.[15] The requirement that an EIS contain a detailed discussion of possible mitigation measures flows both from the language of the Act and, more expressly, from CEQ's implementing regulations. Implicit in NEPA's demand that an agency prepare a detailed statement on "any adverse environmental effects which cannot be avoided should the proposal be implemented," 42 U. S. C § 4332(C)(ii), is an understanding that the EIS will discuss the extent to which adverse effects can be avoided. More generally, omission of a reasonably complete discussion of possible mitigation measures would undermine the "action forcing" function of NEPA. Without such a discussion, neither the agency nor other interested groups and individuals can properly evaluate the severity of

---

15. CEQ regulations define "mitigation" to include:

(a) Avoiding the impact altogether by not taking a certain action or parts of an action.

(b) Minimizing impacts by limiting the degree or magnitude of the action and its implementation.

(c) Rectifying the impact by repairing, rehabilitating, or restoring the affected environment.

(d) Reducing or eliminating the impact over time by preservation and maintenance operations during the life of the action.

(e) Compensating for the impact by replacing or providing substitute resources or environments.

40 C.F.R. § 1508.20 (1987).

the adverse effects. An adverse effect that can be fully remedied by, for example, an inconsequential public expenditure is certainly not as serious as a similar effect that can only be modestly ameliorated through the commitment of vast public and private resources. Recognizing the importance of such a discussion in guaranteeing that the agency has taken a "hard look" at the environmental consequences of proposed federal action, CEQ regulations require that the agency discuss possible mitigation measures in defining the scope of the EIS, 40 CFR § 1508.25(b) (1987), in discussing alternatives to the proposed action, § 1502.14(f), and consequences of that action, § 1502.16(h), and in explaining its ultimate decision, § 1505.2(c).

There is a fundamental distinction, however, between a requirement that mitigation be discussed in sufficient detail to ensure that environmental consequences have been fairly evaluated, on the one hand, and a substantive requirement that a complete mitigation plan be actually formulated and adopted, on the other. In this case, the off-site effects on air quality and on the mule deer herd cannot be mitigated unless nonfederal government agencies take appropriate action. Since it is those state and local governmental bodies that have jurisdiction over the area in which the adverse effects need be addressed and since they have the authority to mitigate them, it would be incongruous to conclude that the Forest Service has no power to act until the local agencies have reached a final conclusion on what mitigating measures they consider necessary. Even more significantly, it would be inconsistent with NEPA's reliance on procedural mechanisms—as opposed to substantive, result-based standards—to demand the presence of a fully developed plan that will mitigate environmental harm before an agency can act. * * *

We thus conclude that the Court of Appeals erred, first, in assuming that "NEPA requires that 'action be taken to mitigate the adverse effects of major federal actions,'" and, second, in finding that this substantive requirement entails the further duty to include in every EIS "a detailed explanation of specific measures which *will* be employed to mitigate the adverse impacts of a proposed action."

The Court of Appeals also concluded that the Forest Service had an obligation to make a "worst case analysis" if it could not make a reasoned assessment of the impact of the Early Winters project on the mule deer herd. * * * In 1986, ... CEQ replaced the "worst case" requirement with a requirement that federal agencies, in the face of unavailable information concerning a reasonably foreseeable significant environmental consequence, prepare "a summary of existing credible scientific evidence which is relevant to evaluating the ... adverse impacts" and prepare an "evaluation of such impacts based upon theoretical approaches or research methods generally accepted in the scientific community." 40 CFR § 1502.22(b) (1987). The amended regulation thus "retains the duty to describe the consequences of a remote, but potentially severe impact, but grounds the duty in evaluation of scientific opinion rather than in the framework of a conjectural 'worst case analysis.' " 50 Fed. Reg. 32237 (1985). * * *

Nor are we convinced that the new CEQ regulation is not controlling simply because it was preceded by a rule that was in some respects more demanding. In *Andrus* v. *Sierra Club*, 442 U.S., at 358, we held that CEQ regulations are entitled to substantial deference. * * * [T]he amendment was designed to better serve the twin functions of an EIS— requiring agencies to take a "hard look" at the consequences of the proposed action and providing important information to other groups and individuals. CEQ explained that by requiring that an EIS focus on reasonably foreseeable impacts, the new regulation "will generate information and discussion on those consequences of greatest concern to the public and of greatest relevance to the agency's decision," 50 Fed. Reg. 32237 (1985), rather than distorting the decisionmaking process by overemphasizing highly speculative harms, 51 Fed. Reg. 15624–15625 (1986); 50 Fed. Reg. 32236 (1985). In light of this well-considered basis for the change, the new regulation is entitled to substantial deference. * * *

In sum, we conclude that NEPA does not require a fully developed plan detailing what steps *will* be taken to mitigate adverse environmental impacts and does not require a "worst case analysis." * * * The judgment of the Court of Appeals is accordingly reversed, and the case is remanded for further proceedings consistent with this opinion. * * *

Methow Valley near Twisp, Washington, from the Methow Valley Citizens' Council, http://www.okanogan1.com/mvcc/index.html (visited Oct. 5, 2004) (photo by George Wooten) (reprinted with permission).

Notes and Questions

1.   "Data gaps" are addressed in 40 C.F.R. § 1502.22, provided below. Does this regulation allow the Forest Service to throw up its collective hands and refuse to collect and assess information, like the development plans of local governments, simply because the information is in the control of another entity? Or because the costs of obtaining it from an outside source

happens to be "exorbitant"? Would you want the government to obtain the information if it could force the developer or project proponent to foot the bill?

---

40 C.F.R. § 1502.22 Incomplete or unavailable information.

When an agency is evaluating reasonably foreseeable significant adverse effects on the human environment in an environmental impact statement and there is incomplete or unavailable information, the agency shall always make clear that such information is lacking.

(a) If the incomplete information relevant to reasonably foreseeable significant adverse impacts is essential to a reasoned choice among alternatives and the overall costs of obtaining it are not exorbitant, the agency shall include the information in the environmental impact statement.

(b) If the information relevant to reasonably foreseeable significant adverse impacts cannot be obtained because the overall costs of obtaining it are exorbitant or the means to obtain it are not known, the agency shall include within the environmental impact statement:

(1) A statement that such information is incomplete or unavailable;

(2) a statement of the relevance of the incomplete or unavailable information to evaluating reasonably foreseeable significant adverse impacts on the human environment;

(3) a summary of existing credible scientific evidence which is relevant to evaluating the reasonably foreseeable significant adverse impacts on the human environment, and

(4) the agency's evaluation of such impacts based upon theoretical approaches or research methods generally accepted in the scientific community. For the purposes of this section, "reasonably foreseeable" includes impacts which have catastrophic consequences, even if their probability of occurrence is low, provided that the analysis of the impacts is supported by credible scientific evidence, is not based on pure conjecture, and is within the rule of reason. * * *

---

2. Does the Nuclear Regulatory Commission have to analyze the likelihood and potential effects of a catastrophic nuclear accident, like the one that occurred at Chernobyl in the former Soviet Union in 1986, when considering a proposal to license a nuclear power plant? *See* 40 C.F.R. § 1502.22(b)(4); Metropolitan Edison Co. v. People Against Nuclear Energy, 460 U.S. 766, 772–73, 103 S.Ct. 1556, 75 L.Ed.2d 534 (1983). As a general rule, speculative impacts need not be discussed in an EIS. Carolina Envtl. Study Group v. United States, 510 F.2d 796 (D.C. Cir. 1975). *See* Edwardsen v. U.S. Dept. of Interior, 268 F.3d 781, 785 (9th Cir. 2001) (an EIS need not include a site-specific oil spill trajectory analysis for an off-shore oil development project but could rely on modeling prepared for a lease in an adjacent area). Why shouldn't an agency be compelled to prepare a "worst case analysis" for an event, even a highly unlikely one, that could have immense ramifications? Wouldn't it be useful to know what the worst, or most environmentally degrading, outcome of a proposal might be? Is a "worst case analysis"

necessary in order to prepare an adequate risk assessment that fully informs the decisionmaker and the public?

3.   Section 404 of the Clean Water Act, 33 U.S.C.A. § 1344, enacted in its present form only a few years after NEPA, requires mitigation when wetlands are destroyed. Why doesn't NEPA require agencies to adopt mitigation plans when their projects will have adverse effects that could be avoided or mitigated, particularly if mitigation would be feasible and cost-effective? In *Methow Valley Citizens Council,* the Supreme Court concluded that NEPA doesn't require a mitigation plan, yet it does require a discussion of possible mitigation options. What good does it do to require a discussion of mitigation options if there's no compulsion to adopt them? *See Methow Valley Citizens Council*, 490 U.S. at 352; Neighbors of Cuddy Mountain v. U.S. Forest Service, 137 F.3d 1372, 1380 (9th Cir. 1998) (finding that a "perfunctory description" of mitigating measures for a timber sale was inadequate).

4.   Following the *Methow Valley Citizens Council* decision, plans to build the ski resort were put on ice, and the "Early Winters" land was eventually sold to R.D. Merrill Co., a Seattle-based timber and real estate company. In 1996, Merrill completed the construction of a luxury lodge, known as the Freestone Inn, located in the shadow of Sandy Butte. In addition, Merrill planned to build a 560–home residential development and golf course, to be named "Arrowleaf," in the Methow Valley near the town of Mazama. Not unexpectedly, these plans gave rise to renewed opposition from the Methow Valley Citizens Council. In 1998, the Valley earned the No. 2 ranking among the state's top 10 "Most Endangered Places," a list compiled by 1,000 Friends of Washington. The Washington Department of Ecology ultimately denied Merrill's application for a water right for the proposed resort, and, in 1999, Merrill withdrew its plans. *See* Chris Solomon, *No Peace in the Valley: Future Uncertain as Resort Plans Unfold*, Seattle Times, Dec. 14, 1999, at A1. For information on Methow Valley and a history of the Lodge's development, *see* Freestone Inn: Our Story, http://www.freestoneinn.com/history.html. For the environmental group's position regarding the project, *see* MVCC Project Updates, http://www.okanogan1.com/mvcc/projects/ arroleaf/resortsummary.htm.

B.   The Council on Environmental Quality and the Environmental Protection Agency

NEPA created the CEQ to advise the President on national environmental policies. 42 U.S.C.A. § 4342. In 1977, President Carter directed the CEQ to promulgate binding regulations to assist the agencies in implementing the provisions of NEPA. Exec. Order No. 11991, 3 C.F.R. 123. The CEQ's regulations, found at 40 C.F.R. §§ 1500–1508, are entitled to "substantial deference." *See* Andrus v. Sierra Club, 442 U.S. 347, 99 S.Ct. 2335, 60 L.Ed.2d 943 (1979).

All Environmental Impact Statements (EISs) prepared by federal agencies are filed with the U.S. Environmental Protection Agency (EPA) pursuant to Section 309 of the Clean Air Act, 42 U.S.C.A. § 7609. If the EPA determines that the action is "unsatisfactory from the standpoint of public health or welfare or environmental quality," it must publish its findings and refer the matter to the CEQ. *Id.* The EPA publishes a Notice of Availability in the Federal Register each week for all of the EISs filed the previous week. This Notice is the official start of the public comment period required by CEQ regulations.

CEQ & EPA Websites

The CEQ's website can be accessed at http://www.whitehouse.gov/ceq/. It provides a link to a site devoted to NEPA, called "NEPA-Net," which serves as a gateway to a variety of national and international resources: http://ceq.eh.doe.gov/nepa/nepanet.htm.

The CEQ's responses to *NEPA's Forty Most Asked Questions, at* http://ceq.eh.doe.gov/nepa/regs/40/40p3.htm, also provide a good resource for anyone who wishes to learn about the NEPA process.

The EPA provides links to Notices of Availability of EISs at http://www.epa.gov/compliance/nepa/current/index.html.

The full-text of Federal Register documents that deal with all aspects of EISs prepared by all federal agencies is maintained on the EPA's Federal Register–Environmental Impact Statements website, http://www.epa.gov/fedrgstr/EPA–IMPACT/.

C. Judicial Review

1. Authority to Review NEPA Cases and Standard of Review

Although the statute does not explicitly provide for judicial review through a citizens' suit provision or otherwise, the federal courts have not hesitated to review agency decisions for NEPA compliance, on grounds that the statute implicitly allows judicial review. *See* Daniel R. Mandelker, NEPA Law and Litigation § 3.01 (2d ed. 1992). In Calvert Cliffs' Coordinating Committee, Inc. v. U. S. Atomic Energy Commission, 449 F.2d 1109 (D.C.Cir. 1971), the D.C. Circuit explained that the courts have the power to require agencies to comply with NEPA.

> Petitioners argue that rules recently adopted by the Atomic Energy Commission to govern consideration of environmental matters fail to satisfy the rigor demanded by NEPA. The Commission, on the other hand, contends that the vagueness of the NEPA mandate and delegation leaves much room for discretion and that the rules challenged by petitioners fall well within the broad scope of the Act. We find the policies embodied in NEPA to be a good deal clearer and more demanding than does the Commission. We conclude that the Commission's procedural rules [precluding consideration of non-radiological environmental issues and other matters] do not comply with the congressional policy. Hence we remand these cases for further rule making.

Id. at 1111–12.

Courts review both the adequacy of an EIS and an agency's decision to forego the preparation of an EIS using the familiar arbitrary and capricious standard of review, discussed in detail in Chapter 3, *supra*. *See* Marsh v. Oregon Natural Resources Council, 490 U.S. 360, 109 S.Ct. 1851, 104 L.Ed.2d 377 (1989); Robertson v. Methow Valley Citizens Council, 490 U.S. 332, 109 S.Ct. 1835, 104 L.Ed.2d 351 (1989). Under this standard, a court will defer to a fully informed and well-considered agency decision, but it will not forgive an agency's clear error of judgment. *See* Metcalf v. Daley, 214 F.3d 1135 (9th Cir. 2000).

In cases where an agency issues an environmental assessment (EA) rather than a full EIS, *see* Section III.E, *infra*; its decision will be upheld if it identifies and takes a "hard look" at all relevant environmental factors and issues a convincing statement of reasons why the environmental impacts will not be significant. Hill v. Boy, 144 F.3d 1446 (11th Cir. 1998); Utah Shared Access Alliance v. U.S. Forest Service, 288 F.3d 1205 (10th Cir. 2002). An EIS will be upheld if it sets forth sufficient information to enable the decision maker to take a "hard look" at the effects, consider the relevant environmental factors and make a reasoned choice between alternatives. *See* Robertson v. Methow Valley Citizens Council, 490 U.S. 332, 109 S.Ct. 1835, 104 L.Ed.2d 351 (1989); Friends of Boundary Waters Wilderness v. Dombeck, 164 F.3d 1115 (8th Cir. 1999); Hughes River Watershed Conservancy v. Johnson, 165 F.3d 283 (4th Cir. 1999); Northwest Resource Info. Ctr., Inc. v. National Marine Fisheries Service, 56 F.3d 1060 (9th Cir. 1995). An agency takes the requisite "hard look" when it obtains opinions from its own experts and from experts outside the agency, gives careful scrutiny to those opinions, and responds to all legitimate concerns that are raised. *See Hughes River Watershed Conservancy,* 165 F.3d at 288. In the event that a "battle of the experts" arises, agencies are entitled to rely on the view of their own experts. *Id.; Oregon Natural Resources Council,* 490 U.S. at 378–85.

2. *Standing and NEPA's Zone of Interests*

In addition to the constitutional requirements for standing, plaintiffs challenging a statutory provision under the Administrative Procedure Act (APA), 5 U.S.C.A. §§ 551 *et seq.,* must satisfy prudential concerns by showing that their injury falls within the "zone of interests" that the statute was designed to protect. See Chapter 3.II.B, *supra.* The following case discusses NEPA's zone of interests in the context of a county's challenge to a decision to designate critical habitat for the northern spotted owl, which had been listed as threatened under the Endangered Species Act.

DOUGLAS COUNTY v. BABBITT
United States Court of Appeals, Ninth Circuit, 1995.
48 F.3d 1495,
cert. denied, 516 U.S. 1042, 116 S.Ct. 698, 133 L.Ed.2d 655 (1996).

* * * [W]e recently stated that:

NEPA was enacted in order "to promote efforts which will prevent or eliminate damage to the environment and biosphere and stimulate the health and welfare of man." 42 U.S.C.A. § 4321 (1988). The purpose of NEPA is to protect the environment, not ... economic interests.... Therefore, a plaintiff who asserts purely economic injuries does not have standing to challenge an agency action under NEPA.

Nevada Land Action Ass'n v. U.S. Forest Service, 8 F.3d 713, 716 (9th Cir. 1993) (citations omitted).

To find that the County's interests do not fall inside the "zone of interests" protected by NEPA, we would have to find that (1) the County's interests are inconsistent with the purposes of NEPA, and that (2) the interests are so inconsistent that it would be unreasonable to assume that Congress intended to permit the suit. * * *

Douglas County asserts that it has standing based on several types of injuries: procedural injury, injury to its proprietary interests, injury to the quality of life of its citizens, injury to wildlife within the county, and injury to its resource management interests. We conclude that the narrow circumstances of this case are sufficient to support procedural standing for Douglas County. This being the case, there is no need for us to address the other alleged bases for standing. * * *

The County has been "accorded a procedural right" because NEPA provides that "local agencies, which are authorized to develop and enforce environmental standards" may comment on the proposed federal action. 42 U.S.C.A. § 4332 (2)(C). The County is such a local agency because an Oregon Statute authorizes counties to "prepare, adopt, amend, and revise" land management plans that contain environmental standards. Or. Rev. Stat. § 197.175 (1993).

The County must also show a "concrete interest" that underlies its procedural interest. That interest must be within the zone of interests NEPA was designed to protect. The County's proprietary interest in its lands adjacent to the critical habitat represents this necessary "concrete interest". The affidavit of Kenneth Hendrick, director of the Land Department for Douglas County, expresses concerns with the proposed critical habitat designation. Hendrick alleges that the land management practices on federal land could affect adjacent county-owned land: "By failing to properly manage for insect and disease control and fire, the federal land management practices threaten the productivity and environment of the adjoining [county] lands." E.R. at 33–34.

These statements describe concrete, plausible interests, within NEPA's zone of concern for the environment, which underlie the County's asserted procedural interests. It is logical for the County to assert that its lands could be threatened by how the adjoining federal lands are managed. It is uncertain whether the findings of an EIS would affect the Secretary's critical habitat designation and when the adjacent county lands would actually be harmed. But under *Lujan*, those concerns are not important: "The person who has been accorded a procedural right to protect his concrete interests can assert the right without meeting all the normal standards for redressibility and immediacy." Lujan [v. Defenders of Wildlife], 112 S. Ct. [2130] at 2142 n.7 [(1992)].

In short, the County meets all of *Lujan*'s strict procedural standing requirements. The County has a procedural right, as well as a concrete interest that could be harmed by the critical habitat designation, and that interest is within the zone of interests protected by NEPA.

Notes and Questions

1.   The merits of the claims raised in *Douglas County* are addressed in the case excerpt included *infra,* Section VI.C.

2.   In Nevada Land Action Ass'n v. U.S. Forest Service, 8 F.3d 713 (9th Cir. 1993), ranchers who held permits to graze livestock on national forest lands challenged the land and resource management plan (LRMP) for the Toiyabe National Forest as violating NEPA and the National Forest Management Act. The court found that the ranchers lacked standing under NEPA:

> NLAA [Nevada Land Action Association] admits that the primary injury suffered by its members is economic, but contends that the LRMP also affects the "human environment" of the NLAA members and has therefore caused "lifestyle loss" as well as economic loss.... NLAA cannot invoke NEPA to prevent "lifestyle loss" when the lifestyle in question is damaging to the environment. Since NLAA's suit is "more likely to frustrate than to further" the objectives of NEPA, ... NLAA lacks standing to challenge the LRMP under NEPA.

Id. at 716 (citations omitted). Similarly, in Rosebud Sioux Tribe v. McDivitt, 286 F.3d 1031 (8th Cir. 2002), cert. denied, 537 U.S. 1188 (2003), a lessee who had planned to operate a pork production facility on tribal land challenged a decision by the Bureau of Indian Affairs to void its lease. The Eighth Circuit dismissed the lessee's NEPA claim for lack of prudential standing, explaining:

> Parties motivated in part by protection of their own economic interests may also challenge agency action as long as their environmental interests are not so insignificant that they should be disregarded altogether. But parties motivated solely by "their own economic self-interest and welfare, are singularly inappropriate parties to be entrusted with the responsibility of asserting the public's environmental interest.... "

Id. at 1038 (internal citations omitted). Douglas County's interest in maintaining its flood control efforts and protecting its proprietary interests seemed predominantly, if not purely, economic in nature. Why, then, did the court find that the county was within NEPA's zone of interests? Are *Nevada Land Action* and *Rosebud Sioux Tribe* distinguishable?

3.   Oil companies were allowed to challenge the Federal Trade Commission's failure to prepare an EIS for its enforcement actions in Mobil Oil Corporation v. Federal Trade Commission, 430 F.Supp. 855 (S.D.N.Y.), *rev'd on other grounds,* 562 F.2d 170 (2nd Cir.1977). The companies, which had been charged by the Commission with violation of antitrust laws, were plainly motivated by economic concerns, but they also alleged that the Commission's requested relief, *i. e.,* divestiture of pipelines and refinery capacity, would

result in depletion of the nation's natural resources. The court concluded that their "financial concerns ... do not at all hinder their standing to raise NEPA issues because they 'have alleged an injury in fact, namely, damage to the environment in which they work and upon which they depend for their livelihood and continued maintenance of the quality of their lives.' " *Id.* at 862 (citation omitted). Is this case analogous to *Douglas County*? Is it distinguishable from *Nevada Land Action* and *Rosebud Sioux Tribe*?

4.   Does NEPA's zone of interests extend to human health concerns? In Hall v. Norton, 266 F.3d 969 (9th Cir. 2001), a local resident argued that the BLM had failed to adequately consider the increase in pollution that could result from its transfer of public lands in Las Vegas Valley to a residential developer. The plaintiff alleged that his respiratory problems would be aggravated by the development that would eventually occur on the transferred lands. The Ninth Circuit found that evidence of a credible threat to the plaintiff's health from airborne pollutants falls "well within" the range of injuries protected by NEPA. It also concluded that his claim would not be defeated simply because the threat of harm from the planned construction lay too far in the future. *Id.* at 976.

5.   How does NEPA's zone of interests differ from the Endangered Species Act's zone of interests, addressed in Bennett v. Spear, Chapter 3.II.B, *supra*, 520 U.S. 154, 117 S.Ct. 1154, 137 L.Ed.2d 281 (1997)? In *Bennett*, the Supreme Court held that ranchers and irrigation districts could proceed with an action under that statute's citizen-suit provision, even though their primary concerns, which stemmed from lost use of reservoir water to protect listed fish species, were economic in nature. *Id.* at 176–177. Is *Bennett* controlling precedent in the NEPA context?

III.   THRESHOLD REQUIREMENTS

This section assesses the threshold requirements of NEPA, all of which must be present before an EIS will be required: (1) an agency; (2) a proposal; (3) major federal action; (4) significantly affecting the human environment. The flow chart below, Figure 1, will help the uninitiated work their way through the process.

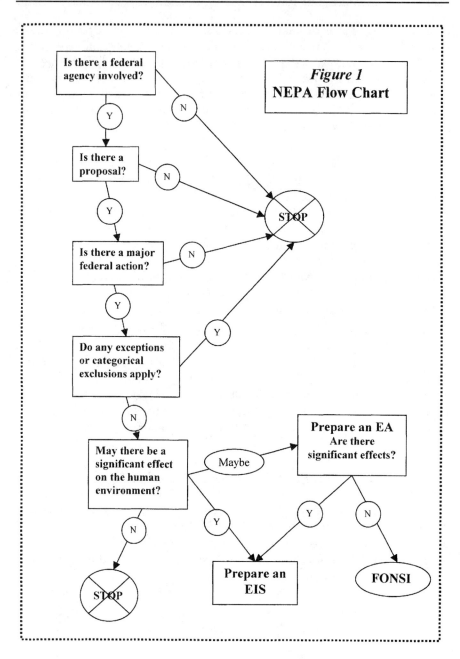

Figure 1
NEPA Flow Chart

A. Is There an Agency?

NEPA imposes responsibilities on "all agencies of the Federal Government." 42 U.S.C.A. § 4332(C). Does it apply to the President, as chief of the executive branch and all its agencies? President Clinton designated dozens of new national monuments during his administration, including the Grand Staircase–Escalante National Monument in Utah (1.9 million acres), Kasha–Katuwe Tent Rocks, New Mexico (4,000 acres), and Buck Island Reef, The Virgin Islands (18,000 acres). As a result, millions of acres of federal public lands were effectively "off limits" for mining and oil and gas development. Not too surprisingly, many of the designations were highly controversial and encountered stiff local opposition. Plaintiffs sued to set certain designations aside on a variety of grounds, including NEPA. Was President Clinton required to issue an EIS for the designation of the Grand Staircase–Escalante or other national monuments? *See* Tulare County v. Bush, 185 F.Supp.2d 18, 28 (D.D.C. 2001) (rejecting a challenge to the designation of the Giant Sequoia National Monument), *aff'd,* Tulare County v. Bush, 306 F.3d 1138 (D.C. Cir. 2002), *cert. denied*, 540 U.S. 813, 124 S.Ct. 63, 157 L.Ed.2d 28 (2003).

---

40 C.F.R. § 1508.12 Federal agency.

"Federal agency" means all agencies of the Federal Government. It does not mean the Congress, the Judiciary, or the President ..... It also includes ... States and units of general local government and Indian tribes assuming NEPA responsibilities under (section 104(h) of the Housing and Community Development Act of 1974).

B.   Is There a Proposal for Action?

The NEPA process must be initiated as early as possible in the decisionmaking process. NEPA's objectives are most likely to be fulfilled if the agency begins to consider alternatives and potential effects before the die has been cast, at a time when the viewpoints of interested persons can be incorporated and the relevant data can provide meaningful guidance to the decisionmakers. *See* 40 C.F.R. § 1501.2.

---

40 C.F.R. § 1501.2 Apply NEPA early in the process.

Agencies shall integrate the NEPA process with other planning at the earliest possible time to insure that planning and decisions reflect environmental values, to avoid delays later in the process, and to head off potential conflicts. Each agency shall:

* * *

(b) Identify environmental effects and values in adequate detail so they can be compared to economic and technical analyses. Environmental documents and appropriate analyses shall be circulated and reviewed at the same time as other planning documents.

* * *

(d) Provide for cases where actions are planned by private applicants or other non-Federal entities before Federal involvement so that:

   (1) Policies or designated staff are available to advise potential applicants of studies or other information foreseeably required for later Federal action.

---

(2) The Federal agency consults early with appropriate State and local agencies and Indian tribes and with interested private persons and organizations when its own involvement is reasonably foreseeable.

(3) The Federal agency commences its NEPA process at the earliest possible time.

How soon is soon enough? An agency must prepare an EIS at "the time at which it makes a recommendation on a proposal for federal action." Aberdeen & Rockfish Railroad Co. v. Students Challenging Regulatory Agency Procedures, 422 U.S. 289, 320, 95 S.Ct. 2336, 2356, 45 L.Ed.2d 191 (1975). In other words, NEPA "kicks in" when an agency proposes a particular course of action. Kleppe v. Sierra Club, 427 U.S. 390, 96 S.Ct. 2718, 49 L.Ed.2d 576 (1976). This generally means that the agency "has a goal and is actively preparing to make a decision on one or more means of accomplishing that goal, and the effects can be meaningfully evaluated." 40 C.F.R. § 1508.23 (1991).

A proposal for federal action may exist where the agency itself intends to take action, or where the agency considers a permit or license application, a lease, or funding authorization for an action by other entities. *See* Scientists' Institute for Public Information, Inc. v. Atomic Energy Com'n, 481 F.2d 1079 (D.C. Cir. 1973). In addition, the expansion or revision of ongoing programs may amount to a proposal for major federal action requiring an EIS or supplemental EIS. Andrus v. Sierra Club, 442 U.S. 347, 363, 99 S.Ct. 2335, 2344, 60 L.Ed.2d 943 (1979). *See* Section V.A, *infra* (When is a Supplemental EIS Required?). The mere contemplation of an action, however, is not a proposal for purposes of NEPA. Agencies are not expected to delve into the possible effects of purely hypothetical projects. National Wildlife Federation v. FERC, 912 F.2d 1471 (D.C. Cir. 1990).

The exact moment at which an agency has a proposal for action is not always easy to pinpoint.

METCALF v. DALEY

United States Court of Appeals, Ninth Circuit, 2000.

214 F.3d 1135.

The Makah, who reside in Washington state on the northwestern Olympic Peninsula, have a 1500 year tradition of hunting whales. In particular, the Makah target the California gray whale ("gray whale"), which annually migrates between the North Pacific and the coast of Mexico. * * *

In 1855, the United States and the Makah entered into the Treaty of Neah Bay, whereby the Makah ceded most of their land on the Olympic Peninsula to the United States in exchange for "the right of taking-fish and of whaling or sealing at usual and accustomed grounds and stations.... " Treaty of Neah Bay, 12 Stat. 939, 940 (1855). Despite their long history of whaling and the Treaty ... , the Makah ceased whaling in the 1920s because widespread commercial whaling had devastated the population of gray whales almost to extinction. * * *

Because the gray whale had become virtually extinct, the United States signed in 1946 the International Convention for the Regulation of Whaling in order "to provide for the proper conservation of whale stocks and thus make possible the orderly development of the whaling industry.... " 62 Stat. 1716, 1717 (1946). The International Convention for the Regulation of Whaling enacted a schedule of whaling regulations ("Schedule") and established the International Whaling Commission ("IWC"), which was to be composed of one member from each signatory nation. *See id.* Furthermore, [it] granted the IWC the power to amend the Schedule by "adopting regulations with respect to the conservation and utilization of whale resources," including quotas for the maximum number of whales to be taken in any one season. *Id.* at 1718–19. * * *

When the IWC was established on December 2, 1946, it took immediate action to protect the beleaguered mammal. Specifically, the IWC amended the Schedule to impose a complete ban on the taking or killing of gray whales. 62 Stat. at 1723. However, the IWC included an exception to the ban "when the meat and products of such whales are to be used exclusively for local consumption by the aborigines." *Id.* This qualification is referred to as the "aboriginal subsistence exception."

In addition to being shielded from commercial whaling under international law, the gray whale received increased protection in 1970 when the United States designated the species as endangered under the Endangered Species Conservation Act of 1969, the predecessor to the Endangered Species Act of 1973 ("ESA"). In 1993, however, NMFS [the National Marine Fisheries Service] determined that the eastern North Pacific stock of gray whales had recovered to near its estimated original population size and was no longer in danger of extinction. As such, this stock of gray whales was removed from the endangered species list in 1994. * * *

After these gray whales were removed from the endangered species list, the Makah decided to resume the hunting of whales who migrated through the Sanctuary.[b] To execute this plan, the Makah turned to the United States government ... for assistance. The Tribe asked representatives from the Department of Commerce to represent it in seeking approval from the IWC for an annual quota of up to five gray whales. * * *

---

b. Most of the whales migrate through the Olympic Coast National Marine Sanctuary, which is adjacent to the Tribe's territory (Neah Bay) on the coast of Washington State. *See Anderson v. Evans* Appendix.

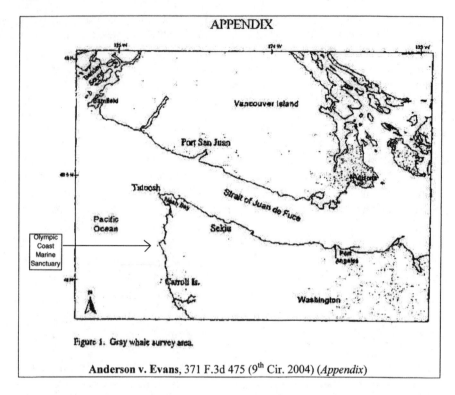

Figure 1. Gray whale survey area.

Anderson v. Evans, 371 F.3d 475 (9th Cir. 2004) (*Appendix*)

* * * [O]n March 22, 1996, NOAA [the National Oceanic and Atmospheric Administration, an entity within the Department of Commerce] entered into a formal written Agreement with the Tribe, which provided that "after an adequate statement of need is prepared ..., NOAA ... will make a formal proposal to the IWC for a quota of gray whales for subsistence and ceremonial use by the Makah Tribe." Furthermore, the Agreement provided for cooperation between NOAA and the Makah Tribal Council ("Council") in managing the harvest of gray whales. * * * Finally, the Agreement provided that within thirty days of IWC approval of a quota, "NOAA will revise its regulations to address subsistence whaling by the Makah Tribe, and the Council will adopt a management plan and regulations to govern the harvest." * * * [T]he United States presented a formal proposal for a quota of gray whales for the Tribe at the IWC annual meeting in June 1996. * * *

In June 1997, an attorney representing the organizations Australians for Animals and BEACH Marine Protection wrote a letter to NOAA and NMFS alleging that the United States Government had violated NEPA by authorizing and promoting the Makah whaling proposal without preparing an EA or an EIS. In response, the Administrator for NOAA wrote to Australians for Animals and BEACH Marine Protection on July 25, 1997, informing them that an EA would be prepared. Twenty-eight days later, on August 22, 1997, a draft EA was distributed for public comment.

On October 13, 1997, NOAA and the Makah entered into a new written Agreement, which, in most respects, was identical to the Agreement signed in 1996. Unlike the earlier Agreement, however, the 1997 Agreement required the Makah to "confine hunting activities to the open waters of the Pacific Ocean outside the Tatoosh–Bonilla Line." Apparently, this provision was added to the Agreement in order to increase the probability that, although the whaling would occur in the Sanctuary, the Makah would hunt only the migratory whales, rather than the Sanctuary's "summer residents." Four days later … NOAA/NMFS issued … a final EA and a Finding of No Significant Impact ("FONSI"). * * *

On April 6, 1998, NOAA issued a Federal Register Notice setting the domestic subsistence whaling quotas for 1998. The Notice stated that the Makah's subsistence and cultural needs had been recognized by both the United States and the IWC. Accordingly, the Notice allowed the Makah to engage in whaling pursuant to the IWC-approved quota and Whaling Convention Act regulations. * * *

* * * NEPA does not set out substantive environmental standards, but instead establishes "action-forcing" procedures that require agencies to take a "hard look" at environmental consequences.… [W]e have observed in connection with the preparation of an EA that "proper timing is one of NEPA's central themes. An assessment must be 'prepared early enough so that it can serve practically as an important contribution to the decisionmaking process and will not be used to rationalize or justify decisions already made.' " [Save the Yaak Committee v. Block, 840 F.2d 714, 718 (9th Cir. 1988)] (quoting 40 C.F.R. § 1502.5 (1987)).

The phrase "early enough" means "at the earliest possible time to insure that planning and decisions reflect environmental values." Andrus v. Sierra Club, 442 U.S. 347, 351 (1979); see also 40 C.F.R. § 1501.2. The Supreme Court in referring to NEPA's requirements as "action forcing," *Andrus*, 442 U.S. at 350, has embraced the rule that for projects directly undertaken by Federal agencies, environmental impact statements "shall be prepared at the feasibility analysis (go-no go) stage and may be supplemented at a later stage if necessary." *Id.* at 351 n.3; see also 40 C.F.R. § 1502.5(a). * * * In summary, the comprehensive "hard look" mandated by Congress and required by the statute must be timely, and it must be taken objectively and in good faith, not as an exercise in form over substance, and not as a subterfuge designed to rationalize a decision already made. * * *

In this case, the Federal Defendants did (1) prepare an EA, (2) decide that the Makah whaling proposal would not significantly affect the environment, and (3) issue a FONSI, but they did so after already having signed two agreements binding them to support the Tribe's proposal. Appellants assert that, in so doing, the Federal Defendants violated NEPA in several ways. Appellants argue that, although NOAA/ NMFS ultimately prepared an EA, they violated NEPA because they prepared the EA too late in the process. According to appellants, "by making a commitment to authorize and fund the Makah whaling plan, and then drafting a NEPA document which simply rubber-stamped the decision ... , defendants eliminated the opportunity to choose among alternatives, ... and seriously impeded the degree to which their planning and decisions could reflect environmental values." * * *

We begin by considering appellants' argument that the Federal Defendants failed timely and in the proper sequence to comply with NEPA. As provided in the regulations promulgated to implement NEPA, "agencies shall integrate the NEPA process with other planning *at the earliest possible time* to insure that planning and decisions reflect environmental values, to avoid delays later in the process, and to head off potential conflicts." 40 C.F.R. § 1501.2 (emphasis added); *see also id.* § 1502.5 ("An agency shall commence preparation of an [EIS] as close as possible to the time the agency is developing or is presented with a proposal.... "). Furthermore, this court has interpreted these regulations as requiring agencies to prepare NEPA documents, such as an EA or an EIS, "before any irreversible and irretrievable commitment of resources." Thus, the issue we must decide here is whether the Federal Defendants prepared the EA too late in the decision-making process, i.e., after making an irreversible and irretrievable commitment of resources. We conclude that they did.

The purpose of an EA is to provide the agency with sufficient evidence and analysis for determining whether to prepare an EIS or to issue a FONSI. 40 C.F.R. § 1508.9. Because the very important decision whether to prepare an EIS is based solely on the EA, the EA is fundamental to the decision-making process. In terms of timing and importance to the goals of NEPA, we see no difference between an EA and an EIS in connection with when an EA must be integrated into the calculus. In the case at bar, the Makah first asked the Federal Defendants to help them secure IWC approval for a gray whale quota in 1995; however, NOAA/NMFS did not prepare an EA until 1997. During these two years, the United States and the Makah worked together toward obtaining a gray whale quota from the IWC. In January 1996, an NOAA representative informed his colleagues that "we now have interagency agreement to support the Makah's application in IWC for a whaling quota of 5 grey whales." More importantly, in March 1996, more than a year before the EA was prepared, NOAA entered into a contract with the Makah pursuant to which it committed to (1) making a formal proposal to the IWC for a quota of gray whales for subsistence and ceremonial use by the Makah and (2) participating in the management of the harvest. To demonstrate the firmness of this commitment, we need only to look at the EA, which says, "In early 1996, [NOAA and the Tribal Council] signed an agreement in which the United States committed to make a formal request to the IWC.... "

The Federal Defendants did not engage the NEPA process "at the earliest possible time." Instead, the record makes clear that the Federal Defendants did not even consider the potential environmental effects of the proposed action until long after they had already committed in writing to support the Makah whaling proposal. The "point of commitment" in this case came when NOAA signed the contract with the Makah in March 1996 and then worked to effectuate the agreement. It was at this juncture that it made an "irreversible and irretrievable commitment of resources." * * * Although it could have, NOAA did not make its promise to seek a quota from the IWC and to participate in the harvest conditional upon a NEPA determination that the Makah whaling proposal would not significantly affect the environment.

Had NOAA/NMFS found after signing the Agreement that allowing the Makah to resume whaling would have a significant effect on the environment, the Federal Defendants would have been required to prepare an EIS, and they may not have been able to fulfill their written commitment to the Tribe. As such, NOAA would have been in breach of contract. Although the United States delegates to the 1996 IWC meeting ultimately withdrew their proposal for a Makah aboriginal subsistence whaling quota, they did so with the Tribe's approval and because the proposal did not have adequate support from other IWC delegations, *not* in order to reconsider environmental concerns. The firmness of the 1996 Agreement became even clearer and more resolute in 1997 when NOAA entered into a new, similar contract with the Tribe to pursue its whaling quota at the 1997 IWC meeting. This Agreement was signed four days *before* the final EA in this case was issued. In the EA, the agencies referred to this second Agreement as having "renewed the cooperative Agreement" signed in 1996. This is strong evidence that NOAA and other agencies made the decision to support the Tribe's proposal in 1996, before the EA process began and without considering the environmental consequences thereof. By the time the Federal Defendants completed the final EA in 1997, the die already had been cast. The "point of commitment" to this proposal clearly had come and gone. [T]he contracts here amounted to a surrender of the Government's right to prevent activity in the relevant area. * * *

It is highly likely that because of the Federal Defendants' prior written commitment to the Makah and concrete efforts on their behalf, the EA was slanted in favor of finding that the Makah whaling proposal would not significantly affect the environment. As the court below noted, "the longer the defendants worked with the Tribe toward the end of whaling, the greater the pressure to achieve this end.... An EA prepared under such circumstances might be subject to at least a subtle prowhaling bias." The EA itself somewhat disingenuously claims in 1997 that the "decision to be made" is "whether to support the Makah Tribe in its effort to continue its whaling tradition," when in point of fact that decision had already been made in contract form. * * * Also, NOAA/ NMFS's statement in the EA that "any perception that the U.S. Government is trying to withdraw its support for Makah whaling would likely plunge the Tribe into a difficult controversy with the United States" strongly suggests that the Federal Defendants were predisposed to issue a FONSI.

NEPA's effectiveness depends entirely on involving environmental considerations in the initial decisionmaking process. *See* 40 C.F.R. § § 1501.2, 1502.5. * * * Here, before preparing an EA, the Federal Defendants signed a contract which obligated them both to make a proposal to the IWC for a gray whale quota and to participate in the harvest of those whales. We hold that by making such a firm commitment before preparing an EA, the Federal Defendants failed to take a "hard look" at the environmental consequences of their actions and, therefore, violated NEPA. * * *

We want to make clear, however, that this case does not stand for the general proposition that an agency cannot begin preliminary consideration of an action without first preparing an EA, or that an agency must always prepare an EA before it can lend support to any proposal. * * * "Council on Environmental Quality (CEQ) regulations actually encourage identification of a preferred course of action during the NEPA process...." Rather, our holding here is limited to the unusual facts and circumstances of this case where the defendants already had made an "irreversible and irretrievable commitment of resources"—i.e., by entering into a contract with the Makah before they considered its environmental consequences and prepared the EA.[3] * * *

Appellees argue that, even if the Federal Defendants did violate NEPA by preparing the EA after deciding to support Makah whaling, the issue is moot because the only relief that the court could order is the preparation of an adequate EA, which, appellees contend, already has been done. [However,] ... appellants contend that the EA is demonstrably suspect because the process under which the EA was prepared was fatally defective—i.e., the Federal Defendants were predisposed to finding that the Makah whaling proposal would not significantly affect the environment. We agree. * * *

Our conclusions about the EA in this case raise an obvious question: Having already committed in writing to support the Makah's whaling proposal, can the Federal Defendants now be trusted to take the clear-eyed hard look at the whaling proposal's consequences required by the law, or will a new EA be a classic Wonderland case of first-the-verdict, then-the-trial? In order to avoid this problem and to ensure that the law is respected, must we—and can we—set aside the FONSI and require the Federal Defendants to proceed directly to the preparation of an Environmental Impact Statement? On reflection, and in consideration of our limited role in this process, we have decided that it is appropriate only to require a new EA, but to require that it be done under circumstances that ensure an objective evaluation free of the previous taint. * * * The manner of ensuring that the process ... is accomplished objectively and in good faith shall be left to the relevant agencies. Should a new EA come back to the courts for additional scrutiny, however, the burden

3. Because we conclude that the Federal Defendants violated NEPA by preparing the EA too late, we need not directly decide whether they also violated NEPA by preparing an inadequate EA, or by issuing a FONSI rather than preparing an EIS.

shall be on the Federal Defendants to demonstrate to the district court that they have complied with this requirement.

Accordingly, we REVERSE and REMAND to the district court. The district court is directed to order the Federal Defendants to set aside the FONSI, suspend implementation of the Agreement with the Tribe, begin the NEPA process afresh, and prepare a new EA. * * * [Dissent omitted]

Notes and Questions

1. Why didn't the court order the government to prepare an EIS for the whaling proposal? Would that have addressed the problem of perceived governmental bias or predisposition to proceed with the proposal?

2. Isn't it likely that the agency will simply incorporate its post hoc rationalization into the new EA? The court agreed that "the EA is demonstrably suspect because the process under which the EA was prepared was fatally defective.... " Should the court have been more concerned about bad faith on the part of the agency? If it were, what options were available to the court in crafting an adequate remedy?

3. Was it appropriate to suspend implementation of the Agreement with the Tribe during the preparation of a new EA or an EIS? Should the Tribes' treaty right be honored regardless of the federal government's obligations under NEPA? The answer may depend, in part, on the precedential hierarchy between federal treaties (international or tribal) and federal statutes. *See* United States v. Dion, 476 U.S. 734, 106 S.Ct. 2216, 90 L.Ed.2d 767 (1986) (specifying an analytical test for determining whether federal statutes abrogate Indian treaties); Chapter Seven, *infra* (Tribal Ownership).

4. Whale-hunting from a cedar canoe is exceedingly difficult, to say the least. It is made even more challenging by protesters who attempt to impede the hunt by throwing objects and discharging fire extinguishers at the canoe. By 2003, the Makah hunters had only taken one whale. The thirty-foot gray whale was harpooned as it surfaced and then executed with a .50–caliber rifle. It was towed back to the beach at Neah Bay, where it was prepared for a traditional potlatch feast and celebration. Meanwhile, the government went back to the drawing board and prepared another EA on the Makah whaling proposal, but it still didn't get it quite right. In Anderson v. Evans, 371 F.3d 475, 490 (9th Cir. 2004), the court concluded that the new EA was deficient for failing to consider potential effects on the local summer whale population, an issue that the court found both uncertain and controversial. The court also expressed concerns that the approval of the Makah proposal could establish a precedent for other actions that may have a cumulative impact on the environment. *Id.* at 493 (citing 40 C.F.R. § 1508.27(b)(6)). It remanded for preparation of an EIS.

5. In Kleppe v. Sierra Club, 427 U.S. 390, 96 S.Ct. 2718, 49 L.Ed.2d 576 (1976), the Supreme Court rejected plaintiff's argument that the agencies responsible for developing coal reserves on federal land should be compelled to prepare an EIS on possible leasing throughout the entire northern Great Plains region. It found that there was no existing or proposed plan for the development of the region, as governmental studies of the area were not parts of an overarching development program and individual projects undertaken or proposed by private industry and public utilities in that part of the country were not integrated into a plan or otherwise interrelated. *Id.* at 401–405. The Court concluded: "A court has no authority to ... determine a point during the germination process of a potential proposal at which an impact statement should be prepared. Such an assertion of judicial authority would leave the agencies uncertain as to their procedural duties under NEPA, would invite judicial involvement in the day-to-day decisionmaking process of the agencies, and would invite litigation." *Id.* at 406. Doesn't this decision encourage agencies to avoid comprehensive planning whenever possible in hopes of avoiding the need to prepare an EIS?

In Focus:

Opposing Viewpoints

The Makah Tribe:

"We are whalers. It is how we are defined between all American tribes," said Ernie Cheeka, a fourteenth generation member of a whaling family.

"By returning to hunting whales, the Makah are literally reaching their hands back and touching ancestors who negotiated the right for them," said Al Ziontz, spokesman for the Makah Whaling Commission.

Paul Watson, President of Sea Shepherd:

"A thunderous explosion [from a Russian vessel] delivered a grenade tipped harpoon at point blank range into the head of the leviathan. . . . The great whale fell back in painful convulsions and rolled and writhed upon the turbulent waves as we watched transfixed with horror and shame. I saw the whale's eye emerge from the sea and gaze upon me. . . . His eye held my eye locked to his gaze . . . [and] I saw pity. Pity not for myself nor for his kind, but pity for us that we could commit such a blasphemous act of cruelty. "

Forks Forum: Tribal and Sea Shepherd
Points of View, http:/www.olypen.com/
aview/whales.html (visited Aug. 16, 2003).

C. Is it a "Major" Federal Action?

NEPA applies to "major federal action." 42 U.S.C.A. § 4332(C). Even seemingly insignificant or routine federal actions may be considered both "major" and "federal", thereby triggering NEPA. Consider each term as defined in the regulation below, 40 C.F.R. § 1508.18.

---

40 C.F.R. § 1508.18

*"**Major Federal action**"* includes actions with effects that may be major and which are potentially subject to Federal control and responsibility. *Major* reinforces but does not have a meaning independent of significantly (§ 1508.27).

Actions include the circumstance where the responsible officials fail to act and that failure to act is reviewable ... under the Administrative Procedure Act or other applicable law as agency action.

(a) ***Actions*** include new and continuing activities, including projects and programs entirely or partly financed, assisted, conducted, regulated, or approved by federal agencies; new or revised agency rules, regulations, plans, policies, or procedures; and legislative proposals (§§ 1506.8, 1508.17). Actions do not include funding assistance solely in the form of general revenue sharing funds ... with no Federal agency control over the subsequent use of such funds. Actions do not include bringing judicial or administrative civil or criminal enforcement actions.

(b) ***Federal actions*** tend to fall within one of the following categories:

> (1) Adoption of official policy, such as rules, regulations * * *; formal documents establishing an agency's policies which will result in or substantially alter agency programs.

> (2) Adoption of formal plans, such as official documents prepared or approved by federal agencies which guide or prescribe alternative uses of federal resources, upon which future agency actions will be based.

> (3) Adoption of programs, such as a group of concerted actions to implement a specific policy or plan; systematic and connected agency decisions allocating agency resources to implement a specific statutory program or executive directive.

> (4) Approval of specific projects, such as construction or management activities located in a defined geographic area. Projects include actions approved by permit or other regulatory decision as well as federal and federally assisted activities.

According to the regulation, the phrase "major federal action" covers actions "potentially subject to Federal control and responsibility." 40

C.F.R. § 1508.18. Courts have construed this provision as requiring the federal agency to have some actual authority over the project. For example, in Sierra Club v. Hodel, 848 F.2d 1068, 1090–91 (10th Cir. 1988), the Bureau of Land Management's involvement in a county road improvement project passing through federal lands was deemed a federal action, where the agency had a statutory duty to determine whether there was a less degrading alternative and, if so, to impose that alternative on the nonfederal actor. Conversely, in Mayaguezanos Por La Salud y El Ambiente v. United States, 198 F.3d 297 (1st Cir. 1999), private shipments of nuclear waste to Japan through the United States' Exclusive Economic Zone were not considered a federal action for purposes of NEPA where the shippers voluntarily notified the Coast Guard of their transit but the Coast Guard had no authority to control the shipments under international or domestic law.

Major federal action can exist when the primary actors are not federal agencies. Macht v. Skinner, 916 F.2d 13 (D.C.Cir.1990). However, if federal involvement is limited to an advisory role, there is no federal action. In other words, "The touchstone of 'major federal action' ... with respect to activity of a nonfederal agency, is a federal agency's authority to influence significant nonfederal activity, and this influence must be more than the power to give nonbinding advice to the nonfederal actor." Sierra Club v. Hodel, 848 F.2d at 1089. *See Ka Makani 'O Kohala Ohana Inc. v. Water Supply*, 295 F.3d 955 (9th Cir. 2002) (concluding that the advisory actions of the U.S. Geological Survey and Department of Housing and Urban Development through the preliminary stages of a Hawaiian water transmission project did not constitute "major Federal action"). The ability to affect the outcome of a project or controversy "by advocacy and negotiation is not synonymous with a federal agency's authority to exercise control over a nonfederal project.... " United States v. Southern Florida Water Management Dist., 28 F.3d 1563, 1572 (11th Cir. 1994). In *Southern Florida Water Management Dist.*, the court determined that a settlement agreement between the United States and the state that committed the state to clean up or prevent nutrient-rich pollutants from degrading a federal refuge and park was not a federal project. *Id.*

Other circuits have agreed that the federal agency must have "actual power to control the project." *See* Ross v. Federal Highway Admin., 162 F.3d 1046, 1051 (10th Cir.1998). This will be found where "termination or modification of the agency involvement would terminate or significantly impact the project." Gettysburg Battlefield Preservation Ass'n v. Gettysburg College, 799 F.Supp. 1571, 1576 (M.D.Pa. 1992), *aff'd*, 989 F.2d 487 (3d. Cir. 1993). In other words, non-federal projects will be considered "federal actions" if they cannot begin or continue without prior approval by a federal agency and the agency possesses authority over the outcome. Sugarloaf Citizens Ass'n v. Federal Energy Regulatory Comm'n, 959 F.2d 508, 513–14 (4th Cir.1992).

Under § 1508.18, can there be a "major" action when the federal nexus or "hook" is minimal, for example, where an agency merely issues a permit or license for a small component of the project in question? In the following case, the Corps of Engineers was required to prepare NEPA analysis for a multi-faceted private development project to take place on a 160 acre site, even though the Corps' only involvement at the site was to issue a permit to place riprap (stones or other solid materials) along the site's boundary to stabilize the river's banks.

COLORADO RIVER INDIAN TRIBES v. MARSH
United States District Court, C.D. California, 1985.
605 F.Supp. 1425.

Developer and Federal Defendants contend that an EIS was unnecessary because federal involvement in the project was minimal and therefore "major federal action" triggering NEPA was lacking. In support of their contention, both rely upon Save the Bay, Inc. v. U.S. Corps of Eng., 610 F.2d 322 (5th Cir.), *cert. denied,* 449 U.S. 900 (1980), and Winnebago Tribe of Nebraska v. Ray, 621 F.2d 269 (8th Cir.), *cert. denied,* 449 U.S. 836 (1980). These cases suggest that … the degree of federal involvement controls the scope of an agency's review of potential impact. Their holdings give independent significance to the word "major" and suggest that the degree of federal involvement is a threshold question in ascertaining the reasonableness of the federal agency's decision not to issue an EIS. This court disagrees … insofar as their rulings stress that "major federal action" is an element that must be met to trigger NEPA and that "major federal action" has significance independent from the element of "significantly affecting the quality of the human environment" in 42 U.S.C.A. § 4332(2)(C).

* * * The circuits have split on the question of whether federal action that significantly affects the environment must also be "major" in an economic or some other nonenvironmental sense to trigger the EIS requirement. We incline to the views expressed in *Minnesota Public Interest Research Group v. Butz,* 8 Cir. *in banc,* 1974, 498 F.2d 1314, 1321–22:

> To separate the consideration of the magnitude of federal action from its impact on the environment does little to foster the purposes of the Act, i.e., to "attain the widest range of beneficial uses of the environment without degradation, risk to health and safety, or other undesirable and unintended consequences." By bifurcating the statutory language, it would be possible to speak of a "minor federal action significantly affecting the quality of the human environment," and to hold NEPA inapplicable to such an action. Yet if the action has a significant effect, it is the intent of NEPA that it should be the subject of the detailed consideration mandated by NEPA; the activities of federal agencies cannot be isolated from their impact upon the environment. (Citations omitted.)

Th[is] is supported by the regulations promulgated under NEPA. As defined by 40 C.F.R. § 1508.18: " 'Major Federal action' includes actions with *effects that may be major* and which are potentially subject to Federal control and responsibility. Major reinforces but does not have a meaning independent of significantly (§ 1508.27) ... " (Emphasis added.) Finally, NEPA's declaration of national environmental policy suggests a concern for the effects of development upon the environment and a commitment to restore and preserve environmental quality * * * To limit the scope to only "major" federal involvement, ignoring the potential for significant impact, seems incongruous to the avowed intent of NEPA to maintain environmental quality. * * *

Notes and Questions

1.   Under *Colorado River Tribes*, the term "major," as used in Section 4332, seems to have little, if any, relevance. Did the court, in effect, read the term right out of the statute? Does the regulation cited by the court, 40 C.F.R. § 1508.18, effectively read the term "major" out of the statute? If so, how does that square with conventional principles of statutory construction? The court disagreed with two cases from different circuits, Save the Bay, Inc. v. U.S. Corps of Eng., 610 F.2d 322 (5th Cir.), cert. denied, 449 U.S. 900, 101 S.Ct. 269, 66 L.Ed.2d 130 (1980), and Winnebago Tribe of Nebraska v. Ray, 621 F.2d 269 (8th Cir.), cert. denied, 449 U.S. 836, 101 S.Ct. 110, 66 L.Ed.2d 43 (1980). Both cases involved projects that predated the current version of 40 C.F.R. 1508.18, which took effect in July 1979. *See* 43 Fed. Reg. 56003 (Nov. 29, 1978). Yet a split in the circuits remains as to whether the term "major" has independent significance, with some courts continuing to follow *Winnebago* and *Save the Bay,* and others following *Colorado River Tribes.*

2.   As a result of *Colorado River Tribes,* the Corps was required to prepare an EIS for the entire development project, even though the magnitude of the Corps' own independent action of granting a permit for shoreline stabilization was minimal. Does this look like a case of "the tail wagging the dog"? If so, is the result antithetical to NEPA's purposes of informed yet pragmatic decisionmaking? Conversely, do you agree with the court's conclusion that NEPA's objectives center on the significance of the effects, not the significance, quantity or magnitude of federal involvement? The court explained, "It is not the degree of federal involvement that influences the standard of living of our society, but is instead, the potential and degree of impact from development that bears upon the overall welfare and enjoyment of our society." 605 F.Supp. at 1432.

3.   Where the federal agency has actual authority over a portion of a multi-jurisdictional project, NEPA applies, but the scope of analysis may be limited. In Winnebago Tribe v. Ray, 621 F.2d 269 (8th Cir.), cert. denied, 449 U.S. 836, 101 S.Ct. 110, 66 L.Ed.2d 43 (1980), the Corps of Engineers was not required to analyze the full range of impacts posed by the construction of a 67–mile long non-federal transmission line over the Missouri River, but was required to consider only the 1 mile portion of the line which crossed navigable waters. The court reasoned that the Corps' authority was limited to navigable waters. As a result, the Corps was able to get by with an EA rather than an EIS. This type of project raises additional questions regarding an agency's segmentation of a project to avoid having to consider significant effects of related facets of the project. For additional information on segmentation, see *infra,* Section IV.C.2.

4. A major federal action cannot be converted into a state or local project for purposes of avoiding NEPA after there has been significant federal involvement. In Ross v. Federal Highway Admin., 162 F.3d 1046 (10th Cir. 1998), the court refused to allow the Federal Highway Administration to discontinue the EIS process for an unfinished segment of a local trafficway, concluding that there was still a "major federal action" even though the state had decided it would not use federal funds to complete the project. It found that the segment in question was initially part of a larger federal demonstration project that could not be converted into a local project after significant federal involvement, notwithstanding the state's right to direct or even refuse the use of additional federal funds. *Id.* at 1054.

D. Does the Action Affect the "Environment"?

NEPA is concerned with the "quality of the human environment." 42 U.S.C.A. § 4332. The "environment," in this context, includes not only the physical environment–air, land, and water—but may also include aesthetic and socio-economic factors. *See* 40 C.F.R. § 1508.14; Metropolitan Edison Co. v. People Against Nuclear Energy, 460 U.S. 766, 772–73, 103 S.Ct. 1556, 75 L.Ed.2d 534 (1983).

---

40 C.F.R. § 1508.14 Human environment.

"Human Environment" shall be interpreted comprehensively to include the natural and physical environment and the relationship of people with that environment. (See the definition of "effects" (§ 1508.8).) This means that economic or social effects are not intended by themselves to require preparation of an environmental impact statement. When an environmental impact statement is prepared and economic or social and natural or physical environmental effects are interrelated, then the environmental impact statement will discuss all of these effects on the human environment.

As section 1508.14 specifies, there must be some effect on the physical environment to trigger NEPA as an initial matter, but once NEPA has been triggered, it requires an assessment of the effects on socio-economic factors as well. In Hanly v. Mitchell, 460 F.2d 640, 647 (2nd Cir. 1972), for example, the court required the General Services Administration to consider the noise, traffic, and crime which could result from the construction of a jail: these factors "affect the urban 'environment' and are surely results of the 'profound influences of ... high density urbanization [and] industrial expansion.' " *Id.* at 647 (citations omitted). It construed the term "environment," as used in NEPA, to encompass quality of life considerations. *Id.*

What if the primary effects of a major federal action are psychological? In *Metropolitan Edison Co.*, 460 U.S. at 779, the Supreme Court rejected a NEPA claim from neighbors of the Three Mile Island nuclear power plants, and held that potential health effects flowing from the community's anxiety about the risks of restarting one of the reactors could only be deemed "environmental" if there was a "reasonably close causal relation" to a change in the physical environment. Although the Court conceded that the operation of the facility was an "event in the physical environment," potential health damage to nearby residents from unrealized risks of a nuclear accident was too far removed from that event to be covered by NEPA. *Id.* at 777.

Notes and Questions

1.   The Bureau of Alcohol, Tobacco and Firearms proposes to allow liquor to be sold in plastic (rather than glass) bottles. Manufacturers of glass bottles challenge the decision on NEPA grounds. Is an EIS required for the adverse economic effects which may be experienced by the plaintiffs? What about potential health risks posed by criminal tampering if injection of poisons into the plastic by third parties is reasonably foreseeable? *See* Glass Packaging Institute v. Regan, 737 F.2d 1083, 1092 (D.C.Cir.) ("We seriously doubt whether Congress fashioned NEPA as an administrative incarnation of the policeman's squad car, roving the streets in search of sporadic criminal activity which may occasionally occur in the aftermath of an agency action, there to arrest the criminal in the name of 'environmental protection.' "), cert. denied, 469 U.S. 1035, 105 S.Ct. 508, 83 L.E.2d 399 (1984).

2.   Is an EIS required for problems associated with overcrowding, vehicular traffic and parking at a proposed high-rise apartment complex? In Chelsea Neighborhood Associations v. U.S. Postal Service, 516 F.2d 378 (2d Cir. 1975), the court found that the Post Office's EIS was deficient for failure to give full consideration to the social effects of apartments that had been proposed by city agencies to be constructed on top of the Post Office's new vehicle maintenance facility. It ordered project planners to consider whether a housing project could become "a human jungle, unsafe at night and unappealing during the day." *Id.* at 388. Is *Chelsea Neighborhood* distinguishable from *Metropolitan Edison Co.* and *Glass Packaging Institute?*

E. Is the Environmental Impact "Significant"?

Many, if not most, NEPA lawsuits turn on the question of significance. Agencies must prepare an EIS when substantial questions are raised as to whether a project will have a significant impact on some human environmental factor. Wetlands Action Network v. United States Corps of Engineers, 222 F.3d 1105 (9th Cir. 2000). The CEQ's definition of the term "significantly" requires considerations of both context and intensity. *See* National Parks and Conservation Association v. Babbitt, 241 F.3d 722, 731 (9th Cir. 2001) (citing 40 C.F.R. § 1508.27). Both beneficial and adverse impacts can count as significant. Significance might also be found if the action affects ecologically critical areas or other unique geographic characteristics or public health or safety. Smith v. United States Forest Serv., 33 F.3d 1072 (9th Cir. 1994).

The question of significance is highly fact specific. As such, it may not be clear at the time of project proposal whether the effects are likely to be significant. Section 1508.27, below, provides a list of criteria to help guide the inquiry.

40 C.F.R. § 1508.27 Significantly.

"Significantly" as used in NEPA requires considerations of both context and intensity:

(a) Context. This means that the significance of an action must be analyzed in several contexts such as society as a whole (human, national), the affected region, the affected interests, and the locality. Significance varies with the setting of the proposed action. For instance, in the case of a site-specific action, significance would usually depend upon the effects in the locale rather than in the world as a whole. Both short- and long-term effects are relevant.

(b) Intensity. This refers to the severity of impact. * * * The following should be considered in evaluating intensity:

(1) Impacts that may be both beneficial and adverse. A significant effect may exist even if the Federal agency believes that on balance the effect will be beneficial.

(2) The degree to which the proposed action affects public health or safety.

(3) Unique characteristics of the geographic area such as proximity to historic or cultural resources, park lands, prime farmlands, wetlands, wild and scenic rivers, or ecologically critical areas.

(4) The degree to which the effects on the quality of the human environment are likely to be highly controversial.

(5) The degree to which the possible effects on the human environment are highly uncertain or involve unique or unknown risks.

(6) The degree to which the action may establish a precedent for future actions with significant effects or represents a decision in principle about a future consideration.

(7) Whether the action is related to other actions with individually insignificant but cumulatively significant impacts. Significance exists if it is reasonable to anticipate a cumulatively significant impact on the environment. Significance cannot be avoided by terming an action temporary or by breaking it down into small component parts.

(8) The degree to which the action may adversely affect districts, sites, highways, structures, or objects listed in or eligible for listing in the National Register of Historic Places or may cause loss or destruction of significant scientific, cultural, or historical resources.

(9) The degree to which the action may adversely affect an endangered or threatened species or its habitat that has been determined to be critical under the Endangered Species Act of 1973.

(10) Whether the action threatens a violation of Federal, State, or local law or requirements imposed for the protection of the environment.

1. The Environmental Assessment (EA)

If in doubt with regard to the significance of an action's effects, an agency may prepare an EA rather than an EIS. Courts have described EAs as "rough-cut, low budget" analyses. Indiana Forest Alliance v. U.S. Forest Service, 325 F.3d 851, 856 (7th Cir. 2003). The regulations define EA as follows:

---

40 C.F.R. § 1508.9 Environmental Assessment.

(a) Means a concise public document for which a Federal agency is responsible that serves to:

(1) Briefly provide sufficient evidence and analysis for determining whether to prepare an environmental impact statement or a finding of no significant impact.

(2) Aid an agency's compliance with the Act when no environmental impact statement is necessary.

(3) Facilitate preparation of a statement when one is necessary.

* * *

The use of EAs to satisfy agencies' NEPA responsibilities is clearly on the rise. In fact, the CEQ concluded that the EA "has evolved to the point where it is the predominant way agencies conduct NEPA analyses." *The National Environmental Policy Act: A Study of its Effectiveness After Twenty–Five Years* 19 (1997), available at http://ceq.eh.doe.gov/nepa/nepa25fn.pdf. Accurate data on the numbers of EAs is not available because, unlike EISs, agencies are not required to report or provide notice of their EAs. A 1993 CEQ survey estimated that about 50,000 EAs were prepared annually, while only 508 EISs, on average, were prepared annually. *Id*. The number of EISs has declined dramatically from their "heyday" in the 1970's, when nearly 2,000 were prepared annually. *Id*. Critics believe that agencies employ EAs rather than EISs to short-circuit public involvement, but the trend may also be due to the perception that the costly and time-consuming EIS process could be the "kiss of death" for the project. *Indiana Forest Alliance*, 325 F.3d at 856.

In Practice:

Number of EISs by Federal Department

Department	1971[1]	1975[1]	1999[2]
Transportation	1293	229	117
Interior	65	67	109
Agriculture	79	189	95

Department	1971[1]	1975[1]	1999[2]
Defense (Army Corps of Engineers)	343	287	52
Commerce	8	13	20
Others	162	225	108
TOTALS	**1950**	**1010**	**501**

[1] *Source: Council for Environmental Quality, The Seventh Annual Report of the Council on Environmental Quality 132 (1976).*

[2] *Source: U.S. EPA, 1999 Environmental Impact Statements Filed with the Environmental Protection Agency, available at http://ceq.eh.doe.gov/ nepa/1999EPAEISData.pdf.*

---

40 C.F.R. § 1501.4 Whether to prepare an environmental impact statement.

* * *

(b) * * * The agency shall involve environmental agencies, applicants, and the public, to the extent practicable, in preparing assessments required by § 1508.9(a)(1).

* * *

(e) Prepare a finding of no significant impact (§ 1508.13), if the agency determines on the basis of the environmental assessment not to prepare a statement.

(1) The agency shall make the finding of no significant impact available to the affected public as specified in § 1506.6.

(2) In certain limited circumstances, ... the agency shall make the finding of no significant impact available for public review ... for 30 days before the agency makes its final determination whether to prepare an environmental impact statement and before the action may begin. The circumstances are:

(i) The proposed action is, or is closely similar to, one which normally requires the preparation of an environmental impact statement under the procedures adopted by the agency pursuant to § 1507.3, or

(ii) The nature of the proposed action is one without precedent.

Agencies are increasingly identifying measures to mitigate the effects of their actions and adopting those measures in their EAs, a phenomenon known as "mitigated FONSIs." *The National Environmental Policy Act: A Study of its Effectiveness After Twenty–Five Years* 19. This practice can save the agencies and project proponents significant time and money, and can result in more environmentally beneficial decisions by identifying potential impacts and ways to avoid them earlier in the process. *See id.* Professor Bradley Karkkainen argues that a mitigated FONSI offers an attractive bargain: in exchange for substantive measures that reduce anticipated environmental impacts below the threshold of "significance," an agency can bypass the burden of producing an EIS. Bradley C. Karkkainen, *Toward a Smarter NEPA: Monitoring and Managing Governments Environmental Performance,* 102 Colum. L. Rev. 903, 908 (2002). By the same token, however, mitigated FONSIs can erode trust in the community and result in less rigorous scientific analysis of both effects and viable alternatives. *The National Environmental Policy Act: A Study of its Effectiveness After Twenty–Five Years* 19.

It appears that the EA trend is likely to continue, at least for the foreseeable future. Agencies should proceed with some caution when they choose to issue EAs, though, as EAs may be more vulnerable to judicial remand than are EISs. Judges sometimes perceive EAs as illicit shortcuts, as is evident in the following case.

COALITION FOR CANYON PRESERVATION v. SLATER

United States District Court, D. Montana, 1999.

33 F.Supp.2d 1276.

This case involves a challenge to a decision by the National Park Service (NPS) to construct a parking lot on the east side of the Going to the Sun Road (GTSR) at the Avalanche Creek area of Glacier National Park. The NPS issued an Environmental Assessment (EA) in April of 1996 for the project. A little over one year later, the service issued a Finding of No Significant Impact (FONSI) in July of 1997. The Coalition seeks a declaratory judgment that defendants have violated the National Environmental Policy Act (NEPA) and the Department of Transportation Act. The Coalition also wants an injunction barring defendants from construction of the proposed parking lot and access road unless and until they have complied with National Environmental Policy Act. * * *

In considering what is contemplated both by the proposed project and the purposes of the environmental laws in question the historical stage needs to be set. As is more fully set forth below, the area of this project has some vegetation, not all of course, that existed in the renaissance period. Some of the trees involved in the area existed shortly after Columbus landed in America. They stem from the time of Machiavelli and the Mona Lisa. They are a part of the crown jewel of national parks, parts that should not be dealt with except in precise conformance with congressional mandate as manifested in the National Environmental Protection Act. For the reasons sets forth below, I am going to grant the injunctive relief the Coalition seeks.

The Avalanche Creek Area is located at the confluence of Avalanche and McDonald Creeks several miles upstream of McDonald Lake adjacent to the Going to the Sun Road (GTSR). Currently, the east side of the Going to the Sun Road in the area contains a campground. It has an asphalt and handicapped accessible boardwalk through the Trail of the Cedars. It is the trailhead for the two mile hike to Avalanche Lake. * * *

The west side of the Going to the Sun Road (toward McDonald Creek) in the Avalanche area has a 12 table picnic area, restrooms, and twenty parking spaces that abut the southbound lane of traffic of the Going to the Sun Road. Because the Trail of the Cedars and the trailhead to Avalanche Lake are on the east side of the road, and the parking to the west, there is considerable pedestrian traffic across the Going to the Sun Road. Additionally, automobiles create road side parking along both shoulders of the Going to the Sun Road in order to visit the popular area. Some of this parked traffic is illegal.

Responding to the increased visitor use and the perceived need to find a long term solution, the National Park Service conducted and completed an Environmental Assessment (EA) for a parking lot on the east side of Going to the Sun Road in 1984. The parking problem was also considered in a Transportation Plan in 1990, that recommended implementing the 1984 plan. The lack of funding meant no action was taken on the 1984 plan.

Finding a solution for the congestion in the Avalanche Creek area was revisited by the National Park Service in 1995–1996. That consideration culminated in the Environmental Assessment and FONSI which are the subject of this case. Because the proposals from 1984 and 1990 were never acted on, the Environmental Assessment that is the subject of this action must stand alone. The Environmental Assessment resulted in the designation of a preferred alternative by the National Park Service which calls for a parking lot on the east side of Going to the Sun Road in the Avalanche Creek area. * * *

The heart of the controversy is the impact the parking lot might have on the vegetation at the site where the proposed alternative is to be constructed. It is a forest classified as cedar-devil's club habitat with trees dating to the year 1517. It is an area with vegetation that the Environmental Assessment admits is rare and vulnerable to extinction. The cedar-devil's club habitat in the Avalanche Creek area is the largest in Montana. It is significant in other ways because it marks the easternmost location of cedar-devil's club habitat in the North American continent. Tree species are numerous, but are dominated by cedar and hemlock. Many of the trees are greater than 40 inches diameter at breast height (dbh).

In considering the location of the proposed parking lot development in 1994, the Assistant Superintendent of Glacier National Park told his Division chiefs that the parking facility had to be built on the west side of Going to the Sun Road due to the "potential for unacceptable resource and visitor experience impacts on the east side of the Going to the Sun Road." (AR 98). The Division chiefs were responsible for developing the Avalanche plan.-

The Draft Environmental Assessment supporting the current proposal characterized the effects of development of the parking facility as follows: "Further permanent loss of this rare and unique habitat, whether it be mature or successional forest, constitutes a long-term significant impact." (AR 196). Curiously, the Final Environmental Assessment omitted this language, but did note that the habitat "is an extremely significant resource due to its age, rarity (and) biogeographic uniqueness." (AR 297). The language of the draft implies the need for an Environmental Impact Statement while the final language is somewhat less demanding but it too implies the need for an EIS to consider the project's impact on an extremely significant resource.

As part of the Environmental Assessment, a Park Service expert stated that plans to increase parking would result in impacts which "are significant in light of the cumulative impacts that have occurred and the extreme rarity of the habitat involved." (AR 92). Public comment on the Environmental Assessment also focused on the anticipated removal of trees from the old-growth forest to accommodate the parking lot. The public comment was nearly universally against the proposed parking lot.

Additionally, the estimate of trees which were slated for removal was underestimated by the National Park Service in the Environmental Assessment and the FONSI. After formally awarding the contract, the Environmental Assessment Interdisciplinary Team Captain admitted that the FONSI was based on a serious discrepancy and that "the down side of this is that we will be cutting more trees than we have stated in our FONSI last July by a significant amount." (AR 600).

The July 1997 FONSI states that only 9 trees greater than 12″ dbh would be removed during construction of the parking lot. The National Park Service estimate in the revised data suggests that the actual number is 47 trees, a five-fold increase. Moreover, additional "hazard trees", those capable of falling into the parking lot and thereby posing threats to visitor safety, would need to be removed in future years. Estimates of the number of hazard trees at risk is close to 200. The National Park Service does not dispute that estimate. The Service admits that hazard tree removal is foreseeable and "could significantly increase the number of large mature trees removed as a result of the new Avalanche parking area." (AR 540)

The Administrative Record is replete with references to significant impacts that would be caused by the preferred alternative, and yet the National Park Service issued a Finding of No Significant Impact. The categorical findings of significant impact on the wealth of this biologically rare and diverse area is incongruous with the Finding of No Significant Impact.

* * * A Finding of No Significant Impact is reviewed under the arbitrary and capricious standard. This standard requires that the "court must ensure that the agency has taken a 'hard look' at the envi-

ronmental consequences of its proposed action." Oregon Natural
Resources Council v. Lowe, 109 F.3d 521, 526 (9th Cir. 1997). * * *

Agencies may reach a FONSI if mitigation measures are proposed
that directly address the impacts identified in the Environmental
Assessment. Here, the National Park Service proposes to remove the
picnic area on the west side of Going to the Sun Road to allow for restoration of the habitat there. It then argues that this undertaking miti-
gates the impacts that will result from constructing the parking lot on
the east side of the road. However, the Environmental Assessment is
deficient in yet another way. There is insufficient scientific analysis that
the area to the west will regenerate, or that its regeneration is sufficient
mitigation to the loss of the habitat to the east. The National Park Service conclusion that it will regenerate is speculative. Finally, there is no
dispute that regeneration, if successful, would take centuries. The measure of mitigation would be nearly half of the next millennium.

Mitigation efforts must be sufficiently detailed to demonstrate that
environmental impacts have been addressed in a meaningful fashion. An
agency's "perfunctory description of mitigating measures is inconsistent
with the 'hard look' it is required to render under NEPA." The mitigation
resolution here proposed does not meet the test. * * *

An Environmental Assessment means there will be either a FONSI
or the preparation of an Environmental Impact Statement. A FONSI
issued by an agency in conjunction with an EA should describe why the
proposed action will not have a significant impact, and it relies on the
Environmental Assessment's scientific analysis and data as its informed
basis and justification. If the agency finds that the proposal may significantly impact the environment, the National Environmental Policy Act
requires that an Environmental Impact Statement must be prepared. 40
C.F.R. § 1501.4.

A hard look in this case shows the FONSI is not supported by the
Administrative Record of this Environmental Assessment. The Administrative Record repeatedly shows that tree removal and other impacts are
significant. Moreover, the type of mitigation listed by the National Park
Service lacks the scientific analysis and supporting data to constitute
sufficient mitigation to support a FONSI. The Park Service's own documents demonstrate and show the significance of the impacts of the proposal. The Finding of No Significant Impact runs counter to the facts
and language of numerous references in the Administrative Record. The
Administrative Record raises substantial questions that this proposal
may have significant impacts on the environment. Consequently, the
lack of an Environmental Impact Statement is unreasonable as a matter
of law. In ignoring the repeated references in the Administrative Record
about the significance of the proposal's impacts, the National Park Service's decision not to perform an Environmental Impact Statement is
arbitrary and capricious. * * *

Plaintiff ... seeks an injunction, and the basis for injunctive relief is irreparable injury and inadequacy of legal remedies. Amoco Production Co. v. Village of Gambell, 480 U.S. 531 (1987). Nothing in the National Environmental Policy Act indicates that Congress intended to restrict a court's equitable jurisdiction. * * * Wherefore, ... the United States Department of Interior and Federal Highway Administration and all persons acting in concert with them, including contractors, are enjoined from implementing the FONSI/RD and further enjoined from authorizing any tree removal or other site preparation in connection with the road access and parking lot at Avalanche Campground, Glacier National Park until such time as an Environmental Impact Statement has been completed in conformance with the National Environmental Protection Act. * * *

Notes and Questions

1.   It isn't often that federal judges draw upon Renaissance figures like Columbus, Machiavelli, and the Mona Lisa to make their point. Did the judge's choice of rhetoric in *Coalition for Canyon Preservation* give you the impression that the judge believed an EIS was *per se* warranted for any impact to the area's ancient vegetation, or was there more to it? Should any federal action that results in alteration of old-growth habitat require an EIS, regardless of other circumstances? *See* 40 C.F.R. § 1508.27.

2.   In 1999, the National Park Service concluded that the Going-to-the-Sun Road must be rehabilitated to preserve its status as a National Historic Landmark and premier visitation site. It issued a DEIS on a comprehensive rehabilitation plan in 2002. The DEIS reported the following:

> Construction of the Going-to-the-Sun Road was a monumental undertaking. The Road was first opened to public travel over Logan Pass in the fall of 1932. During its first year of full operation in 1933, about 40,000 vehicles traveled the Road. Currently about 475,000 vehicles annually travel the Road from June to October and 1.7 million visitors enjoy the Park each year. Since the Road's original construction, traffic volume, avalanches, harsh weather conditions, and inadequate maintenance from a lack of funding and trained staff have all contributed to deterioration of the structural and historic features of the Road. * * * If corrective actions are not taken, historic structures will be lost and adjacent environmental resources may be adversely affected.

Going-to-the-Sun Road Rehabilitation Plan/Draft Environmental Impact Statement S–1 (2002), available at http://www.nps.gov/glac/pdf/gttsroad/Sum.pdf.

Continuing problems persist with respect to traffic patterns and pedestrian crossings "at pullouts, overlooks, and parking areas ... which puts motorists, bicyclists, and pedestrians at risk." *Id.* at S–5. The NPS estimates that the rehabilitation project will take up to eight years to complete and cost between $140 to $170 million. *Id.*-

Tunnel & parapet on east slope of Going-to-the-Sun
Road (July 1933),
http://www.nps.gov/glac/history/photos.htm (visited
July 11, 2003)

3. Significance may be found where a proposal is "highly controversial." 40 C.F.R. § 1508.27(b)(4). Would an EIS be required for the parking lot at issue in *Coalition for Canyon Preservation* simply because of the tremendous public controversy over destruction of old-growth forests? In Indiana Forest Alliance v. U.S. Forest Service, 325 F.3d 851, 857 (7th Cir. 2003), the court concluded that "mere opposition" did not create the type of "high controversy" envisioned by the regulation; if it did, "the EIS outcome would be governed by a 'heckler's veto.' " *Id.* (citations omitted). What type of controversy would trigger the need for an EIS?

4. It may have been possible for the NPS to defend the EA and FONSI for the parking lot at issue in the *Coalition for Canyon Preservation* case if it had been tiered to a comprehensive EIS on rehabilitation and maintenance of the road. For a discussion of tiering, see 40 C.F.R. § 1502.20 and Section IV.C.3, *infra* (Programmatic EISs and Tiering).

5. Is an EIS required when the EA indicates that the effects of the proposal will be wholly beneficial? Courts are split on this question, with some saying "no," Friends of Fiery Gizzard v. Farmers Home Admin., 61 F.3d 501 (6th Cir. 1995), and others at least indicating "yes." Catron County Bd. of Com'rs v. U.S. Fish & Wildlife Service, 75 F.3d 1429 (10th Cir. 1996). Which approach makes more sense, given the overall goals of NEPA? Which is more consistent with the CEQ's regulations, particularly section 1508.27?

2. *Problem: Padre Island National Seashore*[c]

The Padre Island National Seashore is a unit of the National Park System in southern Texas, on the Gulf of Mexico. It was established by

c. This problem is based on fact, but extensive editorial liberties have been taken. No resemblance to actual persons or entities is intended. For background on mineral interests in Padre Island National Seashore, see Dunn–McCampbell Royalty Interest, Inc. v. National Park Service, 112 F.3d 1283 (5th Cir. 1997).

Congress in 1962 "in order to save and preserve, for purposes of public recreation, benefit, and inspiration, a portion of the diminishing seashore of the United States that remains undeveloped." 16 U.S.C.A. § 459d.

Padre Island Seashore Dune Ridge,
http://data2.itc.nps.gov/nature/NaturalFeatures.cfm
?alphacode=pais&loc=4
(Photo by Phil Slattery)

The Seashore represents the only intact ecosystem of its kind on the Gulf, with 130,500 acres of dunes and wetlands. It provides important habitat to threatened and endangered species, such as the Kemps Ridley Sea Turtle, and sensitive native plant species, including the sea oat. It also provides an essential seasonal stop-over for migrating birds. As a barrier island, the Seashore acts as a "buffer zone" to the mainland in the event of hurricanes and other extreme weather conditions. In addition, the Seashore offers unsurpassed birding opportunities and other low impact recreational activities, in stark contrast to the adjacent South Padre Island, a popular resort and "spring break" area, where motorized vehicles and recreational activities of all sorts are allowed.

As is the case in a number of the more recently created national parks, the mineral rights underlying the surface of the Seashore remain in private ownership. The legislative history for the Seashore indicates that the purchase of mineral rights at the time the park was created would have been cost-prohibitive. The co-sponsor of the House bill, Congressman Bailey Hutch, stated that the Seashore would provide an "unparalleled recreational experience for the people of Texas while allowing lucrative oil and gas operations to continue in the area: a win-win scenario."

Under Texas state law, the mineral estate is considered the "dominant estate," and the National Park Service (NPS), like any surface owner, must grant mineral owners reasonable access to their subsurface minerals. NPS regulations, however, require mineral owners to submit operating plans for approval prior to disturbing the federal surface for exploration or development. The submission of an operating plan provides the NPS with notice regarding the location, timing and intensity of the proposed activities. According to NPS regulations, operating plans must include mitigation measures to minimize or avoid adverse effects to surface resources, as well as a reclamation plan to clean up any contaminants and restore site conditions.

Acting pursuant to a lease from the owners of the mineral rights underlying the Seashore, Mondo Oil Company submitted an operating plan to NPS approximately thirty days before it intended to proceed with exploration. Mondo's plan outlines its proposal to conduct a six- to eight-month seismic survey of potential oil deposits underlying the Seashore. The plan calls for the detonation of more than 1,000 dynamite charges along 20 miles of survey lines within the Seashore. The survey lines will be established by crews with up to a dozen crew members, working with off-road vehicles ("ORVs") to cut vegetation, plant the shots of dynamite, and place sound recording equipment. The Seashore's assistant park ranger believes that the ORV tracks and survey lines will be situated in close proximity to essential habitat for the Kemps Ridley turtle. Delays in obtaining plan approval would extend the project into the wet spring season, when the soils and vegetation of the Seashore are most vulnerable to disturbance and when turtles are most likely to be nesting.

NPS has prepared a draft and a final environmental assessment (EA) of the proposed plan. The draft was available on the internet and hard copies of it were circulated to anyone who had expressed an interest in Seashore affairs within the past five years. A thirty-day comment period was provided. Twenty "form" postcards were submitted, all of which stated, "Just Say No to Drilling: Don't Mess with Texas." Only two substantive comment letters were received, one from Mondo Oil and one from the Governor of Texas. Each is described below.

There was virtually no change between the draft and final EA. Given the limited nature of NPS's authorities with regard to the proposal in question, the EA considered only one alternative to Mondo's proposed plan of operations–denial of approval for the plan (the "no action" alternative). It concludes that seismic operations may threaten water quality and fragile dune structure and disrupt recreational bird watching, kayaking and hiking within the Seashore. It states that the measures included in Mondo's reclamation plan will rectify most of the damage, but only after exploration and development activities are completed. If Mondo drills a producing well, reclamation would not occur for years, and perhaps decades. The EA concedes that much of the information necessary to fully assess the impacts on wildlife and birds has not yet been compiled, in large part because NPS lacks the funds to perform detailed biological surveys to determine the presence and distribution of resident and migratory species within the Seashore. The EA referenced a ten-year-old study of sea turtle behavior and population trends, which concluded that around ten percent of the 2,000 adult turtles in existence nest at Padre Island at some point during their reproductive years. Based on this study, the EA concluded that effects on sea turtles would likely be minimal and further study was unwarranted at this time.

Park Superintendent Joe Phillips ultimately issued a Finding of No Significant Impact (FONSI), stating that no EIS would be prepared. Phillips expects to issue a Decision Notice any day, which will approve the plan and allow the project to move ahead. In a confidential email message to his friend, the Superintendent of Big Bend National Park, also located within the state of Texas, Phillips noted that "political expediency" weighed heavily in his decision to recommend approval based on the EA and FONSI. The comment letter submitted by the Governor of Texas urged a speedy turn-around so that Mondo can move forward, thereby giving the local economy a shot in the arm.

In its comments on the draft EA, Mondo objected to NPS's findings regarding potential adverse impacts. Mondo stated that it had incorporated mitigation measures to minimize impacts to the dunes, vegetation and water quality. Its scientists had concluded that the ORVs and dynamite blasts would result in tire tracks, shot holes and scattered debris, but would leave no permanent marks and would likely disappear within the next growing season. Mondo agreed with NPS's ultimate conclusion that an EIS was unnecessary. Meanwhile, Mondo received the Superintendent's okay to do some site-preparation work while waiting for the Decision Notice. It has begun moving temporary housing units, ORVs and seismic equipment onto the Seashore.

Although it did not comment on the draft EA when it was circulated for public comment, Save the Turtles (STT), a national environmental group headquartered in Miami, Florida, filed suit against NPS in federal district court for the Southern District of Texas, seeking to halt the project. STT claims an interest in the conservation of marine species, which it advances through research and litigation. It claims to have hundreds of members, including a few in southern Texas. The complaint alleges violations of NEPA, the Park Service Organic Act, the Endangered Species Act, and the APA. The plaintiff filed a motion for preliminary injunction (PI) with their complaint, and a hearing on the motion has been set for next week.

Mondo Oil has filed a motion to intervene in the lawsuit. Mondo's lawyer contacted Superintendent Phillips to inform him in no uncertain terms that he would be in violation of Federal and Texas state law if he "caves" to those pesky turtle-huggers by denying approval of Mondo's plan or delaying it during the preparation of an EIS.

Notes and Questions

1. The plaintiff's PI motion is based solely on the NEPA claim. To be awarded a PI, plaintiff must establish not only that monetary damages are

inadequate, but also the following four factors: (1) plaintiffs' claim has a substantial likelihood of prevailing on the merits; (2) irreparable harm will result unless the injunction is issued; (3) the injury to the plaintiff outweighs the harm that an injunction may cause the opposing party; and (4) an injunction is not adverse to the public interest. Amoco Production Co. v. Village of Gambell, AK, 480 U.S. 531, 542, 107 S.Ct. 1396, 94 L.Ed.2d 542 (1987); LDDS Communications, Inc. v. Automated Communications, Inc., 35 F.3d 198, 200 (5th Cir. 1994).

2. Make STT's most persuasive arguments on the first factor—the likelihood of success on the merits of its NEPA claim—using all applicable CEQ regulations and pertinent caselaw. Was the issuance of an EA and FONSI appropriate in this case? Is the EA's consideration of environmental effects and reasonable alternatives adequate? Did the NPS improperly ignore the cumulative effects of development on the Seashore along with development on nearby South Padre Island? Does NEPA require the NPS to consider the effects of a possible blow-out or oil spill from future wells and pipelines? In arguing your case, remember that you can only use information that is included in the administrative record, unless you can convince the court to supplement the record with pertinent external evidence.

3. Can STT satisfy the other three elements for obtaining a PI?

4. Change hats for a moment. You just began your new job as a staff attorney for the U.S. Department of Justice. Your supervisor dropped a case file on your desk containing the complaint and the EA in the *STT v. NPS* case. She told you to focus your efforts on responding to the PI motion, in particular, the NEPA arguments set forth in that motion. You must advise your client on the merits of STT's NEPA arguments and any defenses that may be raised, including any possible jurisdictional arguments. You might find Section II.C, *supra* (Judicial Review), helpful as a refresher.

5. Must or should the court allow Mondo to intervene in the case? Fed. R. Civ. P. 24 provides in pertinent part:

(a) Intervention of Right. Upon timely application anyone shall be permitted to intervene in an action: (1) when a statute of the United States confers an unconditional right to intervene; or (2) when the applicant claims an interest relating to the property or transaction which is the subject of the action and the applicant is so situated that the disposition of the action may as a practical matter impair or impede the applicant's ability to protect that interest, unless the applicant's interest is adequately represented by existing parties.

(b) Permissive Intervention. Upon timely application anyone may be permitted to intervene in an action: (1) when a statute of the United States confers a conditional right to intervene; or (2) when an applicant's claim or defense and the main action have a question of law or fact in common. * * * In exercising its discretion the court shall consider whether the intervention will unduly delay or prejudice the adjudication of the rights of the original parties. * * *

5. Assume Judge Grayhat denied STT's motion for PI after she heard oral arguments and considered the briefs. She then entered an order granting Mondo's motion to intervene and requiring all parties to submit to

mediation in an effort to promote settlement. How might a mediator view this case? Consider the complexity and merits of the NEPA claim and any other pertinent legal issues that might be raised if the case were to proceed to a bench trial, as well as any relevant policy matters or equitable concerns. One possible outcome is for NPS to prepare an EIS, which could take up to two years. Would this result put NPS in violation of Texas law, which requires surface owners to provide reasonable and timely access to underlying mineral estates? Laws governing access to leasable minerals, such as oil and gas, are considered in detail in Chapter 12, *infra*. How should the mediator address this potential limitation on federal authority?

IV.　THE ADEQUACY OF THE EIS

A.　The Format and Contents of the EIS

An EIS will be reviewed to ensure that all relevant environmental effects and alternatives were considered. The EIS process typically proceeds through several stages: scoping; draft EIS; final EIS; and Record of Decision. Public comment occurs at several points in this process.

---

40 C.F.R. § 1502.9 Draft, final, and supplemental statements.

Except for proposals for legislation … environmental impact statements shall be prepared in two stages and may be supplemented.

(a) Draft environmental impact statements shall be prepared in accordance with the scope decided upon in the scoping process. The lead agency shall work with the cooperating agencies and shall obtain comments as required in Part 1503 of this chapter.… If a draft statement is so inadequate as to preclude meaningful analysis, the agency shall prepare and circulate a revised draft of the appropriate portion. * * *

(b) Final environmental impact statements shall respond to comments as required in Part 1503 of this chapter. The agency shall discuss at appropriate points in the final statement any responsible opposing view which was not adequately discussed in the draft statement and shall indicate the agency's response to the issues raised. * * *

The first step, scoping, is "an early and open process for determining the scope of issues to be addressed and for identifying the significant issues related to a proposed action." 40 C.F.R. § 1501.7. It can assist the agency in narrowing the scope of the EIS process by identifying and deemphasizing issues that are not particularly significant. *Id.* § 1500.4(g). Scoping provides the public with an important opportunity to help shape the decisionmaking process. It is to occur "as soon as practicable" after the decision to prepare an EIS, at which point the lead agency must publish a notice of intent to begin the scoping process in the Federal Register, inviting "the participation of affected Federal, State, and local agencies, any affected Indian tribe, the proponent of the action, and other interested persons (including those who might not be in accord with the action on environmental grounds)." *Id.* § 1501.7(a)(1). Once scoping occurs, the agency will be ready to begin preparing a draft EIS.

The CEQ regulations provide guidance on the items to be included in the EIS. 40 C.F.R. § 1502.10. The table of contents of any given EIS will look about the same as any other, as most agencies follow the CEQ's recommendations fairly closely.

4040 C.F.R. § 1502.10 Recommended format.

Agencies shall use a format for environmental impact statements which will encourage good analysis and clear presentation of the alternatives including the proposed action. The following standard format ... should be followed unless the agency determines that there is a compelling reason to do otherwise:

(a) Cover sheet.

(b) Summary.

(c) Table of contents.

(d) Purpose of and need for action.

(e) Alternatives including proposed action....

(f) Affected environment.

(g) Environmental consequences....

(h) List of preparers.

(i) List of Agencies, Organizations, and persons to whom copies of the statement are sent.

(j) Index.

(k) Appendices (if any). * * *

B. Alternatives

NEPA's requirement that an agency consider all reasonable alternatives to the proposed action has often been described as the "heart of the EIS." *See* City of Alexandria v. Slater, 198 F.3d 862, 866 (D.C.Cir.1999) (citing 40 C.F.R. § 1502.14, below). Agencies are directed to "[r]igorously explore and objectively evaluate all reasonable alternatives" in an EIS. 40 C.F.R. § 1502.14. There is no prescribed formula as to the number of alternatives to be considered; rather, the agency must consider all alternatives reasonably related to the purposes of the project, however few. Laguna Greenbelt, Inc. v. U.S. Dept. of Transportation, 42 F.3d 517, 524 (9th Cir.1994). The burden is on the party challenging the EIS to offer feasible alternatives. In Department of Transportation v. Public Citizen, 541 U.S. 752, 124 S.Ct. 2204, 2214, 159 L.Ed.2d 60 (2004), challengers forfeited any objections to an EA's failure to discuss potential alternatives to the proposed regulation of Mexican trucks entering the United States when they failed to raise such alternatives in their comments. *See* Morongo Band of Mission Indians v. F.A.A., 161 F.3d 569, 576 (9th Cir. 1998) (plaintiff must make "some showing" that feasible alternatives exist, and cannot simply ask the court "to presume that an adequate alternate site exists somewhere and that the government did not try hard enough to find this site"); River Rd. Alliance, Inc. v. Corps of Eng'rs of United States Army, 764 F.2d 445, 452–53 (7th Cir.1985) ("The Corps was entitled not to conduct a further study of alternatives unless the plaintiffs were prepared to shoulder the burden of showing that [the agencies] had overlooked some plausible alternative site").

---

§ 1502.14 Alternatives including the proposed action.

This section is the heart of the environmental impact statement. * * * [I]t should present the environmental impacts of the proposal and the alternatives in comparative form, thus sharply defining the issues and providing a clear basis for choice among options by the decisionmaker and the public. In this section agencies shall:

(a) Rigorously explore and objectively evaluate all reasonable alternatives, and for alternatives which were eliminated from detailed study, briefly discuss the reasons for their having been eliminated.

(b) Devote substantial treatment to each alternative considered in detail including the proposed action so that reviewers may evaluate their comparative merits.

(c) Include reasonable alternatives not within the jurisdiction of the lead agency.

(d) Include the alternative of no action.

(e) Identify the agency's preferred alternative ... in the draft statement and identify such alternative in the final statement unless another law prohibits the expression of such a preference.

(f) Include appropriate mitigation measures not already included in the proposed action or alternatives.

Courts often describe the decision concerning which alternatives to consider as being bound by a "rule of reason and practicality." Airport Neighbors Alliance, Inc. v. United States, 90 F.3d 426, 432 (10th Cir.1996). A reasonable range of alternatives is typically defined by reference to the agency's stated purpose and need for the project. In other words, agencies are not required to consider alternatives which are "infeasible, ineffective, or inconsistent with the basic policy objectives" for the action at issue. Headwaters, Inc. v. Bureau of Land Management, 914 F.2d 1174, 1180 (9th Cir.1990). In State of S.C. ex rel. Campbell v. O'Leary, 64 F.3d 892, 897 (4th Cir. 1995), the Department of Energy's EA for a proposal to store spent nuclear fuel rods from European research reactors at its Savannah River Site in South Carolina was challenged as inadequate because it "ignored completely or insufficiently discussed" alternatives involving reprocessing rather than storage. The Fourth Circuit disagreed, stating that DOE had considered and rejected reprocessing options as contrary to the government's purpose of effectuating a nonproliferation policy, because reprocessing produces materials that may be used for fabricating weapons. *Id.* at 900.

While the project's purpose is a logical starting point for establishing parameters on the appropriate range of alternatives to be assessed,

the "purpose" of a project is a slippery concept, susceptible of no hard-and-fast definitions. One obvious way for an agency to slip past the structures of NEPA is to contrive a purpose so slender as to define competing "reasonable alternatives" out of consideration (and even out of existence).

Simmons v. United States Army Corps of Eng'rs, 120 F.3d 664, 669 (7th Cir.1997). Although agencies can reject alternatives that do not meet the purpose and need of the project, they cannot define the project so narrowly that it leaves them with only one or two options or otherwise forecloses a reasonable consideration of alternatives. *See* Colorado Envtl. Coalition v. Dombeck, 185 F.3d 1162, 1174–75 (10th Cir.1999); Friends of Southeast's Future v. Morrison, 153 F.3d 1059 (9th Cir. 1998).

CITIZENS' COMMITTEE TO SAVE OUR CANYONS v. U.S. FOREST SERVICE

United States Court of Appeals, Tenth Circuit, 2002.

297 F.3d 1012.

Snowbird owns and operates a ski resort located twenty-five miles southeast of Salt Lake City, Utah. All parties agree that Snowbird is a ski resort of some significance, and during the 1998–99 ski season over 380,000 people visited the resort. The resort itself is comprised of 881 acres of private land (called the Mineral Basin) and 1,674 acres of public land located within the Wasatch–Cache National Forest ("WCNF"). In 1979, the Forest Service issued a special use permit to Snowbird that allowed the resort to establish ski operations on national forest land. Because of its special use permit, Snowbird is required to submit periodically a master development plan outlining its long-range plans for the resort and the public lands it utilizes. * * *

In 1997, Snowbird submitted a master development plan (MDP) to the Forest Service. In the MDP, Snowbird proposed extensive changes to its resort operations. In addition to calling for a general upgrade in operations, increased snowmaking equipment, additional chair lifts, and improved hiking trails, the MDP proposed the construction of a 78,000 square-foot conference center and resort facility on an area known as Hidden Peak, which is within the public property Snowbird uses pursuant to a special use permit. * * *

Because Hidden Peak is located on land owned by the federal government, any substantial structures require Forest Service approval, which, in turn, implicates NEPA. On May 17, 1997, the Forest Service began the NEPA process by announcing its intent to prepare an Environmental Impact Study (EIS) examining Snowbird's proposal and by sending a scoping document, which outlined Snowbird's proposal and solicited public comments, to over 1,000 individuals and organizations. * * *

[I]n October 1998, the Forest Service published a draft EIS (DEIS) that consolidated several possible courses of action, including a no-action alternative, the Snowbird-proposed 78,000 square-foot structure, a considerably smaller, 22,000 square-foot structure, and the preferred alternative, a middle-sized structure ranging from 22,000 to 50,000 square-feet. In addition to discussing the proposed alternatives, the Forest Service outlined, as required by NEPA, alternatives that it had analyzed but not considered in detail. These "rejected alternatives" included a proposal to locate the Hidden Peak development at a different resort area altogether and a proposal to maintain the current sized structure, though with internal upgrades. The Forest Service justified not examining these alternatives in detail on the grounds that they would not meet the needs identified in the MDP. In addition, the DEIS pointed out that the current Hidden Peak buildings violated an existing provision of the WCNF Forest Plan prohibiting structures that might interfere with mountain views from being built on Hidden Peak.[d] * * *

On December 12, 1999, the Forest Service issued a final EIS (FEIS) and a Record of Decision (ROD) authorizing the construction of the Forest Service's preferred alternative, which, among other things, authorized ... "a building not to exceed 50,000 square feet" * * *

Citizens' Committee to Save Our Canyons (SOC), a nonprofit environmental group, soon challenged ... the Hidden Peak structure. * * * [I]t claimed that the Forest Service did not consider an appropriate range of alternatives when examining the Hidden Peak structure. Specifically, SOC argued that the Forest Service should have examined in more detail either constructing a facility smaller than 22,000 feet or not building a structure on Hidden Peak at all. * * *

SOC also challenges that Forest Service's EIS for not considering an appropriate number of alternatives when evaluating Snowbird's proposal for erecting a new Hidden Peak facility. SOC attacks the Forest Service's actions through a two-prong argument. First, SOC contends that the Forest Service inappropriately read the EIS's statement of purpose as focusing exclusively upon building a structure on Hidden Peak. Second, having made this error, SOC alleges, the Forest Service then failed to evaluate the possibility of building a smaller structure on Hidden Peak or, alternatively, placing facilities off peak. We disagree. * * *

One of the key provisions of NEPA and its corresponding regulations is that government agencies must "include in every recommendation or report on proposals" detailed statements analyzing "alternatives to the proposed action." 42 U.S.C.A. § 4332(c)(iii). According to CEQ regulations, considering alternative actions "is the heart of the environmental impact statement." * * * "To comply with the National Environmental Policy Act and its implementing regulations, [agencies] are required to ... give each alternative substantial treatment in the environmental

d. *See* Chapter 6, *infra,* regarding Forest Plans and other National Forest   Management Act (NFMA) requirements.

impact statement." Not only must an agency "rigorously explore and objectively evaluate all reasonable alternatives," agencies must also "briefly discuss the reasons" for having eliminated other alternatives. 40 C.F.R. § 1502.14(a).

As court opinions and the CEQ regulations make clear, however, an agency is only required to consider "reasonable alternatives." Id. § 1502.14. In determining whether an agency considered reasonable alternatives, courts look closely at the objectives identified in an EIS's purpose and needs statement. Where the action subject to NEPA review is triggered by a proposal or application from a private party, it is appropriate for the agency to give substantial weight to the goals and objectives of that private actor. * * *

Once an agency appropriately defines the objectives of an action, "NEPA does not require agencies to analyze 'the environmental consequences of alternatives it has in good faith rejected as too remote, speculative, or ... impractical or ineffective.' " Instead, we apply a "rule of reason test" that asks whether "the environmental impact statement contained sufficient discussion of the relevant issues and opposing viewpoints to enable the Forest Service to take a hard look at the environmental impacts of the proposed expansion and its alternatives." Colo. Envtl. Coalition v. Dombeck, 185 F.3d 1162, 1174 (10th Cir. 1999). Alternatives that "do not accomplish the purpose of an action are not reasonable" and need not be studied in detail by the agency. * * *

In this case, SOC does not directly challenge the Forest Service's stated objectives in evaluating Snowbird's overall master development plan, which included upgrading or replacing outdated facilities, improving circulation throughout the resort, balancing and making more efficient terrain use, and maintaining a "vigorous forest" and "quality recreational experience." Rather, SOC argues that the Forest Service inappropriately restricted the range of alternatives it considered by not fully exploring alternatives that could have accomplished these goals without requiring a large structure on Hidden Peak. All the Forest Service proposals, SOC contends, contained "colossal structures" that would dwarf the existing Hidden Peak structures and obstruct the view of Hidden Peak.

The Forest Service, however, considered alternatives that had differences in size spanning over 56,000 square feet. Besides the no-action alternative, which would have left the smaller existing structures in place with minor alterations, it considered a 22,000 square foot structure, Snowbird's proposal for a 78,000 square foot building, and the preferred alternative, which called for a structure ranging between 22,000 square feet and 50,000 square feet.

Contrary to SOC's claim, the Forest Service did not breach the "rule of reason" by refusing to study in detail alternatives that would have limited the structure's size to between 1,600 square feet and 22,000 square feet or moved the structure off-peak altogether. As the record illustrates, proposals calling for smaller structures on Hidden Peak, or removing the Hidden Peak structure to another location altogether, were impractical and failed to satisfy the objectives of the project. Evidence in the record suggests, for example, that moving the structure to nearby resort areas could have interfered with site-specific plans governing those regions, and that developing another resort would have undercut the investment at Snowbird already made by the Forest Service. According to documents in the record, locating skier services at the base of the resort or in the mid-mountain region, as opposed to the mountain's peak, would not have improved skier circulation, particularly because Hidden Peak is at the center of activity on the mountain and feeds Snowbird's three primary skiing areas, nor would it have met the need to respond to user desires, nor were there available feasible alternative locations. Finally, there is some suggestion in the record that placing the structure at the base of the mountain or in the mid-mountain region could create additional negative visual impacts.

* * * The Service also reasoned that by building on a site where structures already exist, it could minimize environmental impacts in other regions. * * *

Additionally, the Forest Service concluded that anything smaller than 22,000 square foot structure would not "meet skier needs," thereby negating the proposal's goal of increasing efficiency and recreational balance in the area. Having reviewed the record, we cannot conclude that the Forest Service's finding on this score was arbitrary or capricious.

Nor did the Forest Service's consideration of the various alternative structures ignore, as the SOC's argument at times implies, the impact that placing a structure on Hidden Peak would have upon views of the mountain. As maps in the record demonstrate, the Service analyzed in detail how the proposed structures, including the no-action alternative, which would have left the existing structures on the mountain, would have affected the views of Hidden Peak. The Forest Service concluded that the building proposed in the preferred alternative, even though much larger than the existing structures on Hidden Peak, could blend in better with Hidden Peak's ridge line and "could potentially improve the visual impact of the peak." Given that the existing box-shaped structure, which was constructed in 1971, simply sits atop Hidden Peak, while the proposed structure, though larger, would be rounded to blend in with the contour of the Peak, we cannot find the Forest Service's conclusion arbitrary or capricious. Accordingly, we reject SOC's claims that Forest Service considered an impermissible range of alternatives * * * [and] VACATE the injunctions imposed pending appeal.

Notes and Questions

1. A different aspect of this case is addressed subsequently in this chapter, see Section VI.A, *infra* (Categorical Exclusions).

2. A "no action" alternative must be included in every EIS. Does no action necessarily mean *no* action? Not exactly. In *SOC,* the "no action" alternative would have left existing ski resort structures in place. Likewise, in American Rivers v. FERC, 201 F.3d 1186 (9th Cir. 1999), the court found that the no action alternative for a proposed hydropower facility was continued operation under terms and conditions of the original license, rather than non-issuance of the license as argued by environmental groups. *Cf.* Seattle Audubon Soc'y v. Moseley, 80 F.3d 1401 (9th Cir. 1996) (an agency need not follow the "no action" alternative, as long as the agency considers it).

3. Although courts are generally deferential of an agency's judgment on a "reasonable" range of alternatives, agencies can run into trouble when they omit potentially viable alternatives without thorough justification. In Utahns For Better Transp. v. U.S. Dept. of Transp., 305 F.3d 1152 (10th Cir. 2002), the court found an EIS inadequate when the agency omitted an alternative from detailed consideration due to its high costs and adverse impacts on existing development without fully exploring and documenting the costs and impacts in the record.

4. Is an agency required to include an alternative for which it has no authority to implement? *See* Muckleshoot Indian Tribe v. United States Forest Service, 177 F.3d 800 (9th Cir. 1999) (concluding that agencies must assess all reasonable alternatives within the jurisdiction of any part of the federal government).

5. What if the primary purpose of the proposed action is to conserve and protect the natural environment, rather than to develop or harm it? In Kootenai Tribe of Idaho v. Veneman, 313 F.3d 1094 (9th Cir. 2002), the court held that NEPA's requirement that the Forest Service consider alternatives to its proposed Roadless Area Conservation Rule must be interpreted less stringently when the purpose for the Rule was to protect millions of acres of forest land from the adverse effects of road construction. Does the agency's belief that, on balance, the effects of its proposal will be beneficial necessarily justify narrowing the alternatives under consideration?

6. An EA must also consider appropriate alternatives to the proposed project. The range of alternatives in an EA, however, may be more limited than in an EIS. *See* Mt. Lookout–Mt. Nebo Property Protection Ass'n v. F.E.R.C.,143 F.3d 165 (4th Cir. 1998); Friends of the Ompompanoosuc v. FERC, 968 F.2d 1549 (2d Cir.1992); Olmsted Citizens for a Better Community v. United States, 793 F.2d 201 (8th Cir.1986). The CEQ regulations provide that, when an agency determines that an EIS is not necessary, it must "include *brief discussions* of the need for the proposal, of alternatives ..., of the environmental impacts of the proposed action and alternatives, and a listing of agencies and persons consulted." 40 C.F.R. § 1508.9(b) (emphasis added). Did the EA at issue in the Padre Island National Seashore problem, Section III.E.2, *supra,* include an adequate range of alternatives?

C. Effects

An EIS must include an assessment of the consequences of the proposed action and its alternatives. The regulations offer guidance on the types of consequences, or effects, of concern.

---

40 C.F.R. § 1502.16 Environmental consequences.

This section forms the scientific and analytic basis for the comparisons [of alternatives] under § 1502.14. * * * The discussion will include ... any adverse environmental effects which cannot be avoided should the proposal be implemented, the relationship between short-term uses of man's environment and the maintenance and enhancement of long-term productivity, and any irreversible or irretrievable commitments of resources which would be involved in the proposal should it be implemented. * * * It shall include discussions of:

(a) Direct effects and their significance (§ 1508.8).

(b) Indirect effects and their significance (§ 1508.8).

(c) Possible conflicts between the proposed action and the objectives of Federal, regional, State, and local (and in the case of a reservation, Indian tribe) land use plans, policies and controls for the area concerned. (See § 1506.2(d).)

(d) The environmental effects of alternatives including the proposed action. * * *

(e) Energy requirements and conservation potential of various alternatives and mitigation measures.

(f) Natural or depletable resource requirements and conservation potential of various alternatives and mitigation measures.

(g) Urban quality, historic and cultural resources, and the design of the built environment, including the reuse and conservation potential of various alternatives and mitigation measures.

(h) Means to mitigate adverse environmental impacts....

---

1. Direct, Indirect, and Cumulative Effects Caused By Agency Action

The term "effects," which is used interchangeably with "impacts," is defined broadly in the regulations to include the direct, indirect and cumulative effects of agencies' proposals and alternatives. 40 C.F.R. § 1508.8. Direct effects are caused by the proposed action and occur at the same place and time as the action, while indirect effects are a reasonably foreseeable result of the action, but occur later in time or farther away. *Id.* Cumulative impacts are those which result from the impact of the action when added to other past, present, and reasonably foreseeable future actions. *See id.* § 1508.7; Edwardsen v. U.S. Dept. of the Interior, 268 F.3d 781 (9th Cir. 2001).

---

40 C.F.R. § 1508.7 Cumulative impact.

"**Cumulative impact**" is the impact on the environment which results from the incremental impact of the action when added to other past, present, and reasonably foreseeable future actions regardless of what agency (Federal or non-Federal) or person undertakes such other actions. Cumulative impacts can result from individually minor but collectively significant actions taking place over a period of time.

40 C.F.R. § 1508.8 Effects.

"**Effects**" include:

(a) **Direct effects**, which are caused by the action and occur at the same time and place.

(b) **Indirect effects**, which are caused by the action and are later in time or farther removed in distance, but are still reasonably foreseeable. Indirect effects may include growth inducing effects and other effects related to induced changes in the pattern of land use, population density or growth rate, and related effects on air and water and other natural systems, including ecosystems.

Effects and impacts as used in these regulations are synonymous. Effects includes ecological (such as the effects on natural resources and on the components, structures, and functioning of affected ecosystems), aesthetic, historic, cultural, economic, social, or health, whether **direct, indirect, or cumulative**. Effects may also include those resulting from actions which may have both beneficial and detrimental effects, even if on balance the agency believes that the effect will be beneficial.

"NEPA is concerned with all significant environmental effects, not merely adverse ones." Environmental Defense Fund v. Marsh, 651 F.2d 983, 992 (5th Cir. 1981). Accordingly, both detrimental and beneficial effects should be analyzed in an EIS. *See* 40 C.F.R. § 1508.08(b). An EIS may be remanded if the issuing agency inflates the project's benefits in a way that masks or skews the proposal's overall effects. *See* Hughes River Watershed Conservancy v. Glickman, 81 F.3d 437 (4th Cir.1996) (holding that an EIS's use of an inflated estimate of a dam project's economic benefits violated NEPA by impairing fair consideration of the project's adverse environmental effects); Sierra Club v. Sigler, 695 F.2d 957 (5th Cir. 1983) (concluding that, once the Corps chose to trumpet the economic benefits as a "selling point" of an oil terminal and distribution project, NEPA requires full disclosure of related costs).

Indirect and cumulative effects seem to pose the most difficulties for agencies. As specified in section 1508.8(b), the assessment must be thorough and accurate with regard to all reasonably foreseeable effects "caused by" the agency's action. The requisite causal connection between the agency's action and contested environmental effects was the subject of a recent Supreme Court opinion involving a challenge to controversial rules related to the operation of Mexican trucks on United States roadways. DOT v. Public Citizen, 541 U.S. 752, 124 S.Ct. 2204, 159 L.Ed.2d 60 (2004). The Court's NEPA analysis is set forth below.

DEPARTMENT OF TRANSPORTATION
v. PUBLIC CITIZEN

Supreme Court of the United States, 2004.
541 U.S. 752, 124 S.Ct. 2204, 159 L.Ed.2d 60.

JUSTICE THOMAS delivered the opinion of the Court.

In this case, we confront the question whether the National Environmental Policy Act of 1969 and the Clean Air Act (CAA) require the Federal Motor Carrier Safety Administration (FMCSA) to evaluate the environmental effects of cross-border operations of Mexican-domiciled motor carriers, where FMCSA's promulgation of certain regulations would allow such cross-border operations to occur. * * *

FMCSA, an agency within the Department of Transportation (DOT), is responsible for motor carrier safety and registration. See 49 U.S.C. § 113(f). FMCSA has a variety of statutory mandates, including "ensur-[ing]" safety, § 31136, establishing minimum levels of financial responsibility for motor carriers, § 31139, and prescribing federal standards for safety inspections of commercial motor vehicles, § 31142. Importantly, FMCSA has only limited discretion regarding motor vehicle carrier registration: It must grant registration to all domestic or foreign motor carriers that are "willing and able to comply with" the applicable safety, fitness, and financial-responsibility requirements. § 13902(a)(1). FMCSA has no statutory authority to impose or enforce emissions controls or to establish environmental requirements unrelated to motor carrier safety.

* * * In 1982, Congress, concerned about discriminatory treatment of United States motor carriers in Mexico and Canada, enacted a 2–year moratorium on new grants of operating authority. Congress authorized the President to extend the moratorium beyond the 2–year period if Canada or Mexico continued to interfere with United States motor carriers, and also authorized the President to lift or modify the moratorium if he determined that doing so was in the national interest. Although the moratorium on Canadian motor carriers was quickly lifted, the moratorium on Mexican motor carriers remained, and was extended by the President.

In December 1992, the leaders of Mexico, Canada, and the United States signed the North American Free Trade Agreement (NAFTA), 32 I.L.M. 605 (1993). As part of NAFTA, the United States agreed to phase out the moratorium and permit Mexican motor carriers to obtain operating authority within the United States' interior by January 2000. On NAFTA's effective date (January 1, 1994), the President began to lift the trade moratorium by allowing the licensing of Mexican carriers to provide some bus services in the United States. The President, however, did not continue to ease the moratorium on the timetable specified by NAFTA, as concerns about the adequacy of Mexico's regulation of motor carrier safety remained.

The Government of Mexico challenged the United States' implementation of NAFTA's motor carrier provisions under NAFTA's dispute-resolution process, and in February 2001, an international arbitration panel determined that the United States' "blanket refusal" of Mexican motor carrier applications breached the United States' obligations under NAFTA. Shortly thereafter, the President made clear his intention to lift the moratorium ... following the preparation of new regulations governing grants of operating authority to Mexican motor carriers.

In May 2001, FMCSA published for comment proposed rules concerning safety regulation of Mexican motor carriers. One rule (the Application Rule) addressed the establishment of a new application form for Mexican motor carriers that seek authorization to operate within the United States. Another rule (the Safety Monitoring Rule) addressed the establishment of a safety-inspection regime for all Mexican motor carriers that would receive operating authority under the Application Rule.

In December 2001, Congress enacted the Department of Transportation and Related Agencies Appropriations Act, 2002, 115 Stat. 833. Section 350 of this Act ... provided that no funds appropriated under the Act could be obligated or expended to review or to process any application by a Mexican motor carrier for authority to operate in the interior of the United States until FMCSA implemented specific application and safety-monitoring requirements for Mexican carriers. * * *

In January 2002, acting pursuant to NEPA's mandates, FMCSA issued a programmatic EA for the proposed Application and Safety Monitoring Rules. FMCSA's EA evaluated the environmental impact associated with three separate scenarios: where the President did not lift the moratorium; where the President did but where (contrary to what was legally possible) FMCSA did not issue any new regulations; and the Proposed Action Alternative, where the President would modify the moratorium and where FMCSA would adopt the proposed regulations. The EA considered the environmental impact in the categories of traffic and congestion, public safety and health, air quality, noise, socioeconomic factors, and environmental justice. Vital to the EA's analysis, however, was the assumption that there would be no change in trade volume between the United States and Mexico due to the issuance of the regulations. FMCSA did note that § 350's restrictions made it impossible for Mexican motor carriers to operate in the interior of the United States before FMCSA's issuance of the regulations. But, FMCSA determined that "this and any other associated effects in trade characteristics would be the result of the modification of the moratorium" by the President, not a result of FMCSA's implementation of the proposed safety regulations. Because FMCSA concluded that the entry of the Mexican trucks was not an "effect" of its regulations, it did not consider any environmental impact that might be caused by the increased presence of Mexican trucks within the United States.

The particular environmental effects on which the EA focused, then, were those likely to arise from the increase in the number of roadside inspections of Mexican trucks and buses due to the proposed regulations. The EA concluded that these effects (such as a slight increase in emissions, noise from the trucks, and possible danger to passing motorists) were minor and could be addressed and avoided in the inspections process itself. The EA also noted that the increase of inspection-related emissions would be at least partially offset by the fact that the safety requirements would reduce the number of Mexican trucks operating in the United States. Due to these calculations, the EA concluded that the issuance of the proposed regulations would have no significant impact on the environment, and hence FMCSA, on the same day as it released the EA, issued a FONSI.

On March 19, 2002, FMCSA issued ... interim rules. * * * In the regulatory preambles, FMCSA relied on its EA and its FONSI to demonstrate compliance with NEPA. FMCSA also addressed the CAA in the preambles, determining that it did not need to perform a "conformity review" of the proposed regulations ... because the increase in emissions from these regulations would fall below the Environmental Protection Agency's (EPA's) threshold levels needed to trigger such a review. In November 2002, the President lifted the moratorium on qualified Mexican motor carriers. Before this action, however, respondents filed petitions for judicial review * * *

The Court of Appeals concluded that the EA was deficient because it failed to give adequate consideration to the overall environmental impact of lifting the moratorium on the cross-border operation of Mexican motor carriers. According to the Court of Appeals, FMCSA was required to consider the environmental effects of the entry of Mexican trucks because "the President's rescission of the moratorium was 'reasonably foreseeable' at the time the EA was prepared and the decision not to prepare an EIS was made." Due to this perceived deficiency, the Court of Appeals remanded the case for preparation of a full EIS. * * *

Under NEPA, an agency is required to provide an EIS only if it will be undertaking a "major Federal actio[n]," which "significantly affect[s] the quality of the human environment." Under applicable CEQ regulations, "[m]ajor Federal action" is defined to "includ[e] actions with effects that may be major and which are potentially subject to Federal control and responsibility." "Effects" is defined to "include: (a) Direct effects, which are caused by the action and occur at the same time and place," and "(b) Indirect effects, which are caused by the action and are later in time or farther removed in distance, but are still reasonably foreseeable." Thus, the relevant question is whether the increase in cross-border operations of Mexican motor carriers, with the correlative release of emissions by Mexican trucks, is an "effect" of FMCSA's issuance of the Application and Safety Monitoring Rules; if not, FMCSA's failure to address these effects in its EA did not violate NEPA, and so FMCSA's issuance of a FONSI cannot be arbitrary and capricious.

* * * With respect to FMCSA's ability to mitigate, respondents can argue only that FMCSA could regulate emissions from Mexican trucks indirectly, through making the safety-registration process more onerous or by removing older, more polluting trucks through more effective

enforcement of motor carrier safety standards. But respondents fail to identify any evidence that shows that any effect from these possible actions would be significant, or even noticeable, for air-quality purposes. The connection between enforcement of motor carrier safety and the environmental harms alleged in this case is also tenuous at best. Nor is it clear that FMCSA could, consistent with its limited statutory mandates, reasonably impose on Mexican carriers standards beyond those already required in its proposed regulations.

With this point aside, respondents have only one complaint with respect to the EA: It did not take into account the environmental effects of increased cross-border operations of Mexican motor carriers. Respondents' argument that FMCSA was required to consider these effects is simple. Under § 350, FMCSA is barred from expending any funds to process or review any applications by Mexican motor carriers until FMCSA implemented a variety of specific application and safety-monitoring requirements for Mexican carriers. This expenditure bar makes it impossible for any Mexican motor carrier to receive authorization to operate within the United States until FMCSA issued the regulations challenged here. The promulgation of the regulations, the argument goes, would "caus[e]" the entry of Mexican trucks (and hence also cause any emissions such trucks would produce), and the entry of the trucks is "reasonably foreseeable." Thus, the argument concludes, under the relevant CEQ regulations, FMCSA must take these emissions into account in its EA when evaluating whether to produce an EIS.

Respondents' argument, however, overlooks a critical feature of this case: FMCSA has no ability to countermand the President's lifting of the moratorium or otherwise categorically to exclude Mexican motor carriers from operating within the United States. To be sure, § 350 did restrict the ability of FMCSA to authorize cross-border operations of Mexican motor carriers, but Congress did not otherwise modify FMCSA's statutory mandates. In particular, FMCSA remains subject to the mandate of 49 U.S.C. § 13902(a)(1), that FMCSA "*shall* register a person to provide transportation ... as a motor carrier if [it] finds that the person is willing and able to comply with" the safety and financial responsibility requirements established by the Department of Transportation. (Emphasis added.) Under FMCSA's entirely reasonable reading of this provision, it must certify *any* motor carrier that can show that it is willing and able to comply with the various substantive requirements for safety and financial responsibility contained in DOT regulations; only the moratorium prevented it from doing so for Mexican motor carriers before 2001. Thus, upon the lifting of the moratorium, if FMCSA refused to authorize a Mexican motor carrier for cross-border services, where the Mexican motor carrier was willing and able to comply with the various substantive safety and financial responsibilities rules, it would violate § 13902(a)(1). * * *

Respondents must rest, then, on a particularly unyielding variation of "but for" causation, where an agency's action is considered a cause of an environmental effect even when the agency has no authority to prevent the effect. However, a "but for" causal relationship is insufficient to make an agency responsible for a particular effect under NEPA and the relevant regulations. As this Court held in *Metropolitan Edison Co. v. People Against Nuclear Energy*, NEPA requires "a reasonably close causal relationship" between the environmental effect and the alleged cause. The Court analogized this requirement to the "familiar doctrine of proximate cause from tort law." In particular, "courts must look to the underlying policies or legislative intent in order to draw a manageable line between those causal changes that may make an actor responsible for an effect and those that do not."

Also, inherent in NEPA and its implementing regulations is a "rule of reason," which ensures that agencies determine whether and to what extent to prepare an EIS based on the usefulness of any new potential information to the decisionmaking process. Where the preparation of an EIS would serve "no purpose" in light of NEPA's regulatory scheme as a whole, no rule of reason worthy of that title would require an agency to prepare an EIS.

In these circumstances, the underlying policies behind NEPA and Congress' intent, as informed by the "rule of reason," make clear that the causal connection between FMCSA's issuance of the proposed regulations and the entry of the Mexican trucks is insufficient to make FMCSA responsible under NEPA to consider the environmental effects of the entry. * * * Requiring FMCSA to consider the environmental effects of the entry of Mexican trucks would fulfil neither of the[] statutory purposes [of NEPA]. Since FMCSA has no ability categorically to prevent the cross-border operations of Mexican motor carriers, the environmental impact of the cross-border operations would have no effect on FMCSA's decisionmaking—FMCSA simply lacks the power to act on whatever information might be contained in the EIS. Similarly, the informational purpose is not served. The "informational role" of an EIS is to "giv[e] the public the assurance that the agency 'has indeed considered environmental concerns in its decisionmaking process,' *Baltimore Gas & Electric Co.*, and, perhaps more significantly, provid[e] a springboard for public comment" in the agency decisionmaking process itself. The purpose here is to ensure that the "larger audience" can provide input as necessary to the agency making the relevant decisions. * * * But here, the "larger audience" can have no impact on FMCSA's decisionmaking, since, as just noted, FMCSA simply could not act on whatever input this "larger audience" could provide.

It would not, therefore, satisfy NEPA's "rule of reason" to require an agency to prepare a full EIS due to the environmental impact of an action it could not refuse to perform. Put another way, the legally relevant cause of the entry of the Mexican trucks is *not* FMCSA's action, but instead the actions of the President in lifting the moratorium and those of Congress in granting the President this authority while simultaneously limiting FMCSA's discretion. * * *

We hold that where an agency has no ability to prevent a certain effect due to its limited statutory authority over the relevant actions, the agency cannot be considered a legally relevant "cause" of the effect. Hence, under NEPA and the implementing CEQ regulations, the agency need not consider these effects in its EA when determining whether its action is a "major Federal action." Because the President, not FMCSA, could authorize (or not authorize) cross-border operations from Mexican motor carriers, and because FMCSA has no discretion to prevent the entry of Mexican trucks, its EA did not need to consider the environmental effects arising from the entry.

* * * [T]he judgment of the Court of Appeals is reversed, and the case is remanded for further proceedings consistent with this opinion.

Notes and Questions

1.   The Ninth Circuit had found that the EA was "woefully inadequate." As the Supreme Court noted, the EA considered three alternatives and a range of impacts related to public safety and health, noise, air quality and environmental justice. Did the Ninth Circuit have any plausible basis for concluding that the EA was deficient?

2.   The Supreme Court concluded that the FMCSA is not responsible for considering the environmental effects of trucks that it cannot prevent from entering the United States. Is there any reason to limit NEPA's application to those environmental effects that the agency can prevent? On the other hand, wouldn't NEPA's statutory purposes of better governmental decisionmaking and full information disclosure be better served if the agency were to prepare an EIS, even if the power to prevent adverse effects might lie with other agencies or with Congress?

3.   FMSCA estimated that lifting the moratorium could result in 30,000 additional trucks entering the United States, leading to increased emissions from trucks idling during roadside safety inspections. Increased emissions could result in significant effects on air quality. Air pollutants of concern include oxides of nitrogen (NOx) and particulate matter (PM–10), which are emitted with the exhaust fumes of diesel trucks. The Ninth Circuit noted that the petitioners had "pointed to a wealth of government and private studies showing that diesel exhaust and its components constitute a major threat to the health of children, contribute to respiratory illnesses such as asthma and bronchitis, and are likely carcinogenic." 316 F.3d 1002, 1024 (9th Cir. 2003). Under the Clean Air Act, federal agencies may not support activities that violate state air quality implementation plans (SIPs). Did FMCSA act appropriately in deciding not to perform an EIS for increased emissions?

4.   Even when the agency concedes that its action is the proximate cause of environmental effects, issues remain regarding scope of the analysis. Courts have assured the agencies that NEPA does not compel them to venture into the realm of speculation. Even so, assessing cumulative effects of the proposed action, along with other existing and foreseeable future actions in the affected area, often pushes agencies to the very frontiers of scientific knowledge.

[S]cientific uncertainty plagues environmental impact predictions for several reasons. First, the complex nature of the environment involves poorly understood and difficult to determine interactions. Second, the impacts of interest to a decision maker are often those that are impossible to quantify, such as complete loss of a particular area. Third, how and to what extent development will lead to more development is difficult to predict. Finally, an EIS requires analyses of cumulative impacts, which are especially difficult and lead to persistent uncertainty. Specifically, in the NEPA environmental review process, many aspects of both the data used and the decision made involve uncertainty.

Melanie E. Kleiss (Note), *NEPA and Scientific Uncertainty: Using the Precautionary Principle to Bridge the Gap,* 87 Minn. L. Rev. 1215, 1223 (2003) (footnotes omitted).

NATURAL RESOURCES DEFENSE COUNCIL, INC. v. HODEL

United States Court of Appeals, District of Columbia Circuit, 1988.

865 F.2d 288.

Drilling rig in the Gulf of Mexico Oceana, http://northamerica.oceana.org/index.cfm? sectionID=4&fuseaction=news.detail&page ID=1319 (visited Oct. 4, 2004) (photo by the U.S. Department of Interior)

* * * The Outer Continental Shelf Lands Act (OCSLA), 43 U.S.C.A. §§ 1331–1356 (1982), enacted in 1953, authorizes the Secretary of the Interior to sell leases to develop oil and gas deposits in the OCS. * * * [T]he purposes of OCSLA include the "expedited exploration and development of the Outer Continental Shelf in order to achieve national economic and energy policy goals, assure national security, reduce dependence on foreign sources, and maintain a favorable balance of payments in world trade," but these objectives are to be balanced with "protection of the human, marine, and coastal environments." *Id.* § 1802(1)-(2). * * *

[After a series of congressional moratoria against leasing parts of the California OCS and other regions], the Secretary began the development of the five-year [leasing] plan for 1987–1992. * * * [O]n July 2, 1987, Secretary Hodel approved the program at issue in this case. * * *

Petitioners' ... NEPA claim concerns the failure of the FEIS to consider the cumulative impacts of simultaneous development in the Pacific and Alaskan regions on species, particularly whales and salmon, that migrate through the different planning areas. Petitioners contend that the cumulative impact of simultaneous development will be greater than the sum of development in each area considered separately because migratory species will have to swim through each area, with no respite from the harmful effects of OCS development. Because of the "synergistic" effect of this development, petitioners argue, the FEIS should have considered the cumulative impact of simultaneous development on migratory species, and not just the separate effects in each planning area. Had the Secretary done so, they reason, he might have cancelled or deferred some of the lease sales in the two regions so that migratory species would not be exposed to maximum risks throughout their habitat simultaneously.

The Secretary responds simply that the FEIS *does* touch on cumulative impacts. He does not contest petitioners' claim that maximum development in the region will be allowed to occur simultaneously and that cumulative impacts on migratory species may be severe. * * * In this case, the Environmental Protection Agency (EPA) expressed serious concern to the Secretary over the lack of any consideration in the DEIS of inter-regional cumulative impacts. The EPA criticized the DEIS for not analyzing "the cumulative effects on migratory species whose habitat extends into numerous planning basins and regions" and admonished the Secretary to "identify the migratory species of endangered cetaceans, marine mammals, and marine and coastal birds and the full extent of each species' distribution (the full range of their habitat)" and to "include all state and federal oil and gas leasing, oil and gas infrastructure, and non-OCS/non-oil-and-gas activities that fall within their distribution." FEIS, App. E, May 9, 1986 Letter from EPA.

The Secretary asserts that, in response to the EPA's letter, the Department of the Interior added the requisite analysis to the FEIS. Although the FEIS contains sections headed "Cumulative Impacts," in truth, nothing in the FEIS provides the requisite analysis. The FEIS for the most part considers only the impact *within each area* of non-OCS actions plus OCS development and not the impact of simultaneous OCS development in different areas. The few times the FEIS *does* discuss the impact of simultaneous OCS development in different areas, it makes only conclusory remarks, statements that do not equip a decisionmaker to make an informed decision about alternative courses of action or a court to review the Secretary's reasoning. * * * This type of statement does not address the issue raised by the EPA, and which NEPA requires the Secretary to consider: the cumulative impacts of *OCS development* in *different* areas. * * *

The FEIS does devote a few more sentences here to the inter-regional effects on migrating species but these snippets do not constitute real analysis; they merely state (and restate) the obvious:

> Those species which pass through other areas with potentially high risk of an oil spill (such as California) are most vulnerable to high impacts from a spill. For example, the coastal migration routes of the California gray whale which could subject a large segment of the population to an oil spill. [sic] * * * Migrating species are subjected to stresses from anthropogenic sources throughout their range.

FEIS IV.B.7.–33.

The Secretary asserts that this treatment typifies the approach used in the FEIS for the other planning areas.... "Typifies" is an understatement. When the FEIS does address *inter*-regional cumulative impacts, it simply repeats the same boilerplate for each area, varying the language only slightly in each instance. Even under the applicable deferential standard of review, we believe that allowing the Secretary's "analysis" to pass muster here would eviscerate NEPA. In each place in which the FEIS even mentions inter-regional impacts of OCS development, it merely announces that migratory species may be exposed to risks of oil spills and other "impacts" throughout their routes. These perfunctory references do not constitute analysis useful to a decisionmaker in deciding whether, or how, to alter the program to lessen cumulative environmental impacts. * * * We therefore remand this matter to the Secretary for further consideration and any revisions in the five-year program that consideration may warrant.

Notes and Questions

1. The court's examination of the FEIS at issue in *NRDC v. Hodel* convinced it that the Secretary of Interior failed to consider the effect of simultaneous inter-regional oil and gas development on migratory species. As this case illustrates, it is not necessarily enough to look solely at the proposal itself, or to limit the inquiry to the effects of the proposal in the immediate project area.

2. In spite of the deferential standard of review, courts are willing to look behind "boilerplate" or "perfunctory references" to ensure that the agency "shows its work"–a bit like high school algebra–and supports it with thorough and well-reasoned analysis and explication. In Klamath–Siskiyou Wildlands Center v. BLM, 387 F.3d 989 (9th Cir. 2004), the court remanded EAs for two timber sales in the same watershed because they had failed to present more than a "perfunctory" assessment of cumulative effects on water quality and spotted owl habitat. The EAs merely described the effects in various tables and appendices that provided conclusory "checklists" rather than an objective quantification of the degree of impacts. *Id.* at 994. Is there anything inherently wrong with using boilerplate language? Should an agency be forced to "recreate the wheel" every time it prepares an EIS or EA, particularly when it is examining similar activities?

3. Defining the relevant area of analysis can be a challenging job when it comes to assessing indirect and cumulative effects. Exactly how far must the agency go in any given case? The geographic boundaries of an EIS are defined by the scope of the project as well as the physical features of the affected area. Selkirk Cons. Alliance v. Forsgren, 336 F.3d 944, 958 (9th Cir. 2003). The EIS's scope may be defined, for example, by watershed boundaries, Blue Mountains Biodiversity Project v. Blackwood, 161 F.3d 1208, 1214–15 (9th Cir. 1998), *cert. denied*, 527 U.S. 1003, 119 S.Ct. 2337, 144 L.Ed.2d 235 (1999), or by the range of the affected resource. In Kern v. U.S. Bureau of Land Management, 284 F.3d 1062, 1079 (9th Cir.2002), the court held that a cumulative impact analysis must include all "reasonably foreseeable future actions" within the range of the Port Orford Cedar, the affected resource at issue, but in Idaho Sporting Congress, Inc. v. Rittenhouse, 305 F.3d 957, 973 (9th Cir. 2002), the Forest Service's choice of a species' "home range" as the scale of analysis was rejected as arbitrary when its own scientists emphasized that cumulative effects "*must* be addressed at a landscape scale." In some cases, the scope of the impact analysis may be limited to conditions within the proposal's immediate footprint. *See* Muckleshoot Indian Tribe v. U.S. Forest Service, 177 F.3d 800, 809–10 (9th Cir.1999). So long as there is a reasoned basis for the determination (there wasn't in *NRDC v. Hodel*), courts are generally willing to defer to the agency regarding the appropriate geographic region for analysis. *See* Kleppe v. Sierra Club, 427 U.S. 390, 412, 96 S.Ct. 2718, 49 L.Ed.2d 576 (1976) (finding that an EIS for coal leasing was not required for the Great Plains region when the only existing proposals for action were either local or national in scope); Neighbors of Cuddy Mountain v. Alexander, 303 F.3d 1059 (9th Cir. 2002) (holding that an EIS that analyzed cumulative effects of a proposed timber sale in only one area of the forest was adequate, because it took into account all past and proposed sales and concluded that sufficient old growth would remain in the affected area); *Selkirk Cons. Alliance,* 336 F.3d at 959 (finding that an EIS properly excluded an adjacent area in a different watershed with different topography).

4. An EA must take a "hard look" at potential effects, but as is the case with respect to the alternatives analysis, EAs need only provide a "brief discussion" of effects. 40 C.F.R. § 1508.9(b). As a result, EAs need not be as exhaustive as EISs in their treatment of effects. *See Idaho Sporting Congress*, 305 F.3d at 974 (finding that the cumulative effects analysis was inadequate for an EIS, but acceptable for an EA). The use of an EA will not, however, allow agencies to avoid considering indirect and cumulative effects. *See* Native Ecosystems Council v. Dombeck, 304 F.3d 886, 895–96 (9th Cir. 2002) (concluding that an EA had failed to give adequate consideration to the cumulative impacts of the Forest Service's decision to waive its road density standards for a proposed timber sale and for other activities in the project area). And don't forget that the revelation of significant effects on the human environment will warrant a full EIS. Did the EA at issue in the Padre Island National Seashore problem, Section III.E.2, *supra*, take a hard look at the potential environmental effects posed by the proposal to allow oil and gas exploration?

2. *Segmentation*

Connected or closely related actions must be considered in a single EIS. *See* 40 C.F.R. § 1508.25(a)(1); National Wildlife Federation v. FERC, 912 F.2d 1471 (D.C. Cir. 1990). The CEQ regulations preclude segmentation of proposals that:

(i) Automatically trigger other actions which may require environmental impact statements;

(ii) cannot or will not proceed unless other actions are taken previously or simultaneously; or

(iii) are interdependent parts of a large action and depend on the larger action for their justification.

40 C.F.R. § 1508.25(a)(1). *See id.* § 1508.8(a)(1) (defining "connected action" as one that "cannot or will not proceed unless other actions are taken previously or simultaneously"). However, if the proposed actions are merely "similar," but not connected, "agencies 'may wish' to assess them in the same document and 'should do so' when a single document provides 'the best way to assess adequately the combined impacts of similar actions.... ' " Klamath–Siskiyou Wildlands Center v. BLM, 387 F.3d 989 (9th Cir. 2004) (citing 40 C.F.R. § 1508.25(a)(3)).

Forcing an agency to analyze connected actions in a single EIS prevents it from "short-circuiting" NEPA or disguising the cumulative effects of related actions by isolating an individual action that, by itself, may not have a significant environmental impact. Citizens' Comm. to Save Our Canyons v. U.S. Forest Service, 297 F.3d 1012 (10th Cir. 2002). Segmentation into separate analytical parts is prohibited if the project in question will foreclose the opportunity to consider future alternatives or irretrievably commit federal funds for closely related projects. *See* Utahns for Better Transp. v. U.S. Dept. of Transp., 305 F.3d 1152, 1183 (10th Cir. 2002), *modified in part on other grounds,* 319 F.3d 1207 (10th Cir. 2003); Piedmont Heights Civic Club, Inc. v. Moreland, 637 F.2d 430, 439 (5th Cir.1981).

Courts have found that proposed actions are connected when one action could not occur "but for" the occurrence of the other. In Thomas v. Peterson, 753 F.2d 754, 758 (9th Cir. 1985), for example, a timber sale and the construction of a road necessary to access the timber were considered connected actions requiring a single EIS because the timber sales could not proceed without the road. Likewise, in Sierra Club v. United States, 255 F.Supp.2d 1177, 1184 (D.Colo. 2002), the court held that a gravel mining operation and an easement for a road to be used in a proposed expansion of the mine were connected actions because they were inextricably linked: "[b]ut for the road, the mining company could not access the mine site; absent the mine, there is no independent utility for the access road." In contrast, in Northwest Res. Info. Center, Inc. v. National Marine Fisheries Serv., Inc., 56 F.3d 1060, 1069 (9th Cir. 1995), the court concluded that transportation and flow improvement plans could exist without one another, and in *Native Ecosystems Council*, 304 F.3d at 894, it held that each of a dozen timber sales within one national Forest unit could go forward regardless of the others. As a result, each project could be addressed in separate analyses. The EA at issue in *Native Ecosystems Council* was found inadequate, however, for failure to analyze cumulative effects of the sales' impacts on unroaded habitat in the Forest. *Id.* at 895–96. A similar result was reached in *Klamath-Siskiyou Wildlands Center*, 387 F.3d at 997, where the court remanded two EAs for two timber sales in the same watershed because the EAs had failed to present more than a "perfunctory" assessment of cumulative effects, but refused to require the agency to combine the two EAs into one document. *Id.*

Segmentation challenges frequently come up in the context of highways and other transportation projects. The Federal Highway Administration's NEPA regulations provide that a transportation project may be assessed independently if it: (1) has independent utility or significance as a usable passageway and a reasonable expenditure; (2) does not restrict options for other reasonably foreseeable improvements; and (3) connects logical termini and is of sufficient length to address environmental issues on a broad scope. *See* 23 C.F.R. § 771.111(f) (1992). The "logical termini" factor is "designed to weed out projects which are pretextually segmented and for which there is no independent reason to exist[,] ... no life of its own, or is simply illogical when viewed in isolation.... " Macht v. Skinner, 715 F.Supp. 1131, 1135 (D.D.C. 1989). If a highway leads nowhere, it is "a good sign that segmentation is utterly pretextual." Swain v. Brinegar, 542 F.2d 364, 370 (7th Cir. 1976).

The Tenth Circuit Court of Appeals applied the "independent utility" test to an EIS for a development plan for the expansion of a private ski resort on "checkerboard" federal and private lands in Citizens' Comm. to Save Our Canyons v. U.S. Forest Service, 297 F.3d 1012 (10th Cir. 2002) (a different portion of the opinion is provided in section IV.B, above). It found that the EIS had not improperly segmented the proposal from a land exchange between the developer and the Forest Service, because the resort would have grown in accordance with the master development plan regardless of whether additional lands were acquired through the exchange. *Id.* at 1023–24. In other words, the land exchange and the development plan were not dependent upon one another for their justification; they had independent utility. *Id.*

Notes and Questions

1. In Wetlands Action Network v. U.S. Army Corps of Engineers, 222 F.3d 1105 (9th Cir. 2000), cert. denied, 534 U.S. 815, 122 S.Ct. 41, 151 L.Ed.2d 14 (2001), the court held that the Corps did not have to analyze the effects of an entire 1,000 acre development project, which would include residential areas, a marina, hotels, retail establishments, and entertainment venues, in order to grant a permit to fill a 16–acre wetlands portion. It reasoned that the substantive statutes in question gave the Corps jurisdic-

tion over water but not the uplands, which comprised the remainder of the development project, and that the upland portions of the project could proceed without the Corps' permit. *Id.* at 1118. Would the actions have been considered "connected" if the developer chose the site solely because of its proximity to water? Is it ever possible to provide a thorough assessment of cumulative impacts without studying the entire project? *See* 40 C.F.R. § 1508.7-.8 (discussed in Section IV.C.1, *supra*).

2.   In Sierra Club v. Marsh, 769 F.2d 868, 877 (1st Cir. 1985), the First Circuit required the Corps to prepare an EIS for the construction of a major oil terminal to be built by the State of Maine, along with consequential industrial development, even though the Corps' involvement was limited to issuing a permit for a causeway to access the terminal. How can this result be squared with *Wetlands Action*? Is it consistent with *Citizens' Comm. to Save Our Canyons*, 297 F.3d at 1023–24? The court believed that, "once Maine completes the causeway and port, pressure to develop the rest of the island could well prove irreversible." *Sierra Club*, 769 F.2d at 879.

3.   CEQ regulations on connected actions forbid segmentation in the EIS context. Courts have also applied the rule against segmentation to EAs. *See, e.g., Wetlands Action Network*, 222 F.3d at 1118; *Native Ecosystems Council*, 304 F.3d at 894.

3.   *Programmatic EISs and Tiering*

One way to handle interrelated projects is to prepare a "programmatic" EIS covering all aspects of the proposed action and related proposals. The agency can subsequently "tier" its analyses for related individual or site-specific projects to the programmatic EIS without having to "recreate the wheel." Scientists' Inst. for Public Information, Inc. v. Atomic Energy Comm'n, 481 F.2d 1079 (D.C. Cir. 1973). Tiering helps an agency consider environmental effects and alternatives at the earliest possible stage, and allows it to streamline its subsequent analyses when related actions are proposed. *See* 40 C.F.R. § 1502.20.

The downside of programmatic EISs is that their analyses can be quite generic. A generalized assessment is acceptable, however, so long as subsequent analyses of site-specific actions are within the scope of the programmatic EIS and address project alternatives and impacts with specificity. In Park County Resource Council, Inc. v. U.S. Dept. of Agriculture, the court held that a comprehensive EIS was not required for the issuance of an oil and gas lease on national forest land, where a lengthy EA had already been prepared for the agency's leasing program and appropriate restrictions could be required in subsequent permits to drill, which would entail further, more detailed analysis before surface disturbance commenced. Park County Resource Council, Inc. v. U.S. Dept. of Agriculture, 817 F.2d 609 (10th Cir. 1987), *overruled on other grounds by* Village of Los Ranchos De Albuquerque v. Marsh, 956 F.2d 970 (10th Cir. 1992). Conversely, in Pennaco Energy, Inc. v. U.S. Department of Interior, 377 F.3d 1147 (10th Cir. 2004), the Tenth Circuit found that the BLM had failed to prepare an adequate pre-lease analysis on three oil and gas leases for coal bed methane (CBM) development in the Powder River Basin, Wyoming, and that its attempt to rely on two previous EISs was erroneous. A programmatic EIS on the 1985 Resource Management Plan for the area did not contemplate CBM development, which had only recently begun to occur and which raised unique water and air quality concerns. *Id.* at 1157–1159. Further, although a second analysis, the 1999 Wyodak EIS, assessed the impacts of developing CBM properties for approximately 5,000 wells in the area, it related to previously issued leases and did not consider pre-leasing options, such as not leasing an area at all. *Id.* at 1160.

To the extent that tiering is appropriate in any given case, a subsequent EIS or EA can only tier to an analysis which itself was subject to NEPA review. In Kern v. U.S. Bureau of Land Mgmt., 284 F.3d 1062 (9th Cir. 2002), the court held that the EIS for a resource management plan could not tier to the agency's internal mitigation guidelines when the guidelines were never subject to NEPA review.

D. Consideration of Public Comments

NEPA documents are to be written in "plain language ... so that decisionmakers and the public can readily understand them." 40 C.F.R. § 1502.8. EISs and EAs are "unacceptable if they are indecipherable to the public." Klamath–Siskiyou Wildlands Center v. BLM, 387 F.3d 989, 996 (9th Cir. 2004). This "plain language" requirement allows the public to inform and involve itself in the decisionmaking process in a meaningful fashion.

Public comments included in a final EIS are to be regarded as an integral part of the statement. National Helium Corp. v. Morton, 486 F.2d 995, 1003 (10th Cir. 1973), cert. denied, 416 U.S. 993, 94 S.Ct. 2405, 40 L.Ed.2d 772 (1974). *See* 40 C.F.R. § 1502.9 (Section IV.A, *supra*). Failure to consider public comments in a meaningful fashion and to respond to all legitimate concerns can render an EIS inadequate. *See* Public Citizen v. Department of Transportation, 316 F.3d 1002 (9th Cir. 2003), *rev'd on other grounds*, 541 U.S. 752, 124 S.Ct. 2204, 159 L.Ed.2d 60 (2004).

Other agencies, such as the U.S. Environmental Protection Agency, may provide scientific critiques or commentary regarding an EIS's analysis of effects and other pertinent aspects of the proposal. The lead agency must give "serious consideration" to the opinions of other experts, including other agencies with expertise on a relevant issue. In Center for Biological Diversity v. U.S. Forest Service, 349 F.3d 1157, 1168 (9th Cir. 2003), the court held that the Forest Service must respond specifically to a critique by the State Department of Game and Fish regarding key habitat management in the EIS itself; it was not enough to attach a summary of the opposing viewpoints to the EIS. *Id.*

Agencies are entitled to rely on the view of their own qualified experts, and need not defer to others, so long as they articulate a reasoned basis for the disagreement. *See* Texas Committee on Natural Resources v. Marsh, 736 F.2d 262, 268 (5th Cir.1984); *Hughes River Watershed Conservancy,* 165 F.3d at 288 (citing *Oregon Natural Resources Council,* 490 U.S. at 378–85). Courts are especially deferential when reviewing the agency's scientific fact-finding: "We must look at the decision not as the chemist, biologist, or statistician that we are qualified neither by training nor experience to be, but as a reviewing court exercising our narrowly defined duty of holding agencies to certain minimal standards of rationality." Stewart v. Potts, 126 F.Supp.2d 428, 434 (S.D.Tex. 2000), *aff'd,* 34 Fed.Appx. 152, 2002 WL 496389 (5th Cir.2002) (citing Ethyl Corp. v. Environmental Protection Agency, 541 F.2d 1, 36 (D.C.Cir.1976) (en banc) (footnote omitted)).

V. NEW INFORMATION AND SUPPLEMENTAL EISs

After the EIS is issued, a supplemental EIS will be warranted if substantial changes are made in the proposed action, *see* 40 C.F.R. § 1502.9(c)(1); Dubois v. United States Dept. of Agriculture, 102 F.3d 1273 (1st Cir.1996), *cert. denied,* Loon Mountain Recreation Corp. v. Dubois, 521 U.S. 1119, 117 S.Ct. 2510, 138 L.Ed.2d 1013 (1997), or new circumstances or information arises demonstrating that the action will have significant effects on the environment that were not considered in the original EIS, *see* Marsh v. Oregon Natural Resources Council, 490 U.S. 360, 109 S.Ct. 1851, 104 L.Ed.2d 377 (1989). Courts will only set aside an agency's decision not to prepare a supplemental EIS if the decision is "arbitrary and capricious." *See id.* at 376; Ross v. Federal Highway Admin., 162 F.3d 1046 (10th Cir. 1998).

---

§ 1502.9 Draft, final, and supplemental statements.

* * *

(c) Agencies:

(1) Shall prepare supplements to either draft or final environmental impact statements if:

   (i) The agency makes substantial changes in the proposed action that are relevant to environmental concerns; or

   (ii) There are significant new circumstances or information relevant to environmental concerns and bearing on the proposed action or its impacts.

   * * *

(4) Shall prepare, circulate, and file a supplement to a statement in the same fashion (exclusive of scoping) as a draft and final statement unless alternative procedures are approved by the Council.

A. When is a Supplemental EIS Required?

The Supreme Court has explained that an agency's conclusions regarding the significance of new information is a fact-based, technical matter entitled to substantial deference. *Oregon Natural Resources Council*, 490 U.S. at 377. As the following case indicates, courts seem to be somewhat less deferential when agencies fail to prepare supplemental analyses after making major changes in their proposals.

DUBOIS v. UNITED STATES DEPARTMENT OF AGRICULTURE

United States Court of Appeals, First Circuit, 1996.
102 F.3d 1273, *cert. denied*, Loon Mountain Recreation Corp. v. Dubois,
521 U.S. 1119, 117 S.Ct. 2510, 138 L.Ed.2d 1013 (1997).

The defendant-intervenor Loon Mountain Recreation Corporation ("Loon Corp.") operates a ski resort in the White Mountain National Forest in Lincoln, New Hampshire. In order to expand its skiing facilities, Loon Corp. sought and received a permit to do so from the United States Forest Service. Appellant Roland Dubois sued the Forest Service alleging violations of the National Environmental Policy Act ("NEPA"), 42 U.S.C.A. § 4321, et seq. Appellant RESTORE: The North Woods intervened as a plaintiff claiming violations of the same statutes, and appellee Loon Corp. intervened as a defendant. * * *

The White Mountain National Forest ("WMNF") is a public resource managed by the United States Forest Service for a wide range of competing public uses and purposes, including "outdoor recreation, range, timber, watershed, ... wildlife and fish purposes," 16 U.S.C.A. § 528 (1994), and skiing, 16 U.S.C.A. § 497(b) (1994). * * *

Loon Pond is located in the WMNF at an elevation of 2,400 feet. It has a surface area of 19 acres, with shallow areas around the perimeter and a central bowl 65 feet deep. It is unusual for its relatively pristine nature. There is virtually no human activity within the land it drains except skiing at the privately owned Loon Mountain Ski Area. * * *

Loon Corp. owns the Loon Mountain Ski Area, which has operated since the 1960s not far from Loon Pond. Prior to the permit revision that gave rise to this litigation, Loon Corp. held a special use permit to operate on 785 acres of WMNF land. That permit allowed Loon Corp. to draw water ("drawdown") for snowmaking from Loon Pond, as well as from the East Branch of the Pemigewasset River ("East Branch") and from nearby Boyle Brook. * * * In addition to being used as a source of water for snowmaking, Loon Pond has been the repository for disposal of water after it is pumped through the snowmaking system. * * *

In 1986, Loon Corp. applied to the Forest Service for an amendment to its special use permit to allow expansion of its facilities within the WMNF. Pursuant to NEPA, 42 U.S.C.A. § 4332, the Service developed a draft EIS, and a supplement to the draft. Responding to criticism of the adequacy of those documents, the Forest Service issued a revised draft EIS ("RDEIS"), which ... set forth five alternatives to meet the perceived demand for additional alpine skiing. All five were located at the Loon Mountain site. * * *

During the EIS process, Ron Buso, a hydrologist for the WMNF, expressed concern to another Forest Service hydrologist that the proposed drawdown of Loon Pond by twenty feet was likely to have a severe impact on the Pond. * * * According to Buso ..., the increase in the Pond's acidity due to the planned drawdown would change the chemistry of the Pond, cause toxic metals to be released from the sediment, and kill naturally occurring organisms.

Without addressing the issues raised in the Buso memorandum ..., the Forest Service prepared a Final EIS ("FEIS"). The FEIS added a sixth alternative, also on the Loon Mountain site. The new alternative provided for expansion of Loon Corp.'s permit area by 581 acres and for the construction of one new lift and approximately 70 acres of new ski trails, changes designed to accommodate 3,200 additional skiers per day (from the current 5,800 per day). The Forest Service deemed Alternative 6 as the preferred alternative. Under it, Loon Corp. would more than double the amount of water used for snowmaking, from 67 million gallons per year to 138 million gallons. Seventeen million gallons of the increase would be drawn from the East Branch, and 54 million gallons from Loon Pond. In addition, Loon Corp. was authorized to draw the Pond down for snowmaking by fifteen feet, compared to the current eighteen inches. * * * In March 1993, the Forest Service published a Record of Decision (ROD) adopting Alternative 6.

As a mitigation measure to blunt the adverse environmental impact on Loon Pond, the Forest Service required Loon Corp. to pump water from the East Branch to Loon Pond in December and May of each year if the Pond was not otherwise full at those times. In its FEIS, the Forest Service recognized that the ... transfer of East Branch water to Loon Pond ... would introduce pollutants into the Pond. * * * Neither the FEIS nor the ROD set any limits, however, on the level of non-bacterial organisms such as Giardia lambia or on pollutants such as phosphorus that may be present in the transferred water. * * * It did, however, provide a series of restrictions and monitoring requirements for water levels and water quality, including daily testing for turbidity, bacteria, and oil and grease.[4] * * *

Plaintiffs ... appeal the district court's conclusion that the Forest Service was not required, under NEPA, to prepare a supplemental EIS. The question of a supplemental EIS is premised on the dual purposes of the EIS: to assure that the public who might be affected by the proposed project be fully informed of the proposal, its impacts and all major points of view; and to give the agency the benefit of informed comments and suggestions as it takes a "hard look" at the consequences of proposed actions. See Robertson, 490 U.S. at 349, 356; 40 C.F.R. §§ 1502.1, 1502.9(a) (1995).

---

4. In response to an earlier draft EIS, the EPA had expressed the following concern: "While monitoring plans have merit, they should not be considered a substitute for a thorough evaluation of a project and its potential impacts prior to action approval."

An agency "shall" prepare a supplemental EIS if, after issuing its latest draft EIS, "the agency makes substantial changes in the proposed action that are relevant to environmental concerns." 40 C.F.R. § 1502.9(c)(1)(i) (1995). The use of the word "shall" is mandatory, not precatory. * * * Thus, as explained by CEQ, an additional alternative that has not been disseminated previously in a draft EIS may be adopted in a final EIS, without further public comment, only if it is "qualitatively within the spectrum of alternatives that were discussed" in the prior draft; otherwise a supplemental draft is needed. See Forty Most Asked Questions Concerning CEQ's NEPA Regulations, 46 Fed. Reg. 18026, #29b (1981).

Plaintiffs argue that the project proposed as Alternative 6, appearing for the first time in the Final EIS, embodies "substantial changes" from any of the alternatives in the prior drafts of the EIS, and that those changes are "relevant to environmental concerns." See 40 C.F.R. § 1502.9(c)(1)(i). Therefore, plaintiffs assert that, by not describing Alternative 6 in a supplemental EIS—which would give the public an opportunity to comment on it ...—the Forest Service collided with both the public information and the agency guidance objectives of NEPA. In response, defendants argue that ... Alternative 6 is merely a scaled-down modification of Alternative 2 which, as proposed in two phases in the RDEIS, would have been far larger and far more intrusive on the environment than the new Alternative 6. * * *

We conclude, based on the record in this case, that a supplemental EIS was required. The scope of review of a reviewing court is the APA's "arbitrary and capricious" standard. *Marsh*, 490 U.S. at 375–76. The Court in *Marsh* was especially deferential to the "informed discretion of the responsible federal agencies," due to the "high level of technical expertise" required in that case .... In the instant case, however, nothing in the FEIS indicates that any such technically complex scientific analysis would be required in order for this court to determine that Alternative 6 involves a "substantial change" from the prior proposals at Loon Mountain.

Alternative 6, adopted by the Forest Service as its preferred alternative in the final EIS, does not fall "within the spectrum of alternatives" that were considered in previous drafts .... Alternative 6 entails a different configuration of activities and locations, not merely a reduced version of a previously-considered alternative. Phase II of Alternative 2 proposed expanding the ski area primarily on land that is not within the current permit area; in contrast, Alternative 6 squeezes much of its expansion into that current permit area. To accomplish this, Alternative 6 widens existing trails so as to eliminate buffers that currently separate the trails. It also envisions a 28,500–square-foot base lodge facility within the existing permit area. And it develops ski trails, access roads and lifts on land that the prior alternatives had left as a woodland buffer between the old ski area and the proposed expansion area. These are substantial changes from the previously-discussed alternatives, not mere modifications "within the spectrum" of those prior alternatives. It would be one thing if the Forest Service had adopted a new alternative that was actually within the range of previously considered alternatives, e.g., simply reducing the scale of every relevant particular. It is quite another thing to adopt a proposal that is configured differently, in which case public commenters might have pointed out, if given the opportunity ... wholly new problems posed by the new configuration * * *

Nor can it be said that these changes are not "relevant to environmental concerns." They could very well have environmental impacts that the Forest Service has not yet considered, simply based on their more compact physical location. * * * Moreover, the plan selected, Alternative 6 in the FEIS, would require that four million gallons more water be withdrawn annually for snowmaking, compared with the closest alternative among the five previously given detailed consideration. Whether or not viewed in the graphic terms described by plaintiff RESTORE—four million gallons annually is enough water "to create a lake the size of a football field more than eleven feet deep"—this change can be expected to have a significant enough effect on the environment that additional analysis through a supplemental EIS would be required. We conclude, based on the record in this case, that Alternative 6 entails substantial changes from the previously proposed actions that are relevant to environmental concerns, and that the Forest Service did not present those changes to the public in its FEIS for review and comment. Accordingly, the failure to prepare a supplemental EIS was arbitrary and capricious. * * *

Notes and Questions

1. Would the NPS have to prepare a supplemental EA or EIS in the Padre Island Seashore case above, *supra* at Section III.E.2, if a Mondo Oil employee discovers the nest of a rare migratory bird had never seen before in the project area? What if instead a new study was issued by reputable non-governmental scientists just a few days after the FONSI was issued, stating that the population of Kemps Ridley Sea Turtle has declined to only 700 known adults, not 2,000 as previously thought? The report goes on to say that 50% of the turtles, not 20%, nest on or near Padre Island. Is a supplemental analysis required before Mondo may move forward with its plans?

2. Does the obligation to prepare supplemental NEPA analyses extend in perpetuity, throughout the life of a project? In Norton v. Southern Utah Wilderness Alliance, 542 U.S. 55, 124 S.Ct. 2373, 159 L.Ed.2d 137 (2004), the Supreme Court said no. Plaintiffs argued that the Bureau of Land Management must prepare a supplemental EIS on its land use plan for an area that had experienced a dramatic increase in the use of off-road vehicles. The Court rejected the argument on the ground that no "major federal action" had yet to occur; the action was completed when the land use plan was approved in 1991. *Id.* at 2385.

3. If an agency does prepare a supplemental EIS, what factors will the courts consider to determine whether it is adequate? In Mississippi River

Basin Alliance v. Westphal, 230 F.3d 170 (5th Cir. 2000), the Corps of Engineers' supplemental EIS was upheld because it provided sufficiently rigorous consideration of the cumulative impacts of ongoing, proposed, and reasonably foreseeable future actions and alternatives to allow appropriate public assessment of a flood control project. The court explained that the supplement must satisfy the same criteria as an EIS to pass muster. *Id.* at 174.

B. Case Study—Glamis Imperial Gold Mine

Glamis Imperial Gold Mine: Overview of Proposed Mine and Process Area, U.S. Dept. of Interior Bureau of Land Management, Imperial Project FEIS App. L, p.23 (Sept. 2000)

Glamis Imperial Gold Corp. submitted a proposed plan of operations to the Bureau of Land Management (BLM) to construct and operate a huge gold mine on its unpatented mining claims on 1,570 acres in the California Desert Conservation Area in 1995. *See infra* Chapter 12 (discussing requirements of the Mining Law of 1872). As described in the press release below, the BLM prepared multiple analyses on the proposal over the course of the next few years, including a draft EIS, a supplement to the draft EIS, and a final EIS. The final EIS was issued in 2000. It identified five alternatives of varying degrees of intensity, ranging from the proposal for high intensity mining operations to a no action alternative. The high intensity proposal advanced by the company calls for the removal of 450 million tons of rock and ore over the life of the project, along with three large open pits up to 900 feet deep, a heap leach facility (consisting of a heap leach pad and processing ponds), a precious metal recovery plant, an electric substation, and multiple waste rock and soil stockpiles up to 30 stories high.

Numerous commentators, including the Quechan Indian Tribe and the Advisory Council for Historic Preservation, stated that the project's effects on historic and cultural resources in the area would be devastating and could not be mitigated. The U.S. EPA's report on the draft EIS expressed concerns about damage to seasonal wetlands, as well as cultural sites and fossil beds. *See* www.epa.gov/region9/annualreport/00/gg.html. The BLM, in its final EIS, reviewed the comments and concluded that the majority of them were consistent with the no action alternative, *i.e.,* denial of the plan of operations. A Record of Decision was issued in January 2001, in the waning days of the Clinton Administration, denying approval for the plan.

Office of the Secretary   **For Immediate Release: January 17, 2001**

Secretary Babbitt Denies Gold Mine in
Imperial County, California

Citing impacts to nationally significant historic resources and Native American values that cannot be adequately mitigated to meet requirements of Federal law, Secretary of the Interior Bruce Babbitt today signed a decision denying an open pit, cyanide heap leach mining project proposed on public lands in eastern Imperial County, Calif. ***

The decision signed by the Secretary, as recommended by Bureau of Land Management (BLM) which administers the public lands involved, is based upon the following***:

- the proposed project is located in an area determined to have nationally significant Native American values and historic properties and would cause unavoidable adverse impacts to these resources.

- the proposed project will result in unavoidable adverse impacts to visual quality in this substantially undisturbed landscape.

- the impacts of the proposed project cannot be mitigated to the point of meeting the statutory requirement in the 1976 Federal Land Policy and Management Act (FLPMA) that BLM must prevent "undue impairment" of the public lands in the Congressionally designated California Desert Conservation Area (CDCA). ***

- the identified unavoidable and adverse environmental impacts resulting from the project override the possible economic benefits that might be derived from the project.

- the proposed project fails to meet the overall statutory requirement in FLPMA that BLM prevent "unnecessary or undue degradation" of the public land resources.

The determination that the area involved contains nationally significant cultural and historic resources and Native American values critical to the nearby Quechan Indian Tribe is based upon extensive study and documentation supported by findings of the Advisory Council on Historic Preservation (ACHP). The ACHP advised the Department that the project, even with all feasible mitigation measures, would result in "serious and irreparable degradation of the sacred and historic values" in the area and would "effectively destroy" the identified national historic resources. ***

http://www.ca.blm.gov/news/2001/01/nr/imperial_project_rod_nr.html

Months later, officials in the George W. Bush Administration revisited the January 2001 decision and decided to change course, based on new executive policies and a determination that the governing statutes, including FLPMA, did not authorize denial of Glamis's plan of operations. The implications of this determination are discussed below.

Interior rules mine claims valid

By Daschell Phillips, *Imperial Valley Press,* Sept. 30, 2002
http://www.ivpressonline.com/ articles/2002/10/01/export15227.txt

WASHINGTON (MNS)—The U.S. Department of Interior ruled Friday that the claims on a proposed gold mine in eastern Imperial County are valid, bringing development of the mine one step closer despite earlier arguments that it would be harmful to tribal lands. * * *

The move brought protests from American Indian rights supporters. "Once again the Interior Department has demonstrated a callous disregard for Native American culture," said Rep. Nick J. Rahall (D–W.Va.), ranking Democrat on the House Resources Committee. "First the administration revoked the order to protect this sacred area. Now, after ignoring its responsibility to consult with Indian country, the department is paving the way for corporate interests over historic, cultural and religious preservation."

Indian Pass has been named one of the 11 most endangered historical sites in the United States by the National Trust for Historic Preservation. The area is considered a sacred site by the Quechan tribe, which is based at Fort Yuma Indian Reservation in Arizona. * * *

The Department of the Interior's next step is to review the [EIS] ... to determine whether to approve or deny the mine, according to Jan Bedrosian, a spokeswoman for the Bureau of Land Management.* * *

Notes and Questions

1. Opponents of the Glamis project claim that the BLM must prepare an SEIS before it can go forward and grant approval for the plan at this juncture. Is an SEIS warranted? Review 40 C.F.R. § 1502.9(c), *supra.* Is there significant new information or a new or revised proposal that would compel an SEIS? Would it be worthwhile to provide additional time for public comment on the Bush Administration's decision? What if the preferred alternative identified in the initial NEPA documents, prior to 2001, was "no action" (denial of the plan), and public comments had been tailored to that outcome?

2. Would opponents of the project be successful in their challenge to the EIS if the "no action" alternative was not a "no-development" alternative, but instead envisioned some mineral development? Assume that the BLM argues, in defense of this so-called "no action" alternative, that once Glamis had discovered a "valuable mineral deposit" on the federal lands it had a right to proceed with development under the 1872 Mining Law.

3.   It isn't unusual for new administrations to change their stance on discretionary activities or policies adopted by previous administrations. Does NEPA provide any legal basis for prohibiting a new administration from adopting a new position on a mining proposal such as Glamis'? In Fund for Animals v. Norton, *supra,* Chapter 3.III.B.1, 294 F.Supp.2d 92, 105–111 (D.D.C 2003), the Park Service's 2003 decision to allow snowmobiling in Yellowstone National Park came under fire. Just two years earlier, the Park Service had adopted a snowmobiling phase-out. The court concluded that this reversal in policy, with only a cursory explanation, violated both NEPA and the APA.

> This dramatic change in course, in a relatively short period of time and conspicuously timed with the change in administrations, represents precisely the "reversal of the agency's views" that triggers an agency's responsibility to supply a reasoned explanation for the change. * * * The gap between the decision made in 2001, and the decision made in 2003 is stark. In 2001, the rulemaking process culminated in a finding that snowmobiling so adversely impacted the wildlife and resources of the Parks that all snowmobile use must be halted. A scant three years later, the rulemaking process culminated in the conclusion that nearly one thousand snowmobiles will be allowed to enter the park each day. * * * In light of its clear conservation mandate, and the previous conclusion that snowmobile use amounted to unlawful impairment, the Agency is under an obligation to explain this 180 degree reversal. NPS has not met this obligation.

Id. at 105, 107–108. Does *Fund for Animals* help you make a case against the Glamis mining proposal?

VI.   EXCEPTIONS FROM NEPA'S OBLIGATIONS

A.   Categorical Exclusions

CEQ regulations authorize agencies to exclude certain categories of actions from NEPA obligations. *See* 40 C.F.R. § 1508.4. Agencies may adopt a categorical exclusion (CE) for actions that normally do not have a significant impact on the environment. The initial adoption of a CE is subject to public comment and scrutiny by the CEQ. CEs are typically included in regulations, agency handbooks or manuals.

---

40 C.F.R. § 1508.4 Categorical exclusion.

"Categorical Exclusion" means a category of actions which do not individually or cumulatively have a significant effect on the human environment and which have been found to have no such effect in procedures adopted by a Federal agency in implementation of these regulations (§ 1507.3) and for which, therefore, neither an environmental assessment nor an environmental impact statement is required. An agency may decide in its procedures or otherwise, to prepare environmental assessments for the reasons stated in § 1508.9 even though it is not required to do so.

The following case demonstrates an agency's application of a CE to a land exchange that took place in conjunction with the development of a ski resort complex.

CITIZENS' COMMITTEE TO SAVE OUR CANYONS v. U.S. FOREST SERVICE

United States Court of Appeals, Tenth Circuit, 2002.
297 F.3d 1012.

[See Section IV.B., supra, for project background and a discussion of alternatives]

* * * Save Our Canyons ("SOC") challenges the Forest Service's handling of the Interchange [of federal and private lands] on a number of grounds. * * * SOC alleges that the Forest Service acted arbitrarily and capriciously by concluding that the Interchange qualified for a "categorical exclusion" exempting NEPA review. In particular, SOC contends that the Forest Service 1) failed to adequately explain its basis for subjecting the Interchange to a categorical exclusion and 2) misapplied the categorical exclusion it invoked. * * * The district court rejected all of SOC's claims, and we affirm.

* * * Once an agency establishes categorical exclusions, its decision to classify a proposed action as falling within a particular categorical exclusion will be set aside only if a court determines that the decision was arbitrary and capricious. * * *

In this case, the Forest Service, pursuant to its authority under 40 C.F.R. § 1507.3(b)(2)(ii), concluded that the Interchange fell within a categorical exclusion exempting land exchanges from NEPA review "where resulting land uses remain essentially the same." Forest Service Handbook (FSH) 1909.15 § 31.1b(7). * * *

SOC ... contends that the administrative record fails to support the Forest Service's decision to classify the Interchange as falling within the "essentially the same" categorical exclusion. According to SOC, prior to the Interchange, the government's lands were relatively undeveloped. Following the Interchange, however, the federal lands were incorporated into a bustling and burgeoning ski resort, SOC argues. In deciding to go forward with the Interchange, however, the Forest Service rejected this "development" argument, and its reason for doing so is sufficiently supported by the record to prevent reversal under an arbitrary and capricious standard of review. It noted that the existing federal lands were already subject to skiing activity, and, therefore, transferring ownership to Snowbird would not alter its essential use or character. Indeed, according to the Forest Service's assessment, "Prior to the interchange, the federal parcels were undeveloped and proposed to remain undeveloped after the interchange ... Backcountry skiers have used Mineral Basin for years." The Forest Service also noted that, regardless of whether the Interchange occurred, Snowbird intended to develop the surrounding [non-federal] Mineral Basin properties, which constituted the vast majority of land in the Basin and which already engulfed the federal tracts subject to the Interchange. Consequently, irrespective of whether the Interchange transpired, the federal lands would be surrounded by development. Given these facts, we cannot conclude that the Forest Service acted arbitrarily or capriciously when it concluded that activity on the federal lands exchanged in the Interchange would remain "essentially" the same.

Notes and Questions

1. The level of judicial deference seen in *Citizens' Committee to Save Our Canyons* is probably the norm, rather than the exception, when it comes to an agency's application of a duly promulgated CE. In Help Alert Western Kentucky, Inc. v. Tennessee Valley Authority, 191 F.3d 452, 1999 WL 775931 (Table) (6th Cir.1999), the court upheld a decision of the Tennessee Valley Authority (TVA) to allow to timber harvest without preparing an EA or EIS. The TVA authorized a CE for "[m]inor non-TVA activities on TVA property authorized under contract or license ... including ... sale of miscellaneous ... materials from TVA land." *Id.* at *3 (citing 48 Fed.Reg. 19264 (April 28, 1983)). The TVA determined that the project in question, which consisted primarily of selective tree removal on 1.7 percent of the total acreage managed by the TVA, was a "minor" activity. Although the court found the TVA's conclusion "somewhat problematic," it deferred to the agency and allowed the project to go forward. Similarly, in Alaska Center for Environment v. U.S. Forest Service, 189 F.3d 851, 859 (9th Cir. 1999), the court upheld the Forest Service's application of its CE for "minor, short-term special uses of national forest lands" to the issuance and extension of annual permits for helicopter flights utilized in commercially-guided skiing and hiking tours.

2. When should a court reverse an agency's decision to invoke a CE? In Fund for Animals v. Babbitt, 89 F.3d 128 (2nd Cir.1996), the U.S. Fish and Wildlife Service attempted to utilize a CE which covered non-destructive data collection, research, public safety and education to justify its decision to authorize funding for a moose hunt in Vermont. The court held that the moose hunt, designed at least in part to satisfy hunter demand, did not fit within the CE. *Id.* at 133.

B. Emergencies

The CEQ may authorize alternative, streamlined NEPA procedures for emergency situations, even if significant impacts may occur. *See* 40 C.F.R. § 1506.11.

---

40 C.F.R. § 1506.11 Emergencies.

Where emergency circumstances make it necessary to take an action with significant environmental impact without observing the provisions of these regulations, the Federal agency taking the action should consult with the Council about alternative arrangements. Agencies and the Council will limit such arrangements to actions necessary to control the immediate impacts of the emergency. Other actions remain subject to NEPA review.

Emergency procedures are perhaps most often invoked for national security reasons. Although military objectives do not, standing alone, justify emergency treatment or otherwise warrant an exemption from NEPA's requirements, *see* Shiffler v. Schlesinger, 548 F.2d 96 (3d Cir. 1977), the CEQ has treated Department of Defense proposals as emergencies in certain cases. In Valley Citizens for a Safe Environment v. Vest, 1991 WL 330963 (D.Mass.1991), plaintiffs sought an injunction to prevent the Air Force from flying C–5A transport planes from Westover Air Force Base at night. Although an earlier EIS had prohibited nighttime flights at Westover, the Air Force began to fly C–5As on a twenty-four hour schedule in September 1990 when military forces were committed to Operation Desert Storm. Plaintiff requested a supplemental Environmental Impact Statement (SEIS), but the Air Force refused, stating that the crisis in the Middle East constituted an emergency for NEPA purposes. The court agreed with the CEQ and Air Force that an emergency existed, even though the fighting had ceased by the time the case was heard, reasoning that the disruption of Westover operations could create scheduling and supply problems affecting the efficacy of military operations at home and abroad. *Id.* at *5. It approved of the Air Force's plans to prepare a hybrid EA–EIS, which would analyze flight scheduling options, noise impacts, and reduced nighttime operations and provide for a period of public comment, as an appropriate alternative NEPA procedure. *Id.* at *6.

Courts tend to be highly deferential to the CEQ's determination that an emergency exists, even outside the national security context. In National Audubon Society v. Hester, 801 F.2d 405, 407 (D.C.Cir.1986), the D.C. Circuit Court of Appeals found that the U.S. Fish and Wildlife Service (FWS) and the CEQ had properly invoked emergency provisions for the removal of endangered condors from the wild when the species' population began to dip dangerously low. FWS did not prepare an EA or EIS but stated its reasons for the removal in an addendum to an earlier EA. The court found that the agencies had demonstrated a rational basis for the decision to adopt alternative procedures, "given the urgent nature of the Wildlife Service's concerns with condor mortality." *Id.* at 408–409 and n.3.

A remarkably expansive interpretation of Section 1506.11 can be found in Crosby v. Young, 512 F.Supp. 1363 (E.D.Mich.1981). There, the City of Detroit argued that it should be allowed to utilize "alternative arrangements" for environmental review to exercise its eminent domain powers and commence an urban development project involving a new General Motors automobile plant. The City wanted the Department of Housing and Urban Development to commit federal funds before an EIS could be completed. The court agreed with CEQ's determination that the need to relocate the elderly before winter and to address unemployment, crime, the decreasing tax base and Detroit's continuing fiscal crisis constituted an emergency such that it was "impossible to comply with the rigorous obligations of NEPA." *Id.* at 1386–87. The GM project and its long-term effects on surrounding communities are explored in Michael Moore's film, *Roger and Me: A Humorous Look at How General Motors Destroyed Flint, Michigan* (Warner Bros. 1989).

C. Functional Equivalency and Related Exceptions

Agencies do not have to comply with NEPA if their action is taken pursuant to a statute which either explicitly displaces NEPA or is its functional equivalent. Congress has expressly displaced NEPA for certain decisions under the Clean Air Act, 15 U.S.C.A.§ 793(c)(1), and the Clean Water Act, 33 U.S.C.A. § 1371(c)(1) (1994). Congress has also exempted specific projects from NEPA or from judicial review for NEPA compliance. *See* Mount Graham Coalition v. Thomas, 89 F.3d 554 (9th Cir. 1996) (exemption for telescope complex in Arizona); Earth Resources of Alaska v. Federal Energy Regulatory Comm'n, 617 F.2d 775 (D.C.Cir.1980) (exemption for Alaska pipeline system).

Functional equivalence is a doctrine unique to NEPA. Compliance with NEPA obligations is not required where an agency acts pursuant to subsequent legislation that "mandates specific procedures for considering the environment that are functional equivalents of the impact statement process." Alabama ex rel. Siegelman v. U.S. E.P.A., 911 F.2d 499, 504 (11th Cir.1990). Courts have crafted this doctrine to avoid instances where formal compliance with NEPA would be wasteful and redundant.

Many of the EPA's permitting decisions are deemed the functional equivalent of NEPA analysis, which means that the agency need not prepare an EA or EIS before it issues, for example, hazardous waste permits. *See* Alabama ex rel. Siegelman, 911 F.2d at 504. *See also* Warren County v. North Carolina, 528 F.Supp. 276 (E.D.N.C. 1981) (exempting EPA from NEPA for its actions under the Toxic Substances Control Act); Maryland v. Train, 415 F.Supp. 116 (D. Md. 1976) (exempting EPA from NEPA for Ocean Dumping Act permits).

Other agencies have had limited success in escaping NEPA's responsibilities under the functional equivalency doctrine. In Flint Ridge Dev. Co. v. Scenic Rivers Ass'n, 426 U.S. 776, 96 S.Ct. 2430, 49 L.Ed.2d 205 (1976), the Department of Housing and Urban Development was allowed to go forward with the registration of a statement of record under the Interstate Land Sales Full Disclosure Act without an EIS. The Supreme Court held that the preparation of an EIS would create an "irreconcilable and fundamental conflict" with the mandatory duties imposed by the Disclosure Act, which provides that a statement of record becomes effective automatically 30 days after filing. *Id.* at 788. "It is inconceivable that an environmental impact statement could, in 30 days, be drafted, circulated, commended upon, and then reviewed and revised in light of the comments." *Id.* at 788–89.

The following opinion considers whether an EIS is required for actions that maintain the environmental status quo by preventing human interference with the physical environment.

DOUGLAS COUNTY v. BABBITT

United States Court of Appeals, Ninth Circuit, 1995.

48 F.3d 1495 *cert. denied*, 516 U.S. 1042, 116 S.Ct. 698, 133 L.Ed.2d
655 (1996).

Secretary of the Interior Bruce Babbitt (the Secretary) and intervenors, Headwaters, Inc. and Umpqua Valley Audubon Society (Headwaters), appeal the district court's grant of summary judgment in favor of
Douglas County, Oregon (the County), in the County's action alleging
that the Secretary failed to comply with the National Environmental
Policy Act of 1969 (NEPA), 42 U.S.C.A. § 4321 et seq., in designating
certain federal land as critical habitat for the Northern Spotted Owl
pursuant to the Endangered Species Act of 1973 (ESA), 16 U.S.C.A.
§ 1533(a)(3). * * *

Under § 4(a) of the ESA, 16 U.S.C.A. § 1533(a), the Secretary may
list a species as threatened or endangered. When the Secretary lists a
species, he or she must also designate a "critical habitat" for that species. 16 U.S.C.A. § 1533(a)(3). The ESA defines "critical habitat" as the
geographical areas "essential to the conservation of the species." 16
U.S.C.A. § 1532 (5)(A). The Secretary must decide what area to designate as a critical habitat "on the basis of the best scientific data available and after taking into consideration the economic impact, and any
other relevant impact, of specifying any particular area as critical habitat." 16 U.S.C.A. § 1533(b)(2). The ESA requires the Secretary to follow
a clear set of procedures for public notification and comment after he or
she designates a critical habitat. 16 U.S.C.A. § 1533(b)(4)-(6). The effect
of designating an area as a critical habitat is that federal actions that
are likely to destroy or disrupt the habitat are prohibited. 16 U.S.C.A.
§ 1536(a)(2). * * *

On June 26, 1990, in response to litigation brought by a number of
environmental groups, … the Secretary listed the Northern Spotted Owl
as a threatened species pursuant to the ESA. * * *

On May 6, 1991, the Secretary published an initial proposed regulation designating 11,639,195 acres of federal, state and private lands as
"proposed critical habitat." * * * After proposing the critical habitat, the
Secretary held four public hearings at which 364 people testified on the
proposal. As part of his May 6, 1991 announcement, the Secretary concluded that he did not need to prepare an EA (and therefore an EIS) in
conjunction with the designation. The Secretary referred to a policy, that
he first announced in 1983, that determinations made under § 4 of the
ESA were not subject to NEPA. The 1983 policy was based primarily on
(1) the Sixth Circuit's holding in Pacific Legal Foundation v. Andrus, 657
F.2d 829 (6th Cir. 1981), that decisions to list species as threatened or
endangered under the ESA were exempt from NEPA, and (2) a letter
from the Council on Environmental Quality (CEQ) that urged the Secretary to cease preparing EISs in conjunction with actions under § 4 of the
ESA. * * *

The Secretary issued a revised proposed designation of critical habitat on August 13, 1991. The revised designation reduced the critical habitat to 8,240,160 acres by eliminating all privately owned land and most state owned land. The Secretary held another sixty day comment period on the proposed designation and announced another four public hearings. * * * On January 15, 1992, the Secretary issued the final designation of critical habitat. 57 Fed. Reg. 1,796 (1992). The final designation includes 6,887,000 acres, all of which is federal land. The final rule includes a lengthy analysis of all the factors that led to the final critical habitat designation.

* * * The County's primary allegation is that the Secretary failed to comply with NEPA in designating a critical habitat. The district court granted summary judgment on behalf of the County, finding that NEPA did apply to the Secretary's decision to designate a critical habitat [and] entered an order setting aside the final designation of critical habitat until the Secretary complies with NEPA. * * *

On appeal, the Secretary ... argues that NEPA does not apply to designations of critical habitat because the ESA procedures have displaced the NEPA procedures. Headwaters argues that an EIS is not required because the federal action at issue does not change the natural, physical environment, and because requiring an EIS would frustrate the purposes of both NEPA and the ESA. * * *

Whether NEPA applies to a decision of the Secretary to designate a critical habitat under the ESA is a question of first impression. Section 102(2)(C) of NEPA, 42 U.S.C.A. § 4332(2), requires "to the fullest extent possible," that "all agencies of the Federal Government" comply with the EIS requirements when they take "major Federal actions significantly affecting the quality of the human environment." * * * The Supreme Court has interpreted the language "to the fullest extent possible" to be "neither accidental nor hyperbolic." Flint Ridge Dev. Co. v. Scenic Rivers Ass'n, 426 U.S. 776, 787 (1976). Rather, the Court found the language to be a "deliberate command" that the consideration of environmental factors not be "shunted aside" in the "bureaucratic shuffle." *Id.*

Despite the strict language of NEPA, courts have found that some agency actions are not subject to the NEPA requirements. We have noted that "NEPA was not intended to repeal by implication any other statute." Merrell [v. Thomas, 807 F.2d 776, 779 (9th Cir. 1986)] (quoting United States v. Students Challenging Regulatory Agency Procedures (SCRAP), 412 U.S. 669, 694 (1973)). One exception to NEPA's application derives from a statement made by the NEPA conferees. NEPA applies unless "the existing law applicable to such agency's operations expressly prohibits or makes full compliance with one of the directives impossible." H. Conf. Rep. No. 765, 91st Cong., 1st Sess. (1969), *reprinted in* 1969 U.S.C.A.C.A.N. 2767, 2770.

In *Flint Ridge*, 426 U.S. at 788, the Supreme Court, relying on the conferees' language, concluded that requiring the Secretary of the

Department of Housing and Urban Development to prepare an EIS would create an "irreconcilable and fundamental conflict" with his or her duties under the Interstate Land Sales Full Disclosure Act. The Court found that the Secretary could not prepare an EIS and still comply with the statutory duty to allow disclosure statements filed by developers to go into effect within 30 days of filing.

In contrast, the designation of a critical habitat at issue in the instant case does not occur in a highly restrictive time frame. Thus, time constraints alone would not prevent the Secretary from preparing an EIS. [But] ... for the reasons set forth below, we hold that NEPA does not apply to the designation of a critical habitat. * * *

In *Merrell v. Thomas,* 807 F.2d at 778, we found that NEPA did not apply when the EPA registered pesticides under the Federal Insecticide, Fungicide, and Rodenticide Act (FIFRA), 7 U.S.C.A. §§ 136–136y. We traced the legislative history of FIFRA and concluded that because Congress created two different mechanisms in FIFRA and NEPA, and because Congress declined the opportunity to apply NEPA to FIFRA, that it intended that FIFRA procedures replace NEPA for pesticide registration. * * * The legislative history of the ESA at issue in the instant case follows a similar pattern and convinces us that Congress intended that the ESA procedures for designating a critical habitat replace the NEPA requirements. In 1978, ... Congress enacted a set of amendments to the ESA. * * * The [House Committee] report indicates that the committee members wished to introduce some "flexibility" into the stringent requirements of the ESA ... [by] ensuring that the Secretary only makes a critical habitat designation "after a thorough survey of all the available data" and after notice to the affected communities. * * * The procedure Congress chose ... makes the NEPA procedure seem "superfluous." Before the Secretary can issue a final critical habitat designation, he or she must now (1) publish a notice and the text of the designation in the Federal Register; (2) give actual notice and a copy of the designation to each state affected by it; (3) give notice to appropriate scientific organizations; (4) publish a summary of the designation in local newspapers of potentially affected areas; and (5) hold a public hearing if one is requested. 16 U.S.C.A. § 1533(b)(5). This carefully crafted congressional mandate for public participation in the designation process, like the FIFRA procedures reviewed in *Merrell,* displaces NEPA's procedural and informational requirements.

Even if the legislative history suggesting that Congress intended that the ESA procedure for designating a critical habitat displace the NEPA requirements were not as clear, the Secretary would still not be obliged to prepare an EIS when he or she designated a critical habitat under the ESA. We find that the NEPA procedures do not apply to federal actions that do nothing to alter the natural physical environment.

When we consider the purpose of NEPA in light of Supreme Court guidance on the scope of the statute, we conclude that an EA or an EIS is not necessary for federal actions that conserve the environment. * * *

The purpose of NEPA is to "provide a mechanism to enhance or improve the environment and prevent further irreparable damage." * * *

If the purpose of NEPA is to protect the *physical* environment, and the purpose of preparing an EIS is to alert agencies and the public to potential adverse consequences to the land, sea or air, then an EIS is unnecessary when the action at issue does not alter the natural, untouched physical environment at all. * * * The district court found that the argument—that EISs are not required for federal actions that maintain the environmental status quo—could not be determinative, no matter its merits, because it assumed a fact not in evidence. That fact was, that the environment would remain unchanged if designated a critical habitat. The court offered as an example the possibility that the area could acquire more old growth characteristics if it were left alone.

The district court missed the point. Of course a forest, free of human interference, changes all the time—saplings grow, mature trees die, dead trees decay. The touchstone is not *any* change in the status quo, but change effected by humans. Headwaters argues, and we agree, that when a federal agency takes an action that prevents human interference with the environment, it need not prepare an EIS. The environment, of its own accord, will shift, change, and evolve as it does naturally. * * *

We also find that NEPA does not apply to the designation of a critical habitat because the ESA furthers the goals of NEPA without demanding an EIS. NEPA was designed to "promote human welfare by alerting governmental actors to the effect of their proposed actions on the physical environment," *Metropolitan Edison,* 460 U.S. at 772, and "to provide a mechanism to enhance or improve the environment and prevent further irreparable damage." *Pacific Legal Foundation,* 657 F.2d at 837. The ESA is a substantive statute whose goal is to prevent extinction: "the plain intent of Congress in enacting [the ESA] was to halt and reverse the trend toward species extinction, whatever the cost." Tennessee Valley Auth. v. Hill, 437 U.S. 153, 184 (1978). By designating critical habitats for endangered or threatened species, the Secretary "is working to preserve the environment and prevent the irretrievable loss of a natural resource." *Pacific Legal Foundation,* 657 F.2d at 837. Thus the action of the Secretary in designating a critical habitat furthers the purpose of NEPA. Requiring the EPA to file an EIS "would only hinder its efforts at attaining the goal of improving the environment." *Id.*

[In *Pacific Legal Foundation,*] ... the Sixth Circuit gave four reasons why NEPA should not be applied to the Secretary's decision to list species as endangered or threatened under the ESA. We think the analysis applies directly to the facts of the case before us. First, the court in *Pacific Legal Foundation,* 657 F.2d at 835–36, found that if NEPA is applied to the listing of a species the ESA's purpose would be frustrated because the ESA prevents the Secretary from considering environmental impact when listing a species as endangered or threatened. In critical habitat designations the Secretary can only consider "economic impact and any other relevant impact of specifying any particular area as critical habitat." 16 U.S.C.A. § 1533(b)(2). The district court decided that the ESA would not be frustrated by the imposition of NEPA because the language—"any other relevant impact"—could allow the "wide range of impacts required to be analyzed in preparing NEPA documentation." *Douglas County,* 810 F.Supp. at 1479.

The district court did not explain how it decided that the words of the statute were to be given such a broad meaning, and we think its interpretation is misguided. The other impacts that the Secretary may consider must be "relevant" to the designation process. The purpose of the ESA is to prevent extinction of species, and Congress has allowed the Secretary to consider economic consequences of actions that further that purpose. But Congress has not given the Secretary the discretion to consider environmental factors, other than those related directly to the preservation of the species. The Secretary cannot engage in the very broad analysis NEPA requires when designating a critical habitat under the ESA. * * *

[In addition,] … "the Secretary's action in listing a species as endangered or threatened furthers the purpose of NEPA even though no impact statement is filed." * * * As with the decision to list a species under the ESA, the decision to preserve critical habitat for a species protects the environment from exactly the kind of human impacts that NEPA is designed to foreclose. * * *

Fourth, the court in *Pacific Legal Foundation,* 657 F.2d at 840, found that the legislative histories of NEPA and the ESA indicate that Congress did not intend that the Secretary prepare an EIS before listing a species as endangered or threatened under the ESA. … [T]he legislative histories of NEPA and the ESA likewise indicate that Congress did not intend that the Secretary file an EIS before designating a critical habitat. * * *

* * * The old growth forests and the species that inhabit them are unique resources that deserve protection. We are reluctant … to make NEPA more of an "obstructionist tactic" to prevent environmental protection than it may already have become.

Notes and Questions

1. The County argued that NEPA's requirements would be displaced only in cases of "irreconcilable" statutory conflict. The Ninth Circuit rejected that argument, and cited multiple bases for its decision that NEPA does not apply to the designation of critical habitat under the ESA. Which theory do you find most convincing?

2. Although it is well settled that NEPA does not apply to the decision to list a species as endangered or threatened under the ESA, *see* Pacific Legal Foundation v. Andrus, 657 F.2d 829 (6th Cir. 1981), the circuits are split regarding NEPA's application to the designation of critical habitat under the ESA. In Catron County Board of Commissioners v. U.S. Fish and Wildlife Service, 75 F.3d 1429 (10th Cir. 1996), the Court of Appeals for the Tenth Circuit held that the Secretary of Interior must comply with NEPA

when designating critical habitat for the spikedace and loach minnow, two fish species which had been listed as threatened. The Tenth Circuit rejected the reasoning of *Douglas County,* and found that (1) the ESA's procedural requirements for designation only partially satisfied NEPA and did not displace NEPA's more comprehensive requirements for environmental analysis and public involvement; (2) critical habitat designation could have significant actual impacts by preventing the County's flood control efforts; and (3) requiring NEPA analysis would further the goals of the ESA. Which decision best effectuates the goals of NEPA? Of the ESA?

3.   In *Douglas County,* 48 F.3d at 1506, the Ninth Circuit ruled that "when a federal agency takes an action that prevents human interference with the environment, it need not prepare an EIS." Would the case have come out the same way if non-interference could result in degradation of the environment through natural processes, for example, fire or catastrophic flooding? Although it may not have been essential to its holding, the court seemed to believe that non-interference through the designation of critical habitat would in fact be beneficial to the environment, stating that it would "preserve the environment and prevent the irretrievable loss of a natural resource." *Id.* As the Tenth Circuit explained in *Catron County,* however, "[t]he short- and long-term effects of the proposed governmental action ... are often unknown, or, more importantly, initially thought to be beneficial, but after closer analysis determined to be environmentally harmful." 75 F.3d at 1437. Does *Douglas County* give federal agencies too much leeway to decide what is and what is not beneficial? Does it undermine NEPA's premise that it's better to "look before you leap" than to leap first and regret it later?

4.   Is the *Douglas County* opinion consistent with CEQ regulations? *See* 40 C.F.R. 1508.27(b)(1). Is the court necessarily required to follow the CEQ regulation? *See* Andrus v. Sierra Club, 442 U.S. at 358; Chevron U.S.A., Inc. v. Natural Resources Defense Council, Inc., 467 U.S. 837, 104 S.Ct. 2778, 81 L.Ed.2d 694 (1984). The CEQ's role in implementing NEPA is described in Section II.B., *supra* (Administration and Enforcement).

5.   In both the *Douglas County* and *Catron County* cases, the counties feared the economic consequences of critical habitat designation, and probably wanted to avoid designation altogether. It is unusual for plaintiffs whose primary concern is economic in nature to act as NEPA's champions. Although NEPA has long served as a powerful tool for environmental benefit, what are the dangers of NEPA being used as an " 'obstructionist tactic' to prevent environmental protection"? *See Douglas County, supra,* 48 F.3d at 1508.

VII.   NEPA IN SPECIAL CONTEXTS

A.   Proposals for Legislation

NEPA applies to any "proposal for legislation." 42 U.S.C.A. § 4332(2)(C). When a federal agency submits a report or a request for legislation for any substantive program, the submission must be accompanied by an EIS. *See* 40 C.F.R. § 1508.17 (below); Trustees for Alaska

v. Hodel, 806 F.2d 1378 (9th Cir. 1986) (requiring an EIS for statutorily mandated reports to Congress).

---

§ 1508.17 Legislation.

"Legislation" includes a bill or legislative proposal to Congress developed by or with the significant cooperation and support of a Federal agency, but does not include requests for appropriations. The test for significant cooperation is whether the proposal is in fact predominantly that of the agency rather than another source. * * *

Section 1508.17 provides a significant exception from NEPA by stating that agencies' requests for appropriations are not considered legislative proposals. The CEQ believes that the preparation of an EIS is ill-suited to the budget preparation process because of "traditional concepts relating to appropriations and the budget cycle, considerations of timing and confidentiality, and other factors." 43 Fed. Reg. 56004, 55989 (1978). The Supreme Court approved of CEQ's interpretation, explaining that "[a] rule requiring preparation of an EIS on the annual budget request for virtually every ongoing program would trivialize NEPA." Andrus v. Sierra Club, 442 U.S. 347, 359, 99 S.Ct. 2335, 2341, 60 L.Ed.2d 943 (1979) (citations omitted). The Court also found CEQ's position "consistent with the traditional distinction which Congress has drawn between 'legislation' and 'appropriation,' noting that "[t]he rules of both Houses prohibit 'legislation' from being added to an appropriation bill.'" *Id.* at 359–60 (citations omitted). In recent years, however, this particular congressional rule has been waived frequently, allowing enactment of numerous substantive environmental "riders" that have authorized logging, water development projects, telescope complexes and other federal actions. *See* Sandra Zellmer, *Sacrificing Legislative Integrity at the Altar of Appropriations Riders: A Constitutional Crisis,* 21 Harv. Envtl. L. Rev. 457 (1997). Should appropriations requests be exempt from NEPA?

B. National Security

There is no general national defense exemption from NEPA. No GWEN Alliance v. Aldridge, 855 F.2d 1380, 1384 (9th Cir.1988). *See* Natural Resources Defense Council, Inc. v. Evans, 232 F.Supp.2d 1003 (N.D.Cal. 2002) (issuing a preliminary injunction against the Navy's use of a low frequency sonar system for training, testing and routine operations). The military has, however, secured CEQ's approval for alternative, streamlined emergency procedures in some circumstances. *See* Section VI.B, *supra* (Emergencies).

C. Environmental Justice

The Executive Order on Environmental Justice provides that each federal agency shall "to the greatest extent practicable and permitted by law ... make achieving environmental justice part of its mission by identifying and addressing, as appropriate, disproportionately high and adverse human health or environmental effects of its programs, policies, and activities on minority populations and low-income populations.... " Executive Order 12,898 § 1–101, 59 Fed. Reg. 7629 (1994). NEPA can serve as a tool for assessing impacts and considering alternatives to activities that may adversely affect minority or low income populations.

NEPA urges agencies to use "all practicable means" to maintain "an environment which supports diversity and variety of individual choice." 42 U.S.C.A. § 4331(b)(4). The CEQ regulations specify that among the effects that must be considered are "economic, social, or health, whether direct, indirect, or cumulative." 40 C.F.R. § 1508.8(b). The CEQ's guidance documents provide that NEPA analyses must consider effects on minority and low income populations in accordance with the Executive Order. *See* Council on Envtl. Quality, Environmental Justice: Guidance Under the National Environmental Policy Act 9 (1997), *available at* http://ceq.eh.doe.gov/nepa/regs/ej/ej.pdf ("[a]gencies should recognize the interrelated cultural ... factors that may amplify the natural and physical environmental effects of the proposed agency action").

The Executive Order explicitly states, however, that it creates no legal rights or remedies. Exec.Order No. 12,898 § 6–609. In Citizens Concerned About Jet Noise, Inc. v. Dalton, 48 F.Supp.2d 582, 604 (E.D. Va. 1999), *aff'd*, 217 F.3d 838 (4th Cir. 2000), the court rejected arguments that the Navy's EIS failed to adequately assess environmental justice concerns. It concluded that the Executive Order precluded review and that NEPA does not compel an environmental justice analysis. *Id.* As a matter of internal policy, agencies do strive to comply with the Order as a directive from their commander in chief, even if its terms are not legally enforceable. *See, e.g.,* Federal Interagency Working Group on Environmental Justice: Environmental Justice Revitalization Projects, 67 Fed. Reg. 20406 (April 24, 2002) (describing efforts to ensure that federal agencies effectively address environmental justice issues).

D. Extraterritorial Application

As a general rule, courts follow a presumption against the extraterritorial application of domestic statutes. That presumption does not apply, however, where the conduct regulated by the statute in question occurs primarily within the United States.

NEPA has been required for some federal actions that take place outside of the jurisdiction of the United States. In Environmental Defense Fund v. Massey, 986 F.2d 528, 532 (D.C. Cir. 1993), the court held that an EIS was required for a decision involving waste incineration in Antarctica, explaining that the federal agencies' decisionmaking processes were "uniquely domestic" as they took place almost exclusively in this country and involved the workings of the United States government. The court also found that the application of NEPA in this particular context would not infringe on foreign policy or sovereignty because the United States enjoys a great deal of authority in Antarctica, which, like the high seas and outer space, lacks an independent sovereign. *Id.*

at 534. *See* Executive Order 12114 § 2–3(a): Environmental Effects Abroad of Major Federal Actions, 44 Fed.Reg. 1957 (Jan. 4, 1979) (directing agencies to prepare environmental analyses for "major Federal actions significantly affecting the environment of the global commons outside the jurisdiction of any nation (e.g., the oceans or Antarctica)"). NEPA has been applied in a variety of other cases involving extraterritorial activities. *See* Sierra Club v. Adams, 578 F.2d 389 (D.C.Cir.1978) (applying NEPA without remarking on extraterritorial nature of Pan American highway project where the United States had two-thirds of the financial responsibility and control of the project); Natural Resources Defense Council Inc. v. U.S. Dept. of Navy, 2002 WL 32095131 (C.D.Cal.2002) (applying NEPA to the Navy's sonar tests in the Exclusive Economic Zone).

Where the environmental impacts would be felt exclusively within a foreign jurisdiction, however, NEPA analysis will not be required. In Greenpeace USA v. Stone, 748 F.Supp. 749 (D. Hawaii 1990), appeal dismissed, 924 F.2d 175 (9th Cir. 1991), the court held that the Army was not required to prepare an EIS for the movement of obsolete chemical weapons across West Germany. The extraterritorial application of NEPA to the Army's action in that case "would result in a lack of respect for [West Germany's] sovereignty" and encroach on the foreign government's jurisdiction to implement "a political decision which necessarily involved a delicate balancing of risks to the environment and the public.... " *Id.* at 760. The court noted that the Army had prepared an EA for the transoceanic shipment of the munitions and an EIS for the incineration of those munitions at Johnston Atoll, an unincorporated U.S. territory in the Pacific Ocean, but the foreign policy concerns that would be triggered by NEPA's application in West Germany were not implicated by the "global commons" components of the Army's action. *Id.* at 761.

VIII. NEPA'S PROGENY: THE ENVIRONMENTAL POLICY ACTS OF STATES AND OTHER NATIONS

NEPA has been emulated in over half of the states in some way, shape or form. *See* The National Environmental Policy Act: A Study of its Effectiveness After Twenty–Five Years (1997), available at http:// ceq.eh.doe.gov/nepa/nepa25fn.pdf. California, Maryland, Michigan, Minnesota, New York, South Dakota, Virginia, Washington, and Puerto Rico are just a few of the jurisdictions that have adopted environmental review statutes. Most of these "state NEPAs" track the federal NEPA fairly closely. *See* Nicholas A. Robinson, *SEQRA's Siblings: Precedents from Little NEPA's in the Sister States,* 46 Albany L. Rev. 1155, 1157 (1982).

A few state NEPA-like laws go beyond their federal counterpart by adding substantive requirements. The California Environmental Quality Act (CEQA) is perhaps the most well-known of these. See Cal. Pub. Res. Code §§ 21000–21177 (1996). It requires the preparation of environmental impact reports and specifies that "[e]ach public agency shall mitigate or avoid the significant effects on the environment of projects that it carries out or approves whenever it is feasible to do so." Cal. Pub. Res. Code § 21002.1(b) (1996). CEQA and similar statutes have played a significant role in a broad range of state and local proposals, including mining reclamation plans, *see* City of Ukiah v. County of Mendocino, 196 Cal.App.3d 47, 241 Cal.Rptr. 585 (1987); zoning decisions, *see* Boehm v. City of Vancouver, 111 Wash.App. 711, 47 P.3d 137 (2002); and pollution permitting decisions, *see* Minnesota Center for Envtl. Advocacy v. Minnesota Pollution Control Agency, 644 N.W.2d 457 (Minn. 2002).

The movement toward environmental planning and assessment has spread beyond the boundaries of the United States. Many nations have adopted domestic laws modeled on NEPA, including Australia, Canada, Columbia, France, Ghana, Madagascar, Mexico, the Netherlands, New Zealand, South Africa, Thailand, Uganda and Zambia. *See* CHRIS WOOD, ENVIRONMENTAL IMPACT ASSESSMENT: A COMPARATIVE REVIEW 3–4 (1995); UNEP/UNDP JOINT PROJECT ON ENVTL. LAW AND INST. IN AFRICA, FRAMEWORK LAWS AND EIA REGULATIONS (1996 ed. & Supp. 1998).

Transboundary environmental impact assessments (EIAs) are addressed by the World Bank's funding policies as well as by international agreements among nations. The World Bank requires assessments for all projects or operations expected to have adverse environmental impacts that would be significant in terms of the project's type, location, sensitivity or scale and the nature and magnitude of its potential impacts. *See* WORLD BANK OPERATIONAL POLICY 4.01 (1999), available at http://www.worldbank.org. International agreements include the 1992 Rio Declaration and the 2003 Johannesburg World Summit on Sustainable Development, both of which provide for public participation and transparency and accountability in governmental decisionmaking. *See* U.N. Conference on Environment and Development, adopted June 14, 1992, U.N. Doc. A/CONF.151/5/Rev.1, 31 I.L.M. 874 (1992); Report of the World Summit on Sustainable Development 21, U.N. Doc. A/CONF.199/20*, U.N. Sales No. E.03.II.A.1 (2002).

European nations require transboundary EIAs pursuant to a regional convention commonly known as "Espoo"—the Convention on Environmental Impact Assessment in a Transboundary Context, 1989 U.N.T.S. 309 (1997), 30 I.L.M. 800 (1991) (entered into force Sept. 10, 1997). Espoo commits the parties to notify each other and consult on proposals for all major projects likely to have significant transboundary environmental impacts, with the end goal of avoiding or mitigating adverse impacts. Like NEPA, Espoo requires consideration of the potential effects of the project as well as reasonable alternatives. *Id.* App. II, at 323, 30 I.L.M. at 814. But, like most international instruments, Espoo's enforcement mechanisms are relatively weak. Espoo encourages the parties to resolve their differences through negotiations or arbitration. If all else fails, the parties retain the option to take their dispute to the International Court of Justice. *Id.* art. 15, at 318, 30 I.L.M. at 810.

Looking a bit closer to home, the Agreement on Environmental Cooperation, a side agreement to the North American Free Trade Agreement (NAFTA), established a Commission on Environmental Cooperation and charged it with developing recommendations for the assessment and mitigation of proposed projects likely to cause significant adverse transboundary impacts. North American Agreement on Environmental Cooperation, Sept. 14, 1993, 32 I.L.M. 1480 (1993) (entered into force Jan. 1, 1994). The parties have not yet developed a legally binding commitment on EIAs, however, in part because controversial border projects, such as the siting of a state-sponsored low-level radioactive waste facility in Texas, have contributed to deadlock between the parties. One of the major sticking points is whether to extend the EIA obligation to both federal and non-federal projects. Domestic law in Mexico requires EIAs for private hazardous waste facilities, but this would require a much broader commitment from the United States than is required by NEPA. The Agreement on Environmental Cooperation and other international commitments to EIAs are addressed in Angela Z. Cassar & Carl. E. Bruch, *Transboundary Environmental Impact Assessment in International Watercourse Management*, 12 N.Y.U. Envtl. L. J. 169 (2003).

Notes and Questions

1.   Like the Mexican domestic EIA law discussed above, the Espoo Convention imposes an EIA requirement on both public and private projects. Should NEPA be amended to apply not only to major federal actions but also state and private actions? What are the downsides to such an initiative?

2.   Some states, like California, impose substantive requirements to avoid or mitigate environmental harm through their NEPA-like laws. Is NEPA defective because it does not force agencies to prevent adverse effects?

IX. NEPA'S FUTURE

According to Professor Karkkainen, NEPA, "like many erstwhile revolutionaries, ... has now settled into a quiescent and underproductive middle age." Bradley C. Karkkainen, *Toward a Smarter NEPA: Monitoring and Managing Governments Environmental Performance,* 102 Colum. L. Rev. 903, 906 (2002). In spite of over thirty years of experience with the statute, however, litigation over NEPA continues and is as acrimonious as ever. *See* William Snape and John M. Carter, *Weakening the National Environmental Policy Act: How the Bush Administration Uses the Judicial System to Weaken Environmental Protections*, A Report of the Defenders of Wildlife Judicial Accountability Project 7 (2003), available at http://www.defenders.org/publications/nepareport.pdf (identifying trends in the Bush administration's arguments in NEPA cases in federal courts between 2001–2003).

The CEQ has initiated several reviews of NEPA's implementation within the past decade. Its 1997 report identified a variety of criticisms, but ultimately concluded that NEPA has provided an "enduring legacy as a framework for collaboration between federal agencies and those who will bear the environmental, social, and economic impacts of agency decisions." The National Environmental Policy Act: A Study of its Effectiveness After Twenty–Five Years ix (1997), available at http://ceq.eh.doe.gov/nepa/nepa25fn.pdf. It also confirmed that "NEPA has significantly increased public information and input into agency decisionmaking ... in many cases providing the only opportunity for the public to affect these processes." *Id.* at 17. In spite of its costs in terms of time and money, the report found that "NEPA's requirements ... can make it easier to discourage poor proposals, reduce the amount of documentation down the road, and support innovation." *Id.*

The reviewers identified several elements of the NEPA process that are critical to its effective and efficient implementation, one of which is science-based and flexible management approaches for continuing responsiveness once projects are approved. *Id.* at ix. This reflects a broader trend toward adaptive management techniques. Critics consistently point out that NEPA requires only a one-time snapshot of a proposal and its effects on the environment. This snapshot occurs so early in the planning process that solid data, particularly with regard to cumulative effects and anticipated future conditions, is often lacking. Monitoring over the life of the project to ensure that the original assumptions are accurate could address this deficiency. The CEQ regulations require that "a monitoring and enforcement program shall be adopted ... where applicable for any mitigation." 40 C.F.R. § 1505.2(c). They do not require mitigation, however, nor do they specify when monitoring is "applicable" for any particular mitigation measure that is adopted. Several of the major producers of EAs, including the Department of Energy and the Bureau of Land Management, provide monitoring requirements in their own NEPA guidelines, both to adapt project management to changing conditions over time and to gather information for future planning. *The National Environmental Policy Act: A Study of its Effectiveness After Twenty–Five Years* 31.

The adaptive management approach seems to be gathering momentum, and may well be the wave of the future. Of course, requiring the alteration of ongoing projects if monitoring indicates that effects were other than anticipated is an expensive proposition, and a significant departure from NEPA as it currently exists. Even so, "by accepting more uncertainty in their initial analyses (and using adaptive management measures during project implementation), agencies can get projects underway earlier and dramatically reduce costs." *Id.* at 31. Adaptive management is most promising "where resources are not likely to be damaged permanently and there is an opportunity to repair past environmental damage.... " *Id.* at x. You might recall that the U.S. EPA expressed caution about using post-adoption monitoring as a substitute for thorough analysis at the planning stage in *Dubois v. U.S. Dept. of Agriculture*, Section V.A, *supra,* footnote 4.

The chairman of the CEQ under the Bush Administration, James L. Connaughton, has been especially interested in streamlining NEPA. In

2002, he formed a NEPA Task Force and charged its members "to determine opportunities to improve and modernize the NEPA process." The Council on Environmental Quality, Modernizing NEPA Implementation (2003), available at http://ceq.eh.doe.gov/ntf/report/pdftoc.html. The Task Force report, entitled *Modernizing NEPA Implementation*, made recommendations to the CEQ regarding possible revisions to the NEPA regulations and agency guidance. Adaptive management remained a topic of interest in the 2003 Task Force report. The Task Force recommended the consideration of a variety of related issues, including whether and how to integrate adaptive management into EAs, especially when mitigated FONSIs are utilized to prevent significant impacts. *Modernizing NEPA Implementation, Executive Summary* at xi-xii, xiv. The report also advised the CEQ to issue clarifying guidance regarding the use of categorical exclusions, and to encourage agencies to develop categorical exclusions based on broadly defined criteria that provide sufficient flexibility. *Id.* at xiii.

Federal agencies have been eager to climb on the "Modernizing NEPA" band wagon, both with respect to categorical exclusions and mitigated FONSIs. The Healthy Forests Initiative is one area singled out for possible streamlining. *See* James L. Connaughton, *Modernizing the National Environmental Policy Act: Back to the Future*, 12 N.Y.U. Envtl. L. J. 1, 12–13 (2003). To advance the Administration's Healthy Forests Initiative, the Department of Agriculture drafted rules to make NEPA more "efficient" by allowing the Forest Service to prepare EAs or even categorical exclusions, rather than EISs, at the planning stage. *See* Chapter 6, *supra*. The new rules will result in a significant change from current practices, which have been followed since the early 1980's. *See* Matt Jenkins, *Forests Could Lose Environmental Review*, High Country News, Oct. 28, 2002 (below). At the same time, the Forest Service has begun making more expansive use of categorical exclusions for small-scale timber sales, post-fire salvage sales and the construction of timber roads. *See* National Environmental Policy Act: Documentation Needed for Fire Management Activities; Categorical Exclusions, 68 Fed. Reg. 33,814, 33,824 (June 5, 2003); National Environmental Policy Act: Documentation Needed for Limited Timber Harvest, 68 Fed. Reg. 1026 (Jan. 8, 2003). It claims that a streamlined process is necessary to reduce hazardous fuels build-up and reduce the risk of catastrophic forest fires.

In Focus:

High Country News Vol. 34 No. 20, Oct. 28, 2002

Western Roundup

Forests Could Lose Environmental Review

by Matt Jenkins

While the Bush administration has focused its efforts to "streamline" environmental reviews on energy and transportation projects, the next big showdown will take place in the national forests. Tweaking the National Environmental Policy Act is already figuring prominently in Congress' efforts to turn some form of Bush's Healthy Forests Initiative—an emergency forest-thinning plan to reduce the risk of wildfires—into law.... * * * Rep. Scott McInnis, R–Colo., ... would establish "expedited environmental analysis procedures" for hazardous fuels-reduction projects. * * * More significantly, the bill cuts the time frame for challenging thinning projects by more than half, and frees the Forest Service (and Department of Interior agencies like the BLM and Park Service) from having to consider a range of alternatives for any proposed project.

The bill was toned down significantly, thanks in part to the efforts of House Resources Committee members George Miller, D–Calif., and Peter DeFazio, D–Ore., who worked to forge a bipartisan compromise with McInnis. * * *

But the Democrats' compromise effort did not win points with either the Sierra Club or The Wilderness Society, which roundly criticized their longtime allies ... for a similar compromise effort in the Senate. "I'm not putting a hex on cooperation," says The Wilderness Society's Chris Mehl, "(but) we think the underlying bill is so bad you should just blow it up and start over." * * *

Notes and Questions

1.   Environmentalists fear that the Task Force's report may prompt the expanded use of categorical exclusions and FONSIs, and ultimately result in a dramatic weakening of NEPA. *See* Eric Pianin, *Panel Backs Faster Environment Review*, WASH. POST, Sept. 25, 2003, at A31. According to NRDC's Senior Attorney Sharon Buccino, "The Bush administration is all too willing to sacrifice public participation and environmental review to promote its pro-development, pro-industry agenda." *White House Environmental Office Recommendations Could Shut Out Public from Environmental Review Process, Says NRDC* (Sept. 23, 2003), available at http://www.nrdc.org/media/pressreleases/030924.asp. What concerns might arise from the elimination of EISs at the programmatic planning stage in our National Forests? What about the expanded use of categorical exclusions for timber sales and logging roads? Can categorical exclusions be an effective decisionmaking tool in the forest management context? In other contexts?

2.   If the CEQ were to embrace the use of mitigated FONSIs, how could it ensure that the mitigation measures identified in the FONSI as being necessary to avoid significant effects are actually implemented and main-

tained throughout the life of a project? Do environmental groups or other interested parties have sufficient incentives and resources to "watchdog" the action agency over time to make sure that mitigation actually happens, and that it works the way the agency anticipated in the FONSI?

3.   Would adaptive management—which entails less detailed analysis up front but requires monitoring and adaptation throughout the life of the federal action in a dynamic feedback loop—do the trick, or is it just another diversionary tactic to avoid having to prepare an in-depth analysis before the project moves forward?

4.   Professor Karkkainen believes that NEPA must "be retooled to require monitoring, ongoing policy and project reassessment, adaptive mitigation, and an environmental management systems-oriented approach." Karkkainen, *supra,* at 908. If you were a Senator vying to reform NEPA to ensure that the statute endures and ripens into a dignified old age, what would you propose? What measures would help secure NEPA's continuing viability as a cornerstone of environmental protection, rather than just another layer of dreaded bureaucratic red-tape? Consider the lofty goals expressed in section 4331, discussed in Section I, *supra* (Setting the Stage). How might the NEPA process be made more flexible and less onerous while still accomplishing those goals?

*

Part II

OWNERSHIP OF NATURAL RESOURCES

Much of the study and practice and experience of natural resources law revolves around the use and development of a particular resource, along with eventual (and inevitable) government regulation of such use and development. However, resources do not exist in a state where they are first used by humans and then controlled by government. The initial legal pre-condition to both human use and government regulation is "ownership" of the resource. Part II explores this pre-condition—the ownership of the natural resource that sets the stage for its use and management.

Part II was written by Professor Mary C. Wood. The chapters within Part II first introduce us to the importance of ownership as a component of natural resources law, and then concentrate on the various owners of natural resources—the United States, Tribes, States, and Private Parties. Natural resources are regulated and managed differently based on who owns the resource. Part II examines how private parties and government entities have acquired legal ownership interests in natural resources. The chapters within Part II also show us how legal management regimes reflect and shape the differing ownership interests of our nation's natural resources.

Chapter 5

INTRODUCTION TO SOVEREIGN AND INDIVIDUAL OWNERSHIP OF LAND AND RESOURCES

The control of natural resources in this country is a dual function of ownership and governmental regulation. Because law gives owners control over their land, the owner's preference is a strong determinant factor in the condition and use of that land. Owners diverge in their land use preferences. A forested parcel owned by the Nature Conservancy (a non-profit land trust) for the purpose of providing wildlife habitat will be managed differently than a forest owned by a timber company for the purpose of producing revenue to stockholders. Ownership is therefore an important part of natural resources law, because it determines landscape conditions within the broad spectrum of parameters set by regulation.

Traditionally, law schools have given separate course treatment to Property Law, Public Lands Law, Federal Indian Law, Water Law, Wildlife Law, Ocean and Coastal Law, and the like. While all of these courses deal fundamentally with ownership questions, they rarely present a unified ownership construct to guide resolution of natural resources issues. Instead, the different fields of specialty have emerged with little reference to the ownership law of the others. This section of the text focuses exclusively on the *ownership* of natural resources and presents the property foundation that connects the various fields. It describes an overall framework within which to situate federal, tribal, state and individual ownership, and emphasizes the role ownership plays in ecosystem management. Parts III and IV of the casebook provide in-depth coverage of the regulatory aspects of natural resources law.

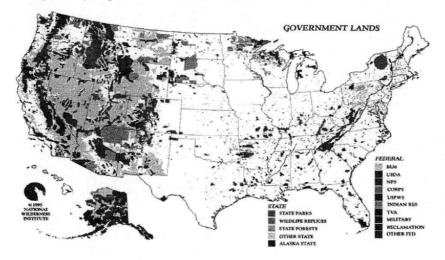

Federal, state, and tribal ownership in the United States; http://www.nwi.org/

Most people are unaware of the complex structure of ownership in the United States. The general public often thinks of ownership in simplistic terms as *private* property ownership. In fact, however, ownership of land and natural resources is both private and public. Individuals and corporations have private ownership, and the federal government, states and tribes have governmental (often termed "sovereign") ownership. The land base of the United States (excluding trust territories like Guam) consists of approximately 2.3 billion acres. Of this, the federal government owns about 29% of the land, or 662 million acres. States own approximately 135 million acres and tribes own about 55 million acres. Governmental entities exert different preferences for land and resource management depending on their public constituencies, bureaucratic makeup, and political factors. Meanwhile, a vast number of non-profit conservation land trusts are gaining property rights in land through consensual transfers by private property owners. Land trusts have protected nearly 6.5 million acres, 2.6 million of which are under conservation easements. Land trust ownership, while not governmental, is quasi-public, because the mission of many land trusts is to benefit the public as a whole.

A picture of ownership in the United States is complicated by the fact that in many instances a parcel of land may have many different strands of ownership. We sometimes think of ownership as absolute and exclusive. The "fee simple" title is, of course, the maximum of legal ownership. But a parcel held in fee may also be subject to express or implied easements allowing others interests in that property. Such encumbrances may benefit other landowners, or the government and its citizens. Throughout history, sovereigns (the federal government, tribes, and states) have conveyed part of their landholdings to other sovereigns or individuals, yet still retained some property rights. In some cases, easements and other encumbrances are implied by courts, sometimes decades after the transfer. These property rights, which could be described categorically as *sovereign servitudes*, operate as easements on the land and can limit current and future property owners' use of the land.

Websources:

For a chart depicting acreage owned by federal, tribal and state governments on a state-by-state basis, see
http://www.nwi.org (National Wilderness Institute)

Retained sovereign property rights are distinct from regulatory mechanisms enforced by governments. Sovereign servitudes may be implied by courts with no legislative expression. Examples of sovereign servitudes include reserved tribal treaty rights (which may provide access by tribal members across public or private lands for fishing and hunting), the federal navigational servitude (which allows the federal government to use private lands on some waterways for the purpose of navigation), and public trust easements (which may allow the public access across certain portions of private land or preclude private property owners from destroying important resources on their lands).

The complex interrelationships involved in ownership of land and resources is more aptly summarized as a "web" of property rights, rather than a "bundle" of rights (the classic metaphor traditionally used in first-year property classes). *See* Craig Anthony Arnold, *The Reconstitution of Property: Property as a Web of Interests,* 26 HARV. ENVTL. L. REV. 281 (2002). The purpose of this chapter is to present this "web" in a way that highlights the interrelationships of ownership among the federal government, tribes, states, and individuals. Understanding this web of property rights is crucial in dealing with present day natural resource conflicts that span broad ecosystems.

Unfortunately, the historic pattern of land conveyance bore little relationship to ecosystem boundaries. In 1785, the federal government established a rectangular survey system under which lands were divided into square townships. Land Ordinance of 1785, *reprinted in* DOCUMENTS OF AMERICAN HISTORY 123 (Henry Steele Commager ed., 7th ed., New York, Appleton–Century–Crofts 1963). Each township was divided into 36 numbered sections, each section containing 640 acres (one square mile). The rectangular survey system formed the reference for all land transactions thereafter, but it has no relation to ecosystem demarcation. Because land transfers have been accomplished according to these unnatural square dimensions, most ecosystems contain a fragmented puzzle of ownership. An action in one part of an ecosystem inevitably affects other parts of the system, creating natural resource conflicts extending well beyond the boundaries of that parcel.

THE PROPERTY CLAUSE: AS IF BIODIVERSITY MATTERED
Dale D. Goble
75 U. COLO. L. REV. 1195, 1196 (2004)

* * * [B]iodiversity is a sprawling thing; it blithely disregards our Euclidean boundaries, moving in response to gravity and wind, biology and whim.

While biodiversity ignores our boundaries, we humans do not—and boundaries foster myopia. As landowners and others concentrate on an individual parcel, they lose sight of the contextual web in which every bounded tract is embedded. This myopia leads to the loss of biological diversity. Consider, for example, coastal wetlands. Between 1950 and 1970, nearly 50 percent of the wetlands along the coasts of Connecticut and Massachusetts were destroyed, not as a result of a conscious decision, but through the conversion of hundreds of small tracts. The fragmentation of ownership, with its resulting focus on individual decisions to develop individual tracts, obscured the overall impact of those decisions.

This is the Tragedy of Fragmentation: boundaries produce fragmentation, and fragmentation, in turn, fosters myopic decisions; these small decisions, however, eventually aggregate to produce a large decision that is never directly made. Although the Tragedy of the Commons is far better known, it is the Tragedy of Fragmentation that poses a far greater risk to biodiversity. * * *

We begin sorting through the puzzle of ownership in Section I, below, which presents a basic historical foundation of title to property in the United States. Section II then reviews the Constitutional framework that governs the property relationships between the various sovereigns and individuals. Section III presents the various types of sovereign ownership in critical public natural resources, such as streambeds, water, and wildlife. Later chapters in this Part II examine in more detail the various categories of ownership and the doctrines that shape how public and private actors exercise their ownership prerogatives.

I. THE HISTORICAL FOUNDATION OF OWNERSHIP: FEDERAL ACQUISITION AND DISPOSITION OF PROPERTY IN THE UNITED STATES

The picture of ownership throughout the history of the United States has been one of constant change since white contact with indigenous peoples. Understanding the broad upheavals and shifts in ownership will provide an orientation for the more detailed materials that follow. The United States government initially acquired land from native nations, European nations, and the original 13 colonies. Treaties, statutes, and executive orders formalized the transfer of native lands to the United States, but also guaranteed retained lands ("reservations") and occasionally easements for continuing tribal use. Many of these instruments promised property rights for tribes "as long as water flows or grass grows upon the Earth." *See* Treaty with the Navajo Indians of 1868, 15 Stat. 667. After the original land acquisitions from the tribes, the federal government embarked on a program of "disposition," transferring lands to states, individuals, and corporations, though it ultimately retained nearly a third of the land base of the United States in federal ownership. Within just a century after making solemn promises of land rights to tribes in the treaties, the federal government broke up about two-thirds of the tribal land base during what is called the Allotment Era (1887–1934), converting much tribal ownership to individual ownership. Indian General Allotment Act, 25 U.S.C. §§ 331–334 (2001).

The modern era has been a period of immense change in sovereign ownership. Numerous land transfers and exchanges are taking place between the federal government, states, and individuals to consolidate ownerships. Many tribes are adding to their land base through purchase or settlement of land claims. Over 1,200 non-profit land trusts in the country are quickly gaining property rights in critical lands and resources. Finally, modern court rulings at the state and federal level are expanding sovereign property rights to water, wildlife, and submersible lands. A layering of various property rights emerges from the significant periods of transition. The materials that follow trace these developments in further detail.

A. Acquisition of Land From European Powers and Native Nations

The origin of title begins with native aboriginal territories. For millennia prior to the onset of European conquest, native peoples lived within defined territories spanning nearly all of what is now the United States. Their societies revolved around use and management of natural resources, with hunting, fishing, gathering (and, in some cases, farming) as central economic enterprises. Relationships of tribes to one another varied, some marked by nearly constant war, and others marked by trade and cultural exchange.

Dating back to medieval times, however, European monarchs asserted a right of conquest over all non-Christian native people in the world. This position, called the "right of discovery," has its origins in the doctrine of the Catholic Church, which was the dominant legal institution of Western Europe. The Pope proclaimed himself the "divinely designated shepherd of Christ's Universal Flock, vested with a supreme spiritual jurisdiction over the souls of all humankind." *See* ROBERT A. WILLIAMS, JR., THE AMERICAN INDIAN IN WESTERN LEGAL THOUGHT: THE DISCOURSES OF CONQUEST 15–21 (Oxford University Press 1990). Catholic legal doctrine extended jurisdiction over all "infidels" to enforce adherence to Christ. These ideas were solidified into a Catholic legal framework that purported to justify conquest of the New World by Christian European monarchs. *Id.*

In 1497, King Henry VII of England issued a charter to the Italian captain John Cabot "to seek out, discover, and find whatsoever isles, countries, regions or provinces of the heathen and infidels whatsoever they be, and in what part of the world [where]ever they be, which before this time have been unknown to all Christians...." *Reprinted in* DOCUMENTS OF AMERICAN HISTORY 5–6 (8th ed., 1968). Cabot landed on the shore of what is now New England in 1497, launching England's colonial rule on the continent. Though Justice Marshall later remarked on how "extravagant the pretension of converting the discovery of an inhabited country into conquest may appear," the U.S. Supreme Court ruled that European "discovery" gave rise to European sovereign property rights overlying the existing aboriginal title. Johnson v. McIntosh, 21 U.S. (8 Wheat.) 543, 5 L. Ed. 681 (1823).

From 1607 to 1732, 13 colonies were formed under charters issued by the British Crown. They became the present states of Virginia, New

Jersey, Massachusetts, New Hampshire, Pennsylvania, New York, Maryland, Connecticut, Rhode Island, Delaware, North Carolina, South Carolina, and Georgia. Each of the colonies entered into treaties with tribes for the purchase of lands. At the same time, other European nations (France, Spain, and Russia) exerted discovery rights over other parts of what is now the United States and established colonial settlements pursuant to charters. These nations also entered into treaties with some tribes for the purchase of Indian lands.

Following the Revolutionary War with England, the new nation of the United States consisted of two sovereigns—the states and the federal government. The newly formed states succeeded to the ownership of land asserted by the predecessor colonies. The infant federal government initially had no land ownership in these states, but seven of the 13 original states relinquished to the new federal government territory they claimed west of their borders extending up to the Great Lakes region. This was the first federal public domain, from which new states were formed.

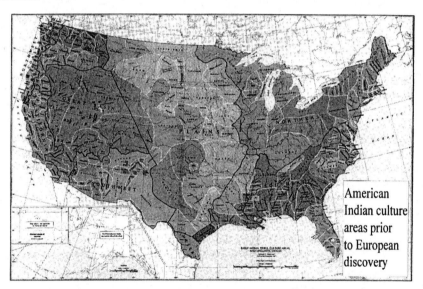

Map of Native territory at time of white contact, U.S. Geological Society, available at http://rockyweb.cr.usgs.gov/outreach/lewisclark/indianlandsmaps.html.

The subsequent process of land acquisition to create the present borders of the United States involved extinguishing claims from two types of sovereigns: native nations that asserted aboriginal title, and European nations that asserted "discovery" rights over that title. In 1800, Spain ceded part of its claims (523 million acres comprising the Louisiana Territory) to France. President Jefferson made the famous Louisiana Purchase from Napoleon, ruler of France, in 1803. Spain surrendered Florida to the United States in 1819. The U.S. annexed Texas in 1845, and in 1846 the federal government gained 180 million acres of land north of California through the Oregon Compromise with Great Britain. The 1848 Treaty of Guadalupe Hidalgo marked the completion of the acquisition of land in the contiguous U.S. by formalizing cessions from Mexico of most of the Southwest, including California. In the latter half of the 19th century, the U.S. acquired Russian claims to Alaska in 1867, and the Republic of Hawaii ceded its sovereignty and its 1.8 million acres to the U.S. in 1898.

Native title still covered most of the land (with a few exceptions, such as where Northeastern tribes had already ceded some of their territory to the colonies). The relationship of European property claims (and, by succession, United States' claims) to aboriginal title was decided in an 1823 Supreme Court case, Johnson v. McIntosh, 21 U.S. (8 Wheat.) 543, 5 L.Ed. 681 (1823). The ruling formed the federal common law foundation for property rights in this country. In *Johnson v. McIntosh,* the Supreme Court ruled that tribes held only a "right of occupancy,"— something less than full fee simple absolute—and that such native title could only be conveyed to the United States as the "discovering" nation. Conveyances by tribes to individuals, therefore, were invalid.

JOHNSON v. MCINTOSH

Supreme Court of the United States, 1823.

21 U.S. (8 Wheat.) 543, 5 L.Ed. 681.

CHIEF JUSTICE MARSHALL delivered the opinion of the Court.

On the discovery of this immense continent, the great nations of Europe were eager to appropriate to themselves so much of it as they could respectively acquire. Its vast extent offered an ample field to the ambition and enterprise of all; and the character and religion of its inhabitants afforded an apology for considering them as a people over whom the superior genius of Europe might claim ascendancy. The potentates of the old world found no difficulty in convincing themselves that they made ample compensation to the inhabitants of the new, by bestowing on them civilization and Christianity, in exchange for unlimited independence. But, as they were all in pursuit of nearly the same object, it was necessary to establish a principle ... that discovery gave title to the government by whose subjects, or by whose authority, it was made, against all other European governments, which title might be consummated by possession.

The exclusion of all other Europeans necessarily gave to the nation making the discovery the sole right of acquiring the soil from the natives, and establishing settlements upon it. * * *

In the establishment of these relations, the rights of the original inhabitants were, in no instance, entirely disregarded; but were necessarily, to a considerable extent, impaired. They were admitted to be the rightful occupants of the soil, with a legal as well as just claim to retain possession of it, and to use it according to their own discretion; but their rights to complete sovereignty, as independent nations, were necessarily diminished, and their power to dispose of the soil at their own will, to whomsoever they pleased, was denied by the original fundamental principle, that discovery gave exclusive title to those who made it.

[T]he different nations of Europe claimed a power to grant the soil, while yet in possession of the natives. These grants have been understood by all to convey a title to the grantees, subject only to the Indian right of occupancy. * * *

No one of the powers of Europe gave its full assent to this principle, more unequivocally than England. * * * So early as the year 1496, her monarch granted a commission to the Cabots, to discover countries then unknown to *Christian people*, and to take possession of them in the name of the king of England. * * *

By the treaty which concluded the war of our revolution ... the powers of government, and the right to soil, which had previously been in Great Britain, passed definitively to these States. * * *

The United States, then, have unequivocally acceded to that great and broad rule by which its civilized inhabitants now hold this country. * * * They maintain, as all others have maintained, that discovery gave an exclusive right to extinguish the Indian title of occupancy, either by purchase or by conquest.... * * *

We will not enter into the controversy, whether agriculturists, merchants, and manufacturers, have a right, on abstract principles, to expel hunters from the territory they possess, or to contract their limits. Conquest gives a title which the Courts of the conqueror cannot deny.... * * * It is not for the Courts of this country to question the validity of this title, or to sustain one which is incompatible with it. * * *

[T]he Indian inhabitants are to be considered merely as occupants, to be protected, indeed, while in peace, in the possession of their lands, but to be deemed incapable of transferring the absolute title to others.

Notes and Questions

1. What was the European "right of discovery" inherited by the United States? How does it mesh with the Indian "right of occupancy?" How do the two rights fit into a classic ownership paradigm? One approach might be to think of the federal and tribal rights as together making up complete title. When the native nations conveyed their title, described as the "right of occupancy," to the United States, their claims to the land were "extinguished." The native "right of occupancy" combined with the federal "right of discovery" became full title (fee simple absolute) vested in the United States, which the government then conveyed to states, individuals, and corporations. In some cases the native transfer of title came with a reservation of easements for hunting and fishing rights. Such easements encumbered the federal "patents" (deeds) to private owners, and continue to provide the basis of tribal rights today. *See* United States v. Winans, 198 U.S. 371, 25 S.Ct. 662, 49 L.Ed. 1089 (1905).

2. Consider one scholar's assessment of *Johnson*:

Johnson's acceptance of the Doctrine of Discovery into United States law represented the legacy of 1,000 years of European racism and colonialism directed against non-Western peoples. White society's exercise of power over Indian tribes received the sanction of the Rule of Law in *Johnson v. McIntosh.* The Doctrine of Discovery's underlying medievally derived ideology—that normatively divergent "savage" peoples could be denied rights and status equal to those accorded to the civilized nations of Europe—had become an integral part of the fabric of United States federal Indian law.... [T]he original legal rules and principles of federal Indian law set down by Marshall in *Johnson v. McIntosh* and its discourse of conquest ensured that future acts of genocide would proceed on a rationalized, legal basis.

Robert A. Williams, Jr., *supra,* at 325–26.

3. The common law rule handed down in *Johnson v. McIntosh* was codified into statute by the Trade and Intercourse Acts of 1790–1834, which prevented the conveyance of any Indian lands without approval of the federal government. 1 Stat. 138, 25 U.S.C. § 177. This prohibition remains operative today. The federal government holds Indian land and resources in "trust" for the tribes. The federal title is described as "naked fee," because the federal government must manage such land solely in the interest of the Indian beneficial owners. United States v. Shoshone Tribe of Indians, 304 U.S. 111, 116, 58 S.Ct. 794, 797, 82 L.Ed. 1213, 1218 (1938). While the system of federal trust ownership has been criticized as paternalistic, it has likely preserved a native land base that otherwise would have been sold off as a result of market pressure. Indeed, some of the east coast tribes have successfully reclaimed title to lands that had been sold to private or state individuals without federal approval in violation of the Trade and Intercourse Acts. *See* Oneida County v. Oneida Indian Nation of New York, 470 U.S. 226, 105 S.Ct. 1245, 84 L.Ed.2d 169 (1985) (upholding federal common law right of action for violation of Trade and Intercourse Act).

The federal process of "extinguishing" Indian title—or the native "right of occupancy"—followed immediately on the heels of acquiring European claims. Until 1871, the federal government extinguished Indian title through use of treaties, a legal tool reserved for establishing sovereign relationships between nations. After 1871 the federal government used statutes, commonly called "treaty substitutes." Indian treaties and treaty substitutes represent the foundational "deeds" to land in most areas within the lower 48 states. They conveyed away the native right of occupancy across those lands ceded to the federal government (called "ceded lands"), and secured reduced areas of land (called "reservations") for tribal homelands.

In some cases the established reservation was part of the original aboriginal territory of the tribe, but in other cases the tribe was removed—often with tragic consequences—to lands far away from its ancestral homeland. Beginning in the late 1700s federal officials began developing a "removal" policy designed to force tribes east of the Mississippi to relinquish their lands in exchange for a permanent Indian territory west of the Mississippi in what is now the state of Oklahoma. The policy culminated in the Removal Act of 1830, Ch. 148, 4 Stat. 411–12 (1830). One of the most studied applications of removal policy involved the Cherokee Nation, which once had aboriginal lands spanning five states east of the Mississippi. President Jackson "removed" the Cherokees from their ancestral lands, forcing over 16,000 Cherokees to travel the "Trail of Tears" to Oklahoma Territory—a genocidal journey during bitterly cold winter conditions in which nearly half (8,000) of the victims died along the way or shortly after arrival.

B. Tribal Lands and Reserved Rights

1. *The Treaty Process*

The use of treaties to formalize native land cessions affirmed the sovereign status of the tribes. But despite the legal characterization of treaties as "contracts between nations," Washington v. Washington State Commercial Passenger Fishing Vessel Ass'n, 443 U.S. 658, 675, 99 S.Ct. 3055, 3069, 61 L.Ed.2d 823, 839 (1979), the treaty process was not nearly as bilateral as the term suggests. Language barriers, coercion, fraud, bribery, and selection of "friendly chiefs" as tribal representatives tainted many treaty negotiations. *See* Charles F. Wilkinson & John M. Volkman, *Judicial Review of Indian Treaty Abrogation: "As Long as Water Flows or Grass Grows Upon the Earth"—How Long a Time is That?*, 63 CAL. L. REV. 601, 608–19 (1975).

In Focus:
Federal Removal of the Wallowa Band of Nez Perce Indians

    The Nee–Me–Poo people ("The People"), known as the Nez Perce Tribe, was comprised of several bands, each having their own leader, and each claiming distinct homelands within an aggregate aboriginal territory encompassing 13 million acres throughout central Idaho, southeastern Washington, and northeastern Oregon. The Wallowa Band of Nez Perce Indians had its ancestral homeland in the beautiful Wallowa Valley of northeastern Oregon. A treaty of 1855 reduced the Nez Perce aboriginal land base to about 7 million acres, but the Wallowa Valley remained in the Band's possession under the leadership of a chief known now as Old Joseph. After gold was discovered in the Nez Perce homeland in the 1860's, settlers and miners swarmed in to claim land and resources. In 1863, the federal government sought a new treaty ceding more lands, and the government negotiators designated Chief Lawyer, a leader who had integrated himself among the whites, as the designated agent to cede land on behalf of all of the Nez Perce Indians.

In Nez Perce governance, however, Chief Lawyer had no authority to act on behalf of the other bands. Despite this lack of authority, Chief Lawyer signed a treaty ceding ninety percent of what remained of the tribal lands—including the Wallowa Valley—to the federal government. Only 750,000 acres of land were retained for the Nez Perce, in Lapwai, Idaho, where Chief Lawyer's band had its home, and where the Nez Perce Reservation remains today. Old Joseph and several other leaders refused to sign the 1863 treaty.

The Wallowa Band of Nez Perces, later led by young Chief Joseph, refused to move from its homeland until tensions with white settlers erupted in 1877 and the United States declared war on the small band. Over the course of four months, Chief Joseph led his people on a grueling 1,300–mile flight towards Canada, where they sought political refuge. The epic retreat ended just 13 miles south of the Canadian border, where the small band was captured by the U.S. Army.

Chief Joseph
www.curtis-collection.com

Hear me my chiefs, I am tired, My heart is sick and sad. From where the sun now stands, I will fight no more forever.

The Wallowa Band of Nez Perces, numbering only 431 after the war, was imprisoned and sent to Fort Leavenworth, Kansas and then later to Indian Territory in Oklahoma. The swampy conditions were deadly, and during exile a quarter of the band died, most from malaria, cholera, and malnutrition. Finally, in 1885 the federal government allowed the 268 remaining Nez Perce prisoners to return to the Pacific Northwest, but not to their homeland in the Wallowa Valley. About half of the band went to the Nez Perce reservation in Lapwai, Idaho. The rest, including Chief Joseph, were sent to Nespelem on the Colville Indian Reservation in central Washington, to join with several bands of Indians from Washington. Many descendents of the band still live there today, but they have no recognized legal rights to their Wallowa aboriginal territory, although their spiritual connection with their ancestral homeland is still strong.

In an unsuccessful appeal to gain return of his people's homeland, Chief Joseph made a speech to Congress in 1879, which remains one of the most compelling portrayals of the treaty process from the perspective of an Indian leader:

> Suppose a white man should come to me and say, "Joseph, I like your horses, and I want to buy them." I say to him, "No, my horses suit me, I will not sell them." Then he goes to my neighbor and says to him: "Joseph has some good horses. I want to buy them, but he refuses to sell." My neighbor answers, "Pay me the money, and I will sell you Joseph's horses." The white man returns to me and says, "Joseph, I have bought your horses, and you must let me have them." If we sold our lands to the Government, this is the way they were bought.

Chief Joseph, *Indian's View of Indian Affairs*, 128 North American Review 419–20 (April 1879).

2. *Tribal Reserved Rights*

The extinguishment of native rights across vast amounts of territory triggered a wave of non-indigenous migration west to the Pacific Ocean. Across the United States, native subsistence economies that had endured for millennia were replaced by dominant Anglo economies centered around agriculture, grazing, mining, forestry, and industry. Towns sprouted up, railroads were built, and the non-native population exploded. Between 1780 and 1869 the United States population increased eleven-fold (from 2,781,000 to 31,443,321) and more than doubled again in the subsequent 30 years, rising to 75,994,575 by 1900. JAMES WILLIAM HURST, LAW AND THE CONDITIONS OF FREEDOM IN THE NINETEENTH CENTURY UNITED STATES (Univ. of Wisconsin Press 1956).

Amidst an unprecedented cultural, demographic, and economic invasion, the reservation lands guaranteed by treaty were the linchpin critical to preserving a traditional way of life for most tribes. As Professor Charles Wilkinson describes, the treaties were designed to create a "measured separatism" for tribes within a growing majority society embracing very different economic and cultural ways:

Implicit ... was not only the expectation that each tribe would remain a people, but also the perception that a homeland, separate and distinct from the surrounding white culture, was a requisite element of that survival. The essence of these laws, then, as viewed both by Indian tribes and by the United States, was to limit tribes to significantly smaller domains but also to preserve substantially intact a set of societal conditions and tribal prerogatives that existed then.

CHARLES F. WILKINSON, AMERICAN INDIANS, TIME, AND THE LAW 18 (Yale Univ. Press 1987).

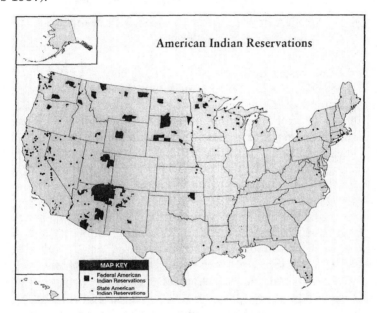

Federal Indian Reservations and state reservations in the United States. Compiled by the Bureau of Census. Available at http://www.census.gov/.

Many treaties contain language reserving to the tribes hunting and fishing rights across the lands ceded to the U.S. government. Tribal leaders realized that the reduced reservation lands could not support the subsistence hunting and fishing necessary to their survival and way of life, so they often insisted on continued access to traditional fishing sites and hunting grounds located off the reservation in ceded lands. *See* Washington v. Washington State Commercial Passenger Fishing Vessel Ass'n, 443 U.S. 658, 666–67, 99 S.Ct. 3055, 3064–65, 61 L.Ed.2d 823, 833–34 (1979). Accordingly, the Stevens treaties of the Pacific Northwest explicitly "secured" the right of taking fish at "usual and accustomed" fishing grounds and stations located off the reservation. Treaties with tribes of the Great Lakes Region also contained promises of continued hunting and fishing. *See* Minnesota v. Mille Lacs Band of Chippewa Indians, 526 U.S. 172, 119 S.Ct. 1187, 143 L.Ed.2d 270 (1999).

In 1905 the Supreme Court interpreted the Stevens treaty language as reserving "easements" underlying later acquired title. United States v. Winans, 198 U.S. 371, 25 S.Ct. 662, 49 L.Ed. 1089 (1905). The opinion plays a key role in establishing the legal property regime in the ceded areas of the Pacific Northwest, because it protects treaty fishing easements as pre-existing sovereign servitudes that take precedence over later-acquired individual private property rights.

UNITED STATES v. WINANS

Supreme Court of the United States, 1905.
198 U.S. 371, 25 S.Ct. 662, 49 L.Ed. 1089.

JUSTICE MCKENNA delivered the opinion of the Court.

* * *

The right to resort to the fishing places in controversy was a part of larger rights possessed by the Indians, upon the exercise of which there was not a shadow of impediment, and which were not much less necessary to the existence of the Indians than the atmosphere they breathed. New conditions came into existence, to which those rights had to be accommodated. Only a limitation of them, however, was necessary and intended, not a taking away. In other words, the treaty was not a grant of rights to the Indians, but a grant of rights from them—a reservation of those not granted. * * * The reservations were in large areas of territory, and the negotiations were with the tribe. They reserved rights, however, to every individual Indian, as though named therein. They imposed a servitude upon every piece of land as though described therein. * * * [The Indians] were given "the right of taking fish at all usual and accustomed places," and the right "of erecting temporary buildings for curing them." The contingency of the future ownership of the lands, therefore, was foreseen and provided for; in other words, the Indians were given a right in the land,—the right of crossing it to the river,—the right to occupy it to the extent and for the purpose mentioned. No other conclusion would give effect to the treaty. And the right was intended to be continuing against the United States and its grantees as well as against the state and its grantees. * * *

The extinguishments of the Indian title, opening the land for settlement, and preparing the way for future states, were appropriate to the objects for which the United States held the territory. And surely it was within the competency of the nation to secure to the Indians such a remnant of the great rights they possessed as 'taking fish at all usual and accustomed places.' Nor does it restrain the state unreasonably, if at all, in the regulation of the right. It only fixes in the land such easements as enable the right to be exercised.* * *

Notes and Questions

1. Many usual and accustomed fishing sites in the Pacific Northwest are located in ceded areas that are now in private ownership. The tribal

right of access to these fishing sites forms a pre-existing servitude binding later acquired private property rights. In the Puget Sound area of Washington State, courts have affirmed the right of tribes to cross private lands in order to harvest shellfish. *See* United States v. State of Washington, 157 F.3d 630 (9th Circuit 1998). Not all treaties encumber private property rights as do the Stevens Treaties of the Pacific Northwest. The relationship between tribal rights and later acquired private property rights turns on specific treaty language and understandings that form the backdrop of the treaties. *See* Chapter 7 for more on treaties.

2. The native claims of Hawaii and Alaska were extinguished outside of the treaty framework, because those states entered the Union long after the treaty practice had ended. Congress recognized Hawaii as an official territory in the Organic Act of 1890 and admitted Hawaii as the 50th state in the union in 1959. *See* NATIVE HAWAIIAN RIGHTS HANDBOOK (Melody Kapilialoha MacKenzie ed., Univ. of Hawaii Press 1991). The system of land and resource rights in Hawaii is quite complex and unique to Hawaii's own history of land tenure. [For discussion see, Neil M. Levy, *Native Hawaiian Land Rights,* 63 CAL. L. REV. 848, 849 (1975).] The Hawai'i Constitution (1978) imposes a duty to protect the subsistence, cultural and religious rights of native Hawaiians. HAW. CONST. art. XII, § 7, and the Hawaii Supreme Court continues to recognize such rights. *See* Public Access Shoreline Hawaii v. Hawai'i County Planning Commission, 79 Haw. 425, 447, 903 P.2d 1246, 1268 (1995), *cert denied,* 517 U.S. 1163, 116 S.Ct. 1559, 134 L.Ed.2d 660 (1996).

3. Native Alaskan aboriginal title was extinguished by the Alaska Native Claims Settlement Act (ANCSA), passed in 1971. P. L. No. 92–203, 85 Stat. 668, 43 U.S.C. § 1601 et. seq. ANCSA revoked all prior reservations that had been set aside for native use and set up a corporate structure under state law to hold native lands. For discussion *see* Benjamin Thompson, *The De Facto Termination of Alaska Native Sovereignty: An Anomaly in an Era of Self–Determination,* 24 AM. INDIAN L. REV. 421 (2000). Alaska native subsistence rights were not mentioned in ANCSA, but in 1980 Congress passed the Alaskan National Interest Lands Conservation Act (ANILCA) which included a provision establishing priority for rural subsistence uses (though not expressly native uses) on federal public lands. 16 U.S.C. § 3114 (2000).

C. The Creation of States and the Disposition of Federal Property

1. The Creation of States

Ownership patterns differ markedly between the eastern and western United States due to the historical context of statehood. The amount of federal public land within states has always been a point of contention embroiled in assertions of state sovereignty. The federal government has huge landholdings amounting to nearly 350 million acres in the eleven continental western states, yet only minimal ownership within the eastern states formed from the original colonies. The admission acts that allowed individual states to enter the Union were often the product of hard-fought compromises concerning the ownership and management of federal public lands.

The 13 states created from the original colonies had no federal land within their borders at the time of creation. The colonies had been the sovereign holders of land, and when the United States was formed, the land passed directly to the successor states, not to the new federal government. The first block of federal public domain came from the cessions made to the federal government by seven of these original 13 states. New states thereafter were carved out of the lands ceded by foreign nations, so initial land ownership in these states was in the federal government. For discussion, *see* PAUL W. GATES, HISTORY OF PUBLIC LAND LAW DEVELOPMENT (1968).

In 1787 the Congress of the Confederation enacted the Northwest Ordinance, which set forth the process by which the territories north of the Ohio River and east of the Mississippi River could become states. Act of July 13, 1787. The Northwest Ordinance contained two provisions that framed sovereign ownership of land within the new states. Article V declared that new states shall be admitted "on an equal footing with the original states, in all respects whatever." Article IV declared that the new states would "never interfere with the primary disposal of the soil by the United States."

2. *The Land Ordinance of 1785*

In 1785, Congress passed a statute to bring order to the disposition of property in the United States. The Land Ordinance of 1785 imposed the "grid" survey system on the public lands, dividing all land into consecutive square townships, each containing 36 sections, following the pattern below.

6	5	4	3	2	1
7	8	9	10	11	12
18	17	16	15	14	13
19	20	21	22	23	24
30	29	28	27	26	25
31	32	33	34	35	36

The grid system was central to the disposition of federal land. The federal government typically made grants of property to states and individuals by reference to the artificial grid imposed upon the topography, not by reference to any ecosystem boundaries (such as a watershed). The grid system still dominates land transactions today, and nearly all surveys and deeds reference the townships and sections. The grid system was a product of the pressing concerns of the time, when Congress was consumed with settling the country and bringing in income to the federal treasury. Settlement was "unquestionably a value in itself; government was under constant, almost invariably successful pressure to bring land to market...." JAMES WILLARD HURST, LAW AND THE CONDITIONS OF FREEDOM IN THE NINETEENTH CENTURY UNITED STATES 35 (Univ. of Wisconsin Press 1956). In retrospect, shaping federal land disposition around an artificial grid system was foolish in the sense that, by dividing up ecosystems, it greatly complicated all natural resource management thereafter. But two centuries ago when ownership patterns began taking shape, resources were plentiful—seemingly inexhaustible—and leaders gave no thought to ecosystem management. Today, natural resource professionals must gain an understanding of the fragmented ownerships and the legal structure governing property rights in order to bring solutions to ecological problems.

In Practice:
Connecting Natural Landscapes with
Property Boundaries

When dealing with any natural resource dispute, whether on a half-acre or two million acres, the natural resource practitioner must understand both the natural features and legal ownerships of a particular landscape. The U.S. Geological Survey has produced maps of most areas of the country. USGS maps are available on the web at http://geography.usgs.gov. Aerial photos of nearly any place in the United States are also available on the USGS website. But such maps and photos do not show ownerships. Many counties have used Geographical Information System (GIS) technology to superimpose property boundaries on overhead photos of the landscape within their jurisdiction. Using this system, a practitioner can find the precise landscape of concern and determine ownerships correlated, typically, with parcel numbers used by the County Tax Assessor's Office. For an example, *see* Clark County, Washington's homepage at www.co.clark.wa.us.

Without these tools, it is often cumbersome and expensive to match property boundaries with landscape features. One can hire a surveyor to make a map of a defined area. The surveyor takes deeds containing legal descriptions of the property and locates iron pipes or features that mark corners of the boundaries of the property. Unfortunately, the standard legal descriptions in surveys reference the grid system in a way that is nearly incomprehensible to the lay person. Should every federal, state, and local jurisdiction make GIS landscape technology available to the general public? How would such technology stimulate on-the-ground conservation partnerships and projects?

---

3.   State Land Grants

When the new states were admitted to the Union, they automatically acquired jurisdiction throughout their territory, but they acquired only those lands as set forth in the admission acts. The federal government typically made two types of land grants to states as part of the admission package. The first type included "in place" grants of specified sections in each township. These lands were to support public education. All states received at least sections 16 and 36 in each township, and some states received far more (for example, Utah, Arizona, Nevada, and New Mexico received four sections from each township). Where a state could not make use of "in place" lands in the designated sections because of prior reservations or conflicting claims, it was entitled to select "in lieu" lands as a replacement. *See* Andrus v. Utah, 446 U.S. 500, 100 S.Ct. 1803, 64 L.Ed.2d 458 (1980). The other type of land grant was for specified purposes (roads, prisons, etc.). These were not limited to particular sections of townships, and they varied in acreage. States could select these lands from available federal lands. States also received land from the federal government after admission to the Union. These grants were for various purposes usually geared towards creating a national infrastructure, such as canals, roads, navigation improvements and schools. Congress also granted away millions of acres of marshes and other wetlands to states under the General Swamp Land Act of 1850.

Montana provides a classic example of mixed sovereign ownership resulting from the acquisition and disposition era.

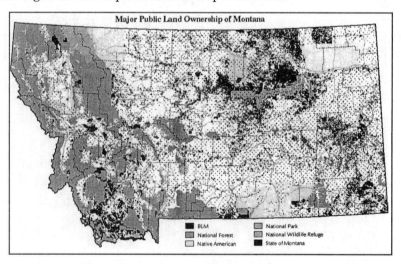

Mixed ownership in Montana: black dots indicate Montana's school trust lands; the Trust Land Management Division of Montana, available at http://nris.state.mt.us/nsdi/nris/ab105.gif.

In aggregate, state land grants created an important category of sovereign ownership in the United States. States own approximately 135 million acres of land. The eleven western states alone own 45 million surface acres of land (an area exceeding all of the New England states). State lands are managed by state land agencies (often called the Department of State Lands). Unfortunately, the method of disbursing land grants across specified sections in each township meant that state lands would be scattered, fragmented and bear an arbitrary relationship to the actual landscape—a condition sometimes referred to as the "blue rash." For example, in Montana, there are over five million acres of state lands, but the acreage is divided into 16,000 separate parcels dispersed through the state. State land grants often form ownership islands (inholdings) within a broader federal management area. For instance, the State of Wyoming holds over seven sections of Grand Teton National Park, amounting to 4,480 acres of land. State lands often provide valuable ecological services, but they also bear the constant pressure of producing income for public education. Intensive resource extraction on state lands may undermine ecological goals of surrounding federal lands. Potential management conflicts abound across landscapes characterized by mixed sovereign ownerships. A leading study of state lands management concludes: "[The] unvarying grant of particular sections in each township ... impose[s] a management burden that was doomed to failure almost from the start." Melinda Bruce & Teresa Rice, *Controlling the Blue Rash: Issues and Trends in State Land Management*, 29 LAND & WATER L. REV. 1, 19 (1994). Chapter 8, *infra*, explores state ownership in further detail.

4. *Land Grants to Individuals and Corporations*

From 1841 on, federal policy promoted the transfer of newly acquired federal lands to small farming families that could build the backbone of a new nation. The government "disposed" of its new lands through a variety of land grants. The General Preemption Act of 1841 (repealed in 1891) gave title to squatters on the public lands as long as they paid $1.25 per acre and met minimal requirements. The Homestead Act of 1862 gave title to 160 acres of land upon proof of settlement and cultivation for 5 years. The Desert Land Act of 1877 authorized the purchase of 640–acre blocks of public land at 25 cents/acre upon showing that such land had been irrigated. The Stock–Raising Homestead Act of 1916 provided for grants of 640–acre tracts of grazing land.

a. Grants to Miners

When gold was discovered in California in 1848, a swarm of miners descended upon the western states. Most simply trespassed on federal lands. There was little law and order, except a rudimentary system of water and mineral allocation that developed in the mining camps and was organized around the principle, "first come first serve." Congress failed to address the situation until 1866 when it passed the first version of a federal mining law, which declared the federal lands free and open to mineral exploration and occupation. Subsequently, Congress passed the Mining Law of 1872, a legal relic that remains in force today. 1872 Mining Law, Ch. 152, §§ 1–16, 17 Stat. 91 (codified as amended in scattered sections of 30 U.S.C. §§ 22–47 (1994)).

Those who discover a "valuable" mineral deposit on federal lands and contribute necessary assessment work towards that claim on an annual basis gain rights to an "unpatented" mining claim. The Mining Law also provides for outright grants of federal lands through issuance of mineral patents (full fee title). Miners can receive patents to the land overlying their claims for $5 an acre (for lode claims), or $2.50 acre (for placer claims). The federal government has issued approximately 65,000 mineral patents, totaling more than three million acres of land. As a result of the Mining Law, much federal land is peppered with mining claims, either unpatented or patented, the latter of which establishes islands of private ownership within the public domain. Some of the patented fee land is within or near national parks or wilderness areas, posing serious conflicts with the ecological values of the surrounding federal lands.

Remarkably, the 1872 law still allows conveyance of fee simple absolute title at the prices of $5 or $2.50 an acre. Since 1994, however, Congress has inserted a rider on the Department of Interior's annual appropriation bill that prevents the government from accepting new patent applications.

> In May 1994, what may have been the most valuable patent application in history ended up on Secretary Babbitt's desk, a consolidated application from American Barrick involving dozens of mining claims covering a huge deposit in Nevada containing an estimated $10 billion dollars worth of gold in place. The Secretary signed the patent, but chose not to do it in the privacy of his office. Instead, he held a press conference where the backdrop was a gigantic check made out to the mining company in the amount of $10 billion and signed 'the American taxpayer,' and he took the opportunity to roundly criticize the Mining Law and the failure of Congress to reform it. A few months later, Congress began the practice of including annual moratoria on new patent applications in the Interior Appropriation bill.

COGGINS, ET. AL., PUBLIC LANDS LAW: CASES AND MATERIALS 618 (5th ed. 2002.). For coverage of mining *see* Chapters 12 and 13.

b. Grants to Railroads

Beginning in 1835, Congress made land grants to railroad companies for the purpose of establishing a national rail transportation system. Cumulatively, the grants total over 100 million acres of formerly public lands. Typically these grants included a right of way for the line itself, as well as odd-numbered square-mile sections along the route for the railroad companies to sell in order to raise capital and encourage settlement. The grants came with the condition that the railroad companies would have to dispose of their lands to homesteaders within a fixed period of time after completing the railroad. The disposition program created huge swaths of checkerboard ownership across the landscape. The railroads owned the odd sections across the 20–80 mile wide route, and the federal government (or the states) owned the even-numbered sections. Huge corporate empires grew from the riches of those early public land grants. Large tracts of the railroad grant lands were retained by the railroad companies and later sold to large timber corporations or spin-off corporations, which proceeded to "liquidate" their holdings by clearcutting the ancient forests. This practice left 1–mile sections in a checkerboard pattern quite obvious in aerial photos. Clearcutting across these landscapes has contributed to the collapse of species such as the marbled murrelet, the spotted owl, and several varieties of native fish. Today, title to those railroad grant lands still generates simmering hostilities, particularly in the forest lands of the western states. *See* DERRICK JENSEN ET AL., RAILROADS AND CLEARCUTS (INLAND EMPIRE PUBLIC LANDS COUNCIL 1995).

5.   *The Allotment Act (Dawes Act) of 1884*

As the available land across the "frontier" was consumed by settlers or squatters, the federal government opened up more land by abrogating Indian treaties and reducing the reservations. Then, in 1884, Congress passed the General Allotment Act (also known as the Dawes Act), which was designed to break up reservations and convert communal tribal land title into individual fee simple absolute. The Act provided for reservation lands to be surveyed and divided into "allotments" (of 160–acre, 80–acre, and 40–acre parcels) to pass to individual Indians in fee simple after a period of 25 years during which the allotments would be held in "trust" for the individual by the federal government. The "surplus" land (all of the land not used for individual allotments) passed to the federal government to augment the land base available for the new immigrants. General Allotment Act, ch. 119, 24 Stat. 388 (1887).

The Allotment Act had devastating consequences for tribes. Surplus lands for the federal government were often chosen from the prime lands on the reservation, leaving the more barren land for the Indian allotments. Though the Act was supposed to nudge Indians into farming pursuits, there was no infrastructure to support farming, and many of the Western lands were far too arid for agriculture. Often, the lands were simply leased out to non-Indian ranchers. When the Indian owners received full title to their individual allotments (after a trust period of 25 years), state taxes began to accrue immediately. With no viable income from their property, the Indian allottees often fell into arrears on the taxes, with the inevitable result that the lands were forfeited to the state and later auctioned off to non-Indians. As a result of the Allotment Act, the total Indian land base dropped from 138,000,000 acres in 1887 to 48,000,000 acres in 1934.

Non–Indians proliferated within and around the borders of the reservations to take up residence on the surplus lands or the lands that defaulted out of the allottees' hands. With the influx of non-Indians, states increasingly asserted jurisdiction within reservation boundaries, intruding on the traditional domain of tribal governments. The Allotment era finally ended in 1934 with the passage of the Indian Reorganization Act of 1934 (IRA), 25 U.S.C. §§ 461–479 (1983). The IRA failed to restore any land, but it extended the trust ownership of individual allot-ments indefinitely, protecting those lands from state taxes. 25 U.S.C. § 462. For a discussion of the Allotment Act and its consequences, *see* Judith V. Royster, *The Legacy of Allotment,* 27 Ariz. St. L. J. 1 (1995).

Overall, allotment had a disparate effect on tribes. Some reserva-tions had not been surveyed prior to the repeal of the Allotment Act and therefore escaped allotment altogether. But on many other reservations, the allotment era left a fragmented land base. Many reservations have a mix of lands, some held in trust by the federal government for the tribe (tribal trust lands), some held in trust by the federal government for individual allottees (allotments), and some held in fee (fee lands) by Indians or, more often, non-Indians who purchased the parcels after the trust period expired.

6. *Modern Federal Ownership and Land Exchanges*

By the late 1800s the disposition policies of the federal government began to give way to a new era in which the government "withdrew" lands from further disposition and created "reservations" of the remain-ing lands to serve unique purposes. The creation of Yellowstone National Park in 1872 marked a turning point as the nation began to value con-servation for its own sake. In 1891 the General Revision Act extended authority to the President to set aside forested lands as public reserva-tions, creating the foundation for what has become an extensive national forest system. *See* Charles Wilkinson, Crossing the Next Meridian: Land, Water, and the Future of the West 122 (Island Press 1992). These and other steps took shape as a new "retention" policy for the remaining fed-eral land that had not been granted to states, individuals, or railroads. The retention policy came about in time to preserve federal ownership over nearly a third of the land in the United States. The great bulk of this land is in the western states, which collectively have a total of 55%, or 364 million acres, of federal public lands within their boundaries. Some states are dominated by federal holdings. For example, the federal government owns 85% of Nevada, 68% of Alaska, 64% of Idaho, and 64% of Utah.

Though the retention era brought an end to the massive federal give-aways of the prior century, it came after a century of conquest and disposition had imposed a property ownership pattern fragmented between various sovereigns and individuals. The natural resource con-flicts of today are in large part the legacy of incompatible property uses resulting from divided ownerships within ecosystems. Not uncommonly, the property management objectives of one owner are undermined by another owner's actions elsewhere in the ecosystem. A stream running off a parcel that has been deforested by a timber corporation may carry so much sediment that it precludes the use of a downstream federal par-cel to sustain fisheries. Or a mine located on private property within a national park (recall federal mining patents) may pollute a stream used as a water source by backpackers in the park. Watercourses connect land in ways that traditional property boundaries ignore. Accordingly, sound ecosystem management (as well as efficient land management) often requires extensive cooperation among owners or consolidation of parcels to eliminate intervening incompatible ownerships.

For these reasons, land exchanges are an increasingly prominent part of the ownership picture nationwide. A land exchange is the voluntary trading of land between two parties. It may be carried out between federal, tribal, and state governments, or between any sovereign and private party (subject to unique limitations if the sovereign is tribal). The Federal Land Policy Management Act (FLPMA) provides authority for the federal government to make such exchanges, as long as they are in the public interest and the lands exchanged are of "equal value." 43 U.S.C. § 1716 (a) (2003). Moreover, federal land exchanges must satisfy the requirements of the National Environmental Policy Act and other federal laws governing agency action. Exchanges between the states and private parties may also be constrained by the federal terms under which the state originally gained title to the property.

In Focus:
The New World Mine Land Exchange

The Clinton administration conducted numerous land exchanges to resolve environmental conflicts in a seemingly "win-win" manner. In some cases, this tool protected national treasures from being despoiled by private activities. In one example, a land exchange induced a mining company to abandon its mineral interests located on private land just outside of Yellowstone National Park. The New World Mine, proposed by Crown Butte Mining, Inc. (CBMI) (a subsidiary of Canadian conglomerate Noranda, Inc.), would have included an underground mine, an ore processing mill, a proposed 106–acre tailings pond, a waste rock storage sight, transmission lines, a work camp, and access roads, all of which threatened the water, wildlife, and recreational assets of Yellowstone Park.

In 1995, after the United Nations World Heritage Committee declared that the New World proposal had placed Yellowstone National Park "in danger," the United States and CBMI signed a Settlement Agreement in which CBMI relinquished its mineral and property interests in exchange for $65 million worth of land in Montana. Mark Mathews, *It Ain't Over Till It's Over*, High Country News, September 30, 1996. For more on the proposed mine, *see* Chapter 6.V.E.

Critics might question whether the federal government should have to trade away millions of dollars of valuable public resources to prevent clear damage to a national asset. Could the government simply have precluded the mining activity through regulatory means?

> Often the regulation fails to prevent ecological damage either because the law is not protective enough or because it is simply not enforced due to political pressure or lack of funding. The Clinton Administration favored political compromises over strong regulation, and land swaps proved a favored mechanism in a variety of high-profile resource conflicts. For discussion, see John H. Cushman, Jr., *U.S. Using Swaps to Protect Land,* NEW YORK TIMES, Sept. 30, 1996, at A1.

While land exchanges are useful in consolidating ownerships to promote ecosystem management, they also have drawbacks. They nearly always entail some losses to communities that have interests in the land slated for trade out of the public domain. Such communities may use the federal land for recreational, cultural, or economic purposes and would be precluded from such use when the area transfers into private ownership. Viewed from this perspective, land swaps are not pure "win-win" solutions. Consider the interests at stake in the following case and the federal procedural protections to safeguard such interests.

MUCKLESHOOT INDIAN TRIBE v. UNITED STATES FOREST SERVICE

United States Court of Appeals, Ninth Circuit, 1999.
177 F.3d 800.

PER CURIAM:

Plaintiffs Muckleshoot Indian Tribe, Pilchuck Audubon Society, and Huckleberry Mountain Protection Society appeal the district court's grant of summary judgment on consolidated challenges to a land exchange between the United States Forest Service and Weyerhaeuser Company. * * *

Huckleberry Mountain, the land subject to the dispute in this case, is located in the Green River watershed in the Mt. Baker–Snoqualmie National Forest ("the Forest") in the state of Washington. The Forest contains sixteen percent of the wilderness in the Pacific Northwest. Thirteen percent (259,545 acres) of the 1,983,774 acres within the National Forest boundary are privately owned, primarily by Weyerhaeuser and other large corporations. Most of the privately-owned lands are in the southern portion of the Forest, and are intermingled with federal lands in a checkerboard pattern of ownership that remains from the federal land grants to railroads a century ago.

Motivated in large part by a desire to unify land ownership, the United States Forest Service ("the Forest Service") and Weyerhaeuser Company ("Weyerhaeuser") began negotiations for a series of land exchanges pursuant to 43 U.S.C. § 1716, which authorizes the exchange of public lands within the National Forest system where "the public interest will be well served" by the exchange. * * * Weyerhaeuser and the Forest Service executed an exchange agreement under which Weyerhaeuser conveyed to the United States 30,253 acres of land in and around Mt. Baker National Forest in return for 4,362 acres of land in the Huckleberry Mountain area. In addition, Weyerhaeuser donated to the United States 962 acres to the Alpine Lakes Wilderness and 1,034 acres for Forest Service management. The National Forest lands that Weyerhaeuser received included old growth, commercial grade timber. The Forest Service also exchanged to Weyerhaeuser intact portions of the Huckleberry Divide Trail, a site important to the Tribe and that the Forest Service found eligible for inclusion in the National Register for Historic Preservation. Weyerhaeuser gave the Forest Service lands that were, for the most part, heavily logged and roaded. Weyerhaeuser intends to log the lands it received in the Exchange. * * *

The Muckleshoot Tribe is made up principally of descendants of tribes or bands that were parties to the Treaty of Point Elliott and the Treaty of Medicine Creek. * * * The Tribe alleges that for thousands of years, the ancestors of present tribal members used Huckleberry Mountain for cultural, religious, and resource purposes—uses that continue to the present day. The Forest Service lands exchanged to Weyerhaeuser were part of the Tribe's ancestral grounds.

Section [106] of [the National Historic Preservation Act (NHPA)] requires that, prior to any federal undertaking, the relevant federal agency "take into account the effect of the undertaking on any district, site, building, structure, or object that is included in or eligible for inclusion in the National Register" and "afford the Advisory Council on Historic Preservation … a reasonable opportunity to comment with regard to such undertaking." 16 U.S.C. § 470f. The Exchange was such an undertaking. 36 C.F.R. § 800.2(o).

We have held that Section 106 of NHPA is a "stop, look, and listen" provision that requires each federal agency to consider the effects of its programs. Under NHPA, a federal agency must make a reasonable and good faith effort to … avoid or mitigate any adverse effects, 36 C.F.R. §§ 800.8(e), 800.9(c). * * * We conclude that the Forest Service has not satisfied NHPA's mitigation requirements. * * *

The Tribe … claims that the Forest Service's attempt to mitigate the adverse effect of transferring a portion of the Divide Trail, an important tribal ancestral transportation route, was inadequate. We agree. * * * The Divide Trail is a 17.5 mile historic aboriginal transportation route. * * * In the proposed Exchange, a portion of the intact trail would be transferred to Weyerhaeuser, where it would likely be logged and rendered ineligible for listing. Transfer and destruction of historic property are "adverse" effects. *See* 36 C.F.R. § 800.9(b).

The regulations offer three options to mitigate an otherwise adverse effect so that it is "considered as being not adverse," two of which are implicated here. 36 C.F.R. § 800.9(c). First, an agency may conduct appropriate research "when the historic property is of value only for its potential contribution to archeological, historical, or architectural research, and when such value can be substantially preserved through the conduct of appropriate research...." 36 C.F.R. § 800.9(c)(1)(emphasis added). Second, an adverse effect becomes "not adverse" when the undertaking is limited to the "transfer, lease, or sale of a historic property, and adequate restrictions or conditions are included to ensure preservation of the property's significant historic features." 36 C.F.R. § 800.9(c)(3)(emphasis added). The Tribe insists that the Forest Service elected the wrong remedy. We agree.

To mitigate the adverse effect of the Exchange, the Forest Service proposed to map the trail using a global positioning system and to photograph significant features along the trail. It rejected an easement or covenant because it concluded that it was too expensive and impractical to monitor Weyerhaeuser's land practices, and because "only" 25 percent of the eligible miles of trail would be transferred out of federal ownership. It also rejected the imposition of conditions to prevent logging and other degradation. * * * The parties agree that the trail is likely to be logged if it is transferred. * * *

The Forest Service did not, and could not, proceed under (c)(1). Under 36 C.F.R. § 800.9(c)(1), research is appropriate mitigation where the historic property is of value only for "its potential contribution to archeological, historical, or architectural research." The Muckleshoots value the Divide Trail for more than its "potential contribution to ... research." * * *

While we do not decide whether the Forest Service's reasons for rejecting deed restrictions were valid, we note that it could have removed the trail from the Exchange. We conclude that documenting the trail did not satisfy the Forest Service's obligations to minimize the adverse effect of transferring the intact portions of the trail. * * *

Notes and Questions

1.   The case demonstrates the mix of property rights on land resulting from the conquest and disposition eras. Here, the Muckleshoot Tribe was the aboriginal owner and continued its use of ceded lands through federal ownership. Could the tribe have asserted treaty rights to continued use of the property once it passed to Weyerhaeuser?

2.   The NHPA is an interesting statute. For the most part, its duties are procedural in nature, much like NEPA (see chapter 4, *supra*). But agencies must be very careful to comply by consulting with state or tribal historic preservation officers and documenting their efforts to avoid or mitigate harm to historic properties (including traditional cultural properties). 16 U.S.C. § 470f; 36 C.F.R. Part 800. Property mechanisms, such as deed restrictions, may be an appropriate means of protecting historic properties. In this case, what "mitigation" would have been adequate for the tribes? If the deed reserves an easement for tribal use, should Weyerhaeuser be allowed to clearcut the surrounding lands, leaving just a narrow trail intact?

II. OWNERSHIP IN A CONSTITUTIONAL FRAMEWORK

As Section I of this chapter explained, the ownership of lands and resources involves a complex interaction between three sovereigns: the federal government, states and tribes. A basic review of the constitutional framework is necessary as a foundation to the more detailed discussion of ownership categories following in Section III. Chapter 3 of this casebook provides additional coverage of constitutional parameters governing the field of natural resources law.

A. The Federal and State Roles in the Constitution

The Supremacy Clause of the Constitution designates the federal government as the supreme sovereign in this country. U.S. CONST. art. VI, cl. 2. But though supreme, the federal government has only limited powers, as spelled out in the Constitution. States are the general sovereigns having the full array of police powers as reserved to them under the 10th Amendment of the Consitution. All federal action must be tied to one of the federal enumerated powers, the most important of which in the natural resources context are: the Enclave Clause, the Property Clause, the Treaty Clause, and the Commerce Clause. Due to liberal interpretation of these powers, federal authority over land and natural resources in this country is extensive. A major restriction against state activity arises from the "dormant Commerce Clause" ("dormant" because the actual language of the Commerce Clause does not address state powers), which has been used to strike down statutes designed to keep natural resources, such as minnows, or natural gas, within a state. *See* West v. Kansas Natural Gas Co., 221 U.S. 229, 255–56, 31 S.Ct. 564, 571, 55 L.Ed. 716, 726–27 (1911).

Not uncommonly, federal and state sovereigns have different priorities in ecosystem or land management. State environmental or natural resource regulations, if enforced on federal lands, may create outcomes that conflict with federal management. The Supreme Court has made clear that where state law conflicts with the federal government's exercise of its enumerated powers, federal law trumps state law under the Supremacy Clause. *See* Kleppe v. New Mexico, 426 U.S. 529, 96 S.Ct. 2285, 49 L.Ed.2d 34 (1976). Thus, where there is a clear federal mandate to manage federal lands or resources in a certain way, state law must recede under a doctrine known as federal preemption. The Court's opinion in California Coastal Comm'n. v. Granite Rock, 480 U.S. 572, 107 S.Ct. 1419, 94 L.Ed.2d 577 (1987), is one of the most comprehensive modern discussions of preemption in the natural resources context. The Court concluded that a state's permit requirement under its Coastal Zone Management Act for operation of an unpatented mining claim on a national forest was not preempted by federal law that allowed mining. The Court made a crucial distinction between permissible state environmental regulation and impermissible land use restriction of a federally permitted activity on federal public lands. *See id.* at 587–593 ("Land use planning in essence chooses particular uses for the land; environmental regulation, at its core, does not mandate particular uses of the land but requires only that, however the land is used, damage to the environment is kept within prescribed limits.").

B. Tribes: The Third Sovereign in the Constitutional Framework

The Constitution says little about the proper role of tribal sovereigns in the governmental framework, specifying only that Congress may regulate commerce with the Indian Tribes. U.S. Const. art. I, § 8, cl. 3. Despite this, courts have created a complex body of federal-Indian law. While this field of law easily consumes an entire law school course, at least the basic governing principles must be familiar to the general practitioner in natural resources law. Chapter 7 deals with federal Indian law in more detail.

A universal starting point of federal Indian law is the understanding that native nations are sovereigns—that is, governments—that pre-existed the United States. Early in the evolution of federal Indian law, the Supreme Court declared that tribes, though not "foreign nations," are "domestic dependant nations" within the United States. Cherokee Nation v. Georgia, 30 U.S. (5 Pet.) 1, 8 L.Ed. 25 (1831). In the landmark case, Worcester v. Georgia, 31 U.S. (6 Pet.) 515, 8 L.Ed. 483 (1832), the Court positioned tribes as the third sovereign within the Constitutional framework, making clear that, as pre-existing sovereigns, tribes were not subordinate to states. The Court also established the enduring principle that Indian relations are solely a matter of federal law, which pre-empts conflicting state law.

Despite the protection from state intrusions, other foundational cases make clear that tribal sovereignty is subject to an overriding federal "plenary power," a doctrine used by courts to justify express Congressional abrogations of native sovereignty. United States v. Kagama, 118 U.S. 375, 6 S.Ct. 1109, 30 L.Ed. 228 (1886). Federal plenary power over tribes is not explicitly indicated in the Constitution, which gives power only to "regulate Commerce ... with the Indian Tribes." U.S. Const., art. I, § 8, cl. 3. Despite the federal plenary power, tribes may exert all powers of sovereignty that have not been extinguished by Congress and that are consistent with their domestic dependent status. As the Court put it in United States v. Wheeler, 435 U.S. 313, 323, 98 S.Ct. 1079, 1086, 55 L.Ed.2d 303, 312 (1978): "The sovereignty that the Indian tribes retain is of a unique and limited character. It exists only at the sufferance of Congress and is subject to complete defeasance. But until Congress acts, the tribes retain their existing sovereign powers."

Recent cases have increasingly limited the ability of tribes to regulate non-Indian activity on non-Indian owned lands within a reservation. *See* Montana v. United States, 450 U.S. 544, 101 S.Ct. 1245, 67 L.Ed.2d 493 (1981) (restricting tribal regulation of non-Indian hunting and fishing on non-Indian lands within the reservation). Suffice it to say, any analysis of natural resource jurisdiction in Indian Country brings forth a quagmire of confusing doctrine.

Treaties are a bedrock source of law because they represent the early understandings between the federal government and individual tribes. Treaties with tribes were executed by the federal government pursuant to the treaty clause of the Constitution. U.S. CONST., art. II § 2, cl. 2. As such, they take a unique position in Constitutional law and are considered the "supreme law of the land." Worcester v. Georgia, 31 U.S. (6 Pet.) 515, 8 L.Ed. 483 (1832). Because treaty negotiations were coercive and one-sided (*see* In Focus: Federal Removal of the Wallowa Band of Nez Perce Indians, Section I.B., *supra*), courts have developed rules of construction to favor the Indian interests. The Supreme Court has said, "Indian treaties are to be interpreted liberally in favor of the Indians, [and] ambiguities are to be resolved in their favor." Minnesota v. Mille Lacs Band of Chippewa Indians, 526 U.S. 172, 200, 119 S.Ct. 1187, 1202, 143 L.Ed.2d 270, 293–94 (1999). Nevertheless, the Supreme Court has construed the federal government's plenary power to include the power to abrogate treaties, as long as Congress makes its intent clear. Minnesota v. Mille Lacs Band of Chippewa Indians, 526 U.S. 172, 202–203, 119 S.Ct. 1187, 1203–04, 143 L.Ed.2d 270, 295–96 (1999). Only Congress may abrogate treaties. Federal agencies lack such authority and must conform their actions to treaty obligations. Where Congress abrogates treaty property rights, compensation is due under the Fifth Amendment of the Constitution. United States v. Sioux Nation of Indians, 448 U.S. 371, 100 S.Ct. 2716, 65 L.Ed.2d 844 (1980).

Notwithstanding the "plenary" federal authority over tribes, courts have imposed a general obligation on the federal government to protect tribal lands, resources, and native interests. Since the beginning of federal-Indian relations, courts have emphasized that the federal government stands in a "trust" relationship with tribes. The trust obligation is a cornerstone of Indian law and has increasing importance in the area of natural resources law as tribal lands and resources face mounting threats from the majority society. *See* Mary Christina Wood, *Indian Land and the Promise of Native Sovereignty: The Trust Doctrine Revisited*, 1994 Utah L. Rev. 1471 (1994).

C. The Constitutional Check Against Sovereign Interference With Private Property

Another parameter in the Constitutional framework surrounding property ownership concerns the protection of individual private property against governmental infringement. The 5th amendment of the Constitution, which applies directly to the federal government and by extension to the states through the 14th amendment, declares: "Nor shall private property be taken for public use, without just compensation." U.S. CONST. amend. V. Courts have uniformly construed the clause to allow governments the power to condemn private property. But the clause also imposes an important limitation on such action. Governments must compensate landowners at fair market value whenever they take private property. Lucas v. South Carolina Coastal Council, 505 U.S. 1003, 112 S.Ct. 2886, 120 L.Ed.2d 798 (1992). The meaning of the word "taken" within the clause has stirred one of the most contentious debates in the modern judicial era and fuels contemporary property rights disputes centered around the concept of "regulatory takings." Private property ownership is subject to regulation by the states and federal government, but in some cases regulation may severely decrease property value or prevent the landowner's preferred use of property. Increasingly, landowners allege a "regulatory taking"—arguing that their property has *effectively* been "taken" because they are deprived of a certain amount of value or type of use.

In Pennsylvania Coal Co. v. Mahon, 260 U.S. 393, 415, 43 S.Ct. 158, 160, 67 L.Ed. 322, 326 (1922), Justice Holmes led the Court out onto a slippery slope by holding that there could be a taking if a regulation "goes too far." The progeny of takings cases since that time has demonstrated, if nothing else, the difficulty of creating a workable standard for regulatory takings. Much of the confusion springs from an unclear and changing notion of what is encompassed in a property right. If a property right does not exist, there can be no taking. As the Court has always held, all private property is subject to reasonable regulation to protect against public harm. *See* Palazzolo v. Rhode Island, 533 U.S. 606, 627, 121 S.Ct. 2448, 150 L.Ed.2d 592 (2001) ("The right to improve property, of course, is subject to the reasonable exercise of state authority."). Preventing the owner from doing something she never had the right to do in the first place is not a taking. This conclusion, however, takes the lawyer only so far, because it begs the question of what regulation is reasonable, a question that continues to befuddle the Supreme Court.

In addition to the regulatory burden that all property must accept, some individual title may be encumbered by pre-existing "sovereign servitudes" that are, by nature, property rights held by government for the public. Examples are treaty rights, the federal navigation servitude, and public trust easements. When these sovereign servitudes underlie individual title, they limit the landowner's ability to make any use of the property that interferes with such public rights. Regulation to prevent an interfering use is inherently not a taking, because the property owner never had the right to put the property to the interfering use in the first place. The judicial conception of sovereign servitudes is an ever-changing one, in some cases growing to meet emerging public needs. As courts expand their notion of sovereign servitudes, the set of takings claims available to private property owners correspondingly retracts. The adjustment between sovereign servitudes and individual property rights is a critical theme that emerges in the next four chapters dealing with federal, tribal, state, and individual property rights. Chapter 9 devotes attention to Constitutional takings jurisprudence.

In Practice:
Finding sovereign servitudes in the chain of title

Where sovereign property rights such as treaty rights, the federal navigational servitude, and public trust easements encumber a particular parcel, such rights form a "cloud" on the title held by individuals. But how does a practitioner determine whether there are underlying sovereign rights on a particular parcel? Unfortunately, there is no streamlined way. When title transfers take place between individuals, the exchange of property rights is "recorded," usually in the county courthouse where the property is located. Searches through title records provide a reliable method for determining individually held title encumbrances, such as easements, future interests, covenants, and the like. But sovereign property interests are typically unrecorded, expressed only through caselaw, treaties, statutes, or executive orders. Therefore, the natural resource practitioner is ill-advised to rely solely on title searches to portray a full picture of ownership. Moreover, title companies, which insure an individual owner's title to property, typically exclude from coverage any encumbrance on title arising from sovereign property rights. So if there are underlying sovereign rights that a purchaser was unaware of at the time of purchase, it is unlikely that the purchaser could later seek recourse for the loss in property value from the title insurance company.

Question: Assume you are a real property lawyer. Under what circumstances should you investigate the possibility of sovereign property rights or unique regulatory concerns? Should you explore the possibility with every parcel, even ones in the middle of a city or farm area? What types of parcels raise "red flags"? River frontage parcels? Ocean beach parcels? Wetland parcels? Others?

III.   THE SOVEREIGN OWNERSHIP OF NATURAL RESOURCES

As Section I described, the federal government, states, and tribes maintain a significant land base, as well as rights in critical natural resources such as wildlife and water. Because these resources play a vital role in sustaining society as a whole, court decisions have set unique limitations on private uses that could harm public interests. This section explores the jig-sawed sovereign ownership of natural resources.

Several early cases establish a bedrock federal common law structure for analyzing federal, tribal and state property rights in resources. These venerable cases include Pollard v. Hagan (1845) (submerged lands); Illinois Central Railroad v. Illinois (1892) (public trust); Geer v. Connecticut (1896) (wildlife); United States v. Winans (1905) (treaty fishing rights easements); and Winters v. United States (1908) (federal reserved water rights). In *Pollard v. Hagan*, the Supreme Court announced fundamental principles of sovereign ownership in the context of submerged lands. The *Pollard* themes are repeated throughout this area of federal common law.

A. Equal Footing Doctrine

Submerged lands are those lands beneath the ordinary high water mark along water bodies.[a] Courts have repeatedly emphasized the importance of submerged lands to the sovereignty of government because they are crucial to navigation, fishing, and commerce. The Court in *Pollard v. Hagan* (excerpted below) articulated what became known as the "equal footing doctrine" to govern ownership of submerged lands. The historical framework surrounding this doctrine was succinctly described in Utah Division of State Lands v. United States, 482 U.S. 193, 195–96, 107 S.Ct. 2318, 96 L.Ed.2d 162 (1987):

> The equal footing doctrine is deeply rooted in history, and the proper application of the doctrine requires an understanding of its origins. Under English common law the English Crown held sovereign title to all lands underlying navigable waters. Because title to such land was important to the sovereign's ability to control navigation, fishing, and other commercial activity on rivers and lakes, ownership of this land was considered an essential attribute of sovereignty. Title to such land was therefore vested in the sovereign for the benefit of the whole people. *See Shively v. Bowlby,* 152 U.S. 1, 11–14 (1894). When the 13 Colonies became independent from Great Britain, they claimed title to the lands under navigable waters within their boundaries as the sovereign successors to the English Crown. Because all subsequently admitted States enter the Union on an *"equal footing"* with the original 13 states, they too hold title to the land under navigable waters within their boundaries upon entry into the Union.

In *Pollard v. Hagan*, the Supreme Court held that title to submerged lands below navigable waterways automatically vested in states upon their admission to the union, without any express language in the

a. The term "submerged lands" is used in a generic sense here. The term as it was traditionally used meant lands sea- ward of the low water mark. *See* ROBERT E. BECK, WATER AND WATER RIGHTS § 30.02(d)(1) (2d ed. 1991).

admission acts. The Court reasoned that these crucial lands were necessary to the sovereign functioning of the new state, and that the new states could not be on "equal footing" with the older states–something promised in the Northwest Ordinance and statehood admissions acts–if they did not own the submerged lands. Submerged lands therefore represent a category of state ownership distinguishable from the express statehood grants described earlier.

Pollard involved a title dispute to submerged lands along the Mobile River in Alabama. The area was within the territory ceded to the federal government by Georgia (one of the original 13 colonies) in 1780. The United States granted plaintiffs title to the tidelands after Alabama became a state. The Court concluded that the United States lost any claim to the land when Alabama entered the Union, and therefore, the federal patent to Pollard was invalid because the federal government could not give what it did not have.

POLLARD v. HAGAN
Supreme Court of the United States, 1845.
44 U.S. (3 How.) 212, 11 L.Ed. 565.

[W]e will now inquire into the nature and extent of the right of the United States to these lands.... This right originated in voluntary surrenders, made by several of the old states, of their waste and unappropriated lands, to the United States, ... to aid in paying the public debt, incurred by the war of the Revolution. The object of all the parties to these contracts of cession, was to convert the land into money for the payment of the debt, and to erect new states over the territory thus ceded; and as soon as these purposes could be accomplished, the power of the United States over these lands, as property, was to cease. * * *

This right of eminent domain over the shores and the soils under the navigable waters, for all municipal purposes, belongs exclusively to the states within their respective territorial jurisdictions, and they, and they only, have the constitutional power to exercise it. To give to the United States the right to transfer to a citizen the title to the shores and the soils under the navigable waters, would be placing in their hands a weapon which might be wielded greatly to the injury of state sovereignty, and deprive the states of the power to exercise a numerous and important class of police powers. But in the hands of the states this power can never be used so as to affect the exercise of any national right of eminent domain or jurisdiction with which the United States have been invested by the Constitution. For, although the territorial limits of Alabama have extended all her sovereign power into the sea, it is there, as on the shore, but municipal power, subject to the Constitution of the United States, and the laws which shall be made in pursuance thereof.

By the preceding course of reasoning we have arrived at these general conclusions: First, the shores of navigable waters, and the soils under them, were not granted by the Constitution to the United States, but were reserved to the states respectively. Secondly, the new states have the same rights, sovereignty, and jurisdiction over this subject as the original states. Thirdly, the right of the United States to the public lands, and the power of Congress to make all needful rules and regulations for the sale and disposition thereof, conferred no power to grant to the plaintiffs the land in controversy in this case.

Notes and Questions

1. The *Pollard* ruling created ribbons of state streambed ownership within blocks of federal lands. In the Minnesota Boundary Waters Wilderness area, for example, the federal government owns 73% of the lands, but the state of Minnesota owns the streambeds. In Minnesota v. Block, 660 F.2d 1240 (8th Cir. 1981), the state objected to the federal government's prohibition on motorboat use within the Boundary Waters Wilderness area and challenged the prohibition as exceeding the federal government's enumerated authority under the Property Clause of the Constitution. The court took a broad view of the Property Clause to uphold federal regulation of activity occurring off federal land.

2. The *Pollard* Court broadly suggested that the federal government could not hold *any* land for itself after the creation of states because doing so would interfere with the states' sovereignty. *See* Pollard v. Hagan, 44 U.S. (3 How.) 212, 224, 11 L.Ed. 565, 571 (1845) ("The object of all the parties to these contracts of cession, was to ... erect new states over the territory thus ceded; and as soon as these purposes could be accomplished, the power of the United States over these lands, as property, was to cease."). Despite that language, cases have limited the *Pollard* ruling to the context of submerged lands. *See* Arizona v. California, 373 U.S. 546, 596–97, 83 S.Ct. 1468, 1496 10 L.Ed.2d 542, 576 (1963).

3. *Pollard* was only the beginning of a line of cases that, pieced together, presents a detailed structure for dealing with questions over ownership of submerged lands. *Pollard* was decided in an era vastly different than the modern one, before population explosion, urbanization, and industrialization. Courts have since recognized the need for some exceptions and limitations to *Pollard's* sweeping rule. The result is a more complex picture of submerged land ownership—one that recognizes federal, tribal and state interests in these vital lands.

Pollard still anchors the framework. There remains a strong presumption that states automatically gained title to submerged lands below navigable waters at the time of statehood. But courts have set limits on the general rule. If the federal government clearly reserved submerged lands beneath navigable waters for itself or for tribes prior to statehood, then title never passed to the new state, but instead stayed with the federal government or the tribe. *See* Utah Div. of State Lands v. United States, 482 U.S. 193, 198, 107 S.Ct. 2318, 2321, 96 L.Ed.2d 162, 170 (1987); Idaho v. United States, 533 U.S. 262, 121 S.Ct. 2135, 150 L.Ed.2d 326 (2001). The Supreme Court recently declared a two-step inquiry in State of Alaska v. United States, 125 S.Ct. 2137, 162 L.Ed.2d 57 (2005):

> We first inquire whether the United States clearly intended to include submerged lands within the reservation. If the answer is yes, we next inquire whether the United States expressed its intent to retain federal title to submerged lands within the reservation.

4. The *Pollard* ruling inevitably created complexities in the tribal area. The treaties often expressly guaranteed the tribe complete use and occupation of the entire reserved area. When states were created, state boundaries formed an overlay to these reservation boundaries. States expected all of the attributes of sovereignty enjoyed by the original 13 colonies and secured by the Equal Footing Doctrine. But venerable principles of federal Indian law protected tribal property rights and jurisdiction within reservation boundaries. Worcester v. Georgia, 31 U.S. (6 Pet.) 515, 8 L.Ed. 483 (1832).

A state's assertion of streambed ownership within an Indian reservation not only presents a sovereign property dispute between the state and tribe, but also threatens deeply rooted tribal jurisdictional prerogatives. If a state owns a streambed within an Indian reservation, that state has grounds for exercising jurisdiction over uses of that streambed. *See* Montana v. United States, 450 U.S. 544, 101 S.Ct. 1245, 67 L.Ed.2d 493 (1981) (tribes divested of their inherent regulatory jurisdiction over non-Indian hunting and fishing on non-tribal submerged lands unless conduct threatens tribe's health and welfare or political or economic integrity).

The resolution of streambed ownership within Indian reservations turns on highly specific factual contexts involving the treaty language and other historical evidence. *See, e.g.*, Choctaw Nation v. Oklahoma, 397 U.S. 620, 90 S.Ct. 1328, 25 L.Ed.2d 615 (1969) (treaties granting reservation lands to the Choctaw, Cherokee, and Chickasaw Nations included the streambeds underlying the Arkansas River); Montana v. United States, 450 U.S. 544, 101 S.Ct. 1245, 67 L.Ed.2d 493 (1981) (Crow Tribe did not own the bed of the Big Horn River, which flows through a reservation set aside by treaty); Idaho v. United States, 533 U.S. 262, 121 S.Ct. 2135, 150 L.Ed.2d 326 (2001) (Coeur d'Alene Tribe owns the lakebed of that portion of Lake Coeur d'Alene that is within the reservation set aside by Executive Order).

In Focus:

The County Supremacy Movement's Revival of Pollard

In the 1990s, a "County Supremacy" movement—essentially a replay of the Sagebrush Rebellion in the late 1970s—ignited across the western states. A coalition of mining, timber and ranching interests, resentful of increasing protections limiting extractive uses on the public lands, resurrected *Pollard* to suggest that the federal government did not really own its public lands. They invoked the sweeping language of *Pollard* to argue that the federal government should have transferred its landholdings to each of the western states upon admission to the union, and that failure to do so violated the Equal Footing Doctrine. They went so far as to pass local ordinances—nearly 100 in all—declaring county or state ownership of federal public lands. Violence erupted in some places.

UNREST IN THE WEST
Erik Larson
TIME, Oct. 23, 1995

Sitting on a bale of barley destined for his cattle, Dick Carver gets just a little misty eyed as he recalls the moment that propelled him to leadership of a rebellion now sweeping the West. Usually mild mannered and affable, the Nevada rancher and Nye County commissioner reached a point last year when he had had enough. To him, federal intrusion into the daily life of his county had simply grown too great, so on July 4, 1994—Independence Day—he took the law into his own hands. His weapon of choice: a rusting, yellow D–7 Caterpillar bulldozer. * * *

Carver had climbed aboard the Caterpillar to bulldoze open a weather-damaged road across a national forest. The hitch was, he wanted to do so without federal permission. Although plainly illegal, in Carver's mind it was an act of civil disobedience—a frontier Boston Tea Party—warranted by the tyranny he and his fellow citizens in Nye had long endured. But in this case, the purported tyrant was the U.S. government. The incident immediately made Carver a leading voice in the so-called county-supremacy movement now gaining momentum throughout the West. It also triggered a major federal lawsuit seeking to assert once and for all the government's ownership of federal lands in Nye County and, by legal inference, its possession of public lands that cover one-third of the nation's ground. The Justice Department estimates that at least 35 counties, primarily in Arizona, New Mexico, Nevada and California, have declared authority over federal lands within their boundaries. Other estimates put the number far higher. * * * The new rebelliousness has created a breeding ground for violence, especially in the austere rural settlements that bracket the Continental Divide. * * *

The forces powering the Nye County rebellion are those resculpting the political and social landscape of America at large. They just happened to have converged with their greatest intensity in the West, where private and public interests clash directly and daily, typically over such visceral issues as land and water. The angry rebels range from ranchers fed up with bureaucrats' telling them when and where to graze their cattle to developers denied crucial water rights. * * *

The third largest county in America, Nye is an immense wedge covering more than 18,000 sq. mi., about the size of Vermont and New Hampshire combined, but is occupied by only 20,000 people—plenty of elbow room, except for the fact that the Federal Government owns 93% of the land. The Bureau of Land Management (BLM) controls most of the valleys, the U.S. Forest Service most of the uplands. The Defense Department too claims huge chunks of the county, including the Nevada Test Site, where it detonated hundreds of nuclear devices, and the Tonopah Test Range, the darling of paranormal buffs, who know it by the nickname Dreamland and suspect that all manner of spooky events have occurred there. Even the airspace over Nye is largely restricted to military aircraft. Jet fighters scream up Carver's Big Smoky Valley, occasionally roaring past cars at sage top altitude. * * * The ultimate metaphor for federal intrusion is the Energy Department's hotly controversial proposal to use Yucca Mountain, in Nye, for the nation's first high-level radioactive-waste dump. * * *

Dawn broke on the D–7 caterpillar draped in an American flag. ** Two forest officials arrived, David Young, a law-enforcement agent, and David Grider, then the district ranger. When the crowd saw that Young was armed, some 50 people by Carver's count, strapped on their own handguns. * * *

Young did not interfere until Carver began plowing a roadbed outside the existing right-of-way. Suddenly, he stepped in front of the bulldozer and unfurled a sign, stating STOP! DISTURBANCE NOT AUTHORIZED! But Carver kept going, at one point brandishing his Constitution. * * * The event ended without violence. Word of the Jefferson Canyon Road affair spread quickly through the West and immediately drew the ire of the Justice Department. The government filed its lawsuit against the county in March. * * *

History runs through the case like a strand of barbed wire. * * * Distilled to its bare essence, Nye County's argument is this: Under the "equal footing" doctrine, new states admitted to the Union were to enter with all the dignity and sovereignty of the original 13. By retaining so much of Nevada's land, the government gave it second-class status, in violation of the equal-footing doctrine. * * *

The district court of Nevada put an end to the local assertion of land ownership in United States v. Nye County, 920 F. Supp. 1108 (D. Nev. 1996). The court rejected the County's equal footing argument, asserting that it could find no historical precedent for implied transfer of dry land to the states upon statehood. A year after *Nye County* was decided, the Ninth Circuit stifled any last whimper of county supremacy in United States v. Gardner, 107 F.3d 1314 (9th Cir. 1997). The case involved Nevada ranchers who grazed their cattle illegally on federal public lands, claiming that the federal government did not own the land under *Pollard*. The court stated:

> [T]he Supreme Court has declined to extend the Equal Footing Doctrine to lands other than those underneath navigable waters or waters affected by the ebb and flow of the tides. * * * The Equal Footing Doctrine, then, does not operate to reserve title to fast dry lands to individual states. Moreover, the Supreme Court has long held that the Equal Footing Doctrine refers to "those attributes essential to [a state's] equality in dignity and

power with other states." *Coyle v. Smith*, 221 U.S. 559, 568 (1911). * * * The Equal Footing Doctrine, then, applies to political rights and sovereignty, not to economic or physical characteristics of the states. * * * Therefore, the Equal Footing Doctrine would not operate, as Gardners argue, to give Nevada title to the public lands within its boundaries.

Gardner, 107 F.3d at 1319.

For an insightful article exploring the impact of *Pollard* in modern state assertions of sovereignty, *see* Paul Conable, *Equal Footing, County Supremacy, and the Western Public Lands,* 26 ENVTL. L. 1263 (1996). For a background of western land use politics, *see* John Leshy, *Unraveling the Sagebrush Rebellion: Law, Politics, and Federal Lands,* 14 U.C. DAVIS L. REV. 317 (1980). The conflict over federal lands in western states is further explored in Chapter 3, section I.

In Practice:
Putting Together Submerged Land Ownership Rules

Ownership of submerged lands is complicated, with the various rules fitting together like a puzzle. When analyzing submerged lands beneath *navigable* waters, apply the *Pollard* rule of state ownership, as modified by the "clear reservation" cases above that allow federal or tribal ownership in exceptional circumstances. When dealing with submerged lands below *non*-navigable waterways, a different rule applies. Those lands did *not* automatically vest with the state upon statehood, but remained in federal ownership (of course such lands may later have been transferred to private individuals). *See* DAN TARLOCK, LAW OF WATER RIGHTS AND RESOURCES (3d ed. 1988); ROBERT E. BECK, WATER AND WATER RIGHTS (2d ed. 1991). The ownership question thus turns on whether the waterway was navigable-in-fact at the precise time the state entered the union. A standard federal navigability test is used for this purpose: waterways are "navigable in fact when they are used, or are susceptible of being used, in their natural and ordinary condition, as highways for commerce, over which trade and travel are or may be conducted in the customary modes of trade and travel on water...." United States v. Holt State Bank, 270 U.S. 49, 56, 46 S.Ct. 197, 199, 70 L.Ed. 465, 469 (1926). Submerged lands subject to influence of the tide are treated differently because of the unique sovereign interests in such waters. The general rule is that states have ownership of all lands subject to the ebb and flow of the tide inland regardless of whether such waters are navigable. Phillips Petroleum Co. v. Mississippi, 484 U.S. 469, 108 S.Ct. 791, 98 L.Ed.2d 877 (1988). These submerged tidelands automatically passed to states under the Equal Footing doctrine. United States v. Alaska, 521 U.S. 1, 4, 117 S.Ct. 1888, 1891, 138 L.Ed.2d 231, 242 (1997). Courts have held

that the United States owns title to offshore land, because of its
supreme national interests in maintaining the borders. United States
v. California, 332 U.S. 19, 67 S.Ct. 1658, 91 L.Ed. 1889 (1947). In
1953, however, Congress passed the Submerged Lands Act of 1953, 43
U.S.C. §§ 1301–1315, in which it conveyed to the states title to
coastal submerged lands up to three miles offshore. Any state claiming title to submerged coastal lands within the three-mile belt, therefore, must base its claim on the Submerged Lands Act. *See Alaska,*
521 U.S. at 6.

B.   The Public Trust Doctrine

The public trust doctrine is a common law doctrine that imposes
sovereign fiduciary responsibilities in certain types of land and resources
that are critical to the public. Sovereign property rights implicated by
the public trust doctrine may affect title held by private landowners,
posing an important limitation on the private uses of property. As a
foundation for environmental law, the role of the public trust doctrine
cannot be overemphasized. The doctrine first took root in this country in
the context of streambed ownership. Since that time, however, some
courts have greatly expanded the public trust doctrine to protect sovereign property rights in other critical resources, including water, dry sand
beaches, wetlands, parks, and wildlife.

The landmark case announcing the doctrine was Illinois Central
Railroad Co. v. Illinois, 146 U.S. 387, 13 S.Ct. 110, 36 L.Ed. 1018 (1892).
The State of Illinois, acting through its legislature, conveyed submerged
lands along Chicago's waterfront on Lake Michigan to Illinois Central
Railroad (a private company). During that era, fraud and corruption
were prevalent, and the grant to Illinois Central had been made under
dubious circumstances. The legislature later tried to revoke the grant
and reclaim the contested area. A suit was brought by the Illinois Attorney General to invalidate the prior grant.

ILLINOIS CENTRAL RAILROAD CO. v. ILLINOIS
Supreme Court of the United States, 1892.
146 U.S. 387, 13 S.Ct. 110, 36 L.Ed. 1018

JUSTICE FIELD delivered the opinion of the Court.

The object of the suit is to obtain a judicial determination of the title
of certain lands on the east or lake front of the city of Chicago....

The state of Illinois was admitted into the Union in 1818 on an
equal footing with the original states, in all respects. * * * [T]he state
holds the title to the lands under the navigable waters of Lake Michigan,
within its limits, in the same manner that the state holds title to soils
under tide water, by the common law ... ; and that title necessarily carries with it control over the waters above them, whenever the lands are
subjected to use. But it is a title different in character from that which
the state holds in lands intended for sale. It is different from the title

which the United States hold in the public lands which are open to pre-emption and sale. It is a title held in trust for the people of the state, that they may enjoy the navigation of the waters, carry on commerce over them, and have liberty of fishing therein, freed from the obstruction or interference of private parties. The interest of the people in the navigation of the waters and in commerce over them may be improved in many instances by the erection of wharves, docks, and piers therein, for which purpose the state may grant parcels of the submerged lands; and, so long as their disposition is made for such purpose, no valid objections can be made to the grants. It is grants of parcels of lands under navigable waters that may afford foundation for wharves, piers, docks, and other structures in aid of commerce, and grants of parcels which, being occupied, do not substantially impair the public interest in the lands and waters remaining, that are chiefly considered and sustained in the adjudged cases as a valid exercise of legislative power consistently with the trust to the public upon which such lands are held by the state. But that is a very different doctrine from the one which would sanction the abdication of the general control of the state over lands under the navigable waters of an entire harbor or bay, or of a sea or lake. Such abdication is not consistent with the exercise of that trust which requires the government of the state to preserve such waters for the use of the public. The trust devolving upon the state for the public, and which can only be discharged by the management and control of property in which the public has an interest, cannot be relinquished by a transfer of the property. The control of the state for the purposes of the trust can never be lost, except as to such parcels as are used in promoting the interests of the public therein, or can be disposed of without any substantial impairment of the public interest in the lands and waters remaining. It is only by observing the distinction between a grant of such parcels for the improvement of the public interest, or which when occupied do not substantially impair the public interest in the lands and waters remaining, and a grant of the whole property in which the public is interested, that the language of the adjudged cases can be reconciled. * * * A grant of all the lands under the navigable waters of a state has never been adjudged to be within the legislative power; and any attempted grant of the kind would be held, if not absolutely void on its face, as subject to revocation. The state can no more abdicate its trust over property in which the whole people are interested, like navigable waters and soils under them, so as to leave them entirely under the use and control of private parties, except in the instance of parcels mentioned for the improvement of the navigation and use of the waters, or when parcels can be disposed of without impairment of the public interest in what remains, than it can abdicate its police powers in the administration of government and the preservation of the peace. In the administration of government the use of such powers may for a limited period be delegated to a municipality or other body, but there always remains with the state the right to revoke those powers and exercise them in a more direct manner, and one more conformable to its wishes. So with trusts connected with public property, or property of a special character, like lands under navigable waters; they cannot be placed entirely beyond the direction and control of the state.

The harbor of Chicago is of immense value to the people of the state of Illinois, in the facilities it affords to its vast and constantly increasing commerce; and the idea that its legislature can deprive the state of control over its bed and waters, and place the same in the hands of a private corporation ... is a proposition that cannot be defended. * * *

Surely an act of the legislature transferring the title to its submerged lands and the power claimed by the railroad company to a foreign state or nation would be repudiated, without hesitation, as a gross perversion of the trust over the property under which it is held. So would a similar transfer to a corporation of another state. It would not be listened to that the control and management of the harbor of that great city—a subject of concern to the whole people of the state—should thus be placed elsewhere than in the state itself. * * *

Any grant of the kind is necessarily revocable, and the exercise of the trust by which the property was held by the state can be resumed at any time. Undoubtedly there may be expenses incurred in improvements made under such a grant, which the state ought to pay; but, be that as it may, the power to resume the trust whenever the state judges best is, we think, incontrovertible. The position advanced by the railroad company in support of its claim to the ownership of the submerged lands, and the right to the erection of wharves, piers, and docks at its pleasure, or for its business in the harbor of Chicago, would place every harbor in the country at the mercy of a majority of the legislature of the state in which the harbor is situated.

We cannot, it is true, cite any authority where a grant of this kind has been held invalid, for we believe that no instance exists where the harbor of a great city and its commerce have been allowed to pass into the control of any private corporation. But the decisions are numerous which declare that such property is held by the state, by virtue of its sovereignty, in trust for the public. The ownership of the navigable waters of the harbor, and of the lands under them, is a subject of public concern to the whole people of the state. The trust with which they are held, therefore, is governmental, and cannot be alienated, except in those instances mentioned, of parcels used in the improvement of the interest thus held, or when parcels can be disposed of without detriment to the public interest in the lands and waters remaining.

This follows necessarily from the public character of the property, being held by the whole people for purposes in which the whole people are interested. * * * The legislature could not give away nor sell the discretion of its successors in respect to matters, the government of which, from the very nature of things, must vary with varying circumstances. The legislation which may be needed one day for the harbor may be different from the legislation that may be required at another day. Every legislature must, at the time of its existence, exercise the power of the state in the execution of the trust devolved upon it. We hold, therefore, that any attempted cession of the ownership and control of the state in and over the submerged lands in Lake Michigan ... was inoperative to affect, modify, or in any respect to control the sovereignty and dominion of the state over the lands.... There can be no irrepealable contract in a conveyance of property by a grantor in disregard of a public trust, under which he was bound to hold and manage it.

Notes and Questions

1. At the outset of its opinion the Court noted that the state of Illinois acquired the submerged lands upon statehood under *Pollard v. Hagan.* Recall that *Pollard,* like *Illinois Central,* also dealt with a grant of submerged lands to a private party. The *Pollard* Court emphasized the significance of submerged lands to the sovereignty of the state:

> To give to the United States the right to transfer to a citizen the title to the shores and the soils under the navigable waters, would be placing in their hands a weapon which might be wielded greatly to the injury of state sovereignty, and deprive the states of the power to exercise a numerous and important class of police powers.

Pollard, 44 U.S. at 230.

Did the *Illinois Central* Court essentially apply this same reasoning? How are the submerged lands critical to the sovereign functioning of the state? What role did submerged lands play in sustaining the fishing, navigation, and commerce so vital to 19th century society?

2. If the public trust doctrine is the mechanism to protect public interests in lands that are vital to sovereign functioning, is the doctrine limited to the context of submerged lands? Are there other categories of land and resources that are equally crucial to modern society? What about the last strongholds of habitat for endangered species, or parks and other open spaces, recharge areas for diminishing aquifers, floodplains, or wetland areas? Did the Court invite expansion of the doctrine as societal needs emerged? Consider the Court's statement: "So with trusts connected with public property, *or property of a special character*, like lands under navigable waters, they cannot be placed entirely beyond the direction and control of the State." (Emphasis added.) Some courts in fact have expanded the public trust doctrine both in terms of geographic scope and the public interests it protects. Chapter 8.II, infra, explores the doctrine in its modern form.

3. Consider the relationship between sovereign and individual property rights in public trust resources. The submerged lands at issue in *Illinois Central* entered state ownership through the equal footing doctrine as a "trust" to benefit the public. The Court explained that, though the lands may be transferred to private parties, the public "trust" could not be relinquished by the State. The trust encumbers the land even after it is transferred into private property ownership. As the Court explained, "[a]ny grant of the kind is necessarily revocable, and the exercise of the trust by which the property was held by the state can be resumed at any time." *Illinois Central,* 146 U.S. at 455. Private property owners acquiring title to such trust property, then,

actually acquire a property interest that has a significant encumbrance in the form of an antecedent public property right. This public property right has an important interplay with Constitutional takings doctrine under the Fifth Amendment, which provides that no private property can be taken by the state or federal government without compensation. According to public trust theory, when the state exerts its pre-existing public trust property rights, even to revoke a prior grant, it is not taking away any private property rights that the landowner ever had, because the landowner's rights were always encumbered by a public trust. *See* Richard J. Lazarus, *Changing Conceptions of Property and Sovereignty in Natural Resources: Questioning the Public Trust Doctrine,* 71 Iowa L. Rev. 631, 648–49 (1986). This subject is further explored in Chapter 9.II.B.

4.   The *Illinois Central* Court placed limits on the public trust doctrine. Consider the following statement:

> The trust with which [submerged lands] are held, therefore, is governmental and cannot be alienated, *except* in those instances mentioned, of parcels used in the improvement of the interest thus held, or when parcels can be disposed of without detriment to the public interest in the lands and waters remaining.

Illinois Central Railroad Co, 146 U.S. at 455–56 (emphasis added).

Does this language create a broad exception to the general rule against alienability? What if a parcel is initially alienated without detriment to the remaining trust lands, but then *becomes* necessary for the public many years later? Is the public trust a dormant property right that can support revocation at any time the parcel is used in a manner harmful to the remaining public trust property? These and many other questions frame the modern doctrinal development of the public trust. *See* Chapter 8.II.

C.   Waters

Water is vital to life itself, and conflicts over water abound. In every basin there is a finite quantity of water available for the competing demands of municipalities, farmers, industries, recreationalists, and species. In many basins, excessive water withdrawals literally de-water the streams, pushing fisheries towards extinction and unraveling entire aquatic ecosystems. Because of the crucial role water plays in sustaining human life and the environment, the ownership scheme governing this resource is of preeminent importance. Water is also one of the most complex areas of natural resources law, because of the myriad public and private needs that require balancing. Like other resource allocation schemes, rights in water law operate on both the sovereign and individual levels. While Chapter 14 covers the subject in far more detail, this section presents a brief overview of water ownership.

1.   *Individual Ownership of Water Rights: Riparianism and Prior Appropriation*

Citizens gain water rights through the law of the state in which the water is located. *See* California Oregon Power Co. v. Beaver Portland

Cement Co., 295 U.S. 142, 55 S.Ct. 725, 79 L.Ed. 1356 (1935). Such individual water rights originate in the common law of the state, but most states now have detailed permit systems governing the allocation of water to individuals. A water right is a unique type of property right. Because of the vital importance of water to the public as a whole, sovereign property interests significantly encumber individual water rights.

Two distinct systems of water rights operate in the United States. East of the 100th meridian, a system of riparian law governs. This system vests a property right to water in all owners of land along a waterway. Such riparian landowners may make reasonable use of the water but cannot use it to the detriment of other riparian owners. Riparian owners have rights to continued flow of water passing by or through their lands. In each state west of the 100th meridian, a system of "prior appropriation" governs surface water use and allocation wholly or in part. A pure prior appropriation system gives water rights only to "appropriators" who actually divert the water out of the stream. In the arid West, this system allows more land to benefit from water, but it can also result in tremendous environmental damage to waterways that are de-watered by diversions. Under this system, a riparian landowner has no inherent rights to a flow of water by or through her land. Nine western states follow a pure prior appropriation system: Colorado, Alaska, Arizona, Idaho, Montana, Nevada, New Mexico, Utah, and Wyoming. In addition to the two "pure" versions of riparian and appropriation law, ten states have a hybrid combination of riparian and appropriation doctrine: California, Kansas, Mississippi, Nebraska, North Dakota, Oklahoma, Oregon, South Dakota, Texas, and Washington.

The western system of prior appropriation was formed in the mining camps in the mid–1800s. It became customary to divert water from a stream to another location. The prior appropriation system is a rudimentary legal scheme formalizing a "first-come, first-serve" approach. Water rights arise from actual diversions of water out of the stream for "beneficial" uses, a term defined by state law. This system prioritizes the water rights according to the date of first use. A log mill, for example, may have a water right to withdraw 100 cfs (cubic feet per second, a standard measure of the water right) with a priority date of 1910. The log mill would have priority over a junior appropriator who begins diverting water at a later date. If a farmer began appropriating 80 cfs in 1920, the farmer's (or her successor's) water right is junior to the mill's (or its successor's) right, but senior to all rights acquired thereafter. In times of scarcity, senior appropriators take their water first, and junior appropriators often forgo. The junior appropriator located upstream of the senior appropriator must let the water pass to allow the senior appropriator her full beneficial use. When appropriators do not get water because of their junior position in the priority scheme, their rights are described as "paper rights." In flood years, when water levels exceed those of average years, such paper rights may actually be watered. In practice, the administration of the prior appropriation system is exceedingly complicated, but the basic principle of "first in time, first in right" is simple. Protracted proceedings in state courts (called "adjudications") quantify and validate appropriation rights throughout a basin. Water adjudications often involve complex settlements among the various parties with competing claims to the water.

2. *Interstate Allocation*

Because many waterways cross state boundaries, the matter of interstate water allocation is critical to a stable water regime. There are three ways of accomplishing interstate allocation. The first is through Congressional apportionment, which results in a statute. In 1990, for example, Congress passed a statute apportioning Lake Tahoe and the Truckee and Carson Rivers between California and Nevada. PL 101–618, 104 Stat. 3289, Title II (1990). The second method is through interstate compacts, provided for by Article I, section 10, clause 3 of the Constitution. This tool allows states to enter into agreements over allocation of water, but requires Congressional approval of such agreements in order to protect the national interest in the waterway. Compacts normally are implemented through separate state legislation in each of the party states. Examples include the 1922 Colorado River Compact between Colorado River Basin states and the 1949 Pecos River Compact between Texas and New Mexico. The third method is through federal litigation. In interstate water allocation suits brought by states, the Supreme Court serves as the court of original jurisdiction and applies federal common law. In a dispute between Kansas and Colorado over the waters of the Arkansas River, the Court described its role in adjudicating interstate waters:

> One cardinal rule, underlying all the relations of the States to each other, is that of equality of right. Each State stands on the same level with all the rest. It can impose its own legislation on no one of the others, and is bound to yield its own views to none. Yet, whenever ... the action of one State reaches, through the agency of natural laws, into the territory of another State, the question of the extent and the limitations of the rights of the two States becomes a matter of justiciable dispute between them, and this court is called upon to settle that dispute in such a way as will recognize the equal rights of both and at the same time establish justice between them. In other words, through these successive disputes and decisions this court is practically building up what may not improperly be called interstate common law.

Kansas v. Colorado, 206 U.S. 46, 97–98, 27 S.Ct. 655, 667, 51 L.Ed. 956 (1907).

3. *Reserved Water Rights for Federal Lands and Tribes*

The states primarily control the ownership of water within the United States, and allocate water rights to individuals. An exception to this is reserved water rights held by the federal government and Indian tribes. Within the model of prior appropriation, federal courts have carved out a water right to benefit federal and tribal lands, many of which are located in the arid reaches of the West and would be rendered worthless if not served by water. The water right is a property right deemed implicitly "reserved" at the time the reservation of land was formalized. A landmark case, Winters v. United States, 207 U.S. 564, 28 S.Ct. 207, 52 L.Ed. 340 (1908), introduced the concept of federally reserved water rights. The doctrine of implied tribal water rights was further shaped in Arizona v. California, 373 U.S. 546, 600, 83 S.Ct. 1468, 10 L.Ed. 542 (1963), which held that Indian reservations carry an implied water right of a quantity sufficient "to irrigate all the practicably irrigable acreage" on the reservations. In United States v. Adair, 723 F.2d 1394 (9th Cir. 1983), the Ninth Circuit recognized an instream water right to support tribal fisheries. The *Adair* litigation is discussed in Chapter 7.

The *Winters* doctrine provides for federal reserved water rights to benefit any type of federal reservation, not just lands reserved for tribes. In the last two centuries, the federal government has also reserved lands for military posts, wildlife refuges, national forests, national parks, national monuments, and wilderness areas. Such reservations of land carry implied federally reserved water rights. *Arizona v. California*, 373 U.S. at 601. Indian reserved water rights and other federal reserved water rights fit into the state system of prior appropriation in the same way. Both types of water rights have a priority date set at the date the reservation was created. Therefore, a reservation that was established in 1855 would carry a water right having a priority date of 1855. By attaching a priority date to what is essentially a riparian water right benefiting land, the reserved water rights doctrine creates a federal water right that fits directly into the western system of prior appropriation. The priority date attached to the reserved rights makes them senior to all later acquired water rights, but junior to any previously acquired water rights. Since Indian reservations were established to make way for settlement by non-Indians, they often carry the earliest priority dates, which makes the tribal rights senior to most if not all other rights in a basin. In the case of other federal reservations, particularly ones just recently established, the priority date may render the federal water rights relatively junior and therefore ineffectual. Moreover, in United States v. New Mexico, 438 U.S. 696, 98 S.Ct. 3012, 57 L.Ed.2d 1052 (1978), the Court emphasized that the quantity of federally reserved water is that amount necessary to fulfill only the *primary* purposes of the reservation. Secondary uses, while important, do not carry reserved water rights.

Global Perspective:

Commodification of the World's Water Supplies

Increasingly, there is a global movement to "privatize" water, taking it out of the hands of sovereign control. Consider the following views on water issues that played a central role in the second World Summit on Sustainable Development held in Johannesburg, South Africa, in September, 2002.

WHO OWNS WATER?
Maude Barlow & Tony Clarke
THE NATION, Sept. 2, 2002

"Water promises to be to the 21st century what oil was to the 20th century: the precious commodity that determines the wealth of nations."—Fortune

* * * [An] increasing number of voices—including human rights and environmental groups, think tanks and research organizations, official international agencies and thousands of community groups around the world—are sounding an alarm. The earth's fresh water is finite and small, representing less than one half of 1 percent of the world's total water stock. Not only are we adding 85 million new people to the planet every year, but also our per capita use of water is doubling every twenty years, at more than twice the rate of human population growth. A legacy of factory farming, flood irrigation, the construction of massive dams, toxic dumping, wetlands and forest destruction, and urban and industrial pollution has damaged the Earth's surface water so badly that we are now mining the underground water reserves far faster than nature can replenish them.

The earth's "hot stains"—areas where water reserves are disappearing—include the Middle East, Northern China, Mexico, California and almost two-dozen countries in Africa. Today thirty-one countries and over 1 billion people completely lack access to clean water. Every eight seconds a child dies from drinking contaminated water. The global freshwater crisis looms as one of the greatest threats ever to the survival of our planet. * * *

Faced with the suddenly well-documented freshwater crisis, governments and international institutions are advocating a Washington Consensus solution: the privatization and commodification of water. Price water, they say in chorus; put it up for sale and let the market determine its future. For them, the debate is closed. Water, say the World Bank and the United Nations, is a "human need," not a "human right." These are not semantics; the difference in interpretation is crucial. A human need can be supplied many ways, especially for those with money. No one can sell a human right.

So a handful of transnational corporations, backed by the World Bank and the International Monetary Fund, are aggressively taking over the management of public water services in countries around the world, dramatically raising the price of water to the local residents and profiting especially from the Third World's desperate search for solutions to its water crisis. Some are startlingly open; the decline in freshwater supplies and standards has created a wonderful venture opportunity for water corporations and their investors, they boast. The agenda is clear: Water should be treated like any other tradable good, with its use determined by the principles of profit.

* * * According to *Fortune*, the annual profits of the water industry now amount to about 40 percent of those of the oil sector and are already substantially higher than the pharmaceutical sector, now close to $1 trillion. But only about 5 percent of the world's water is currently in private hands, so it is clear that [there is] huge profit potential as the water crisis worsens. * * * They are aided by the World Bank and the IMF, which are increasingly forcing Third World countries to abandon their public water delivery systems and contract with the water giants in order to be eligible for debt relief. * * *

At the same time, governments are signing away their control over domestic water supplies to trade agreements such as the North American Free Trade Agreement, its expected successor, the Free Trade Area of the Americas (FTAA), and the World Trade Organization. These global trade institutions effectively give transnational corporations unprecedented access to the freshwater resources of signatory countries. Already, corporations have started to sue governments in order to gain access to domestic water sources and, armed with the protection of these international trade agreements, are setting their sights on the commercialization of water. * * *

If we allow the commodification of the world's freshwater supplies, we will lose the capacity to avert the looming water crisis. We will be allowing the emergence of a water elite that will determine the world's water future in its own interest. In such a scenario, water will go to those who can afford it and not to those who need it. * * *

Water must be declared and understood for all time to be the common property of all. In a world where everything is being privatized, citizens must establish clear perimeters around those areas that are sacred to life and necessary for the survival of the planet. Simply, governments must declare that water belongs to the earth and all species and is a fundamental human right. No one has the right to appropriate it for profit. Water must be declared a public trust, and all governments must enact legislation to protect the freshwater resources in their territory. An international legal framework is also desperately needed. * * *

Notes and Questions

1. Should water be a public commodity or a private commodity? What are the advantages and disadvantages of each approach?

2. Does the domestic legal model for water allocation allow privatization in the United States? Would the public trust doctrine allow complete privatization of water? Is public trust theory at the core of the global water "commons" proposed by the authors? Is a property rights framework, one that affirms sovereign rights to public resources, essential to preserving water and sustaining life on the planet?

3. For legal analysis of emerging global water issues, *see Access to Water*, SUSTAINABLE DEVELOPMENT AND POLICY, vol. V, issue 1 (Winter 2005), *available at* http://www.wcl.American.edu/org/sustainabledevelopment. For a broad study on the global water crisis, *see* MAUDE BARLOW, BLUE GOLD: THE GLOBAL WATER CRISIS AND THE COMMODIFICATION OF THE WORLD'S WATER SUPPLY (1999).

D.   The Federal Navigational Servitude

The federal government retains a unique property interest, known as the federal navigational servitude, in navigable waters and their streambeds. The servitude allows the federal government to carry out its power under the Commerce Clause to maintain such waterways for navigation. As a property law concept, the servitude can be thought of as an incident of sovereignty that is distinctly federal in nature, necessary to secure the national interest in navigation. As an encumbrance on title, it defeats any tribal, state, or individual property interest that conflicts with the overriding purpose of navigation. Accordingly, the servitude allows the government to infringe upon private property when necessary to achieve navigation purposes without compensation under the Fifth Amendment of the Constitution. As the Court explained in United States v. Chicago, M., St. P. & P.R. Co., 312 U.S. 592, 596–97, 61 S.Ct. 772, 775, 85 L.Ed. 1064, 1070 (1941):

> The dominant power of the federal Government, as has been repeatedly held, extends to the entire bed of a stream, which includes the lands below ordinary highwater mark. The exercise of the power within these limits is not an invasion of any private property right in such lands for which the United States must make compensation. The damage sustained results not from a taking of the riparian owner's property in the stream bed, but from the lawful exercise of a power to which that property has always been subject.

The scope of the federal navigation servitude reaches to streambeds of both navigable waterways and also tributary non-navigable waterways where there is an effect on navigation. United States v. Grand River Dam Authority, 363 U.S. 229, 80 S.Ct. 1134, 4 L.Ed.2d 1186 (1960). The servitude also reaches to secure the flow of the water in navigable waterways and non-navigable tributaries, prohibiting private parties from water withdrawals that would compromise navigability. U.S. v. Rio Grande Dam & Irrigation Co., 174 U.S. 690, 703 (1899). While exercise of the servitude must relate to the core interest of navigation, courts have generously construed that purpose. Lewis Blue Point Oyster Cultivation Co. v. Briggs, 229 U.S. 82, 87, 33 S.Ct. 679, 680, 57 L.Ed. 1083, 1085 (1913) (the dominant right of navigation "must include the right to use the bed of the water for every purpose which is in aid of navigation."); *but see* Kaiser Aetna v. United States, 444 U.S. 164, 172, 100 S.Ct. 383, 388, 62 L.Ed.2d 332, 341 (1979) ("[T]his Court has never held that the navigational servitude creates a blanket exception to the Takings Clause whenever Congress exercises its Commerce Clause authority to promote navigation....").

How does the servitude relate to other sovereign property interests held by the states and tribes? Because the federal government is the supreme sovereign within the Constitutional structure, its navigational servitude trumps property rights held by the other sovereigns, but only if the purpose of navigation so requires. The federal navigation servitude, for example, may preclude the state governments from issuing rights to water in a stream (a right normally conferred on states) if doing so interferes with navigation: "[A] State cannot, by its legislation, destroy the right of the United States ... to the continued flow of its waters.... [I]t is limited by the superior power of the general government to secure uninterrupted navigability of all navigable streams within the limits of the United States." *Rio Grande Dam & Irrigation Co.,* 174 U.S. at 703. The navigation servitude also supercedes the ownership interests states and tribes have in their streambeds. *See* United States v. Cherokee Nation, 480 U.S. 700, 107 S.Ct. 1487, 94 L.Ed.2d 704 (1987).

In Practice:
Carrying out the Federal Navigational Servitude

The federal agency charged with primary responsibility for maintaining the navigational capacity of rivers is the U.S. Army Corps of Engineers. *See* http://www.usace.army.mil/. The Corps operates a total of 383 dams across the country, most of which serve a navigational purpose. *See* Services for the Public, U.S. Army Corps of Engineers, *available at* http://www.usace.army.mil/public.html#Flood. Many of these operations interfere with native fisheries and create complex issues under the Endangered Species Act. *See e.g.* National Wildlife Federation v. National Marine Fisheries Service, 254 F.Supp.2d 1196 (D.Or. 2003). A national dam removal movement has focused public attention on dams with the worst environmental consequences. *See* Michael T. Pyle, *Beyond Fish Ladders: Dam Removal as a Strategy for Restoring America's Rivers*, 14 STAN. ENVTL. L. J. 97 (1995).

The Corps also plays a *regulatory* role in assuring the navigable capacity of the nation's waterways. It has authority under an old statute, the Rivers and Harbors Act, to maintain the waterways free of obstructions. 39 U.S.C. § 401 *et seq.* (2003). In addition, the Corps implements section 404 of the Clean Water Act, which regulates the fill of wetlands. 33 U.S.C. § 1251 (2003).

E. Wildlife

Wildlife in a state of freedom is classified as *ferae naturae*. Every government in the world has *ferae naturae* within its borders, and many governments share interests in migratory populations of wildlife. Moreover, nearly all landowners have some part of the animal kingdom on their property. Though human conditions have always depended for survival on *ferae naturae*, modern analysis for situating this resource in the broader context of property rights remains in a remarkably undeveloped state. The four characteristics of this natural resource as living, transient, beyond human control, and irreplaceable create vexing complexities for the law. In the United States, modern courts have a tendency to distill rights to wildlife into regulatory terms, applying the myriad of statutes that govern activities affecting wildlife. Yet a time-revered set of property-based principles is gaining a resurgence. Both approaches are covered in detail in Chapter 14.

Washington State officials collaring a deer with a radio locating device. Available at http://wdfw.wa.gov/gallery.

1. *The Sovereign Trust in Wildlife Resources*

Common law recognizes a property-based sovereign trust interest in wildlife populations that live within, or pass through, a sovereign's borders. Such judicial recognition arose out of an early need to establish public rights to wildlife in a pre-possessory state. The doctrinal body of law recognizing a sovereign trusteeship over wildlife joins a rich and ancient body of jurisprudence applying a "public trust" in other natural resources such as air and water. The principles are so fundamental to the functioning of government that they are manifest in the law of several other nations and trace back to ancient legal regimes predating the United States.

The landmark decision Geer v. Connecticut, 161 U.S. 519, 16 S.Ct. 600, 40 L.Ed. 793 (1896), comprehensively articulated the sovereign property interest in wildlife. The immediate issue in that case was whether the state of Connecticut could forbid game taken within the state from entering into interstate commerce despite restrictions emanating from the Commerce Clause of the Constitution. As a predicate to the constitutional issue, the Court delved into the more fundamental question of whether any sovereign may assert property rights in *ferae naturae*. Resting its conclusion on reasoning dating back through English common law to the law of ancient Greece, the Court set forth a principle of sovereign trusteeship in wildlife that endures to this day.

GEER v. CONNECTICUT

Supreme Court of the United States, 1896.
161 U.S. 519, 16 S.Ct. 600, 40 L.Ed. 793

JUSTICE WHITE delivered the opinion of the Court.

From the earliest traditions the right to reduce animals ferae naturae to possession has been subject to the control of the law-giving power. * * * Pothier in his treatise on Property speaks as follows:

"In France, as well as in all other civilized countries of Europe, the civil law has restrained the liberty which the pure law of nature gave to every one to capture animals who, being in naturali laxitate, belong to no person in particular. The sovereigns have reserved to themselves ... the right to hunt all game, and have forbidden hunting to other persons. * * * The civil law it is said cannot be contrary to the natural law. This is true as regards those things which the natural law commands or which it forbids; but the civil law can restrict that which the natural law only permits." * * *

It is for this reason, although by the pure law of nature, hunting was permitted to each individual, the prince had the right to reserve it in favor of certain persons and forbid it to others. * * * In tracing the origin of the classification of animals ferae naturae, as things common, Pothier moreover says:

"The first of mankind had in common all those things which God had given to the human race. * * * The human race having multiplied, men partitioned among themselves the earth and the greater part of those things which were on its surface. That which fell to each one among them commenced to belong to him in private ownership, and this process is the origin of the right of property. Some things, however, did not enter into this division, and remain therefore to this day in the condition of the ancient and negative community. * * * These things are those which the jurisconsults called res communes. Marcien refers to several kinds—the air, the water which runs in the rivers, the sea and its shores.... As regards wild animals, ferae naturae, they have remained in the ancient state of negative community." * * *

The practice of the government of England from the earliest time to the present has put into execution the authority to control and regulate the taking of game. Undoubtedly this attribute of government to control the taking of animals ferae naturae, which was thus recognized and enforced by the common law of England, was vested in the colonial governments [and] passed to the States with the separation from the mother country, and remains in them at the present day, in so far as its exercise may be not incompatible with ... the rights conveyed to the Federal government by the Constitution. * * * In most of the States laws have been passed for the protection and preservation of game. * * *

[T]he power or control pledged in the State, resulting from this common ownership, is to be exercised, like all other powers of government, as a trust for the benefit of the people, and not as a prerogative for the advantage of the government, as distinct from the people, or for the benefit of private individuals as distinguished from the public good. Therefore, for the purpose of exercising this power, the State ... represents its people, and the ownership is that of the people in their united sovereignty. * * * "[The] ownership of wild animals, so far as they are capable of ownership, is in the State, not as a proprietor but in its sovereign capacity as the representative and for the benefit of all its people in common." * * *

[T]he ownership of the sovereign authority is in trust for all the people of the State, and hence by implication it is the duty of the legislature to enact such laws as will best preserve the subject of the trust and secure its beneficial use in the future to the people of the State.... * * *

Aside from the authority of the State, derived from the common ownership of game and the trust for the benefit of its people which the State exercises in relation thereto, there is another view of the power of the State in regard to the property in game, which is equally conclusive. The right to preserve game flows from the undoubted existence in the State of a police power to that end.... Indeed, the source of the police power as to game birds ... flows from the duty of the State to preserve for its people a valuable food supply. * * *

Notes and Questions

1. *Geer* refers to the sovereign ownership of wildlife as a "trust." Many courts and commentators have treated the wildlife trust as a branch of the public trust doctrine, with its roots in the same foundational principles that frame all sovereign property rights in natural resources. *See* Gary D. Meyers, *Variation on a Theme: Expanding the Public Trust Doctrine to Include Protection of Wildlife,* 19 ENVTL. L. 723, 728 (1989); Deborah G. Musiker, Tom France, Lisa A. Hallenbeck, *The Public Trust and Parens Patriae Doctrines: Protecting Wildlife In Uncertain Times,* 16 PUB. LAND L. REV. 87 (1995). The *Geer* Court referred to governmental control over the take of wildlife as an "attribute of government." Does this language have an analogue in the streambed cases upholding the public trust doctrine? Recall Pollard v. Hagan, 44 U.S. (3 How.) 212, 11 L.Ed. 565 (1845), and Illinois Central Railroad Co. v. Illinois, 146 U.S. 387, 13 S.Ct. 110, 36 L.Ed. 1018 (1892), where the Court emphasized that streambeds were critical to public welfare and, hence, to

state sovereignty. At the time of the *Geer* decision, did wildlife play an equally significant role with respect to public welfare? Does it today?

2. The *Geer* Court's framework presents a clear delineation between the rights in wildlife acquired by individuals and the rights held by governments on behalf of the public. Within this property framework, individuals may gain property rights in animals only through license by the government. Such regulation to preserve wildlife "deprive[s] no person of his property, because he who takes or kills game had no previous right to property in it, and when he acquires such right by reducing it to possession, he does so subject to such conditions and limitations as the legislature has seen fit to impose." *Geer*, 161 U.S. at 533. Once an individual takes an animal pursuant to a government license, that animal ceases to be a part of *ferae naturae,* or the living, free wildlife resource owned in common by the public. When the governmental property interest ends, the animal becomes the private property of the person who captured it.

3. Prior to *Geer*, there was an already well-settled doctrine of property law that governed conflicts between *individuals* competing for wildlife. The classic case, Pierson v. Post, 3 Cai. R. 175 (N.Y. Sup. Ct. 1805), which still finds its way into most first-year property courses, had already established ownership principles on the individual level. The case gave rise to an enduring principle in property law that, in cases of individual claims to wildlife, possession gives rise to a property interest, and efforts short of possession or capture produce no legal entitlement.

Pierson v. Post established the requirement of possession or capture as a condition precedent to acquiring *individual* rights in wildlife. But it did not answer the question of whether all individuals have an equal right to pursue wildlife and take from the commons, or whether there is an underlying *sovereign* property interest that may serve as the basis for allocating rights in *ferae naturae. Geer*, decided nearly a century after *Pierson v. Post,* embarked on this new level of property analysis. It found antecedent sovereign property rights to wildlife in a free state.

4. One forceful aspect of the trust doctrine articulated in *Geer* is that it mandates protection of the "corpus" of the trust for future generations. The *Geer* Court stated: "[I]t is the duty of the legislature to enact such laws as will best preserve the subject of the trust, and secure its beneficial use in the future to the people of the state." 161 U.S. at 534. What is the corpus of the trust? Is it just the wildlife populations themselves, or does it also include the habitat upon which such populations rely? For an argument that both populations and the habitat make up the "wildlife capital" comprising the public's trust asset, *see* Mary Christina Wood, *The Tribal Property Right to Wildlife Capital (Part 1): Applying Principles of Sovereignty to Protect Imperiled Wildlife Populations,* 37 IDAHO L. REV. 1, 43–45 (2000).

5. If the wildlife trust corpus does include habitat, do landowners suffer takings under the 5th Amendment when the government imposes regulation to protect wildlife habitat on their property? Is that habitat encumbered by an antecedent property right in favor of the public? Recall that the classic public trust doctrine may provide a barrier to takings claims in certain circumstances. Some scholars have explored this line of doctrinal analysis in the context of wildlife regulation. *See, e.g.* Hope M. Babcock, *Should*

Lucas v. South Carolina Coastal Council Protect Where the Wild Things Are? Of Beavers, Bob–O–Links, and Other Things that go Bump in the Night, 85 IOWA L. REV. 849 (2000); Patrick A. Parenteau, *Who's Taking What? Property Rights, Endangered Species, and the Constitution*, 6 FORDHAM ENVTL. J. 619 (1995); Oliver A. Houck, *Why Do We Protect Endangered Species and What Does that Say About Whether Restrictions on Private Property to Protect Them Constitute "Takings?"* 80 IOWA L. REV. 297 (1995).

6. *Geer* suggests that the sovereign has two roles with respect to wild-life: a proprietary role stemming from ownership theory and a police power role stemming from legislative power. How do the two differ in the context of wildlife regulation? Why is it important to emphasize the property basis of wildlife regulation? Does the wildlife trust theory, because it is rooted in the public trust doctrine, trigger a judicial check on the legislative branch? Chapter 8.II.B explores that question.

7. Is the modern legislative scheme adequate to protect wildlife? Several federal statutes, most notably the ESA, are designed to protect species, and each state has a statutory body of wildlife law as well. However, critics point out that the effectiveness of such statutes is hindered by lack of funding, lack of enforcement, and weak standards—all, perhaps, a result of political pressure against regulation. *See* Oliver A. Houck, *The Endangered Species Act and Its Implementation by the U.S. Departments of Interior and Commerce,* 64 U. COLO. L. REV. 277, 326–27 (1993) (extensive review of Endangered Species Act implementation).

Mounting species extinctions shed doubt on the effectiveness of current statutory laws. A 1990 report issued by the Council on Environmental Quality (CEQ) concludes that a total of 9,000 U.S. plant and animal species may currently be at risk of extinction, noting: "The problem is national in scope, with every region of the country reporting losses of native species ... more than species are being lost. Whole plant and animal communities—integrated, resilient systems—are threatened." COUNCIL ON ENVIRONMENTAL QUALITY, ENVIRONMENTAL QUALITY, 21ST ANNUAL REPORT 137 (1990).

2. *The State Ownership Doctrine*

Another part of the *Geer* decision addressed the Commerce Clause, which restricts states from impairing the interstate flow of commerce. U.S. CONST. art. I § 8, cl. 3. The law forbidding export of game in *Geer* was clearly protectionist, presumably designed to keep an important food source within the state. But the *Geer* Court relied upon the state "ownership" of wildlife to hold that there was no effect on interstate commerce. Under its reasoning, because the state had full property rights in the wildlife resource, it could transfer less than a full property right to individuals when it issued licenses to hunt. In the Court's view, the state restriction against transporting the birds out of state represented a property right the state held back from the hunter. Because the restriction prohibited transport outside the state, no Interstate Commerce was implicated:

The common ownership imports the right to keep the property, if the sovereign so chooses, always within its jurisdiction for every purpose. The qualification which forbids its removal from the State necessarily entered into and formed part of every transaction on the subject, and deprived the mere sale or exchange of these articles of that element of freedom of contract and of full ownership which is an essential attribute of commerce. * * *

Geer, 161 U.S. at 530–531.

During the century following *Geer*, this Commerce Clause analysis eroded. *See* George C. Coggins, *Wildlife and the Constitution: The Walls Come Tumbling Down*, 55 WASH. L. REV. 295 (1980). Finally the Supreme Court expressly overturned *Geer* in Hughes v. Oklahoma, 441 U.S. 322, 99 S.Ct. 1727, 60 L.Ed.2d 250 (1979), a case challenging an Oklahoma law prohibiting the transportation of minnows caught within the state for sale outside the state. *Hughes* struck down the law, definitively holding that the "fiction" of state ownership could not overcome the Commerce Clause prohibition against impairing interstate commerce. But *Hughes* also had some qualifying language:

> The overruling of *Geer* does not leave the States powerless to protect and conserve wild animal life within their borders. Today's decision makes clear, however, that States may promote this legitimate purpose only in ways consistent with the basic principle that ... when a wild animal becomes an article of commerce, its use cannot be limited to the citizens of one State to the exclusion of citizens of another State.

441 U.S. at 335–36.

The fundamental wildlife trust principles in *Greer* have endured despite *Hughes*. *See* GOBLE AND FREYFOGLE, WILDLIFE LAW, CASES AND MATERIALS 437–45 (Foundation Press, 2002); Mary Christina Wood, *The Tribal Property Right to Wildlife Capital (Part I): Applying Priciples of Sovereignty to Protect Imperiled Wildlife Populations*, 37 IDAHO L. REV. 1, 52–53 (2000) ("[W]hile the state ownership doctrine has fallen sway to greater constitutional interests, the core property-based principles of sovereign trusteeship over *ferae naturae* underlying the doctrine endure to add a critical dimension to modern wildlife issues").

3. Tribal Property Rights to Wildlife

Geer's characterization of the property interest in *ferae naturae* as an attribute of sovereignty was equally, if not more, compelling in the context of tribal sovereigns. *See* Mescalero Apache Tribe v. New Mexico, 630 F.2d 724, 734–35 (10th Cir. 1980), *aff'd* New Mexico v. Mescalero Apache Tribe, 462 U.S. 324, 103 S.Ct. 2378, 76 L.Ed.2d 611 (1983) (recognizing wildlife trusteeship applicable to tribes). For millennia prior to white settlement and conquest, native nations pursued subsistence economies, depending entirely on fish, wildlife, and plants for survival. When tribes entered into treaties with the federal government, they were forced to relinquish the vast territories necessary to maintain their subsistence lifestyle. But many tribes expressly secured rights in the treaties to fish and hunt on these ceded lands.

Treaty clauses have generated an extensive body of federal common law. *United States v. Winans, supra,* found an easement across private property in the Pacific Northwest for tribes to access traditional fishing sites. This early case provided the property law foundation for later interpretation of treaty hunting and fishing rights. It is well-established that treaty harvest rights are property rights that are subject to Fifth Amendment compensation when they are taken by the federal government. Whitefoot v. United States, 293 F.2d 658 (Ct. Cl. 1961), *cert. denied,* 369 U.S. 818, 82 S.Ct. 829, 7 L.Ed.2d 784 (1962). This area of common law fits together with other cases establishing sovereign servitudes and interests in favor of federal and state sovereigns. In the most recent Supreme Court ruling on treaty harvest rights, the Court made clear that the exercise of tribal treaty rights is not incompatible with state sovereignty and that there is no implied termination of treaty rights upon statehood. Minnesota v. Mille Lacs Band of Chippewa Indians, 526 U.S. 172, 204, 207, 119 S.Ct. 1187, 1204, 1206, 143 L.Ed.2d 270 (1999) ("Although States have important interests in regulating wildlife and natural resources within their borders, this authority is shared with the Federal Government when the Federal Government exercises one of its enumerated constitutional powers, such as treaty making.... There is nothing inherent in the nature of reserved treaty rights to suggest that they can be extinguished by *implication* at statehood.").

Because particularly strong promises were made in treaties executed with tribes in the Pacific Northwest and Great Lakes Regions, several cases from those regions tend to be the leading ones interpreting treaty harvest rights. The Supreme Court has interpreted the Northwest treaty fishing clause as reserving half of the available harvest of salmon for the tribes. Washington v. Washington State Commercial Passenger Fishing Vessel Ass'n, 443 U.S. 658, 676–79, 99 S.Ct. 3055, 3069–71, 61 L.Ed.2d 823 (1979).

In the modern era of extinction, nearly all species face extraordinary pressure from human activity, and many of those species supporting treaty hunting and fishing rights are imperiled. The need for environmental protection of treaty species gives rise to an entirely new set of issues that courts and natural resource professionals must face in the coming years. Unfortunately, treaty harvest rights remain much of an enigma to many natural resource practitioners. Instead of being situated within the overall framework governing sovereign property interests, treaty rights tend to receive separate treatment as a specialized area. Chapter 7.V. explores treaty harvest rights.

Global Perspective:
Declining Species Worldwide

E.O. Wilson, renowned Harvard biologist, estimates that the world is losing 27,000 species per year (3 per hour). E.O Wilson, THE DIVERSITY OF LIFE 280 (1992). The World Conservation Union (IUCN) produces a "red list" of threatened species worldwide, organized by country. The 2000 report found that, globally, approximately 30% of all fishes, 20% of all amphibians, and 25% of reptile species, are threatened. Consult www.iucn.org. World Wildlife Fund (WWF) examines ecosystems on a global scale and presents trends in species loss. Its 2000 report concludes that "the Earth's natural ecosystems have declined by about 33 per cent over the last 30 years [while] the ecological pressure of humanity on the Earth has increased by about 50 per cent over the same period." WWF LIVING PLANET REPORT 2000 1; www.worldwildlife.org. WWF presents indexes to measure changes in species abundance over time in three separate categories: forest species, freshwater species, and marine species. Its 2000 report presented a dramatic decline in all three categories over the period 1970–99: freshwater species (–50%), marine species (–35%), and forest species (–12%).

F. Review

The ownership of land and natural resources in this country is something of a jigsaw puzzle. As this chapter has demonstrated, ownership occurs on the sovereign level between the federal government, states, and tribes. Where conflicts exist, the issue becomes one of primacy. An interest may be supreme over other interests because it is an antecedent interest or because the Constitutional organization of the sovereign powers requires supremacy under those circumstances. Sovereigns, in turn, transfer significant property interests in land and natural resources to individuals and corporations. But often, the sovereigns maintain implied ownership interests that may trump private property rights. The following table summarizes the sovereign ownership interests discussed in this chapter.

Type of Resource	Sovereign Interest	Explanation	Major Cases[b]
Submerged lands below navigable waterways	State, tribe, or federal government owns	Ownership of submerged lands passes to states automatically upon statehood under Equal Footing Doctrine, but may be reserved by federal government for its own purposes or for a tribe prior to statehood.	Pollard v. Hagan Utah Div. of State Lands v. United States Choctaw Nation v. Oklahoma Montana v. United States Idaho v. United States
Inland tidelands (shoreward of low water mark) navigable or not	State or tribe owns (unless reserved by federal government)	Ownership of inland tidelands passes to states automatically upon statehood under the Equal Footing Doctrine (but could be reserved for tribes by the federal government).	Phillips Petroleum Co. v. Mississippi
Offshore lands (seaward of low water mark) within three miles of coastline	State owns unless reserved by federal government from operation of Submerged Lands Act	The federal government owned as matter of national sovereignty, but conveyed to states under Submerged Lands Act of 1953.	United States v. California United States v. Alaska
Offshore lands beyond three mile coastline	Federal government owns	The federal government owns under common law as incident of national sovereignty; land not conveyed to states in Submerged Lands Act.	United States v. California United States v. Alaska
All navigable waterways	Federal government owns a navigational servitude to keep the waterway suitable for navigation	The servitude, as an inherent attribute of sovereignty, is impliedly reserved from all grants, and is carried out under the Commerce Clause of the Constitution.	United States v. Chicago United States v. Cherokee Nation

    b. All cases are Supreme Court cases unless otherwise noted.

Type of Resource	Sovereign Interest	Explanation	Major Cases
Submerged lands	State may own public trust easement to protect waterways for fishing, navigation, commerce and potentially other public purposes (recreation, biodiversity, etc.)	The public trust doctrine attaches to all waterways gained pursuant to the Equal Footing Doctrine. States may impliedly reserve a public trust easement when they convey the land to private parties; the public trust doctrine has been extended in some states to include water, wetlands, and dry sand beaches.	Illinois Central Railroad Co. v. Illinois
Aboriginal fishing and hunting grounds	Tribes of some regions retain treaty rights to access historic fishing/hunting/gathering sites	Some tribal rights of access act as an encumbrance on federal, state and private property.	United States v. Winans
Water	State water rights	States own water and have authority to allocate water rights (under riparian, prior appropriation, or mixed systems) to individuals.	California Oregon Power v. Beaver Portland Cement Co Kansas v. Colorado
Water	Tribal reserved water rights	Tribes have implied reserved water rights in quantities sufficient for "practicably irrigable acreage" on their reservations; and, where applicable, an instream right to benefit fisheries; tribal water rights supercede rights of all junior appropriators.	Winters v. United States Arizona v. California United States v. Adair)(9th Cir.)

Type of Resource	Sovereign Interest	Explanation	Major Cases
Water	Federal reserved water rights	The federal government has implied reserved water rights to fulfill primary (but not secondary) purposes of federal reservations, with a priority date as of the date of the reservation.	Winters v. United States Cappaert v. United States United States v. New Mexico
Wildlife	State trusteeship	States have trust ownership interest in wildlife populations; states allocate wildlife harvest rights through licenses to their citizens.	Geer v. Connecticut
Wildlife	Tribal treaty (or treaty equivalent) and access harvest rights	Tribes have property rights to wildlife populations as determined by language of the treaty or treaty equivalent; tribes allocate harvest rights to their members.	Washington v. Washington State Commercial Passenger Fishing Vessel Assn. Minnesota v. Mille Lacs Band of Chippewa Indians

Exercise:

The following hypothetical illustrates the various property interests that can arise in one parcel as result of historical property transfers on both the sovereign and individual levels. Try to identify the ownership interests that could have bearing on this conflict.

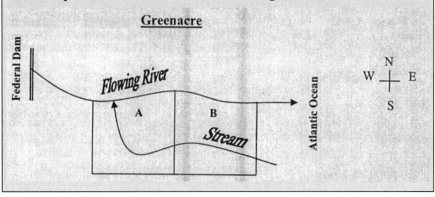

Greenacre consists of 10 acres of heavily forested property with streams and wetlands located along the Flowing River, a major navigable waterway, that flows to the Atlantic Ocean. Before white contact, the site was an Indian fishing camp. In 1795, the tribes ceded the area to the federal government but reserved rights in their treaties to fish along the Flowing River at their usual and accustomed fishing sites. The federal government, in turn, conveyed Greenacre to a private homesteader (Greene) in a federal patent. Statehood for this area was attained in 1799.

Greene used the entire property for a fish hatchery. A stream, which is a tributary to the Flowing River, flows across the property from east to west. In historic times, the fish migrated from the Flowing River up the entire length of the stream to spawn. In 1950, the hatchery business folded, and Greene's descendants (successor owners) divided Greenacre into Tracts A (the western half) and B (the eastern half). The Greene family kept tract B, and sold Tract A to Smith, retaining water rights to benefit Tract B. Over time, the property became residential, and one small cottage was built on each tract by the respective owners, but the natural resources on both parcels remained largely intact.

Between 1950 and 2000, the salmon populations in the Flowing River dropped precipitously due to dams, habitat degradation, and over-fishing. The shoreline all around Greenacre became built up with subdivisions and commercial development. The water levels on the shore of the Flowing River became subject to fluctuation as a result of federal water releases at a dam built upstream. Now, Greenacre (both Parcels A and B) provides the only remaining habitat left on the river for the imperiled salmon, listed as threatened under the Endangered Species Act (ESA).

In 2000, the Greene Family conveyed a conservation easement on Tract B to a Land Trust to protect their parcel in perpetuity as salmon habitat. They also conveyed the tidelands on Tract B in fee simple absolute to the State Department of Fish and Wildlife, which manages the salmon recovery effort. The current owner of Tract A wishes to clearcut his parcel, replace the cottage with a mansion, and put in a spacious lawn (using water from the stream for the sprinkler system). These actions are likely to harm salmon habitat.

Questions: What sovereign and individual property rights are present? Setting aside any potential regulatory issues for the moment, could any property rights be used to protect the salmon habitat from development? Who would have legal standing to assert such rights? Related regulatory issues are addressed in Chapters 14 (Water) and 15 (Wildlife).

Chapter 6

FEDERAL OWNERSHIP OF PUBLIC LANDS

I.   INTRODUCTION

Nearly a third of the land base of the United States is owned by the federal government. Most of it is concentrated in the Western states and Alaska. The focus of this chapter is the overall management regime for federal public lands; much of the detail involved in timber contracts, mineral rights, and the like, is treated in Part III of this text. As you study the materials in this chapter, bear in mind this Part's overarching theme that ownership of lands and resources is the greatest determinative factor as to their use. Consider in each highlighted case whether the outcome would be different if the disputed resource fell under the management of another federal agency with a different mission and statutory authority, or a tribal government, state government, land trust, or private party. Different biases and objectives inherent in each category of ownership present themselves across the physical landscape.

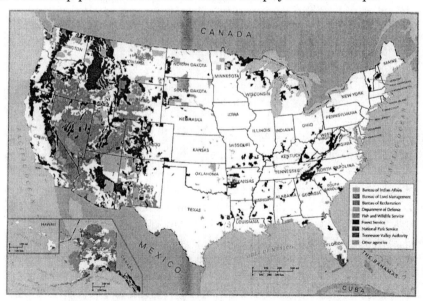

Map of federal public lands, http://nationalatlas.gov/fedlands/fedlands2.gif.

A. The Land Management Agencies

Federal lands management is divided among four primary agencies: the Forest Service, the Bureau of Land Management, the U.S. Fish and Wildlife Service, and the National Park Service. Each agency is subject to a different set of "organic" laws which designate the management objectives for the particular land base. Past experience in controlling these lands has engendered different bureaucratic personalities in these agencies as well as divergent outside constituencies exerting constant pressure, legally and politically, to gain access to public resources.

The United States Forest Service, housed within the U.S. Department of Agriculture, is the primary agency responsible for the nation's 155 national forests and 20 grasslands. Comprising approximately 191 million acres of land, the national forests constitute nearly 8.5% of the total land area of the United States. The Bureau of Land Management (BLM), within the U.S. Department of Interior, manages 262 million acres of surface land, and approximately another 300 million acres of subsurface mineral resources. Nearly two-thirds of BLM lands are located in Alaska; the remainder primarily consists of arid lands found within the other eleven Western states. The U.S. Fish and Wildlife Service (USFWS), also within the Department of Interior, administers the National Wildlife Refuge System. The Refuge System encompasses over 95 million acres and includes over 540 national wildlife refuges and game ranges as well as 69 National Fish Hatcheries. The National Park Service (NPS), within the Department of Interior, manages over 84 million acres of land, about 49 million of which are designated as National Parks. The NPS also manages a holding of monuments, historic sites, battlefields, seashores, lake shores and recreation areas.

In addition, each of these federal agencies manages various areas designated as wilderness. An agency gains oversight of a particular wilderness area through the law that created the wilderness. For example, Congress designated the U.S. Forest Service as the land manager of the 585,238–acre Teton Wilderness Area in Wyoming, gave the National Park Service authority over the Craters of the Moon Wilderness in Idaho, authorized the U.S. Fish & Wildlife Service to manage the Okefenokee Wilderness in Georgia, and directed BLM to administer the Mesquite Wilderness pursuant to the California Desert Protection Act of 1994.

Websources:

USDA Forest Service: http://www.fs.fed.us

Bureau of Land Management: http://www.blm.gov

U.S. Fish and Wildlife Service: http://www.fws.gov

National Park Service: http://www.nps.gov

Because public lands issues involve conflicting rights and obligations created by common law, statute, or regulation, a starting point for understanding nearly any modern dispute is learning the history of the ownership and designation of the land in question, or "tracing the title." Nearly all public lands originated in native ownership and were "extinguished" by treaty, statute, or executive order. *See* Chapter 5. Most of the current holdings have been in federal ownership since initial extinguishment, but some public land has entered the federal inventory through purchase, land exchange, or condemnation after an intervening period of state or private ownership. Once in the federal inventory, land is subject to the comprehensive federal laws dealing with public lands. It is often a challenge for the natural resources practitioner to determine what statutes applied to the land at what time. Statutes in effect long ago may have since been repealed but nevertheless support grandfathered rights (*see,* for example, the discussion below regarding R.S. 2477 claims of public "highways" across federal lands). In this regard, two management tools are important to understand: withdrawal and reservation.

"Withdrawal" is a legal tool used by the federal government to take particular public lands out of the scope of the generally applicable disposition statutes, such as the early homesteading laws and the General Mining Law of 1872. Until land is "withdrawn," it is open for exploitation under any general laws that apply. Of course, the early homesteading laws have long since been repealed, but the General Mining Law of 1872 still applies to grant claimants mineral rights as well as private title ("patents") to federal land where they have established a valid mining claim. "Reservation" follows withdrawal and refers to designating the land for a particular purpose, such as a refuge, monument, national forest, or park. The lands owned by the federal government are generally classified as either "public domain" or "reserved" lands. The public domain lands are those that are still open to disposition under the federal public land laws and are not exclusively dedicated to any specific governmental or public purpose. *See, e.g.,* Federal Power Commission v. Oregon, 349 U.S. 435, 75 S.Ct. 832, 99 L.Ed. 1215 (1955); United States v. Minnesota, 270 U.S. 181, 46 S.Ct. 298, 70 L.Ed. 539 (1926). Public domain lands are, for the most part, managed by the United States Department of the Interior through its BLM. (Newcomers to the field of public lands law should be advised that many natural resource practitioners call the BLM public domain lands "public lands," which is quite confusing since *all* federally owned lands—not just BLM public domain lands—are "public lands.") Nearly all BLM lands are open to mining claims under the General Mining Law of 1872.

"Withdrawals" are critically important because they protect the land base from further ownership claims that would otherwise be permitted by disposition statutes still in effect such as the General Mining Law. It is important to determine exactly when a withdrawal was made, in order to determine whether any ownership interests vested prior to that time. Moreover, withdrawals may be narrow or broad, and it is crucial to know their scope. Withdrawals can take the land out of the purview of all disposition statutes, or just some disposition statutes, or they can even create a very limited carve-out from just certain parts of some disposition statutes. In that respect, withdrawals are a very flexible tool. For example, the Common Varieties Act of 1955 withdrew all federal lands from the operation of the General Mining Law only insofar as common types of minerals (such as sand and gravel) were concerned, leaving the lands subject to the operation of the General Mining Law for hardrock minerals. 30 U.S.C. § 611 (1955). *See* United States v. Coleman, 390 U.S. 599, 88 S.Ct. 1327, 20 L.Ed.2d 170 (1968); JOHN LESHY, THE MINING LAW: A STUDY IN PERPETUAL MOTION 130–135 (1987). Moreover, though national forests are "reserved lands," their withdrawal still left them within the purview of the General Mining Act, so national forests are still open to mining claims. *See* Forest Service Organic Act of 1897, 30 Stat. 1.

Withdrawals can be made by Congress or the Executive. For most of the nation's history, Congress acquiesced to the President's decision to withdraw huge tracts of land from various disposition statutes, and the Supreme Court interpreted this acquiescence as implied authority for the President. *See* United States v. Midwest Oil Co., 236 U.S. 459, 35 S.Ct. 309, 59 L.Ed. 673 (1915) (upholding President Taft's decision to withdraw federal lands from the mining act to preserve oil reserves). The Pickett Act, 43 U.S.C. § 141 (1976) (passed in 1910), provided explicit Presidential withdrawal authority. It was repealed in 1976 by the Federal Land Management Act (FLPMA), 43 U.S.C. §§ 1701 *et seq.* (1970), which set forth the modern process for withdrawals. The Antiquities Act also provides a separate means of executive withdrawals for national monuments. *See* Chapter 6.V. (discussing Antiquities Act). Not surprisingly, because withdrawal is such a potent tool for the preservation of land, withdrawal actions are often politically contentious. The legal issues surrounding withdrawal authority are complicated both in a statutory sense and a constitutional sense, as they permeate the basic division of authority between Congress and the Executive. The FLPMA provisions, which involve an unusual interaction between the Congressional and the Executive branch, may be Constitutionally problematic. For analysis, *see* Robert L. Glicksman, *Severability and the Realignment of the Balance of Power Over the Public Lands: The Federal Land Policy and Management Act of 1976 After the Legislative Veto Decisions,* 36 HAST. L.J. 1 (1984); Ronald J. Athmann, *FLPMA § 204(E): A Constitutional Infirmity,* 8 TUL. ENVTL. L.J. 505 (1995).

In Practice: Tracing Title to Federal Public Lands

Many a natural resource practitioner has lamented his or her failure to gain a comprehensive picture of ownership before launching into a dispute, only to be surprised at a hidden vested right that determines the legal outcome. The history of federal land ownership and designation is not easy to research, because in many cases there has been no practice to "record" federal parcels or tracts of land through the standard county title processes that apply in the private realm. But public lands management agencies typically have the resources available to determine the title and management history of their land base. Most have administrative sections and personnel exclusively devoted to realty matters, and many offer publications addressing their ownership history. The landmark court cases dealing with various categories of public lands (forests, wilderness areas, BLM lands, refuges, monuments, and parks) often contain detailed ownership history as well.

Where title disputes involve interests of the United States, claimants may challenge the United State's title to real property in court under the Quiet Title Act (QTA) of 1972, 28 U.S.C. § 2409a, in which Congress waived federal sovereign immunity in order to resolve controverted claims to title. The QTA is the exclusive means by which such claims against the United States may be resolved. Block v. North Dakota, 461 U.S. 273, 103 S.Ct. 1811, 75 L.Ed.2d 840 (1983). For all claimants except states, the QTA bars suits not filed within 12 years of the time an action accrued (the date a claimant "knew or should have known of the claim of the United States."). 28 U.S.C. § 2409a (g).

B.   The Statutory Framework of Public Lands Law: An Overview

The field of public lands law consists of a myriad of statutes that frame the agencies' responsibilities. It is helpful to think of the statutory structure as a "ladder," with statutes forming multiple overlays of mandates. Some statutes apply to all federal agencies in the same way; others are unique to particular agency. Understanding the common statutory structure provides some coherence to the field. In very general terms, the statutes fall into four categories, all of which apply to modern agency action: 1) organic laws; 2) planning statutes; 3) environmental statutes; and 4) administrative statutes. The depiction below includes only the leading statutes; the entire array of public lands statutes is vast.

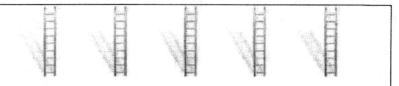

PUBLIC LANDS STATUTORY LADDER

ADMINISTRATIVE STATUTES
Federal Advisory Committee Act, 5 U.S.C. App. 1-15 (1972)
Equal Access to Justice Act, 28 U.S.C. § 2412 (1980)
Administrative Procedure Act, 5 U.S.C. §§ 501-706 (1946)

ENVIRONMENTAL STATUTES
Clean Air Act, 42 U.S.C. §§ 7401-7671 (1970)
Clean Water Act, 33 U.S.C. §§ 1251-1387 (1972)
Resource Conservation and Recovery Act, 42 U.S.C. §§ 6901-6992 (1976)
Endangered Species Act, 16 U.S.C. §§ 1531-1544 (1973)
National Environmental Policy Act, 42 U.S.C. §§ 4321-4370 (1969)

PLANNING STATUTES
National Forest Management Act, 16 U.S.C. §§ 1600-1614 (1976)
Federal Lands Policy Management Act, 43 U.S.C. §§ 1701-1784 (1976)
National Parks and Recreation Act of 1978, 16 U.S.C. § 1a-7(b) (1978)
Refuge Improvement Act of 1997, 16 U.S.C. §§ 668dd-ee (1997)

ORGANIC LAWS
Organic Act (Forest) of 1897, 16 U.S.C. §§ 472-82 (1897)
National Park Service Organic Act of 1916, 16 U.S.C. §§ 1-3 (1916)
Taylor Grazing Act of 1934, 443 U.S.C. § 315 (1934)
General Mining Law of 1872, 30 U.S.C. §§ 22-39 (1872)
National Wildlife Refuge Administration Act of 1966, 16 U.S.C. §§ 668dd-ee(1)
(1966)

The "organic law" of a land management agency is a statute that sets forth a general charter for the agency and describes its administrative structure and mission. Each of the four land management agencies has such an "organic" act. Organic acts for the Forest Service, Park Service, and BLM were passed relatively early in the history of public lands law, in the late 1800s and early 1900s. The Forest Service Organic Act of 1897 establishes the purposes of national forests "to improve and protect the forest within the boundaries [and to] secur[e] favorable conditions of water flows, and to furnish a continuous supply of timber.... " 16 U.S.C. § 475. The Taylor Grazing Act of 1934 (which directs the BLM grazing program) calls for the establishment of grazing districts and requires the agency to "preserve the land and its resources from destruction or unnecessary injury [and] to provide for the orderly use, improvement, and development of the range.... " 43 U.S.C. § 315a. The Park Service Organic Act of 1916 directs the Park Service to manage national parks and monuments "to conserve the scenery and the natural and historic objects and the wild life therein and to provide for the enjoyment of the same in such manner and by such means as will leave them unimpaired for the enjoyment of future generations." 16 U.S.C. § 1. Meanwhile, the General Mining Law of 1872 applies to the hardrock mineral resources across federal public lands, making them "free and open to exploration and purchase, by citizens of the United States.... " 30 U.S.C. § 22. It vests administrative duties in the Department of the Interior.

These initial statutes are rather bare-bones, their lack of detail reflecting the era out of which they emerged. They were designed to set forth the use of newly acquired public lands for various utilitarian purposes, including logging, mining, grazing, and recreation, but also conservation. The "organic" act for the U.S. Fish and Wildlife Service was a latecomer, passed in 1966 after most of the refuges and protected areas under the agency's jurisdiction had already been established. The 1966 National Wildlife Refuge Administration Act was the first statute to organize such lands into a system with the purpose of "conservation of fish and wildlife." 16 U.S.C. § 668dd. The simple terms of these organic acts set forth the basic purposes for which the lands are to be administered. Though not repealed by later statutes, their lack of specificity makes them less useful than the more modern statutes.

The modern planning statutes came with the tide of legislation Congress passed in the 1970s to create sweeping reform in the area of natural resources law. The reforms were largely in response to public pressure to change the direction of public lands management from dominant, extractive use (grazing, timber, mining) to multiple use accommodating a broader variety of public interests. All of the planning statutes contain much more detail than the initial organic statutes. *See* the National Forest Management Act, 16 U.S.C. §§ 1600–1614; the Federal Land Policy Management Act, 43 U.S.C. §§ 1701–1784; amendments to the National Park Service Organic Act, 16 U.S.C. § 1a–7(b) (1978); and the Refuge Improvement Act of 1997, 16 U.S.C. §§ 668dd-ee. For analysis, *see* Robert Fischman, *The National Wildlife Refuge System and the Hallmarks of Modern Organic Legislation*, 29 ECOLOGY L.Q. 457, 510–511, 538–541 (2002). The importance of these planning statutes can hardly be over-estimated. They all require the agencies to engage in a land-use planning process for the public lands. The land-use plans (called various names by the different agencies) are usually in effect for 10–15 years and set the agenda for the agency's management. The public has played a central role in development of these plans, through comment and appeal procedures. The conservation community has generally tried to hold the agencies' feet to the fire in carrying out obligations set forth in plans by bringing litigation where there is a perceived failure to meet substantive or procedural requirements. As the Supreme Court's recent decision in Norton v. Southern Utah Wilderness Alliance, 542 U.S. 55, 124 S.Ct. 2373, 159 L.Ed.2d 137 (2004) (excerpted in Chapter 3, *supra*) demonstrates, however, the role of land use planning on federal lands may be undergoing a dramatic shift.

Environmental laws form a third statutory level in the ladder. Congress passed a set of laws in the late 1960s and 1970s designed to create a full system of environmental protection. These include the National Environmental Policy Act (NEPA), 42 U.S.C. §§ 4321–4370, the Endangered Species Act (ESA), 16 U.S.C. §§ 1531–1544, and pollution control and remediation statutes such as the Clean Water Act, 33 U.S.C. §§ 1251–1387, the Clean Air Act, 42 U.S.C. §§ 7401–7671, the Resource Conservation and Recovery Act, 42 U.S.C. §§ 6901–6992, and the Comprehensive Environmental Response, Compensation and Liability Act, 42 U.S.C. §§ 9601–9675. While not directly geared towards public lands issues, these statutes apply to all federal agencies. NEPA and the ESA have gained enormous prominence in the public lands area and deserve particular mention. Detailed coverage of these statutes is provided in Chapter 4 and 15, respectively.

NEPA, a statute designed to promote environmental protection and environmental democracy, has revolutionized public lands management. Applicable only to federal agencies, its major force lies in a procedural mandate requiring each federal agency to prepare an Environmental Impact Statement (EIS) before undertaking any major "action" that "significantly affect[s] the quality of the human environment.... " 42 U.S.C. § 4332 (2)(C). An EIS is a thorough document that explores the effects of a proposed action and alternatives to it. An agency may undertake an Environmental Assessment (EA) to determine whether any major action it proposes rises to the level of significance that requires a full EIS. Because NEPA is triggered by federal "actions," the statute brings a multitude of public lands activities within its scope. The promulgation of land use plans (required under the modern planning statutes), the issuance of permits, and the undertaking of projects all trigger NEPA analysis. Moreover, NEPA's public notice and comment provisions provide an avenue for the broader public to influence agency decisions.

The ESA was passed to protect imperiled wildlife. Species listed under the act as "threatened" or "endangered" receive protection from direct "take" (defined as killing, harming, or harassing a species) and habitat destruction. 16 U.S.C. § 1538 (a)(1)(B); Babbitt v. Sweet Home Chapter of Communities for a Great Oregon, 515 U.S. 687, 115 S.Ct. 2407, 132 L.Ed.2d 597 (1995). A central provision, Section 7, applies only to federal agencies, and, like NEPA, is triggered by federal "action." Section 7 requires every federal agency to "insure that any action authorized, funded, or carried out by such agency ... is not likely to jeopardize the continued existence" of any listed species, or result in the "destruction or adverse modification" of the species' designated critical habitat. 16 U.S.C. § 1536(a)(2). Virtually every land use plan, permit, lease or project on public lands can implicate section 7 of the ESA if a listed species is present. Because listed species are found on nearly all federal lands, Section 7 has a sweeping effect across the full realm of public lands management.

The provision is carried out through consultation with one of two agencies, each commonly referred to as the "Service." The U.S. Fish and Wildlife Service (USFWS) implements the act for terrestrial species, and the NOAA Fisheries Service (formerly the National Marine Fisheries Service, or NMFS) implements the act for marine mammal species.

Through a detailed process set forth in the statute, the "Service" issues a Biological Opinion (BO) indicating whether the proposed action would jeopardize a species. Section 7's prohibition is strict and has a significant effect on land management, occasionally halting entire timber, grazing, or recreation programs. Many a federal manager complains that the ESA vests the Services with superior authority that trumps the land agency's traditional role. Citizens can enforce the ESA through the statute's citizen suit provision.

The administrative statutes form an important fourth rung in the statutory ladder. They are applicable to every federal agency and play a significant role in public land management. The Administrative Procedure Act (APA) requires federal agencies to provide public notice and opportunity for comment when passing regulations to implement federal statutes. 5 U.S.C. § 553. The APA waives the federal government's sovereign immunity and authorizes courts to overturn agency actions that are "arbitrary, capricious, an abuse of discretion, or otherwise not in accordance with law." 5 U.S.C. § 706 (2)(A). The importance of this provision cannot be overstated; nearly every public lands law case includes APA claims. Since neither the public lands statutes nor NEPA have citizen suits provisions, the only "ticket" into court is through the APA. The Equal Access to Justice Act (EAJA) provides support for public lands litigation by providing for attorneys fees to any party that "prevail[s]" against the federal government "unless the court finds that the position of the United States was substantially justified or that special circumstances make an award unjust." 28 U.S.C. § 2412 (d)(1)(A). Finally, the Federal Advisory Committee Act (FACA) sets forth general procedures advisory committees must follow, such as providing public notice and records of meetings, to reduce the potential for back-door politicking with the agencies. 5 U.S.C. App. 2, §§ 1 et seq. These procedures have assumed more importance in recent years as a result of reforms made during the Clinton administration that established new advisory committees in the areas of forest and range management. *See* Dover A. Norris-York, *The Federal Advisory Committee Act: Barrier or Boon to Effective Natural Resource Management?* 26 ENVTL. L. 419 (1996).

C. Public Lands Law Litigation

By the time the modern planning and environmental laws were enacted, an agency culture favoring mineral, logging, and grazing interests—what Professor Charles Wilkinson calls "the Lords of Yesterday"—was already entrenched. CHARLES F. WILKINSON, CROSSING THE NEXT MERIDIAN: LAND, WATER, AND THE FUTURE OF THE WEST (1992). Over the course of a century or more, those interests gained a substantial foothold in the bureaucracy and still exert considerable pressure on the agencies to promote extractive outcomes on federal public lands. Not uncommonly, public lands managers confront direct Congressional pressure in their decisions. Traditionally, this Congressional interest has been generated by powerful western Senators who receive political backing and financial support from the extractive interests. Political pressure combined with lack of agency funding sometimes sway agencies to take actions that violate their statutory mandates.

Beginning in the 1980s, a wave of litigation ensued against federal land agencies, challenging a broad variety of management actions as violating the modern planning statutes, as well as NEPA and the ESA. Environmental groups challenged forest plans, rangeland plans, mining, timber sales and grazing permits. Most challenges were framed around the APA's standard of "arbitrary, capricious, or not in accordance with law," 5 U.S.C. § 706 (2)(A), or "unlawfully withheld," action, 5 U.S.C. § 706 (1).

Successful litigation may have a sweeping, immediate effect on public lands management. The broader the challenged agency "action," the broader is the scope of potential injunctive relief. Suits challenging land use plans for failure to consult under section 7 of the ESA, for example, resulted in blanket injunctions across entire national forests or BLM districts. *See* Lane County Audubon Society v. Jamison, 958 F.2d 290 (9th Cir. 1992) (enjoining timber sales on BLM lands in coastal old growth spotted owl habitat pending consultation under the ESA); Pacific Rivers Council v. Thomas, 30 F.3d 1050, 1056 (9th Cir. 1994) (requiring Forest Service to undergo ESA consultation before proceeding with timber sales and other projects on the Wallowa–Whitman and the Umatilla National Forests); Silver v. Babbitt, 924 F.Supp. 976, 989 (D. Ariz. 1995) (enjoining timber harvest activities pending consultation pursuant to section 7(a)(2) of ESA).

Public lands litigation is the quintessential "complex litigation," because it involves so many different statutes, agencies, and legal issues. Basic constitutional and administrative requirements such as ripeness, standing, and exhaustion of administrative remedies must be satisfied. *See* Chapter 3, *supra*; Lujan v. National Wildlife Fed'n., 497 U.S. 871, 110 S.Ct. 3177, 111 L.Ed.2d 695 (1990) (standing requirements); Ohio Forestry Ass'n v. Sierra Club, 523 U.S. 726, 737, 118 S.Ct. 1665, 1672, 140 L.Ed.2d 921, 931 (1998) (ripeness). In many public lands cases, procedural issues overshadow the substantive issues emanating from statutory mandates. Moreover, contested land management usually gives rise to litigation on several fronts. Various groups may bring different suits against an agency using different statutes. The administrative context framing litigation in this area is complex, typically involving an array of various plans, guidance documents, regional studies and NEPA documents. As litigation continues through a decade or more, a complicated "law of the case" often develops through the various court decisions, appeals, remands to the agency, and administrative processes. The novice practitioner would be hard-pressed to understand a forest litigation case from the Pacific Northwest, Texas, or Alaska in light of the multitude of court decisions, agency regulations, regional plans, Congressional riders and environmental studies that have come to bear upon those heated controversies.

As noted earlier, the basic statutory authority for bringing suits against federal agencies is the Administrative Procedure Act. In 2004, the Supreme Court issued an opinion in *Norton v. Southern Utah Wilderness Alliance* which may have a chilling effect on efforts to reform public lands management through litigation, especially in the context of enforcing commitments made by the agencies in their land use plans. While the case involved a BLM land use plan, the ramifications of the opinion ripple across all of federal public lands law. What enforcement options remain when an agency fails to implement statutory requirements? You may wish to review the opinion, provided in Chapter 3.III.C.

D.   Ownership Complexities and Access Issues in Public Lands Law

The management regime of federal public lands is riddled with ownership complexities. Few blocks of federal public land have exclusively federal interests. Most of the Indian reservations in the West are bordered by federal lands that were at one time aboriginal territory. Tribes may have treaty rights to wildlife and water on federal land and may also access sacred sites. States own the streambeds of most navigable waterways within federal lands. As a result of the historic state land grants, they may also own blocks of land interspersed with federal land. Private "inholdings" are often found within federal borders because private settlement occurred prior to many federal reservations. In some areas, the lands originally granted to the railroads fracture the federal ownership in a checkerboard pattern made obvious today by timber clear-cutting or other development. Most federal lands are also peppered with private mining claims allowed under the General Mining Law of 1872. Even some wilderness areas have active mining claims that were established prior to protective designation. The Frank Church River of No Return Wilderness in Idaho, for example, is known for its "cherry stems"—mining access roads that intrude into the desolate wilderness.

Land exchanges are a tool commonly used by federal agencies to consolidate ownerships. Lands exchanged must be of "equal value," and the exchange must be in the public interest. *See* FLPMA, 16 U.S.C. § 1716. One of the most notable land exchanges involved a swap of state lands for federal acreage in Utah to correct the cumbersome checkerboard pattern of state ownership left over from the state grant era. *See* The Utah Schools and Land Exchange Act of 1998, 16 U.S.C. § 431. For further treatment of land exchanges *see* Chapter 5.I.C.6. *See also* Anderson, *Public Land Exchanges, Sales, and Purchases Under the Federal Land Policy and Management Act of 1976*, 1979 UTAH L. REV. 657. The Western Land Exchange Project has written a citizens' manual on federal land exchanges, *available at* www.westlx.org.

Access issues also form a complex layer to federal land ownership. Generally, private inholdings within the boundaries of the National Forest System have a right of access across federal lands. *See* Montana Wilderness Ass'n v. United States Forest Service, 655 F.2d 951 (9th Cir.

1981), *cert. denied,* 455 U.S. 989, 102 S.Ct. 1612, 71 L.Ed.2d 848 (1982) (interpreting access provision of Alaska National Interest Lands Conservation Act, to apply to all national forest lands including those outside of Alaska). Access to private inholdings across BLM lands is governed by FLPMA, which provides for right-of-way permits if certain conditions (such as environmental protection measures) are met. 43 U.S.C. § 1761.

A statutory relic passed by Congress in 1866 and later repealed in 1976 gives rise to additional access claims across public lands. The statute, called R.S. 2477 (43 U.S.C. § 932), granted non-federal entities the ability to create and own "rights-of-ways for the construction of highways" over public lands that had not yet been reserved for specific purposes. Such rights-of-way were subject only to state law and did not require specific federal approval. Subsequent reservation of a federal parcel did not extinguish previously established rights-of-way, but did foreclose any further access rights under R.S. 2477. United States v. Jenks, 129 F.3d 1348 (1997). In 1976, Congress passed FLPMA, which repealed the R.S. 2477 and replaced it with a detailed provision governing grants of rights-of-way. 43 U.S.C. §§ 1761–1771. Those seeking rights of way after 1976 must obtain permission from the federal government and, in most cases, pay fair market value for such rights.

FLPMA's repeal of R.S. 2477, however, did not extinguish pre-existing rights of way. Valid rights of way may exist if claimants can prove an R.S. 2477 claim pre-dating 1976. Fitzgerald v. United States, 932 F.Supp. 1195 (D. Ariz. 1996); United States v. Garfield County, 122 F.Supp.2d 1201, 1241 (D. Utah 2000). Of course, even valid R.S. 2477 access rights are subject to federal environmental regulation, as are all property rights. *See* Mountain States Legal Foundation v. Espy, 833 F.Supp. 808 (D. Idaho 1993) (upholding restrictions on access to protect endangered species).

Disputed R.S. 2477 route across sensitive desert stream on BLM land in Arch Canyon, Utah. Available at http://www.suwa.org. Photo by Scott Groene.

R.S. 2477 claims have moved center-stage in public lands policy. As described in a leading citizen conservation handbook, "The statute [R.S. 2477] is used to try to establish that dirt tracks, stream bottoms, livestock trails, and other faint paths are 'highways' and thereby defeat conservation-oriented actions, such as wilderness designation." ERIK SCHLENKER–GOODRICH, A CITIZEN'S GUIDE TO OFF–ROAD VEHICLE MANAGEMENT AND YOUR BUREAU OF LAND MANAGEMENT PUBLIC LANDS 76 (The Wilderness Society, 2002). Assertions of old claims by non-federal parties may result in the construction of roads across vast portions of the federal land base, including pristine areas in national forests, wildlife refuges, national parks, national monuments, and even wilderness. Such roads could preclude Wilderness Study Areas from being included in the national wilderness system. The prospect of R.S. 2477 claims also gives pause to private property owners who may be surprised to find that they took title from the federal government subject to such claims. *See* Theo Stein, *Old Law Pits Landowners, 'Road' Users,* DENVER POST, Aug. 19, 2003 at B–01.

For a comprehensive overview of the legislative and administrative history surrounding R.S. 2477, *see* CRS REPORT FOR CONGRESS, HIGHWAY RIGHTS OF WAY ON PUBLIC LANDS: R.S. 2477 AND DISCLAIMERS OF INTEREST (2003). For citizen strategies on challenging R.S. 2477 claims, *see* SCHLENKER-GOODRICH, A CITIZEN'S GUIDE, *supra* at 77. The interested student may wish to browse web photo galleries of alleged R.S. 2477 "highways" *at* http://www.suwa.org or http://members.aol.com/gshiker999/index.html.

E. Beyond Boundaries: Ecosystem Management of Federal Public Lands

Perhaps the greatest challenge across the field of natural resources law is the management of ecosystems split between various types of ownership. As one author observes:

> Spillovers from one parcel to another are not the only, or even the most interesting, aspect of the spillover problem. Ecologists have pointed to a more ubiquitous factor of interconnections: not only water, but air, wildlife, soil moisture regimes, indeed the whole landscape or ecosystem can perhaps be best understood as a series of physical and biological relationships that transcend property boundaries. Many have argued that those fundamental ecological interconnections are destroyed by our system of private and public property and the notion of ownership of specific parcels.

Sally K. Fairfax *et al.*, *The Federal Forests Are Not What They Seem: Formal and Informal Claims to Federal Lands,* 25 ECOLOGY L.Q. 630, 632, 633–641 (1999).

The following excerpt explores the modern trend in public lands management to address ecosystem protection.

A NEW ERA FOR THE WESTERN PUBLIC LANDS: BEYOND THE BOUNDARY LINE: CONSTRUCTING A LAW OF ECOSYSTEM MANAGEMENT

Robert B. Keiter

65 U. Colo. L. Rev. 293, 294–296, 300–301, 302–304, 318–319, 320–322, 323 (1994)

Whether the controversy involves spotted owls in the Pacific Northwest, visibility on the Colorado Plateau, or grizzly bears in Greater Yellowstone, the solution being espoused today is to manage the ecosystem as an entity. Indeed, each of the principal federal land management agencies—the Forest Service, Bureau of Land Management, National Park Service, and U.S. Fish & Wildlife Service—is openly touting ecosystem management as the panacea for today's natural resource controversies. * * *

The concept of ecosystem management, though still often misunderstood, has now been defined with sufficient precision to constitute a viable natural resource management policy. Drawing heavily upon ecological and biological sciences, particularly the field of conservation biology, ecosystem management views the land and resource base in its entirety, as a holistic or integrated entity. Management focuses on entire ecosystems, not just individual resources such as timber and forage. Recognizing that natural systems often cross jurisdictional boundaries, ecosystem management emphasizes the need for inter-jurisdictional coordination to ensure ecological integrity and sustainable resource systems. The policy is designed to maintain and restore natural processes, including biodiversity levels and natural disturbance regimes. And because ecological systems evolve over time, often unpredictably, ecosystem management is intended to accommodate such instability and change. * * *

The existing legal system governing public lands and resources does not expressly endorse the concept of ecosystem management. In fact, by relying upon politically-determined boundary lines to define ownership responsibilities, federal public land law runs directly counter to ecosystem management principles, which envision management based upon often-changing, ecologically-defined boundaries. Furthermore, most federal natural resource laws are anything but holistic in scope or intent when they establish separate legal regimes governing management and production of individual resources such as timber and minerals. But several relatively new laws, including the Endangered Species Act, National Environment Policy Act, National Forest Management Act, and Federal Land Policy and Management Act, are beginning to break down traditional boundary limitations and excessive legal compartmentalization. These laws ... obligate federal land managers to broaden their management perspective; they also vest managers with sufficient authority to experiment with ecosystem management concepts. In the shadow of the law, therefore, a new era in public land management is beginning to take shape. * * *

For additional analysis of federal ecosystem management, *see* Chapter 2.II.B (Landscape Linkages) and 2.IV.A (Ecosystem Management), *supra*; Oliver A. Houck, *On the Law of Biodiversity and Ecosystem Management*, 81 Minn. L. Rev. 869 (1997). For a discussion of the shift from the dominant, extractive use of public lands to recreation and conservation, *see* Jan G. Laitos & Thomas A. Carr, *The Transformation on Public Lands*, 26 Ecology L. Q. 140 (1999).

F.   The Pacific Northwest's Ancient Forest Controversy: A Case Study in Unstable Management of Federal Public Lands

One of the greatest hurdles to effective public lands management is the inability of the present legal system to support a stable regime. Political interests are engaged in a constant tug-of-war over the public lands. As the materials in this chapter indicate, consistent policy is undercut by changes in Presidential administrations, court rulings, and Congressional intervention through appropriations riders. One of the clearest examples of management instability involves the northern spotted owl and its habitat in the old growth forests of the Pacific Northwest. This case study provides a glimpse of both the forces at play in public lands management and the complexity of practice in this area.

The Pacific Northwest's northern spotted owl; Photo by U.S. Department of Transportation, Federal Highway Administration.

THE BUSH ADMINISTRATION'S SWEETHEART
SETTLEMENT POLICY:
A TROJAN HORSE STRATEGY FOR ADVANCING COMMODITY
PRODUCTION ON PUBLIC LANDS
Michael C. Blumm

34 ENVTL. L. REP. 10397, 10409–10411 (May 2004)

* * * The origins of the Northwest Forest Plan lie in the unsustainable timber harvesting that characterized Northwest public forests in
the 1970s and 1980s, when it appeared that the federal government
aimed to liquidate the last of the region's remaining old growth forests.
Environmentalists became aware of the precarious state of the northern
spotted owl, and they challenged the small islands of habitat protection
the Forest Service provided for the spotted owl that biological studies
increasingly showed were inadequate.

Litigation over Northwest public timber harvests began in the mid–
1980s, when environmentalists obtained an injunction halting logging in
the Suislaw National Forest for violating NEPA by failing to consider the
risk of landslides and their effects on water quality and fish populations.
Sen. Mark Hatfield (R–Or.) responded to the injunction in 1985 by introducing the first of what became a series of appropriation riders to overturn court injunctions. A complicated interplay between the courts
ensued, with courts enjoining federal timber harvests for violating environmental laws while the riders attempted to withdraw the courts' jurisdiction or suspend the underlying laws. Although the Court ratified Congress' ability to change the underlying laws via appropriation riders,
Congress allowed the riders to expire after 1990, and the lower courts
reinstated the injunctions even before the Court handed down its ruling,
largely because the Forest Service and the BLM failed to consider and
publicly disclose the latest scientific information concerning the northern spotted owl and its habitat requirements. Then, after the court-
ordered listing of the owl in 1990, the Endangered Species Act (ESA)
took center stage.

The listing, combined with NEPA and National Forest Management
Act (NFMA) injunctions, led to the formation of an interagency task
force that recommended that the Forest Service and the BLM set aside
roughly eight million acres in spotted owl habitat reserves in which logging would be prohibited and road building discouraged. The Forest Service accepted this approach, but the BLM resisted, eventually seeking
and obtaining a rare and controversial ESA exemption in 1992 that
allowed limited logging in some spotted owl habitat areas that was later
withdrawn by the Clinton Administration. But broad-based court injunctions were affirmed by the Ninth Circuit in early 1993 on non-ESA
grounds, and the listing of the northern spotted owl promised additional
logging restrictions.

Faced with the prospect that the ESA would add to an already stale-
mated timber supply situation, the Clinton Administration attempted to
fashion a compromise. After convening a widely publicized "Forest Sum-

mit" in Portland, Oregon, in 1993, the Administration considered a variety of alternatives in developing what became known as the Northwest Forest Plan, covering over 20 million acres of federal forests west of the Cascades, stretching from northern California to the Canadian border. The alternative selected was the most timber productive of those studied, establishing a goal of an annual harvest of 1.1 billion board-feet of timber, a target that was subsequently reduced to 805 million annual board-feet of timber. This 1994 plan, which amended 19 Forest Service and 7 BLM land management plans, also promised to protect and restore large tracts of public forest to provide for the viability of mobile species like the northern spotted owl. The plan was the first large-scale ecosystem management plan and consequently sought watershed restoration on a unprecedented scale; among the species it sought to protect were Pacific salmon, which themselves were the subject of ESA listings.

Under the plan, the timber harvests would come from approximately 30% of the remaining old growth in Northwest public forests available for logging on some 4.6 million acres between reserves. But before logging those areas, the plan required the Forest Service and the BLM to undertake watershed analysis aimed at protecting streams via buffers or other mitigation measures and to conduct surveys for rare and relatively less mobile forest-dependent species such as red tree voles, which are an important prey for owls. These "aquatic conservation" and "survey and manage" requirements were crucial to the plan's legality. According to the reviewing court: "If the plan as implemented is to remain lawful, the monitoring, watershed analysis, and mitigation steps called for by [it] will have to be faithfully carried out." The court ruled that the plan provided only the minimum amount of protection demanded by the ESA and other federal laws, stating that "any more logging sales than the plan contemplates would probably violate the laws."

But the ink was barely dry on the Northwest Forest Plan when Congress once again resorted to authorizing timber harvests by appropriation rider. After the Republican takeover of Congress in the 1994 elections, a 1995 appropriation bill contained a provision that became known as the Timber Salvage Rider, which contained a series of exemptions from environmental law for public timber harvests, two of which were focused on the harvests within the range of the Northwest Forest Plan. The 1995 rider was but a temporary victory for the timber industry, as public outcry prevented its renewal when it expired in 1996. Even with the 1995 rider, the annual timber production target in the Northwest Forest Plan never materialized, largely due to the inability of the Forest Service to carry out its aquatic conservation and survey duties and still find suitable areas to harvest. Ironically, the timber industry, which fought the Northwest Forest Plan, began to embrace the plan, at least in terms of its projected annual timber harvest.

But there were many other parts of the Northwest Forest Plan to which the industry objected, especially after the courts declared that the provisions of the plan were enforceable. First, in 1999, Judge William L. Dwyer of the U.S. District Court for the Western District of Washington ruled that the federal land management agencies' failure to complete surveys for over 70 species, especially the red tree vole, violated the plan. Later that year, Judge Barbara J. Rothstein of the same court again enforced the requirements of the Northwest Forest Plan, this time its aquatic conservation requirements, despite the National Marine Fisheries Service's determination that proposed logging would not violate the ESA. In each case, the result was to stop public timber harvests.

Thus, when the Bush Administration assumed office in early 2001, the timber industry viewed the Northwest Forest Plan as a broken promise, largely (but not exclusively) due to its survey and manage and aquatic conservation requirements that had resulted in decreased timber harvest. The industry decided to pursue a multifaceted, comprehensive approach to transform the Northwest Forest Plan into a plan for achieving a prescribed level of timber harvest, much like in the 1980s, when harvest levels were set in appropriation riders. The vehicle to accomplish this transformation was a series of lawsuits in which the industry challenged various aspects of the Northwest Forest Plan under the watch of a sympathetic Administration. The result was several settlement agreements designed to make the Northwest Forest Plan much more user-friendly to the timber industry.

In Practice: Be Alert to Appropriation Riders

Appropriation riders are the "sneaker waves" of public lands law.

Historically, riders were used only occasionally by both Democrat and Republican legislators to influence public lands law. Over the past decade, however, there has been a surge in the use of riders to such an extent that dealing with riders is a predictable part of public lands law practice today. To those legislators who craft them, a primary appeal of riders is that they avoid democratic processes and are largely hidden from the public. Appropriations riders do not go through the normal committees that generate substantive public lands legislation. Instead, these bills are tacked on to huge appropriations packages that have little relationship to the substance of the bill. Riders are difficult to find amidst hundreds of pages of an appropriations package.

The natural resource practitioner must be on a constant look-out for riders that may affect implementation of important laws. Often riders are drafted in the wake of public lands litigation to avoid the outcome. The most practical way to monitor for riders is to keep in close touch with public interest or industry groups that have lobbyists in Washington D.C., or with Congressional staff that are involved with the issue. Newsletters and email alerts from national organizations also provide news about pending riders.

Notes and Questions

1. What are the major destabilizing forces in the Pacific Northwest Ancient Forest controversy? The Northwest Forest Plan was one of the first attempts in the nation to institute an "ecosystem management" policy that would endure over time. How long did the plan last before it was undercut? What legal mechanisms subverted the plan? Is Congress a leading culprit in the destabilization of public lands management? Or are the courts? What is the difference between each branch's effect on public lands policy? How can public lands mangers and policy makers create stability in an area fraught with such controversy? For a discussion of the efficacy of federal ecosystem policies, see Chapter 2.IV.A, *supra*.

2. One of the newest phenomena in public lands litigation involves "friendly settlements." In his article, Professor Blumm describes settlements made by the Bush administration in lawsuits that had challenged the government's forest policy in the Pacific Northwest. He finds comparisons with other settlements in the natural resources area and concludes:

> [T]he [Bush] Administration changed the course of public land law by responding (or not responding) to a series of lawsuits brought by commodity interest groups against Clinton Administration policies. Instead of defending its predecessor's policy initiatives, the Bush Administration often settled the lawsuits, promising to adopt reforms advocated by the commodity interest litigators. This "get sued and supply a sweetheart settlement" policy was complemented in one case ... by a closely related strategy of virtually failing to litigate at all. Indeed, it seemed as if the Administration was pursuing a "Trojan Horse" approach to changing public land policy: first inviting litigation from industry; then, once a case was filed, avoiding a court decision on the merits through settlement agreements that gave the industry everything it could have hoped for through litigation, while undermining environmental controls in the process. This sweetheart settlement process was accomplished behind closed doors without public participation or any change in legislation. This use of litigation without judicial decision would surprise those who, in an earlier generation, advocated litigation to advance environmental and civil rights issues in order to overcome legislative inertia. A generation later, the use of public law litigation in the service of rolling back environmental protection, in large measure through governmental acquiescence, must be viewed by its early advocates as a cruel irony.

Blumm, supra, 34 ENVTL. L. REP. 10397, 10398.

Government lawyers are supposed to represent the government's interest zealously. Who defines what their position should be when a new administration reverses the policy of the former administration? Is there any normative standard to guide government attorneys involved in public lands litigation? Are "friendly settlements" an ethical abuse or political fact of life?

3. Appropriations riders are now constantly used by Congress to affect public lands management. Though Presidents have the constitutional power to veto legislation, they find themselves "over the barrel" when faced with riders, because the appropriations packages to which the riders are attached are often necessary for continued federal funding. While the constitutional-

ity of riders has not been fully litigated, the Supreme Court upheld one of the most notorious timber riders in Robertson v. Seattle Audubon Soc'y, 503 U.S. 429, 112 S.Ct. 1407, 118 L.Ed.2d 73 (1992). The "section 318 rider" set an annual harvest level for northwest forests, thereby changing the law that was subject to ongoing federal court cases. Department of the Interior and Related Agencies Appropriations Act for Fiscal Year 1990, Pub. L. No. 101–121, § 318, 103 Stat. 701, 745–50 (1989). One of the most far-reaching riders was the "Salvage Rider" of 1995, spearheaded by Sen. Mark Hatfield of Oregon, who was Chair of the Senate Appropriations Committee. Emergency Supplemental Appropriations for Additional Disaster Assistance, for Anti-terrorism Initiatives, for Assistance in the Recovery from the Tragedy that Occurred at Oklahoma City, and Rescissions Act, 16 U.S.C. § 1611. The law mandated salvage sales across the country in forest stands that were "imminently susceptible to fire or insect attack"—language that was sufficiently broad to cover most timber sales the Forest Service wanted to implement. The bill exempted such sales from virtually every environmental law, eliminated the public's right to administrative appeals, and restrained judicial injunctive relief pending court appeals. *See* Michael Axline, *Salvage Logging: Point & Counterpoint: Forest Health and the Politics of Expediency*, 26 ENVTL. L. 613 (1996). For commentary on public lands riders, *see* Sandra Zellmer, *Sacrificing Legislative Integrity at the Altar of Appropriations Riders*, 21 HARV. ENVTL. L. REV. 457 (1997).

4. The harvest cutbacks resulting from the Northwest Forest Plan caused resentment that continues to simmer in timber communities. A notice in Idaho's Star–News, June 26, 2003 (a decade after the plan was finalized) read:

Warren gets Ready for Spotted Owl Shoot

Celebrate the Fourth of July by helping out the Warren Fire and Rescue Fund at the Warren Spotted Owl shoot on Friday, July 4. Warren is located about 40 miles north of McCall.... It is unlikely any of the controversial birds will be seen, much less shot, but the fun will nonetheless begin at noon with the final round of shooting to follow at noon Saturday, July 5.

5. Public opinion is a vital part of public lands management, yet it is difficult to find adequate in-depth press coverage of this area. Standard newspapers and television newscasts devote little time to the complexities inherent in most public lands issues, so there is a tendency toward bi-polar simplifications such as "spotted owls versus jobs"—a characterization that makes great headlines but perpetuates misunderstandings and engenders hostility. Two specialized newspapers provide focused analysis of public lands issues: Cascadia Times, www.times.org; and High Country News, www.hcn.org. Reading these periodicals gives the novice quick footing in the field and keeps seasoned practitioners up to date.

The materials that follow focus individually on different categories of land management in the public lands inventory. They cover national forests, BLM lands, national refuges, parks, and monuments. The chapter concludes with brief coverage of mining as an overlay to all of these federal land categories. As you will discover, though all of these land categories represent federal public ownership, the character of the managing federal agency very much determines how such ownership translates into on-the-ground resource uses.

This chapter provides extensive treatment of forestry law as an entrée into the other public lands categories. Among all of the sub-fields of public lands law, forest law is by far the most complex and evolved. It has been the subject of extensive rule-makings that have shifted dramatically between administrations. Forest controversies have generated complex litigation in multiple regions, most notably Alaska, the Pacific Northwest, the Rocky Mountain Region, the Southeast, and in Wisconsin, Texas and Ohio. Because forest litigation weaves together various planning mandates with NEPA and the ESA, it has pushed the field of public lands law into a far more complicated realm than anyone might have imagined back when the National Forest Management Act and other planning statutes were passed. Moreover, forest law demonstrates patterns of agency behavior, Presidential and Congressional politics, and citizen responses that ripple across every area of public lands law.

II. THE NATIONAL FORESTS

A. The Political and Physical Landscape

The national forest system has its origin in the Forest Reserve Act of 1891, which authorized the President to designate forest reservations on federal public lands. Act of March 3, 1891, ch. 561, 26 Stat. 1095, 1103 (repealed 1976). There are now 155 national forests in the United States managed by the U.S. Forest Service, which is part of the Department of Agriculture. The national forests are among the most popular natural areas of the United States, attracting over 214 million visitors every year (double the number of visitors to national parks). Comprising 192 million acres, or 8.5% of the total area of the United States, the vast majority of national forest land (87%) is located in the West. Beyond meeting a growing recreational demand, forests provide a host of essential ecosystem services. They serve as vital buffer areas for national parks and wilderness areas, provide a source of water for wild and scenic rivers, provide habitat for imperiled species, supply a source for municipal drinking water, filter air pollution, and serve an important role in flood control, soil formation, climate control, and nutrient cycling. Many national forests are storehouses for biodiversity, the benefits of which scientists are only beginning to recognize.

In Practice:
Understanding the Bureaucratic Structure

The Forest Service is directed by the Chief of the Forest Service. The agency is divided into nine regions, each headed by a Regional Forester. Each region contains several national forests, each of which is headed by a Forest Supervisor. Each national forest, in turn, is

> divided into ranger districts (over 600 nationwide), each led by a district ranger. Each district typically manages an area of 50,000 to 1 million acres. The agency maintains a website at http://www.fs.fed.us/ with links providing specific information on each of the 155 national forests. Many national forests have their own websites as well.

While many a forest visitor has been shocked to find that public national forests are logged for private commercial purposes, the timber output of national forests has long been the dominant factor shaping forest policy. *See* CHARLES F. WILKINSON, CROSSING THE NEXT MERIDIAN: LAND, WATER, AND THE FUTURE OF THE WEST, Ch. 4 (1992). Gifford Pinchot, who became the first head of the Forest Service in 1898, had a decidedly utilitarian vision of the forest, and to a large extent the agency culture still reflects that orientation today. In the years following World War II, the timber production from many national forests surged to levels far beyond what was sustainable. The Forest Service instituted the practice of "clearcutting" (now called "even aged management" by the agency), an efficient technique used by industry on private lands to harvest vast areas of forest in a short period of time, leaving a landscape bare of trees. As one court described:

> For nearly half a century following its creation in 1905, the National Forest System provided only a fraction of the national timber supply with almost ninety-five per cent coming from privately owned forests. During this period the Forest Service regarded itself as a custodian and protector of the forests rather than a prime producer, and consistent with this role the Service faithfully carried out the provisions of the Organic Act with respect to selective timber cutting. In 1940, however, with private timber reserves badly depleted, World War II created an enormous demand for lumber and this was followed by the post-war building boom. As a result the posture of the Forest Service quickly changed from custodian to a production agency. It was in this new role that the Service initiated the policy of even-aged management in the national forests, first in the West and ultimately in the Eastern forests, including the Monongahela.

West Va. Div. of Izaak Walton League, Inc. v. Butz, 522 F.2d 945, 954 (4th Cir. 1975).

In national forests across the country, the Forest Service also punched in roads to serve the timber sales. Approximately 385,000 miles of roads crisscross the national forests—more than ten times the U.S. Interstate Highway System and enough to circle the globe seventeen times. U.S. Dept. of Agriculture, Forest Service, *Fiscal Year 1999 Road Accomplishment Report* (1999). Attempts to halt road building, even temporarily, have been met with opposition from the logging industry as well as from local communities that have economies based on timber production. As roads intrude into previously untouched areas, such areas fall off the roadless area inventory, which has historically been the object of wilderness preservation efforts.

As part of the agency's shift after World War II, Forest Service policy in some regions turned towards "liquidating" the old growth ancient forests. *See, e.g.,* Sierra Club v. Hardin, 325 F.Supp. 99, 122–24 (D. Alaska 1971) (describing Forest Service's "policy of liquidation of the old growth forests in southeastern Alaska.... "). Harvest of these towering stands– some of them several hundred years old—was justified on the basis that they were "overmature." Their rate of growth had slowed with age, and retaining them was perceived as a decadent use of space that could otherwise be used for fast growing young trees arranged in mono-culture industrial tree plantations. *See* George Cameron Coggins, Charles F. Wilkinson, & John D. Leshy, Federal Public Land and Resources Law 4d. 671 (2001). Harvest rates escalated in the 1980s, and in clearcut after clearcut, the ancient forests gave way to tree plantations. Scientists warned that at current logging rates, all of the unprotected old-growth forest in the Pacific Northwest would be destroyed by 2020. *See* Paul Hirt, A Conspiracy of Optimism: Management of the National Forests Since World War II (1994). Today, less than 10% of the ancient forest remains in the Pacific Northwest. The Wilderness Society, *National Forests Factsheet,* January 24, 2000, http://www.wilderness.org/Library/ Documents/loader.cfm?url=/commonspot/security/getfile.cfm& PageID=3014.

Timber sales are fiscally evaluated according to the receipts they bring in versus the costs incurred by the agency to manage them. Evaluated in these terms (not accounting for environmental damage caused by some timber practices), many sales are "below cost," meaning that the Forest Service spends more money on the sale than it receives in income. The federal subsidy to timber companies is justified by the Forest Service for the economic benefits timber sales bring to local communities located near federal forests. Such communities typically desire a continuous supply of timber to keep mills operating. One of the most publicized cases of subsidy comes from the Tongass National Forest in Alaska where, in 1988 alone, nearly half a billion board feet of old growth forest was cut and sold at a price that gave the Forest Service as little as 8 cents on the dollar. *See* Oliver A. Houck, *On the Law of Biodiveristy and Ecosystem Management,* 81 Minn. L. Rev. 869, 901 (1997). A study conducted by the General Accounting Office reported that the Forest Service claimed losses from timber sales in excess of $2 billion from 1992–1997. General Accounting Office, Forest Service: Amount of Timber Offered, Sold, and Harvested, and Timber Sales Outlays, Fiscal Years 1992 Through 1997, RCED–99–174, June 15, 1999.

On a national level, the resource damage from the Forest Service timber sale program has been considerable. The widespread practice of clear-cutting, especially on steep slopes, has caused massive soil erosion and damage to salmon habitat. *See* 62 Fed. Reg. 24588, 24593 (May 6, 1997) (final rule listing the coho salmon as threatened in S. Oregon & N. California). The thousands of miles of roads constructed to facilitate timber harvest cause further erosion, landslides, and additional destruction of riparian habitat. *See generally* USDA, COMMITTEE OF SCIENTISTS, SUSTAINING THE PEOPLE'S LANDS: RECOMMENDATIONS FOR STEWARDSHIP OF THE NATIONAL FORESTS AND GRASSLANDS INTO THE NEXT CENTURY (March 15, 1999). As harvested lands are replanted with single-tree species to maximize timber output, the resulting plantations lack not only the aesthetic qualities of ancient forests, but also crucial species diversity. *Id.*

Clearcuts on the Willamette National Forest. Photo by James Johnston.

Public opposition to forest practices intensified in the 1980s as more clearcuts appeared across the national landscape. Citizens increasingly became involved in challenges to timber sales at the local grassroots level, largely because NEPA provided them the opportunity to examine timber sale documents and environmental analysis. Groups such as the Sierra Club launched campaigns to increase citizen activism in forest policy. As Professor Federico Cheever sums up, "[e]xercise of the discretion guarded in NFMA's legislative process has gotten the Forest Service a political battering that no one could have predicted.... Smokey Bear receives death threats. The Forest Service is attacked from both ends of the political spectrum and pleases almost no one." Federico Cheever, *Four Failed Forest Standards: What We Can Learn From the History of the National Forest Management Act's Substantive Timber Management Provisions,* 77 OR. L. REV. 601, 703 (1998). In response to criticism, the Forest Service created a public relations strategy to temper the tone of information released to the public. At least one commentator found the Forest Service's new terminology amusingly transparent.

DAMAGE CONTROL:
A FIELD GUIDE TO IMPORTANT EUPHEMISMS
IN ENVIRONMENTAL LAW
Oliver A. Houck
15 TUL. ENVTL. L. J. 129 (2001)

One of the reasons environmental law is difficult is that it can be so embarrassing. It is one thing to say that you picked up a speeding ticket or had to pay back taxes. It is another to admit that you are using the Hudson River for a sewer or that you cut loose fourteen hundred tons of toxins over Los Angeles last year. The result is the rise of a new vocabulary to soften the blow. Just as military experts talk of collateral damage to describe the impact of weapons gone awry, so virtually every agency and industry that whacks the environment has developed its own language of damage control.

The language is not accidental. Some years ago the U.S. Geological Survey's mining chief, smarting under the disclosure requirements of the National Environmental Policy Act, wrote to his environmental personnel objecting to their characterization of mined lands as "disturbed." Certainly, he went on, "there should be a better word then (sic) 'disturbed' to describe land utilized and altered in the production of coal." Fully warm to the task, his memo concluded:

> When the Geological Survey has the lead in preparing environmental statements, inflammatory words such as disturbed, devastated, defiled, ravaged, gouged, scarred and destroyed should not be used. These are the words used by the Sierra Club, Friends of the Earth, environmentalists, homosexuals, ecologists and other ideological Eunuchs opposed to developing natural resources.

Well said! Most of these conversations go unseen, of course, except for the results they produce, a set of euphemisms intended to blur the effects of strip mining, channel dredging, clearcutting, waste dumping and other dark features we would like to imagine were otherwise. Here are a few of the more important ones: * * *

"Even–Aged Management." When is a forest even-aged? When all the trees are cut down at the same time. Leftist sympathizers call the practice "clearcutting."[a] The phrase "even aged" has a friendlier ring to it, like the 7–to–8 and 9–to–11–year-old divisions in your child's little league. * * *

"Multiple Use." Whatever use has the most clout, rendering it, apparently, multiple. According to a consistent string of judicial decisions, there is no imaginable dedication to a single use that is not in fact "multiple." Indeed, one court found that committing 99.5% of the largest forest in America to timber farming was multiple use. The more money you stand to make from public resources, the more you like multiple use management. * * *

---

a. Author's note: This chapter uses the terms "clearcut" and "clearcutting" to comport with the terminology used by Congress in NFMA, 16 U.S.C. § 1604(g).

"Overmature." When are you overmature? When you have achieved your maximum growth rate, maybe as late as age fifteen? But probably earlier. At which point it is time to kill you before you take up the space of some youngster who is really putting on useful pounds. Some forests are full of overmature trees, many of them tall, some of them older than your uncle! These kinds of trees are also known as "waste." As stated in the original Tongass National Forest Plan, our mission is to eliminate the waste from "decadent" stands of "overmature" trees. * * *

In Practice:
Silviculture Vocabulary

The natural resource practitioner must become familiar with a new technical vocabulary for virtually any area in which s/he chooses to practice. Several of the key terms used in forestry are listed here, while others are provided in Chapter 11 (Timber).

> *Even-aged harvest ("clearcutting")* removes all trees of all ages from the site.

> *Seed tree harvest* leaves approximately 10 trees an acre which produce seeds for future generations of trees.

> *Shelterwood harvest* leaves approximately 20 trees an acre to produce seeds and shade for future generations of trees. Ultimately an "even-aged forest" also results from shelterwood and seed tree methods, as the few remaining trees after such harvest are isolated and often fall to high winds or are removed in a future cut.

> *Selective harvest* removes only certain trees of harvestable quality, leaving the majority in the stand.

> *Diameter at Breast Height (DBH)* refers to the size of a tree, measured by the diameter at 4 1/2 feet off the ground.

> *Sale Area* is the area in which a timber sale occurs; not all lands within this area are cut.

The materials in this section present the statutory and regulatory framework of national forest law. The extraordinary value of national forests—both to the public and to timber interests—makes them subject to a political tug-of-war, the result of which is tremendous instability in the legal regime governing Forest Service activities. The environmental reform era of the 1970s created a new set of protections for national forests and gave the public a legal handle in how the forests were managed. But the ESA, NEPA, and NFMA did nothing to deflate the political forces that had grown around a massive timber output. The Forest Service sometimes ignored the important mandates embodied in these new laws. Environmentalists sought relief in the courts, gaining sweeping injunctions that shut down entire national forests. *See, e.g.,* Pacific Rivers Council v. Thomas, 30 F.3d 1050 (9th Cir. 1994); Silver v. Babbitt, 924 F.Supp. 976 (D. Ariz. 1995). In turn, the timber industry sought relief from court decisions in the offices of individual Senators, who intervened to push riders exempting forest practices from the restrictive laws that caused grid-lock of federal forests. And so the pattern goes on even to this day, leading to tremendous instability and failure in long-range forest planning. For case studies that reveal the complex triangle of power between the Executive Branch, Congress, and the courts in forest policy, *see* Oliver A. Houck, *On the Law of Biodiversity and Ecosystem Management*, 81 MINN. L. REV. 869, 892–930 (1997).

Beyond the extraordinary dynamics resulting from conflicts between the three branches of government, forest policy has swung wildly between presidential administrations. President Clinton instituted a variety of "reforms" designed to bring ecosystem management to the realm of forest policy. *See* George Frampton, *Ecosystem Management in the Clinton Administration*, 7 DUKE ENVTL. L. & POL'Y F. 39 (1996). Though the details in the new approach were often not well-received in the environmental community, the general policy direction towards sustainable management was favored by conservation groups. The Clinton reforms were barely in place when the second Bush administration took office and embarked on an overhaul of forest policy, geared towards bringing "reform" of a different nature. On January 24, 2001, the new administration suspended the Clinton regulations, including implementation of the new forest management rules and the "roadless rule" (a hallmark of President Clinton's public lands policy) that prohibited construction of new roads in roadless areas. *See* 66 Fed. Reg. 8899 (Feb. 5, 2001). On August 22, 2002, President Bush launched the Healthy Forests Initiative, a package of regulatory measures designed to eliminate some of the public comment and appeal rights and significantly narrow NEPA requirements for many activities on national forests. U.S. FOREST SERVICE, DEP'T OF AGRIC., HEALTHY FORESTS: AN INITIATIVE FOR WILDFIRE PREVENTION AND STRONGER COMMUNITIES (2002). The Healthy Forests Initiative culminated in passage of the Healthy Forest Restoration Act (HFRA) by Congress in December, 2003. Pub. L. 108–148, 117 Stat. 1887. The new law is designed to carve out "hazardous fuels reduction" projects from the scope of applicable NFMA and NEPA requirements.

The Forest Service's new measures answered the long-time complaints of the timber industry that environmentalists were abusing NEPA and NFMA processes to slow down the rate of harvest on national forests. Indeed, by the turn of the 21st century, conservation groups had successfully used NEPA, NFMA, and the ESA in nearly every region of the country to dramatically reduce cutting on national forests, from the peak of 12 billion board feet (3 million loaded log trucks) nationally per year under President Reagan, to approximately 2 billion board feet (500,000 loaded log trucks) under President Clinton. The Forest Service has long complained that the laws create a regulatory straight jacket impeding their work as land managers. But conservation groups point out that reduced timber outputs simply bring forest policy more in line with a sustainable rate of harvest to compensate for the massive over-cutting of the 1980s that led to species loss and severe watershed degra-dation. An influential paper prepared by the Forest Service presented the rationale for the Bush II administration's regulatory reforms, many of which are explored in this section.

THE PROCESS PREDICAMENT:
HOW STATUTORY, REGULATORY, AND ADMINISTRATIVE FACTORS AFFECT NATIONAL FOREST MANAGEMENT 5, 10 (2002)
USDA Forest Service

Despite a century of devotion to conservationism, the Forest Service today faces a forest health crisis of tremendous proportions:

- 73 million acres of national forests are at risk from severe wildland fires that threaten human safety and ecosystem integrity.

- Tens of millions of acres in all ownerships are threatened by dozens of different insects and diseases.

- Invasive species are spreading at an accelerated rate, degrading an increasing proportion of forests, rangelands, and riparian habitats.

Unfortunately, the Forest Service operates within a statutory, regu-latory, and administrative framework that has kept the agency from effectively addressing rapid declines in forest health. This same frame-work impedes nearly every other aspect of multiple-use management as well. Three problem areas stand out:

1. Excessive analysis—confusion, delays, costs, and risk manage-ment associated with the required consultations and studies;

2. Ineffective public involvement—procedural requirements that create disincentives to collaboration in national forest manage-ment; and

3. Management inefficiencies—poor planning and decision-making, a deteriorating skills base, and inflexible funding rules, problems that are compounded by the sheer volume of the required paperwork and the associated proliferation of opportu-nities to misinterpret or misapply required procedures.

These factors frequently place line officers in a costly procedural quagmire, where a single project can take years to move forward and where planning costs alone can exceed $1 million. Even non-controversial projects often proceed at a snail's pace.

Forest Service officials have estimated that planning and assess-ment consume 40% of total direct work at the national forest level. That would represent an expenditure of more than $250 million per year. Although some planning is obviously necessary, Forest Service officials have estimated that improving administrative procedures could shift up to $100 million a year from unnecessary planning to actual project work to restore ecosystems and deliver services on the ground. * * *

Statutory, regulatory, and administrative requirements impede the efficient, effective management of the National Forest System. * * *

Notes and Questions

1. The *Process Predicament* paper favors collaborative decision-making instead of outcomes that result from litigation. *See id.* at 39. Under collaborative processes, do conservation groups and industry groups play on an even field? Who benefits from litigation, and who benefits from collaboration?

2. In the 1990s, the Forest Service began to package a majority of timber sales in many regions as "treatments" for undesirable forest conditions such as insect infestations or disease. Yet many such sales have a significant "green tree" component, consisting of live trees unaffected by disease or insects. *See* the Salvage Rider of 1996, 16 U.S.C. § 1611 (allowing cutting of "associated trees" in addition to dead, diseased, and insect-infested trees). These are commercially valuable trees often coveted by commercial logging interests. How can an astute practitioner distinguish between treatments that are truly needed to address forest health and those that are not? Is it enough in this age of political battles over scarce resources to simply take the agency at its word? What challenges does the new vocabulary create for lawyers seeking to explain a forest program to a judge, or to the public in an opinion-editorial? Does the growing complexity of forest management favor commercial or public interests?

3. There are often serious disagreements over the appropriate response to an insect or disease problem in a forest. Insect infestations can leave miles and miles of dead trees in their wake in a relatively short period of time. Such trees become fuel for wildfire. The industry decries the waste of such trees, arguing for early removal of stands that are diseased or infested to keep the problem from spreading. Conservationists, on the other hand, point out that insects and disease are part of the natural cycle of most forests. Logging these areas can have adverse effects on other forest resources, such as streams that support fisheries. Should the public be involved in these complex management decisions, and, if so, how? For discussion of the conflicts over salvage logging, *see* Marc Fink, *Logging After Wildfire: Salvaging Economic Value or Mugging A Burn Victim*, 19 J. ENVTL. L. & LITIG. 193 (2004).

4. In the 1990s, the Sierra Club launched a campaign to end commercial logging on national forests. *See* http://www.sierraclub.org/forests. The Sierra Club reasons that the costs of subsidized commercial timber sales on national forests outweigh the economic benefits. It also asserts that taxpayers should not finance the hidden costs associated with degraded watersheds and adverse impacts on wildlife. What are the advantages and disadvantages of ending commercial logging on national forests? Should the forests be used for other commercial purposes such as recreation and sustainable harvest of forest products like mushrooms, berries, and ferns? What benefits accrue to the public under either scenario? Is it fair to nearby forest commu-

nities to cut off a supply of federal timber? Where should the balance be struck between local and national interests?

5. The Forest Service's budget is greatly determined by the level of cut it gets out. *See* Sierra Club v. Thomas, 105 F.3d 248, 251 (6th Cir. 1997) (describing budget process). Some argue that this provides the driving incentive for Forest Service policy: "Deep Throat told us to 'follow the money.' When it comes to the Forest Service we should certainly follow that advice. Budgetary incentives play an enormous role in determining what the Forest Service, or any other federal agency, decides to do. Changing budgetary incentives can change agency conduct." Federico Cheever, *Four Failed Forest Standards: What We Can Learn From the History of the National Forest Management Act's Substantive Timber Management Provisions,* 77 OR. L. REV. 601, 704 (1998). What budgetary reforms could you propose? Would industry and conservation groups propose different reforms? Would they share any common ground? For a discussion of the budgetary influences on the Forest Service, *see* RANDAL O'TOOLE, REFORMING THE FOREST SERVICE 122 (1988).

B. A Statutory Overview

National forest law is governed by three primary laws: The Organic Act of 1897, 15 U.S.C. § 473; the Multiple Use Sustained Yield Act of 1960 (MUSY), 16 U.S.C. §§ 528–531; and the National Forest Management Act (NFMA), 16 U.S.C. §§ 1600–1614 (1976), which remains the dominant statute today. The Organic Act articulated the purpose of national forests (then called forest reserves): "to improve and protect the forest within the boundaries, or for the purposes of securing favorable water flows, and to furnish a continuous supply of timber for the use and necessities of citizens of the United States." It authorized the sale of "dead, matured, or large growth trees ... as may be compatible with the utilization of the forests thereon," but mandated that such trees be individually "marked and designated" prior to harvest. After World War II, the Forest Service used this authorization to step up harvest on national forests.

In 1960, Congress passed MUSY to force the Forest Service to shift management of national forests to a broader spectrum of uses. MUSY declared that federal forest lands "shall be administered for outdoor recreation, range, timber, watershed, and wildlife and fish purposes," in the combination that "will best meet the needs of the American people." It ended with a caveat that such purposes "are declared to be supplemental to, but not in derogation of" the purposes set forth in the Organic Act. 16 U.S.C. §§ 528, 531. MUSY also declared that the national forests be administered to produce "sustained yield." 16 U.S.C. § 529. While MUSY's purposes were lofty, it was a poorly crafted statute with no process for implementation, and no clear statement as to how to balance the various uses of the forest. Nor did it distinguish how much of each use is necessary for a forest to meet the standard of "multiple use." Arguably, using 95% of the forest for timber harvesting and 5% for recreation is "multiple use." As the Ninth Circuit Court of Appeals put it, the language of MUSY "breathes discretion in every pore." Perkins v. Bergland, 608 F.2d 803, 806 (9th Cir.1979)

Not surprisingly, courts interpreted MUSY as granting considerable discretion to the Forest Service to choose appropriate forest uses. In the Tongass National Forest of southeast Alaska, the MUSY mandate did not preclude the Forest Service from embarking on a plan to log all but .006% of 4.5 million acres of commercial forestland and selling 8.7 billion board feet of timber to U.S. Plywood–Champion Papers for the company's exclusive harvest over a 50–year contract period. The district court of Alaska dismissed a MUSY challenge brought by the Sierra Club, finding that the Forest Service need only give "due consideration" to the various MUSY values: "While the material undoubtedly shows the overwhelming commitment of the Tongass National Forest to timber harvest objectives in preference to other multiple use values, Congress has given no indication as to the weight to be assigned each value and it must be assumed that the decision as to the proper mix of uses within any particular area is left to the sound discretion and expertise of the Forest Service." Sierra Club v. Hardin, 325 F.Supp. 99, 123 (D. Alaska 1971). On appeal, the Ninth Circuit remanded the case in an unpublished opinion with only an obscure caution that the "due consideration" requirement fashioned by the district court "can hardly be satisfied by a showing of knowledge of the consequences and a decision to ignore them." Sierra Club v. Butz, 3 E.L.R. 20292 (9th Cir. 1973). The MUSY experiment, which announced broad goals without articulating precise, objective, enforceable standards, merely affirmed the Forest Service's discretion, which was already bent on producing a high timber output. Scholars have criticized MUSY: "The multiple use, sustained yield statutes … represent congressional buck-passing, and they allow bureaucratic lawmaking. They give managers a latitude that would be deemed undue in other more visible areas of the law." *See* George C. Coggins, *Of Succotash Syndromes and Vacuous Platitudes: The Meaning of "Multiple Use, Sustained Yield" for Public Land Management*, 53 U. Colo. L. Rev. 229 (1981).

As the public's forests continued to fall to clearcuts in the decade and a half following MUSY, the environmental community and timber interests were at loggerheads over national forest policy. Citizens lost confidence in the Forest Service's stewardship abilities and sought a statutory regime that would limit the discretion of the agency. In 1971, a Congressional subcommittee led by Frank Church of Idaho held hearings on Forest Service practices. These hearings received condemning testimony against the Forest Service's clear-cutting, and the committee issued a report which included the "Church Committee guidelines" on harvest practices. Those guidelines became the "seminal text" that engendered the standards incorporated into NFMA five years later. *See* Federico Cheever, *Four Failed Forest Standards, supra* at 620.

In 1975, a surprising decision from the Fourth Circuit interpreting the Organic Act of 1897 gave citizens the clout they needed to seek reform in Congress. West Virginia Div. of Izaak Walton League, Inc. v. Butz, 522 F.2d 945 (4th Cir. 1975). The Izaak Walton League had challenged three timber sales allowing clearcuts on 428 acres of the Monongahela National Forest of West Virginia. *Id.* at 946. The court held that clearcutting violated a sleeper provision in the Organic Act that allowed cutting of only "dead, matured or large growth" trees, and required marking of individual trees prior to harvest. *Id.* at 948–951. Contrary to the selective harvest method mandated by the Organic Act, clearcut harvest methods entail marking only the outside boundaries of a sale rather than individual trees. *Id.* at 946–47. The precedential value of the case as applied to other forests created the impetus for Congressional action and spurred passage of the National Forest Management Act (NFMA) in 1976.

Through NFMA, Congress attempted to bridle the Forest Service's vast discretion by imposing an extensive new mandate comprised of two parts: planning and substantive standards. First, NFMA requires the Forest Service to develop Land and Resource Management Plans (LRMPs) to govern all activities on a forest. Such plans were to be developed with extensive public involvement provided under the previously enacted National Environmental Policy Act. (Also in 1976, Congress imposed a similar land management planning process on the BLM through FLPMA, 43 U.S.C. §§ 1711–1712, 1751–1753). Second, NFMA set forth a series of substantive standards designed to protect the forest resources while still allowing timber harvest. It repealed the key provisions of the Organic Act that prevented clear-cutting, but substituted other standards that were intended to restrict the agency's use of the practice. 16 U.S.C. § 1604(g)(3). As Senator Hubert Humphrey stated,

> The days have ended when the forest may be viewed only as trees and trees viewed only as timber. The soil and water, the grasses and the shrubs, the fish and the wildlife, and the beauty that is the forest must become integral parts of the resources managers' thinking and actions.

122 Cong. Rec. 5619 (1976).

For analysis of NFMA, *see* CHARLES F. WILKINSON & H. MICHAEL ANDERSON, LAND AND RESOURCE PLANNING IN THE NATIONAL FORESTS (1987); Charles F. Wilkinson, *The National Forest Management Act: The Twenty Years Behind, the Twenty Years Ahead,* 68 U. COLO. L. REV. 659 (1997).

In addition to NFMA, the ESA and NEPA play a central role in forest management. Modern forest law must be viewed as an intricate meshing of all three statutes. Both the ESA and NEPA are triggered by federal "actions," which include Forest Service planning activities and projects. The recent passage of the Healthy Forest Restoration Act, Pub. L. 108–148, 117 Stat. 1887, described more fully in section F below, presents another layer of statutory law. The HFRA essentially carves out certain "hazardous fuel reduction projects" from the standard processes of NEPA, although it leaves intact the operation of NFMA and the ESA for such projects.

C. NFMA's Mandate

1. *Planning Under NFMA*

The forest plans (LRMPs) are critical documents because they guide all forest activities for their duration (up to 15 years). Congress wanted the Forest Service to incorporate the full myriad of forest values into the planning process, so it required the agency to develop the plans using an interdisciplinary team and a "systematic interdisciplinary approach to achieve integrated consideration of physical, biological, economic, and other sciences." 16 U.S.C. § 1604(b), (f)(3). Congress also required the Forest Service to incorporate the requirements of "multiple use" under MUSY into the plans. 16 U.S.C. § 1604(e).

LRMPS are, essentially, zoning plans for the forest, performing three essential functions. First, they identify uses and management priorities for particular areas of the forest. NFMA specifically requires the Forest Service to identify areas suitable and not suitable for timber production, "considering physical, economic, and other pertinent factors." 16 U.S.C. § 1604 (k). A typical forest plan divides the forest into different management areas. For example, the George Washington National Forest, located in Virginia, has 18 management areas. Management Area 17 is devoted to timber production. Other management areas are dedicated to recreation, wilderness study, remote habitat for wildlife, and other uses. USDA, *George Washington National Forest Final Revised Land and Resource Management Plan* (January 1993).

Second, the plans project harvesting levels (informally called an "allowable cut") for the forest and set forth a planned timber sale program, along with "probable methods of timber harvest.... " 16 U.S.C. §§ 1604(e)(2), (f)(2). The allowable cut is determined in light of "the availability of lands and their suitability for resource management." 16 U.S.C. § 1604(e)(2). In lay terms, this means that the harvest levels must correlate with the amount of land suitable for harvest. A forest encompassing one million acres, for example, will not have suitable commercial timber land across all one million acres. Some areas may be rocky, or have steep slopes, or may be better managed for wildlife habitat. In an attempt to shift the agency away from unsustainable logging, NFMA requires that harvest levels be set in accordance with principles of sustained yield, as previously set forth under MUSY, and that trees reach their "culmination of mean annual increment of growth" (a level of maturity) prior to harvest. 16 U.S.C. §§ 1604(e), (m)(1).

Third, NFMA requires that the LRMPs incorporate certain substantive standards geared towards protecting soils, watersheds, fish and wildlife, and designed to prevent automatic use of clearcutting as a harvest method. 16 U.S.C. § 1604(g). Many of these standards are fleshed out in the Forest Service's regulations contained in 36 C.F.R. Part 219 (1999). These standards, explained in further detail below, are incorporated in the LRMPs for the purpose of constraining the Forest Service's discretion as it plans and carries out projects on the forests. In the past, such standards have often been quite specific, such as setting particular road densities or establishing tree retention requirements (even to the detail of number of trees per acre, and clump formation). These "musts and shalls" in the LRMPs have typically been the fodder for enforcement by forest conservation groups, but recent regulatory amendments have eliminated prescriptive standards for revised plans. *See* Final Rule, National Forest System Land and Resource Management Planning, 70 Fed. Reg. 1022, 1025 (Jan. 5, 2005), amending 36 C.F.R. Part 219. For a comprehensive description of NFMA land management plans, *see* Michael J. Gippert & Vincent L. DeWitte, *The Nature of Land and Resource Management Planning Under the National Forest Management Act,* 3 ENVTL. L. 149 (1996).

Additional standards are often developed at the regional level. For example, a regional directive in the Uinta National Forest attempts to halt the spread of noxious weeds by applying specific prevention and control measures including treatment with chemical, biological, mechanical, cultural, and manual methods. INTERMOUNTAIN REGION, U.S. FOREST SERVICE, SUPPLEMENT NO. R4 2000–2001–1 TO THE FOREST SERVICE MANUAL 2000, ZERO CODE 2080: NOXIOUS WEED MANAGEMENT (2001). Sometimes, but not always, such directives trigger amendments to the LRMPs.

NFMA requires that the LRMPs be revised every 15 years, or earlier if conditions significantly change. 16 U.S.C. § 1604(f)(5). The revision constitutes a major overhaul of the LRMP. The revision process is distinct from the amendment process, which is used to make adjustments from time to time within the 15–year life of the plan. Nearly all forest plans undergo several amendments before the next revision. In some regions, the rate of ecological destruction is so rapid that forest plans are quickly outdated by new requirements triggered by species listings under the ESA.

In several instances, the Forest Service has responded to ESA listings with broad regional habitat plans covering several forests. In the Pacific Northwest, for example, the Forest Service developed the Northwest Forest Plan, which provided protection for the northern spotted owl across 24.5 million acres of owl habitat and incorporated a detailed "Aquatic Conservation Strategy" geared towards habitat protection for ESA listed salmon. In the Pacific Southwest region, a regional effort known as the Sierra Nevada Ecosystem Project sought to protect owl habitat across national forests in the Sierra Nevada mountain range. In the southern region, the Forest Service issued a plan for management of the red-cockaded woodpecker and its habitat across multiple forests. As the Forest Service increasingly takes an ecosystem-wide approach to management, these regional plans may become more common for particular species. Such broad habitat plans form a new regulatory layer to the LRMPs and are administratively handled as amendments to the LRMPs. The Northwest forest Plan, for example, amended 19 individual LRMPs at once. The specific management prescriptions of these region-wide habitat plans trump the less protective management criteria of the LRMPs that they amend, but the rest of the LRMP remains operative. As "actions" undertaken by a federal agency, the regional habitat plans must comply with section 7 of the Endangered Species Act, 16 U.S.C. § 1536, and must be promulgated in accordance with NEPA. Accordingly, they are often the subject of litigation. *See, e.g.,* Seattle Audubon Society v. Lyons, 80 F.3d 1401 (9th Cir. 1996) (reviewing Northwest Forest Plan).

Despite the sea-change in forest law brought about by the ESA, the standard LRMPs are still very important for determining the overall use of the forest. The first generation of LRMPs was completed in the 1980s. These plans have either just recently been revised or are now currently in the process of revision. While NFMA requires that the plans be revised no later than 15 years after initial promulgation, 16 U.S.C. § 1604(f)(5), Congress passed an appropriations rider on Nov. 5, 2001 that extended the deadline for plans that had not yet been revised. P.L. 107–63, § 327; 115 Stat. 414 (107th Cong. 1st Sess, 2001).

It would be hard to overstate the importance of the second-generation plans, as they will determine the forest management regime for the next 15 years. The tension over these plans is great. Environmental advocates have approached the second-generation revisions as an opportunity to employ the NFMA planning process to create a set of clear prescriptions to bridle Forest Service discretion. They often push for very specific management standards, having learned from the MUSY experience that imprecise standards leave too much room for agency discretion and thwart judicial enforcement. The Forest Service, however, places a premium on retaining discretion and feels that mandatory standards in plans preclude much needed management flexibility and invite litigation. On January 5, 2005, the Forest Service issued a sweeping new planning rule that changed the fundamental character of NFMA plans from a set of enforceable standards to non-enforceable desired conditions. It is discussed below in Section C.3.c.

2. *NFMA's Substantive Standards*

Congress included a set of substantive standards in NFMA to constrain the Forest Services's discretion in managing the national forests. The statute reads in relevant part:

[T]he Secretary shall ... promulgate regulations ... that set out the process for development and revision of the land management plans.... The regulations shall include: * * *

(3) specifying guidelines for land management plans developed to achieve the goals of the Program which— * * *

(B) provide for diversity of plant and animal communities based on the suitability and capability of the specific land area in order to meet overall multiple-use objectives, and within the multiple-use objectives of a land management plan ... provide, where appropriate, to the degree practicable, for steps to be taken to preserve the diversity of tree species similar to that existing in the region controlled by the plan. * * *

(E) insure that timber will be harvested from National Forest System lands only where—

> (i) soil, slope, or other watershed conditions will not be irreversibly damaged;

> (ii) there is assurance that such lands can be adequately restocked within five years after harvest;

> (iii) protection is provided for streams, streambanks, shorelines, lakes, wetlands, and other bodies of water from detrimental changes in water temperatures, blockages of water courses, and deposits of sediment, where harvests are likely to seriously and adversely affect water conditions or fish habitat; and

> (iv) the harvesting system to be used is not selected primarily because it will give the greatest dollar return or the greatest unit output of timber; and

(F) insure that clearcutting, seed tree cutting, shelterwood cutting, and other cuts designed to regenerate an even-aged stand of timber will be used as a cutting method on National Forest System lands only where—

> (i) for clearcutting, it is determined to be the optimum method, and for other such cuts it is determined to be appropriate, to meet the objectives and requirements of the relevant land management plan; * * *

> (iii) cut blocks, patches, or strips are shaped and blended to the extent practicable with the natural terrain;

> (iv) there are established according to geographic areas, forest types, or other suitable classifications the maximum size limits for areas to be cut in one harvest operation, including provision to exceed the established limits after appropriate public notice and review by the responsible Forest Service officer one level above the Forest Service officer who normally would approve the harvest proposal: *Provided*, That such limits shall not apply to the size of areas harvested as a result of natural catastrophic conditions such as fire, insect and disease attack, or windstorm; and

> (v) such cuts are carried out in a manner consistent with the protection of soil, watershed, fish, wildlife, recreation, and esthetic resources, and the regeneration of the timber resource.

16 U.S.C. § 1604(g).

While in 1976 these substantive standards seemed quite specific and enforceable, Congress left an ambiguity that triggered considerable litigation: whether the standards amount to on-the-ground requirements restricting the Forest Service's discretion, or whether their only role is to guide development of the LRMPs. Section E below addresses this issue. Most of the attention has been on the diversity standard, the clearcutting standards, and the re-stocking standard.

3. *NFMA Regulations*

Despite the detailed prescriptions of NFMA, the force of any statute depends on the implementing regulations fashioned by the agency. It should come as no surprise that incoming Presidential administrations often craft new regulations when they want to steer policy in a different direction. The implementing regulations of NFMA are found at 36 C.F.R. Part 219. Attuned to the importance of regulatory prescriptions, Congress included a unique provision in NFMA that required the Secretary of Agriculture to enlist the assistance of a Committee of Scientists in drafting the original regulations "to assure that an effective interdisciplinary approach is proposed and adopted." 16 U.S.C. § 1604(h)(1). The initial NFMA regulations were passed in 1979 and amended in 1982. They reflected a scientific approach that prioritized species protection, and, notably, they incorporated precise standards for agency behavior. An effort by the agency at revising the regulations in 1995 was turned back by public opposition. *See* 60 Fed. Reg. 18886 (April 13, 1995) (proposed rule). In 2000, the Clinton Administration overhauled the regulations, and in 2005 the pendulum took another abrupt swing when the Bush II administration issued a broad new planning rule. Final Rule, National Forest System Land and Resource Management Planning, 70 Fed. Reg. 1022 (Jan. 5, 2005). Because first generation LRMPs are still governed by the 1982 regulations, and because most litigation thus far has occurred under them, they continue to form the foundation for legal analysis.

a. **The 1982 Diversity Regulations**

One of the most important regulatory standards is expressed in the 1982 "diversity regulation," which is thought to be even more protective than the ESA, as it is geared towards all native and other desirable fish and wildlife species on the national forests (not just ESA listed ones) and requires "viable populations." The regulation provides:

> Fish and wildlife habitat shall be managed to maintain viable populations of existing native and desired non-native vertebrate species in the planning area. For planning purposes, a viable population shall be regarded as one which has the estimated numbers and distribution of reproductive individuals to insure its continued existence is well distributed in the planning area. In order to insure that viable populations will be maintained, habitat must be provided to

support, at least, a minimum number of reproductive individuals and that habitat must be well distributed so that those individuals can interact with others in the planning area.

36 C.F.R. § 219.19 (1998).

ON THE LAW OF BIODIVERSITY AND ECOSYSTEM MANAGEMENT
Oliver A. Houck
81 MINN. L. REV. 869 (1997)

The litigation over the diversity standard has been extensive, perhaps because the 1982 regulation (36 CFR pt. 219) contained some of the most precise prescriptions aimed towards preserving species and biodiversity on federal forests. * * *

In 1976, diversity planning was boosted forward by the "most adventurous congressional incursion" into the activities of the Forest Service, * * * the National Forest Management Act (NFMA). 16 U.S.C. §§ 1600–1614 (1994). Buried within the Act's many compromises over competing uses of forest resources was the nation's first and only explicit statutory provision for the protection of biological diversity. * * *

Left to its own devices, [Section 1604(g)(3)(B)] would not travel very far. At first blush its language reads almost as a parody of law, qualified by no fewer than two provisos: "where appropriate" and "to the degree practicable," and, were anything left, by the eviscerating "in order to meet overall multiple-use objectives," a standard that has consistently failed to limit agency decisions. * * * The legislative history of this section, however, tells a quite different story about what was intended and, indeed, said. The diversity provision of NFMA was a seriously debated and conscious attempt by the Act's leading sponsors to curb the conversion of hardwoods to other species and to forestall monoculture forestry. * * * In context, the use of the term "multiple-use objectives" was intended to limit the reduction of forest diversity to a few dominant species. * * * Departures from the principle of species diversity would be allowed only where justified on the basis of "overall" multiple-use objectives, that is to say, objectives other than timber. * * * The burden of this justification lay on the Service. * * * When Congress said "multiple-use" in Section 1604(g)(3)(B), it was not thinking license; it was thinking constraint.

Congress went one step further. In order to make the new limitations on timber management a reality, Congress directed the appointment of a Committee of Scientists to assist the Forest Service in developing regulations that would flesh out these provisions and become, in effect, the law of NFMA. *See* 16 U.S.C. § 1604(h) (1994). The Committee's recommendations on managing for diversity were to become the state-of-the-art. * * *

The Forest Service's final biological diversity requirements are contained in two sections of its planning regulations. Section 219.27, entitled "Management Requirements," provides the goal and the baseline:

> (g) Diversity. Management prescriptions, where appropriate and to the extent practicable, shall preserve and enhance the diversity of plant and animal communities, including endemic and desirable naturalized plant and animal species, so that it is at least as great as that which would be expected in a natural forest and the diversity of tree species similar to that existing in the planning area. 36 C.F.R. § 219.27(g) (1996).

Granting the modifiers and the qualifiers, there is no escaping that the goal is the diversity of the natural forest. The regulation continues:

> Reductions in diversity of plant and animal communities and tree species from that which would be expected in a natural forest, or from that similar to the existing diversity in the planning area, may be prescribed only where needed to meet overall multiple-use objectives. *Id.*

Departures from the goal of natural forest diversity face a heavy burden of proof. The second requirement is contained in Section 219.19, entitled "Fish and wildlife resource." 36 C.F.R. § 219.19 (1996). It is specific and prescriptive: Habitat "shall be managed to maintain viable populations" of existing species; that is, populations with sufficient numbers and distribution "to insure" that the species remains "well-distributed in the planning area." *Id.* The standard is both numerical, "a minimum number of reproductive individuals," and spatial, habitat that is "well distributed" to facilitate interaction and breeding. *Id.* Notable here is the obligation "to insure" the viability of these populations, language that would seem to call for cautious assumptions in favor of the species. * * * Notable also is the absence of qualifiers and escape clauses. The standard may be difficult, but it is plain. * * *

In the world envisioned by the Committee and the regulations, the protection of these species and their habitat needs would have become goals of proactive forest planning, with each species identified and monitored to ensure, in turn, a diverse forest ecosystem. In the more mundane world of a commodity-driven forest program, they became instead a defensive, biology-based bottom line—and a legal battleground. * * *

In Practice:
Sorting Through Species Classifications on
National Forests

The Forest Service manages species using a variety of classifications, the terminology of which can be confusing. *Endangered* or *threatened species* refers to species listed under the ESA. These species have special, enforceable protections under that statute. *Sensitive species* are species typically designated by the Forest Service on a regional level as being potentially imperiled but not yet ESA-listed. Forest Service protection of sensitive species comes from the diversity mandate of NFMA. Many sensitive species ultimately become ESA-listed species. *Management Indicator (MI) species* are species with habitat needs generally representative of other species in the ecosystem; thus, management of the MI species is, in theory, supposed to protect the other many species in the forest. 36 C.F.R. § 219.19. Sometimes the choice of MI species is challenged. *See, e.g.,* Oregon Natural Resources Council v. Lowe, 109 F.3d 521 (9th Cir. 1997).

The various classifications of species, in turn, gives rise to different documentation associated with actions affecting habitat. A *biological assessment* (BA) is an assessment mandated under the ESA for listed endangered or threatened species. A *biological evaluation* is a document the Forest Service prepares to assess the impacts of its actions on sensitive species. Where a listed species is "likely to be affected by" a Forest Service action, as determined by the BA, the Forest Service must engage in formal consultation with the U.S. Fish and Wildlife Service (in the case of terrestrial species) or the NOAA Fisheries Service (in the case of marine species) to determine whether the proposed action will jeopardize the existence of the species. 16 U.S.C. § 1536 (a)(2).

b. The Clinton 2000 Regulations

In 1997, the Secretary of Agriculture under the Clinton Administration convened a second Committee of Scientists to review Forest Service policy and recommend changes to planning and practices under NFMA. The Committee steered the focus of forest planning to ecosystem management and declared the goal of sustainability to be the "guiding star for stewardship of the national forests and grasslands." COMM. OF SCIENTISTS, U.S. DEP'T OF AGRIC., SUSTAINING THE PEOPLE'S LANDS: RECOMMENDATIONS FOR STEWARDSHIP OF THE NATIONAL FORESTS AND GRASSLANDS INTO THE NEXT CENTURY 175 (1999).

Following the Committee's direction, the Forest Service issued a new set of regulations in 2000 to replace the 1982 version. 65 Fed. Reg. 67,514 (Nov. 9, 2000). The wording reflected the Committee's overall direction, declaring sustainability as the "overall goal of management of the National Forest System." 36 C.F.R. Parts 217, 219 (2000). Emphasizing the ecological interconnectedness of all forest resources, the new regulations combined the previously separate management standards pertaining to vegetation, fish and wildlife, water and soil resources into one regulatory provision dealing with ecological sustainability. 36 C.F.R. § 219.20 (2000). But despite their feel-good ecosystem approach, some environmental analysts criticized the regulations for replacing the detailed standards of the 1982 regulations with guidelines that lacked enough precision to be enforceable in court. One of the most significant changes between the 1982 and Clinton 2000 regulations had to do with species viability. In contrast to the 1982 regulation stating that "[f]ish and wildlife habitat *shall* be managed to maintain viable populations ... in the planning area" (§ 219.19)(1982), the Clinton 2000 regulations merely required the Forest Service to maintain ecological conditions that "provide a high likelihood ... of supporting ... the viability of ... species ... within the plan area." *Id.* § 219.20(b)(2)(i)(2000). To the environmental critics, the 2000 regulations were a return to the days of MUSY, where broad standards vested the Forest Service with more discretion and precluded judicial enforcement. Professor Oliver Houck had warned of this possibility: "In its definitions without meanings, processes without standards, and replacement of objectivity with generalities, the Service would eliminate any commitment to diversity qua diversity. In the name of 'ecosystem management,' it would reinvent multiple use." Houck, *supra*, at 928.

c.   The Healthy Forest Initiative (HFI) Planning Rules

The Clinton 2000 regulations had a short life. In May, 2001, the Forest Service dispensed with the Clinton regulations and reinstated the 1982 regulations as an interim step towards a new NFMA planning rule. 66 Fed. Reg. 27552. On January 5, 2005, the Forest Service promulgated a final new NFMA planning rule. Final Rule, National Forest System Land and Resource Management Planning, 70 Fed. Reg. 1022, 1025 (Jan. 5, 2005). While many environmental organizations had not favored the Clinton approach to NFMA planning, they found even more to dislike in the new planning rule, which eliminated any requirement to provide for viable populations of plant and animal species. The preamble to the final rule stated:

> The species viability requirement was not adopted for several reasons. First, the experience of the Forest Service under the 1982 planning rule has been that ensuring species viability is not always possible. For example, viability of some species ... may not be achievable because of species-specific distribution patterns ... or when the reasons for species decline are due to factors outside the control of the agency (such as habitat alteration in South America causing decline of some Neotropical birds), or when the land lacks the capability to support species (such as a drought affecting fish habitat).

> Second, the number of recognized species present on ... the National Forest System is very large. It is clearly impractical to analyze all species, and previous attempts to analyze the full suite of species via groups, surrogates, and representatives have had mixed success in practice.

> Third, focus on the viability requirement has often diverted attention and resources away from an ecosystem approach to land management that, in the Department's view, is the most efficient and effective way to manage for the broadest range of species with the limited resources available for the task.

Requirements for species population monitoring are not included in this final rule. * * * [I]n compliance with NFMA, the ecological sustainability provisions in the final rule provide the foundation for the plan to provide for diversity of plant and animal communities. The final rule provides a complementary ecosystem and species diversity approach for ecological sustainability.

70 Fed. Reg. at 1029.

Another major change brought about in the 2005 planning regulation is the elimination of "shalls" and "musts," which in effect precludes specific (and enforceable) standards in land management plans. Instead, plans will contain five broad principle components: desired conditions, objectives, guidelines, suitability of areas, and special areas. 70 Fed. Reg. at 1025. The planning rule also requires each national forest to develop and implement a standardized "environmental management system" developed and used widely by industry to track environmental conditions on a land base. *Id.* at 1029. The preamble to the rule explains:

[P]lans under this final rule will be more strategic and less prescriptive in nature than under the 1982 planning rule. * * * [T]he agency has concluded that plans are more effective if they include more detailed descriptions of desired conditions, rather than long lists of prohibitive standards or guidelines or absolute suitability determinations developed in an attempt to anticipate and address every possible future project or activity and the potential effects they could cause. * * *

Desired conditions are the social, economic, and ecological attributes toward which management of the land and resources ... is to be directed. Desired conditions are long-term in nature and aspirational, but are neither commitments nor final decisions approving projects and activities. * * *

[I]n line with and to clarify the strategic nature of the plans, this final rule instead adopts the term "guidelines" and has removed the term "standards" as a plan component. The Department decided to employ the term "guideline" to reflect a more flexible menu of choices consistent with the nature of plans set forth in this rule. * * * A Responsible Official has the discretion to act within the range of guidelines, as well as the latitude to depart from guidelines when circumstances warrant it. * * *

70 Fed. Reg. at 1024–26.

As noted earlier, forest conservation groups have been heavily involved in the forest plan revision process with the goal of attaining as many definite prescriptive standards as possible. Judicial review is much more difficult without measurable standards, because courts are inclined to view the agency action as discretionary. The new planning rule, by dramatically broadening agency discretion, reflects the philosophy expressed in the agency's *Process Predicament* paper, *supra,* that courts have become too involved with the Forest Service's land management. *See id.* at 36. The Supreme Court itself seems to agree, if *Norton v. Southern Utah Wilderness Alliance*, discussed in Section I, *supra*, is viewed as a reluctance to enforce all but the most prescriptive plan standards.

D. NFMA, NEPA and the HFI

The natural resource practitioner must have considerable familiarity with the National Environmental Policy Act, covered in depth in Chapter 4. NEPA has an enormous impact on forest management. The initial Council of Environmental Quality (CEQ) regulations implementing NEPA are found at 40 C.F.R. §§ 1500–1508.28 (1978). The Forest Service procedures for NEPA compliance at the project level are contained in 36 C.F.R. Part 215. The Forest Service Manual (FSM) sets forth detailed NEPA responsibilities in Chapter 1950. The Forest Service Handbook (FSH), http://www.fs.fed.us/im/directives, contains an even more detailed description of NEPA procedures.

NEPA is designed to inform agency decision-making and allow the public a say in federal decisions that affect the environment. 42 U.S.C. § 4342. *See* Robertson v. Methow Valley Citizens Council, 490 U.S. 332, 109 S.Ct. 1835, 104 L.Ed.2d 351 (1989). The Council on Environmental Quality called NEPA the "foundation of modern American environmental protection." CEQ, THE NATIONAL ENVIRONMENTAL POLICY ACT: A STUDY OF ITS EFFECTIVENESS AFTER TWENTY-FIVE YEARS (1997).

In the area of forest law, citizens have used NEPA effectively to gain access to information, require the agency to look at alternatives for proposed actions, and to appeal actions to higher venues within the agency, or in court. But just as NEPA has proved indispensable to citizen involvement in forest policy, NEPA processes have greatly frustrated federal officials as well as the timber industry. *See Process Predicament, supra,* at 16 ("[E]nvironmental studies are … now complex, often costly and time consuming and sometimes redundant…. Decision-making is complicated by the extensive environmental and public involvement procedures developed under NFMA, NEPA, ESA, FACA, and the Forest Service appeals process.)." Many blame NEPA for delaying timber sales by creating red tape and grounds for appeal. *See* Stark Ackerman, *Observations on the Transformation of the Forest Service: The Effects of the National Environmental Policy Act on U.S. Forest Service Decision Making,* 20 ENVTL. L. 703, 711 (1990).

By the time of the second Bush administration, substantial political pressure from industry and within the agency itself had mounted to eliminate some of the basic NEPA requirements from forest management. The Bush II administration responded with a number of regulatory measures that dramatically shrank NEPA processes for several types of Forest Service decisions. Understanding the impact of the these changes requires a basic knowledge of the framework of NEPA, detailed in Chapter 4, *supra*.

The core mandate of NEPA is the requirement that agencies prepare an Environmental Impact Statement (EIS) for major actions "significantly affecting ... the environment." 42 U.S.C. § 4332(c). To determine whether an action "significantly" affects the environment, agencies undertake Environmental Assessments (EAs), which are shorter, less detailed, documents than EISs. If the agency believes there is no "significant" environmental effect, the agency issues a Finding of No Significant Impact (FONSI), along with a Record of Decision (ROD) implementing the action. If, on the other hand, the agency determines there are significant impacts, the agency prepares an EIS, which explores both alternatives to the proposed action and all significant environmental effects.

While the ultimate result of NEPA is not a substantive one, NEPA often changes the course of an agency's actions through public scrutiny or appeal. NEPA provides the public with an opportunity to comment on an EIS. 40 C.F.R. § 1506.6(b); 1503.1. The public comment period allowed by the Forest Service for EISs is 45 days. 36 C.F.R. § 215.6(a)(1)(ii). NEPA and the CEQ regulations do not provide an explicit public comment opportunity on EAs, but the Forest Service Appeals Reform Act requires the agency to provide a thirty-day comment period on all proposed actions implementing land and resource management plans. 16 U.S.C. § 1612(a). The timing of this comment period is crucial because it determines how much information the public will have on the proposal. The Appeals Reform Act does not specify when the 30–day comment period must take place, but until 2003, the Forest Service regulations had provided that it would commence upon issuance of draft EAs. 36 C.F.R. § 215.5 (1993). The comment period for draft EAs was an important procedural opportunity heavily used by the public to provide input, especially on proposed timber sales that the Forest Service did not believe warranted full-blown EISs.

Under the Bush II reforms, the public's comment opportunities shrank. The Forest Service eliminated the fixed period for public comment on EAs and substituted a much looser standard that gives the district ranger discretion to decide when to provide a 30–day public comment opportunity on any proposed action requiring an EA. *See* 36 C.F.R. § 215.5(a)(2)(2003). This change triggered concern among public interest groups that district rangers may use their discretion to allow comment on proposed decisions only at the earliest "scoping" stage, prior to development of a draft EA. At this very early point in time, the agency typically identifies, in general terms, a proposed action and requests input on potential environmental issues and alternatives. Under this approach, the public lacks the specific information needed to fully evaluate the proposal.

The Forest Service also shrank the NEPA process by expanding the use of Categorical Exclusions for many of its activities. The NEPA statute itself does not provide for categorical exclusions, but the CEQ regulations allow agencies to "categorically exclude" certain actions "which do not individually or cumulatively have ... significant effects on the

human environment." 40 C.F.R. § 1508.4 (2003). The regulatory consequences of creating a CE are great, because the CE effectively removes
any action falling within that category from subsequent mandatory environmental analysis or public review. 40 C.F.R. § 1508.4. CEs are justified on the basis that some categories of action typically are so minor
that they virtually never, or very rarely, have significant environmental
effects, so it would be a waste of time and resources to subject them to
environmental review under NEPA. NEPA analysis is required, however,
where "extraordinary circumstances" may create a significant environmental effect from an otherwise categorically excluded action. 40 C.F.R.
§ 1508.4; California v. Norton, 311 F.3d 1162, 1170 (9th Cir. 2002). For
example, the Forest Service's use of a CE was held "arbitrary and capricious" when it increased a prior harvest limit for live trees two-and-a-
half-fold and for salvage timber ten-fold without sufficient explanation
and in the face of a contrary task force recommendation. Heartwood, Inc.
v. U.S. Forest Service, 73 F.Supp.2d 962 (S.D. Ill. 1999).

Until the Bush II administration, forest conservationists did not pay
much heed to CEs, as the Forest Service had generally reserved this
regulatory device for minor "painting the campground outhouse" decisions. See 7 C.F.R. § 1b.3 (a)(1)-(2) (2003) (noting CEs for routine personnel and administrative activities); see also FSH ch. 30, § 31.1a. As part
of the Healthy Forests Initiative, however, the Forest Service created
sweeping new categorical exclusions, described below. Such CEs remove
all environmental analysis (including EAs) for the covered actions, leaving only a thin requirement to document in a "memorandum" that the
project will have no significant or cumulative impacts. See FSH ch. 30,
§ 18.1.

In a new regulation, the Forest Service explicitly exempted CEs
from public notice, comment, and appeal. 36 C.F.R. §§ 215.4(a), 215.12
(f); 68 Fed. Reg. 33582 (June 4, 2003). The agency further paved the way
for categorically excluded action by promulgating a rule that certain
"extraordinary" circumstances, such as the presence of endangered species or roadless areas, will not automatically preclude an action from
being categorically excluded. 67 Fed. Reg. 54622 (Aug. 23, 2002). The
rule has been challenged in Wildlaw et al. v. U.S. Forest Service, Case
No. CV–03–T–682–N (M.D. Ala.)(June 30, 2003). These regulations create a new procedural device to handle entire categories of action without
the environmental analysis or public process traditionally required by
NEPA. The Forest Service also created entire new categories of CEs to
tap into this reduced NEPA process. The new CEs encompass actions
that had formerly required a full EIS, or at least an EA to determine
whether they had significant environmental effects.

On the planning level, the Forest Service has proposed that all
LRMP revisions be categorically excluded from NEPA analysis. See Final
Rule, National Forest System Land and Resource Management Plan-
ning, 70 Fed. Reg. 1022, 1032 (Jan. 5, 2005); National Environmental
Policy Act Documentation Needed for Developing, Revising, or Amending

Land Management Plans, 70 Fed. Reg. 1062 (Jan. 5, 2005). Categorically excluding land management plan revisions removes nearly all environmental analysis associated with plan revisions and eliminates the traditional public notice, comment, and appeals associated with the revisions. The proposal to treat LRMP revisions as CEs sent a shock wave through the forest conservation community, as revisions (which occur by law every 15 years) typically have detailed EISs, considerable public comment, and extensive appeals. Conservation groups have traditionally poured enormous energy into studying and commenting on Forest Plans, and making the most of the full NEPA process. The public has pressed for clear, specific, mandatory standards in such plans (and plan revisions) so that courts would find such standards enforceable. *See, e.g.,* Neighbors of Cuddy Mountain v. U.S. Forest Service, 137 F.3d 1372 (9th Cir. 1998); *infra* section E (NFMA enforcement).

The Forest Service, on the other hand, is clearly steering its administrative practice in a different direction. Viewing administrative appeals and court litigation as severe impediments to land management planning (*see Process Predicament, supra,* at p. 463), the agency is creating for itself far more discretion through its regulatory changes. The Forest Service now views its LRMPs as strategic documents oriented towards establishing a broad vision of future forest management. Under this view, the plans are an inappropriate vehicle for specific prescriptions relating to on-the-ground practices. *See* 70 Fed. Reg. at 1031 ("This final rule clarifies that plans will be strategic rather than prescriptive.... "). Accordingly, the new planning rule emphasizes that forest plan revisions will not contain specific, enforceable, standards. *See id.* at 1025 ("[T]he agency has concluded that plans are more effective if they include more detailed descriptions of desired conditions, rather than long lists of prohibitive standards or guidelines.... "). The proposed CE status for plan revisions dovetails with this new view of land management plans. As the Forest Service explains in its final planning rule, *id.* at 1031, 1033:

> At the time of plan approval, the Forest Service does not have detailed information about what projects and activities will be proposed over the 15–year life of a plan, how many projects will be approved, where they will be located, or how they will be designed. * * * [T]he agency's experience with planning has demonstrated the need to clarify what plans, in fact, actually do. * * * In essence, a plan simply is a description of a vision for the future that, coupled with evaluation, provides a starting point for project and activity NEPA analysis. * * * The categorical exclusion proposed in connection with this final rule clarifies that plan development, plan amendment or plan revisions .... do not significantly affect the environment, and thus are categorically excluded from further NEPA analysis, unless extraordinary circumstances are present. * * *

On the project level, the Forest Service created a total of five new categories of CEs through two rulemakings. 68 Fed. Reg. 33814 (June 5,

2003); 68 Fed. Reg. 44598 (July 29, 2003). Interestingly, the CEs are not published in the Code of Federal Regulations but rather are additions to the Forest Service Handbook, FSH 1909.15, § 31.2 (10)-(14). An additional categorical exclusion was statutorily created by the Healthy Forests Restoration Act, explained in more detail below, to allow "Applied Silvicultural Assessments" which entail up to 1,000 acres of logging to control insects and disease. HFRA § 404, Pub. L. 108–148, 117 Stat. 1887, codified at 16 U.S.C. § 6554. All of the new CEs have limitations and must be studied carefully to determine their precise scope. Briefly, the new regulatory CEs promulgated as part of President Bush's Healthy Forest Initiative are:

1. Hazardous Fuels Reduction Activities CE (§ 31.2 (10)): Allows up to 4,500 acres of burning or 1,000 acres of mechanical treatments, which may include logging.

2. Post–Fire Rehabilitation Activities CE (§ 31.2 (11)): Allows up to 4,200 acres of post-fire rehabilitation activities within three years after a wildfire.

3. Live Tree Harvest CE (§ 31.2 (12)): Allows up to 70 acres of logging with incidental live tree removal, but prohibits clear-cutting.

4. Salvage Logging CE (§ 31.2 (13)): Allows up to 250 acres post-fire logging of dead or dying trees.

5. Sanitation Harvest CE (§ 31.2 (14)): Allows up to 250 acres of "sanitation" logging to control insects or disease, with incidental live tree removal for certain purposes.

Notes and Questions

1. Are the new Healthy Forest Initiative CEs large enough to drive several logging trucks through, or are they more on the scale of "painting the campground outhouse?" Can you expect "significant" environmental impacts from 1,000 acres of logging for "fuels reduction"? *See* FSH § 31.2 (10). Under the traditional analytical framework, the presence of significant impacts kicks the action out of a categorical exclusion. How will the new "extraordinary circumstances" rule, 67 Fed. Reg. 54622 (Aug. 23, 2002), affect this analysis? Given that a regulation cannot amend a statute, and that NEPA does not provide any exceptions for categorical exclusions, is the rule likely to hold up in court?

2. Do you agree with the Forest Service's rationale behind its proposed CE for forest plan revisions? If forest plans are to be "strategic," rather than prescriptive, will they have any significant environmental effects? Will the new plans carry out NFMA's planning mandate, contained in 16 U.S.C. § 1604(g)? *See supra,* pp. 408–410.

3. Traditionally, NEPA has provided the public a strong voice in the management of public lands. Has the Healthy Forests Initiative stripped the public of considerable input by categorically excluding (as proposed) plan revisions and five categories of on-the-ground action? If so, should these changes be accomplished by amending the statute? Are administrative rules

less visible? How might public interest watchdog groups adapt their strategy to these regulatory changes?

4. The Healthy Forests Initiative (HFI) has fundamentally changed NEPA practice in the context of forest law. Now a practitioner must categorize NEPA documentation into three separate realms: 1) the standard EAs and EISs for on-the-ground projects that are not affected by the HFI; 2) CE documentation (minimal) for forest plan revisions (now a proposed rule) and for on-the-ground activities falling into the five CE categories described above; and 3) reduced NEPA documentation for Healthy Forest Restoration Act (HFRA) activities (*see* section F below).

5. Even before the new Healthy Forests Initiative rules, commenting on timber sale EAs was no easy task. Such documents routinely exceed 100 pages and include an enormous amount of technical and "boilerplate" language. Sprinkled with euphemisms such as "treatment" to describe logging, a college-educated citizen might read through an entire EA without realizing that it was proposing to cut trees. Giving weight to NEPA's purpose of engaging the public, the CEQ regulations call for clear, plain language. *See* 40 C.F.R. § 1502.8 ("Environmental impact statements shall be written in plain language so that decision makers and the public can readily understand them"); 40 C.F.R. § 1500.2(b) ("Environmental impact statements shall be concise, clear, and to the point.... "). Because Forest Service documents are usually difficult to understand, groups such as the Sierra Club provide standard NEPA comment checklists for timber-related projects to help citizens provide input into the process. *See, e.g.,* SIERRA CLUB FOREST WATCH TRAINING MANUAL (March 2004).

6. An important part of public participation in forest policy is the right to appeal decisions administratively. The Appeals Reform Act provides citizens the right to file administrative appeals of any "projects and activities implementing land and management plans." Pub. L. 102–381, Title III, § 322(a). 16 U.S.C.S. § 1612. Administrative appeals are avenues for the public to seek review beyond the most immediate supervisor, who typically has an attachment to the decided outcome. Such appeals do not require the representation of a lawyer and entail only minimal expense. Exhaustion of administrative appeals is generally required in order to bring an action in court. *See, e.g.,* 7 U.S.C. § 6912 (2004); Kleisser v. U.S. Forest Service, 183 F.3d 196 (3d Cir. 1999). Most citizen appeals challenge the proposed action as not complying with the forest plan, or the NFMA regulations, or NEPA. Between January 2001 and July 2002, 48 percent of all Forest Service mechanical fuels reduction projects were appealed. Useful as they may be to the public, the Forest Service views the appeal process as an albatross, delaying sometimes urgent management actions. A central part of the Bush II administration's Healthy Forests Initiative was directed towards limiting appeals. The appeals regulations were overhauled to restrict citizen standing, clarify that no appeals exist for CEs, allow for immediate implementation of some logging projects that could entail "emergency" economic loss if appealed, and push the appeal decision down to the supervisory level just above the decision-maker. *See* 36 C.F.R. Part 215, 68 Fed. Reg. 33582 (June 4, 2003). Whether the new regulation complies with the Appeals Reform Act remains to be seen.

In Practice:
Staying Informed of Forest Service Decisions

Natural resource practitioners traditionally relied on the required public notice of EAs and EISs to stay informed of Forest Service activities. With the elimination of many notice requirements through the categorical exclusions, the practitioner must resort to other means. Early notice of decisions is more crucial than ever, because many Forest Service decisions now allow public comment at only the very earliest "scoping" stage. To stay informed, the practitioner can use any of the following methods:

1) *Regular phone calls to the District Ranger or NEPA coordinator:* This is a time-tested method. Many an environmental lawyer will say that the best research tool is the telephone.

2) *Newspaper of record*: Each National Forest is required to identify its "newspaper of record" where it will publish all notices and opportunity for comment. The newspaper may be a very small rural one. Natural resource practitioners often subscribe to the ones they wish to monitor.

3) *Quarterly Schedule of Proposed Actions ("SOPA"):* The Forest Service publishes a schedule of proposed actions for every forest. Anyone may write to the National Forest and request to be put on the mailing list. Note, however, that the agency can document and commence a CE project in the time frame between the quarterly SOPAs, so notice through this means may not be timely.

4) *Mailing list request:* Write to the District Ranger's Office of the National Forest of interest and ask to be placed on the mailing list for all logging and prescribed fire activities, as well as any projects implemented under the HFRA.

5) *Freedom of Information Act Request:* The Freedom of Information Act provides the legal venue for accessing agency records. 5 U.S.C. § 552(a)(4)(B). This is a relatively cumbersome means of acquiring information. Requests are made to the Forest's Information Officer. The Sierra Club provides a sample FOIA request letter as part of its Forest Watch Training Manual, available from the Washington D.C. office of the Sierra Club. *See also* http://www.rcfp.org/foiact/index.html.

Adapted with permission from: Sierra Club, Healthy Forest Initiative Action Guide, March 2004.

E. Enforceability of NFMA

Has NFMA done much to change Forest Service practices on the ground? Many denuded steep slopes and scoured streambeds within the national forests provide evidence that the agency often disregarded NFMA's provisions in its push to "get the cut out." *See* Seattle Audubon Society v. Evans, 771 F.Supp. 1081, 1090 (W.D. Wa. 1991), *aff'd* 952 F.2d 297 (9th Cir. 1991) (noting Forest Service's "deliberate and systematic refusal" to comply with the law and enjoining further timber sales). Indeed, as is the case with any law, NMFA is only as effective as its enforcement regime. Unlike regulatory laws, there is no "super-agency" such as the Environmental Protection Agency or the U.S. Fish and Wildlife Service to enforce the requirements of NFMA. Only citizens can enforce the requirements, through the Administrative Procedure Act (APA), 5 U.S.C. § 701, et seq. Judicial enforcement is not only expensive, but requires satisfaction of elaborate administrative and Constitutional requirements such as standing, ripeness, and exhaustion of administrative remedies, *see* Chapter 3, *supra*. Nevertheless, due to the persistent efforts of national and grassroots environmental groups, there is a voluminous body of caselaw interpreting NFMA. Many of the initial cases subsequently mushroomed into complex litigation comprised of multiple independent challenges under various laws (NEPA, the ESA, and the Clean Water Act) focusing on particular forests or regions. For a description of complex litigation involving the forests in the Pacific Northwest, Alaska, Wisconsin, and Texas, *see* Oliver A. Houck, *On the Law of Biodiversity and Ecosystem Management*, 81 MINN. L. REV. 869, 892–930 (1997).

NFMA enforcement occurs on three levels: 1) challenges to the LRMPs; 2) challenges to sales as not conforming to LRMPs; and 3) challenges to sales as not conforming to NFMA's statutory and regulatory requirements. Under the APA, a court may set aside any action that is "arbitrary, capricious, ... or otherwise not in accordance with law." 5 U.S.C. § 706. Generally speaking, where the agency violates an explicit mandate set forth in the statute or regulations, plaintiffs allege that the action is "otherwise not in accordance with law." Where the action does not violate an explicit directive, plaintiffs allege the action is "arbitrary [and] capricious." The latter challenges are often directed towards an agency action that turned on a technical decision, such as the amount of protected habitat provided for a sensitive species. Not surprisingly, the former type of challenge is more apt to meet with success. Judges find it easier to enforce a clear mandate, such as a statutory deadline, than to substitute their judgment for the agency's technical determination. Federal courts still faithfully adhere to an established doctrine of administrative law affording deference to agency action, particularly in matters falling within the agency's technical expertise. As one commentator put it:

> The proliferation of administrative agencies emerging from the New Deal reflected a faith that modern social and economic problems required an expert's attention: "Those who rationalized the New Deal's regulatory initiatives regarded expertise and specialization as the particular strengths of the administrative process." That exper-

tise was not shared by judges, since it "springs only from that continuity of interest, that ability and desire to devote fifty-two weeks a year, year after year, to a particular problem. A month of experience will be worth a year of hearings."

RONALD A. CASS ET AL., ADMINISTRATIVE LAW: CASES AND MATERIALS 2D 141 (1987) (citation omitted).

As the cases in this section indicate, the deference doctrine has proved a formidable barrier to citizen enforcement of NFMA.

1. *Challenges to LRMPs*

The first round of LRMPs produced a host of challenges, though not many successful ones. The second round of plans (15–year revisions) is expected to produce an equally massive litigation effort by citizen groups. Recall, however, that the Healthy Forests Initiative proposes treating the revisions as categorical exclusions that will not have environmental analysis or administrative appeals. (*See* Section D above). Aside from regulatory developments, the legal context for plan appeals changed dramatically as a result of Ohio Forestry Association, Inc. v. Sierra Club, 523 U.S. 726, 118 S.Ct. 1665, 140 L.Ed.2d 921 (1998) (excerpted in Chapter 3.II.D, *supra*). There, the Sierra Club challenged the forest plan for Ohio's Wayne National Forest on the ground that the plan permitted too much logging and clearcutting. The Court concluded that the controversy was not ripe for judicial review. The decision precludes legal challenges to a forest plan before a specific, discrete project begins. In other words, plaintiffs must wait until the Forest Service has taken action to implement the plan on the ground, after which time some would say "the die is cast."

By limiting review of the forest plan to the stage at which it is implemented on the ground, does the Court create a situation where reviewing district courts will "fail to see the forest for the trees?" Will the specific challenged project take the focus away from a broad look at the forest plan? The Court placed much emphasis on the fact that individual project actions will help a court focus on how a forest plan will operate on the ground. But given that there are a multitude of projects, each with unique site-specific impacts, is any one project likely to be representative of the plan's effect on the ground across the whole forest? The Court found that the Sierra Club did not have much to lose by waiting to challenge the plan until the implementation stage. Is a reviewing court likely to go back and scrutinize the entire forest plan at the time it is implemented? What practical problems might a public interest group face in the wake of *Ohio Forestry Association*?

Does the Court leave open the possibility that a group could challenge the EIS prepared for the forest plan under NEPA at a pre-implementation stage? Is there a difference, in terms of ripeness considerations, between NFMA and NEPA claims? Note that the Forest Service has proposed eliminating NEPA review and comment at the plan stage by treating plan revisions as categorical exclusions. *See supra* Section D (NFMA, NEPA and the HFI).

Many of the challenges to first generation forest plans were brought prior to *Ohio Forestry*. In one notable case, the Sierra Club tried to force the Forest Service to use the science of conservation biology in developing forest plans for two national forests in Wisconsin. Sierra Club v. Marita, 46 F.3d 606 (7th Cir. 1995). The court rejected the challenge, stating, "[T]he Service acted well within its regulatory discretion." *Id.* at 621. Many other challenges to forest plans fell to the formidable deference doctrine, particularly when the challenge was directed to the technical parts of the plan. *See, e.g.,* Oregon Natural Resources Council v. Lowe, 109 F.3d 521 (9th Cir. 1997) ("While the ONRC has presented evidence suggesting that habitat guidelines ... should be revised to insure species viability, it has not met the burden of establishing that the Forest Service acted arbitrarily and capriciously in establishing these guidelines.").

2.   *Challenges to Sales as Not Conforming to LRMPs*

A second level of NFMA enforcement involves challenges to timber sales on the basis that they don't comply with the specific prescriptions of the forest plan (LRMP). NFMA litigation has been most successful in this context. NFMA explicitly states that site-specific decisions must "be consistent" with plans, 16 U.S.C. § 1604(i). This language seemingly makes the standards of forest plans enforceable. *See* Ohio Forestry Ass'n v. Sierra Club, 523 U.S. 726, 730, 118 S.Ct. 1665, 140 L.Ed.2d 921 (1998) (noting that NMFA requires all "forest uses to conform to forest plans"). Are they still enforceable following *Norton v. Southern Utah Wilderness Alliance*, excerpted in Chapter 3.III.C?

Many of the "first generation" forest plans, such as the Payette LRMP in the case below, had specific technical mandates that allowed little room for agency discretion. The Forest Service, however, has recently taken a new direction rejecting prescriptive standards that could limit its discretion. As noted earlier, under the new planning rule, the revised plans will not contain the "shalls and musts" of former plans. Some scholars have warned against giving the Forest Service more discretion. *See* Houck, *supra,* at n.366 ("The code words fool no one involved: more 'discretion' means that industry gets to cut more timber."). As you read *Cuddy Mountain* below, consider how a more discretionary LRMP would have affected the outcome of the case. Also consider how the Supreme Court's decision in *Norton v. Southern Utah Wilderness Alliance*, excerpted in Chapter 3.III.C, changes the legal terrain.

NEIGHBORS OF CUDDY MOUNTAIN v. UNITED STATES FOREST SERVICE
United States Court of Appeals for the Ninth Circuit, 1998.
137 F.3d 1372.

Plaintiffs seek to enjoin the sale of timber in the Cuddy Mountain area of Payette National Forest. They claim that the United States Forest Service (Forest Service), in determining whether such a sale could go forward, violated the National Forest Management Act (NFMA), 16 U.S.C. § 1600 *et seq.* * * *

The NFMA creates a statutory framework for the management of our national forests. It provides a two-step process for forest planning. The NFMA first requires the Forest Service to develop a Land Resource Management Plan (LRMP) and an EIS for the entire forest. *Id.*; 36 C.F.R. § 219.10(a), (b). A LRMP and EIS were prepared for Payette in May, 1988. Implementation of the LRMP occurs at the site-specific level. Thus, once the LRMP is in place, site-specific projects, such as the Grade/Dukes timber sale, are assessed by the Forest Service. *Id.*; 36 C.F.R. § 219.10(e). * * *

The NFMA imposes substantive requirements at both stages, such as the need to insure biological diversity. *See* 36 C.F.R. § 219, *et seq.* A site-specific decision, such as one to sell timber, must be consistent with the LRMP for the larger area. *See Inland Empire*, 88 F.3d at 757; 16 U.S.C. § 1604(i) ("Resource plans and permits, contracts, and other instruments for the use and occupancy of National Forest System lands shall be consistent with the land management plans"); 36 CFR § 219.10(e).

Neighbors' claims are based on alleged failures of the Forest Service to abide by the procedural and substantive requirements of the NFMA and NEPA in conducting the analysis for the Grade/Dukes sale. * * * Neighbors is particularly concerned that the Grade/Dukes sale, alone and in combination with other timber sales in the Cuddy Mountain Roadless area, will greatly deplete the small amount of old growth habitat that remains in the Payette. * * * Neighbors is also concerned with the impact of this sale on fisheries in the area. We agree that the Forest Service has violated the NFMA by failing to insure that the Grade/Dukes sale is consistent with the Payette LRMP. * * *

The Payette LRMP, developed in 1988, requires that a certain percentage of old growth habitat be retained in Payette. A number of species in Payette rely on old growth habitat, including the pileated woodpecker, flammulated owl, great gray owl, and northern goshawk. The pileated woodpecker is the "management indicator species" for old growth habitat. A management indicator species "is used as a bellwether ... for the other species that have the same special habitat needs or populations characteristics." Thus, by studying the result of the sale on the habitat for the pileated woodpecker, the Forest Service can estimate the effect of the sale on other old growth-dependent species. *See* 36 C.F.R. § 219.19(a)(1).

With regard to the specific percentage of old growth that must be retained in Payette, the Payette LRMP states:

> Retain a minimum of 5 percent old growth or mature forest, of which 2.5 percent must be old growth habitat ... *within each theoretical pileated woodpecker home range* .... Old growth stands must be at least 30 acres in size. * * *

Thus, to prove that the Grade/Dukes sale would be consistent with the Payette LRMP, the Forest Service should have shown that after the sale, there would be at least 5/2.5 percent of old growth "within each theoretical pileated woodpecker home range." The Forest Service has failed to do so. In fact, the Forest Service provides no information whatsoever regarding how many woodpecker home ranges there are within the sale area, or how many home ranges would be affected by the timber sale. Having failed to do so, it certainly could not have demonstrated that after the sale, a sufficient percentage of old growth would remain in each affected pileated woodpecker home range. Instead, the Forest Service recited the results of a survey to the effect that after the sale, there will be at least 5/2.5 percent of old growth in the Grade/Dukes sale area as a whole. * * * The "analysis area" appears to be the Grade/Dukes sale area, and not the woodpecker home range(s), as required. Indeed, in quoting from the Payette LRMP, the Forest Service inexplicably deleted from that portion of the statement describing the percentage of old growth that must be retained, the phrase that specifies the geographic scope that must be analyzed, i.e., the pileated woodpecker home range.

Thus, the Forest Service did not comply with the requirements of the LRMP in so far as the Forest Service evaluated the "analysis area" rather than the "home range" of the pileated woodpecker. As such, it did not demonstrate that the Grade/Dukes project would be consistent with the Payette LRMP, and thus it failed to comply with the NFMA.

Notes and Questions

1. For other examples of cases discussing plans, *see* National Audubon Society v. Hoffman, 132 F.3d 7 (2nd Cir. 1997) (road building consistent with forest plan); Friends of Southeast's Future v. Morrison, 153 F.3d 1059 (9th Cir. 1998) (proposed timber sale violated Tongass forest plan); Neighbors of Cuddy Mountain II v. Alexander, 303 F.3d 1059 (9th Cir. 2002) (reversing district court's dismissal of claim that timber sale was inconsistent with old growth standards in Payette Forest plan); Forest Guardians v. U.S. Forest Serv., 180 F.Supp.2d 1273 (D. N.M. 2001) (determining species population through habitat trend data violated forest plan); Idaho Sporting Cong. v. Rittenhouse, 305 F.3d 957 (9th Cir. 2002) (implementation of Boise forest plan did not comply with NFMA).

2. In his thorough review of NFMA, Professor Houck warns of the danger of removing firm standards in second-generation LRMPs:

[It] is hard not to sympathize with the Service as it proposed to run for cover from its planning regulations ... in the next round of forest decisions. In so doing, the Service would make a major strategic mistake. As onerous as rules and the prospect of judicial review may be, they are nothing to the contorting influence on agency life of economic interests and politics. One of the few things in life that can stand up to a bullying committee chairman is law. When the agency cuts itself loose from the specific requirements of species-based planning, in favor of amorphous, unenforceable concepts of ecosystem management, it throws its biologists, field managers, and forest rangers to the dogs. They may pick up a lot of apparent discretion, but they will have no shield when the pressure comes on. And when it comes to decisions that will affect large amounts of real estate, these pressures are always on.

Houck, *supra,* at 928–929.

3. *Enforcement of NFMA's Substantive Standards*

As noted at the outset of this section, NFMA sets forth a series of standards in 16 U.S.C. § 1604(g)(3)(B), (E), and (F) that deal with wild-life protection and use of clear-cutting and other even-aged harvest methods. The standards, set forth on pp. 471–472, are often referred to as the "substantive standards" of NFMA. Section 1604(g)(3)(B) is commonly known as the "diversity" standard because it requires the Forest Service to "provide for diversity of plant and animal communities." The standards dealing with timber harvest practices are found in § 1604(g)(3)(B) (requiring the Service to "insure" timber harvest will be undertaken only where soil, slope and watershed conditions will not be damaged, adequate protection is provided for streams, and there is assurance that the land will be restocked within five years); and § 1604(g)(3)(F) (limiting clearcutting to where it is the "optimum method" and other even-aged cuts where it is "appropriate" to meet the objectives of the plan).

Despite the clarity of some of the standards, Congress left an obvious ambiguity as to their precise legal role. The statute directs the Service to "specif[y] guidelines for land management plans" which meet the listed standards. 16 U.S.C. § 1604 (g)(3). In his thorough review of litigation under the timber harvest standards, Professor Federico Cheever notes a serious "point of compliance" issue created by this ambiguity:

> NFMA mandated a forest planning process and contemplated that, under the umbrella of that process, specific actions—like timber sales—would take place. But ... it did not specify whether the timber management standards applied to the planning process, the site-specific processes, or both. Neither did it specify exactly what sort of agency action constituted compliance. These omissions have generated extensive confusion.

> The Forest Service has asserted that the standards applied to the planning process.... [P]laintiffs have generally asserted that the standards had to be satisfied at both levels. [P]laintiffs suffered more significant reverses in this area than in any other because Congress had not spoken to this issue.

Federico Cheever, *Four Failed Forest Standards: What We Can Learn From the History of the National Forest Management Act's Substantive Timber Management Provisions,* 77 Or. L. Rev. 601, 696 (1998).

From a strategic litigation perspective, how important is it that courts consider NFMA's standards enforceable on the ground apart from the forest plan requirements and NFMA regulations? Do NFMA's substantive standards gain more importance in light of the recent changes to the planning regulations, which eliminate the clear species diversity parameters and other requirements? Interpreting caselaw in this area is difficult because most plaintiffs have challenged Forest Service activities as not complying with the regulations, rather than NFMA's statutory standards. For a sampling of relevant litigation, *see* Forest Guardians v. U.S. Forest Serv., 180 F.Supp.2d 1273 (D.N.M. 2001) (concluding that NFMA and the implementing regulations apply to site-specific projects); Inland Empire Pub. Lands Council v. U.S. Forest Serv., 88 F.3d 754, 760 n.6 (9th Cir. 1996) (rejecting argument that diversity regulation applies only to promulgation of forest plans and not to site-specific projects); Sierra Club v. Martin, 168 F.3d 1, 6 (11th Cir. 1999) (regulation applies to specific actions); Sierra Club v. Peterson, 185 F.3d 349, 373 (5th Cir. 1999) ("NFMA and its associated regulations require the Forest Service to comply with the law on-the-ground rather than merely issuing standards and guidelines as part of its LRMPs"), *vacated and remanded on other grounds*, 228 F.3d 559 (5th Cir. 2000) (en banc); Sharps v. U.S. Forest Serv., 28 F.3d 851, 855 (8th Cir. 1994) (NFMA regulation applied only to regional guides and forest plans).

The harvest standards and diversity standards of NFMA have generated considerable litigation, much of it summarized in Cheever, *supra,* and Houck, *supra*. Because the implementation of the NFMA standards through plans and regulations often turns on technical judgment, a major obstacle to such enforcement is the deference doctrine. The district court opinion below indicates an aggressive judicial approach towards enforcing NFMA's clearcutting standards in the context of a challenge to multiple timber sales in Texas national forests. The opinion was overturned by the Fifth Circuit on appeal, so it does not hold precedential value. It remains, however, useful to examine for its approach to agency deference and the court's reviewing role.

SIERRA CLUB v. ESPY

United States District Court, Eastern District of Texas, 1993.
822 F.Supp. 356, 359–370, *rev'd* 38 F.3d 792 (5th Cir. 1994).

* * * Plaintiffs contend that the defendants' even-aged logging agenda is illegal in that the agency has not complied with the constraints on the Service's choice of even-aged management techniques contained in that Act. * * *

While it is generally accepted that federal agencies are entitled to a presumption of good faith and regularity in arriving at their decisions, Sierra Club v. Costle, 657 F.2d 298, 334 (D.C. Cir. 1981), the presumption is not irrebuttable. Federal courts would be abdicating their Constitutional role were they to simply "rubber stamp" agency decisions in the face of complex issues, rather than insuring that such decisions accord with clear congressional mandates. As Judge J. Skelly Wright so aptly put it: "[T]he judicial role ... is to see that important legislative purposes, heralded in the halls of Congress, are not lost or misdirected in the vast hallways of the federal bureaucracy." * * *

Defendants have taken the extreme, and untenable, position that there is no provision of the APA or the NFMA allowing the plaintiffs to judicially challenge actual, on-the-ground practices of the Forest Service. Defendants have argued to the Court that the NFMA is a mere "planning statute," *i.e.,* with *no* substantive component (in contrast, they say, to the Endangered Species Act (ESA), 16 U.S.C. § 1531 *et seq.,* for example). However, the NFMA does erect unambiguous, substantive "outer boundaries" on the Forest Service's discretion in terms of forest management valuations (*i.e.,* the setting of agency goals, or "ends") and concomitant, consistent practices. * * *

The NFMA addresses *wildlife* management, for example, on several levels. * * * This Court is presently most concerned with the quite specific NFMA requirement that even-aged cuts ... "are carried out in a manner *consistent with* the *protection of* soil, watershed, fish, wildlife, recreation, and aesthetic resources, and the regeneration of the timber resource." 16 U.S.C. § 1604(g)(3)(F)(v) (emphasis added). The mandate of this Section is amplified by the NFMA's Section 1604(g)(3)(B), which states that the Service Planners must manage to "provide for diversity of plant and animal communities." * * *

Specifically, the NFMA mandates that the Service "insure," by *means* of regulation promulgation, this essential *end:* that even-aged management practices be used in the national forests *only when* "consistent with the *protection of* soil, watershed, fish, wildlife, recreation, and aesthetic resources, and the regeneration of the timber resource." 16 U.S.C. § 1604(g)(3)(F)(v) (emphasis added). The NFMA thus contemplates that even-aged management techniques will be used only in exceptional circumstances. Yet, the defendants appear to utilize even-aged management logging as if it comprised the statutory "rule," rather than the exception. The Service in fact utilizes *uneven-aged* management techniques very rarely—*i.e.,* as an exception to *even-aged* logging. [P]ursuant to the 1987 Plan one hundred percent (100%) of the timber base of the East Texas National Forests, or eighty-two percent (82%) of the entire forest was under even-aged management. * * *

The mandate of Section 1604(g)(3)(F)(v) could not be more clearly expressed.... * * * Section 1604(g)(3)(F)(v) states that the Service can use even-aged logging practices only in the exceptional circumstance— *i.e.,* only when such is insured to be consistent with the protection of the forests' natural resources. * * *

History illuminates the NFMA's clear substantive mandate. During the sixteen (16) years following enactment of the Multiple–Use Sustained Yield Act of 1960 (MUSY), Congress imposed only *one* major substantive restriction on the Forest Service's discretion in wildlife matters, and that was the one reflected in the Endangered Species Act of 1973 (ESA), 16 U.S.C. § 1536(a)(2). * * * As to all other [non ESA-listed] species, the Service possessed virtually absolute, unreviewable managerial discretion. * * * Public outcry over the use, or abuse, of that discretion, if not the broad agency discretion itself, led Congress to intervene in the Service's operations ... through enactment of the NFMA. The public and Congress were concerned that, left to its own essentially unbridled devices, the Service would manage the national forests as mere monocultural "tree farms." * * *

[T]he actual discretion for which the defendants argue amounts to nothing less than a bald attempt ... to return to "the bad old days" which were supposed to be left behind by the NFMA. * * * The Court cannot 'rubber stamp' the clearly overly-restrictive interpretation of the NFMA the defendants advocate * * * The failure to comply with the NMFA's substantive, forest resource protection requirement is clearly an act "not in accordance with law," or "in excess of statutory jurisdiction, authority, or limitations, or short of statutory right." *See* 5 U.S.C. § 706 (2)(A) & (C). * * *

The federal courts have an obligation to insure that the agencies obey valid congressional prescriptions. When a federal court fails to prevent and correct statutory violations by excessively self-aggrandized, run-amok executive agencies, Congress' (and the people's) purposes are frustrated, and, more generally, the rule of law itself is subverted. Judicial refusals to enjoin such violations abdicate, for one thing, the courts' affirmative role in the Constitution's system of checks and balances. * * * Were the Court to abdicate to the agency defendants its Constitutional responsibility to hold them to their duty to enforce unambiguous environmental laws, the Court would effectively "repeal" the oft-times "last chance" environmental protection validly championed into the United States Code by the citizenry.

Notes and Questions

1.   What is the court's view of the Forest Service's role, and of its own role? How does the court view the purposes of NFMA? How does the court view the role of agency discretion under NFMA?

2.   The district court decision was promptly reversed by the Fifth Circuit in Sierra Club v. Espy, 38 F.3d 792, 800 (5th Cir. 1994), which expressed a different view of NFMA's clearcutting standards: "NFMA does not bar even-aged management or require that it be undertaken only in exceptional circumstances.... The district court used "exceptional" as a decisional standard–and hence it upset the balance struck [by Congress]." The Texas Forest saga continued when a subsequent round of litigation resulted in injunctions against timber harvesting for failure to comply with soil and watershed standards. Sierra Club v. Glickman, 974 F.Supp. 905 (E.D. Tex. 1997). On appeal, that decision was affirmed by Sierra Club v. Peterson, 185 F.3d 349 (5th Cir. 1999), but the appellate panel's opinion was vacated by an *en banc* panel of the Fifth Circuit. Sierra Club v. Peterson, 228 F.3d 559 (5th Cir. 2000) (finding plaintiffs did not challenge identifiable final agency action).

3.   In Sierra Club v. Thomas, 105 F.3d 248 (6th Cir. 1997), the Sixth Circuit expressed a view of NFMA's clear-cutting provision similar to the one held by the Texas district court in *Sierra Club v. Espy*. Though the decision was reversed by the Supreme Court on other grounds (ripeness) in Ohio Forestry Ass'n v. Sierra Club, 523 U.S. 726, 118 S.Ct. 1665, 140 L.Ed.2d 921 (1998), the opinion demonstrated a hard crack in the shell of deference. Finding that the forest plan for the Wayne National Forest allowed too much clearcutting, the Chief Judge of the Sixth Circuit wrote:

The National Forest Management Act was enacted as a direct result of congressional concern for Forest Service clearcutting practices and the dominant role timber production has historically played in Forest Service policies. Congress was concerned that, if left to its own essentially unbridled devices, the Forest Service would manage the national forests as mere monocultural "tree farms." * * * [The] formal planning process was designed to curtail agency discretion and to ensure forest preservation and productivity. Substantively, the Act imposes extensive limitations on timber harvesting by restricting the use of clearcutting to situations in which clearcutting is the optimum method for harvesting. * * *

Although the Forest Service has the benefit of the presumption of good faith and regularity in agency action, we have attempted to ascertain whether the plan has been improperly skewed. We conclude that the planning process was improperly predisposed toward clearcutting. The resulting plan is arbitrary and capricious because it is based upon this artificial narrowing of options. * * *

The National Forest Management Act ... contemplates that even-aged management techniques will be used only in exceptional circumstances. Yet, the defendants would utilize even-aged management logging as if it were the statutory rule, rather than the exception. * * *

Created, in part, to ensure a reliable timber supply, the Forest Service has a history of preferring timber production to other uses. Rather than being a neutral process which determines how the national forests can best meet the needs of the American people, forest planning, as practiced by the Forest Service, is a political process replete with opportunities for the intrusion of bias and abuse. Because national forests are located near rural communities, foresters make management decisions to support perceived needs in the communities. * * * The dependency of these communities on timber production causes over-harvesting and destructive harvesting methods. The relationship of the Forest Service to the timber industry also constrains the Forest Service's planning freedom. Rural constituencies reliant on timber sale revenues may provoke politicians to place pressure on the Forest Service to sustain that revenue. Consequently, the Forest Service becomes trapped: cutting off timber sales would cause loss of employment and revenue in local communities but continued timber sales risk over-harvesting and below-cost sales.

The Forest Service budgeting process, which allows the Forest Service to keep a percentage of the funds it realizes from timber sales, provides an incentive for the Forest Service to sell timber below cost or at a loss. * * * Again, conflicting interests lead to perverse results: clearcutting provides the Forest Service with a higher congressional subsidy because the Forest Service can request preparation and administrative costs. Consequently, decisions may be made, not because they are in the best interest of the American people but because they benefit the Forest Service's fiscal interest.

Each of these biases undermines even the facial neutrality of the National Forest Management Act [and causes] the Forest Service to manage primarily to maximize timber outputs.

The public nature of the planning process and the public's right to appeal timber sales were intended by Congress to be a check on the Forest Service's power and discretion. Judicial review of planning decisions is intended to be a further check. Accordingly, ... we find the Forest Service has failed to comply with the protective spirit of the National Forest Management Act.

Sierra Club v. Thomas, 105 F.3d 248, 249–252 (6th Cir. 1997); *see also* House v. U.S. Forest Serv., 974 F.Supp. 1022, 1026 (E.D. Ky. 1997) (quoting *Sierra Club v. Thomas*). The concurring judge in *Sierra Club v. Thomas* took umbrage at the "majority's largely undocumented broadside against the Forest Service," noting, "Our speculation about the motives and biases of the Forest Service, even if accurate, is unnecessary, and therefore, ought not to be voiced in this opinion." Sierra Club v. Thomas, 105 F.3d at 252 (Batchelder, J., concurring).

As you review the history of Forest Service management as well as management by other federal agencies in subsequent sections of this chapter, it is useful to bear in mind that the tug-of-war over public lands is largely played out as a conflict over appropriate levels of deference given to the agencies. For commentary on the problematic role of the deference doctrine in insulating politicized agency action from judicial review, *see* Mary Christina Wood, *Reclaiming the Natural Rivers: The Endangered Species Act as Applied to Endangered River Ecosystems*, 40 ARIZ. L. REV. 197, 255–268 (1998) (suggesting procedural approach to overcome the deference doctrine).

4.   Professor Cheever thoroughly inventories the litigation under NFMA's timber practice standards and concludes that NFMA was a "resounding failur[e]," largely because the standards were not written in a precise enough way to preclude agency discretion that favors a high timber output. Cheever, *supra*, at 601. Professor Houck comes to a similar conclusion in the context of NFMA's diversity provision. *See* Houck, *supra*, at 892 ("On reflection, Congress took the first wrong turn in assuming, with unrealistic optimism, that the Service could offset decades of timber-first training and continuing pressures to keep the cut high with precatory language about diversity goals and multiple use.").

F.   Fire Policy and the Healthy Forest Restoration Act

Wildfires are a natural part of forest ecosystems to which the plant and animal communities have adapted. Fire clears the understory and recycles nutrients that are locked up in woody matter. But fires play very different roles in different ecosystems. For instance, the thick bark of mature ponderosa pine and sequoia can protect trees from flame. In those forests, fire may allow for larger, more widely spaced trees. In other forests, however, such as lodge pole pine and high elevation spruce fir, fires are often stand-replacing, leaving aspen forests to grow in their place.

Wildfires are perceived by many to pose an increasing threat to national forests. Whether the threat is as great as the perception is a matter of debate. After almost a century of wildfire suppression, considerable fuel has accumulated in many national forests. Fires in those forests may burn hotter and faster than natural low-intensity fires. Some scientists believe that global warming exacerbates the problem by creating climate conditions that lead to catastrophic fires. INTERGOVERNMENTAL PANEL ON CLIMATE CHANGE, IPCC SPECIAL REPORT ON THE REGIONAL IMPACTS OF CLIMATE CHANGE: AN ASSESSMENT OF VULNERABILITY (1997). The 2002 fire season, one of the worst in recorded history, burned more than 7.1 million acres.

Wildfires are a growing concern because they can create severe impacts for human communities. In 2002, wildfires burned 550 homes in

Colorado and Arizona. Much of the problem is that homes are increasingly located in forested areas naturally prone to fire. The presence of neighborhoods up against forests or grasslands creates what wildfire managers call a "wildland-urban interface" (WUI) or a "red zone." As population growth explodes throughout the West and more homes are constructed in desirable remote areas, the WUI expands, creating severe problems for fire management. One policy question gaining more attention is the extent to which federal tax dollars should be spent to preserve isolated subdivisions from wildfire.

Fire threatens a home near Durango, Colorado, during the 2002 fire season. Barry Gutierrez, reprinted by permission from The Rocky Mountain News. Available at http:// www.hcn.org.

In 2000, Congress directed the Secretaries of Interior and Agriculture to develop a comprehensive approach to wildland fire. Pub. L. 106–291 (2000). The agencies developed the National Fire Plan, which contained strategies to reduce fuels in the forest and improve prevention and suppression, with local assistance and coordination. U.S. FOREST SERVICE ET AL., A COLLABORATIVE APPROACH FOR REDUCING WILDLAND FIRE RISKS TO COMMUNITIES AND THE ENVIRONMENT: 10–YEAR COMPREHENSIVE STRATEGY (2001). Despite the fact that long-term fire suppression may sometimes create conditions leading to catastrophic fires, both the BLM and the Forest Service suppress most wildfires, rejecting a "let it burn" policy because of the risks it entails. The national firefighting effort has created what many now call the "industrial fire complex," costing $1.6 billion in 2002 alone.

In August 2002, President Bush proposed the Healthy Forests Initiative, involving the regulatory measures described in sections C–D, above. The Healthy Forests Initiative culminated in Congress's enactment of the Healthy Forest Restoration Act (HFRA) in 2003, which creates streamlined procedures for "authorized hazardous fuel reduction projects" on both national forests and BLM's forest lands. Pub. L. 108–

148, 117 Stat. 1887, 16 U.S.C. § 6501 *et seq.* Though the statute was enacted to protect national forests from catastrophic wildfire, conservation groups are concerned that it will allow increased logging in the name of fire risk reduction.

THE FAR SIDE®   By GARY LARSON

"And see this ring right here, Jimmy? ... That's another time when the old fellow miraculously survived some big forest fire."

HFRA adds an additional layer of complexity to forest law. On a broad level, it is important to keep in mind that, unless the Forest Service characterizes a particular project as a HFRA project, all of the NFMA standard laws and regulations described above apply to the particular activity. For HFRA projects, however, Congress diminished NEPA's application and changed the administrative review process. So while HFRA is significant in the overall realm of forest management, it in no way overhauled forest law.

Congress authorized $760 million per fiscal year for projects under HFRA. 16 U.S.C. § 6517(b). The Forest Service must allocate at least half of the funds to projects in "wildland-urban interface" areas. 16

U.S.C. § 6513(d)(1)(A). The overall acreage subject to the act is capped at 20 million acres, leaving the Forest Service with discretion as to where to locate projects. 16 U.S.C. § 6512(c).

The first level of HFRA analysis is determining where it applies. HFRA projects are limited to specific categories of land, defined by reference to technical reports and prior agency assessments. *See* 16 U.S.C. § 6512(a)(1)-(5). One such category is federal land in wildland-urban interface areas. HFRA projects are not authorized on wilderness lands, wilderness study areas, or on federal land protected by statute or Presidential proclamation. 16 U.S.C. § 6512(d).

HFRA essentially creates a streamlined set of NEPA procedures and appeal procedures for authorized projects. It expressly leaves intact all other statutes and regulations otherwise applicable to such projects. *See* 16 U.S.C. § 6512(b). The primary effect of HFRA is that it removes the alternatives analysis that has been described as the "heart" of NEPA. 40 C.F.R. § 1502.14. Projects inside the wildland-urban interface, for example, require only one action alternative in addition to the proposed action; the Forest Service need not analyze a "no action" alternative. 16 U.S.C. § 6514(d)(2). [For certain HFRA authorized projects outside the wildland-urban interface, if] citizens want the Forest Service to consider a management alternative as part of the NEPA process, they must be involved at an early stage to suggest the alternative, because the agency is under no obligation to develop this second action alternative on its own. The HFRA does not change, however, all other NEPA requirements that apply to any project. The act requires that all authorized projects be accompanied by the standard NEPA environmental assessments or EISs. 16 U.S.C. § 6514(g). *See* Chapter 4, *supra*.

The HRFA statute includes a surprising provision geared towards protecting the old growth forest that could be harmed by fuels reduction projects. Prior to 2003, no general forest statute had recognized old growth as a special natural asset. HFRA states, "In carrying out a covered project, the Secretary shall fully maintain, or contribute toward the restoration of, the structure and composition of old growth stands…. " 16 U.S.C. § 6512(e). The requirement applies to all fuels reduction projects except those on federal land affected by blowdown, ice storms, or insect infestation. *Id.* Outside of old growth areas, the statute provides direction to protect large trees, stating that projects should focus "largely on small diameter trees [and] maximiz[e] the retention of large trees…. " 16 U.S.C. § 6512(f).

HFRA eliminates the standard appeal process for authorized projects. It establishes instead a new "pre-decisional administrative review process" as the sole means through which a citizen may seek review of a project. 16 U.S.C. § 6515(a)(1). Regulations implementing this process are found at a new part 218, subpart A. Citizens may bring pre-decisional "objections" before the agency only if they had previously submitted specific comments relating to the project during the NEPA scoping or public comment period. 16 U.S.C. § 6515(a)(3). Moreover, only those citizens who exhausted this administrative process are eligible to bring actions in court challenging the decision. 16 U.S.C. § 6515 (c). In a nutshell, HFRA allows limited citizen involvement, but puts a premium on early participation—something that is often difficult for the general public.

Apart from the standard "authorized hazardous fuels reduction project," the HFRA creates a special category of project called an "applied silvicultural assessment," which does away with all NEPA review on land that the Secretary determines is "at risk of infestation by, or infested with, forest-damaging insects." 16 U.S.C. § 6554(a). Despite the innocuous ring of the term "assessment," such projects can include full-scale logging and even clearcutting. As long as the Forest Service limits the project to less than 1,000 acres, the action is categorically excluded from NEPA so that no environmental analysis is required. 16 U.S.C. § 6554(d)(1). The Forest Service must provide public notice of the "assessment" and an opportunity for comment, but the statute avoids detailing the process. 16 U.S.C. § 6554(c). A total of 250,000 acres may be categorically excluded under this section. 16 U.S.C. § 6554(d)(3). The statute preserves, however, the "extraordinary circumstances" exception to the categorical exclusion. 16 U.S.C. § 6554(d)(2)(B). Applied silvicultural assessment projects cannot be undertaken in wilderness areas, other areas protected by statute or Presidential proclamation, or in areas where the activities "would be inconsistent with" the applicable LRMP. 16 U.S.C. § 6554(b)(1).

In Practice:
Finding Resources for Citizen Forest Monitors

Over the last decade, many forest conservation groups have enlisted citizens to monitor activities on federal forests for compliance with NFMA, NEPA, and other environmental laws. The overhaul of forest law brought about by the Healthy Forests Initiative in recent years has challenged the "forest watch" citizenry, because new standards are complicated for even the experienced forest practitioner to understand. Forest conservation groups have responded by producing educational materials geared towards citizens. Several forest conservation groups have the full text of the HFRA, a legal analysis of its provisions, and updates of regulatory developments on their websites. Wildlaw has published a Legal Action Plan Under the Healthy Forests Restoration Act of 2003, *available at* www.wildlaw.org. The Sierra Club has produced a Healthy Forest Initiative Action Guide: How To Protect Our National Forests Under The New Rules of the Bush Administration (March 2004) as well as a Forest Watch Training Manual: Using the Law to Monitor and Guard Our National Forests (March 2004). Also available from the Sierra Club is a table of all of the regulatory changes (with citations to the Federal Register and Code of Federal Regulations) proposed or finalized by the Bush II administration in the area of public forest management.

G.　The Roadless Policy

The national forests have some of the last wild, unroaded areas in the country that are not yet protected as wilderness. *See* H. Michael Anderson & Aliki Moncrief, *America's Unprotected Wilderness,* 76 Denv. U. L. Rev. 413 (1999). But these areas also contain some of the last large stands of timber coveted by industry. Not surprisingly, the fight over such areas has intensified in recent years. One of the most dramatic measures taken by the Clinton administration was the promulgation of a "roadless rule" designed to protect a third of the acreage of the national forest system from further road-building. Special Areas; Roadless Area Conservation, 66 Fed. Reg. 3244 (Jan. 12, 2001). The rule would preserve the roadless characteristics of those areas for potential future wilderness inclusion. The rule has traveled on a rocky legal path through the courts, complicated greatly by the fact that a new administration with a vastly different public lands agenda fell into the position of defending the rule in court. Professor Blumm reveals the important legal and political nuances of this saga.

THE BUSH ADMINISTRATION'S SWEETHEART SETTLEMENT POLICY: A TROJAN HORSE STRATEGY FOR ADVANCING COMMODITY PRODUCTION ON PUBLIC LANDS
Michael C. Blumm
34 Envtl. L. Rptr. 10397, 10406–10407 (May 2004)

A.　*The Idaho Suit*

* * * Challenges to the [roadless] rule did not even await its final promulgation: days after President William J. Clinton signed the rule the state of Idaho, Boise Cascade, the Kootenai Tribe of Idaho, several snowmobile and off-road vehicle organizations, two livestock companies, and two counties filed suit, seeking an injunction barring implementation of the rule. In what would prove to be a significant development, environmental groups intervened on the side of the government. Six other suits followed, including suits by the states of Alaska, Utah, and Wyoming.

The incoming Bush Administration wasted little time in addressing the roadless rule, which was scheduled to take effect on March 12, 2001: it suspended the rule's application for 60 days on its first day in office. Although U.S. Attorney General John Ashcroft claimed at his confirmation hearing that he would defend and enforce the rule, the U.S. Department of Justice failed to defend the rule on its merits in the Idaho case, claiming that the Administration had the rule under review ....

Judge Edward Lodge of the U.S. District Court for the District of Idaho ... enjoined implementation of the rule, ... conclud[ing] that [it violated NEPA.] * * *

The Bush Administration chose not to appeal the Lodge decision, but the intervening environmental groups did. On December 12, 2001, a divided panel of the U.S. Court of Appeals for the Ninth Circuit ...

reversed the district court, rejecting claims that the roadless rule was promulgated without proper process. * * * The court therefore ... reinstated the roadless rule. At least for a time.

B.   *The Alaska Settlement*

The roadless rule had particular effect in Alaska, protecting over nine million acres of the Tongass National Forest in Southeast Alaska and some five million acres of the Chugach National Forest in the south central part of the state. These are the nation's two largest national forests, and together they account for around one-quarter of the roadless acreage affected by the roadless rule. The Tongass ... has the country's largest old growth trees scheduled for timber harvest, with some 663,000 acres of low-elevation, old growth slated for timber harvest in 49 timber sales under the Forest Service's current plan. In an effort to ensure that this old growth is in fact harvested, the state of Alaska filed a challenge to the roadless rule in the Alaska district court, claiming that the roadless rule violated numerous federal statutes, including the Alaska National Interest Lands Conservation Act, which the state claimed forbids establishing new reserves in Alaska without congressional consent. * * *

As in the appeal of the Idaho case, the Bush Administration decided not to defend the roadless rule, choosing instead to settle the case. On June 9, 2003, the Administration announced that it had reached an agreement with the state, promising that it would amend the roadless rule to exempt the Tongass from its application. The Administration also announced that it would allow any governor to apply for an exemption from the roadless rule on several grounds, including fire protection and wildlife habitat restoration. * * *

C.   *The Wyoming Injunction*

A month after the Bush Administration announced its settlement with the state of Alaska, a Wyoming district court issued a nationwide injunction against the roadless rule, ruling that it not only violated NEPA (as Judge Lodge held in the Idaho decision) but also * * * violated the Wilderness Act by usurping the U.S. Congress' exclusive power to designate wilderness areas. * * * [J]udge Brimmer thought the roadless rule was "a thinly veiled attempt to designate 'wilderness areas' in violation of the clear and unambiguous process established by the Wilderness Act...." This Wilderness Act ruling was more damaging to roadless area protection than the NEPA ruling because by requiring congressional approval, it would foreclose even the Bush Administration's halfhearted attempts to amend or re-promulgate some form of the roadless rule.

Due to these Wilderness Act and NEPA violations the court issued a permanent, nationwide injunction against the roadless rule. * * * As in the case of the Idaho decision, the Bush Administration chose not to appeal the Wyoming decision, although intervening environmental groups did. * * *

Notes and Questions

1.   Typically the government, through the U.S. Department of Justice, defends its rules when challenged in court. But as Professor Blumm's account demonstrates, the defense can be influenced by a new administration's agenda. How important is it in this context that citizen groups have standing to defend public lands rules in court?

2.   The issue of roadless areas is related to wilderness protection, a topic covered in depth in Chapter 15. For a cogent argument that Judge Brimmer was wrong in concluding that roadless area protection violates the Wilderness Act, *see* Sandra Zellmer, *A Preservation Paradox: Political Prestidigitation and an Enduring Resource of Wildness*, 34 Envtl. L. 1015, 1079–81 (2004). On the virtues of the roadless rule more generally, *see* Robert L. Glicksman, *Traveling in Opposite Directions: Roadless Area Management under the Clinton and Bush Administrations*, 34 Envtl. L. 1143 (2004).

3.   Subsequent to the *Wyoming* district court decision, the Bush II administration amended the roadless rule, 70 Fed. Reg. 25654 (May 13, 2005), 36 C.F.R. Part 294. Under the new rule, governors have 18 months to make a request to the Forest Service for roadless protection in their state. The Secretary of Agriculture will consider the requests and make final decisions. If a state does not affirmatively seek such roadless protection, the Forest Service will not provide it. After the amended rule was issued, the Tenth Circuit dismissed the *Wyoming* case as moot. *See* Wyoming v. U.S.D.A., 2005 WL 1607932 (10th Cir. 2005). For a description of the rule and the governors' responses, *see* Feds Pass Roadless Headache to States, HIGH COUNTRY NEWS, Aug. 16, 2004, at 3. Should states be the gatekeepers when it comes to protection of federal lands?

Exercise:

You have been asked to provide advice to a citizen group seeking to challenge a proposed timber sale (called the Silver Bullet sale) in a national forest in Wyoming. The group, Forest Champions, has learned from the most recent Schedule of Proposed Actions (SOPA) that the sale involves "even-aged" management on 3,000 acres for the purpose of controlling insect infestation that could lead to extreme fire danger. The forest provides habitat for several ESA-listed species as well as species classified as sensitive under the Forest Plan. The Forest Plan is undergoing the initial stages of revision. An internal order issued by the Forest Supervisor eight years ago prohibits the cutting of old growth on the Forest. The proposed Silver Bullet sale is in an area of the forest designated as "roadless" under the Clinton Roadless Rule. No NEPA documents have yet been prepared for the sale. Please advise the Forest Champions on possible challenges, administrative and judicial, to the sale, and chart out a course of action to maximize the group's chance of success on both levels. Consider the recent changes to forest policy effectuated by the Forest Service and Congress. Identify any additional information that must be gathered.

Global Perspective:

The Right of Future Generations to Forest Resources

Globally, forest resources are in crisis. Approximately half of the world's original forest is gone, and another 30% is degraded or fragmented. THE WORLDWATCH INSTITUTE, VITAL SIGNS 2002 104 (2002). In 1993, the Supreme Court of the Philippines handed down a remarkable decision to protect forest resources for future generations.

JUAN ANTONIO OPOSA ET AL., v. THE HONORABLE FULGENCIO S. FACTORAN, JR., G.R.

No. 101083, July 30, 1993.

(en banc) DAVIDE, JR., J:

[T]his petition bears upon the right of Filipinos to a balanced and healthful ecology which the petitioners dramatically associate with the twin concepts of "inter-generational responsibility" and "inter-generational justice." Specifically, it touches on the issue of whether the said petitioners have a cause of action to "prevent the misappropriation or impairment" of Philippine rainforests and "arrest the unabated hemorrhage of the country's vital life-support systems...."

* * * The principal plaintiffs ... are all minors duly represented and joined by their respective parents.... The complaint ... alleges that the plaintiffs "are all citizens of the Republic of the Philippines, taxpayers, and entitled to the full benefit, use and enjoyment of the natural resource treasure that is the country's virgin tropical rainforests." * * * The minors further asseverate that they "represent their generation as well as generations yet unborn." Consequently, it is prayed for that judgment be rendered:

" ... ordering [the government] to—

(1) Cancel all existing timber license agreements in this country; [and]

(2) Cease and desist from receiving, accepting, processing, renewing or approving new timber license agreements." * * *

The complaint starts off with the general averments that the Philippine archipelago of 7,100 islands has a land area of thirty million (30,000,000) hectares and is endowed with rich, lush and verdant rainforests in which varied, rare and unique species of flora and fauna may be found; these rainforests contain a genetic, biological and chemical pool which is irreplaceable; they are also the habitat of indigenous Philippine cultures which have existed, endured and flourished since time immemorial; scientific evidence reveals that in order to maintain a balanced and healthful ecology, the country's land area should be utilized on the basis of a ratio of fifty-four per cent (54%) for forest cover and forty-six per cent (46%) for agricultural, residential, industrial, commercial and other uses; the distortion and disturbance of this balance as a consequence of deforestation have resulted in a host of environmental tragedies, such as (a) water shortages, ... (c) massive erosion and the consequential loss of soil fertility and agricultural productivity, ... (d) the endangering and extinction of the country's unique, rare and varied flora and fauna, (e) the disturbance and dislocation of cultural communities, including the disappearance of the Filipino's indigenous cultures, ... and (k) the reduction of the earth's capacity to process carbon dioxide gases which has led to perplexing and catastrophic climatic changes such as the phenomenon of global warming, otherwise known as the "greenhouse effect."

* * * As their cause of action, they specifically allege that: * * *

8.   Twenty-five (25) years ago, the Philippines had some sixteen (16) million hectares of rainforests constituting roughly 53% of the country's land mass.

9.   Satellite images taken in 1987 reveal that there remained no more than 1.2 million hectares of said rainforests or four per cent (4.0%) of the country's land area.

10.   More recent surveys reveal that a mere 850,000 hectares of virgin old-growth rainforests are left, barely 2.8% of the entire land mass of the Philippine archipelago and about 3.0 million hectares of immature and uneconomical secondary growth forests. * * *

12.   At the present rate of deforestation, i.e. about 200,000 hectares per annum or 25 hectares per hour–nighttime, Saturdays, Sundays and holidays included–the Philippines will be bereft of forest resources after the end of this ensuing decade, if not earlier. * * *

14.   The continued allowance by defendant of [timber license agreement] holders to cut and deforest the remaining forest stands will work great damage and irreparable injury to plaintiffs–especially plaintiff minors and their successors–who may never see, use, benefit from and enjoy this rare and unique natural resource treasure. This act of defendant constitutes a misappropriation and/or impairment of the natural resource property he holds in trust for the benefit of plaintiff minors and succeeding generations.

15.   Plaintiffs have a clear and constitutional right to a balanced and healthful ecology and are entitled to protection by the State in its capacity as the parens patriae. * * *

18.   The continued failure and refusal by defendant to cancel the [timber license agreements] is an act violative of the rights of plaintiffs, especially plaintiff minors who may be left with a country that is desertified (sic), bare, barren and devoid of the wonderful flora, fauna

and indigenous cultures which the Philippines has been abundantly blessed with. * * *

20. Furthermore, defendant's continued refusal to cancel the afore-mentioned [timber license agreements] is contradictory to the Constitutional policy of the State to ... 'protect and advance the right of the people to a balanced and healthful ecology in accord with the rhythm and harmony of nature.' (Section 16, Article II, id.)

21. Finally, defendant's act is contrary to the highest law of humankind—the natural law—and violative of plaintiffs' right to self-preservation and perpetuation. * * *

[T]he respondents aver that the petitioners failed to allege in their complaint a specific legal right violated by the respondent Secretary for which any relief is provided by law. They see nothing in the complaint but vague and nebulous allegations concerning an "environmental right" which supposedly entitles the petitioners to the "protection by the state in its capacity as parens patriae." Such allegations, according to them, do not reveal a valid cause of action. They then reiterate the theory that the question of whether logging should be permitted in the country is a political question which should be properly addressed to the executive or legislative branches of Government. They therefore assert that the petitioners' recourse is not to file an action in court, but to lobby before Congress for the passage of a bill that would ban logging totally. * * *

This case ... has a special and novel element. Petitioners minors assert that they represent their generation as well as generations yet unborn. We find no difficulty in ruling that they can, for themselves, for others of their generation and for the succeeding generations, file a class suit. Their personality to sue in behalf of the succeeding generations can only be based on the concept of intergenerational responsibility insofar as the right to a balanced and healthful ecology is concerned. Such a right, as hereinafter expounded, considers the "rhythm and harmony of nature." Nature means the created world in its entirety. * * *

Needless to say, every generation has a responsibility to the next to preserve that rhythm and harmony for the full enjoyment of a balanced and healthful ecology. Put a little differently, the minors' assertion of their right to a sound environment constitutes, at the same time, the performance of their obligation to ensure the protection of that right for the generations to come. * * *

We do not hesitate to find for the petitioners ... The complaint focuses on one specific fundamental legal right—the right to a balanced and healthful ecology which, for the first time in our nation's constitutional history, is solemnly incorporated in the fundamental law. Section 16, Article II of the 1987 Constitution explicitly provides:

"SEC. 16. The State shall protect and advance the right of the people to a balanced and healthful ecology in accord with the rhythm and harmony of nature."

This right unites with the right to health ...:

"SEC. 15. The State shall protect and promote the right to health of the people and instill health consciousness among them."

While the right to a balanced and healthful ecology is to be found, under the Declaration of Principles and State Policies and not under the Bill of Rights, it does not follow that it is less important than any of the civil and political rights enumerated in the latter. Such a right belongs to a different category of rights altogether for it concerns nothing less than self-preservation and self-perpetuation—aptly and fittingly stressed by the petitioners—the advancement of which may even be said to predate all governments and constitutions.

As a matter of fact, these basic rights need not even be written in the Constitution for they are assumed to exist from the inception of humankind. If they are now explicitly mentioned in the fundamental charter, it is because of the well-founded fear of its framers that unless the right to a balanced and healthful ecology and to health are mandated as state policies by the Constitution itself, thereby high-lighting their continuing importance and imposing upon the state a solemn obligation to preserve the first and protect and advance the second, the day would not be too far when all else would be lost not only for the present generation, but also for those to come—generations which stand to inherit nothing but parched earth incapable of sustaining life.

The right to a balanced and healthful ecology carries with it the correlative duty to refrain from impairing the environment.... A denial or violation of that right by the other who has the correlative duty or obligation to respect or protect the same gives rise to a cause of action. Petitioners maintain that the granting of the [timber license agreements], which they claim was done with grave abuse of discretion, violated their right to a balanced and healthful ecology; hence, the full protection thereof requires that no further [timber license agreements] should be renewed or granted. * * *

The foregoing considered, Civil Case No. 90–777 cannot be said to raise a political question. Policy formulation or determination by the executive or legislative branches of Government is not squarely put in issue. What is principally involved is the enforcement of a right vis-à-vis policies already formulated and expressed in legislation. * * *

[The] Petition is hereby GRANTED....

Question

Is the Court essentially announcing a public trust doctrine for the protection of forest resources? Could such a doctrine apply to the remaining old growth in some forests in the United States? For in-depth coverage of the public trust doctrine, *see infra,* Ch. 8.II.

III. PUBLIC RANGELAND MANAGEMENT

Grazing has traditionally been one of the primary uses of federal land in the West. The Bureau of Land Management (BLM) manages approximately 262 million acres of land in the western states, including Alaska, Arizona, California, Colorado, Idaho, Montana, Nevada, New Mexico, Oregon, Utah, and Wyoming. Another 101 million acres of National Forest land is managed for grazing. While the higher reaches of the Western landscape feature snowcapped peaks, alpine lakes, and dense forests, much of the BLM lower-elevation land base is arid, supporting grassland and shrub-steppe ecosystems. These lands typically have a variety of grasses, forbes, and shrubs, but few trees. Historically, these areas supported buffalo, antelope, and a diversity of other animal and plant species. With the settlement of the West, immigrant families moved into these remote reaches and struck up a living as ranchers before the federal government had much of a presence there. *See* R. White, "It's Your Misfortune and None of My Own:" A History of the American West (1991). Today, much of the Western landscape is still dotted with private ranches engaged in livestock production. But the vast federal landholdings support relatively few cattle because of harsh vegetative and climate conditions. It is said that while a cow can live off about 1/2 an acre in the East, it requires about 10–200 acres of land in the arid West (areas receiving less than 14" rainfall a year). Accordingly, only 6% of the livestock producers in the 17 states west of the Mississippi River—about 23,600 ranchers—use federal land for grazing. Kenneth H. Mathews Jr., K. Ingram, J. Lewandrowski, & J. Dunmore, Public Lands and Western Communities 19, Agricultural Outlook, Economic Research Service, USDA (June–July 2002).

Nevertheless, there are few areas of public lands management that incite more controversy—and churn up more vexing ownership issues—than rangeland management. The controversy is a product of modern times. Until the past few decades, much of the federal rangeland was considered "wasteland," not valuable for any use other than grazing. But increased public recreational interest in these lands combined with a more sophisticated understanding of their ecosystem function and value has led to new views over appropriate use and management. BLM lands contain a wealth of ecological resources, including 23 million acres of riparian and wetland habitat, 2.7 million acres of lakes, 116,000 miles of fish-bearing streams, 182 million acres of big game habitat, 213 million acres of small game habitat, and 30 million acres of waterfowl habitat. The Wilderness Society, A Conservationist's Guide to BLM Planning and Decision–Making 1 (2003). Today, public rangeland issues are permeated with concerns over endangered species management and watershed protection.

Ranchers are unique users of the public lands, because in many cases their use goes back many generations. Their ancestors came out West in the early settlement rush of the 19th century and established homesteads under the Homestead Act or other land-grant statutes that conveyed fee title to a certain amount of acreage (160 acres or more) for farming. *See* Chapter 5.I.C.4. Early pioneer families naturally chose to locate along creeks and streams, as they needed the water supply for domestic use, subsistence farming, and raising forage for cows. Through this use they established some of the early water rights (though still junior to Indian water rights) in the western basins. But because the harsh conditions of the West require expansive amounts of land to run a cattle operation—far beyond the limited amount of fee acreage gained through federal land grants—ranchers made a practice of grazing their cattle on adjacent unclaimed federal lands during certain times of the year.

A typical family ranch operation in the 1800s used the water rights and fee land (called "base property") for the production of hay to tide the cattle over in the winter. In the early summer when the snow melted from the mountains, the family drove the herd up to the higher elevations on public land where there was fresh grass. In the fall a great "round-up" and cattle drive brought the herd back to the base property or nearby federal lands for the winter, where temperatures were less extreme. In winter months the cattle subsisted off the food grown during the summer and drank from the lower-elevation streams. To a great extent, the same pattern of business still continues on many small ranches.

The use of federal land to support a cattle operation was an integral part of the family enterprise, and encouraged by federal policy. Until 1934, such grazing was entirely unregulated. The Supreme Court determined early on that Congress's acquiescence to the grazing constituted an implied license for the activity. Buford v. Houtz, 133 U.S. 320, 10 S.Ct. 305, 33 L.Ed. 618 (1890). The ranchers' use, though never a property right in the classic sense, was for all practical purposes intertwined with two solid property rights—fee title to base property and corollary senior water rights. Because proximity of additional grazing land to fee land is a vital component of the Western ranching enterprise, the ranchers' dependence on federal land continues today. Terminating grazing on public lands may drive many family ranches out of business, as there is typically little available private rangeland to absorb a relocation off of federal lands. Many counties in the West have considerable federal ownership, some even exceeding 80%.

Thus, compared to other public lands users such as the weekend recreationalist, the migrant logger, or the mining executive, the rancher's expectations of continuing his or her use are based on much greater historical reliance and are more connected to family cohesiveness and tradition. The uncertain and desolate life of a ranching family instilled a common spirit of perseverance and ruggedness (some would say "bull-headedness") that endures today and permeates rangeland politics in the West. Many ranching families cling to their lifestyle in spite of daunting challenges brought on by a volatile global beef market, costly environmental compliance, and changing communities. For the most part, small family ranchers that survive off the public lands have little or no profit margin, staying in the business only for the way of life and spiritual fulfillment gained from leaving a longstanding legacy to the next generation. Indeed, ranching provides one of the few remaining examples in the nation of non-native land-dependent family enterprise.

Today, the future of the traditional Western ranching culture is threatened as corporate enterprise and a millionaire class buys out small family ranches. Huge corporate cattle operations gain the same subsidies and benefits from federal lands that their predecessors had, but with none of the same justifications. Increasingly, as more and more family ranchers face crushing debt and encroaching urban development, they subdivide and sell their lands as "ranchettes" for wealthy newcomers. As development metastasizes through rural areas, entire ranching communities transform to playgrounds for the well-heeled in a matter of a few years. Both modern demographic pressures and the historical context are important to keep in mind when studying the controversial area of public rangeland management.

This section of the text focuses on the BLM as the primary agency managing public rangeland. Housed within the Department of Interior, BLM is predominantly involved in rangeland management under two primary statutes, the Taylor Grazing Act, 43 U.S.C. § 315–315r, and the Federal Land Management and Policy Act (FLPMA), 43 U.S.C. § 1701 *et. seq.* The Forest Service also administers grazing permits and leases on federal forests. The Organic Act of 1897 provides basic authority to the Forest Service to manage the "occupancy and use" of national forests, which broadly includes the allowance of grazing. 16 U.S.C. § 551. Land use plans developed under the National Forest Management Act (NFMA) may designate grazing as a use of some forest areas and provide management prescriptions. 16 U.S.C. § 1600 *et. seq.* The Forest Service's issuance of grazing permits on federal forests must comply with FLPMA's grazing permit provisions, expressly made applicable to the Forest Service. 43 U.S.C. § 1752.

In Practice:
Understanding the Bureaucratic Structure

The BLM administrative hierarchy has its headquarters in Washington D.C. The BLM land base is administered by 12 state offices, each run by a State Director. State offices are divided into districts. At the lowest rung of the ladder are field offices. BLM is considered to be a highly decentralized agency, with considerable planning and decision-making carried out at the field office level.

An important corollary to the BLM structure is the Interior Board of Land Appeals (IBLA), an administrative adjudicative office that hears appeals on BLM decisions. The IBLA is located within the Interior's Office of Hearings and Appeals (OHA). Administrative Law Judges (ALJs) hear the appeals that fall within the jurisdiction of the IBLA. Another important office is the Department of Interior's Office of the Solicitor. That office provides legal advice to BLM in all of its program areas (including grazing, forestry, mining, and wilderness) and represents the agency in appeals to the IBLA. The Office of Solicitor has eight regional offices, each headed by a Regional Solicitor. The United States Solicitor provides opinions, called "Solicitor's Opinions," that interpret the laws governing BLM and other land management agencies within the Department of Interior (such as the Park Service, the Bureau of Reclamation, the Bureau of Indian Affairs, and the U.S. Fish and Wildlife Service). The Solicitor is a political appointee, and not surprisingly, Solicitor's Opinions often vary between presidential administrations to provide a legal slant most favorable to the political bent of the particular administration. Solicitor's Opinions may be found at http://www.doi.gov/sol/. A directory of BLM offices can be found on the internet at http://www.blm.gov/nhp/directory/index.htm. For an organizational chart of the BLM departments, *see* http://www.blm.gov/nhp/directory/BLM_Org_Chart.pdf.

An excellent guide to the BLM and its processes is: THE WILDERNESS SOCIETY, A CONSERVATIONIST'S GUIDE TO BLM PLANNING AND DECISION–MAKING (2003), *available at* http://www.wilderness.org/Library/Documents/BLM_Citizens_Guide.cfm.

A.   The Statutory Framework for BLM Rangeland Management

The Taylor Grazing Act (TGA) was passed in 1934 to respond to a crisis brought about by unregulated use of the federal lands for grazing. The public domain had become a classic "tragedy of the commons," in which every rancher had the incentive to graze as much as possible before his neighbor's cows arrived on the range. *See generally* W. GARD, FRONTIER JUSTICE 81–149 (1949). The overgrazing left vast landscapes in a devastated condition with severe damage to grasslands and soils. Even the ranchers were horrified, having to face the prospect of an unsustainable resource if the ways of implied license continued.

The TGA brought regulation to the range, with a stated goal to promote the "highest use of the public lands," "preserve the land and its resources from destruction or unnecessary injury," and "to provide for the orderly use, improvement, and development of the range." 43 U.S.C. §§ 315, 315a. It vested authority in the Department of Interior to establish grazing "districts" and to issue permits to graze livestock within those districts, charging "reasonable fees" for use of the land. 43 U.S.C. §§ 315, 315a, 315b. Areas isolated from a district could be leased for grazing purposes under the same system that applied to permits. The TGA specified the class of individuals eligible to receive permits, as well as a preference system for allocating the grazing privileges. Under the TGA, only "bona fide settlers, residents, and other stock owners" are eligible for grazing permits. 43 U.S.C. § 315b. Preference is given to "those within or near" a grazing district who are "landowners engaged in the livestock business, bona fide occupants or settlers, or owners of water or water rights." 43 U.S.C. § 315b. By 1937 the BLM passed regulations to implement the preference system. As described by the Supreme Court:

> Those rules recognized that many ranchers had long maintained herds on their own private lands during part of the year, while allowing their herds to graze farther afield on public land at other times. The rules consequently gave a first preference to owners of stock who also owned "base property," *i.e.*, private land (or water rights) sufficient to support their herds, *and* who had grazed the public range during the five years just prior to the Taylor Act's enactment. They gave a second preference to other owners of nearby "base" property lacking prior use. And they gave a third preference to stock owners without base property, like the nomadic sheep herder. Since lower preference categories divided capacity left over after satisfaction of all higher preference claims, this system, in effect, awarded grazing privileges to owners of land or water.

Public Lands Council v. Babbitt, 529 U.S. 728, 734–35, 120 S.Ct. 1815, 1819–20, 146 L.Ed.2d 753, 761 (2000).

The TGA charged the Interior Department with an enormous administrative task that entailed surveying the boundaries of the public range, creating grazing districts (37 in all), estimating grazing capacity, and dividing the forage among eligible applicants. Back in the early 1930s when the western range was a far and remote place isolated from Washington D.C. bureaucrats, the agency needed local expertise to perform its task. The TGA provided for local "advisory" boards comprised of ranchers in the districts to advise BLM on implementing a permit system. *See* W. Calef, Private Grazing and Public Lands 60 (1960) (describing the advisory boards as "the effective governing and administrative body of each grazing district."). These local advisory boards had tremendous influence over the agency's local decisions from the beginning— some contend too much influence. The boards formed the grassroots organizational base for a political lobby over national rangeland politics that continues today through the National Cattleman's Association. As part of a comprehensive "Rangeland Reform" initiative, the Clinton Administration attempted to bring more diverse perspectives to BLM's rangeland management by creating a set of advisory boards called "Resource Advisory Councils" (RACs for short). *See* 60 Fed. Reg. 9894 (Feb. 22, 1995).

Regulation under the TGA was fairly minimal, and the public range continued to experience overgrazing, erosion, and habitat loss. In 1976, as part of a greater wave of environmental legislation, Congress passed the Federal Land Policy and Management Act (FLPMA), which contains provisions directing BLM's management of rangelands and other public lands. 43 U.S.C. §§ 1711–1712; 1751–1753. In 1978, Congress enacted another statute, the Public Rangeland Improvement Act (PRIA), 43 U.S.C. § 1901, requiring BLM to maintain an inventory of range conditions and record of trends. Broadly speaking, FLPMA mirrors some of the provisions applicable to the Forest Service through NFMA, also passed in 1976. Like NFMA, FLPMA requires BLM to develop land use plans that direct agency activities. 43 U.S.C. §§ 1712, 1732(a). The agency calls these plans Resource Management Plans (RMPs). Much of the required planning focuses on "allotments" as a basic land unit. An allotment may encompass any number of acres, and several, or just one, permit or lease. While traditionally nearly all allotments were grazed, today it is not uncommon for BLM to temporarily suspend or permanently retire the use of some allotments for conservation or recreation.

Plans developed under FLPMA must incorporate requirements of multiple use and sustained yield, the same mandates announced in the Multiple Use Sustained Yield Act of 1960 (MUSY). Recall that these mandates were also incorporated into NFMA to steer the Forest Service towards more environmentally responsible management. 43 U.S.C. § 1702 (c), (h). *See supra* Section II. While MUSY has had little impact on forest management, the mandate of "multiple use" has had some effect in the grazing context. In 1997 the Interior Board of Land Appeals decided a case (called "Comb Wash" by many practitioners) brought by Arizona State Law Professor Joe Feller and the National Wildlife Federation challenging the renewal of a grazing permit for an area that included five canyons of scenic value. National Wildlife Federation v. BLM, 140 IBLA 85 (1997). The Board drew from Sierra Club v. Butz, 3 E.L.R. 20,292–93 (9th Cir. 1973), a case involving the Tongass National Forest in Alaska, to find that the multiple use mandate requires that the various " 'values in question be informedly and rationally taken into balance.' " 140 IBLA at 99. The Board concluded that BLM violated FLPMA's multiple use mandate because:

> it failed to engage in any reasoned or informed decisionmaking process concerning grazing in the canyons in the allotment. That process must show that BLM has balanced competing resource values to ensure that the public lands in the canyons are managed in the manner that will best meet the present and future needs of the American people.

Id. at 101.

In contrast to NFMA's detailed land management plan standards, FLPMA's standards are minimal. Beyond requiring multiple use and sustained yield, as well as compliance with applicable pollution laws, the primary planning standards are:

(3)　give priority to the designation and protection of areas of critical environmental concern (ACEC) (defined in 43 U.S.C. § 1702(a) as "areas within the public lands where special management attention is required ... to protect and prevent irreparable damage to important historic, cultural, or scenic values, fish and wildlife resources or other natural systems or processes...."); * * *

(5)　consider present and potential uses of the public lands;

(6)　consider the relative scarcity of the values involved and the availability of alternative means ... and sites for realization of those values;

(7)　weigh long-term benefits to the public against short-term benefits.

43 U.S.C. § 1712 (c).

Given the latitude courts have granted the Forest Service even within the more detailed structure of NFMA, it is perhaps not surprising that courts are reluctant to overturn BLM land use plans for non-compliance with FLPMA, a statute announcing only the broadest parameters of management. As in the forest context, the primary obstacle in challenging BLM plans is the administrative deference doctrine. In one of the more notable cases, Natural Resources Defense Council, Inc. v. Hodel, 624 F.Supp. 1045, 1058–59 (D. Nev. 1985), *aff'd,* 819 F.2d 927 (9th Cir. 1987), the court upheld a plan that was challenged on the basis that it allowed overgrazing in the Reno area:

> Plaintiffs argue that FLPMA and PRIA provide "standards" against which the court can determine whether the [plan] is "arbitrary, capricious or contrary to law." The declarations of policy and goals in [FLPMA] contain only broad expressions of concern and desire for improvement. They are general clauses and phrases which "can hardly be considered concrete limits upon agency discretion. Rather, it is language which 'breathes discretion at every pore.'" Perkins v. Bergland, 608 F.2d at 806, *quoting* Strickland v. Morton, 519 F.2d 467, 469 (9th Cir. 1975). Although I might privately agree with plaintiffs that a more aggressive approach to range improvement would be environmentally preferable, or might even be closer to what Congress had in mind, the Ninth Circuit has made it plain that "the courts are not at liberty to break the tie choosing one theory of range management as superior to another." *Perkins,* 608 F.2d at 807. The modest plans adopted by the BLM for dealing with range conditions in the Reno area are not "irrational" and thus cannot be disturbed by the court.

While FLPMA's land use planning process may seem rudderless, two potentially powerful substantive standards can be distilled from the statute. One is the "unnecessary or undue degradation" standard (known as the "UUD standard" by practitioners). FLMPA states:

In managing the public lands the Secretary [of the Interior] shall, by regulation or otherwise, take any action necessary to prevent unnecessary or undue degradation of the lands. 43 U.S.C. § 1732(b).

Could a court interpret this UUD language as an affirmative mandate to protect the environment? The UUD standard dovetails with another provision that requires BLM to undertake multiple use "without permanent impairment of the productivity of the land and the quality of the environment with consideration being given to the relative values of the resources...." 43 U.S.C. § 1702(c) (definition of "multiple use"). Does the "permanent impairment" standard set a bottom line for "undue degradation?" Or is the former watered down by "consideration" of other values? There is limited caselaw on these provisions. In the mining context, a court stated, "[I]n enacting FLPMA, Congress's intent was clear: Interior is to prevent, not only unnecessary degradation, but also degradation that, while necessary to mining, is undue or excessive." *See* Mineral Policy Center v. Norton, 292 F.Supp.2d 30, 42 (D. D.C. 2003) (excerpted in Chapter 3.B, *supra*). The Clinton and Bush II administrations took different views of the standard in promulgating regulations to carry out § 1732(b). *See* discussion in Section VI.B., *infra*.

A second potentially strong protection buried in FLPMA requires BLM to "give priority to the designation and protection of areas of critical environmental concern...." 43 U.S.C. § 1712(c)(3). The section defining "Areas of Critical Environmental Concern (ACEC)" describes ACECs as "areas within the public lands where special management attention is required ... to protect and prevent irreparable damage to important [listed] values." 43 U.S.C. § 1702(a). Does this language imply a "no irreparable damage" management standard for ACEC's? If so, does that standard have any teeth? In practice, the BLM has largely ignored such areas, but a leading citizen handbook concludes:

> ACECs are likely inadequate to protect entire landscapes, but they could be effectively used to protect core areas or especially vulnerable sites such as riparian corridors, wetlands, fragile soils, wildlife habitat, etc.... Once established, an ACEC provides a mechanism and justification for closing the land to high-impact recreational use such as ORVs [off-road vehicles]....

THE WILDERNESS SOCIETY, A CONSERVATIONIST'S GUIDE TO BLM PLANNING AND DECISION–MAKING 36–37 (2003). Designating the ACECs is the first step towards gaining agency protection for such areas.

BLM's land use planning and implementation of projects triggers other environmental laws that could have a significant impact on the ground. As in the forest context, developing a land use plan is an "action" under NEPA that requires environmental analysis, typically a full EIS. 42 U.S.C. § 4332(2)(C). Moreover, the same action triggers consultation under the Endangered Species Act for any listed species. 16 U.S.C. § 1536(a)(2). In Pacific Rivers Council v. Thomas, 936 F.Supp. 738 (D. Idaho. 1996), the court enjoined livestock grazing in areas that could affect listed salmon species pending consultation with the National Marine Fisheries Service on BLM's land management plan. Grazing decisions must also comply with the Clean Water Act, 33 U.S.C. § 1341, and other pollution laws. *See* Peter M. Lacy, *Addressing Water Pollution from Livestock Grazing After ONDA v. Dombeck: Legal Strategies Under the Clean Water Act*, 30 ENVTL. L. 617 (2000).

Another statute, the Wild and Scenic Rivers Act (WSRA), 16 U.S.C. §§ 1271–1284, may prove to be a formidable restraint to grazing in wild and scenic river corridors. Section 1281(a) states: "Each component of the national wild and scenic rivers system shall be administered in such manner as to protect and enhance the values which caused it to be included in said system...." The WSRA requires the managing agency to develop a management plan to protect the values for which the river was designated. 1624 U.S.C. § 1274(d)(1). This planning mandate is a separate statutory requirement from FLPMA's land use planning mandate, and it results in a separate management plan, though BLM can certainly coordinate the processes. The WSRA plan, like a FLPMA plan, is a federal "action" that triggers NEPA. The WSRA has been used to eliminate grazing entirely from the Owyhee Canyon area in Oregon along river stretches designated "wild" under that statute. In *Oregon Natural Desert Association v. Singleton,* below, the BLM had initiated work on a plan to protect the wild and primitive characteristics of segments of the Owyhee River and its tributaries, designating several areas as "areas of concern" that had experienced negative effects from grazing. (To clear up any confusion, these "areas of concern" were designated under the WSRA, not under FLPMA as ACECs). The environmental plaintiffs challenged BLM's failure to comply with NEPA in developing the WSRA plan. After entering summary judgment for the plaintiffs on NEPA grounds and giving BLM an opportunity to arrive at a plan to avoid an injunction against grazing (an opportunity BLM declined), a frustrated court permanently enjoined all grazing in the "areas of concern" identified by the WSRA plan.

OREGON NATURAL DESERT ASS'N v. SINGLETON

United States District Court, District of Oregon, 1999.

75 F.Supp.2d 1139.

Redden, District Judge.

This is an action brought by environmental groups (collectively "ONDA"), against the Bureau of Land Management ("BLM").... ONDA challenges the BLM's management of the Main, West Little, and North Fork Owyhee River corridors, alleging that the BLM failed to prepare an environmental impact statement ("EIS") analyzing the effect of cattle grazing on the area, as required by the National Environmental Policy Act ("NEPA"), 42 U.S.C. §§ 4321–4370a, and that its management plan violates the BLM's mandate under the Wild and Scenic Rivers Act ("WSRA"), 16 U.S.C. § 1271–1284.

On November 3, 1998, the court entered summary judgment in ONDA's favor, concluding that the BLM's management plan failed to consider whether cattle grazing was consistent with the WSRA's objectives and ordering the BLM to prepare an EIS. The court then turned to ONDA's request [to] enjoin all cattle grazing in the river corridor. The court expressed reservations about entering a complete injunction against all cattle grazing, but also stated its misgivings about continuing the status quo in the "areas of concern" identified by the BLM while the EIS was being developed. * * * The court might be more inclined to maintain the status quo if it were persuaded that continuation of the BLM's current grazing management practices could lead to restoration of the areas of concern. However, the BLM has not demonstrated that its current practices have led to any significant improvement in the areas of concern over the past seven years, and the court concludes that the continued degradation of the areas of concern can be remedied only by closing these areas entirely to cattle grazing.

The BLM has previously closed certain areas to grazing but then allowed the affected permittees to add their herds to those grazing in other areas. The court therefore concludes that only the complete elimination of permits for a certain number of animal unit months ("AUMs") will prevent the possibility that cattle will be removed from one degraded area only to increase grazing pressure elsewhere.

The court now permanently enjoins cattle grazing in the "areas of concern" identified by the BLM.... The permits for those AUMs are to be eliminated, rather than shifted to more lightly grazed areas. * * *

Congress has classified the three river segments as "wild," the most restrictive of three WSRA classifications. A wild river area is defined under the WSRA as "free of impoundments and generally inaccessible except by trail, with watersheds or shorelines essentially primitive and waters unpolluted." 16 U.S.C. § 1273(b). The public interest also includes the public policy stated by Congress of preserving these rivers in as pristine and unpolluted a condition as possible.

It has been almost seven years since the BLM recognized that cattle grazing was creating noticeable negative effects on the rivers' values in some parts of the corridor. The BLM found that grazing conflicted with recreational values where livestock congregated, grazed and defecated around campsites; that the visual impact of livestock trailing and grazing affected scenic and recreation values; and that the ecological condition of upland and riparian areas was being degraded by livestock grazing, trampling and defecation. The BLM designated specific areas of concern in 1993 ....

* * * [T]he evidence shows that, with the exception of the areas around Deary Pasture, grazing in the areas of concern has been neither reduced nor otherwise regulated. The same observations of heavy grazing, trampling, and bank erosion reported in 1993 have continued well into 1999. The persistent degradation of these areas and the BLM's

apparent inability to manage cattle grazing in a manner which would repair and restore the areas of concern has serious negative consequences for the recreational, scenic and ecological values of the designated rivers. These negative effects have existed for many years and there is no indication that they will change significantly in the future. * * * The Bureau of Land Management is enjoined to eliminate, permanently, domestic sheep and cattle grazing from all of the areas of concern identified in the 1993 Plan....

Notes and Questions

1. In the grazing context as well as any other natural resource context, the effectiveness of judicial review is a paramount factor in determining agency behavior. In the *ONDA* case, Judge Redden perceived a recalcitrant agency that had not taken any action to improve the condition of identified areas of concern. He responded by issuing a permanent injunction against grazing throughout all identified areas of concern, on the basis that any lesser injunction would prompt the agency to shift the grazing to other areas.

Contrast the court's orientation in NRDC v. Hodel, 624 F.Supp. 1045, 1062 (D. Nev. 1985) where, in refusing to disturb a BLM land use plan for the Reno area, the judge stated:

> Plaintiffs are understandably upset at what they view to be a lopsided and ecologically insensitive pattern of management of public lands at the hands of the BLM, a subject explored at length by many commentators. Congress attempted to remedy this situation through FLPMA, PRIA and other acts, but it has done so with only the broadest sorts of discretionary language, which does not provide helpful standards by which a court can readily adjudicate agency compliance.

> [T]his is a case in which plaintiffs ask me to become—and defendants urge me not to become—the rangemaster for about 700,000 acres of federal lands in western Nevada. For some reason, over the past 15 years or so, I and many of my Article III colleagues have become or have been implored to become forestmasters, roadmasters, schoolmasters, fishmasters, prisonmasters, watermasters, and the like. * * *

> [T]he primary reason for the large scale intrusion of the judiciary into the governance of our society has been an inability or unwillingness of the first two branches of our governments—both state and federal—to fashion solutions for significant societal, environmental, and economic problems in America. Frankly, I see little likelihood that the legislative and executive branches will take the statutory (and occasional constitutional) steps which would at least slow, if not reverse, this trend. Fortunately, for reasons set out in this opinion which (to me) are legally correct, I am able to resist the invitation to become western Nevada's rangemaster.

NRDC v. Hodel, 624 F.Supp. at 1062.

Which is the better judicial approach towards agency action? Are courts becoming more equipped to become "rangemasters?" Are they gaining expertise that is useful in analyzing agency action? If the courts refuse to scrutinize agency action on the basis that it is too technical for the court's expertise, does the deference doctrine in effect insulate agency behavior that is illegal? Or does the doctrine protect against judicial encroachment into areas properly reserved for the executive? Consider the separation of powers between the three branches of government. Given that the courts must enforce the law in order to preserve that delicate balance between the branches, what is the best use of the deference doctrine in administrative cases?

2. Examine again the requirements for BLM's land use plans. Unlike the forest context, BLM plans have rarely been challenged in court. Is that because the standards are so vague? How could a court decide whether a plan "weigh[s] long-term benefits to the public against short-term benefits?" 43 U.S.C. § 1712(c)(7). Most commentators agree that the provision with the most force is the requirement that BLM designate and protect areas of critical environmental concern (ACEC). 43 U.S.C. § 1712(c)(3). But the statute fails to set forth any process or standards for protecting these areas. In reality, BLM still allows grazing—even harmful grazing—in many ACECs. How might a court enforce this provision? Does the statute leave protection of these areas entirely to the discretion of BLM?

Does the *ONDA* opinion excerpted above create any useful precedent for fashioning a remedy to protect areas designated by BLM? Note that the *ONDA* decision dealt with "Areas of Concern" that BLM designated under the WSRA planning process. Such areas have no administrative relationship to the ACECs mentioned in FLPMA. BLM, in fact, has performed its FLPMA and WSRA planning for the Owyhee area on separate administrative tracts. Even though the *ONDA* decision dealt with a different statute, might the court's rationale in creating a strict remedy have some application to the FLPMA context? Could you envision an anti-grazing group seeking to prohibit grazing in areas identified as ACECs in a Resource Management Plan?

3. Recall that in Ohio Forestry Association v. Sierra Club, 523 U.S. 726, 118 S.Ct. 1665, 140 L.Ed.2d 921 (1998), the Court found that a challenge to a forest plan was not ripe for review prior to action implementing the plan on the ground. *See* section II.E, *supra*. Given the similar nature of the land use planning mandate, does this decision apply with the same force to FLPMA plans? Natural resource professionals must bear in mind that procedural decisions such as the *Ohio Forestry* case can have cross-cutting effects across the entire field of public lands law.

4. Conflicts abound over the use of off-road vehicles (ORVs) on BLM lands. It is estimated that 42 million Americans now engage in recreational ORV use, double what it was just two decades ago. *See* Norton v. Southern Utah Wilderness Alliance, 542 U.S. 55, 124 S.Ct. 2373, 2377, 159 L.Ed.2d 137, 147 (2004). ORV use can harm wildlife, destroy sensitive riparian areas, and incite the rage of quiet recreationalists. It is often opposed by ranchers as well, because ORVs can interfere with cattle grazing. BLM has ORV regulations that apply to all of the land it administers. 43 C.F.R. § 8340.0–8. For an excellent guide to the BLM ORV regulatory process, *see* ERIK SCHLENKER–GOODRICH, A CITIZEN'S GUIDE TO OFF–ROAD VEHICLE MANAGEMENT AND YOUR BUREAU OF LAND MANAGEMENT PUBLIC LANDS (The Wilderness Society,

April 2002). Citizen groups have tried to limit ORV use on BLM lands through litigation seeking to enforce land use plans, FLMPA standards, and NEPA. In Norton v. Southern Utah Wilderness Alliance, 542 U.S. 55, 124 S.Ct. 2373, 159 L.Ed.2d 137 (2004), the Supreme Court dealt a blow to such claims by interpreting the Administrative Procedure Act, FLMPA's land use planning mandate, and NEPA's supplementation requirement in a restrictive manner. *See* section I.C, *supra*.

Exercise:

Imagine a hypothetical ACEC in Montana called "Silver Gulch" that encompasses 5,000 acres of prime hiking and backpacking territory and draws over twenty thousand visitors a year. Grazing there pollutes the streams and detracts from the recreational experience of visitors. Draft an argument seeking injunctive relief against grazing in the area. If you cite to the *ONDA* case, be sure to acknowledge the WSRA context in which that injunction was issued.

B. Grazing Permits

The provisions of the Taylor Grazing Act (TGA) and FLPMA, together with the set of regulations BLM devised to implement the statutes (called the Rangeland Code) set forth a structure for grazing permits. Permits under the TGA are valid for 10 years, subject to renewal with a preference given to the permit holder. 43 U.S.C. § 315b. Permits must specify numbers of stock and seasons of use, as well as other "terms and conditions as [BLM] deems appropriate for management of the permitted or leased lands." 43 U.S.C. § 1752(e).

The grazing privileges in a permit or lease are quantified in terms of "animal unit months," or "AUMs," which is the amount of forage needed to sustain one cow (or alternatively, five sheep) for one month. BLM has authority to develop an "Allotment Management Plan" (AMP) to incorporate into grazing permits and leases as well. 43 U.S.C. § 1752 (d). An AMP is a document that contains more detailed prescriptions for managing and improving the land in order to meet objectives of multiple use and sustained yield. 43 U.S.C. § 1702 (k). It is prepared in consultation with the permittee(s). Because issuance of a permit or lease is a federal "action," NEPA requires environmental analysis. 42 U.S.C. § 4332(2)(C).

Section 315b of the Taylor Grazing Act expressly makes clear that the issuance of a permit "shall not create any right, title, interest, or estate in or to the lands," a provision emphasized by the Supreme Court in its most recent opinion on BLM grazing management, Public Lands Council v. Babbitt, 529 U.S. 728, 733–34, 120 S.Ct. 1815, 1819–20, 146 L.Ed.2d 753, 760–61 (2000); *see also* United States v. Fuller, 409 U.S. 488, 494, 93 S.Ct. 801, 805, 35 L.Ed.2d 16, 22 (1973) (finding clear the congressional intent that "no compensable property right be created in the permit lands themselves as a result of the issuance of the permit."). However, if a permit or lease is cancelled as a result of BLM's decision to devote the land to another purpose, the permittee is entitled to compensation for his or her interest in improvements made on the rangeland. 43 U.S.C § 1752 (g).

FLPMA contains an important environmental safeguard allowing BLM to adjust grazing levels set forth in permits in response to range conditions. 43 U.S.C. § 1752 (e). Courts are likely to review reductions in grazing with considerable deference to the agency. *See, e.g.,* Perkins v. Bergland, 608 F.2d 803 (9th Cir. 1979) (rancher failed to show decision was arbitrary or capricious); McKinley v. United States, 828 F.Supp. 888 (D. N.M. 1993) (same); *but see* Hinsdale Livestock Co. v. United States, 501 F.Supp. 773 (D. Mont. 1980) (overruling BLM's decision to reduce grazing levels in response to drought conditions).

FLPMA and the TGA both make clear that the BLM has authority to cancel, suspend, or modify a grazing permit. *See Public Lands Council,* 529 U.S. at 735. This can happen if the permittee overgrazes, loses control of the base property, fails to use the permit, fails to comply with the Range Code, or if the Secretary reduces the amount of grazing for such time as necessary in response to environmental conditions or range depletion. The permittee may also lose a permit or lease if the land use plan changes to reclassify the land for another use, though BLM must give the permittee two years' notice for such permit cancellations. 43 U.S.C. § 1752(a), (g). Barring all of these circumstances, an existing permit holder has first priority for renewing his or her permit. 43 U.S.C. § 1752(c). The statutory regime therefore establishes security for existing permit holders vis-a-vis other permittees, but also allows BLM flexibility to change the land use designation or impose new conditions. To avoid rancher reliance, each permit or lease must contain a revocation clause as specified in 43 U.S.C. § 1752(a).

C. Clinton's Rangeland Reform

In 1995, under the Clinton administration, BLM adopted a set of regulations informally known as "Rangeland Reform '94," 60 Fed. Reg. 9894 (Feb. 22, 1995) (Final Rule). The reform was aimed at incorporating ecosystem and other public values in BLM permit decisions under the TGA and FLPMA. The new regulations established environmental standards to guide permit decisions. These standards are discussed below. Other parts dealt with the permit preference system, permit eligibility requirements, title to improvements on public lands, and creation of Resource Advisory Councils.

One of the lightning rods in the Rangeland Reform regulations concerned conservation use of grazing permits. Several years prior to the Clinton administration, grazing reform organizations had devised a private scheme to protect land from grazing within the existing permit system of FLPMA and the TGA. They purchased ranches (fee lands), gained the federal grazing permits that attached to the fee land, and then rested the land from grazing for the duration of the permit (up to 10 years). Such actions challenged a long-standing regulatory presumption that land within BLM's grazing districts would be primarily used for grazing. *See* 43 U.S.C. § 315 (lands within district are "chiefly valuable for grazing"). Bruce Babbitt, Secretary of Interior under the Clinton administration, seemed to give a go-ahead to such conservation efforts by including a provision in Rangeland Reform expressly allowing grazing permits to be used for conservation use. *See* 43 C.F.R. § 4130.2 (1995) (establishing conservation use as an allowable permit or lease use and noting that forage used for conservation purposes would not be available to other livestock operators); § 4140.1 (conservation use not a prohibited act). Ranching communities saw this regulatory move as a first step in an agenda to end all grazing on public lands. Anti-grazing organizations had made their intent clear in prior years with calls to arms such as "no moo '92" and "cow free 93." While the Clinton administration had never expressed this position, the ranching communities reacted to Rangeland Reform with considerable hostility.

The Public Lands Council and other ranching related organizations challenged 10 of the regulations in Clinton's Rangeland Reform package in federal court as exceeding the authority of the Taylor Grazing Act. The district court overturned four of the 10 regulations, including the conservation use rule. Public Lands Council v. Interior, 929 F.Supp. 1436, 1450–1451 (D. Wyo. 1996). On appeal, the Tenth Circuit reversed the district court as to three of those rules, but the circuit court agreed that the conservation use rule was contrary to the Taylor Grazing Act and therefore invalid:

> The TGA authorizes the Secretary to establish grazing districts comprised of public lands "which in his opinion are chiefly valuable for grazing and raising forage crops." 43 U.S.C. § 315. When range conditions are such that reductions in grazing are necessary, temporary non-use is appropriate and furthers the preservation goals of the TGA, FLPMA, and PRIA, even when that temporary non-use happens to last the entire duration of the permit. BLM may impose temporary reductions, *see* 43 C.F.R. § 4110.3–2 (1994), or permittees may voluntarily reduce their grazing levels. The presumption is, however, that if and when range conditions improve and more forage becomes available, permissible grazing levels will rise. * * * The Secretary's new conservation use rule reverses that presumption. Rather than annually evaluating range conditions to determine whether grazing levels should increase or decrease, as is done with temporary non-use, the Secretary's conservation use rule authorizes placement of land in non-use for the entire duration of a permit. This is an impermissible exercise of the Secretary's authority under section three of the TGA because land that he has designated as "chiefly valuable for grazing livestock" will be completely excluded from grazing use even though range conditions could be good enough to support grazing. Congress intended that once the Secretary established a grazing district under the TGA, the primary use of that land should be grazing.

Public Lands Council v. Babbitt, 167 F.3d 1287, 1308–9 (10th Cir. 1999).

The Court of Appeals' decision as to the conservation use rule was not appealed to the Supreme Court. Thus, that rule remains invalid. The three other rules upheld by the Tenth Circuit were subsequently appealed to the Supreme Court. One of those, which dealt with "eligibility" requirements for grazing permits, skirted close to the terrain trod by the invalid conservation use rule. In a resounding affirmation of BLM's discretionary authority to promulgate rules under the Taylor Grazing Act and FLPMA, the Supreme Court upheld all three of the challenged rules. The portion of the opinion dealing with the eligibility requirements is excerpted below.

PUBLIC LANDS COUNCIL v. BABBITT

Supreme Court of the United States, 2000.
529 U.S. 728, 120 S.Ct. 1815, 146 L.Ed.2d 753.

JUSTICE BREYER delivered the opinion of the Court.

* * * The Taylor act ... grants the Secretary of the Interior authority to divide the public range lands into grazing districts, to specify the amount of grazing permitted in each district, to issue leases or permits "to graze livestock," and to charge "reasonable fees" for use of the land. It specifies that preference in respect to grazing permits "shall be given ... to those within or near" a grazing district "who are landowners engaged in the livestock business, bona fide occupants or settlers, or owners of water or water rights." § 315b. And, as particularly relevant here, it adds:

> So far as consistent with the purposes and provisions of this subchapter, grazing privileges recognized and acknowledged shall be adequately safeguarded, but the creation of a grazing district or the issuance of a permit ... shall not create any right, title, interest, or estate in or to the lands. * * *

The ranchers' ... challenge focuses upon a provision of the Taylor act that limits issuance of permits to "settlers, residents, and other *stock owners*...." 43 U.S.C. § 315b (emphasis added). In 1936, the Secretary, following this requirement, issued a regulation that limited eligibility to those who "ow[n] livestock." But in 1942, the Secretary changed the regulation's wording to limit eligibility to those "engaged in the livestock business," 1942 Range Code § 3(a), and so it remained until 1994. The new regulation eliminates the words "engaged in the livestock business," thereby seeming to make eligible otherwise qualified applicants even if they do not engage in the livestock business. *See* 43 CFR § 4110.1(a) (1995).

The new change is not as radical as the text of the new regulation suggests. The new rule deletes the entire phrase "engaged in the livestock business" from § 4110.1, and seems to require only that an applicant "own or control land or water base property...." *Ibid.* But the omission, standing alone, does not render the regulation facially invalid, for the regulation cannot change the statute, and a regulation promulgated to guide the Secretary's discretion in exercising his authority under the

Act need not also restate all related statutory language. Ultimately it is *both* the Taylor act and the regulations promulgated thereunder that constrain the Secretary's discretion in issuing permits. The statute continues to limit the Secretary's authorization to issue permits to "bona fide settlers, residents, and *other stock owners*." 43 U.S.C. § 315b (emphasis added).

Nor will the change necessarily lead to widespread issuance of grazing permits to "stock owners" who are not in the livestock business. Those in the business continue to enjoy a preference in the issuance of grazing permits. The same section of the Taylor act mandates that the Secretary accord a preference to "landowners engaged in the livestock business, bona fide occupants or settlers." *Ibid.* And this statutory language has been extremely important in practice. * * *

The ranchers' underlying concern is that the qualifications amendment is part of a scheme to end livestock grazing on the public lands. They say that "individuals or organizations owning small quantities of stock [will] acquire grazing permits, even though they intend not to graze at all or to graze only a nominal number of livestock—all the while excluding others from using the public range for grazing." The new regulations, they charge, will allow individuals to "acquire a few livestock, ... obtain a permit for what amounts to a conservation purpose and then effectively mothball the permit."

But the regulations do not allow this. The regulations specify that regular grazing permits will be issued for livestock grazing, or suspended use. See 43 CFR §§ 4130.2(a), 4130.2(g) (1998). New regulations allowing issuance of permits for conservation use were held unlawful by the Court of Appeals and the Secretary did not seek review of that decision. * * *

Notes and Questions

1. In light of the Court of Appeal's decision and the Supreme Court's reasoning in the excerpted portion above, conservation permits are clearly not allowed. *See* 68 Fed. Reg. 68452, 68454 (Dec. 8, 2003) (proposed rule eliminating conservation permits to comport with judicial rulings). Nevertheless, as is often the case in public lands law, legal rulings sometimes have an unexpected life on the ground. Some grassland conservation groups still successfully engage in conservation non-use of permits. The regulation currently allow for three years of temporary non-use for the convenience of the rancher. 43 C.F.R. § 4130.2(g)(2). Many ranchers rely on this provision when personal or financial circumstances prevent use of the permit. Some conservation organizations that have purchased land with corollary federal grazing permits have had little trouble resting the federal land during this three-year regulatory period. After that expires, they may try to prevail upon BLM to place the permit's AUMs in a status of "suspended non-use" to protect the resource. This means that the permittee has paper rights to the forage, but may not enjoy those rights during the period of suspension.

Another conservation strategy is to "buy out" permits and leases. This entails paying a rancher to permanently not graze and relinquish his/her permit, then gaining from BLM a redesignation of the allotment to non-grazing use. In 2002, the United States Solicitor wrote a legal opinion, later followed by a memorandum, making clear that the decision to expire grazing on an allotment within a district requires an amendment to the land use plan. *See* USDOI, Office of the Solicitor, Memorandum Re/ Clarification of M–37008 (May 13, 2003). Ultimately, however, even buyouts accompanied by land use plan changes do not effectuate permanent protection. As the Solicitor's Opinion makes clear, grazing retirement decisions are subject to reconsideration and reversal during subsequent land use planning processes, so permanent conservation can be achieved only through Congressional action. *See* www.publiclandsranching.org (discussing proposed legislation for voluntary buyout program).

2.   What is "livestock"? *See* 40 C.F.R. § 4100.0–5 (defining as "species of domestic livestock—cattle, sheep, horses, burros, and goats"). If Grand Canyon Trust wanted to graze a few llama or perhaps an ostrich or two rather than cattle, could it? Would such a strategy circumvent the restriction on conservation use?

3.   The *Public Lands Council* opinion affirmed two other regulations that were part of Clinton's Rangeland Reform. One redefined grazing "preference" to eliminate reference to any quantity of AUMs. *See* 43 C.F.R. § 4100.0–5 (1995) (defining preference as "a superior or priority position against others for the purpose of receiving a grazing permit or lease."). The other regulation granted the United States title to permanent structural improvements made pursuant to cooperative agreements authorized in the TGA. *Id.* at 748–49.

4.   Overall, the Rangeland Reform regulations challenged at the Supreme Court level in *Public Lands Council* did not represent a dramatic departure in the way BLM implemented its permit system. The significance of the *Public Lands Council* opinion lies perhaps more in its resounding affirmation of BLM's authority to protect the range under the TGA, and its overall premise that ranchers, as users of the public lands, do not have fixed rights in grazing levels. *See id.* at 741 (citing Taylor Grazing Act's qualification that "the issuance of a permit pursuant to the provisions of this sub-chapter shall not create any right, title, interest or estate in or to the lands," 43 U.S.C. § 315(b)). In retrospect, from the perspective of the ranchers, was it wise to challenge the regulations? Do you suppose the ranchers hoped for a dramatic decision announcing that they have legitimate expectations of private property rights on public lands? If so, did the strategy backfire?

5.   For an analysis of the *Public Lands Council* opinion, *see* Joseph M. Feller, *Back to the Present: The Supreme Court Refuses to Move Public Range Law Backward, But Will the BLM Move Public Range Law Forward?* 31 ENVTL. L. REP. 10021 (2001). For treatment of the Rangeland Reform rules, *see* Joseph H. Feller, *Till the Cows Come Home: The Fatal Flaw in the Clinton Administration's Public Lands Grazing Policy,* 25 ENVTL. L. 703 (1995).

6.   Another approach used by the anti-grazing movement is to create pressure to raise the fees charged by BLM for public forage. FLPMA mandates that BLM "receive fair market value of the use of the public lands and their resources." 43 U.S.C. § 1701(a)(9). Fees are set by the Secretary of

Interior according to a formula established in the grazing regulations. 43 C.F.R. § 4130.8–1. The fee is currently at $1.35 per AUM. Environmental interests point out that this fee is well below the market rate on private lands (which tends to fall between $6–$15/AUM). A hike in grazing fees can potentially drive a large number of family ranchers into debt and force sales of their private fee lands. Not surprisingly, ranchers vociferously oppose fee increases. While anti-grazing groups aim shrill criticism towards what they perceive as subsidized grazing through low fees, federal permittees contend that the fee represents the market value of federal lands. Federal lands, they point out, have none of the amenities associated with leases of private lands, including proximity to water sources, quality of forage, herd monitoring and veterinary care. For analysis, *see* BETSY CODY, CRS REPORT FOR CONGRESS: 96006: GRAZING FEES AND RANGELAND MANAGEMENT (Dec. 4, 1998).

Even if the grazing fees are below the market rate, do they amount to anything more than a drop in the bucket as compared with the massive give-aways to mining companies? As section VI., *infra,* explains, hard rock mining companies extract billions of dollars of minerals from U.S. lands at absolutely no charge—often leaving toxic dumps in their wake that cost the public enormous amounts of money to clean up. Is the focus on low grazing fees actually prompted by economic concerns, or is it motivated instead by a desire to eliminate ranching on public lands?

In Practice:
The Agency Appeals Process

    Like other land management agencies, BLM has an administrative appeals process for its decisions. In general, BLM appeals are divided into two categories: appeals of land use plan (RMP) decisions and appeal of decisions implementing the RMPs.

    Appeals of RMPs are called "protests" and are submitted to the Director of the BLM. 43 C.F.R. § 1610.5–2(a)(1). Strict standing requirements limit the category of persons who can bring such appeals to those that have both participated in the planning process and will be or may be adversely affected by the plan decision. 43 C.F.R. § 1610.5–2(a). Protests are limited in scope to those issues that were submitted for the record during the agency planning process. *Id.* Thus, it is crucial for interested parties to submit comments during the planning process in order to preserve grounds for appeal.

    Appeals of implementation decisions are made to the Interior Board of Land Appeals (IBLA), a separate office within the Department of Interior. Many of the appeals rules are contained within 43 C.F.R. Part 4. In some cases, the appellant must first bring a request to BLM to reconsider a decision before taking the appeal to the IBLA. IBLA appeals might be heard by one administrative law judge (ALJ) or a panel of judges, depending on the type of action appealed. The IBLA may not hear appeals on planning decisions, including the designation of Areas of Critical Environmental Concern, which BLM considers a planning decision. *See* U.S. DEPARTMENT OF THE INTERIOR

BUREAU OF LAND MANAGEMENT, LAND USE PLANNING HANDBOOK APPENDIX F. The natural resource practitioner may search IBLA decisions in a database of cases found at http://hearingsandappeals.doi.gov/Lands.html.

During the process of the appeal, the contested decision might be implemented on the ground. *See, e.g.* 43 C.F.R. § 4.21(a)(2) (decision effective upon expiration of time period for appeal); 43 C.F.R. § 4160.3(f) (effective date of certain grazing decisions). To protect against this, appellants may seek a "stay" of the decision pending appeal by submitting a "Petition for a Stay." 43 C.F.R. § 4.21(a)(2).

The appeals process is riddled with procedural requirements, any one of which can present a legal pitfall. An excellent description of the appeals process, along with flowcharts and tips to navigate through the maze of jurisdictional, venue, and timing requirements, is found in THE WILDERNESS SOCIETY, A CONSERVATIONIST'S GUIDE TO BLM PLANNING AND DECISION–MAKING 118–134 (2003), *available at* http://www.wilderness.org/Library/Documents/BLM_Citizens_Guide.cfm.

D. Environmental Issues Surrounding Grazing

Grazing on the public lands involves a full spectrum of environmental issues, but one should avoid the pitfalls of presuming that all grazing permits trigger the same set of environmental concerns; each grazing allotment is unique. Broadly speaking, environmental concerns over grazing generally fall into four categories. The first involves the impact of grazing on recreational resources. As population soars in the West, the recreational use of public lands continues to grow and expand into areas historically unnoticed by the general public. For example, the spectacular Owyhee canyon land of Oregon, where grazing has dominated for the last century, is now appreciated for its wilderness recreational qualities and glorious scenic features.

Upper Owyhee River Area, http://itd.idaho.gov/byways/online.brochure/120/owyhee.htm.

Recreationalists object to cows trampling through campsites, pounding sensitive riparian areas, and defecating along trails and in the streams. Public pressure to end grazing in areas such as the Owyhee is mounting, forcing BLM to weigh the traditional grazing benefits accruing only to a few small ranching families against the broad public benefits of recreation. But, is public lands grazing as a whole incompatible with recreation? Certainly many grazing allotments—perhaps even the majority—are in areas with little or no current recreation.

A second environmental concern focuses on the grassland or shrub-steppe ecosystem itself. Long ignored by the public, these lands are in fact a complex biotic system comprised of grasses, forbes (flowering plants), and shrubs. Grazing degrades the soil composition, destroys native grasses such as bluestem and bunch grass, and invites non-native invasive species such as cheat grass, detested by hikers because it works its way deep into the socks and boots. Grazing may also change the natural fire regime of an area by encouraging the proliferation of grasses that spread flame more rapidly. Overgrazing has occurred for so long on the public lands that there are few remaining examples of natural grassland landscapes. Most of the public rangelands are, in Edward Abbey's fine words, "cowburnt." *See* Edward Abbey, *Even the Bad Guys Wear White Hats,* HARPERS, Jan. 1986, at 51. Consider the proposal below to preserve "old growth" grasslands.

FROM OLD–GROWTH FORESTS TO OLD–GROWTH GRASSLANDS: MANAGING RANGELANDS FOR STRUCTURE AND FUNCTION
Joseph M. Feller & David E. Brown
42 ARIZ. L. REV. 319 (2000)

Public forest managers in the United States recognize that forests serve important ecological and social functions other than timber production and that mature forests provide certain benefits that cannot be obtained from younger forests. Cutting mature forests therefore can result in a severe loss of values, regardless of whether the cut forests regenerate into young forests of the same tree species. In order to avoid this loss, recent forest management decisions provide for reduced rates of timber harvest and designate substantial areas of public forests to be retained in a natural state.

For the most part, public rangeland management has not undergone a similar development. Although agency policies nominally recognize some of the ecological and social functions of rangelands other than forage production, actual rangeland management practices still reflect an implicit assumption that loss of forage productivity is the only potential negative impact of livestock grazing. * * * Other rangeland values that may be compromised by grazing, such as wildlife habitat, water quality, and scenic beauty, are generally ignored. * * *

We propose an agenda for a reformed public rangeland management that respects the structure and function of grasslands. Borrowing concepts from modern developments in forest management, this agenda includes a moratorium on construction of new livestock water developments in areas where grazing has so far been limited by lack of water, creation of reserves that are protected from livestock grazing, and extended rotations and reduced stocking levels in areas where grazing continues. * * *

The first lesson is to avoid degrading or destroying remaining ecosystems ... that still retain a large measure of their original structure and function. * * * At first glance, it would appear that it is far too late to protect old-growth grasslands from livestock grazing. Grazing is already permitted on virtually all public rangelands; indeed, grazing on almost all of these lands predates the existence [of BLM]. There are, nonetheless, portions of the public rangelands that have been spared many of the impacts of grazing. These include areas that are too distant from water sources, either natural or artificial, to receive regular livestock use. In the arid climate of the American West, livestock cannot travel more than a few miles from drinkable water; most livestock use is concentrated within one or two miles of water sources. Water developments are to livestock grazing what roads are to logging; just as the roadless areas are where most of the remaining old-growth forests occur, the waterless areas are where most of the remaining intact grasslands are found. * * *

BLM and Forest Service range managers view livestock water developments as a near-universal solution to problems of overgrazing, particularly in riparian areas. * * * The result is the systematic elimination of America's last remaining old-growth grasslands. * * *

Therefore, as a first step in the development of a management policy that recognizes the importance of maintaining the structure and function of rangelands, we propose a moratorium on the construction of new livestock water developments on public rangelands. * * *

Cattle grazing along creek bottom in the Dry Creek Wilderness Study Area in the BLM Vale District in Oregon. Available at www.blm.gov.

A third category of environmental concern arises over the extreme riparian damage caused by cattle. In the hot and dry Western climate, cows naturally gravitate to water and, if left to their own devices, often spend the entire day bathing in the streams or lounging on the stream banks. This behavior can ruin a riparian system. Cattle hooves squash sensitive riparian plants and sometimes cause massive soil erosion and discharge into the creeks. Cows also defecate in the creeks, causing obvious pollution. All of these impacts contribute to the loss of fisheries habitat. Consider the description of grazing effects in the John Day Basin of Oregon:

> [T]he John Day is home to one of the few remaining exclusively wild runs of spring Chinook salmon and summer steelhead trout in the world. The John Day is distinguished by the largest and most diverse native fish populations in Oregon, including redband trout, bull trout, and west slope cutthroat trout.
>
> With 500 miles of undammed waters, the John Day is the second-longest free-flowing river in the continental United States. With some of its headwaters protected as wilderness, the John Day seems like the ideal place to nurture wild salmon. And it would be if it weren't for grazing-caused damage in most of its headwaters and dewatering the lower river.
>
> In the headwaters, the river and its tributaries are much shallower, wider, [and] warmer.... Bathtub-like water temperatures upwards of 75 degrees led the late grazing reform advocate Denzel Ferguson to observe, "The only way a steelhead can make it down the Middle Fork of the John Day is on a motorcycle at midnight."

Paul Koberstein, *Double Trouble for Wild Fish*: Cascadia Times, Fall 2002, at 18–19.

In response to this type of damage, many permits require riparian protection along waterways. This usually entails construction of a fence to keep cows out of the sensitive areas. But cows clearly require an alternative water source; if one is not readily available to them, they may trample the fence. At least three options are used on a regular basis. The first is to set breaks in the fence—called water gaps—to allow concentrated access to limited sections of the waterway. The second option is to divert an amount of the water from the stream through a pipe to a stock tank located outside of the riparian zone. A third option is to develop multiple upland water sources at naturally occurring springs. None of these options works perfectly, and in some cases they simply shift the impacts away from the immediate riparian zone to other sensitive areas.

One of the most far-reaching riparian improvement efforts has occurred in the Gila Basin of New Mexico and Arizona. A lawsuit brought by Forest Guardians and the Center for Biological Diversity ended in a settlement agreement in April 1998, forcing the removal of 15,000 cows from 230 miles of riparian zone on Forest Service lands.

Tony Davis, *Healing the Gila*, HIGH COUNTRY NEWS, October 22, 2001. Congress allocated $400,000 to install fences along the waterways and to provide new watering stations for cows. In just three years the riparian system began to show signs of restoration, including new growth of grass and willows along the river banks. However, anti-grazing advocates contend that the relocation of cows to upland areas has shifted damage to sensitive springs. More litigation has ensued to protect those and other parts of the Gila Basin. For discussion, *see* Paul Koberstein, *The Big Dry: Gila River*, CASCADIA TIMES, Fall, 2002 at 18.

A fourth concern associated with grazing arises over habitat for imperiled species. Rangelands support a broad variety of riparian species, such as salmon, trout, minnows, and chubs, many of which are in decline as a result of grazing. Beyond the riparian-dependant species, the pigmy rabbit, sage sparrow, Townsend pocket gopher, harvest mouse, kit fox, Southwest willow flycatcher, black-tailed prairie dog, yellow-billed cuckoo, spotted bat, western jumping mouse, and many others all depend on ecosystems found on BLM lands. The sage grouse, dubbed the "spotted owl" of rangeland, is in serious decline across BLM lands in the 11 Western states where it still exists. The sage grouse relies on sagebrush habitat that is degraded by numerous ranching activities, including herbicide applications, mechanical removal of sagebrush, introduction of exotic species, and alteration of plant communities and fire regimes through grazing. Even so, in 2005, the U.S. Fish and Wildlife Service made a preliminary finding denying petitions to list the sage grouse under the ESA as "not warranted." *See* Proposed Rule, 70 Fed. Reg. 2243 (Jan. 12, 2005).

Mounting concern over the environmental harm caused by grazing on BLM lands, coupled with increased pressure to comply with federal statutes such as the Endangered Species Act and Clean Water Act, prompted the Clinton Administration to set a new environmental mandate for BLM management of its rangelands. The heart of the Rangeland Reform regulations is 43 C.F.R § 4180.1, which sets forth the "Fundamentals of Rangeland Health." The Fundamentals present a desired environmental condition for BLM lands. Section 4180.2 requires each BLM state director to make progress towards the Fundamentals by developing "standards and guidelines" that apply to the permit and lease administration process. The standards and guidelines must address matters such as watershed function, nutrient cycling and energy flow, water quality, and species habitat. 43 C.F.R. § 4180.2(d). Using a classic "hammer" regulatory strategy, the rules also set "fallback" standards that would take effect in the event state standards and guidelines were not completed by February, 1997. *See* 60 Fed. Reg. 9899 (Feb. 22, 1995). BLM was directed to "take appropriate action as soon as practicable but not later than the start of the next grazing year" to implement the standards by reducing livestock rates, adjusting the season or duration of livestock use, or modifying or relocating range improvements. 43 C.F.R. § 4180.2(c); 60 Fed. Reg. 9899. A Ninth Circuit decision gave the regu-

lations considerable bite. *See* Idaho Watersheds Project v. Hahn, 187
F.3d 1035, 1037 (9th Cir. 1999) ("The plain language of the regulation
[43 C.F.R. § 4180.2(c)] requires taking action that results in progress
toward fulfillment of ecological standards and guidelines by the start of
the next grazing year."). A proposed rule-making by the Bush II administration would extend somewhat the deadline for taking action on the
ground to comply with the standards and guidelines. 68 Fed. Reg. 68452,
68466 (Dec. 8, 2003) (to be codified at 43 C.F.R. pt. 4100). For discussion
of the Rangeland Reform standards, *see* Bruce M. Pendery, *Reforming
Livestock Grazing on the Public Domain: Ecosystem Management–Based
Standards and Guidelines Blaze a New Path for Range Management*, 27
ENVTL. L. 513 (1997); CATHY CARLSON & JOHANNA WALD, RANGELAND REFORM
REVISITED (2000).

E. Ranching to Preserve Western Open Spaces

Apart from the statutes and regulations pertaining to grazing, natural resource practitioners must deal with policy positions on a daily
basis. Because of the environmental issues associated with ranching,
some call for an end of ranching altogether on the western lands. A book
by Professor Debra L. Donahue argues that cattle should be removed
from BLM lands where there is a mean annual precipitation of 12 inches
or less. She contends that maintaining cattle on those lands compromises biodiversity concerns. DEBRA L. DONAHUE, THE WESTERN RANGE
REVISITED (1999). Another influential book, WELFARE RANCHING: THE SUBSI-
DIZED DESTRUCTION OF THE AMERICAN WEST (George Wuerthner & Mollie
Matteson, eds.) (Island Press. 2002) makes the same argument by presenting photos showing destroyed riparian areas and grasslands.

But not all environmentalists agree that grazing should end on federal public lands in the West. Grazing issues divide the environmental
community, because many believe that ranching helps protect the landscape against sprawl, deemed a far more serious threat to open space,
watershed and wildlife resources. The position of pro-grazing conservationists builds on the unique triangle of interests involved in ranching:
federal permits, base fee lands, and water rights. When a ranch loses a
federal permit or lease, it may no longer be a viable economic operation.
In that event, the rancher must sell the private fee lands and associated
water rights. Developers may buy up these lands and water rights and
create subdivisions. The result is suburban sprawl. Cities such as Boise,
Denver, Salt Lake City, Bend, and Reno typify the exploding growth
across the West—a boom from 17 million people in 1945 to over 57 million today. Urbanization pushes asphalt into areas formerly punctuated
by fences and a few outbuildings. Pro-grazing environmentalists contend
that the "uglified" landscape, water depletion, air and water pollution,
congestion, soil destruction, toxic waste, and a myriad of other impacts
are far more destructive than ranching to the natural landscape. Believing that ranchers are the last stronghold against the developers' predation on the West, this camp of environmentalists disagrees with

the cattle-free campaign to end grazing on public lands. Amidst these emerging factions of the conservation movement, a growing number of land trusts seek to protect the ranching way of life—and open space—in perpetuity through use of conservation easements.

COW-FREE CROWD IGNORES SCIENCE, SPRAWL
Ed Marston
HIGH COUNTRY NEWS, Dec. 9, 2002

The West is tiny when pitted against our imagining of it. We imagined the buffalo would never be extinguished. We imagined the beaver would never be trapped out. We imagined big trees would always stand over the next ridge. But in a short time, the mountain men and buffalo hunters and loggers rolled over this alleged vastness.

Now comes a new group of dreamers: the cattle-free movement. It believes sprawl can never conquer the West's million square miles. * * * Eighty-five percent of the federal land managed by the Forest Service and Bureau of Land Management is grazed. That's 406,000 square miles. Another estimated 170,000 square miles of private range land is attached to the public grazing lands. Together, 21,000 public land ranchers use 576,000 square miles of land.

As this land goes, so will go the 1 million square mile West. This land is going somewhere. Ranchers have been on short rations and hard times since the beginnings of the Anglo West, but never more so than now. They are an aging group, and about half of the public-land ranchers work off the ranch. If they don't come to ranching with a fortune, they usually just squeeze by.

For some, it's the only life they know. But most stick to it because it's a job that is also their play. That is part of what brings them into such fierce conflict with their fellow recreationists: the cattle-free people. * * *

The cattle-free movement is small but fierce. Among those pitted against it are reformers, some of whom are ranchers, like the Malpai Borderlands Group, which want its industry to change, and some of whom are environmentalists, like The Nature Conservancy, which believes ranching is better for habitat and wildlife than development. * * *

[Cattle-free proponents] maintai[n] that no time should be lost in removing livestock from the public's land. Once the cows are gone, [they] argue, the vegetation and wildlife will come back. The land will "rewild." [Cattle-free proponents] are able to believe in "rewilding" because they maintain a tight focus. [They] don't worry about what other interests might move onto the public land once ranchers are gone. They ignore the fact that ranchers are environmentalists' only allies in the fight against coalbed methane and off-road vehicles. * * *

One reason for the single-mindedness of the cattle-free movement is the personal bitterness created by recent history. For a century, ranchers and the West's elected officials ran the federal lands as if they were private lands, located in a separate nation called The West. * * * [T]hey used their political power to subvert the laws that should have protected the health of the land. Relicts of that lawless era are not hard to find.

* * * Given this sorry history, why should the rest of us care if 21,000 families are bought out or forced off the public land? We have 170,000 reasons to care. That is the square miles of private land—roughly Utah and Idaho put together—that may become useless as ranchland if cows are forced off the public land. This land was chosen by homesteaders because it has the deepest soils and the most water and biodiversity. It is winter range to wildlife and open space to communities. The land they didn't homestead—what is now the public land—is thin soiled, high elevation, arid. Undeveloped private ranchland is what keeps the West from becoming New Jersey with bumps.

[The cattle-free movement] rejects this argument. It argues that while cows vs. condos may be valid close to metro areas, it is invalid in most of the vast West. Unfortunately, no matter what the location, once the private ranchland has been shorn of their federal grazing allotments, someone will be willing to pay more for that private land than the rancher can to graze cows. Close to urban areas, the buyer may be a subdivider. Farther out, the demand will be for 10–acre ranchettes. And way out, it will be someone looking for 40 acres for a trailer, outbuildings and sheds.

Think of the demand for land. * * * Arizona's population grew in the 1990s by 40 percent, Colorado's and Utah's by 30 percent, and New Mexico's by 20 percent. Land use grew faster. From 1960 to 1990, Colorado's population grew at 3 percent a year, but developed land increased 8 percent. In Idaho, the figures were 1.9 percent and 7.8 percent. Like galaxies in the outer reaches of our universe, sprawl is accelerating. * * *

Sprawl can't be stopped by ranchers alone. The protection of wide open spaces is a job for all of us, from federal land managers to fire experts to rural planning commissions to land trusts. And finally, it's also up to the cattle-free people, who must become reformers and co-operators before it is too late for the West.

CATTLEMEN MAKE USE OF A CONSERVATION TOOL
Adam Burke
HIGH COUNTRY NEWS, June 21, 1999

GUNNISON, Colo.—Frost gilds the branches of the elder and cottonwood trees bordering the Redden family's pastureland as Brett Redden climbs into a tractor at dawn and delivers hay to 300 cattle. Then he goes to his "regular" job with the fire and rescue crew at Gunnison Airport. Some months he'll pick up extra work driving cattle trucks and building roads.

Redden's wife, sister, brother-in-law and mother also juggle jobs to keep the family ranch going. "At times, each one of us was working one, two, or even three jobs besides ranch work," he says, "and we were still sinking deeper and deeper into debt."

His is a familiar predicament for ranchers. Perched on the southern toes of Colorado's central mountains, Gunnison is close to national forest trails and the bustling resort town of Crested Butte, 28 miles to the north. Brett Redden has seen great swaths of grazing land around him go under the developer's knife as ranchers have sold out.

A few years ago, Redden himself considered selling the ranch to subdividers. Then, thanks to an innovative cattlemen's organization, he sold the rights to develop the ranch and saved his business. In 1997, Redden Ranches Inc. sold a conservation easement on 995 acres of the Ohio Creek Valley ranch for almost $660,000, erasing the potential for development and giving the family a sizeable tax break because the family also donated some land to the land trust. Eventually, Redden hopes to be able to quit his airport job and focus on ranching.

Redden's story marks a recent shift throughout Colorado, as agricultural landowners turn toward conservation easements as a way to stem real estate pressure and stay in business. Urban environmentalists may have developed the tool of conservation easements to preserve open space, but that tool is now firmly in the mainstream of Colorado's ranching community. * * *

Convincing cattlemen to use conservation easements has not been easy—even though easements allow ranchers to keep ranching and few land trusts require landowners to meet water-quality or rangeland standards. What convinced some was the growing pressure from several fronts. Over the last decade, many have gone out of business from mortgage debt, encroaching subdivision development, property and inheritance taxes, low beef prices and high production costs. According to the Colorado Agricultural Statistic Service, the state has lost 1.5 million acres of productive agricultural land since 1987, and 200,000 of those acres disappeared in 1996 alone.

To counter the decline, the Colorado Cattlemen's Association, a beef industry advocacy group founded 132 years ago, formed a land trust in 1995. The Colorado Cattlemen's Agricultural Land Trust, it focuses on educating ranchers about the value of conservation easements and also helps coordinate local efforts.

The problem, explains Lynne Sherrod, the group's executive director, is that ranchers are "dirt-rich and dollar-poor." Ranchland is worth a tremendous amount to developers, particularly around resort communities such as Steamboat Springs, where the land trust is based. But few ranchers have the money to pay rising property taxes, and hefty inheritance taxes—which can add up to more than 50 percent of the land's value—make it difficult to pass the land on to their children. * * * By granting the Cattlemen's Land Trust a conservation easement, ranchers guarantee that the land—and the taxes—will be valued as agricultural, not as future subdivisions. Easements also ensure that water rights stay with the land instead of being sold off to cities or developers, and that heirs can farm the land if they choose to. * * *

The Gunnison group enjoys support from the local environmental community. The High Country Citizens' Alliance runs a "Cows not Condos" campaign to emphasize its support for ranching in Gunnison County. * * *

"It's in our interest to keep ranchers in business because, at least locally, they are the best means of preserving open space," alliance president Dennis Hall asserts. "This coming together of ranchers and ecologists in Gunnison over the last few years is a sign of the times—a reaction to bigger enemies which threaten us both."

Notes and Questions

1. Some anti-grazing advocates believe that development is a threat only near growing metropolitan areas, resort towns, and retirement communities, where demand for housing is soaring. But doesn't that describe large parts of West? Are isolated areas with little housing demand the exception or the rule? How will circumstances be different 50 years into the future? Will population growth, internet access, and innovative technology (such as solar power and satellite communication) transform places previously deemed uninhabitable into magnets for settlement and, thus, development?

2. In the cows v. condos debate, pro-ranching conservationists nearly always assert that local land use controls will fail to prevent development of land that moves from ranchers' hands into other private ownership. Does their position have merit? Can local land use control prevent sprawl from overtaking the West? For an in-depth article on development threats to private rangeland in the West, *see* Jon Christensen, *Who Will Take Over the Ranch: As a Real Estate Frenzy Grips the West, Conservationists Scramble to Save a Disappearing Landscape,* HIGH COUNTRY NEWS, March 29, 2004.

3. The Nature Conservancy has developed a range program called "grassbanking" where it exchanges forage for conservation practices. For example, on its Matador Ranch in north-central Wyoming, the Nature Conservancy allows neighboring ranchers to graze for reduced grazing fees on the condition that those ranchers will maintain sound conservation practices on their own ranches. The 60,000–acre working cattle ranch is serving as the nucleus for improved management of over a quarter of a million acres in the county. For more information about this project, *see* http://nature.org/wherewework/northamerica/states/montana/preserves/art10062.html.

4. The American Farmland Trust has identified "Strategic Ranch Land at Risk in the Rocky Mountain West," to direct priorities in gaining conservation easements in ranch country. The map is located at www.farmland.org. The subject of conservation easements on private lands is addressed in Chapter 9.III.

IV. NATIONAL WILDLIFE REFUGES

Another category of public lands is the National Wildlife Refuge System, comprised of over 92 million acres of federal lands divided into

509 units located across the 50 states. Managed by the U.S. Fish and Wildlife Service (USFWS), the system includes wildlife refuges, areas for the protection of endangered species, game ranges, wildlife management areas, and waterfowl production systems. The first protective land designation came in 1868 when President Grant set aside islands in Alaska as a reserve for the northern fur seal. Subsequent designations occurred in no coherent fashion through various statutes, executive orders, and administrative declarations. These original designation documents (referred to as "establishment documents") are important, because they set forth individual purposes for which each particular area was established. Such stated purposes vary greatly, ranging from narrow, single-species missions to broad goals designed to fulfill international migratory treaty obligations. *See* Robert L. Fischman, *The National Wildlife Refuge System and the Hallmarks of Modern Organic Legislation*, 29 ECOLOGY L. Q. 457 (2002).

A. Wildlife Refuge Management Acts

Not until 1966 did Congress organize these scattered "lands, waters, and interests" into a consolidated system to be administered for the conservation of fish and wildlife. The Refuge Administration Act, 16 U.S.C. § 668dd, imposed a central requirement limiting permissible secondary uses of refuge lands to those "compatible with" the major purposes for which such areas were established. 16 U.S.C. § 668dd(d)(1)(A). This "compatibility standard" derived from and carried forth a requirement from an earlier act, the Refuge Recreation Act of 1962, that allows recreational use of refuges to the extent such uses are "not inconsistent with" and do "not interfere with" the primary purposes for which the protected areas were established. 16 U.S.C. § 460k. The inquiry of whether a particular secondary use is "compatible" with the purposes of the refuge requires analysis of the establishment document creating the refuge. Because the seemingly generic "compatibility" standard of the 1966 Act bootstraps to the widely variable purposes expressed in individual establishment documents, it actually detracts from a coherent national management approach towards refuge lands. For litigation over secondary refuge uses, *see* Defenders of Wildlife v. Andrus (Ruby Lake II), 455 F.Supp. 446 (D. D.C. 1978) (Secretary's rule permitting boating in refuge violated Refuge Recreation Act because use was not compatible with, and interfered with, the primary purpose of the refuge); National Audubon Society v. Babbitt, No. C92–1641 (W.D. Wash.) (consolidated compatibility challenges across multiple refuges) (settlement agreement filed Oct. 22, 1993).

In Practice:
Understanding the Bureaucratic Structure

The U.S. Fish and Wildlife Service (USFWS) is an agency within the U.S. Department of Interior. Policy driving the agency's management practices comes from the Secretary of Interior, who also oversees BLM, the Bureau of Reclamation, the National Park Service, and the Bureau of Indian Affairs (BIA). The Solicitor of the United States provides legal advice to all of these agencies. It is important to understand that sometimes the missions of the Interior agencies are mutually incompatible with respect to shared resources. This is particularly true in the area of water rights. In the Klamath Basin of Oregon, for example, the USFWS competes with the Bureau of Reclamation and the Klamath Tribe (represented by BIA) for water rights to serve four refuges. *See generally* Reed Benson, *Giving Suckers (and Salmon) an Even Break: Klamath Basin Water and the Endangered Species Act*, 25 TUL. ENVTL. L. J. 197 (2002). As a practical matter, the Secretary of Interior resolves these inter-agency disputes politically, reconciling them into a unified Interior priority that guides the U.S. Department of Justice in its representation of the federal government in water rights adjudications. *See* Robert L. Fischman, *The National Wildlife Refuge System and the Hallmarks of Modern Organic Legislation*, 29 ECOLOGY L. Q. 457, 576 n. 659 (2002). The refuges are often lower on the priority ladder and fail to receive sufficient water during low flow conditions. *See* Michael Milstein, *Klamath Refuges Go Thirsty: Life Sustaining Wetlands for Migrating Birds Are Drying Up at Alarming Rates*, THE OREGONION, July 13, 2001, at 1. The federal government's "one voice" approach to water issues can be frustrating to the many constituencies represented by different missions of the federal agencies. Behind the scenes, the political maneuvering between the various agency heads, the Secretary of Interior, the Solicitor, and the Department of Justice can be fierce. To be effective, the modern natural resource practitioner must be plugged into these dynamics.

In 1989 the General Accounting Office delivered a stinging report on USFWS's management of the refuge system, concluding that the agency was allowing harmful secondary uses—such as boating, grazing, timber harvest, and public use—on 59% of the refuges. *See* U.S. GENERAL ACCOUNTING OFFICE, NATIONAL WILDLIFE REFUGES: CONTINUING PROBLEMS WITH INCOMPATIBLE USES CALL FOR BOLD ACTION, GAO/T–RCED–89–196 (1989). In response, President Clinton issued Executive Order 12,996 in 1996 to reform refuge management and establish an overriding mission to manage the lands and waters for conservation. The action was in step with a broad set of environmental reforms the Clinton Administration pursued in the context of public lands management.

Prompted into action by the Executive Order, Congress enacted a foundational statute for the management of refuge lands in 1997. Passed as amendments to the 1966 Refuge Administration Act, the Refuge Improvement Act takes its place with FLPMA and NFMA as a primary land management statute. It establishes an overriding mission for the USFWS "to administer a national network of lands and waters for the conservation, management, and where appropriate, restoration of the fish, wildlife, and plant resources and their habitats within the United States for the benefit of present and future generations of Americans." 16 U.S.C. § 668dd(a)(2). Like other land management statutes, it requires the USFWS to develop land use plans (called "comprehensive conservation plans") to direct activities within the managed area. Such plans must be revised every 15 years, or earlier if "conditions that affect the refuge or planning unit have changed significantly." 16 U.S.C. § 668dd(e). The planning requirement triggers NEPA and also the ESA if listed species are located within the planning area. The statute makes clear that the final plans create binding management prescriptions: "[T]he Secretary shall manage the refuge or planning unit in a manner consistent with the plan." 16 U.S.C. § 668dd(e)(1)(E).

The compatibility standard continues to play a central role in the amended act. 16 U.S.C. § 668dd(d)(1)(A) (allowing only refuge uses that are "compatible with the major purposes for which [refuges] were established."). The Act defines "compatible use" as a "wildlife-dependent recreational use or any other use of a refuge that, in the sound professional judgment of the [USFWS] will not materially interfere with or detract from the fulfillment of the mission of the System or the purposes of the refuge." 16 U.S.C. § 668ee(1). In a provision that adds flesh to the standard, Congress required USFWS to make a compatibility determination before initiating or permitting a new use of a refuge or expanding, renewing, or extending an existing use. 16 U.S.C. § 668dd(d)(3)(A). Compatibility determinations must be made in writing, subject to public input. § 16 U.S.C. 668dd(d)(3)(B).

The Act also sets forth a preferred use of "compatible wildlife-dependent recreation," which must receive priority consideration over general uses in refuge planning. 16 U.S.C. §§ 668dd(a)(3)(A),(B),(C); (a)(4)(H). Wildlife-dependent recreation is defined as "a use of a refuge involving hunting, fishing, wildlife observation and photography, or environmental education and interpretation." 16 USC § 668ee(2). Beyond prioritizing this type of recreation as a refuge use, the USFWS must facilitate and provide opportunities for such recreation. 16 U.S.C. § 668dd(a)(3)(D). The recreation must, of course, meet the compatibility standard.

In mandatory language, the Act directs the USFWS to administer the refuge system according to 14 explicit standards, four of which focus on prioritizing wildlife-dependent recreational use. Significant others are excerpted below.

In administering the System, the Secretary shall—

(A) provide for the conservation of fish, wildlife, and plants, and their habitats within the System;

(B) ensure that the biological integrity, diversity, and environmental health of the System are maintained for the benefit of present and future generations of Americans;

(C) plan and direct the continued growth of the System in a manner that is best designed to accomplish the mission of the System, to contribute to the conservation of the ecosystems of the United States ... ;

(D) ensure that the mission of the System and the purposes of each refuge are carried out...; * * *

(F) assist in the maintenance of adequate water quantity and water quality to fulfill the mission of the System and the purposes of each refuge;

(G) acquire, under State law, water rights that are needed for refuge purposes; * * *

(N) monitor the status and trends of fish, wildlife, and plants in each refuge.

16 U.S.C. § 668dd(a)(4).

In 2000, USFWS issued final compatibility regulations under the amended statute. *See* Final Compatibility Regulations Pursuant to the National Wildlife Refuge System Improvement Act of 1997, 65 Fed. Reg. 62458 (Oct. 18, 2000). The agency also issued a "biological integrity, diversity, and environmental health policy" as an addition to the USFWS Manual, to provide guidance on carrying out the environmental health standard of § 668dd(a)(4)(B), above. 66 Fed. Reg. 3,810 (Jan. 16, 2001); USFWS Manual, 601 FW 3, *available at* http://policy.fws.gov. In his leading commentary on the Refuge Improvement Act, Professor Robert Fischman describes why this standard, as interpreted by the agency in its policy, is a vanguard of public lands management.

THE NATIONAL WILDLIFE REFUGE SYSTEM AND THE HALLMARKS OF MODERN ORGANIC LEGISLATION
Robert L. Fischman
29 ECOLOGY L. Q. 457, 563, 568–70, 620 (2002)

[T]the Improvement Act's ecological mandate to ensure the maintenance of "biological integrity, diversity, and environmental health" catapults the Refuge System to the front lines of conservation biology. * * * No other organic mandate employs such unconditional, specific ecological criteria to constrain management and promote conservation. * * *

An important new manual provision states that "refuge managers should address" threats to biological integrity, diversity, and environmental health that originate from actions that occur outside of the refuge boundary. The manual advises refuge managers to seek redress before local planning and zoning boards, and state administrative and regulatory agencies if voluntary or collaborative attempts to forge solutions do not work. Though tempered by cautionary language, these are nonetheless bold instructions for a traditionally timid agency.

The external threat to public lands is one of the most serious challenges facing conservation. Moreover, because so many refuges are at the lower reaches of watersheds, compared to national forests and national parks, the Refuge System faces particularly difficult problems that necessitate work outside of boundaries to stem degradation. For instance, chemical run-off and soil erosion from upstream farm practices threaten refuge conservation in the Upper Mississippi River refuge. The state of Louisiana has issued a fish consumption advisory for the Upper Ouachita National Wildlife Refuge due to mercury levels in the fish. Oil and gas development, industrial effluent, and contaminated sediment runoff are all likely external sources of the mercury. * * * How the Service responds to these external threats will be an early indication of the effectiveness of the strong language in the refuge policy to secure biological integrity, diversity and environmental health. * * *

The mandate to maintain biological integrity, diversity, and environmental health establishes a path-breaking precedent for public land management. * * * This is an overdue statutory recognition that public lands play central roles in providing the ecosystem services (such as pollination and nutrient cycling) on which humans are utterly dependent. The mandate is also a recognition of the value of natural diversity and ecological health as ends in themselves, even if we cannot trace their direct benefit to our welfare. As a substantive management criterion supporting the Refuge System mission, this mandate reflects a change in the relative importance that the functioning of nature plays in our public land use decisions.

Pelican Island National Wildlife Refuge, Florida. *Source*: USWFS, http://images.fws.gov/.

Notes and Questions

1. Are the new statutory standards, or "criteria," in the Refuge Improvement Act, 16 U.S.C. § 668dd(a)(4), enforceable? How do they relate to the land use plans mandated by the same statute? Consider Professor Fischman's analysis of the Act's criteria:

The criteria help shape plans but apply to refuge activities irrespective of the plans. A specific management action, even if consistent with a plan, may still run afoul of the Improvement Act if it would violate a substantive management criterion. * * *

The criteria are also important because they will be footholds for litigation over management of the System. Given the tradition of deference to the proprietary discretion of federal land management agencies, these substantive footholds are crucial in spurring courts to review federal resource management decisions.

Id. at 544–45.

The refuge standards are at least as explicit as many found in NFMA. In light of the experience under NFMA, how do you think courts will respond to citizen efforts seeking to enforce the refuge standards?

2.   Note the mandate in 16 U.S.C. § 66dd(a)(4)(C) to grow the Refuge System. How can USFWS accomplish that? Beyond funding, will it need to devise innovative approaches to gaining property rights on behalf of the public? Increasingly the USFWS is receiving conservation easements over private property to protect habitat values. Such conservation easements create an overlay of public property rights on private fee land, allowing a refuge system to expand out towards ecosystem boundaries without the full conversion of private land into public land. Easements can be essential where private property adjoining a refuge could be used in a manner harmful to refuge values. Such easements may or may not provide for public access, depending on the landowner's preference and the agency's goals. Conservation easements are discussed in Chapter 9.III.

3.   Water depletion is a classic external threat affecting many reservations. Standard (G) above requires the USFWS to affirmatively act to acquire water rights on behalf of the refuges. 16 U.S.C. § 66dd(a)(4)(G). Professor Fischman calls this "the only affirmative trust mandate of its kind in U.S. organic legislation." Fischman, *supra,* at 591. Refuge water rights are recognized under the doctrine of federally reserved water rights, explained in Chapters 5.III and 14. The 1966 Refuge Administration Act treats water rights as a key part of the wildlife refuges. *See* 16 U.S.C. § 668dd(a)(1) (consolidating "all lands, waters, and interests therein administered ... as wildlife refuges...."). But acquiring water rights in scarce conditions is a challenge. This is particularly true since most federal reserved water rights are determined as part of a state adjudication in a forum not necessarily receptive to federal interests. *See* 43 U.S.C. § 666 (2003) (allowing federal government to be joined as a party in state court water rights adjudications). In United States v. Idaho, 135 Idaho 655, 23 P.3d 117 (2001), the Idaho Supreme Court denied federally reserved water rights for the Deer Flat National Wildlife Refuge, consisting of 95 islands distributed along 110 miles of the Snake River. Dewatering the islands allows predators to access critical nesting habitat for migratory birds. The court reasoned that the primary purpose of the refuge was to protect birds from hunters:

Hunting is still prohibited and migratory birds still have a sanctuary without a federally reserved water right. Without water there would be no island, but there would [still] be a sanctuary.... One can assume that there was an expectation that the islands would remain surrounded by water, but that does not equate to an intent to reserve a federal water right to accomplish that purpose.

Id. at 126.

The court found that the purposes of providing isolation from predators, proximity to open water, and riparian habitat were "secondary" and would not support a federally reserved water right under United States v. New Mexico, 438 U.S. 696, 702, 98 S.Ct. 3012, 3015, 57 L.Ed.2d 1052, 1058 (1978). *Idaho*, 23 P.3d at 128.

4. Recreational conflicts on wildlife refuges are explored in detail in Chapter 15 (Preservation and Recreation).

> ***Exercise:***
>
> Assume you work for the U.S. Department of Interior as an attorney advising the USFWS on refuge management. A national wildlife refuge in Wisconsin, established primarily to provide habitat for migratory water-fowl, is located adjacent to a private duck hunting reserve called Mal-lard's Way. Lead shot was allowed at Mallard's Way for several decades and has severely contaminated the ponds that the ducks use. The con-tamination has spread to a stream that flows onto the refuge. Provide advice on what duty, if any, the USFWS has to address the situation and whether the USFWS is subject to citizen enforcement under the Adminis-trative Procedure Act (APA) for failure to address this threat.

B. Cooperative Federalism in the Wildlife Refuge System

Because wildlife is migratory, the USFWS must often coordinate refuge management with other sovereigns. The case below, which has the most comprehensive treatment of the Refuge Improvement Act to date, explores federal-state tensions.

WYOMING v. UNITED STATES

United States Court of Appeals, Tenth Circuit, 2002.

279 F.3d 1214.

Once again a federal court is called upon to unravel a congressionally-legislated Federal–State standoff. The National Elk Ref-uge (NER), a part of the National Wildlife Refuge System (NWRS), encompasses approximately 24,700 acres of wilderness north of Jackson Hole, Wyoming, in the greater Yellowstone area. Brucellosis, a serious disease that causes miscarriage, is endemic to free-ranging elk in the greater Yellowstone area and a threat to Wyoming's domestic cattle industry. Plaintiff State of Wyoming and the United States Fish and Wildlife Service (FWS) ... disagree over how best to manage brucellosis on the NER. Specifically, the State challenges the FWS's refusal to per-mit the State to vaccinate elk on the NER with a brucellosis vaccine known as "Strain 19." According to the FWS, after several years of research and study, the biosafety and efficacy of Strain 19 vis-a-vis elk remain unproven. The State disagrees.

Resolution of this matter ultimately rests upon our construction of the National Wildlife Refuge System Improvement Act of 1997 (NWR-SIA)(codified at 16 U.S.C. §§ 668dd–668ee). Unfortunately, the NWR-SIA does not (nor does any federal law) directly address the problem of brucellosis in wildlife, or establish clear priority between wildlife and domestic livestock when interests involving the two conflict. In the jurisdictionally-fragmented Yellowstone area, however, one thing is certain: Wildlife management policies affecting the interests of multiple sovereigns demand a high degree of inter-governmental cooperation. Such cooperation is conspicuously absent in this case. * * *

Authorities first detected brucellosis in elk in the greater Yellowstone area around 1930. Today, brucellosis infects approximately thirty percent of the elk in western Wyoming. Thus, significant levels of brucellosis still occur in the [elk] population on the NER. Experts estimate that the annual elk calf loss due to brucellosis-related abortions on the NER is seven percent of the calf crop.

The concentration of free-ranging elk herds on Wyoming and NER winter feed grounds appears to perpetuate brucellosis. The feed grounds, which host around 25,000 elk each winter, are prime locations for the transmission of brucellosis because the herds are in close contact during the critical birthing period. Because natural winter habitat in the region is not adequate to sustain the elk herds at their current numbers, closing the feed grounds would foster competition, which appears to increase the risk of brucellosis transmission.

The primary significance of brucellosis-related abortions in Wyoming's elk herds is the potential for transmission of the disease to domestic cattle. Elk and other wildlife in the greater Yellowstone area do not respect jurisdictional boundaries. Instead, wildlife wanders freely across the region's public and private lands. Experts explain that the creation of artificial barriers to separate domestic cattle from wild elk is not feasible. * * *

Thus, the impetus behind Wyoming's desire to eradicate brucellosis in elk is the potential for economic loss to its domestic cattle industry. Experts estimate that from 1951 to 1981, brucellosis cost the nation's cattle industry $1.6 billion. Another estimate places that cost at $100 million annually. * * *

We ... focus on whether the FWS's decision was "arbitrary, capricious, an abuse of discretion, or otherwise not in accordance with law." 5 U.S.C. § 706(2)(A). * * *

The provisions of the APA are applicable except to the extent that— (1) statutes preclude judicial review; or (2) agency action is committed to agency discretion by law. 5 U.S.C. § 701(a). * * *

Congress undoubtedly did not intend its call for "effective coordination, interaction, and cooperation with owners of land adjoining refuges and the fish and wildlife agenc[ies] of the State," 16 U.S.C.

§ 668dd(a)(4)(e), a theme running throughout the NWRSIA, to constitute merely a recommendation which the FWS might ignore with impunity. [W]e reject any suggestion that Congress "committed to agency discretion by law" the FWS's decision to deny the State of Wyoming's request. * * * Simply put, "[t]here is law to apply" in this case. Congress throughout the NWRSIA has indicated an intent to circumscribe the FWS's discretion. The requirement that the FWS in developing a conservation plan for each refuge comply with State policies and objectives to the "extent" or "maximum extent practicable," *id.* §§ 668dd(e), undoubtedly places limits on the agency's discretion. *See Random House Dictionary* 1517 (2d ed.1987) (defining "practicable" as "capable of being done, effected, or put into practice, with the available means").

Additionally, in determining whether a proposed "use" of a refuge constitutes a "compatible use," *i.e.,* a use that "will not materially interfere with or detract from the fulfillment of the mission of the System or the purposes of the refuge," the NWRSIA directs the Secretary to exercise "sound professional judgment." 16 U.S.C. § 668ee(1). The NWRSIA defines the phrase "sound professional judgment" as "a finding, determination, or decision that is consistent with principles of sound fish and wildlife management and administration, available science and resources, and adherence to the requirements of this Act and other applicable laws." *Id.* § 668ee(3). * * *

Clearly then, nothing in the NWRSIA or its legislative history indicates that Congress sought to preclude judicial review of the FWS's decision in this case. * * * Accordingly, we conclude that § 701(a) of the APA does not preclude judicial review of the FWS's decision to deny the State of Wyoming's request to vaccinate elk on the NER with Strain 19. * * *

[W]e have little difficulty concluding that the State of Wyoming states a claim for relief .... If, as the State suggests, the Strain 19 vaccine is a safe and effective means of containing brucellosis in freeranging elk, and the FWS has no viable alternative means of reducing the high rate of brucellosis-infected elk on the NER, then the FWS decision to deny the State's request to vaccinate elk on the NER with Strain 19 may very well be "arbitrary, capricious, an abuse of discretion, or otherwise not in accordance with law." 5 U.S.C. § 706(2)(A). Thus, we conclude that the district court erred in dismissing Count III for failure to state a claim upon which relief may be granted. * * *

As we recently recognized, "[h]abitat management is a delicate venture." To make matters worse, jurisdictional allocation regarding wildlife management within the NWRS is a legal quagmire. Unfortunately, the NWRSIA with its broad language and general directives is not particularly helpful in resolving any particular conflict, especially where resolution of that conflict, whether agreed upon or court ordered, will inevitably affect the interests of dual sovereigns. To that extent, wildlife management is inherently political. Thus, wildlife managers simply cannot view wildlife management in isolation, as the FWS appears to be doing in this instance. * * * Given the NWRSIA's repeated calls for a "cooperative federalism," we find inexcusable the parties' unwillingness in this case to even attempt to amicably resolve the brucellosis controversy or find any common ground on which to commence fruitful negotiations.

To be sure, deference to agency action is appropriate "where that action implicates scientific and technical judgments within the scope of agency expertise." The problem is that after an extended period of time, the FWS still appears unable or unwilling to make any judgment regarding the biosafety and efficacy of Strain 19 as applied to free-ranging elk. But the law requires answers. For instance, the FWS has never explained why the State's proposal would "stand as an obstacle to the accomplishment and execution" of federal objectives. Due to health and safety concerns, the FWS effectively pulled the plug on the State's vaccination of elk on the NER after a trial run from 1989–1991. That was over a decade ago and the FWS has yet to resolve these concerns. * * *

We reverse the district court's dismissal of Count III ... and remand this matter to the district court for "full plenary review" of the FWS's decision.... * * *

Notes and Questions

1.   In an earlier portion of the opinion, the court addressed the matter of Constitutional authority over wildlife. The State had argued that it had the power to manage the wildlife on federal public lands under the Tenth Amendment of the Constitution, which provides: "The powers not delegated to the United States by the Constitution, nor prohibited by it to the States, are reserved to the States respectively...." The 10th Circuit solidly rejected this argument, applying Kleppe v. New Mexico, 426 U.S. 529, 96 S.Ct. 2285, 49 L.Ed.2d 34 (1976):

> Historically, States have possessed "broad trustee and police powers over the ... wildlife within their borders, including ... wildlife found on Federal lands within a State." But those powers are not constitutionally-based. The Property Clause of the United States Constitution delegates to Congress (thus the Tenth Amendment does not reserve to the States) "the Power to dispose of and make all needful Rules and Regulations respecting the Territory or other Property belonging to the United States." U.S. Const. art. IV, § 3, cl. 2. * * *

> Notably, Congress' power in this regard is "plenary." State jurisdiction over federal land "does not extend to any matter that is not consistent with full power in the United States to protect its lands, to control their use and to prescribe in what manner others may acquire rights in them." If Congress so chooses, federal legislation ... necessarily override[s] and preempt[s] conflicting state laws, policies, and objectives under the Constitution's Supremacy Clause, U.S. Const. art. VI, cl. 2. * * *

> In our view, *the "complete power" that Congress has over public lands necessarily includes the power to regulate and protect the wildlife living there.*

Wyoming v. United States, 279 F.3d 1214, 1226–28 (10th Cir. 2002) (some citations omitted) (emphasis in original).

By concluding that the " 'complete power' that Congress has over public lands necessarily includes the power to regulate and protect the wildlife living there," does the court imply that the federal government has an ownership interest in the wildlife itself, not just in the lands supporting the wildlife? Basic ownership questions underlie the vast reach of wildlife law, which is covered in Chapter 14, *infra*.

2. As the *Wyoming* case demonstrates, migratory wildlife patterns give rise to some of the most vexing questions of sovereign authority. Like the elk in Wyoming, bison in Montana have generated considerable litigation because of the potential of carrying disease across borders. When the bison herd in Yellowstone National Park exceeds the Park's carrying capacity of about 2,500 bison, the herd typically migrates outside the Park in search of additional forage, creating the same sort of federal-state conflict that was center-stage in the Wyoming case. The general solution has been a cooperative plan between the National Park Service and the state of Montana for "boundary management" of the herd, a major component of which is killing bison that migrate outside Park boundaries. During the harsh winter of 1996–97, 1,100 bison were killed by federal personnel. For litigation involving bison, *see* Intertribal Bison Coop. v. Babbitt, 25 F.Supp.2d 1135 (D. Mont. 1998), *aff'd* 175 F.3d 1149 (9th Cir. 1999) (upholding 1996 Interim Plan as consistent with both NEPA and the APA); Greater Yellowstone Coalition v. Babbitt, 952 F.Supp. 1435 (D. Mont. 1996), *aff'd* 108 F.3d 1385 (9th Cir. 1997) (denying request to enjoin the capture and removal of bison within the park); Fund for Animals v. Clark, 27 F.Supp.2d 8 (D. D.C. 1998) (granting preliminary injunction against organized bison hunt on federal lands).

3. In 1980, the federal government took a hands-off approach to the state of Alaska's "wolf-kill program" that entailed gunning down from aircraft 170 wolves for the purpose of increasing moose herds. The program included substantial wolf kill on federal lands over which BLM exercised control under FLPMA. In Defenders of Wildlife v. Andrus, 627 F.2d 1238, 1243–44 (D.C. Cir. 1980), the D.C. Circuit held that the federal government's inaction in failing to prevent the wolf kill on federal land did not trigger NEPA.

> Our discussion ... centers around the fact that, while the plain language of [NEPA] calls for an impact statement when there is "major Federal action," here it is the Secretary's *inaction* which is complained of. * * * [I]n no published opinion of which we have been made aware has a court held that there is "federal action" where an agency has done nothing more than fail to prevent the other party's action from occurring.

Does this opinion take a superficial approach to the difficult issue of inter-sovereign control over wildlife populations? Could you make an argument that the federal government has an affirmative *duty* to protect the wolf population on federal lands, either because it has a sovereign trust ownership interest in the wolf population, or because wolves are an integral part of the property over which the federal government has ownership and control under the Property Clause? If such an ownership interest and concomitant duty of protection exist, does failure to carry out an affirmative duty fall into the same category as other "inaction" under NEPA? Does FLPMA raise such a duty? How would that duty be enforced, following Norton v. Southern Utah Wilderness Alliance, 542 U.S. 55, 124 S. Ct. 2373, 159 L.Ed.2d 137 (2004)?

4. Sovereign issues over wildlife are not limited to the federal and state governments. Increasingly, tribes assert a historic interest in wildlife populations on and off federal lands. A tribe may have an interest in a species found on federal lands because that land was part of the tribe's aboriginal territory and the species played an important role in the tribe's culture and/or economy, or it may have an interest in preserving habitat on federal lands for a species currently harvested. Over the last decade, the federal government has taken initiatives to involve tribes in species co-management off the reservations. The 1994 Tribal Self–Governance Act allows tribes to receive annual funding agreements for programs, services and functions administered by Department of Interior agencies, including USFWS. 25 U.S.C. §§ 458aa–458hh. The program must be in an area of "specific geographic, historical, or cultural significance" to the tribe. 25 U.S.C. § 458cc(c). In April 2003, the Secretary identified 34 National Parks and 19 National Wildlife Refuges, hatcheries, and similar operations that could be eligible for tribal funding agreements. 67 Fed. Reg. 16431 (April 5, 2002).

C. The Artic National Wildlife Refuge—A Special Case

Caribou Herds Crossing the Arctic National Wildlife Refuge. *Source:* USFWS, http://arctic.fws.gov/scenes.html.

Tucked in the northeast corner of Alaska, the Arctic National Wildlife Refuge (ANWR) encompasses 19.8 million acres and spans six different ecological zones, all above the Arctic Circle. Established in 1960 by Public Land Order 2214 for the purpose of "preserving unique wildlife, wilderness and recreational values," ANWR initially contained 8.9 million acres. The balance of ANWR lands was added with the passage of the Alaska National Interest Lands Conversation Act (ANILCA) in 1980, 16 U.S.C. §§ 3101–3233. Long thought of as the last American wilderness, ANWR is an intact ecosystem hosting a spectacular array of mammals, including grizzly bear, polar bear, muskoxen, dall sheep, wolverine, snowshoe hare, arctic fox, lynx, and gray wolf. ANWR's coastal plain, an exceptionally verdant 100–mile long strip of land wedged between the Brooks range and the Beaufort Sea, is the calving grounds for the huge Porcupine caribou herd, which migrates between the Refuge and the Yukon and Northwest Territories. ANWR also serves as a breeding ground or migration stop for 180 bird species. ANWR is the homeland of native cultures, including the Inupiat Eskimos and the Athabascan Indians.

In addition to the biological wealth of ANWR, the area contains potentially valuable oil reserves that the oil industry has long coveted. *See* Chapter 2.I.A. and III, *supra*. In ANILCA, Congress explicitly barred oil and gas leasing, development, and production from ANWR "until authorized by (a separate) Act of Congress." ANILCA, Sec. 1003, 16 U.S.C. § 3143. However, Congress recognized at least the potential for oil and gas production in ANWR and authorized exploratory activity within the coastal plain. ANILCA, Sec. 1002(a), 16 U.S.C § 3142(a). Such exploratory activity is to occur only "in a manner that avoids significant adverse effects on the fish and wildlife and other resources." *Id.* If oil and gas exploration, development, or production does occur, the Secretary of the Interior is required to work closely with the State of Alaska and with representatives of indigenous populations to evaluate impacts on wildlife populations. The Secretary must also coordinate with Canadian authorities to evaluate impacts "particularly with respect to the Porcupine caribou herd." ANILCA, Sec. 1005, 16 U.S.C. § 3145(a). Advocates for opening ANWR to further exploration and subsequent oil production have urged that such activities can be done without undue disruption to wildlife or wilderness values, but wildlife researchers and conservationists warn that ANWR energy development could endanger caribou and other species such as polar bears, bowhead and beluga whales, and bearded, ringed, and spotted seals.

For two decades after ANILCA was passed, the politics did not align to open up ANWR to oil drilling. But early in the Bush II administration, President George W. Bush, a former Texas oilman, and Vice President Cheney (former CEO of one of the world's largest oil services companies) declared their intention to open ANWR to oil development. The announcement triggered nation-wide opposition among conservation groups. *See* Justin Blum, *Senate Backs Drilling in Wild Alaska Refuge,* Washington Post, March 17, 2005. ANWR's singularly wild features now hang in the balance of Congressional politics. Is oil and gas development the type of activity that would be considered "compatible" with this refuge, or with the system as a whole, per 16 U.S.C. § 668dd(d)(1)(A)?

For commentary, *see* Robert W. Corbisier, *The Arctic National Wildlife Refuge, Correlative Rights, and Sourdough: Not Just for Bread Anymore,* 19 Alaska L. Rev. 393 (2002). For a helpful guide to ANILCA, *see* The Wilderness Society, Alaska National Conservation Act Citizen's Guide

(2001). For updates on the ANWR developments, consult the USFWS web page on ANWR, at http://arctic.fws.gov.

Chapter 2.I.A and III, *supra*, describe the divergent national, state, and native perspectives on the issue. The articles below provide additional detail. As you read them, consider how the various ownership interests bear upon this controversy.

A FIERCE FIGHT FOR ALASKA'S RICHES
Marego Athans
BALTIMORE SUN, May 6, 2001, at A1

Here on the edge of the Arctic National Wildlife Refuge on Alaska's North Slope, the temperature 30 below zero on this sunny day on the cusp of spring, people seem content to operate in a separate orbit from the rest of the country.

But now, this remote and isolated spot, closer to the North Pole than Washington, D.C., finds itself in the midst of a national debate. On one side, oil companies clamor to tap the billions of barrels of oil said to lie beneath the refuge. On the other side, environmentalists say drilling will despoil one of North America's last pristine ecosystems. This is land where 129,000 caribou migrate each year to their calving grounds, where polar bears come to den, and wolves, wolverines, arctic foxes, geese, millions of migratory birds and many other species come to feed on an explosion of growth that emerges after the winter freeze on the Arctic tundra. * * *

One reason so many Alaskans favor opening ANWR is that they have a vested interest in future oil production. Thanks to oil, each of the state's 626,000 residents gets a $2,000 annual check, just for living here, from the state's $26 billion Permanent Fund, fed by revenues collected from Prudhoe Bay oil. Thanks to oil, they pay no income tax, no state sales tax.

But that bounty is threatened because Prudhoe Bay's production is declining after nearly a quarter-century of pumping—from a peak of 2 million barrels a day in 1988 to just half that today—and the Permanent Fund is edging into the red, paying out more than it's earning.

For decades, Alaska's economy has depended on the extraction of natural resources: oil and gas drilling, logging, fishing, mining and hunting. But most of all oil, which contributed $2.4 billion to state coffers last year, financing 80 percent of the state budget. Oil has made possible a busy network of air travel—jets, bush planes, float planes—that transports ordinary citizens around a vast state, one-fifth the size of the continental United States and much of it devoid of roads. Oil has turned this wild and remote place into a modern society, with satellite dishes in rural villages and money to send high school basketball teams on chartered planes to basketball tournaments at more than $10,000 a trip. Anchorage, population 260,000, has a $70 million performing arts center, a municipal library, a convention center and arena—all built by state money amid the oil boom.

If the oil dividends can make life almost cushy, they also foster a certain dependency in a state that proclaims its rugged independence. Despite the extreme climate they endure, Alaskans have become among the most cosseted of Americans. They get more money from the federal government per capita than the residents of any other state—$8,521, according to a census survey last year. This is partly because so much of the state (68 percent) is made up of federal lands ....

* * *

How much oil lies beneath ANWR is in dispute. * * * Even under the most optimistic projection, the North Slope would account for only about 10 percent of the United States' current consumption of about 20 million barrels of crude oil and petroleum products daily. * * *

TWO SIDES OF THE OIL DRILLING DEBATE
Marego Athans
BALTIMORE SUN, May 7, 2001, at A1

* * * Here, just south of the Arctic National Wildlife Refuge, live 125 Gwich'in Indians, people who for centuries have lived off the caribou that migrate through their land each year on their way to and from calving grounds in the refuge. In many ways, the Gwich'in still live as their ancestors did, in houses that have no running water or indoor heating. Plumbing is basically an indoor outhouse system, employing what are euphemistically called "honey buckets." There are no roads in and out, only a small, snow-covered landing strip. Most significantly at the moment, there are no oil dividends—and that's fine for a tribe that resists being tainted by the modern world.

On the other side of the Brooks Range, on the Arctic Ocean, live the Inupiat Eskimos of Kaktovik, population 250, another group of Native Alaskans struggling to maintain their centuries-old language and traditions against the onslaught of the 21st century. Just a generation or so away from the nomadic hunter's life, the Inupiat have reaped a fortune from the oil that flows from the vast Prudhoe Bay oil fields to the west— and now have a fire station, a community center, a police department, a water plant, a power plant, a municipal services building and a modern school that recently spent $11,000 to send its basketball teams on a chartered plane to a regional tournament.

The two Native Alaskan groups stand on opposite sides of the debate over drilling in the remote refuge. They are living symbols of what stands to be lost, and gained, from drilling in the fragile Arctic tundra— whether a lifestyle long intertwined with the wanderings of a caribou herd can be sustained, or whether that must give way to America's energy needs by accepting drilling in the ANWR, as the refuge is commonly called.

For centuries, the Gwich'in have relied on the Porcupine caribou herd, now 129,000 strong. Caribou meat, skin, fur and bones have been a primary source of food, clothing and shelter here, and the animal is a cultural and spiritual symbol. The Gwich'in people, as well as many scientists and environmentalists, fear that opening the refuge to oil interests will harm the delicate ecosystem and disrupt the caribou's migration pattern, which takes the herd from the Porcupine River Valley in Canada's Yukon Territory to its summer calving grounds in ANWR.

"To make people in the Lower 48 understand what caribou mean to us—it's like their house, their job. To me, it's part of living, just like water, air, breathing, that basic human feeling about living," said Arctic Village resident Calvin Tritt, who grew up watching his grandfather train a telescope on the Brooks Range each July and remembers the excitement in the village when the tribal elder announced the first caribou coming over the mountain on their way south from the coastal plain.

In Kaktovik, to the north on the Arctic Ocean, people are wedded to a modern lifestyle, and they are worried that without a boost in new oil revenue, the village buildings and infrastructure will deteriorate. "It's an easy life, not like it used to be," said Isaac Akootchook, 79, an Inupiat elder and Presbyterian minister who lived in a sod house as a child and remembers spending much of his day hauling ice for drinking water and wood for fire. * * *

[The] 7,000 Gwich'in Indians living in Alaska and Northwest Canada in small villages along the Porcupine caribou's migratory route, say that greed has driven the Inupiat and other Native Alaskans to sell out. * * * On advice from the tribe's elders, the Gwich'in opted out of the Alaska Native Claims Settlement Act of 1971, refusing to give up their claims to 1.8 million acres on the edge of ANWR. Under the act, most Native Alaskans, including the Inupiat, yielded tribal claims to state and federal land in Alaska in return for a cash settlement of $965 million and stock in native-owned corporations, which gained title to some land and the underlying mineral deposits. Some of these corporations foundered, but others have flourished, paying dividends to native shareholders. The Inupiat of Kaktovik received title to more than 92,000 acres, most of it in ANWR. * * *

The Gwich'in have opposed opening ANWR each time the idea has come up over the years. Now that it has become a full-scale political and public relations war in Washington, the village is getting new visitors.

"We've had senators and congressmen come to Arctic Village and say, 'You'll all be rich if you just support us opening ANWR,'" said Evon Peter, the 25-year-old elected village chief, who—with short-cropped hair, a hooded sweatshirt and camouflage pants, looks like a university student.

"They say, 'We can guarantee you all six-figure incomes. * * * We usually just give them a plate of caribou meat and say, 'Enjoy.'"

"One way to look at it is a human rights issue," Peter said. "Caribou—we live off the meat, the clothing, the skin, the fur. Our life is tied to them. * * * A threat to them is a threat to us...."

On a larger scale—and speaking from his own experience studying the history of Native Americans—Peter relates the drilling effort to "colonization, subjugation and enslavement."

"They've taken it to a new, modern, technical, politically correct level," he said, "but the push is to find resources that create more wealth for them and displace the indigenous people."

V. PARKS AND MONUMENTS

The National Park Service (NPS) manages a system of lands that covers 83 million acres and includes national parks, monuments, historic sites, seashores, lakeshores, and recreation areas. The creation of Yellowstone National Park in 1872 launched a national preservation effort directed towards some of the most stunningly scenic and historically significant places in the United States, including places such as Yosemite, Zion, the Grand Canyon, the Grand Tetons, Death Valley, the Sonoran Desert, and Alaska's Glacier Bay. As Congress stated in the statute organizing the various lands into one national park system: "[T]hese areas, though distinct in character, are united ... as cumulative expressions of a single national heritage." 16 U.S.C. § 1a–1. This section of the chapter focuses on national parks and monuments as part of the overall coverage of federal public lands, and in particular explores ownership-related issues such as sacred sites and external threats from property outside federal boundaries. Chapter 15 covers preservation and recreation within the National Park System (NPS) in more detail.

A. Creation of National Parks and Monuments

National parks and monuments are designated in different ways, involving different branches of government. National parks are created by Congress alone. National monuments are designated either by Congress or through Presidential Proclamation under authority of the Antiquities Act of 1906, which says:

> The President of the United States is authorized, in his discretion, to declare by public proclamation historic landmarks, historic and prehistoric structures, and other objects of historic or scientific interest that are situated upon the lands owned or controlled by the Government of the United States to be national monuments, and may reserve as a part thereof parcels of land, the limits of which in all cases shall be confined to the smallest area compatible with the proper care and management of the objects to be protected.

16 U.S.C. § 431.

National parks and monuments are closely intertwined. All parks and most monuments are managed by the National Park Service as part of one National Park System. Both designations involve "withdrawal" of the federal land from the extractive laws such as the General Mining Law of 1872, though such withdrawals do not extinguish prior valid mining or other claims already established within such areas. National parks and monuments are both managed for the same general purposes of conservation and public enjoyment, explored in more detail below.

The designation process is the major difference between the two types of federal reservations. The Antiquities Act gives the President enormous discretion to accomplish the same protection for national monuments that Congress extends in designating national parks. The Antiquities Act represents an express Congressional delegation of authority to the President to make withdrawals and reservations and thereby allows the President to protect outstanding areas on federal public lands from imminent threats. The authority has been used by nearly every President—except Nixon, Reagan, George H. W. Bush and George W. Bush—to designate a total of 141 national monuments. In 1978, President Carter proclaimed 56 million acres of Alaska as national monuments, which provided a bridge of protection until Congress enacted the Alaska National Interest Lands Conservation Act two years later, establishing permanent protective designation of the lands. In 1996 President Clinton invoked the Antiquities Act to designate the Grand Staircase–Escalante National Monument in Utah, consisting of 1.9 million acres of federal land described in the Proclamation as a "high, rugged, and remote region, where bold plateaus and multi-hued cliffs run for distances that defy human perspective." Proclamation No. 6920, 61 Fed. Reg. 50,223 (Sept. 18, 1996). In a notable departure from past practice, the Bureau of Land Management (rather than the Park Service) was designated to manage that monument. *See* Ann E. Halden, *The Grand Staircase–Escalante National Monument and the Antiquities Act*, 8 FORDHAM ENVTL. L. J. 713 (1997). During the last part of his term, President Clinton designated 18 new national monuments, including the Giant Sequoia National Monument in California consisting of 300,000 acres containing 34 groves of giant sequoia trees, which can live for millennia and reach skyscraper heights. Giant Sequoia National Monument, California–Proclamation No. 7295, 65 Fed. Reg. 24095 (Apr. 25, 2000).

As a practical matter, Presidential proclamations under the Antiquities Act are enduring. Congress has never taken away a designation made under the Antiquities Act. In fact, many national monuments have later been re-designated by Congress as National Parks. Though Congress certainly has the authority to pass legislation overturning a monument designation, once a proclamation is announced the public quickly gains a strong interest in the land. For all practical purposes, the proclamation blankets the area with political protection beyond its legal force. Most Congressmen would be loathe to risk the political fallout of undoing a proclamation, though many fight hard to prevent them. (Sen. Orrin Hatch, R–Utah, protested the Grand Staircase–Escalante Monument as the "mother of all land grabs.") Julie Cart, *Amid Drought, a Range War Erupts in Utah Over Grazing Restrictions; Ranchers are Fuming over Federal Efforts to Restore the Land of Grand Staircase–Escalante*, L.A. TIMES, Dec. 26, 2000, at A5. A provision in FLPMA likely precludes a president from reversing a proclamation made by an earlier president under the Antiquities Act. *See* FLPMA 43 U.S.C. § 1714(j).

Though the Antiquities Act expressly limits the monument designation to "historic landmarks, historic and prehistoric structures, and other objects of historic or scientific interest that are situated upon the [federal] lands," and limits the protection to the "smallest area compatible with the proper care and management of the objects to be protected," 16 U.S.C. § 431, presidents have used the authority to create sweeping protection for enormous landscapes. Courts have taken a liberal approach towards affirming the proclamations, giving tremendous deference to the President. In Cameron v. United States, 252 U.S. 450, 456, 40 S.Ct. 410, 411, 64 L.Ed. 659, 660 (1920), the Supreme Court upheld President Roosevelt's designation of Grand Canyon National Monument on the basis that it is the "greatest eroded canyon in the United States, if not in the world, is over a mile in depth, has attracted wide attention among explorers and scientists, affords an unexampled field for geologic study, is regarded as one of the great natural wonders, and annually draws to its border thousands of visitors." The court in State of Wyoming v. Franke, 58 F.Supp. 890 (D. Wyo. 1945), rejected a claim that the President misused authority under the Act to designate Jackson Hole National Monument. The plaintiff accused the President of "substitut-[ing], through the Antiquities Act, a National Monument for a National Park, the creation of which is within the sole province of the Congress." *Id.* at 892. The court brushed aside the claim, stating: "[I]f there be evidence in the case of a substantial character upon which the President may have acted in declaring that there were objects of historic or scientific interest included within the area, it is sufficient upon which he may have based a decision." *Id.* at 895. In Tulare County v. Bush, 306 F.3d 1138 (D.C. Cir. 2002), the D.C. Circuit rejected a challenge to President Clinton's Proclamation designating the Giant Sequoia National Monument. Plaintiffs had claimed that the President failed to include in his proclamation sufficient detail demonstrating that the area encompassed objects of historic or scientific interest under the Act. The court stated:

> The Proclamation lyrically describes "magnificent groves of towering giant sequoias," "bold granite domes, spires, and plunging gorges," "an enormous number of habitats," "limestone caverns and ... unique paleontological resources documenting tens of thousands of years of ecosystem change," as well as "many archaeological sites recording Native American occupation ... and historic remnants of early Euroamerican settlement." Proclamation at 24,095. By identi-

fying historic sites and objects of scientific interest located within the designated lands, the Proclamation adverts to the statutory standard.

Id. at 1141.

In response to a second claim that the President made no meaningful investigation or determination of the "smallest area" needed to protect any specifically identified objects of historic or scientific interest, the court said, "[T]he Antiquities Act does not impose upon the President an obligation to make any particular investigation." *Id.* at 1142. On the same day the D.C. Circuit upheld six other Antiquities Act Proclamations made by President Clinton. *See* Mountain States Legal Foundation v. Bush, 306 F.3d 1132, 1137 (D.C. Cir. 2002) (noting that the Antiquities Act confers broad discretion on the President, and separation of powers concerns are alleviated through judicial review). Presidential proclamations under the Antiquities Act do not require NEPA review as long as the designation is initiated by the President and not an agency. *See* Alaska v. Carter, 462 F.Supp. 1155, 1159–60 (D. Alaska 1978). For analysis of the designation process, *see* Christine A. Klein, *Preserving Monumental Landscapes Under the Antiquities Act,* 87 CORNELL L. REV. 1333 (2002); Richard M. Johannsen, *Public Land Withdrawal Policy and the Antiquities Act,* 56 WASH. L. REV. 439 (1981).

B. Management Directives

The National Park Service Organic Act of 1916 designated the National Park Service (NPS) to oversee lands within the National Park System. It established the following management directive:

> [C]onserve the scenery and the natural and historic objects and the wild life therein and to provide for the enjoyment of the same in such manner and by such means as will leave them unimpaired for the enjoyment of future generations. 16 U.S.C. § 1.

The directive contains a dual purpose of preservation and public use. Not infrequently the two conflict, and the Park Service must use its discretion to find an appropriate balance. The attraction of most national parks and monuments is their primitive character. Providing "for the enjoyment" of these sensitive areas is made difficult by the sheer number of visitors as well as their expectations for material comfort. This gives rise to management dilemmas. For example, should the Park Service provide rustic cabins or a modern motel for lodging? Should it allow 500 or 5,000 visitors to raft a river in a given week? For a discussion of these dilemmas, *see generally* JOSEPH L. SAX, MOUNTAINS WITHOUT HANDRAILS: REFLECTIONS ON THE NATIONAL PARKS (1980); Robert W. Winks, Symposium, *The National Park System: The National Park Service Act of 1916: "A Contradictory Mandate?,"* 74 DENV. U. L. REV. 575, 610 (1997).

In 1978 Congress amended the Park Service Organic Act to impose a land use planning requirement on the Park Service similar to that of other federal agencies. The Park Service's "General Management Plans," as they are called, are federal "actions" that trigger NEPA and receive public comment. Such plans set forth a mechanism through which the Park Service evaluates different levels and types of public use, among other things. Plans must discuss:

1.   Measures for the preservation of the area's resources;

2.   Indications of types and general intensities of development (including visitor circulation and transportation patterns, systems and modes) associated with public enjoyment and use of the area....

3.   Identification of and implementation commitments for visitor carrying capacities for all areas of the unit; and

4.   Indications of potential modifications to the external boundaries of the unit, and the reasons therefore. 16 U.S.C. § 1a–7.

Traffic Jam in Yosemite National Park. Photo by Joe Easty, http:// members.virtualtourist.com/m/374e1/b8c57/8/.

C. Public Use Conflicts

Much of the controversy over national parks and monuments involves conflicts between different types of public use. These issues are more intense today due to market inventions in motorized recreational vehicles such as snowmobiles, jet skis, and ATVs. To those who use these mechanized toys, national parks and monuments are the ultimate play-ground. But to the multitude of cross-country skiers, hikers, canoeists, birdwatchers and others, they represent an outrageous intrusion into the solitude that makes these places unique. The noise of one motor carries far in primitive areas, slicing the quiet of an entire canyon, forest, or lake area, and ruining the solace sought by others who visit. Motorized recreational vehicles also emit substantial pollution and cause extensive damage to sensitive terrain. The Park Service must resolve such issues in the land use planning process with little direction from the statute, which simply sets forth a directive to conserve but also to provide for the public "enjoyment" of the lands. 16 U.S.C. § 1. Challenges to Park Service determinations are made through the Administrative Procedure Act (APA). The vast discretion afforded the Park Service makes it difficult to show that planning decisions are "arbitrary, capricious, or an abuse of discretion." 5 U.S.C. § 706(2)(A).

In Conservation Law Foundation of New England v. Secretary of Interior, 864 F.2d 954 (1st Cir. 1989), conservationists challenged a General Management Plan for the Cape Cod National Seashore, contending that the plan's allowance for restricted use of off-road vehicles (ORVs) violated the statute establishing the Seashore. The court upheld the plan, but the concurring Judge Breyer (then a circuit court judge) said the question was a "close one:"

> The Conservation Law Foundation, in its brief, notes that recreational "vehicles are used by less than 2.5 percent of the summertime visitors to the Seashore." The government, in its brief, says that it has set aside 8 miles, of 48 Cape Cod National Seashore beachfront miles, or 16 percent of the beach, for ORV use. Although it seems fairly obvious that those who use ORVs need a length of coastline in which to use them, it is also fairly obvious that their use is often incompatible with the quiet enjoyment of the seashore that the Cape Cod National Seashore Act contemplated the vast majority of visitors would seek. At some geographical point, reserving miles of coastline for ORVs would amount to taking too much from too many for the enjoyment of too few. We here hold only that, giving full and appropriate weight to the judgment of the administrators, we cannot say, on the basis of the record before us, that 16 percent actually crosses the line marked by the statutory word "arbitrary."

Id. at 961.

Does the Park Service Organic Act impliedly prohibit most use of motorized recreational vehicles? Read section 1 of the Organic Act, *supra*, at p. 493, carefully. Is the Park Service under a mandate to provide for maximum access and every form of enjoyment within national parks and monuments? Or is the "enjoyment" integrally tied to the scenery, natural and historic objects, and wildlife? If you conclude the latter, do jet skis, snowmobiles, and ATVs meet that test? Does the vehicle in any way enhance the enjoyment of the characteristics which caused these places to be designated as national parks or monuments, or is most of the enjoyment associated with the characteristics of the vehicle itself (speed, noise, power, image)?

Approaching the issue from another angle, are some visitors precluded from their "enjoyment" of the scenery by the presence of motorized recreational vehicles? The remote and undeveloped quality of parks and monuments is usually a central factor in their protective designation. Does the designation carry an implicit expectation of "quiet enjoyment" associated with the solitude of the area? Can silence be deemed one of the major resources associated with the landscape? Think about the characteristics of a pristine "soundshed," analogous to a pristine "viewshed" and "watershed." In such a soundshed a visitor might hear the rustle of leaves in the breeze, the chirping of birds, and the lapping of water. If so, are these characteristics destroyed by the buzz of a motorized vehicle? Is this unacceptable noise pollution?

On the other hand, do motorized recreational vehicles allow access to places within parks and monuments that otherwise would not be accessible to the ordinary person? Would eliminating motorized recreational vehicle use constitute undue favoritism towards hardy hikers, and discrimination towards the elderly or people with disabilities? And how does sheer laziness factor into "enjoyment" offered by the statute? To what extent should the Park Service make access as easy as possible for as many people as possible? These are the dilemmas the Park Service must grapple with on a regular basis.

Two executive orders deal with motorized recreational use of federal lands. Executive Order 11644, issued by President Nixon in 1972, found that such use must be consistent with "the protection of the resources of the public lands, promotion of the safety of all users of those lands, and minimization of conflicts among the various uses of those lands." Exec. Order 11644 § 1, 37 Fed. Reg. 2877 (Feb. 8, 1972). It allows motorized vehicle trails in the National Park System only "if the [agency] determines that off-road vehicle use in such locations will not adversely affect their natural, aesthetic, or scenic values." *Id.* § 3(a)(4). Exec. Order 11989, issued by President Carter in 1977, further provides:

> Whenever [the Park Service] determines that the use of off-road vehicles will cause or is causing considerable adverse effects on the soil, vegetation, wildlife habitat or cultural or historic resources of particular areas or trails of the public lands, [it must] immediately close such areas or trails to the type of off-road vehicle causing such effects until such time as [it] determines that such adverse effects have been eliminated and that measures have been implemented to prevent future recurrence.

E.O. 11989 § 9(a), 42 Fed. Reg. 26,959 (May 24, 1977).

In Focus:
Snowmobiles in Yellowstone National Park

Snowmobiles and Bison in Yellowstone National Park, National Park Service, www.nps.gov/yell/press/images/issues/smblmtns.jpg.

One of the most contentious disputes surrounding motorized vehicle use concerns snowmobiling in Yellowstone National Park. The key cases, *Fund for Animals v. Norton,* 294 F.Supp.2d 92 (D. D.C 2003), and *Int'l Snowmobile Manufacturers Ass'n v. Norton,* 340 F.Supp.2d 1249 (D. Wyo. 2004), are provided in Chapter 3.III.B.1, *supra,* to illustrate the arbitrary and capricious standard of review. The following account by Professor Michael Blumm highlights the power struggle between Congress, the Executive, and courts over this issue. You will be surprised to find in this controversy an ecological thread back to the slaughter of bison, discussed in section IV.B of this chapter.

THE BUSH ADMINISTRATION'S SWEETHEART SETTLEMENT POLICY: A TROJAN HORSE STRATEGY FOR ADVANCING COMMODITY PRODUCTION ON PUBLIC LANDS
Michael C. Blumm
34 ENVTL. L. RPTR. 10397 (May 2004)

Yellowstone National Park, the crown jewel of the National Park System, has been the scene of considerable conflict over the use of snowmobiles. * * *

In 1990, in response to ... increased [snowmobile] use, the NPS completed a winter use plan for Yellowstone.... But this plan did little to protect wildlife, erroneously predicted that there would be no air quality problems, and its estimate for increased use over the next decade was exceeded in just three years. * * * Meanwhile, the harsh winter of 1996–1997 produced a snowfall 150% above normal and ice that prevented the park's bison from reaching the grass beneath the snow. Consequently, numerous bison migrated out of the park in search of food, mostly into Montana, many on snowmobile roads. Since some park bison carry brucellosis that, if transmitted to cattle, can cause aborted calves, the state of Montana slaughtered most of the bison leaving the park—over 1,000 head in all. This slaughter amounted to roughly one-third of the park's herd.... The bison slaughter prompted a suit from the Fund for Animals, objecting to the NPS' failure to write an EIS and to engage in ESA biological consultation on the park's winter use program. * * *

A. *The 2000 Winter Use Plan*

In October 1997, the government settled the EIS/ESA case in an agreement that called for a new winter use plan by October 2000. While the planning was ongoing, in early 1999, a coalition of environmental groups ... petitioned the NPS to ban snowmobiles in all 28 park units where they were allowed. * * *

The preferred alternative called for eliminating snowmobiling in Yellowstone, allowing access only by mass transit snowcoach. However, due to a 2000 appropriations rider that forbade any changes in snowmobile use in any NPS unit before the end of the 2001–2002 season, the NPS opted for a phase-in of the snowmobile ban; a complete ban would not go into effect until the 2003–2004 season.

The basis of the ban lay in the NPS' interpretation of its responsibilities under the NPS Organic Act, which requires conservation of park resources and values and avoiding "impairment" to park resources. * * *

The NPS acknowledged that public access to park resources was an important purpose of the park system, and that snowmobiling in Yellowstone evolved to make winter use experiences available to a wider range of people than the most physically fit. But the agency maintained that the ongoing adverse affects of snowmobiling on wildlife, air quality, and natural soundscapes and odors made it impossible to fulfill its obligation to avoid impairment of Yellowstone's resources and values. * * * Even before the agency implemented the plan through an administrative rule, the International Snowmobile Manufacturers Association and the state of Wyoming sued the NPS, alleging that the EIS violated NEPA and the Organic Act.

Six weeks after the filing of the suit, on January 21, 2001, in one of the last acts of the Clinton Administration, the NPS promulgated a rule [that] would have prohibited snowmobiling in Yellowstone, effective for the 2004–2005 season, at which point the only motorized transport in the park would be mass transit snowcoach. * * *

B.   The 2001 Settlement Agreement and the 2003 Winter Use Plan

The Bush Administration wasted no time in suspending the snowmobile phaseout just a week after it was promulgated. Then, in June 2001, the Administration reached a settlement with the snowmobile manufacturers in which the NPS promised to reconsider the snowmobile ban and to prepare a supplemental EIS, incorporating significant new information, including new snowmobile technology. * * *

The NPS issued the final supplemental EIS in February 2003, which included a preferred alternative not considered in the draft that would authorize 950 snowmobilers per day in the parks. That was the alternative officially adopted by the agency one month later in its record of decision.... * * *

The NPS maintained that new snowmobiles, which became available in the three years between 2000 and 2003, and the new four-stroke engines are "substantially cleaner than standard two-stroke engines." * * *

C.   The 2003 District of Columbia District Court Decision

A coalition of environmental groups ... filed suit against the Bush Administration's 2003 plan, charging that its willingness to continue snowmobiling and trail grooming in light of the NPS' earlier finding of impairment of park resources and values amounted to arbitrary decisionmaking in violation of the Administrative Procedure Act (APA). *Fund for Animals v. Norton,* 294 F. Supp. 2d 92, 97, 34 ELR 20010 (D. D.C. 2003). * * *

On December 16, 2003, Judge Emmet Sullivan of the D.C. District Court, a President Clinton appointee, agreed with the environmentalists and set aside the 2003 plan. Judge Sullivan acknowledged that although the standard of judicial review of agency action was highly deferential, there was "a slight wrinkle" when an agency reverses an earlier decision: it must supply "a reasoned analysis for the change beyond that which may be required when an agency does not act in the first instance." *Id.* at 104. In short, the court must be convinced that the agency has not "deliberately changed" or "casually ignored" prior precedents and standards. *Id.* Judge Sullivan was not persuaded that the Bush Administration had supplied such a reasonable explanation for the turnabout it promulgated. * * *

The court concluded that the NPS' explanation of its administrative flip-flop was "weak, at best," lacking a "cogent, supported explanation," and therefore a "quintessentially arbitrary and capricious" decision, particularly in light of the agency's conservation mandate and its earlier impairment finding. Consequently, Judge Sullivan ...

enjoined the Bush Administration's proposal to resume snowmobiling in Yellowstone, [and] reinstated the Clinton phaseout plan. Then, eight weeks after Judge Sullivan's decision, the U.S. District Court for the District of Wyoming enjoined the Clinton plan.

D. The 2004 District of Wyoming Court Decision

After unsuccessfully seeking a stay of Judge Sullivan's decision from the D.C. Circuit, Wyoming and the snowmobile manufacturers turned their attention to the Wyoming judge who had approved the 2001 settlement that allowed snowmobiling to continue. * * * Judge Brimmer, who earlier had issued the injunction against the roadless rule, and who once enjoined significant parts of former DOI Secretary Bruce Babbitt's rangeland reform regulations, [issued] a preliminary injunction against the implementation of the Clinton snowmobile ban. * * * He thought the balance of harms clearly favored the snowmobile industry ... * * * [H]e remanded the issue to the NPS to promulgate "fair and equitable rules" that would include limiting snowmobile use to four-stroke engines. The NPS immediately promulgated rules allowing up to 780 snowmobiles in Yellowstone and more in Teton National Park, not all of which had to meet best available technology standards, but all of which must be commercially guided.

Question: How would you reconcile the two Yellowstone National Park cases?

Exercise:

Assume you are an attorney advising the National Park Service. Propose a rule to manage motorized recreational vehicle use. Would the rule allow some use "integral" to the enjoyment of the park or monument, such as transportation of visitors to areas that are otherwise not readily accessible? Would the rule limit the speed and/or pollution emissions of such vehicles? See 36 C.F.R. 7.52–7.53 (allowing snowmobile use in Cedar Breaks and Black Canyon of the Gunnison National Monuments only when "snow depth prevents regular vehicular travel," and then only on certain designated paved or gravel roads). Develop criteria that can be applied to a multitude of situations and vehicles (snowmobiles, ORVs, jet skis, etc.). In doing so, reference the language of the Organic Act of 1916. Also reference the National Park Service's 2001 Management Policy, which provides:

> Congress, recognizing that the enjoyment by future generations of the national parks can be ensured only if the superb quality of park resources and values is left unimpaired, has provided that when there is a conflict between conserving resources and values and providing for enjoyment of them, conservation is to be predominant.

National Park Service, 2001 Management Policies at 1.4.1. Does your rule depart from, or expand upon, the executive orders quoted supra?

D. Commercial Use of Parks and Monuments

While national parks and monuments managed by the Park Service are far more protected from commercial exploitation than national forests or BLM public lands, the statutory scheme does allow some use. For example, though the National Park Mining Regulation Act of 1976, 16 U.S.C. § 1901 et seq., effectively withdrew all national parks and monuments from location and entry under the General Mining law of 1872, valid existing rights established prior to the law's enactment on Sept. 28, 1976, are recognized. Access and mining operations are regulated by the Secretary of Interior "as he deems necessary or desirable for the preservation and management of those areas." 16 U.S.C. § 1902. The regulations, implemented by the Park Service, are found at 36 C.F.R. §§ 9.1–9.18. The Park Service reports 12,428 unpatented claims, and an additional 746 mining patents, in the national park system. *See* Duane A. Thompson, CRS Report 96–161: Mining in National Parks and Wilderness Areas (1996). Hunting and trapping is banned in all units of the National Park System unless specifically allowed by Congress in the individual establishment acts. *See* National Rifle Ass'n v. Potter, 628 F. Supp. 903 (D. D.C. 1986) (upholding ban).

Logging is permissible under certain conditions. While section 1 of the National Park Service Organic Act mandates that the park system be managed for conservation, section 3 allows the NPS to "sell or dispose of timber in those cases where in [its] judgment the cutting of such timber is required in order to control the attacks of insects or diseases or otherwise conserve the scenery or the natural or historic objects in any such park, monument, or reservation." 16 U.S.C. § 3. The same provision allows for grazing when "such use is not detrimental to the primary purpose for which such park, monument, or reservation was created." *Id.*

On January 4, 2004, the Forest Service announced it would allow commercial logging in the Giant Sequoia National Monument in California. 69 Fed. Reg. 2593. The decision triggered widespread opposition from the conservation community and put center-stage the issue of management discretion over national monuments. The monument contains two-thirds of all of the giant sequoia trees in the world (most of the remaining trees are in the adjacent Sequoia National Park). President Clinton parted with tradition when he designated the Forest Service, rather than the Park Service, as the managing agency with jurisdiction over the monument and directed the Forest Service to come up with a management plan for the area. Giant Sequoia National Monument, California–Proclamation No. 7295, 65 Fed. Reg. 24,095 (Apr. 15, 2000). The following article, which reports on the 2003 draft plan, provides context for the logging decision.

SCOPE OF LOGGING IN SEQUOIA MONUMENT
PLAN ANGERS CRITICS
Bettina Boxall
L. A. TIMES, Jan. 28, 2003, at A1

When 34 groves of giant sequoias and 300,000 surrounding acres were named a national monument by President Clinton during his final year in office, a long fight over protection of some of Earth's most majestic trees appeared to end.

It didn't. Last month, the U.S. Forest Service released a proposal for managing the Giant Sequoia National Monument that has flabbergasted environmentalists and revived their quarrel with the agency's stewardship of sequoias, which can live for millennia and reach skyscraper heights. Though the monument designation bans commercial logging, the management blueprint would allow, in the name of reduced fire risk, the cutting of enough commercial timber to fill 3,000 logging trucks a year. It would permit the felling of trees, including sequoias, as much as 30 inches in diameter—a size the Forest Service is now barred from cutting in much of the rest of the Sierra Nevada. * * *

The Forest Service describes the proposal as the best and fastest way to address pressing issues in the monument .... * * * One is the risk of a catastrophic wildfire, highlighted last summer when a 150,000–acre blaze burned for weeks in the forest, coming within half a mile of one of the monument's groves. The other is a long-term decline in sequoia regeneration caused by suppression of the natural cycle of frequent, small fires that sequoias need to reproduce.

Conservationists agree that the fire risk needs to be addressed. But they say that, by allowing so much logging, the Forest Service would be thumbing its nose at the monument charter, which prohibits removal of trees unless "clearly needed for ecological restoration and maintenance or public safety." * * *

Under the plan, about 10 million board feet of lumber a year could be cut by commercial loggers contracting with the Forest Service. That is as much timber as was logged in the entire Sequoia National Forest in 1998, before the monument's establishment in 2000.

Art Gaffrey, supervisor of the monument and the national forest, dismisses the criticism of the logging plan as unwarranted political spin. "No longer do we manage this public land based on market demands," Gaffrey said. "It will be to maintain forest health and protect objects of interest from wildfire."

For additional reporting on the draft plan, *see* Matt Weiser, *Giant Sequoias Could Get the Ax,* HIGH COUNTRY NEWS 4, June 9, 2003. After receiving 16,500 public comments on the draft management plan, the Forest Service reduced the amount of logging by about a third, to 7.5

million board feet/year (equating to 2,000 logging trucks a year). *See* Bettina Boxall, *Sequoia Plan Trims Timber Cutting; Environmentalists See a "Mixed Bag" in the U.S. Forest Service's Final Management Plan for the National Monument in the Southern Sierra,* L.A. TIMES, Jan. 17, 2004. The Sierra Club and other conservation organizations immediately filed suit challenging the logging.

As the materials in this chapter demonstrate, each public lands agency approaches its job with a defined—often entrenched—sense of mission. Is the Forest Service using the "healthy forests" rationale as a reason to rationalize logging the giant sequoias? Or is it making the best management decision under circumstances of extreme fire danger? Would the Park Service have more credibility as a managing agency? If commercial logging were allowed in the Giant Sequoia National Monument, what precedent would that establish for other protective areas with huge timber reserves, such as Yosemite National Park and Yellowstone National Park?

President Clinton experimented with different management regimes in some of his monument designations. He gave authority to BLM to manage 15 new monuments, including the Grand Staircase–Escalante National Monument in Utah, the Sonoran Desert National Monument in Arizona, and Cascade–Siskyou National Monument in Oregon. The monuments, combined with the other protected areas BLM already managed, were designated as the National Landscape Conservation System during the second term of the Clinton Administration. For more detail, *see The BLM Limps Into a New Era,* HIGH COUNTRY NEWS, Apr. 14, 2003, at 12. Why do you suppose he broke with tradition by giving monument authority to agencies other than the Park Service? Was that a good idea?

The most widespread commercial use in the National Park System is by concessionaires such as hotel operators, restaurants, and recreational outfitters. Concessions are governed by the Organic Act, 16 U.S.C. § 3, and the National Park Service Concessions Management Act of 1998, 16 U.S.C. §§ 5951–5966. This topic is covered in Chapter 15.II.B, *infra.*

E.   External Threats to Parks and Monuments

The national parks have been the focus of an extensive inquiry into external threats to federal property. *See* Robert B. Keiter, *On Protecting the National Parks from the External Threats Dilemma,* 20 LAND & WATER L. REV. 355 (1985); George C. Coggins, *Protecting the Wildlife Resources of the National Parks from External Threats,* 22 LAND & WATER L. REV. 1 (1987). Logging, air pollution, mining, and urban encroachment outside federal boundaries all pose serious threats to the National Park System. In Sierra Club v. Dept. of Interior I, 376 F.Supp. 90 (N.D. Cal. 1974), a district court fashioned what appeared to be a public trust responsibility to protect federal lands from outside threats. Clearcutting across adjacent private lands left the Redwood National Park vulnerable to high winds, landslides, mudslides and stream siltation. The Sierra Club sought a court order directing the Department of the Interior to use its authority to abate logging along the periphery of the park's borders. The court drew such a duty from the National Park System Organic Act, 16 U.S.C. § 1, as well as a specific provision in the establishment statute for the Redwood National Park. A section of that act authorized the Secretary to acquire interests in land on the periphery of the park and to enter into contracts and cooperative agreements with private landowners to assure that the private forestry operations would not damage the Park. 16 U.S.C. § 79c(e). Beyond reference to these statutory duties, the court described the Secretary's responsibility in managing the park as a "trust responsibility." It concluded that the statutes "impose[d] a legal duty on the Secretary to utilize the specific powers given to him whenever reasonably necessary for the protection of the park, and that any discretion vested in the Secretary ... is subordinate to his paramount legal duty imposed, not only under his trust obligation but by the statute itself, to protect the park." *Sierra Club*, 376 F.Supp. at 95–96. In a subsequent case, the same court found that the Secretary failed to carry out his duty:

> [T]he conduct of the Secretary must be considered in the light of a very unique statute—a statute which did more than establish a national park; it also expressly vested the Secretary with authority to take certain specifically stated steps designed to protect the Park from damage caused by logging operations on the surrounding privately owned lands. * * * Out of its concern that continued logging operations on those privately owned lands could cause damage within the Park, the Congress expressly invested the Secretary with these specific powers to take administrative action designed to protect it. * * * [T]here is, in addition to these specific powers, a general trust duty imposed upon the National Park Service, Department of the Interior, by the National Park System Act, 16 U.S.C. § 1 et. seq., to conserve scenery and natural and historic objects and wildlife ... and to provide for the enjoyment of the same in such manner and by such means as will leave them unimpaired for the enjoyment of future generations. * * * [T]he ... defendants unreasonably, arbitrarily and in abuse of discretion have failed, refused and neglected to take steps to exercise and perform duties imposed upon them by the National Park System Act, 16 U.S.C. § 1, and the Redwood National Park Act, 16 U.S.C. 79a, and duties otherwise imposed upon them by law....

Sierra Club v. Department of Interior II, 398 F.Supp. 284, 286–293 (N.D. Cal. 1975).

The Redwoods cases conjure up—but don't really answer— fundamental questions concerning the duties of federal land managers. Do federal land agencies hold the public lands in a "trust" akin to federal ownership of Indian lands or state ownership of streambeds? If so, is there a federal duty to affirmatively protect the corpus of the trust?

See Light v. United States, 220 U.S. 523, 537, 31 S.Ct. 485, 55 L.Ed. 570 (1911) (describing Congress's power over the public lands in trust terms).

Certainly Congress has the Constitutional power under the Property Clause to protect federal land from damage arising outside federal boundaries. *See* Camfield v. United States, 167 U.S. 518, 17 S.Ct. 864, 42 L.Ed. 260 (1897) (U.S. has power to compel removal of fence erected by defendants on private lands, where fence enclosed about 20,000 acres of public lands); Minnesota v. Block, 660 F.2d 1240 (8th Cir. 1981), *cert. denied,* 455 U.S. 1007, 102 S.Ct. 1645, 71 L.Ed.2d 876 (1982) ("Congress' power must extend to regulation of conduct on or off the public land that would threaten the designated purpose of federal lands"). Do federal *agencies* have this power—or even a duty—as an inherent part of their administrative authority? Is an affirmative trust obligation to protect federal lands from outside threats enforceable as a matter of common law? While the Redwoods cases hinted at a trust responsibility, the holdings rested largely on the explicit statutory language of the Redwoods Park Act. A later case rejected the idea that the National Park Service has a common law trust duty apart from any express statutory duty. *See* Sierra Club v. Andrus, 487 F.Supp. 443 (D. D.C. 1980), *aff'd on other grounds*, Sierra Club v. Watt, 659 F.2d 203 (D.C. Cir. 1981).

Review the language of the Refuge Improvement Act, 16 U.S.C. § 668dd(a), discussed above in section IV.A. Can you find any trust duties implicit in that statute?

In Focus:
Mining Threats to Yellowstone National Park

In the 1990s, a huge cyanide heap leach mine (the New World Mine) was proposed on private lands just three miles outside of Yellowstone National Park. Acid drainage from the mine would have threatened three watersheds, including Soda Butte Creek, which flows into one of the most breathtaking valleys in Yellowstone Park. The mine also would have created an enormous impoundment consisting of 5.5 tons of tailings in Fisher Creek valley, next to Yellowstone Park. This triggered concerns that the intense seismic activity and landslides in the valley could cause the impoundment to burst, sending a toxic river of waste into the Clark Fork River. *See* Fen Montaigne, *A Gold Mine in Montana is a Lode of Controversy*, PHILADELPHIA INQUIRER, Oct. 2, 1995. A New York Times editorial concluded:

> The threat arises from a Canadian conglomerate, Noranda Inc., which plans to hollow out a mountain that sits above Yellowstone, a scant three miles from the parks' border. The mountain is said to contain $500 million in gold, silver and copper. The company promises that poisonous wastes from the mine will not seep into the surrounding streams and the park. But the troubled

history of Western mining sends a different message entirely: This project poses a clear long-term threat to the water, wildlife and general sanctity of the 2.2 million acre preserve. * * *

Noranda promises a pollution-proof project. The company says it can pull eight million tons of ore out of the mountain, fill a 77–acre lake 10 stories deep with waste and seal it for eternity. That sort of technological confidence chills the blood. Man-made structures have a way of deteriorating over time, especially in harsh climates. The Noranda site is 10,000 feet above sea level, and enjoys only 30 frost-free days a year.

No Mines Near Yellowstone, The New York Times, Aug. 29, 1994.

In response to national public pressure, President Clinton averted the proposed mine through a federal buyout, costing taxpayers $65 million. *See New World Mining District Response and Restoration Project Summary*, USDA, 2001, http://206.127.65.86/newworld/documents/Projsum_ 01.pdf. The land-exchange component of the buy-out is described above in Chapter 5.I.D.6. Due to the extraordinary costs of mining buyouts, this solution is rarely feasible.

Recall the early public trust case, *Illinois Central Railroad v. Illinois*, excerpted in Chapter 5.III.B. Could one argue that the mining rights were encumbered by a public trust protective of Yellowstone National Park? If so, would there be any duty to compensate the mining company for its loss of mineral rights? Does the answer depend on whether the mineral rights were established before the national park? For analysis of the public trust doctrine, *see* Chapter 8.II.

One of the classic external threats to parks and monuments involves water rights. Parks and monuments generally have corollary federally reserved water rights in a quantity necessary to fulfill the purposes of the reservation, with a priority date as of when the reservation was established. *See* Cappaert v. United States, 426 U.S. 128, 96 S.Ct. 2062, 48 L.Ed.2d 523 (1976) (upholding water rights for Devil's Hole National Monument); *see also* Chapter 5.III.C. A recent district court order dealing with reserved water rights for the Black Canyon of the Gunnison National Park in Colorado suggests an affirmative duty on the part of the federal government to protect the water rights reserved at the time of the reservation. High Country Citizens' Alliance v. Norton, Civ. Action No. 03–WY–1712–CB, Order Denying Defendants' Motion to Dismiss (D. Colo. April, 19, 2004). In that case the National Park Service had asserted a water right with a 1933 priority date for the park, and a state court had recognized the right. In 2003, however, the Secretary of Interior entered into an agreement with the State of Colorado in which it relinquished the federally reserved right of 1933 and, in exchange, took a state-based water right with a junior priority date of 2003 (essentially, a mere paper right). Environmental groups challenged the action as an illegal give-away of federal property. The court denied the government's motion to dismiss in language that underscores a trust-like duty, enforceable under the Administrative Procedure Act, to preserve the property of the United States: "The Park Service Act [establishes] a non-discretionary duty to protect and preserve the natural resources, including the water rights, of the Black Canyon." *Id.*

Fundamental questions of federal duties associated with sovereign ownership are bound to persist as long as there are competing claims to the resources on public lands. Procedurally, consider how such issues will come before the courts following the Supreme Court's decision in Norton v. Southern Utah Wilderness Alliance, 542 U.S. 55, 124 S.Ct. 2373, 159 L.Ed.2d 137 (2004). How (and when) could such duties be enforced?

F.   Sacred Sites and Native Interests on Federal Lands

As chapter 5 described, the boundaries of national parks, monuments, and other federal reserves were carved from aboriginal territory. These new borders legally separated Indian reservations from many of the sacred sites native people had been accessing for hundreds or even thousands of years. Yet in many cases, native people continued to cross boundaries to perform sacred rituals, quests, and prayers in a pattern of clandestine and continuous use. Use of these areas today remains central to traditional tribal lifeways. But increased logging, mining, and recreation now threatens many of these native practices either by destroying lands central to the religion or by interfering with the practice itself. Government management of sacred sites triggers the First Amendment, which provides that "Congress shall make no law respecting an establishment of religion or prohibiting the free exercise thereof...." U.S. CONST. amend. I. Both the Establishment Clause and the Free Exercise Clause of the First Amendment arise in public lands management decisions involving sacred sites.

In 1988, the Supreme Court decided Lyng v. Northwest Indian Cemetary Protective Association, 485 U.S. 439, 108 S.Ct. 1319, 99 L.Ed.2d 534 (1988), which sets forth the Constitutional standard for sacred sites protection on federal land. The case involved a challenge to a road proposed through the Chimney Rock section of the Six Rivers National Forest, an area used for religious ceremonies by the Yurok, Karok, and Tolowa Indians of California. A Forest Service study had recommended not constructing the road on the basis that it would "cause serious and irreparable damage to the sacred areas which are an integral and necessary part of the belief systems and lifeway of Northwest California Indian peoples." *Id.* at 442. Nevertheless, the Court refused to require the government to produce a "compelling" justification for its road. Justice O'Connor wrote for the majority:

> It is true that this Court has repeatedly held that indirect coercion or penalties on the free exercise of religion, not just outright prohibitions, are subject to scrutiny under the First Amendment. * * * This does not and cannot imply that incidental effects of government

programs, which may make it more difficult to practice certain religions but which have no tendency to coerce individuals into acting contrary to their religious beliefs, require government to bring forward a compelling justification for its otherwise lawful actions. * * * The first Amendment must apply to all citizens alike, and it can give to none of them a veto over public programs that do not prohibit the free exercise of religion. * * * No disrespect for these [native ceremonial] practices is implied when one notes that such beliefs could easily require de facto beneficial ownership of some rather spacious tracts of public property. * * * Whatever rights the Indians may have to the use of the area, however, those rights do not divest the Government of its right to use what is, after all, *its* land.

Id. at 450–53 (emphasis in original).

Sacred sites protection has become a pervasive issue in federal lands management today. One of the most notable conflicts surrounds Devils Tower National Monument in Wyoming.

Devils Tower Monument, National Park Service, http://www.nps.gov/deto/.

This towering rock formation, known in native communities as Bear's Lodge, has been a sacred site for nearby plains tribes since time immemorial. More recently, it has become a climber's mecca. To reconcile the conflicting interests, the National Park Service called for a climbing ban during the month of June, an important month for native ceremonies. The climbing ban was challenged by climbing guide Andy Petefish and his associates in the following case.

BEAR LODGE MULT. USE ASSN. v. BABBITT (*BEAR LODGE II*)

United States District Court, District of Wyoming, 1998.
2 F.Supp.2d 1448, 1449–1457 *aff'd on other grounds*, 175 F.3d 814
(10th Cir. 1999), *cert. denied*, 529 U.S. 1037, 120 S.Ct. 1530, 146
L.Ed.2d 345 (2000).

The United States Department of the Interior, National Park Service ("NPS") issued a Final Climbing Management Plan ("FCMP") / Finding of No Significant Impact for Devils Tower National Monument in February of 1995. * * * The FCMP [provides] that "[i]n respect for the reverence many American Indians hold for Devils Tower as a *sacred* site, rock climbers will be asked to *voluntarily* refrain from climbing on Devils Tower during the culturally significant month of June." (Emphasis added). The FCMP does not identify any other reason for the June "voluntary closure."

The NPS represents that it will not enforce the voluntary closure, but will instead rely on climbers' self-regulation and a new "cross-cultural educational program" "to motivate climbers and other park visitors to comply." The NPS has also placed a sign at the base of the Tower in order to encourage visitors to stay on the trail surrounding the Tower. Despite the FCMP's reliance on self-regulation, it also provides that if the voluntary closure proves to be "unsuccessful," the NPS will consider taking several actions including: (a) revising the climbing management plan; (b) reconvening a climbing management plan work group; (c) instituting additional measures to further encourage compliance; (d) change the duration and nature of the voluntary closure; (e) converting the June closure to mandatory; and (f) writing a new definition of success for the voluntary closure. * * * The NPS, however, states that the voluntary closure will be "fully successful" only "when every climber personally chooses not to climb at Devils Tower during June out of respect for American Indian cultural values."

The NPS plans to fully comply with its own June closure by not allowing NPS staff to climb on the tower in June except to enforce laws and regulations or to perform emergency operations. * * *

In this case Plaintiffs ... allege that the NPS's plan wrongfully promotes religion in violation of the establishment clause of the first amendment. * * *

Voluntary Climbing Ban: The Establishment Clause of the First Amendment states that "Congress shall make no law respecting an establishment of religion...." (U.S. Const. amend. I). * * * [T]he United States Supreme Court has concluded that this provision prohibits laws "which aid one religion, aid all religions, or prefer one religion over another." * * * In Lemon v. Kurtzman, 403 U.S. 602, 91 S.Ct. 2105, 29 L.Ed.2d 745 (1971), the court established a three part test for delineating between proper and improper government actions. According to this test a governmental action does not offend the Establishment Clause if it (1) has a secular purpose, (2) does not have the principal or primary effect of advancing or inhibiting religion, and (3) does not foster an excessive entanglement with religion. * * *

Balanced in the analysis of the permissibility or impermissibility of the Government's actions is the ability of government to accommodate religious practices. The Supreme Court "has long recognized that the government may (and sometimes must) accommodate religious practices and that it may do so without violating the Establishment Clause." The Constitution actually "mandates accommodation, not merely tolerance, of all religions, and forbids hostility toward any." Lynch v. Donnelly, 465 U.S. 668, 673, 104 S.Ct. 1355, 1359, 79 L.Ed.2d 604, 610 (1984). * * *

[*Purpose:*] In this case the Defendants contend that the climbing plan was designed, in part, to eliminate barriers to American Indian's free practice of religion. They argue that this type of accommodation is particularly appropriate in situations like this where impediments to worship arise because a group's sacred place of worship is found on property of the United States. Defendants assert that their actions are also aimed at fostering the preservation of the historical, social and cultural practices of Native Americans which are necessarily intertwined with their religious practices. While the purposes behind the voluntary climbing ban are directly related to Native American religious practices, that is not the end of the analysis. The purposes underlying the ban are really to remove barriers to religious worship occasioned by public ownership of the Tower. This is in the nature of accommodation, not promotion, and consequently is a legitimate secular purpose.

Effect: Accommodation also plays a role in considering whether the principal effect of a policy is to advance religion. The Supreme Court has said, "[a] law is not unconstitutional simply because it *allows* churches to advance religion, which is their very purpose. For a law to have forbidden 'effects' under *Lemon,* it must be fair to say that the government itself has advanced religion through its own activities or influence." * * * Appropriate accommodation does not have a principal effect of advancing religion. * * * Actions step beyond the bounds of reasonable accommodation when they force people to support a given religion. * * *

In the context of the Free Exercise Clause, the Tenth Circuit drew a line demarcating impermissible accommodation in the area of public lands ruling that the "[e]xercise of First Amendment freedoms may not be asserted to deprive the public of its normal use of an area." Badoni v. Higginson, 638 F.2d 172, 179 (1980). The record clearly reveals that climbing at the Devils Tower National Monument is a "legitimate recreational and historic" use of Park Service lands. If the NPS is, in effect, depriving individuals of their legitimate use of the monument in order to enforce the tribes' rights to worship, it has stepped beyond permissible accommodation and into the realm of promoting religion. The gravamen of the issue then becomes whether climbers are allowed meaningful access to the monument. Stated another way, is the climbing ban voluntary or is it actually an improper exercise of government coercion?

* * * Although the NPS has stated that an unsuccessful voluntary ban may lead it to make the ban mandatory, that is far from an inevitable result. * * * [T]he remote and speculative possibility of a mandatory ban found in this case is insufficient to transform the Government's action into a coercive measure.

Excessive Entanglement: The Court concludes that the voluntary climbing ban also passes muster when measured against the excessive entanglement test. * * * The organizations benefited by the voluntary climbing ban, namely Native American tribes, are not solely religious organizations, but also represent a common heritage and culture. As a result, there is much less danger that the Government's actions will inordinately advance solely religious activities. * * * The government is merely enabling Native Americans to worship in a more peaceful setting. In doing so, the Park Service has no involvement in the manner of worship that takes place, but only provides an atmosphere more conducive to worship. * * *

[T]he voluntary climbing ban ... constitutes a legitimate exercise of the Secretary of the Interior's discretion in managing the Monument.

Notes and Questions

1. Initially, the NPS had issued a mandatory climbing ban on commercial climbers during June to accommodate tribal religious practices. A preliminary injunction was issued against that ban as a violation of the Establishment Clause in Bear Lodge Multiple Use Assoc. v. Babbitt (*Bear Lodge I),* No. 96–CV–063–D (D. Wyo. June 8, 1996). The NPS then revised its plan and issued a wholly voluntary ban on all types of climbers. This plan was the subject of *Bear Lodge II,* excerpted above. Why did the NPS allude to the possibility of a mandatory ban in the revised plan? On appeal, the Tenth Circuit found that the plaintiffs lacked standing to challenge the revised plan.

2. As the Bear's Lodge conflict demonstrates, there is a fine line between the Establishment Clause and the Free Exercise Clause in the context of public lands management. How far can the federal government go to avoid destroying sacred sites or religious practices at such sites before it runs headlong into the Establishment Clause? Can the government prohibit logging in a certain area to protect a sacred site? Is this different from prohibiting visitors from using an area?

3. In 1996, President Clinton issued an Executive Order dealing with the accommodation of sacred sites on federal lands. Exec. Order 13007—Indian Sacred Sites, 61 Fed. Reg. 26,771 (May 24, 1996). The order requires each land management agency "to the extent practicable, permitted by law ... (1) accommodate access to and ceremonial use of Indian sacred sites by Indian religious practitioners and (2) avoid adversely affecting the physical integrity of such sacred sites." The Order also requires agencies to develop procedures for protecting sacred sites. The Order, however, explicitly provides that it creates no new legally enforceable rights. *Id.* § 4.

4. For extensive analysis of protecting sacred sites on public lands, *see* Sandra B. Zellmer, *Sustaining Geographies of Hope: Cultural Resources on*

Public Lands, 73 U. Colo. L. Rev. 413, 417–18 (2002); Erik B. Bluemel, *Accommodating Native American Cultural Activities on Federal Public Lands,* 41 Idaho L. Rev. 2 (2005). For a list of religious features and structures in the National Park System, *see* http://www.sacredland.org/sacred_lands.html.

5. In an effort to promote tribal participation in the management of National Parks and Monuments, the 1994 Self Governance Act allows tribes to receive funding from agencies within the Department of Interior to carry out programs, services, functions and activities that are of "special geographic, historical, or cultural significance" to a self-governance tribe. 25 U.S.C. § 458cc(c). The Department of Interior has identified 34 units of the National Park System as eligible for such agreements where a tribe can show "geographical, cultural, or historical connections" to the land area. 67 Fed. Reg. 16431 (Apr. 5, 2002). The units include such well-known areas as Glacier Bay National Park (Alaska), Redwood National Park (California), Glacier National Park (Montana), Olympic National Park (Washington), and Mount Rainier National Park (Washington). A provision of the National Park Service Organic Act also allows the Park Service to enter into cooperative agreements with tribes for carrying out Park Service programs. *See* 16 U.S.C. § 1g. For more on tribal co-management, *see* Chapter 7.VI.

VI. MINING ON PUBLIC LANDS

Websources:

USDA Forest Service
> http://www.fs.fed.us/

Bureau of Land Management
> http://www.blm.gov/nhp/facts/index.htm

The Mineral Policy Center
> http://www.mineralpolicy.org/ewa/home.cfm

Mineral Policy Institute
> http://www.mpi.org.au/

Mineral claims add another layer of ownership to federally owned public lands. While Chapter 12 deals with the details of mining and mineral leasing law, this section briefly explores the role of hardrock mining claims in overall federal public lands ownership and management. The General Mining Law of 1872 allows citizens to stake claims on the public lands, take the minerals for free, and receive a federal "patent," or deed to the land, for the price of $2.50 or $5.00 an acre, depending on the type of claim. 30 U.S.C. § 22. The law creates a stepped-up system of property rights on federal lands. An unpatented mining claim is a private property right to the minerals discovered. A patented claim creates a private property right to the land as well as the minerals. The Department of Interior has authority to determine whether a claim is valid and issue a patent for claims on federal land. Individual federal land management agencies have regulatory authority over mining activities conducted on lands within their jurisdiction.

The General Mining Law has peppered federal public lands with mining claims. While withdrawn lands, such as wilderness areas, national parks, monuments, and refuges, are protected from future claims, past mining claims are considered valid property rights and still burden those specially designated lands. Many a backpacker has stumbled upon a mining claim in remote wilderness—or more likely, has encountered the toxic contamination flowing from a claim. Rights to explore for minerals occur on any land that has not been withdrawn, which includes most BLM and Forest Service lands that are not protected by special designation. Approximately 400 million acres of federal lands still remain open to mining under the General Mining Law. It is estimated that there are 235,948 active mining claims and thousands of abandoned mines on federal land. *See* Marc Humphries & Carol Hardy Vincent, *Mining on Federal Lands*, CRS Issue Brief for Congress IB89130 (July, 2004); U.S. Geological Survey, *The USGS Abandoned Mine Lands Initiative, available at* http://www.usgs.gov/themes/factsheet/095–99/index.html. Since 1872, more than 3.3 million acres of federal land, an area the size of Connecticut, has been patented and turned over to mining claimants. *Id.*

The give-aways associated with the General Mining Law are enormous. The federal government charges nothing for the value of hard rock minerals taken from public lands. The Department of the Interior (DOI) estimated the value of production in year 2000 alone to be approximately $1.0 billion (the value reached $1.8 billion in 1993). *Id.* at 8. Because the patented lands are still conveyed for $2.50 or $5.00 per acre, the federal government also suffers a hefty loss in property value when it conveys mining patents. In 1989, the General Accounting Office reviewed 20 patents and found that the federal government had received less than $4,500 for lands valued between $13.8 million and $47.9 million. U.S. GENERAL ACCOUNTABILITY OFFICE, THE MINING LAW OF 1872 NEEDS REVISION 24, GAO/RCED–89–72 (March 1989).

The scattered private ownership within federal property holdings resulting from the Mining Law makes ecosystem management extraordinarily difficult. The ownership of mining claims usually comes with access rights that burden federal public lands. But even more consequential is the environmental contamination that mining sites produce. Hardrock mining releases massive quantities of hazardous substances, including mercury, cyanide gas, arsenic, and heavy metals, into the environment. *See* Mineral Policy Center v. Norton, 292 F.Supp.2d 30, 33 (D.D.C. 2003) (excerpted in Chapter 3.III.B.2, *supra*) ("The emission of such chemicals affects water quality, vegetation, wildlife, soil, air purity, and cultural resources."). Contamination spreads across watersheds far from the point of origin to wreak ecological havoc on lands and resources owned by the public, tribes, and individuals. Some rivers, like the Alamosa River in Colorado, have stretches that are ecologically dead for several miles. A New York Times report describes that site:

> [H]igh in the San Juan range of the Rocky Mountains ... another Canadian company has left the Government with a $100 million cleanup job. After extracting 280,000 ounces of gold from the Summitville mine, Galactic Resources of Vancouver, British Columbia, declared bankruptcy in 1992 and left Colorado.

> It left behind a leaking, toxic soup of cyanide and heavy metals; the waste has killed 17 miles of streams and polluted water supplies in lower valleys, infuriating farmers and fishermen. The Environmental Protection Agency is spending more than $40,000 a day to contain the disaster.

> The West is full of dead rivers, rust colored from mine waste, a legacy of the fact that the 1872 mining law has no cleanup or reclamation requirements. There are more than 10,000 miles of dead streams, by one Federal estimate.

Timothy Egan, *New Gold Rush Stirs Fears of Exploitation,* THE NEW YORK TIMES, Aug. 14, 1994.

In 2004, the Environmental Protection Agency (EPA) released hardrock mining statistics for 2002, indicating the industry accumulated 1.3 billion pounds of toxic waste, including 384 million pounds of arsenic, 350 million pounds of lead, and 4 million pounds of mercury. *See* EPA's Toxic Release Inventory, at http://www.epa.gov/tri/. The releases are so great that EPA has ranked the hardrock mining industry as the nation's leading emitter of toxic pollution. *See Mineral Policy Center,* 292 F. Supp.2d at 33. The agency reported that mining has polluted stream reaches in the headwaters of more than 40% of western watersheds. U.S. EPA, LIQUID ASSETS 2000: AMERICA'S WATER RESOURCES AT A TURNING POINT, EPA 840–B–00–001, May 2000, at 10.

The estimated costs of cleaning up past mining damage range from $32–72 billion. *See* http://www.earthworksaction.org/aml.cfm. The costs of cleaning up the Summitville mine, described above, are estimated to exceed $170 million. *See* Roger Flynn & Jeffrey C. Parsons, *The Right to Say No: Federal Authority Over Hardrock Mining on Public Lands,* 16 J. ENVTL. L. & LITIG. 249, 250–52 (2001). In Montana alone, cleanup of mining sites has exceeded the bond amounts posted by miners by at least $24.6 million. *Id.*

The following excerpt describes in more detail modern industrial mining practices and their environmental effects. Efforts to regulate mining operations are described in subsection B. below.

STATE OF THE WORLD 2003–
ECOSYSTEMS, PEOPLE, AND MINES
WORLDWATCH INSTITUTE, JANUARY 2003, P. 116–118

In the last century ... lower energy costs and [new] mining technologies have made it possible to transform landscapes completely. Earthmoving equipment is used to literally move mountains in order to get to a mineral deposit. These technological advancements have led to two trends: the extraction of minerals from lower-grade ores—ores that contain very small amounts of mineral—and the development of surface mines instead of underground ones. * * *

The amount of wastes generated by mines is staggering.... For every usable ton of copper, 110 tons of wasterock and ore are discarded, and another 200 tons of overburden earth are moved. For gold [the amount] translates into roughly 3 tons of waste per gold wedding ring. * * *

Chemical innovations have also contributed to the dual trends in low grading and surface mines. In the late 1800s, U.S. chemists patented cyanide heap-leaching as a method of separating gold from ore. Today, gold mines everywhere from South Africa to Nevada use this technique. Cyanide is mixed with water and then is poured or sprayed over heaps of crushed ore in order to dissolve bits of gold. Once the usable gold is removed, the stacks of crushed ore–known as tailings–are treated to reduce cyanide concentrations, although the chemical is never entirely diluted. When gold prices shot up in the early 1980s, this method gained new popularity as miners rushed to extract gold from deposits containing even tiny amounts of the metal. Between 1983 and 1999, U.S. consumption of crystalline sodium cyanide more than tripled, reaching 130 kilograms—about 90 percent of which was used in gold mining. A teaspoon containing a 2 percent cyanide solution can kill an adult.

Where do these chemical-laced wasted end up? They are piled into heaps [and are] walled into constructed holding areas (called dams).... Tailings dams are typically built by stacking piles of wastes above ground or in freshwater ponds. * * * [M]ine wastes ... have spilled out of waste sites and poisoned drinking water supplies and aquatic habitat. In the U.S. West, mining has contaminated an estimated 26,000 kilometers of streams and rivers.

There is no reliable way to dispose of billions of tons of materials discreetly. Catastrophic spills of mine wastes in recent years have resulted in enormous fish kills, soil and water pollution, and damage to human health. In 2000, for instance, a tailings dam split open at the Baia Mare mine in Romania. This accident sent some 100,000 tons of wastewater and 20,000 tons of sludge contaminated with cyanide, copper, and heavy metals into the Tisza River, and eventually into the Danube—destroying 1,240 tons of fish and polluting the drinking water supplies of 2.5 million people. * * * Of the hundreds of mining-related environmental incidents since 1975, about 75 percent have involved tailings dam ruptures. * * *

Mining's effects frequently persist after an operation is closed. Acid drainage is an especially long-lived problem. This happens when a mining operation excavates rock that contains sulfide minerals. When these materials are exposed to oxygen and water, they react to form sulfuric acid. This acid will continue to form, and to drain out of the rock, as long as the rock is exposed to air and water and the sulfides have not been depleted—a process that can take hundreds or thousands of years. The Iron Mountain mine in northern California, for instance, has been closed since 1963 but continues to drain sulfuric acid, along with heavy metals such as cadmium and zinc, into the Sacramento River. The river's bright orange water is completely devoid of life, and has a pH of minus 3—which is 10,000 times more acidic than battery acid. Experts report that the mine may continue to leach acid for another 3,000 years.

In Practice:
The Role of the GAO in Public Lands Management

One of the most reliable sources of information on the management of public lands by federal agencies comes from the General Accountability Office (GAO), formerly the General Accounting Office. The GAO, often referred to as the investigative arm of Congress, is independent and nonpartisan. It studies how the federal government spends taxpayer dollars and advises Congress and the heads of executive agencies about ways to make government more effective and responsive. Contrary to what its name suggests, the GAO engages in review of agency practices extending far beyond mere "accounting" matters to implementation of statutory duties. As an independent branch of Congress, GAO tends to be an aggressive investigator of agency practices. GAO reports are widely considered to be credible and "official" sources of information. They are highly influential in Congressional hearings, court decisions, and the press. GAO investigations can be requested by any member of Congress, but priority is given to requests from committee chairpersons and ranking minority members.

In 1986, the GAO began an investigation into mining practices, requested by Congressman Nick Rahall and others. *See* Andrew P. Morriss, Roger E. Meiners, & Andrew Dorchak, *Between a Hard Rock and a Hard Place: Politics, Midnight Regulations, and Mining*, 55 ADMIN. L. REV. 551, 570 (2003). The GAO issued a series of hard hitting reports that focused on the General Mining Law and BLM's implementation of it. *See, e.g.,* U.S. GENERAL ACCOUNTING OFFICE, PUBLIC LANDS: INTERIOR SHOULD ENSURE AGAINST ABUSES FROM HARDROCK MINING, GAO/RCED–86–48 (1986); U.S. GENERAL ACCOUNTING OFFICE, FEDERAL LAND MANAGEMENT: LIMITED ACTION TO RECLAIM HARDROCK MINE SITES, GAO/RCED–88–21 (1987); U.S. GENERAL ACCOUNTING OFFICE, FEDERAL

LAND MANAGEMENT: AN ASSESSMENT OF HARDROCK MINING DAMAGE, GAO/
RCED–88–123BR (1988); U.S. GENERAL ACCOUNTING OFFICE, FEDERAL
LAND MANAGEMENT: THE MINING LAW OF 1872 NEEDS REVISION, GAO/
RCED–89–72 (1989). GAO reports are available at www.gao.gov/
index.html.

A. Property Rights Under the Mining Act

The General Mining Law was passed in another era to encourage
economic activity on a vastly different scale than occurs today in the
mining sector. The law was written to provide a means for individual
settlers to stake out claims and gain title to the land for $2.50 or $5.00
an acre. Yet the basic provisions of the law apply today to huge mining
corporations, many of them foreign, with operations that can encompass
thousands of acres. *See* Flynn & Parsons, *supra*, at 250–252. The modern pitfalls associated with large-scale mining will surely test the limits
of this antiquated act.

The General Mining Law of 1872 provides:

[A]ll valuable mineral deposits in lands belonging to the United
States ... shall be free and open to exploration and purchase, and
the lands in which they are found to occupation and purchase, by
citizens of the United States and those who have declared their
intention to become such, under regulations prescribed by law, and
according to the local customs or rules of miners in the several mining districts....

30 U.S.C. § 22 (2003).

Stated quite simply, mining rights divide into three stages: 1) exploration; 2) the unpatented mining claim; and 3) the patented mining
claim. The 1872 mining law establishes size limits for the two types of
claims: "lode" claims, which are claims to mineral veins within hard
rock, and "placer" claims, which is the right to take loose material. A
valid "unpatented" mining claim allows the miner to take the minerals
from federal land without paying anything, but the miner does not have
ownership of the land underlying the claim. Some mining companies
prefer to keep their claims "unpatented" instead of seeking patents to
the land. Why might this be? To establish a valid "unpatented" mining
claim, the miner must make a "discovery" of the minerals and comply
with various marking, location, recording, and annual fee requirements
deriving from federal and state law. *See, e.g.* 30 U.S.C.A. § § 28, 28f
(2003). Moreover, the mineral must be "valuable" under the express language of the Mining Act. Two dove-tailing tests apply to determine if
there is a "valuable" mineral deposit. Under the "prudent person" test, a
mineral is "valuable" if a prudent person would be justified in developing the mineral, in light of the expense of doing so. Watt v. Western
Nuclear, Inc., 462 U.S. 36, 58, 103 S.Ct. 2218, 2231, 76 L.Ed.2d 400, 417
(1983). The closely associated "profitability test" requires a showing that

the mineral can be removed at a profit, taking into account all of the costs of removal. Hjelvik v. Babbitt, 198 F.3d 1072, 1074 (9th Cir. 1999), citing United States v. Coleman, 390 U.S. 599, 602, 88 S.Ct. 1327, 20 L.Ed.2d 170 (1968). If the costs of removing the mineral exceed the potential market value of the mineral, arguably there is no valid unpatented mining claim.

A miner may receive a "patent" to the federal land underlying a valid claim. This comes at the whopping price of $5.00 per acre for lode claims and $2.50 per acre for placer claims. 30 U.S.C. § 37. Because conveyance of the patent by the Department of Interior is considered a non-discretionary act under the General Mining Law, it does not trigger NEPA requirements. *See* South Dakota v. Andrus, 614 F.2d 1190 (8th Cir. 1980). A patent essentially transforms the acreage from federal public land to private land, at which point there are few federal limits (outside of environmental regulation) on the activities that can occur there.

The General Mining Law provides an associated right to "mill site" claims. These are claims to non-mineral land needed for the processing of the mining claim. 30 U.S.C. § 42 (mill sites may be located on "non-mineral land not contiguous to the vein or lode."). The size of these claims is statutorily limited to five acres. *Id.* Another secondary right is access to the claim.

The ownership rights of unpatented mining claims were clarified by the Surface Resources Act (SRA) of 1955, which stated that, although miners have the right to uses "reasonably incident" to their claim, the United States retains the right "to manage and dispose of" the vegetative and other surface resources of unpatented mining claims. 30 U.S.C. § 612. *See* United States v. Richardson, 599 F.2d 290 (9th Cir. 1979) (enjoining mineral prospecting that damaged surface resources). The act also made clear the right of the government and citizens to "use so much of the surface [of the claim] thereof as may be necessary" for their purposes, including access to adjacent land. 30 U.S.C. § 612. *See* United States v. Curtis–Nevada Mines, 611 F.2d 1277 (9th Cir. 1980) (unpatented mining claim subject to public recreational access).

To limit industrial mining, conservation groups increasingly focus on two provisions within the General Mining Law: the millsite provision and the "valuable" mineral requirement. *See* Roger Flynn, *The 1872 Mining Law as an Impediment to Mineral Development on Public Lands: An 19th Century Law Meets the Realities of Modern Mining*, 34 LAND & WATER L. REV. 301 (1999).

The millsite provision—The Clinton Administration dusted off this little noticed provision of the General Mining Law in an effort to restrict huge cyanide heap leach operations. The land needed for processing material and disposing of waste rock in large-scale industrial mining may range from several hundred to several thousand acres. *See* JOHN D. LESHY, THE MINING LAW, A STUDY IN PERPETUAL MOTION 439 (1987). The millsite provision, however, expressly limits the allowable millsite acreage to five acres—plenty for the pioneer operations the law was designed to promote, though meager by today's industrial standards. The Solicitor of Interior in the Clinton Administration (John Leshy, who also happens to be the foremost legal scholar on mining law) issued a Solicitor's Opinion in 1997 calling attention to the five-acre limit. Solicitor's Opinion M–36988, Limitations on Patenting Millsites under the Mining Law of 1872 (Nov. 7, 1997). Interpreted strictly, the limit could grind to a halt many plans for huge industrial mines that simply cannot operate on a small footprint. Critics charged that the millsite opinion was "an attempt by [Secretary] Babbitt to aggressively remake the General Mining Law of 1872 without legislative changes." *See* Andrew P. Morris, *et al, Between a Hard Rock and a Hard Place: Politics, Midnight Regulations and Mining*, 55 ADMIN. L. REV. 551, 575–577 (2003). Congress reacted in 1999 by passing an appropriations rider that grandfathered in prior patent applications and operations. Interior and Related Agencies Appropriations Act for FY2000, P.L. 106–113, § 337(a). The millsite Solicitor's Opinion was quickly discarded by the Bush II administration, and a new regulation was issued on October 24, 2003, broadly interpreting the millsite provision to allow modern industrial mining. 68 Fed. Reg. 61406, 61054. Though the new millsite regulation has not yet been challenged in court, the millsite language lingers in the statute as a possible impediment to industrial mining operations, and its meaning will doubtless be fleshed out in future litigation.

"Valuable" minerals, environmental regulation, and the profitability test—The General Mining Law gives away only "valuable mineral deposits." 30 U.S.C. § 22. The provision has been interpreted to require a showing that the mineral can be mined at a profit. Conservationists argue that many mining companies cannot meet the "profitability" test because the environmental costs associated with their operations are so high. They assert that mining has been profitable in the past only because such costs were thrust onto the public as externalities. BLM is charged with making profitability determinations, but until recently the agency has failed to aggressively explore the profitability of mining operations in light of modern environmental costs.

In 1998, the Interior Board of Land Appeals issued a decision that directly addressed the interplay of environmental costs and the profitability test:

> [I]n determining whether a discovery exists, the costs of compliance with all applicable Federal and State laws (including environmental laws) are properly considered in determining whether or not the mineral deposit is presently marketable at a profit, *i.e.,* whether the mineral deposit can be deemed to be a valuable mineral deposit within the meaning of the mining laws. If the costs of compliance render the mineral development of a claim uneconomic, the claim, itself, is invalid and any plan of operations therefor is properly rejected. Under no circumstances can compliance be waived merely because failing to do so would make mining of the claim unprofitable. Claim validity is determined by the ability of the claimant to

show a profit can be made after accounting for the costs of compliance with all applicable laws, and, where a claimant is unable to do so, BLM must, indeed, reject the plan of operations and take affirmative steps to invalidate the claim....

Great Basin Mine Watch et. al., 146 IBLA 248, 256 (1998); *see also* United States v. Kosanke Sand Corp., 12 IBLA 282, 299 (1973) ("To the extent federal, state, or local law requires that anti-pollution devices or other environmental safeguards be installed and maintained ... [these expenses] may be properly be considered ... [with respect to] the issue of marketability...."). Would it be reasonable for a BLM official to incorporate the potential costs of cleanup and natural resource damages under the Comprehensive Environmental Response, Cleanup and Liability Act (CERCLA) into the profitability equation? Would it be reasonable not to? If one incorporates potential natural resource damages available through CERCLA (explained in more detail in subsection B below), many operations may not be profitable. Would the mining company argue that such costs are speculative? What approach should the agency use in making a reasonable determination as to probability of environmental damage?

In Practice:
The Role of the BLM, the Forest Service, and
Other Federal Agencies

   Mining law can be quite confusing to the natural resource practitioner because it does not fall within the exclusive purview of one agency. The General Mining Law of 1872 provides for the basic mining rights on federal lands. The Department of Interior is responsible for conveying patents to land and determining the validity of claims. In short, the Department is responsible for administering the system of mining "rights." Each land management agency is responsible for regulating activities, including mining, on its designated lands. BLM and the Forest Service have a huge mining regulation workload because most of their lands have not been withdrawn from the purview of the General Mining Act. The U.S. Fish and Wildlife Service and the Park Service also regulate mining on their lands, under their separate authorities. Mining regulation is further complicated by the fact that the land management statutes give agencies different statutory authority over their surface resources. The Forest Service has tied its mining regulations back to the Organic Act. 16 U.S.C. § 551. BLM regulates mining under the authority of the Federal Land Policy Management Act. 43 U.S.C. § 1732(b). FLPMA provides an important statutory overlay to the General Mining Act, because it requires BLM to prevent "unnecessary or undue degradation" to the public lands. *Id.*

   In addition to the agencies that have land management authority over mining, other federal agencies might become involved when a mining plan of operations is subject to review for approval. The NOAA

Fisheries Service or U.S. Fish and Wildlife Service must consult under Section 7 of the ESA when an ESA listed species may be affected. The U.S. Environmental Protection Agency has jurisdiction under the Clean Water Act over any discharges of pollutants to navigable waters. 33 U.S.C. § 1131(a). Also, the U.S. Army Corps of Engineers has jurisdiction over any "fill" of wetlands associated with mining operations. 33 U.S.C. § 1344. In practice, however, these statutes rarely provide a complete brake on mining.

Notes and Questions

1. *Patents*—The patent process gives away federal land for $2.50 or $5.00 per acre, depending on the type of mining claim. Once the land is held in fee, there is no requirement that it be used for mining. Beginning in 1994, Congress passed annual appropriations riders placing a moratorium upon the issuance of patents by the Department of Interior. *See* Department of Interior and Related Agencies Appropriations Act of September 30, 1994, P.L. 103–332, 108 Stat. 2499, § 12. A 1996 rider, however, imposed a rigorous schedule on the Department of Interior to process 90 percent of "grandfathered" patent applications (those submitted prior to the 1994 rider) within a five-year period. Omnibus Consolidated Rescissions and Appropriations Act of 1996, Pub. L. No. 104–134, 110 Stat. 1321 (1996). For discussion, *see* Randy Hubbard, *The 1872 Mining Law: Past, Present, and Future?*, 17 NAT. RESOURCES & ENV'T. 149 (2003).

2. *Withdrawals*—The environmental consequences of mining make the issue of public land withdrawals all the more important in today's world. Land that has been "withdrawn" from the effect of the Mining Law is protected from new mining claims. The President has the power to make withdrawals under FLPMA. *See* 43 U.S.C. § 1714. See Section I.A., supra. The Antiquities Act also provides a separate means of executive withdrawals. *See* Section V.A., *supra* (discussing Antiquities Act).

3. A leading study of the mining law is JOHN LESHY, THE MINING LAW: A STUDY IN PERPETUAL MOTION (1987). For a comprehensive treatise of mining law, *see* ROCKY MOUNTAIN MINERAL LAW FOUNDATION, AMERICAN LAW OF MINING 2D (1984). For investigative inquiry into the effects of mining in the West, *see* *The Mining of the West: Profit And Pollution on Public Lands*, SEATTLE POST-INTELLIGENCER, June 11–14, 2001.

B. Regulation of Mining

Mining industry officials often assert that there is an "absolute" right to mine under the General Mining Law. They premise their contention on the basis that a mining right—even an unpatented mining claim—is a private property right. But like all property rights, mining is subject to regulation. The General Mining Law expressly makes the right to mine subject to "regulations prescribed by law." 30 U.S.C. § 22.

The land management statutes vest the Forest Service and the BLM with regulatory responsibilities over unpatented mining claims within their respective jurisdictions. The Organic Act gives the Forest Service the power to regulate the "occupancy and use" of the national forests and to "preserve the forests ... from destruction." 16 U.S.C. § 551. Under this statutory authority, the Forest Service regulations require mining claimants to submit and gain approval for a "plan of operations" if the mining would "likely cause significant disturbance of surface resources." 36 C.F.R § 228.4(a)(2001). The plan of operations is the framework document that regulates the particular activity at the site. As part of this regulatory process, the agency may demand strong protections for public resources. Whether such regulation is "reasonable," of course, depends on the relative burden on the claimant and the harm sought to be prevented by the regulation. In Clouser v. Espy, 42 F.3d 1522, 1530 (9th Cir. 1994), the Ninth Circuit upheld a Forest Service restriction that prohibited motorized access to a claim and allowed only pack-mule hauling of equipment: "[T]here can be no doubt that the Department of Agriculture possesses statutory authority to regulate activities related to mining—even in non-wilderness areas—in order to preserve the national forests." *Id.*

BLM's regulatory authority over mining comes from FLPMA, 43 U.S.C. § 1732(b), which directs the Secretary of Interior to "take any action necessary to prevent *unnecessary or undue degradation* of the public lands." (Emphasis added). In effect, this "UUD" standard creates a protective overlay to the General Mining Law's broad allowance for mining. *See* Mineral Policy Center v. Norton, 292 F.Supp.2d 30, 33 (D. D.C. 2003). Conservationists increasingly contend that the modern industrial cyanide heap-leach mining fails to meet the UUD statutory standard. BLM has promulgated regulations, referred to as the "3809 regulations," to implement the UUD standard. Under this authority, mining activities (with some exceptions for ones causing minimal ground disturbance) must be approved in a plan of operations. 43 C.F.R. § 3809.11, .21 (2001).

The Clinton Administration seized the UUD authority to issue new 3809 regulations (referred to as the "2000 regulations") which defined "undue or unnecessary degradation" to include "conditions, activities, or practices that result in *substantial irreparable harm* to significant scientific, cultural, or environmental resource values of the public lands that cannot be effectively mitigated." 65 Fed. Reg. 70,115 (Nov. 21, 2000) (emphasis added). The new regulations provided authority to deny mining plans of operation based on the harm the mining activity would cause to the land or other resources—a position that had never been taken by BLM at any prior time. The "substantial irreparable harm" (SIH) standard threatened the mining industry, whose cyanide heap-leach practices arguably cause "substantial irreparable harm" in many (perhaps most) instances. The Bush II administration wasted no time in doing away with the SIH standard in new 3809 regulations issued October 30, 2001 (called the "2001 regulations"). 66 Fed. Reg. 54, 860 (Oct. 30, 2001). Moreover, a new Solicitor's Opinion interpreted the UUD standard in FLPMA in a restrictive fashion as prohibiting only activities that were not "necessary" for mining, reading away the "undue" language in the statute. The 2001 regulations were challenged in Mineral Policy Center v. Norton, 292 F. Supp.2d 30 (D. D.C. 2003), which is excerpted in Chapter 3.III.B.2, *supra.* The court upheld BLM's reversal of the SIH standard, but in sweeping language that may provide fodder for future litigation, it interpreted the "unnecessary or undue degradation" standard of FLPMA in fairly broad terms underscoring the ability of BLM to deny mining plans of operations.

For an account of the dramatic regulatory changes between the Bush–Clinton–Bush administrations, *see* Randy Hubbard, *The 1872 Mining Law: Past, Present, and Future?,* 17 NAT. RESOURCES & ENV'T 149 (2003); and Morris, *et al, supra,* at 583–606.

In addition to the land management statutes, the full panoply of federal and state environmental laws also applies to mineral activity. For analysis of the environmental regulation of mining, *see* Roger Flynn & Jeffrey C. Parsons, *The Right to Say No: Federal Authority Over Hardrock Mining on Public Lands,* 16 J. ENVTL. L. & LITIG. 249 (2001). Even though strict environmental requirements would seemingly thwart many mining proposals, in practice, regulators have a difficult time saying no, and the strongly worded standards often fizzle in the implementation stage, as the Hecla Grouse Creek Mine case study below demonstrates.

In Focus:
The Grouse Creek Mine in Idaho

The Grouse Creek Mine, with its 65-acre cyanide lake perched above the headwaters of the Salmon River in Idaho. Photo courtesy of Paul Koberstein.

POISON IN SALMON COUNTRY:
EMERGENCY ACTION ORDERED FOR REMOVAL
OF CYANIDE LAKE IN IDAHO
Paul Koberstein
CASCADIA TIMES, May 2000

Federal officials say they will issue an emergency order forcing a gold mining company to remove a lake of cyanide that is contaminating salmon habitat in Idaho.... The lake is perched on a bench almost directly above the Yankee Fork of Idaho's famous Salmon River, at the edge of the Frank Church–River of No Return Wilderness. The Salmon River and its tributaries are key to the Northwest's billion-dollar salmon restoration effort. Once home to some of the most abundant salmon runs of any tributary in the Columbia Basin, its fish have been decimated since the construction of federal dams on the Columbia and Snake. Federal officials worry that the cyanide spilling into the Salmon's headwaters is making survival all the more difficult for endangered salmon, steelhead and bull trout.

The government intends to move quickly on removing the 65–acre lake, which contains 500 million gallons of cyanide-laced wastewater, plus 4.3 million tons of tailings—all from the defunct Grouse Creek open-pit gold mine. Cyanide has been detected in ground or surface water near the mine almost continuously since it opened in 1994. But the government's biggest fear now is that eventually the lake could overflow in a major storm, sending torrents of poison down a mountainside into the Yankee Fork, potentially killing all living things for many miles. The dam holding back the lake could also become unstable because of earthquakes, bad weather or leaks.

"We have a problem on our hands," said Helen Hillman of the National Oceanic and Atmospheric Administration in Seattle.... NOAA is involved because it manages Idaho's salmon under the Endangered Species Act. "If we don't do something about it, it could get worse," Hillman said. "The amazing thing was this mine was permitted in the first place. Eventually it would overflow, and you would have highly toxic water flowing right into the Yankee Fork. It would kill everything in the Yankee Fork for miles."

One federal official likened the situation to a Romanian gold mine spill that devastated 300 miles of the Danube and its tributaries. The top of a dam broke and released an estimated 100,000 cubic meters of cyanide-laced wastewater within 11 hours. Now, in Idaho, with every heavy spring rain, agencies and conservationists watching the cyanide lake at Grouse Creek worry that a similar disaster could happen in Idaho.

"We are facing a tradeoff between the low level of damage from cyanide release, and the potential for a catastrophic spill," said Nick Iadanza, a National Marine Fisheries Service biologist who has reviewed cleanup plans. "In Romania we had the same kind of situation. A tailings impoundment didn't fail—it overflowed. There was a massive fish kill. If this mine at Grouse Creek would fail, that would be pretty catastrophic."

[T]he government's plan for removing the lake is risky.... They plan to drain all of the contaminated water from the lake, treat it, and then dump it directly into the Yankee Fork. Given the high levels of contamination, the EPA believes that removing all the pollution from the water may not be possible at any price within Hecla's ability to pay. However, federal officials say the river will dilute the pollution enough to make it safe for fish—a point that some conservationists dispute. They are concerned that toxic levels of pollution will be discharged directly in the path of migrating salmon for however long it takes to empty the lake, most likely for three or more years. * * *

But while officials hurry to head off a catastrophic spill, they must also deal with chronic cyanide poisoning of salmon habitat that appears to be getting worse as water levels in the lake rise. The EPA says the lake recently was found to be leaking at a new point. And as the waters rise, the downward pressure forcing contaminated water out from the bottom of the lake also increases. Water levels in the lake have risen about 10 feet in the last three years, with about 20 feet to go before water reaches the top of the dam.

[T]he dam was built on top of an old landslide, and another federal official reviewing the problem said the lake is not in a secure place and was never designed to hold as much water as it does now. * * *

The poisons would enter the Yankee Fork just upstream from a million-dollar salmon recovery project operated by the Shoshone–Bannock Tribe, which is working to restore salmon runs to the area, where the tribe has reserved fishing rights. * * *

Hecla is opposed to federal proposals calling on it to remove and treat the wastewater to a high standard, insisting instead on a much less rigorous cleanup. * * * Hecla carries a $7 million bond, an amount that probably won't come close to covering cleanup costs at Grouse Creek. Hecla also has environmental cleanup liabilities at seven other sites in Idaho, including Superfund sites at Bunker Hill and the South Fork Coeur D'Alene River. If Hecla walks away from these obligations, the responsibility to pay for them would shift to taxpayers, officials say. * * *

Historically throughout the West, mines have been major polluters, but the mining industry claims to have made big strides in environmental protection at newer sites. That's why this spill is so troublesome. Grouse Creek was billed as a modern, open-pit mine using "state of the art" technology by its owner, Idaho politicians and even the EPA. Its main defense against a spill was a supposed to be a plastic liner placed under the lake, and a 12–inch layer of compacted clay beneath that. The liners failed long ago.

Rick Johnson, executive director of the Idaho Conservation League, contends that the troubling situation at Grouse Creek demonstrates beyond doubt that open-pit cyanide mines, no matter how carefully constructed, pose unacceptable risks to the environment. "This is modern mining at its best—bleeding cyanide into the river," he said. The events at Grouse Creek have disillusioned even some of the mine's boosters. "I used to hold this mine up as a mine run well," the EPA's Ceto said. * * *

[A]ppalling to some is the fact that the EPA, U.S. Forest Service, National Marine Fisheries Service and the state of Idaho granted permits allowing the Grouse Creek mine to be built on top of endangered salmon in the first place. * * *

Notes and Questions

1. Did it make sense to situate a cyanide heap leach mine directly above the headwaters that are essential to a billion-dollar regional salmon restoration effort? Why was the mine sited in this location in the first place? What does the damage caused by Hecla mean for other commercial sectors that impact salmon? Will ranchers, loggers, fishermen, and federal dam operators have to absorb a greater burden of conservation to compensate for Hecla's action? Since the burden of conservation across a huge watershed such as the Columbia River Basin can hardly be quantified, will Hecla suffer no legal recourse for its damage to fish habitat?

2. A separate section of the story details, by name, the individuals responsible for the Grouse Creek Mine, including both Hecla and federal officials. Did the Supervisor of the Salmon–Challis National Forest carry out his statutory duties under the Organic Act in permitting the mine? The National Marine Fisheries Service is in charge of implementing the Endangered Species Act (ESA). The agency concluded that the mine, perched above vital habitat for the Snake River salmon, would pose no jeopardy to the species. When the problems arose just a few years later, the agency changed its tune. What dynamics influence agency officials in the permitting process? Why did multiple agencies approve this mine? Linda Stone, a conservationist who opposed the mine, said in the story, "Hecla called the shots. The Forest Service, state agencies, and politicians kowtowed to the mining company." Are there systemic flaws in the nature of modern agency functioning that could be revealed by case-studies such as this one?

3. As the article mentions, Hecla has a history of mining in Idaho. It is one of the major defendants in the Coeur d'Alene litigation described below. Would it be arbitrary and capricious for the Forest Service to consider a company's environmental history and financial obligations from its other mining sites in the approval process?

> 4. Mining companies often claim that new modern technology, such as plastic lining systems, will prevent hazardous substances from migrating into watersheds. It is well-known to hazardous waste practitioners, however, that liners are not inviolate; even the best may ultimately fail. *See* JEFFREY G. MILLER & CRAIG N. JOHNSTON, THE LAW OF HAZARDOUS WASTE DISPOSAL AND REMEDIATION 10 (1996). The Grouse Creek Mine was touted for having state-of-the-art liner containment technology. How can government regulators rationally assess the probability of environmental damage without having to rely on data from mining officials, who naturally have every incentive to downplay the dangers?
>
> 5. How should bonding requirements incorporate costs of prospective environmental damage that may not occur for 50 or 100, or even 300 plus years? BLM's bonding regulations are contained at 43 C.F.R. §§ 3809.500–.599. Forest Service bonding regulations are at 36 C.F.R. § 228.13. Typically, agencies require only minimal bonds that fall many millions of dollars short of the cleanup costs for mining pollution.

The Comprehensive Environmental Response, Cleanup, Liability Act (CERCLA) applies to mining activity, but its forceful provisions come into play only after the environmental damage is done. CERCLA imposes strict liability on individuals and corporations for the costs of cleanup from their release of hazardous substances into the environment. 42 U.S.C. § 9607 (1994). Moreover, CERCLA contains a "natural resource damage" provision that allows the federal government, states, and tribes to recover damages for natural resources destroyed by the release of hazardous substances. CERCLA, 42 U.S.C. § 9607 (1994). Because mining activity causes the discharge of "hazardous substances" covered by the act—heavy metals, acid mine drainage, cyanide, and other substances—the CERCLA liability scheme would, in theory, give assurance that someone will pay the costs for the damage done. Even if some of the responsible parties are insolvent, courts have sometimes imposed joint and several liability, so the remaining defendants may be on the hook for the entire cleanup cost. New York v. Shore Realty Corp., 759 F.2d 1032 (2d Cir. 1985). The problem is that the cleanup costs are often so staggering that they far surpass most companies' ability to pay. Many CERCLA cleanups force the companies into bankruptcy. Also, many mining corporations are foreign entities with subsidiaries in the United States that are not well-capitalized to pay for the damage. Accordingly, much of the cleanup bill for the damage from mining falls on the American taxpayers. For discussion of CERCLA in the mining context, *see* Jan G. Laitos, *CERCLA Liability For Abandoned Mines,* 23 COLO. LAW. 371 (1994); Marilyn G. Alkire, *CERCLA Liability for Mining and Milling Operations,* 30 ROCKY MTN. MIN. L. INST. 7–1, 7–6 to 7–12 (1984).

The biggest CERCLA case ever to go to trial involves mining pollution throughout the Lake Coeur d'Alene Basin in Idaho and Washington. More than 100 companies mined for silver, gold, copper, cadmium, zinc, and lead high up in the watershed from the 1880s on. Approximately 72 million tons of toxic metals were discharged into the Coeur d'Alene River, which transported the poisons down to Lake Coeur d'Alene and then into the Spokane River. The bed of Lake Coeur d'Alene now has 83 million tons of sediment containing cadmium, lead and zinc. The contamination is so pervasive in the Coeur d'Alene Basin that health advisories warn people not to swim in waterways even several miles from the lake, including the Spokane River. Fish sampled throughout the Spokane River have elevated levels of lead. The estimated cost of cleanup from the mining and associated smelter operations is $1 billion. For information on mining contamination in the Basin, *see* Paul Koberstein, *Out of the Earth, Into our Lungs,* CASCADIA TIMES 8, Nov.-Dec. 2000.

The federal government brought a CERCLA cost-recovery and natural resource damages suit against the companies that were still solvent. The Coeur d'Alene Tribe brought a separate action for natural resource damages, and the cases were consolidated. In 2003, the court issued an opinion finding defendant mining companies liable for natural resource damages resulting from their historic mining practices. Coeur d'Alene Tribe v. Asarco, 280 F.Supp.2d 1094 (D. Idaho 2003). Phase II of the litigation will establish the amount of damages and resolve other pending issues. For a discussion of the Coeur d'Alene litigation, *see* Michael R. Thorp & Kristen Bamford Wynne, *The Coeur d'Alene Case: Breathing New Life Into Old Defenses,* 17 NAT. RES. & ENV'T. 158 (2003). For documents pertaining to the CERCLA cleanup, *see* the EPA's Coeur d'Alene Basin web site, at http://www.epa.gov/region10.

The tribal ownership role in the Coeur d'Alene CERCLA action demonstrates the increasingly broad reach of tribal sovereigns in natural resource issues. Tribes are eligible as natural resource trustees under CERCLA and can sue to recover damages to resources. *See* CERCLA, 42 U.S.C. § 9607(f)(1). The Supreme Court has ruled that the Tribe owns the southern third of the lakebed of Lake Coeur d'Alene, rejecting the State of Idaho's claim of ownership under the Equal Footing Doctrine. *See* Idaho v. United States, 533 U.S. 262, 282, 121 S.Ct. 2135, 2147, 150 L.Ed.2d 326, 342 (2001) (discussed in Chapter 5.III.A). The ruling put the Tribe in the position of a natural resource trustee that can sue for damage to that portion of the lakebed. *See Coeur d'Alene,* 280 F. Supp.2d at 1117. In addition, the Tribe has usufructory property rights in water, fisheries and wildlife that may form a basis for additional natural resource damages, a matter to be decided in phase II of the *Coeur d'Alene* natural resource damage litigation.

Given the potential for multi-million dollar liability, one might think that mining companies would exercise the utmost caution in conducting their operations. Yet hundreds of mining sites—including some of the newest "state of the art" mines—have caused releases of hazardous substances. Why hasn't CERCLA been a more effective tool in preventing contamination? The following case study, involving Glamis Gold Ltd.'s mining plan, provides an opportunity to consider the imposition of preventative measures on a proposed mine *before* the damage occurs. Various aspects of the proposal are discussed in Chapter 4.V.B (NEPA) and Chapter 12.V. (minerals).

In Focus: The Glamis Imperial Project and Quechan Sacred Sites

One of the most controversial ongoing mining proposals is the Glamis Imperial Project in south-eastern California. The large-scale open pit mine is proposed on BLM lands in an area that has extraordinary cultural and historic value to the Quechan and other tribes of the area. The Quechan's sacred Trail of Dreams, prayer circles, rock rings, and other spiritual features of great religious significance crisscross Glamis' mining claims. The proposed mine would involve excavating 300 million tons of waste rock, digging an 880–foot pit, and leaving two huge waste dumps and a 280–foot heap leach pad on site.

After seven years of consideration involving two draft EISs and a final EIS, Interior Secretary Babbitt (under the Clinton administration) denied the mining company's plan of operations. Record of Decision for the Imperial Project Gold Mine Proposal, 10-11 (Jan. 17, 2001). The denial was based in part on a special provision in FLPMA for the California Desert Conservation Area (CDCA), and in part on the Clinton 3809 mining regulations (promulgated in 2000) that provided authority to disapprove a proposed plan of mining operations to protect cultural resources from substantial irreparable harm. *See* Section VI.B., *supra*.

When the Bush II administration came into office, the new Secretary of Interior, Gale Norton, rescinded both the Clinton regulations and the Jan. 17, 2001 Record of Decision that had denied the Imperial Project plan of operations. For discussion, *see* Roger Flynn & Jeffrey C. Parsons, *The Right To Say No: Federal Authority Over Hardrock Mining On Public Lands,* 16 J. Envtl. L. & Litig. 249, 326–29 (Fall 2001). But Secretary Norton did not take action to approve the mine.

The saga then took an interesting turn into state and international law. The Tribe seized the period of administrative limbo to take action in another forum—the California Legislature. In 2003, the legislature passed a new mining law (S.B. 22) requiring open pit metal mines to be completely backfilled as part of the reclamation process—an exceedingly expensive requirement that would for all practical purposes preclude the Imperial Project. *See* Pub. Res. Code 2773.3. For background, *see* Julie Cart, *New Rule Imperils Mining, Firms Say*, L.A. Times, April 15, 2003, at B6. Whether the California law is preempted by federal law is an interesting question that finds its boundaries in the landmark *California Coastal Commission* opinion. *See* California Coastal Commission v. Granite Rock Co., 480 U.S. 572, 107 S.Ct. 1419, 94 L.Ed.2d 577 (1987). The mining company has responded by seeking relief (using its Canadian parent corporation) through international processes provided in the North American Free Trade Agreement (NAFTA), filing an action claiming that it has suffered an impermissible "expropriation" under Chapter 11 of the treaty. North American Free Trade Agreement, Dec. 17, 1992, Can.-U.S.-Mex., 32 I.L.M. 605, 639 (1993). *See* Evelyn Iritani, *Gold Firm Plans Suit Under NAFTA*, L.A. TIMES, Aug. 20, 2003, at C1. Glamis demands $50 million in compensation. Glamis and the U.S. State Department have agreed to arbitration of the claim. For discussion, *see* Mike McGee, *Skirting the Law Under NAFTA, Foreign Companies Can Avoid American Courts*, 2004 ALM Properties, Inc., The Recorder (February 24, 2004), *available at* http://www.law.georgetown.edu/gelpi/papers/recordernafta.pdf.

Exercise:

You represent a mining company, called "Goldstrike," with claims on BLM lands in Utah. Goldstrike is a subsidiary of a foreign corporation located in Canada. Goldstrike seeks to develop a cyanide heap-leach mine to extract gold. The proposed operation would be in a pristine watershed that is part of the critical habitat for an ESA-listed fish. The company has agreed to install a containment liner, but even so, by the company's own account, its cyanide pond will leach contaminants into a stream flowing onto an Indian reservation located 1/2 mile from the proposed mine. Goldstrike expects the mine to operate 10 years. Provide advice to the company on the various ownership interests implicated by this proposal, as well as any potential liabilities associated with its proposed operations.

Chapter 7

TRIBAL OWNERSHIP

This Part of the casebook has focused on different types of ownership as a determinative factor in how land and natural resources are managed. The category of tribal ownership invokes a totally different set of laws than federal, state, and individual ownership, and often reflects values quite different from those influencing ownership prerogatives in the other categories. Chapter 5 provides the fundamental background underlying federal Indian law, including principles pertaining to the federal trust obligation, tribal treaty rights, inherent tribal sovereignty, and jurisdictional questions. This chapter delves into more specific issues regarding tribal natural resources management.

Websources:

Several organizations and inter-tribal commissions deal with tribal natural resource and treaty issues. The websites of a few are listed below:

Native American Rights Fund: http://www.narf.org

Indigenous Environmental Network: http://www.ienearth.org

National Tribal Environmental Council: http://www.ntec.org

Native American Water Association: http://www.nawainc.org

Council of Energy Resource Tribes: http://www.certredearth.com

Intertribal Timber Council: http://www.itcnet.org

Native American Fish and Wildlife Society: http://www.nafws.org

---

I. INDIAN COUNTRY TODAY

Indian Country is occupied by numerous tribes diverse in their geographic location, cultural background, and history. At present, there are over 562 federally recognized tribes and at least 169 more tribes lacking federal recognition. There are approximately 300 federally administered Indian reservations, most located in the west, totaling about 55 million acres. *See* AMERICAN INDIAN DIGEST: CONTEMPORARY DEMOGRAPHICS OF THE AMERICAN INDIAN: FACTS ABOUT TODAY'S AMERICAN INDIANS, Appendix D–1 (1996). Roughly half of the American Indian population lives on or near reservations, while the other half lives primarily in urban areas. Reservations play a vital role in serving as the homelands and cultural enclaves for tribal people and in producing revenue for tribal communities. Professor Charles Wilkinson has described reservation lands as "islands of Indianness" within the larger society where tribal prerogatives, culture, tradition, and values prevail. CHARLES F. WILKINSON, AMERICAN INDIANS, TIME, AND THE LAW 122 (1987). Yet the reservations vary tremendously in size and resource abundance. The Navajo Nation has the largest reservation land base, encompassing 16 million acres of land in Arizona, New Mexico, and Utah. The Yakama, Colville, Hualapai, Blackfeet, and Jicarilla reservations each have roughly a million acres of land. California tribes have only tiny "rancherias," Alaska native corporations have "villages," and some tribes have no lands spared from federal conquest.

The makeup of property ownership within Indian reservations also varies considerably. Recall that during the Allotment period, the federal government breached treaties and split up many Indian lands, allocating parcels to individual Indians or families in fee simple. *See supra*, Chapter 5. The parcels passed to individuals after a 25–year period in which the government held them in trust for the individual allottees. More often than not, the crushing burden of state taxes precluded the allottee from holding the property after the trust period expired, and non-Indians gained substantial ownership of land within the outer boundaries of reservations by buying up allotments lost through state foreclosure. When the Indian Reorganization Act was passed in 1934, 48 Stat. 984 (codified at 25 U.S.C. §§ 461–479 (2001)), it extended the trust status of those individual allotments that had not yet been transferred in fee simple to the Indian owners, leaving some lands perpetually in trust for individual Indians. 25 U.S.C. § 462. Accordingly, reservations today may have three types of land ownership within their boundaries: land held in trust by the federal government (usually called trust lands), land held in trust by the federal government for individual allottees (usually called allotments), and land held in fee simple absolute (called "fee" lands).

The resulting picture may be a very fragmented one, with reservations divided into scattered parcels of non-Indian and Indian ownership. On many reservations, the tribe is a minority landowner. The 770,000–acre Nez Perce Reservation in Idaho, for example, contains only 115,500 acres of tribally owned and Indian allotment lands. By contrast, the San Carlos Tribe's 1,826,541–acre reservation in Arizona is 100% tribally owned.

Tribes differ greatly in their economic status and pursuits. The 750–member Mashantucket Pequot Tribe, located in northeast Connecticut, has enjoyed wealth unparalleled in Indian Country as a result of its Foxwoods Casino, one of the largest in the world, estimated to have drawn over $8 billion in revenue since it opened in 1993. The Oglala Lakota Sioux Pine Ridge Reservation, on the other hand, is impoverished due to a nearly 85% unemployment rate. *See* Peter Kilborn, *Clinton, Amid the Despair on a Reservation, Again Pledges Help*, THE N.Y. TIMES, July 8, 1999, at A16. Although the proliferation of gaming has helped lift many tribes out of dire economic straits, a large number of tribes located in parts of the country too remote to support the operation of viable casinos remain economically desperate. Some of these tribes have used their land and natural resources to open hotels and resorts, or to produce timber, oil, gas, and other minerals. Yet others succumb to outside offers to locate hazardous and even nuclear waste facilities on their reservations. On many of the larger reservations and in Alaska, a subsistence economy still plays an important part in sustaining the cultural heritage of the tribe and supplying food to its members. Reservation plants (roots, berries and medicinal plants) and wildlife (deer, elk, caribou, fish, and game) are vital to sustaining these traditional economies. The dire economic conditions across a vast expanse of Indian Country creates profound dilemmas surrounding the use of reservation land and resources.

Many tribes are adding to their land base to provide more opportunities for economic development or traditional enterprise. Most restoration efforts focus on lands lost through treaty abrogation, allotment or termination. A few tribes, particularly those that were terminated and later regained recognition, have had some lands restored as a result of Congressional action. The expansion of Indian Country gives even more reason for natural resource professionals to understand the basic principles of Indian law.

In Focus:

The Proposal to Restore Lands of the Confederated Tribes of Coos, Lower Umpqua and Siuslaw

The Confederated Tribes of Coos, Lower Umpqua and Siuslaw (aggregated together as one tribal government by the United States) inhabited the coastal regions of Oregon, claiming aboriginal holdings collectively amounting to about 1.6 million acres of land. The government never performed on a treaty promise to provide the tribes with a reservation, nor did it compensate the tribes for loss of their land. Instead, the tribes were imprisoned on another reservation, where approximately half of the population died of starvation, disease, and exposure while their lands were settled by non-Indians. Upon release after 19 years of confinement, the landless tribes returned to their homeland region and established a formal government in 1916, which has continued to the present. In 1954, the tribes were terminated over their strong opposition, and federal assistance ended. Federal recognition was restored in 1984, but the tribes continued to suffer economically. Over time, the tribal confederation collected a few isolated parcels for a reservation (6.2 acres), a tribal office (9.7 acres), low-income housing units (18 acres) and a planned casino (98 acres). In 1999, the 720–member confederation developed a detailed proposal for return of approximately 100,000 acres of forest land located in the Siuslaw National Forest (managed by the U.S. Forest Service). In March, 2003, Senator Gordon Smith announced his intention to introduce a bill restoring 63,000 acres of forestland to the tribe. *See* Scott Maben, *Bill Offers Coast Forest Homeland to Tribes,* THE EUGENE REGISTER–GUARD, Mar. 8, 2003. The tribal proposal states in part:

> [R]eacquir[ing] a portion of the Tribes' ancestral homelands is vital to restoration of Tribal culture. It will enable a spiritual and physical reconnecting to the land which Tribal ancestors inhabited for centuries.

> [It will provide] a place to restore cultural practices and beliefs which bond Indian people forever to the land and teach lifeways which are in harmony and at peace with the natural world.
>
> * * * Many Tribal members still walk through these lands to pray, camp, pick berries, hunt, and fish. When we do these things, we know our ancestors walked here before us doing these things, for uncounted generations. * * *
>
> Restoration [will] be accomplished by [legislative] re-designation of a portion of the ... Siuslaw National Forest as Indian trust land. [The] federal lands, [which are] presently managed by the Forest Service, will be taken into trust for the Tribes by the Secretary of the Interior and managed by the Bureau of Indian Affairs and Tribes.
>
> CONFEDERATED TRIBES OF COOS, LOWER UMPQUA AND SIUSLAW INDIANS, RESERVATION PLAN AND FOREST LAND RESTORATION PROPOSAL 24, 51 (1999). As of 2006, the legislation had not passed.

Exercise:

The Confederated Tribes' restored land would come from what is currently a national forest managed under the National Forest Management Act (NFMA) (detailed in Chapter 6.II). Given that the tribe intends to use the forest partly for harvesting timber, what ecosystem protections will be in place if the tribe acquires the land? NFMA will no longer apply, but the tribe promises to manage the land in accordance with standards applied to adjacent federal land managed under NFMA. Assume you are an attorney for a forest conservation organization. What position would you take on the restoration plan? Would you urge that the legislation authorizing the restored lands contain enforceable standards? Outline the standards and enforcement mechanisms you might propose.

II. LAND AND RESOURCE ETHICS

One can hardly consider the role of tribes in natural resources law without reflecting on the traditional perspectives that have guided tribal interaction with the environment for millennia. The unique land ethic common to most indigenous communities stands in stark contrast to that of the majority society. While tribal council decisions today sometimes depart from these traditional values, the indigenous approach is still sufficiently alive and so frequently expressed by tribal policy makers that it is gaining increasing importance in non-Indian land policy. Native scholar and activist Winona LaDuke describes what she believes are fundamental differences between "indigenous thinking" and "industrial thinking."

VOICES FROM WHITE EARTH: GAA-WAABAABIGANIKAAG
Winona LaDuke
Thirteenth Annual E.F. Schumacher Lectures,
Oct. 1993, Yale University
at http://www.schumachersociety.org/lec-lad.html

* * * Indigenous people continue their ways of living based on generations and generations of knowledge and practice on the land. [T]he perspective of indigenous peoples is entirely different from that of the dominant society in this country.

Indigenous peoples believe fundamentally in natural law and a state of balance. We believe that all societies and cultural practices must exist in accordance with natural law in order to be sustainable. We also believe that cultural diversity is as essential as biological diversity to maintaining sustainable societies. Indigenous peoples have lived on earth sustainably for thousands of years, and I suggest to you that indigenous ways of living are the only sustainable ways of living. * * *

Indigenous people have taken great care to fashion their societies in accordance with natural law, which is the highest law. * * * Most indigenous ceremonies, if you look to their essence, are about the restoration of balance. That is our intent: to restore, and then to retain, balance. Nature itself continually tries to balance, to equalize.

According to our way of living and our way of looking at the world, most of the world is animate. * * * Looking at the world and seeing that most things are alive, we have come to believe, based on this perception, that they have spirit. They have standing on their own. Therefore, when I harvest wild rice on our reservation up north, I always offer *asemah*, tobacco, because when you take something, you must always give thanks to its spirit for giving itself to you, for it has a choice whether to give itself to you or not. * * *

And so we are always very careful when we harvest. * * * We also say that when you take, you must take only what you need and leave the rest. Because if you take more than you need, that means you are greedy. You have brought about imbalance; you have been selfish. To do this in our community is a very big disgrace. It is a violation of natural law. * * *

We have tried to retain this way of living and this way of thinking in spite of all that has happened to us over the centuries. I believe we do retain most of these practices to a great extent in many of our societies. In our community they are overshadowed at times by industrialism, but they still exist.

I would like to contrast ... indigenous thinking with what I call "industrial thinking." * * * Industrial thinking is characterized by several ideas which run counter to indigenous ideas. First, instead of believing that natural law is preeminent, industrial society believes that humans are entitled to full dominion over nature. It believes that man—

and it is usually man of course—has some God-given right to all that is around him, that he has been created superior to the rest. Second, instead of modeling itself on the cyclical structure of nature, this society is patterned on linear thinking. * * * And certain values permeate this way of thinking, such as the concept of progress. Industrial society wants to keep making progress as it moves down the timeline, progress defined by things like technological advancement and economic growth. This value accompanies linear thinking.

Third, there is the attitude toward what is wild as opposed to what is cultivated or "tame." This society believes it must tame the wilderness. It also believes in the superiority of civilized over primitive peoples, a belief which also follows a linear model: that somehow, over time, people will become more civilized. Also related of course is the idea behind colonialism: that some people have the right to civilize other people. My experience is that people who are viewed as "primitive" are generally people of color, and people who are viewed as "civilized" are those of European descent. This prejudice still permeates industrial society and in fact even permeates "progressive" thinking. It holds that somehow people of European descent are smarter—they have some better knowledge of the world than the rest of us. I suggest that this is perhaps a racist worldview, that it has racist implications. * * *

Fourth, [i]ndustrial language has changed things from being animate, alive, and having spirit to being inanimate, mere objects and commodities of society. When things are inanimate, "man" can view them as his God-given right. He can take them, commodify them, and manipulate them in society. * * *

Fifth ... is the idea of capitalism itself. * * * The capitalist goal is to use the least labor, capital, and resources to accumulate the most profit. The intent of capitalism is accumulation. So the capitalist's method is always to take more than is needed. Therefore, from an indigenous point of view capitalism is inherently out of harmony with natural law.

Based on this goal of accumulation, industrial society practices conspicuous consumption. Indigenous societies, on the other hand, practice what I would call "conspicuous distribution." We focus on the potlatch, the giveaway, an event which carries much more honor than accumulation does. In fact, the more you give away, the greater your honor. * * *

Over the past five hundred years the indigenous experience has been one of conflict between the indigenous and the industrial worldviews. * * * Indigenous people understand clearly that this society, which has caused the extinction of more species in the past hundred and fifty years than the total species extinction from the Ice Age to the midnineteenth century, is the same society that has caused the extinction of about two thousand different indigenous peoples in the Western Hemisphere alone. We understand intimately the relationship between extinction of species and extinction of peoples, because we experience both. * * *

Notes and Questions

1. LaDuke ends the passage with this statement: "A common set of values is needed to live together sustainably on the land." Do you agree?

2. Tribal governments often express strong conservation values in their natural resource management. As sovereigns, they frequently stand in marked contrast to their state and federal partners, which typically do not express an ethic towards the land, much less one based on spiritual mandates. Do tribal sovereigns carry the potential to influence their state and federal counterparts, or are their governing philosophies too far apart to have any influence?

3. In 2003, the Navajo Nation released to the public its traditional and spiritual laws in written form. *See* Robert Yazzie, *Air, Light/Fire, Water and Earth/Pollen: Sacred Elements That Sustain Life,* 18 J. ENVTL. L. & LITIG. 191 (2003). Section 5(G) of the code states: "It is the duty and responsibility of the Dine' to protect and preserve the beauty of the natural world for future generations." For a full text of the code, *see* Native Web, http://www.nativeweb.org/pages/legal/navajo_ law.html.

4. Does the indigenous worldview provide any practical direction towards sustainability in the face of a modern economy dominated by the corporate structure? How do corporations arrive at decisions that significantly impact natural resources? Do they take into consideration the harm their actions may have on human communities or on environmental sustainability, or do short-term profit motives form the primary yardstick for decisions?

5. Some tribal councils have allowed strip mining, clearcutting, and the siting of waste dumps on their land. Has the indigenous cultural norm of traditional "natural law" been eroded by assimilation with the majority society and its industrial viewpoint? Or do these choices reflect the economic despair in Indian Country? A combination of the two? For discussions of native environmental values, *see* Rebecca Tsosie, *Tribal Environmental Policy in an Era of Self–Determination: The Role of Ethics, Economics, and Traditional Ecological Knowledge,* 21 VT. L. REV. 225 (1996).

III. LAND AND RESOURCE MANAGEMENT IN INDIAN COUNTRY

While Indian land comprises only a small fraction of the land base in the United States, its role in broader ecosystem terms is often crucial. Yet many natural resource professionals have little understanding of how land and resource management decisions are made in Indian Country, or what sovereigns exercise jurisdiction over land-based activities. This lack of awareness is not surprising, because natural resource issues within Indian Country invoke one of the most complicated areas of the law. Generally, it is useful to take a two-fold approach to such issues.

First, it is essential to ask who owns the land or resource in question. As previously explained, land within reservation boundaries might be held by the federal government in trust for the tribe, or in trust for an Indian allottee, or it might be held in fee ownership by a private party. If the land is held in fee ownership, decisions as to management are made by the owner, just as such decisions would be made by owners of private property outside of Indian Country. But if the land is held in trust for the tribe by the federal government, there are two sovereigns involved: the federal government and the tribe. The federal government's role is determined by its trust responsibility towards the tribe. *See* Chapter 5.II.B., *supra*. In the case of allotted lands, the federal government is still trustee, but the beneficial owner is the individual member of the tribe. Section A below provides an overview of the four primary areas of economic activity on Indian lands: agricultural and grazing leasing, mineral development, forest management, and commercial leasing. Because the federal government's role with respect to tribal trust and allotted lands is one of a trustee, questions of liability loom over the government's land management actions in each of these categories. Four Supreme Court cases provide the parameters for the government's trust liability, an area explored in section B.

After sorting through the mix of ownership issues involved with land management decisions, the second level of analysis is determining the regulatory jurisdiction that applies to any given situation. Suppose, for example, a tribe wants to engage in forest operations on its reservation. What laws pertain to that activity, and which sovereign enforces them? Or suppose an owner of fee land within a reservation decides to build a housing subdivision on the land. Does the tribe, or the state, have land use regulatory authority over the proposal? These are complicated questions that involve an accommodation of three sovereigns: the federal government, the tribes, and the states. Section C provides the jurisdictional framework for approaching these questions.

A. Land Management Decisions on Trust Lands Within Indian Country

The Supreme Court has declared the ownership of Indian trust lands analogous to "one existing under a common law trust, with the United States as trustee, the Indian tribes or individuals as beneficiaries, and the property and natural resources managed by the United States as the trust corpus." Dep't of Interior v. Klamath Water Users Protective Ass'n, 532 U.S. 1, 121 S.Ct. 1060, 149 L.Ed.2d 87 (2001). Generally speaking, Indian tribes are the beneficial owners of all of the natural resources upon their lands, including the forest and mineral resources. United States v. Shoshone Tribe of Indians, 304 U.S. 111, 58 S.Ct. 794, 82 L.Ed. 1213 (1938). Since the beginning of federal-Indian relations, Congress has prohibited private individuals or local governments from acquiring property interests in tribal lands without federal approval. Nonintercourse Act, 25 U.S.C. § 177 (1834). This approval role derives from the federal government's trust ownership of all Indian lands and resources, a concept first introduced in Johnson v. McIntosh, 21 U.S. 543, 5 L.Ed. 681 (1823); *see also Shoshone*, 304 U.S. at 116 (as trustee, United States holds "naked fee" title to Indian land, and tribes hold the beneficial interest).

The BIA's land management role is governed by several statutes, explained in more detail below. Historically, this federal role has been all-encompassing, but in recent years, tribes have gained more control over their lands and resources. Provisions in the Indian Self–Determination and Education Assistance Act of 1975 and the Tribal Self Governance Act of 1994 allow tribes to enter into contracts, cooperative agreements and funding agreements with the federal government to manage reservation programs. *See* 25 U.S.C. § 450e–1 (grants and cooperative agreements); 25 U.S.C. § 450f (self-determination contracts); 25 U.S.C. § 450h (grants to tribal organizations or tribes); 25 U.S.C. § 458cc (funding agreements). Even where a tribe takes advantage of these mechanisms, however, the federal government retains supervisory authority, and leases of Indian land to non-Indians still require federal approval under the Nonintercourse Act, 25 U.S.C. § 177; *see also* 25 U.S.C. § 415. For discussion, *see* Reid Payton Chambers & Monroe E. Price, *Regulating Sovereignty: Secretarial Discretion and Leasing of Indian Lands,* 26 Stan. L. Rev. 1061 (1974).

1. *Agricultural and Grazing Leasing*

The Indian Long–Term Leasing Act of 1955, 25 U.S.C. § 415, allows leases of up to 25 years for farming purposes and leases of up to 10 years for grazing. In 1990, Congress passed the American Indian Agricultural Resources Management Act (AIARMA) to promote grazing and farming of Indian lands and to support increased tribal management of those uses. 25 U.S.C. § 3701 et seq. AIARMA provides for 10–year agricultural resources plans, which may be developed and implemented by the tribe or by the federal government (in consultation with the tribe). *See* 25 U.S.C. § 3711(b). The plans inventory the resources, define tribal goals and objectives, and create steps towards those goals. 25 U.S.C. § 3711(b)(1). In general, the statute requires that management of agricultural lands be in compliance with tribal cultural, environmental, and land use laws unless inconsistent with federal trust obligations or federal law. 25 U.S.C. § 3712(b). Moreover, farming and grazing must be consistent with principles of sustained yield management and conservation principles. *See* 25 C.F.R. § 162.231. For an overview of the statutory and regulatory context of grazing, *see* Handbook of Federal Indian Law, Ch. 17 (2005 ed.).

2. *Mineral Development*

Indian tribes are, in the aggregate, the third largest owners of mineral resources in the United States. The two primary statutes governing mineral development on Indian land are the Indian Mineral Leasing Act of 1938 and the Indian Mineral Development Act of 1982. The 1938 Act established initial procedures for leasing tribal lands. Mineral leases required both tribal consent and the approval of the Secretary of the Interior. 25 U.S.C. § 396a–g. A major drawback to the statute was that it allowed leases to continue under the original terms "as long thereafter as minerals are produced in paying quantities," *id.,* leaving many tribes with deficient royalties and less than optimal terms. Moreover, the tribes had no authority to control management decisions or impose environmental protections.

In 1982, Congress set out to reform the mineral leasing system on Indian lands by enacting the Indian Mineral Development Act (IMDA), 25 U.S.C. § 2101. The IMDA was designed to give tribes more control over mineral leasing and increase their financial return. Under the IMDA, tribes can negotiate their own mineral agreements, though such agreements are subject to the Secretary's approval to ensure that they are "in the best interest of the Indian Tribe." 25 U.S.C. § 2103(b). Through mineral agreements, tribes can negotiate royalty rates or other conditions favorable to the tribe, and impose management criteria and environmental standards. In deciding whether to approve the lease, the Secretary must consider the potential economic benefits as well potential "environmental, social, and cultural effects" on the tribe. *Id.* A downside of the IMDA is that once the mineral agreement is final, the tribe loses its ability to cancel it, though the Secretary retains authority to cancel in the event of violations.

Environmental effects of mining may be acute and long-lasting. On Navajo lands, uranium mining that began in the 1940s has left 1300 abandoned mines. Radioactive tailings continue to cause radiation sickness among Navajo people and threaten drinking water supplies. *See* Peter H. Eichstaedt, If You Poison Us: Uranium and Native Americans (Red Crane Books 1994). In 2005, the Navajo Nation Tribal Council enacted a tribal law banning any further uranium mining. *See Coming Clean on Uranium at Navajo,* Indian Country Today, April 28, 2005. The 27,000-square-mile reservation, which spreads across parts of Arizona, Colorado, New Mexico and Utah, sits upon one of the world's largest deposits of uranium ore.

For more on tribal mineral development, *see* Handbook of Federal Indian Law, Ch. 17 (2005 ed.); Judith V. Royster, *Mineral Development in Indian Country: The Evolution of Tribal Control Over Mineral Resources,* 29 Tulsa L. J. 541 (1994).

In Focus:

The Northern Cheyenne's Battle Against Mineral Leasing

A BREATH OF FRESH AIR: SURROUNDED BY A MASSIVE INDUSTRIAL BUILDUP, THE NORTHERN CHEYENNE TRIBE DEFENDS ITS HOMELAND
Bob Struckman and Ray Ring
High Country News, Jan. 20, 2003

* * * In southeast Montana, the Northern Cheyenne Reservation is an island. The tribe has been nearly surrounded by no less than five

huge strip mines, as well as the Colstrip power plant, haulage rail-roads and transmission lines.* * * And a few miles east of the reservation, in the only direction still undeveloped, the Montana state government has allied with industry seeking to create a new strip mine, and possibly build another power plant and railroad.

Yet for 30 years, the Northern Cheyenne—a relatively small and isolated tribe—have fought powerful corporations that want to develop the coalbeds that underlie almost every inch of the reservation. They have done what many other tribes have been unable to do: protected their land and culture, and repeatedly reached beyond their borders to battle development off the reservation. * * *

The Northern Cheyenne Indian reservation is not large. Over the years, its boundaries have been adjusted, and now it encompasses about 707 square miles of rugged, semi-arid country, rising up to Badger Peak's 4,422–foot elevation. Ponderosa pines dot the long red ridges, and sagebrush, skunkweed and prairie grasses fill the narrow valleys. The Tongue River meanders along the eastern border.

"We had to fight for it, with our spirit (and) our determination to continue and survive as a people on our land," says Joe Little Coyote, the tribe's economic development planner.

During community meetings, old men still rise to expound on the lessons learned at Little Bighorn…. Generations since have faced tough times, trying to survive on small-scale ranching, logging and federal assistance, far from any city, airport or interstate highway.

Yet under the reservation's surface lie arguably the biggest coal reserves held by any tribe—an estimated 20 to 50 billion tons, part of a coal belt that stretches from southeast Montana into Wyoming. The coal tends to be low-sulfur, relatively clean-burning and desirable as a fuel for power plants. Large-scale strip mining began on land near the reservation in 1968, and when the Arab oil embargo sparked an energy crisis in the early 1970s, the coal companies ramped up production.

At first, the tribe saw this as an opportunity. From 1966 to 1971, the tribal council signed coal leases with a half-dozen corporations and speculators, including Peabody Coal, Consolidated Coal, and Amax Coal.

The federal Bureau of Indian Affairs acted as trustee for the tribe, theoretically watching out for the tribe's interests. But the BIA didn't even complete an environmental impact statement, and the leases covered more than half the reservation. The agency sold the exploration rights for about $9 per acre, and the tribe would have received royalties of no more than 17.5 cents a ton for any coal mined.

"The BIA had sold our coal for less than gravel," says Gail Small, the outspoken leader of Native Action, a Northern Cheyenne activist group.

"The federal and tribal representatives were clearly overmatched" in those lease negotiations, says Jason Whiteman Jr., a Northern Cheyenne who has worked in the tribe's environmental program since the 1970s. "We had no idea what the impacts would be," he says, and the terms of the deal were "unconscionable."

The Northern Cheyenne began to understand the implications as the corporations drilled thousands of exploration holes and announced plans to build power plants on the reservation. Such development would threaten more than the tribe's cattle ranches and crops. It would strike at the underlying tribal culture. "I remember seeing blueprints for boomtowns of 30,000 people on the reservation—we would've been a minority here," says Whiteman. * * *

Claiming the BIA had violated laws and neglected its role as trustee, the Northern Cheyenne presented a 600–page petition to then-Secretary of Interior Rogers C.B. Morton. It was a bold move. Working the highest levels of federal government, within a few years the tribe got all those coal leases canceled, forced the corporations to pay about $10 million in damages, and gained control of another 7,000 acres one corporation had bought for mining. * * *

Throughout the 1970s, Tribal Chairman Rowland helped foster a younger generation of budding activists and leaders, who were so inspired and empowered by early victories that they have retained a sense of mission and optimism ever since. * * * Among the innovative steps taken by Rowland in those days was a youth program in which local kids traveled by bus to visit coal mines in Wyoming and on the Navajo Reservation in Arizona. Gail Small recalls sitting for a photograph with about 20 fellow students in a huge mechanical shovel near Gillette, Wyo., and feeling awed by the immense power of the mining operation.

"We were sent out as scouts, and on the way home we talked about it. We got fired up. We knew that, given the chance, we would be exploited," says Small....

As industry pressures increased, the Northern Cheyenne continued to stand tough in courts and gain concessions from corporations in savvy negotiations. The tribe voided industry-friendly coal leases made on three sides of the reservation by the Reagan administration's secretary of Interior, James Watt, in 1982, and canceled the permit for the Montco mine just east of the reservation in 1997. The Northern Cheyenne also cancelled the allotment of much of the reservation's subsurface mineral rights to individual tribal members and heirs— something coal speculators had hoped to take advantage of. Now the tribe effectively retains ownership of all the subsurface rights on the reservation. * * *

"The companies will never leave us alone," says Whiteman. "They will always be knocking at the door."

3. *Forest Resources*

Tribal forest lands are often part of a broader ecosystem comprised of mixed ownerships. There are 16 million acres of forested land on 214 Indian reservations in 23 states. In addition to their timber value, Indian forest lands provide tribes with fish, wildlife, berries, medicinal plants, firewood, and forage for stock. They also provide recreational opportunities, support watersheds, and contain cultural, spiritual and archeological resources.

A statute passed in 1910 gave the Secretary of Interior the power to sell timber from Indian land. 25 U.S.C. § 407. Regulations required tribal consent for all timber sales. 25 C.F.R. § 163.14(a). Over the following two decades, concerns mounted over the Bureau of Indian Affair's (BIA's) clear-cutting practices—or, in the words of one official, the "slaughtering of Indian timber lands." *See* United States v. Mitchell, 463 U.S. 206, 221 n.21, 103 S.Ct. 2961, 2970, 77 L.Ed.2d 580, 594 (1983) *(Mitchell II)* (quoting John Collier, Commissioner of Indian Affairs). In 1934, Congress enacted the Indian Reorganization Act (IRA), which included a provision requiring the Secretary to manage Indian forest lands on the basis of "sustained yield." 25 U.S.C. § 466. Nevertheless, BIA continued to convert old growth forests to tree plantations on Indian reservations, causing environmental damage.

In 1990, Congress enacted the National Indian Forest Resource Management Act (NIFRMA). 25 U.S.C. § 3102. This was a comprehensive forest management statute designed to provide tribes with a more active role in management and to encourage more sustainable forestry. NIFRMA emphasizes the management of the forest as a whole, expanding the focus beyond timber to a whole host of "forest products," defined to include not only timber, but also fuel wood, nuts, berries, roots, mushrooms, herbs, Christmas trees, and "other marketable material." 25 U.S.C. § 3103(6). The regulations require Secretarial approval as well as tribal authorization before forest products may be sold from reservation lands. 25 C.F.R. § 163.14(a). In a sharp departure from the timber-dominant emphasis of past management directives, NIFRMA requires management of tribal forest land in its natural state when the tribe determines that the recreational, aesthetic, cultural, or traditional values of the land represent "the highest and best use." 25 U.S.C. § 3104(b)(5). Further, NIFRMA imposes management objectives to regulate water runoff, minimize soil erosion, and protect wildlife, fisheries, grazing, recreation, aesthetic, cultural, and traditional values. 25 U.S.C. § 3104(b)(6). NIFRMA refined the sustained yield mandate of earlier forest laws by requiring management of forest land "in a perpetually productive state in accordance with principles of sustained yield." 25 U.S.C. § 3104(b)(1). It also defines "sustained yield" in broad fashion to support continuous production of "forest products" as a whole. 25 U.S.C. § 3103(14).

Reflecting Congress' overall faith in forest planning (recall NFMA, explained in Chapter 6.II), NIFRMA imposes a forest planning requirement in Indian country, too. The Act calls for the Secretary of Interior to develop forest management plans (FMPs) with full tribal consultation and participation. 25 U.S.C. § 3104(b)(2). FMPs link into (and must be consistent with) a broader type of plan known as a "tribal integrated resource management plan" that comprehensively covers management of all of the tribe's natural resources. See 25 U.S.C. § 3103(4)(B), (5), (15), § 3104(b)(2). All timber harvests must be "consistent with" the FMP, see Silver v. Babbitt, 924 F.Supp. 976, 984 (D. Ariz. 1995), and comply with all applicable tribal laws. 25 U.S.C. § 3108. The provision is important, as tribes are increasingly developing detailed codes to govern natural resources management.

4. Commercial Leasing

Commercial leasing of tribal lands by non-Indians is conducted under the Long–Term Leasing Act of 1955, 25 U.S.C. § 415. That section authorizes leases up to 25 years (with an option to renew for another 25 years) for "public, religious, educational, recreational, or business purposes...." The Secretary of Interior retains the authority to cancel a lease in case of violation of lease terms. 25 C.F.R. § 162.619. In Rosebud Sioux Tribe v. McDivitt, 286 F.3d 1031 (2002), the Eighth Circuit found that a company who had a lease for a hog farm on tribal lands had no standing to challenge the government's cancellation of the lease.

The lease approval function of the federal government takes place against a complex modern political framework. The current BIA policy is to defer to tribal councils in making approval decisions. See 25 C.F.R. § 162.107(a). Yet many proposals to lease Indian lands, particularly those geared towards mining and waste disposal, carry long-term or permanent environmental consequences and are vigorously opposed by many members of the tribe. Occasionally, proposals approved by one tribal council are then repudiated by a newly elected tribal council— unless it is too late. In Rosebud Sioux Tribe, supra, for example, the tribal council initially approved the hog farm lease, but a reconstituted council later disfavored it. Federal approval authority is often viewed as an encroachment on tribal sovereignty, yet at the same time such approval may be the only check against losing a tribal land base to industrial interests. The excerpts below explores this complex federal role.

INDIAN LAND AND THE PROMISE OF NATIVE SOVEREIGNTY: THE TRUST DOCTRINE REVISITED
Mary Christina Wood
1994 Utah L. Rev. 1471

* * * The majority society in the United States has always had an insatiable demand for land. If history has any predictive value, the pressure to exploit the remaining 56.6 million acres of native-owned land

likely will continue.... * * * A barrage of recent development proposals directed to tribes starkly demonstrates an intense modern pressure to develop and industrialize Indian Country. In [this era], land grabbing is likely to take subtle forms [such as] leasing and development. Most Indian tribes have established tribal corporations and are poised to enter the capitalist economy; indeed, many tribes have already established themselves as economic partners with non-Indian industrial interests. Tribal councils across the country are entertaining offers by private non-Indian corporations to lease tribal lands for mines, industrial sites, waste dumps, residential and commercial developments, and incinerators.

Waste disposal issues provide a revealing glimpse of the intense market pressures on tribes, through their tribal councils, to accommodate non-Indian activity on their land. Due to the scarcity of waste disposal facilities, the reluctance of most non-Indian communities to host new facilities, and the prospect of relaxed regulation in Indian Country, waste disposal interests have aggressively targeted Indian lands as sites for the nation's next generation of waste facilities. Nearly every Indian tribe has been asked by industry or government, or both, to accept waste produced by the non-Indian sector. * * *

The rush to develop Indian land and resources has ignited fierce opposition within Indian Country. * * * Tribal decisions that involve long-term or permanent commitment of tribal lands and resources to non-Indian industrial development increasingly pit the tribal councils against factions or individual members of the tribe. By virtue of its approval authority, the federal government is placed in the position of a potential arbiter of a decision made in the first instance by the tribal council to sell or lease tribal resources. In such cases, the federal government's duty to safeguard tribal resources is particularly weighty, given the typically high stakes regarding land and the controversial nature of the decisions. However, in the modern Self–Determination era, the federal government is likely simply to defer to the tribal council's decision in determining whether to approve the particular transaction. * * *

The decisions of many tribal governments to develop reservation lands for permanent, non-Indian industrial use over the objections of a substantial part of the tribal population raise difficult questions concerning the federal government's trust responsibility in approving tribal land transactions and a court's duty in reviewing the federal decision. On the one hand, conflict over development is not uncommon in other governments, and the existence of conflict alone may not justify judicial interference. Self-determination can flourish on reservations only if the federal government leaves tribes to set their own priorities. [P]art of the price of sovereignty may be improper or unwelcome management by tribal governments. * * *

[On the other hand], [e]ven in the earliest dealings with Indian nations, the trust obligation encompassed the duty to preserve the Indian land base from market encroachments by the majority society.

The Nonintercourse Act was passed to prevent wholesale disposition of Indian lands to private, non-Indian interests—a result that, as history bears out, is inevitable when there is no operative restraint on the sale of Indian lands. The Act's restriction against purchase of Indian lands was viewed not as an intrusion into tribal sovereignty, but rather as a restraint on the majority society—particularly its hungry entrepreneurs—designed to preclude destruction of the tribal entity and homeland through predictably irresistible forces of capitalism. Such a restraint was, and arguably still is, an integral part of a separatist paradigm.

Many believe that without a continuing restraint on transfer of Indian lands, tribal lands and resources will ultimately convert to assets in the portfolios of non-Indian firms. * * * The federal approval requirement may be the only external check against the transfer of native lands to private parties through [lease and joint ventures]. The approval authority in this context is a direct outgrowth of the same concerns which prompted passage of the Nonintercourse Act two centuries ago. * * *

Notes and Questions

1.   When the BIA is asked to approve a lease on Indian lands, to whom is the trust obligation owed? The Court in Seminole Nation v. United States, 316 U.S. 286, 62 S.Ct. 1049, 86 L.Ed. 1480 (1942), directed the duty to both the tribe and its individual members. As a district court later explained:

> The [BIA] is charged not only with the duty to protect the rights and interest of the tribe, but also the rights of the *individual* members thereof. And the duty to protect these rights is the same whether the attempted infringement is by non-members or members of the tribe.

United States v. Camp, 169 F.Supp. 568, 572 (E.D. Wash. 1959) (emphasis added).

2.   Offers of hazardous waste disposal are prevalent in Indian Country. Corporate officials typically seek out Indian lands because rigorous state regulations may not apply, and reservations are more isolated from citizen NIMBY ("not in my backyard") complaints. For an examination of the tribal dynamics that may lead to tribal acceptance of hazardous waste, *see* Scott Morrison & LeAnne Howe, *The Sewage of Foreigners: An Examination of the Historical Precedent for Modern Waste Disposal on Indian Lands*, 39 Fed. B. News & J. 370 (1992). The authors begin their analysis by observing:

> Corporate waste brokers proposing landfill and disposal factories on 20th century tribal reservations are not unlike the caravans of English, French, and Spanish traders in the 18th and 19th centuries who were led into town by Indian leaders on horseback. Today, the Chief pulls up in a black Cadillac with tinted windows flanked by his non-Indian financial manager.

3.   When BIA faces a lease approval decision, how should it define its trust obligation? Should environmental considerations take precedence over economic considerations? Should BIA consider the consequences to just the

present generation, or to generations to come? Should BIA consider the effect on culture and sovereignty? For an analysis of these issues, *see* Mary Christina Wood, *Protecting the Attributes of Native Sovereignty: A New Trust Paradigm for Federal Actions Affecting Tribal Lands and Resources*, 1995 UTAH L. REV. 109.

In Focus: Proposed Nuclear Waste Site on the Groshute Reservation

One of the most poignant conflicts over Indian lands involves the nation's search for a disposal site for its nuclear waste. In 1987, Congress charged the Department of Energy (DOE) with finding a temporary 40 to 50 year repository for nuclear waste pending consideration and construction of a permanent facility at Yucca Mountain, Nevada. Nuclear Waste Policy Amendments Act of 1987, 42 U.S.C. §§ 10101–10266 (1988). The Office of the Nuclear Waste Negotiator was created to find a willing host for the temporary facility, known as the Monitored Retrievable Storage ("MRS") facility. *Id.* at §§ 10241–10250. No states seriously considered the proposal, but 16 tribes, including the Goshute Tribe of Utah, applied for initial grants. In 1994, DOE feasibility grants for the MRS were discontinued, and in 1995, the Office of Nuclear Negotiator was shut down for lack of funding, having found no host for the waste.

The tribal council for the Mescalero Apache Tribe, which had been pursuing site feasibility studies for the MRS in cooperation with the federal government, then formed an independent partnership with 33 utilities to site nuclear waste on the reservation. The tribal council's decision triggered a response by local dissidents. In January 1995, the Mescalero Apache tribal membership voted to reject the tribal council's plan to accept the nuclear waste. But just two months later, in a surprising reversal, the tribal membership voted in a second referendum to proceed with plans to accept the waste. Ultimately, the tide turned again, and the Mescalero Apache Tribe rejected the $250 million offer to site the waste storage facility on reservation land. This decision prompted the utilities to find an alternative waste disposal site. Jay Price, *CP & L Nuclear Storage Ok'd*, THE NEWS AND OBSERVER, December 22, 2000, at A1. The consortium initiated negotiations with the Skull Valley Band of Goshutes in Utah, leading to a stunning replay of the tribal dynamics that had framed the Mescalero Apache controversy.

FAMILY FEUD: SKULL VALLEY GOSHUTES FIGHT AN INTERNAL BATTLE OVER THE LUCRATIVE NUCLEAR WASTE STORAGE PROPOSAL

Judy Fahys

THE SALT LAKE TRIBUNE

August 18, 2002, at A1

* * * Five years have passed since leaders of the Skull Valley Band of the Goshutes offered to make tribal land an open-air parking lot for 44,000 tons of the nation's highly radioactive power-plant waste just 45 miles southwest of Salt Lake City. The shock wave split the tiny tribe and rolled its way to Washington, D.C., where the reverberations have never ceased.

The consortium of eight utility companies advocating the storage site has fought for it in courts, in political arenas and in the arena of public opinion. * * * The deal has been attacked by Utah political leaders, whose constituents do not use nuclear power. With bitter memories of the government's deadly atomic-testing in the 1950s and '60s, Utah is increasingly uneasy in its potential role as one of the nation's dumping grounds.

In Skull Valley, the 121 Goshutes have watched their dream of reclaiming their tribal identity fractured by infighting over money, power and the future itself.

The waste project deal, which could bring unimaginable wealth to the tribe, has triggered a tribal election scandal, subpoenas from a federal grand jury, a regulatory tug of war, a half-dozen lawsuits and a plea for help to Interior Secretary Gale Norton.

"They are waving this like it's economic development, like it's a really good deal, when it has poisoned us ...," says Margene Bullcreek, a tribal member who is opposed to the project. "Everybody is going to say, 'We don't want this' later. But it's going to be too late." * * *

[G]oshute Chairman Leon Bear ... champions the reservation as a storage site. Everyone knew from the outset the consortium had deep pockets and Bear's backing.

Two years before the Goshute waste contract was signed in 1997, the Mescalero Apaches in New Mexico agreed with the utilities to host a facility half as big. Mescalero leaders said the project would be a $250 million boon to the tribe, but their people vetoed it.

Goshute leaders will not say how closely their deal mirrors the Mescaleros' deal. But even if the Goshutes merely matched that windfall, the sum would exceed $2 million for each Skull Valley member, whose average income is about $8,000 a year. * * *

Terms of the contract are secret, known only to Bear's inner circle and the principals at Private Fuel Storage (PFS), a limited liability corporation representing eight utilities with 33 nuclear reactors dotting the East Coast, California and points in between. * * * The utility consortium plans to use Skull Valley for up to 40 years as a way station for 4,000 concrete-and-steel waste casks.

The amount of waste proposed for Skull Valley is equal to all the power plant waste ever produced by commercial reactors in the United States. PFS and Bear insist the project poses virtually no health or safety risk, a claim the state flatly rejects.

The project will cost PFS an estimated $3.1 billion. And supporters say it is a smart way for the Goshutes to make money from one of their few assets—reservation land. * * *

Bear claims that the Tribal Council, constituted of all the adult members of the Skull Valley Band of Goshutes, understands and approves of the deal. Tribal critics say that is nonsense; they accuse the Executive Committee of operating in secret. Bear heads the three-person Executive Committee that manages tribal business and signs all the checks. * * *

Bullcreek, Bear's neighbor and chief antagonist, has attempted, through news media conferences and anti-nuclear meetings all over the nation, to rally opposition. * * * Last fall, dissidents asked the Interior Board of Indian Appeals to throw out the BIA's pivotal decision to approve the waste-site lease. They later asked Interior to get involved, but neither has responded. * * *

Even the NRC [Nuclear Regulatory Commission] has stepped into the fray, temporarily blocking a[n] order issued by the Atomic Safety and Licensing Board, which screens nuclear-facility license applications for the NRC. Last winter, the board ordered Bear to account for the waste project money in light of the corruption allegations raised by dissident Goshutes. But the NRC intervened on grounds that financial disclosure might violate tribal sovereignty. * * *

Notes and Questions

1. How are arguments of tribal sovereignty used by the project proponents and by the project opponents? Would federal disapproval of the waste storage proposal encroach on tribal sovereignty?

2. Is this project an example of native economic resurgence in the Self-Determination era? Or does it represent the opposite—sheer exploitation of economically desperate circumstances? What choices do the Goshutes have for economic survival? If they had a choice between clean industry and a nuclear waste facility, would they willingly choose the latter?

3. Does the Goshute case study offer any insights into tribal governance? Not uncommonly, tribes have competing groups that claim governmental authority, and the federal government recognizes only one. Abuse of process and fraud taint some tribal elections and may lead to ill-constituted governments. Much of the instability of some tribal governments traces back

to the passage of the Indian Reorganization Act of 1934, in which Congress created a new model of tribal government that departed from traditional leadership models. 25 U.S.C. § 476 (1988). *See* George S. Esber, Jr., *Shortcomings of the Indian Self–Determination Policy, in* STATE AND RESERVATION: NEW PERSPECTIVES ON FEDERAL INDIAN POLICY, 212 (George P. Castile & Robert L. Bee eds., 1992).

4.   The federal government has continued to recognize Bear as the leader of the Goshutes despite challenges by dissidents that he has no authority to act for the tribe under their system of governance. For an account, *see* Judy Fahys, *Feds Recognize Bear as Goshute Leader: Indian Affairs Will Deal With Embattled Chairman,* SALT LAKE TRIBUNE, April 2, 2002, at B2; Patty Henetz, *Elections Attempt Fails,* SALT LAKE TRIBUNE, Nov. 20, 2004.

What interest does the federal government have in this dispute? The matter of short-term nuclear storage is a pressing problem for the federal government. Does the federal government have an incentive to recognize tribal leadership that will welcome such waste? Who has the authority to identify valid governing bodies? Ultimately, the courts resolve competing claims for power on Indian reservations. *See* Oneida Indian Nation v. Clark, 593 F.Supp. 257 (N.D. N.Y. 1984); Harjo v. Kleppe, 420 F.Supp. 1110 (D. D.C. 1976) (Creek Nation conflict).

5.   How does the trust doctrine apply to this situation? What federal decisions trigger the responsibility? Individual members of the Goshute Tribe brought a lawsuit against Secretary of Interior Gail Norton challenging the BIA's conditional approval of the lease between the tribe and the consortium. Blackbear v. Norton, Civil No: 2:01–CV–317–PGC (D. Utah); *see also* Judy Fahys, *supra.* The case was dismissed because the members failed to exhaust their administrative remedies. 93 Fed.Appx. 192, 2004 WL 407037 (10th Cir. 2004). The State of Utah filed a separate lawsuit, seeking to intervene in the BIA's lease approval process for the facility. The Tenth Circuit found that the action was not ripe for review, because BIA's lease approval was conditioned on the completion of an EIS and the issuance of a license by the NRC, neither of which had occurred when the state filed its lawsuit. Utah v. United States, 210 F.3d 1193 (10th Cir. 2000). On September 9, 2005, the U.S. Nuclear Regulatory Commission issued a license for the facility. *See* Shankar Vedantam, *Storage Plan Approved for Nuclear Waste,* THE WASHINGTON POST, Sept. 10, 2005, at A2.

6.   The state of Utah is staunchly opposed to the waste site. The waste would be transported through the state to reach the reservation, and any release of nuclear material could affect the population center of Salt Lake City, just 45 miles away from the reservation. Should a tribe of 121 members be able to bring that kind of risk to the state? Is tribal sovereignty that powerful? Or is this, in essence, a federal decision couched behind the mask of tribal sovereignty?

7.   Environmental racism is a relatively new concept that has gained the attention of policy-makers over the last decade. On February 11, 1994, President Clinton issued an executive order mandating that agencies shall "[t]o the greatest extent practicable and permitted by law ... achiev[e] environmental justice as part of [their] mission by identifying and addressing, as

appropriate, disproportionately high and adverse human health or environ-mental effects of [their] programs, policies, and activities on minority popu-lations and low-income populations in the United States." Exec. Order No. 12,898. How does the concept of environmental racism apply to this situa-tion? Is it environmentally racist to site nuclear waste on the Goshute lands, or is it environmentally racist to deny the project if the tribal council wants it? For an analysis of nuclear waste disposal as it affects tribes, *see* Alex T. Skibine, *High Level Nuclear Waste on Indian Reservations: Pushing the Tribal Sovereignty Envelope to the Edge,* 21 J. LAND RESOURCES & ENVTL. L. 287 (2001).

Exercise:

Assume you are the BIA official charged with deciding whether to approve the Goshute lease for a nuclear waste facility. How do you define your trust obligation towards the tribe? Are you supposed to pro-tect cultural, economic, and governmental interests of the tribe? Or are you supposed to protect the land base? Do classic principles of trust law have any bearing on this situation? Consider the venerable property principle that prohibits trustees from allowing "waste" to the property. 93 C.J.S., *Waste*, section 3. Does the approval of a nuclear waste facil-ity amount to "waste" of tribal lands? What are the long-term conse-quences to the tribal land base flowing from approval of the facility? Does it matter that the facility is supposed to be temporary (40 years)? Given the extreme safety hazards involved in transporting the material and the cost of constructing a permanent facility, is there a chance that the Goshute facility will end up as the permanent repository for waste that will remain radioactive for over 10,000 years? Prepare a document that sets forth your decision and explains how the decision carries out the trust obligation. You might want to revisit this decision when you've had a chance to study federal trust liabilities in the next section.

B. Federal Trust Liability for Mismanaging Indian Lands and Resources

Many tribes have successfully sued BIA for damages for failure to manage their lands and resources according to the fiduciary standards of a trustee. *See, e.g.,* United States v. White Mountain Apache Tribe, 537 U.S. 465, 123 S.Ct. 1126, 155 L.Ed.2d 40 (2003) (holding the govern-ment liable for failing to maintain buildings located on land held in trust for the tribe but occupied by the government); White Mountain Apache Tribe v. United States, 11 Cl. Ct. 614, 681 (1987) (government liable for damages from mismanagement of tribal range and timberland), *aff'd,* 5 F.3d 1506 (Fed. Cir. 1993) *cert. denied,* 114 S. Ct. 1538 (1994). Claims for damages are brought in the Court of Federal Claims under the Indian Tucker Act, 28 U.S.C. § 1505 (1988), or the Tucker Act, 25 U.S.C. § 1491, and can be appealed to the Federal Circuit. Such claims are quite different than the claims tribes may make under the Administra-tive Procedure Act (APA) for injunctive relief against on-going agency action. *See infra* section IV. Both the APA and the Tucker Acts waive the government's sovereign immunity, but the Tucker Act is far more restrictive. The Tucker Act waives sovereign immunity for any "claim against the United States founded either upon the *Constitution, or any Act of Congress or any regulation* of an executive department, or upon any express or implied contract with the United States...." 28 U.S.C. § 1491(a)(1) (emphasis added). By the explicit terms of the statute, claims must be grounded in a positive expression of law in the Constitution, statute, regulation, or contract. By contrast, the APA contains a broad waiver of sovereign immunity against federal agencies for "a person suffering legal wrong because of agency action...." 5 U.S.C. § 702, 706 (1988).

A trust claim for damages under the Tucker Act must be based on an independent source of law that creates a federally recognized substantive right and that can be fairly interpreted as mandating compensation for violation of the right. United States v. Mitchell, 463 U.S. 206, 216, 103 S.Ct. 2961, 2967–68, 77 L.Ed.2d 580, 590–91 (1983) (*Mitchell II*). In United States v. Mitchell, 445 U.S. 535, 100 S.Ct. 1349, 63 L.Ed.2d 607 (1980) (*Mitchell I*), and *Mitchell II, supra,* the Court issued two landmark rulings setting the terrain for tribal claims for damages under the Tucker Act. The Quinault Tribe and Quinault Indian allottees brought an action against the United States for mismanagement of forests on allotted lands within the Quinault Indian reservation in Washington. The plaintiffs contended that the government was bound by a trust duty to manage forests on allotted lands in compliance with fiduciary standards.

In *Mitchell I*, the Court found that the General Allotment Act, despite its language placing allotted lands "in trust," created merely a "limited trust" relationship and imposed no obligation on the government to manage forest resources on the property. Instead, the allotment scheme contemplated that the allottee, rather than the government, would manage the land. In *Mitchell II*, however, the Court found a trust obligation on two bases. It first found that the Indian forest management statutes imposed a trust duty because they envisioned a detailed management role for the executive branch, though, interestingly, they lacked express trust language. *Mitchell II*, 463 U.S. at 225. The Court also suggested that, even apart from statutory implication, a fiduciary relationship arises whenever the executive branch maintains extensive control over Indian property. Noting that the Department of the Interior "exercises literally daily supervision over the harvesting and management of tribal timber," the Court concluded:

> [A] fiduciary relationship necessarily arises when the Government assumes such elaborate control over forests and property belonging to Indians. All of the necessary elements of a common-law trust are present: a trustee (the United States), a beneficiary (the Indian allottees), and a trust corpus (Indian timber, lands, and funds).

Id. at 225 (citation omitted).

Taken together, the *Mitchell* opinions indicate that, in the context of monetary claims against the government, the existence of a fiduciary obligation giving rise to liability will be determined on a case-specific basis largely dependent on the framework of the statutes involved. In 2003, the Court applied the trust doctrine in two other Tucker Act cases involving federal management on tribal lands. In United States v. Navajo Nation, 537 U.S. 488, 123 S.Ct. 1079, 155 L.Ed.2d 60 (2003), the Court found no compensable fiduciary duty in managing Indian mineral resources, but in United States v. White Mountain Apache Tribe, 537 U.S. 465, 123 S.Ct. 1126, 155 L.Ed.2d 40 (2003), it found a compensable trust obligation in the federal government's control over buildings on the reservation.

As more tribes gain control over their own resource management in this modern era of tribal self-determination, BIA's role as land manager correspondingly declines. Will this declining role have implications for the federal government's trust liability? Do tribes face a dilemma in asserting more control over their resources, because such control might remove any active trustee role for the federal government and therefore reduce the chances of recovering damages if a mistake is made? For commentary on the government's trust obligation in managing Indian property, *see* HANDBOOK OF FEDERAL INDIAN LAW, Ch. 5 (2005 ed.); Gregory C. Sisk, *Yesterday and Today: Of Indians, Breach of Trust, Money, and Sovereign Immunity,* 39 TULSA L. REV. 313 (2003).

The government also faces liability in managing tribal money funds. In 1996, a lawsuit was filed by Indian plaintiffs seeking $10 billion in damages for mismanaged individual trust accounts. Cobell v. Babbitt, 91 F.Supp.2d 1 (D. D.C. 1999) (finding that the government breached its trust obligations), *aff'd* Cobell v. Norton, 240 F.3d 1081 (D.C. Cir. 2001). The lawsuit is proceeding slowly through the damages phase of the case.

Global Perspective: Rights of Indigenous Peoples Worldwide

Increasingly, native nations across the world are uniting in a global effort to protect their lands and natural resources, as well as sovereignty and cultural autonomy, against encroachment from industrialized nations. In 1994, the United Nations Working Group on Indigenous Populations issued a Draft United Nations Declaration on the Rights of Indigenous Peoples. U.N. Doc. E/CN.4/1995/2; E/CN.4/Sub.2/1994/56. The declaration, though still under discussion, reflects directions in thinking about indigenous land issues. Part VI is excerpted below.

Article 26
Indigenous peoples have the right to own, develop, control and use the lands and territories ... which they have traditionally owned or otherwise occupied or used. * * *

Article 27
Indigenous peoples have the right to the restitution of the lands, territories and resources which they have traditionally owned or other-

wise occupied or used.... Where this is not possible, they have the right to fair and just compensation. * * *

Article 28
Indigenous peoples have the right to the conservation, restoration and protection of the total environment and the productive capacity of their lands, territories and resources. * * * States shall take effective measures to ensure that no storage or disposal of hazardous materials shall take place in the lands and territories of indigenous peoples. * * *

Article 30
Indigenous peoples have the right to determine and develop priorities and strategies for the development or use of their lands ... including the right to require that States obtain their free and informed consent prior to the approval of any project affecting their lands, territories and other resources.... Pursuant to agreement with the indigenous peoples concerned, just and fair compensation shall be provided for any such activities and measures taken to mitigate adverse environmental, economic, social, cultural or spiritual impacts.

For discussion, *see* Robert A. Williams, Jr., *Encounters on the Frontiers of International Human Rights Law: Redefining the Terms of Indigenous Peoples' Survival in the World,* 1990 DUKE L. J. 660.

C.   The Regulatory Regime Within Indian Country

1.   *State and Tribal Regulation*

Few practitioners of federal Indian law would deny the muddled state of doctrine governing state and tribal jurisdiction across reservations. Nevertheless, there are a few clear guiding concepts. The jurisdictional analysis turns on questions of who is being regulated (Indian or non-Indian) and the underlying ownership of the land on which regulated activities take place. First, it is generally the case that tribes have authority over their members' activities within their territory, unless Congress has otherwise stated. *See* HANDBOOK OF FEDERAL INDIAN LAW, Ch. 6 (2005 ed.); *see also* White Mountain Apache Tribe v. Bracker, 448 U.S. 136, 100 S.Ct. 2578, 65 L.Ed.2d 665 (1980). The complications come into play with respect to non-Indians, or activities on non-Indian (fee) owned land within a reservation. There, the practitioner has to ask whether the tribe, or the state, or *both* have jurisdiction. In some cases, the two sovereigns may exercise concurrent jurisdiction.

As a basic starting point, there are two distinct, primary bases for keeping state jurisdiction out of Indian Country: the inherent authority of tribes, and federal preemption in the area of Indian affairs. *See* McClanahan v. Arizona State Tax Comm'n, 411 U.S. 164, 172, 93 S.Ct. 1257, 1262, 36 L.Ed.2d 129, 135 (1973) (noting that "the trend has been away from the idea of inherent Indian sovereignty as a bar to state jurisdiction and toward reliance on federal pre-emption"). As the Court stated in Williams v. Lee, 358 U.S. 217, 223, 79 S.Ct. 269, 3 L.Ed.2d 251

(1959): "Essentially, absent governing Acts of Congress, the question has always been whether the state action infringed on the right of reservation Indians to make their own laws and be ruled by them." Resolution of jurisdictional questions turns on a number of factors. As the Court summarized in White Mountain Apache Tribe, 448 U.S. at 142–45:

> When on-reservation conduct involving only Indians is at issue, state law is generally inapplicable, for the State's regulatory interest is likely to be minimal and the federal interest in encouraging tribal self-government is at its strongest. More difficult questions arise where, as here, a State asserts authority over the conduct of non-Indians engaging in activity on the reservation. In such cases we have examined the language of the relevant federal treaties and statutes in terms of both the broad policies that underlie them and the notions of sovereignty that have developed from historical traditions of tribal independence. This inquiry is not dependent on mechanical or absolute conceptions of state or tribal sovereignty, but has called for a particularized inquiry into the nature of the state, federal, and tribal interests at stake, an inquiry designed to determine whether, in the specific context, the exercise of state authority would violate federal law.

Thus, while state jurisdiction over non-Indian activities within reservations is not presumed, neither is it absolutely precluded in cases where the state demonstrates a strong regulatory interest.

After considering state jurisdiction, the next level of analysis is whether tribes have jurisdiction over non-members within reservation boundaries. It is settled that tribes do not have criminal authority over non-Indians within the reservation. Oliphant v. Suquamish Indian Tribe, 435 U.S. 191, 98 S.Ct. 1011, 55 L.Ed.2d 209 (1978). As to civil authority, the outcome often depends on whether the conduct is on fee lands or tribal trust lands within the reservation. Tribes are in a fairly strong position for regulating non-Indian activities on trust lands within the reservation. In New Mexico v. Mescalero Apache Tribe, 462 U.S. 324, 103 S.Ct. 2378, 76 L.Ed.2d 611 (1983), the Court affirmed tribal jurisdiction over non-Indian hunting and fishing on trust lands. The Court also refused to allow state concurrent jurisdiction over the activities, stating:

> Several considerations strongly support the … conclusion that the Tribe's authority to regulate hunting and fishing pre-empts state jurisdiction. It is important to emphasize that concurrent jurisdiction would effectively nullify the Tribe's authority to control hunting and fishing on the reservation. * * * The State would be able to dictate the terms on which nonmembers are permitted to utilize the reservation's resources. The Tribe would thus exercise its authority over the reservation only at the sufferance of the State. The tribal authority to regulate hunting and fishing by nonmembers, which has been repeatedly confirmed by federal treaties and laws … would

have a rather hollow ring if tribal authority amounted to no more than this.

Id. at 338.

But in *Montana,* below, the Court made clear that tribal civil authority over the activities of non-Indians on fee lands within the reservation has been implicitly divested as a result of the tribes' domestic dependant status, subject to two important exceptions. The case has sweeping implications for tribal natural resource management across reservations with mixed private/tribal ownership.

MONTANA v. UNITED STATES
Supreme Court of the United States, 1981.
450 U.S. 544, 101 S.Ct. 1245, 67 L.Ed.2d 493.

JUSTICE STEWART delivered the opinion of the Court.

This case concerns the sources and scope of the power of an Indian tribe to regulate hunting and fishing by non-Indians on lands within its reservation owned in fee simple by non-Indians. * * *

[T]hrough their original incorporation into the United States as well as through specific treaties and statutes, the Indian tribes have lost many of the attributes of sovereignty. [We have] distinguished between those inherent powers retained by the tribes and those divested: "The areas in which such implicit divestiture of sovereignty has been held to have occurred are those involving *the relations between an Indian tribe and nonmembers of the tribe....*" * * *

Thus, in addition to the power to punish tribal offenders, the Indian tribes retain their inherent power to determine tribal membership, to regulate domestic relations among members, and to prescribe rules of inheritance for members. But exercise of tribal power beyond what is necessary to protect tribal self-government or to control internal relations is inconsistent with the dependent status of the tribes, and so cannot survive without express congressional delegation. Since regulation of hunting and fishing by nonmembers of a tribe on lands no longer owned by the tribe bears no clear relationship to tribal self-government or internal relations, the general principles of retained inherent sovereignty did not authorize the Crow Tribe to [exercise jurisdiction over non-members]. * * *

To be sure, Indian tribes retain inherent sovereign power to exercise some forms of civil jurisdiction over non-Indians on their reservations, even on non-Indian fee lands. A tribe may regulate, through taxation, licensing, or other means, the activities of nonmembers who enter consensual relationships with the tribe or its members, through commercial dealing, contracts, leases, or other arrangements. A tribe may also retain inherent power to exercise civil authority over the conduct of non-Indians on fee lands within its reservation when that conduct threatens or has some direct effect on the political integrity, the economic security, or the health or welfare of the tribe. * * *

No such circumstances, however, are involved in this case. Non–Indian hunters and fishermen on non-Indian fee land do not enter any agreements or dealings with the Crow Tribe so as to subject themselves to tribal civil jurisdiction. And nothing in this case suggests that such non-Indian hunting and fishing so threaten the Tribe's political or economic security as to justify tribal regulation. The complaint ... did not allege that non-Indian hunting and fishing on fee lands imperil the subsistence or welfare of the Tribe. Furthermore ... the Crow Tribe has traditionally accommodated itself to the State's "near exclusive" regulation of hunting and fishing on fee lands within the reservation. [M]ontana's statutory and regulatory scheme does not prevent the Crow Tribe from limiting or forbidding non-Indian hunting and fishing on lands still owned by or held in trust for the Tribe or its members. * * *

Notes and Questions

1. Despite the analytical challenge of reconciling *Montana* with the prior body of Supreme Court doctrine, the natural resource practitioner must extract from the decision some black letter law principles. *Montana* has been interpreted as a denial of tribal jurisdiction over non-Indians on *fee* lands subject to two exceptions: 1) the consensual relations test; and 2) the political integrity/economic security/health and welfare test.

2. What is the scope of the second *Montana* exception? Can there be *any* environmental, wildlife, or land use regulation that is *not* geared towards conduct that affects the "political integrity, the economic security, or the health or welfare of the tribe?" What weight should be given the Court's notation that the non-Indian fishing in *Montana* would not "imperil the subsistence or welfare of the Tribe?" Could the regulatory framework change in the future if harvested populations decline on the reservation?

3. The Supreme Court in *Montana* focused on the underlying ownership of the lands as a point of departure for its analysis, acknowledging that the tribe "may prohibit nonmembers from hunting or fishing on land belonging to the Tribe...." 450 U.S. at 557. The non-Indian hunting and fishing activities in question occurred on the bed of the Big Horn River. A predicate issue to the jurisdictional issue, then, was ownership of the underlying bed. The State of Montana argued that it held ownership to the bed under the equal footing doctrine, and the Court agreed. The case demonstrates that modern disputes may still turn on seemingly archaic questions of land ownership, although ownership is not always determinative. *See* Wisconsin v. Environmental Protection Agency, 266 F.3d 741 (7th Cir. 2001) (state ownership of streambeds does not preclude tribe from regulating waters under approved tribal program under the Clean Water Act).

4. By setting up different jurisdictional rules for fee lands and tribal trust lands, the Court has in effect created a checkerboard system of regulation. This can make land use and environmental regulation quite cumbersome. Was the Supreme Court aware of this? Does *Montana* cut against the grain of modern efforts to unify jurisdictions in their regulation of broad ecosystems?

5. *Montana* has been followed by other significant Supreme Court cases. In 1989, the Court decided Brendale v. Confederated Tribes and Bands of the Yakima Nation, 492 U.S. 408, 109 S.Ct. 2994, 106 L.Ed.2d 343 (1989). The issue in that case was whether the Yakama Nation[a] had exclusive zoning authority over two non-Indian fee parcels. One parcel was within a "closed" part of the reservation that was primarily owned by the tribe and was generally not open to non-members. The other parcel was in an "open" part of the reservation which was primarily owned in fee by non-Indians. The case resulted in a plurality opinion with no real consensus, although all of the Justices applied *Montana*. As to the closed area, a majority held that the tribe retained exclusive authority to zone fee lands. As to the open area, a majority held that the county had exclusive zoning authority over the fee lands. The opinion is a confusing foray into both state and tribal jurisdictional issues. For subsequent cases in this area, *see* South Dakota v. Bourland, 508 U.S. 679, 113 S.Ct. 2309, 124 L.Ed.2d 606 (1993); Strate v. A–1 Contractors, 520 U.S. 438, 117 S.Ct. 1404, 137 L.Ed.2d 661 (1997); Atkinson Trading Co. v. Shirley, 532 U.S. 645, 121 S.Ct. 1825, 149 L.Ed.2d 889 (2001). The area of state and tribal jurisdiction is summarized in the HANDBOOK OF FEDERAL INDIAN LAW Ch. 6 (2005 ed.).

6. While the practitioner should avoid over-simplifying jurisdiction in Indian Country, the following chart may be helpful in providing a structure in which to analyze the issues. The chart depicts the rules of common law governing jurisdictional questions. In particular instances, of course, Congress may have delegated authority to the tribes. *See* section III.C.2.c. below (discussing tribal environmental programs).

Regulatory (Non–Criminal) Jurisdiction Within Indian Country

	Indians	**Non-Indians**	
Tribal Jurisdiction	Full jurisdiction over members and internal relations	**On fee lands** (*Montana*)	**On tribal lands** (*Mescalero*)
		No tribal jurisdiction unless activity falls into either exception:	Tribal jurisdiction traditionally presumed
		1) is pursuant to consensual relations with tribe; or 2) affects political integrity, economic security, or health or welfare of the tribe	
State Jurisdiction	Presumption against jurisdiction (*McClanahan, White Mountain Apache Tribe*)	Presumption against state jurisdiction (because of inherent tribal sovereignty and federal preemption, *Williams*), but presumption can be overcome by particularized inquiry into the nature of the state, federal, and tribal interests at stake (*White Mountain Apache Tribe*)	

a. Since *Brendale*, the Tribe changed the spelling of its name to "Yakama" to reflect the historic spelling.

2. *Federal Regulation*

In the late 1960s and 1970s, Congress passed a complex set of federal environmental laws to address the problem of ecosystem deterioration nationwide. Applying such laws to Indian Country invokes both the background principles of tribal jurisdiction discussed above and complex questions of statutory interpretation. Some general principles come into play. As a basic matter, federal laws apply to tribes unless Congress excluded Indian lands, the law interferes with a tribe's self-government, or the law conflicts with treaty rights. Donovan v. Coeur d'Alene Tribal Farm, 751 F.2d 1113, 1116 (9th Cir. 1985). (In the case of treaty conflict, the proper analysis is whether Congress intended to use its plenary power to abrogate treaty rights. *See* section V.A.4.b. *infra*). While many federal statutes affect Indian Country, the ones with the most pervasive effect are the National Environmental Policy Act (NEPA), the Endangered Species Act (ESA), and the federal pollution control laws. Each warrants a separate analysis.

a. NEPA

The National Environmental Policy Act (NEPA), 42 U.S.C. § 4321 *et. seq.*, addressed in detail in Chapter 4, is designed to inform federal agency decision-making and allow the public a say in federal decisions that affect the environment. The core mandate of NEPA is the requirement that federal agencies prepare an Environmental Impact Statement (EIS) for actions "significantly affecting ... the environment." 42 U.S.C. § 1332(C).

NEPA applies to all federal agencies, including the Bureau of Indian Affairs (BIA). It is well-settled that NEPA comes into play with federal decisions approving leases and other resource uses on Indian land. *See* Davis v. Morton, 469 F.2d 593, 597 (10th Cir. 1972). Courts have found that if the BIA approves a lease or similar agreement without first complying with NEPA, the agreement is invalid and the lessee gains no property right in the agreement. Sangre de Cristo Dev. Co. v. United States, 932 F.2d 891 (10th Cir. 1991); *see also* Rosebud Sioux Tribe v. McDivitt, 286 F.3d 1031 (8th Cir. 2002). BIA has developed detailed procedures for incorporating NEPA into its decisions. *See* Bureau of Indian Affairs NEPA Handbook, 30 BIAM Supp. 1. For analysis of how NEPA applies to resource management in Indian Country, *see* Handbook of Federal Indian Law, Ch. 17 (2005 ed.).

NEPA regulations require the lead agency to solicit comments from the governing tribe when there are on-reservation effects from the proposed federal action. 40 C.F.R. §§ 1503.1(a)(2)(ii). Of course, where the federal action at hand is simply BIA's approval of a tribal council's decision to lease land or to promulgate a resource management plan, such formal tribal commentary will typically be non-critical. NEPA processes, however, may afford an outlet for dissident members of the tribe opposed to the tribal council's decision. Where the federal action is undertaken by an agency other than BIA, such as where the EPA approves a permit for a waste dump on fee lands within a reservation, the comments from the tribe should have a powerful effect in framing the federal agency's trust obligation to the tribe.

Some tribes are developing their own Tribal Environmental Policy Acts (TEPAs) to provide environmental review of actions within the reservation. While these TEPAs do not derive from NEPA, they are roughly modeled after NEPA's structure. For discussion, *see* Dean B. Suagee & Patrick A. Parenteau, *Fashioning a Comprehensive Environmental Review Code for Tribal Governments: Institutions and Processes,* 21 AM. INDIAN L. REV. 297 (1997). Tribal governments typically lack the "sunshine laws" that apply to federal, state, and local governments, so there is often no legal duty that forces tribal leaders to share information with their membership or the general public. Where TEPAs provide for public notice and comment, they may partially allay the commonly expressed concerns of non-Indian residents within reservations that they have no input into tribal decisions.

While the ultimate result of NEPA is not a substantive one, NEPA often changes the course of agency actions through public scrutiny or appeal. NEPA litigation may delay projects long enough that political winds shift on the reservation. In *Davis v. Morton, supra,* the tribal council executed a 99–year lease of 5,400 acres of reservation land to a development company in 1970, and the BIA approved the decision. The project was stalled by the 10th Circuit's decision imposing NEPA requirements on federal approval. By 1976, after an environmental study was completed, the tribal council changed leadership and the new council requested that BIA void the lease, which it did.

In Practice:
Incorporating Environmental
Justice into NEPA Processes

Many federal decisions have the potential to impose disparate impacts on minority populations, including tribal populations. In 1994, President Clinton issued an Executive Order requiring all federal agencies to incorporate environmental justice considerations into their decision-making. Executive Order 12898: Federal Actions to Address Environmental Justice in Minority Populations and Low–Income Populations, 59 Fed. Reg. 7629 (1994). The Order applies specifically to Indian tribes. *See* 59 Fed. Reg. 7632. In 1997, the Council on Environmental Quality issued a guidance document that specifically directs federal agencies to seek tribal participation in federal decisions consistent with the trust responsibility and treaty obligations. U.S. Council on Environmental Quality, Environmental Justice: Guidance Under the National Environmental Policy Act 1, 9 (Dec. 10, 1997), http://ceq.eh.doe.gov/nepa/regs/ej/justice.pdf. The document notes that environmental justice implications may arise from cultural and economic impacts to tribal populations.

b. ESA Regulation

As society continues to eradicate wildlife habitat, more imperiled species find their last refuges within the boundaries of Indian Country. Accordingly, several provisions of the Endangered Species Act (ESA) are implicated by management of Indian lands. Indian forest and range-lands provide critical habitat for a growing number of species listed as threatened or endangered under the ESA. 16 U.S.C. §§ 1531, 1544. *See* Sandi Zellmer, *Indian Lands as Critical Habitat for Indian Nations and Endangered Species,* 43 S.D. L. REV. 381 (1998). Section 7 of the ESA prohibits federal agencies from taking action that will "jeopardize the continued existence" of any listed species, or that will destroy or modify "critical habitat" designated for listed species. 16 U.S.C. § 1536(a). One court has held that BIA approvals of a tribal forest management plan and timber sales are federal "actions" subject to section 7's consultation requirement and jeopardy prohibition. *See* Silver v. Babbitt, 924 F.Supp. 976, 984, 986 (D. Ariz. 1995) (enjoining BIA timber sales on Navajo reservation).

Other provisions of the ESA also address habitat for protected species. Section 9 prohibits any person from "taking" a listed species, a term that includes habitat degradation. Babbitt v. Sweet Home Chapter of Communities for a Great Oregon, 515 U.S. 687, 698–699, 115 S.Ct. 2407, 2413–14, 132 L.Ed.2d 597, 611–12 (1995). Section 9 applies to Indian land. *See* Donovan v. Coeur d'Alene Tribal Farm, 751 F.2d 1113, 1116 (9th Cir. 1985). Section 10 of the ESA authorizes some "incidental take" of species under conditions specified in an approved conservation plan. 16 U.S.C. § 1539(a). Several tribes are developing habitat conservation plans to govern timber harvest on reservation lands that provide habitat for listed species. *See generally* http://endangered.fws.gov/hcp/index.html#about.

Recognizing the increasing role of ESA regulation in tribal natural resource management, the Secretaries of the Departments of the Interior and Commerce signed a joint secretarial order in 1997 outlining procedures and principles to guide their agencies in implementing the ESA on Indian lands. Secretarial Order 3206: American Indian Tribal Rights, Federal–Tribal Trust Responsibilities, and the Endangered Species Act (1997), *reprinted in* Charles Wilkinson, *The Role of Bilateralism in Fulfilling the Federal–Tribal Relationship: The Tribal Rights–Endangered Species Secretarial Order,* 72 WASH. L. REV. 1063, 1089–1107 (1997). The Order requires consultation with affected tribes at all steps in the ESA process. *See* Sandi Zellmer, *Conserving Ecosystems Through the Secretarial Order on Tribal Rights,* 14 NAT. RESOURCES & ENV'T. 162 (2000).

c. Pollution Control Regulation and TAS Programs

Tribal pollution control is quickly becoming a specialized sub-field of federal Indian law and natural resources law, particularly because tribal standards may have an impact on off-reservation polluting activities. *See infra* section VI.A. Congress has passed four primary laws to regulate polluting activities: the Clean Water Act (CWA); the Clean Air Act (CAA); the Safe Drinking Water Act (SDWA); and the Resource Conservation Recovery Act (RCRA). Figuring out how these laws apply to Indian Country entails a statutory analysis against the backdrop of basic jurisdictional principles.

A starting point to the analysis is that federal laws of general applicability typically apply to Indian Country. *See* Phillips Petroleum Co. v. U.S. Environmental Protection Agency, 803 F.2d 545 (10th Cir. 1986); Blue Legs v. U.S. Bureau of Indian Affairs, 867 F.2d 1094 (8th Cir. 1989). The U.S. Environmental Protection Agency (EPA) is charged with implementing environmental statutes nationwide. All of the four primary pollution statutes create a "cooperative federalism" model in which EPA is the supreme regulator, but states may assume regulatory authority to carry out federal laws within their jurisdictions. To do so, states must receive EPA approval of their programs. States may create standards that exceed federal minimums, but they may not drop below the national standards.

As the third sovereigns within the constitutional democracy, tribes were somewhat of an afterthought in this federal-state structure of statutory environmental law. EPA has long taken the position that, absent express statutory language, states have no authority to implement their programs within Indian Country in light of the general presumptions against state authority explored above. *See* EPA Policy for the Administration of Environmental Programs on Indian Reservations (1984), http://www.epa.gov/indian/1984.htm. None of the environmental statutes initially provided such jurisdiction. In State of Washington Dept. of Ecology v. U.S. Environmental Protection Agency, 752 F.2d 1465 (9th Cir. 1985), the Ninth Circuit confirmed EPA's jurisdictional approach. Therefore, EPA is left as the agency implementing federal environmental law in Indian Country. *See e.g.* 40 C.F.R. § 123.1(h) (Clean Water programs).

In the mid–1980s, Congress began to amend the environmental statutes to provide for tribal programs similar to state programs. Today, the Clean Water Act, the Clean Air Act and the Safe Drinking Water Act all have "Treatment as State" (TAS) provisions allowing tribes to develop programs to implement the federal statutes within their reservations. *See* CWA, 33 U.S.C. § 1377(e); CAA, 42 U.S.C. § 7601(d); SDWA, 42 U.S.C. § 300j–11(a). The Comprehensive Environmental Response, Compensation, and Liability Act (CERCLA), 42 U.S.C. § 9601, while not a pollution-control statute, also has a TAS provision and designates tribes as eligible to recover natural resource damages from releases of hazardous substances, 42 U.S.C. § 9607(f)(1). The Resource Conservation Recovery Act is the only major statute that still lacks a TAS provision, and the D.C. Circuit has held that the EPA has no authority to treat tribes as states under that Act. Backcountry Against Dumps v. Environmental Protection Agency, 100 F.3d 147 (D.C. Cir. 1996). Apart from RCRA, however, tribes may have inherent tribal jurisdiction in many instances to regulate waste disposal within their reservation boundaries. Nevertheless, many commentators advocate for amending RCRA to include a TAS provision. *See* Fred E. Breedlove, *Implementing the Resource Conservation and Recovery Act (RCRA) in Indian Country and Approaches for Amending RCRA to Better Serve Tribal Interests,* 26 VT. L. REV. 881 (2002).

The administrative journey towards gaining federal environmental program approval under the other three statutes is not easy. A tribe must apply to the EPA for a determination that it is eligible for TAS treatment, which means meeting specific criteria outlined in the particular statute. *See* Montana v. U.S. Environmental Protection Agency, 137 F.3d 1135 (9th Cir. 1998) (upholding EPA's approval of a TAS program for the Flathead Indian Reservation). For a detailed analysis of this complex area, *see* Jane Marx et. al, *Tribal Jurisdiction Over Reservation Water Quality and Quantity,* 43 S.D. L. REV. 315 (1998).

Exercise:

The Siskyit Tribe ("Tribe") is located in Wyoming on a 5,000–acre reservation. Approximately half of the reservation is owned in fee by non-Indians as a result of the Allotment Era. A company called Veg–It owns 20 acres of fee land within the reservation. Veg–It recently began a composting operation on the land, using garbage hauled in from off the reservation. The operation is just 500 yards away from a stream that provides drinking water for tribal residents and supports a tribal fishery. Recently tribal members have been complaining about the intolerable stench from the huge compost pile. They also complain that the company keeps bright lights on all night at the facility, which can interfere with religious practices. Company officials say the stench and nighttime lighting is unavoidable.

The tribal council has recently passed two ordinances. One prohibits night-time lighting, and the other prohibits operations resulting in offensive odors. A long established tribal ordinance prohibits any pollution in the waterways that would interfere with drinking, ceremonial, and fisheries uses of the reservation waters. The company refuses to comply with the ordinances, claiming that the state, not the tribe, has authority over its lands. The state has no equivalent light or odor regulations, but does have a general program implementing the Clean Water Act.

You are an attorney working for the tribe. The tribal council has asked you to evaluate whether it has jurisdiction over these operations and whether it should pursue the possibility of TAS program authority under any federal environmental statutes. It currently has no TAS authority.

IV. INCIDENTAL FEDERAL ACTION AFFECTING INDIAN COUNTRY

In the last half-century, a myriad of federal agencies burgeoned with the growth of the administrative state. Today such agencies have a profound impact on tribal lands and resources through their "incidental action" in carrying out general public lands laws and environmental statutes. For example, polluting activities permitted by the U.S. Environmental Protection Agency (EPA) under the various federal environmental statutes degrade reservation lands, airsheds, and water supplies. Similarly, federal programs designed to allocate or manage shared resources, such as water and wildlife, often affect a tribe's ability to support a reservation-based tribal economy. There is a disturbing pattern of failing to regulate non-Indian threats to species and then imposing a disproportionate conservation burden on the tribes. *See* Sandi Zellmer, *Conserving Ecosystems Through the Secretarial Order on Tribal Rights*, 14 NAT. RESOURCES & ENV'T. 162 (2000). Moreover, a host of activities carried out on federal public lands or at federal facilities—such as mining, timber harvest, oil and gas production, recreation, hazardous waste disposal, and defense operations—may seriously impact the culture, economy, and environment of nearby reservations. All of these actions potentially implicate the fiduciary relationship between the federal government and tribes—one of the primary cornerstones of Indian law. Because the trust responsibility applies to all federal agencies, natural resource professionals must understand its role in the broader context of administrative law. Chapter 5.II.B. explores the origins of the federal trust responsibility towards tribes.

A. The Federal Trust Obligation in Administrative Law

Courts have consistently found that the trust obligation applies to all federal agencies in carrying out their statutory mandates. *See, e.g.,* Okanogan Highlands Alliance v. Williams, 236 F.3d 468 (9th Cir. 2000) (Forest Service); Skokomish Indian Tribe v. FERC, 121 F.3d 1303, 1308 (9th Cir. 1997) (Federal Energy Regulatory Commission); Morongo Band of Mission Indians v. FAA, 161 F.3d 569, 574 (9th Cir. 1998) (Federal Aviation Administration); Nance v. Environmental Protection Agency, 645 F.2d 701, 710–711 (9th Cir. 1981) (EPA).

In its most fundamental form, the trust responsibility towards tribes is simply a duty of protection towards tribal lands, treaty rights, and other tribal interests. In Seminole Nation v. United States, 316 U.S. 286, 297, 62 S.Ct. 1049, 1054–55, 86 L.Ed. 1480, 1490–91 (1942), the Supreme Court declared that federal agencies would be held to the "most exacting fiduciary standards" in their dealings with tribes. As straightforward as that may seem, the enforcement of the trust responsibility is quite complex. It is helpful to separate the two separate spheres of federal action into the trustee and incidental action contexts. When acting as trustee for Indian lands and resources, the federal government (through the BIA) is held to specific statutory requirements typically requiring management in the "best interests" of the tribe or its members; in this context there are usually no other competing beneficiary interests. *See* Section III. A. & B., *supra*. The "incidental action" context involves a host of federal agencies carrying out general statutes that fail to address specific Indian needs. Such agencies regularly confront competing interests of tribes and other public constituencies in implementing general mandates.

In this latter "incidental action" context, the analysis involves folding the common law trust responsibility into complex statutes such as the Endangered Species Act, the National Forest Management Act, the Clean Water Act, and other statutes regulating land, water, and wildlife. It is important to keep in mind that the trust obligation cannot override clear statutory mandates. Because agencies have no authority to disregard Congressional directives, the trust responsibility may guide agencies only when there are statutory gaps that Congress intended to be filled by agency discretion. *See* Skokomish Indian Tribe, 121 F.3d at 1309 (where tribe's application for hydropower facility was barred by regulations, "the federal trust responsibility does not compel its acceptance").

Trust claims seeking injunctive relief are most often brought as part of a package of statutory challenges under the APA, which allows courts to set aside an action that is "arbitrary, capricious, an abuse of discretion, or otherwise not in accordance with law." 5 U.S.C. § 706(2)(A). Courts have incorporated trust analysis into statutory claims brought under the APA. *See* Northwest Sea Farms v. United States Army Corps of Engineers, 931 F.Supp. 1515 (W. D. Wash. 1996); *but see* Gros Ventre Tribe v. United States, Order, CV 00–69–M–DW at 13 (D. Mont. Oct. 22, 2004) (cautioning that judicial review under the APA is contingent on a final agency action, and that any trust arguments must be brought within the framework of a statutory law that triggered such final action). In all cases seeking to enforce the trust obligation against administrative agencies, the first task is to identify the "pocket of discretion" that the agency has available within the statutory parameters. Agencies may not violate clear statutory mandates, but most natural resource statutes leave tremendous discretion to the agencies to carry out general standards.

One of the clearest declarations of the administrative trust responsibility was made by the court in Pyramid Lake Paiute Tribe of Indians v. Morton, 354 F.Supp. 252 (D. D.C. 1972). There, the Tribe challenged the amount of water allocated by the Secretary of Interior out of the Truckee River to non-Indian interests. The water diversions were harming tribal fisheries on the reservation. The court applied the trust responsibility as an interstitial obligation that filled gaps in statutory law left by Congress. The court found that, when an agency has discretion to choose from a variety of outcomes, the trust obligation requires that it make a decision adequately protective of tribal interests, and particularly, tribal property (including treaty harvest rights and water rights). The court stated:

> The Tribe contends that the regulation delivers more water to the District than required by applicable court decrees and statutes, and improperly diverts water that otherwise would flow into nearby Pyramid Lake located on the Tribe's reservation. This Lake has been the Tribe's principal source of livelihood. * * * The Tribe contends that the Secretary's action is an arbitrary abuse of discretion in that the Secretary has ... failed to fulfill his trust responsibilities to the Tribe ... * * *
>
> In order to fulfill his fiduciary duty, the Secretary must insure, to the extent of his power, that all water not obligated by court decree or contract with the District goes to Pyramid Lake. The United States, acting through the Secretary of Interior, "has charged itself with moral obligations of the highest responsibility and trust. Its conduct ... should therefore be judged by the most exacting fiduciary standards." *Seminole Nation v. United States*, 316 U.S. 286, 297 (1942). * * *
>
> The Secretary was obliged to formulate a closely developed regulation that would preserve water for the Tribe. He was further obliged to assert his statutory and contractual authority to the fullest extent possible to accomplish this result. * * * Possible difficulties ... could not simply be blunted by a "judgment call" calculated to placate temporarily conflicting claims to precious water. The Secretary's action ... fails to demonstrate an adequate recognition of his fiduciary duty to the Tribe. This also is an abuse of discretion and not in accordance with law. * * *

Pyramid Lake Paiute Tribe of Indians, 354 F.Supp. at 256–57.

Other cases decided after *Pyramid Lake* also invoke the trust obligation to protect native lands and resources against damage by non-Indian interests. *See* Northern Cheyenne Tribe v. Hodel, 12 Indian L. Rep. 3065 (D. Mont. Oct. 8, 1985) (mem.) (finding violation of trust responsibility by Department of Interior in issuing coal leases on public lands adjacent to Cheyenne Reservation); Klamath Tribes v. U.S. Forest Service, No 96–381–HA (D. Or. Oct. 2, 1996) (enjoining timber sales that could adversely affect treaty hunted deer herds, finding that Forest Service has a "substantive duty to protect 'to the fullest extent possible' the tribes' treaty rights, and the resources on which those rights depend."); Northwest Sea Farms v. U.S. Army Corps of Engineers, 931 F.Supp. 1515, 1520 (W.D. Wash. 1996) ("In carrying out its fiduciary duty, it is [the federal agencies'] responsibility to ensure that Indian treaty rights are given full effect."); Parravano v. Babbitt, 70 F.3d 539 (9th Cir. 1995) (upholding, under the trust responsibility, emergency ocean harvest regulations issued by Department of Commerce to protect Hoopa Valley and Yurok Tribes' fishing rights); Klamath Water Users Protective Ass'n v. Patterson, 204 F.3d 1206, 1213 (9th Cir. 2000) ("[The] United States, as trustee for the Tribes, has a responsibility to protect their rights and resources."). This body of law is collected and analyzed in Mary Christina Wood, *Indian Land and the Promise of Native Sovereignty: The Trust Doctrine Revisited,* 1994 UTAH L. REV. 1513–1535.

But more recent cases have muddled the distinction between trust standards and general statutory standards, finding the trust obligation automatically discharged by the agency's compliance with its statutory mandates. *See e.g.* Morongo Band of Mission Indians v. Federal Aviation Administration, 161 F.3d 569, 574 (9th Cir. 1998) (rejecting claim that the Federal Aviation Administration had violated its trust obligation by allowing a flight path over the reservation, stating, "[U]nless there is a specific duty that has been placed on the government with respect to Indians, this responsibility is discharged by the agency's compliance with general regulations and statutes not specifically aimed at protecting Indian tribes."); Gros Ventre Tribe v. United States, 344 F.Supp.2d 1221, 1226, (D. Mont. 2004); Pit River Tribe v. Bureau of Land Management, 306 F.Supp.2d 929 (E.D. Cal. 2004); Pacific Coast Federation of Fishermen's Associations v. Yurok Tribe, Civ. No. C02–02006 SBA (N.D. Cal., March 7, 2005). The first case to reflect this approach was North Slope Borough v. Andrus, 642 F.2d 589 (D.C. Cir. 1980). There, members of the Inupiat native community challenged the Secretary of Interior's decision to issue oil leases in the Beaufort Sea region, which serves as migratory habitat for the bowhead whale, an endangered species that provides subsistence for Inupiat people. The Inupiat challenged the lease decision under both the trust doctrine and section 7 of the ESA, which prohibits a federal agency from taking action that is "likely to jeopardize" the continued existence of any listed species. 16 U.S.C. § 1536(a)(2). The court rejected the challenge, finding the ESA satisfied and interpreting the trust duty as coextensive with ESA protection:

> [W]here the Secretary has acted responsibly in respect of the environment, he has implemented responsibly, and protected, the parallel concerns of the Native Alaskans. In sum, the substantive interests of the Natives and of their native environment are congruent. The protection given by the Secretary to one, as we have held, merges with the protection he owes to the other.

North Slope Borough, 642 F.2d at 612.

In general, are statutory standards designed with Indian interests in mind? Does ESA protection, designed only to prevent species from going extinct, ensure protection of whale populations sufficient to allow for hunting by the Inupiat people? The recent cases finding the trust obligation satisfied by statutory standards have been criticized in Mary Christina Wood, *The Indian Trust Responsibility: Protecting Tribal Lands and Resources Through Claims of Injunctive Relief Against Federal Agencies,* 39 TULSA L. REV. 355 (2003) and Mary Christina Wood, *Protecting the Attributes of Native Sovereignty: A New Trust Paradigm for Federal Actions Affecting Tribal Lands and Resources,* 1995 UTAH L. REV. 109, 120 (urging courts to resist any approach that "merely assimilates the trust doctrine—and the unique interests it protects—into the broader statutory framework designed to further the often minimalist interests of the majority society").

In Focus: The Klamath Basin and Trust Obligations

An on-going conflict in the Klamath Basin of Oregon illustrates the trust obligation and its application in a complex water dispute involving numerous conflicting interests. The basin is the aboriginal home of the Yurok, Klamath, Hoopa Valley, and Karuk Tribes, all of which continue their ages-old reliance on fish. Early in the 20th Century, a huge Bureau of Reclamation project transformed the hydrology of the basin to provide irrigation water to farmers who settled the area. Diverting water from the rivers that serve as habitat to fish, the project has imperiled native fish species, and triggered their listing under the Endangered Species Act (ESA). Federal practices in the basin have prompted a set of lawsuits within a complicated legal structure consisting of the ESA, treaty rights, water appropriation doctrine, and federal reclamation laws. For background, *see* Reed D. Benson, *Giving Suckers (and Salmon) an Even Break: Klamath Basin Water and the Endangered Species Act*, 15 Tul. Envtl. L. J. 197 (2002).

In the fall of 2001, the Klamath Basin experienced an extreme drought, and the federal government withheld water from agricultural diversion to protect fish listed under the ESA. In a challenge brought by irrigators, the district court of Oregon found that the Bureau of Reclamation acted properly in carrying out both the requirements for ESA-listed fish and the trust obligation to the tribes. *See Klamath Water Users Ass'n v. Patterson*, 15 F.Supp.2d 990, 996 (D. Or. 1998) *aff'd*, 204 F.3d 1206, 1213–14 (9th Cir. 2000) ("[T]he United States, as a trustee for the Tribes ... has a responsibility to divert the water and resources needed to fulfill the Tribes' rights, rights that take precedence over any alleged rights of the Irrigators."). Later, in a symbolic show of rebellion against federal control, protestors from farming communities stormed a canal headgate in Klamath Falls, Oregon, bringing national attention to the basin's water crisis by illegally releasing water into the canals. The next year, the government reversed its position and allowed Klamath River water levels to drop severely, which in turn likely contributed to a massive fish kill of over 33,000 salmon. *See* Michelle Cole, *With Deep Ties to Fish, Tribes Mourn Die–Off*, The Sunday Oregonian, Oct. 6, 2002, at A17. In a recent decision now on appeal before the Ninth Circuit, a district court rejected a trust claim against the government for the fish kill, based on the *Morongo Band* line of cases: "In the absence of ... a specific duty, the government's general trust responsibilities to the Tribe are discharged by compliance with generally applicable regulations and statutes." Pacific Coast Federation of Fishermen's Associations v. Yurok Tribe, Civ. No. C02–02006 SBA, slip op. at 17 (N.D. Cal., March 7, 2005).

> While the controversies over the Klamath water are divisive, all parties seem to agree that history gave rise to too many claims on a limited ecosystem—a theme repeated in basin after basin across the United States.

> **Exercise:**
> Assume you represent a tribe in a challenge to BLM's approval of a mine just off the reservation. Your client claims that the mine would have harmful impacts to waters and wildlife on the reservation. The government contends that, by complying with the Federal Land Policy Management Act (FLPMA), it is automatically carrying out its trust obligation toward tribes, even though FLPMA gives no mention of tribal interests. What approach will you take? Will you challenge the action under purely statutory standards, or argue for an enhanced trust standard within the FLPMA framework? Review the statutory standards applicable to mining under FLPMA, discussed in Chapter 6.VI. Were these standards created with the unique property interests of tribes in mind? If not, does compliance with them ensure protection of native lands and resources? Outline your arguments, incorporating the widely varying precedent in this area.

B. Incorporating the Trust Obligation Into the Administrative Framework

President Clinton took important steps to integrate the trust obligation into the administrative framework and to create a new era of government-to-government relations with tribes when he issued a Memorandum entitled, "Government-to-Government Relations With Native American Tribal Governments." 59 Fed. Reg. 22951 (Apr. 29, 1994). The memorandum attempted to clarify the trust responsibility by outlining principles that executive agencies must follow in their interactions with tribes. It requires federal agencies to ensure that they operate "within a government-to-government relationship" with tribes, consult with tribes prior to taking actions that affect tribes, assess agency plans, programs and activities for their impacts on tribes, and tailor federal programs to address unique tribal needs. While the memorandum is not enforceable by tribes in court, it is an important first step in creating a process to carry out the sovereign trust relationship between the federal government and tribes. Following the Memorandum, federal agencies began to develop trust policies to establish protocol for dealing with tribal interests in the implementation of statutes. During the Clinton administration nearly all federal departments and agencies having authority over natural resources and the environment developed either draft or final policies. For analysis, *see* Mary C. Wood, *Fulfilling the Executive's Trust Responsibility Toward the Native Nations on Environmental Issues: A Partial Critique of the Clinton Administration's Promises and Performance,* 25 Envtl. L. 733, 799–800 (1995). In 1998, President Clinton issued an executive order strengthening his mandate to agencies, and in 2000 he revised the order, excerpted below.

CONSULTATION AND COORDINATION WITH INDIAN TRIBAL GOVERNMENTS
Executive Order 13175
65 Fed. Reg. 67249
Nov. 6, 2000

Sec. 2. Fundamental Principles

In formulating or implementing policies that have tribal implications, agencies shall be guided by the following fundamental principles:

(a) The United States has a unique legal relationship with Indian tribal governments.... The Federal Government has enacted numerous statutes and promulgated numerous regulations that establish and define a trust relationship with Indian tribes.

(b) * * * As domestic dependent nations, Indian tribes exercise inherent sovereign powers over their members and territory. * * *

(c) The United States recognizes the right of Indian tribes to self-government and supports tribal sovereignty and self-determination.

Sec. 3. Policymaking Criteria.

In addition to adhering to the fundamental principles set forth in section 2, agencies shall adhere, to the extent permitted by law, to the following criteria when formulating and implementing policies that have tribal implications:

(a) Agencies shall respect Indian tribal self-government and sovereignty, honor tribal treaty and other rights, and strive to meet the responsibilities that arise from the unique legal relationship between the Federal Government and Indian tribal governments. * * *

Sec. 5. Consultation.

(a) Each agency shall have an accountable process to ensure meaningful and timely input by tribal officials in the development of regulatory policies that have tribal implications. * * *

Sec. 10. Judicial Review.

This order is intended only to improve the internal management of the executive branch, and is not intended to create any right, benefit, or trust responsibility, substantive or procedural, enforceable at law by a party against the United States, its agencies, or any person.

Notes and Questions

1. While the Executive Order has prompted agencies to formulate a government-to-government relationship with tribes, has it done anything to clarify the trust obligation towards tribes or define its meaning? Does the reference to statutory and regulatory standards in section 2(a) clarify or confuse matters?

2. Does the educational value of the Executive Order surpass its legal value to tribes? Without an order of this kind, would agency officials engaged in activities having consequences to tribes understand the sovereign nature of tribes, the federal trust obligation, and the tribal role in the Constitutional structure of the United States?

3. In some cases, tribes proactively take the lead in suggesting appropriate trust standards of protection by negotiating with the Executive Branch on a program-by-program basis. For example, in 1997, tribes and the Secretaries of Interior and Commerce negotiated an agreement that would guide the two departments in carrying out the Endangered Species Act in conformance with the trust obligation. The federal agencies had recognized that they have significant discretion in implementing the ESA, and that the historical exercise of that discretion has failed to protect tribal interests. The negotiations resulted in a detailed Secretarial Order designed to establish an agency process to ensure compliance with trust duties. *See* Departments of Interior and Commerce, *American Indian Tribal Rights, Federal–Tribal Trust Responsibilities, and the Endangered Species Act,* Secretarial Order No. 3206 (June 5, 1997).

V. INDIAN TREATY RIGHTS

Indian treaties are, fundamentally, deeds in which the tribes relinquished lands and retained certain rights. Many tribes in the Pacific Northwest, Great Lakes area, and other regions retained harvest rights across ceded lands directed at wild game, fish, or plants and berries. Access rights associated with treaty harvest clauses vary depending on the specific treaty language. In the Pacific Northwest, access rights to "usual and accustomed" fishing grounds are generally valid notwithstanding the fact that they lie on what is now private property. United States v. Winans, 198 U.S. 371, 25 S.Ct. 662, 49 L.Ed. 1089 (1905). In contrast, the Seventh Circuit has construed the Chippewa treaty rights in the Great Lakes Region as not encumbering private lands. *See* Lac Courte Oreilles Band of Chippewa Indians v. Voigt, 700 F.2d 341, 365 (7th Cir. 1983). In addition to harvest rights, treaties carry implied reserved water rights. Winters v. United States, 207 U.S. 564, 28 S.Ct. 207, 52 L.Ed. 340 (1908). As described in Chapter 13, *infra* (Water), reserved Indian water rights are often the most senior in the basin, above all other water users.

The landmark case, *United States v. Winans*, made clear that "the treaty was not a grant of rights to the Indians, but a grant of rights from them—a reservation of those not granted." *Winans*, 198 U.S. at 381. Therefore, tribes retain rights not granted away. The Supreme Court has noted on many occasions that "Indian treaties are to be interpreted liberally in favor of the Indians, [and] ambiguities are to be resolved in their favor." Minnesota v. Mille Lacs Band of Chippewa Indians, 526 U.S. 172, 200, 119 S.Ct. 1187, 1202, 143 L.Ed.2d 270, 293 (1999). Courts have sometimes inferred harvest rights even where a treaty does not explicitly mention them. *See* Menominee Tribe of Indians v. United States, 391 U.S. 404, 406, 88 S.Ct. 1705, 1707, 20 L.Ed.2d 697 (1968) (construing treaty language "to be held as Indian lands are held" as including a right to fish and hunt). Congress may abrogate treaty rights, but only if it makes its intention plain and clear. United States v. Dion, 476 U.S. 734, 106 S.Ct. 2216, 90 L.Ed.2d 767 (1986). A treaty abrogation is a taking of property subject to the 5th Amendment's requirement of compensation. *Menominee, supra.*

Tribes without recognized treaties may have significant harvest rights as well. Treaties were used as a mechanism for dealing with tribes only until 1871, and many reservations in the lower 48 states were created by statute or executive order rather than a treaty. Courts have taken a liberal approach in interpreting these instruments to infer many of the same types of harvest and water rights that were reserved in treaties with other tribes. *See* Parravano v. Babbitt, 70 F.3d 539, 545 (9th Cir. 1995) (Hoopa Valley and Yurok tribes have federally reserved fishing rights associated with executive orders and statutes creating their reservation). However, treaty rights may differ from rights created by "treaty equivalents" in terms of the compensation required if they are extinguished. *See* Sioux Tribe of Indians v. United States, 316 U.S. 317, 62 S.Ct. 1095, 86 L.Ed. 1501 (1942) (rights created by executive order without Congressional ratification amount to unrecognized title that does not require compensation upon extinguishment).

Alaska and Hawaii natives did not enter into treaties with the federal government, but their traditional hunting, fishing, and gathering rights have some limited protection through statutes and court decisions. Alaska native subsistence falls within the Alaska National Interest Lands Conservation Act (ANILCA), which Congress passed in 1980. ANILCA protects subsistence use (by native and rural non-native individuals) on public lands in Alaska. *See* 16 U.S.C. §§ 410hh–3233 (1980); Alaska v. Babbitt, 72 F.3d 698 (9th Cir. 1995), *cert. denied*, 517 U.S. 1187, 116 S.Ct. 1672, 134 L.Ed.2d 776 (1996). Traditional Hawaiian harvest and gathering rights are protected on undeveloped lands under the Hawaii Constitution and state statutes. *See* Public Access Shoreline Hawaii (PASH) v. Hawai'i County Planning Commission, 79 Hawai'i 425, 903 P.2d 1246–1271 (1995); Kalipi v. Hawaiian Trust Co., 66 Haw. 1, 656 P.2d 745 (1982). An excellent summary of Alaska native subsistence rights is found in GETCHES, WILKINSON, & WILLIAMS, CASES AND MATERIALS ON FEDERAL INDIAN LAW, 4ed. 924–928 (West 1998). *See also* Jeremy D. Sacks, *Culture, Cash or Calories: Interpreting Alaska Native Subsistence Rights,* 12 ALASKA L. REV. 247 (1995). For commentary on Hawaiian native rights, *see Symposium: Managing Hawai'i's Public Trust Doctrine,* 24 HAWAII L. REV. 21 (2001).

A. Treaty Harvest Rights

1. *Historic and Modern Cultural Framework of Treaty Rights*

The modern exercise of treaty fishing rights is an outgrowth of a traditional cultural lineage extending back, in some cases, several thousand years. One of the most studied contexts of Indian fishing rights is the Pacific Northwest. *See* FAY COHEN, TREATIES ON TRIAL: THE CONTINUING CONTROVERSY OVER NORTHWEST INDIAN FISHING RIGHTS (1986); ROBERTA ULRICH, EMPTY NETS: INDIANS, DAMS, AND THE COLUMBIA RIVER (1999). Because the Pacific Northwest has been at the epicenter of treaty rights litigation, the materials in this section focus on that region, but other treaty rights settings are equally important and rival the Northwest in complexity.

A tribal fisherman, Jaime Pinkham, extends a traditional dip net to catch salmon returning to spawn at a Nez Perce treaty fishing site in ceded territory, Rapid River, Idaho. Photo courtesy of Alvin A. Pinkham, Sr.

From 1854–1855, Isaac Stevens, Superintendent of Indian Affairs for the Washington Territory, negotiated six treaties with tribes across the Pacific Northwest. The Stevens treaties all contained a similar clause stating: "The right of taking fish, at all usual and accustomed grounds and stations, is further secured to said Indians, in common with all citizens of the Territory...." *See* Washington v. Washington State Commercial Passenger Fishing Vessel Assoc., 443 U.S. 658, 674, 99 S.Ct. 3055, 3069, 61 L.Ed.2d 823, 839 (1979). An extensive description of Indian fishing is found in a district court decision commonly known as the "Boldt decision" (after the judge who decided the case) upholding treaty fishing rights in Washington State. The opinion, 203 pages in length, contains considerable evidence showing the Indians' likely understanding of the treaty language. This evidence is important because one of the primary canons of treaty construction is that language be interpreted as the Indians would have understood it at the time. *See Passenger Fishing Vessel*, 443 U.S. at 676. The district court found:

> * * * [O]ne common cultural characteristic among all of these Indians was the almost universal and generally paramount dependence upon the products of an aquatic economy, especially anadromous fish, to sustain the Indian way of life. These fish were vital to the Indian diet, played an important role in their religious life, and constituted a major element of their trade and economy. * * *

At the treaty council the United States negotiators promised, and the Indians understood, that the Yakimas would forever be able to continue the same off-reservation food gathering and fishing practices as to time, place, method, species and extent as they had or were exercising. The Yakimas relied on these promises and they formed a material and basic part of the treaty and of the Indians' understanding of the meaning of the treaty. * * *

The treaty-secured rights to resort to the usual and accustomed places to fish were a part of larger rights possessed by the treating Indians, upon the exercise of which there was not a shadow of impediment, and which were not much less necessary to their existence than the atmosphere they breathed.

U.S. v. Washington, 384 F.Supp. 312 (W.D Wash. 1974) (emphasis added).

While the right to fish was necessary for sheer physical survival at treaty times, fishing still forms a central part of the native way of life across the Pacific Northwest. Tribal people still fish for traditional, subsistence, and commercial purposes. Modern tribal leaders emphasize that the continued existence of salmon—and the continued exercise of treaty fishing rights—is essential to tribal cultural survival.

Treaty rights bring up a set of complex issues that can be categorized as follows: access, allocation, regulation, and conservation. Access issues are particularly pronounced when the treaty activity is asserted on private lands. Because treaty rights may still be exercised after periods of dormancy, they may come as a surprise to private landowners. In the Pacific Northwest, where treaty rights encumber private property along waterways with usual and accustomed fishing sites, new development proposals may encounter complex treaty access issues. Allocation issues involve the division of harvest rights between tribal and state sovereigns. Regulation of treaty harvest creates complex questions of state, federal, and tribal jurisdiction. Finally, questions of broad conservation duties are gaining a front-seat role in treaty harvest issues. The majority society can swiftly reduce formerly harvestable populations to numbers hovering around extinction, provoking the obvious question of whether the treaty right incorporates an implicit right to protect the species. The following materials explore these dimensions of treaty rights, using the Pacific Northwest as a case study.

2. Access Issues

The following article explores a controversy over access rights deriving from the landmark case, *United States v. Winans, supra.*

RIVER LAND FOR RIVER PEOPLE
Marla Williams
LAND & PEOPLE MAGAZINE (spring 1999)

Gulls circle and shriek, diving from low-flying clouds to the surging, slate-colored river below. On the cliffs rising from the river, a man skids across slick basalt before leaping recklessly from a wet rock to a warped wood platform high above the water. * * * The makeshift structure shudders as he lifts a massive angle of fishing net. The 20–foot-long dip net gathered on a pine rim about four feet in diameter, dangles from the end of an unwieldy pole. Leaning far out over swirling eddies below, the man lowers the huge net into the river—combing the current for fish in the ancient way of the River People. He is Klickitat, descended from a race that 10,000 years earlier heard its name called out by gulls chasing salmon up the Columbia River.

* * * Just up the hill, below a grassy swell of land that hides the fisherman from sight, is a large for-sale sign announcing "Klickitat Landing"—a 33–lot luxury subdivision overlooking the river at Lyle Point, Washington about 80 miles east of Vancouver, Washington, on scenic Highway 14. * * * River and earth are bound together here, old friends steadying each other against change as constant and unruly as the wind. Now a low, blue metal gate set in stone announces a barrier—not only between Native Americans and the river that flows through their history, but to all who seek a quiet place along the river where they might contemplate what was and what will be.

When the prospective developers, Columbia Gorge Investors Ltd., bought Lyle Point in 1991 from Burlington Northern, a strong and favorable wind was blowing in their direction. An international destination for windsurfers and other recreationists, the Columbia Gorge receives more than 2 million visitors a year. Affluent windsurfers in pursuit of five-foot swells and 40–mile-per-hour winds were descending en masse on river towns ready to receive them. Developers saw a chance to buy into the boom at Lyle Point—one of the few remaining pieces of prime, undeveloped riverfront in the Columbia Gorge. There are no houses on the property yet, but there are roads and lot markers and utility boxes. Tennis courts, a swimming pool, and a windboard launch are promised amenities. * * *

The Native American name for this place is Nanainmi Waki 'Uulktt, or "place where the wind blows from two directions." Crossing an open field at Lyle Point, Chief Johnny Jackson walks slowly—not with age, but respect. The traditional chief of the Cascade Klickitat Band, Jackson believes his ancestors are buried at Lyle Point—their bones embedded in the ground as surely as their memory is fixed in his heart. * * *

When explorers Meriwether Lewis and William Clark arrived at Lyle Point in 1805, they found a thriving indigenous population living largely on fish. * * * By 1855, Stevens had coerced a number of tribes to sign treaties ceding their lands and confining them to reservations. * * * Among them were the Klickitat, who had lost nearly all their land but retained the right to fish in the Columbia. A decade later, pioneer James O. Lyle settled at Klickitat Landing on Lyle Point with his family. With westward expansion, a town sprang up and, fed by steamboat and railroad, grew rapidly. * * *

* * * In the fall of 1993, as the salmon returned to the Columbia, the River People returned to Lyle Point. Days before, over the objections of Native Americans and the Columbia Gorge Audubon Society, county officials had granted developers final approval for the subdivision. Now the River People pitched tipis, built a sweat lodge, trucked in portable toilets, and settled in for what would be a long, tense occupation.

"I am a quiet person. I do not like to fight," says Margaret Flintknife Saluskin, a Wishcum and a member of the Yakama Nation. It was Saluskin who led the protest. "I could not permit a blue metal gate to separate me from my ancestors, my way of life."

Developers assured tribal members that they would have access to the Columbia, and that their right under the Yakamas' Treaty of 1855 to fish from riverbanks would be respected. But Saluskin and others questioned whether the owners of new luxury houses would tolerate Indians cleaning fish and camping next door. "The salmon is our 'first food,' given to us by the Creator," Saluskin explains. "Our rights to fish cannot depend on the kindness of strangers." * * *

Notes and Questions

1. Would the presence of condos or McMansions impair the Indian treaty fishing right at Lyle Point? The developer would have allowed continued tribal access, so technically speaking, the Indians could have continued to fish at the site. But, is culture so inextricably connected with the treaty harvest right that it must be considered a part of the overall tribal property right? How do you go about defining contextual protection of these treaty rights? Recall that the *Winans* case described the Yakama's right of access under the treaty as an easement. *See* Chapter 5.I.C., *supra*. In practical terms, how do you establish an appropriate geographic buffer for the fishing easement in order to protect the cultural dimensions implicit in the exercise of the treaty right? How does western property law address questions of cultural context?

2. For nearly two years, the treaty Indians, along with the Columbia Gorge Audubon Society, maintained a teepee occupation of Lyle Point and kept a sacred fire burning on the bluff overlooking the Columbia River. The Yakama Nation and other tribes sued in federal district court to protect treaty fishing rights at Lyle Point. Prior to a decision in the case, the Trust For Public Lands (TPL) negotiated an option to buy the property. The tribe also reached a settlement with the developer in which the Yakamas purchased a small strip of the riverfront property. In March 2000, TPL purchased the remaining property to protect it from development, and the organization now seeks to sell the property to a conservation buyer who will protect it in perpetuity. This case study illustrates the importance of land trusts in the fast changing area of natural resources law. For background on land trusts, *see* Chapter 9.III.

3. Assume the property had not been purchased by TPL and the matter had proceeded to litigation. If you were a law clerk for the federal judge handling the case and were asked to write a bench memo analyzing the right of access in this context, how would you structure your analysis? Refer to the *Winans* case, *supra*.

4. In the 1990s, tribes in the Puget Sound area began to assert their treaty rights to shellfish, most of which are located on private lands. Many of these encumbered parcels are luxury shoreline estates owned by people who had not thought about treaty rights at the time they purchased the property. In a continuation of the *United States v. Washington* litigation, the Ninth Circuit Court of Appeals upheld the right of the treaty fishermen to assert their *Winans* right of access across private lands to harvest shellfish. *See* United States v. Washington, 135 F.3d 618 (9th Cir. 1998). This exercise of treaty rights on private land triggered a new round of hostility towards the tribes. *See* Ross Anderson, *Look Who's Clamming in My Yard—Rulings Pit Tribes Against Landowners*, THE SEATTLE TIMES, Feb. 15, 1998; Mariel J. Combs, *United States v. Washington: The Boldt Decision Reincarnated*, 29 ENVTL. L. 683 (1999).

Exercise:

Assume you are the Trust For Public Lands project manager for the newly acquired Lyle Point site. What management strategy will you have for the site until you find a buyer who can hold the site in conservation for the long-term? What role will the tribe have at the site, and what processes will you use to involve the tribe? What role will the public have? What kind of buyer will you seek, and what protections, if any, will you include in a sale agreement to ensure that tribal cultural interests are protected? Prepare an outline of a strategy to present to your director.

---

3.   Quantifying Ownership in a Shared Resource

In nearly all cases involving treaty rights, states make competing demands on the same wildlife resource. One of the most difficult challenges for courts has been to allocate a shared wildlife resource between states and tribes. In Washington v. Washington State Commercial Passenger Fishing Vessel Association, 443 U.S. 658, 99 S.Ct. 3055, 61 L.Ed.2d 823 (1979), the Court affirmed Judge Boldt's interpretation of the fishing clause in the Northwest treaties to require a 50–50 division of the harvestable fish.

WASHINGTON v. WASHINGTON STATE COMMERCIAL PASSENGER FISHING VESSEL ASS'N.
Supreme Court of the United States, 1979.
443 U.S. 658, 99 S.Ct. 3055, 61 L.Ed.2d 823.

JUSTICE STEVENS delivered the opinion of the Court.

* * * One hundred and twenty-five years ago when the relevant treaties were signed, anadromous fish were even more important to most of the population of western Washington than they are today. At that time, about three-fourths of the approximately 10,000 inhabitants of the area were Indians. * * * Their usual and accustomed fishing places were numerous and were scattered throughout the area, and included marine as well as fresh-water areas. * * *

It is perfectly clear ... that the Indians were vitally interested in protecting their right to take fish at usual and accustomed places, whether on or off the reservations, and that they were invited by the white negotiators to rely and in fact did rely heavily on the good faith of the United States to protect that right. * * *

The Indians understood that non-Indians would also have the right to fish at their off-reservation fishing sites. But this was not understood as a significant limitation on their right to take fish. * * * [I]t is fair to conclude that when the treaties were negotiated, neither party realized or intended that their agreement would determine whether, and if so how, a resource that had always been thought inexhaustible would be allocated between the native Indians and the incoming settlers when it later became scarce. * * *

The [treaty] provide[s]: "The right of taking fish, at all usual and accustomed grounds and stations, is further secured to said Indians, in common with all citizens of the Territory ..." * * * [T]he State of Washington [argues] that it was merely access that the negotiators guaranteed. It is equally plausible to conclude, however, that the specific provision for access was intended to secure a greater right—a right to harvest a share of the runs....

[T]he treaty must ... be construed, not according to the technical meaning of its words to learned lawyers, but in the sense in which they would naturally be understood by the Indians. * * *

Governor Stevens and his associates were well aware of the "sense" in which the Indians were likely to view assurances regarding their fishing rights. During the negotiations, the vital importance of the fish to the Indians was repeatedly emphasized by both sides, and the Governor's promises that the treaties would protect that source of food and commerce were crucial in obtaining the Indians' assent. It is ... inconceivable that either party deliberately agreed to authorize future settlers to crowd the Indians out of any meaningful use of their accustomed places to fish. That each individual Indian would share an "equal opportunity" with thousands of newly arrived individual settlers is totally foreign to the spirit of the negotiations. Such a "right," along with the $207,500 paid the Indians, would hardly have been sufficient to compensate them for the millions of acres they ceded to the Territory.

It is true that the words "in common with" may be read either as nothing more than a guarantee that individual Indians would have the same right as individual non-Indians or as securing an interest in the fish runs themselves. If we were to construe these words by reference to 19th-century property concepts, we might accept the former interpretation.... But we think greater importance should be given to the Indians' likely understanding of the other words in the treaties and especially the reference to the "right of *taking* fish"—a right that had no special meaning at common law but that must have had obvious significance to the tribes relinquishing a portion of their pre-existing rights to the United States in return for this promise. This language is particularly meaningful in the context of anadromous fisheries ... because of the relative predictability of the "harvest." In this context, it makes sense to say that a party has a right to "take"—rather than merely the "opportunity" to try to catch—some of the large quantities of fish that will almost certainly be available at a given place at a given time.

This interpretation is confirmed by additional language in the treaties. The fishing clause speaks of "securing" certain fishing rights, a term the Court has previously interpreted as synonymous with "reserving" rights previously exercised. *Winans*, 198 U.S. at 381. [Since] the Indians had always exercised the right to meet their subsistence and commercial needs by taking fish from treaty area waters, they would be unlikely to perceive a "reservation" of that right as merely the chance, shared with millions of other citizens, occasionally to dip their nets into the territorial waters. * * * Because it was the tribes that were given a right in common with non-Indian citizens, it is especially likely that a class right to a share of fish, rather than a personal right to attempt to land fish, was intended. * * *

[A]n equitable measure of the common right should initially divide the harvestable portion of each run that passes through a "usual and accustomed" place into approximately equal treaty and nontreaty shares, and should then reduce the treaty share if tribal needs may be satisfied by a lesser amount. * * * It bears repeating, however, that the 50% figure imposes a maximum but not a minimum allocation. ... [T]he central principle here must be that Indian treaty rights to a natural resource that once was thoroughly and exclusively exploited by the Indians secures so much as, but no more than, is necessary to provide the Indians with a livelihood—that is to say, a moderate living. Accordingly, while the maximum possible allocation to the Indians is fixed at 50%, the minimum is not; the latter will, upon proper submissions to the District Court, be modified in response to changing circumstances. If, for example, a tribe should dwindle to just a few members, or if it should find other sources of support that lead it to abandon its fisheries, a 45% or 50% allocation of an entire run that passes through its customary fishing grounds would be manifestly inappropriate because the livelihood of the tribe under those circumstances could not reasonably require an allotment of a large number of fish.

Notes and Questions

1.   The *Passenger Fishing Vessel* Court interpreted the treaty language to require a 50–50 allocation of the harvestable fish between states and tribes. Due to the nearly identical language used in the fishing clauses of the other Stevens treaties executed throughout the Pacific Northwest, courts apply the same allocation principles to all nine of the Stevens treaties. Because the 50–50–allocation rule is tied to specific treaty language, it is not controlling in cases involving different treaty language.

2.   The Court in *Passenger Fishing Vessel* made clear that the 50% figure represented a cap on the tribal share, and that the tribal allocation would be reduced to that amount necessary to support a "moderate living" if circumstances changed. Is this "moderate living" standard evident from the treaty language? What if the tribes require more than 50% of the harvestable runs to support a moderate living? The Court's emphasis that "the 50% figure imposes a maximum" seems to foreclose anything more. Do you think the tribal negotiators contemplated this outcome?

In reality, the Court's "moderate living" standard has never been applied in the context of Pacific Northwest fisheries. The salmon fishery is in steep decline, due to hydroelectric development, pollution, irrigation, urban development and poor forestry and grazing practices—nearly all the fault of non-Indian society. While, historically, up to 16 million fish returned to the Columbia River Basin, returns have dropped over 90%, and scientists believe that at least 100 salmon stocks have gone extinct throughout the Basin and another 50 are at risk of extinction. The harvestable portion of each fishery is so small that a 50% allocation does not approach the numbers to sustain even the most conservative interpretation of "moderate living." Tribal officials estimate that tribal take (approximately 50,000 fish per year) is only 1% of historic take levels. For a discussion of the salmon fishery and the tribal role in recovering populations, *See* Mary Christina Wood, *Reclaiming the Natural Rivers: The Endangered Species Act as Applied to Endangered River Ecosystems,* 40 Arizona L. Rev. 197, 226–229 (1998).

3. Judge Boldt's initial allocation decision, which held that the tribes were entitled to a 50% share of the harvestable portion of the fish runs, triggered a series of events that presented nearly unparalleled challenges to federal court authority. State courts repudiated Judge Boldt's rulings, necessitating him to assume direct federal judicial supervision over harvest management. Though the challenges were finally put to rest with the *Passenger Fishing Vessel* opinion, that decision did little to calm the racial animosity towards Indian fisherman that erupted into violent episodes during the Northwest's "Fish Wars."

In his book, Messages from Frank's Landing, Professor Charles Wilkinson presents a compelling portrayal of the historical context leading up to the landmark Boldt decision and the Indian fishermen who carried the struggle. Frank's Landing, a six-acre home site of tribal fisherman Billy Frank and his family on the Nisqually River, became a "focal point" for tribal assertion of treaty rights in the Northwest.

> [D]uring the runs, Frank's Landing was hyperactive, white hot. The surveillance was continuous. There were scores of raids, many of them—preserved both in front-page photographs and a great amount of film footage—ugly, heartrending brawls. In time, the banks of the Nisqually merged with the school-house steps of Little Rock, the bridge at Selma, and the back of the bus in Montgomery.

> The game wardens—a dozen to more than fifty—would descend the banks in a stone-faced scramble toward a few Nisqually men in a canoe or skiff unloading salmon from a gillnet. Usually the Nisqually would give passive resistance—dead weight—and five officers or more would drag the men up the rugged banks toward the waiting vehicles. The dragging often got rough, with much pushing and shoving, many arms twisted way up the back, and numerous cold-cock punches. The billy clubs made their thuds. Sometimes the Indian men struck back. Sometimes Indian people on the banks threw stones and sticks at the intruders. The stench of tear gas hung in the air.

Charles F. Wilkinson, Messages from Frank's Landing: A Story of Salmon, Treaties, and the Indian Way 38 (2000).

4. A remarkable aspect of federal Indian law is that it enforces treaties made over 150 years ago, negotiated in a geographical and political context much different than what we know today. As Professor Charles Wilkinson pointed out in his landmark work, American Indians, Time, and the Law 32 (1987), "The modern cases reflect the premise that tribes should be insulated

against the passage of time." *See also* United States v. Washington, 384 F.Supp. 312, 406–07 (W.D. Wash. 1974) ("[T]he mere passage of time has not eroded, and cannot erode, the rights guaranteed by solemn treaties that both sides pledged on their honor to uphold."). Are these treaty rights secure against the passage of time over the next 150 years?

5. Judicial enforcement of treaty harvest clauses in the Great Lakes region (particularly in Minnesota, Michigan and Wisconsin) has generated a voluminous body of ongoing case law dealing with allocation, regulation, and management issues similar to those in the Pacific Northwest litigation. *See e.g.,* United States v. Michigan, 653 F.2d 277 (6th Cir. 1981); Lac Courte Oreilles Band of Chippewa Indians v. Voigt, 700 F.2d 341 (7th Cir. 1983); Mille Lacs Band of Chippewa Indians v. Minnesota, 124 F.3d 904 (8th Cir. 1997), *aff'd,* 526 U.S. 172, 119 S.Ct. 1187, 143 L.Ed.2d 270 (1999). For a review of the Great Lakes litigation, *see* GETCHES, WILKINSON & WILLIAMS, CASES AND MATERIALS ON FEDERAL INDIAN LAW 4D 881–82, 893–901 (West 1998); GOBLE AND FREYFOGLE, WILDLIFE LAW, CASES AND MATERIALS 629–630 (Foundation Press, 2002).

6. For more discussion of treaty harvest rights, *see* Robert J. Miller, *Native Rights: Indian Hunting and Fishing Rights,* 21 ENVTL. L. 1291 (1991); Mason D. Morisset, *The Legal Standards for Allocating the Fisheries Resource,* 22 IDAHO L. REV. 609 (1986).

4. *Regulation of Tribal Treaty Harvest Rights*

An entire body of common law has grown around regulation of Indian treaty harvest. Because tribes are sovereigns with authority over their members' conduct both on and off the reservation, tribes have clear regulatory authority over their members' harvest activities. New Mexico v. Mescalero Apache Tribe, 462 U.S. 324, 330, 103 S.Ct. 2378, 2384, 76 L.Ed.2d 611, 617 (1983). Tribes in their sovereign capacity issue fishing, hunting, and gathering privileges to their citizens and develop and enforce regulations with respect to harvest. Settler v. Lameer, 507 F.2d 231, 232–33, 239 (9th Cir. 1974). Tribal regulation of members' harvest extends off the reservation. *Id.*; Lac Courte Oreilles Band of Lake Superior Chippewa Indians v. Wisconsin, 668 F.Supp. 1233, 1241 (W.D. Wis. 1987); United States v. Michigan, 471 F.Supp. 192, 274 (W.D. Mich. 1979), *aff'd,* 653 F.2d 277 (6th Cir. 1981).

a. State Regulation of Off–Reservation Tribal Treaty Harvest

Quite apart from the body of Indian law, states have a traditional regulatory role over wildlife harvest within their borders. *See* Geer v. Connecticut, 161 U.S. 519, 16 S.Ct. 600, 40 L.Ed. 793 (1896). Such regulation can conflict with tribal exercise of treaty rights, particularly where the states single out tribal harvest to absorb an undue burden of conservation. State regulation of tribal harvest has engendered bitter conflicts in the Pacific Northwest and Great Lakes regions. It is clear that the traditional state authority to regulate wildlife is subject to federal preemption. *See* Hughes v. Oklahoma, 441 U.S. 322, 99 S.Ct. 1727,

60 L.Ed.2d 250 (1979). Because Indian treaty rights are federal rights, courts have imposed important restrictions on state regulation of Indian harvest. The Court in Minnesota v. Mille Lacs Band of Chippewa Indians, 526 U.S. 172, 204, 119 S.Ct. 1187, 1204, 143 L.Ed.2d 270, 296 (1999) declared:

> [A]n Indian tribe's treaty rights to hunt, fish, and gather on state land are not irreconcilable with a State's sovereignty over the natural resources in the State. Rather, Indian treaty rights can coexist with state management of natural resources. Although States have important interests in regulating wildlife and natural resources within their borders, this authority is shared with the Federal Government when the Federal Government exercises one of its enumerated constitutional powers, such as treaty making (citation omitted).

The restrictions on state regulation vary according to whether the harvest is on or off the reservation. When tribal members are exercising their treaty rights on the reservation, the state's ability to exercise concurrent authority is extremely limited. The Supreme Court has held that such regulation is warranted only in "exceptional circumstances." New Mexico v. Mescalero Apache Tribe, 462 U.S. 324, 331–332, 103 S.Ct. 2378, 2385, 76 L.Ed.2d 611, 619 (1983).

Off the reservation, however, a different rule applies. In Puyallup Tribe v. Dept. of Game, 391 U.S. 392, 88 S.Ct. 1725, 20 L.Ed.2d 689 (1968) (*Puyallup I*), the Court held that the state could regulate Indian treaty fishing off the reservation only if the state regulation was "in the interest of conservation" and did not "discriminate against the Indians." *See also* United States v. Michigan, 653 F.2d 277, 279 (6th Cir. 1981); Lac Courte Oreilles Band of Lake Superior Chippewa Indians v. Wisconsin, 740 F.Supp. 1400, 1421–1422 (W.D. Wis. 1990). In a subsequent case, Dept. of Game v. Puyallup Tribe, 414 U.S. 44, 94 S.Ct. 330, 38 L.Ed.2d 254 (1973) (*Puyallup II*), the Court determined that the State of Washington's ban on all net fishing was, in fact, discriminatory, because virtually all Indian fishermen used nets, and the state allowed the hook-and-line form of fishing engaged in by non-Indians.

The application of the *Puyallup* standards has engendered a more specific set of "conservation necessity" standards that courts have imposed on states to justify regulation of Indian treaty fishing. Two are particularly forceful and have been adopted both in the Pacific Northwest and the Great Lakes contexts. The first is that the state regulation of the tribes must be the least restrictive alternative method available to achieve the necessary conservation. *See* United States v. Oregon, 769 F.2d 1410, 1416 (9th Cir. 1985); United States v. Michigan, 653 F.2d 277, 279 (6th Cir. 1981); Lac Courte Oreilles Band of Lake Superior Chippewa Indians v. Wisconsin, 668 F.Supp. 1233, 1236 (W.D. Wis. 1987). The second is that the state must show it is not able to achieve its conservation goals by regulating only the non-treaty users. *See* Antoine v. Washington, 420 U.S. 194, 207, 95 S.Ct. 944, 952, 43 L.Ed.2d 129, 139 (1975); United States v. Washington, 520 F.2d 676, 685–686 (9th Cir.

1975); Lac Courte Oreilles Band of Lake Superior Chippewa Indians v. Wisconsin, 668 F.Supp. 1233, 1236 (W.D. Wis. 1987).

Does the anti-discrimination requirement of the *Puyallup* cases, as detailed through these "conservation necessity" standards, really protect Indian treaty fishing? Salmon and all other species follow a lifecycle that is heavily impacted by numerous factors, including habitat degradation, predation, and other take. Indian fishing occurs at the end of the life-cycle as the fish are spawning. By that time, if the run is diminished, it is difficult to regulate anything but Indian fishing in a last-ditch effort to save the run. The failure of state and federal government to regulate non-Indian sources of mortality may create a recurring cycle in which collapsing runs justify regulation of Indian fishing despite *Puyallup's* anti-discrimination standard. *See* Mary Christina Wood, *Fulfilling the Executive's Trust Responsibility Toward the Native Nations on Environmental Issues: A Partial Critique of the Clinton Administration's Promises and Performance,* 25 ENVTL. L. 733–800 (1995) ("Where an agency fails to affirmatively regulate non-Indian causes of mortality to the extent that it *creates* a situation of biological crisis, thereby leaving just the option of regulating a tribal activity, the tribal use is arguably the subject of discrimination.").

b. Federal Regulation of Indian Treaty Harvest

While off-reservation wildlife regulation has traditionally fallen to the states, increasingly federal agencies assert regulatory jurisdiction over imperiled species under the Endangered Species Act (ESA). The National Marine Fisheries Service and U.S. Fish and Wildlife Service implement the ESA. Section 9 of the ESA, which prohibits take of endangered species without an incidental take permit, pertains to any tribal harvest of listed species. 16 U.S.C. § 1538. Section 10 of the act allows "incidental take" of species if authorized by the Services. 16 U.S.C. § 1539. Procedurally, the Services may opt to treat the tribal sovereign harvest as a federal action under section 7 of the ESA, in which case the Services must determine whether the harvest is "likely to jeopardize" the continued existence of the species. 16 U.S.C. § 1536(a).

Although statutes of general applicability such as the ESA generally apply to tribal activities, the ESA's application to tribal harvest may be problematic if it goes so far as to abrogate treaty rights. In United States v. Dion, 476 U.S. 734, 106 S.Ct. 2216, 90 L.Ed.2d 767 (1986), the Supreme Court determined that federal statutes do not abrogate treaty rights unless there is "clear evidence" that Congress considered the conflict between the statute and tribal treaty rights, and intended to abrogate the treaties. *Id.* at 740. In that case, defendant Dion, a member of the Yankton Sioux Tribe, was convicted of shooting four bald eagles on the Yankton Sioux Reservation in South Dakota in violation of both the Endangered Species Act and Eagle Protection Act. The Court found that the Eagle Protection Act implicitly abrogated treaty rights, but did not reach the issue of whether the ESA meets the abrogation test.

UNITED STATES v. DION

Supreme Court of the United States, 1986.
476 U.S. 734, 106 S.Ct. 2216, 90 L.Ed.2d 767.

JUSTICE MARSHALL delivered the opinion of the Court.

* * * We have required that Congress' intention to abrogate Indian treaty rights be clear and plain. * * * Indian treaty rights are too fundamental to be easily cast aside. * * *

Explicit statement by Congress is preferable for the purpose of ensuring legislative accountability for the abrogation of treaty rights. We have not rigidly interpreted that preference, however, as a *per se* rule; where the evidence of congressional intent to abrogate is sufficiently compelling, "... intent can also be found by a reviewing court from clear and reliable evidence in the legislative history of a statute." What is essential is clear evidence that Congress actually considered the conflict between its intended action on the one hand and Indian treaty rights on the other, and chose to resolve that conflict by abrogating the treaty. * * *

The Eagle Protection Act renders it a federal crime to "take, possess, sell, [and] purchase ... any bald eagle commonly known as the American eagle or any golden eagle, alive or dead, or any part, nest, or egg thereof." 16 U. S. C. § 668(a). * * * The Act, however, authorizes the Secretary of the Interior to permit the taking, possession, and transportation of eagles "for the religious purposes of Indian tribes," ... 16 U.S.C. § 668a.

Congressional intent to abrogate Indian treaty rights to hunt bald and golden eagles is certainly strongly suggested on the face of the Eagle Protection Act. The provision allowing taking of eagles under permit for the religious purposes of Indian tribes is difficult to explain except as a reflection of an understanding that the statute otherwise bans the taking of eagles by Indians, a recognition that such a prohibition would cause hardship for the Indians, and a decision that that problem should be solved not by exempting Indians from the coverage of the statute, but by authorizing the Secretary to issue permits to Indians where appropriate.

The legislative history of the statute supports that view. * * *

We therefore read the statute as having abrogated [Dion's] treaty right.

Dion also asserts a treaty right to take bald eagles as a defense to his Endangered Species Act prosecution. * * * [H]e asserts that he is immune from Endangered Species Act prosecution because he possesses a treaty right to hunt and kill bald eagles. We have held, however, that Congress in passing and amending the Eagle Protection Act divested Dion of his treaty right to hunt bald eagles. He therefore has no treaty right to hunt bald eagles that he can assert as a defense to an Endangered Species Act charge.

We do not hold that when Congress passed and amended the Eagle Protection Act, it stripped away Indian treaty protection for conduct not expressly prohibited by that statute. But ... Dion here asserts a treaty right to engage in precisely the conduct that Congress, overriding Indian treaty rights, made criminal in the Eagle Protection Act. That statute, we hold, removed Dion's treaty shield for that conduct, and Congress' failure to discuss that shield in the context of the Endangered Species Act did not revive that treaty right.... * * * (citation omitted).

Notes and Questions

1. The *Dion* test has been tagged the "consideration and choice" test by those in the field. *See Dion, supra* ("What is essential is clear evidence that Congress actually considered the conflict between its intended action on the one hand and Indian treaty rights on the other, and chose to resolve that conflict by abrogating the treaty."). In *Dion*, the Court found evidence of Congressional intent to abrogate treaty rights from the structure of the Eagle Protection Act which provided a special permit process for native use of eagle feathers and its legislative history. Express legislative recognition of treaty rights in the statute is not required.

2. It is unclear, under *Dion's* "consideration and choice" test, whether the ESA abrogates treaty rights. The Supreme Court failed to reach the issue. The ESA itself contains no language specific to Indian treaty rights. But like the Eagle Protection Act, it does contain an exemption directed towards native use. The key difference is that the ESA exemption is directed only towards Alaska natives, *see* 16 U.S.C. § 1539(e), whereas the permit provision in the Eagle Protection Act was much broader, directed towards "Indian tribes." Alaska Natives do not have treaty rights to begin with. One court applied this distinction to a similar Alaska Native exemption in the Migratory Bird Treaty Act and found insufficient evidence of abrogation. *See* United States v. Bresette, 761 F.Supp. 658, 663–65 (D. Minn. 1991). Another district court, however, analyzed the ESA in the context of the Seminole's treaty right to hunt the ESA-listed black panther and found abrogation. *See* United States v. Billie, 667 F.Supp. 1485 (S.D. Fla. 1987). Suffice it to say, the issue is far from settled. For discussion, *see* Robert Laurence, *The Abrogation of Indian Treaties by Federal Statutes Protective of the Environment,* 31 Nat. Resources J. 859 (1991).

3. What is the effect of abrogation of a treaty right? The *Dion* Court implied that the right vanishes upon a finding of Congressional abrogation. The Court held that the abrogation effectuated by the Eagle Protection Act "divested" Dion of any further treaty right that could be asserted as a defense to the ESA. Theoretically, then, abrogation seems to be an all out taking of a treaty right, akin to a Fifth Amendment taking under the Constitution. Because treaty rights are deemed property rights, abrogation appears to warrant compensation. *See* Menominee Tribe of Indians v. United States, 391 U.S. 404, 88 S.Ct. 1705, 20 L.Ed.2d 697 (1968).

But did the Court really think through its analysis of abrogation? What if the eagle populations recover (as they have since *Dion* was decided) and the eagle is de-listed under both the Eagle Protection Act and the ESA? Did the Supreme Court ever consider this possibility? Should the Yankton Sioux lose their treaty right forever just because that treaty right was regulated during a period of low populations? Did the Court really need to frame the question as one of abrogation? Couldn't the Court have simply framed the question as whether Congress intended the Eagle Protection Act to *regulate* treaty rights? Theoretically, regulation may occur without abrogation. At least one court has applied the *Puyallup* conservation standards, rather than *Dion's* abrogation standard, to federal wildlife regulation of treaty rights. *See* Anderson v. Evans, 371 F.3d 475 (9th Cir. 2004) (Marine Mammal Protection Act).

4. In 1997, the Secretaries of Commerce and Interior issued a Joint Secretarial Order addressing how the ESA will be implemented when it affects tribes. *See Secretarial Order 3206: American Indian Tribal Rights, Federal–Tribal Trust Responsibilities, and the Endangered Species Act* (1997), *available at* http://endangered.fws.gov/tribal/Esatribe.htm. The Order requires the Services to consult with tribes before enforcing the ESA against the exercise of tribal harvest rights. As a prerequisite for such enforcement, the Order also requires the Services to determine that tribal conservation measures are inadequate, that sufficient conservation cannot be achieved through regulation of non-Indians, and that the regulation of the tribal activity is the least restrictive means available to accomplish the conservation goals–all a fairly clear importation of the conservation standards that had been applied to the state context by *Puyallup* and later fishing cases. For commentary, *see* Charles Wilkinson, *The Role of Bilateralism in Fulfilling the Federal–Tribal Relationship: The Tribal Rights–Endangered Species Secretarial Order*, 72 WASH. L. REV. 1063, 1071 (1997); Sandi B. Zellmer, *Conserving Ecosystems Through the Secretarial Order on Tribal Rights*, 14 NAT. RESOURCES & ENV'T. 162 (2000).

Exercise:

You are an attorney for NMFS, which has regulatory jurisdiction over actions affecting the ESA listed salmon in the Columbia Basin. The Columbia River Tribes have treaty rights to take salmon migrating up the Columbia and Snake Rivers. Because of low fish populations, NMFS seeks to prohibit all tribal fishing during a spring run of salmon. The tribes claim that the prohibition would preclude a ceremonial fishery of tremendous religious significance. NMFS continues to allow coastal non-Indian fishing and dam operations to go on substantially unchanged even though both activities result in killing protected salmon.

Advise NMFS on the following:

1) Whether it is obligated, as a matter of Indian law, to regulate other non-Indian activities so as to protect treaty rights to salmon.

2) Whether the Tribes would be successful in a lawsuit to enjoin NMFS from interfering with their harvest.

5. *Environmental Conservation as a Treaty Right*

In the face of declining species, tribes increasingly contend that their treaty rights include a right of environmental protection. The article below examines the nature of the treaty wildlife asset in the context of Columbia River fisheries.

THE TRIBAL PROPERTY RIGHT TO WILDLIFE CAPITAL
Mary Christina Wood
37 Idaho L. Rev. 1, 32, 42–45 (2000) (Part I);
25 Vt. L. Rev. 355, 355–448 (2001) (Part II)

The history of salmon law suggests that a great impediment to species recovery is a failure to define and enforce on a broad level mutual obligations of the federal government, tribes, and states in sustaining the fishery. Environmental devastation of salmon runs has rendered nearly moot the traditional judicial approach of defining tribal treaty rights in terms of harvest alone. * * * [S]overeign rights to harvestable returns are no longer an overriding issue because there are so few fish returning to harvest sites. Rather, the critical issue is whether tribes have rights to maintain healthy runs of fish. The inquiry demands a reconceptualization of the wildlife resource as a whole. * * *

Much like a financial asset, the salmon asset consists of two major components: capital and yield. The capital component contains those elements necessary to maintain the fishery as a whole in perpetuity. The yield component represents the amount of fish that can be harvested each year without diminishing the natural capital over time. In the financial world, a capital asset in an account produces income (or yield) on a perpetual basis. If a financial manager depletes the capital, the yield will diminish accordingly. So it is with the natural world as well. Capital and yield are both composite parts of the asset as a whole, but proper management (whether financial or environmental) requires a clear delineation between them so as to ensure perpetual returns.

[The] capital component of wildlife is further dichotomized into two basic elements. The first consists of robust populations which can produce future generations of the species. * * * Applied to the salmon fishery, the population component of capital consists both of the juvenile fish which migrate out to sea and a portion of the returning adults which spawn and replenish the species. * * *

The second component of wildlife capital consists of natural production areas. These are areas with natural conditions necessary to support the species throughout its entire life cycle. Natural production areas are every bit as critical to the wildlife asset as, for example, a production facility is to a manufacturing process, or land is to a crop. * * * The salmon species rely on natural production areas which embrace spawning and rearing habitat, migratory habitat, and ocean habitat. * * *

It is elementary that both components of wildlife capital are necessary to maintain the natural asset over time. * * * If the populations are over-harvested below the minimum viable population threshold, the species will go extinct despite adequate natural production areas. By the same token, if the habitat is destroyed, the species will go extinct despite the ample size of a returning generation of spawners. These principles were designed by evolutionary process and represent inalterable "natural laws" which govern the resource as a whole. * * *

The [*Washington Passenger Fishing Vessel* opinion], while celebrated as a landmark in federal Indian law, had a tragic element of mistaken focus. For while courts were defining and enforcing a tribal property right to the yield component of the treaty fisheries, industrial forces were rapidly decimating the salmon capital, and the tribal victories rang ever more hollow in subsequent years as the salmon moved toward extinction. In retrospect, courts should have defined the tribal property interest as one in salmon capital as well as yield. * * *

Until present, only one case has addressed whether treaty rights implicitly include a broad duty of environmental protection. United States v. Washington *(Phase II),* 506 F.Supp. 187 (W.D. Wash. 1980), *vacated on procedural grounds,* United States v. Washington, 759 F.2d 1353 (9th Cir. 1985) (en banc). In that case, the United States sued the state of Washington on behalf of several tribes, seeking a declaratory judgment that the tribes' fishing right includes the right to have treaty fish protected from environmental degradation. *Id.* at 202. The claim was a sweeping one, extending across the full landscape of salmon habitat located within the district court's jurisdiction. It was the second phase in the landmark litigation in which Judge Boldt had earlier ruled that the Washington treaty tribes were entitled to one-half of the harvestable salmon. Judge Orrick succeeded Judge Boldt in handling the *U.S. v. Washington* litigation, and issued the opinion in *Phase II.* Because the United States, tribes, and Washington were direct parties to the *Phase II* litigation, the case presented an unparalleled opportunity for a court to define inter-sovereign obligations to protect the natural production areas essential to the shared fishery.

UNITED STATES v. STATE OF WASHINGTON (PHASE II)

United States District Court, Western District of Washington, 1980.

506 F.Supp. 187.

This opinion constitutes but the most recent link in a long chain of opinions construing the following 27 words: "The right of taking fish, at all usual and accustomed grounds and stations, is further secured to said Indians, in common with all citizens of the Territory." * * *

The quoted clause appears in six treaties negotiated between the United States and several Pacific Northwest Indian tribes in 1854 and 1855. * * * [The] issue presently before the Court is the legal question whether the tribes' fishing right includes the right to have treaty fish protected from environmental degradation. Plaintiffs' pending motion for partial summary judgment does not reach the additional questions whether the State is violating the tribes' alleged environmental right and what relief may be warranted. * * *

At the outset, the Court holds that implicitly incorporated in the treaties' fishing clause is the right to have the fishery habitat protected from man-made despoliation. Virtually every case construing this fishing clause has recognized it to be the cornerstone of the treaties and has emphasized its overriding importance to the tribes. The Indians understood, and were led by Governor Stevens to believe, that the treaties entitled them to continue fishing in perpetuity and that the settlers would not qualify, restrict, or interfere with their right to take fish.

The most fundamental prerequisite to exercising the right to take fish is the existence of fish to be taken. In order for salmon and steelhead trout to survive, specific environmental conditions must be present. A fisheries study prepared jointly by the State and the federal government identifies at least five such conditions: "(1) access to and from the sea, (2) an adequate supply of good-quality water, (3) a sufficient amount of suitable gravel for spawning and egg incubation, (4) an ample supply of food, and (5) sufficient shelter." It is undisputed that "alteration of even one of these essential, finely-balanced requirements will affect the production potential." It is also undisputed that these conditions have been altered and that human activities have seriously degraded the quality of the fishery habitat. * * *

[I]t is well established that the treaty negotiators specifically assured the tribes that they could continue to fish notwithstanding the changes that the impending western expansion would certainly entail. * * *

It has been stated repeatedly that neither party to the treaties, nor their successors in interest, may act in a manner that destroys the fishery. * * * The only significant difference between the holding here and prior decisions is that the general rule that neither party may impair the other's fishing right is applied to the particular situation of impairment by environmental degradation rather than by physical device, by otherwise-burdened access to the fishery, by discriminatory regulation, or by discriminatory application of neutral regulations.

The conclusion that the treaty-secured fishing right incorporates an environmental right is consonant with the implied-reservation-of-water doctrine that is often employed in the construction of Indian treaties. In *Winters v. United States*, 207 U.S. 564 (1908), the seminal case in this area, the Supreme Court held that when the treaty creating the Fort Belknap Indian Reservation was signed, the parties impliedly reserved a sufficient quantity of water to irrigate the arid reservation land. Without that water, the purpose of creating the Reservation to enable the tribe to give up its nomadic existence and sustain itself on a relatively small tract of land would be incapable of fulfillment.

In this case, there can be no doubt that one of the paramount purposes of the treaties in question was to reserve to the tribes the right to continue fishing as an economic and cultural way of life. It is equally beyond doubt that the existence of an environmentally-acceptable habitat is essential to the survival of the fish, without which the expressly-reserved right to take fish would be meaningless and valueless. Thus, it is necessary to recognize an implied environmental right in order to fulfill the purposes of the fishing clause. Indeed, courts have already recognized implied water rights for the specific purpose of preserving fish. * * *

The State argues at some length that it is not necessary to imply an environmental right because there currently exist numerous federal and State programs designed to protect the fish habitat. * * * However, the fact that there may be means of at least partially protecting the fish habitat does not negate the existence of the right. An environmental right must be implied in order to fulfill the purposes of the fishing clause. Whether existing means of enforcing that right are adequate (as the State contends), or whether supplementary means must be adopted (as plaintiffs request), is a separate issue to be addressed at the remedial stage of this litigation. * * *

As the parties approach the relief stage, of critical concern will be the precise scope of the State's environmental duty. * * * The treaties reserve to the tribes a sufficient quantity of fish to satisfy their moderate living needs, subject to a ceiling of 50 percent of the harvestable run. *Washington Phase I, supra*, 443 U.S. at 686–687. That is the minimal need which gives rise to an implied right to environmental protection of the fish habitat. Therefore, the correlative duty imposed upon the State (as well as the United States and third parties) is to refrain from degrading the fish habitat to an extent that would deprive the tribes of their moderate living needs. * * *

Notes and Questions

1. In an en banc decision, the Ninth Circuit vacated Judge Orrick's path-breaking *Washington Phase II* opinion. United States v. Washington, 759 F.2d 1353 (9th Cir. 1985). The court held that a declaratory judgment was not warranted because there was insufficient evidence linking state actions to fish decline. *Id.* at 1357. In the two decades since that opinion, however, an enormous amount of scientific information has been produced as a result of the ESA listings of Pacific salmon up and down the West Coast. Extensive reports and studies on salmon needs, produced as part of the ESA's recovery planning process, now establish a sound factual basis for any contemporary litigation. In 1995, amidst a serious collapse of fish populations, the tribes threatened to resurrect the *Phase II* litigation to secure more favorable environmental conditions for fish. An assistant attorney general for the state of Washington called such potential treaty litigation the "800–pound gorilla in the closet." Neil Modie, *Tribes Seek to Rescue Salmon*, Seattle Post–Intelligencer, June 16, 1995, at B1.

In January, 2001, the tribes finally released the gorilla. Washington treaty fishing tribes that were parties in the Washington Phase II litigation re-initiated the case, but this time with a narrow complaint. *See* Request for Determination, U.S. v. Washington, Civ. No. C70–9213 (W.D. Wash. 2001). The tribes maintain that their treaties incorporate an environmental right of protection that is being violated by the state's maintenance of fish-blocking culverts. Obviously, the factors contributing to salmon decline extend far beyond culverts. Why do you think the tribes limited the action to culverts? If the tribes prevail in the "culverts litigation," what kind of precedent will that set? Is a court more likely to grant relief in a case limited to discrete harm as opposed to a case seeking redress for all of the potentially harmful actions across the basin? After a protracted period of negotiations, efforts to settle the case have failed, and the case is moving to trial.

2. Other courts have addressed aspects of the environmental question and have recognized some form of implied duty of environmental protection towards the tribes. For a full review of these cases, *see* Michael C. Blumm & Brett M. Swift, *The Indian Treaty Piscary Profit and Habitat Protection in the Pacific Northwest: A Property Rights Approach,* 69 U. COLO. L. REV. 407 (1998). The district court of Idaho, however, refused to recognize an environmental duty in the context of a damages action brought by the Nez Perce Tribe against a power company. *See* Nez Perce Tribe v. Idaho Power Co., 847 F.Supp. 791 (D. Idaho 1994). The case does not offer an analysis of inter-sovereign environmental obligations, as the defendant was a private party, not a sovereign.

3. Assume a court finds a treaty right to environmental protection. How would that right be enforced? While a court could set the parameters of an environmental treaty right, any judicial remedy would likely use a settlement process to allow the federal, tribal, and state agencies to agree on a recovery plan to implement the treaty rights. Co-management over harvest aspects of fisheries has generally been successful in the Columbia River Basin, *see infra* section VI. Does the complicated nature of environmental protection and restoration lend itself to a similar co-management approach between the various sovereigns? The Columbia River tribes have produced an extensive recovery plan for the salmon. *See* COLUMBIA RIVER INTER–TRIBAL FISH COMM'N, WY–KAN–USH–MI, WA–KISH–WIT, SPIRIT OF THE SALMON: THE COLUMBIA RIVER ANADROMOUS FISH RESTORATION PLAN OF THE NEZ PERCE, UMATILLA, WARM SPRINGS AND YAKAMA TRIBES 2–4 (1995). Should such a plan take a front-seat role in settlement negotiations? How would a court structure settlement negotiations?

4. For further discussion of treaty rights to environmental protection, *see* Mary Christina Wood, *The Tribal Property Right to Wildlife Capital (Part I): Applying Principles of Sovereignty to Protect Imperiled Wildlife Populations,* 37 IDAHO L. REV. 1 (2000); Mary Christina Wood, *The Tribal Property Right to Wildlife Capital (Part II): Asserting a Sovereign Servitude to Protect Habitat of Imperiled Species,* 25 VT. L. REV. 355 (2001); Blumm & Swift, *supra.*

B. Tribal Reserved Rights to Water

Treaties carry implied reserved water rights which add an important ownership component to the mix of natural resources law. This section briefly describes Indian water rights as part of the overall scheme of water allocation. Chapter 13 deals more fully with water rights.

The landmark case Winters v. United States, 207 U.S. 564, 28 S.Ct. 207, 52 L.Ed. 340 (1908), established the reserved water rights doctrine, holding that Indian reservations carry water rights with a priority date as of the date the reservation was established. In 1963, the Court quantified such rights in Arizona v. California, 373 U.S. 546, 83 S.Ct. 1468, 10 L.Ed.2d 542 (1963), stating that tribes were entitled to an amount equal to the "practicably irrigable acreage" on their reservations. Indian water rights are typically the most senior in the basin because reservations were established prior to the time most other non-Indian uses of water began. At the heart of the *Winters* reserved water rights doctrine is the rationale that water rights are necessary, and therefore implied, to make use of the retained tribal lands, or reservations, for farming. Another branch of the Indian water rights doctrine has developed to protect the fisheries subject to tribal harvest. This instream water right can be thought of as a component of a treaty right to environmental protection, explored above.

UNITED STATES v. ADAIR

United States Court of Appeals, Ninth Circuit, 1983.
723 F.2d 1394, *cert. denied*, 467 U.S. 1252, 104 S.Ct. 3536,
82 L.Ed.2d 841 (1984).

In 1975 the United States filed suit in district court, pursuant to 28 U.S.C. § 1345 (1976), for a declaration of water rights within an area whose boundaries roughly coincide with the former Klamath Indian Reservation. * * * The major feature of the subject area is a large flat valley historically known as the Klamath Marsh. * * *

The Klamath Indians have hunted, fished, and foraged in the area of the Klamath Marsh and upper Williamson River for over a thousand years. In 1864 the Klamath Tribe entered into a treaty with the United States whereby it relinquished its aboriginal claim to some 12 million acres of land in return for a reservation of approximately 800,000 acres in south-central Oregon. * * * Article I of the treaty gave the Klamath the exclusive right to hunt, fish, and gather on their reservation. * * *

The issue presented for decision in this case is whether, as the district court held, these hunting and fishing rights carry with them an implied reservation of water rights. * * *

First, water rights may be implied only "[w]here water is necessary to fulfill the very purposes for which a federal reservation was created," and not where it is merely "valuable for a secondary use of the reservation." *New Mexico,* 438 U.S. at 702. Second, the ... doctrine "reserves only that amount of water necessary to fulfill the purpose of the reservation, no more." *Cappaert,* 426 U.S. at 141.

The question, therefore, is whether securing to the Indians the right to hunt, fish, and gather was a primary purpose of the Klamath Reservation. * * * The State and individual appellants argue that the intent of the 1864 Treaty was to convert the Indians to an agricultural way of life. The Government and the Tribe argue that an equally important purpose of the treaty was to guarantee continuity of the Indians' hunting and gathering lifestyle. * * * It is apparent that a second essential purpose in setting aside the Klamath Reservation, recognized by both the Tribe and the Government, was to encourage the Indians to take up farming.

Neither *Cappaert* nor *New Mexico* requires us to choose between these activities or to identify a single essential purpose which the parties to the 1864 Treaty intended the Klamath Reservation to serve. * * * We therefore have no difficulty in upholding the district court's finding that at the time the Klamath Reservation was established, the Government and the Tribe intended to reserve a quantity of the water flowing through the reservation not only for the purpose of supporting Klamath agriculture, but also for the purpose of maintaining the Tribe's treaty right to hunt and fish on reservation lands. * * *

[T]he right to water reserved to further the Tribe's hunting and fishing purposes is unusual in that it is basically non-consumptive. The holder of such a right is not entitled to withdraw water from the stream for agricultural, industrial, or other consumptive uses (absent independent consumptive rights). Rather, the entitlement consists of the right to prevent other appropriators from depleting the streams' waters below a protected level in any area where the non-consumptive right applies. * * *

[The Tribe's] water rights necessarily carry a priority date of time immemorial. The rights were not created by the 1864 Treaty, rather, the treaty confirmed the continued existence of these rights. * * * To assign the Tribe's hunting and fishing water rights the later, 1864, priority date argued for by the State and individual appellants would ignore one of the fundamental principles of prior appropriations law—that priority for a particular water right dates from the time of first use. * * *

This does not mean, however, as the individual appellants argue, that the former Klamath Reservation will be subject to a "wilderness servitude" in favor of the Tribe. Apparently, appellants read the water rights decreed to the Tribe to require restoration of an 1864 level of water flow on former reservation lands now used by the Tribe to maintain traditional hunting and fishing lifestyles. We do not interpret the district court's decision so expansively.

In its opinion discussing the Tribe's hunting and fishing water rights, the district court stated "[t]he Indians are still entitled to as much water on the Reservation lands as they need to protect their hunting and fishing rights." We interpret this statement to confirm to the Tribe the amount of water necessary to support its hunting and fishing rights as currently exercised to maintain the livelihood of Tribe members, not as these rights once were exercised by the Tribe in 1864. We find authority for such a construction ... in *Washington v. Fishing Vessel Ass'n,* 443 U.S. 658 (1979). There, [the] court stated "that Indian treaty rights to a natural resource that once was thoroughly and exclusively exploited by the Indians secures so much as, but not more than, is necessary to provide the Indians with a livelihood—that is to say, a moderate living." 443 U.S. at 686. Implicit in this "moderate living" standard is the conclusion that Indian tribes are not generally entitled to the same level of exclusive use and exploitation of a natural resource that they enjoyed at the time they entered into the treaty reserving their interest in the resource, unless, of course, no lesser level will supply them with a moderate living. As limited by the "moderate living" standard enunciated in *Fishing Vessel,* we [find] that the Klamath Tribe is entitled to a reservation of water, with a priority date of immemorial use, sufficient to support exercise of treaty hunting and fishing rights.

Notes and Questions

1. How did the court use the moderate living standard, first announced in the *Washington Passenger Fishing Vessel* decision? What is the interplay between the moderate living standard and the priority date of "time immemorial?"

2. The Klamath water rights context was further complicated by the fact that the Tribe was terminated in 1954 and lost its reservation lands. The *Adair* court held, however, that the tribe's water rights survived the Termination Act. *See Adair*, 723 F.2d at 1412. An earlier case had found that the treaty hunting and fishing rights survived termination. *See* Kimball v. Callahan (*Kimball I*), 493 F.2d 564, 568–69 (9th Cir. 1974).

3. The *Adair* case is now proceeding through a second stage of litigation to quantify the water rights according to the standards set forth by the Ninth Circuit. *See* United States v. Adair (*Adair II*), 187 F. Supp. 2d 1273 (D. Or. 2002).

4. Other courts have also upheld an instream water right to benefit tribal fisheries. For discussion of these and other cases, *see* Michael C. Blumm, *Unconventional Waters: The Quiet Revolution in Federal and Tribal Minimum Streamflows,* 19 ECOLOGY L. Q. 445 (1992).

5. For a detailed analysis of native water rights, *see* JUDITH V. ROYSTER & MICHAEL C. BLUMM, NATIVE AMERICAN NATURAL RESOURCES LAW, Ch. VII (Carolina Academic Press 2002).

6. Hawaiian native water rights arise in an entirely different legal context than the traditional reserved rights doctrine. In McBryde Sugar Co. v. Robinson, 54 Haw. 174, 504 P.2d 1330 (1973), the Supreme Court of Hawaii held that the state holds all of the water resources in a public trust for the benefit of its people. For a discussion of native Hawaiian water rights, *see* Elizabeth Ann Ho'oipo Kala'ena'auao Pa Martin *et al., Cultures in Conflict in Hawai'i: The Law and Politics of Native Hawaiian Water Rights,* 18 HAW. L. REV. 71 (1996).

VI. TRIBAL CO–MANAGEMENT OF NATURAL RESOURCES

As the previous materials show, tribes have extensive interests in resources located outside of reservation boundaries including wildlife, waters, roots, berries, medicinal plants and cultural resources such as sacred sites and artifacts. When treaties, statutes, and executive orders reduced tribal aboriginal borders to current reservations, most of these crucial resources were left on "ceded" lands open to new owners: the federal government, states, or private parties. This new ownership has created enormous problems for tribes seeking to maintain traditional lifestyles that depend on the continuing viability of subsistence and cultural resources. Increasingly, tribes are seeking innovative ways to exercise their sovereign prerogatives across lands and waters located in aboriginal territory and/or cultural use areas. The challenge for tribes, of course, is that they now lack jurisdiction in these areas. Modern legal mechanisms create a foothold, though rarely a direct authority role, in managing shared resources. Tribal "co-management" has evolved as a descriptive term encompassing a broad spectrum of tribal efforts to assert native sovereign prerogatives in resource management off the reservation.

A. Co-Management Roles

The term "co-management" could imply four distinct roles. The first is setting objectives and standards for environmental health in areas off the reservation, or asserting the right to define the desired "environmental condition." Establishing standards relating to flow levels in rivers, pollutant loading of airsheds, riparian area protection criteria, and fish recovery objectives are all examples of this kind of involvement. Because the sovereign borders do not allow direct tribal authority over such decisions, tribal influence is often indirect. Nevertheless, several modern environmental processes open the door for tribal input. The National Environmental Policy Act (NEPA) and other statutes allow for tribal comment on proposed federal decisions affecting the environment. *See* NEPA, 42 U.S.C. §§ 4321–4347; *see also* Northwest Power Act, 16 U.S.C. § 839b(h)(1)(A), (h)(10)(A) (Council's plan for managing the Columbia River hydrosystem to protect species must be based in part on tribal recommendations). Moreover, most federal agencies dealing with natural resources have developed Indian trust policies that provide a government-to-government consultation process with tribes. *See* Executive Order 13007, *Indian Sacred Sites*, 61 Fed. Reg. 26771 (May 24, 1996); Executive Order 13175, *Consultation and Coordination with Indian Tribal Governments* (Nov. 6, 2000); Executive Order 12898, *Federal Actions To Address Environmental Justice in Minority Populations and Low–Income Populations*, 59 Fed. Reg. 7629 (Feb. 11, 1994); Secretarial Order 3206: American Indian Tribal Rights, Federal–Tribal Trust Responsibilities, and the Endangered Species Act (1997). Furthermore, court decisions involving treaty rights may result in consent decrees affording tribes a direct co-management role in off-reservation resources. *See* United States v. Oregon, 699 F.Supp. 1456, 1459 (D. Or. 1988), *aff'd,* 913 F.2d 576 (9th Cir. 1990) (decree governing Columbia River harvest co-management). Finally, the Clean Water Act and other federal pollution statutes allow tribes to set standards on their reservations as part of a tribal pollution control program authorized under "Treatment as States" (TAS) provisions. The Environmental Protection Agency (EPA) has authority to enforce such standards off the reservation where, for example, an upstream polluter would violate tribal water quality standards. For discussion, *see* Edmund J. Goodman, *Indian Tribal Sovereignty and Water Resources: Watersheds, Ecosystems and Tribal Co-Management*, 20 J. LAND RESOURCES AND ENVTL. L. 185 (2000).

The second type of co-management is implementation of environmental standards on the ground. For example, decisions involving individual pollution permits, timber sales, grazing licenses, and dam operations all fall into this category. This facet of co-management does not involve asserting a desired environmental condition, but does involve applying substantial scientific or technical discretion in determining how to carry out the established condition. The Self–Governance Act of 1994, 25 U.S.C. § 458cc, explored below, may allow tribes to engage in this level of co-management by delegating to tribes programs managed by the U.S. Department of Interior.

A third co-management role involves the non-discretionary aspects of implementing projects or programs. Building or maintaining a visitor center on federal public land, conducting a public educational program, carrying out a prescriptive fire burn, or monitoring wildlife populations are all examples of this type of co-management. Tribes are increasingly involved at this level through contracts, cooperative agreements, and annual program funding agreements authorized by the Self–Governance Act of 1994.

A fourth type of co-management is enforcing standards and regulations pertaining to the protection of resources. This may involve, for example, the authority to issue citations to visitors to National Parks for violating park rules, or arresting poachers for illegal take of regulated species. An enforcement role is problematic because it invokes the jurisdictional limitations of tribal governments over non-Indians. *See* Oliphant v. Suquamish Indian Tribe, 435 U.S. 191, 98 S.Ct. 1011, 55 L.Ed.2d 209 (1978) (tribes lack criminal jurisdiction over non-Indians). Enforcement against tribal members, however, is appropriate in most cases. *See* Settler v. Lameer, 507 F.2d 231 (9th Cir. 1974) (affirming rights of tribes to manage tribal fishing off the reservation); United States v. Michigan, 471 F.Supp. 192 (W.D. Mich. 1979) (same).

The term "co-management," therefore, may be used in the broadest sense to capture the wide variety of roles that tribes currently play in resource management. As tribes become increasingly visible "third sovereigns" in the management of resources, it will be important for the natural resource practitioner to appreciate the jurisdictional and political implications of these distinct roles.

B. Cooperative Agreements, Contracts, and Programs Under the Tribal Self–Governance Act

A variety of authorities allow for tribes to enter into cooperative agreements with state or federal agencies for the management of off-reservation resources or lands. *See, e.g.,* The Indian Self–Determination and Education Assistance Act (ISDEAA), 25 U.S.C. § 450f; Fish and Wildlife Coordination Act of 1984, 16 U.S.C. § § 661 et seq.; National Park Service Organic Act, 16 U.S.C. § 1g. But the most far-reaching statutory co-management directive came in 1994, when Congress passed the Tribal Self–Governance Act (as an amendment to the ISDEAA), which allows tribes to receive annual funding to administer programs, services, and functions under the jurisdiction of Department of Interior agencies (other than BIA) in areas "which are of specific geographic, historical, or cultural significance" to them. 25 U.S.C. § 458cc(c); P.L. 103–414, 108 Stat. 4272. This provision is directly aimed towards providing tribes a foothold in management of areas outside their current jurisdiction in which they have an aboriginal interest or nexus.

The Secretary of Interior's decision to delegate these program functions is discretionary, and eligibility is limited to "self-governance" tribes or tribal organizations (there are currently about 80 who have entered into "self-governance agreements" with the BIA). The Act allows tribal assumption of activities within the jurisdiction of the National Park Service, U.S. Fish and Wildlife Service, the Bureau of Land Management, the Bureau of Reclamation, the Minerals Management Service, and the U.S. Geological Survey. In 2003, the Secretary identified 34 National Parks and 15 National Wildlife Refuges that could be eligible for tribal funding agreements. 67 Fed. Reg. 16431 (April 5, 2002). In 2004, the Department of Interior tapped its statutory authority by negotiating an agreement with the Confederated Salish and Kootenai Indian tribes to undertake biological, fire, maintenance and visitor management activities in the 18,500–acre National Bison Range Complex operated in Montana by the U. S. Fish and Wildlife Service. The agreement is available at http://mountainprairie.fws.gov/cskt-fws-negotiation.

A thorny issue arising from the nexus program is the extent to which tribes can make discretionary decisions in resource management. At the very least, the Act enables tribes to perform the ministerial aspects of program implementation, such as providing tourism services within National Park areas, conducting scientific data-gathering for the U.S. Fish and Wildlife Service, and engaging in fire suppression activities on BLM lands. In some cases, these types of on-the-ground tribal activities may result in significant impacts to overall management, but such impacts will be collateral, not direct. A host of discretionary actions lie within the programs administered by Interior agencies—such as BLM's decision whether to issue grazing permits, USFWS's determination as to the optimal elk population within the Wyoming Elk Refuge, the Park Service's decision on how to best manage grizzly bear activity in Glacier National Park, and the Bureau of Reclamation's decision whether to release water from projects for fish enhancement purposes. These are the types of decisions in which tribes often have a direct stake, but typically no voice. Environmental groups fear having less input if authority is transferred from federal agencies to tribes. A central issue is the extent to which the tribes can assert their vision of the desired environmental condition in nexus areas.

Resolution of this issue turns on a provision in the Self–Governance Act that prohibits the delegation of "inherently federal" functions to tribes: "Nothing in this section is intended ... to authorize the Secretary to enter into any agreement ... with respect to functions that are inherently Federal...." 25 U.S.C. § 458cc(k). "Inherently federal," however, is not defined in the statute, and the question is bound to be the focus of every nexus program agreement. The article below provides context for program delegation by exploring the Salish–Kootenai agreement, which is now final.

INDIAN TRIBES AIM TO MANAGE BISON REFUGE: SALISH AND KOOTENAI SEEK TO CONTINUE ANCESTORS' EFFORTS TO PROTECT ONCE–ENDANGERED SPECIES
Mark Mathews
THE WASHINGTON POST, July 8, 2003, at A15

PABLO, Mont.—Fred Matt, tribal chairman of the Confederated Salish and Kootenai Indian tribes has a special passion—the American bison. "We had a long cultural history and connection with the bison," he said. "In the 1870s, our ancestors brought back a half-dozen calves to the Mission Valley from the plains when they saw the bison were being slaughtered to extinction." By 1900, the free-ranging herd numbered about 1,000 in this valley hemmed by craggy mountains and Flathead Lake. But government officials had other plans for the "Flathead" Indians who inhabited this 1.2 million-acre reservation.... In 1906, government officials forced tribal members to sell the bison to make way for homesteading. The beasts were shipped to Canada. In 1908, the federal government allocated 160–acre plots to each tribal member, then sold the rest of the land to non-Indians. That same year, ... President Theodore Roosevelt create[d] a refuge for the nearly extinct species. The government "cut 18,000 acres out of the heart of the reservation," said Matt, and paid the tribes $1.56 an acre. "Then, they bought back some of the same animals that had been relocated to Canada." The tribes now want to contract with the U.S. Fish and Wildlife Service to manage the National Bison Range. [R]egulations require a Fish and Wildlife manager to remain in charge, and the agency must maintain oversight of all inherently governmental duties. * * *

While the Fish and Wildlife Service agrees the Salish and Kootenai have the necessary cultural and historic ties to the refuges, "the major impediments are determining what are the inherently federal functions that must remain under Fish and Wildlife Service authority," [an Inte-

rior official] said. The tribes have committed to maintaining the current
refuge workforce, but employees remain wary. They worry about job
security and advancement opportunities. * * *

Tribal Chairman Matt insists the tribes have consistently shown a
strong commitment to conservation. The Salish and Kootenai were the
first tribes to set aside a reservation wilderness area—89,000 acres that
cover much of the west flank of the Mission Mountain front. During the
summer, even tribal members are denied access to more than 10,000
acres of wilderness to protect grizzly bears.

The tribes also have managed reintroduction programs for threatened peregrine falcons, trumpeter swans and leopard frogs. * * * Still,
the proposal to transfer management of the bison range to the tribes has
met stiff opposition from some in the local community—where non-
Indians outnumber tribal members about 6 to 1. * * *

Notes and Questions

1. What are the parameters for defining "inherently federal" functions? What are the Constitutional limitations? What are the statutory limitations?

2. What are the public's concerns in handing over management to a
tribe? Non-tribal citizens have no procedural input into the decisions of
tribes, and often have no direct way of acquiring information regarding
tribal decisions. Accordingly, environmental groups often oppose tribal management of "public" resources. What environmental laws may protect the
public's interest? NEPA provides procedural protections, but its applicability
within the context of tribal co-management is unclear, because NEPA only
applies to federal actions. NEPA, 42 U.S.C. § 4331 (1969).

3. Annual funding agreements are a subject of negotiation between the
tribe and the Department of Interior. What should the agreements contain?
What milestones should they set? Try to outline the parameters of such an
agreement in the National Bison Range context. Pay particular attention to
defining "inherently federal" functions in the agreement. Approach the task
from the perspective of a government official, an environmental group attorney, and a tribal leader. What interests does each party have? Where are
they congruent, and where are they at odds?

4. Fifty-one tribes are members of the InterTribal Bison Cooperative
(ITBC), an organization with a mission "to restore bison to Indian Nations
in a manner that is compatible with their spiritual and cultural beliefs and
practices." http://www.intertribalbison.org. The organization has a collective
herd of over 8,000 bison on tribal lands and is working to reestablish more
herds to promote "cultural enhancement, spiritual revitalization, ecological
restoration, and economic development." *Id.*

5. At least 70 of the 560 federally recognized tribes have established
natural resource programs, and many engage in cooperative projects to
restore wildlife resources in ceded territory. While the Endangered Species
Act funds state programs, it contains no funding for tribal programs. Organizations such as the Defenders of Wildlife and the National Wildlife Fed-

eration have helped fund tribal programs, recognizing that tribes are often able to take restoration initiatives more decisively than the federal or state governments, which are sometimes paralyzed by bureaucracy. A growing number of success stories emerge from such initiatives. *See* Michelle Nijhuis, *Wildlife Management Blossoms on the Reservations,* HIGH COUNTRY NEWS (Feb. 26, 2001).

In Focus: Nez Perce Co–Management of Wolf Recovery

RETURN OF THE NATIVES
Michelle Nijhuis
HIGH COUNTRY NEWS
February 26, 2001

When Horace Axtell was a boy in the 1920s and '30s, his grandmother would take him on fishing and berry-gathering trips in the Idaho mountains. Like most Nez Perce, they would often work in the forest for two or three weeks at a time. It was on one of those long trips that he heard a wolf howl. * * *

In 1974, the wolf landed on the federal endangered species list.

Axtell, 76, lives with his wife in a small house on the edge of this placid timber town, 15 miles from the Nez Perce Reservation where he grew up. * * *

And he has lived to see his tribe bring wolves back to Idaho.

In 1995, after the state Legislature barred the Idaho Fish and Game Department from cooperating with the federal wolf recovery program, the Nez Perce went to the federal government and volunteered to take the place of the state.

The program has since become one of the most successful wildlife recovery efforts ever. The wolves are multiplying with gusto—almost 200 are roaming free in the state—and the population may soon reach the goals set by the feds.

Thanks to the state legislators' stubbornness, the Nez Perce are the first and only tribe to oversee the statewide recovery of an endangered species. The tribal wildlife department works side-by-side with the federal government, tracking wolves in the vast wilderness lands that once belonged to the tribe. It's a deliciously ironic opportunity, and the tribe is making the most of it. The wolf program is now just one of many Nez Perce projects on and off the reservation, all aimed at strengthening tribal sovereignty and recovering the lands, livelihood and culture stolen during U.S. expansion. Like wolves released from their cages, the Nez Perce are energetically turning the tables on their own bitter history.

The Nez Perce and the gray wolf have a lot in common. Both were chased from their homes and pushed to the edge of annihilation by Westward expansion. Both still suffer the prejudice of the dominant culture. And both have managed to survive. * * * Though the wolf isn't as central to Nez Perce culture as the salmon, wolves symbolize wisdom, strength and family loyalty in tribal legend. * * *

So the Nez Perce were paying close attention in 1991, when Congress directed the Fish and Wildlife Service to develop a recovery strategy for wolves in the Northern Rockies. * * *

Opposition in Idaho was fierce. * * * Idaho ranchers, facing low meat prices, thought wolf predation would mean the end of their businesses. Hunters hated the idea of sharing their prey with wolves, and state officials, … spoke vehemently against wolf recovery. * * * [I]n 1995 [the Idaho state legislature] overwhelmingly voted to prohibit Idaho Fish and Game from having anything to do with wolf recovery. * * * [But] [t]he federal plan had to go forward, with or without the state, so Fish and Wildlife Service staffers started looking for someone else to take on the state's local management role. * * * Levi Holt, who was on the tribal council at the time, says it was a scary decision for the Nez Perce. Wolf recovery was controversial and high-profile, federal funding was tight, and there was no guarantee of success. Some feared the tribe risked a backlash from the state government, and many worried that failure could have repercussions for wildlife restoration projects throughout Indian Country. * * *

[T]ribal wildlife program staffers jumped into the game: They wrote a management plan for the wolves. * * * In 1996, they helped oversee the second wolf release. * * *

The federal agency gradually gained confidence in the tribe. Now, with a $300,000 annual budget from the Fish and Wildlife Service, two full-time biologists and their four- to six-person seasonal staff monitor all of the radio-collared wolves, keep tabs on pack behavior and reproduction, and relocate wolves that attack cattle or sheep. As local ambassadors for the wolves, they also meet with ranchers and others in the area to calm fears and build support.

"They've been a godsend," says Ed Bangs, who runs the gray wolf recovery program for the Fish and Wildlife Service. Since tribal wildlife department staffers live in the recovery area, he explains, they can respond quickly to problems and win the trust of locals. "I don't think the program would have been as successful without them," he says. The Fish and Wildlife Service found it easier to relax when wolf numbers boomed beyond all expectations. * * * Surveys in 2000 estimate 191 wolves, with 18 packs producing 16 litters of pups this past season. * * *

When the state of Idaho gave up its role in wolf management, it unwittingly strengthened the sovereignty of the Nez Perce, altering the complicated relationships between states, tribal and federal governments. It's given the tribe political confidence—and a precedent to build on.

Some state officials would like the tribe to retreat back within reservation boundaries when the wolves are recovered, but it may not be that simple. Though Nez Perce officials know that the political geometry will change with delisting, they want to maintain a long-term role in the program....

Co-Management Exercise:

Assume you are a tribal attorney asked to provide advice in creating a tribal co-management role in the three scenarios below. Identify the type of co-management implicated by each of the three actions and propose a strategy for tribal involvement drawing from the materials above. Be sure to identify potential stumbling blocks and sources of likely opposition. Consider the perspectives of federal and state land and resource managers.

1. The tribe wants to initiate a reintroduction program for the sage grouse both on tribal lands and ceded lands in BLM ownership. The species has been proposed for ESA listing, but USFWS has not yet decided to list it. Reintroduction would require significant habitat restoration and protection and may negatively impact grazing practices. Ranchers with grazing leases on these public lands oppose tribal co-management.

2. The tribe wants to develop an educational program for Devils Tower National Monument, managed by the National Park Service (NPS). The program would educate visitors on the native religious and cultural interests in the monument, the history of federal-tribal relations, and the ecosystem values associated with the monument.

3. The tribe wants to co-manage huckleberry resources on a national forest, located in ceded territory adjacent to the reservation. Gathering rights are not expressly mentioned in the tribe's treaty with the federal government, but gathering has occurred since time immemorial, and the berries continue to form a central part of the cultural and subsistence needs of the tribe. Because logging practices, fire suppression policy, and pesticide use all impact the resource, the tribe seeks a decision role in Forest Service management decisions. The tribe also wants to regulate the amount of huckleberries taken by non-Indian recreational and commercial gatherers on the national forest.

Chapter 8

STATE LANDS OWNERSHIP

State lands comprise a significant category of land ownership, consisting of approximately 135 million acres, which is about 6% of the total United States land base. The eleven western states alone own or manage at least 45 million surface acres, and Colorado manages more land than that found in the entire state of Connecticut. State lands are used for a variety of purposes, including timber harvest, grazing, mining, commercial and residential leasing, urban development, recreation, and preservation. *See* Melinda Bruce & Teresa Rice, *Controlling the Blue Rash: Issues and Trends in State Land Management,* 29 LAND & WATER L. REV. 1 (1994).

Websources:

Most state lands offices have a website. The websites often give great detail as to the history of the land grants, the pertinent constitutional or statutory language creating the land grants, an inventory of the state lands, their current uses, and the administrative structure governing state lands management. For a sampling, *see:*

• Arkansas Commissioner of State Lands, http://www.state.ar.us/land/land.html

• Maine Department of Conservation, Bureau of Parks and Lands, http://www.state.me.us/doc/parks

• Maryland Department of Natural Resources, http://www.dnr.state.md.us/sw_ index_ flash.asp

---

> • Minnesota Department of Natural Resources, http://www.dnr.state.mn.us/index.html
>
> • Nevada Division of State Lands, Department of Conservation and Natural Resources, http://www.lands.nv.gov/
>
> • Texas General Land Office, http://www.glo.state.tx.us

State lands generally fall into three categories. The first is the "grant lands" or "trust lands." As part of the process of creating states in the Union, the federal government granted specific sections of each township to states. These lands were to be sold or managed to provide revenue for the state's public schools. The government made grants of additional parcels to support hospitals, prisons, military institutes, and other purposes. Beginning with Ohio in 1803 and ending with Alaska in 1959, the federal government made land grants as a part of admission for 34 states. A total of 330,000,000 acres were granted to the states for all purposes. Of that, 78,000,000 acres were given in support of schools. *Id.* The school trust lands are the focus of most legal doctrine pertaining to state grant lands.

Today's state grant land issues are oriented almost entirely to the western states. The eastern states largely opted to sell their school lands rather than retain and manage them. Those states put the sales proceeds into permanent funds which are managed to generate income for the state schools. *See* JON A. SOUDER & SALLY K. FAIRFAX, STATE TRUST LANDS: HISTORY, MANAGEMENT, AND SUSTAINABLE USE 6 (University Press of Kansas 1996). The 22 states presently managing trust lands are: Alabama, Alaska, Arizona, California, Colorado, Hawaii, Idaho, Louisiana, Minnesota, Montana, Nebraska, Nevada, New Mexico, North Dakota, Oklahoma, Oregon, South Dakota, Texas, Utah, Washington, Wisconsin, and Wyoming. Jon A. Souder, Sally K. Fairfax & Larry Ruth, *Sustainable Resources Management and State School Lands: The Quest For Guiding Principles,* 34 NAT. RESOURCES J. 271, n. 45 (1994). Section I below explores the history and management of these lands.

The second category of state land ownership is submersible lands. It is estimated that the western coastal states alone own 7.1 million acres of submerged lands. Submersible land ownership does not derive from any express grant, but rather from the implied grant that resulted from the landmark ruling in Pollard v. Hagan, 44 U.S. 212, 11 L.Ed. 565 (1845). In that case the Supreme Court determined that states entered the Union on "equal footing" with other states and gained title to their streambeds along navigable waterways as a necessary aspect of sovereignty. *See* Chapter 5.III.A. From the ownership of submersible lands springs the public trust doctrine, a foundational doctrine in environmental law. Framed by the early case, Illinois Central R.R. Co. v. Illinois, 146 U.S. 387, 13 S.Ct. 110, 36 L.Ed. 1018 (1892), that doctrine has expanded in several states to provide protection to waterways, dry sand areas, and other resources. *See* Chapter 5.III.B. Section II of this chapter provides more detailed treatment of the public trust doctrine.

The third category of state lands consists of those lands and interests acquired after admission for various purposes. Increasingly, states across the country are gaining through purchase, gift, or exchange more lands for parks, recreation, and wildlife habitat. Many state agencies are also acquiring conservation easements across private property for the protection of endangered and threatened species. The statutory mandates for acquisition and subsequent management of such lands vary tremendously between land categories and between states. Generally speaking, the primary problem plaguing these lands and easements is lack of funding for management.

Considered in their totality, state lands hold an impressive array of natural resources valuable for mining, grazing, logging, and development. But as two commentators describe:

> Besides having development value, state lands under all types of agency ownership in the West offer a rich variety of recreational, natural, biological, cultural and historical value. Lands possessing natural and biological value include the Tonto Natural Bridge (the largest travertine bridge in the world), a virgin limestone cave (one of the few such caves still "living" ...), two of the ten largest Giant Sequoia trees, ancient redwood stands, a desert wilderness park of more than 600,000 acres, old growth forests, hundreds of miles of Pacific dry sand beach and wetlands, tidelands, lake and ocean islands, the headwaters of the Missouri River, one of the largest freshwater springs in the world (producing 338 million gallons of water a day), and wilderness areas.

Bruce & Rice, *supra,* at 12–13.

As a sub-field of natural resources law and policy, state lands ownership presents many challenges. First, unlike the field of federal public lands law, which is fragmented along federal agency lines, much of the diversity from this field comes from the divergent culture and history of the states themselves. Each state has its own cases, regulations, and policies pertaining to state lands management. Much of this law traces back to the original state constitutions and enabling acts. While cross-cutting doctrines are evident, the astute practitioner must take into account individual state differences.

A second challenge arises from the distinct nature of state land categories. State grant or "trust" lands are managed according to strict trust principles benefiting schools. By contrast, public trust lands (submersible lands, waters, and other areas subject to the public trust) are managed according to a much broader mandate generally benefiting the public as a whole. The law generated around these two categories is markedly different in origin, but both combine features of federal and state law. Mandates applicable to grant lands refer back to specific language in the state's constitution or enabling act, as interpreted by court decisions. Mandates applicable to submersible lands come largely in the form of a judicially created public trust doctrine. In many states, that doctrine has jumped from the judicial arena to the legislative and administrative realm as states attempt to codify and further define or limit it, in various fashions. Confusion often results from the common use of the term "trust" with respect to trust (grant) lands and submersible public trust lands. Most states do not apply the public trust doctrine to grant lands, viewing the latter as subject to a stringent, narrowly defined express "trust" in favor of school interests.

A third challenge comes from the scattered nature of the state lands across a broader geography. State lands are notoriously fragmented into different parcels of varying size, often forming ownership islands amidst blocks of other federal or private property. For example, Montana's 5.2 million acres are scattered into sixteen thousand separate parcels. *See* Bruce & Rice, *supra,* at 6–7. Many states have no complete inventory of their landholdings. *See id.* at 35–37.

The origin of state ownership was bound to create management problems. In the case of submersible lands, the states' streambeds form ribbons of ownership within larger blocks of land owned by other sovereigns or private parties. In the case of grant lands, the state's ownership was doled out as separate one-square mile sections of each township. The 1785 Land Ordinance created a rectangular grid for the survey and sale of the ceded territory. *See* Chapter 5.I.D.2. Section 16 in each township was reserved for public schools within the township. As later states entered the union, the federal government increased the number of sections granted to states for educational and other purposes, as explained below. The practice of granting square-mile sections within each township created square stamps upon the landscape sometimes called the "blue rash" (a term coined from the federal maps that show state ownership in blue). The isolated and scattered nature of the tracts creates tremendous challenges for finding income-producing uses on those lands, as well as forging an ecosystem-wide approach to natural resource problems. *See* Bruce & Rice*, supra*, at 19.

As you read the materials below, contrast the different management mandates developed for grant lands versus public trust lands. In the materials dealing with state grant lands, you will find numerous threads back to federal lands management as well. Ask how the state management prerogatives differ from the management schemes for surrounding federal and private lands, and explore the overall ecosystem effect of fragmented ownership on land health and natural resources sustainability.

In Practice:
The Bureaucracy of State Lands Management

State lands management is typically governed by a state land commission or a board, which may be elected or appointed. The structure of state lands governance differs considerably from state to state.

Typically, the board oversees a lands agency, often called the Division of State Lands, or the Department of State Lands. The practitioner will find a useful resource in the Western States Land Commissioners Association Directory, which compiles all of the agencies and boards. The Directory is available at http://www.wslca.org/contents/Western_States_Contact_Report.pdf.

A helpful summary of the land grants, acres granted, and dates of admission to the union, is found in Table 1–1 of SOUDER & FAIRFAX, STATE TRUST LANDS, *supra*, at 20–21.

The practitioner should be aware that, though submersible lands and grant lands are often held by the state lands board, park lands and wildlife habitat may be held by other state agencies, typically the state parks department or the state fish and wildlife department. Moreover, some states vest management authority over forest lands in the state forestry department, even though the title to the land is held by the lands board. To further complicate matters, many state lands agencies hold title to vast mineral resources beneath lands managed by other state agencies, the federal government or private parties. The lack of coordination between the various state land agencies is a notorious problem in the field of state lands management.

I.   STATE GRANT LANDS

A.   The Land Grant Process and the Original Grant Documents

STATE SCHOOL LANDS: DOES THE FEDERAL TRUST MANDATE PREVENT PRESERVATION?
Alan V. Hager
12 NAT. RESOURCES & ENV'T 39 (1997)

* * * In Virginia and the other original colonies, as well as Vermont, Kentucky, and Tennessee, there was no federal public domain. Lands were either under private ownership or owned by the states themselves. These lands provided a fertile source of revenue for the public education that the states were to provide for their citizenry. In most of the remaining states, the United States retained virtually all of the unappropriated lands. Federal lands provided no tax base for the support of public education, and states without a revenue source for public education would not be on an equal footing with the original states. * * *

The need for a solution to the problem of providing financial support for public education in the new states was first presented in 1802 when Ohio was to be carved from the Northwest Territory and admitted as a state. Drawing upon the Land Ordinance of 1785, which reserved Lot

No. 16 in every township for the maintenance of schools, and the Northwest Ordinance of 1787, which encouraged the establishment and perpetuation of schools in the new territory but prohibited the taxing of property of the United States, Congress fashioned a compromise. That compromise became part of the Ohio Enabling Act and the enabling acts of every other state to be admitted except Maine, Texas, West Virginia, and Hawaii. (Texas and Hawaii were independent nations before they were admitted to the Union and owned their public domain by virtue of their sovereignty. Maine and West Virginia were created from existing states.) Under the compromise, the new state would pledge not to tax federal lands and, in exchange, would receive from Congress a grant of federal lands within its borders for the support of public education. These agreements were characterized by the United States Supreme Court as solemn compacts between the states and the federal government in which Congress imposed and the states accepted a binding and perpetual obligation to use the granted lands and the revenue generated from them for public schools.

The federal lands to be granted to the states upon their admission were specified sections in each federally surveyed township. The number of these sections granted to the states increased with time. The earlier admitted states, those that had been part of the Northwest Territory and those that became part of the Confederacy, received section 16 of every township. States admitted in and after 1850 that comprise the bulk of the plains and western states received sections 16 and 36 of every township. Utah, New Mexico, and Arizona, which were among the last to be admitted, received sections 2, 16, 32 and 36 of every township. The increase in the amount of lands granted to the states may have been merely a product of increasing congressional generosity. However, the fragility and limited usefulness of lands in the arid West required substantially larger grants to give the states in this region a revenue source comparable to that of their midwestern and southern counterparts. The larger grants coupled with the larger land areas of the western states and the penchant of the midwestern and southern states immediately to sell substantial portions of their lands gave the western states by far the largest inventory of lands to manage. * * * In the arid West, there was no ready market for land, so selling vast quantities of school lands was not always an option.

Typical of the enabling acts pursuant to which Congress granted school lands to the western and plains states is Washington's. It grants "sections numbered sixteen and thirty-six in every township ... for the support of the common schools...." It permits Washington to grant easements or rights in the lands provided that the disposition is "in pursuance of general laws providing for such disposition, [and] ... the full market value ... has been paid or safely secured to the State." The state constitutions usually incorporate the language of the enabling acts and often provide that the granted lands and/or the revenues from them are held in trust. The Washington Constitution states that "the public lands granted to the state are held in trust for all the people...." The constitutions of Idaho, Montana, and Utah provide that all lands granted to the state by the federal government shall be held in trust for the people and are to be disposed of only for the purposes for which they have been granted. Nebraska's Constitution contains an explicit statement of the trust to which the funds from school lands are subject. It says that these funds "shall be deemed trust funds held by the state ... [which] are solemnly pledged to the purposes for which they are granted...."

The trust concept did not appear in any enabling act until Congress passed the New Mexico–Arizona Enabling Act in 1910. Congress stated explicitly that the school lands granted to New Mexico and Arizona were to be held in trust.... The New Mexico–Arizona Enabling Act also contained significant restrictions on the disposition and leasing of the lands, including a directive that no lands be sold or leased for less than their fair market value. Congress also required these states to establish a separate fund for all revenues generated by the trust lands ... and authorized the Attorney General of the United States to enforce the terms of the grant. * * *

In Practice: The Original Documents

When analyzing current issues pertaining to state grant lands, it is important to consult the state constitution and enabling act, because both set forth standards governing management and disposition of the grant lands.

The language of the various state constitutions and enabling acts differ markedly, with a clear trend towards more specific language restricting the use of grant lands as Congress progressed in admitting new states to the union. The earlier grants were expressed in just a few sentences. The specificity culminated in the New Mexico–Arizona Enabling Act, which jointly dealt with the admissions of those two states to the Union. That act contained by far the most stringent grant language (still, the provision consumes less than two pages). *See* Pub. L. No. 61–310, 36 Stat. 557 (1910). Though the language is found in no other enabling acts or constitutions, it has formed the basis for considerable Supreme Court precedent on state lands. *See* Lassen v. Arizona, ex rel. Arizona Highway Dept., 385 U.S. 458, 87 S.Ct. 584, 17 L.Ed.2d 515 (1967), excerpted below; Ervien v. United States, 251 U.S. 41, 40 S.Ct. 75, 64 L.Ed. 128 (1919). A useful table compiling citations to the statutes and constitutions, with a summary of pertinent language, is found in Bruce & Rice, *supra*, at Table 3. For additional background on the state land grants, *see* Paul W. Gates, History of Public Land Law Development (Public Land Law Review Comm. 1968).

Notes and Questions

1. Alaska and Hawaii have considerable state landholdings, but they result from a different process than that described above. As two leading state trust land scholars explain:

> After a forty-two-year interlude, Congress voted to admit Alaska and Hawaii to the Union in 1958 and 1959, respectively. * * *
>
> Throughout the pendency of Alaska's statehood quest, the federal government continued to own more than 99 percent of Alaskan land. * * * Instead of granting sections in townships, the statehood bill for Alaska gave the state twenty-five years to choose 102.5 million acres of unreserved land and fifty years to select an additional 800,000 acres of national forest land near communities. The value of those selection rights was significantly reduced when state selections were halted and both the federal government and the state's Native Americans moved to the front of the land-grab queue with almost 200 million acres of selection rights, as a result of the Alaska Native Claims Selection Act. [Ed. note: Alaska ended up with 86 million acres of surface land in state ownership.]
>
> Hawaii joined the United States after half a century as an independent constitutional monarchy and another 50 years as a territory of the United States. The statehood act ratified a trust established on royal lands to support schools and returned to the new state all the lands held by the U.S. at the time of statehood. Hence, Hawaii has a school land trust, but it is not based on the cadastral system so familiar in the lower forty-eight, finding its roots and traditions rather in the Great Mahale of 1848.

SOUDER & FAIRFAX, STATE TRUST LANDS, *supra,* at 23–24.

2. Scholars have uniformly proposed consolidation of state trust lands as a solution to the overwhelming hurdles involved in managing scattered landholdings. The mechanism for consolidation typically involves a land exchange between the state and the federal government, whose landholdings often surround the state holdings. One of the most ambitious land exchange programs took place in Utah:

> [T]he creation of the controversial Grand Staircase–Escalante National Monument actually made possible a land exchange that both Congress and Utah had been seeking for years. The controversy that led to the exchange began when, during the 1996 presidential campaign, President Clinton created the Grand Staircase–Escalante National Monument out of valuable resource lands in southern Utah. The monument caused a local outcry; so, in an effort to appease those upset by its creation, Clinton promised to exchange state trust lands trapped inside the new federal reservation. This … resulted in the exchange of 376,739 acres of state trust lands for more than 139,000 acres of federal land and $50 million. [The] exchange was part of a long history of attempts by Utah to exchange many of its trust parcels for more manageable, larger blocks of land. * * *

Wade R. Budge, *Changing the Focus: Managing State Trust Lands in the Twenty–First Century*, 19 J. LAND, RES. & ENVTL. L. 223, 238 (1999). *See* Utah Schools and Lands Exchange Act of 1998, Pub. L. No. 105–335, 112 Stat. 3139 (1998). For more on land exchanges, *see* Chapter 5.I.D.6, *supra*.

3. The Lincoln Institute of Land Policy and the Sonoran Institute Joint Venture on State Trust Lands have produced a comprehensive report detailing the legal background and current management of trust lands in the West. *See* PETER W. CULP, CYNTHIA C. TUELL, & DIANE CONRADI, TRUST LANDS IN THE AMERICAN WEST: A LEGAL OVERVIEW AND POLICY ASSESSMENT (2005).

B. Trust Principles and the Maximization of Revenue

School trust lands provide a fascinating glimpse into public trust law. The lands are widely deemed to be held in trust by the states for the narrow purpose of providing revenue for schools. While other uses of the land, such as for conservation, might maximize public benefit in other ways, state land managers uniformly believe that the "sacred trust" requires them to prioritize revenue-maximizing uses for the state school lands. *See* Bruce & Rice, *supra* at 29–31. Accordingly, a parcel that is well-suited for a public park might be leased for mining purposes in order to maximize revenue to serve the "trust." In that way, school trusts are distinct from lands held broadly to promote common public purposes. Ironically, such grant lands contribute an "insignificant percentage" to the school budget in most states, due to poor administration and low lease returns. *See id.* at 30.

Management to achieve maximum revenue often compromises critical ecosystem values of state lands, and in some cases unravels conservation gains made by other land managers on adjacent property. Many scholars have grappled with how the narrow trust construct came to be applied to state lands. Only one enabling act, pertaining jointly to New Mexico and Arizona, expressly declares that the lands are to be held "in trust." *See* New Mexico–Arizona Enabling Act, Pub. L. No. 61–310, § 28, 36 Stat. 557, 574 (1910) ("[A]ll lands hereby granted ... shall be by the said State held in trust...."). Two leading commentators provide an interesting glimpse into how a case interpreting the New Mexico–Arizona Enabling Act, *Lassen v. Arizona Highway Dept.*, excerpted below, became the transformative case in the field.

Workers adjust coal mining machinery underneath Utah State Lands, http://
www.energy.utah.gov/newdata/StatAbstract/Coal2.0/CoalImages/deer_creek_CM1.JPG.

STATE TRUST LANDS: HISTORY, MANAGEMENT,
AND SUSTAINABLE USE
Jon A. Souder & Sally K. Fairfax
33–36 (University Press of Kansas 1996)

Because of the trust mandate, school trust lands are unique among
public resources. It is reasonable to wonder how this doctrine came to be
applied to the lands. The notion of a "trust" was not present at the
beginning and did not become a clear part of the federal/state bargain ...
until the Arizona and New Mexico accession. Yet all these lands are currently referred to as "trust lands." * * * In state cases from the 1920s
and 1930s, state courts did not find either state constitutional *or*
enabling act provisions ... to bar state agencies from using school lands
for diverse state purposes. * * *

The worm turned radically in 1966, when the U.S. Supreme Court
[decided *Lassen v. Arizona Highway Department.*] *Lassen* is the starting
point for a series of modern cases that rely on trust principles to answer
ancient issues about the granted lands. * * *

Once the Supreme Court decided *Lassen*, state courts all over the
west, irrespective of the language of their particular enabling act or
state constitution, fell into line. Thus the least typical of the accession
bargains has become central in defining all of them. * * *

Two familiar judicial procedures have inclined the decisions ... to simplify around a few tractable themes. * * * First, one effect of school lands obscurity has been a blurring of the distinctions that arose historically and a tendency for the familiar (the trust principles) to dominate the unfamiliar (the peculiarities of public lands history and policy). Second, normal deference to U.S. Supreme Court decisions has given this blurring a particular flavor in the school lands setting. Unique provisions in the Arizona and New Mexico Enabling Act authorized the U.S. Attorney General to enforce the provisions of the act. Cases from Arizona and New Mexico have, therefore, dominated Supreme Court discussion of school lands, and precedents from Arizona and New Mexico have become central in interpreting the grants in other jurisdictions. * * *

Trust principles ... have come to dominate judicial understanding of school grants.... [T]he standard reliance on precedent and higher court rulings [has] erode[d] appreciation of differences in state accession bargains. A gradual process of accreting judicial decisions has rounded the angles and left the courts with the operating assumption that the grants are trusts that are basically the same. * * *

LASSEN v. ARIZONA HIGHWAY DEPARTMENT

Supreme Court of the United States, 1967.
385 U.S. 458, 87 S.Ct. 584, 17 L.Ed.2d 515.

JUSTICE HARLAN delivered the opinion of the Court.

This action was brought as an original proceeding in the Supreme Court of Arizona by the [State Highway Department]. The Department seeks to prohibit the application by the State Land Commissioner of rules governing the acquisition of rights of way and material sites in federally donated lands held in trust by the State. The Commissioner's rules provide in pertinent part that "Rights of Way and Material Sites may be granted ... for an indefinite period ... after full payment of the appraised value ... has been made to the State Land Department." * * * The Supreme Court of Arizona held that it may be conclusively presumed that highways constructed across trust lands always enhance the value of the remaining trust lands in amounts at least equal to the value of the areas taken. It therefore ordered the Commissioner to grant without actual compensation material sites and rights of way upon trust lands.

The lands at issue here are among some 10,790,000 acres granted by the United States to Arizona in trust ... * * * The terms under which the United States provided these lands were included in the New Mexico–Arizona Enabling Act. 36 Stat. 557. The Act describes with particularity the disposition Arizona may make of the lands and of the funds derived from them, but it does not directly refer to the conditions or consequences of the use by the State itself of the trust lands for purposes not designated in the grant. * * * We ... [conclude] that the terms and purposes of the grant do not permit Arizona to diminish the actual compensation ... payable to the trust by the amount of any enhancement in the value of the remaining trust lands.

The Enabling Act unequivocally demands both that the trust receive the full value of any lands transferred from it and that any funds received be employed only for the purposes for which the land was given. First, it requires that before trust lands or their products are offered for sale they must be "appraised at their true value," and that "no sale or other disposal ... shall be made for a consideration less than the value so ascertained...." * * * Second, it imposes a series of careful restrictions upon the use of trust funds. * * * The Act thus specifically forbids the use of "money or thing of value directly or indirectly derived" from trust lands for any purposes other than those for which that parcel of land was granted. It requires the creation of separate trust accounts for each of the designated beneficiaries, prohibits the transfer of funds among the accounts, and directs with great precision their administration. "Words more clearly designed ... to create definite and specific trusts and to make them in all respects separate and independent of each other could hardly have been chosen." *United States v. Ervien*, 246 F. 277, 279. All these restrictions in combination indicate Congress' concern both that the grants provide the most substantial support possible to the beneficiaries and that only those beneficiaries profit from the trust. * * * Nothing in these restrictions is explicitly addressed to acquisitions by the State for its other public activities.... * * *

We hold therefore that Arizona must actually compensate the trust in money for the full appraised value of any material sites or rights of way which it obtains on or over trust lands. * * *

Notes and Questions

1. In essence, the *Lassen* Court held that state grant lands must be used for the narrow purposes expressed in the state enabling act, rather than a broader set of public purposes. As Souder and Fairfax note, state courts all over the West have applied the *Lassen* decision to their school trust lands even though their enabling acts do not contain the same restrictive language as that of the New Mexico–Arizona Enabling Act. Is this an example of doctrinal laziness, or is there a federal strand of trust law implicit in these statehood grants that threads together all state school land grants despite the express language in the original documents? One commentator has noted that the post-*Lassen* decisions combine to form a modern "school land trust doctrine." Sean E. O'Day, *School Trust Lands: The Land Manager's Dilemma Between Educational Funding and Environmental Conservation, A Hobson's Choice?* 8 N.Y.U. ENVTL. L. J. 163, 165 (1999). The application of *Lassen* to states beyond Arizona and New Mexico has been criticized for restricting conservation use of trust lands. *See* Hager, *State School Lands, supra,* at 80 ("[L]and managers should have the discretion to determine that certain parcels should be preserved forever in their natural state, not merely the discretion to determine how best to exploit the land and its resources.").

2. Consider the differences between federal lands management, explored in Chapter 6, and state lands management under the *Lassen* doctrine. Do the two management regimes result in substantially different out-

comes? Professor Fairfax suggests that trust principles derived from the state context might inform federal land management.

> Federal managers are told to manage the lands in the "combination of uses that best meets the needs of the American people." This flaccid direction is translated into volumes of procedural guidance, but gives relatively little direction as to substantive priorities or goals to be obtained. In contrast the state trust lands are managed like private property that a trustee directs to be maintained for the benefit of a specified beneficiary. This trust mandate [has] clarity, accountability, enforceability, and perpetuity. * * *

> Without belaboring the obvious, [the state lands trust] mandate is significantly different from the rather mushy commands and Byzantine procedural requirements that afflict the federal land management agencies. * * *

Sally K. Fairfax, *Thinking the Unthinkable: States as Public Land Managers*, 3 HASTINGS W–NW. J. ENVTL L. & POL'Y 249, 250, 259 (1996).

3. Leading commentators have noted that the role of courts is markedly different in the two contexts of state trust lands and federal public lands. In the eyes of the courts, state lands agencies are deemed trustees, while federal land management agencies are considered administrators acting pursuant to broad statutory discretion. The distinction is consequential.

> The administrator's advantage arises from the fact that the Court must respect agency discretion: it cannot substitute its judgment for the administrator's, and it must defer to the administrator's expertise. * * * The shoe is on the other foot in the case of a trustee. The court seeks specifically to assess whether the trustee has met the "prudent person" standard: did the trustee act with prudence in handling the trust assets? The effect of any apparent or alleged expertise on the part of the trustee is not to insulate his or her decision from scrutiny, but rather to require him or her to meet higher and higher standards of prudence. * * * [This] provides the trust added protection from self-serving or politically or legislatively harassed administrators.

Jon A. Souder, Sally K. Fairfax & Larry Ruth, *Sustainable Resources Management and State School Lands: The Quest for Guiding Principles,* 34 NAT. RESOURCES J. 271, 295–96 (1994).

Consider again the universal problem of politically influenced federal public lands managers and the administrative deference doctrine that often serves as a shield against enforcement of federal statutory mandates. Can the trust principle suggested by Souder et. al. provide a check against too much deference to agencies? Could public interest litigators argue that the federal agencies are held to some general trust standards? If trust principles have spread from the New Mexico–Arizona context to other state contexts, can a generic form of trustee's loyalty to the public arise in the context of federal lands management? If so, does it necessarily bring with it the concomitant principle requiring maximization of revenue?

The case below explores modern standards for trust management of state lands.

NATIONAL PARKS AND CONSERVATION ASSOCIATION v. BOARD OF STATE LANDS

Supreme Court of Utah, 1993.
869 P.2d 909.

National Parks and Conservation Association (NPCA) appeals ... rulings issued by the Division of State Lands and Forestry (Division) in connection with the Division's decision to exchange a section of state school trust land for lands owned by Garfield County. NPCA contends that ... the patent conveying the school land section to the County should be rescinded.

The school trust land at issue ... lies within the boundaries of Capitol Reef National Park. The State of Utah acquired section 16 from the federal government pursuant to the Utah Enabling Act, which provided that the state was to receive at statehood four sections in every township "for the support of common schools." The Constitution of Utah provides that lands conveyed to the state pursuant to the Enabling Act "shall be held in trust for the people ... for the respective purposes for which they have been or may be granted." UTAH CONST. art. XX, § 1.

Garfield County applied to the Division to exchange county land for section 16.... The County wanted to acquire section 16 so that it could pave part of a dirt road known as the Burr Trail to improve public access to the resplendent scenery of the area. * * *

The central issue of this case is whether the scenic, aesthetic, and recreational values of school trust land should be given preference over maximization of income. * * * The Director ruled that the Division could not give priority to non-monetary values because of its fiduciary duty to manage school trust land for the exclusive economic benefit of the common schools. * * * NPCA contends that the Director erred in ruling that it could not give preference to scenic, aesthetic, and recreational values. This issue goes to the heart of the nature of the school land trust. * * *

The state of Utah accepted these lands and agreed to hold them in trust for the purposes for which they were given. Article XX, § 1 of the Utah Constitution provides:

All lands of the State that have been ... granted to the State by Congress ... are hereby accepted, and declared to be the public lands of the State; and shall be held in trust for the people, to be disposed of as provided by law, for the respective purposes for which they have been granted....

In administering the school trust lands, the state, through the Board and the Division, acts as a trustee. * * * All trustees owe fiduciary duties to the beneficiaries of the trust. The duty of loyalty requires a trustee to act only for the benefit of the beneficiaries and to exercise prudence and skill in administering the trust.... These are legally binding duties, enforceable by those with a sufficient interest in school trust lands to have standing....

The United States Supreme Court has made clear that the value of school trust lands cannot be used to further other legitimate governmental objectives, even if there is some indirect benefit to the public schools. [*See Lassen, supra*]. * * * State courts have also consistently held that school trust lands must be administered for the benefit of the public schools. * * * *State v. University of Alaska*, 624 P.2d 807 (Alaska 1981) dealt with an issue similar to the one at hand. There the state contended that the use of school land as a park for recreational purposes was justified. The Supreme Court of Alaska held that the school land could not be used for recreational purposes without compensating the trust. The court stated: ... "The implied intent of the grant was to maximize the economic return from the land for the benefit of the university. This intent cannot be accomplished if the use of the land is restricted to any significant degree." *Id*. at 813.

In short, trust beneficiaries do not include the general public or other governmental institutions, and the trust is not to be administered for the general welfare of the state. As the Eighth Circuit stated in *United States v. Ervien*, 246 F. 277, 280 (8th Cir. 1917), *aff'd*, 251 U.S. 41 (1919):

> Congress did not intend that the lands granted and confirmed should collectively constitute a general resource or asset like ordinary public lands held broadly in trust for the people, or that the proceeds should constitute a fund like money raised by taxation for "general purposes."

NPCA relies on the "emerging public trust doctrine" in arguing that school trust land is public land "held in trust for *citizens*." (Emphasis added.) NPCA confuses the public trust that applies to sovereign lands with school trust land. The "public trust" doctrine ... protects the ecological integrity of public lands and their public recreational uses for the benefit of the public at large. The public trust doctrine, however, is limited to sovereign lands and perhaps other state lands that are not subject to specific trusts, such as school trust lands.... Thus, the beneficiaries and the purposes of the public trust and the school land trust are different. * * *

We have emphasized the duty of the trustee to maximize the monetary return of school trust lands. We turn now to an issue that is of great importance to this state. Located on some state school lands are unique scenic, archeological, and paleontological sites. Such treasures are legacies of past millennia whose true value could never be expressed in monetary terms. The question is, can such treasures be preserved without violating the terms of the school trust? We think so. * * *

Although the primary objective of the school land trust is to maximize the economic value of school trust lands, that does not mean that school lands should be administered to maximize economic return in the short run. The beneficiaries of the school land trust, the common schools, are a continuing class, and the trustee must maximize the income from school lands in the long run. *Scott on Trusts*, § 232. Certainly it would be as much a violation of the state's fiduciary obligations to immediately sell all state school lands as it would be to use the proceeds from the lands for a nontrust purpose.

The Division should recognize that some school lands have unique scenic, paleontological, and archeological values that would have little economic value on the open market. In some cases, it would be unconscionable not to preserve and protect those values. It may be possible for the Division to protect and preserve those values without diminishing the economic value of the land. For example, with appropriate restrictions it may be possible for livestock grazing and perhaps even mineral extraction to occur on a school section without damaging archaeological and paleontological sites. But when economic exploitation of such lands is not compatible with the noneconomic values, the state may have to consider exchanging public trust lands or other state lands for school lands. Indeed, it might be necessary for the state to buy or lease the school lands from the trust so that unique noneconomic values can be preserved and protected and the full economic value of the school trust lands still realized.

In this case, the Division did consider aesthetic and recreational values in deciding to exchange section 16 for Garfield County's lands. NPCA's argument is not that the Division totally failed to consider these values, but that the Division should have given priority to those values over the state's duty to maximize economic return. For the reasons stated above, that position is contrary to the duties imposed on the state and the Division under the school land trust. We hold that the Board did not breach its trust duties by refusing to give priority to the scenic, aesthetic, and recreational values of section 16 over economic values when it approved the land exchange. * * *

DURHAM, JUSTICE, concurring in the result:

[I] disagree with the suggestion that the state must *always* give the economic interests of the school trust priority over all other considerations in managing trust lands. The majority is correct that the state has a significant duty to the beneficiaries of the school trust, which ordinarily will prevail, but I believe that in some situations it is permissible for the state to give priority to factors besides economic gain to the school trust.

The majority reasons that (1) the state holds section 16 in trust for the school system, (2) the state is subject to the same duties as a private trustee, and (3) a private trustee has a duty of undivided loyalty to the beneficiaries of a trust, therefore (4) the state has a duty of undivided loyalty to the school system, and (5) economic gain to the school system is the only proper consideration in managing section 16. This reasoning is faulty in treating a state exactly the same as a private trustee. A state has powers and duties far beyond those of an ordinary citizen. It has ... the responsibility to legislate in the interest of its citizens. A state can never have "undivided loyalty" to a single interest group; it must consider the health, safety, and welfare of all its people. It also has the duty to manage and preserve public lands for the benefit of present and future generations. These responsibilities may occasionally conflict with the duty to maximize income for the school trust. While the state's duties to the school system are important, they cannot and do not override every other obligation. * * *

The majority opinion acknowledges that failure to preserve scenic, paleontological, or archaeological values may occasionally be "unconscionable," but the alternatives it proposes are inadequate. The majority concludes that in such a situation, the state may have to consider either exchanging other state lands for school trust lands or leasing or buying the lands from the trust. Neither of these options would be satisfactory. * * *

Notes and Questions

1. The court notes that it would be "unconscionable" not to protect and preserve some unique scenic and historical values. Yet, does the court provide a clear line for when those values must override the goal to maximize profits from trust lands? Is there room for a broader public trust mandate? For further discussion of Utah's state school lands, *see* Wayne McCormack, *Land Use Planning and Management of State School Lands,* 1982 UTAH L. REV. 525. The concurring opinion implies that there may be other more desirable management alternatives. What might they be?

2. Several other cases have applied *Lassen* to define the trust responsibility in the context of school lands. *See e.g.,* Alamo Land & Cattle Co., Inc. v. Arizona, 424 U.S. 295, 96 S.Ct. 910, 47 L.Ed.2d 1 (1976); United States v. 78.61 Acres of Land in Dawas and Sioux Counties, 265 F.Supp. 564 (D. Neb. 1967); County of Skamania v. State of Washington, 102 Wash.2d 127, 685 P.2d 576 (1984); Oklahoma Educ. Assn. v. Nigh, 1982 Ok. 22, 642 P.2d 230 (1982); Havasu Heights Ranch and Dev. Corp. v. State Land Dept., 158 Ariz. 552, 764 P.2d 37 (1988); United States v. 111.2 Acres of Land in Ferry County, 293 F.Supp. 1042 (E.D. Wash. 1968), *aff'd* 435 F.2d 561 (9th Cir. 1970); State v. University of Alaska, 624 P.2d 807 (Alaska 1981); In re Conflicting Lease Application for Wyo. Agr. Lease No. 1–7027, 972 P.2d 586 (Wyo. 1999).

3. A Washington case suggests liability to neighboring landowners associated with timber harvest on adjacent state lands. In Dickgieser v. Washington, 153 Wash.2d 530, 105 P.3d 26 (2005), landowners sued the state for inverse condemnation when logging on upslope state trust lands caused flooding of the landowners' property. Experts testified that the landowners would continue to suffer "repeated, permanent, and chronic flooding of their property as a result of the logging." 105 P.3d at 28. The Supreme Court of Washington held that the claim could go forward. If the state is liable under the state's constitution, which prohibits the taking of private property for public use without just compensation, must state lands managers incorporate such potential liability in their determination as to what activity will maximize revenues on state lands? Clearcutting state forest-

lands in Washington has long been a volatile issue. In September, 2004, the Washington State Board of Natural Resources increased the harvest on state lands by 23% from the prior level. *See* CULP, TUELL, & CONRADI, *supra*, at 152.

4. Grazing is a prominent use of state grant lands in the West. In order to protect environmentally sensitive state lands from intensive grazing, some environmental groups are buying leases on state grasslands and then resting the lands for the duration of the lease. In Idaho Watersheds Project, Inc. v. State Board of Land Commissioners, 918 P.2d 1206 (Idaho 1996), the Supreme Court of Idaho held that where a conservation group made the sole bid for a state lands lease at an auction, the state land board must award the lease to the group rather than to the rancher who previously held the lease. For discussion, *see* O'Day, *School Trust Lands supra,* at 227–28 (concluding, "When an environmental group is the highest bidder and the conservation use of that lease does not interfere with long-term financial returns, a state's refusal to allow an environmental group to bid on a lease is a breach of the trust"). Quite ironically, while the *Idaho Watersheds Project* court required the Board to issue the lease to an environmental organization for conservation use of the property, the federal government is prohibited from conservation use of its own grazing lands. Although the Clinton Administration had promulgated a regulation allowing conservation use as part of its Rangeland Reform initiative, the rule was overturned as contrary to the Taylor Grazing Act. *See* Public Lands Council v. U.S. Dept. of Interior, 929 F.Supp. 1436, 1450–1451 (D. Wyo. 1996), discussed in Ch. 6.III. *supra.*

In Focus: Colorado State Grant Lands

In Colorado, voters passed an initiative known as Amendment 16 to amend Colorado's Constitutional provisions regarding the management of the school lands. One provision declared a principle of "sound stewardship" that should guide school land management:

[The] economic productivity of all lands held in public trust is dependent on sound stewardship, including protecting and enhancing the beauty, natural values, open space and wildlife habitat thereof, for this and future generations. In recognition of these principles, the board shall be governed by the standards set forth in this section ... in the discharge of its fiduciary obligations....

The initiative was challenged in Branson School District RE–82 v. Romer, 161 F.3d 619 (10th Cir. 1998). The plaintiff school district contended that Amendment 16 created a mission that injected a conflict of interest into the state's trustee duties by diverting the state from the sole purpose of supporting education. The court found that a federal trust applied to the school lands, but that the "sound stewardship" principle was consistent with the trust management:

> Rather than reading this provision as changing the exclusive purpose of the school lands trust, as the plaintiffs argue, we believe that the "sound stewardship" principle merely announces a new management approach for the land trust. The additional requirement to consider beauty, nature, open space, and wildlife habitat as part of the whole panoply of land management considerations simply indicates a change in the state's chosen mechanism for achieving its continuing obligation to manage the school lands for the support of the common schools. A trustee is expected to use his or her skill and expertise in managing a trust, and it is certainly fairly possible for a trustee to conclude that protecting and enhancing the aesthetic value of a property will increase its long-term economic potential and productivity. The trust obligation, after all, is unlimited in time and a long-range vision of how best to preserve the value and productivity of the trust assets may very well include attention to preserving the beauty and natural values of the property.

Id. at 638.

II. THE PUBLIC TRUST DOCTRINE

A. The Foundation and Scope of the Doctrine

One of the most fundamental underpinnings of modern conservation law is the public trust doctrine, a common law principle that has its seeds in the state ownership of submerged lands along navigable waters. The early Supreme Court case, *Pollard v. Hagan*, established that state ownership of streambeds was crucial for state sovereign functioning, since these lands support fishing, navigation, and commerce. 44 U.S. 212, 229, 11 L.Ed. 565, 573 (1845). Accordingly, the Court determined that the states impliedly acquired ownership of submersible lands from the federal government upon statehood. *See* Chapter 5.III, *supra*.

This equal footing doctrine created the legal platform for the public trust doctrine, which governs both the uses that can be made of submersible lands, and the private property rights that can be acquired from the state in such lands. The lodestar case for interpreting the public trust doctrine is Illinois Central Railroad Co. v. Illinois, 146 U.S. 387, 13 S.Ct. 110, 36 L.Ed. 1018 (1892), excerpted in Chapter 5. In that case, the Supreme Court announced that an implied public trust encumbered submersible lands along navigable waterways: "It is a title held in trust for the people of the state that they may enjoy the navigation of the waters, carry on commerce over them, and have liberty of fishing therein freed from the obstruction or interference of private parties." *Id.* at 452. The Court held that, even if the state conveys the submersible lands to private parties, such lands are encumbered by a public trust easement restricting the uses that the property owner can make of the lands. *See id.* at 453 ("The control of the State for the purposes of the trust can never be lost. ... "). More recent Supreme Court recognition of the doctrine came in Phillips Petroleum Co. v. Mississippi, 484 U.S. 469, 108 S.Ct. 791, 98 L.Ed.2d 877 (1988). The Court found that states acquired all tidelands, navigable or not, upon admission to statehood, and that the public trust attached to such tidelands.

The premise of the public trust doctrine is simple: some natural resources are so important to the public's well-being that they should not be destroyed by the present generation, but should instead be retained in "trust" by the sovereign for the continued welfare of future generations. *See* Arizona Center for Law in the Pub. Interest v. Hassell, 172 Ariz. 356, 367, 837 P.2d 158, 169 (1991) ("The beneficiaries of the public trust are not just present generations but those to come. The check and balance of judicial review provides a level of protection against improvident dissipation of an irreplaceable res."). The sovereign government has special trustee duties to preserve the natural trust. While theoretically this public trust principle could apply to any sovereign government, the doctrine has found its fullest expression at the state level. Because the public trust doctrine emanates from property ownership on behalf of the public, the duties and powers to preserve the trust are distinct from the states' legislative police powers.

Interestingly, though federal common law determines ownership of submersible lands and sets forth the fundamental public trust principle associated with sovereign ownership, the Supreme Court has allowed the parameters of the doctrine to develop on a state-by-state basis. *See Arizona Center*, 837 P.2d at 167 ("[E]ach state must develop its own jurisprudence for the administration of the lands it holds in public trust."). There are now over 100 cases interpreting the public trust doctrine on the state level, an indication that the doctrine is fast becoming a distinct body of law within the broader framework of natural resources law.

As with any doctrine that develops through the state courts, variations in state law are inevitable. Forty states have announced the public trust doctrine, and ten have not. Washington asserted a public trust doctrine fairly recently in 1987. *See* Orion Corp. v. State, 109 Wash.2d 621, 747 P.2d 1062 (Wash. 1987), *cert. denied*, 486 U.S. 1022 (1988). Other states, such as Wisconsin, have public trust cases on the books dating as far back as the 1800s. *See* Priewe v. Wisconsin State Land and Improvement Co., 93 Wis. 534, 67 N.W. 918 (1896).

Some states have taken an expansive approach to the doctrine, while others have been more restrictive. The varied state approaches can be measured by how far they have evolved from the traditional focus of the trust as announced in *Illinois Central*. The geographic focus of that case was submersible lands along navigable waterways. The interests protected by the trust doctrine in that era were limited to fishing, navigation, and commerce. As the materials in this section demonstrate, many courts have expanded the public trust doctrine to meet the changing needs of society. *See, e.g.,* R.W. Docks & Slips v. State of Wisconsin, 244 Wis.2d 497, 628 N.W.2d 781 (2001) (public trust doctrine includes protection of recreational and aesthetic interests); Cinque Bambini Partnership v. Mississippi, 491 So.2d 508, 512 (Miss.1986) ("[T]he purposes of the trust have evolved with the needs and sensitivities of the people...."); Kootenai Envtl. Alliance v. Panhandle Yacht Club, 105 Idaho 622, 625, 671 P.2d 1085, 1088 (1983) ("The trust is a dynamic, rather than static, concept and seems destined to expand with the development and recognition of new public uses."); Marks v. Whitney, 6 Cal.3d 251, 259, 491 P.2d 374, 380 (1971) ("In administering the trust the state is not burdened with an outmoded classification favoring one mode of utilization over another."). Others, however, have remained steadfast to the three traditional public trust interests and the geographic scope of the doctrine. *See* Groves v. Dept. of Natural Resources, 1994 WL 89804 (Del. Super. Ct. 1994) (no public trust rights in walking or recreational activities); Bell v. Town of Wells, 557 A.2d 168, 174 (Me. 1989) (public trust interests limited to fishing, fowling, and navigation); Douglaston Manor v. Bahrakis, 89 N.Y.2d 472, 678 N.E.2d 201, 655 N.Y.S.2d 745 (1997) (refusing to extend public trust to non-navigable waters)*; see also* Anderson Columbia Co. v. Board of Trustees, 748 So.2d 1061 (Fla. Dist. Ct. App. 1999) (state cannot assert public trust rights in filled lands previously granted to private owners by state legislature).

One begins a public trust analysis with the premise that the doctrine applies only to lands of a special character necessary for the public welfare. *See* Illinois Central, 146 U.S. at 454 ("So with trusts connected with public property, or property of a *special character*, like lands under navigable waters; they cannot be placed entirely beyond the direction and control of the State.") (emphasis added). Most often, such "special" land has been associated with water, because water plays an essential role in society. Not only are waterways important for the traditional public trust interests of fishing, navigation and commerce, but they are vital for more modern concerns such as biodiversity, wildlife habitat, aesthetics and recreation. Accordingly, the doctrine has been applied to submersible lands along navigable waterways, non-navigable waterways, tidelands, wetlands, dry sand beach areas and water itself. *See* Richard J. Lazarus, *Changing Conceptions of Property and Sovereignty in Natural Resources: Questioning the Public Trust Doctrine*, 71 Iowa L. Rev. 631, 648 (1986). While a sound argument might be made that the public trust doctrine should apply to other areas of special character, such as old growth forests, aquifer recharge zones, or critical wildlife habitat, courts have not made that leap.

The juxtaposition of the public trust doctrine with state land and water ownership can be quite confusing. At one level, the doctrine originated in the state ownership of streambeds, so it is a doctrine that seems to have property rights at its core. Certainly the public trust most clearly applies to submersible lands along navigable waterways that were impliedly granted to the state upon admission to the union. On the other hand, as noted above, in some states the doctrine has crept out of these narrow boundaries to apply to dry sand areas and submersible lands along non-navigable waterways. Matthews v. Bay Head Improv. Assoc., 95 N.J. 306, 322, 471 A.2d 355, 363 (1984) (dry sand area); National Audubon Society v. Superior Court, 33 Cal.3d 419, 437, 658 P.2d 709, 721 (1983) (non-navigable tributaries); Robinson v. Ariyoshi, 65 Haw. 641, 674, 658 P.2d 287, 310 (1982) (water quality); United Plainsmen Ass'n. v. North Dakota State Water Conservation Comm'n., 247 N.W.2d 457, 462 (N.D. 1976) (water supply). Some of the lands now encompassed within the public trust doctrine may never have entered into state ownership, having been granted directly from the federal government to farmers, homesteaders, miners, or railroad companies. As the public trust doctrine expands to reflect true ecological needs rather than fixed property boundaries, the title origins become more murky and courts resort to a more generalized sovereign power.

Public trust cases generally arise in three different contexts, and while the underlying trust theory remains constant, these contexts are becoming more distinct as the overall body of law advances. The first context is where the state still holds its public trust lands and seeks to manage them. Often states will want to engage in exploitative uses of the property (such as mining or construction). The public trust doctrine can operate as a management principle limiting potentially damaging uses. *See, e.g.,* Sacco v. Department of Public Works, 352 Mass. 670, 673, 227 N.E.2d 478, 480 (1967) (state agency cannot fill pond to widen highway); Robbins v. Department of Public Works, 355 Mass. 328, 332, 244 N.E.2d 577, 580 (1969) (state cannot extend interstate over meadows); Morse v. Oregon Division of State Lands, 285 Or. 197, 209, 590 P.2d 709, 715 (1979) (state did not adequately demonstrate public need to fill tidelands for airport). Some courts have developed an affirmative duty to protect trust lands and resources that are still held by the state and to seek compensation for injury to them. *See, e.g.,* State, Dept. of Environmental Protection v. Jersey Central Power & Light Co., 336 A.2d 750, 759 (N.J. Super.Ct.App.Div. 1975), *rev'd on other grounds,* 351 A.2d 337 (N.J. 1976) ("The State has not only the right but also the affirmative fiduciary obligation to ... seek compensation for any diminution in [the] trust corpus."); *see also* Deborah G. Musiker et al., *The Public Trust and Parens Patriae Doctrines: Protecting Wildlife in Uncertain Political Times,* 16 PUB. LAND L. REV. 87, 89–109 (1995) (noting courts' expectation that the state will act to protect public rights in the trust corpus).

The second context is where the state seeks to grant away rights to public trust lands through conveyance of fee title or leases. Courts increasingly review such actions carefully under the public trust doctrine. *Kootenai Envtl. Alliance,* 671 P.2d at 1092 (review of leases); Lake Michigan Federation v. U.S. Army Corps of Engineers, 742 F.Supp. 441, 445 (N.D. Ill. 1990) (review of land grant). The Supreme Court in *Illinois Central* did not preclude all conveyances of public trust lands. Instead, it left open the possibility of conveyances of land out of the public trust where such conveyances are made "for the improvement of the navigation and use of the waters, or when parcels can be disposed of without impairment of the public interest in what remains...." *Illinois Central*, 146 U.S. at 453. Modern cases struggle with defining the circumstances under which a state legislature may alienate public trust resources and the extent to which a court should serve as a check on such state legislative action.

The third context involves public trust land that was once in state ownership but is now in private hands. As the Supreme Court made clear in *Illinois Central*, private property owners that acquire title to public trust lands do not acquire full title (assuming the land was not properly excised from the trust), but take subject to an implied easement held by the state in favor of the public beneficiaries. *See Illinois Central*, 146 U.S. at 453 ("The trust devolving upon the state for the public ... cannot be relinquished by a transfer of property."); *Marks*, 491 P.2d at 380 ("[Tidelands are] subject to a reserved easement in the state for trust purposes."). At its most extreme, the public trust doctrine can force reacquisition of these lands without compensation to the owner. *See Illinois Central*, 146 U.S. at 455 ("Any grant of the kind is necessarily revocable, and the exercise of the trust by which the property was held by the State can be resumed at any time."). In its more moderate iteration, the public trust doctrine might simply form a limit on the uses the private property owner can make of the property, in order to protect the public's rights. Just v. Marinette County, 201 N.W.2d 761, 768 (1972) (upholding wetlands fill restriction against takings claim, noting "[a]n owner of land has no absolute and unlimited right to change the essential natural character of his land so as to use it for a purpose for which it was unsuited in its natural state and which injures the rights of others."); *Marks*, 491 P.2d at 380 (restricting fill of tidelands, noting, "one of the most important public uses of the tidelands—a use encompassed within the tidelands trust—is the preservation of those lands in their natural state...."). In between these poles, the public trust doctrine might allow public access along these lands. *See id.* at 381 (noting public's right to "assert the public trust easement for hunting, fishing and navigation in privately owned tidelands"); *Matthews*, 471 A.2d at 366 (recognizing right of public access on private dry sand beach); Stevens v. City of Cannon Beach, 854 P.2d 449, 456 (Or. 1993) (recognizing public access on Oregon beaches under doctrine of custom, closely related to public trust doctrine). The Constitutional right of compensation under the Fifth Amendment may not provide any remedy for the public's intrusion into private property ownership in public trust lands because, as the theory goes, the private property owners never received full title in the first place. At the time of transfer from state ownership to private ownership, the state impliedly withheld a "stick in the bundle of rights"—a stick that may remain dormant several decades until a court recognizes the pre-existing sovereign property right. The relationship between Fifth Amendment takings law and the public trust doctrine is explored in Chapter 9.II.B.1.

The public trust doctrine is one of the most fascinating areas of natural resources ownership, because it tests the separation of powers between the branches of government. Generally, courts defer to legislative action. In at least some public trust cases, however, courts assume a powerful veto role over the legislature, invalidating legislative conveyances of property out of the public trust. *Illinois Central*, 146 U.S. at 460 (submerged lands previously conveyed to railroad); *Lake Michigan*, 742 F.Supp. at 445 (Illinois Legislature had no authority to convey submersible lands held in the public trust to Loyola University, a private educational institution). This suggests the power of a constitutional principle, but courts have been unclear about the precise underpinnings of the public trust authority. Not surprisingly, the public trust doctrine has sparked considerable debate over the judicial role in the broader context of our democratic system. Increasingly, there is an obvious tug-of-war between the state courts and legislatures. In at least three states (Idaho, Mississippi and Arizona), a judicial declaration of a public trust doctrine was swiftly followed by legislative action creating a statute that partially invalidated the doctrine or limited its reach. See Michael C. Blumm, Harrison C. Dunning & Scott W. Reed, *Renouncing the Public Trust Doctrine: An Assessment of the Validity of Idaho House Bill 794*, 24 ECOLOGY L.Q. 461, 466 (1997); John Alton Duff & Kristen Michele Fletcher, *Augmenting the Public Trust: The Secretary of State's Efforts to Create a Public Trust Ecosystem Regime in Mississippi*, 67 MISS. L.J. 645, 653 (1998), Joseph M. Feller, *Equal Footing, the Public Trust, and Arizona's Rivers*, ARIZONA RIPARIAN COUNCIL NEWSL. 1 (ASU June 2001). In Arizona, the courts returned a volley, holding that the state could not invalidate the public trust doctrine. Arizona Center for Law in the Public Interest v. Hassell, 837 P.2d 158, 173 (Ariz. 1991). Thus, the public trust doctrine presents a rather extraordinary area of jurisprudence, testing which branch of government has the final say in determining whether critical lands and natural resources will remain intact for future generations. While the state legislatures are clearly the more obvious "trustees" acting for government, judges may be more immune to the processes that cause legislatures to squander valuable resources on present generations.

B. The Implications of the Public Trust Doctrine: Pro & Con

Scholars have debated the origins of the public trust doctrine as well as its role in modern natural resources law. The following articles give a sense of some of the vexing questions that characterize this area.

LIBERATING THE PUBLIC TRUST DOCTRINE FROM ITS HISTORICAL SHACKLES
Joseph L. Sax
14 U.C. DAVIS L. REV. 185, 186–193 (1980)

* * * At its heart, the public trust doctrine is not just a set of rules about tidelands, a restraint on alienation by the government or an his-

torical inquiry into the circumstances of long-forgotten grants. And neither Roman Law nor the English experience with lands underlying tidal waters is the place to search for the core of the trust idea.

The essence of property law is respect for reasonable expectations. * * * [I]nsofar as expectations underlie strong and deeply held legal-ethical ideals, they are not limited to title ownership. * * *

[S]tability, and the protection of stable relationships, is one of the most basic and persistent concerns of the legal system. * * * Of course, stability does not mean the absence of change, [but it] does mean a commitment to evolutionary rather than revolutionary change, for the rate of change and the capacity it provides for transition are precisely what separate continuity and adaptation from crisis and collapse. * * * The disappearance of various species from the earth in the natural, evolutionary process is totally different from the disappearance of species over a short time. The key difference is not the *fact* of change, but the *rate* of change. * * *

The central idea of the public trust is preventing the destabilizing disappointment of expectations held in common but without formal recognition such as title. * * * [T]he public trust doctrine should be employed to help us reach the real issues—expectations and destabilization—whether the expectations are those of private property ownership, of a diffuse public benefit from ecosystem protection or of a community's water supply. * * *

Our task is to identify the trustee's obligation with an eye toward insulating those expectations that support social, economic and ecological systems from avoidable destabilization and disruption. * * *

THE HEADWATERS OF THE PUBLIC TRUST:
SOME OF THE TRADITIONAL DOCTRINE
Charles F. Wilkinson
19 ENVTL. L. 425, 425–472 (1989)

* * * The public trust doctrine is complicated—there are fifty-one public trust doctrines in this country alone; timely—the judicial, legislative and scholarly work on the doctrine is proceeding apace; and arcane—the roots of the public trust doctrine go back literally for millennia. * * *

Both the implied transfer [of submersible lands to states] and the overlying trust in favor of public access are now settled parts of our jurisprudence. There are powerful state interests—powerful enough to induce the implied transfer in the first place—and strong national interests—strong enough to impress an implicit trust on these highly valued natural resources. It does not make sense that a state could abdicate a federally and constitutionally imposed trust completely. As Justice Field put it in *Illinois Central*, if there were no trust at all, such a situation 'would place every harbor in the country at the mercy of a majority of the legislature of the State in which the harbor is situated.' At the same time, there is plainly broad state discretion; *Illinois Central* recognized the propriety both of state transfers consistent with navigation and of nonnavigation related transfers that did not substantially impair the trust. * * *

The traditional trust allows the states wide latitude, but the states are federally prohibited from abrogating the public trust entirely. * * * [T]he most principled analysis leads to the conclusion that the public trust has minimum requirements set by the Constitution. The states have such broad discretion to fashion their own individual bodies of trust law that the constitutional standards will seldom be called into play. * * *

Court decisions and legislation in most states have supplemented the traditional federal doctrine, and most of the remaining states are likely to follow eventually. The … major developments are these. First, some states have extended the coverage of the trust beyond those watercourses navigable for title to all, or nearly all, waters of the state. * * * Second, cases have extended the trust beyond the traditional purposes of commerce, navigation, and fishing, with the most common "new" purposes being various forms of recreation. Third, various cases have extended the reach beyond watercourses per se …. to dry sand beaches, wildlife, and state parks. * * * Last … a number of state courts have moved into the area of appropriation of water. These courts hold or suggest that water rights obtained under the prior appropriation doctrine might be curtailed if such appropriations substantially impair watercourses navigable for title. * * *

The trust, whether invoked by courts or legislatures, can play a principled part in structuring a system that really does reflect the vitality, diversity, and sacredness of both our ever-changing society and our inspiring, magnificent river systems. * * *

CHANGING CONCEPTIONS OF PROPERTY AND SOVEREIGNTY IN NATURAL RESOURCES: QUESTIONING THE PUBLIC TRUST DOCTRINE
Richard J. Lazarus
71 Iowa L. Rev. 631, 650–655 (1986)

* * * Advocates of the public trust doctrine have been concerned primarily with the ability of the doctrine to impose enforceable restrictions on the authority of the sovereign to act in a manner potentially harmful to the trust resource. Predictions that the doctrine would provide courts with the needed legal basis to restrict such governmental acts have borne out. Still, the doctrine's precise meaning to those courts has varied considerably. Some courts diverge from the mainstream to find that the doctrine places an affirmative duty on the government to

protect or conserve trust resources in the first instance. Most, however, find it restricts governmental actions that adversely affect trust concerns. Within this latter category, courts differ considerably over the precise standards to apply to the challenged governmental action. The decisions gravitate around three types of standards: (1) a requirement that the challenged governmental action satisfy a public trust purpose; (2) a requirement that the disputed action occur only after consideration of any adverse impact on the trust resource and then only if such impact is either minimal or necessary; and (3) a requirement that if the action challenged is that of an executive branch agency, the proposed action has specific legislative authorization. * * *

For some courts, the requirement of some public trust purpose is satisfied quite easily. These courts simply look for some relationship between the proposed governmental action and a legitimate public purpose. This standard apparently does not require significantly more than would the normal police power inquiry for a valid public purpose. Other courts, however, have gone further and required the public purpose to have some connection with the substantive concerns of the trust doctrine. For some judges, this means a relation to the traditional public trust purposes—commerce, navigation, and fishing. For others, the requirement extends further and calls for a relation to the resource in its natural condition. * * *

The most meaningful construction the courts have given the public trust doctrine has been to require the government to consider the adverse impacts of a proposed action on trust resources. The impact of this consideration requirement is at its greatest when coupled with the additional mandate that only minimal or "necessary" harm is permissible. Courts have held that consideration of trust concerns occurs in advance of proposed governmental action, requires prior comprehensive resource planning or specific cost/benefit balancing, and includes a continuing duty to reconsider when circumstances and knowledge change. * * *

Some courts add the restriction that the government is always barred from inflicting more than a modicum of harm to trust interests. * * * Most courts, borrowing language from the *Illinois Central* decision, have required that there be no "substantial impairment" of the trust resource. * * * The courts, in more recent decisions, have recognized that destruction of trust resources is sometimes necessary, and therefore, they will impose a public trust standard that calls for heightened administrative justification for the action. This standard is implemented, for instance, by ... allowing only "necessary" harmful activities, or requiring that the government take all "reasonable" or "feasible" steps to minimize the harm. Each of these standards by their terms stops short of declaring an absolute environmental quality standard. * * *

The third type of public trust standard ... requires strict statutory construction of legislative delegations of authority to administrative agencies. * * * The underlying substantive thrust of this standard holds that only the legislature can properly decide to have the government take action that may substantially harm trust resources, because the legislature most closely mirrors the will of the public. Although a few courts have interpreted this mandate literally and have stated that only the legislature can interfere with trust interests, most permit the power to be delegated.... The general test is whether the legislative delegation of authority to the agency is clear, express, and specific. * * *

Notes and Questions

1. What is the origin of the public trust doctrine? Elsewhere in his article, Professor Wilkinson notes that variations of the doctrine were apparent in the ancient societies of Europe, the Orient, Africa, Moslem countries, and Native America. Wilkinson, *supra* at 429–30. He concludes: "The real headwaters of the public trust doctrine, then, arise in rivulets from all reaches of the basin that holds the societies of the world." *Id.* at 431. Does the doctrine express a fundamental attribute of sovereignty that every government implicitly has—ownership and control over resources that are vital to the public welfare? In the United States, is the doctrine constitutional in nature because of its association with the Equal Footing Doctrine that provides the seeds of ownership for public trust theory? Or is it a common law doctrine arising out of property law? Why does it matter? Does a constitutional doctrine allow the courts more authority to override a legislative action that destroys part of the trust? Can a non-Constitutional common law doctrine easily be displaced by statutes? Does the origin of the doctrine get at the heart of the separation of powers between the courts and legislatures?

2. As Professor Wilkinson points out, the doctrine seems to be hybrid in the sense of having both federal and state characteristics. The broad contours of the doctrine seemingly arise from federal law, but the states may develop rules to implement their trust duties. Indeed, states have developed many variations of the doctrine, some expanding it, and some interpreting it narrowly. Despite these differences, would a state be free to entirely disregard public trust obligations over submersible lands on navigable waterways? Could a suit be brought in federal court asserting the minimal public trust duty against a state legislature that disregarded any trust duty?

3. In 1970, Professor Sax wrote a groundbreaking law review article on the public trust doctrine. Joseph L. Sax, *The Public Trust Doctrine in Natural Resource Law: Effective Judicial Intervention*, 68 Mich L. Rev. 471 (1970). The commentary generated a surge in public trust litigation over the following two decades. Over a hundred cases have applied the public trust doctrine in states across the nation, indicating the potential strength of the doctrine. But Professor Lazarus has criticized growing reliance on the public trust doctrine to achieve environmental protection of key resources:

> Assessment of the future value of the public trust doctrine must start with the candid premise that the doctrine rests on legal fictions. Notions of "sovereign ownership" of certain natural resources and the "duties of the sovereign as trustee" to natural resources are simply judicially created shorthand methods to justify treating differently governmental transactions that involve those resources.

Instead of immediately casting the fiction aside, recognizing the fictional nature of the trust doctrine is necessary to frame the debate on the doctrine's continued usefulness in natural resources law. Just as the need for legal fictions arises in the wake of changing circumstances that strain existing legal norms, so too the need dissipates when, over time, the fabric of the law is woven in a more coherent and systematic fashion in response to those initial changes. * * *

[T]he day of "final reckoning" for the doctrine is here, or soon will be, and reliance upon it is no longer in order.... [T]he law of standing, tort law, property law, administrative law, and the police power have all evolved in response to ... environmental and natural resources problems and are weaving a new and unified fabric for natural resources law. * * * [M]uch of what the public trust doctrine offered in the past is now, at best, superfluous and, at worst, distracting and theoretically inconsistent with new notions of property and sovereignty developing in the current reworking of natural resources law.

Lazarus, *Changing Conceptions, supra* at 656–658.

Why did Professor Lazarus describe the public trust doctrine as a "fiction?" Are doctrines expressing the federal navigational servitude, the equal footing doctrine, the wildlife trust, and the federal Indian trust responsibility equally fictitious because they have no express reference in the Constitution? Does "fiction" refer to the courts' development of common law to protect society's new, evolving expectations? If so, is that a legitimate function of the common law?

4. Do you agree that the public trust doctrine is superfluous now that environmental law and natural resources law have become heavily statutory? Are there flaws in a purely statutory system of law such as lax enforcement, politicized agency implementation, and resistance by private property owners? How does the public trust doctrine respond to these deficiencies?

5. Many have speculated whether the public trust doctrine applies to the federal government. The doctrine is discussed only briefly in Chapter 6.V.E., as there is scant case law on the subject. *See* Light v. United States, 220 U.S. 523, 31 S.Ct. 485, 55 L.Ed. 570 (1911) (implying federal trust obligation for public lands); United States v. 1.58 Acres Situated in the City of Boston, 523 F.Supp. 120, 125 (D. Mass. 1981) (finding public trust doctrine applicable to both federal government and state as co-trustees of land below low water mark in Boston Harbor); In re Complaint of Steuart Transp. Co., 495 F.Supp. 38, 40 (E.D. Va. 1980) (allowing federal government to recover damages for destroyed migratory waterfowl under public trust theory); Sierra Club v. Department of Interior I, 376 F.Supp. 90 (N.D. Cal. 1974) (finding trust responsibility in managing national park); Palila v. Hawaii Dept. of Land and Natural Resources, 471 F.Supp. 985, 995 n.40 (D. Haw. 1979) (implying federal property interest in wildlife populations); District of Columbia v. Air Florida, Inc., 750 F.2d 1077, 1083 (D.C. Cir. 1984) (posing question of federal trust but not resolving it); *but see* Sierra Club v. Andrus, 487 F.Supp. 443 (D. D.C. 1980), *aff'd on other grounds* Sierra Club v. Watt, 659 F.2d 203 (D.C. Cir. 1981) (rejecting argument that National Park Service has common law trust duty in managing national park). If the trust arises as an attribute of sovereignty, should it apply to any sovereign government?

For an argument that the federal government holds a supreme, but residuary, sovereign trust over wildlife populations, *see* Mary Christina Wood, *The Tribal Property Right to Wildlife Capital (Part I): Applying Principles of Sovereignty to Protect Imperiled Wildlife Populations*, 37 IDAHO L. REV. 1, 79 (2000).

In an in-depth examination of whether the public trust doctrine applies to the federal government's management of its public lands, Professor Charles Wilkinson concludes:

> * * * [T]here is an imposing and growing body of case law suggesting that the public trust doctrine applies to the public lands. * * * The public trust doctrine is rooted in the precept that some resources are so central to the well-being of the community that they must be protected by distinctive, judge-made principles. * * * Anglo–American jurisprudence is rife with judicially developed doctrines that reflect the deeply held convictions of our society. In natural resources law generally, the unique qualities of some resources have impelled courts to apply the public trust doctrine as a flexible, loosely connected set of rules that allow maximum public utilization. The increasing use of trust language in public lands cases indicates an awareness that the special values of the federal lands, like other resources on which the trust has been impressed, have been gradually but indelibly imprinted on our national consciousness. * * *

Charles F. Wilkinson, *The Public Trust Doctrine in Public Land Law,* 14 U.C. DAVIS L. REV. 269, 277–316 (1980).

6.   While common law expression of a federal trust is in its infancy, statutory recognition of federal trust duties is well-established. Natural resource damages provisions found in numerous environmental statutes reflect the sovereign trustee power of the federal government, tribes, and states, and express a duty to seek compensation for damage to public trust assets. *See* CERCLA, 42 U.S.C. § 9607(f)(1)(2004); Oil Pollution Act of 1990 (OPA), 33 U.S.C. § 2706(a)(2004); Clean Water Act, 33 U.S.C.A. § 1319 (2004); Marine Protection, Research and Sanctuaries Act (MPRSA), 16 U.S.C.A. § 1375 (2004).

7.   The power of the public trust doctrine is evident by the fact that courts will apply trust restrictions to private property owners even after the doctrine has long been dormant. The sovereign interest cannot be lost by adverse possession, laches, or any other equitable doctrine. Courts have little sympathy for property owners' objections that they have been paying full taxes on property that is later held to be less than the classic fee. *See Phillips Petroleum Co. v. Mississippi*, 484 U.S. 469, 484, 108 S.Ct. 791, 98 L.Ed.2d 877 (1988) ("[T]he fact that petitioners have ... long paid taxes on these lands does not change the outcome"); Secretary of State v. Wiesenberg, 633 So. 2d 983, 987, 989 (Miss. 1994) ("[P]roperty expectations of the [owners] who had occupied and paid taxes on property bordering [a river] were not significant enough (not a higher purpose) to warrant overriding the public trust doctrine in order to grant fee simple ownership to the [owners].").

C.   Legislative Alienation of Public Trust Resources and the Court's Role

The materials below explore the intriguing role of the public trust doctrine as a judicial check on state legislative and agency action. As you read them, consider the strengths and drawbacks of judicial activism in this area. Who benefits and who loses? How does the doctrine fit within well-established principles regarding the separation of powers? Do courts have the ultimate final say in critical natural resource distribution? If so, how is the judicial role confined?

THE PUBLIC TRUST: A FUNDAMENTAL DOCTRINE OF AMERICAN PROPERTY LAW
Harrison C. Dunning
19 ENVTL. L. 515, 515–525 (1989)

* * * The public trust is a fundamental doctrine in American property law.... Courts currently use the doctrine with regard to a significant range of natural resources associated with navigable water. For those resources the doctrine represents recognition of important public property rights, and as a consequence, the doctrine also represents severe limitations on private property rights. More indicative of the doctrine's fundamental nature, however, is the way the courts, the originators of the doctrine in this country, have in some states concluded that the doctrine is so entrenched as to be immune from legislative abolition. In those states the public trust doctrine has assumed the character of an implied constitutional doctrine, much like the related equal footing doctrine in federal law. * * *

Important questions [surround] that acknowledged responsibility to protect "common heritage" or public trust resources. Why is fulfillment of this duty not left to the legislatures' discretion? A legislature's exercise of the police power is an enormously powerful tool today, even though it was poorly developed in 1892 when the Supreme Court decided *Illinois Central*. What justifies the insistence that the state recognize a public property right, and further that the courts be able to limit legislative abolition or modification of that property right? * * *

The key to answering these difficult questions may lie in the physical characteristics of public trust resources. Navigable bays, lakes, and rivers share, in addition to scarcity, a natural suitability for common use. * * * Common use by the general population serves as the basis to characterize these natural resources as common heritage or public trust assets. * * * [A] public trust resource is, as Justice Holmes once wrote of a river, "more than an amenity, it is a treasure."

Those courts that recognize the public trust interest as not subject to legislative abolition typically do not provide theoretical support for their conclusions. On the one hand, they must believe that the public trust doctrine is more than a conventional notion of the common law, for such rules are fully subject to legislative modification or abrogation. On the other hand, it is difficult to conclude that they believe that no public trust asset could ever be removed from the protection of the doctrine. For example, the courts would never conclude that, as a matter of principle, no navigable bay or lake or part thereof could ever be filled or drained, and devoted to other purposes, regardless of how pressing the need. What they may be saying instead is that the public trust doctrine limits legislative freedom because it is an implied state constitutional doctrine, one that springs from a fundamental notion of how government is to operate with regard to common heritage natural resources. That is, government must protect public access to such resources unless there is a solemn decision to the contrary.

Federal law has for many years articulated a related, implied, constitutional concept that addresses the relationship between government and property: the equal footing doctrine. This doctrine accords equivalent status to all states in the Union. [T]his doctrine is ... the basis for rulings long ago that the federal government holds the beds of navigable rivers in territories in trust for future states, and that upon admission to the Union, states take title to those beds. The equal footing doctrine thus links state sovereignty to property rights. * * *

[The] public trust doctrine illustrates a fascinating and significant intersection of property rights and constitutional concepts. It provides a dramatic example of how common heritage natural resources, given constitutional protection, can inspire a unique property rights regime. It is a regime more heavily weighted toward public rights than we usually find in our property law.... * * *

THE PUBLIC TRUST DOCTRINE IN NATURAL RESOURCE LAW: EFFECTIVE JUDICIAL INTERVENTION
Joseph L. Sax
68 MICH. L. REV. 471, 558–66 (1970)

* * * Public trust problems ... occur in a wide range of situations in which diffuse public interests need protection against tightly organized groups with clear and immediate goals. * * *

Understandably, courts are reluctant to intervene in the processes of any given agency. Accordingly, they are inclined to achieve democratization through indirect means—either by requiring the intervention of other agencies, which will serve to represent under-represented interests, or by calling upon the legislature to make an express and open policy decision on the matter in question. * * * This relationship suggests that democratization is essentially the function which the courts perceive themselves as performing, and that even those courts which are the most active and interventionist in the public trust area are not interested in displacing legislative bodies as the final authorities in setting resource policies. * * *

In the ideal world, legislatures are the most representative and responsive public agencies; and to the extent that judicial intervention moves legislatures toward that ideal, the citizenry is well served. Certainly even the most representative legislature may act in highly unsatisfactory ways when dealing with minority rights, for then it confronts the problem of majority tyranny. But that problem is not the one which arises in public resource litigation. Indeed, it is the opposite problem that frequently arises in public trust cases—that is, a diffuse majority is made subject to the will of a concerted minority. For self-interested and powerful minorities often have an undue influence on the public resource decisions of legislative and administrative bodies and cause those bodies to ignore broadly based public interests. Thus, the function which the courts must perform and have been performing, is to promote equality of political power for a disorganized and diffuse majority by remanding appropriate cases to the legislature after public opinion has been aroused. * * *

[C]ourts have an important and fruitful role to play in helping to promote rational management of our natural resources. Courts have been both misunderstood and underrated as a resource for dealing with resources. It is usually true that those who know the least about the judicial process are often the most ready to characterize the courts as doctrinaire and rigid.... * * *

[I]t is demonstrable that the courts in their own intuitive way–sometimes clumsy and cumbersome–have shown more insight and sensitivity to many of the fundamental problems of resource management than have any of the other branches of government. [T]he judiciary can be expected to play an increasingly important and fruitful role in safeguarding the public trust.

LAKE MICHIGAN FEDERATION v. UNITED STATES ARMY CORPS OF ENGINEERS

United States District Court, Northern District of Illinois, 1990.
742 F.Supp. 441.

* * * The Lake Michigan Federation ("Federation") has filed this action ... against Loyola University of Chicago ("Loyola") [and] the United States Army Corps of Engineers.... The Federation seeks an injunction restraining Loyola from constructing a twenty acre lakefill on its Lake Shore campus in Chicago, Illinois. Because we find that the property to be used for this project was conveyed in violation of the public trust, we grant the Federation's motion for injunctive relief.

Loyola is a private educational institution organized as a not-for-profit corporation. Among Loyola's campuses in the Chicago area is its Lake Shore campus bordering Lake Michigan on the north side of the city. In 1988, Loyola decided to expand this campus. Loyola determined that it would not be feasible to expand onto adjacent land. Instead, it developed plans to construct a lakefill of approximately twenty acres in the waters of neighboring Lake Michigan. * * *

The plans developed by Loyola called for a lakefill of about 18.5 acres. Along the perimeter of the lakefill, Loyola intended to construct a stone revetment, as well as bike and walking paths, a seawall, and lawn areas. The public would have unrestricted access to these areas, which comprise about 2.1 acres of lakefill. In the interior portion of the lakefill, Loyola plans to build athletic facilities, including a running track, a women's softball field, and multi-purpose athletic fields. The public would have access to these areas, but subject to Loyola's right of ownership. * * * Loyola sought and received legislative and municipal approval of this project. [T]he Illinois Legislature conveyed approximately 18.5 acres of the lakebed to Loyola for the purpose of expansion. In this act, the legislature acknowledged that it holds the title of submerged lands in trust for the people of Illinois. However, because the public would benefit from the lakefill in various ways, the legislature reasoned that it had the power to convey the land to Loyola. * * *

The classic statement of the public trust doctrine was promulgated in *Illinois Central R.R. Co., v. Illinois,* 146 U.S. 387 (1892). In this case, the Supreme Court invalidated the transfer of 1000 acres of submerged lands in Lake Michigan to the Illinois Central Railroad. The Court explained that dominion and sovereignty over submerged lands belong to the State in which the land is found. *Id.* at 435. However, the title to these submerged lands is "different in character from that which the State holds in lands intended for sale." *Id.* at 452. "It is a title held in trust for the people of the State that they may enjoy the navigation of the waters, carry on commerce over them, and have liberty of fishing therein freed from the obstruction or interference of private parties." *Id.* "The State can no more abdicate its trust over property in which the whole people are interested, like navigable waters and the soils under them, so as to leave them entirely under the use and control of private parties ... than it can abdicate its police powers in the administration of government and the preservation of peace." *Id.* at 453. * * *

Three basic principles can be distilled from [the] body of public trust case law. First, courts should be critical of attempts by the state to surrender valuable public resources to a private entity. Second, the public trust is violated when the primary purpose of a legislative grant is to benefit a private interest. Finally, any attempt by the state to relinquish its power over a public resource should be invalidated under the doctrine.

Applying these criteria to the legislative grant of the lakebed to Loyola, it is apparent that the transfer violates the public trust doctrine. First, while the project has some aspects which are beneficial to the public, the primary purpose of the grant is to satisfy a private interest. * * * [The] inescapable truth is that the lakebed property will be sacrificed to satisfy Loyola's private needs. Under the public trust doctrine, such a sacrifice cannot be tolerated.

Not only does the challenged legislation give away public trust property to satisfy a private interest, but it also constitutes an attempt to relinquish state power over this property. Upon completion of the project, Loyola will become the owner of 18.5 acres of land that previously belonged to the state. Accordingly, the state will relinquish its ... ability to safeguard the interests of the public as to this land.

Loyola contends that the limitations placed on its ownership by the State are sufficient to constitute state control over the property. By the terms of the conveyance, Loyola is not allowed to construct buildings or parking areas on the lakefill. The state also has a right of reentry should Loyola attempt to transfer the property to any entity which does not operate as a nonprofit educational institution. In addition, the legislation provides "[s]ubject to Loyola University's rights and obligations of ownership ... public use and enjoyment of ... the lakefill shall not be unreasonably denied."

It remains to be seen whether these restrictions are more than illusory. For example, subsequent legislation could be passed which lifts the restrictions placed on the conveyance. Alternatively, the State of Illinois could choose not to exercise its right of re-entry or otherwise enforce the restrictions which are to be placed on the quitclaim deed.

However, even if we accept the proposition that the conditions of conveyance constitute bonafide restrictions, we do not agree that these restrictions are sufficient to constitute retention of public control over the lakefill. Although Loyola would lack the complete discretion over the use of its property, it is undeniable that its rights would be superior to those of the public. The enabling legislation gives Loyola the power to control public access to the property. However, as the property currently exists, citizens have access to Lake Michigan, free "from the obstruction or interference of private parties." *Illinois Central Railroad Company v. Illinois*, 146 U.S. at 452. The discretion vested in Loyola by the legislature is precisely the type of restriction which the public trust doctrine is intended to proscribe.

Loyola suggests that we should not apply the public trust doctrine because the lakefill will increase the public's opportunity to enjoy that portion of the lakefront. Loyola observes that the existing shoreline is privately owned by Loyola, with no right of public access. * * * Therefore, Loyola reasons that if it is allowed to complete the lakefill, the public will be in a better position to enjoy the lake because of the aesthetic improvement to the coastline and the property on the whole.

This argument is seriously flawed. Loyola ignores the fact that the public will have to sacrifice 18.5 acres of publicly held land in order to obtain a coastline to which it has unlimited access. Moreover, it glosses over the fact that the public is actually gaining nothing. The public currently has unrestricted access to the submerged lands which will become the new coastline. In reality, the public is losing its right of access to the portion of the lake which would become the interior portion of the lakefill. * * *

Loyola also argues that we should be deferent to the Illinois legislature's determination that the grant at issue did not violate the public trust. [T]he legislature acknowledged that it held the lakebed in trust for the public and declared that the grant would not violate this trust because of the project's numerous public benefits. According to Loyola, we should yield to this specific legislative consideration of public interest. However, this claim is incorrect both as a matter of logic and precedent. The very purpose of the public trust doctrine is to police the legislature's disposition of public lands. If courts were to rubber stamp legislative decisions, as Loyola advocates, the doctrine would have no teeth. The legislature would have unfettered discretion to breach the public trust as long as it was able to articulate some gain to the public. Moreover, Illinois courts have acknowledged that courts are not encumbered by legislative expressions of public interest. * * * Therefore, we find that the legislative determination that the lakefill would serve the public is no obstacle to our conclusion that the grant was in breach of the public trust.

What we have here is a transparent giveaway of public property to a private entity. The lakebed of Lake Michigan is held in trust for and belongs to the citizenry of the state. The conveyance of lakebed property to a private party—no matter how reputable and highly motivated that private party may be—violates this public trust doctrine. This improper conveyance is not made any more palatable by attaching cosmetic conditions to the conveyance which permit restricted public access to the private property. Because the conveyance of [the] lakebed to Loyola violated the public trust doctrine, Loyola is permanently enjoined from placing any fill material in the lake or proceeding, in any manner, with further construction of the lakefill. * * *

KOOTENAI ENVIRONMENTAL ALLIANCE, INC. v. PANHANDLE YACHT CLUB, INC.

Supreme Court of Idaho, 1983.
671 P.2d 1085.

* * * By this appeal we are asked to determine whether the "public trust doctrine" precludes a grant by the Idaho Department of Lands of a lease to a private club for the construction, maintenance and use of private docking facilities on a bay in a navigable lake. * * * In April, 1978, an application for a permit to make an encroachment on Lake Coeur d'Alene was filed with the Department of Lands [by] Panhandle Yacht Club. The application was ... for the purpose of constructing 112 sailboat slips with pilings, waterways and related facilities for the use of the yacht club members. The permit was for issuance of a ten-year lease, with right to apply for successive ten-year terms.

The leasehold area was to encompass a five-acre area of surface water enclosed by a floating-log breakwater. * * * Lake Coeur d'Alene is approximately seventy square miles in size and thus the encroachment impedes navigation on about .01% (.0001) of the lake area. * * *

The State of Idaho holds title to the beds of all navigable bodies of water below the natural high water mark for the use and benefit of the public. The power to direct, control and dispose of the public lands is vested in the State Board of Land Commissioners.... * * *

Illinois Central R.R. Co. v. Illinois, 146 U.S. 387 (1892), is the seminal case on the scope of the public trust doctrine and remains the primary authority today. That decision established the principle that a state, as administrator of the trust in navigable waters on behalf of the public, does not have the power to abdicate its role as trustee in favor of private parties. * * * [T]he court stated:

> * * * The interest of the people in the navigation of the waters and in commerce over them may be improved in many instances by the erection of wharves, docks, and piers therein, for which purpose the state may grant parcels of the submerged lands; and, so long as their disposition is made for such purpose, no valid objections can be made to the grants. It is grants ... in aid of commerce, and grants of parcels which, being occupied, *do not substantially impair the public interest in the lands and waters remaining,* that are ... a valid exercise of legislative power consistently with the trust to the public upon which such lands are held by the state. (emphasis supplied.)

And, the court in discussing the legislative power, went on to state:

> A grant of all the lands under the navigable waters of a state has never been adjudged to be within the legislative power; and any attempted grant of the kind would be held, if not absolutely void on its face, as subject to revocation. The state can no more abdicate its trust over property in which the whole people are interested, like navigable waters and soils under them, so as to leave them entirely under the use and control of private parties, *except in the instance of parcels mentioned for the improvement of the navigation and use of the waters, or when parcels can be disposed of without impairment of the public interest in what remains,* than it can abdicate its police powers in the administration of government and the preservation of the peace. * * *

Therefore, a two part test emerges to determine the validity of the grant of public trust property. One, is the grant in aid of navigation, commerce, or other trust purposes, and two, does it substantially impair the public interest in the lands and waters remaining? * * *

Before we apply the rule in *Illinois Central* to the facts of this case we will review the evolution of the public trust doctrine in other jurisdictions. Massachusetts, Wisconsin and California are the three states with the wealth of authority on the subject. * * *

[The] Massachusetts court[s] ... requir[e] a strong showing of direct legislative intent to alienate public trust resources before [upholding] such alienation. [The] legislature must identify the land and there must appear in the legislation not only a statement of the new use but a statement or recital demonstrating legislative awareness of the existing public use. * * * We do not agree that public trust resources may only be alienated by *express legislative* mandates. Such a requirement would impose an undue burden on a legislature which at the present time meets only a few months each year. However, we do follow the substance of the Massachusetts approach–that public trust resources may only be alienated or impaired through open and visible actions, where the public is *in fact* informed of the proposed action and has substantial opportunity to respond to the proposed action before a final decision is made thereon. Moreover, decisions made by non-elected agencies rather than by the legislature itself will be subjected to closer scrutiny than will legislative decision making. In the present case, this standard has been complied with. Notice of the proposed permit was published in the Coeur d'Alene press, and public hearings were held before the State Department of Lands. * * * In addition, this controversy did not remain confined to examination by the Department of Lands. Concerned citizens brought the permit application and their opposition to it to the attention of the Board of Land Directors. * * *

We take the following guidance from the approach adopted by the Wisconsin court[s]. Final determination whether the alienation or impairment of a public trust resource violates the public trust doctrine will be made by the judiciary. This is not to say that this court will supplant its judgment for that of the legislature or agency. However, it does mean that this court will take a "close look" at the action to determine if it complies with the public trust doctrine and it will not act merely as a rubber stamp for agency or legislative action. In making such a determination the court will examine, among other things, such factors as the degree of effect of the project on public trust uses, navigation, fishing, recreation and commerce; the impact of the individual project on the public trust resource; the impact of the individual project when examined cumulatively with existing impediments to full use of the public trust resource, *i.e.* in this instance the proportion of the lake taken up by docks, moorings or other impediments; the impact of the project on the public trust resource when that resource is examined in light of the primary purpose for which the resource is suited, *i.e.* commerce, navigation, fishing or recreation; and the degree to which broad public uses are set aside in favor of more limited or private ones.

[T]wo rules developed in California: (1) The state may make an absolute grant of tidelands to private parties when to do so is to promote navigation and commerce; and (2) Grants to private persons not for this purpose do not pass title free of the trust, but rather title is taken subject to the trust.

* * * Under the California rule statutes alienating public trust resources will be construed in light of the public trust doctrine requirements. The public trust doctrine takes precedent even over vested water rights. * * * Grants to individuals of public trust resources will be construed as given subject to the public trust doctrine unless the legislature explicitly provides otherwise.

This case involves the granting of a permit for an encroachment, and not the grant of property in fee simple, to private parties. The property has not been placed entirely beyond the control of the state and the legislature has not given away or sold the discretion of its successors. The Department of Lands has determined that the use of the public trust property by the yacht club for the purpose of constructing sailboat slips does not violate the public trust in the resource at this time. After a thorough examination of the record in this case ... we agree. However, the grant remains subject to the public trust. Under the California rule herein adopted, the state is not precluded from determining in the future that this conveyance is no longer compatible with the public trust imposed on this conveyance. * * *

It is clear ... that the Department of Lands acting as the representative of the State Land Board has the power to dispose of public lands. This power is not absolute, however, and is subject to the limitations imposed by the public trust doctrine. As before stated, we do not construe the public trust doctrine in this state to allow public trust resources to be alienated only legislatively. Nor do we construe it to prohibit the State Land Board from delegating its authority to make such decisions to the State Department of Lands. However, it must again be emphasized that mere compliance by these bodies with their legislative authority is not sufficient to determine if their actions comport with the requirements of the public trust doctrine. The public trust doctrine at all times forms the outer boundaries of permissible government action with respect to public trust resources. * * *

The hearing officer [concluded] ... that a navigational or economic necessity or justification has been established and that little or no adverse effect will be registered against property, navigation, fish and wildlife habitat, aquatic life, recreation, aesthetic beauty or water quality.

[We] hold that the issuance of this encroachment ... does not violate the public trust doctrine. * * * We note, however, the grant remains subject to the "public trust." * * *

Notes and Questions

1.   What is the difference between the approaches of the *Kootenai* court and the *Lake Michigan* court in allowing trust resources to be conveyed to private parties? What tests are fashioned by these courts? Compare these tests with the approach expressed in the California case, *Marks v. Whitney*:

> [T]he state through the Legislature may find and determine that such [trust] lands are no longer useful for trust purposes and free them from the trust. When tidelands have been so freed from the trust—and if they are not subject to the constitutional prohibition forbidding alienation— they may be irrevocably conveyed into absolute private ownership.... It is a political question, within the wisdom and power of the Legislature, acting within the scope of its duties as trustee, to determine whether public trust uses should be modified or extinguished and to take the necessary steps to free them from such burden.

491 P.2d 374, 380 (Cal. 1971).

The Mississippi Supreme Court has fashioned this test: "The only way public trust lands can be disposed of is if it is done pursuant to 'a higher public purpose,' while at the same time not being detrimental to the general public. [Public trust lands] may be alienated from the State only upon the authority of legislative enactment and then only consistent with the public purposes of the trust." Secretary of State v. Wiesenberg, 633 So.2d 983, 987 (Miss. 1994). The Mississippi court upheld the conveyance of over 150 acres of submerged land to a developer. *Id.* at 993. Under the scheme, 47% of the developed area was used for "public purposes" such as golf-courses, beaches, parks, greenbelts, waterways, schools, churches, marinas, streets, drainage, and similar facilities. *Id.* The remaining 53% was used for residential, commercial and resort development. *Id.* The court found that there was a "higher purpose in accommodating an expanding population, commerce, tourism and recreation." *Id.* The court noted, "If the totality of the development promotes the public interest in general, the incidental private ownership of individual lots does not negate the comprehensive public purpose." *Id.* How would these facts fare in the *Lake Michigan* court? Under this "higher purpose" approach, could any private development obtain public trust lands as long as it provided some public access?

2.   Do the *Kootenai* and *Lake Michigan* courts take a different view of their role as guardians of the public trust resources? Do they differ in terms of their judicial ability to override legislative action conveying resources out of the public trust? As a policy matter, what are the dangers of using the public trust doctrine to override state legislative action? What are the dangers of *not* allowing courts the final say in trust alienation? Do most legislatures truly protect present resources for tomorrow's generations, or do they allow present exploitation that will harm future generations? Are courts in the best position to guard the critical resources that make up the public trust? Should a judicial veto be limited to certain compelling circumstances, and if so, what factors define those circumstances?

3.   Responding to the scholarship of Professors Sax, Dunning, and others, Professor James Huffman wrote a strong criticism of the courts' use of the public trust doctrine to remedy perceived flaws in the democratic process:

> [Professor Sax's] central thesis is that democracy sometimes does not work.... According to Sax, "[t]he public trust concept is ... a technique by which courts may mend perceived imperfections in the legislative and administrative process." * * * [The] doctrine is "a medium for democratization." * * * Unanswered is the question of why the judiciary, an elitist institution with few democratic credentials, should be in a position to second-guess the actions of a legislature and its administrators.

James L. Huffman, *Trusting the Public Interest to Judges: A Comment on the Public Trust Writings of Professors Sax, Wilkinson, Dunning and Johnson,* 63 DENVER UNIV. L. REV. 565, 572 (1986).

4.   In some states, the state legislature has enacted legislation to curb judicial application of the trust. *See* Michael C. Blumm, Harrison C. Dunning & Scott W. Reed, *Renouncing the Public Trust Doctrine: An Assessment of the Validity of Idaho House Bill 794,* 24 ECOLOGY L. Q. 461, 466 (1997); John Alton Duff & Kristen Michele Fletcher, *Augmenting the Public Trust:*

The Secretary of State's Efforts to Create a Public Trust Ecosystem Regime in Mississippi, 67 MISS L. J. 645, 653 (1998); Joseph M. Feller, *Equal Footing and the Public Trust, and Arizona's Rivers,* 14 ARIZ. RIPARIAN COUNCIL NEWSLTR. 1 (ASU June 2001). Does the legislature ever have the last word on public trust issues? Recall the statement in *Illinois Central* that grants of public trust property must necessarily be revocable, or "every harbor in the country [would be] at the mercy of a majority of the legislature of the State in which the harbor is situated." Illinois Central Railroad Co. v. Illinois, 146 U.S. 387, 455, 13 S.Ct. 110, 119, 36 L.Ed. 1018, 1043 (1892). Is the doctrine of a judicial veto so firmly embedded in federal public trust jurisprudence that it amounts to a reserved principle that could come into play even after a state legislature restricted a judicial determination of the public trust? Arizona courts have twice struck legislative attempts to restrict the trust. *See* Arizona Center for Law in the Pub. Int. v. Hassell, 172 Ariz. 356, 371, 837 P.2d 158, 173 (1991); Defenders of Wildlife v. Hull, 199 Ariz. 411, 426, 18 P.3d 722, 737 (2001).

In Focus: Mississippi Land Exchange

In 1996, Mississippi's Secretary of State exchanged 6.73 acres of public trust tidelands for 4,225 acres of undisturbed uplands. The 6.73 acres of tidelands consisted of filled tidelands, tidelands that were slated to be filled, and tidelands that would remain in their natural state. The Secretary of State proposed the swap to replace the tidelands that would soon be filled and lose their natural value, and to help the developer avoid the time-consuming process of legislatively alienating the public trust properties. The Secretary of State's action has been applauded by two commentators who conclude: "The transaction serves to augment the amount of land in the state's public trust corpus in an effort to better secure and preserve the state's public trust tidelands and their ecosystems." *See* Duff & Fletcher, *supra* at 654. But is a land swap of this sort a valid measure under the public trust doctrine? Does an exchange obviate public trust analysis because it is not a standard "alienation," or does it have enough of an alienation component to merit review? What is the status of the acquired land? Can it be deemed public trust land?

D. Applying the Trust to Private Lands and Water Rights

The public trust doctrine involves an intriguing intersection between private property rights and public property rights. The cases in this section explore an expansion of the doctrine to reach private dry sand beaches and water rights. As you read the cases, consider how evolving societal interests are transformed into public property rights through judicial use of the doctrine.

MATTHEWS v. BAY HEAD IMPROVEMENT ASS'N
Supreme Court of New Jersey, 1984.
471 A.2d 355.

* * * The public trust doctrine acknowledges that the ownership, dominion and sovereignty over land flowed by tidal waters, which extend to the mean high water mark, is vested in the State in trust for the people. The public's right to use the tidal lands and water encompasses navigation, fishing and recreational uses, including bathing, swimming and other shore activities. Borough of Neptune City v. Borough of Avon-by-the-Sea, 61 N.J. 296, 309, 294 A.2d 47 (1972). In *Avon* we held that the public trust applied to the municipally-owned dry sand beach immediately landward of the high water mark. The major issue in this case is whether, ancillary to the public's right to enjoy the tidal lands, the public has a right to gain access through and to use the dry sand area not owned by a municipality but by a quasi-public body. * * *

Bay Head consists of a fairly narrow strip of land, 6,667 feet long (about 1 1/4 miles). A beach runs along its entire length adjacent to the Atlantic Ocean. There are 76 separate parcels of land that border the beach. All except six, are owned by private individuals. Title to those six is vested in the [Bayhead Improvement Association] [whose] purposes are ... cleaning, policing and otherwise making attractive and safe the bathing beaches in [the Borough of Bayhead]....

Nine streets in the Borough, which are perpendicular to the beach, end at the dry sand. The Association owns the land commencing at the end of seven of these streets for the width of each street and extending through the upper dry sand to the mean high water line, the beginning of the wet sand area or foreshore. In addition, the Association owns the fee in six shore front properties, three of which are contiguous and have a frontage aggregating 310 feet. Many owners of beachfront property executed and delivered to the Association leases of the upper dry sand area. * * * The Association controls and supervises its beach property between the third week in June and Labor Day. * * * Membership is generally limited to residents of Bay Head. * * *

Except for fishermen, who are permitted to walk through the upper dry sand area to the foreshore, only the membership may use the beach between 10:00 a.m. and 5:30 p.m. during the summer season. The public is permitted to use the Association's beach from 5:30 p.m. to 10:00 a.m. during the summer and, with no hourly restrictions, between Labor Day and mid-June.

No attempt has ever been made to stop anyone from occupying the terrain east of the high water mark. During certain parts of the day, when the tide is low, the foreshore could consist of about 50 feet of sand not being flowed by the water. The public could gain access to the foreshore by coming from the Borough of Point Pleasant Beach on the north or from the Borough of Mantoloking on the south. * * * There is also a public boardwalk, about one-third of a mile long, parallel to the ocean on the westerly side of the dry sand area. The boardwalk is owned and maintained by the municipality. * * *

In *Avon,* Justice Hall reaffirmed the public's right to use the waterfront as announced in *Arnold v. Mundy.* He observed that the public has a right to use the land below the mean average high water mark where the tide ebbs and flows. These uses have historically included navigation and fishing. In *Avon* the public's rights were extended "to recreational uses, including bathing, swimming and other shore activities." 61 N.J. at 309, 294 A.2d 47. The Florida Supreme Court has held:

> The constant enjoyment of this privilege [bathing in salt waters] of thus using the ocean and its fore-shore for ages without dispute should prove sufficient to establish it as an American common law right, similar to that of fishing in the sea, even if this right had not come down to us as a part of the English common law, which it undoubtedly has. [White v. Hughes, 139 Fla. 54, 59, 190 So. 446, 449 (1939).]

It has been said that "[h]ealth, recreation and sports are encompassed in and intimately related to the general welfare of a well-balanced state." * * * Extension of the public trust doctrine to include bathing, swimming and other shore activities is consonant with and furthers the general welfare. The public's right to enjoy these privileges must be respected.

In order to exercise these rights guaranteed by the public trust doctrine, the public must have access to municipally-owned dry sand areas as well as the foreshore. The extension of the public trust doctrine [in *Avon*] to include municipally-owned dry sand areas was necessitated by our conclusion that enjoyment of rights in the foreshore is inseparable from use of dry sand beaches. * * * The [*Avon*] Court impliedly [held] that full enjoyment of the foreshore necessitated some use of the upper sand, so that the latter came under the umbrella of the public trust.

In *Avon* ... our finding of public rights in dry sand areas was specifically and appropriately limited to those beaches owned by a municipality. We now address the extent of the public's interest in privately-owned dry sand beaches. This interest may take one of two forms. First, the public may have a right to cross privately owned dry sand beaches in order to gain access to the foreshore. Second, this interest may be of the sort enjoyed by the public in municipal beaches under *Avon* and *Deal,* namely, the right to sunbathe and generally enjoy recreational activities.

Beaches are a unique resource and are irreplaceable. The public demand for beaches has increased with the growth of population and improvement of transportation facilities. Furthermore the projected demand for saltwater swimming will not be met "unless the existing swimming capacities of the four coastal counties are expanded." * * *

Exercise of the public's right to swim and bathe below the mean high water mark may depend upon a right to pass across the upland beach. Without some means of access the public right to use the foreshore would be meaningless. To say that the public trust doctrine entitles the public to swim in the ocean and to use the foreshore in connection therewith without assuring the public of a feasible access route would seriously impinge on, if not effectively eliminate, the rights of the public trust doctrine. This does not mean the public has an unrestricted right to cross at will over any and all property bordering on the common property. The public interest is satisfied so long as there is reasonable access to the sea.

Judge Best, in his dissent in *Blundell v. Catterall* (K.B.1821), stated that passage to the seashore was essential to the exercise of that right. He believed that bathing in the tidal waters was an essential right similar to that of navigation and served the general welfare by promoting health and the ability to swim. * * * Judge Best would have held on principles of public policy "that the interruption of free access to the sea is a public nuisance...."

The touchstone of Judge Best's reasoning is that the particular circumstances must be considered and examined before arriving at a solution that will accommodate the public's right and the private interests involved. Thus an undeveloped segment of the shore may have been available and used for access so as to establish a public right-of-way to the wet sand. Or there may be publicly-owned property, such as in *Avon,* which is suitable. Or, as in this case, the public streets and adjacent upland sand area might serve as a proper means of entry. The test is whether those means are reasonably satisfactory so that the public's right to use the beachfront can be satisfied.

The bather's right in the upland sands is not limited to passage. Reasonable enjoyment of the foreshore and the sea cannot be realized unless some enjoyment of the dry sand area is also allowed. The complete pleasure of swimming must be accompanied by intermittent periods of rest and relaxation beyond the water's edge. The unavailability of the physical situs for such rest and relaxation would seriously curtail and in many situations eliminate the right to the recreational use of the ocean. * * *

We see no reason why rights under the public trust doctrine to use of the upland dry sand area should be limited to municipally-owned property. It is true that the private owner's interest in the upland dry sand area is not identical to that of a municipality. Nonetheless, where use of dry sand is essential or reasonably necessary for enjoyment of the ocean, the doctrine warrants the public's use of the upland dry sand area subject to an accommodation of the interests of the owner. * * *

[W]e perceive the public trust doctrine not to be "fixed or static," but one to "be molded and extended to meet changing conditions and needs of the public it was created to benefit." *Avon,* 294 A.2d 47. Precisely what privately-owned upland sand area will be available and required to satisfy the public's rights under the public trust doctrine will depend on the circumstances. Location of the dry sand area in relation to the foreshore, extent and availability of publicly-owned upland sand area, nature and extent of the public demand, and usage of the upland sand land by the owner are all factors to be weighed and considered in fixing the contours of the usage of the upper sand.

Today, recognizing the increasing demand for our State's beaches and the dynamic nature of the public trust doctrine, we find that the public must be given both access to and use of privately-owned dry sand areas as reasonably necessary. While the public's rights in private beaches are not co–extensive with the rights enjoyed in municipal beaches, private landowners may not in all instances prevent the public from exercising its rights under the public trust doctrine. The public must be afforded reasonable access to the foreshore as well as a suitable area for recreation on the dry sand.

NATIONAL AUDUBON SOCIETY v. SUPERIOR COURT OF ALPINE COUNTY, DEP'T OF WATER AND POWER OF L.A. ("MONO LAKE")

Supreme Court of California, 1983.
658 P.2d 709, 711–732.

* * * Mono Lake, the second largest lake in California, sits at the base of the Sierra Nevada escarpment near the eastern entrance to Yosemite National Park. The lake is saline; it contains no fish but supports a large population of brine shrimp which feed vast numbers of nesting and migratory birds. Islands in the lake protect a large breeding colony of California gulls, and the lake itself serves as a haven on the migration route for thousands of Northern Phalarope, Wilson's Phalarope, and Eared Greve. Towers and spires of tufa on the north and south shores are matters of geological interest and a tourist attraction. * * *

Five freshwater streams ... arise near the crest of the range and carry the annual runoff to the west shore of the lake. In 1940, however, the Division of Water Resources, the predecessor to the present California Water Resources Board, granted the Department of Water and Power of the City of Los Angeles (hereafter DWP) a permit to appropriate virtually the entire flow of four of the five streams flowing into the lake. * * *

As a result of these diversions, the level of the lake has dropped; the surface area has diminished by one-third; one of the two principal islands in the lake has become a peninsula, exposing the gull rookery there to coyotes and other predators and causing the gulls to abandon the former island. [B]oth the scenic beauty and the ecological values of Mono Lake are imperiled. Plaintiffs filed suit in superior court to enjoin the DWP diversions on the theory that the shores, bed and waters of Mono Lake are protected by a public trust. * * *

This case brings together for the first time two systems of legal thought: the appropriative water rights system which since the days of the gold rush has dominated California water law, and the public trust doctrine which, after evolving as a shield for the protection of tidelands, now extends its protective scope to navigable lakes. Ever since we first recognized that the public trust protects environmental and recreational values (*Marks v. Whitney*, 491 P.2d 374 (1971)), the two systems of legal thought have been on a collision course. They meet in a unique and dramatic setting which highlights the clash of values. Mono Lake is a scenic and ecological treasure of national significance, imperiled by continued diversions of water; yet, the need of Los Angeles for water is apparent, its reliance on rights granted by the board evident, the cost of curtailing diversions substantial. * * *

The water rights enjoyed by DWP were granted ... without any consideration of the impact upon the public trust. An objective study and reconsideration of the water rights in the Mono Basin is long overdue. The water law of California—which we conceive to be an integration including both the public trust doctrine and the board-administered appropriative rights system—permits such a reconsideration; the values underlying that integration require it. * * *

[C]ases amply demonstrate the continuing power of the state as administrator of the public trust, a power which extends to the revocation of previously granted rights or to the enforcement of the trust against lands long thought free of the trust. Except for those rare instances in which a grantee may acquire a right to use former trust property free of trust restrictions, the grantee holds subject to the trust, and while he may assert a vested right to the servient estate (the right of use subject to the trust) and to any improvements he erects, he can claim no vested right to bar recognition of the trust or state action to carry out its purposes.

Since the public trust doctrine does not prevent the state from choosing between trust uses, the Attorney General of California [argues that] "trust uses" encompass all public uses, so that in practical effect the doctrine would impose no restrictions on the state's ability to allocate trust property. We know of no authority that supports this view of the public trust. * * * [T]he public trust is more than an affirmation of state power to use public property for public purposes. It is an affirmation of the duty of the state to protect the people's common heritage of streams, lakes, marshlands and tidelands, surrendering that right of protection only in rare cases when the abandonment of that right is consistent with the purposes of the trust. * * *

As we have seen, the public trust doctrine and the appropriative water rights system administered by the Water Board developed independently of each other. * * * To embrace one system of thought and reject the other would lead to an unbalanced structure, one which would either decry as a breach of trust appropriations essential to the economic development of this state, or deny any duty to protect or even consider the values promoted by the public trust. Therefore, seeking an accommodation ... we reach the following conclusions:

a. The state as sovereign retains continuing supervisory control over its navigable waters and the lands beneath those waters. This principle, fundamental to the concept of the public trust, applies to rights in flowing waters as well as to rights in tidelands and lakeshores; it prevents any party from acquiring a vested right to appropriate water in a manner harmful to the interests protected by the public trust.

b. As a matter of current and historical necessity, the Legislature, acting [through] the Water Board, has the power to grant usufructuary licenses that will permit an appropriator to take water from flowing streams and use that water in a distant part of the state, even though this taking … may unavoidably harm the trust uses at the source stream. The population and economy of this state depend upon the appropriation of vast quantities of water for uses unrelated to in-stream trust values. * * *

c. The state has an affirmative duty to take the public trust into account in the planning and allocation of water resources, and to protect public trust uses whenever feasible. * * * As a matter of practical necessity the state may have to approve appropriations despite foreseeable harm to public trust uses. In so doing, however, the state must bear in mind its duty as trustee to consider the effect of the taking on the public trust and to preserve, so far as consistent with the public interest, the uses protected by the trust. Once the state has approved an appropriation, the public trust imposes a duty of continuing supervision over the taking and use of the appropriated water. [T]he state is not confined by past allocation decisions which may be incorrect in light of current knowledge or inconsistent with current needs. * * * It is clear that some responsible body ought to reconsider the allocation of the waters of the Mono Basin. No vested rights bar such reconsideration. * * *

This opinion is but one step in the eventual resolution of the Mono Lake controversy. We do not dictate any particular allocation of water. Our objective is to resolve a legal conundrum in which two competing systems of thought—the public trust doctrine and the appropriative water rights system—existed independently of each other suggest[ing] opposite results. We hope by integrating these two doctrines to clear away the legal barriers which have so far prevented either the Water Board or the courts from taking a new and objective look at the water resources of the Mono Basin. The human and environmental uses of Mono Lake—uses protected by the public trust doctrine—… should not be destroyed because the state mistakenly thought itself powerless to protect them. * * *

Mono Lake, near Lee Vining, California. Photo by Sandi Zellmer.

Notes and Questions

1. What does the *Matthews* decision portend for individual owners of private property along New Jersey beaches? Did the court indicate whether the public trust doctrine would expand to allow public access on beaches not held by an association? On July 26, 2005, the Supreme Court of New Jersey extended the *Mathews* decision to private property. Raleigh Avenue Beach Assoc. v. Atlantis Beach Club, 185 N.J. 40, 879 A.2d 112 (2005). For background, *see* Robert Schwaneberg, *Justices Can Draw a Line in the Sand With Ruling in Landmark Access Case,* NEWARK STAR–LEDGER (Jan. 17, 2005).

2. The *Mono Lake* and *Matthews* cases represent expansions of the public trust doctrine with respect to both its geographic reach and the interests protected. Traditionally, the public trust doctrine protected only fishing, navigation and commerce interests. What interests were expressed in the *Mono Lake* and *Matthews* cases? Do modern interests protected by the public trust doctrine reflect core societal needs, similar to fishing, navigation and commerce in the early 19th century? Or are some of them frivolous? What about the recreational interests in the *Matthews* case? Note the court's reference to a New Jersey opinion finding that "health, recreation and sports are encompassed in and intimately related to the general welfare of a well-balanced state." N.J. Sports & Exposition Authority v. McCrane, 119 N.J.Super. 457, 488, 292 A.2d 580 (N.J. Super. Ct. Law Div. 1971), *aff'd*, 61 N.J. 1, 292 A.2d 545. What is the difference between use of the trust doctrine to protect the public's interest in sun-bathing on a New Jersey beach, and the public's interest in protecting a recharge zone for a sole-source aquifer used for municipal drinking water? Should the public trust doctrine protect only core societal interests, or should it extend to other less essential, but nevertheless important, amenities of life as well? Where does one draw the line? Is your opinion influenced by how far the doctrine reaches into private property rights? Is it influenced by how much power a court exercises to override legislative will?

3. In his comprehensive survey of public trust cases, Professor Lazarus notes that the geographic reach of the doctrine has expanded beyond the

traditional streambed/tideland context to water resources, marine life, dry sand areas, rural parklands, wildlife, a historic battlefield, archaeological remains, and even a downtown area. *See* Lazarus, *supra* at 649–50. What unifying thread brings these various resources together under the public trust umbrella? Consider this original language in *Illinois Central*: "So with trusts connected with public property, or property of a special character, like lands under navigable waters, they cannot be placed entirely beyond the direction and control of the State." Illinois Central Railroad Co. v. Illinois, 146 U.S. 387, 454, 13 S.Ct. 110, 118, 36 L.Ed. 1018, 1043 (1892). Does that language suggest that the public trust doctrine should be strictly limited to the submerged lands underlying navigable waters, or does it imply a much broader geographic reach? Do some of the modern applications of the public trust doctrine go beyond the appropriate reach of the public trust doctrine? If you were a judge, would you apply the public trust doctrine to protect one of the last remaining forest habitat areas for the red-cockaded woodpecker? Would you apply it to prohibit mining activities outside the border of Yellowstone National Park if such activities could seriously pollute a river flowing into the park? *See In Focus*, Chapter 6.V.E (New World Mine). Where should the courts draw the line to ensure doctrinal development faithful to the original *Illinois Central* opinion?

4. A close cousin of the public trust doctrine is the ancient doctrine of custom, which provides for the public's right of continued access to a place upon a showing of seven explicit factors including that "[t]he land has been used in this manner so long 'that the memory of man runneth not to the contrary.'" *See* Oregon ex. rel. Thorton v. Hay, 254 Or. 584, 595, 462 P.2d 671, 677 (1969); Stevens v. Cannon Beach, 317 Or. 131, 854 P.2d 449 (1993), *supra*, at Ch. 9.II.B.2. Like the public trust doctrine and treaty access rights, the doctrine of custom forms a defense to Fifth Amendment takings claims asserted by private property owners. The doctrine is not nearly as broad as the public trust doctrine, because it protects only access to places traditionally accessed by the population. It is broader than treaty rights in that it benefits the public as a whole rather than tribal members in particular. In Hawaii, however, the doctrine of custom is well established to protect the rights of native Hawaiians. *See* Public Access Shoreline Hawaii v. Hawaii County Planning Comm'n, 79 Haw. 425, 903 P.2d 1246 (1995).

5. A significant expansion of the public trust doctrine involves the area of water rights, which are addressed in detail in Chapter 13, *infra*. The *Mono Lake* precedent launched other cases in the West challenging water diversions. *See* San Carlos Apache Tribe v. Superior Court of Arizona, 193 Ariz. 195, 972 P.2d 179 (1999) (invalidating legislation that precluded water adjudication proceedings from taking public trust into account); In re Water Use Permit Applications, 94 Haw. 97, 9 P.3d 409, 447–48 (2000) (public trust doctrine applies to all water resources, including groundwater); Shokal v. Dunn, 109 Idaho 330, 336, 707 P.2d 441, 447 n.2 (1985) ("Any grant to use the state's waters is 'subject to the trust and to action by the State necessary to fulfill its trust responsibilities.'"); Ordean Parks v. Cooper, 2004 S.D. 27, 41, 676 N.W.2d 823, 838 (2004) (water over privately owned lakebeds is public trust asset); *but see* Postema v. Pollution Control Hearings Board, 142

Wn.2d 68, 98–99, 11 P.3d 726, 744 (2000) (department may not use public trust doctrine as criterion in considering applications to appropriate water).

In *Mineral County v. State Dep't of Conservation and Natural Resources*, 117 Nev. 235, 244–49, 20 P.3d 800, 806–809 (2001), the Nevada Supreme Court referred the question of whether a public trust applied to Nevada water rights to a federal district court handling a pending water adjudication. A stirring opinion by concurring justices indicated the rising prominence of the doctrine:

> * * * [The] existence of the public trust doctrine in Nevada appears to be beyond debate. * * * It is not just the water appropriators who have a vested interest in the water from the Walker River, but every citizen of Nevada as well. It is this water that will dictate whether Walker Lake survives in its present state or becomes a dry lake bed. * * * The public expects this unique natural resource to be preserved and for all of us to always be able to marvel at this massive glittering body of water lying majestically in the midst of a dry mountainous desert. * * *

> If the [law] does not clearly direct the [water] engineer to continuously consider ... the public's interest in Nevada's natural water resources, then the law is deficient. It is then appropriate, if not our constitutional duty, to expressly reaffirm the engineer's continuing responsibility as a public trustee to allocate and supervise water rights so that the appropriations do not "substantially impair the public interest in the lands and waters remaining." *Illinois Central*, 146 U.S. at 452. * * * Our dwindling natural resources deserve no less.

Despite the California Supreme Court's clear statement in Mono Lake, *supra*, that water rights are not fully vested property rights, but are rather continually subject to the public trust, one case has found that California water users suffered a Constitutional taking under the Fifth Amendment when the federal government cut off flows of contracted water to save imperiled fish species under the regulatory authority of the Endangered Species Act. *Tulare Lake Basin Water Storage District v. United States*, 49 Fed. Cl. 313 (2001). The court acknowledged that the public trust doctrine sets a limit on the acquisition of property rights to water in California, but stated:

> While under California law, the title to water always remains with the state, the right to the water's use is transferred first by permit to [the state Department of Water Resources], and then by contract to end-users, such as the plaintiffs. Those contracts confer on plaintiffs a right to the exclusive use of prescribed quantities of water, consistent with the terms of the permits. That right remains in place until formally changed by administrative process. Thus, we see plaintiff's contract rights in the water's use as superior to all competing interests.

Tulare, 49 Fed. Cl. at 318; *see also later proceeding,* Tulare Lake Basin Water Storage District v. United States, 59 Fed. Cl. 246 (2003) (awarding California water users damages). *But see* Rith Energy, Inc. v. United States, 44 Fed. Cl. 108 (1999) (upholding denial of mining permit against takings claim finding that potentially affected groundwaters were held by the state in public trust); In re Water Use Permit Applications, 94 Haw. 97, 9 P.3d 409 (2000) (finding no taking from deprivation of water because water is a public trust resource and does not inhere in landowners' titles).

The *Tulare* ruling was not appealed by the federal government. Instead, the government settled the case by agreeing to pay California water districts $16.7 million for water diverted to help the rare fish. The decision to settle the case was controversial. The California attorney general's office, the National Marine Fisheries Service, and Senator Dianne Feinstein (D–Cal.) had all urged the government to appeal the decision because it could set a precedent for other water contracts that must suffer cutbacks to benefit endangered species. *See* Bettina Boxall, *U.S. to Pay $16 Million in Water Rights Case,* Los Angeles Times, Dec. 22, 04.

Nevertheless, the precedential effect of the *Tulare* case seems limited. Bureau of Reclamation contracts usually include a provision that shields the government from liability for failure to deliver a full supply of water. Courts have interpreted these provisions as authorizing the government to reduce contract water deliveries if necessary to comply with the ESA. O'Neill v. United States, 50 F.3d 677, 681–84 (9th Cir. 1995); Rio Grande Silvery Minnow v. Keys, 333 F.3d 1109, 1138 (10th Cir. 2003), vacated on other grounds, 355 F.3d 1215 (10th Cir. 2004). *See* Brian Gray, *The Property Right in Water,* 9 Hastings W-NW. J. Envtl. L. & Pol'y 1, 26 (2002). In a case decided after *Tulare, supra,* the U.S. Court of Federal Claims found that water users could not assert a takings claim for deprivation of private property under the Fifth Amendment when their water use was curtailed to meet obligations under the ESA. Klamath Irrigation District v. United States, 67 Fed. Cl. 504 (2005). In a thorough review of the water rights in question, the court concluded that any remedy would arise from a contract claim, not a takings claim, but cautioned that the contracts in question had language limiting the government's liability for water curtailments. Noting that the Tulare court had failed to consider such limiting contract language, or state doctrine that might limit water rights in order to protect fish and wildlife, the Klamath court concluded, "[w]ith all due respect, Tulare appears to be wrong on some counts, incomplete in others and, distinguishable, at all events." *Id.* at 538.

Chapter 9

PRIVATE LAND OWNERSHIP

Private ownership accounts for about 65% of the land base of the United States. These lands contain critical wetlands, aquifers, coastal areas, forests, species habitat, and other sensitive areas. Land health across the country depends in large part upon practices within private boundaries, yet these activities are governed by laws that are almost completely separate from those pertaining to federal, state, and tribal ownership. Use of privately owned land falls within state property and land use laws, discussed in Chapter 10.

In his famous article, *Tragedy of the Commons,* excerpted in Chapter 1.IV.A. *supra,* Garrett Hardin indicates that private property rights can prevent overuse of common resources, such as grasslands or fisheries. But by and large, state property laws have failed to safeguard important natural resources. Ecosystem destruction is increasing throughout the United States, to the point that the nation faces the loss of hundreds of natural ecosystems. *See* Reed F. Noss & Robert L. Peters, *Endangered Ecosystems: A Status Report on America's Vanishing Habitat and Wildlife,* ix–x (1995), *available at*: http://www.defenders.org/pubs/

endangeredeco.pdf. Already, the United States has lost 117 million acres of wetlands (over 50 percent of what was present at white contact); the Pacific region has lost 25 million acres (90%) of its ancient forest; California alone has lost 22 million acres of native grassland; and aquatic communities are degraded throughout the United States. *Id.* at viii. The loss of ecosystems is the leading cause of species extinctions in the U.S. and around the world, and more than half of all U.S. species listed as threatened or endangered rely exclusively on private lands. *See id.* at 46; DEFENDERS OF WILDLIFE, BUILDING ECONOMIC INCENTIVES INTO THE ENDANGERED SPECIES ACT vii (Wendy E. Hudson ed., 2d ed. 1993).

Congress addressed deficiencies in state law by passing a number of federal environmental statutes, two of which in particular have tremendous bearing on private land practices. The Endangered Species Act (ESA), 16 U.S.C. §§ 1531–1544, has been interpreted to limit alteration of listed species' habitat on private land. Babbitt v. Sweet Home Chapter of Communities for a Great Oregon, 515 U.S. 687, 115 S.Ct. 2407, 132 L.Ed.2d 597 (1995). The Clean Water Act limits fill of wetlands on private lands. 33 U.S.C. § 1344. Increasingly, states are passing more land use schemes to protect important natural and cultural resources.

The modern federal and state environmental statutory framework implicates an area of constitutional law known as regulatory takings. The 5th amendment of the Constitution (which limits federal action and also state action, through the 14th amendment) declares that no private property may be taken by the government without compensation to the owner. U.S. CONST. amend. V. Private property owners increasingly make the claim that their property is effectively "taken" when regulations prohibit a desired use. This is one of the thorniest areas of natural resources law, because the doctrines are muddled and in a constant state of flux due to recent Supreme Court opinions. It is an area that the natural resource practitioner cannot ignore because the interpretation of takings under the Constitution defines in large part what amount of regulation the states and federal government can impose without having to compensate landowners. A duty to compensate constrains the government's ability to regulate because government budgets typically are inadequate to pay landowners for regulatory burdens.

The area of takings churns up the most fundamental ownership questions because it forces an inquiry into what an individual acquires in the way of property rights when gaining title to land. If the bundle of property rights does not include the right to engage in action prohibited by a regulation, the owner's property has not been "taken" by the government when the regulation prohibits the activity; thus, no compensation is due. As the following materials and cases make clear, private property rights are very much bounded by public ownership rights, but the delineation between those two sets of rights is a matter of much debate.

Section I begins with a look at the institution of private property—its origins and changing directions. Section II presents a series of modern Supreme Court cases that frame the area of Constitutional takings. Section III explores the burgeoning use of conservation easements to protect community features and environmental values associated with legacy property. By enabling the acquisition of conservation rights through consensual transactions involving traditional property mechanisms, conservation easements create solutions that protect the environment without confronting the takings dilemma. This new form of ownership represents an important component in the field of natural resources law.

I. CHANGING CONCEPTIONS OF PROPERTY RIGHTS

Throughout history, sovereigns have structured property rights regimes in dramatically different ways. For example, the classic Anglo system of property rights vests "fee simple absolute" title in the owner, accompanied by a right to exclude all others from using the property. The concept of ownership as full dominion and control over property is reflected in the early thinking of John Locke and William Blackstone, scholars whose work exerted considerable influence over the development of property law in the United States. Blackstone began with a description of property as "[t]hat sole and despotic dominion which one man claims and exercises over the external things of the world, in total exclusion of the right of any other individual in the universe." WILLIAM BLACKSTONE, COMMENTARIES ON THE LAWS OF ENGLAND 2 (1979 ed.) (1865–69). Locke wrote that property rights emerged from the combining of labor with land:

> Though the earth and all inferior creatures be common to all men, yet every man has a property in his own person; this nobody has any right to but himself. The labor of his body and the work of his hands, we may say, are property his. Whatsoever then he removes out of the state that nature has provided and left it in, he has mixed his labor with, and joined to it something that is his own, and thereby makes it his property. * * * Thus the grass my horse has bit, the turfs my servant has cut, and the ore I have digged in any place where I have a right to them in common with others, become my property without the assignation or consent of anybody.

JOHN LOCKE, SECOND TREATISE OF GOVERNMENT 17–18 (Bobbs–Merrill ed. 1952) (original publication 1690).

Traditional property rights established by native governments were substantially different than the Lockean concept. As Professor Joseph Singer describes:

> [M]any American Indian nations developed property systems that were far more oriented to sharing than are non-Indian property systems. * * * The tribe itself would have mechanisms for assigning specific pieces of land to individuals or families, and if needs changed, the tribal government might reallocate assignments. Thus,

property was not generally sold in a way that gave as full powers to owners as exist in non-Indian systems. Moreover, property rights were not exclusive; rather, uses of property would overlap. Thus, while a particular family might use a piece of land to plant crops, this would not preclude other tribal members from trespassing or gathering nonagricultural food on such lands.

JOSEPH SINGER, PROPERTY LAW: RULES, POLICIES, AND PRACTICES, 12 (2d ed. 1997) (citing WILLIAM CRONIN, CHANGES IN THE LAND).

A. American Property Law: Individual Rights and Ecological Interest

Individualistic notions of private property became firmly embedded in American legal tradition. After wresting land from tribes, the U.S. government and states transferred considerable land to private individuals and corporations, carving up the landscape along boundaries that made little sense in ecological terms. In the popular American culture, land ownership is a simplistic concept, implying full rights to do what one pleases within the boundaries of one's property. What is the consequence of that ideology to the broader ecological landscape?

Let's start by imagining a fine Persian carpet and a hunting knife. The carpet is twelve feet by eighteen, say. That gives us 216 square feet of continuous woven material.... We set about cutting the carpet into thirty-six equal pieces, each one a rectangle, two feet by three.... When we're finished cutting, we measure the individual pieces, total them up—and find that, lo, there's still nearly 216 square feet of recognizably carpet like stuff. But what does it amount to? Have we got thirty-six nice Persian throw rugs? No. All we're left with is three dozen ragged fragments, each one worthless and commencing to come apart.

Now take the same logic outdoors and it begins to explain why ... the red fox, *Vulpes vulpes*, is missing from Bryce Canyon National Park. It suggests [why] myriad other creatures are mysteriously absent from myriad other sites. An ecosystem is a tapestry of species and relationships. Chop away a section, isolate that section, and there arises the problem of unraveling. * * * Plink, plink, plink, extinctions occur, steadily but without any evident cause. Species disappear. Whole categories of plants and animals vanish.

Dale D. Goble, *The Problem of Unraveling: Biodiversity and Private Property in Land*, 38 IDAHO L. REV. 291, 291 (2002).

Modern ecological understandings place greater importance on the relationship of individual parcels to the natural context in which they are situated. In the following essay, Professor Eric T. Freyfogle examines simplistic assumptions that still permeate American views of property and urges a more multi-faceted understanding of land.

THE CONSTRUCTION OF OWNERSHIP
Eric T. Freyfogle
1996 U. ILL. L. REV. 173, 173–76

Like many cultural artifacts, the institution of private land ownership today is weighted down by contradictions. * * * Consider the important matter of land *value*. Where does a land parcel's value come from, according to the thinking of the modern landowner? In the mind of that person, value means market value, the value that land would fetch when sold for cash. The landowner thinks that if he paid for the land, he gave rise to its value: he created it, and by rights, the value is his to enjoy and consume. But does this view of value make sense when we open the doors and head out onto the land itself? Outside, where plants grow and animals search for food, value has a far different meaning. Value lies not in exchange, but in use, not in land from which the most can be taken, but in land that vibrates in its health. Is the soil fertile? Are the plants and animals prosperous? Is the water clean and suitable for drinking? In the natural order, value is an intensely practical concern, based on the land's lasting ability to meet life's essential needs.

Consider the matter of land *uses*, a second point on which sensitive land stewards and the mainstream landowner hold contradictory thoughts. According to the now-dominant line of thought, land uses by definition are human uses. When humans are not actively using the land, we call it unused, even wasted. Parts of the land that are not directly beneficial to humans are, by this conceit, useless. When a farm field is converted to a golf course, the land has shifted to a higher use. When a tree dies and decays, falling in time with gravity, the tree is wasted; we have failed to put it to any use. When water in an arid land is allowed to flow into the sea, uninterrupted by irrigators and thirsty cities, we have failed to use it efficiently.

Opposing this myopic definition of use is an older and broader one, the understanding that sees how a woodpecker uses a dying tree to supply food and shelter, and how an owl might use the same tree as a perch to watch and listen. Under this more attentive definition, a river uses its surrounding wetlands to hold storm water to regulate flooding and limit siltation. A mole uses the topsoil to grow earthworms for dinner. * * * Far from being wasted or useless, water left in a stream helps sustain fish and other aquatic life.

There is also the matter of land *boundaries*. * * * For a single landowner, boundary lines set limits on responsibility. At the boundary line, my responsibility ends, or so thinks the modern mind. My land, the developer says, is a discrete thing, separate from the rest of the world. If nature has carefully knitted my land to surrounding acres, those links are unimportant. In my calculations of costs and benefits, only costs incurred within the boundaries are added to the ledger; only benefits captured on my tract are taken into account. * * *

Are there boundaries on the land, boundaries that are more than human creations? Indeed there are, although they rarely have the precision of the surveyor's azimuth.... Watersheds establish boundaries, and they do count. Where forest meets field, another boundary exists, and edge-loving animals are glad of it. Where ocean meets beach, where forest soil gives way to prairie soil, where flat land turns upward into hillside—all of these are boundaries of sorts. In its encrusted, artificial wisdom, landed property rights as we know them overlook these natural boundaries; only human-drawn lines gain the law's respect.

Finally, we need to consider the matter of land *health*. To the modern mind, dominated by economics, liberal individualism, and inherited ideas of land ownership, what does it mean for the land to be healthy? In this mode of ordering the world, land is an object, valuable only in terms of its utility to the owner. * * * If a farmer wants his huge tractor in the field early in the spring, and cannot stand the thought of puddles and mud that linger into May, then his field is healthy when it is underlain with drainage tiles—dumping water into rivers unnaturally fast, accelerating spring river flows, eroding river banks, increasing spring flooding, and lowering water tables in mid-summer.

Opposed to this utilitarian, individualistic understanding of land health is the one that we draw upon when surveying the land in more wholesome terms. Because all terrestrial life depends on the soil, land health begins there, with soil that is fertile and of good structure. Waterways are healthy when they provide clean water to drink and sound habitat for fish and mussels and muskrats. Forests are healthy when species are naturally diverse and when the tree population in a landscape includes trees of all ages, from seedling to rotted log. * * *

On all four of these points—land value, land use, boundaries, and land health—a disorienting gap exists between land as the artificial thing [and] land as part of an ecological community.... Land [as] property law conceives of it in its simplifying abstraction, is a thing that we humans have constructed.

Suburban encroachment on agricultural land.
Photo by Don Grim.

As history demonstrates, property rights are not set in stone. Defined by legislatures and courts, they are a product of a constantly changing society. *See* Morton J. Horwitz, *The Transformation in the Conception of Property*, *in* TRANSFORMATION OF AMERICAN LAW, 1780–1860 (1977). A fundamental role of property rights in society is to allocate scarce land and resources. As the environment becomes more degraded, population increases, and resources become increasingly scarce, societal needs change. Consider the effects of water scarcity, global warming, wildlife extinction, and wetlands depletion on community needs. Is the Lockean/Blackstone notion of private property suited to a world that bears little relationship to the one that formed the context of their thinking? Should government continue to reward "total dominion" over nature by allowing individuals to use their property in ways that deplete increasingly needed resources? The following essays explore new directions in property law.

SOME THOUGHTS ON THE DECLINE
OF PRIVATE PROPERTY
Joseph L. Sax
58 WASH. L. REV. 481, 484–94 (1983)

We have endowed individuals and enterprises with property because we assume that the private ownership system will allocate and reallocate the property resource to socially desirable uses. Any such allocational system will, of course, fail from time to time. But when the system regularly fails to allocate property to "correct" uses, we begin to lose faith in the system itself. Just as older systems of property, like feudal tenures, declined as they became nonfunctional, so our own system is declining to the extent it is perceived as a functional failure. Since such failures are becoming increasingly common, the property rights that lead to such failures are increasingly ceasing to be recognized.

[In] modern situations such as open space preservation or coastal protection, there is widespread agreement that non-development is the correct result.... * * * Why are values changing, and why does the property system not automatically adapt to them? One important explanation may lie in the difference between the different kinds of benefits flowing from property—"exclusive" and "nonexclusive" consumption benefits. In a case of exclusive consumption (a residence or a shopping center, for example), virtually all benefits flow exclusively to those who occupy and use the land. In such a case, where there are no significant externalities, one expects the direct users to be able to organize, calculate and bid for the opportunity to enjoy those benefits. In general, the community as a whole is content to have the property allocated to whomever among such competing exclusive use bidders is willing to make the highest bid. The conventional property system is organized to facilitate such allocations, and such allocations only.

If, however, the "competitors" include those who benefit from maintenance of an existing historic building, the consumption is nonexclusive. That is to say, the number of people who will potentially benefit is much greater: Benefits are not limited to actual occupants.... * * *

When nonexclusive consumption benefits are very small by comparison to exclusive consumption values, the traditional system of allocation functions well. But as nonexclusive benefits rise in importance, the capacity of traditional private property transactions to allocate satisfactorily diminishes, and in such circumstances one should not be surprised to see diminishing confidence in the property system as an engine of allocation. * * *

[F]or substantial areas of land the content of private ownership rights that we have long relied on is misallocating the land, and that what was long viewed as exceptional (government intervention to allocate correctly) is becoming commonplace. This change cannot help but impose enormous pressure upon our conception of the role that private ownership in land should play.

We have already seen some remarkable transformations, of which the rise of historic preservation ordinances is but one example. The perceived dominating importance of nonexclusive uses of shoreline has already given rise in the last decade to a greatly revived public trust doctrine. In that instance, the path of a judicially led transformation was paved by a long—though largely moribund—tradition of government retention of public rights in submerged shoreland that were never transferred into private ownership. The tradition was often ignored in the mid-nineteenth century, especially in places like California where vast acreages of submerged shoreline were passed into private ownership to encourage development.

At the time, the private ownership of these lands seemed absolute. As the need for nonexclusive uses of the lands rose in the last decade, and as the availability of such lands shrank, we witnessed some remarkable judicial pyrotechnics. For instance, recent California Supreme Court decisions have redefined the nature of the grants made by the legislature in the 1860's, questioned longstanding property rights in water, and explicitly reversed previous decisions holding that absolute private rights had been granted, thereby reinstating the public right of nonexclusive use on the inventive theory of implicit reservations in grants made more than a century ago.

However shocking such results may be to conventional legal sensibilities, they reveal a trend that is equally obvious in a range of other areas [such as] open space, coastal and wetland zoning. * * *

[U]nwillingness to compensate property owners reflects a desire to bring about some redistribution.... In withdrawing developmental rights (as opposed to existing uses), the legislatures and the courts are in fact leaving in place some long-existing uses, such as open space, coastal access, recreational opportunities, and historic structures. What is changing is not the quantum of de facto nonexclusive benefits, but the quantum of rights to destroy those benefits. Public privileges, long enjoyed, are becoming public rights.

THE PARTICULARS OF OWNING
Eric T. Freyfogle
25 Ecology L. Q. 574, 584–85 (1999)

What one sees today, in the case of many environmentally motivated laws, are efforts to achieve property's core values in ways that are more respectful of the health of nature. Lawmakers make mistakes—of that there is no doubt. But the complaint that environmental laws trample on core property values is greatly exaggerated. What is happening is that land health has joined the ranks of widely embraced communal goals. It is an important new goal, and with its arrival it is only appropriate that property's other, older aims move over some to make room.

Many environmental laws do nothing more than require landowners to internalize some of the harms that they have traditionally shoved on neighbors. Laws of this type do diminish landowner options, but hardly to a degree that personal privacy is threatened or investments are likely to end. Other environmental laws have the effect of tailoring individual rights so that land use patterns are respectful of the land's natural features. Examples here include familiar laws restricting the uses of wetlands and regulations protecting wildlife habitat. These laws, by and large, are designed to deal with particular problems, considered in isolation. Taken as a whole, however, such laws do evidence a distinct new trend, probably the most important trend now taking place in property law.

A century ago, landowner rights were largely conceived in abstract terms. There was the hypothetical Blackacre and the abstract bundle of rights that its owner possessed. In thinking this way, the law paid little attention to the land itself, as if the natural features of a land parcel had no impact on the owner's land use options. Thankfully, that kind of ecological blindness is slowly coming to an end. Slowly, painfully, people are coming to think that landowner rights should somehow depend on the natural features of the parcel owned. They are finally giving nature a chance to participate in the lawmaking process. Before land is put to an intensive use, certain questions are becoming essential: How is nature using the land? For what uses is the land naturally suited? How can human uses better respect nature's ways?

This new tendency to tailor property rights to the land is not all that well understood. It is therefore misinterpreted as a wide-ranging attack on landed property rights. If the law can ban house-building on a fragile barrier island, critics wonder, can it ban houses everywhere? The question is a sensible one, but only if one fails to recognize why barrier islands are ill suited for houses and why the property rights of an island owner might rightly differ from the rights of an owner of stable, drier land. This trend of tailoring rights to the land poses little real threat to the core values of property. Once people see what is going on, once they realize that property rights now depend in part on the land itself, expectations can be adjusted and life can go on, with as much economic growth, personal privacy, and civic harmony as ever before.

Notes and Questions

1. Do Sax and Freyfogle suggest that a new law of property is organizing around a more refined notion geared towards the unique values of land? If so, would you characterize their musings as "pie in the sky" optimism? Few would deny that a development frenzy is in full swing today. In just a matter of decades, the real estate and construction industry has converted millions of acres of farms, wetlands, forests, and other prime natural areas to subdivisions, strip malls, and "McMansion" communities. The rate of development in the United States has soared in the last half-century. The amount of urban land area nearly quadrupled between 1954 and 1997, from 18.6 million acres to about 74.0 million acres in the contiguous 48 states. U.S. Envtl. Protection Agency, E.P.A. 231–R–01–002, Our Built and Natural Environments: A Technical Review of the Interactions Between Land Use, Transportation, and Environmental Quality 4 (2001), available at:

http://www.smartgrowth.org/library/built.html. As development has increased, so has loss of natural habitat. *See Noss & Peters, supra.*

Is it curious that American society calls such destruction of land and natural resources "development?" The term "development" implies good progress with no associated detriments. Does this nomenclature relate back to a notion that land is wasted unless combined with human labor, an essentially Lockean construct? Is such a notion outdated in today's world? Standard development practices still involve tearing vegetation from the land, draining wetlands, diverting or eliminating streams, and covering rich soils with asphalt. Should such land "developers" instead be considered land "abusers?" Is there still a cultural inhibition embedded in property law tradition against taking developers to task for destructive practices? Consider Prof. Freyfogle's comments:

> [T]here is a ... foundational issue at stake: the matter of individual responsibility and discipline. It should be obvious to almost anyone, but apparently is not, that sapping soil of its fertility is harmful. It should be obvious, but still is not, that eroding a hillside, and leaving no room for wildlife, and polluting a waterway, are all harmful acts. When a law restricts these activities it merely asks landowners to become responsible community members–a fair and meager enough request, one should think. But if requests like these are so modest, why as a community do we have such problems uttering them and enforcing them? Why do we seem to pay so much heed to the barely veiled greed of land abusers, who in the name of private rights claim the power to continue their destructive ways and who express outrage at the mere thought of facing limits? * * *

> It is merely a specific application of this strand of modern thought for a landowner to assert, when his land use simply harms

the community at large, that the community has no right to intervene unless it pays him or her to stop.

Eric Freyfogle, *The Construction of Ownership, supra*, at 182–185.

2. Proponents of traditional private property rights decry modern environmental laws as an illegal encroachment into "natural rights" of humans. They reach back to the teachings of Locke and Blackstone to suggest that exclusive property rights are set in stone and cannot be altered by government. Professor Joan McGregor explains:

> Arguing that they follow John Locke's path, these critics [of property regulation] support their views by claiming individual "natural rights" that are prior to and independent of the government. * * * Locke's theory of property rights is grounded in ... the premise that God intends that the earth should serve the preservation of mankind. * * * Locke argues that individuals ... have a natural right to property, a right not given by the monarchy or government, but by God.

Joan L. McGregor, *This Land is Your Land, This Land is My Land: A Philosophical Reflection on Natural Rights to Property and Environmental Regulations*, 12 J. ENVTL. L. & LITIG. 87, 87–93 (1997).

In contrast to the Lockean theory of "natural rights," Professor Freyfogle joins several other leading property law scholars to emphasize that property rights are created by the state, and can and should be changed to meet evolving societal needs:

> [P]rivate property as a cultural institution is very much a human creation. To say that a person owns land means little unless we know when and in what culture the person lived, and what ownership meant at that moment in time and place. As nature created it, the land of seventeenth-century New England was the same for native inhabitant and arriving settler. As it existed in the minds of the people, however, land as object of ownership varied widely.

> This observation carries with it a vital corollary. If private property is a human creation, a mere mental abstraction, then it is something that a culture can change if and when it so chooses. * * * [P]roponents of the many types of land exploitation would have us believe ... that property ownership is a God-given construct, an idea ... inked on some unassailable parchment. But this is simply not so. Since our nation was founded, ownership norms have shifted significantly, and they must continue to shift. Although our Constitution protects "property" rights, it wisely does not explain what those rights are or what private ownership is all about. Rightly understood, the Constitution does not stand as a roadblock to the reconstruction of a more ecologically sound, more community-minded scheme of private property rights.

Eric Freyfogle, *The Construction of Ownership, supra*, at 173, 177–178.

3. Traditional property law makes no distinction in ownership rights flowing from parcels with different natural features. Is this an extreme failure of the law? Does it make sense to treat a parcel of land containing rare wetlands or species habitat in the same way as a paved parking lot located

in the heart of a commercial zone? Does a residential parcel with a mani-
cured lawn carry the same community value as a forested parcel? Does an
ocean shoreline parcel equate with a cornfield in the middle of Nebraska?
Should property law impose differing obligations according to the natural
importance of the parcel?

On the other hand, don't most pieces of private property provide at least
some ecological functions that contribute to community land health? Consider the often quoted statement of Aldo Leopold:

> If the land mechanism as a whole is good, then every part is good,
> whether we understand it or not. If the biota, in the course of aeons, has
> built something we like but do not understand, then who but a fool
> would discard seemingly useless parts? To keep every cog and wheel is
> the first precaution of intelligent tinkering.

Aldo Leopold, Conservation, Round River, 146–7 (Luna B. Leopold, ed., 1953).

Professor Holly Doremus has advocated conserving the "ordinary" parcels of land, as well as the extraordinary parcels, in order to preserve
national biodiversity:

> As we did in the earliest days of conscious nature protection, we
> continue to concentrate on setting aside special places and protecting
> dwindling special resources against exhaustion. Given today's condi-
> tions, that strategy is not likely to achieve our current goal of protect-
> ing a wide range of biotic resources over a long period of time. If we
> are to succeed in protecting biodiversity, we must find ways to focus
> the law and the public on ordinary nature rather than merely the
> obviously special or unique aspects of nature. * * * Carlos David-
> son's description of nature as a tapestry, out of which human activity
> is pulling thread after thread, helps demonstrate the distinction.
> * * * [T]he goal of biodiversity protection is nothing less than pres-
> ervation of the entire tapestry.... The loss of every thread dimin-
> ishes the picture, but no thread is so special that its removal will
> cause the entire picture to disappear. Protecting the tapestry is a
> very different task than protecting the best, the most striking, or the
> most important individual threads or parts of the overall picture. We
> simply cannot save the whole by identifying and saving the most spe-
> cial parts.

Holly Doremus, *Biodiversity and the Challenge of Saving the Ordinary*, 108
Idaho L. Rev. 325, 325–29 (2002).

4. Professor Carol Rose has urged attention to a different category of
property that is neither private property nor public property. She identifies
the genre of "limited common property" or LCP, which is "property held as a
commons among the members of a group, but exclusively vis-à-vis the outside world ... a property type that is neither entirely individualistic nor
entirely public." Carol M. Rose, *The Several Futures of Property: Of Cyber-
space and Folk Tales, Emission Trades and Ecosystems*, 83 Minn. L. Rev. 129,
132 (2002). As she explains, "[A] hybrid property regime begins by establishing a regulatory 'cap' on total use of a given resource; then within the
capped allowable amount, the regime allocates individual portions to persons or entities...." *Id.* at 164–165.

In Focus:
Vancouver, Washington's Tree Ordinance

How would you achieve protection of "ordinary" parcels as suggested by Prof. Doremus? A beginning point might be protecting the vegetation on private property. Some cities have moved in that direction by passing tree protection ordinances that prohibit landowners from cutting trees without a permit. For example, the City of Vancouver, Washington, has a tree ordinance that recognizes the functions of privately owned wooded areas in providing "habitat, cover, food supply and corridors for a diversity of fish and wildlife.... " Vancouver Municipal Code, § 20.96.010. The tree ordinance states: "When there are feasible and prudent location alternatives on site for proposed building structures or other site improvements, wooded areas and trees are to be preserved." *Id.* § 20.96.070(D)(2).

Many private property owners would resist such regulation, arguing that they own the trees and that the trees' benefits are limited to their own property. Increasingly, however, natural resource practitioners are pointing out the community environmental benefits flowing from such resources on private lands. American Forests, a conservation organization, has developed computer technology called "City Green Analysis" to assess the value of trees to a community. An Urban Ecosystem Analysis conducted in several cities demonstrates the costly effects of losing trees across a region. The analysis for the Willamette/Lower Columbia Region concluded that between 1972 and 2000 the heavy tree canopy in Vancouver, Washington decreased 90.6%, and the moderate canopy decreased 84.5%. *See* www.americanforests.org. It concludes that the current tree canopy in Vancouver is providing $2,296,882 annually in stormwater benefits and $1,213,291 in air pollution removal.

Exercise:

Traditionally, property law professors and scholars have referred to property rights as a "bundle of sticks." As interest grows in re-conceptualizing private property rights, some members of the legal academy are urging other metaphors to reflect modern thinking in property law. Assume you are a property law professor preparing for the first day of class. Read the materials that follow and prepare remarks to the class explaining why you prefer a particular metaphor—the traditional bundle of sticks, the bundle with a "public cord," or the "web of interests"—for explaining property law concepts.

RECONCEIVING THE BUNDLE OF STICKS:
LAND AS A COMMUNITY–BASED RESOURCE
Myrl L. Duncan
32 ENVTL L. 773, 774 (2002)

The law has long used the metaphor of the bundle of sticks as a way to describe and think about the nature of property, especially land. * * * Using separate sticks to represent different estates also graphically demonstrates the "arithmetic of estates," the principle that collectively the various estates must at all times add up to the whole bundle, a fee simple. * * * The problem is that while it is a useful device for thinking about the rights that exist in a piece of land—the various sticks that make up the bundle—the metaphor's focus on individual parts fosters a disregard of the parcel as a whole. Further, the metaphor treats a landowner's collection of rights only in the abstract. By considering the bundle complete in and of itself, the metaphor ignores the fact that landowners, and thus bundles, interact not only with neighboring landowners but also with the public at large in ways that affect society's desire and need for a healthy environment. The metaphor also fails to account for the fact that parcels of land interact with each other within the nonhuman world. * * *

Completing the Bundle: The Public Cord

Today land ownership encompasses interconnectedness, context, correlativity and the public interest among its core values. Because the purpose of the bundle metaphor is to provide a way to conceptualize the nature of ownership, it follows that the metaphor must be expanded to acknowledge those values. * * * Put another way, we must openly acknowledge that in addition to affording private rights based in antiquity, land ownership today means shouldering public responsibilities inherent in an intensely interconnected and ever-changing world. * * * By incorporating into the bundle the cord that represents the community at large, the public interest, we complete the bundle metaphor. We also critically transform it—and thus the way we think about property. Instead of reinforcing the Lockean notion that the sticks, which represent private property, exist separate and apart from the community, we explicitly acknowledge that without the bonds of community there would be no bundle. Rights in private property do not exist in the absence of law; they exist only because the community recognizes them and is willing to enforce the claims of rights holders. Determining which rights the community is willing to recognize thus involves balancing private and community interests. [The] complete bundle metaphor provides the framework for considering that balancing process. * * *

> ## RECONSTITUTION OF PROPERTY
> ### Craig Anthony Arnold
> 26 HARV. ENVTL. L. REV. 281, 285, 333–58, 356–64 (2002)
>
> [T]he modern concept of property as a bundle of rights diminishes the importance of the natural environment and the human relationship with the natural environment.... * * * The [metaphor] is incompatible with two essential principles of environmentalism, perhaps best represented by Aldo Leopold's land ethic: (1) the interconnectedness of people and their physical environment and (2) the importance of the unique characteristics of each object.
>
> [We] should come to think of property as a web of interests. The web is a set of interconnections among persons, groups, and entities each with some stake in an identifiable (but either tangible or intangible) object, which is at the center of the web. All of the interest-holders are connected both to the object and to one another. * * * As a functional and contextual tool, the web of interests metaphor focuses attention on the nature and characteristics of the object of property interests, the relationships between interest holders and the object, and the relationships among the interest holders, including society's stake in the object. * * * The web of interests is a way of seeing *property* as vital, distinctive, adaptive, and functional, as well as a way of seeing *people* connected not only to one another but also to the objects of their property interests.

B. Expanding Concepts of Nuisance

Some scholars are reconceiving property law by focusing on an expanded and more sophisticated view of "harm." The traditional property law doctrine of nuisance incorporates the no-harm rule as a limit on a landowner's right to use her property: *sic utere tuo ut alienum non laedas* (use your property so as not to injure the rights of your neighbor). Consider the view of Professor Freyfogle, urging attention to this aspect of property law.

THE CONSTRUCTION OF OWNERSHIP
Eric T. Freyfogle
1996 U. ILL. L. REV. 173, 178–87

[T]he absolute-ownership myth simply makes no sense when we apply it to an actual piece of land. Am I the "absolute owner" of my home if an adjacent landowner can set up a cement factory, pounding rocks and spewing dust, thereby rendering my home uninhabitable? * * * Unless I can halt inconsistent uses by neighbors, I have few rights that really count. Yet, if I can limit what my neighbors do, have not their "absolute" rights been constricted? And if I can limit what they do, cannot they in fairness similarly limit what I do as well?

To put the matter in plain terms, a landowner's rights at any given time include two distinct components—a right to use the land and a right to halt inconsistent uses by neighboring landowners. * * * In some manner, an ownership scheme needs to mix the right to use and the right to halt inconsistent uses. * * *

In nineteenth-century America, the mix between these two categories of rights shifted considerably, in ways that have proven decidedly harsh for the natural landscape. Early in the century most landowners engaged in relatively sensitive uses—farming, grazing, minor handicrafts, and the like. * * * Owners had rights to use the land, but they also enjoyed substantial rights to complain when an uphill neighbor drained his land unnaturally or when a railroad steam engine scared a horse and caused it to break a leg.

As the nineteenth century wore on, American values changed. As a culture, we came to favor industrial development. In the belching smokestacks and polluted waterways we saw progress, or at least what we took to be the necessary and tolerable by-products of progress. What was happening, in property ownership terms, was that landowners were gaining greater rights to *use* the land intensively, but at the same time they were yielding the right to complain about what their neighbors did. * * * In today's era of environmental controls, [l]andowners are slowly being nudged to curtail their most destructive resource-use practices; they are being pushed to abide by limits that look at least vaguely like some of the common-law rules in place a century and a half ago. * * *

[This] is not a reduction in property rights, but rather a reconfiguration of those rights. The right to use the land ... is surely being curtailed. But ... there comes with that reduction an increased right to halt similar activity by surrounding landowners. [Thus] the overall bundle of rights is no smaller in size, only different in composition. * * * The principal beneficiaries of land-use controls are not the public at large, but other landowners.... [L]and-use restrictions do not so much limit property rights as they do promote and protect them. * * *

Notes and Questions

Liability for nuisance is generally imposed if there is a finding that: (1) the defendant has unreasonably interfered with the plaintiff's use and enjoyment of her property; and (2) the plaintiff has incurred substantial harm as a result of the defendant's interference. Are you convinced that nuisance law should evolve beyond these basic elements to reflect modern ecological understanding? If so, who would the landowner's duty of "no harm" extend to? Just adjacent neighbors, or the community as a whole, or some larger population? Consider Professor Freyfogle's response:

> A landowner's duty is not just to refrain from harming land owned by others, it is to refrain from harming the land that is his. Harm is harm, even though its ill consequences will be felt by future generations, for they too are moral beings, only slightly removed and slightly different from ourselves. Harm is harm, even though it is widespread and even though its destructive ripples are difficult even for the trained ecologist to trace. A landowner simply cannot be per-

mitted to look away when the harm he causes is imposed, not on some single neighbor who comes over the fence to complain, but on a hundred or a thousand landowners miles downstream or downwind, who lack the time and ability to trace the problem back. * * * *Id.* at 178–87.

II. THE SHIFTING ACCOMMODATION BETWEEN PRIVATE PROPERTY RIGHTS AND PUBLIC WELFARE: THE FIFTH AMENDMENT TAKINGS DOCTRINE

The Fifth Amendment of the Constitution states, "nor shall private property be taken for *public use* without just compensation." U.S. CONST. amend. V (emphasis added). Modern takings jurisprudence is riddled with complexity, but at a very basic level, the field can be divided into three types of takings: physical takings, regulatory takings, and hybrid takings, which combine features of the first two.

Websources:

Georgetown Environmental Law and Policy Institute (GELPI) publishes on-line summaries of important cases and developments in Fifth Amendment takings law. Subscribers can receive regular updates through email. *See* http://www.law.georgetown.edu/gelpi/.

A. Physical Takings

Courts originally interpreted the Takings Clause of the Constitution to allow compensation for only clear physical invasions of property. A physical invasion occurs, for example, when a state puts a highway through a property owner's land, or when a city condemns an easement for a recreational path. Physical invasions may be far less dramatic to require compensation under modern caselaw; the Supreme Court has emphasized that any "permanent physical occupation," no matter how small, requires compensation. Loretto v. Teleprompter Manhattan CATV Corp., 458 U.S. 419, 102 S.Ct. 3164, 73 L.Ed.2d 868 (1982) (law that required landlords to allow cable television companies to install cable boxes on their property was a taking).

A preliminary question in physical takings cases is whether the taking is for "public use." In recent years, this public use limitation has proved "rather toothless." DAVID A. DANA & THOMAS W. MERRILL, PROPERTY TAKINGS (2002). In Hawaii Hous. Auth. v. Midkiff, 467 U.S. 229, 241, 104 S.Ct. 2321, 2329, 81 L.Ed.2d 186, 198 (1984), the Supreme Court declared: "[W]here the exercise of the eminent domain power is rationally related to a conceivable public purpose, the Court has never held a compensated taking to be proscribed by the Public Use Clause." But the meaning of the Public Use Clause is particularly stretched in cases involving condemnation for redevelopment. Many cities seek to promote redevelopment of blighted urban areas, yet private redevelopment corporations are often unable to convince all of the private property owners in the area to sell. Without acquiring all property in the proposed redevelopment area, the corporation cannot carry out a comprehensive renewal plan. In such cases, many courts have allowed public condemnation of the private properties and subsequent transfer to the private development corporation on the theory that there is public benefit from the condemnation in the form of economic progress and a wealthier tax base. In Poletown Neighborhood Council v. City of Detroit, 410 Mich. 616, 304 N.W.2d 455 (1981), the Michigan Supreme Court allowed the City of Detroit to condemn 465 acres of land and convey it to General Motors Corporation for a new auto manufacturing plant, stating that "public use" included job creation and tax revenues. Yet such condemnation strikes at the heart of the individual's expectation of stability in property ownership. As one property owner faced with condemnation in Lakewood, Ohio, put it, "They're taking one piece of private property, taking it away from us and giving it to someone else who is a private individual. And that's not fair." Anne Thompson, *Ohio Couple Accuses City of Grabbing Land,* NBC News (Jan. 31, 2005), *http://www.msnbc.msn.com/id/ 6891224/.* In 2004, the Michigan Supreme Court overruled *Poletown,* signaling that it would give greater scrutiny to such cases. Wayne v. Hathock, 471 Mich. 445, 481, 684 N.W.2d 765, 786 (2004) ("After all, if one's ownership of private property is forever subject to the government's determination that another private party would put one's land to better use, then the ownership of real property is perpetually threatened by the expansion plans of any large discount retailer, 'megastore,' or the like.").

In 2005, the Supreme Court handed down a ruling that gives government considerable leeway to condemn private property for redevelopment. In Kelo v. City of New London, 125 S.Ct. 2655, 162 L.Ed.2d 439 (2005), the city of New London pursued a large scale urban rejuvenation plan for a waterfront area surrounding a new Pfizer pharmaceutical research facility. The city, which had an unemployment rate twice that of the rest of Connecticut, pledged $7 million to clean up the area and provide more public services, hoping to "build momentum for the revitalization of downtown" through a waterfront hotel, marinas, a riverwalk, and office and retail space. *Id.* at 2659. Much to the chagrin of city officials, seven of the 90 existing landowners in the area refused to sell out. In the end, the Supreme Court, in a 5–4 ruling, upheld the city's exercise of eminent domain power to condemn the homes of the hold-outs. It explained that the "public use" requirement had been satisfied: "The City has carefully formulated an economic development plan that it believes will provide appreciable benefits to the community, including ... new jobs and increased tax revenue.* * * [W]e decline to second-guess the City's considered judgments about the efficacy of its development plan [and] we also decline to second-guess the City's determinations as to what lands it needs to acquire in order to effectuate the project." *Id.* at 2665, 2668. Justice O'Connor, writing for the dissent, lamented, "The beneficiaries are likely to be those citizens with disproportionate influence and power in the political process, including large corporations and development firms." *Id.* at 2677.

Texas columnist Molly Ivins, known for her staunch support of civil rights and her distinct brand of liberal humor, wrote a scathing review:

> "Jobs, jobs, jobs," is the eternal cry of the economic development lobby, which always stands to profit from whatever abomination is about to be foisted on the public. * * * [L]ocal governments are likely to seize on any chance to increase their tax base. * * * Those who naively trust local governments to make wise decisions clearly haven't been paying attention. * * * Look, a Wal–Mart brings in more tax dollars than 10 mom-and-pop stores. A chemical plant[] brings in more than the local shrimpers, especially after it kills off all the shrimp. Just like Monopoly, your house is worth more with a hotel on it than a home. * * * If you can convince any elected official in Texas that there is a higher good than "a healthy bidness climate," you let me know about it. The rivers and bays, the aquifers, the air we breathe—none of that has ever stood in the way of economic development in this state.

Molly Ivins, *Justices Aren't Paying Attention*, Sioux City J., July 2, 2005, at A8. Do you agree with Ivins? No doubt, most of us would if it were our home in question. But where would it leave cities like New London, which are struggling to rejuvenate their blighted downtown areas, if they could not wield the power of condemnation over the few hold-outs who might otherwise thwart a large-scale redevelopment plan?

There is a *per se* rule for compensation in the case of a physical invasion of property. Much force behind this rule comes from the notion that the power to exclude others has traditionally been considered "one of the most treasured strands in an owner's bundle of property rights." *Loretto, supra,* at 435. There are two clear exceptions, however, to the per se rule of compensation in physical invasion cases. One is where public necessity forces the invasion. *See* Miller v. Schoene, 276 U.S. 272, 48 S.Ct. 246, 72 L.Ed. 568 (1928) (no duty of compensation to the owner of cedar trees that the government ordered destroyed to prevent a disease from spreading to economically valuable apple trees); Bowditch v. Boston, 101 U.S. 16, 25 L.Ed. 980 (1880) (state has no liability for destruction of property "in cases of actual necessity" to prevent the spreading of fire or forestall threats to lives and property of others). The other situation is where the governmental action is merely carrying out underlying, antecedent public ownership rights. Where the parcel is encumbered by treaty rights, the public trust doctrine, or the federal navigational servitude, for example, governmental action effectuating those rights does not amount to a taking of private property, because the owner had no property right to interfere with the antecedent public property rights in the first place. *See, e.g.* Illinois Central Railroad Co. v.

Illinois, 146 U.S. 387, 13 S.Ct. 110, 36 L.Ed. 1018 (1892) (submersible lands encumbered by public trust are subject to revocation by legislature without compensation where private owner uses lands in manner inconsistent with public interest in navigation, fishing, or commerce); Lewis Blue Point Oyster Cultivation Co. v. Briggs, 229 U.S. 82, 87, 33 S.Ct. 679, 680, 57 L.Ed. 1083, 1085 (1913) (no right to compensation for destruction of oyster bed in course of government's dredging of a channel: "[T]he owner of the bed of navigable waters holds subject absolutely to the public right of navigation....").

Global Perspective—Public Access in England

ENGLISH LAW TO GIVE WALKERS NEW ACCESS
Allan Cowell
New York Times, April 7, 2002

LONDON—ALMOST 70 years ago, hundreds of British ramblers embarked on what turned out to be one of the most decisive episodes of a long-running contest for access to their nation's swaths of wild, uncultivated but privately owned land.

On April 21, 1932, the walkers converged on the Peak District in northwestern England, braving bailiffs, police and gamekeepers to demand free access to Kinder Scout, a boggy, high plateau that landowners had sought to close off as an exclusive preserve of upper-crust grouse shooters. The walkers, by contrast, came mostly from working-class sections of industrial Manchester at a time when Britain's class divisions were far less subtly cloaked than they are today. There was more than a whiff of class struggle in the air. * * * Ramblers scuffled with gamekeepers and the police. * * * One of them, Benny Rothman, a labor unionist, Communist and avid rambler who died in January, became the emblem of an enduring effort to grant walkers a statutory right to roam at will on land defined as "mountain, moor, heath or down or registered common land."

This year, British ramblers plan to hold a ramble marking the 70th anniversary of the Mass Trespass, and they will have something to celebrate. For the first time since Mr. Rothman's early protests, a law has been passed enshrining the right to roam for British walkers wherever they choose on stretches of nonfarmland. * * * [T]here is still some resistance. Owners of moorland used for grouse shooting have not been willing to see legions of ramblers tramping across their domains. * * * Of course, whole areas of Britain are open to the public in national parks, National Trust estates and other places....

The new English legislation promises to open 4,000 square miles of land currently closed to the public by the time mapping is complete and landowners have had time to register objections before the end of 2005. [The] new law offers landowners a right to close off access for 28 days and possibly longer each year. * * * The main worry among landowners ... is that the new laws offer no compensation for financial losses—such as broken fencing or damage to nesting flocks of grouse and other game birds, which are expensive to raise for the benefit of hunters. Landowners are lobbying for recognition of these issues and some sort of compromise in the law, but so far the problems are unresolved.

Question: How would a "roaming rights" statute fare under the Fifth Amendment of the U.S. Constitution? Is it good public policy? How did such a statute pass in Britain, when it would be virtually unimaginable in the U.S.? Was the idea equally far-fetched 70 years ago in Britain?

B. Regulatory Takings

In 1922, Justice Holmes led the Court onto what would prove a very slippery slope when he stated in Pennsylvania Coal Co. v. Mahon that "while property may be regulated to a certain extent, if regulation goes too far it will be recognized as a taking." 260 U.S. 393, 415, 43 S.Ct. 158, 160, 67 L.Ed. 322, 326 (1922). This decision gave birth to the complex field of regulatory takings. As the Court emphasized in *Mahon*, most average regulation will not trigger a compensation requirement because "[g]overnment hardly could go on" if it had to pay every property owner for diminishment in property values caused by regulation. *Id.* at 413. Nevertheless, the Court has struggled with drawing the line between acceptable regulation and regulation that is so severe as to amount to a taking. Supreme Court cases rendered in the past decade and a half throw this area into a state of considerable flux.

The traditional regulatory takings rule is an ad-hoc, factual inquiry. Known as the "Penn Central test," three factors are balanced to evaluate a takings claim: 1) the economic impact of the regulation; 2) its interference with reasonable investment backed expectations; and 3) the character of the government action. *See* Pennsylvania Central Transportation Co. v. City of New York, 438 U.S. 104, 98 S.Ct. 2646, 57 L.Ed.2d 631 (1978) (upholding historic preservation law against takings challenge); *see also* Hodel v. Virginia Surface Mining and Reclamation Assoc., 452 U.S. 264, 295, 101 S.Ct. 2352, 2370, 69 L.Ed.2d 1, 28 (1981). In 1992, however, the Supreme Court decided Lucas v. South Carolina Coastal Council, 505 U.S. 1003, 112 S.Ct. 2886, 120 L.Ed.2d 798 (1992), which carved out an exception to the circumstances in which the *Penn Central* test applies. The Court found that where a regulation denies the property owner of all "economically viable use" of her property, there is a *per se* compensation requirement unless the regulatory restrictions "inhere" in the title to the property by virtue of the state's "background principles" of nuisance and property.

The beach in front of the Lucas lots, Isle of Pines, South Carolina. Photo by William Fischel, http://www.dartmouth.edu/[]wfischel/lucasessay.html.

1. *"Per Se" Regulatory Takings*

LUCAS v. SOUTH CAROLINA COASTAL COUNCIL

Supreme Court of the United States.
505 U.S. 1003 (1992).

JUSTICE SCALIA delivered the opinion of the Court.

In 1986, petitioner David H. Lucas paid $975,000 for two residential lots on the Isle of Palms in Charleston County, South Carolina, on which he intended to build single-family homes. In 1988, however, the South Carolina Legislature enacted the Beachfront Management Act, which had the direct effect of barring petitioner from erecting any permanent habitable structures on his two parcels. A state trial court found that this prohibition rendered Lucas's parcels "valueless." This case requires us to decide whether the Act's dramatic effect on the economic value of Lucas's lots accomplished a taking of private property under the Fifth and Fourteenth Amendments requiring the payment of "just compensation." U.S. CONST. amend. V.

Prior to Justice Holmes's exposition in *Pennsylvania Coal Co. v. Mahon*, 260 U.S. 393 (1922), it was generally thought that the Takings Clause reached only a "direct appropriation" of property, or the functional equivalent of a "practical ouster of [the owner's] possession." Justice Holmes recognized in *Mahon*, however, that if ... the uses of private property were subject to unbridled, uncompensated qualification under the police power, "the natural tendency of human nature [would be] to extend the qualification more and more until at last private property disappeared." These considerations gave birth in that case to the oft-cited maxim that, "while property may be regulated to a certain extent, if regulation goes too far it will be recognized as a taking." *Id.*

Nevertheless, our decision in *Mahon* offered little insight into when, and under what circumstances, a given regulation would be seen as going "too far" for purposes of the Fifth Amendment. In 70-odd years of succeeding "regulatory takings" jurisprudence, we have generally eschewed any " 'set formula' " for determining how far is too far, preferring to "engage in ... essentially ad hoc, factual inquiries." *Penn Central Transportation Co. v. New York City*, 438 U.S. 104 (1978). We have, however, described at least two discrete categories of regulatory action as compensable without case-specific inquiry into the public interest advanced in support of the restraint. The first encompasses regulations that compel the property owner to suffer a physical "invasion" of his property. [N]o matter how minute the intrusion, and no matter how weighty the public purpose behind it, we have required compensation. * * *

The second situation in which we have found categorical treatment appropriate is where regulation denies all economically beneficial or productive use of land. As we have said on numerous occasions, the Fifth Amendment is violated when land-use regulation "... *denies an owner economically viable use of his land.*"[7]

We have never set forth the justification for this rule. Perhaps it is simply, as Justice Brennan suggested, that total deprivation of beneficial use is, from the landowner's point of view, the equivalent of a physical appropriation. "For what is the land but the profits thereof[?]" 1 E. Coke, Institutes, ch. 1, § 1 (1st Am. ed. 1812). Surely, at least, in the extraordinary circumstance when *no* productive or economically beneficial use of land is permitted, it is less realistic to indulge our usual assumption that the legislature is simply "adjusting the benefits and burdens of economic life," in a manner that secures an "average reciprocity of advantage" to everyone concerned, *Pennsylvania Coal Co. v. Mahon*, 260 U.S. at 415.

[R]egulations that leave the owner of land without economically beneficial or productive options for its use—typically, as here, by requiring land to be left substantially in its natural state—carry with them a heightened risk that private property is being pressed into some form of public service under the guise of mitigating serious public harm. * * *

---

7. Regrettably, the rhetorical force of our "deprivation of all economically feasible use" rule is greater than its precision, since the rule does not make clear the "property interest" against which the loss of value is to be measured. When, for example, a regulation requires a developer to leave 90% of a rural tract in its natural state, it is unclear whether we would analyze the situation as one in which the owner has been deprived of all economically beneficial use of the burdened portion of the tract, or as one in which the owner has suffered a mere diminution in value of the tract as a whole.... The answer to this difficult question may lie in how the owner's reasonable expectations have been shaped by the State's law of property—*i.e.*, whether and to what degree the State's law has accorded legal recognition and protection to the particular interest in land with respect to which the takings claimant alleges a diminution in (or elimination of) value. * * *

The South Carolina Supreme Court [found that] the Beachfront Management Act was no ordinary enactment, but involved an exercise of South Carolina's "police powers" to mitigate the harm to the public interest that petitioner's use of his land might occasion.... In the court's view, [this] brought petitioner's challenge within a long line of this Court's cases sustaining against ... Takings Clause challenges the State's use of its "police powers" to enjoin a property owner from activities akin to public nuisances. * * *

[The] distinction between "harm-preventing" and "benefit-conferring" regulation is often in the eye of the beholder. It is quite possible, for example, to describe in *either* fashion the ecological, economic, and esthetic concerns that inspired the South Carolina Legislature in the present case. One could say that imposing a servitude on Lucas's land is necessary in order to prevent his use of it from "harming" South Carolina's ecological resources; or, instead, in order to achieve the "benefits" of an ecological preserve.... Whether one or the other of the competing characterizations will come to one's lips in a particular case depends primarily upon one's evaluation of the worth of competing uses of real estate....[12] * * *

Where the State seeks to sustain regulation that deprives land of all economically beneficial use, we think it may resist compensation only if the logically antecedent inquiry into the nature of the owner's estate shows that the proscribed use interests were not part of his title to begin with. * * * It seems to us that the property owner necessarily expects the uses of his property to be restricted, from time to time, by various measures newly enacted by the State in legitimate exercise of its police powers; "as long recognized, some values are enjoyed under an implied limitation and must yield to the police power." *Pennsylvania Coal Co. v. Mahon*, 260 U.S. at 413. [But] we think the notion pressed by the Council that title is somehow held subject to the "implied limitation" that the State may subsequently eliminate all economically valuable use is inconsistent with the historical compact recorded in the Takings Clause that has become part of our constitutional culture.

Where "permanent physical occupation" of land is concerned, we have refused to allow the government to decree it anew (without compensation), no matter how weighty the asserted "public interests" involved ... —though we assuredly *would* permit the government to assert a permanent easement that was a pre-existing limitation upon the landowner's title. Compare *Scranton v. Wheeler*, 179 U.S. 141, 163

---

12. In JUSTICE BLACKMUN's view, even with respect to regulations that deprive an owner of all developmental or economically beneficial land uses, the test for required compensation is whether the legislature has recited a harm-preventing justification for its action. Since such a jus-tification can be formulated in practically every case, this amounts to a test of whether the legislature has a stupid staff. We think the Takings Clause requires courts to do more than insist upon artful harm-preventing characterizations.

(1900) (interests of "riparian owner in the submerged lands ... bordering on a public navigable water" held subject to Government's navigational servitude), with *Kaiser Aetna v. United States*, 444 U.S. at 178–180 (imposition of navigational servitude on marina created and rendered navigable at private expense held to constitute a taking). We believe similar treatment must be accorded ... regulations that prohibit all economically beneficial use of land: Any limitation so severe cannot be newly legislated or decreed (without compensation), but must inhere in the title itself, in the restrictions that background principles of the State's law of property and nuisance already place upon land ownership. A law or decree with such an effect must, in other words, do no more than duplicate the result that could have been achieved in the courts—by adjacent landowners (or other uniquely affected persons) under the State's law of private nuisance, or by the State under its complementary power to abate nuisances that affect the public generally, or otherwise.[16]

On this analysis, the owner of a lakebed, for example, would not be entitled to compensation when he is denied the requisite permit to engage in a landfilling operation that would have the effect of flooding others' land. Nor the corporate owner of a nuclear generating plant, when it is directed to remove all improvements from its land upon discovery that the plant sits astride an earthquake fault. Such regulatory action may well have the effect of eliminating the land's only economically productive use, but it does not proscribe a productive use that was previously permissible under relevant property and nuisance principles. The use of these properties for what are now expressly prohibited purposes was *always* unlawful, and ... it was open to the State at any point to make the implication of those background principles of nuisance and property law explicit.... * * * When, however, a regulation that declares "off-limits" all economically productive or beneficial uses of land goes beyond what the relevant background principles would dictate, compensation must be paid to sustain it.

The "total taking" inquiry we require today will ordinarily entail (as the application of state nuisance law ordinarily entails) analysis of, among other things, the degree of harm to public lands and resources, or adjacent private property, posed by the claimant's proposed activities, the social value of the claimant's activities and their suitability to the locality in question, and the relative ease with which the alleged harm can be avoided through measures taken by the claimant and the government (or adjacent private landowners) alike. The fact that a particular use has long been engaged in by similarly situated owners ordinarily imports a lack of any common-law prohibition (though changed circumstances or new knowledge may make what was previously permissible

16. The principal "otherwise" that we have in mind is litigation absolving the State (or private parties) of liability for the destruction of "real and personal property, in cases of actual necessity, to prevent the spreading of a fire" or to forestall other grave threats to the lives and property of others. Bowditch v. Boston, 101 U.S. 16, 18–19 (1880).

no longer so). So also does the fact that other landowners, similarly situated, are permitted to continue the use denied to the claimant.

It seems unlikely that common-law principles would have prevented the erection of any habitable or productive improvements on petitioner's land; they rarely support prohibition of the "essential use" of land. The question, however, is one of state law to be dealt with on remand. We emphasize that to win its case South Carolina must do more than proffer the legislature's declaration that the uses Lucas desires are inconsistent with the public interest.... Instead, as it would be required to do if it sought to restrain Lucas in a common-law action for public nuisance, South Carolina must identify background principles of nuisance and property law that prohibit the uses he now intends in the circumstances in which the property is presently found. * * *

JUSTICE KENNEDY, concurring in the judgment:

* * * Where a taking is alleged from regulations which deprive the property of all value, the test must be whether the deprivation is contrary to reasonable, investment-backed expectations. * * *

In my view, reasonable expectations must be understood in light of the whole of our legal tradition. The common law of nuisance is too narrow a confine for the exercise of regulatory power in a complex and interdependent society. The State should not be prevented from enacting new regulatory initiatives in response to changing conditions.... The Takings Clause does not require a static body of state property law; it protects private expectations to ensure private investment. I agree with the Court that nuisance prevention accords with the most common expectations of property owners who face regulation, but I do not believe this can be the sole source of state authority to impose severe restrictions. Coastal property may present such unique concerns for a fragile land system that the State can go further in regulating its development and use than the common law of nuisance might otherwise permit. * * *

Notes and Questions

1. *Harm / benefit distinction*—Why did the *Lucas* majority reject the harm/benefit distinction that had governed prior regulatory takings analysis? Is the distinction truly in the "eye of the beholder," or is there a normative approach to identifying whether a governmental action prevents harm or confers a benefit? The South Carolina legislature found that the natural beach and dune system protected by the Beachfront Management Act served a vital function in "protect[ing] life and property by serving as a storm barrier...." in hurricanes and other storms. *See Lucas, supra,* n. 10 (citing statute). Isn't that statute aimed towards preventing a harm? Perhaps the trouble lies more in the fact that many statutes that have harm prevention as their central goal also confer corollary benefits. In *Lucas*, the legislature had also found that the statute, by preserving the shoreline, would support tourism. *See id.* If tourism is deemed a benefit, does the existence of this benefit erase any fundamental harm-preventing nature of the statute?

2. *Denial of all economically viable use*—In another part of his concurring opinion, Justice Kennedy questioned the South Carolina trial court's

determination that Mr. Lucas had been left with no economically viable use of the parcel after the regulation. *See Lucas*, 505 U.S. at 1034 ("I share the reservations of some of my colleagues about a finding that a beachfront lot loses all value because of a development restriction."). Does it appear that the trial court focused on Lucas's type of development use only? Is this too narrow a focus? Could Mr. Lucas sell his property to the county or state as a public park? Or conversely, could he sell it to the neighbors to augment their parcels (and would they be induced to buy the parcel simply to prevent it from becoming a public park)? Could Mr. Lucas place an environmental education center on the property, using temporary structures? Could he keep the parcel as speculative property for the future on the possibility that the legislation will be someday be amended to remove the restrictions? Are developers under any obligation to explore creative uses of property?

In Palazzolo v. Rhode Island, 533 U.S. 606, 121 S.Ct. 2448, 150 L.Ed.2d 592 (2001), the petitioner initially planned a 74-acre lot residential subdivision, valued at $3,150,000, on 20 acres of land, most of which was salt marsh subject to tidal flooding. A regulation protecting the marsh ecosystem precluded the development on all but an upland portion of the parcel, leaving petitioner with a land value of $200,000. The Court found that the value of the upland area defeated a finding of no economically viable use under *Lucas*. *Id.* at 632 ("A regulation permitting a landowner to build a substantial residence on an 18-acre parcel does not leave the property 'economically idle.' ") (citing *Lucas*).

3. *Lucas* created a fork in the road for regulatory takings analysis by injecting a threshold inquiry: whether the regulation in question deprives the property of "all economically viable use." If it does not, the *Penn Central* three-factor test applies. If the regulation does deprive the property of all economically viable use, there is a *per se* compensation requirement unless the court finds that the restrictions "inhere[d] in the title." Does the new categorical rule announced in *Lucas* create an artificial distinction between a 95% and 100% decline in value? *See Lucas*, *supra* at 1064 (Stevens, J., dissenting) ("[T]he Court's new rule is wholly arbitrary. A landowner whose property is diminished in value 95% recovers nothing while an owner whose property is diminished 100% recovers the land's full value.").

4. *"Inhering in the title"*— What restrictions "inhere in the title?" Does that mean that precise restrictions have to be expressed prior to the owner's purchase of the parcel? Or does the phrase refer to a more generalized power of the state that may result in different restrictions over time? Does the *Lucas* opinion leave flexibility for the legislature to respond to new environmental problems? *See id.* at 1035 (Kennedy, J., concurring) ("[T]he state should not be prevented from enacting new regulatory initiatives in response to changing conditions...."). How important was the fact that all other beachfront lots had already been developed for residential housing by Lucas's nieghbors?

5. *Post-enactment purchaser: the Palazzolo holding*—A purchaser's reasonable expectations bear considerable weight in the traditional takings analysis. Following *Lucas*, there was some doubt as to whether landowners that purchased the property *after* a regulation had been passed could ever bring a regulatory takings claim, because it could be argued that regulatory

restrictions already in force "inhered in" the title acquired. The Supreme Court directly addressed the situation of so-called "post-enactment purchasers" in *Palazzolo v. Rhode Island*, 533 U.S. 606, 121 S.Ct. 2448, 150 L.Ed.2d 592 (2001), finding there was no bar to a takings claim.

> The theory underlying the argument that post-enactment purchasers cannot challenge a regulation under the Takings Clause seems to run on these lines: Property rights are created by the State. So, the argument goes, by prospective legislation the State can shape and define property rights and reasonable investment-backed expectations, and subsequent owners cannot claim any injury from lost value. After all, they purchased or took title with notice of the limitation.

> The State may not put so potent a Hobbesian stick into the Lockean bundle. * * * Were we to accept the State's rule, the postenactment transfer of title would absolve the State of its obligation to defend any action restricting land use, no matter how extreme or unreasonable. A State would be allowed, in effect, to put an expiration date on the Takings Clause. * * *

> We have no occasion to consider the precise circumstances when a legislative enactment can be deemed a background principle of state law .... It suffices to say that a regulation that otherwise would be unconstitutional ... is not transformed into a background principle of the State's law by mere virtue of the passage of title. * * *

Palazzolo, 533 U.S. at 627–630.

6. *Background principles*—"[B]ackground principles [of] property and nuisance" amount to two different exceptions to the categorical rule in *Lucas. See Lucas, supra,* at 1029. Are these exceptions to *Lucas* likely to expand over time as state courts realize the importance of protecting public needs? Are the exceptions likely to develop differently in the various states? One scholar has suggested a third "background principle" arising from a case decided long before *Lucas*. In Just v. Marinette County, 56 Wis.2d 7, 201 N.W.2d 761 (1972), a developer brought a takings claim when a shoreline regulation restricted development of his property, which contained substantial wetlands. The court denied the takings claim, setting forth what Professor Craig Arnold calls a "natural use" doctrine that, along with the public trust doctrine and the nuisance doctrine, may "inhere" in the title of landowners and limit the categorical compensation rule of *Lucas. See* Craig Anthony Arnold, *The Reconstitution of Property: Property as a Web of Interests,* 26 HARV. ENVT. L. REV. 281, 349–50 (2002). The *Just* court stated:

> In the instant case we have a restriction on the use of a citizens' property, not to secure a benefit for the public, but to prevent a harm from the change in the natural character of the citizens' property. We start with the premise that lakes and rivers in their natural state are unpolluted and the pollution which now exists is man made. The state of Wisconsin under the trust doctrine has a duty to eradicate the present pollution and to prevent further pollution in its navigable waters. This is not, in a legal sense, a gain or a securing of a benefit by the maintaining of the natural *status quo* of the environment.

[S]wamps and wetlands serve a vital role in nature, are part of the balance of nature and are essential to the purity of the water in our lakes and streams. * * *

An owner of land has no absolute and unlimited right to change the essential natural character of his land so as to use it for a purpose for which it was unsuited in its natural state and which injures the rights of others. The [zoning] is not an unreasonable exercise of that power to prevent harm to public rights by limiting the use of private property to its natural uses. * * *

Just, supra, at 767–68.

Does the "natural use" approach of *Just* clarify the harm/benefit distinction that Justice Scalia eschewed in *Lucas*? Many scholars are trying to situate the *Just* holding within the spectrum of the Court's more recent takings cases. State courts define the property rights protected by the Fifth Amendment. In states that choose to follow the "natural use" doctrine of *Just*, what lands are likely to be subject to a strict test for compensation? Or does *Lucas* foreclose the *Just* doctrine in takings law? *See* Joseph L. Sax, *Property Rights and the Economy of Nature: Understanding Lucas v. South Carolina Costal Council*, 45 Stan. L. Rev. 1433, 1441–42 (1993) (characterizing *Lucas* as a rejection of *Just's* natural use doctrine).

7.   What consequences will result if the area of regulatory takings greatly expands? Will government be able to pay for all takings? Will government still be able to regulate? Will the public interest be promoted or harmed? How will private property interests be affected?

8.   Suppose you work in the City Attorney's office. The permit department has stopped imposing mandatory development restrictions required by the land use code because the staff is worried such restrictions will give rise to takings claims. In a broad sense, how does the takings doctrine interact with police power functions? Does the staff have the constitutional authority *not* to implement the land use code when it has been enacted as binding law? What advice will you give to the staffers?

9.   Suppose a landowner is denied a federal permit to construct a house in a wetland area and files a successful takings claim under *Lucas*, gaining the full value of the lot (assume $200,000). Suppose that, two years later, a new Presidential administration changes the wetlands regulations, thereby allowing development on the lot. The landowner is able to build as originally planned. Does the *Lucas* opinion provide for this windfall? Did the *Lucas* majority even think of this? Is there a problem, conceptually, with compensating a landowner for the value of property (under the notion that the property was "functionally" taken by the government) yet not vesting title in the government? In South Carolina, for example, the legislature amended the restriction that had prevented Lucas's development just two years after its initial enactment to allow special permits for construction seaward of the coastal baseline. *See Tahoe–Sierra Preserv. Council, Inc. v. Tahoe Reg'l. Planning Agency,* 535 U.S. 302, 347 (2002) (Rehnquist, J., dissenting) ("The 'permanent' prohibition that the Court held to be a taking in *Lucas* lasted less than two years ... because the law, as it often does, changed.").

10.   For commentary on *Lucas, see* Sax, *supra*; Richard A. Epstein, *Lucas v. South Carolina Coastal Council: A Tangled Web of Expectations,* 45

STAN. L. REV. 1369 (1993); Frank I. Michelman, *Property, Federalism, and Jurisprudence: A Comment on Lucas and Judicial Conservatism,* 35 WILLIAM AND MARY L. REV. 301 (1993).

11. Lingle v. Chevron U.S.A. Inc., 125 S.Ct. 2074, 161 L.Ed.2d 876 (2005), represents the latest word on the prong of the *Penn Central* inquiry regarding the character of the government action at issue. Chevron challenged a Hawaii statute limiting the rent that oil companies could charge dealers leasing company-owned service stations. The Ninth Circuit held that the Hawaii law did not substantially advance a legitimate state interest in lowering consumer gasoline prices, and therefore a regulatory taking had occurred. 363 F.3d 846 (2004). The Supreme Court reversed, emphasizing that the relevant inquiry is whether the action affects property interests through some public program adjusting benefits and burdens of economic life to promote the common good, but not whether it "substantially advances legitimate state interests." 125 S.Ct. at 2087. Rather, the "legitimate state interests" test relates to due process claims, and is not an appropriate test for determining whether a government action is a Fifth Amendment taking. *Id.* Of course, the economic impact of the regulation and the extent to which regulation has interfered with distinct investment-backed expectations remain highly relevant in a takings case. But what is left of inquiry into the character of the government action? What evidence should a claimant attempt to submit on this aspect of a takings claim?

> **Exercise:**
>
> What factors are relevant to the nuisance inquiry that forms one of the background principles referenced in *Lucas*? Who decides whether there is a nuisance that prevents compensation in a takings case? Is there much predictability with the nuisance exception?
>
> Consider the following scenario. The state of Cascadia has a rich body of nuisance law. Several old cases find a nuisance where a landowner's diversion of water floods a neighbor's property. Recently, the state adopted a regulation restricting construction in flood plains because development may aggravate flood conditions and damage public and private resources. A developer who purchased property before the new regulation is challenging it as a taking under *Lucas*. There are no nuisance cases on point dealing with construction in flood plains. Formulate an argument for the developer that the application of the regulation is a taking. Then formulate a counter argument for the State. Which position is stronger under *Lucas*? Is there a credible argument that *Lucas* doesn't apply?

---

2. The Public Trust Doctrine

Takings law seeks to protect the individual's private property interests against regulation advancing societal interests. By contrast, the public trust doctrine (explored in Chapter 8.II) protects the public's broad ecological needs by defining certain public property rights as taking precedence over private property rights. The intersection between the public trust doctrine and the takings doctrine is one of the most fascinating—and fluctuating—areas of natural resources ownership law.

ESPLANADE PROPERTIES v. CITY OF SEATTLE
United States Court of Appeals for the Ninth Circuit.
307 F.3d 978 (2002).

Plaintiff Esplanade Properties, LLC ("Esplanade") challenges the legality of the City of Seattle's ("the City's") denial of its application to develop shoreline property on Elliot Bay in Seattle, Washington. Esplanade contends that the City's action resulted in a complete deprivation of economic use of its property, constituting an inverse condemnation in violation of federal and state constitutional law....

In 1992, Esplanade began a long, and ultimately unsuccessful, process of attempting to secure permission to construct single-family residential housing on and over tidelands located below Magnolia bluff, near both a large city park and a large marina. The property ... is submerged completely for roughly half of the day, during which time it resembles a large sand bar. Esplanade purchased the property for $40,000 in 1991, and quickly retained a development team to design and secure permits for nine waterfront homes, each to be constructed on platforms supported by pilings. * * * None of [its permit] applications were ever approved. * * *

The Takings Clause of the Fifth Amendment prohibits the government from taking "private property ... for public use, without just compensation." U.S. CONST. amend. V. This clause prohibits "Government from forcing some people alone to bear public burdens which, in all fairness and justice, should be borne by the public as a whole." *Penn. Cent. Transp. Co. v. City of New York*, 438 U.S. 104, 123. * * * [U]nder the "categorical" takings doctrine articulated in *Lucas*, . . . [w]here a regulation "denies all economically beneficial or productive use of land," the multi-factor analysis established in *Penn Central* is not applied, and a compensable taking has occurred *unless* "the logically antecedent inquiry into the nature of the owner's estate shows that the proscribed use interests were not part of his title to begin with." *Lucas*, 505 U.S. at 1027. In other words, for a government entity to avoid liability, any "law or decree" depriving the property owner of all economically beneficial use of her property "must inhere in the title itself, in the restrictions that background principles of the State's law of property and nuisance already place upon land ownership." 505 U.S. at 1029.

Here, the district court found ... that the background principles of Washington law, specifically the public trust doctrine, burdened plaintiff's property and precluded Esplanade from prevailing in a takings action against the City. * * *

In this case, the "restrictions that background principles" of Washington law place upon such ownership are found in the public trust doctrine. As the Washington Supreme Court recently explained, the "state's ownership of tidelands and shorelands is comprised of two distinct aspects—the *jus privatum* and the *jus publicum.*" *State v. Longshore*, 5 P.3d 1256, 1262 (Wash. 2000). Relevant here, the "jus publicum, or public trust doctrine, is the right 'of navigation, together with its incidental rights of fishing, boating, swimming, water skiing, and other related recreational purposes generally regarded as corollary to the right of navigation and the use of public waters.' " *Id*. The "doctrine reserves a public property interest, the jus publicum, in tidelands and the waters flowing over them, despite the sale of these lands into private ownership." * * *

It is beyond cavil that "a public trust doctrine has always existed in Washington." *Orion Corp.*, 747 P.2d at 1072 (citing *Caminiti*, 732 P.2d at 994). The doctrine is "partially encapsulated in the language of [Washington's] constitution which reserves state ownership in 'the beds and shores of all navigable waters in the state.' " The doctrine is also reflected in Washington's Shoreline Management Act ("SMA"), adopted in 1971. RCW §§ 90.58.010–.930.[3] Following a long history "favoring the sale of tidelands and shorelands," resulting in the privatization of approximately 60 percent of the tidelands and 30 percent of the shorelands originally owned by the state, *Caminiti*, 732 P.2d at 996, the Washington legislature found that the SMA was necessary because "unrestricted construction on the privately owned or public owned shorelines ... is not in the best public interest." RCW 90.58.020.

The public trust doctrine, reflected in part in the SMA, unquestionably burdens Esplanade's property. We agree with the district court ... that Washington's public trust doctrine ran with the title to the tideland properties and alone precluded the shoreline residential development proposed by Esplanade. In *Orion*, the plaintiff corporation, prior to the enactment of the SMA, ... proposed dredging and filling of [Padilla] Bay to create a significant residential community. In addressing plaintiff's challenge to subsequent local and state environmental regulations, ... the court decided that the tidelands of the Bay were burdened by the public trust doctrine prior to the enactment of the SMA. At the time of Orion's purchase, "Orion could make no use of the tidelands which would substantially impair the [public] trust." 747 P.2d at 1073. * * * We find that the development proposed by Esplanade would suffer the same fate under the public trust doctrine as the project proposed by Orion Corp.

Esplanade's argument that *Orion* lacks authority, following the Court's decision in *Lucas*, is without merit. *Lucas*, while articulating an expansive concept of what constitutes a regulatory taking, effectively

---

3. The district court erred in stating that "whatever public trust doctrine existed prior to the enactment of the SMA has been superceded and the SMA is now the declaration of that doctrine." The doctrine itself is reflected *in* the SMA, but is not superseded *by* it, as made clear by the Washington Supreme Court in *Orion*, 747 P.2d at 1073 n. 11 ("We have observed that trust principles are *reflected* in the SMA's underlying policy....") (emphasis added).

recognized the public trust doctrine: "Any [regulation that prohibits all economically beneficial use of land] ... must inhere in the title itself, in the restrictions that background principles of the State's law of property and nuisance already place upon land ownership." 505 U.S. at 1029, n. 16. *Lucas* does nothing to disturb *Orion's* application of Washington's public trust doctrine. * * *

As the district court correctly noted, "Esplanade ... took the risk," when it purchased this large tract of tidelands in 1991 for only $40,000, "that, despite extensive federal, state, and local regulations restricting shoreline development, it could nonetheless overcome those numerous hurdles to complete its project and realize a substantial return on its limited initial investment. Now, having failed ... it seeks indemnity from the City." The takings doctrine does not supply plaintiff with such a right to indemnification. * * *

STEVENS v. CITY OF CANNON BEACH
Supreme Court of Oregon.
317 Ore. 131, 854 P.2d 449 (1993).

* * * Plaintiffs own two vacant lots in the dry sand area of the City of Cannon Beach (city). They applied to defendants city and Oregon Department of Parks and Recreation (department) for permits to build a seawall as part of the eventual development of the lots for motel or hotel use. City and department denied the application on a number of grounds. Plaintiffs then brought this inverse condemnation action, alleging ... a taking of plaintiff's property rights in violation of the Fifth Amendment of the United States Constitution. * * * [The decision of this court in *State ex. Rel. Thornton v. Hay*, 462 P.2d 671 (Or. 1960) stated]:

> The disputed area [dry sand area] is *sui generis*. While the fore-shore is "owned" by the state, and the upland is "owned" by the pat-entee or record title holder, neither can be said to "own" the full bundle of rights normally connoted by the term "estate in fee simple." * * * The rule in this case, based upon custom, is salutary in confirming a public right, and at the same time it takes from no man anything which he has had a legitimate reason to regard as exclusively his.

* * * [P]laintiffs argue that ... because they acquired their property before this court's 1969 decision in *Thornton*, the rule from *Thornton* may not be applied retroactively to them.[1] * * * Defendants argue that, because under the state property law doctrine of custom, the proscribed use interests in this case were not part of plaintiffs' title, there is no taking under *Lucas*. * * * *Thornton*, defendants argue, did not create a new legal principle, but merely applied an existing legal principle of easement by custom grounded in Oregon's property law. * * *

---

1. The date of the *Thornton* decision is not relevant. Rather, the question is when, under *Thornton's* reasoning, *the public rights came into being*. The answer is that that they came into being long before plaintiffs acquired any interests in their land.

The parties recognize, and we agree, that *Thornton* is directly on point. The issue, therefore, is the viability of *Thornton's* rule of law in the light of *Lucas*. * * * The facts in this case and in *Thornton* are remarkably similar. In each case, the landowners wished to enclose the dry sand area of their Cannon Beach properties, thereby excluding the public from that portion of the ocean shore. In *Thornton*, this court held that the state could prevent such enclosures because, throughout Oregon's history, the dry sand area customarily had been used by the public:

> The dry-sand area in Oregon has been enjoyed by the general public as a recreational adjunct of the wet-sand or foreshore area since the beginning of the state's political history. The first European settlers on these shores found the aboriginal inhabitants using the foreshore for clam digging and the dry-sand area for their cooking fires. The newcomers continued these customs after statehood. Thus, from the time of the earliest settlement to the present day, the general public has assumed that the dry-sand area was a part of the public beach, and the public has used the dry-sand area for picnics, gathering wood, building warming fires, and generally as a headquarters from which to supervise children or to range out over the foreshore as the tides advance and recede. * * *

> Perhaps one explanation for the evolution of the custom of the public to use the dry-sand area for recreational purposes is that the area could not be used conveniently by its owners for any other purpose. The dry-sand area is unstable in its seaward boundaries, unsafe during winter storms, and for the most part unfit for the construction of permanent structures. *Thornton, supra.* * * *

We now turn to the determination of what effect the Supreme Court's opinion in *Lucas* has on Oregon's well-established policy of public access to and protection of its ocean shores.... * * *

The *Lucas* Court addressed a state's sudden elimination of all economically valuable use of land without compensation, holding that:

> Any limitation so severe [as to prohibit all economically beneficial use of land] cannot be newly legislated or decreed (without compensation), but must inhere in the title itself, in the restrictions that background principles *of the State's law of property* and nuisance already place upon land ownership. *Id.*, 120 L Ed 2d at 821 (emphasis added). * * *

Applying the *Lucas* analysis to this case, we conclude that the common-law doctrine of custom as applied to Oregon's ocean shores in *Thornton* is not "newly legislated or decreed"; to the contrary, to use the words of the *Lucas* court, it "inhere[s] in the title itself, in the restrictions that background principles of the State's law of property and nuisance already placed upon land ownership." *Id.* at 821. Plaintiffs' argument that a "retroactive" application of the *Thornton* rule to their property is unconstitutional, is not persuasive. *Thornton* did not create a new rule of law and apply it retroactively to the land at issue in that case.... *Thornton* merely enunciated one of Oregon's "background principles of * * * the law of property." *Lucas, supra*, 120 L Ed 2d at 821. * * *

When plaintiffs took title to their land, they were on notice that exclusive use of the dry sand areas was not a part of the "bundle of rights" that they acquired, because public use of dry sand areas "is so notorious that notice of the custom on the part of persons buying land along the shore must be presumed." *Thornton, supra*, 254 Or. at 598. * * * We, therefore, hold that the doctrine of custom as applied to public use of Oregon's dry sand areas is one of "the restrictions that background principles of the State's law of property * * * already place upon land ownership." *Lucas, supra*, 120 L Ed 2d at 821. We hold that plaintiffs have never had the property interests that they claim were taken by defendants' decision and regulations.

Notes and Questions

1. As society destroys more wetlands, water sources, and species habitat, will the need for ecological services on remaining lands increase? If so, will the public trust doctrine expand to protect these parcels? How will that expansion affect takings law under *Lucas*?

2. Many courts have emphasized the need for flexibility to allow the public trust doctrine to adjust to new societal needs; thus the doctrine is often applied to newly arising circumstances that have no close precedent in the caselaw. *See* Chapter 8.II. Do the *Esplanade* and *Stevens* cases indicate that courts will allow new iterations of the public trust doctrine to defeat takings claims?

3. The U.S. Supreme Court rejected certiorari in the *Stevens* case. In his dissent to the Court's denial of certiorari, Justice Scalia acknowledged that "the Constitution leaves the law of real property to the States," but declared that a state may not invoke "nonexistent rules of state substantive law" to defeat a takings claim: "Our opinion in *Lucas* * * * would be a nullity if anything that a state court chooses to denominate 'background law'— regardless of whether it is really such—could eliminate property rights." 114 S.Ct. at 1334. Did the Supreme Court of Oregon have a principled basis upon which to find that the doctrine of custom applied to the open sandy beach along the Pacific Ocean or did the court simply draw new law out of thin air?

4. For an argument that the wildlife trust joins the public trust doctrine in defeating takings claims under *Lucas, see* Hope M. Babcock, *Should Lucas v. South Carolina Coastal Council Protect Where the Wild Things Are? Of Beavers, Bob-o-Links, and Other Things that Go Bump in the Night*, 85 Iowa Law Rev. 849 (2000).

5. Professor James Huffman has criticized use of the public trust doctrine as a tool to defeat takings claims. *See* James L. Huffman, *Avoiding the*

Takings Clause Through the Myth of Public Rights: the Public Trust and Reserved Rights Doctrines at Work, 3 J. LAND USE & ENVTL. L. 171, 211–212 (1987):

> [T]he public interest will be served by reliance on a private property system for the allocation of scarce resources. * * * To the extent that we believe that private decisions will optimize the social benefits we can derive from our scarce resources, we should be concerned about judicial doctrines which alter private rights with impunity. * * *
>
> The central concern should be with the public trust doctrine which threatens to grow out of control. * * * Rather than a protection of long-recognized public rights, which it was, it has become a means for the states to regulate and take private property without having to give even passing consideration to the fifth amendment. The takings clause is circumvented by relying on the fiction that newly created public rights existed prior to the vesting of any private rights.
>
> If the state can take private rights without compensation by relying on the myth of the public trust doctrine, there will be little reason for the courts to insist on compensation when the state pursues the same ends through the police power. The next logical step will surely be to equate the state's police power with its responsibilities as a trustee and thus avoid the fifth amendment entirely.

3. *Partial Takings: The Tahoe–Sierra Holding*

A core inquiry in both the *Lucas* and *Pennsylvania Central* test is determining the proportionate amount of land affected by the regulation. This is often called the "denominator problem." *See* Keystone Bituminous Coal Ass'n v. DeBenedictis, 480 U.S. 470, 497, 107 S.Ct. 1232, 1249, 94 L.Ed.2d 472, 498 (1987) ("[O]ur test for regulatory taking requires us to compare the value that has been taken from the property with the value that remains in the property, [and] one of the critical questions is determining how to define the unit of property whose value is to furnish the denominator of the fraction."). If, for example, a landowner has a 20-acre parcel, and a wetlands regulation prohibits development on five of those 20 acres, should the court consider the entire parcel as a whole in assessing the impact of the regulation, or should it focus on merely the part affected? The inquiry makes a critical difference in takings analysis. If the parcel as a whole is analyzed, then the regulation affects just 25% of it, leaving 75% of it available for development. *Lucas* would not apply because, under this analysis, there is no deprivation of *all* economically viable use. And under the *Penn. Central* test, the first factor (diminution in value) could focus on the 75% remaining usable land. If, however, the court totally disregarded the portion of developable land remaining and just focused on the five acres affected, the takings analysis would find total deprivation of economic use of those five acres, and *Lucas* would automatically apply with its *per se* rule of compensation. Under this approach to the takings inquiry, virtually all property regulation would be captured in *Lucas's* "categorical takings" net. The urge to disregard the parcel as a whole and focus on just the part affected has become known as "partial takings analysis."

Partial takings analysis was squarely rejected by the Supreme Court in *Penn Central*, where Justice Brennan wrote:

> Taking jurisprudence does not divide a single parcel into discrete segments and attempt to determine whether rights in a particular segment have been entirely abrogated. In deciding whether a particular governmental action has effected a taking, this Court focuses rather both on the character of the action and on the nature and extent of the interference with rights in the parcel as a whole....

Penn Cent. Transp. Co. v. City of New York, 438 U.S. 104, 131–32, 98 S.Ct. 2646, 2662–63, 57 L.Ed.2d 631, 652–53 (1978).

See also Concrete Pipe & Products of California, Inc. v. Construction Laborers Pension Trust for Southern California, 508 U.S. 602, 644, 113 S.Ct. 2264, 2290, 124 L.Ed.2d 539, 578 (1993) ("[I]n *Penn Central Transp. Co. v. New York City,* we held that [a claimant's parcel of property could not first be divided into what was taken and what was left] for the purpose of demonstrating the taking of the former to be complete and hence compensable.... [T]he relevant question ... is whether the property taken is all, or only a portion of, the parcel in question."). Nevertheless, Professor Richard Epstein has persistently urged a partial takings analysis:

> [T]he issue of partial restrictions on land use looms, unresolved, on the horizon. * * * Only one thing is relevant: The greater the taking, the greater the payment. What is taken is what counts; what is retained, or the ratio between retained and taken property, is irrelevant.... [The] line between total and partial takings is relevant only to the question of how much compensation is required, not to whether there is a basic obligation to compensate. * * * [O]nce the Court lets it be known that a value deprivation of 95% requires no compensation, what legislature will be foolish enough to take an entire plot of land? Consequently, the Court has provided an effective blueprint for confiscation that budget-conscious state legislators will be eager to follow to the letter.

Richard A. Epstein, *Lucas v. South Carolina Coastal Council: A Tangled Web of Expectations*, 45 Stan. L. Rev. 1369, 1375–77 (1993).

Despite the Court's earlier pronouncements rejecting partial takings analysis, the theory seemed to gain favor with at least some justices on the Supreme Court. Footnote 7 of Justice Scalia's opinion in *Lucas, supra,* alluded to the theory. But in Palazzolo v. Rhode Island, 533 U.S. 606, 121 S.Ct. 2448, 150 L.Ed.2d 592 (2001), the Court refused to "conceptually sever" the burdened portion of the parcel from the remaining portion. The Court stated:

> Petitioner [argued] that the upland parcel is distinct from the wetlands portions, so he should be permitted to assert a deprivation

limited to the latter. This contention asks us to examine the difficult, persisting question of what is the proper denominator in the takings fraction. Some of our cases indicate that the extent of deprivation effected by a regulatory action is measured against the value of the parcel as a whole, *see, e.g., Keystone Bituminous Coal Assn.* v. *DeBenedictis,* 480 U.S. 470, 497 (1987); but we have at times expressed discomfort with the logic of this rule, see *Lucas, supra,* at 1016–1017, n. 7.... Whatever the merits of these criticisms, we will not explore the point here. * * * The case comes to us on the premise that petitioner's entire parcel serves as the basis for his takings claim, and, so framed, the total deprivation argument fails. * * *

533 U.S. at 631–32. *See* Michael C. Blumm, *Palazzolo and the Decline of Justice Scalia's Categorical Takings Doctrine,* 30 B.C. ENVTL. AFF. L. REV. 137, 138–39 (2002) ("*Palazzolo* ... signals that the categorical approach to takings cases championed by Justice Scalia in his *Lucas* decision no longer commands a majority of the Court.").

In 2002, the Supreme Court squarely addressed the partial takings theory in the context of a temporary moratorium on development near Lake Tahoe. The district court's opinion described the context at some length. The court noted that Lake Tahoe was "uniquely beautiful," 34 F.Supp.2d 1226, 1230 (D. Nev. 1999); the clarity of its waters was " 'not *merely* transparent, but dazzlingly, brilliantly so.' " *Id.* (quoting Mark Twain, ROUGHING IT 174–175 (1872)). Lake Tahoe's exceptional clarity was attributed to a lack of algae that fouls the waters of many other lakes. The court noted, however, that the lake's pristine state had deteriorated significantly over the past 40 years due to increased land development in the Lake Tahoe Basin. The upsurge of development caused "increased nutrient loading of the lake largely because of the increase in impervious coverage of land in the Basin.... " *Id.* Indeed, "unless the process is stopped, the lake will lose its clarity and its trademark blue color, becoming green and opaque for eternity." *Id.* To address these problems, a regional planning agency imposed a development moratorium, which was challenged in the case below. Chapter 10.IV.B describes the Tahoe planning process in more detail.

TAHOE–SIERRA PRESERVATION COUNCIL v. TAHOE REGIONAL PLANNING AGENCY
Supreme Court of the United States.
535 U.S. 302 (2002).

JUSTICE STEVENS delivered the opinion of the Court.

The question presented is whether a moratorium on development imposed during the process of devising a comprehensive land-use plan constitutes a *per se* taking of property requiring compensation under the Takings Clause of the United States Constitution. This case actually involves two moratoria ordered by respondent Tahoe Regional Planning Agency (TRPA) to maintain the status quo while studying the impact of development on Lake Tahoe and designing a strategy for environmentally sound growth. * * * As a result of these two directives, virtually all development on a substantial portion of the property subject to TRPA's jurisdiction was prohibited for a period of 32 months. * * *

The petitioners include the Tahoe Sierra Preservation Council, a nonprofit membership corporation representing about 2,000 owners of both improved and unimproved parcels of real estate in the Lake Tahoe Basin, and a class of some 400 individual owners of vacant lots.... * * *

Petitioners make only a facial attack on Ordinance 81–5 and Resolution 83–21. They contend that the mere enactment of a temporary regulation that, while in effect, denies a property owner all viable economic use of her property gives rise to an unqualified constitutional obligation to compensate her for the value of its use during that period. Hence, they "face an uphill battle" that is made especially steep by their desire for a categorical rule requiring compensation whenever the government imposes such a moratorium on development. Under their proposed rule, there is no need to evaluate the landowners' investment-backed expectations, the actual impact of the regulation on any individual, the importance of the public interest served by the regulation, or the reasons for imposing the temporary restriction. For petitioners, it is enough that a regulation imposes a temporary deprivation—no matter how brief—of all economically viable use to trigger a *per se* rule that a taking has occurred. * * *

When the government physically takes possession of an interest in property for some public purpose, it has a categorical duty to compensate the former owner, regardless of whether the interest that is taken constitutes an entire parcel or merely a part thereof. * * * But a government regulation that merely ... bans certain private uses of a portion of an owner's property ... does not constitute a categorical taking. * * * Land-use regulations are ubiquitous and most of them impact property values in some tangential way—often in completely unanticipated ways. Treating them all as *per se* takings would transform government regulation into a luxury few governments could afford. By contrast, physical appropriations are relatively rare, easily identified, and usually represent a greater affront to individual property rights. * * *

[Petitioners] rely principally on our decision in *Lucas v. South Carolina Coastal Council,* 505 U.S. 1003 (1992)—a regulatory takings case that, nevertheless, applied a categorical rule—to argue that the *Penn Central* framework is inapplicable here. * * * As we noted in *Lucas,* it was Justice Holmes' opinion in *Pennsylvania Coal Co. v. Mahon* ... that "if regulation goes too far it will be recognized as a taking." * * *

[O]ur decision in *Lucas* is not dispositive of the question presented. * * * The categorical rule that we applied in *Lucas* states that compensation is required when a regulation deprives an owner of "*all* economically beneficial uses" of his land. *Id.* at 1019. Under that rule, a statute that "wholly eliminated the value" of Lucas' fee simple title clearly qualified as a taking. But our holding was limited to "the extraordinary circumstance when *no* productive or economically beneficial use of land is permitted." *Id.* at 1017. The emphasis on the word "no" in the text of the opinion was, in effect, reiterated in a footnote explaining that the categorical rule would not apply if the diminution in value were 95% instead of 100%. *Id.* at 1019, n. 8. Anything less than a "complete elimination of value," or a "total loss," the Court acknowledged, would require the kind of analysis applied in *Penn Central.* * * *

Petitioners seek to bring this case under the rule announced in *Lucas* by arguing that we can effectively sever a 32–month segment from the remainder of each landowner's fee simple estate, and then ask whether that segment has been taken in its entirety by the moratoria. Of course, defining the property interest taken in terms of the very regulation being challenged is circular. With property so divided, every delay would become a total ban; the moratorium and the normal permit process alike would constitute categorical takings. Petitioners' "conceptual severance" argument is unavailing because it ignores *Penn Central's* admonition that in regulatory takings cases we must focus on "the parcel as a whole." 438 U.S. at 130–131. We have consistently rejected such an approach to the "denominator" question. * * * Thus, the District Court erred when it disaggregated petitioners' property into temporal segments corresponding to the regulations at issue and then analyzed whether petitioners were deprived of all economically viable use during each period. The starting point for the court's analysis should have been to ask whether there was a total taking of the entire parcel; if not, then *Penn Central* was the proper framework. * * *

Logically, a fee simple estate cannot be rendered valueless by a temporary prohibition on economic use, because the property will recover value as soon as the prohibition is lifted. * * *

In rejecting petitioners' *per se* rule, we do not hold that the temporary nature of a land-use restriction precludes finding that it effects a taking; we simply recognize that it should not be given exclusive significance one way or the other. * * * [M]oratoria like Ordinance 81–5 and Resolution 83–21 are used widely among land-use planners to preserve the status quo while formulating a more permanent development strategy. In fact, the consensus in the planning community appears to be that moratoria, or "interim development controls" as they are often called, are an essential tool of successful development. * * *

The interest in facilitating informed decision making by regulatory agencies counsels against adopting a *per se* rule that would impose such severe costs on their deliberations. Otherwise, the financial constraints of compensating property owners during a moratorium may force officials to rush through the planning process or to abandon the practice altogether. To the extent that communities are forced to abandon using moratoria, landowners will have incentives to develop their property quickly before a comprehensive plan can be enacted, thereby fostering inefficient and ill-conceived growth. * * *

It may well be true that any moratorium that lasts for more than one year should be viewed with special skepticism. But given the fact that the District Court found that the 32 months required by TRPA to formulate the 1984 Regional Plan was not unreasonable, we could not possibly conclude that every delay of over one year is constitutionally unacceptable. Formulating a general rule of this kind is a suitable task for state legislatures. In our view, the duration of the restriction is one of the important factors that a court must consider in the appraisal of a regulatory takings claim, but with respect to that factor as with respect to other factors, the "temptation to adopt what amount to *per se* rules in either direction must be resisted." *Palazzolo,* 533 U.S. at 636 (O'CONNOR, J., concurring). * * * We conclude, therefore, that the interest in "fairness and justice" will be best served by relying on the familiar *Penn Central* approach when deciding cases like this, rather than by attempting to craft a new categorical rule.

[Dissents omitted]

Notes and Questions

1.   Though the Supreme Court in *Tahoe–Sierra* dealt with the issue of partial takings on the temporal scale, did it also put to rest the issue of partial takings as measured on the physical scale (referred to as the "denominator" problem)? After *Tahoe–Sierra*, can a developer who is precluded from destroying 20 acres of wetlands claim a total taking of that 20 acres if she has 10 remaining acres available for development activities?

2.   Could a savvy developer who is knowledgeable about takings doctrine create a takings claim by sub-dividing his lot into two pieces—one piece consisting of the acreage burdened by the regulation, and the other consisting of the unburdened acreage? Does the doctrine account for such conceivable manipulation?

3.   For different perspectives on *Tahoe–Sierra* from leading scholars in the takings field, *see* Richard J. Lazarus, *Celebrating Tahoe–Sierra*, 33 ENVTL. L. 1 (2003); and Richard A. Epstein, *The Ebbs and Flows in Takings Law: Reflections on the Lake Tahoe Case,* SHO25 ALI–ABI 247 (2002).

In Focus: Oregon's Takings Statute—Measure 37

The State of Oregon has long been viewed as a leader in land use planning and "smart growth." But in November, 2004, Oregon voters passed Measure 37, the most extreme regulatory takings measure in the nation. The measure provides a right of compensation for partial takings and waives the land use restriction if compensation is not paid. The official ballot statement accompanying Measure 37 explained:

[T]he owner of private real property is entitled to receive just compensation when a land use regulation is enacted after the owner or a family member became the owner of the property if the regulation restricts the use of the property and reduces its fair market value. If a property owner proves that a land use regulation restricts the use of the owner's property, and reduces its value, then the government responsible for the regulation will have a choice: pay the owner of the property an amount equal to the reduction in value or modify, change or not apply the regulation to the owner's property.

The editorial below summarizes objections to Measure 37.

GUEST VIEWPOINT: OREGONIANS WILL REGRET MEASURE 37

Liam Sherlock

THE EUGENE REGISTER–GUARD, Feb. 3, 2005

[M]indless strip malls and endless subdivisions mutate landscapes throughout much of the rest of this country. * * * [Yet, Oregon] create[d] the most advanced land-use system in the nation. These laws upheld ... livable communities, public participation, fairness, and a high quality of life.

Proponents of Ballot Measure 37 won last November by arguing that a person whose property loses value as a result of any zoning laws enacted in the past, present or future should be compensated. Voters probably thought this sounded reasonable. What got lost in the rhetoric, however, is that most towns and counties can't afford to pay the compensation that will be demanded by Measure 37 claimants. Local governments will then have to waive enforcement of the zoning law at issue.

Measure 37 will benefit few and harm many. Our much lauded and respected approach to community planning and natural resource protection will soon start to unravel like a moth-eaten sweater. * * * Measure 37 claims ... are unfair to neighbors, are destructive to our communities and natural resources, and are offensive to the commonweal of Oregonians.

For example, under Measure 37, a couple that has lived and raised a family in a small-town neighborhood for the last 15 years may wake up one morning to find that a neighbor is, without notice or warning, converting his property into a commercial dog kennel. He can do this because he bought his property 30 years ago—before the residential zone was created. Because the town could not afford to pay his Measure 37 claim for compensation, it was forced to grant him a waiver of the residential restrictions. The couple then discovers that, with the kennel, their property value (and that of the six other families on the block) has plummeted by 30 percent.

But Measure 37 does not speak to their losses. One benefits, all the rest suffer.

Another terrible cost of Measure 37 is the dismantling of public participation in Oregon's land use system. In accord with our best democratic traditions, Oregon's prior land-use process allowed competing views to be heard and evaluated before decisions were made. Today's Measure 37 claimants had an equal opportunity to argue against the adoption of land-use laws they can now circumvent simply by writing a claim letter to the enforcing jurisdiction.

In contrast, Measure 37 includes no due-process requirement that potentially affected neighbors receive notice of compensation claims or zoning waiver requests. Unless local governments, the state Legislature or the courts correct this unfair omission, neighbors of Measure 37 claimants will have no opportunity to weigh in on whether a town or county should pay compensation or grant a waiver to allow an incompatible land use.

Measure 37 also has a profound chilling effect on future planning laws and regulations. If any city or county now enacts an ordinance to protect natural resources, open spaces and scenic and historic areas, a whole new series of Measure 37 claims will spring into being. We are unlikely to see the enactment of new land use laws, even if community needs or circumstances cry out for them. * * *

By providing retroactive windfalls to property owners who happened to buy their land before the enactment of land-use laws, we have created a Frankenstein's monster. Under Measure 37, we taxpayers will either have to pay ... to Measure 37 claimants, thereby forfeiting funds needed for public services such as schools, road repair, libraries and parks [or] else we can watch as claimants build incompatible developments that diminish the livability and property values of neighborhoods and communities.

Notes and Questions

1. Recall Justice Holmes' often quoted statement from Pennsylvania Coal Co. v. Mahon, 260 U.S. 393, 415, 43 S.Ct. 158, 160, 67 L.Ed. 322, 326 (1922), that "[g]overnment hardly could go on" if it had to pay every property owner for diminishment in property values caused by regulation. *Id.* at 413. State and local government will not be able to afford the compensation required by Measure 37. What then? Under Measure 37, regulation ends with respect to those parcels subject to claims. Can government so abdicate its police powers to protect the health and welfare of its citizens through regulation? One circuit court judge has held Measure 37 invalid, partly because it impairs the legislative body's inherent police power to govern. MacPherson v. Dept. of Administrative Services, Case No. 00C15769, slip op. at 10–12 (Cir. Ct. Or. Oct. 15, 2005) ("Measure 37 requires the goverment to pay if it wants to enforce valid, previously enacted, land use regulations, i.e. it must pay to govern.") The decision, which has been appealed, is available at http://www.ojd.state.or.us/mar/documents/measure37_ 000.pdf.

2. Shortly after the measure took effect, a flood of claims inundated city and county offices across Oregon. In Hood River County, for example, an orchard owner submitted a $57 million claim to build homes on 842 acres of pear orchards. Some cities, such as Eugene, Oregon, have responded to Measure 37 with a surprising twist: they have created (in their Measure 37 implementing ordinances) a private cause of action allowing neighbors to sue developers for damages and legal costs in instances where their property is devalued as a result of development arising from Measure 37 claims. *See* Alan Pittmann, *Unraveling Measure 37*, EUGENE WEEKLY 14 (Dec. 2, 2004).

3. Strongly held views of individual liberty permeate the Measure 37 debate in Oregon. In Yamhill County, one County Commissioner declared during a claims hearing: "Measure 37 restores a right.... In the United States, in our free country, most people would agree rights are not subject to the permission of a governing body. Rights are not subject to community approval, either." *See* Laura Oppenheimer, *Measure 37 Exposes Nerves*, THE OREGONIAN, Feb. 02, 2005 (quoting Commissioner Kathy George). Does this statement truly reflect the legal tradition of the United States or is it exaggerated rhetoric?

4. Chapter 10.III, *infra*, on Land Use Regulation, provides the full text of Measure 37.

C. Hybrid Takings

Apart from physical and regulatory takings, a third category of cases can be pulled from the Court's tangled takings jurisprudence. These cases might be called "hybrid" cases because they involve physical exactions of property, or core sticks of the property bundle, as a condition for allowing development within a regulatory scheme. Consider a property owner who wants to develop two acres for home sites and applies for a permit from the City. Assume the City could deny the permit in full based on impacts to wetlands, but instead decides to allow the development on the condition that the landowner conveys to the City an easement allowing public access across a portion of the wetlands. The conveyance of an access easement amounts to a conveyance of a core stick in the bundle and seemingly implicates the Court's physical takings jurisprudence. But because the conveyance is a condition of the City's application of its regulations, there is a fair dose of regulatory takings as well. The combination of the exaction and the regulatory framework makes this a hybrid situation. Though the Court has not specifically used the term "hybrid" to earmark these cases, it has formulated very specific rules in this context through two landmark opinions, Nollan v. California Coastal Comm'n, 483 U.S. 825, 835, 107 S.Ct. 3141, 3148, 97 L.Ed.2d 677, 688 (1987) and Dolan v. City of Tigard, 512 U.S. 374, 114 S.Ct. 2309, 129 L.Ed.2d 304 (1994).

NOLLAN v. CALIFORNIA COASTAL COMMISSION

Supreme Court of the United States.

483 U.S. 825 (1987).

JUSTICE SCALIA delivered the opinion of the Court.

The Nollans own a beachfront lot in Ventura County, California. A quarter-mile north of their property is Faria County Park, an oceanside public park with a public beach and recreation area. Another public beach area, known locally as "the Cove," lies 1,800 feet south of their lot. A concrete seawall approximately eight feet high separates the beach portion of the Nollans' property from the rest of the lot. The historic mean high tide line determines the lot's oceanside boundary. The Nollans [sought] to demolish [their] bungalow and replace it. In order to do so, ... they were required to obtain a coastal development permit from the California Coastal Commission. [The] Commission staff ... recommended that the permit be granted subject to the condition that [the Nollans] allow the public an easement to pass across a portion of their property bounded by the mean high tide line on one side, and their seawall on the other side. This would make it easier for the public to get to Faria County Park and the Cove. * * *.

[T]he Commission ... found that the new house would increase blockage of the view of the ocean, thus contributing to the development of "a 'wall' of residential structures" that would prevent the public "psychologically ... from realizing a stretch of coastline exists nearby that they have every right to visit." The new house would also increase private use of the shorefront. These effects of construction of the house, along with other area development, would cumulatively "burden the public's ability to traverse to and along the shorefront." Therefore the Commission could properly require the Nollans to offset that burden by providing additional lateral access to the public beaches in the form of an easement across their property. * * *

Had California simply required the Nollans to make an easement across their beachfront available to the public on a permanent basis in order to increase public access to the beach, rather than conditioning their permit to rebuild their house on their agreeing to do so, we have no doubt there would have been a taking. * * * Indeed, one of the principal uses of the eminent domain power is to assure that the government be able to require conveyance of just such interests, so long as it pays for them. * * * Given, then, that requiring uncompensated conveyance of the easement outright would violate the Fourteenth Amendment, the question becomes whether requiring it to be conveyed as a condition for issuing a land-use permit alters the outcome. We have long recognized that land-use regulation does not effect a taking if it "substantially advance[s] legitimate state interests" and does not "den[y] an owner economically viable use of his land," *Agins* v. *Tiburon*, 447 U.S. 255, 260 (1980). * * *

The Commission argues that among these permissible purposes are protecting the public's ability to see the beach, assisting the public in overcoming the "psychological barrier" to using the beach created by a developed shorefront, and preventing congestion on the public beaches. We assume, without deciding, that this is so—in which case the Commission unquestionably would be able to deny the Nollans their permit outright if their new house ... would substantially impede these purposes, unless the denial would interfere so drastically with the Nollans' use of their property as to constitute a taking. *See Penn Central Transportation Co.* v. *New York City, supra.*

The Commission argues that a permit condition that serves the same legitimate police-power purpose as a refusal to issue the permit should not be found to be a taking if the refusal to issue the permit would not constitute a taking. We agree. Thus, if the Commission attached to the permit some condition that would have protected the public's ability to see the beach notwithstanding construction of the new house—for example, a height limitation, a width restriction, or a ban on fences—so long as the Commission could have exercised its police power (as we have assumed it could) to forbid construction of the house altogether, imposition of the condition would also be constitutional. Moreover (and here we come closer to the facts of the present case), the condition would be constitutional even if it consisted of the requirement that the Nollans provide a viewing spot on their property for passersby with whose sighting of the ocean their new house would interfere. Although such a requirement, constituting a permanent grant of continuous access to the property, would have to be considered a taking if it were not attached to a development permit, the Commission's assumed power to forbid construction of the house in order to protect the public's view of the beach must surely include the power to condition construction upon some concession by the owner, even a concession of property rights, that serves the same end. * * *

The evident constitutional propriety disappears, however, if the condition substituted for the prohibition utterly fails to further the end advanced as the justification for the prohibition. * * * [T]he lack of nexus between the condition and the original purpose of the building restriction converts that purpose to something other than what it was. The purpose then becomes, quite simply, the obtaining of an easement to serve some valid governmental purpose, but without payment of compensation. Whatever may be the outer limits of "legitimate state interests" in the takings and land-use context, this is not one of them. In short, unless the permit condition serves the same governmental purpose as the development ban, the building restriction is not a valid regulation of land use but "an out-and-out plan of extortion." * * *

The Nollans' new house, the Commission found, will interfere with "visual access" to the beach. * * * It is quite impossible to understand how a requirement that people already on the public beaches be able to walk across the Nollans' property reduces any obstacles to viewing the beach created by the new house. * * * If [California] wants an easement across the Nollan's property, it must pay for it.

Reversed.

In Focus: The Malibu Beach Conflict—A Takings Case Study

IN A BATTLE OVER ACCESS, COASTAL PANEL ORDERS AN END TO POSTINGS AND GUARDS AT BROAD BEACH
Kenneth R. Weiss
LOS ANGELES TIMES, July 10, 2004

Launching a summer campaign on behalf of public sunbathing, the California Coastal Commission has targeted one of Malibu's most exclusive strands, Broad Beach ... The commission, established decades ago to protect public beach access, has demanded that homeowners remove the "Private Property, Do Not Trespass" signs in the sand. It has also demanded the community discontinue motorized beach patrols.

And the commission took the unusual step this week of posting aerial photos with lot-by-lot descriptions on its website, detailing precisely the public access easements where beachgoers can legally drape their towels and plant their umbrellas.

The fight over Broad Beach is emerging as a classic clash between public access and private property rights of the area's homeowners, who include celebrities.... * * * Earlier this year, the homeowners group, the Trancas Property Owners Assn., filed a lawsuit challenging some of the public access easements, which it claimed were extracted by "coercion" in a manner that "shocks the conscience." * * *

The commission has begun its first wave of enforcement by sending letters to eight homeowners, asking each of them to remove the "Private Property" sign on the beach in front of their homes. * * * In one case, the property owner had agreed not to post any signs on his land [in] exchange for commission permission to demolish a home and build a new one four years ago. In the seven other cases, the signs are on properties on which the owners have granted easements providing public access in exchange for permits to build or remodel their homes. The public easements typically cover a swath of dry sand that extends 25 feet inland from the mean high-tide line. Everything seaward of that line [essentially the surf zone and the wet sand] allows unfettered public access because it is state tidelands. * * *

The battle at Broad Beach is different from skirmishes involving public access at other beaches. More common in California are disputes over "vertical" easements, which are paths across private prop-

erty to allow the public to get from the nearest road to the shoreline.
* * *

By contrast, getting to Broad Beach is easy. Its two county-owned pathways from the road were part of the original subdivision. Those narrow corridors set off by chains are virtually the only places on dry sand where the public can be without fear of being rousted.

The fight has centered on the "lateral" easements, which run along the shore and across the seaward edge of homeowners' yards. So far, 52 of the 108 lots at Broad Beach have such public easements, strips often 25 feet wide beginning at the mean high tide. They are intermittent, though, creating a confusing patchwork of public beach.
* * *

In its lawsuit, the Trancas Property Owners Assn., representing Broad Beach homeowners, claims the public easements are illegal. The lawsuit seeks to apply a 1987 U.S. Supreme Court decision that calls the commission's old requirements for these easements "an out-and-out plan of extortion." The court limited the demand for such easements to cases in which development could infringe on public access, such as a seawall built close to the surf.

In response to that ruling, the commission changed its practice. It offered property owners a choice: Voluntarily grant public easements to the state or go through the costly, time-consuming process of conducting studies that prove their proposed developments will not interfere with public access.

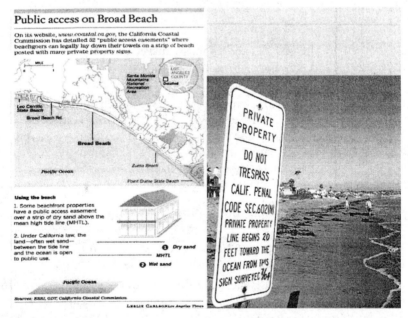

California Coastal Commission website explaining public access easements and picture of Broad Beach, reproduced by Los Angeles Times, July 10, 2004.

Notes and Questions

1.   According to the *Nollan* Court, the easement dedication did not meet the essential "nexus" test, which requires a direct, logical relationship between the easement and the purpose of the restriction. Could any other sort of easement have satisfied the essential "nexus" test?

2.   Could the Commission have denied the Nollan's permit application outright without risking a taking?

3.   Why didn't the Supreme Court in *Nollan* announce a rule barring *any* physical exactions as conditions for a building permit?

4.   Did the public have any pre-existing right to walk along the beach in the *Nollan* case? Explain in precise terms any rights the public had. Then, using the *Nollan* framework, analyze the California Coastal Commission's more recent campaign (*In Focus, above*) to provide public access to Broad Beach in Malibu. The Malibu conflict is further considered in In Focus, Chapter 10.V.

5.   If the *Nollan* case had occurred in Oregon instead of California, and the Coastal Commission had sought a recorded easement for the public to walk along the dry sand beach, how would you analyze the case, applying *Stevens v. Cannon Beach, supra*?

6.   In 1994, the Supreme Court added a second requirement to the hybrid takings test. Dolan v. City of Tigard, 512 U.S. 374, 114 S.Ct. 2309, 129 L.Ed.2d 304 (1994), involved a city's required dedication of land for flood control and traffic abatement as part of a condition for a building permit. The Court applied *Nollan* to find that the essential nexus existed between the dedication and the purposes of the permit. It then added:

> [O]ur analysis requires us to determine whether the degree of the exactions demanded by the city's permit conditions bears the required relationship to the projected impact of petitioner's proposed development. * * * We think a term such as "rough proportionality" best encapsulates what we hold to be the requirement of the Fifth Amendment. No precise mathematical calculation is required, but the city must make some sort of individualized determination that the required dedication is related both in nature and extent to the impact of the proposed development.

Dolan, supra, at 389. Following *Dolan*, government bears the initial burden of showing that the required dedication is "rough[ly] proportiona[l]" to the impacts of the proposed activity. This requirement seemingly applies across the broad spectrum of *hybrid* regulatory exactions occurring under local, state, and federal land use and environmental laws.

7.   In City of Monterey v. Del Monte Dunes, 526 U.S. 687, 702, 119 S.Ct. 1624, 1635, 143 L.Ed.2d 882, 900 (1999), the Court made clear that the *Nollan/Dolan* analysis does not apply to standard regulation, but is limited to the special context of exactions. *See id.* at 703 (noting the *Dolan* test was not designed to address, and is not readily applicable to, a case in which the "landowner's challenge is based not on excessive exactions but on denial of development").

8. Where do conservation easements fall in the realm of takings analysis? Assume the federal government conditions an incidental take permit (ITP) under section 10 of the Endangered Species Act on the conveyance of a conservation easement protecting certain parts of the habitat from development in perpetuity. Would you analyze this situation under *Nollan* and *Dolan*? It certainly would appear to fall under those cases, because the conservation easement removes a core stick in the bundle of property rights. One recent state court case, however, found that a required dedication of a conservation easement was not properly analyzed under those cases. *See* Smith v. Town of Mendon, 4 N.Y.3d 1, 789 N.Y.S.2d 696, 822 N.E.2d 1214 (2004) (reasoning that *Nollan* and *Dolan* apply only to conditions that affect the owner's right to exclude). The dissent argued, "[t]he majority is ... simply wrong when it asserts that the Town is not requiring a dedication of property to public use by mandating that the [owners] grant it a conservation easement, which is perpetual in duration, runs with the land, and is recorded." *Id.* at 20.

D. From Hobbesian Sticks to Lockean Bundles[a] and Beyond: Pulling it All Together

As you have no doubt noticed, takings jurisprudence is riddled with complexities. There is no dearth of commentary. For a sampling, *see* Joseph Sax, *Takings and the Police Power,* 74 YALE L. J. 36 (1964); Frank Michelman, *Property, Utility, and Fairness: Comments on the Ethical Foundations of "Just Compensation" Law*, 80 HARV. L. REV. 1165 (1967); RICHARD EPSTEIN, TAKINGS, PRIVATE PROPERTY AND THE POWER OF EMINENT DOMAIN (1985); Margaret Jane Radin, *The Liberal Conception of Property: Cross Currents in the Jurisprudence of Takings,* 88 COLUM. L. REV. 1667, 1676 (1988); Carol Rose, *Property Rights, Regulatory Regimes and the New Takings Jurisprudence—An Evolutionary Approach,* 57 TENN. L. REV. 577 (1990); Marc R. Poirier, *The Virtue of Vagueness in Takings Doctrine,* 24 CARDOZO L. REV. 93 (2002); Holly Doremus, *Takings and Transitions,* 19 J. LAND USE & ENVTL. L. 1 (2003); and Stewart E. Sterk, *The Federalist Dimension of Regulatory Takings Jurisprudence,* 114 YALE L. J. 203 (2004).

To provide a framework for understanding the field, the chart below summarizes the major holdings. But charts are naturally oversimplifications, and the one below is no substitute for the hard work of legal analysis, which requires reading all of the landmark cases in their entirety, some several times over.

---

a. *Palazzolo*, 533 U.S. at 627.

Type of Taking	Supreme Court Cases	Rule	

Physical	Loretto
	Miller v. Schoene
	Winans
	Illinois Central
	Lewis Blue
	  Point Oyster
	  Cultivation Co.
		Per se compensation requirement unless:
		1) public necessity; or
		2) antecedent sovereign property rights (such as treaty rights, public trust, navigational servitude)	

Regulatory	Pennsylvania Central Lucas	If regulation deprives land of "all economically beneficial use," apply *Lucas* to find per se taking *unless* the restrictions inhere in the title itself through background principles of nuisance or property law (public trust doctrine, navigational servitude, treaty rights, doctrine of custom)	If regulation does not deprive land of all economically viable use, apply *Pennsylvania Central* three-part balancing test: 1) character of the government action 2) diminution in property value 3) extent of interference with reasonable, investment-backed expectations
	Palazzolo	Post-enactment purchasers are not barred from asserting takings claims	
	Tahoe-Sierra	Temporary moratoriums are not per se takings	
	Lingle	*Penn Central* balancing test does not turn on whether the regulation in question "substantially advances" legitimate state interests	
Hybrid	Nollan	Essential "nexus" required between the legitimate state interest and the permit condition exacted by the government	
	Dolan	Exaction must be "roughly proportional" to the impact of the proposed development	

Exercise:

The Zollans own a 20–acre lot along a lovely river. It was densely forested when they bought the property, but they cleared 3 acres for a dwelling site. After building their house, members of the public habitually stopped on the road behind the house to look through the remaining clearing for a view of the river. Recently the Zollans submitted an application for a building permit to expand their house. The permit scheme has as one of its purposes "to preserve public views of waterways." The Zollan's expansion would cut off the public's view. The local agency has said it will grant the permit on the condition that the Zollans provide an easement for a narrow walking path alongside their house for the public to access the river from the road. There is no feasible alternative for a smaller expansion to preserve the view. The Zollans object to the easement condition and claim a taking. They point out that the public never had a view of the river before they created it by clearing trees and contend that the public has lost only the windfall created as a result of the Zollan's initial clearing.

Using analysis from *Nollan* and *Dolan*, *supra*, develop arguments on behalf of both the Zollans and the local agency.

III. CONSERVATION EASEMENTS

The failure of regulation to adequately protect natural resources on private lands, coupled with a growing threat of takings lawsuits fueled by the property rights movement, has spurred a dramatic growth in the use of property-based mechanisms to achieve conservation on private lands. Non-profit land trusts and governmental agencies are increasingly accepting fee title or conservation easements to protect private land in perpetuity. The grant of such fee or easements on the part of the landowner is entirely voluntary, often induced by significant tax incentives. In the case of a conservation easement, the property owner retains title to the land and may use it for any purpose not inconsistent with the easement. The easement represents an important "stick" in the bundle of property rights. The primary right acquired by the holder is the right to prevent certain uses on the property (for example, mining, construction, logging, and such). The holder typically also acquires limited rights of access to the property for purposes of inspection.

Conservation easements are flexible tools that are drafted to respond to the individual conservation needs of the parcel as well as the preferences of the owner. They may, but need not, provide public access. They may allow limited ground-disturbing activity such as grazing, farming and certain forms of logging if those uses are not inconsistent with the purposes of the easement. The easement may provide the holder the right to be directly involved in managing the property, or it may simply provide the right to enforce against specified activities on the land. The proliferation of conservation easements has resulted in specialized documents with myriad provisions tailored to the protection of wildlife habitat, rangeland, forests, and historic areas.

A. The Rise in Conservation Easements

Private conservation tools are now so prevalent that they amount to a "second generation" of environmental law, following the first generation of command and control regimes. Conservation trust strategies cause significant changes in the ownership of natural resources. Some land trusts transfer land they acquire in fee to a federal, state, or local public agency, thereby increasing the amount of public holdings in the United States.

Where a land trust retains fee title to property it acquires, the ownership amounts to a public/private ownership. It is private in the sense that it is not managed by any governmental agency. However, it is public in the sense that it must be managed according to the conservation purposes which are set out in the state law that makes the land trust a qualified holder of the property interest in the first place. The land trust's board of directors manages the property or easement in accordance with the trust's conservation mission. That ownership is much different than corporate ownership, which manages land for profit, or individual ownership, which is geared towards individual preferences.

If current growth rates are any indicator, land trusts will soon comprise a significant ownership sector in nearly every area of the nation. Land trust growth boomed in the 1980s and continued through the 1990s at an unprecedented rate. Between 1990 and 1994 alone, local and regional land trusts in the United States increased by 23.3%, averaging one new land trust per week. Today, there are more than 1,200 land trusts nationwide. By the end of year 2000, these land trusts had protected nearly 6.5 million acres of land. Of that total, 2.6 million acres is protected by conservation easements, which represents a marked increase over the amount of land (450,000 acres) protected by conservation easements in 1990. The number of easements represented by the currently protected acreage is 11,670, indicating the usefulness and popularity of this conservation tool. Through 1998, land trusts had transferred 2,487,000 acres of land to third parties, typically governmental agencies or other land trusts. The land trust movement has achieved dramatic conservation successes in particular states. In Vermont, 25 land trusts have collectively conserved over 7% of the entire state.

Land trusts represent a wide range of geographic scope and interest. Some are local, such as the McKenzie River Land Trust in Oregon, the Tennessee River Gorge Trust in Tennessee, the Desert Foothills Land Trust in Arizona, the Leelanau Conservancy in Michigan, and many others. Some are regional, such as the Natural Lands Trust in Pennsylvania, the Pacific Forest Trust in California, and the Appalachian Trail Conference Land Trust in West Virginia. Still others, such as The Nature Conservancy (TNC) and Trust for Public Lands (TPL), are national.

Websources:

The land trust movement is still very much a grassroots movement with little infrastructure. However, a national organization, the Land Trust Alliance (LTA), provides an umbrella of support and information and represents the interests of land trusts on national policy issues.

> The LTA also holds an annual land trust "rally" that features panels addressing practical topics ranging from enforcement to negotiation of documents, appraisal techniques, and finding a donor base. Much of the statistical information regarding the land trust movement is gained from an LTA survey performed in 2000, called the LTA Census, 2000. The website for the Land Trust Alliance is found at *www.lta.org*.

The explosion of land trusts in recent decades is attributable to new legislation on the state level. The common law simply did not recognize negative easements such as view easements and conservation easements. *See* Federico Cheever, *Public Good and Private Magic in the Law of Land Trusts and Conservation Easements: A Happy Present and a Troubled Future*, 73 Denv. U. L. Rev. 1077 (1996). A conservation easement, then, is generally valid only if it is recognized as a form of enforceable property right through state legislation. In 1981, the Uniform Conservation Easement Act (UCEA) was adopted by the National Conference on Uniform State Laws to stimulate conservation easement enabling legislation at the state level. By 1997, 16 states had adopted the UCEA outright, and several adopted a modified version. Some states had statutes that predated the UCEA. Today, only two states, North Dakota and Wyoming, have not adopted any conservation easement legislation at all.

In Practice:
State Variation in Conservation Easements

Overall, the state statutes vary considerably in what they allow conservation easements to protect. Some statutes are quite broad, spanning resources from air quality to architectural sites, to open spaces and natural areas. Others allow only limited protection for specified resources, such as agricultural land, historic sites, and water. *See* Todd D. Mayo, Protecting the Land: Conservation Easements, Past, Present, and Future 28–30 *Table 2.1* (Julie Ann Gustanski & Roderick H. Squires eds., Island Press 2000). The natural resource practitioner must consult state law to determine the parameters of a valid conservation easement (CE) in a particular state. The Uniform Conservation Easement Act states that a conservation easement can be for the following purposes: retaining or protecting natural, scenic, or open-space values; assuring the availability of agricultural, forest, or recreational use; protecting natural resources; maintaining or enhancing air or water quality; or preserving the historical, architectural, archaeological, or cultural aspects of real property. Uniform Conservation Easement Act § 1(1), 12 U.L.A. 170 (1996).

CORRALLING SPRAWL
Richard Mahler
LAND & PEOPLE 19–25
(Trust For Public Lands, April 26, 2002)

Jim Macfarlane stabs his index finger toward a honeycomb of condominiums that almost fills a secluded mountain canyon. "This is exactly what we do not want our ranch to become," the Salt Lake City businessman declares emphatically, as we drive past dozens of pastel-colored boxes that climb the steep hillsides. * * *

Within a few minutes, we have crossed the fence line separating Jeremy Ranch—a once-rustic homestead now filled with high-end condos, an upscale restaurant, and an 18–hole golf course—from the Macfarlanes' Peaceful Valley Ranch. The 7,300–acre property looks much the same as it did in 1847 when Brigham Young led the first party of Mormon settlers through this notch in the Wasatch Mountains east of Salt Lake City. Much of the craggy landscape is drop-dead beautiful: forested slopes, snow-capped peaks, and verdant valleys watered by rock-strewn streams. Leaving suburban development behind, we turn a corner and see a herd of elk browsing a sun-dappled meadow.

Hundreds of land-rich, cash-poor ranchers throughout the West have seen the unimaginable come true, finding themselves forced to sell land that has sustained their families for generations. They have watched helplessly as almost overnight their former pastures sprout houses, shopping centers, gas stations, and other fixtures of suburban life. The story is increasingly familiar: a landowner (or the landowner's heirs), faced with high taxes, hefty operating expenses, and declining livestock revenues, sells out to a developer, who quickly turns agricultural property into residential "ranchettes," which are then sold to eager buyers—many of them affluent urbanites eager to escape the crowded city. Such developments are often inappropriate for their environments and yield the same kind of urban sprawl that newcomers found so distasteful in the places they left. Such sprawl often changes dramatically the traditional economies and pastoral character of rural lands, while damaging the watershed function of the terrain, destroying wildlife habitat, and undermining traditional uses the land may have served for hunters, fishers, and woodcutters.

It's a growing phenomenon in the West. According to the most recent estimate of the U.S. Department of Agriculture, in 1997 agricultural land was being developed at a rate of 1.2 million acres annually, double the rate of only five years earlier. "Many of the West's big, family-owned ranches are on the brink of disappearing," says Deborah Frey-Love, Trust for Public Land's New Mexico state director, who oversaw the Peaceful Valley Ranch easement transaction two years ago. "It's make it or break it time for these folks," Love emphasizes. But there is hope. For an increasing number of these properties, an innovative and powerful tool is being used to thwart sprawl and preserve working ranches that honor conservation goals. By selling (rather than donating) "development rights" in perpetuity to a local public entity, such as a nonprofit land trust or government agency, a landowner can lower tax liabilities, receive enough money to stay in business, and protect land from the kinds of uses most likely to endanger its natural resources and ability to sustain a traditional way of life. Title to the property remains with the owner, whose ranching practices are subject to oversight by the holder of the conservation easement.

* * * The conservation easement on the [Peaceful Valley] ranch is held by the state's Department of Natural Resources, which works with [the family] in balancing the interests of livestock and the environment. Pasture rotation, for example, has helped the elk population grow large enough to justify selected culling by hunters, who pay for the privilege, thus helping sustain the ranch's cattle herd. * * *

Besides preserving a much-loved traditional way of life, preventing the break-up of large working ranches will protect an impressive view-shed, vital wildlife travel corridors, and prime habitat for elk, pronghorn, and raptors. * * *

For ranchers who don't have other sources of income, the fear of losing what they most care about is very real. "We know what the future holds if we don't act soon," says Randy Rusk, gesturing toward the new 35–acre ranchettes that line the southern border of his family's 1,553–acre Rusk Hereford Ranch. Not long ago, cattle grazed in pastures that are now front lawns and flowerbeds. An irrigation ditch flows past barbecues and swing sets, whose owners now complain about "intruding" cowboys and "smelly" manure. As Rusk sees it, the sale of development rights is "the last best chance" for him and other ranchers who wish to preserve a bucolic landscape and a neighborly way of life that are a vital part of the region's heritage. * * *

Rancher with privately owned cattle in Valles Caldera National Preserve, New Mexico, http://www.vallescaldera.gov/ranching.

B. Incentives Surrounding Conservation Easements

A unique blend of financial and emotional incentives typically combines to prompt landowners to convey conservation easements. Yet these incentives may fade over several generations and create pressure on the easement. Professor Federico Cheever explores these dynamics through a colorful hypothetical.

PUBLIC GOOD AND PRIVATE MAGIC IN THE LAW OF LAND TRUSTS AND CONSERVATION EASEMENTS: A HAPPY PRESENT AND A TROUBLED FUTURE
Federico Cheever
73 Denv. U. L. Rev. 1077, 1087–93 (1996)

Laura Deadlock wakes up one morning and realizes that she is not as young as she used to be. Seventy years of raising cattle on the Deadlock ranch and fighting with the federal government about public land grazing have taken their toll. She loves her family and hopes they will stay in the ranching business. She loves her Colorado mountain ranch and the idea of seeing it carpeted with condominiums fills her with dismay. She owns a thousand acres, worth $1 million in a real estate market inflated by developers and perhaps half that much ($500,000) as a going concern. * * * Laura has an honest son, Martin, who works at a university a few hours drive away. She would be happy to leave him the ranch and he would be happy to have it. However, Laura is aware of the federal estate tax and knows that if she leaves Martin the ranch in her will there may be more estate tax to pay than he can afford on his university salary.[b]

In a recent issue of High Country News, Laura read an article about ranchers in another part of the state "preserving" their ranch by granting conservation easements to public interest land trusts. Laura calls someone she knows in town who puts her in touch with the president of the Local Area Land Trust. A few days later the land trust president drives out and gives Laura the good news. First, if she grants the land trust an easement [a]ny restrictions ... will "run with the land"—bind future owners. * * * If Laura wishes, the easement can be "perpetual," protecting the land forever. Second, by donating the easement to the land trust Laura loses nothing she values (just development rights) and gains a potentially large charitable tax deduction. * * * The value of the charitable deduction will be the "value" of the restriction. The value of the restriction is generally the difference between the value of the land unburdened by the restriction and its value subject to restriction.

In Laura's case, her land is worth $500,000 as a cattle ranch and $1 million for development. If she grants away all development rights not associated with maintaining her ranching operation, she can assert that

---

b. Federal estate tax laws have been overhauled since this article was written; as a result, the tax burden has diminished substantially. Congress is also revisiting the charitable tax deduction associated with conservation easements, discussed *infra*. For updates, *see www.lta.org*.

she has reduced the value of her land by one-half ($500,000). Under the federal tax code, she may deduct the lesser of the value of the easement or 30% of her adjusted gross income each year for a total of six years until the value of the gift is depleted. [T]he deduction is likely to save her a great deal of money.

If Laura needs cash, the land trust may be able to find some and enter into a "bargain sale" whereby Laura sells the easement to the trust at a price below its "fair market value." She gets a charitable income tax deduction for the difference between fair market value and the sale price, and some money. * * *

Third, by donating the easement, Laura effectively reduces the value of her land, thereby sheltering her estate from federal and estate tax and, perhaps, local property tax. * * *

Fourth, the arrangement will be a private transaction between Laura and the Local Area Land Trust: no "red tape" or government approval required. * * * Having lived most of her life in the area, she may also place an additional premium on the local nature of the transaction. Chances are good that the Local Area Land Trust is a small organization concerned only with a small area of the state and that its president is a volunteer. * * *

Laura grants the easement to the Local Area Land Trust and leaves the burdened possessory estate—the Deadlock Ranch—to her son, Martin. During his tenure he respects her [and] gets along well with the people from the Local Area Land Trust. Three decades pass. Martin dies and his daughter, Nora, receives the ranch through his will. By now, the potential economics of the ranch have changed. As a result of continued declines in the price of beef, the ranch is still worth $500,000 for the uses allowed by the easement. Ranching is now less common in the area and a buyer who intends to ranch might be hard to find. However, if the easement did not exist, the ranch would be worth $15 million for development.

Nora ... grew up in town. She has no interest in ranching and barely remembers her grandmother Deadlock. She cannot imagine any reasonable grandmother would have wanted to deprive her of a life of cultural enrichment and leisure just to preserve a thousand acres of scrubby ranchland. She goes to a lawyer [who] tells her the bad news. The easement that her grandmother granted to the Local Area Land Trust "runs with the land" and binds all future owners, regardless of their feelings on the subject. The restrictions are perpetual, and, therefore, neither Nora nor her heirs have any hope of outlasting them. * * *

In Nora's eyes the easement is privatized regulation. The voluntariness of the transaction, so important to her grandmother, is insignificant to Nora. * * * The people who run the Local Area Land Trust, strangers to Nora, value "her" ranch as open space and wildlife habitat and can summon the government's assistance in the form of court action to ensure that Nora preserves the ranch for those purposes. [This] "public" law, in the form of legislation and courts, ... separates Nora from her millions. * * * Nora [may] decide to cast the dice, venturing a significant sum in litigation fees in an attempt to "break" the easement [and develop] the unburdened ranch.

First, Nora may attack the status of the Local Area Land Trust as a "charitable" organization. State conservation easement statutes require that a land trust be a "charitable" organization in order to qualify as a holder of a conservation easement. The federal tax code requires that a land trust pass a series of tests to qualify as a "charitable" organization. If Nora successfully argues that the Local Area Land Trust no longer qualifies as a "charitable" organization, a judge can decide not to enforce the terms of the easement.

Second, Nora could attack the circumstances of the easement. * * * Some states require that easements are "appropriate" for conservation purposes. Nora could argue that the doctrine of changed conditions should apply to conservation easements. The doctrine of changed conditions allows a court to terminate or alter a servitude or covenant when the circumstances in or around the burdened land no longer serve the original purpose of the restriction. [In] fifty years Nora's property could be an island of ranchland surrounded by a heavily populated city. It would be absurd to ranch in these conditions.... * * *

Third, Nora could break the terms of the easement and hope that the Local Area Land Trust takes no action until the statute of limitations runs out. In many states the statute of limitations for property and contractual claims is very short. * * * [T]he Local Area Land Trust may not be up for the court battle against Nora. Local land trusts typically have a fraction of the financial resources that private landowners like Nora are willing to spend in litigation to remove the easement. * * *

[T]he perpetual nature of conservation easements makes them precarious. The real property system favors alienability, relying on market forces to provide the best use of the land. * * * The specificity and the durability of the restrictions the easement imposes are among its greatest virtues, but ultimately they may also provide a persuasive argument for invalidating it.

Notes and Questions

1. The Uniform Conservation Easement Act states in § 3(b) that a court retains the power to modify or terminate a conservation easement in accordance with the principles of law or equity. Unif. Conservation Easement Act § 3(b), 12 U.L.A. 177 (1996). Does this provision threaten the "permanent" nature of the conservation easement? What sort of factors might a court look at in determining whether to modify or terminate a conservation easement? Who might bring such a claim to the court? Because conservation easements are such a recent phenomenon, there are few court cases addressing this issue. *C.f.* Turner v. Taylor, 268 Wis.2d 628, 673 N.W.2d 716 (App. 2003) (Wisconsin easements may be extinguished if not recorded in past 30 years, unless owner was on notice of easement).

2. One of the most interesting statutory provisions on termination comes from Maine. The Maine statute allows a court to "deny equitable enforcement of a conservation easement when it finds that change of circumstances has rendered that easement no longer in the public interest," but "[n]o comparative economic test may be used to determine ... if a conservation easement is in the public interest." 33 Me. Rev. Stat. Ann. § 478(3) (1998). The comment to that section states: "It is intended that the court will not define public interest in terms of a higher economic value or return for the land." *Id.*, Comment. Presumably in Maine, placing a conservation easement on property relieves that property of ever again being valued according to the traditional approach that views land in terms of highest developable value. Could this signal a beginning of the transformation of property law into a system that recognizes community values in land?

3. The federal tax code provides incentives for donations of property interests to land trusts through charitable deduction. To receive a federal tax deduction for a conservation easement under I.R.C. section 170(h), the conservation easement must be granted "in perpetuity." I.R.C. § 170 (h)(2)(C)(1994). Moreover, to qualify for the deduction, the conservation easement must protect one of four different "conservation purposes" expressed in the tax code: 1) preservation of land areas for outdoor recreation by, or the education of, the general public; 2) the protection of relatively natural habitat of fish, wildlife, plants, or similar ecosystem; 3) the preservation of open space (including farmland or forestland) where such preservation is for the scenic enjoyment of the general public, or pursuant to a clearly delineated federal, state, or local governmental conservation policy, and will yield a significant public benefit; or 4) the preservation of a certified historic area or historically important land area. *Id.* § 170(h)(4).

For detailed analysis of these tax incentives, *see* Nancy A. McLaughlin, *The Role of Land Trusts in Biodiversity Conservation on Private Lands*, 38 Idaho L. Rev. 453, 466–67 (2002); Stephen J. Small, *An Obscure Tax Code Provision Takes Private Land Protection into the Twenty–First Century, in* Protecting the Land, *supra*, at 55, 65.

4. While it is possible to convey "term" conservation easements that last for specific periods of time, such as 20, 50, or 100 years, most landowners prefer to grant easements "in perpetuity." Part of the reason for this is that a federal tax deduction is available only for perpetual easements, as described above in Note 3. But also, many landowners enjoy the feeling that they are creating a lasting regime of ecological stewardship for the lands that they love. For the same reason, however, certain sectors of the development community oppose the land trust movement on the grounds that it takes prime development land out of the market. Indeed, "perpetuity" has come under criticism by some scholars who argue that conservation easements will be costly to future generations and limit their options, in effect, giving "dead hand control" to present generations over the actions of future generations. *See* Julia D. Mahoney, *Perpetual Restrictions on Land and the Problem of the Future*, 88 Va. L. Rev. 739 (2002). Prof. McLaughlin refutes the argument: "[C]oncerns about 'dead hand' control in the context of conservation easements may be misplaced given that the degradation and destruction of ecosystems as a result of development often is substantially irrevers-

ible, while those who restrict development through easements actually keep options open for future generations." McLaughlin, *The Role of Land Trusts, supra,* at 466–67 (2002); *see also* Barton H. Thompson Jr., *The Trouble with Time: Influencing the Conservation Choices of Future Generations,* 44 NAT. RES. J. 601 (2004). On balance, is "perpetuity" a good thing in the land conservation context?

5. The Uniform Conservation Easement Act allows a "holder" of a conservation easement to be:

(i) a governmental body empowered to hold an interest in real property under the laws of this State or the United States; or

(ii) a charitable corporation, charitable association, or charitable trust, the purposes or powers of which include retaining or protecting the natural, scenic, or open-space values of real property, assuring the availability of real property for agricultural, forest, recreational, or open-space use, protecting natural resources, maintaining or enhancing air or water quality, or preserving the historical, architectural, archaeological, or cultural aspects of real property.

Unif. Conservation Easement Act § 1(2)(i-ii), 12 U.L.A. 170 (1996).

How flexible is the second category? Would it include a state Cattlemen's Association seeking to protect ranchland? If so, must the Cattlemen's Association require ranch owners to operate in an ecologically sustainable manner? In other words, does the provision require that holders of an easement protecting agricultural land also protect other values of real property like habitat values? Should the definition be more strict, or does it allow for necessary flexibility in circumstances that vary considerably nationwide?

6. It is important to note that conservation easements cannot be conveyed simply by the sheer will of the landowner. Many lands that deserve protection are not protected by this tool simply because there is no receiving entity. There may be no land trust available to accept an easement. Government entities may reject acquisition for a number of reasons, including inadequate resources. Or the land may simply not fit the strategic priorities of the government or local land trust. Moreover, land must be quite special in terms of natural or historic characteristics to qualify for a federal conservation easement deduction. Easements over neighborhood backyards won't meet the criteria.

Nevertheless, there have been abuses by those who seek to gain tax breaks. In 2003, Washington Post reporters uncovered stories of developers who had donated easements on golf courses, profiting from tax deductions gained through characterizing the protected courses as "open space." Joe Stephens & David B. Ottaway, *Developers Find Payoff in Preservation, Donors Reap Tax Incentive by Giving to Land Trusts, but Critics Fear Abuse of System,* WASH. POST, Dec. 21, 2003. Such questionable transactions have marred an otherwise rosey reputation of the land trust movement, and have since chilled many land trusts in their acquisitions. Land trusts that facilitate such dubious transactions likely constitute a very small minority of the movement as a whole. However, even a reputable national land trust, The Nature Conservancy (TNC), received heated criticism after reporters discovered several transactions involving TNC trustees and supporters that allowed substantial development in sensitive areas. *See* David B. Ottaway & Joe Stephens, *Nonprofit Land Bank Amasses Billions, Charity Builds Assets on Corporate Partnerships*, WASH. POST, May 4, 2003, and associated articles, May 3–6, 2003.

7. While the land trust movement is now in the acquisition phase, it will mature into an enforcement phase as property transfers to a new generation of owners who may not feel as comfortable with the restrictions on the property. Currently there are few cases dealing with enforcement of such easements. *See, e.g.,* Big Meadows Grazing Ass'n v. U.S., 344 F.3d 940 (9th Cir. 2003) (government not required to obtain participating landowner's assent to implement conservation plans pursuant to easement conveyed under Wetland Reserve Program); Racine v. U.S., 858 F.2d 506 (9th Cir. 1988) (interpreting scenic easement to permit dude ranching structures which do not impair scenic, natural, historic, pastoral, and wildlife values); Madden v. Nature Conservancy, 823 F.Supp. 815 (D. Mont. 1992) (construing parties' intent to reserve and retain conservation rights in property). Most land trusts think carefully about enforcement before they decide to accept an easement into their holdings. They often require a stewardship fee to contribute to a general endowment for funding legal enforcement in the future. Such fees are typically paid by the landowner, even in the case where the landowner donates the value of the easement.

A valuable tool in the enforcement realm is the baseline study. This study, typically performed by the land trust at the time of easement acquisition, inventories the natural baseline condition of the property through photos, surveys, descriptions, and occasionally more elaborate scientific data collection. Annual monitoring of the property by the land trust refers back to baseline conditions. With an adequate baseline study, it is possible to determine what conditions have changed since the beginning of the easement.

8. Note the interplay between regulations and conservation easements. Conservation easements are generally more stringent than the existing regulations. Conservation easements do not trump regulations; they simply provide private rights to enforce certain duties iterated in the easement. Conservation easements granted in perpetuity are far more durable than regulations, which may change with the political winds. If the regulations change to impose fewer restrictions on the property, the conservation easement may act as a private net to achieve conservation that is no longer mandatory through regulation. Note also that a particular piece of property may, over time, be subject to more than one conservation easement. Imagine an instance in which an owner grants an easement with specific land use limitations but no public access. Ten years later the same owner, or a successor owner, might convey another conservation easement that provides for public access and some affirmative habitat recovery obligations. That later easement will amount to another layer of restriction on the property. Over time, such "layering" may greatly complicate matters for real estate lawyers and natural resource practitioners.

9. For in-depth analysis of conservation easements, *see* PROTECTING THE LAND, *supra*; SALLY K. FAIRFAX & DARLA GUENZLER, CONSERVATION TRUSTS (University Press of Kansas, 2001).

In Practice:
Drafting a Conservation Easement

A conservation easement is uniquely tailored to the conditions of the land, the preferences of the landowner, and the priorities of the receiving land trust. The document must be flexible enough to provide durability over time between parties with potentially changing values. Beyond addressing land-specific duties and prohibited actions, it should address procedural issues, such as notification to the parties, assignment of rights, indemnification for liability, and other foreseeable matters. A useful starting point in drafting is the Model Conservation Easement, published in THE CONSERVATION EASEMENT HANDBOOK (Trust for Public Land, 1988). The Model Easement contains sample provisions that may be modified to suit particular circumstances. The Model Easement does not carry any force of law, but is rather an early attempt by conservation trust practitioners to set forth a structure for conservation easements.

The Model Easement is accompanied by this drafting advice in the introductory commentary:

[T]he goals of the parties in all likelihood will diverge over time. * * * [There is an] absolute need for clarity and precision in the document that establish[es] the restrictions of the property. * * * This instrument, we must remember, is to control Greenacre's fate over time and is to govern the behavior of people who are not present at the outset. Not only Greenacre is at stake. Whether or not the relationships among those future participants are to be peaceful or stormy, efficient or costly, privately resolved or the basis for expensive strife, will also be fundamentally affected by the quality of the original grant of the conservation easement. * * *

Precision in the document for the particular transaction requires clarity of thinking among the parties as well as drafting skill; fuzziness in legal phrasing can emanate from failing to think carefully and patiently enough about just what might happen. * * * [P]erpetutity counsels flexibility—the need for a mechanism for adapting to the unforeseen—a capacity for stretch. An easement is more than the sum of its restrictions; it is [the] right to protect certain values. The more drafters focus on the future, which cannot be known, the more emphasis they place on articulating those values in the easement. As critical for an easement's long-term enforceability as its express restrictions, the thinking goes, is the clarity with which its purpose and intent are set out. *Id. at* 147–48.

> **Exercise:**
>
> There is a common assumption that regulation alone is sufficient to protect natural resources. This assumption often undercuts support for financing the purchase of conservation easements. To acquire funding for a conservation project, a natural resource practitioner must be able to clearly explain the flaws in the existing regulatory structure designed to protect the resource. Assume you work for a city trying to acquire funding to hold a conservation easement on a densely forested parcel that provides important habitat for a fish listed under the state's Endangered Species Act. The Act prohibits any individual from "taking" the fish, including any activities that cause forseeable harm to the species through habitat destruction. The committee charged with allocating public funding for fish protection has asked you to explain why a conservation easement is necessary. How would you respond? What provisions would you want to see in the easement?

C. The Role of Land Trusts in National Conservation Efforts

Land trust mechanisms play a special role in the national conservation effort because they are uniquely tailored to achieving conservation on private lands. Until the last few decades, conservation efforts were focused largely on federal lands. Yet around 65% of land in the contiguous United States is in private ownership. In many regions, a conducive market, combined with friendly local regulators, can fuel a building frenzy that converts valuable natural resources to urban infrastructure in a strikingly short period of time. Between 1982 and 1992, over one million hectares of pasture was transformed to residential and industrial development, roads, and shopping areas. Richard L. Knight, *Private Lands: The Neglected Geography*, 13 CONSERVATION BIOLOGY 223, 223–24 (1999). Between 1990 and 2000, development on nonfederal lands increased by 18%.

This land rush has a devastating impact on wildlife populations. It is estimated that more than half of all threatened and endangered species in the United States rely on habitat located exclusively on private lands. An additional 20% of listed species spend approximately half their time using habitat on private lands. Peter Morrisette, *Conservation Easements and the Public Good: Preserving the Environment on Private Lands*, 41 NAT. RESOURCES J. 373, 374 (2001). Moreover, some ecosystems are found primarily, or in some cases entirely, on non-federal lands. For example, most wetlands and grasslands in the lower 48 states are in private or state ownership. *See* David W. Crumpacker, et. al., *A Preliminary Assessment of the Status of Major Terrestrial and Wetland Ecosystems on Federal and Indian Lands in the United States*, 2 CONSERVATION BIOLOGY 103, 107–12 (1988).

Much of the growth in conservation easements is targeted towards saving remaining viable habitat for imperiled wildlife. Approximately 42% of conservation easements have wildlife protection as their primary

purpose. *Land Trust Alliance Summary Data*, NATIONAL LAND TRUST CEN-
SUS, *available at* http://www.lta.org/newsroom/census_summary_data
.htm. How effective can the land trust movement be in protecting biodiversity, and what advantages do conservation easements offer over the
traditional regulatory tools in protecting wildlife habitat? What are the
disadvantages? The excerpt below explores these questions.

THE ROLE OF LAND TRUSTS IN
BIODIVERSITY CONSERVATION ON PRIVATE LANDS
Nancy A. McLaughlin
38 IDAHO L. REV. 453, 460–68 (2002)

* * * Conservation easements acquired by land trusts generally are
not well suited to the protection of biodiversity in core areas. The proper
level of biodiversity protection in core areas often can be achieved only if
the landowner agrees to refrain from most or all uses of the land or to
actively manage the land for biodiversity protection purposes. In most
cases landowners are not willing to accept such restrictions or responsibilities. However, conservation easements acquired by land trusts may
be particularly well-suited to the protection of areas considered to be
"buffer zones" around core areas, where the landowners' retained rights
to use the land are compatible with biodiversity protection goals. In such
cases, acquiring a conservation easement may be as beneficial, more cost
effective, and more feasible than obtaining fee title to the land.

Even in a situation where a conservation easement does little more
than restrict the development of the land to which it relates and, thus,
may allow continued uses of the land that are not compatible with biodiversity protection goals, such an easement can be viewed as an important first step in the protection of the land. Nothing in the sale or donation of a conservation easement to a land trust prevents the layering of
additional restrictions on the use of the land subject to the easement,
whether those additional restrictions are imposed by regulation or purchased from or donated by the current or a successive owner of the land.

The voluntary nature of the sale or donation of conservation easements to land trusts, the numerous conservation purposes for which
deductible easements may be donated under section 170(h), and the
myriad of land trusts with diverse objectives that acquire easements
make it difficult to incorporate such easements into an coordinated
biodiversity conservation initiative. However, the existence of a myriad
of non-governmental organizations that often are staffed and supported
by community members is precisely what may make the sale or donation
of a conservation easement to a land trust an attractive option to some
landowners who otherwise would not voluntarily protect their lands.

In addition, although land trusts sometimes acquire easements in a
reactive manner, letting landowner requests, imminent sales or threats
of development determine which easements they accept, an increasing
number of land trusts engage in strategic planning in an effort to target

their limited resources to the protection of key parcels that fit within the broader programs of landscape preservation. As the land trust movement matures, there appears to be an increasing recognition on the part of many of its members of the importance of protecting entire ecosystems, and that ad hoc, piecemeal protection of parcels will not accomplish long-term habit and ecosystem protection goals.

It is arguable that the public funds expended on the conservation easements acquired by land trusts, at least those easements that have habitat protection as their conservation purpose, would be better spent in programs that more effectively plan for biodiversity protection by targeting land with the highest conservation value and in most critical need of protection. However, as discussed by Holly Doremus, it is becoming increasingly apparent that a biodiversity conservation approach that focuses only on the protection of reserves likely will not be successful over the long term because such an approach ignores and, in some respects, exacerbates the growing disconnect in our society between humans and nature. Holly Doremus, *Biodiversity and the Challenge of Saving the Ordinary*, 38 IDAHO L. REV. 325 (2002). Recognizing that "the more completely we isolate our daily lives from nature, the more tenuous our commitment to protecting nature is likely to become," Doremus argues for finding ways to "focus the law, and the public, on protecting ordinary nature." *Id.* at 342.

Land trusts, and the conservation easements they acquire, provide a means through which individuals, families, and communities can participate in the protection of ordinary nature—the working farms, the family homesteads, the public trails and parks, the urban gardens. The variety of missions pursued by individual land trusts and the broad conservation purposes for which deductible easements may be granted under section 170(h) allow land trusts to cast a much wider net of land protections than is found in more targeted land conservation programs.... * * *

Although lacking the "flash and glamour" associated with the protection of large parcels that have undeniable scenic or habitat value, the ordinary parcels protected by land trusts constitute a significant portion of the national landscape. Their protection should be part of any biodiversity conservation initiative that recognizes the benefit of fostering connections between people and nature and the futility of relying solely on government regulation and government land acquisition.

An equally important role that land trusts and the conservation easements they acquire can play in biodiversity conservation is that of facilitating a transition from the prevailing view of private property . . . to a view of private property in which individual parcels of land are seen as part of a larger landscape and landowners are deemed to owe obligations to both the natural and human community.... One of the more difficult tasks facing proponents of this latter view of private property is that of discovering a means of adopting it without unfairly hurting existing property owners. Conservation easements may offer just such means. * * *

In Focus: The South Carolina Low–Country

[In] the South Carolina low-country, landowners have joined with state and federal agencies to protect more than 160,000 acres of land since 1987, almost half through donated conservation easements. Dana Beach, the Executive Director of the South Carolina Coastal Conservation League (www.scccl.org), explains part of the Ashepoo/ Combahee/Edisto (ACE) basin initiative:

> One protected property in the ACE is the 12,325–acre Cheeha–Combahee Plantation. With 21 miles of magnificent river/marsh frontage, dramatic topography and no local land use regulations, Cheeha–Combahee was a perfect candidate for a high-end golf course or equestrian development in the style of Hilton Head, just 30 miles to the south.

> In 1993, eight families purchased Cheeha–Combahee and donated a perpetual conservation easement to Ducks Unlimited. The easement allows only 10 subdivisions with no parcel smaller than 600 acres. In contrast, the most restrictive zoning in South Carolina limits subdivision to 25 acre lots or larger. * * * Forty-four of South Carolina's 46 counties have "rural" zoning codes with minimum lot sizes of one acre, or they have no zoning at all. Unfortunately, South Carolina is no exception. Throughout the Southeast, where biodiversity is among the highest in the nation, rural zoning is a prescription for sprawl. Leaving rural land protection in the hands of counties and states would consign most of the wildlife habitat in the nation to oblivion.

> Critics contend that easements often deliver large tax benefits to individual donors with questionable public benefits in return. The Cheeha–Combahee easement was valued at approximately $2.8 million. It provided an income tax benefit to the owners, and a cost to the taxpayer, of less than $1 million, or approximately $80.00 per acre. In its protected state, the property provides enormous value for wildlife, water quality, and other ecological services. It has also facilitated a growing eco-tourism industry of kayakers and canoeists, along with traditional hunters and anglers who enjoy the benefits of a protected watershed and riparian vistas. Most importantly Cheeha–Combahee lies between state and federal wildlife preserves.

Dana Beach, *Create More Incentives for Easements,* OPEN SPACE 13 (Summer, 2004).

*

Part III

LAND USE AND COMMODITY RESOURCES

Historically, natural resources can be broken down into two classes—(1) those which have been used as "commodities," for their economic and marketplace value, and (2) those which are valuable in their natural state primarily for non-economic reasons. The chapters within Part III focus on the so-called "commodity" resources. Throughout the 19th and most of the 20th centuries, natural resources were thought to be important only if they had economic worth. During the latter part of the 20th century, and certainly within the 21st century, many natural resources have been recognized as valuable and useful irrespective of their economic attributes. These non-commodity resources are the topic of Part IV.

Chapter 10, written by Professor Dan Cole, addresses the most common natural resource commodity of all—land (including wetlands). This chapter focuses on land owned by private parties, and used for economic benefit, such as production of agricultural resources. Chapter 10 also examines government regulation of private land use. Chapter 11, written by Professor Sandra Zellmer, is on timber, a renewable resource with enormous commodity value. Forests also have tremendous ecological value, and regulation of the timber resource reflects this tension between timber both as a commodity and non-commodity resource. Chapter 12, written by Professors Cole and Jan G. Laitos, takes up the topic of mineral resources. Minerals are a commodity when they are used for energy purposes (oil, gas, coal, coalbed methane gas), as precious hardrock minerals (gold, copper, molybdenum, and diamonds), or as building materials (rock, stone, sand, gravel). Chapter 12 examines the different types of mineral resources, their ownership, and their regulation. Chapter 13, written by Professors Laitos and Zellmer, addresses the final commodity resource—water. As a commodity, water is used in multiple ways, where each use is meant to be consistent with a legal regime which determines (1) who owns the right to use the water, and (2) what legal consequences follow from such use. Like timber, water is also valuable "in place," as a non-commodity resource. This aspect of water is considered in other chapters, particularly Chapters 14 (Wildlife) and 15 (Preservation and Recreation).

Chapter 10

LAND

Every chapter in this book concerns the land resource in some way, shape, or form. Most obviously, public land laws such as NFMA and FLPMA directly regulate the use of lands owned by the United States government and managed, respectively, by the Forest Service and BLM. Less obviously, but just as importantly, water law affects land uses by determining the availability of water for domestic, agricultural, or industrial purposes, while wildlife law affects land use activities that modify or destroy habitat. This chapter describes the vast legal systems governing the use of *private* lands in both urban and rural areas. It dovetails with Chapter 9 (Private Ownership), but looks at land use issues from a regulatory standpoint.

I. OVERVIEW

A. The Land Resource and Its Many Uses

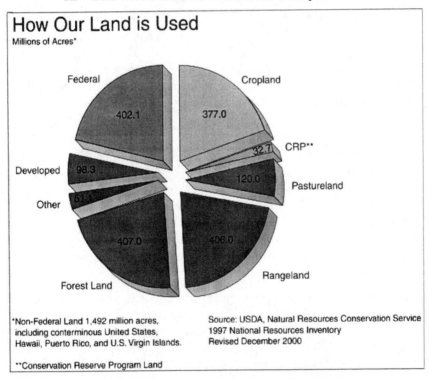

How Our Land is Used
Millions of Acres*

Federal 402.1
Cropland 377.0
CRP** 32.7
Pastureland 120.0
Developed 98.3
Other 51.4
Forest Land 407.0
Rangeland 406.0

*Non-Federal Land 1,492 million acres, including conterminous United States, Hawaii, Puerto Rico, and U.S. Virgin Islands.

**Conservation Reserve Program Land

Source: USDA, Natural Resources Conservation Service 1997 National Resources Inventory Revised December 2000

PRESENT LAND USE AND LAND COVER IN THE USA
Consequences: The Nature and Implications of
Environmental Change 24–33 (1995)
William B. Meyer

Land use is the way in which, and the purposes for which, human beings employ the land and its resources: for example, farming, mining, or lumbering. *Land cover* describes the physical state of the land surface: as in cropland, mountains, or forests. The term land cover originally referred to the kind and state of vegetation (such as forest or grass cover), but it has broadened in subsequent usage to include human structures such as buildings or pavement and other aspects of the natural environment, such as soil type, biodiversity, and surface and groundwater. A vast array of physical characteristics—climate, physiography, soil, biota—and the varieties of past and present human utilization combine to make every parcel of land on the nation's surface unique in the cover it possesses and the opportunities for use that it offers. For most practical purposes, land units must be aggregated into quite broad categories, but the frequent use of such simplified classes should not be allowed to dull one's sense of the variation that is contained in any one of them.

Land cover is affected by natural events, including climate variation, flooding, vegetation succession, and fire, all of which can sometimes be affected in character and magnitude by human activities. Both globally and in the United States, though, land cover today is altered principally by direct human use: by agriculture and livestock raising, forest harvesting and management, and construction. There are also incidental impacts from other human activities such as forests damaged by acid rain from fossil fuel combustion and crops near cities damaged by tropospheric ozone resulting from automobile exhaust. * * *

Where Are We?

The United States, exclusive of Alaska and Hawaii, assumed its present size and shape around the middle of the 19th century. Hawaii is relatively small, ecologically distinctive, and profoundly affected by a long and distinctive history of human use; Alaska is huge and little affected to date by direct land use. In this review assessment, we therefore survey land use and land cover change, focusing on the past century and a half, only in the coterminous or lower 48 states. Those states cover an area of almost 1900 million acres, or about 3 million square miles.

How land is *used*, and thus how *land cover* is altered, depends on who controls the land and on the pressures and incentives shaping the behavior of the owner. Some 400 million acres in the coterminous 48 states—about 21% of the total—are federally owned. The two largest chunks are the 170 million acres in Western rangeland controlled by the Bureau of Land Management and the approximately equal area of the National Forest System. Federal land represents 45% of the area of the twelve western states, but is not a large share of any other regional total. There are also significant land holdings by state governments throughout the country.

Most of the land of the United States is privately owned, but under federal, state, and local restrictions on its use that have increased over time. The difference between public and private land is important in explaining and forecasting land use and land cover change, but the division is not absolute, and each sector is influenced by the other. Private land use is heavily influenced by public policies, not only by regulation of certain uses but through incentives that encourage others.... The large government role in land use on both government and private land means that policy, as well as economic forces, must be considered in explaining and projecting changes in the land....

There is no standard, universally accepted set of categories for classifying land by either use or cover, and the most commonly used, moreover, are hybrids of land cover and land use. Those employed here, which are by and large those of the U.S. National Resources Inventory conducted every five years by relevant federal agencies, are cropland, forest, grassland (pasture and rangeland), wetlands, and developed land.

- *Cropland* is land in farms that is devoted to crop production; it is not to be confused with total farmland, a broad land-use or land-ownership category that can incorporate many forms of land cover.

- *Forest land* is characterized by a predominance of tree cover and is further divided by the U.S. Census into timberland and non-timberland. By definition, the former must be capable of producing 20 cubic feet of industrial wood per acre per year and remain legally open to timber production.

- *Grassland* as a category of land cover embraces two contrasting Census categories of use; pasture (enclosed and what is called improved grassland, often closely tied to cropland and used for intensive livestock raising), and range (often unenclosed or unimproved grazing land with sparser grass cover and utilized for more extensive production).

- *Wetlands* are not a separate Census or National Resources Inventory category and are included within other categories: swamp, for example, is wetland forest. They are defined by federal agencies as lands covered all or part of the year with water, but not so deeply or permanently as to be classified as surface water *per se*.

- The U.S. government classifies as *developed* land urban and built-up parcels that exceed certain size thresholds. "Developed" or "urban" land is clearly as use rather than a cover category. Cities and suburbs as they are politically defined have rarely more than half of their area, and often much less, taken up by distinctively "urban" land cover such as buildings and pavement. Trees and grass cover substantial areas of the metropolitan United States; indeed, tree cover is greater in some settlements than in the rural areas surrounding them.

By the 1987 U.S. Natural Resources Inventory, non-federal lands were divided by major land use and land cover classes as follows: cropland, about 420 million acres (22% of the entire area of the 48 states); rangeland about 400 million (21%); forest, 390 million (21%); pasture, 130 million (7%); and developed land, 80 million (4%). Minor covers and uses, including surface water, make up another 60 million acres.... The

401 million acres of federal land are about half forest and half range. Wetlands, which fall within these other Census classes, represent approximately 100 million acres or about five percent of the national area; 95 percent of them are freshwater and five percent are coastal.

These figures, for even a single period, represent not a static but a dynamic total, with constant exchanges among uses. Changes in the area and the location of cropland, for example, are the result of the *addition* of new cropland from conversion of grassland, forest, and wetland and its *subtraction* either by abandonment of cropping and reversion to one of these less intensive use/cover forms or by conversion to developed land. The main causes of forest *loss* are clearing for agriculture, logging, and clearing for development; the main cause of forest *gain* is abandonment of cropland followed by either passive or active reforestation. Grassland is converted by the creation of pasture from forest, the interchange of pasture and cropland, and the conversion of rangeland to cropland, often through irrigation.

Change in wetland is predominantly loss through drainage for agriculture and construction. They also include natural gain and loss, but the growing possibilities for wetland creation and restoration are implicit in the Environmental Protection Agency's "no net loss" policy.... Change in developed land runs in only one direction: it expands and is not, to any significant extent, converted to any other category. * * * Regional patterns within the U.S. (using the four standard government regions of Northeast, Midwest, South, and West) display ... variety. The Northeast, though the most densely populated region, is the most heavily wooded, with three-fifths of its area in forest cover. It is also the only region of the four in which "developed" land, by the Census definition, amounts to more than a minuscule share of the total; it covers about eight percent of the Northeast and more than a quarter of the state of New Jersey. Cropland, not surprisingly, is by far the dominant use/cover in the Midwest, accounting for just under half of its expanse. The South as a whole presents the most balanced mix of land types: about 40 percent forest, 20 percent each of cropland and rangeland, and a little more than ten percent pasture. Western land is predominantly rangeland, with forest following and cropland a distant third. Wetlands are concentrated along the Atlantic seaboard, in the Southeast, and in the upper Midwest. Within each region, of course, there is further variety at and below the state level.

Where Have We Been?

* * *

Cropland

Total cropland rose steadily at the expense of other land covers throughout most of American history. It reached a peak during the 1940s and has subsequently fluctuated in the neighborhood of 400 million acres, though the precise figure depends on the definition of cropland used. Long-term regional patterns have displayed more variety. Cropland abandonment in some areas of New England began to be significant ... by the middle of the nineteenth century. Although total farmland peaked in the region as late as 1880 (at 50%) and did not decline sharply until the turn of the century, a steady decline in the sub category of cropland and an increase in other farmland covers such as woodland and unimproved pasture was already strongly apparent. The Middle Atlantic followed a similar trajectory, as, more recently, has the South. Competition from other, more fertile sections of the country in agricultural production and within the East from other demands on land and labor have been factors; a long-term rise in agricultural productivity caused by technological advances has also exerted a steady downward pressure on total crop acreage even though population, income, and demand have all risen.

Irrigated cropland on a significant scale in the United States extends back only to the 1890s and the early activities in the West of the Bureau of Reclamation. Growing rapidly through about 1920, the amount of irrigated land remained relatively constant between the wars, but rose again rapidly after 1945 with institutional and technological developments such as the use of center-pivot irrigation drawing on the Ogallala Aquifer on the High Plains. It reached 25 million acres by 1950 and doubled to include about an eighth of all cropland by 1980. Since then the amount of irrigated land has experienced a modest decline, in part through the partial depletion of aquifers such as the Ogallala and through competition from cities for water in dry areas.

Forests

At the time of European settlement, forest covered about half of the present 48 states. The greater part lay in the eastern part of the country, and most of it had already been significantly altered by Native American land-use practices that left a mosaic of different covers, including substantial areas of open land.

Forest area began a continuous decline with the onset of European settlement that would not be halted until the early twentieth century. Clearance for farmland and harvesting for fuel, timber, and other wood products represented the principal sources of pressure. From an estimated 900 million acres in 1850, the wooded area of the entire U.S. reached a low point of 600 million acres around 1920.... It then rose slowly through the postwar decades, largely through abandonment of cropland and regrowth on cutover areas, but around 1960 began again a modest decline, the result of settlement expansion and of higher rates of timber extraction through mechanization. The agricultural censuses recorded a drop of 17 million acres in U.S. forest cover between 1970 and 1987 (though data uncertainties and the small size of the changes relative to the total forest area make a precise dating of the reversals difficult). At the same time, if the U.S. forests have been shrinking in area they have been growing in density and volume. The trend in forest biomass has been consistently upward; timber stock measured in the agricultural censuses from 1952 to 1987 grew by about 30%.

National totals of forested areas again represent the aggregation of varied regional experiences. Farm abandonment in much of the East has translated directly into forest recovery, beginning in the mid- to late-nineteenth century.... Historically, lumbering followed a regular pattern of harvesting one region's resources and moving on to the next; the once extensive old-growth forest of the Great Lakes, the South, and the Pacific Northwest represented successive and overlapping frontiers. After about 1930, frontier-type exploitation gave way to a greater emphasis on permanence and management of stands by timber companies. Wood itself has declined in importance as a natural resource, but forests have been increasingly valued and protected for a range of other services, including wildlife habitat, recreation, and streamflow regulation.

Grassland

The most significant changes in grassland have involved impacts of grazing on the Western range. Though data for many periods are scanty or suspect, it is clear that rangelands have often been seriously over-grazed, with deleterious consequences including soil erosion and compaction, increased streamflow variability, and floral and fauna biodiversity loss as well as reduced value for production. The net value of grazing use on the Western range is nationally small, though significant locally, and pressures for tighter management have increasingly been guided by ecological and preservationist as well as production concerns.

Wetland

According to the most recent estimates, 53% of American wetlands were lost between the 1780s and the 1980s, principally to drainage for agriculture. Most of the conversion presumably took place during the twentieth century; between the 1950s and the 1970s alone, about 11 million acres were lost. Unassisted private action was long thought to drain too little; since mid-century, it has become apparent that the opposite is true, that unfettered private action tends to drain too much, i.e., at the expense of now-valued wetland. The positive externalities once expected from drainage—improved public health and beautification of an unappealing natural landscape—carry less weight today than the negative ones it produces. These include the decline of wildlife, greater extremes of streamflow, and loss of a natural landscape that is now seen as more attractive than a human-modified one. The rate of wetland loss has now been cut significantly by regulation and by the removal of incentives for drainage once offered by many government programs.

Developed Land

As the American population has grown and become more urbanized, the land devoted to settlement has increased in at least some degree. Like the rest of the developed world, the United States now has an overwhelmingly non-farm population residing in cities, suburbs, and towns and villages. Surrounding urban areas is a classical frontier of rapid and sometimes chaotic land-use and land cover change. Urban impacts go beyond the mere subtraction of land from other land uses and land covers for settlement and infrastructure; they also involve the mining of building materials, the disposal of wastes, the creation of parks and water supply reservoirs, and the introduction of pollutants in air, water, and soil. Long-term data on urban use and cover trends are unfortunately not available. But the trend in American cities has undeniably been one of residential dispersal and lessened settlement densities as transportation technologies have improved; settlement has thus required higher amounts of land per person over time.

Where Are We Going?

The most credible projections of changes in land use and land cover in the United States over the next fifty years have come from recent assessments produced under the federal laws that now mandate regular inventories of resource stocks and prospects. The most recent inquiry into land resources, completed by the Department of Agriculture in 1989 ... , sought to project their likely extent and condition a half-century into the future, to the year 2040. The results indicated that only slow changes were expected nationally in the major categories of land use and land cover: a loss in forest area of some 5% (a slower rate of loss than was experienced in the same period before); a similarly modest decline in cropland; and an increase in rangeland of about 5% through 2040. Projections are not certainties, however: they may either incorrectly identify the consequences of the factors they consider or fail to consider important factors that could alter the picture. Because of the significant impacts of policy and of market forces, the role of policy—notoriously difficult to forecast and assess—demands increased attention, in both its deliberate and its inadvertent effects. * * *

Why Does It Matter?

Land-use and land-cover changes, besides affecting the current and future supply of land resources, are important sources of many other forms of environmental change. They are also linked to them through synergistic connections that can amplify their overall effect.

Loss of plant and animal biodiversity is principally traceable to land transformation, primarily through the fragmentation of natural habitat. Worldwide trends in land-use and land cover change are an important source of the so-called greenhouse gases, whose accumulation in the atmosphere may bring about global climate change. As much as 35% of the increase in atmospheric CO_2 in the last 100 years can be attributed to land-use change, principally through deforestation. The major, known sources of increased methane—rice paddies, landfills, biomass burning, and cattle—are all related to land use. Much of the increase in nitrous oxide is now thought due to a collection of sources that also depend upon the use of the land, including biomass burning, cattle and feedlots, fertilizer application, and contaminated aquifers.

Land-use practices at the local and regional levels can dramatically affect soil condition as well as water quality, and water supply. And finally, vulnerability or sensitivity to existing climate hazards and possible climate change is very much affected by changes in land use and cover. * * *

Notes and Questions

1. Professor Meyer points out that developed (built-upon) land constitutes only a small fraction of the total land area of the United States. However, the rate of land development increased during the second half of the nineteenth century and accelerated throughout the twentieth century, as the US population grew and moved in ever greater numbers from farms into towns and cities. Figure 2 shows the growth of developed land (represented by the white shaded area) in and around the City of Baltimore, Maryland, over a two hundred year period from 1792 to 1992. Note particularly the exponential growth in the years since World War II. Is this merely a reflection of a growing population, or is there something more at work?

Figure 2: Growth of the City of Baltimore, 1792 – 1992

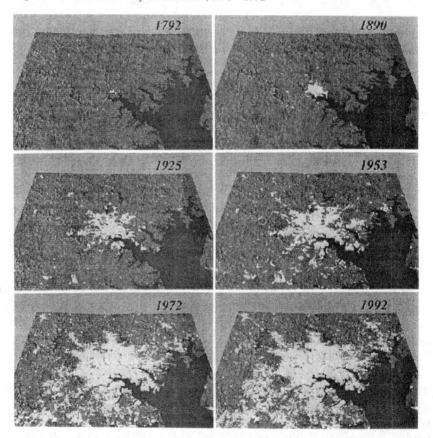

2. The growth of cities and towns—commonly referred to as the problem of "urban sprawl"—has become one of the most important issues in

land-use planning. That problem will be explored later in this chapter. The following section explores what historically has been the primary focus of local land-use planners: segregating incompatible land uses within urban and suburban areas.

B. Why Plan for Land Use?

In the United States, most decisions about the use of resources are left to the discretion of private owners, on the assumption that they rationally will seek to maximize the value of the assets they own, and thereby maximize the social product, making society as a whole better off. American society typically relies on markets to allocate among private owners the power to decide how and when natural resources will (or will not) be developed and used. A great wealth of empirical, as well as theoretical, evidence supports the view that markets allocate resources more effectively than "central planners." Yet governmental land-use planning constitutes an obvious socialistic limitation on market-based land development. Why do we tolerate it? Why do we rely, at least some of the time, on central planners, rather than land markets, to decide how and when land development takes place?

As with many environmental issues addressed throughout this book, land-use planning is premised on the notion of *market failure* (as described in Chapter 1). Land markets allegedly fail to allocate land resources, including development rights, to either prevent or minimize the costs of conflicts. Nuisance law constitutes one common-law remedy for land use conflicts; but nuisance suits are typically brought after a conflict has arisen, that is, after costs have been incurred. The goal of land-use planning is to prevent socially costly land-use conflicts from arising in the first place. *See* D.B. Lee, *Land Use Planning as a Response to Market Failure*, in The Land Use Policy Debate in the United States 149 (J. de Neufville ed., 1981).

The market failure justification for government intervention in land development is virtually taken for granted. But, as Ronald Coase has cautioned, it is myopic to focus only on *market failures* as if *government failures* never happen. Ronald H. Coase, *The Problem of Social Cost*, 3 J.L. & Econ. 1 (1960). As noted in Chapter 1, governments also fail to efficiently allocate entitlements to resources. So, the mere fact that markets sometimes allocate land development rights inefficiently is not a sufficient justification for government land use planning and zoning. From an economic perspective, zoning is justified only if it generates net benefits for social welfare, *i.e.*, benefits in excess of its costs. Expressed in Coasian terms, government allocation is justified only when it is expected to produce fewer social costs (thereby maximizing the social product) than market allocation. As Robert Ellickson noted more than 30 years ago, "[t]he total public and private administrative costs of zoning are far from insubstantial. These costs, when added to the high prevention costs zoning is likely to involve, may be so great that an entire zoning ordinance is inefficient; that is, the reduction in nuisance costs is less than the concomitant prevention and administrative costs." Robert C. Ellickson, *Alternatives to Zoning: Covenants, Nuisance Rules, and Fines as Land Use Controls*, 40 U.Chi. L.Rev. 681, 699 (1973). Whether or not this is the case is an empirical question. Ellickson postulates that government land use regulations are likely to be "the most efficient device for dealing with a few pervasive land use problems," but may be a relatively inefficient tool for dealing with other problems. *Id.*

In addition to efficiency concerns, government regulations of land development often raise equity issues, especially in cases where those regulations operate to exclude outsiders from entering a certain market. Growth controls, for example, are likely to reduce the availability of housing for would-be residents in two ways: (1) by directly limiting the amount of development that can occur within town boundaries; and (2) by increasing the scarcity, and thereby raising the prices, of existing housing stocks. Such controls are likely to have disproportionate impacts on low-income individuals and families. Consequently, the system of public land use planning, as practiced in the United States, does not lack for critics. *See, e.g.*, Ellickson, *supra*.

II. LOCAL LAND USE PLANNING

A. Comprehensive Planning

Most land use planning takes place at the level of local governments. Local planners designate the type, design, nature, and location of physical facilities that serve residential, commercial, industrial, agricultural, and general business needs. These governmentally imposed conditions on the use of land can affect where, how, and the extent to which natural resources may be developed.

1. The Plan

A local or county government commission drafts a land use plan—referred to alternatively as "master plan," "development plan," "comprehensive plan," or just plain "plan"—to reflect its view of how the community should grow and develop. The plan is often nothing more than a color-coded map of the metropolitan area, which specifies where different types of development might occur. Local government authority to formulate land use plans and impose zoning regulations comes from state enabling statutes, adopted in every state, and modeled after the Standard City Planning Enabling Act of 1928 (SCPEA), a uniform statute proposed by the U.S. Department of Commerce.

The plan serves as a policy guide to officials responsible for overseeing an area's physical development. In most states, the plan is merely a recommendation, having no legal effect unless and until an appropriate local legislative body, such as the city council or board of county commissioners, adopts it and implements it through zoning or other regulations. *See* Creative Displays, Inc. v. City of Florence, 602 S.W.2d 682 (Ky.

1980); Cochran v. Planning Board of the City of Summit, 87 N.J.Super. 526, 210 A.2d 99 (1965).

The essential elements of a plan are that it be comprehensive, general, and long-range. "Comprehensive" means that all geographic parts of the community must be encompassed in the plan, as well as the infrastructure elements such as roadways and utilities that will affect the community's development. The "general" requirement means that the plan must summarize policies for growth, but need not specify locations for that growth. The plan's "long-range" goal reflects the need to look 20 to 30 years ahead. Because increasing populations and economic development bear on the provision of public services, including water supplies, sewers, and roads, planners today pay attention not only to private land development but also to changing transportation needs and the provision of community facilities, including schools, solid waste sites, and water treatment plants.

2. The Planning Commission

The SCPEA created the concept of a planning commission, a local agency with a planning staff answerable to the local legislative body (city council or county commissioners). The planning staff prepares a land use plan with guidance from the planning commission, which subsequently refers the plan to the legislative body for adoption. The legislative body refers all other proposals for a community's spatial development to the planning commission for action, while retaining the authority to override the commission's recommendations. Appeals from a planning commission action may take one of two routes. A person challenging the action may go to the city council or board of county commissioners and then to the courts; alternatively, the challenger may appeal to the county's board of adjustment (or zoning board of appeals) and then to the courts. Boards of adjustment or appeals are administrative appeal agencies located within a community's planning department or commission.

B. Implementing the Plan

Land use plans, by themselves, accomplish nothing unless and until they are implemented (however imperfectly) through zoning regulations, subdivision regulations, special use permits, planned unit developments, or growth controls. To be valid (*i.e.*, legal), any such implementing measure must constitute a valid exercise of the police power, and not amount to an unconstitutional taking.

1. Zoning

a. General Structure

Zoning is the most common form of public land use regulation. Local zoning is authorized by state statutes patterned after the Department of Commerce's 1927 Standard Zoning Enabling Act (SZEA) which itself was based on a 1917 New York State zoning enabling law. Most states now have such a law, which in effect grants the state's police power to local governments. In some states, however, local governments have "home rule" authority directly from the state's constitution, which obviates the need for any explicit, statutory grant of police power from the state. Whether the source of the local government's authority is a constitutional "home rule" provision or a state zoning enabling act, zoning ordinances are only lawful if they are enacted pursuant to that authority. Moreover, zoning ordinances must be valid exercises of the police power and they must satisfy the Fifth Amendment "takings" clause. Taking claims are addressed at Section IV.B.4. of this chapter, as well as in Chapter 9.111, *supra*.

Under the SZEA, zoning is defined as the division of a government unit into districts. Within these districts the following elements are regulated:

1.   the height and bulk of buildings;

2.   the land area that can be occupied and that must remain open;

3.   the density of the population or intensity of use;

4.   the use of a structure for a particular purpose—such as commercial, industrial, agricultural, mineral extractive, or residential.

Beyond specifying physical design and purpose, zoning is intended to separate incompatible land uses and to preserve the economic value of existing properties in light of new developments. For example, a sand and gravel quarry should be isolated from a residential community because its activities could cause subsidence of neighboring residential land, thereby reducing residential property values. *See* Stephan & Sons, Inc. v. Municipality of Anchorage, 685 P.2d 98 (Alaska 1984).

b. Constitutionality of Land Use Planning and Regulation

In the minds of some scholars (and a few judges), *all* zoning constitutes an unconstitutional taking of private property because the government is restricting the rights of landowners to develop their lands as they see fit. *See* RICHARD A. EPSTEIN, TAKINGS: PRIVATE PROPERTY AND THE POWER OF EMINENT DOMAIN (1985). However, the United States Supreme Court long ago upheld the general constitutionality of comprehensive zoning.

VILLAGE OF EUCLID v. AMBLER REALTY CO.
United States Supreme Court, 1926.
272 U.S. 365, 47 S.Ct. 114, 71 L.Ed. 303.

JUSTICE SUTHERLAND delivered the opinion of the Court.

* * *

Building zone laws are of modern origin. They began in this country about twenty-five years ago. Until recent years, urban life was compara-

tively simple; but with the great increase and concentration of population, problems have developed, and constantly are developing, which
require, and will continue to require, additional restrictions in respect of
the use and occupation of private lands in urban communities. Regulations, the wisdom, necessity, and validity of which, as applied to existing
conditions, are so apparent that they are now uniformly sustained, a
century ago, or even half a century ago, probably would have been
rejected as arbitrary and oppressive. Such regulations are sustained,
under the complex conditions of our day, for reasons analogous to those
which justify traffic regulations, which, before the advent of automobiles
and rapid transit street railways, would have been condemned as fatally
arbitrary and unreasonable....

The ordinance now under review [which set forth the various uses—
residential, commercial, industrial—to which different parcels of land in
Euclid, Ohio could be put], and all similar laws and regulations, must
find their justification in some aspect of the police power, asserted for
the public welfare. The line which in this field separates the legitimate
from the illegitimate assumption of power is not capable of precise
delimitation. It varies with circumstances and conditions. A regulatory
zoning ordinance, which would be clearly valid as applied to the great
cities, might be clearly invalid as applied to rural communities. * * *

[T]he question whether the power exists to forbid the erection of a
building of a particular kind or for a particular use, like the question of
whether a particular thing is a nuisance, is to be determined, not by an
abstract consideration of the building or the thing considered apart, but
by considering it in connection with the circumstances of the locality....
A nuisance may be merely a right thing in the wrong place—like a pig in
the parlor instead of the barnyard. If the validity of the legislative classification for zoning purposes be fairly debatable, the legislative judgment must be allowed to control. * * *

There is no serious difference of opinion in respect of the validity of
laws and regulations fixing the height of buildings within reasonable
limits, the character of materials and methods of construction, and the
adjoining area which must be left open, in order to minimize the danger
of fire or collapse, the evils of over-crowding, and the like, and excluding
from residential sections offensive trades, industries and structures
likely to create nuisances.... * * * .... If it be a proper exercise of the
police power to relegate industrial establishments to localities separated
from residential sections, it is not easy to find a sufficient reason for
denying the power because the effect of its exercise is to divert an industrial flow from the course which it would follow to the injury of the residential public if left alone, to another course where such injury will be
obviated. It is not meant by this, however, to exclude the possibility of
cases where the general public interest would so far outweigh the interest of the municipality that the municipality would not be allowed to
stand in the way.

We find no difficulty in sustaining restrictions of the kind thus far reviewed. The serious question in the case arises over the provisions of the ordinance excluding from residential districts, apartment houses, business houses, retail stores and shops, and other like establishments. This question involves the validity of what is really the crux of the more recent zoning legislation, namely, the creation and maintenance of residential districts, from which business and trade of every sort, including hotels and apartment houses, are excluded. Upon that question, this Court has not thus far spoken. The decisions of the state courts are numerous and conflicting; but those which broadly sustain the power greatly outnumber those which deny altogether or narrowly limit it; and it is very apparent that there is a constantly increasing tendency in the direction of the broader view.... * * *

The matter of zoning has received much attention at the hands of commissions and experts, and the results of their investigations have been set forth in comprehensive reports. These reports, which bear every evidence of painstaking consideration, concur in the view that the segregation of residential, business, and industrial buildings will make it easier to provide fire apparatus suitable for the character and intensity of the development in each section; that it will increase the safety and security of home life; greatly tend to prevent street accidents, especially to children, by reducing the traffic and resulting confusion in residential sections; decrease noise and other conditions which produce or intensify nervous disorders; preserve a more favorable environment in which to rear children, etc. With particular reference to apartment houses, it is pointed out that the development of detached house sections is greatly retarded by the coming of apartment houses, which has sometimes resulted in destroying the entire section for private house purposes; that in such sections very often the apartment house is a mere parasite, constructed in order to take advantage of the open spaces and attractive surroundings created by the residential character of the district. Moreover, the coming of one apartment house is followed by others, interfering by their height and bulk with the free circulation of air and monopolizing the rays of the sun which otherwise would fall upon the smaller homes, and bringing, as their necessary accompaniments, the disturbing noises incident to increased traffic and business, and the occupation, by means of moving and parked automobiles, of larger portions of the streets, thus detracting from their safety and depriving children of the privilege of quiet and open spaces for play, enjoyed by those in more favored localities,—until, finally, the residential character of the neighborhood and its desirability as a place of detached residences are utterly destroyed. Under these circumstances, apartment houses, which in a different environment would be not only entirely unobjectionable but highly desirable, come very near to being nuisances.

If these reasons, thus summarized, do not demonstrate the wisdom or sound policy in all respects of those restrictions which we have indicated as pertinent to the inquiry, at least, the reasons are sufficiently cogent to preclude us from saying, as it must be said before the ordinance can be declared unconstitutional, that such provisions are clearly arbitrary and unreasonable, having no substantial relation to the public health, safety, morals, or general welfare.... * * *

Decree reversed.

Notes

1. This ruling was so significant that comprehensive zoning afterwards came to be known as "Euclidian zoning." In the *Euclid* case, the Supreme Court upheld the *general* constitutionality of comprehensive zoning, but it did not rule that any and every zoning ordinance is constitutional. Each individual zoning ordinance remains subject to constitutional review to ensure that it does not exceed the local government's police power or impinge too much on private property rights, including the reasonable, investment-backed expectations of developers. *See, e.g.,* Pennsylvania Coal Co. v. Mahon, 260 U.S. 393, 43 S.Ct. 158, 67 L.Ed. 322 (1922); Penn Central Transportation Co. v. City of New York, 438 U.S. 104, 98 S.Ct. 2646, 57 L.Ed.2d 631 (1978); Lucas v. South Carolina Coastal Council, 505 U.S. 1003, 112 S.Ct. 2886, 120 L.Ed.2d 798 (1992). However, zoning ordinances are only rarely overturned on constitutional grounds. On the takings implications of zoning and other forms of government regulation, *see* Chapter 9 on Individual Ownership.

2. Zoning districts are designated by use. Originally, the highest designated use was single-family residential, after that came multi-family residential, commercial, and industrial (the lowest designated use). Today, in many cities, open-space uses such as parks, have a higher designation than even residential uses, and other intermediate categories have been added. For example, the single-family residential classification may be split into separate categories for detached residences and attached residences (such as duplexes). In 2003, Pittsburgh, Pennsylvania (Urban Zoning Code 902.02) listed 15 zoning districts:

A. Hillside (H)

B. Park and Open Space (PO)

C. Residential Single–Unit Detached (R1D)

D. Residential Single–Unit Attached (R1A)

E. Residential Two–Unit (R2)

F. Residential Three–Unit (R3)

G. Residential Multi–Unit (RM)

H. Neighborhood Office (NDO)

I. Local Neighborhood Commercial (LNC)

J. Neighborhood Industrial (NDI)

K. Urban Neighborhood Commercial (UNC)

L. Highway Commercial (HC)

M. Educational/Medical Institution (EMI)

N. Urban Industrial District (UI)

O. General Industrial (GI)

One interesting point worth noting about Pittsburgh's list of zoning districts is the absence of agricultural areas, signifying the complete lack of agricultural land within the City's jurisdiction. In cities and towns with agricultural lands, those lands generally have status higher than or equal to single-family residential lands. Agricultural land use regulations, and mechanisms for preserving agricultural lands, are treated in some detail later in Sections III.D. and IV of this chapter.

3. Zoning is *cumulative* in that higher uses are generally allowed in areas zoned for lower uses, but not *vice versa*. So, in Pittsburgh, single-family detached residences are allowed in areas zoned for single-family attached residences, residential multi-unit, or even commercial. But neither commercial uses nor residential multi-unit dwellings are generally allowed in areas zoned single-family residential. Technically, single-family attached dwellings should not be built in areas zoned for single-family detached residences.

4. In addition to controlling the types of uses to which land may be put, zoning ordinances regulate many other facets of development, including building height, location of buildings with respect to property boundaries, even fence height. Figure 3 illustrates the multitude of zoning restrictions that may apply to an individual plot of land zoned single-family residential.

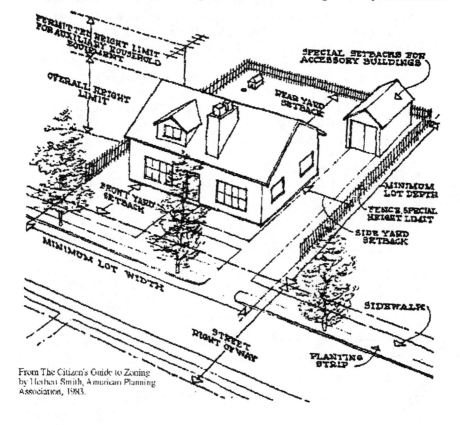

From The Citizen's Guide to Zoning
by Herbert Smith, American Planning
Association, 1983.

5. *Historic zoning.* In addition to preventing land-use conflicts, zoning ordinances in many cities pay special attention to preserving buildings and areas of historic significance from alterations or new development that might significantly detract from their historical value. Such ordinances may create special commissions with authority, among other things, to approve or reject proposals to add-on to or alter the structure of an historic building or even to change the color of its exterior paint. Historic zoning is generally constitutional. *See, e.g.,* Penn Central Transportation Co. v. City of New York, 438 U.S. 104, 98 S.Ct. 2646, 57 L.Ed.2d 631 (1978);

6. Nearly every city in the United States now has zoning. Among larger cities, only Houston, Texas, has failed to enact a comprehensive system of zoning ordinances. Meanwhile, in many rural counties of the United States, little or no land planning takes place. The reason is simple: those counties are virtually devoid of development pressure; they are located too far from population centers to be attractive locations for residential, industrial, or commercial developers, and their populations are not growing.

Even though Euclidean zoning is generally constitutional, individual zoning ordinances and other land use regulations may be unconstitutional if they either physically deprive the landowner of property or greatly diminish the value of property rights (or reasonable investment-backed expectations). *See* Pennsylvania Coal Co. v. Mahon, 260 U.S. 393, 43 S.Ct. 158, 67 L.Ed. 322 (1922); Penn Central Transportation Co. v. City of New York, 438 U.S. 104, 98 S.Ct. 2646, 57 L.Ed.2d 631 (1978); Lucas v. South Carolina Coastal Council, 505 U.S. 1003, 112 S.Ct. 2886, 120 L.Ed.2d 798 (1992). When land-use regulations are held unconstitutional, the government must either compensate the landowner or withdraw the regulation. For a more general and more detailed discussion of takings and just compensation law, *see* Chapter 9.

Zoning ordinances may also be invalid if they are not "consistent" with the local government's comprehensive plan. *See, e.g.,* Lazy Mountain Land Club v. Matanuska–Susitna Borough Bd. of Adjustment and Appeals, 904 P.2d 373 (Alaska 1995). In City of Cape Canaveral v. Cuberta Mosher, 467 So.2d 468 (Fla. App. 1985), the court explained what it means for zoning to be "consistent" (or "inconsistent") with the plan:

> The word "consistent" implies the idea or existence of some type or form of model, standard, guideline, point, mark or measure as a norm and a comparison of items or actions against that norm. Consistency is the fundamental relation between the norm and the compared item. If the compared item is in accordance with, or in agreement with, or within the parameters specified, or exemplified, by the norm, it is "consistent" with it but if the compared item deviates or departs in any direction or degree from the parameters of the norm, the compared item or action is not "consistent" with the norm.

City of Cape Canaveral at 471.

In Practice:

The requirement that zoning be consistent with a comprehensive plan imposes little practical burden on planners. Courts tend to uphold regulations so long as they are not patently *inconsistent* with the comprehensive plan, and the burden of proving inconsistency falls on the party challenging the regulation. *See, e.g.,* Gregory v. Alachua, 553 So.2d 206 (Fla.App. 1989). In some states, plan consistency is not even required. *See, e.g.,* Urrutia v. Blaine County, Idaho, 134 Idaho 353, 2 P.3d 738, 742–3 (2000) ("a comprehensive plan does not operate as legally controlling zoning law, but rather serves to guide and advise the governmental agencies responsible for making zoning decisions"); 1350 Lake Shore Assocs. v. Casalino, 352 Ill.App.3d 1027, 1047, 287 Ill.Dec. 708, 816 N.E.2d 675, 693 (2004) ("a comprehensive plan is only a factor to be considered in determining the validity of an ordinance").

c. Protection and Amortization of Pre-existing, Nonconforming Uses

It is one thing for local governments to regulate the development of vacant land; it is quite another for them to outlaw a valid, pre-existing use of land that does not conform to the subsequently adopted zoning ordinances. In some jurisdictions, such pre-existing, non-conforming uses cannot be zoned out of existence without payment of just compensation for a taking. *See, e.g.,* PA Northwestern Distributors, Inc. v. Zoning Hearing Board, 526 Pa. 186, 584 A.2d 1372 (1991). In those states, if regulators want to avoid paying compensation, they must allow the pre-existing, nonconforming use to live out its natural life, and wait for its abandonment, destruction, or replacement. In a slight majority of states, however, local governments can lawfully zone out pre-existing, nonconforming uses through a process known as *amortization*. Daniel R. Mandelker, Land Use Law § 5.70 (3d ed. 1993). Amortization gives pre-existing, non-conforming uses a "reasonable" period of time to recoup expenses and earn profits, before those uses are terminated (in that area) by operation of law. So long as the time period for amortization is reasonable, no valid taking claim arises under the federal constitution. *See, e.g.,* Board of Zoning Appeals, Bloomington, Indiana v. Leisz, 702 N.E.2d 1026 (In. 1998). What constitutes a reasonable time period, however, is dependent on the circumstances and the jurisdiction. "For any given use, one can find cases upholding, and other cases invalidating, periods ranging from 1 to 30 or more years." Jesse Dukeminier and James E. Krier, Property 982 (5th ed. 2002).

d. Special Use Permits, Variances, Rezoning, and Spot Zoning

Local governments would prefer all land development activities to proceed in strict accordance with comprehensive plans and zoning ordinances. But the real world always turns out to be messier than planning maps. As a practical matter, zoning ordinances need to be flexible enough to provide for exceptional circumstances. They do so in multiple ways, two of the more important of which are the special use permit (or special exception) and the variance.

Special use permits are not really deviations from zoning; they are contemplated by planners and usually explicitly listed in zoning ordinances as *possible* land uses that *may* be permitted under certain circumstances. A zoning ordinance for a rural area, for example, might list sand and gravel mining as a special use, that is, a use that *may* be, but is not automatically, permitted under the zoning ordinance. In order to lawfully engage in mining activities, mine operators first have to acquire a special use permit, which they could do upon a showing that their proposed use would conform in all respects with local zoning and not pose any threat to public health, safety or welfare. Upon such a showing, local permitting authorities in most states have no discretion to deny the special use permit. *See, e.g.*, Martin Marietta Aggregates v. Board of County Commissioners, 5 Kan.App.2d 774, 625 P.2d 516 (1981). However, those local authorities do have the power to impose conditions on the special use to ensure that no harm is caused to neighboring properties. For example, special use permits for mining operations virtually always include conditions protecting against subsidence of buildings on neighboring properties and requiring reclamation.

The variance is another tool designed to increase the flexibility of zoning. It is, however, quite different from the special use permit. "[A] variance is authority extended to a landowner to use his property in a manner prohibited by the ordinance (absent such variance) while a special exception allows him to put his property to a use which the ordinance expressly permits." Stucki v. Plavin, 291 A.2d 508, 511 (Me. 1972). Because variances allow activities otherwise prohibited by zoning ordinances, they are more difficult than special use permits to obtain. An applicant for a variance must show that the land for which they seek the variance is uniquely suited to the non-conforming use, and that they will, therefore, suffer special and undue hardship if the permit is not granted. Undue hardship, which must not be self-imposed, is a condition for obtaining the variance because the purpose of variances, from the local government's point of view, is to avoid possible takings claims for imposing too great a burden on individual landowners. *See* Daniel R. Mandelker, *Delegation of Power and Function in Zoning Administration*, 1963 WASH. U.L. Q. 60, 62–3. As the New York Court of Appeals explained in Otto v. Steinhilber, 282 N.Y. 71, 24 N.E.2d 851 (1939):

> The object of a variance granted by the Board of Appeals in favor of property owners suffering unnecessary hardship in the operation of a zoning law is to afford relief to an individual property owner laboring under restrictions to which no valid general objection may be made. Where the property owner is unable reasonably to use his land because of zoning restrictions, the fault may lie in the fact that the particular zoning restriction is unreasonable in its application to a certain locality or the oppressive result may be caused by conditions peculiar to a particular piece of land…. In order to prevent the oppressive operation of the zoning law in particular instances, when the zoning restrictions are otherwise generally reasonable, the zoning laws usually create a safety valve under the control of a Board of Appeals, which may relieve against "unnecessary hardship" in particular instances.

Otto, 24 N.E.2d at 852.

Because variances may pose a threat to neighboring lands, especially when the uses they allow are incompatible with neighboring uses permitted by the zoning ordinances, conditions are typically attached to variances to ensure that no harm is caused to neighboring properties. Many states do not allow zoning boards to grant variances if those variances might harm neighboring properties or otherwise "alter the essential character of the locality." *Id.* at 853.

Variances are an administrative (quasi-judicial) tool. Rezoning (a.k.a., zoning amendment) is a legislative mechanism for achieving greater flexibility in land use regulation. Indeed, it is the obvious way of making large-scale changes in zoning. However, rezoning often is used to change the status of an individual parcel of land. In that circumstance, known as "spot zoning," the zoning amendment achieves the same purpose as a variance, but through a legislative rather than administrative procedure. Spot zoning is illegal if: (a) "a small parcel of land is singled out for special and privileged treatment;" (b) "the singling out is not in the public interest but only for the benefit of the landowner;" *and* (c) "the action is not in accord with a comprehensive plan." Donald G. Hagman and Julian C. Juergensmeyer, Urban Planning and Land Development Control Law 136–7 (2d ed. 1986). Spot zoning is perfectly legal if any one of these three factors is lacking.

2. *Growth Controls*

All zoning ordinances are designed, in substantial part, to control growth. In recent years, however, some communities have gone to unusual lengths to limit growth and development, using measures ranging from quotas on housing permits to restrictions on the extension of city services (police, fire, water, and sewer). While several cities and a couple of states have experimented with various forms of urban growth control, the most famous such system is the Urban Growth Boundary that Portland, Oregon, instituted in 1979.

URBAN MECCA: PORTLAND, ORE., SHOWS NATION'S CITY PLANNERS HOW TO GUIDE GROWTH CRUCIAL FACTOR IN ITS SUCCESS IS A REGIONAL APPROACH, ESPECIALLY TO LAND USE

SUBURBAN SPRAWL LINGERS ON

Bob Ortega

The Wall Street Journal

Tuesday, December 26, 1995

PORTLAND, Ore.—In the 22 years since Oregon declared war on urban sprawl, the Portland area has become a mecca for city planners from Vermont to Southern California. They admire its pedestrian malls, parks and light-rail line.

But few trek out to the suburb of Beaverton. Outside Mayor Rob Drake's office windows there is a typical suburban scene: Traffic snarled around a mishmash of shopping malls, fast-food chains and used-car lots. "This is our original downtown, but people don't usually know that," he says, almost apologetically.

Such are the two aspects of the struggle to get a grip on growth. In the past two decades, Portland has succeeded perhaps more than any other Western city in controlling urban sprawl, fostering public transportation and revitalizing the inner city. However, it hasn't gotten rid of congestion, soaring housing costs and strip-mall suburbs such as Beaverton. Yet for a region desperate to tame surging growth, "Portland's answer is as good as you're going to get," says Anthony Downs, a senior fellow at the Brookings Institution in Washington.

Finding ways to handle the population surge in the West has become a major issue for cities such as Denver, Las Vegas and Salt Lake City. In November, seven cities in the Rocky Mountain region alone considered ballot measures calling for caps on building permits or other restrictions on growth; about half passed.

Most cities have reacted by absorbing outlying areas. Between 1970 and 1990, Phoenix nearly doubled its urbanized area to 741.4 square miles. Denver's has grown 77% since 1973, to more than 550 square miles. But many planners blame such sprawling development for the decline in downtown areas and for increased pollution and traffic congestion as commuters drive farther to work.

"All we have to do is look at Los Angeles to see how many people want to leave it because it's a sprawling, violent, congested, smoggy, unlivable city," says Dick Lamm, a former Colorado governor who failed in three efforts to push statewide planning laws through the legislature. "So what are we doing? Not a damn thing different than they did in L.A."

However, things are different in Portland, which in two decades has added just two square miles to its urban area. In the early 1970s, the city was much like others in the West. Downtown businesses were fleeing to the suburbs. ... [h]omeowners worrying about declining property values. Air pollution violated federal clean-air standards an average of 100 days a year. The state's transportation plans called for 54 new freeways and expressways in the region.

But in 1973, an odd coalition of farmers, timber interests, environmentalists and an activist governor pushed through the country's first statewide land-use law, which gave Portland a framework to channel growth rather than trying to halt it.

In 1979, Portland-area governments banned development outside a boundary ringing the city. Voters established the country's first elected regional government, called Metro, and gave it control over planning for the 24 municipalities and three counties in the metropolitan area. "Because developers can't just pick up and move out to the cheap farmlands, we've had the leverage and incentive to redevelop" areas, says Gussie McRobert, mayor of suburban Gresham and chairwoman of Metro's growth advisory committee.

Money earmarked for a new freeway was funneled instead into a light-rail system and improved bus service. New regulations required new downtown buildings to devote at least 50% of their frontage to retail space with windows or other displays. "So, instead of fortress architecture," says Charlie Hales, a developer and Metro commissioner, "there's life and activity downtown all day long." * * * The number of downtown jobs has doubled since 1975 without the city adding a single parking space, widening roads or building new ones. Traffic still gets congested, but with 40% of downtown workers commuting on light rail or buses, according to the city's transit authority, Portland hasn't had any air-quality violations since 1991. The ambitious future goal: to reduce auto traffic and parking spaces 20% during the next few decades.

In the suburbs, new regional planning channels large retail and commercial developments along public-transit lines. Instead of separating residential, business and retail areas, "mixed-use" zoning encourages projects such as Fairview Village, a 600–unit housing development reminiscent of a traditional New England town and now under construction just inside Portland's eastern growth boundary. Near a $5 billion computer-chip plant being built by LSI Logic Corp., the project includes single-family homes, town houses, row houses and buildings with shops at street level and apartments above. All will be within walking distance of a retail and civic center, city hall, post office and elementary school. The single-family homes sit on 5,000–square-foot lots, half the typical development size, but they look out on parks, bike paths and broad sidewalks.

"We do get people saying, 'This is too tight for me. Where am I going to put my motor home?' " says the developer, Rick Holt. "But it isn't just another subdivision with small lots. It's a whole village."

Henry Richmond, a lawyer and cofounder of 1000 Friends of Oregon, a watchdog group, says such development—if built around mass transit and not the automobile—is the solution to a rapidly growing population. "West Germany is roughly the same size as Colorado or Oregon, and it has 65 million people and magnificent countryside and beautiful pedestrian cities," he says. Colorado, Oregon and other Western states, he adds, "can easily handle three times the population they have today ... unless they keep doing things the way they have for the last 30 years."

As Metro drafts a plan to guide growth through the year 2040, the debate centers on whether to accommodate the expected 1.1 million new residents within the current boundary or to expand the boundary by 9,000 acres—a bit under 4%. By contrast, just two of the 12 new developments going up near Phoenix this year will take up more than 14,000 acres of desert.

"We're looking 40 years ahead and talking about a few thousand acres," Mr. Richmond says. "That isn't happening anywhere else in the country." Such results attract attention: Seven states—Florida, New Jersey, Washington, Maine, Vermont, Georgia and Rhode Island—have adopted planning laws or growth-management programs modeled on Oregon's. Other states are studying them.

The key to Portland's success is a regional approach. Every community had to establish growth boundaries and draw up comprehensive plans for leaving farm and forest areas undeveloped. And they can be legally forced to stick to the plans.

Meanwhile, the 1973 law and subsequent regulations give Oregon developers many advantages. Communities are generally barred from capping development and must plan and zone for anticipated growth. An appeals board dedicated solely to land-use issues halved the eight months it had taken courts to rule on appeals. Neighborhoods are encouraged to get involved in the planning process but have little input when building permits are issued. "If it's zoned for apartments, it doesn't matter how many neighbors show up and say they don't want apartments there," Metro's Mr. Hales says. "We follow our plan."

There are problems, of course. Many Oregonians initially thought that a growth boundary, by itself, would suffice. But it didn't halt the hyperdevelopment of suburbs such as Beaverton. Driving through a nearby apartment complex, Jon Chandler, general counsel of Portland's home builders' association, notes that "20 years ago, we thought it made sense to put apartments out here on the edge of the urban-growth boundary so neighbors wouldn't yell at you—even though high density out here, far from jobs and mass transit, doesn't make much sense."

And, as Beaverton illustrates, strip malls and the like aren't ended by the boundary; they just arise inside it unless cities take an active role in planning.

The boundary also has forced local and regional governments to change zoning codes so that more high-density housing will be built to meet growth needs. That often upsets current homeowners. A recent planning proposal to add thousands of housing units through "infill" developments in Portland's Albina area was scaled back drastically after residents protested. A similar plan in Portland's southeast fringe is also under attack.

Meanwhile, developers complain that planners push for higher density while regulations continue to "encourage 'Leave It to Beaver' housing," concedes John Fregonese, Metro's director of growth management. But Mr. Hales, the commissioner, notes that "attached" dwellings—duplexes, town houses, row houses and condominiums—constituted 12% of Portland housing going on the market in the first half of this year, up from 3% in the late 1980s. Today, he says, "I'd say the demand now is at least twice that."

Even as lots and homes get smaller, Portland's once-modest housing prices have doubled since 1988, to $132,000, says Pat Ritz, president of Oregon Title Insurance Co. Many developers blame the growth boundary, but how much of the rise is due to it isn't clear; home prices have soared all over the West. In Denver, they are up 44% in the past four years, compared with 26% in Portland.

The housing squeeze is worst at the bottom end of the market, says Howard Nolte, who runs a nonprofit group that tries to reclaim decayed inner-city areas by rebuilding homes. Driving into the Eliot neighborhood, where forlorn shacks sit near four new houses, he says, "Two years ago, we were paying $2,000 for a lot here. Last month, we paid $20,000 for a 5,000–square-foot lot with a house we had to tear down." Six years ago, his group's new houses in the area sold for $50,000 to $60,000, but now the minimum price is $85,000 because of rising land costs.

Out in Beaverton, Mayor Drake seems confident that the transformation in Portland will reach his town and the rest of the outskirts. Beaverton's planners fell behind as its population doubled to 63,000 in the past 10 years, he says, but with a light-rail line opening next year, the city can finally begin to carry out a six-year-old plan to redesign its downtown and other areas.

Crawling through traffic, Mayor Drake * * * warms to the pitch: Here will be sidewalks, there a new esplanade, on this side a retail center and residential development, on that a park. "This will finally give us a downtown," he says. "It happened in Portland. It can happen here."

––––––––––––

Portland's efforts to control urban sprawl have been fairly successful. As noted in this 1995 Wall Street Journal article, Portland has controlled the expansion of its boundaries far better than other cities with fast-growing populations, while maintaining open space and other amenities better than most. But critics—including, not surprisingly, land developers—complain about the cost of this achievement, particularly in terms of housing prices. It stands to reason that if new housing is limited by restrictions on land use, while demand for housing is increasing because of population in-flows, the price of existing housing must rise. However, the "first rigorous" economic analysis of the relationship between Portland's Urban Growth Boundary (UGB) and housing prices found that "[w]hile the UGB has likely imposed upward pressure on prices, ... the effect has been fairly modest." For the most part, housing price increases in Portland are consistent with increases in other fast-growing western cities that do not have UGBs. Justin Phillips and Eban Goodstein, *Growth Management and Housing Prices: The Case of Portland, Oregon*, 18 CONTEMP. ECON. POLICY 334, 341–2 (2000).

Suburban Sprawl in New Jersey

Today, Portland's Urban Growth Boundary and Oregon's entire system of land-use regulation is threatened with obliteration by a new property rights initiative recently enacted by public referendum. That initiative, known as "Measure 37," is addressed in the next section.

III.   STATE LAND USE PLANNING AND REGULATION

Traditionally, state governments left land-use regulation to city and county governments. In recent decades, however, the states have become more directly involved in controlling land development and use. Just a few years after the City of Portland initiated its Urban Growth Boundary (UGB) scheme, for example, the State of Oregon mandated that every other municipality in the state establish its own UGB. Nearly half the states now have some form of state-level land use planning, with a wide variety of goals and methods of implementation. Some states, as in

Oregon's case, seek to bridle growth; others use the planning process to facilitate economic development, for example by providing tax breaks to developers who create economic opportunities by developing land in "enterprise zones," which are usually designated in blighted or economically depressed urban areas.

A. Statewide Land Use Plans

In a comprehensive state plan, a legislatively appointed commission usually classifies all state lands into several areas, each of which must conform to statewide goals. This designation process directly affects people's use of their own property. For example, a person who owns land in an area designated as "critical" may be precluded from boring a mine shaft that would allow economic prosperity but risk instability to the surrounding terrain.

A commission charged with developing such a plan may take into account the following factors: (1) demography and projected growth of the state; (2) the types of industry and commerce within the state; (3) comprehensive housing data; (4) geological and ecological characteristics of state lands, reflecting the fact that in some areas development should be restricted because of potential for flooding or erosion; (5) existing capital infrastructure, including highways, navigation projects, parks, schools, and airports; and (6) areas which are of special environmental, scientific, archeological, or historical significance, and would be adversely affected by development.

Policies set forth in the state plan must be approved legislatively. The policies set forth in the plan are usually written in broad-brush terms. This generalized nature is due partly to the political influences exerted during plan formulation and partly to the difficulty of applying the same standards to diverse regions of the same state. For example, when devising a plan for natural resource exploitation, a state commission may be at the center of a battle between environmentalists and extractive industries. Adding to the tension are the conflicting interests of population growth centers, with their accompanying airports, highways, and sub-developments, and low-density population regions, including forests, open spaces, and agricultural areas. Typically, the commission must also decide whether the plan will encompass developments of a purely physical nature, such as a plant generating electricity, or will take into account societal needs, such as the pollution that the electric plant will emit. In addition, state land use plans often come into conflict with the policies of other state agencies, including departments of transportation, commerce, health, and environmental protection.

State land use plans come in various shapes and sizes. Examples from Oregon, Vermont and Hawaii should suffice to give a flavor of the wide variety of plans in existence.

Oregon—As previously noted, Oregon has been a frontrunner in the area of state level planning. Oregon law authorizes a state Land Conservation and Development Commission to set statewide goals with which local (city and county) planning commissions must comply. Ore.Rev.Stat. 197.005. These goals address:

a. Land use planning

b. Agricultural lands

c. Forest lands

d. Open spaces, scenic and historic areas and natural resources

e. Air, water and land resources quality

f. The state economy

g. Transportation

h. Coastal shorelands

i. Ocean resources

The Commission provides local governments with guidelines to aid in designing plans to conform with the State's goals. After the city, county, or special district develops such a plan, the Commission may "amend and administer" the local plan to ensure compliance. *See* Maresh v. Yamhill County, 68 Or.App. 471, 683 P.2d 124 (1984) (sustaining the Commission's invalidation of a county ordinance rezoning a site from agricultural-forestry to mineral). Local planning agencies have a degree of latitude in planning to conform to the State's goals. This enables diverse counties, including those in the eastern farming districts and those in western coastal areas, to devise plans that conform to the State plan. However, the State Commission has substantial oversight authority to ensure that local planning agencies do not violate those goals. A local comprehensive plan, and any actions in accordance with that plan, which fail to meet state standards may be void. *See* Willamette University v. Land Conservation and Development Commission, 45 Or.App. 355, 608 P.2d 1178 (1980).

Oregon's focus has led to uniform, statewide application of its statutory goals. The goals are comprehensive and affect virtually all areas of state land use planning. The attention given to the protection of the environment, to the land's economic utility, and its cultural, historical, and aesthetic amenities makes the Oregon approach the most advanced state planning endeavor in the country.

In Focus:

Oregon's Land Use Planning Effort

Today, Oregon's entire system of land use planning, including Portland's Urban Growth Boundaries (discussed above) is under threat from Measure 37, an initiative enacted in a public referendum in November 2004, which ostensibly requires the State to either pay compensation for all regulatory impositions on private landowners or exempt their lands from regulation.

MEASURE 37

The following provisions are added to and made a part of ORS chapter 197:

(1) If a public entity enacts or enforces a new land use regulation or enforces a land use regulation enacted prior to the effective date of this amendment that restricts the use of private real property or any interest therein and has the effect of reducing the fair market value of the property, or any interest therein, then the owner of the property shall be paid just compensation.

(2) Just compensation shall be equal to the reduction in the fair market value of the affected property interest resulting from enactment or enforcement of the land use regulation as of the date the owner makes written demand for compensation under this act.

(3) Subsection (1) of this act shall not apply to land use regulations:

(A) Restricting or prohibiting activities commonly and historically recognized as public nuisances under common law. This subsection shall be construed narrowly in favor of a finding of compensation under this act;

(B) Restricting or prohibiting activities for the protection of public health and safety, such as fire and building codes, health and sanitation regulations, solid or hazardous waste regulations, and pollution control regulations;

(C) To the extent the land use regulation is required to comply with federal law;

(D) Restricting or prohibiting the use of a property for the purpose of selling pornography or performing nude dancing. Nothing in this subsection, however, is intended to affect or alter rights provided by the Oregon or United States Constitutions; or

(E) Enacted prior to the date of acquisition of the property by the owner or a family member of the owner who owned the subject property prior to acquisition or inheritance by the owner, whichever occurred first.

(4) Just compensation under subsection (1) of this act shall be due the owner of the property if the land use regulation continues to be enforced against the property 180 days after the owner of the property makes written demand for compensation under this

section to the public entity enacting or enforcing the land use regulation.

(5) For claims arising from land use regulations enacted prior to the effective date of this act, written demand for compensation under subsection (4) shall be made within two years of the effective date of this act, or the date the public entity applies the land use regulation as an approval criteria to an application submitted by the owner of the property, whichever is later. For claims arising from land use regulations enacted after the effective date of this act, written demand for compensation under subsection (4) shall be made within two years of the enactment of the land use regulation, or the date the owner of the property submits a land use application in which the land use regulation is an approval criteria, whichever is later.

(6) If a land use regulation continues to apply to the subject property more than 180 days after the present owner of the property has made written demand for compensation under this act, the present owner of the property, or any interest therein, shall have a cause of action for compensation ... and ... shall be entitled to reasonable attorney fees, expenses, costs, and other disbursements reasonably incurred to collect the compensation.

(7) A metropolitan service district, city, or county, or state agency may adopt or apply procedures for the processing of claims under this act, but in no event shall these procedures act as a prerequisite to the filing of a compensation claim under subsection (6) of this act, nor shall the failure of an owner of property to file an application for a land use permit with the local government serve as grounds for dismissal, abatement, or delay of a compensation claim under subsection (6) of this act.

(8) Notwithstanding any other state statute or the availability of funds under subsection (10) of this act, in lieu of payment of just compensation under this act, the governing body responsible for enacting the land use regulation may modify, remove, or not to apply the land use regulation or land use regulations to allow the owner to use the property for a use permitted at the time the owner acquired the property.
* * *

(10) Claims made under this section shall be paid from funds, if any, specifically allocated by the legislature, city, county, or metropolitan service district for payment of claims under this act. * * * If a claim has not been paid within two years from the date on which it accrues, the owner shall be allowed to use the property as permitted at the time the owner acquired the property.

(11) Definitions—for purposes of this section:
* * *

(B) Land use regulation shall include:

(i) Any statute regulating the use of land or any interest therein;

(ii) Administrative rules and goals of the Land Conservation and Development Commission;

(iii) Local government comprehensive plans, zoning ordinances, land division ordinances, and transportation ordinances;

(iv) Metropolitan service district regional framework plans, functional plans, planning goals and objectives; and

(v) Statutes and administrative rules regulating farming and forest practices.

* * *

(12) The remedy created by this act is in addition to any other remedy under the Oregon or United States Constitutions, and is not intended to modify or replace any other remedy. * * *

The enactment of Measure 37 in Oregon demonstrates that there are political as well as constitutional limits on public land use planning and regulation. The precise effects of the measure remain to be seen. In the first place, the law may face legal challenges.[a] Second, the Oregon legislature may consider amendments to, or replacement legislation for, Measure 37. *See* Laura Oppenheimer and Ashbel S. Green, *Challenges to Land Law Face Slim Prospects*, The Oregonian, Nov. 12, 2004. It remains to be seen whether the enactment of Measure 37 represents the beginning of a national trend.

PROPERTY RIGHTS LAW MAY ALTER OREGON LANDSCAPE
Felicity Barringer
The New York Times
November 26, 2004 Friday

PORTLAND, Ore., Nov. 20

Over the past three decades, Oregon has earned a reputation for having the most restrictive land-use rules in the nation. Housing was grouped in and near the cities, while vast parcels of farmland and for-

a. Just as this book was going to press, on February 21, 2006, the Oregon Supreme Court ruled that Measure 37 did not violate either the state or federal constitutions. MacPherson v. Department of Administrative Services, Case No. S52857, available on the World Wide Web at http://www.publications.ojd.state.or.us/S52875.htm.

ests were untouched by so much as a suburban cul-de-sac. Environmentalists and advocates for "smart growth" cheered the ever-growing list of rules as visionary, while some landowners, timber companies and political allies cried foul.

But in a matter of days, the landowners will get a chance to turn the tables. Under a ballot measure approved on Nov. 2, property owners who can prove that environmental or zoning rules have hurt their investments can force the government to compensate them for the losses—or get an exemption from the rules.

Supporters of the measure, which passed 60 percent to 40 percent, call it a landmark in a 30-year battle over property rights. "I've been getting calls from California, Idaho, Washington, Alaska and Wisconsin," said Ross Day, a Portland lawyer for the conservative group Oregonians in Action who co-wrote the law, Ballot Measure 37. "They all want to find out what our secret recipe was to get it passed."
* * *

Richard J. Lazarus, a professor at the Georgetown University Law Center who specializes in environmental law, called the measure a blunt instrument that could undermine all zoning and environmental protections and undercut land values. "If you can build a little Houston anywhere, or a gravel pit or a shopping center next to your home, you don't have maximization of property values," Professor Lazarus said.

"If you fail to regulate now, you're reducing property values for future Oregonians," he continued. "A lot of what government is doing in environmental protection is at least trying to balance the needs of present and future generations."

The new law, Professor Lazarus said, "is one of those very simple solutions, but, boy, did they open a can of worms."

Conservatives across the country have championed the idea of compensation for aggrieved landowners since at least the mid-1990's and the 1994 Republican "Contract With America." Four states have laws dating from that period that provide some compensation for affected property owners.

"In Oregon, they're serious," said Michael M. Berger, a partner in the Los Angeles law firm of Manatt, Phelps & Phillips. "It helps make people sit up and take notice that this is something they have to deal with. This is a big shock to the body politic—it's a very red-state thing to do, and Oregon is very blue, so this shows it cut across everyone."

Both sides expect the measure to survive judicial scrutiny, and the state and local governments are to start fielding claims on Dec. 2. If claims are found to be valid and the government will not or cannot pay, it must instead waive any restrictions that went into force after the owners—or their parents or grandparents—acquired the land.

Some fear that the state will be unable to pay and that hillsides in the Cascades now bristling with fir trees and pear orchards could sprout a crop of McMansions, Wal–Marts or resort condominiums in a few years.

The supporters of the new law successfully depicted the current plight of property owners in a campaign with a decidedly populist edge. One advertisement showed a woman penalized for cutting blackberry bushes—potential wildlife habitat—in her backyard in Portland.

Another woman, Dorothy English, 92, was a fixture on drive-time radio advertisements in the final week of the campaign. Ms. English bought land in the hills west of Portland in 1953 and is still fighting for the right to carve several lucrative building lots out of the 20 acres she has left. "They've made fools of people in this state," she said last Wednesday. "I've always been fighting the government and I'm not going to stop."

The Hood River Valley, 60 miles east of Portland and the source of more than a third of the nation's Bosc pears, is one of the places that could be most affected. Many of the farmers are the third or fourth generations of their families to work the same land. Most land-use regulation came after their families did, so their claims could be extensive and expensive. The valley nestles along the Columbia River Gorge, a strong draw for windsurfers; the development pressure is strong.

Sitting in their living room in the town of Hood River, overlooking fields newly planted in cherries, John Benton and his wife, Julie, both 57, said that their income was eroding and that their 100–acre farm had "barely supported us." The Bentons, whose family ownership dates to 1910, said that orchard farmers like themselves could not make a living without an infusion of cash from selling land for home construction.

By contrast, their neighbor Fritz VonLubken, who is 69 and bought his orchards from a grandfather who came to the area in 1912, said he believed that farmland needed to be preserved. "You zone for industrial districts," Mr. VonLubken said. "Well, farming is an industry. It needs to be protected. We're a high-value business, and this is the best location for us."

Mike McCarthy, whose 250 acres scattered on the northeastern apron of Mount Hood produce a plentiful crop of pears, said, "These are the most productive soils in Oregon," and, as such, were irreplaceable.

The success of the ballot measure has led advocates of planning to do some soul searching. It won a majority in all 35 of the state's counties except the one that encompasses Corvallis and Oregon State

University and got a thin majority even in the progressive city of Portland.

"It definitely calls into question a lot of the mechanisms we have now," said David Bragdon, the president of the Metro Council, which sets the growth parameters for 460 square miles in three metropolitan Portland counties. "And it undermines the mechanisms we have."

* * *

Each county has established "urban growth boundaries" around its cities and has tried to keep most development to areas within them. On farmland, houses can be built only under strict conditions—for instance, the buyer must show that he can generate $80,000 in annual gross income from farming for a period of years before he can build. Nonfarm dwellings are allowed only in areas with poor soil. In return, farmers receive substantial property tax breaks; their land may be assessed at as little as 0.5 percent of land where development is encouraged.

Even if they succeed, farmers who fight to have the urban growth boundary extended to their lands must pay a one-time tax amounting to perhaps 7.5 percent of the land's new value—in addition to federal and state capital gains taxes on the sale of the property. Thanks to such tight policies, suburban sprawl has been largely banished in Oregon.

Gov. Theodore R. Kulongoski, a Democrat who opposed the compensation measure, said last week that he would push to have claims paid rather than tear holes in the state's land-use system. But, like many other states, Oregon is strapped. To pay the claims, some pro-planning forces suggest setting high taxes on the profits on newly developable land. If, instead, the government grants exemptions to land-use rules, many property owners might want to sell for the ready profit.

Mr. VonLubken, like Professor Lazarus, said he believed that the first wave of farmland sales would be the most lucrative and that those new residents, having paid a premium for bucolic splendor, would support regulation to help keep a second wave of newcomers away.

The state's population grew 20.4 percent in the 1990's, to about 3.4 million people in 2000. * * * [s]tate, tribal and federal lands constitute about 55 percent of the state's total acreage. Of the remaining 27.7 million acres of privately held land, 56 percent is farmland.

Others states that allow for compensation for aggrieved property owners are Florida, Texas, Louisiana and Mississippi. But they set a threshold, for instance a 25 percent reduction in a property's value, and will pay only for losses caused by new land-use rules. The retroactive feature of the Oregon law could affect many more people. Until the claims start, though, no one will hazard a guess at just how much land will be affected, and at what cost.

"It's no coincidence that they passed this Measure 37 in a state that has prided itself on having the most extensive planning and regulatory scheme for rural lands," said J. David Breemer, a staff lawyer with the Pacific Legal Foundation, a conservative advocacy organization. "This type of initiative and legislation will be more common now."

The planners, however, are still flying their flags. "Quality of life is something that is shared," said Robert Liberty, a former president of 1,000 Friends of Oregon, an ardent pro-planning group, who was just elected to the board of the Portland regional planning agency. * * * "One of the best things about the planning process is that it makes a better community for everyone, regardless of income." * * *

Whatever else it may do, Oregon's Measure 37 demonstrates that land use planners are constrained not only by the Constitution's takings clause, but also by political institutions, including both public referenda and ordinary legislation. In recent years, the General Assemblies of several states, including Texas, Florida, Louisiana, and Mississippi, have enacted *takings statutes*, which, on paper at least, afford greater protection to private property owners than the 5th Amendment's takings clause as presently interpreted by the U.S. Supreme Court.

For example, Lousiana's 1995 Right to Farm and Forest Act, La.Rev.Stat.Ann. 3:3601 *et seq*, grants a cause of action to owners of agricultural or forest lands to sue state or local government agencies for regulatory impositions that reduce the value of the property by 20 percent or more. The government has the option of paying compensation or rescinding the regulatory imposition. Are these types of state laws a good idea? Are you more comfortable with initiatives like Measure 37, passed by voter referendum, than those that originate with the legislative? On state takings laws generally, *see* Mark W. Cordes, *Leapfrogging the Constitution: The Rise of State Takings Legislation*, 24 Ecol. L.Q. 187 (1997); Larry Morandi, *Evaluating the Effects of State Takings Legislation*, 23 State Legis. Rep. (Jan. 1998), available on the World Wide Web at http://www.ncsl.org/programs/esnr/slr232.htm.

Vermont—Vermont's Land Use Development Act, 10 Vt.Stat.Ann. § 6001 *et seq.*, was enacted in response to a growing number of recreational facilities and vacation homes being built in rural and previously undeveloped areas. It requires that a state permit be obtained for the development of ten or more acres for commercial, industrial, or governmental purposes. A permit must also be obtained for developments at elevations above 1500 feet, since such areas are deemed environmentally sensitive and prone to irreversible damage 10 Vt.Stat.Ann. § 6086. Pursuant to the Act, Vermont is divided into nine geographic districts, each monitored by a district commissioner appointed by the governor. Before a development permit will be issued, the developer must comply with certain statutory criteria and conditions relating to air and water pollution, water supplies, soil erosion, transportation facilities, and provision of public services. Local governments in Vermont retain control over all other aspects of zoning.

Hawaii—In Hawaii, a state land use commission classifies land by its traditional use: urban, rural, agricultural, or conservation. Hawaii Rev. State §§ 205–1, 205–2. Conservation districts include watersheds, scenic and historic areas, beaches and wilderness. Rural districts are those which combine low-density residential (one dwelling per one-half acre) with small farms. Agricultural districts are areas characterized by the cultivation of crops, orchards, forestry, and animal husbandry. Urban districts are designated by county ordinance or regulation.

Hidden within this system are several problems, which should serve as a warning to state planners. First, the relatively stable prices of Hawaii's cash crops, including pineapples and sugar cane, compared with the high cost of real estate, has created friction between the state commission, which administers the agricultural districts, and the counties, which administer the urban districts. The agricultural lands would undoubtedly yield a higher return on investment if converted to a more intensive use, such as high-rise apartment dwellings; but, at the same time, Hawaii's traditional agricultural economy would be decimated. This same problem plagues virtually all states with sizeable agricultural industries, including those that do not take Hawaii's traditional use-based approach to state land-use classifications.

Another source of friction between state planners and counties in Hawaii is that land designated as "conservation" consists of the residue of lands that do not fit easily into one of the other categories. Fast-growing counties seek to re-designate "conservation" lands as "urban" so as to proceed with development, while the state prefers to preserve the land's natural assets in the conservation designation. This county-state conflict is illustrative of the difficulties planners everywhere have in finding a proper fit between the "highest and best" use of land as determined by the market, and what administrators consider to be an "acceptable" use of land. If Hawaii can experience such problems, given its limited size and number of counties, one can imagine the problems of planning in much larger, more populous states. Counties with high-density growth do not want the same treatment as those that are predominantly agricultural. Thus, the battle lines are drawn between environmentalists, farmers, and developers.

B. Farmland Preservation and Regulation

Agriculture remains the dominant land use in the United States. More acres of land are devoted to growing crops or pasturing livestock than any other use. However, in many states—especially those with fast growing urban areas—agricultural lands are being converted to non-agricultural uses at a rapid rate. While urban sprawl is typically blamed for the fast rate of farmland conversion, analysts dispute both the extent and the causes of agricultural land losses. Nevertheless, in response to pressures from agricultural and other interests, states have instituted various measures to preserve agricultural lands in agricultural use, including right-to-farm laws and conservation easements.

1. The "Problem" of Farmland Loss

FARMING ON THE EDGE
American Farmland Trust, Saving American
Farmland: What Works 3–9 (1997)

[E]very state in the nation is sacrificing irreplaceable agricultural resources to urban sprawl. We are converting a total of about 1 million acres a year, and while the quantity of top-quality agricultural land being lost varies from state to state, the process of conversion increases the pressures on agriculture even beyond the acres that are actually taken out of production....

Farming is what distinguishes land as farmland. Along with sunshine and water, we need land to grow food, fiber and oilseed crops. But not all of it is equally well-suited to production. Fertile soils take millions of years to develop. Creating them takes a combination of climate, geology, biology, and good luck; so far, no one has found a way to manufacture these. Productive agricultural land is a finite and indispensable resource.

* * * Roughly 56 percent of our crops are grown on prime farmland, yet according to the U.S. Department of Agriculture, these are the very soils most likely to be converted to nonagricultural use. Most of our population centers are surrounded by high quality farmland. Between 1990 and 1994, 84 percent of non-metropolitan counties next to metropolitan areas gained population. This helps explain the conversion of 4 million acres of prime farmland and the conversion of another 266,000 acres of unique farmland in 10 years.

Economic opportunity, environmental protection, community infrastructure and quality of life are among the most compelling reasons to save farmland. Saving farmland is a good investment in the future of our country. Yet despite its importance to our nation and communities, our most valuable farmland is at risk, imperiled by complex forces of conversion that can take 20 or more years to be fully realized on the landscape. Conversion is fueled by rising real estate values and property taxes, declining agricultural profitability, conflicts between farmers and their non-farming neighbors, stricter environmental regulations and a decline in farmers' satisfaction with agriculture as a way of life.

Meeting the Challenges of Farming in an Urban Age

The frontier spirit drove Americans to settle the wilderness. The early settlers transformed the landscape by clearing forests and draining swamps. They took advantage of productive soils and built towns and cities near rivers and in fertile valleys. Farming was often the basis of wealth and trade. America's most profitable agriculture still takes place near population centers. More than half of the value of American agricultural production comes from counties in and around urban areas. These areas provide 85 percent of our fresh fruits and vegetables, 79 percent of our dairy products and nearly half of our meat and grain. Urban-influence counties [counties including or adjacent to metropolitan areas with at least 25 people per square mile] account for 56 percent of our gross agricultural sales and 91 percent of our specialty crops.

Yet population growth in counties with the highest agricultural productivity is more than twice the national average. For example, in the last generation, Pittsburgh, Chicago, Cleveland, St. Louis and Detroit lost an average of 37 percent of their central city populations while suburban land use soared. And during the 1980s, many urban centers reached out of their borders and developed "edge cities," often with suburbs of their own.

Historically, an abundance of land, coupled with the development of long-distance transportation systems, encouraged American farmers to move west to avoid non-farm population encroachment. In the 19th century, federal policies such as the Homestead Act made western lands available for agriculture. However, since World War II, the government has stimulated the conversion of farmland to residential and commercial uses with little regard for the quality of the natural resource base or the land use preferences of states and municipalities. Chief among federal policies that encourage conversion are highway construction, the income tax deduction for home mortgage interest and facilities construction.

The effects of these policies were felt first on the coasts, especially in California and in the mid-Atlantic and northeastern states. These areas continue to experience losses, but the threat is spreading. Today, our top-producing agricultural states also are in jeopardy. For example, from 1982 to 1992, Texas lost more of its best-quality farmland than any other state. Florida, several other Southeastern states and much of the Midwest also converted significant acreage of prime and unique soils.

When people move out of cities, they often do so to escape noise, pollution, deteriorated neighborhoods and crime. However, this leads to further decline in our city centers and often begins a process of re-creating urban problems in the country. As suburbs close to cities become crowded with homes, shopping malls, convenience stores and commuters, people seek homes farther and farther out into rural communities.[a] This scattershot expansion creates demand for subdivisions,

---

   a. Revisit the evolving footprint of the City of Baltimore, Figure 3, above.

public services, retail businesses and professional jobs in areas that were once devoted to resource-based industries such as farmer, logging and fishing.

Increasingly, farmers and ranchers in rural areas are facing the same problems as those in more developed areas. Improvements in computer technology are allowing professionals to live in more isolated communities and "telecommute" to distant offices. The strong economy of the 1980s and 1990s fueled demand for vacation homes in traditional ranching areas such as Colorado, Montana and Utah and near the working dairy farms of Vermont's Lake Champlain. * * * Farmers and ranchers are being forced to compete for land and resources, which can reduce or eliminate profits. To challenge these forces, we must find a way to stabilize the land base, to support the economics of agriculture and, increasingly, to protect our natural resources....

Saving Farmland Ensures Food Security and Creates Economic Opportunities

The dominant role of U.S. agriculture in the global economy has been likened to OPEC's position in the field of energy. Agriculture accounts for nearly 16 percent of the U.S. gross domestic product and provides 18 percent of civilian jobs. The market value of our agricultural commodities was $162 billion in 1992, and domestic demand for food and fiber products generated $950 billion in 1992. Our farmland supports the world's most productive food and farming system.

With a rapidly increasing world population and expanding international markets, saving farmland is a wise investment in global food security and economic opportunity. While food shortages are unlikely to threaten American consumers in the short term, our population is predicted to grow by 50 percent in the next 50 years, with farmers and ranchers having to make do with 13 percent fewer acres of high quality agricultural land. If we do not take measures to save our best-quality resources for the future, domestic food production—and certainly food prices—could become an issue for the next generation.

The United States produces half of the world's grain exports. The current world human population of 5.7 billion is growing by more than 88 million people a decade. Meanwhile, global food production seems to be declining in relation to world population. In 1990, the USDA reported that grain consumption had exceeded production for three years in a row. The 1996 World Food Summit of the United Nations reported that to adequately feed the world, global food production must quadruple on the next 50 years.

Developing nations in Africa, Asia and Latin America are already concerned about food security. Even as worldwide demand for food rises, many countries are paving over their arable land for commercial growth to support rapidly expanding economies. These countries are expected to be larger consumers of U.S. agricultural products in the future.

Our agricultural exports are an important part of the food supply of many industrialized countries. Currently, the Japanese are our most important customers, accounting for nearly 20 percent of our total agricultural exports. Japan is increasingly purchasing American specialty crops as well as grains. According to the Wall Street Journal, Japanese imports of vegetables grew by 66 percent in 1994. Forty-four percent of the increase was in American-grown vegetables, especially broccoli, asparagus and onions.

The diversity and versatility of American agriculture can ensure our continuing preeminence in world markets. But if we do not develop an investment strategy that preserves our assets, including agricultural land, we will not have resources readily available to supply rapidly changing global demand. * * *

Saving Farmland Protects Our Natural Resources

With 945 million acres in production, agriculture is the dominant land use in the United States. So it is not surprising that farming has significant ecological impact. Since most farmers live close to the land, it is in their best interest to protect the environment that sustains them. Yet, ever since the publication of Rachel Carson's *Silent Spring* more than three decades ago, environmentalists have called attention to the negative consequences of some of the inputs associated with modern agricultural practices.

* * *

A new tide of federal regulations has imposed environmental restrictions on agricultural practices. The first wave came in the early 1970s, first with the Clean Air Act and then with the Clean Water Act and the reauthorization of the Federal Insecticide, Fungicide, and Rodenticide Act [FIFRA].... Since the 1985 Farm Bill, the agricultural community has begun to address the ecological and economic costs of conventional agriculture. The 1990 and 1996 Farm Bills included new agricultural policies that emphasize resource conservation.

The Conservation Reserve Program was authorized by the 1985 Farm Bill. It pays landowners not to cultivate highly erodible cropland and sensitive areas like streamside buffers, critical wildlife habitat and wetlands. The program is administered by the USDA Farm Services Agency with technical assistance from the Natural Resources Conservation Service [NRCS]. Approximately $1.95 billion was spent on this program in fiscal year 1996, protecting about 34 million acres under 10-year contracts. In the past, the focus was on curbing soil erosion, particularly in the Great Plains. Changes made by the 1996 Farm Bill increase emphasis on protecting sensitive aquatic resources, by allowing continuous signup for farmers who use practices such as filter strips, buffers along rivers and contour grass strips.

The Wetlands Reserve Program [WRP] was authorized by the 1990 Farm Bill and is administered by the NRCS. The WRP pays for perpetual and long-term conservation easements, as well as shorter-term agreements that call for restoration and protection of formerly cultivated wetlands. Since the program began, the NRCS has spent $274 million to restore and protect 325,833 acres of wetlands nationwide. Program rules tend to favor areas where there are extensive, low-cost wetlands such as the Mississippi Delta, but anticipated changes will make the program more attractive in the East and far West where land is more expensive and wetlands more isolated.

* * *

According to the USDA, it is hard to overestimate the importance of the non-market goods and services that agriculture provides. Well-managed farmland protects soil and water resources and can prevent flooding. It absorbs and filters wastewater and provides groundwater recharge. New energy crops even have the potential to replace fossil fuels. From wetland management to on-farm composting for municipalities, farmers are finding ways to improve environmental quality.

Saving Farmland is an Investment in Community Infrastructure

To many people, the most compelling reasons for saving farmland are local and personal, and much of the political support for farmland protection is driven by grassroots community efforts. Agriculture contributes to local economies directly, through sales, job creation, support services and businesses, and also by supplying lucrative secondary markets such as food processing. Distinctive agricultural landscapes may be magnets for tourism. Farmland offers a hedge against fragmented suburban development while supporting a diversified economic base. Increasingly, people view natural resources, including agricultural land, as vital for the well-being of our communities, rather than as "free" material to be disposed of at will.

Privately owned and managed farmland generates more tax revenues than it costs in services. * * * [c]areful examination [by the American Farmland Trust] of local budgets has shown that farm, forest and open land more than pay for the municipal services they require, while taxes on residential uses consistently fail to cover costs.* * *

Saving Farmland Sustains Our Quality of Life

Sometimes the most important qualities are the hardest to quantify. This is true of the role that farmland plays in contributing a sense of place. Farm and ranch land maintains scenic, cultural and historic landscapes. It offers beautiful views and managed open space, which can provide opportunities for hunting, horseback riding, fishing and other recreational activities. Farms and ranches create indentifiable and unique community character and add to our quality of life.

These qualities are appreciated by visitors as well. * * * In Lancaster, Pa., agriculture is still the leading industry, but with Amish and Old Order Mennonites working in the fields, tourism is not far behind. Napa Valley, Calif., is another place known as a destination for "agrotourism." Tourists have become such a large part of most Napa Valley wineries that many vintners have hired hospitality staff. Both the valley and the wines have gained name recognition, and the economy is thriving.

Finally, farming is an integral part of our heritage and our identity as a people. American democracy is rooted in our agricultural past and founded on the principle that all people can own property and earn a living from the land. Our ongoing relationship with the agricultural landscape connects us to our history and to the natural world. Our land is our legacy, both as we look back to the past and as we consider what we have of value to pass on to future generations.

* * *

The Process of Conversion

Farmers generally sell their land out of agriculture for two reasons: weak farm profitability and the high value of land for nonfarm development. These two factors underlie the complex process of farmland conversion.

Declining farm profitability has many causes. Among them, rising land values and property taxes play a significant role by increasing the costs of agriculture. Expensive land also increases opportunity costs: Selling lots for development is generally more lucrative than raising crops or livestock. As municipalities change from rural to suburban—and then from suburban to urban—the pressures mount on producers to sell their land. * * *

Rural land is cheap for suburban developers, who are willing to pay landowners far more than agricultural value for the flat, well-drained land they prefer for building. As people from surrounding urban and suburban areas move into rural communities, large land parcels are divided and prices soar far beyond their economic value for agriculture. Farmland, which requires few public services, is typically converted to subdivisions filled with residents who require education, utilities and other costly amenities. High land costs make it difficult for new farmers to enter agriculture or for existing producers to buy or rent land to expand operations. Inflated land values make it too expensive for farmers to compete in agricultural markets. Transferring land from one generation to the next also becomes difficult. Federal and state inheritance taxes are assessed at the time of death and are based on the highest and best use of property. Without solid estate planning and a farm transfer strategy, heirs often find they cannot pay inheritance taxes without selling all or a portion of their land.

Scattered development increases the likelihood of conflict between farmers and ranchers, and their neighbors. Large land parcels are divided into smaller and smaller tracts, which more people can afford to buy. The remaining operations become separated by housing developments inhabited by people with little understanding of agriculture as a business or way of life. New residents may appreciate the agricultural landscape, but they frequently resent farm chemicals and the smell of manure, noisy machinery and slow-moving vehicles. Often they complain; sometimes they sue. Complaints can lead to new ordinances that restrict agricultural practices. Production costs rise as losses due to trespassing, pilfering, harassment of livestock and vandalism increase.

In the last 20 years, the public has demanded higher environmental performance from agriculture. Concern about conserving soil and water has expanded to include nonpoint source pollution, wetland protection and biodiversity. Environmental regulations on agriculture have become stiffer, and farmers have had to find alternatives to conventional practices. New techniques may not be as well researched, proven or profitable as the methods that have been promoted and used for 50 years. These demands add to production costs.

The combination of these forces threaten the viability of agriculture. When farmers and ranchers sell out, the economic foundation of rural communities is weakened. Local seed and feed distributors and equipment dealers go out of business, and the remaining producers must travel longer distances and pay higher prices to purchase supplies and services. Communities that were once tight-knit become fragmented and farmers become stressed. Discouraged, they may reduce long-term investments in their operations. Without pro-farming public policies and political support, the snowballing process of scattered development, falling profits and rising property taxes can result in an "impermanence syndrome," in which farmers' expectation of decline may actually stimulate it.

As agriculture loses ground, farmers and ranchers become a minority and often lose influence in their communities. This weakens their political voice, especially in local planning and zoning decisions. While zoning bylaws can be drafted to support agriculture and limit the forces that cause decline, without vision and attention to the needs of the agricultural community, new ordinances can be hostile to commercial production.

MONOCULTURE

The clash of urban and rural cultures is personal as well as economic and political. Although they are entrepreneurs, most farmers and ranchers work the land because they love it. They are as motivated by family, faith and feeling as they are compelled to make a profit. Many have farmed or ranched for their entire lives.* * * Failing to address the issues of urban influence and conversion pressure may mean an end to their way of life. We must address the challenges together to secure the land base, support agriculture and maintain a high quality of life in our communities.

———————

The American Farmland Trust paints a bleak picture of agricultural lands under threat from urban and suburban encroachment, threatening our food supply, the national economy, and our very way of life. Many analysts, however, do not accept the premise that farmland is under substantial threat from development, let alone the grave consequences that supposedly flow from that threat.

———————

"THE SPRAWLING OF AMERICA" POLICY STUDY NO. 251

Reason Public Policy Institute (February 1999)
Samuel R. Staley

* * *

A. Historical Trends in Farmland

For many, the loss of farmland is best illustrated by the loss of farms. Most states have experienced a persistent drop. Nationally, the number of farms fell from 6.4 million in 1910 to 2.0 million in 1997, a 67.8 percent drop. The largest decline occurred during the 1950s when 1.6 million farms disappeared. The dramatic decline in the number of farms is misleading, however, because the average farm size has increased. Many farms disappeared through consolidation within the industry.

Land in farms, potentially a more direct indicator of open-space loss, fell from 1.2 billion acres in 1950 to 968 million acres in 1997. At first glance, this decline might seem startling: farmers are growing food on about 20 percent less land. A more detailed analysis of farmland-loss trends is less alarming.

The most significant losses occurred during the 1960s. The nation lost 7.3 million acres of farmland annually that decade. ... After the 1970s, farmland loss moderated. The nation lost about 6.3 million acres per year in the 1970s and 5.2 million acres in the 1980s. Annual farmland loss was cut almost in half during the 1990s, averaging 2.6 million acres lost each year.-

Thus, projections of future farmland losses based on historical patterns are unreliable. Take the case of Michigan. Michigan had 12.7 million acres in farmland in 1970. During the 1960s, the state lost 2.7 million acres of farmland. If this acreage loss had been sustained, Michigan would have run out of farmland within 50 years. Farmland losses moderated to 1.3 million acres during the 1970s. At that pace, Michigan would have run out of farmland within 100 years. Now, at 1990s acreage loss rates, Michigan has more than two centuries of farmland left. Of course, even characterizing trends in this way is not meaningful. Rates of decline may continue to slow, or even reverse. Ironically, farmland loss was moderating while newspaper headlines in Michigan were highlighting the effects of urban sprawl and a governor's task force recommended legislative action to protect farmland from land development.

Similar trends are evident nationally. While farmland loss is highly variable, a general trend toward moderation is evident. Nationally, the amount of land in farms fell by 6.2 percent during the 1960s, then moderated to 5.8 percent in the 1970s, 5.0 percent in the 1980s, and to 2.7 percent in the 1990s. * * *

Farmland loss varies significantly by individual state. Farmland loss increased through the 1980s for California and then dropped to 3.7 percent in the 1990s. In Minnesota, land in farms fell by almost 5 percent in the 1960s, but declined by just 1 percent in the 1980s and 1990s. * * *

The continued moderation in farmland loss is important. If farmland loss is moderating, predictions about future losses will be biased if they assume no change in current trends. This is clear when a simple mathematical extension of previous loss rates is projected into the future. Farmland loss rates were projected for eleven states based on the decline in the number of acres in farms during each decade. These acreage losses were then projected into the future using 1990 as the base year.

In Minnesota, farm acreage losses experienced in the 1960s would have resulted in the complete disappearance of all farmland in 200 years. With loss rates similar to the 1990s, Minnesota has 1,500 years left. In California, loss rates equivalent to the 1960s would eliminate all farmland (using 1990 as base year) in 140 years. Losses equivalent to those in the more moderate 1990s extend the year of "zero farmland" to almost 400 years. In Colorado, farm acreage losses were dramatic in the 1970s and 1980s, but moderating losses in the 1990s push the year of "zero farmland" to more than 550 years. Thus, historical patterns of farmland loss are not reliable predictors of future farmland loss.

B.   Farmland Loss and Urbanization

While conventional wisdom claims urbanization is the primary culprit in farmland loss, the reality may be quite different. Urbanized land area increased by 8.3 million acres in the United States from 1982 to 1992, a 17.4 percent increase. Total cropland, grasslands, and pasture declined by 14.4 million acres during the same period. Even if all land converted from farmland went to urban uses (*not* parks, forests, or other recreational uses), urbanization would account for a little more than half (57.8 percent) of the nation's farmland loss. If the national decline in harvested forests is included as another "victim" of urbanization—adding 8.5 million acres to the total lost rural space—urbanization could account for 36.2 percent of the loss in rural space. An analysis of cropland trends from 1949 to 1992 by Ohio State University economist Luther Tweeten found that 26 percent of the decline in cropland could be explained by urbanization. Changes in the economic fortunes of the agricultural industry accounted for 74 percent of the decline. * * * Suggestions that urbanization is the primary "threat" to farmland preservation are not clearly supported by land-use trends at the national or state level. * * * From 1949 to 1992, for example, land in urban uses increased by 39.7 million acres to 57.9 million. Land in rural parks and wildlife areas increased by 59.2 million acres to 86.9 million during the same period. Thus, on a national level, the nation protected one-third more land than it developed.

* * * Similar trends are evident when acreage loss rates are compared among states. In some cases (e.g., California and Colorado), land devoted to cropland and pasture increased while land simultaneously was converted to urban uses. In states where farmland declined, urbanization accounted for a relatively small part of the loss. In Indiana, for example, farm-related land uses fell by 645,000 acres while urbanization used 139,000 acres (about 22 percent).

* * *

State-level data on farmland loss do not capture the local effects of the loss of farmland and open space. Many people are less interested in the fate of farms on the other side of the state than the farm in their own backyard. Even if a state is not facing significant farmland loss overall, in urbanizing areas the losses can be severe. The case of Washtenaw County, Michigan is instructive. Washtenaw County has been urbanizing at rapid rates for more than two decades, a consequence in part of economic growth spun off from the University of Michigan in Ann Arbor and continuing out-migration from nearby Detroit. As more and more people moved to the Ann Arbor area, land was developed for residential and commercial uses. As farmland was converted to urbanized forms of development, county commissioners responded to grassroots citizen concerns about preserving open space by placing on a countywide ballot an initiative to purchase the development rights of farmland by increasing the local sales tax. The measure was defeated at the ballot box, but the case provides an important reminder of concerns about lost open space and land development.

* * *

Changes in cropland vary significantly from period to period. While conventional wisdom paints a direct relationship between agricultural and urban uses, cropland—the land used to grow food—changes from period to period, sometimes increasing and sometimes declining depending on the demand for food.

Cropland declined from 1954 to 1964, then increased by 6.3 percent from 1964 to 1969. Cropland then declined again by 1.5 percent from 1969 to 1974, increased from 1974 to 1978 (a period of significant out-migration from central cities) and then fell modestly through 1992. Despite rapid urbanization, the agricultural industry has not been prevented from adjusting cropland to meet other needs. * * *

The Washtenaw County initiative occurred despite the fact Michigan, while one of the most urbanized states in the nation, has substantial amounts of open space available, even in metropolitan areas. About 10 percent of Michigan's land is developed. Overall, 22.7 percent of Michigan's land is classified as a special use (i.e., highways, state and federal parks, mining, airports, industrial parks in non-urban areas, etc.). Counties with central cities, such as Ann Arbor in Washtenaw County, devote less than 45 percent of their land to urban and other non-rural uses. In other words, even in central-city counties, more than half of the land is devoted to pasture, cropland, forest, or water. Counties that are part of metropolitan areas, but do not include central cities, still have more than 60 percent of the land in rural and agricultural uses on average.

C. Prime Farmland

Another concern raised by many is the loss of prime and unique farmland. Prime farmland is highly productive as a result of irrigation, location, soil type, and a variety of other criteria. "Land classified as prime farmland," notes the U.S. Department of Agriculture, "has the growing season, moisture supply, and soil quality needed to sustain high yields when treated and managed according to modern farming methods." Nationally, 24 percent of rural nonfederal land and half of all cropland is classified as prime. About 28 percent of urbanization uses prime farmland. One-third of converted land is nonprime forestland, and another 24 percent is nonprime farmland.

Designation as prime farmland, however, does not necessarily imply it is economically productive. Some of the nation's most productive farmland is not prime. "Florida and Arizona," the U.S. Department of Agriculture observed recently, "have little prime farmland ... but these areas rank among the most economically productive in the Nation." A number of factors influence the productivity of agriculture, including weather, erosion, the use of fertilizers, pesticides, irrigation, and other technologies. In fact, the nation's agricultural output has increased tremendously in recent years, largely as a result of better harvesting techniques and new technology. Capital equipment accounts for more than two-thirds of agriculture's productivity while land accounts for 20 percent and is declining.

D.   Farmland Loss and the Food Supply

Concern about the loss of farmland is tied—often explicitly—to agricultural production. A recent Michigan State University study warned: "[Farmland acreage trends] should assure that Michigan citizens will have sufficient land for food production to the year 2010, but future generations may not be able to produce enough food if the population continues to grow." * * * Growth-management laws also explicitly address these concerns in their state planning goals. South Carolina's County Planning Act lists "protecting the food supply" as one of nine justifications for comprehensive county-wide planning. * * *

Fears of future food shortages are greatly exaggerated and run contrary to trends in cropland, production, and food availability. Despite small declines in land in farms and virtually constant amount of land devoted to cropland, food production and productivity have increased dramatically. World output for meats, rice, and fish has increased by more than one-third since 1980. From 1950 to 1992, worldwide grain production per person increased 154.5 percent. These increases were largely a product of the ongoing technological revolution in agriculture.

The U.S. Department of Agriculture's index of national farm output—how much food is actually produced—rose from 73 in 1970 to 92 in 1980 to 108 in 1993, a 17.4 percent increase over 1980 levels and 47.9 percent increase since 1970. Moreover, the nation continues to be a net exporter of agricultural products. Total farm income increased by 63 percent from 1980 to 1994, according to the U.S. Bureau of Economic Analysis. Indeed, recent projections of a drop in farm income are the result of declining exports.

Not surprisingly, the U.S. Department of Agriculture's Economic Research Service concluded in a 1997 report "losing farmland to urban uses does not threaten total cropland or the level of agricultural production which should be sufficient to meet food and fiber demand into the next century."

In fact, higher yields and stocks have allowed a new industry to emerge. Corn and other crops are now used for industrial and other non-feed uses such as fuel alcohol and energy from biomass. Hydroponics—growing crops in a nutrient-rich, water-based solution—is also commercially viable (without subsidies), dramatically reducing the importance of land in food production. Whether nonfood uses create significant new demand for crops will depend on market factors such as the scarcity of other energy sources. * * *

E.   Farm Output, Land Prices, and the Real–Estate Market

If farmers can grow more food on less land, more land is available for other uses such as open space, commercial development, or housing. In fact, the U.S. Department of Agriculture recently found that, although cropland acreage has undergone little net change since 1945, whether cropland is harvested, idle, or lays fallow depends on federal programs and economic markets. Strong export markets fueled expansions of cropland in the 1970s and 1980s, but cropland fell as millions of acres were diverted into federal programs. Idle cropland, for example, has varied from 20.5 percent of the total used for crops in 1987 to 5.5 percent in 1982. In 1992, 56 million acres, or 16.6 percent of the total amount used for crops, was idle. An analysis of the causes of farmland loss between 1949 and 1992 by Ohio State University agricultural economist Luther Tweeten found the "lack of farm economic viability rather than urban encroachment" was the principal reason for cropland loss.

Changes in the relative importance of land are evident in real-estate markets. More urbanized states have higher land prices overall, and agricultural land values reflect this competition. The nation's most urbanized state, New Jersey, has the highest agricultural-land value ($6,221 in 1995). States with the lowest land values typically are the most rural.... The ten most-urbanized states—located mostly in the Northeast—have average land values exceeding $1,000 per acre. Of the remaining 38 states, only five—California, Iowa, North Carolina, Ohio, and Vermont—had farmland values exceeding $1,000 per acre. In contrast, with the exception of Idaho, the ten least-urbanized states had average land values well under $500 per acre. The relationship between urbanization and agricultural land values is strikingly direct: the more competition by other uses, the higher agricultural land prices are.

Agricultural land often cannot compete economically, prompting the conversion of farmland to urban or other uses. In Portland, Oregon, the assessed value (taxed) of an acre of farmland is $954 while an urbanized acre is valued at $67,135. More importantly, perhaps, agricultural land prices were unable to keep pace with the growth of prices for urban land. From 1992 to 1996, the value of vacant urban land increased 61 percent while the average increase for farmland was 52 percent. The value of agricultural production cannot generate the economic value necessary to compete effectively with alternative uses, such as housing, office space, roads, or even a shopping mall.

F. Conclusion

Concerns that farmland loss will cripple the agricultural industry or significantly reduce the nation's food supply are not supported by the evidence. Farmland loss has moderated significantly in recent years, and world population growth is expected to level off well before a crisis in food production emerges. * * *

Farmland conversion indicates changing priorities and competition in real-estate markets. Given the rapid increases in agricultural productivity, the value of farmland relative to other uses—including forest use, open space, housing, and commercial development—is falling. * * *

Notes and Questions

1. Which of the preceding two articles do you find more persuasive? Why?

2.   The author of the second article, *The Sprawling of America*, admits

> Although urban sprawl does not appear to be "gobbling up" land
> at unprecedented rates, this does not imply that land development is
> benign. Even if farmland preservation were not an issue, concerns
> over the environmental impacts of development and the costs of pro-
> viding services to new residential and commercial subdivisions would
> be important issues that might justify public attention.

How would you address these concerns if you were a state or local legislator?

———————

Whether or not farmland conversion is a legitimate and significant
social concern, state legislatures throughout the United States have
responded to political pressure from farming interests with legislation
designed to protect agricultural land uses. The earliest state efforts took
the form of "right-to-farm" laws, which protected farming operations
from nuisance suits brought by neighbors.

2.   *Right-To-Farm Laws*

Many urbanites and suburbanites move to farm country to escape
the noise, odors, pollution, and congestion of the cities and suburbs. But
those expecting a quiet, bucolic existence in farm country are often
unpleasantly surprised to discover the unique sounds and smells of agricultural operations: the pungent odors of manure and pesticides; clouds
of dust from tilling the soil; bothersome insects and rodents; and loud
machines harvesting crops late into the night. These facets of agricultural production sometimes lead to legal conflicts between farmers and
their newly arrived neighbors, which can significantly increase the cost
of farming and ranching.

SPUR INDUSTRIES v. DEL E. WEBB DEVELOPMENT CO.

Arizona Supreme Court, 1972.
108 Ariz. 178, 494 P.2d 700.

VICE CHIEF JUSTICE CAMERON delivered the opinion of the Court.

From a judgment permanently enjoining the defendant, Spur Industries,
Inc., from operating a cattle feedlot near the plaintiff Del E. Webb Development Company's Sun City, Spur appeals. Webb cross-appeals.
Although numerous issues are raised, we feel that it is necessary to
answer only two questions. They are:

1.   Where the operation of a business, such as a cattle feedlot is
lawful in the first instance, but becomes a nuisance by reason of a
nearby residential area, may the feedlot operation be enjoined in an
action brought by the developer of the residential area?

2.   Assuming that the nuisance may be enjoined, may the developer
of a completely new town or urban area in a previously agricultural area

be required to indemnify the operator of the feedlot who must move or cease operation because of the presence of the residential area created by the developer?

*   *   *

In 1956, Spur's predecessors in interest, H. Marion Welborn and the Northside Hay Mill and Trading Company, developed feedlots, about 1/2 mile south of Olive Avenue, in an area between the confluence of the usually dry Agua Fria and New Rivers. The area is well suited for cattle feeding and in 1959, there were 25 cattle feeding pens or dairy operations within a seven mile radius of the location developed by Spur's predecessors. In April and May of 1959, the Northside Hay Mill was feeding between 6,000 and 7,000 head of cattle and Welborn approximately 1,500 head on a combined area of 35 acres.

In May of 1959, Del Webb began to plan the development of an urban area to be known as Sun City. For this purpose, the Marinette and the Santa Fe Ranches, some 20,000 acres of farmland, were purchased for $15,000,000 or $750.00 per acre. This price was considerably less than the price of land located near the urban area of Phoenix, and along with the success of Youngtown was a factor influencing the decision to purchase the property in question.

*   *   *

Accompanied by an extensive advertising campaign, homes were first offered by Del Webb in January 1960 and the first unit to be completed was south of Grand Avenue and approximately 2 1/2 miles north of Spur. By 2 May 1960, there were 450 to 500 houses completed or under construction. At this time, Del Webb did not consider odors from the Spur feed pens a problem and Del Webb continued to develop in a southerly direction, until sales resistance became so great that the parcels were difficult if not impossible to sell. * * *

By December 1967, Del Webb's property had extended south to Olive Avenue and Spur was within 500 feet of Olive Avenue to the north. * * * Del Webb filed its original complaint alleging that in excess of 1,300 lots in the southwest portion were unfit for development for sale as residential lots because of the operation of the Spur feedlot.

Del Webb's suit complained that the Spur feeding operation was a public nuisance because of the flies and the odor which were drifting or being blown by the prevailing south to north wind over the southern portion of Sun City. At the time of the suit, Spur was feeding between 20,000 and 30,000 head of cattle, and the facts amply support the finding of the trial court that the feed pens had become a nuisance to the people who resided in the southern part of Del Webb's development. The testimony indicated that cattle in a commercial feedlot will produce 35 to 40 pounds of wet manure per day, per head, or over a million pounds of wet manure per day for 30,000 head of cattle, and that despite the admittedly good feedlot management and good housekeeping practices by Spur, the resulting odor and flies produced an annoying if not unhealthy situation as far as the senior citizens of southern Sun City were concerned. There is no doubt that some of the citizens of Sun City were unable to enjoy the outdoor living which Del Webb had advertised and that Del Webb was faced with sales resistance from prospective purchasers as well as strong and persistent complaints from the people who had purchased homes in that area. * * *

It is noted, however, that neither the citizens of Sun City nor Youngtown are represented in this lawsuit and the suit is solely between Del E. Webb Development Company and Spur Industries, Inc.

MAY SPUR BE ENJOINED?

The difference between a private nuisance and a public nuisance is generally one of degree. A private nuisance is one affecting a single individual or a definite small number of persons in the enjoyment of private rights not common to the public, while a public nuisance is one affecting the rights enjoyed by citizens as a part of the public. To constitute a public nuisance, the nuisance must affect a considerable number of people or an entire community or neighborhood.

Where the injury is slight, the remedy for minor inconveniences lies in an action for damages rather than in one for an injunction.

Thus, it would appear from the admittedly incomplete record as developed in the trial court, that, at most, residents of Youngtown would be entitled to damages rather than injunctive relief.

We have no difficulty, however, in agreeing with the conclusion of the trial court that Spur's operation was an enjoinable public nuisance as far as the people in the southern portion of Del Webb's Sun City were concerned.

§§ 36–601, subsec. A reads as follows: * * *

"A. The following conditions are specifically declared public nuisances dangerous to the public health:

"1.   Any condition or place in populous areas which constitutes a breeding place for flies, rodents, mosquitoes and other insects which are capable of carrying and transmitting disease-causing organisms to any person or persons."

By this statute, before an otherwise lawful (and necessary) business may be declared a public nuisance, there must be a "populous" area in which people are injured:

"* * * [I]t hardly admits a doubt that, in determining the question as to whether a lawful occupation is so conducted as to constitute a nuisance as a matter of fact, the locality and surroundings are of the first importance. (citations omitted) A business which is not per se a public nuisance may become such by being carried on at a place where the health, comfort, or convenience of a populous neighborhood is affected. * * * What might amount to a serious nuisance in one locality by reason of the density of the population, or character of the neighborhood affected, may in another place and under different surroundings be deemed proper and unobjectionable. * * *."

MacDonald v. Perry, 32 Ariz. 39, 49–50, 255 P. 494, 497 (1927).

It is clear that as to the citizens of Sun City, the operation of Spur's feedlot was both a public and a private nuisance. They could have successfully maintained an action to abate the nuisance. Del Webb, having shown a special injury in the loss of sales, had a standing to bring suit to enjoin the nuisance The judgment of the trial court permanently enjoining the operation of the feedlot is affirmed.

MUST DEL WEBB INDEMNIFY SPUR?

A suit to enjoin a nuisance sounds in equity and the courts have long recognized a special responsibility to the public when acting as a court of equity:

§§ 104. Where public interest is involved.

"Courts of equity may, and frequently do, go much further both to give and withhold relief in furtherance of the public interest than they are accustomed to go when only private interests are involved. Accordingly, the granting or withholding of relief may properly be dependent upon considerations of public interest. * * *." 27 Am.Jur.2d, Equity, page 626.

In addition to protecting the public interest, however, courts of equity are concerned with protecting the operator of a lawfully, albeit noxious, business from the result of a knowing and willful encroachment by others near his business.

In the so-called "coming to the nuisance" cases, the courts have held that the residential landowner may not have relief if he knowingly came into a neighborhood reserved for industrial or agricultural endeavors and has been damaged thereby:

"Plaintiffs chose to live in an area uncontrolled by zoning laws or restrictive covenants and remote from urban development. In such an area plaintiffs cannot complain that legitimate agricultural pursuits are being carried on in the vicinity, nor can plaintiffs, having chosen to build in an agricultural area, complain that the agricultural pursuits carried on in the area depreciate the value of their homes. The area being *primarily agricultural*, any opinion reflecting the value of such property must take this factor into account. The standards affecting the value of residence property in an urban setting, subject to zoning controls and controlled planning techniques, cannot be the standards by which agricultural properties are judged.

"People employed in a city who build their homes in suburban areas of the county beyond the limits of a city and zoning regulations do so for a reason. Some do so to avoid the high taxation rate imposed by cities, or to avoid special assessments for street, sewer and water projects. They usually build on improved or hard surface highways, which have been built either at state or county expense and thereby avoid special assessments for these improvements. It may be that they desire to get away from the congestion of traffic, smoke, noise, foul air and the many other annoyances of city life. But with all these advantages in going beyond the area which is zoned and restricted to protect them in their homes, they must be prepared to take the disadvantages." *Dill v. Excel Packing Company*, 183 Kan. 513, 525, 526, 331 P.2d 539, 548, 549 (1958). See also *East St. Johns Shingle Co. v. City of Portland*, 195 Or. 505, 246 P.2d 554, 560–562 (1952).

And:

"* * * a party cannot justly call upon the law to make that place suitable for his residence which was not so when he selected it. * * *." *Gilbert v. Showerman*, 23 Mich. 448, 455, 2 Brown 158 (1871).

Were Webb the only party injured, we would feel justified in holding that the doctrine of "coming to the nuisance" would have been a bar to the relief asked by Webb, and, on the other hand, had Spur located the feedlot near the outskirts of a city and had the city grown toward the feedlot, Spur would have to suffer the cost of abating the nuisance as to those people locating within the growth pattern of the expanding city:

"The case affords, perhaps, an example where a business established at a place remote from population is gradually surrounded and becomes part of a populous center, so that a business which formerly was not an interference with the rights of others has become so by the encroachment of the population * * *." *City of Ft. Smith v. Western Hide & Fur Co.*, 153 Ark. 99, 103, 239 S.W. 724, 726 (1922).

We agree, however, with the Massachusetts court that:

"The law of nuisance affords no rigid rule to be applied in all instances. It is elastic. It undertakes to require only that which is fair and reasonable under all the circumstances. In a commonwealth like this, which depends for its material prosperity so largely on the continued growth and enlargement of manufacturing of diverse varieties, 'extreme rights' cannot be enforced. * * *." *Stevens v. Rockport Granite Co.*, 216 Mass. 486, 488, 104 N.E. 371, 373 (1914).

There was no indication in the instant case at the time Spur and its predecessors located in western Maricopa County that a new city would spring up, full-blown, alongside the feeding operation and that the developer of that city would ask the court to order Spur to move because of the new city. Spur is required to move not because of any wrongdoing on the part of Spur, but because of a proper and legitimate regard of the courts for the rights and interests of the public.

Del Webb, on the other hand, is entitled to the relief prayed for (a permanent injunction), not because Webb is blameless, but because of the damage to the people who have been encouraged to purchase homes in Sun City. It does not equitably or legally follow, however, that Webb, being entitled to the injunction, is then free of any liability to Spur if Webb has in fact been the cause of the damage Spur has sustained. It does not seem harsh to require a developer, who has taken advantage of the lesser land values in a rural area as well as the availability of large tracts of land on which to build and develop a new town or city in the area, to indemnify those who are forced to leave as a result.

Having brought people to the nuisance to the foreseeable detriment of Spur, Webb must indemnify Spur for a reasonable amount of the cost of moving or shutting down. It should be noted that this relief to Spur is limited to a case wherein a developer has, with foreseeability, brought into a previously agricultural or industrial area the population which makes necessary the granting of an injunction against a lawful business and for which the business has no adequate relief.

It is therefore the decision of this court that the matter be remanded to the trial court for a hearing upon the damages sustained by the defendant Spur as a reasonable and direct result of the granting of the permanent injunction. * * *

Notes and Questions

1. The *Spur* case is best known for the court's innovative remedy enjoining the defendant's feedlot but requiring the plaintiff to compensate the defendant for reasonable costs of complying with the injunction. The court made the plaintiff *purchase* the injunction because it found that the plaintiff was largely responsible for its own harm. That is, Del Webb was guilty of "coming to the nuisance." Does this remedy seem appropriate?

2. In *Spur*, the court suggests that if Del Webb had been the only party affected by the flies and odors from Spur's feedlot, it would have denied the plaintiff any relief. Indeed, the court notes that the plaintiff, in essence, received the benefit of its bargain. It purchased real estate in a predominantly agricultural region, rather than in some already developed area such as Scottsdale, because the agricultural land was cheaper. Land is less expensive in agricultural areas, in part, because agricultural land uses entail pests and odors. People are not willing to pay as much for land with pests and odors as they are willing to pay for pest- and odor-free land. Despite this, of course, the court in *Spur* enjoined the pre-existing nuisance out of concern for the residents of Sun City. But if Del Webb came to the nuisance, the residents of Sun City, all of whom purchased lots from Del Webb, certainly came to the nuisance as well. Weren't they, like Del Webb, precompensated for the nuisance by the relatively low prices they paid for their lots?

3. Into the nineteenth century, a plaintiff guilty of "coming to the nuisance" had no remedy against a pre-existing nuisance. As an English court explained in the early case of Rex v. Cross [1812], 2 C & P 483, 172 Eng. Rep. 219 (Nisi Prius):

If a certain noxious trade is already established in a place remote from habitations and public roads, and persons afterwards come and build houses within the reach of the noxious effects; or if a public road be made so near to it that the carrying on of the trade becomes a nuisance to the persons using the road; in those cases the party would be entitled to continue his trade, because his trade was legal before the erection of the houses in the one case, and the making of the road in the other.

Even before the end of the nineteenth century, however, the coming-to-the-nuisance doctrine had evolved (at least in America) from a "decision rule," that is, a rule determining the outcome of the case, to merely one factor for the courts to consider in deciding the extent (if any) of a defendant's culpability. *See, e.g.*, Hurlbut v. McKone, 55 Conn. 31, 10 A. 164, 167 (1887) ("A man is not to be precluded from building and living on his own land because the adjoining proprietor first erected a nuisance."); United States v. Luce, 141 F. 385, 410 (C.C.D.Del. 1905) ("It is well settled that the mere fact that one voluntarily 'comes to a nuisance' will not preclude him from complaining of and obtaining relief against it.").

4. Does the result in the *Spur* case seem fair to the defendant? The court attempts to be fair to Spur by forcing the plaintiff to purchase the injunction. But note the incentive effect of the court's ruling for agricultural land users:

The court enjoined Spur's feedlot as a nuisance in an agricultural area dominated by feedlots. If a feedlot is a nuisance in that location, it must be a nuisance everywhere. But feedlots are not socially undesirable. Society (with the exception of vegetarians) wants its steaks and hamburgers, which means it wants feedlots. But where? The court's ruling in *Spur* creates substantial uncertainty for those who already own feedlots and for those who might enter that business. That uncertainty increases the cost of doing business.

DANIEL H. COLE AND PETER Z. GROSSMAN, PRINCIPLES OF LAW AND ECONOMICS 131 (2004).

Largely in response to decisions like *Spur*, agricultural interests lobbied state legislatures to enact laws to insulate farmers and ranchers from nuisance suits. Every state now has a "right-to-farm" statute that reduces the nuisance liability of agricultural land users. In 1963 Kansas enacted the nation's first right-to-farm act, which expressly insulated feedlots from liability so the *Spur* case could not have arisen in that state. It arose in Arizona, however, which had no right-to-farm law in 1972. The Arizona legislature enacted one nine years after the case. The provisions of Arizona's 1981 statute are fairly typical of right-to-farm laws:

A. Agricultural operations conducted on farmland that are consistent with good agricultural practices and established prior to surrounding nonagricultural uses are presumed to be reasonable and do not constitute a nuisance unless the agricultural operation has a substantial adverse effect on the public health and safety.

B. Agricultural operations undertaken in conformity with federal, state and local laws and regulations are presumed to be good agricultural practice and not adversely affecting the public health and safety.

Ariz. Rev. Stat. Ann. §§ 3–111 to 3–112 (1995).

With right-to-farm laws in place, it has become more difficult for residential developers and owners to complain of nuisances from pre-existing agricultural operations, such as feedlots. *See* Shatto v. McNulty, 509 N.E.2d 897 (Ind.App. 1987) (holding that under Indiana's right to farm statute, Ind. Code § 32–30–6–9, residents could not move to an established agricultural area and then complain about the ordinary smells associated with pre-existing hog farming activities); Holubec v. Brandenberger, 111 S.W.3d 32 (Tex. 2003) (holding that farming operations existing for more than a year before a complaint is filed are protected under Texas's Right-to-Farm Statute, Tex. Agric. Code § 251.004(a)). However, a farmer or feedlot operator might still be liable for nuisance if they *expand* or significantly change their operations, after the arrival of residential neighbors. *See* Payne v. Skaar, 127 Idaho 341, 900 P.2d 1352 (1995) (holding that Idaho's right-to-farm statute, I.C. §§ 22–4501 to 22–4504, does not protect an established feedlot from nuisance suits if the nuisance arises from expansion of the agricultural activity).

Some right-to-farm laws go farther than others in seeking to insulate farming operations from nuisance suits. In the following case, the Iowa Supreme Court concluded that a state "right to farm" law that insulated *all* non-negligent agricultural activities, including those that *post*-dated neighboring land uses, constituted an unconstitutional taking of plaintiffs' property rights without just compensation.

BORMANN v. BOARD OF SUPERVISORS
Supreme Court of Iowa.
584 N.W.2d 309 (1998) (en banc).

JUSTICE LAVORATO delivered the opinion of the Court.

In this appeal we are asked to decide whether a statutory immunity from nuisance suits results in a taking of private property for public use without just compensation in violation of federal and Iowa constitutional provisions. * * *

The facts are not in dispute. In September 1994, Gerald and Joan Girres applied to the Kossuth County Board of Supervisors for establishment of an "agricultural area" that would include land they owned as well as property owned by [other applicants]. *See Iowa Code § 352.6* (1993). The real property involved consisted of 960 acres. On November 10, 1994, the Board denied the application....

Two months later, in January 1995, the applicants tried again with more success. The Board approved the agricultural area designation by a 3–2 vote—one of which was based on the "flip [of] a nickel." In granting the designation, the Board this time found that the application to create the agricultural area designation "complies with *Iowa Code section 352.6* and that the adoption of the proposed agricultural area is consistent with the purposes of Chapter 352."

In April 1995, several neighbors of the new agricultural area filed a writ of certiorari and declaratory judgment action in district court.

The plaintiffs, Clarence and Caroline Bormann and Leonard and Cecelia McGuire (neighbors), challenged the Board's action in a number of respects. The neighbors alleged the Board's action violated their constitutionally inalienable right to protect property under the Iowa Constitution, deprived them of property without due process or just compensation under both the federal and Iowa Constitutions, denied them due process under the federal and Iowa Constitutions, ran afoul of res judicata principles, and was "arbitrary and capricious." * * *

A.   The parties' contentions.

The Board's approval of the agricultural area here triggered the provisions of *Iowa Code section 352.11(1)(a)*. More specifically, the approval gave the applicants immunity from nuisance suits. The neighbors contend that the approval with the attendant nuisance immunity results in a taking of private property without the payment of just compensation in violation of federal and state constitutional provisions.

The neighbors concede, as they must, that their challenge to section 352.11(1)(a) is a facial one because the neighbors have presented neither allegations nor proof of nuisance. However, the neighbors strenuously argue that in a facial challenge context courts have developed certain bright line tests that spare them from this heavy burden. Specifically, the neighbors say, these bright line tests provide that a governmental action resulting in the condemnation or the imposition of certain specific property interests constitutes automatic or per se takings.

Here, the neighbors argue further, that the section 352.11(1)(a) immunity provision gives the applicants the right to create or maintain a nuisance over the neighbors' property, in effect creating an easement in favor of the applicants. The creation of the easement, the neighbors conclude, results in an automatic or per se taking under a claim of regulatory taking.

The Board and applicants respond that a per se taking occurs only when there has been a permanent physical invasion of the property or the owner has been denied all economically beneficial or productive use of the property. They insist the record reflects neither has occurred. Thus, they contend, the court must apply a balancing test enunciated in *Penn Central Transportation Co. v. City of New York, 438 U.S. 104, 98 S. Ct. 2646, 57 L. Ed. 2d 631 (1978)*. They argue that under that balancing test the neighbors lose.

B.   The relevant constitutional and statutory provisions.

The Fifth Amendment to the Federal Constitution pertinently provides that "no person shall be ... deprived of life, liberty, or property without due process of law; nor shall private property be taken for public use, without just compensation." The Fourteenth Amendment to the Federal Constitution prohibits a state from "depriving any person of life, liberty, or property without due process of law." The Fourteenth Amendment makes the Fifth Amendment applicable to the states and their political subdivisions. *Chicago B. & Q. R.R. v. City of Chicago, 166 U.S. 226, 234–35, 17 S. Ct. 581, 584, 41 L. Ed. 979 (1897).*

Article I, section 9 of the Iowa Constitution pertinently provides that "no person shall be deprived of life, liberty, or property, without due process of law." Article I, section 18 of the Iowa Constitution provides:

> Eminent domain—drainage ditches and levees. Private property shall not be taken for public use without just compensation first being made, or secured to be made to the owner thereof, as soon as the damages shall be assessed by a jury.

Iowa Code section 352.6 sets forth the procedure for obtaining an agricultural area designation. * * * This provision also prescribes the conditions under which a county board of supervisors may designate farmland as an agricultural area. *Id.* An agricultural area includes, among other activities, raising and storing crops, the care and feeding of livestock, the treatment or disposal of wastes resulting from livestock, and the creation of noise, odor, dust, or fumes. *Iowa Code § 352.2(6).*

Iowa Code section 352.11(1)(a) provides the immunity from nuisance suits:

> A farm or farm operation located in an agricultural area shall not be found to be a nuisance regardless of the established date of operation or expansion of the agricultural activities of the farm or farm operation. This paragraph shall apply to a farm operation conducted within an agricultural area for six years following the exclusion of land within an agricultural area other than by withdrawal as provided in section 352.9.

The immunity does not apply to a nuisance resulting from a violation of a federal statute, regulation, state statute, or rule. *Iowa Code § 352.11(1)(b).* Nor does the immunity apply to a nuisance resulting from the negligent operation of the farm or farm operation. *Id.* Additionally, there is no immunity from suits because of an injury or damage to a person or property caused by the farm or farm operation before the creation of the agricultural area. *Id.* Finally, there is no immunity from suit "for an injury or damage sustained by the person [bringing suit] because of the pollution or change in condition of the waters of a stream, the overflowing of the person's land, or excessive soil erosion into another person's land, unless the injury or damage is caused by an act of God." *Id.*

* * *

C. The framework of analysis.

As the neighbors point out, the federal and state constitutional provisions we set out earlier provide the following framework for a "takings" analysis: (1) Is there a constitutionally protected private property interest at stake? (2) Has this private property interest been "taken" by the government for public use? and (3) If the protected property interest has been taken, has just compensation been paid to the owner? The neighbors contend there is a constitutionally protected private right which the Board has taken from them without paying just compensation. That taking, the neighbors contend, results from the Board's approval of the agricultural area triggering the nuisance immunity in section 352.11(1)(a). The Board and the applicants concede the neighbors have received no compensation so we need not concern ourselves with the third step of the analysis: Has just compensation been paid to the owner? * * *

Textually, the federal and Iowa Constitutions prohibit the government from taking property for public use without just compensation. Property for just compensation purposes means "the group of rights inhering in the citizens' relation to the physical thing, as the right to possess, use and dispose of it." *United States v. General Motors Corp., 323 U.S. 373, 378, 65 S. Ct. 357, 89 L. Ed. 311, 318 (1945)*. In short, property for just compensation purposes includes "every sort of interest the citizen may possess." *Id.; see also Liddick v. Council Bluffs, 232 Iowa 197, 221–22, 5 N.W.2d 361, 374 (1942)* ("Property is not alone the corporeal thing, but consists also in certain rights therein created and sanctioned by law, of which, with respect to land, the principal ones are the rights of use and enjoyment....").

State law determines what constitutes a property right. *Webb's Fabulous Pharmacies, Inc. v. Beckwith, 449 U.S. 155, 161, 101 S. Ct. 446, 451, 66 L. Ed. 2d 358, 362 (1980)*.

The property interest at stake here is that of an easement, which is an interest in land. Over one hundred years ago, this court held that the right to maintain a nuisance is an easement. *Churchill v. Burlington Water Co., 94 Iowa 89, 93, 62 N.W. 646, 647 (1895)*. *Churchill* defines an easement as a privilege without profit, which the owner of one neighboring tenement [has] of another, existing in respect of their several tenements, by which the servient owner is obliged to suffer, or not do something on his own land, for the advantage of the dominant owner. *Id.*

Churchill's holding that the right to maintain a nuisance is an easement and its definition of an easement are consistent with the Restatement of Property:

An easement is an interest in land which entitles the owner of the easement to *use* or enjoy land in the possession of another.... It may entitle him to do acts which he would otherwise not be privileged to do, or it may merely entitle him to prevent the owner of the land subject to the easement from doing acts which he would otherwise be privileged to do. An easement which entitles the owner to do acts which, were it not for the easement, he would not be privileged to do, is an affirmative easement.... [The easement] may entitle [its] owner to do acts on his own land which, were it not for the easement, would constitute a nuisance.

Restatement of Property § 451 cmt. a, at 2911–12 (1944)....

Another feature of easements is that easements run with the land:

The land which is entitled to the easement or service is called a dominant tenement, and the land which is burdened with the servitude is called the servient tenement. Neither easements nor servitudes are personal, but they are accessory to, and run with, the land. The first with the dominant tenement, and the second with the servient tenement.

Dawson v. McKinnon, 226 Iowa 756, 767, 285 N.W. 258, 263 (1939).

Thus, the nuisance immunity provision in section 352.11(1)(a) creates an easement in the property affected by the nuisance (the servient tenement) in favor of the applicants' land (the dominant tenement). This is because the immunity allows the applicants to do acts on their own land which, were it not for the easement, would constitute a nuisance. For example, in their farming operations the applicants would be allowed to generate "offensive smells" on their property which without the easement would permit affected property owners to sue the applicants for nuisances. * * *

Easements are property interests subject to the just compensation requirements of the Fifth Amendment to the Federal Constitution. *United States v. Welch, 217 U.S. 333, 339, 30 S. Ct. 527, 527, 54 L. Ed. 787, 788 (1910).* Easements are also property interests subject to the just compensation requirements of our own Constitution. *Simkins v. City of Davenport, 232 N.W.2d 561, 566 (Iowa 1975).*

* * * [T]he state cannot regulate property so as to insulate the users from potential private nuisance claims without providing just compensation to persons injured by the nuisance. The Supreme Court firmly established this principle in *Richards,* holding that "while the legislature may legalize what otherwise would be a public nuisance, it may not confer immunity from action for a private nuisance of such a character as to amount in effect to a taking." *Richards,* 233 U.S. at 553....

* * *

As mentioned, the Board's approval of the applicants' application for an agricultural area triggered the provisions of section 352.11(1)(a). The approval gave the applicants immunity from nuisance suits. (Significantly, section 352.2(6) allows an agricultural area to include activities such as the creation of noise, odor, dust, or fumes.) This immunity resulted in the Board's taking of easements in the neighbors' properties for the benefit of the applicants. The easements entitle the applicants to do acts on their property, which, were it not for the easement, would constitute a nuisance. This amounts to a taking of private property for public use without the payment of just compensation in violation of the Fifth Amendment to the Federal Constitution. This also amounts to a taking of private property for public use in violation of article I, section 18 of the Iowa Constitution.

In enacting section 352.11(1)(a), the legislature * * * has exceeded its authority by authorizing the use of property in such a way as to infringe on the rights of others by allowing the creation of a nuisance without the payment of just compensation. The authorization is in violation of the Fifth Amendment to the Federal Constitution and article I, section 18 of the Iowa Constitution.

The district court erred in concluding otherwise.

D.   The remedy. * * *

Here the neighbors seek no compensation. Rather, they seek only invalidation of that portion of section 352.11(1)(a) that provides immunity against nuisance suits. We therefore need not concern ourselves with damages for any temporary taking. Accordingly, we hold unconstitutional and invalidate that portion of section 352.11(1)(a) that provides for immunity against nuisance suits. * * *

We reverse and remand for an order declaring that portion of *Iowa Code section 352.11(1)(a)* that provides for immunity against nuisances unconstitutional and without any force or effect.

Notes and Questions

1.   Did the court in *Bormann* invalidate right-to-farm laws generally? The Iowa statute held unconstitutional in that case did not merely codify the "coming to the nuisance" doctrine, but went much farther, seeking to insulate from liability any agricultural operation in an agricultural area, even if that operation was not first in time. It is doubtful that the Iowa Supreme Court would have found the statute unconstitutional if the statute had limited its protection to pre-existing nuisances that resulted from normal, pre-existing, and non-negligent agricultural operations that use "best agricultural practices" as defined in the locality. *See* Steven J. Laurent, *Michigan's Right to Farm Act: Have Revisions Gone Too Far?*, 2002 L. Rev. M.S.U.–D.C.L. 213 (contrasting Michigan's Right to Farm Act with the Iowa statute held unconstitutional in the *Bormann* case).

2.   Right to farm laws typically do not seek to protect any and all pre-existing agricultural activities against nuisance suits. To be insulated from liability, the existing use must: (a) be unchanged, (b) not have been a nuisance when it started, and (c) be non-negligent (e.g., in accordance with best agricultural practices of the community and in conformity with all state and local permits and other requirements). *See, e.g.*, Shatto v. McNulty, 509 N.E.2d 897, 900 (Ind.App. 1987).

3. Other Tools of Farmland Preservation: Agricultural Zoning

PRESERVATION OF AGRICULTURAL LANDS THROUGH LAND USE PLANNING TOOLS AND TECHNIQUES
Elisa Paster
44 NAT. RESOURCES J. 283–318 (2004)

* * *

A. Agricultural Zoning

Courts validated zoning as a legitimate exercise of a municipality's police power in the seminal case of Village of Euclid, Ohio v. Ambler Realty Company. Since that time, local governments have used zoning to achieve fulfillment of general health and welfare goals, including the preservation of agricultural lands. Indeed, zoning is the most utilized technique for preserving agricultural and rural lands in part because zoning land exclusively for agricultural use prevents residential subdivisions while simultaneously creating a holding zone to restrict urban expansion. While some zoning regulations have fallen to takings claims ... courts have consistently upheld agricultural zoning against takings claims because agricultural zoning permits some economic use of the land (i.e., farming).

1. Area Based

Area based zoning ordinances allow a fixed amount of development per a specified number of acres, for example one nonfarm lot per 50 acres. These ordinances operate to preserve agricultural land by limiting incompatible development within agricultural areas. For instance, in sliding scale zoning ordinances, the number of dwelling units permitted varies with the size of the tract. Owners of smaller parcels may divide their land into more lots on a per-acre basis than owners of larger parcels. Sliding scale zoning may also be used by qualitatively assessing land. For example, Clinton County, Indiana, allows denser development on lands with poor soil quality and prohibits development on lands with fertile soil. Sliding scale zoning operates as an agricultural preservation technique by promoting development on smaller tracts that are on less valuable soil while prohibiting development on fertile, soil rich lands.

Conservation easements are used in many communities to restrict development once maximum densities are reached. Communities that do not require conservation easements or some other type of deed restriction will be in danger of losing the land to non-agricultural uses in the future. The other potential problem with area-based zoning is that, as with other types of zoning ordinances, area-based zoning is only as good as the political will to maintain and enforce it. * * *

On the other hand, area-based zoning is a very inexpensive way to protect land because little public expenditure is necessary. Compared to other programs, such as transfer of development rights and purchase of development rights, area based zoning can be implemented very quickly and cheaply. The public is also familiar with area-based zoning, making adaptation and implementation of these programs less susceptible to public controversy.

2. Large Lot Zoning

Some communities have tried to slow rapid growth patterns by requiring that rural land be subdivided into a minimum of five-acre lots, with the intention that larger parcels will maintain lower density and rural character. As a general rule, the minimum lot size created is the amount of land necessary to carry on a successful farming operation; thus, lot sizes reflect the economic reality of agriculture.

Though large lot zoning was a traditional strategy to protect farmland in the 1970s and 1980s, the resulting development of subdivisions has suggested that it may not be the most effective strategy. The main problem is that the lot size is not large enough to discourage development, yet it is too small for effective agriculture. Large lot zoning, therefore, is widely criticized for promoting sprawl and the degradation of farmland. * * * Property owners find large lot zoning objectionable because only the rich can afford the large prices that are commensurate with large lots. Other critics have renamed large lot zoning "snob zoning" and the residents of these areas "cappuccino cowboys."

3. Cluster

Cluster zoning allows development on part of a property while the remainder is retained for open space or agricultural uses. Cluster zoning encourages creativity in urban site design and enables the protection of on site amenities and environmentally sensitive areas. Cluster zoning and cluster subdivisions are known by many names: open space zoning or density zoning and cluster developments, conservation subdivisions, open space, or open land subdivisions, respectively.

Clustering may be accomplished though the use of a particular zoning district, which establishes a fixed or sliding scale area-based dwelling unit allocation and requires clustering on a portion of the site. Alternatively, clustering may be used in conjunction with existing zoning and allowed as an optional or density bonus. For example, the Hammocks, a residential development in Florida, was built using cluster zoning paired with density incentives, thereby increasing the average net density to 11.5 units per acre and creating green spaces and lakes for the community.

Cluster zoning may require that the landowner of a tract of land identify the building lots and the open space to be preserved, or it may simply require that a certain percentage of land remain as open space or agricultural land. The protected land is usually owned and maintained by a homeowners association. Specifically allowed land uses are either identified in the existing zoning or limited by cluster development regulations. For example, one model ordinance permits residential and open space uses. * * * Possible open space uses include agricultural ones such as farming (crops, the and raising and sale of livestock) and Christmas tree farming and sales, and passive recreational spaces for wildlife sanctuaries and nature preserves. Communities like Larimer County, Colorado, offer a system of incentives and benefits that gives local administrators the option of adopting regulations that fit the specific needs of parcels on a case-by-case basis.

The most effective clustering regulations are those that are mandatory. As stated by one agricultural preservation expert, when clustering and open space preservation are left optional, only a small percentage of developers will choose to take advantage of this approach. * * * The community is still left with conventional development patterns repeated over fields and woodlands.

Though cluster zoning can keep land available for smaller agricultural operations or open space, it is generally not a viable technique for commercial agriculture. The protected land is normally owned by a homeowners association, and, while homeowners may lease it back to local farmers, some residents may object to allowing agricultural production because of noise, dust, and odors related to commercial farming. * * * In general, cluster zoning has been used most successfully to protect environmentally sensitive lands or to create intermediary areas between agricultural areas and housing.

Critics of cluster zoning argue that it actually results in "clustered sprawl" and that farmland within clustered residential areas can only realistically be used for low-value crops because of incompatible use issues. Critics also argue that cluster zoning is environmentally unsound because cluster development works best with urban infrastructure although the remote location requires onsite septic tanks. Failing septic systems require the extension of water and sewer lines, which opens farmland up to more development. Finally, cluster development is criticized because mixing residences and farming simply does not work.

While critics of clustering worry that this technique will cause loss of exurban or rural character, subdivisions designed with these concerns in mind can mitigate, if not eliminate, such concerns. A clustered subdivision should be located as near to the major roads in the area as possible to allow for easy access. Instead of having separate driveways onto the arterial roads, creating a more urban feel, a subdivision should be designed so the entire tract is set back from the main road with only one access point to the road and houses accessing a loop or network of small streets. These streets should be gravel and narrower then traditional urban subdivision streets to create a rural neighborhood feel. Clustered subdivisions should also be buffered from the street with extensive landscape—hopefully so well buffered that passing motorists will not even realize the houses exist.

4. Buffering

Buffering is the physical separation of farms from incompatible uses including landscape and acreage. Buffers are narrow bands of land planted with permanent vegetation that are located in and around areas of intensive agricultural production. Buffers safeguard farms from vandals and trespassers and protect adjacent homeowners from the negative impacts of commercial farming. Several types of buffers exist including field borders, riparian grass buffers, contour grass strips, grassed waterways, and vegetative bordersn86 and range in size from 50 feet to 800 feet. All have the same function: to minimize conflicts between residential and agricultural users.

Buffers can be mandatory or voluntary. In Suffield, Connecticut, an individual farmer may request a buffer with a width of 30 to 100 feet. The buffer is located on the parcel that the developer will develop. The law also requires that lot owners be notified that they are responsible for buffer maintenance * * * Other communities have voluntary buffers between farm and non-farm uses. The Georgia Model Code requires that any non-agricultural use located next to an agricultural use provide a 150–foot agricultural buffer. The buffer must consist of native trees, hedges, and naturally occurring elements "so that they provide a more or less opaque screen" between the agricultural and nonagricultural uses.

A significant challenge with buffers is enforcement. Though ordinances may require buffers, the ordinances are not always enforced. Buffering ordinances can be effective as long as local government has subdivision review authority to impose the buffer requirement and provided local government enforces the buffers once in place. Placing the buffer restriction in the landowners' title will assure adequate legal notice to the individual landowner responsible.

Successful buffer ordinances cannot be standard; each buffer must be site based and locally determined. Mandatory buffers that require maintenance are most effective. * * * While buffers themselves do not protect farmland, they reduce incompatibility problems, which lead to pressure on farmers ... to stop farming.

5. Overall Benefits and Drawbacks of Agricultural Zoning

Overall, the aforementioned zoning techniques are an inexpensive way to protect large areas of agricultural land because little public expenditure is necessary to implement zoning ordinances. Communities also favor agricultural zoning ordinances because they are easy and quick to implement as compared to development rights programs and easy to explain to the public, who are accustomed to zoning ordinances. * * *

Critics of agricultural zoning suggest that these programs are not permanent. While flexibility is beneficial, it is also a drawback because large agricultural parcels may quickly be converted to developable parcels with a simple zone change. Moreover, agricultural preservation ordinances do not prevent annexation by municipalities (unless annexation is forbidden on agricultural lands), so lands may quickly lose protection from development. One solution is for agricultural zoning programs to include mandatory deed restrictions or easement requirements to prevent conversion and annexation. Unfortunately, mandatory ordinances generally decrease land values, which decrease farmer's equity in land, so many farmers are opposed to agricultural zoning. Finally, these programs may be difficult to monitor and enforce on a day-to-day basis. Municipalities must be willing to devote economic and human resources to agricultural zoning programs to ensure their success.

B. Non–Zoning Techniques

* * *

2. Agricultural Districting

Agricultural districts are special areas where commercial agriculture is encouraged and protected through a broad array of measures such as bans on local government laws that restrict farming, enhanced protection from private nuisance lawsuits, eligibility for differential tax assessment, and limiting non-farm development around active agricultural areas and conservation easement programs. Agricultural districting is distinct from zoning in that the latter only addresses particular land uses and is one tool that might be used in an agricultural district. An agricultural district encompasses a wider range of tools for farmers that include land use policies, taxing mechanisms, and zoning and conservation techniques.

Agricultural districts are generally state-level programs. As of 1997, 16 states have enacted agricultural district laws. * * * Benefits exist because agricultural districts are flexible and local in nature; stabilize the land base at a low public cost; provide multiple benefits to farmers; help protect large blocks of land; and have voluntary enrollment, which makes the program popular with farmers. The drawbacks of the program are the following: sanctions for withdrawing land are minimal and do not deter conversion; limits on non-farm development may not prohibit the development of urban infrastructure in agricultural areas; and, in some states, benefits are not a strong enough incentive for farmers to enroll and the procedure for creating the districts is long and cumbersome. States may overcome the drawbacks by developing strong incentives and penalties....

3. Land Evaluation Systems

The land evaluation and site assessment system (LESA) was launched in 1981 by the U.S. Soil Conservation Service to make objective ratings of the agricultural suitability of lands against the demands for other uses. LESA effectively rates a tract's potential for agricultural as well as social and economic factors. * * * LESA is a two-part system consisting of land evaluation and site assessment that can be used as part of an agricultural preservation program by assisting implementation of the Farmland Protection Policy Act (FPPA), selecting appropriate lands to be included in the program, and establishing minimum parcel sizes for farm subdivisions in agricultural districts. The land evaluation part of LESA is usually designed by the federal Soil Conservation Service (SCS) and local Soil and Water Conservation Districts (SWCD). * * * Site assessment factors include parcel size, on-farm investment, characteristics external to the parcel of land, such as nearby land uses, zoning, and other farmland protection measures.

LESA is a flexible system designed to accommodate differences among states, counties, or areas. * * * LESA is effective in selecting lands for development rights programs, choosing land for preservation, identifying appropriate locations for infrastructure, assessing environmental impacts, and developing guidelines determining which uses should be permitted for land conversion to nonagricultural use.

A 1990–1991 study identified 212 local and state governments in 31 states as active or former users of LESA. Of these 212 jurisdictions, 138 local and state governments were still using the system in 1994. Those who abandoned the system found it too complicated or time consuming, while others noted a lack of interest or support by landowners or planners. * * * Approximately 79 percent of respondents were satisfied with LESA.

C.   Land and "Less-Than-Fee" Acquisition Programs

  1.   Conservation Easements

A conservation easement (or conservation restriction) is a voluntary legal agreement between a landowner and a land trust or government agency that permanently limits uses of the land to protect its conservation values. The landowner sells the right to develop all or part of the land to the conservation organization for non-agricultural or non-open space uses, but the landowner may continue to own and use the land and may sell it or pass it on to heirs. Each easement is tailored to meet the landowner's personal management objectives and goals for the property so that current uses may continue.

Placing an easement may result in property tax savings and can be essential for passing land on to the next generation. By removing the land's development potential, the easement lowers its market value, thereby lowering estate taxes. Whether the easement is donated during life or by will, it can make a critical difference in the heirs' ability to keep the land intact. * * *

Granting conservation easements as an exaction and using conservation easements in tandem with other techniques is becoming popular. In the city of Agoura Hills, the developer of a large subdivision dedicated 63 acres of land at the gateway of the Santa Monica Mountains in exchange for cluster zoning. The city was in favor of the dedication because it did not cost money and reaped the same benefits. The developer favored the dedication because tax benefits were available, cluster zoning provided more density, and the open space was a desirable amenity to the development.

2. Purchase of Development Rights and Purchase of Conservation Easements

In a typical purchase of development rights (PDR) program, the government purchases the owner's right to develop specific parcels of land.... One form of PDR commonly used for agricultural preservation is the purchase of conservation easements (PACE). Landowners voluntarily sell conservation easements to governments or other private conservation agencies. The price of the development right is generally equal to the diminution in the market value of the land resulting from the removal of the development rights and, thus, is the difference between the value of the land for agricultural use or open space and the land's current value. In return for the payment, the landowner agrees to use the land for open space or agriculture in perpetuity, although some programs allow termination of the condition under certain restrictions. PDR programs are similar to conservation easements with one critical difference: in PDR programs the development rights can be sold to another landowner while conservation easements do not transfer a development right.

PDR programs may be independent or cooperative state and local programs. * * * Cooperative state and local governmental programs are advantageous because they allow the state to set broad policies and implement regional planning strategies, while local governments, with their specific knowledge of the area, identify land suitable for PDR programs and monitor the programs. Cooperative programs are also beneficial because of the increased levels of funding available.

PDR programs are popular with farmers because they offer enticing incentives including the availability of real capital without having to mortgage land, lower real property taxes reflecting the decrease in the value of the land once the development rights have been sold, and potential estate or inheritance tax benefits. PDR programs are also advantageous because they offer a more permanent solution than does zoning, while avoiding Fifth Amendment takings challenges that might hamper zoning efforts.

Some landowners reject PDR programs because they are perceived as "tying the hands" of the landowners' heirs, who may wish to sell the land for its development value. PDR programs may not work because, although buying development rights is less expensive than buying land in fee simple, the program is still cash intensive. In communities where taxes and fees are already levied for schools, public safety, parks, infrastructure, and community programs, agricultural preservation may fall by the wayside unless there is heightened community awareness as to the necessity of preserving agricultural lands.

Successful PDR programs must be carefully designed to include a set of criteria that prioritizes which land the development rights should purchase. The criteria must take into account the location and surrounding uses of the land. PDR programs make sense if hundreds of acres can be preserved (either through contiguous smaller parcels or a few large parcels) because it is more likely that larger commercial farms will be successful. * * *

3. Transfer of Development Rights

Transfer of Development Rights (TDR) allows for planning on an area-wide basis by allowing landowners in restricted areas (sending areas) to transfer densities and other development rights to landowners in areas appropriate for higher density development (receiving areas). Landowners in receiving areas are allowed to develop their land but only if they purchase development rights from the agricultural or environmentally sensitive lands, thereby directing development away from threatened lands to areas better equipped to deal with heavy development.

TDR programs are popular not only because they give governments an alternative to purchasing land outright in fee simple and ameliorate the harshness of restrictive zoning, but also because the goal is to have an "everyone wins" outcome. The sending area landowner is able to continue farming without development pressures and benefits from the sale of the rights. The receiving area landowner is able to build at a greater density and realizes the market value of the land. Other benefits to government are the ability to make full use of public infrastructure, ease in providing affordable housing through higher densities, preservation of land, and legal defensibility. * * *

The transfer of development rights is not an ordinary part of the bundle of rights associated with land ownership. State governments must enact specific legislation to enable a local government to legalize the sending of development rights from one parcel to another. * * * Some state statutes enable localities to authorize and implement TDR programs while others merely provide for the adoption of an ordinance under planning and zoning powers.

D. Taxation Programs

1. Agricultural Tax Programs Generally

The disparity between the market value of agricultural land for farming and other uses and high property taxes are two reasons farmers are "forced" to sell their farms. To reduce the temptation or need to sell due to the tax burden, many states have enacted legislation giving real property tax deferments, preferences, or exemptions to the owners of agricultural or eligible land. * * * The purpose of agricultural tax programs is to help farmers economically by reducing their real property taxes by basing tax value on agriculture instead of on its value for development. * * * Unfortunately, tax programs cannot ensure long-term protection of farmland and are criticized because they inadvertently provide a subsidy to real estate speculators who keep their land in agriculture pending development. Although tax incentives do reduce the tax pressure, they do not reduce development pressure, and the capital gains for land development may still outweigh the property tax incentive in some markets. Nonetheless, tax programs are beneficial because they correct inequities in the tax system created by development pressures and help farmers stay in business.

2. Differential Assessment

Differential tax programs provide incentives for landowners to keep their land in agriculture by assessing agricultural land at its current or farm value rather than its fair market value. Agricultural value represents what farmers would pay to buy land in light of the net farm income they can expect to receive from it, while fair market value represents what a willing buyer would pay to develop the land. * * *

The taxation programs are designed to target commercial agricultural land rather than hobby farms used for recreation or land that is vacant pending development. To achieve this goal, landowners may be required to sign restrictive agreements (California) or restrictive covenants (Georgia, Hawaii, New York, and Pennsylvania). The restrictive agreements must be signed as a condition precedent to the value assessment. In Minnesota, this goal is achieved by having fairly restrictive eligibility criteria: lots must be at least ten acres and must meet an ownership and production test. * * *

3. Land Conversion Tax

A land conversion tax is a fee to convert farmland from agricultural to non-agricultural uses and is best demonstrated by California's Williamson Act. Under the Act, participating landowners sign a ten-year contract with the county that renews annually and gives the landowners a substantial tax break. In return, the landowner agrees to use the land only for agricultural purposes. If the landowner wants to get out of the program, he or she may initiate the nine-year non-renewal process. During the nonrenewal process, the annual tax assessment gradually increases. At the end of the period, the contract is terminated. To approve a tentative contract cancellation, a county or municipality must make specific findings that are supported by substantial evidence. The existence of an opportunity for another use of the property is not sufficient reason for cancellation. * * * The landowner must pay a cancellation fee equal to 12 and one-half percent of the cancellation valuation of the property.

E. Infrastructure Fees

* * * Impact fees are mandatory payments imposed by local governments at the time of development approval that are calculated to be the proportionate share of the capital cost of providing a development with major infrastructure such as roads, schools, sewer and water lines, and emergency services. The charges differ from taxes in that impact fees constitute a single payment, unlike periodic payments of taxes. The developer is only required to pay his "fair share," or the cost that the new development will impose on the community. Governments favor impact

fees because they reduce the reliance on bonds to finance infrastructure and because the community avoids paying the high costs of development on the fringe or in areas without existing infrastructure. Impact fees exist in some form or other in every state.

The courts have upheld the legality of impact fees if there is a rational relationship between the demands of new development and assessments against it. There are two prongs in this rational nexus test: first, there must be a need for an additional public facility or service created by the new development and the fee must not exceed the cost of providing the facility; and second, the development charged the fee must derive some benefit from the new facility. Impact fees that do not meet this test are considered unconstitutional takings, entitling the property owner to monetary damages.

* * * While impact fees have not traditionally been used as a direct tool to protect agricultural land, they have been used as part of an overall growth management policy that may have a strong preservation component. * * *

A new type of impact fee, called an environmental mitigation fee or simply a mitigation fee, is a hybrid between an impact fee and the marketbased environmental mitigation models. In the context of agricultural preservation, municipalities identify agricultural and natural resource lands that are in danger of conversion through a comprehensive planning process. The comprehensive plan guides the assessment of impact of any development. A developer would be charged based on an established formula and may choose one of three options: pay and proceed with the project, reduce the adverse impact and pay a reduced fee, or pay another firm to mitigate adverse environmental impact elsewhere. In essence, mitigation fees require that developers permanently protect open space or agricultural land in exchange for permission to convert other land to urban uses. The money generated through mitigation fees can be funneled into agricultural preservation programs such as PDR ... and TDR or into local budgets for monitoring and enforcement....

F. Comprehensive Planning

Timing and sequencing development to coincide with the provision of public facilities was first implemented in an innovative plan in Ramapo, New York, and was upheld by the courts in the landmark case of Golden v. Planning Board of Town of Ramapo. The basic idea is that all residential development must proceed according to the provision of adequate municipal facilities as established by a long-term comprehensive and capital improvement program. The importance of the Ramapo plan is the recognition of the fundamental constitutional principle that development on the urban fringe can be controlled by linking the development with the planned extension of capital improvements over a reasonable time.

A tier system utilizes the Ramapo principle by providing for the delineation of functional areas within the region for the identification of goals and objectives and the implementation of growth management techniques. The number of tiers will vary according to the current and desired pattern of the urban area but will generally include a downtown area or urban core, existing residential areas within the urban area and older suburban areas, a developing area, rural and agricultural lands that are inappropriate or premature for development, and environmental and agricultural zones that warrant preservation or protection through environmental protection. * * *

Tier ... systems preserve agricultural lands by directing development to existing urban areas and by prioritizing lands to be given over to development based on infrastructure and LOS standards. These systems do not concentrate on one particular sector of a city but instead concentrate on planning for the entire area. The result is that agricultural and open space preservation are given due consideration and are seen as an important resource for the entire community.

* * *

Notes and Questions

1. Do any of the tools described above represent a "magic bullet" for farmland preservation? Are any of them worthwhile, when balanced against other local and regional priorities and budgetary constraints? Do you favor mandatory or voluntary approaches?

2. Landowners' perspectives on conservation easements are discussed in Chapter 9.III.C. (Private Ownership). *See also* DANIEL H. COLE, POLLUTION AND PROPERTY: COMPARING OWNERSHIP INSTITUTIONS FOR ENVIRONMENTAL PROTECTION 60–66 (2002).

IV. FEDERAL LAND USE REGULATION

Historically, the federal government has been much less involved than state and local governments in the regulation of private land uses. But over the past half-century, the federal government's level of direct involvement in local land use decisions has increased, particularly with respect to issues relating to environmental protection and natural resources conservation.

A. Federal Planning and Siting Laws

For the most part, the federal government leaves planning and regulation of private land-uses, leaving such activities to state and local governments. Nevertheless, the U.S. government's presence is often felt. Obviously, properties under federal jurisdiction, such as military installations and national parks, are automatically subject to federal planning unless such authority is delegated to state or local bodies. With respect to other lands, the federal influence may be more limited and indirect, but that does not mean it is necessarily insignificant. For example, federal environmental regulations, including those under NEPA, the Clean Air Act, and the Clean Water Act, can affect state and local land use planners as well as developers by imposing environmental standards and, in some cases, permitting requirements on new developments. Compliance with such standards and requirements can slow development and add to developers' costs.

For certain kinds of developments, such as hydroelectric dams and hazardous waste treatment facilities, the federal government is directly involved in location site permitting. Under the 1920 Federal Power Act, 16 U.S.C. §§ 791–828c, as amended in 1935 (49 Stat. 803), all non-federal hydroelectric dams must receive a license from the Federal Energy Regulatory Commission (formerly the Federal Power Commission) if they: (1) are located within the United States; (2) are located in navigable waters; (3) use water or water power from a government dam; and (4) affect interstate commerce. FERC jurisdiction is thus limited to issuing licenses to private citizens, corporations, utilities, or state and municipal governments. Federally owned hydro-projects are authorized and regulated under project-specific federal statutes.

An even more extensive federal permitting and regulatory program governs the development of hazardous waste treatment, storage, and disposal facilities (TSDFs) under the federal Resource Conservation and Recovery Act of 1976, as amended in 1984 (also known as the Solid Waste Disposal Act), 42 U.S.C. §§ 6901 to 6992k. No such facility can be constructed or accept waste deliveries without a permit from the federal government. 42 U.S.C. § 6925. To receive and maintain a permit, a TSDF must abide by myriad pre-construction, construction, operational, closure, and post-closure requirements. Hazardous wastes cannot be treated, stored, or disposed of at any TSDF that does not have a valid permit.

Only a few federal regulatory programs, however, directly regulate the use of private residential or agricultural lands. Those that do are among the most politically controversial of all federal regulatory programs. They include the Endangered Species Act, which restricts private land development to protect endangered and threatened species and their habitat, and the Clean Water Act's wetlands permitting program. The limitations on private land development under the Endangered Species Act are addressed extensively in Chapter 15 on Wildlife Law. The present discussion will focus on wetlands permitting under the Clean Water Act.

B. Federal Wetland Protection

Wetlands are defined as "areas that are inundated or saturated by surface or ground water at a frequency and duration sufficient to support, and that under normal circumstances do support, a prevalence of vegetation typically adapted for life in saturated soil conditions." 33 C.F.R. § 328.3(b). People used to call such places swamps, bogs, and marshes, and they did not like them. Wetlands were considered unhealthful wastelands of bad air and putrid water, infested with disease-carrying vermin and insects. Such areas, according to prevailing thought, could only be rendered productive through reclamation, that is, by conversion to drylands through the process of dredging and filling.

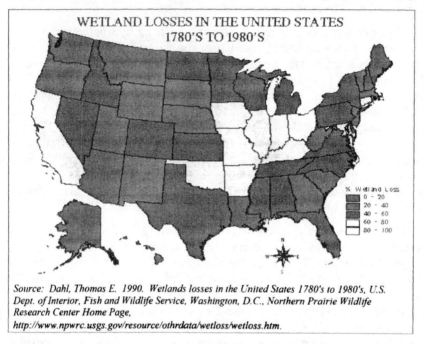

WETLAND LOSSES IN THE UNITED STATES
1780'S TO 1980'S

Source: Dahl, Thomas E. 1990. Wetlands losses in the United States 1780's to 1980's, U.S. Dept. of Interior, Fish and Wildlife Service, Washington, D.C., Northern Prairie Wildlife Research Center Home Page,
http://www.npwrc.usgs.gov/resource/othrdata/wetloss/wetloss.htm.

Over time, however, scientists began to realize that wetlands provide a variety of valuable functions. A wetland might serve as home for fish and fowl, as well as habitat for their predators. Depending upon their geographical setting, wetlands may form a natural storm-break for mainland structures, soaking up heavy rains to prevent flooding. A wetland's lush plant life also purifies the air and water by filtering out pollutants. Unfortunately, by the time all of this became well understood, the majority of all wetlands in the United States had been destroyed, most of them intentionally. When Europeans first arrived in America, total wetland acreage in what became the lower 48 United States amounted to more than 220 million acres, or about 5% of the total land area. By 1997, total wetland acreage had been cut by more than half to about 105.5 million acres. U.S. Department of the Interior, U.S. Fish and Wildlife Service, *Status and Trends of Wetlands in the Coterminous United States 1986–1997* (2000).

Wetlands are easily destroyed, even unintentionally, because they are so fragile. The slightest dredging or filling activity may alter the water level. A change in the water level in turn affects plant life, which requires alternating periods of inundation and dryness. Wild animals near wetlands depend on the plants' nourishment so wildlife, too, may be jeopardized by any abrupt excavation. Equally damaging to wetlands areas is the inevitable air and water pollution that comes with economic development. As wetlands are destroyed or converted to drylands, they no longer serve as natural pollution filters or as sponges to soak up flood waters during periods of heavy rain, which thereby exacerbates local pollution and flooding problems. The social costs of wetlands destruction, consequently, can be very high.

1. *The Scope of Federal Jurisdiction Over Wetlands*

In its 1977 Amendments to the 1972 Clean Water Act (CWA), 33 U.S.C.A. § 1251, Congress established a permitting program, operated by the U.S. Army Corps of Engineers and overseen by the federal Environmental Protection Agency, to control the destruction of wetlands. The CWA's general purpose is to reduce national water pollution problems, but Section 404, 33 U.S.C.A. § 1344, has the special purpose of preserving wetlands from intentional or unintentional destruction. It is in the nature of a resource conservation measure, but it relates directly to the CWA's broader mission of pollution control. Congress perceived that by preserving wetland resources, § 404 would contribute to the CWA's larger goal of improving water quality.

The source of Congress's authority to regulate water pollution stems from the Commerce Clause of the Constitution, according to which all navigable coastal and inland waters may be subject to federal legislation. But how can "wetlands" possibly be defined as "navigable" in keeping with this constitutional limitation? First, the Clean Water Act defines "navigable waters" broadly as "the waters of the United States, including the territorial seas." 33 U.S.C. § 1362(7). And the EPA and the Army Corps have, by regulation, defined "waters of the United States" to include:

(1)   ... all waters which are subject to the ebb and flow of the tide;

(2)   All interstate waters including interstate wetlands;

(3)   All other waters such as intrastate lakes, rivers, streams (including intermittent streams), mudflats, sandflats, wetlands, sloughs, prairie potholes, wet meadows, playa lakes, or natural ponds, the use, degradation or destruction of which could affect interstate or foreign commerce ... ; * * *

(7)   Wetlands adjacent to waters (other than waters that are themselves wetlands) identified in ... this section.

33 C.F.R. § 328.3(a).

In the following case, the U.S. Supreme Court upheld this regulation and the § 404 permitting program generally.

UNITED STATES v. RIVERSIDE BAYVIEW HOMES, INC.

Supreme Court of the United States, 1985.
474 U.S. 121, 106 S.Ct. 455, 88 L.Ed.2d 419.

JUSTICE WHITE, delivered the opinion for a unanimous Court.

This case presents the question whether the Clean Water Act (CWA), *33 U. S. C. § 1251 et seq.*, together with certain regulations promulgated under its authority by the Army Corps of Engineers, authorizes the Corps to require landowners to obtain permits from the Corps before discharging fill material into wetlands adjacent to navigable bodies of water and their tributaries.

I

.... [A]ny discharge of dredged or fill materials into "navigable waters"—defined as the "waters of the United States"—is forbidden unless authorized by a permit issued by the Corps of Engineers pursuant to § 404, *33 U. S. C. § 1344.* ... [T]he Corps construed the Act to cover all "freshwater wetlands" that were adjacent to other covered waters. A "freshwater wetland" was defined as an area that is "periodically inundated" and is "normally characterized by the prevalence of vegetation that requires saturated soil conditions for growth and reproduction." 33 CFR § 209.120(d)(2)*(h)* (1976). In 1977, the Corps refined its definition of wetlands by eliminating the reference to periodic inundation and making other minor changes. The 1977 definition reads as follows:

> "The term 'wetlands' means those areas that are inundated or saturated by surface or ground water at a frequency and duration sufficient to support, and that under normal circumstances do support, a prevalence of vegetation typically adapted for life in saturated soil conditions. Wetlands generally include swamps, marshes, bogs and similar areas."

33 CFR § 323.2(c) (1978).

In 1982, the 1977 regulations were replaced by substantively identical regulations that remain in force today. See *33 CFR § 323.2* (1985).

Respondent Riverside Bayview Homes, Inc. (hereafter respondent), owns 80 acres of low-lying, marshy land near the shores of Lake St. Clair in Macomb County, Michigan. In 1976, respondent began to place fill materials on its property as part of its preparations for construction of a housing development. The Corps of Engineers, believing that the property was an "adjacent wetland" under the 1975 regulation defining "waters of the United States," filed suit ... seeking to enjoin respondent from filling the property without the permission of the Corps.

The District Court held that the portion of respondent's property lying below 575.5 feet above sea level was a covered wetland and enjoined respondent from filling it without a permit. * * * [T]the Sixth Circuit reversed. The court construed the Corps' regulation to exclude from the category of adjacent wetlands—and hence from that of "waters of the United States"—wetlands that were not subject to flooding by adjacent navigable waters at a frequency sufficient to support the growth of aquatic vegetation. The court adopted this construction of the regulation because, in its view, a broader definition of wetlands might result in the taking of private property without just compensation. The court also expressed its doubt that Congress, in granting the Corps jurisdiction to regulate the filling of "navigable waters," intended to allow regulation of wetlands that were not the result of flooding by navigable waters. Under the court's reading of the regulation, respondent's property was not within the Corps' jurisdiction, because its semiaquatic characteristics were not the result of frequent flooding by the nearby navigable waters. Respondent was therefore free to fill the property without obtaining a permit. * * *

II

The question whether the Corps of Engineers may demand that respondent obtain a permit before placing fill material on its property is primarily one of regulatory and statutory interpretation: we must determine whether respondent's property is an "adjacent wetland" within the meaning of the applicable regulation, and, if so, whether the Corps' jurisdiction over "navigable waters" gives it statutory authority to regulate discharges of fill material into such a wetland. In this connection, we first consider the Court of Appeals' position that the Corps' regulatory authority under the statute and its implementing regulations must be narrowly construed to avoid a taking without just compensation in violation of the Fifth Amendment.

We have frequently suggested that governmental land-use regulation may under extreme circumstances amount to a "taking" of the affected property.... [B]ut * * * the mere assertion of regulatory jurisdiction by a governmental body does not constitute a regulatory taking.... The reasons are obvious. A requirement that a person obtain a permit before engaging in a certain use of his or her property does not itself "take" the property in any sense: after all, the very existence of a permit system implies that permission may be granted, leaving the landowner free to use the property as desired. Moreover, even if the permit is denied, there may be other viable uses available to the owner. Only when a permit is denied and the effect of the denial is to prevent "economically viable" use of the land in question can it be said that a taking has occurred.

If neither the imposition of the permit requirement itself nor the denial of a permit necessarily constitutes a taking, it follows that the Court of Appeals erred in concluding that a narrow reading of the Corps' regulatory jurisdiction over wetlands was "necessary" to avoid "a serious taking problem." ...

III

Purged of its spurious constitutional overtones, the question whether the regulation at issue requires respondent to obtain a permit before filling its property is an easy one. The regulation extends the Corps' authority under § 404 to all wetlands adjacent to navigable or interstate waters and their tributaries. Wetlands, in turn, are defined as lands that are "inundated *or saturated* by surface *or ground water* at a frequency and duration sufficient to support, and that under normal circumstances do support, a prevalence of vegetation typically adapted for life in saturated soil conditions." *33 CFR § 323.2(c)* (1985) (emphasis added). The plain language of the regulation refutes the Court of Appeals' conclusion that inundation or "frequent flooding" by the adjacent body of water is a *sine qua non* of a wetland under the regulation. Indeed, the regulation could hardly state more clearly that saturation by either surface or ground water is sufficient to bring an area within the category of wetlands, provided that the saturation is sufficient to and does support wetland vegetation.

*   *   *

Without the nonexistent requirement of frequent flooding, the regulatory definition of adjacent wetlands covers the property here. The District Court found that respondent's property was "characterized by the presence of vegetation that requires saturated soil conditions for growth and reproduction," ... and that the source of the saturated soil conditions on the property was ground water. * * * In addition, the court found that the wetland located on respondent's property was adjacent to a body of navigable water, since the area characterized by saturated soil conditions and wetland vegetation extended beyond the boundary of respondent's property to Black Creek, a navigable waterway. * * * Together, these findings establish that respondent's property is a wetland adjacent to a navigable waterway. Hence, it is part of the "waters of the United States" as defined by *33 CFR § 323.2* (1985), and if the regulation itself is valid as a construction of the term "waters of the United States" as used in the Clean Water Act, a question which we now address, the property falls within the scope of the Corps' jurisdiction over "navigable waters" under § 404 of the Act.

IV

A

An agency's construction of a statute it is charged with enforcing is entitled to deference if it is reasonable and not in conflict with the expressed intent of Congress.... Accordingly, our review is limited to the question whether it is reasonable, in light of the language, policies, and legislative history of the Act for the Corps to exercise jurisdiction over wetlands adjacent to but not regularly flooded by rivers, streams, and other hydrographic features more conventionally identifiable as "waters."

On a purely linguistic level, it may appear unreasonable to classify "lands," wet or otherwise, as "waters." Such a simplistic response, however, does justice neither to the problem faced by the Corps in defining the scope of its authority under § 404(a) nor to the realities of the problem of water pollution that the Clean Water Act was intended to combat. In determining the limits of its power to regulate discharges under the Act, the Corps must necessarily choose some point at which water ends and land begins. Our common experience tells us that this is often no easy task: the transition from water to solid ground is not necessarily or even typically an abrupt one. Rather, between open waters and dry land may lie shallows, marshes, mudflats, swamps, bogs—in short, a huge array of areas that are not wholly aquatic but nevertheless fall far short of being dry land. Where on this continuum to find the limit of "waters" is far from obvious.

Faced with such a problem of defining the bounds of its regulatory authority, an agency may appropriately look to the legislative history and underlying policies of its statutory grants of authority. Neither of these sources provides unambiguous guidance for the Corps in this case, but together they do support the reasonableness of the Corps' approach of defining adjacent wetlands as "waters" within the meaning of § 404(a). Section 404 originated as part of the Federal Water Pollution Control Act Amendments of 1972, which constituted a comprehensive legislative attempt "to restore and maintain the chemical, physical, and biological integrity of the Nation's waters." CWA § 101, *33 U.S.C. § 1251.* This objective incorporated a broad, systemic view of the goal of maintaining and improving water quality: as the House Report on the legislation put it, "the word 'integrity' ... refers to a condition in which the natural structure and function of ecosystems [are] maintained." H. R. Rep. No. 92–911, p. 76 (1972). Protection of aquatic ecosystems, Congress recognized, demanded broad federal authority to control pollution, for "[water] moves in hydrologic cycles and it is essential that discharge of pollutants be controlled at the source." S. Rep. No. 92–414, p. 77 (1972).

In keeping with these views, Congress chose to define the waters covered by the Act broadly. Although the Act prohibits discharges into "navigable waters," ... the Act's definition of "navigable waters" as "the waters of the United States" makes it clear that the term "navigable" as used in the Act is of limited import. In adopting this definition of "navigable waters," Congress evidently intended to repudiate limits that had been placed on federal regulation by earlier water pollution control statutes and to exercise its powers under the Commerce Clause to regulate at least some waters that would not be deemed "navigable" under the classical understanding of that term....

Of course, it is one thing to recognize that Congress intended to allow regulation of waters that might not satisfy traditional tests of navigability; it is another to assert that Congress intended to abandon traditional notions of "waters" and include in that term "wetlands" as well. Nonetheless, the evident breadth of congressional concern for protection of water quality and aquatic ecosystems suggests that it is reasonable for the Corps to interpret the term "waters" to encompass wetlands adjacent to waters as more conventionally defined. Following the lead of the Environmental Protection Agency, see *38 Fed. Reg. 10834 (1973),* the Corps has determined that wetlands adjacent to navigable waters do as a general matter play a key role in protecting and enhancing water quality:

"The regulation of activities that cause water pollution cannot rely on ... artificial lines ... but must focus on all waters that together form the entire aquatic system. Water moves in hydrologic cycles, and the pollution of this part of the aquatic system, regardless of whether it is above or below an ordinary high water mark, or mean high tide line, will affect the water quality of the other waters within that aquatic system.

"For this reason, the landward limit of Federal jurisdiction under Section 404 must include any adjacent wetlands that form the border of or are in reasonable proximity to other waters of the United States, as these wetlands are part of this aquatic system."

42 Fed. Reg. 37128 (1977).

We cannot say that the Corps' conclusion that adjacent wetlands are inseparably bound up with the "waters" of the United States—based as it is on the Corps' and EPA's technical expertise—is unreasonable. In view of the breadth of federal regulatory authority contemplated by the Act itself and the inherent difficulties of defining precise bounds to regulable waters, the Corps' ecological judgment about the relationship between waters and their adjacent wetlands provides an adequate basis for a legal judgment that adjacent wetlands may be defined as waters under the Act.

This holds true even for wetlands that are not the result of flooding or permeation by water having its source in adjacent bodies of open water. The Corps has concluded that wetlands may affect the water quality of adjacent lakes, rivers, and streams even when the waters of those bodies do not actually inundate the wetlands. For example, wetlands that are not flooded by adjacent waters may still tend to drain into those waters. In such circumstances, the Corps has concluded that wetlands may serve to filter and purify water draining into adjacent bodies of water, see *33 CFR § 320.4(b)(2)(vii)* (1985), and to slow the flow of surface runoff into lakes, rivers, and streams and thus prevent flooding and erosion, see §§ 320.4(b)(2)(iv) and (v). In addition, adjacent wetlands may "serve significant natural biological functions, including food chain production, general habitat, and nesting, spawning, rearing and resting sites for aquatic ... species." § 320.4(b)(2)(i). In short, the Corps has concluded that wetlands adjacent to lakes, rivers, streams, and other bodies of water may function as integral parts of the aquatic environment even when the moisture creating the wetlands does not find its source in the adjacent bodies of water. Again, we cannot say that the Corps' judgment on these matters is unreasonable, and we therefore conclude that a definition of "waters of the United States" encompassing all wetlands adjacent to other bodies of water over which the Corps has jurisdiction is a permissible interpretation of the Act. Because respondent's property is part of a wetland that actually abuts on a navigable waterway, respondent was required to have a permit in this case.

B

Following promulgation of the Corps' interim final regulations in 1975, the Corps' assertion of authority under § 404 over waters not actually navigable engendered some congressional opposition. The controversy came to a head during Congress' consideration of the Clean Water Act of 1977, a major piece of legislation aimed at achieving "interim improvements within the existing framework" of the Clean Water Act. H. R. Rep. No. 95–139, pp. 1–2 (1977). In the end, however, as we shall explain, Congress acquiesced in the administrative construction.

Critics of the Corps' permit program attempted to insert limitations on the Corps' § 404 jurisdiction into the 1977 legislation: the House bill ... proposed a redefinition of "navigable waters" that would have limited the Corps' authority under § 404 to waters navigable in fact and their adjacent wetlands (defined as wetlands periodically inundated by contiguous navigable waters).... The bill reported by the Senate Committee on Environment and Public Works, by contrast, contained no redefinition of the scope of the "navigable waters" covered by § 404, and dealt with the perceived problem of over-regulation by the Corps by exempting certain activities (primarily agricultural) from the permit requirement.... On the floor of the Senate, however, an amendment was proposed limiting the scope of "navigable waters" along the lines set forth in the House bill....

In both Chambers, debate on ... proposals to narrow the definition of navigable waters centered largely on the issue of wetlands preservation.... * * * In the House, the debate ended with the adoption of a narrowed definition of "waters"; but in the Senate the limiting amendment was defeated and the old definition retained. The Conference Committee adopted the Senate's approach: efforts to narrow the definition of "waters" were abandoned; the legislation as ultimately passed, in the words of Senator Baker, "[retained] the comprehensive jurisdiction over the Nation's waters exercised in the 1972 Federal Water Pollution Control Act."

The significance of Congress' treatment of the Corps' § 404 jurisdiction in its consideration of the Clean Water Act of 1977 is twofold. First, the scope of the Corps' asserted jurisdiction over wetlands was specifically brought to Congress' attention, and Congress rejected measures designed to curb the Corps' jurisdiction in large part because of its concern that protection of wetlands would be unduly hampered by a narrowed definition of "navigable waters." Although we are chary of attributing significance to Congress' failure to act, a refusal by Congress to overrule an agency's construction of legislation is at least some evidence of the reasonableness of that construction, particularly where the administrative construction has been brought to Congress' attention through legislation specifically designed to supplant it....

Second, it is notable that even those who would have restricted the reach of the Corps' jurisdiction would have done so not by removing wetlands altogether from the definition of "waters of the United States," but only by restricting the scope of "navigable waters" under § 404 to waters navigable in fact *and their adjacent wetlands....* * * * Thus, even those who thought that the Corps' existing authority under § 404 was too broad recognized (1) that the definition of "navigable waters" then in force ... was reasonably interpreted to include adjacent wetlands, (2) that the water quality concerns of the Clean Water Act demanded regulation of at least some discharges into wetlands, and (3) that whatever jurisdiction the Corps would retain over discharges of fill material after passage of the 1977 legislation should extend to discharges into wetlands adjacent to any waters over which the Corps retained jurisdiction. These views provide additional support for a conclusion that Congress in 1977 acquiesced in the Corps' definition of waters as including adjacent wetlands. * * *

C

We are thus persuaded that the language, policies, and history of the Clean Water Act compel a finding that the Corps has acted reasonably in interpreting the Act to require permits for the discharge of fill material into wetlands adjacent to the "waters of the United States." The regulation in which the Corps has embodied this interpretation by its terms includes the wetlands on respondent's property within the class of waters that may not be filled without a permit; and, as we have seen, there is no reason to interpret the regulation more narrowly than its terms would indicate. Accordingly, the judgment of the Court of Appeals is *Reversed*.

Notes and Questions

1. The Supreme Court, in *Riverside Bayview Homes*, decided that "adjacent" wetlands, even those that are never inundated by the waters to which they are adjacent, are subject to federal regulations under the § 404 permitting program. As a result, the developer was required to obtain a federal permit and comply with its terms, as well as all requirements of state and local law, before proceeding with its housing development on the shores of Lake St. Clair. Are you convinced that the phrase "navigable waters" in the CWA should be construed so broadly?

2. What about "isolated" wetlands, that is, wetlands that have no apparent connection to any adjacent navigable waterbody? In the following case, the Supreme Court established a clear limit on federal authority to regulate such wetlands.

SOLID WASTE AGENCY OF NORTHERN COOK COUNTY v. UNITED STATES ARMY CORPS OF ENGINEERS, ET AL.

Supreme Court of the United States, 2001.
531 U.S. 159, 121 S.Ct. 675, 148 L.Ed.2d 576.

CHIEF JUSTICE REHNQUIST delivered the opinion of the Court.

Section 404(a) of the Clean Water Act (CWA or Act), 86 Stat. 884, as amended, *33 U.S.C. § 1344*(a), regulates the discharge of dredged or fill material into "navigable waters." The United States Army Corps of Engineers (Corps) has interpreted § 404(a) to confer federal authority over an abandoned sand and gravel pit in northern Illinois which provides habitat for migratory birds. We are asked to decide whether the provisions of § 404(a) may be fairly extended to these waters, and, if so, whether Congress could exercise such authority consistent with the Commerce Clause, U.S. Const., Art. I, § 8, cl. 3. We answer the first question in the negative and therefore do not reach the second.

Petitioner, the Solid Waste Agency of Northern Cook County (SWANCC), is a consortium of 23 suburban Chicago cities and villages that united in an effort to locate and develop a disposal site for baled nonhazardous solid waste. The Chicago Gravel Company informed the municipalities of the availability of a 533–acre parcel, bestriding the Illinois counties Cook and Kane, which had been the site of a sand and gravel pit mining operation for three decades up until about 1960. Long since abandoned, the old mining site eventually gave way to a successional stage forest, with its remnant excavation trenches evolving into a scattering of permanent and seasonal ponds of varying size (from under one-tenth of an acre to several acres) and depth (from several inches to several feet).

The municipalities decided to purchase the site for disposal of their baled nonhazardous solid waste. By law, SWANCC was required to file for various permits from Cook County and the State of Illinois before it could begin operation of its balefill project. In addition, because the operation called for the filling of some of the permanent and seasonal ponds, SWANCC contacted ... the Corps, to determine if a federal landfill permit was required under § 404(a) of the CWA, *33 U.S.C. § 1344*(a).

Section 404(a) grants the Corps authority to issue permits "for the discharge of dredged or fill material into the navigable waters at specified disposal sites." *Ibid.* The term "navigable waters" is defined under the Act as "the waters of the United States, including the territorial seas." § 1362(7). The Corps has issued regulations defining the term "waters of the United States" to include

> "waters such as intrastate lakes, rivers, streams (including intermittent streams), mudflats, sandflats, wetlands, sloughs, prairie potholes, wet meadows, playa lakes, or natural ponds, the use, degradation or destruction of which could affect interstate or foreign commerce...." *33 CFR § 328.3(a)(3)* (1999).

In 1986, in an attempt to "clarify" the reach of its jurisdiction, the Corps stated that § 404(a) extends to intrastate waters:

> "a. Which are or would be used as habitat by birds protected by Migratory Bird Treaties; or

> "b. Which are or would be used as habitat by other migratory birds which cross state lines; or

"c. Which are or would be used as habitat for endangered species; or

"d. Used to irrigate crops sold in interstate commerce." *51 Fed. Reg. 41217.*

This last promulgation has been dubbed the "Migratory Bird Rule."

The Corps initially concluded that it had no jurisdiction over the site because it contained no "wetlands," or areas which support "vegetation typically adapted for life in saturated soil conditions," *33 CFR § 328.3(b)* (1999). However, after the Illinois Nature Preserves Commission informed the Corps that a number of migratory bird species had been observed at the site, the Corps reconsidered and ultimately asserted jurisdiction over the balefill site pursuant to subpart (b) of the "Migratory Bird Rule." The Corps found that approximately 121 bird species had been observed at the site, including several known to depend upon aquatic environments for a significant portion of their life requirements. Thus, on November 16, 1987, the Corps formally "determined that the seasonally ponded, abandoned gravel mining depressions located on the project site, while not wetlands, did qualify as 'waters of the United States' ... based upon the following criteria: (1) the proposed site had been abandoned as a gravel mining operation; (2) the water areas and spoil piles had developed a natural character; and (3) the water areas are used as habitat by migratory bird *[sic]* which cross state lines." ... During the application process, SWANCC made several proposals to mitigate the likely displacement of the migratory birds and to preserve a great blue heron rookery located on the site. Its balefill project ultimately received the necessary local and state approval. By 1993, SWANCC had received a special use planned development permit from the Cook County Board of Appeals, a landfill development permit from the Illinois Environmental Protection Agency, and approval from the Illinois Department of Conservation.

Despite SWANCC's securing the required water quality certification from the Illinois Environmental Protection Agency, the Corps refused to issue a § 404(a) permit. The Corps found that SWANCC had not established that its proposal was the "least environmentally damaging, most practicable alternative" for disposal of nonhazardous solid waste; that SWANCC's failure to set aside sufficient funds to remediate leaks posed an "unacceptable risk to the public's drinking water supply"; and that the impact of the project upon area-sensitive species was "unmitigatable since a landfill surface cannot be redeveloped into a forested habitat." ...

Petitioner filed suit under the Administrative Procedure Act, *5 U.S.C. § 701 et seq.*, in the Northern District of Illinois challenging both the Corps' jurisdiction over the site and the merits of its denial of the § 404(a) permit. * * * Petitioner argued that respondents had exceeded their statutory authority in interpreting CWA to cover nonnavigable, isolated, intrastate waters based upon the presence of migratory birds and, in the alternative, that Congress lacked the power under the Commerce Clause to grant such regulatory jurisdiction.

The Court of Appeals began its analysis with the constitutional question, holding that Congress has the authority to regulate such waters based upon "the cumulative impact doctrine, under which a single activity that itself has no discernible effect on interstate commerce may still be regulated if the aggregate effect of that class of activity has a substantial impact on interstate commerce." *191 F.3d 845, 850 (CA7 1999)*. The aggregate effect of the "destruction of the natural habitat of migratory birds" on interstate commerce, the court held, was substantial because each year millions of Americans cross state lines and spend over a billion dollars to hunt and observe migratory birds.... The Court of Appeals then turned to the regulatory question. The court held that the CWA reaches as many waters as the Commerce Clause allows and, given its earlier Commerce Clause ruling, it therefore followed that respondents' "Migratory Bird Rule" was a reasonable interpretation of the Act. * * * We granted certiorari ... and now reverse.

Congress passed the CWA for the stated purpose of "restoring and maintaining the chemical, physical, and biological integrity of the Nation's waters." *33 U.S.C. § 1251*(a). In so doing, Congress chose to "recognize, preserve, and protect the primary responsibilities and rights of States to prevent, reduce, and eliminate pollution, to plan the development and use (including restoration, preservation, and enhancement) of land and water resources, and to consult with the Administrator in the exercise of his authority under this chapter." § 1251(b). Relevant here, § 404(a) authorizes respondents to regulate the discharge of fill material into "navigable waters," *33 U.S.C. § 1344*(a), which the statute defines as "the waters of the United States, including the territorial seas," § 1362(7). Respondents have interpreted these words to cover the abandoned gravel pit at issue here because it is used as habitat for migratory birds. We conclude that the "Migratory Bird Rule" is not fairly supported by the CWA.

This is not the first time we have been called upon to evaluate the meaning of § 404(a). In *United States v. Riverside Bayview Homes, Inc., 474 U.S. 121, 88 L. Ed. 2d 419, 106 S. Ct. 455 (1985)*, we held that the Corps had § 404(a) jurisdiction over wetlands that actually abutted on a navigable waterway. In so doing, we noted that the term "navigable" is of "limited import" and that Congress evidenced its intent to "regulate at least some waters that would not be deemed 'navigable' under the classical understanding of that term." *Id. at 133*. But our holding was based in large measure upon Congress' unequivocal acquiescence to, and approval of, the Corps' regulations interpreting the CWA to cover wetlands adjacent to navigable waters. See *474 U.S. at 135–139*. We found that Congress' concern for the protection of water quality and aquatic ecosystems indicated its intent to regulate wetlands "inseparably bound up with the 'waters' of the United States." 474 U.S. at 134.

It was the significant nexus between the wetlands and "navigable waters" that informed our reading of the CWA in *Riverside Bayview Homes*. Indeed, we did not "express any opinion" on the "question of the authority of the Corps to regulate discharges of fill material into wetlands that are not adjacent to bodies of open water...." 474 U.S. at 131–132, *n. 8*. In order to rule for respondents here, we would have to hold that the jurisdiction of the Corps extends to ponds that are *not* adjacent to open water. But we conclude that the text of the statute will not allow this.

Indeed, the Corps' *original* interpretation of the CWA, promulgated two years after its enactment, is inconsistent with that which it espouses here. Its 1974 regulations defined § 404(a)'s "navigable waters" to mean "those waters of the United States which are subject to the ebb and flow of the tide, and/or are presently, or have been in the past, or may be in the future susceptible for use for purposes of interstate or foreign commerce." 33 CFR § 209.120(d)(1). The Corps emphasized that "it is the water body's capability of use by the public for purposes of transportation or commerce which is the determinative factor." § 209.260(e)(1). Respondents put forward no persuasive evidence that the Corps mistook Congress' intent in 1974.

Respondents next contend that whatever its original aim in 1972, Congress charted a new course five years later when it approved the more expansive definition of "navigable waters" found in the Corps' 1977 regulations. In July 1977, the Corps formally adopted *33 CFR § 323.2(a)(5)* (1978), which defined "waters of the United States" to include "isolated wetlands and lakes, intermittent streams, prairie potholes, and other waters that are not part of a tributary system to interstate waters or to navigable waters of the United States, the degradation or destruction of which could affect interstate commerce." Respondents argue that Congress was aware of this more expansive interpretation during its 1977 amendments to the CWA. Specifically, respondents point to a failed House bill, H. R. 3199, that would have defined "navigable waters" as "all waters which are presently used, or are susceptible to use in their natural condition or by reasonable improvement as a means to transport interstate or foreign commerce." 123 Cong. Rec. 10420, 10434 (1977). * * * The failure to pass legislation that would have overturned the Corps' 1977 regulations and the extension of jurisdiction in § 404(g) to waters "other than" traditional "navigable waters," respondents submit, indicate that Congress recognized and accepted a broad definition of "navigable waters" that includes nonnavigable, isolated, intrastate waters.

Although we have recognized congressional acquiescence to administrative interpretations of a statute in some situations, we have done so with extreme care. "Failed legislative proposals are 'a particularly dangerous ground on which to rest an interpretation of a prior statute.'" ... A bill can be proposed for any number of reasons, and it can be rejected for just as many others. * * *

We conclude that respondents have failed to make the necessary showing that the failure of the 1977 House bill demonstrates Congress' acquiescence to the Corps' regulations or the "Migratory Bird Rule," which, of course, did not first appear until 1986. Although respondents cite some legislative history showing Congress' recognition of the Corps' assertion of jurisdiction over "isolated waters," as we explained in *Riverside Bayview Homes*, "in both Chambers, debate on the proposals to narrow the definition of navigable waters centered largely on the issue of wetlands preservation." *474 U.S. at 136*. Beyond Congress' desire to regulate wetlands adjacent to "navigable waters," respondents point us to no persuasive evidence that the House bill was proposed in response to the Corps' claim of jurisdiction over nonnavigable, isolated, intrastate waters or that its failure indicated congressional acquiescence to such jurisdiction. * * *

We thus decline respondents' invitation to take what they see as the next ineluctable step after *Riverside Bayview Homes*: holding that isolated ponds, some only seasonal, wholly located within two Illinois counties, fall under § 404(a)'s definition of "navigable waters" because they serve as habitat for migratory birds. As counsel for respondents conceded at oral argument, such a ruling would assume that "the use of the word navigable in the statute ... does not have any independent significance." ... We cannot agree that Congress' separate definitional use of the phrase "waters of the United States" constitutes a basis for reading the term "navigable waters" out of the statute. We said in *Riverside Bayview Homes* that the word "navigable" in the statute was of "limited effect" and went on to hold that § 404(a) extended to nonnavigable wetlands adjacent to open waters. But it is one thing to give a word limited effect and quite another to give it no effect whatever. The term "navigable" has at least the import of showing us what Congress had in mind as its authority for enacting the CWA: its traditional jurisdiction over waters that were or had been navigable in fact or which could reasonably be so made....

Respondents ... contend that, at the very least, it must be said that Congress did not address the precise question of § 404(a)'s scope with regard to non-navigable, isolated, intrastate waters, and that, therefore, we should give deference to the "Migratory Bird Rule." See, *e.g.*, *Chevron U.S.A. Inc. v. Natural Resources Defense Council, Inc., 467 U.S. 837, 81 L. Ed. 2d 694, 104 S. Ct. 2778 (1984)*. We find § 404(a) to be clear, but even were we to agree with respondents, we would not extend *Chevron* deference here.

Where an administrative interpretation of a statute invokes the outer limits of Congress' power, we expect a clear indication that Congress intended that result.... This requirement stems from our prudential desire not to needlessly reach constitutional issues and our assumption that Congress does not casually authorize administrative agencies to interpret a statute to push the limit of congressional authority.... This concern is heightened where the administrative interpretation alters the federal-state framework by permitting federal encroachment upon a traditional state power.... Thus, "where an otherwise acceptable construction of a statute would raise serious constitutional problems, the Court will construe the statute to avoid such problems unless such construction is plainly contrary to the intent of Congress." * * *

Twice in the past six years we have reaffirmed the proposition that the grant of authority to Congress under the Commerce Clause, though broad, is not unlimited. See *United States v. Morrison, 529 U.S. 598, 146 L. Ed. 2d 658, 120 S. Ct. 1740 (2000); United States v. Lopez, 514 U.S. 549, 131 L. Ed. 2d 626, 115 S. Ct. 1624 (1995)*. Respondents argue that the "Migratory Bird Rule" falls within Congress' power to regulate intrastate activities that "substantially affect" interstate commerce. They note that the protection of migratory birds is a "national interest of very nearly the first magnitude," *Missouri v. Holland, 252 U.S. 416, 435, 64 L. Ed. 641, 40 S. Ct. 382, 18 Ohio L. Rep. 61 (1920)*, and that, as the Court of Appeals found, millions of people spend over a billion dollars annually on recreational pursuits relating to migratory birds. These arguments raise significant constitutional questions. For example, we would have to evaluate the precise object or activity that, in the aggregate, substantially affects interstate commerce. This is not clear, for although the Corps has claimed jurisdiction over petitioner's land because it contains water areas used as habitat by migratory birds, respondents now, *post litem motam*, focus upon the fact that the regulated activity is petitioner's municipal landfill, which is "plainly of a commercial nature." ... But this is a far cry, indeed, from the "navigable waters" and "waters of the United States" to which the statute by its terms extends.

These are significant constitutional questions raised by respondents' application of their regulations, and yet we find nothing approaching a clear statement from Congress that it intended § 404(a) to reach an abandoned sand and gravel pit such as we have here. Permitting respondents to claim federal jurisdiction over ponds and mudflats falling within the "Migratory Bird Rule" would result in a significant impingement of the States' traditional and primary power over land and water use.... Rather than expressing a desire to readjust the federal-state balance in this manner, Congress chose to "recognize, preserve, and protect the primary responsibilities and rights of States ... to plan the development and use ... of land and water resources...." *33 U.S.C. § 1251*(b). We thus read the statute as written to avoid the significant constitutional and federalism questions raised by respondents' interpretation, and therefore reject the request for administrative deference.

We hold that *33 CFR § 328.3(a)(3)* (1999), as clarified and applied to petitioner's balefill site pursuant to the "Migratory Bird Rule," *51 Fed. Reg. 41217 (1986)*, exceeds the authority granted to respondents under § 404(a) of the CWA. * * *

Notes and Questions

1. What is the scope of federal jurisdiction over wetlands after *SWANCC*? Did the Court overrule or merely delimit its earlier rule from *Riverside Bayview Homes*? The *SWANCC* Court held that there must be a

"significant nexus" between the wetlands and some navigable water body. Some circuit courts, since *SWANCC*, have adopted broad definitions of "significant nexus," upholding even slight or intermittent hydrological connections as "significant." *See, e.g.*, United States v. Deaton, 332 F.3d 698 (4th Cir.2003), cert. denied, 541 U.S. 972, 124 S.Ct. 1874, 158 L.Ed.2d 466 (2004) (roadside ditch covered); United States v. Rapanos, 376 F.3d 629 (6th cir. 2004) (hydrologically connected wetlands covered, even absent "direct abutment" to navigable water); Headwaters, Inc. v. Talent Irrigation District, 243 F.3d 526 (9th Cir. 2001) (irrigation canals covered). "The emerging majority rule among the federal courts ... is that any surface water connection to waters that are navigable in the traditional sense—however intermittent, convoluted, or human-made the connection might be—is sufficient to confer CWA jurisdiction over a water body." Robin Kundis Craig, *Beyond SWANCC: The New Federalism and Clean Water Act Jurisdiction*, 33 ENVTL. L. 113, 132 (2003).

2. *SWANCC* interprets the Clean Water Act as asserting less than the full extent of possible federal jurisdiction. Isolated wetlands, that is, wetlands with no "significant nexus" to any navigable water body, are not subject to § 404 dredge and fill permitting. As a consequence of this interpretation, according to some estimates, between 30 and 60 percent of the nation's wetlands are unprotected by the CWA. *See* Jon Kusler, The SWANCC Decision and State Regulation of Wetlands, *available at* www.aswm.org/fwp/swancc/aswm-int.pdf.

Websources:

U.S. Army Corps of Engineers, http://www.usace.army.mil
State Wetlands Programs at http://www.aswm.org/swp/states.htm

---

3. Even though the federal government is precluded from regulating isolated wetlands, such wetlands still may be protected under state law. State governments have independent regulatory authority to limit dredging and filling of wetlands. Indeed, the Court characterized the states' authority as a "traditional state power," and expressed its concern that the Corps' expansive interpretation of federal power would have "alter[ed] the federal-state framework." *SWANCC, supra*. To date, however, according to the Association of State Wetland Managers, only 16 states—Connecticut, Florida, Maine, Maryland, Massachusetts, Michigan, Minnesota, New Hampshire, New Jersey, New York, Oregon, Pennsylvania, Rhode Island, Vermont, Virginia, and Wisconsin—have wetland regulatory programs.

Wisconsin's 2001 Act 6 is notable as a direct response to the U.S. Supreme Court's ruling in *SWANCC*. Act 6 regulates only "non-federal" wetlands, which are defined as wetlands no longer subject to U.S. Army Corps of Engineers jurisdiction because of federal court decisions (*i.e., SWANCC*). Act 6 is available at http://www.legis.state.wi.us/2001/data/ acts/01Act6.pdf. *See also* Wisconsin Legislative Council Legal Memorandum, Water Quality

Certification for Nonfederal Wetlands (2001 Wisconsin Act 6), available at http://www.legis.state.wi.us/lc/ jlc01/LM_ 2001_ 4.pdf.

4. Bills have been introduced in Congress that would overturn the *SWANCC* decision by amending the Clean Water Act to broaden the scope of federal jurisdiction, but none has been enacted. *See* Jeffrey Z. Zinn and Claudia Copeland, Wetland Issues, Congressional Research Service Issue Brief for Congress, IB97014 (Updated August 12, 2004). What, if any, action should Congress and/or the Executive branch take in response to SWANCC?

2. *The Federal Permitting Program*

With respect to those wetlands that remain subject to federal jurisdiction, § 404 of the CWA authorizes the Army Corps of Engineers to issue permits for applicants to discharge dredged or fill materials into navigable waters at particular locations. 33 U.S.C.A. § 1344(a). A "discharge of a pollutant" triggering § 404 includes changing the bottom elevation of a stream, United States v. Zanger, 767 F.Supp. 1030 (N.D. Cal. 1991), and the movement of indigenous materials into waters of the United States. Rybachek v. U.S. EPA, 904 F.2d 1276, 1286 (9th Cir. 1990). Resuspension of indigenous sediments through "incidental fall-back" during dredging, however, is not considered an addition (or discharge) under § 404. National Min. Ass'n v. U.S. Army Corps of Engineers, 145 F.3d 1399, 1407 (D.C. Cir. 1998).

The Corps can only issue the permit if it finds that the dredge and fill activity would not significantly degrade the nation's waters and no practicable alternative exists that would be less damaging to the aquatic environment. An "alternative" is "available" if it is "capable of being done after taking into consideration cost, existing technology, and logistics in light of overall project purposes." 40 C.F.R. § 230.10(a)(2). The burden is on the applicant to prove that there is no available alternative. Applicants must also agree to take practicable measures to avoid or minimize impacts, and compensate for wetland destruction or damage by undertaking activities to restore or create wetlands. Wetlands mitigation is addressed below in Section IV.B.6.

There are two types of § 404 permits. "Individual permits" are required for dredge and fill activities that are likely to have significant impacts on wetlands, and they can be awarded only after public notice and comment. For activities that are likely to have only minimal adverse impacts on wetlands, the Corps may issue "general permits," which apply on a national, regional, or state-wide basis for particular categories of activities (such as road maintenance). The dual permitting process is designed to focus attention on projects with significant effects on wetlands, while expediting review and approval of permits for cases involving only minor impacts to wetlands.

"Normal" farming and silvaculture activities do not require § 404 permits, 33 U.S.C.A. § 1344(f)1)(A), unless those activities would constitute a new use or impair the flow of navigable waters. United States v. Larkins, 852 F.2d 189 (6th Cir. 1988); United States v. Akers, 785 F.2d

814 (9th Cir. 1986); Avoyelles Sportsmen's League, Inc. v. Marsh, 715 F.2d 897 (5th Cir. 1983). What if a farmer uses a tractor to pull metal prongs through the soil to prepare fields for a new crop? In Borden Ranch v. U.S. Army Corps of Engineers, 261 F.3d 810 (9th Cir. 2001), *aff'd* 537 U.S. 99, 123 S.Ct. 599, 154 L.Ed.2d 508 (2002), the court held that "deep ripping" was covered by Section 404, and required the rancher to get a permit before he could convert his pasture to vineyards.

Review of dredge and fill permit applications under the Clean Water Act involves a balancing test. "The decision whether to issue a permit will be based on the probable impact of the proposed activity and its intended use on the public interest.... The benefits which reasonably may be expected to accrue from the proposal must be balanced against its reasonably foreseeable detriments." 33 C.F.R. § 320.4. Is the use of such a balancing test advisable when dealing with ecologically fragile areas such as wetlands? How likely is it that economic or political pressure would be used to tip the scales in favor of development?

If the Corps decides that granting a permit would be in the public interest, the Environmental Protection Agency can still veto that decision, if it concludes that (1) there are less detrimental alternatives to the proposed dredge and fill activity, Bersani v. U.S. EPA, 850 F.2d 36 (2d Cir. 1988), *cert. denied*, 489 U.S. 1089, 109 S.Ct. 1556, 103 L.Ed.2d 859 (1989) or (2) the permitted activity would have an unreasonable effect upon water supplies, fish, wildlife, or recreation areas. Alameda Water and Sanitation Dist. v. Reilly, 930 F.Supp. 486 (D.Colo. 1996). However, in the case of James City County v. EPA, 758 F.Supp. 348 (E.D.Va. 1990), *aff'd in relevant part*, 955 F.2d 254 (4th Cir. 1992), the court held that EPA could not veto a Corps permit based on a mere *presumption* that there are alternatives to the proposed dredge and fill operation. Although EPA's subsequent veto of the James County permit (due to unacceptable environmental impacts) was ultimately upheld, *see* James city County v. U.S. EPA, 12 F.3d 1330 (4th Cir. 1993), as a practical matter, EPA vetoes of Corps permits are rare.

The Corps processes approximately 85,000 permits each year. More than 90 percent of these are general, as opposed to individual, permits. Because the vast majority of permits are general, average processing time is relatively short, taking less than 60 days from application to issuance. Applications for individual permits often take up to 120 days to process. Less than 0.2 percent of permits are denied, although most individual permits have conditions attached to them. In Fiscal Year 2002, the Corp issued permits affecting a total of 24,650 acres of wetlands, but those same permits required the restoration, creation, or enhancement of 57,820 acres of wetlands. Jeffrey A. Zinn and Claudia Copeland, Wetland Issues, CRS Issue Brief for Congress CRS–5 (Updated August 12, 2004).

3.   *NEPA Implications of § 404 Permitting*

Issuance of a § 404 permit constitutes a major federal action requiring environmental analysis under NEPA (addressed in detail in Chapter

4). The Corps must assess the environmental impacts of the specific activity requiring the permit. 33 C.F.R. Part 325, Appendix B § 7(b). Does this mean that the Corps must consider all of the impacts of a larger project of which the § 404 permitted activity is only a small part? Some courts have said no. *See* Wetlands Action Network v. US Army Corps of Engineers, 222 F.3d 1105 (9th Cir. 2000), *cert. denied,* 534 U.S. 815, 122 S.Ct. 41, 151 L.Ed.2d 14 (2001) (requiring NEPA review for permit application to fill 120 acres of wetlands, but not for the entire 1,000 acre development project to which the application related), when the remainder of the project area affected only uplands). For discussion, see Chapter 4.IV.C.2, *supra* (NEPA Effects—Segmentation).

4. *Takings Implications of § 404 Permitting*

Section 404 reaches a vast array of private activities on private lands. Can denial of a dredge and fill permit application give rise to a takings claim under the 5th Amendment?

LLOYD A. GOOD v. UNITED STATES
United States Court of Appeals for the Federal Circuit, 1999.
189 F.3d 1355.

SENIOR CIRCUIT JUDGE SMITH delivered the opinion of the Court.

* * * Lloyd A. Good, Jr. sued the federal government on the basis that it effectively took his property without just compensation when the U.S. Army Corps of Engineers denied him permission to dredge and fill on land he owns in the Florida Keys. The U.S. Court of Federal Claims granted summary judgment to the United States. We affirm.

Facts

Lloyd A. Good, Jr. ("Good") … purchased a forty-acre tract of undeveloped land on Lower Sugarloaf Key, Florida, in 1973, as part of a much larger real estate purchase. The tract, known as Sugarloaf Shores, consists of thirty-two acres of wetlands (a combination of salt marsh and freshwater marsh) and eight acres of uplands. The sales contract for the land stated that:

> The Buyers recognize that certain of the lands covered by this contract may be below the mean high tide line and that as of today there are certain problems in connection with the obtaining of State and Federal permission for dredging and filling operations.

Good's efforts to develop the property began in 1980, when he hired Keycology, Inc., a land planning and development firm, to obtain the federal, state, and county permits necessary to develop Sugarloaf Shores into a residential subdivision. In their contract, Good and Keycology acknowledged that "obtaining said permits is at best difficult and by no means assured."

Good submitted his first permit application to the U.S. Army Corps of Engineers ("Corps") in March 1981. The Corps permit was required for dredging and filling navigable waters of the United States, including wetlands adjacent to navigable waters, under the Rivers and Harbors Act of 1899 and under § 404 of the Clean Water Act. Good proposed filling 7.4 acres of salt marsh and excavating another 5.4 acres of salt marsh in order to create a 54-lot subdivision and a 48-slip marina. The Corps granted the requested permit in May 1983. Good modified the permit in response to county environmental concerns and the modified permit was issued January 6, 1984. Under both permits, the authorized work had to be completed within five years. See *33 CFR § 325.6* (1998).

Good and Keycology were also pursuing the required state and county permits. In February 1983, the state Department of Environmental Regulation issued a permit for the requested dredging and filling. The state permit was conditioned, however, on Good obtaining county approval for the project.

On May 10, 1983, Good applied for county approval of the dredge-and-fill proposal that had been approved by the federal and state permits. The county determined that the plan was a "major development" subject to a more stringent environmental review than under standard procedures. * * * [but ultimately] granted Good's permit ... [under standard procedures].

At this point, Good had received federal, state, and county approval to develop the property. Florida law, however, presented one more hurdle, in the form of the Environmental Land and Water Management Act, *FLA. STAT. ANN. § § 380.012* to 380.12 (West 1997). The Act created a statutory regime for regulating development in Areas of Critical State Concern, including the entire Florida Keys. Under the Act, the Florida Department of Community Affairs ("DCA") reviews local land development orders in Areas of Critical State Concern and may appeal those orders to the Florida Land and Water Adjudicatory Commission ("FLAWAC"). See *FLA. STAT. ANN. § 380.07* (West 1997). On September 10, 1984, the DCA appealed the county's approval of Good's dredge-and-fill project. FLAWAC held that the county had erred in subjecting Good's plan only to the standard review, and on May 29, 1986 ordered the county to review the project as a "major development."

Making matters worse for Good, the county in the meantime had adopted a new land use plan and new development regulations. The new regulations prohibited dredging to provide access to docks, prohibited filling of salt marsh for building sites, and limited filling of salt marsh to 10% of the salt marsh on a parcel. MONROE COUNTY, FLA. CODE, art. II, § 9.5–345 (1986). Since Good's plan involved dredging to provide boat access between the proposed marina and Upper Sugarloaf Sound, and required filling roughly 25% of the parcel's salt marsh to provide building sites, Good's project would not have been allowed under the new regulations.

Good filed suit in state court, alleging that the state had taken his property without just compensation and that FLAWAC's order was an unreasonable exercise of police power. That suit was settled on October 22, 1987. The consent decree provided that Good's application would be evaluated under the repealed major development review standard but that any future development of Sugarloaf Shores would be subject to later-enacted land use regulations.

Good's efforts to get state and county approval for his project had used up most of the five-year time limit on the federal permits issued in 1983 and 1984. Good therefore requested that the Corps extend the time limits of the permits. The Corps denied Good's request to reissue the permits without changes, but granted a new permit allowing substantially the same development on October 17, 1988.

* * * Final county approval... was subject to fifteen conditions, the most significant of which was approval of the project by the South Florida Water Management District (SFWMD). SFWMD notified Good that its staff recommended denying the application, based on "the unmitigated loss of wetlands, the loss of habitat for the endangered species within them [i.e., the state-listed mud turtle and Lower Keys marsh rabbit] and the lack of reasonable assurance that future unmitigated wetlands destruction will not occur due to the lack of the above-requested dedication. * * * Good ... never obtained SFWMD approval for his project.

Apparently despairing of ever obtaining approval for his 54–lot plan, Good submitted a new, scaled-down plan to the Corps in July 1990. * * * Good proposed building only sixteen homes, together with a canal and tennis court. Although the new plan greatly reduced the overall number of houses, it located all of them in the wetlands area. The overall wetlands loss, therefore, was only reduced from 10.53 acres to 10.17 acres.

Between the time the Corps issued Good's 1988 permit and the time he applied for the 1990 permit, the Lower Keys marsh rabbit was listed as an endangered species under the Endangered Species Act ("ESA"). See *16 U.S.C. § 1533* (1994); *55 Fed. Reg. 25,588* (June 21, 1990). The Corps was therefore required to consult with the Fish and Wildlife Service ("FWS") to insure that issuing the requested permit would not place the continued existence of the species in jeopardy. See *16 U.S.C. § 1536* (a)(2) (1994).* * * FWS concluded that the project proposed in Good's 1990 permit application would not jeopardize the continued existence of the marsh rabbit. Nevertheless, it recommended denial of the permit based on the development's overall environmental impact.

The FWS biological opinion also instructed the Corps to notify Good not to proceed under his 1988 permit. The 1988 permit had been issued before the marsh rabbit was listed as an endangered species and proposed a different project than the 1990 permit application. Therefore, the FWS "no jeopardy" finding did not apply to the earlier permit, and development pursuant to the 1988 permit could violate the ESA.

On May 14, 1991, the Corps notified FWS that Good intended to proceed with the project allowed by the 1988 permit. The Corps also noted that it did not believe the project would jeopardize the marsh rabbit, but noted that the silver rice rat had been listed as an endangered species subsequent to the FWS biological opinion on the 1990 permit application. See *56 Fed. Reg. 19,809* (April 30, 1991).

In response, FWS initiated consultation under the ESA and notified the Corps that it would prepare a new biological opinion evaluating the effect of Good's 1988 plan on both endangered species. On December 18, 1991, FWS released its new biological opinion, concluding that both the 1988 and 1990 plans jeopardized the continued existence of both the Lower Keys marsh rabbit and the silver rice rat. FWS recommended that the Corps deny the 1990 application and modify the 1988 permit to include FWS's "reasonable and prudent alternatives," which included locating all homesites in upland areas and limiting water access to a single communal dock.

The Corps denied Good's 1990 permit application on March 17, 1994. At the same time, the Corps notified Good that his 1988 permit had expired. The Corps based its denial on the threat that either project posed to the endangered rat and rabbit. * * *

On July 11, 1994, Good filed suit, alleging that the Corps' denial of his permit worked an uncompensated taking in violation of the Fifth Amendment. * * * [T]he Court of Federal Claims granted summary judgment in favor of the government. The court held that the Corps' denial of Good's permit did not constitute a "per se" taking under *Lucas v. South Carolina Coastal Council, 505 U.S. 1003, 120 L. Ed. 2d 798, 112 S. Ct. 2886 (1992)*, because the ESA did not require that the property be left in its natural state and because the government had shown that the property retained value, either for development or for sale of transferrable development rights (TDRs), after the permit denial. * * *

The court also held that there had been no taking under the ad hoc analysis of *Penn Central Transportation Co. v. New York City, 438 U.S. 104, 124, 57 L. Ed. 2d 631, 98 S. Ct. 2646 (1978)*. The court held that Good lacked reasonable, investment-backed expectations since federal and state regulations imposed significant restrictions on his ability to develop his property both at the time he purchased it and at the time he began to develop it. Finding the lack of reasonable expectations determinative, the court held that no taking had occurred. * * *

Analysis

* * *

For any regulatory takings claim to succeed, the claimant must show that the government's regulatory restraint interfered with his investment-backed expectations in a manner that requires the government to compensate him. See *Loveladies Harbor, 28 F.3d at 1179*. The requirement of investment-backed expectations "limits recovery to owners who can demonstrate that they bought their property in reliance on the non-existence of the challenged regulation." ... These expectations must be reasonable....

Reasonable, investment-backed expectations are an element of every regulatory takings case. See *Loveladies Harbor, 28 F.3d at 1179*. See also *id. at 1177* ("In legal terms, the owner who bought with knowledge of the restraint could be said to have no reliance interest, or to have assumed the risk of any economic loss. In economic terms, it could be said that the market had already discounted for the risk, so that a purchaser could not show a loss in his investment attributable to it.")....

Good argues that the Supreme Court has eliminated the requirement for reasonable, investment-backed expectations, at least in cases where the challenged regulation eliminates virtually all of the economic value of the landowner's property. In support, Appellant cites *Lucas, 505 U.S. at 1015,* and argues that *Loveladies Harbor* should be reversed as contrary to *Lucas*.

However, we agree with the *Loveladies Harbor* court that the Supreme Court in *Lucas* did not mean to eliminate the requirement for reasonable, investment-backed expectations to establish a taking. It is true that the Court in *Lucas* set out what it called a "categorical" taking "where regulation denies all economically beneficial or productive use of land." *505 U.S. at 1015.* * * * [But] [i]n Lucas, there was no question of whether the plaintiff had satisfied that criterion. See *505 U.S. at 1006–1007* ("In 1986, petitioner David H. Lucas paid $975,000 for two residential lots ... In 1988, however, the South Carolina Legislature enacted the Beachfront Management Act, ... which had the direct effect of barring petitioner from erecting any permanent habitable structures on his two parcels.").

In addition, it is common sense that "one who buys with knowledge of a restraint assumes the risk of economic loss. In such a case, the owner presumably paid a discounted price for the property. Compensating him for a 'taking' would confer a windfall." ...

Appellant alternatively argues that he had reasonable, investment-backed expectations of building a residential subdivision on his property. Appellant reasons that the permit requirements of the Rivers and Harbors Act and the Clean Water Act are irrelevant to his reasonable expectations at the time he purchased the subject property, because he obtained the federal dredge-and-fill permits required by those acts three times, and was only denied a permit, based on the provisions of the Endangered Species Act ("ESA"), when two endangered species were found on his property. Therefore, since the ESA did not exist when he bought his land, he could not have expected to be denied a permit based on its provisions.

Appellant's position is not entirely unreasonable, but we must ultimately reject it. In view of the regulatory climate that existed when Appellant acquired the subject property, Appellant could not have had a reasonable expectation that he would approval to fill ten acres of wetlands in order to develop the land.

In 1973, when Appellant purchased the subject land, federal law required that a permit be obtained from the Army Corps of Engineers in order to dredge or fill in wetlands adjacent to a navigable waterway. Even in 1973, the Corps had been considering environmental criteria in its permitting decisions for a number of years. See *Deltona Corp. v. United States, 228 Ct. Cl. 476, 657 F.2d 1184, 1187 (Ct. Cl. 1981)* ("On December 18, 1968, in response to a growing national concern for environmental values and related federal legislation, the Corps [announced that it] would consider the following additional factors in reviewing permit applications: fish and wildlife, conservation, pollution, aesthetics, ecology, and the general public interest."). * * *

In addition to the federal regulations, development of the subject land required approval by both the state of Florida and Monroe County. At the time he bought the subject parcel, Appellant acknowledged both the necessity and the difficulty of obtaining regulatory approval. The sales contract specifically stated that "the Buyers recognize that ... as of today there are certain problems in connection with the obtaining of State and Federal permission for dredging and filling operations." Appellant thus had both constructive and actual knowledge that either state or federal regulations could ultimately prevent him from building on the property. Despite his knowledge of the difficult regulatory path ahead, Appellant took no steps to obtain the required regulatory approval for seven years.

During this period, public concern about the environment resulted in numerous laws and regulations affecting land development. For example:

- In December 1973, the Endangered Species Act was enacted. *16 U.S.C. § 1531* et seq. (1994). * * *

- In 1975, the Corps of Engineers issued regulations broadening its interpretation of its § 404 authority to regulate dredging and filling in wetlands. See *United States v. Riverside Bayview Homes, 474 U.S. 121, 123–124, 88 L. Ed. 2d 419, 106 S. Ct. 455 (1985).* In 1977, the Corps further broadened its definition of wetlands subject to § 404's permit requirements. *See id.*

- Also in 1977, Florida enacted its own Endangered and Threatened Species Act, *FLA. STAT. ANN. § 372.072* (West 1997), further emphasizing the public concern for Florida's environment. In 1979, the Florida Keys Protection Act was enacted, designating the Keys an Area of Critical State Concern. *FLA. STAT. ANN. § 380.0552* (West 1997).

Thus, rising environmental awareness translated into ever-tightening land use regulations. Surely Appellant was not oblivious to this trend.

The picture emerges, then, of Appellant in 1973 acknowledging the difficulty of obtaining approval for his project, then waiting seven years, watching as the applicable regulations got more stringent, before taking any steps to obtain the required approval. When in 1980 he finally retained a land development firm to seek the required permits, he acknowledged that "obtaining said permits is at best difficult and by no means assured."

While Appellant's prolonged inaction does not bar his takings claim, it reduces his ability to fairly claim surprise when his permit application was denied. * * * In light of the growing consciousness of and sensitivity toward environmental issues, Appellant must also have been aware that standards could change to his detriment, and that regulatory approval could become harder to get.

We therefore conclude that Appellant lacked a reasonable, investment-backed expectation that he would obtain the regulatory approval needed to develop the property at issue here. We have previously held that the government is entitled to summary judgment on a regulatory takings claim where the plaintiffs lacked reasonable, investment-backed expectations, even where the challenged government action "substantially reduced the value of plaintiffs' property." ... Appellant's lack of reasonable, investment-backed expectations defeats his takings claim as a matter of law.

* * *

Notes and Questions

1. The Court in *Good* did not hold that Corp rejections of § 404 permit applications can never constitute compensable takings; it merely concluded that Mr. Good lacked the reasonable, investment-backed expectations necessary to support a takings claim based on denial of the permit. Under what circumstances might a court find that a permit applicant has "reasonable" expectations of developing land that cannot developed without a permit to which they have no vested right?

2. Unlike in Lucas v. South Carolina Coastal Council, 505 U.S. 1003, 112 S.Ct. 2886, 120 L.Ed.2d 798 (1992), the § 404 permitting program predated Mr. Good's purchase of the property; and unlike in Nollan v. California Coastal Commission, 483 U.S. 825, 107 S.Ct. 3141, 97 L.Ed.2d 677 (1987), and Dolan v. City of Tigard, 512 U.S. 374, 114 S.Ct. 2309, 129 L.Ed.2d 304 (1994), *Good* was not an exaction case (*see* Chapter 9.11.C. *supra*). The Corps did not condition the grant of a § 404 permit on a conveyance of land to the public, it merely denied a permit to which Mr. Good had no pre-existing right.

3. In Palazzolo v. Rhode Island, 533 U.S. 606, 121 S.Ct. 2448, 150 L.Ed.2d 592 (2001), the U.S. Supreme Court held that *state* wetlands regulations that prevented a landowner from developing coastal marshlands *might* amount to a compensable takings, even though the landowner purchased the land *after* the state regulations had taken effect, *if* the landowner could demonstrate reasonable, investment-backed expectations of developing the marshlands. The Court remanded the case to the Rhode Island state

courts for further proceedings, but without suggesting what might constitute reasonable, investment-backed expectations in such a case.

4. For another case denying regulatory takings claims based on rejections of applications for § 404 permits, *see* Walcek v. United States, 303 F.3d 1349 (Fed. Cir. 2002).

5. Section 401 Certification

The states play an important role in federal wetlands permitting program. Section 401(a) of the CWA provides:

> Any applicant for a Federal license or permit to conduct any activity ... which may result in any discharge into the navigable waters, shall provide the licensing or permitting agency a certification from the State in which the discharge originates or will originate ... that any such discharge will comply with the applicable provisions ... of this title.... No license or permit shall be granted until the certification required by this section has been obtained or has been waived.... No license or permit shall be granted if certification has been denied by the State....

33 U.S.C.A. § 1341(a).

In addition to giving states veto power over § 404 permits, § 401(d) authorizes them to impose "any ... limitations, and monitoring requirements necessary to assure ... compl[iance] with any applicable effluent limitations or other limitations ... of this title.... " Such imposed limitations become "a condition on any Federal license or permit.... " 33 U.S.C.A. § 1341(d).

Efforts to minimize state authority under § 401 have been unsuccessful. In PUD No. 1 Jefferson County v. Washington Dept. of Ecology, 511 U.S. 700, 114 S.Ct. 1900, 128 L.Ed.2d 716 (1994), the Supreme Court upheld state-imposed minimum stream flow requirements as a condition for § 401 certification, of a proposed hydroelectric project, and in Howard W. Heck & Associates v. United States, 37 Fed.Cl. 245 (Ct.Cl. 1997), the court ruled that plaintiff's taking claim for denial of a § 404 permit was not ripe because the plaintiff had not obtained § 401 state certification, which is prerequisite to obtaining a § 404 permit.

6. Mitigating Wetlands Loss

Section 404 regulations prohibit filling of wetlands "unless appropriate and practicable steps have been taken which will minimize potential adverse impacts of the discharge on the aquatic ecosystem." 40 C.F.R. § 230.10(d). This regulation has been interpreted to require mitigation of wetlands losses by creating, restoring or enhancing wetlands. For years, the Corps and the EPA disagreed about the extent to which mitigation could be used as justification for approving dredge and fill permits. The Corps was perfectly willing to issue permits on the assumption that mitigation activities would compensate for lost or damaged wetlands. *See, e.g.*, Bersani v. United States E.P.A., 850 F.2d 36 (2d Cir. 1988). The EPA, by contrast, preferred to *avoid* and *minimize* wetland losses, preferring mitigation only as a last resort. In 1990, the EPA and Corp finally agreed on a Mitigation Policy.

MEMORANDUM OF AGREEMENT
BETWEEN THE ENVIRONMENTAL PROTECTION AGENCY AND THE DEPARTMENT OF THE ARMY CONCERNING THE DETERMINATION OF MITIGATION UNDER THE CLEAN WATER ACT SECTION 404(b)(1) GUIDELINES
February 6, 1990 (55 Fed. Reg. 9210)

A. The Council on Environmental Quality (CEQ) has defined mitigation in its regulations at 40 CFR 1508.20 to include: avoiding impacts, minimizing impacts, rectifying impacts, reducing impacts over time, and compensating for impacts. The Guidelines establish environmental criteria which must be met for activities to be permitted under Section 404. The types of mitigation enumerated by CEQ are compatible with the requirements of the Guidelines; however, as a practical matter, they can be combined to form three general types: avoidance, minimization and compensatory mitigation.

   1. Avoidance. Section 230.10(a) allows permit issuance for only the least environmentally damaging practicable alternative. The thrust of this section on alternatives is avoidance of impacts. Section 230.10(a) requires that no discharge shall be permitted if there is a practicable alternative to the proposed discharge which would have less adverse impact on the aquatic ecosystem, so long as the alternative does not have other significant adverse environmental consequences.... Compensatory mitigation may not be used as a method to reduce environmental impacts in the evaluation of the least environmentally damaging practicable alternatives for the purposes of requirements under Section 230.10(a).

   2. Minimization. Section 230.10(d) states that appropriate and practicable steps to minimize the adverse impacts will be required through project modifications and permit conditions.

   3. Compensatory Mitigation. Appropriate and practicable compensatory mitigation is required for unavoidable adverse impacts which remain after all appropriate and practicable minimization has been required. Compensatory actions (e.g., restoration of existing degraded wetlands or creation of man-made wetlands) should be undertaken, when practicable, in areas adjacent or contiguous to the discharge site (on-site compensatory mitigation). If on-site compensatory mitigation is not practicable, off-site compensatory mitigation should be undertaken in the same geographic area if practicable (i.e., in close physical proximity and, to the extent possible, the same watershed). * * *

Mitigation banking may be an acceptable form of compensatory mitigation under specific criteria designed to ensure an environmentally successful bank. Simple purchase or "preservation" of existing wetland resources may in only exceptional circumstances be accepted as compensatory mitigation. * * *

* * *

B. In achieving the goals of the CWA, the Corps will strive to avoid adverse impacts and offset unavoidable adverse impacts to existing aquatic resources. Measures which can accomplish this can be identified only through resource assessments tailored to the site performed by qualified professionals because ecological characteristics of each aquatic site are unique. Functional values should be assessed by applying aquatic site assessment techniques generally recognized by experts in the field and/or best professional judgment of federal and state agency representatives, provided such assessments fully consider ecological functions included in the Guidelines. The objective of mitigation for unavoidable impacts is to offset environmental losses. Additionally for wetlands, such mitigation should provide, at a minimum, one for one functional replacement (i.e., no net loss of values), with an adequate margin of safety to reflect the expected degree of success associated with the mitigation plan, recognizing that this minimum requirement may not be appropriate and practicable, and thus may not be relevant in all cases. In the absence of more definitive information on the functions and values of specific wetlands sites, a minimum of 1 to 1 acreage replacement may be used as a reasonable surrogate for no net loss of functions or values. However, this ratio may be greater where the functional values of the area being impacted are demonstrably high and the replacement wetlands are of lower functional value or the likelihood of success of the mitigation project is low. Conversely, the ratio may be less than 1 to 1 for areas where the functional values associated with the area being impacted are demonstrably low and the likelihood of success associated with the mitigation proposal is high.

* * *

The effectiveness of "replacing" and "banking" wetlands has been questioned, and this aspect of the 404 program remains controversial. Compare the following two excerpts.

THE CLINTON WETLANDS PLAN: NO NET GAIN IN WETLANDS PROTECTION
Michael C. Blumm
9 J. Land Use Envtl. L. 203, 226–28 (1994)

Mitigation banking is a kind of transferable development right program that enables a developer to create, restore, or enhance wetlands to compensate for future projects that will destroy other wetlands.

The Bush Administration endorsed mitigation banking in its 1991 wetlands plan, and a number of mitigation banks have been established, mostly by large developers and state highway departments. * * *

Developers have long advocated the use of mitigation banks to add flexibility to wetlands permitting. They claim that banks will provide high value, low cost wetlands for mitigation and will encourage creation of large wetlands areas that have a higher success rate and are easier to monitor than smaller projects. They further claim success is ensured because mitigation is required in advance of development and because creation and management responsibilities are assigned to the bank rather than the developer.

Environmentalists have been wary of wetlands banking, claiming that it encourages: (1) off site mitigation that cannot replace many wetlands values which are site specific; (2) an excess of certain kinds of wetlands, such as marshes and shrub wetlands, because they are easier and cheaper to create than other wetlands types; and (3) issuance of fill permits based on wetlands creation when avoidance and minimization alternatives exist. Some of the environmentalists' concerns are not unique to banks; they pertain to the woeful state of compensatory mitigation generally. For example, one study in Florida indicated that only about one-quarter of projects undertaking compensatory mitigation successfully produced functional wetlands. Worse, more than one-third of the projects requiring compensatory mitigation as a permit condition failed even to attempt compensation, and six in ten failed to satisfy the permit conditions. With such a sorry success rate, a mitigation banking program that requires compensation in advance and relieves developers of creation, restoration, and management responsibilities appears to be an attractive alternative.

The Clinton plan endorsed mitigation banking wholeheartedly, but subjected its use to two conditions. First, the plan made satisfaction of mitigation sequencing required by the Mitigation Memorandum of Agreement a prerequisite to banking. Second, the plan required that mitigation be established before permit issuance. The Corps' interim guidance issued concurrently with the Clinton plan emphasized the availability of banking credits only after a demonstration that impacts associated with a project have been avoided and minimized "to the extent practicable," and required mitigation banks "generally" to be in place before banked credits could be used to offset wetlands losses. The guidance stressed that bank sites should generally be in the same watershed as the wetlands losses, required formal written agreements with federal authorities to establish banks, and encouraged the establishment of private banks. All use of bank credits must be authorized and enforced by the 404 permit process.

Widespread use of mitigation banking will certainly add flexibility, long sought by developers, to wetlands regulation. If it is not employed to undermine the 404(b) guidelines' policy of favoring avoidance and minimization of impacts over compensation for wetlands losses, banking can also produce wetlands preservation benefits by bringing third party expertise to wetlands creation, restoration, and management. Well operated banks could relieve overburdened regulators from overseeing mitigation projects, and could foster the Clinton plan's goal of increasing the quantity and quality of the nation's wetlands by (1) establishing greater than 1:1 ratios of credit acreage to lost acreage, and (2) focusing primarily on restoring wetlands such as those converted to farm land, rather than relying on the uncertain science of wetlands creation. The devil will be in the details.

RESTORED WETLANDS FLUNK REAL–WORLD TEST
David Malakoff
280 Sci. 371–2 (April 1988)

To the untrained eye, a roadside salt marsh 8 kilometers south of downtown San Diego may look like any other urban wetland: a lush carpet of tall grass teeming with fish and birds. In fact, the 12–hectare plot in the Sweetwater National Wildlife Refuge is a kind of ecological counterfeit, created in 1985 to replace natural wetlands destroyed by construction projects. But restoration ecologists were unable to fool Nature. After intense scientific scrutiny, U.S. Fish and Wildlife Service (FWS) officials last January determined that the ersatz marsh has failed to attract light-footed clapper rails—an endangered bird for which it was supposed to provide habitat—and ordered the owner of the land, the California transportation department (Caltrans), to undertake further restoration work. "It was a mistake to assume that a constructed wetland would become equivalent to a natural system," says ecologist Joy Zedler of the University of Wisconsin, Madison, whose 10-year study of the Sweetwater marsh led to FWS's ruling.

Setbacks at Sweetwater and many other sites came under the spotlight last week at a tidal wetlands meeting here that questioned the assumptions now driving a wetlands restoration boom in the United States. The U.S. Department of Agriculture estimates that since 1982, restoration and creation projects have added more than 400,000 hectares of fresh- and saltwater wetlands to the nation's inventory. And last February, the Clinton Administration unveiled a clean-water initiative that calls for government agencies to aid efforts to create 80,000 hectares of new wetlands each year over the next decade. The plan says new marshes should be "functionally equivalent" to natural systems, meaning they should be as good as undisturbed wetlands at processing nutrients, storing floodwaters, and sheltering wildlife.

But ecologists are still debating whether it will be possible to churn out wetlands that work like the real thing. Some, including Zedler, worry that many wetlands engineers have failed to learn from past mistakes. Others are more optimistic, saying that projects considered failures today may still prove successful in time.

Such natural healing was the idea behind the Sweetwater marsh. Caltrans wetland designers assumed that once the site had been graded to the right slope and tidal flow had been restored, nature would slowly mold the marsh into a form that would support three endangered species—the clapper rail, the least tern, and the bird's beak, a small plant—that were being driven to extinction by Caltrans development. But it didn't work out that way. For one thing, Zedler and her research team, then at San Diego State University, discovered that Spartina cordgrass—transplanted from nearby wetlands to provide nesting sites for the clapper rail—refused to grow to 90 centimeters, the bird's preferred height. The problem ... was the marsh's sandy, nutrient-poor soil. To fix that [the team] ... added nitrogen fertilizer, which spurred the grass to grow taller. But unpredictably, the added nutrients allowed pickleweed, another marsh plant, to outgrow the desired grass.

Zedler's team also found that Sweetwater accumulated less nitrogen and produced less organic matter than nearby "reference" wetlands. Overall, using 11 criteria—such as grass height and invertebrate counts—the researchers concluded in 1990 that the created wetland was at best less than 60% equivalent to a natural marsh. * * * [They] predict it will take at least 20 more years for the new marsh to match the reference sites for just one criterion: soil nitrogen. * * *

Based on Zedler's findings, FWS faulted the project for producing stunted grass—a violation of an agreement between FWS and Caltrans requiring the wetland to have the tall vegetation favored by the clapper rail. To compensate for the flaw, Caltrans must now restore other potential rail habitat on the Sweetwater refuge by removing debris that has clogged tidal channels. But the restored marsh, Zedler believes, will "never provide tall grass habitat for clapper rails, because the soils are too coarse to hold nitrogen."

Some wetland experts, however, argue that time is on Sweetwater's side. "A tidal wetland constructed on sand is going to take more than just a decade to approach natural function," says Ed Garbisch of Environmental Concern Inc., a nonprofit wetlands restoration group in St. Michaels, Maryland. Zedler's reference wetlands, he argues, "do not provide a legitimate comparison—she should compare her site to natural wetlands that are being created on [similar] mineral soils," such as those found at some river mouths.

Three years ago, the need for such one-to-one comparisons led ecologist William Mitsch of Ohio State University, Columbus, to launch one of the largest wetland experiments in the nation by building two identical 1–hectare freshwater wetlands along the Olentangy River in Columbus, Ohio. Mitsch believes that the two marshes—one stocked with plants and animals by hand, the other by nature—will eventually be indistinguishable. At the meeting, he presented data suggesting they are becoming just that, with both plots showing similar growth patterns. * * *

But perhaps the largest current test of nature's ability to reclaim lost wetlands with just a nudge from people is currently playing out along the Delaware Bay in New Jersey. There, an electric utility—Public Service Electric and Gas Company—is using heavy equipment to breach dikes protecting farmland and surrender it back to the sea. By the end of 1999, the company—forced by regulators to undertake the $100 million project—hopes to re-create 2500 hectares of tidal marsh in an attempt to boost the bay's seafood stocks and replace millions of fish killed by operations at one of its nuclear power plants. Such megaprojects, which typically include long-term monitoring programs, should help settle longtime debates over how best to restore tidal marshes, Zedler and others say. * * * "Regulators typically want creation and replacement right away but it's going to take time for Mother Nature and Father Time to do their work."

C. Coastal Zone and Shoreland Management

Thirty states border an ocean or one of the Great Lakes. During the twentieth century, the development of offshore oil refineries, shoreline urbanization, and residential communities increasingly threatened coastal areas in those states. Because coastal areas have important recreational and environmental values, federal and state governments enacted planning and regulatory laws to protect them.

1. The Federal Coastal Zone Management Act of 1972

The federal government created incentives for states to protect their coastal zones in the Coastal Zone Management Act of 1972 (CZMA), 16 U.S.C.A. § 1451. This statute does not regulate coastal areas directly. Rather, it seeks to accomplish its goal of rational use of coastal lands and waters by providing monetary assistance to coastal states that develop management plans consistent with the Act's standards. The federal standards require that state plan (1) designate the geographical zone to be regulated, (2) describe permissible uses of land and water resources within this zone, and (3) provide sufficient authority for the plan's implementation. In addition, the CZMA requires that state coastal zone management programs address energy facility siting within their coastal zones. States may delegate primary authority for program implementation to local governments. Interestingly, the primary responsibility for approving and funding state programs belongs not to the EPA or some federal resource agency but to the U.S. Department of Commerce.

Although coastal states are not required to adopt coastal zone legislation pursuant to the CZMA, the Act contains several incentives for state participation. These incentives have been so attractive that all coastal states have taken some action toward preparing coastal zone plans. After a plan receives approval, the state qualifies for federal grants that pay up to 80% of the cost of administering the program. Second, approval triggers a "federal consistency" provision in the CZMA which requires federal agencies, permittees, and lessees to demonstrate that their proposed developments in the coastal zones will comply with state program requirements. Federal agencies may not approve proposed projects that are inconsistent with a coastal state's program, except upon a finding by the Secretary of Commerce that the project is consistent with the purposes of the Act or is necessary for national security. 16 U.S.C.A. § 1456.

The consistency provision of the CZMA has been particularly relevant with respect to federally authorized oil and gas developments on the Outer Continental Shelf. Section 307(c)(1) of the Act provides that "[e]ach Federal agency conducting or supporting activities directly affecting the coastal zone shall be in a manner which is ... consistent with approved state management programs." An approved coastal zone management plan gives the state a measure of control over federal actions "directly affecting the coastal zone." Is the Department of the Interior's sale of oil and gas leases on the Outer Continental Shelf an activity "directly affecting" a state's coastal zone? In Secretary of the Interior v. California, 464 U.S. 312, 104 S.Ct. 656, 78 L.Ed.2d 496 (1984), the Supreme Court ruled that lease sales do not "directly affect" a state's coastal zone because they do not involve exploration or development of the lease tracts. However, in 1990, Congress expressly overturned that ruling in amendments to the Coastal Zone Management Act. 16 U.S.C.A. § 1456(c)(1). *See* California v. Norton, 311 F.3d 1162, 1172–73 (9th Cir. 2002).

2. Subsidiary State Regulation of Coastal Zones, Shorelines, and Beaches

States with coastal zone plans under the CZMA split roughly into two groups. The first consists of those states that, through legislation, have identified a set of development activities that require a permit if carried on in a coastal zone. Permit review occurs at the state agency level and is somewhat analogous to site planning. *See* Section III.B of this chapter. Such a program costs less to initiate because it requires no comprehensive plan for development. It also provides the state with more flexibility than a comprehensive plan. The major drawbacks, however, are a lack of specificity and statewide uniformity. States along the eastern seaboard generally use the permit system. The second group of states are those that have enacted comprehensive coastal plans which provide land development controls for coastal areas. The following three states have adopted comprehensive coastal plans:

California—In 1972, voters approved the California Conservation Act which established the California Coastal Commission to prepare a comprehensive plan for the state's coastal zone resources. The constitutionality of the Act was upheld in CEEED v. California Coastal Zone Conservation Commission, 43 Cal.App.3d 306, 118 Cal.Rptr. 315 (1974). In 1975, the Commission submitted its plan to the legislature for approval, and a year later the California Coastal Act, West's Ann.Cal.Pub.-Res.Code § 30103(a), was enacted to implement the Commission's plan. The California Coastal Act was found to comply with the CZMA in American Petroleum Institute v. Knecht, 609 F.2d 1306 (9th Cir. 1979). Under the Act, any person seeking to develop property within a designated coastal area must obtain a permit from an appropriate regional commission. Commission decisions denying permits for coastal development, or imposing conditions on such permits, may be subject to takings claims. *See* Nollan v. California Coastal Commission, 483 U.S. 825, 107 S.Ct. 3141, 97 L.Ed.2d 677 (1987) (excerpted in Chapter 9.II.C. *supra*) (holding that a permit condition requiring public dedication or "exaction" of private lands constituted a compensable taking because the exaction did not substantially further a legitimate governmental interest); *but see*

Frisco Land & Mining Co. v. State, 74 Cal.App.3d 736, 141 Cal.Rptr. 820 (1978), *cert. denied* 436 U.S. 918, 98 S.Ct. 2263, 56 L.Ed.2d 758 (1978) (holding that restrictions on private property rights created by the California Coastal Act did not constitute compensable taking). Meanwhile, local decisionmakers may still adopt measures to protect the coastal zone. *See* Yost v. Thomas, 36 Cal.3d 561, 205 Cal.Rptr. 801, 685 P.2d 1152 (1984) (the Coastal Act does not preclude a referendum on a local land use measure affecting the coastal zone).

Washington—The Washington State Shoreline Management Act of 1971, Rev.Code Wash. Ch. 90.58.020 *et seq*, enables local governments to devise "master programs" which are then reviewed for approval by the State Department of Ecology. These local programs form the basis for comprehensive shoreline and coastal zone management. The Act also divides all shorelines into two categories: "shorelines" and "shorelines of statewide significance." For the second category, the Act provides more explicit and exacting requirements for development and use. *See* Nisqually Delta Assoc. v. DuPont, 103 Wn.2d 720, 696 P.2d 1222 (1985) (designation of shoreline as "of statewide significance" does not prevent all development but merely provides greater procedural safeguards prior to development); Friends and Land Owners Opposing Development v. Washington State Department of Ecology, 38 Wn.App. 84, 684 P.2d 765 (1984).

South Carolina—South Carolina's Beachfront Management Act is among the more well known of state coastal area protection laws because of the famous *Lucas* case excerpted in Chapter 9.II.B. In that case, the U.S. Supreme Court held that South Carolina had to compensate Mr. Lucas for "taking" his land because the Beachfront Management Act deprived him of all economically beneficial uses. *Lucas*, 505 U.S. at 1015. In the following excerpt, Vicki Been explains the history and structure of the Act.

LUCAS v. THE GREEN MACHINE: USING THE TAKINGS CLAUSE TO PROMOTE MORE EFFICIENT REGULATION?
in PROPERTY STORIES 221–257
Vicki Been
(G. Korngold and A. Morriss eds., 2004)

* * *

The South Carolina Beachfront Management Act of 1988:

In 1977, six years before Lucas sought to develop the lots, the South Carolina legislature adopted the Coastal Zone Act [1977 S.C. Acts 123, S.C. Code Ann. §§ 48–39–10 to 48–39–220. Responding both to growing concerns about the erosion of the state's beaches and to the incentives the Federal Coastal Zone Management Act of 1972 gave states to plan for coastal development, South Carolina's Coastal Zone Act established the South Carolina Coastal Council ("the Council") and directed it to develop a comprehensive coastal management program. The legislation empowered the Council to designate areas of "critical state concern" within the coastal zone and to regulate both development and the use or erosion control devices within those zones.

The Coastal Act did not, however, give the Council jurisdiction landward of the "primary front row dune." Many property owners took advantage of that crucial limitation by building structures just a foot or two back from the high tide line. Further, the Council routinely granted permits for erosion control structures, and those structures proliferated even as evidence mounted that they actually caused, rather than prevented, significant erosion.

Several events in the mid-1980s convinced the Council that a different strategy was needed to protect the state's beaches. In 1984, the U.S. Environmental Protection Agency and the South Carolina Sea Grant Program sponsored a program that drew public attention to the dangers that the rising sea levels projected to result from global warming (among other factors) would pose for South Carolina's shoreline and barrier islands. In addition, storms in the winter of 1986–87 resulted in significant damage to sea walls, buildings, and pools close to the beach. The Council responded both by tightening its permitting practices and by commissioning a Blue Ribbon Committee to study erosion control and recommend reforms to the Coastal Zone Act. The Committee recommended an expansion of the Council's jurisdiction over erosion areas behind the dunes. It also advocated a "retreat" program to move new development, as well as the rebuilding of damaged structures, back from the beach. After considerable public debate, the South Carolina General Assembly enacted the Beachfront Management Act of 1988 ("the BMA") ... to implement the Committee's recommendations.

The BMA's preamble notes that the Coastal Zone Act did not enable the Coastal Council "to effectively protect the integrity of the beach/dune system" and that "consequently ... development unwisely has been sited too close to the [beach/dune] system ... [and] has jeopardized the stability of the beach/dune system, accelerated erosion, and endangered adjacent property." After finding that "it is in both the public and private interests to protect the system from this unwise development," the BMA sought "a gradual retreat from the [beach/dune] system over a forty-year period." The BMA accordingly required the Council to establish "a baseline" for inlet erosion zones at "the most landward point of erosion at any time during the past forty years." The BMA then required the Council to establish "setback lines" landward of the baseline at a distance equaling 40 times the annual erosion rate, or a minimum of twenty feet. The BMA therefore allowed the Council to regulate not just the existing beachfront, but the area in which the beach and dunes were projected to move over the next forty years given the natural forces of erosion.

The BMA prohibited the construction of any new structures in a "dead zone" twenty feet landward of the baseline, except for "grandfathered" projects for which the property owner had already obtained a building permit or planned development approval and had begun construction prior to March 1988. The BMA then limited construction in the area between the dead zone and the forty-year setback line to homes no larger than 5000 square feet, placed as far landward on the lot as possible. The BMA also prohibited owners of structures damaged or destroyed by fire or natural causes from rebuilding in the dead zone, and limited rebuilding between that zone and the setback line to the size of the original structure.

The general constitutionality of South Carolina's Beachfront Management Act was upheld by the 4th Circuit U.S. Court of Appeals in *Esposito v. South Carolina Coastal Council*, 939 F.2d 165 (4th Cir. 1991), even though a year later the Supreme Court ruled in *Lucas v. South Carolina Coastal Council*, 505 U.S. 1003, 112 S.Ct. 2886, 120 L.Ed.2d 798 (1992), that the Act, as applied to Mr. Lucas's land, worked an unconstitutional taking without just compensation.

* * *

Section 305(b)(7) of the CZMA, 16 U.S.C.A. § 1451, requires that the management plan for each coastal state include "a definition of the term 'beach' and a planning process for the protection of, and access to, public beaches and other public coastal areas...." Public rights in beaches, particularly access to beaches, are historically grounded upon roman and common law doctrines. Some states rely on a prescriptive rights/implied dedication theory. *See Moody v. White*, 593 S.W.2d 372 (Tex.Civ.App. 1979); *Gion v. Santa Cruz*, 2 Cal.3d 29, 84 Cal.Rptr. 162, 465 P.2d 50 (1970). Courts in Oregon, Florida, and Hawaii have upheld public beach access under the doctrine of custom. *See State ex rel. Thornton v. Hay*, 254 Or. 584, 462 P.2d 671 (1969); *City of Daytona Beach v. Tona–Rama*, 294 So.2d 73 (Fla. 1974); *In re Ashford*, 50 Hawaii 314, 440 P.2d 76 (1968). New Jersey has held that the state's beaches are a "public trust" to which private property rights must give way. *See Matthew v. Bay Head Improvement Association*, 95 N.J. 306, 471 A.2d 355 (1984); *Borough of Neptune City v. Borough of Avon-by-the-Sea*, 61 N.J. 296, 294 A.2d 47 (1972). Many states have enacted statutes which establish public rights to beaches, or regulate the building of structures on beaches, even private beaches. *See* Ga.Ann. Code § 12–5–230, upheld in *Rolleston v. State*, 245 Ga. 576, 266 S.E.2d 189 (1980). Public access rights are described in detail in Chapter 8.II, *supra*.

In Focus:

Recently, the issue of public beach access has become heated, as owners of beachfront lots in California have asserted a right to prevent members of the public from crossing the beach in front of their homes.

OWNERS OF MALIBU MANSIONS
CRY, 'THIS SAND IS MY SAND'
By Timothy Egan
The New York Times
August 25, 2002

It started as another golden California day, the shoreline aglow in the haloed light of midmorning. Rob LeMond was teaching children in his surfing camp, passing on nearly a half-century of knowledge about riding the waves of the Pacific.

Then a nearby homeowner complained that Mr. LeMond's surfing students had crossed the line onto his beach property. The sheriff was called. A long argument followed over which strip of sand belonged to the public and which was private.

"Finally, this homeowner turned to me and said something I thought I'd never hear on a California beach," said Mr. LeMond, 54, of Malibu. "He said he did not like to look out his window and see people swimming, because it blocked his view."

Skirmishes over surf and sand have become particularly intense up and down the Southern California coast this summer. To some people, the fight is about a California birthright: public access to every inch of the state's 1,160–mile shoreline. By law, there is no such thing as private beach in California. In a state where 80 percent of the 34 million people live within an hour of the coast, it is no small fight.

Others see a gold coast of hypocrisy. Some of Hollywood's and the Democratic Party's biggest contributors to liberal causes, like David Geffen, have turned into conservative property-rights advocates because the battle is taking place in their sandy backyards. * * * A court fight, initiated by Mr. Geffen, the entertainment mogul, could take the question of beach access well beyond the shores of Malibu. Last month, he filed suit seeking to block public access to a narrow walkway that goes by his Malibu compound. He promised access 19 years ago, but the path has never been opened, and Mr. Geffen now says it would be unsafe, dirty and impractical to allow people to walk by his home to the beach.

Mr. Geffen contends in the lawsuit that the access way amounts to a "taking of property without compensation," an argument that conservatives have used in environmental fights for years. If the suit is successful, it could make it much harder for state and federal agencies to open paths to public beaches throughout the United States, or even to acquire open space for wildlife or recreation, some experts say.

"This could keep the public away from a lot of beaches," said Robert Ritchie, director of research at the Huntington Library in San Marino, who is writing a book on beach culture. "And because a very significant percentage of the United States population now lives in counties facing the ocean, the pressure for public access has become enormous. At the same time, you have these homeowners fighting to keep the hordes back."

The stand taken by beachfront owners here in Malibu, long a Democratic Party stronghold, has infuriated another sector of party supporters—environmentalists.

"Here you have the superrich wanting to have a private beach in a state that decided long ago it would not allow any private beaches," said Carl Pope, executive director of the Sierra Club. "It's a huge land grab. By blocking access, they want to lock up the coast."

Further complicating the issue, a prominent environmental philanthropist, Wendy McCaw, has vowed to take her lawsuit against beach access to the United States Supreme Court, making many of the same arguments as Mr. Geffen.

Ms. McCaw, the billionaire owner of The Santa Barbara News–Press, is trying to block access to a 500–foot strip of beach below her 25–acre estate on a bluff in Santa Barbara County. The easement was granted by a previous owner, and Ms. McCaw says it does not apply to her. She has already paid $460,000 in fines in her fight to prevent access. She says if the state is going to require an access path from her private property, then she should be compensated.

"There needs to be more effort toward protecting the embattled wildlife calling our beaches home, rather than focusing on how to pack more humans with their destructive ways into those sensitive habitats," Ms. McCaw said.

In most states, beaches that are covered by water at high tide but are relatively dry at low tide are public. The entire West Coast falls under this mean high tide doctrine. But some states, notably New York, Massachusetts and Maine, are more restrictive, allowing fences in the water and private ownership of tidelands.

California voters, in a populist campaign 30 years ago, took the additional step of guaranteeing "access" to beaches, and empowered the California Coastal Commission to fight on the public's behalf.

Since then, the state has reached more than 1,300 access deals with private property owners, but many of those have a time limit and are set to expire within a few years.

"Development shall not interfere with the public right of access to the sea," reads a section of the California Coastal Act.

Beachfront owners in Malibu have surveyed the tide lines and posted signs warning people that it is trespassing to walk within a zone they have claimed from their houses to the ocean. The coastal commission says these private surveys are meaningless because the definition of what a public beach is changes daily, with the tides. Still, homeowners in parts of Malibu have hired private security forces to roam the beach on three-wheeled vehicles, herding people away from areas they consider private property.

A 1987 Supreme Court ruling, *Nollan v. California Coastal Commission,* limited the commission's authority to insist on public access, saying it had power only over new developments. Mr. Geffen and Ms. McCaw are trying to expand the *Nollan* ruling.

Mr. Geffen's spokesman ... said the *Nollan* ruling should be applied retroactively to Mr. Geffen ... [because] the public access promise Mr. Geffen made in 1983 was "extorted" from him as a condition to expand his beach property with maid quarters and other improvements. * * *

... [T]he coastal commission says that it has granted hundreds of access points that are no more than footpaths next to mansions, and that they operate without lifeguards or bathrooms and have few problems.

The path by Mr. Geffen's estate is blocked by a locked gate. In front of the house is a 275-foot stretch of beach, which is open to the public at low tide, but requires a 20-minute hike to reach now. * * *

The city of Malibu, a 27-mile strip of beach castles and hillside homes along each side of the Pacific Coast Highway with a population of 13,000, has joined Mr. Geffen in his lawsuit.

Jeff Jennings, the mayor of Malibu, said the city was concerned about safety and garbage pickup if the access point at Mr. Geffen's house was not properly maintained ... "I have no interest in keeping the public off public land," Mr. Jennings said. "But most people who come to the beaches are not experts in water safety. It can be a highly dangerous situation."

Veteran surfers, who rely on the narrow public paths to get to some of the best waves of the Pacific, say they do not need lifeguards or bathrooms. But they would like to bring back an earlier era.

"In the old days, it was live and let live," said Kurt Lampson, a surfing instructor who grew up on Malibu's beaches. "Now you got these guards going around saying sit here, don't walk there. It's depressing."

None of the cases mentioned in the New York Times article has yet worked its way through the court system. How do you think they should be resolved? California law takes an expansive view of public rights under the common law public trust doctrine and more specific provisions related to coastal areas. *See* Chapter 8.II, *supra* (State Ownership). Some states however, are much more restrictive, even to the point of allowing private land owners to erect fences in the water to keep the public out. If you were a legislator in a coastal state, how could you craft a statute that would balance the interests of landowners and members of the beach-going public, while protecting coastal resources?

Chapter 11

TIMBER

I. FOREST RESOURCES IN THE UNITED STATES

No other economic and geographical factor has so profoundly affected the development of the country as the forest.[a]

Even before Henry David Thoreau published *Walden* in 1854, forests had been an integral part of American life. Lacking the great cathe-

---

a. MICHAEL WILLIAMS, AMERICANS AND THEIR FORESTS: A HISTORICAL GEOGRAPHY 3 (1989) (citing Raphael Zon, *The Vanishing* *Heritage*, National Archives—Forest Service Papers GRG 95).

838

drals and castles of Europe, forests and mountains became America's most significant antiquity. Thoreau and other nineteenth century authors, along with artists like Thomas Cole, Alfred Bierstadt and Thomas Moran, promoted the public's fascination with nature through their dramatic and even spiritual depictions of forested landscapes. BARBARA NOVAK, NATURE AND CULTURE 4, 158, 164–65 (Oxford Press1995). Of course, popular characters like Johnny Appleseed and Babe the Blue Ox, Paul Bunyan's constant companion, didn't hurt.

The tension between resource extraction—logging—and preservation of the forests, their inhabitants and their natural amenities is a persistent theme in modern forest management. The drama has been writ large in recent times in the battleground states of the Pacific Northwest, where the spotted owl, salmon and other imperiled species have found themselves on center stage, playing the antagonist to the forest industry and communities dependent on forestry jobs. But this tension is not a new phenomenon. Thoreau found solitude and strength in his use of the ax to make himself a dwelling place, but at the same time he mourned the lost trees.

This chapter explores issues surrounding both production and preservation on our nation's forestlands. It focuses primarily on non-federal lands, as the National Forest System and other public lands are addressed in Chapter 6, while tribal lands are covered in Chapter 7, *supra*. A brief snapshot of state and National Forest management is included in the last section of this chapter for comparative purposes.

A.   Historic Forest Resources and Forestry Practices

When Europeans began settling along the east coast of present-day United States, nearly half of all land in this country was covered with forests. Most of this forestland—over 80%—was located east of the Great Plains, particularly in the Great Lakes region, New England, the Atlantic coastal region, and the southeast. Only 20% was situated in the Pacific states and the Rocky Mountain region. As settlers spread westward, dramatic changes in the landscape followed. The settlers cut, burned or toppled trees to clear the land for agriculture, to construct homes, fences and ships, and to provide fuel to heat their homes and later to power steam-boats and trains. Lumber and other wood products became a leading export from the American colonies in the eighteenth and nineteenth centuries. MICHAEL WILLIAMS, AMERICANS AND THEIR FORESTS: A HISTORICAL GEOGRAPHY 3–4, 157–58, 222–28 (1989).

Timeless Timber, Virgin Growth Timber: A Piece of History For The Future, http://www.timelesstimber.com/about/ContentPlus.asp?cmd=CONTENT&articleID=71 (visited Aug. 4, 2004).

Logging mills dotted the shorelines of the lakes and rivers of North America throughout the nineteenth century. Thousands of lumberjacks felled millions of virgin trees, some well over 1,000 years old. Species in demand included red birch, walnut, maple, red cypress, beech, red oak, white pine, and ponderosa pine. The amount of timber harvested rose from 0.5 billion board feet (bbf) in 1801 to 46 bbf in 1906. MICHAEL WILLIAMS, DEFORESTING THE EARTH: FROM PRE–HISTORY TO GLOBAL CRISIS 317 (2003). By the 1920's, forests in the United States had been reduced by nearly half. WILLIAMS, AMERICANS AND THEIR FORESTS, *supra*, at 4. *See* JAMES WILLARD HURST, LAW AND ECONOMIC GROWTH: THE LEGAL HISTORY OF THE LUMBER INDUSTRY IN WISCONSIN 1836–1915, 571–91 (1964) (chronicling Wisconsin's attempts to prevent deforestation in the early 1900's). The rate of logging across the nation began to decline, however, and per capita consumption of wood products dropped significantly as production and use of alternative products such as concrete, steel, plastic, and petroleum grew. *Williams, supra*, at 5, 487–88.

During the nineteenth century, an expedient form of transporting logs was to tie them onto rafts and float them to the mills for processing. Many logs were lost when they became waterlogged in transit and settled to the bottom of the lake or river. These sunken timbers, or "sinkers", have remained below the cold, deep waters of the Great Lakes and other major waterbodies of North America for over a century. In the 1990's, methods were designed to recover and dry them so that they could be processed into high-end wood products. Today, around two million board feet of submerged lumber is recovered each year. Some of the trees have distinguishing marks showing the logging company's name or other data that allows the salvager to determine the identity of the sawmill and the year the log was cut down. *Timeless Timber, Virgin Growth Timber: A Piece of History For The Future*, http://www.timelesstimber.com/about/ContentPlus.asp?cmd=CONTENT&articleID=71 (visited Aug. 4, 2004).

Sinkers have tremendous commercial value. Virgin hardwood species matured very slowly, accumulating up to 40 to 50 rings per inch, largely because they grew under a thick canopy of evergreen trees and had to compete for limited nutrients and sunlight. Old-growth trees are finely grained and provide wood of exceptional quality. In comparison, hardwood trees grown today typically mature much more rapidly, and create wood that is much less dense, averaging only 5 to 10 rings per inch. Currently, most of the nation's commercial forests are comprised of trees less than 50 years old, and very few forests are over 175 years old.

JURASSIC BARK—SALVAGING ANCIENT LOGS
SUNK IN LAKE SUPERIOR

Scott Patterson

Mother Earth News (Oct/Nov. 1998), http://www.findarticles.com/p/
articles/mi_m1279/is_n170/ai_21211707/print

* * * Several years ago, Scott Mitchen, co-founder along with Robert "Buz" Holland of the Superior Water–Logged Lumber Co., Inc. ... discovered that hundreds of thousands—if not millions—of logs lie preserved on the bed of Lake Superior, remnants of logging operations that stretch back over 300 years. Transported in chain-boomed rafts to sawmills, 20% to 30% of the timber became water-logged and fell to the lake bed ... until treasure hunter and shipwreck salvager Scott Mitchen and his team of divers get hold of it. * * *

Mitchen, who has described the lost logs as the "Jurassic Park of wood," is harvesting red oak, flaming red birch, maple, cherry, elm, walnut, and more—all of which have slumbered for centuries in the cold silences of the Great Lake. * * * The low temperatures and oxygen content of the lake preserved the logs, some nearly 700 years old, embalming them like mummies from a lost civilization. * * *

Superior Water–Logged is using the salvaged wood to build furniture, handicrafts, and musical instruments. Marketed under the trademark Timeless Timber, many of these items are crafted by locals in the Ashland area. One can purchase a walking stick made from a century-old hard maple for $135, wood carvings starting at $140, or a hand-carved decoy for $1,500. * * *

The furniture is assembled with old-fashioned woodworking techniques, such as pegs in place of nails, and pinned mortise and tenon joinery. Craftsmen who use the wood first had to rediscover and learn these largely antiquated methods.

* * * Microsoft mogul Bill Gates used paneling made from the old wood in the library of his mansion. Other notable sites that have incorporated the wood are the Boeing Building in Seattle and the Saddledome, home of the Calgary Flames hockey team. * * *

The wood is also ideal for musical instruments. * * * The water of the lake chemically altered the fibers of the logs, giving the wood an added resonance for musical instruments. * * * "When we look at the infrared spectrum, we find this wood from Lake Superior is very similar to that used in a cello by Antonio Stradivari," says Dr. Joseph Nagyvary of the Department of Biochemistry at Texas A & M University. * * *

[A]fter the company started showing financially promising results, a swarm of other prospective old-log harvesters came out of the woodwork. "We had a gold rush-type situation on the permits," says Mitchen. "It put a scare in everybody that the whole bottom [of the lake] would be ripped up." * * *

Notes and Questions

1. Timeless Timber promotes its products as sustainably-harvested timber: "By recovering the vast amount of logs that sunk during the logging boom of yesteryear, we are able to help reduce the need to harvest existing forests to meet the current demand for wood. Timeless Timber logs are retrieved without damage to wildlife habits. Every site is carefully assessed to prevent disturbing existing fish and wildlife habits." Timeless Timber, Mission, http://www.timelesstimber.com/About/ContentPlus.asp?cmd=CONTENT&articleID=126 (visited Aug. 4, 2004).

What, if any, downsides are there to this type of harvest? Is it truly "sustainable", as the company claims? If you were a state regulator in Wisconsin or Minnesota, how would you manage the demands of treasure hunters who attempt to salvage ancient logs? Would you allow immediate harvest to get these rare and precious products to market and fulfill consumer demand, or would you impose some limits? Should the federal government, rather than the states, step in and control the harvest? Note that, in Scott Mitchen's view, "government red tape" imposed by State and Federal agencies poses a significant impediment to harvesting.

2. Who should get the revenues from the sale of ancient logs: the treasure hunter who discovers the logs, the salvager who recovers them, the owner of the submerged lands (presumably the state), or the descendants or successors of the logging companies that initially harvested the forests? Should the citizens of the state share the revenues from this scarce, exhaustible resource? Consider whether the law of "capture" should apply (see Pierson v. Post, chapter 14, *infra*), or the rules applicable to "lost property," or something else entirely.

B. A Snapshot of Forest Resources and Forestry Practices Today

Today, approximately 747 million acres of land (over one million square miles) in the United States are classified as forestland. This represents one-third of all land in the United States. The greatest percentage of this land is privately owned. In the forests of the Northeast–Maine, New Hampshire, New York and Vermont—22 of 26 million acres of forestland are owned privately, while in the South, about 90% of forestland is privately owned. Stephen D. Blackmer, *Of Wilderness and Commerce: A Historical Overview of the Northern Forest,* 19 Vt. L.Rev. 263, 264 (1995). Land ownership patterns in the Northwest are quite different. There, the federal government owns more than half of the commercial timberland.

"Commercial" forestland is that which is available for, and capable of, growing trees used to produce lumber and other forest products. *See* California Forest Practices Act, Cal. Pub. Res. Code § 4526 (West 1984). Approximately two-thirds of all forested lands in the United States are considered commercial. U.S. Forest Service, An Analysis of the Timber Situation in the United States (1980). About 58% of commercial forestland is owned by private individuals, two-thirds of whom are small, nonindustrial owners, such as farmers. *See* THOM MCEVOY, LEGAL ASPECTS OF OWNING AND MANAGING WOODLANDS 1 (1998); Society of American Foresters, Forest Facts, http://www.safnet.org/aboutforestry/facts.cfm.

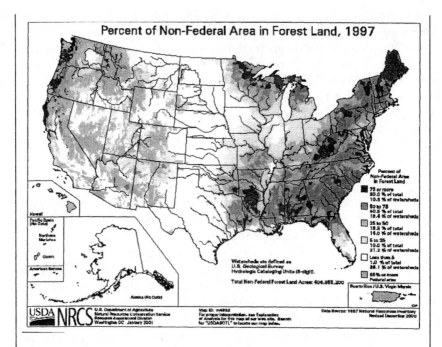

Percent of Non-Federal Area in Forest Land, 1997

This map, provided by the U.S.D.A. Natural Resources Conservation Service, shows the distribution of non-Federal forestland. Areas with 75% or more non-federal forestlands are black; areas with less than 5% non-federal forestlands are white. Areas comprised of 95% or more of federal lands are gray. For purposes of the map, forestland is land that is at least 10 percent stocked by trees of any size that will be at least 4 meters (13 feet) tall at maturity, with canopy cover of 25 percent or greater. USDA, Percent of Non-Federal Area in Forestland, 1997, http://www.nrcs.usda.gov/technical/land/mappdfs/m4982.pdf.

Nationwide, about 30% of all forestland is federally owned. *See National Wilderness Institute, State by State Government Land Ownership,* http://www.nwi.org/Maps/LandChart.html (visited Dec. 1, 2004). Indian reservations contain about 2%, or 16 million acres of forests, about 6 million of which is considered commercial timberland. James D. Hill and Howard G. Arnett, *Understanding Indian Tribal Timber Sales,* 9 Nat. Resources & Env't 38, 39 (1995). The balance of forestland in the United States is owned by state and local governments, which together own approximately 30 million acres of commercial forestland. Celia Campbell–Mohn, Barry Breen, and J. William Futrell, Environmental Law From Resources to Recovery 412 (1993).

In Focus:

Forestlands: Quantity, Type, and Ownership

One third of the United States is forested. In other words, of our nation's 2.3 billion acres of land, almost 750 million acres are forestlands.

Commercial forestlands make up 66 percent of the total. Nearly three-fourths of these commercial forestlands are located in the eastern United States.

Non-commercial forestlands are classified as either "incapable" or "unavailable" for harvest. About 90% of all non-commercial forestlands are considered incapable of growing sufficient wood fiber to make them profitable to harvest. Most of these lands are located in Alaska.

About 10% of the non-commercial lands are classified as either reserved or deferred. These lands are capable of growing trees for harvest but are not available because they are within Parks, Wilderness areas, and other single-use restrictions.

See Demand the Appalachian Standard,
http://www.appalachianwood.org/forestry/quantity.htm.

Eastern forests have supported commercial logging operations for over 100 years, and, consequently, consist of young forests with relatively small timber inventories. Many private forests in the east are managed to supply the paper and pulp industry. On the other hand, western regions account for approximately two-thirds of the nation's "sawtimber" inventory (tree species large enough to yield large logs) because of the many mature trees in the old-growth forests of the Rocky Mountains and Pacific Northwest.

Tree species vary among regions. The western forests consist almost entirely of softwoods (redwoods and conifers, such as fir, pine and spruce), which produce high quality lumber and plywood. Eastern forests produce mainly hardwoods such as oak, hickory, and maple. Southern pines are a source of pulp for the paper products industry. A typical Southern pine is considered fully mature and ready for harvest in thirty to thirty-five years after planting. In contrast, maturity cycles of fifty to eighty years are not uncommon for western softwood forests.

Forestlands provide vital ecosystem services, such as wildlife habitat for a broad range of species and water filtration. Trees help prevent soil erosion by providing windbreaks and by slowing the movement of water and stabilizing the soil with their roots and fallen leaves. Farmland produces 1,000 to 50,000 tons of sediment per square mile every year, and land stripped for construction generates 25,000 to 50,000 tons, while forestland produces only about 50 tons. 2 Rathkopf's The Law of Zoning and Planning § 20:8 (4th ed.) (database updated October 2004), *citing* Edwin Clark, III, Eroding Soils: The Off–Farm Impact (1985). Trees also clear our air by acting as carbon "sinks." One mature tree absorbs about 13 pounds of carbon dioxide annually. For every ton of wood grown in a forest, 1.47 tons of carbon dioxide are removed and replaced with 1.07 tons of oxygen. *See* Forest Facts, *supra;* John P. Caspersen et al., *Contributions of Land–Use History to Carbon Accumu-*

lation in U.S. Forests, 290 Science 1148–1151, Nov. 10, 2000.

In Practice:

Society of American Foresters

The non-profit Society of American Foresters represents the forestry profession in the United States. The Society, which is the largest professional society for foresters in the world, was founded in 1900 by Gifford Pinchot. Its mission is "to advance the science, education, technology, and practice of forestry; to enhance the competency of its members; to establish professional excellence; and, to use the knowledge, skills, and conservation ethic of the profession to ensure the continued health and use of forest ecosystems and the present and future availability of forest resources to benefit society."

Society of American Foresters, About SAF, http://www.safnet.org/who/whoweare.cfm.

The Society's on-line Journal of Forestry Professional Resource Guide provides information and web links to forestry products and services. The Society also offers several periodicals, including the *Journal of Forestry*, which is billed as the premier scholarly journal in forestry. The Journal is designed to keep forestry professionals informed about significant developments in forest science and policy.

According to the Society of American Foresters, the timber industry ranks among the top 10 employers in 40 of the 50 states. Society of American Foresters, Forest Facts, http://www.safnet.org/aboutforestry/facts.cfm (visited Dec. 7, 2004). Until the 1990's, the industry had been the largest employer in the Oregon. Lundmark, *supra*, at 803. From the late 1980's through the 1990's, however, thousands of timber-related jobs were lost as lumber mills closed throughout the west. Restrictions imposed to protect spotted owl habitat and other environmental requirements have taken a toll, but the true culprits appear to be the rise of automation in the timber industry and the decline in prices for U.S. lumber caused in part by imports of duty-free Canadian lumber. Matt Jenkins, *U.S. Mills Fall Under the Canadian Ax*, High Country News, Mar. 26, 2001 (discussing effects of 1996 U.S.-Canada Softwood Lumber Agreement).

THE FAR SIDE®   BY GARY LARSON

"You know what I'm sayin'? ... Me, for example. I couldn't work in some stuffy little office. ... The outdoors just calls to me."

Solid-wood products (lumber and plywood) comprise one of the most volatile manufacturing industries in the American economy. Because much of its output flows directly into the housing industry, demand fluctuates with the volume of home building (which fluctuates widely). THOMAS MICHAEL POWER, LOST LANDSCAPES AND FAILED ECONOMIES: THE SEARCH FOR THE VALUE OF PLACE 139–140 (1996). As a result of this volatility, workers in the wood products sector are far more likely to be displaced than other types of American workers. *Id.* at 141. But the lack of job stability is not the only concern facing forestry workers:

> Forestry is one of the most dangerous occupations around. No other has a higher injury and mortality rate. The rate of disabling injuries in the lumber and wood products industry is 40 percent higher than in the construction industry and three times higher than in mining and manufacturing.

Id. at 146.

Timber resources pose unique challenges from a production stand-point as well. For many natural resources, the amount available for development is fixed—there are finite amounts of coal or oil in the ground. In contrast, trees are renewable, but growth rates vary tremendously based on the type of tree, precipitation, soil types, nutrients, and many other factors. The length of time required for a seedling to grow into a merchantable product can complicate business planning. In order to determine the types and numbers of trees to plant in any given year, the forester must predict both growth rates and the demand for timber decades or more in the future. Further complicating the job is the fact that a forest can physically depreciate in value over time, as older trees die and decay. Entire forests can be lost through fire, disease, insect infestation, and catastrophic storms. Yet leaving trees in place until they become mature or even old-growth forests is highly desirable in terms of economic returns as well as social and ecological values.

Timber management strategies at national, regional, and local levels, on both private and public lands, are influenced significantly by management directives for the National Forest System, which covers over 190 million acres of land.

[T]he federal timber harvest amount, an integral aspect of forest planning, is the gauge from which private harvesting is measured. Reductions or increases in the federal harvest amount can dictate the level of private production. Nationally, reductions in the federal harvest in the Pacific Northwest … have led to a heightened demand for southern timber. As a result, production in and profits from southern forests, particularly private holdings, have increased.

Kelly Murphy, *Cutting Through the Forest of the Standing Doctrine: Challenging Resource Management Plans in the Eighth and Ninth Circuits*, 18 U. Ark. Little Rock L.J. 223, 224–225 (1996).

The following sections of this chapter address the law's response to the benefits, detriments, and overall challenges posed by the ownership and management of timber resources on private, state, federal, and tribal lands. The definitions provided below will help the reader sort through the ecological, economic and legal issues.

In Practice: Silvicultural Vocabulary

Commercial (or Suitable) Timberland—land available for timber production and capable of growing commercially valuable wood products. A common benchmark is growth of at least 20 ft³/acre of timber a year.

Forest land—Land at least 10 percent stocked by trees of any size, or formerly having such tree cover and not currently developed for nonforest uses.

Log—A section of a tree at least 8 feet long, sufficiently straight enough to yield at least an 8–foot board.

Lumber—Wood that is cut and prepared for use as building material.

Sawtimber trees—Trees large enough to yield at least one 12–foot log or two 8–foot logs. This includes softwood trees 9.0 inches and larger in diameter at breast heighth (dbh), and hardwood trees 11.0 inches and larger.

Silviculture—The field of managing forest vegetation to accomplish specified objectives, which may include timber, wildlife, water, recreation, aesthetics, or any combination of these or other forest uses. This discipline studies forest establishment, composition, quality, growth, and harvest.

Stumpage—Timber in standing trees, sold at a fixed price per tree or per stump. Stumpage may also be used to refer to the value of standing timber. Stumpage rates vary tremendously depending on tree species and region. Rates are influenced by supply and demand, as well as the tree's quality and potential use (*e.g.,* fine furniture, lumber for building, pulpwood for paper or fuel, or specialty products like Christmas trees), the distance to processing mills, accessibility, and other site factors.

Thousand Board Feet (MBF)—A unit of measurement equal to 1,000 feet of wood 1 inch thick.

Timber—A general term applied to forest products. It may also mean trees that are grown for wood to be used in building, or, even more specifically, sawed lumber more than 4 by 4 inches in breadth and thickness.

Woodland—Forest land incapable of yielding commercially valuable wood because of adverse site conditions.

Sources: USDA Forest Service, INTERIM RESOURCE INVENTORY GLOSSARY (June 14, 1989); USDA Southern Research Station Forest Inventory and Analysis, http://srsfia2.fs.fed.us/publicweb/; Merriam–Webster Online, http://www.m-w.com/. More silviculture terms, including harvest methods, are found in Chapter 6.

II. PRIVATE FORESTRY LAW

The laws related to timber management vary depending on whether it takes place on private, state, tribal, or federal lands. Private timber law is a combination of property, tort, and contract law. State timber laws regulate the forestry industry by requiring practices designed to minimize water pollution, soil erosion, and fire danger, and by encouraging or requiring reforestation. Federal environmental statutes also affect forestry practices. In comparison, development on federal and state timber lands is controlled by government contract law, as well as statutes governing long-term planning, environmental protection, and wildlife conservation.

A. Private Timber as Property

1. *Interests in Timber: Conveyances and Contracts*

Because many of the privately owned forests are small and the capital investment necessary for development is high, most small, non-industrial owners sell their timber to timber companies. This transaction can be accomplished in a number of ways. The landowner who desires to retain the most control over timber development will cut the trees and then sell the wood. Many private landowners do not have the resources to do this. A more cost-effective way to manage a private forest may be to execute a timber sales contract, lease, or *profit a prendre*, under which the timber company buys the right to cut certain trees for a specified amount of time. Alternatively, the landowner might sever the timber rights from the land, giving the timber company ownership of all timber resources through a deed or other appropriate instrument, while retaining ownership of the land and the right to use the land for all non-timber purposes. In other words, trees can be severed from the land and conveyed as a separate estate, just as minerals can be conveyed separately from the surface estate. *See* JAN LAITOS, NATURAL RESOURCES LAW 338–349 (West 2002).

Timber may be considered either real or personal property, depending on context. The distinction is important in determining whether the doctrine of conversion or trespass applies to the unlawful cutting of trees, whether the Statute of Frauds applies to a sale of the trees, and other matters such as sales or excise taxes, recording requirements, and the applicable statute of limitations.

At common law, trees are considered part of the land on which they are growing, and treated as realty until they are severed from the soil. Walters v. Sheffield, 75 Fla. 505, 78 So. 539 (1918); Owens v. Lewis, 46 Ind. 488 (1874); D.W. Alderman & Sons Co. v. Kirven, 209 S.C. 446, 40 S.E.2d 791 (1946). Exceptions may include nursery stock intended for sale and transportation, Dennison v. Harden, 29 Wash.2d 243, 186 P.2d 908 (1947), and standing trees sold with the intention of immediate harvest and severance from the soil. Elmonte Inv. Co. v. Schafer Bros. Logging Co., 192 Wash. 1, 72 P.2d 311 (1937). Generally speaking, the common law treats a conveyance of standing trees as a conveyance of an interest in real property, subject to the requirements governing a real estate transaction. Once the trees are severed, they become personalty under common law.

J. W. MAILLIARD, III, ET AL., DOING BUSINESS AS GERMAN CREEK PROPERTIES v. WILLOW CREEK RANCH CO.

Court of Appeal, First District, California, 1969.
273 Cal.App.2d 370, 78 Cal.Rptr. 139.

De-forested pasture near Jenner, CA (Jan. 3, 2005). Photo by S. Zellmer.

[P]laintiffs-respondents are the assignees of the grantees of a timber grant executed on June 2, 1958 by one Baxman and wife to respondents' assignors. The purchase price was $30,000 and the grant was recorded on June 4, 1958. The subject timber is on a 3600–acre tract located near Jenner, Sonoma County, and the land and timber were owned, prior to the above sale of the timber, by the Baxmans. The land will be referred to herein as the Baxman Ranch.

The timber grant provided that Baxman and wife granted to respondents' assignors 'all of the merchantable timber on grantors' ranch,' including 'the right to clear cut the area down to Any size diameter grantees deem merchantable' * * * Grantees have eight years in which to remove the timber provided that if the timber is not all removed in eight years, then Grantees may have Additional time to remove it upon paying to Grantors the sum of $250.00 for each additional year necessary or desirable.' * * *

On or about February 20, 1961 the original grantees under the timber grant assigned all of their interest therein to respondents. This assignment was recorded on February 23, 1961. On December 28, 1962 the Baxmans sold the subject land to the appellants, who had actual and constructive knowledge of said timber grant and its terms.

On January 16, 1964 appellants' attorney wrote to respondents, questioning the validity of respondents' timber grant and their right to harvest any of the timber on the subject property except that which was merchantable as of the time of the original 1958 grant. * * *

The judgment appealed from holds: (1) that respondents are the owners of all of the timber on the subject property and have the right to 'clear cut' and remove the same regardless of the size thereof. * * *

When the grant is, as here, of 'all the merchantable timber' on the grantors' land, the courts will first look to the grant itself for a definition of what the parties intend the term 'merchantable timber' to mean. In the instant case the parties provided that such term was intended to include trees of any size diameter grantees deem merchantable. Hence, there is no point in discussing cases in which the term 'merchantable timber' is unqualified or not defined in the agreement or grant in question. It is obvious that the parties here intended to leave it up to the grantees as to what trees they deemed merchantable.

Baxman testified in substance that he desired to turn the subject property into a sheep ranch and that he wanted the land as clear of trees as was possible in order to increase the growth of grass for grazing purposes. This was his objective in granting the right to 'clear cut' the entire area and, in doing so, allowing the grantees to cut 'down to any size diameter grantees deem merchantable.'[1]

We have concluded that the trial court correctly interpreted the timber grant and that there is substantial evidence to support its finding that said grant conveyed to and was intended to convey to the grantees thereunder the 'right to remove all the timber from the said real property, Regardless of size.'

Respondents did not acquire a right to the timber on the subject property in Perpetuity. They expressly conclude this, stating that their ownership of such timber is 'subject to their right to remove it within a certain number of years. * * * If they cannot remove the timber within that time (8 years plus 8 years), the same reverts to the landowners.' In making this concession, respondents have effectively precluded themselves and any of their successors from ever making any 'perpetuity claim.' Respondents likewise disclaim any interest in any trees that were not in existence on June 2, 1958. * * *

Appellants contend that respondents are restricted in their cutting of trees to those of a size which the original grantees cut during the period from June 2, 1958 to February 20, 1961, when the timber grant was transferred to respondents. This would indeed be a strained interpretation of the terms of the grant and one that neither the trial court nor we deem reasonable. It is understandable that the original grantees

---

1. * * *

THE COURT: [Y]ou were making your money off of the sheep and the more that they could cut of the timber the more grass

you would have and the more sheep you could run? * * *

[Baxman]: That's the way I felt.

would select the most profitable trees at the outset and recoup their capital investment as soon as possible. That they did so does not destroy their right, under the clear terms of the grant, 'to clear cut the area down to any size diameter grantees deem merchantable.' The mere fact that in the early years of the grant period the larger trees were selected for cutting does not mean that the grantees were abandoning their right to cut smaller trees in the future. * * *

Appellants [contend] ... that respondents were only entitled to the merchantable timber on the subject property at the time of the timber grant, June 2, 1958. This contention is, of course, motivated by the fact that trees which appellants contend were not 'merchantable' on June 2, 1958, would grow sufficiently during the life of the timber grant to become 'merchantable.'

In Buffum [v. Texaco, Inc. (1996)], 241 Cal.App.2d 732, 50 Cal.Rptr. 852, the owner of timber land (Tompkins) deeded to Humboldt Milling Co. "all of the timber standing, lying and contained" on said land. The court said: 'It is generally held that the word 'timber' unless modified or controlled by other expressions in an instrument means trees fit to be used for lumber in building or construction.' The court held that when Tompkins granted 'all of the timber' he intended to convey to Humboldt and the latter intended to acquire, 'all of the Merchantable timber then on the property.'

In the instant case, the timber grant expressly defines merchantable timber as trees of 'any size diameter grantees deem merchantable.' Therefore, the definition of timber set forth in the *Buffum* case is not applicable here because, in the language of *Buffum*, the word 'timber' was 'modified or controlled by other expressions in an instrument.'

Judgment affirmed.

Notes and Questions

1. On appeal, the appellant-landowner argued that "merchantable" timber meant that which was at least 18 inches in diameter breast high (about 4 ½ feet above the ground). What did the original parties to the transaction intend "merchantable" to mean in this case? Should the successors to the grantees be able to cut any trees they can sell at a profit, regardless of size or condition? If the contract or grant were silent, and extrinsic evidence were not allowed, what would the grantees be allowed to cut? Should timber be deemed "merchantable" if it can only be used for pulp and paper, rather than furniture or housing material?

2. If the parties simply refer to "timber," would all trees standing at the time of the contract as well as trees grown through the end of the contract period be included? The answer may turn on the duration of time provided for harvesting. How long did the purchaser have in *Mailliard* case to cut and haul the timber? Only a reasonable period of time? What is reasonable? Would the outcome be different if Baxman, the original landowner, hadn't intended to raise livestock on the property but had some other plans?

3.　All states except Louisiana have adopted some version of the Uniform Commercial Code to govern transactions for the sale of goods. Harry J. Haynsworth, The Unified Business Organizations Code: The Next Generation, 29 Del. J. Corp. L. 83, 110 (2004).[b] The 1972 version of Uniform Commercial Code § 2–107 treats a contract for the sale of timber or crops as a contract for a sale of goods, regardless of whether the timber or crop is be harvested by the buyer or the seller. In contrast, the 1962 version of section 2–107 treats standing timber as a "good" only if it will be severed by the seller. If instead the buyer were required to cut the timber according to the terms of the contract, the transaction would be considered one involving real property under the earlier version. See Baxter v. Lyttle, 465 N.E.2d 198 (Ind. App. 1984). What reason could the drafters of the 1962 version have had to make this distinction? Why did the 1972 version take a different approach? Which approach is most likely to provide adequate notice to prospective purchasers or mortgagees of the land? Which is most likely to facilitate the necessary financing for the transaction? Note that the 1972 version of section 2–107 retains the distinction between buyer-severance and seller-severance for minerals, including oil and gas, and characterizes minerals as real property only if they are to be severed by the seller. Why are minerals treated differently than timber? You might find the court's discussion in Bonds v. Carter, 75 S.W.3d 192 (Ark. 2002), *infra*, helpful.

4.　If the sale is governed by the UCC, the trees must be harvested within a reasonable period of time to prevent abandonment of the right to harvest. See Fischer v. Zepa Consulting AG., 710 N.Y.S.2d 830, 95 N.Y.2d 66, 732 N.E.2d 937 (2000), *citing* McKinney's Uniform Commercial Code §§ 2–107, 2–309(1). In *Fischer*, the court concluded that the conveyance of a right to "[a]ll hardwood and softwood, timber, and trees now or hereafter lying, being and situate on or in" a specified tract of land, "together with a right of way and easement in perpetuity, to and for the benefit of the grantee," for purpose of "inspecting, cutting, skidding, piling and removing" timber, was a transfer of a perpetual interest in land rather than a sale of goods. Accordingly, the New York version of the UCC did not apply. Does that necessarily mean the buyer can cut the trees at his leisure? Would the Rule Against Perpetuities restrict or prohibit a conveyance that gives an interest in timber "in perpetuity", or "for so long as the trees shall grow"?

2.　Trespass and Adverse Possession

A trespass is an invasion of a legally protected possessory interest in property. The elements of a trespass claim are: (1) plaintiff was in possession or was the owner of property; (2) defendant made an unauthorized, intentional entry upon said property; and (3) plaintiff suffered damage as a result of the invasion of her possessory rights. Barnard v. Rowland, 132 N.C.App. 416, 512 S.E.2d 458 (1999); Northern P.R. Co. v. Lewis, 162 U.S. 366, 16 S.Ct. 831, 40 L.Ed. 1002 (1896). Liability for trespass may be imposed for intentional or voluntary acts, reckless conduct, or abnormally dangerous activities. See Teasley v. Roberson, 149

---

b.　Even Louisiana, a civil law state,　　Haynsworth, *supra*, at 110.
has adopted many of the UCC's provisions.

Miss. 188, 115 So. 211 (1928) (imposing liability on a defendant who admitted branding plaintiff's trees by mistake); Clinchfield Coal Corp. v. Hayter, 130 Va. 711, 108 S.E. 854 (1921) (liability may be imposed for the value of timber cut down on the land of another, even though the action occurred under a mistake of fact and in good faith). *See also* Sterling v. Velsicol Chemical Corp., 647 F.Supp. 303, 319 (W.D. Tenn. 1986), *aff'd* in relevant part, 855 F.2d 1188 (6th Cir. 1988) (imposing trespass liability for "incursion" of chemical waste onto plaintiffs' property). The requisite intent for trespass is the intent to complete the physical act. Mere nonfeasance does not suffice. *See* Robin C. Larner, 75 Am. Jur. 2d Trespass §§ 29, 74 (2004).

You may be liable for trespass if you cut down a tree in your backyard and it falls on your neighbor's garage roof. You may also be liable for trespass if you set fire to a brush pile on your land and it engulfs your neighbor's wood lot or her house. These are both volitional acts, and it is no defense that you acted in good faith and did not intend to commit a trespass. If you simply allowed limbs from a tree in your backyard to grow naturally over the property line of your neighbor's lot, resulting in injury when one limb fell on your neighbor's garage roof, have you engaged in an intentional act for purposes of trespass liability?

Some states have enacted specific statutes imposing criminal penalties for willful injury or destruction of trees standing or growing on the property of another. An early version of the Nebraska Criminal Code provided that any persons who "willfully and maliciously, and without lawful authority," injured or destroyed another person's trees worth thirty-five dollars or more "shall be imprisoned in the penitentiary, and kept at hard labor not more than ten years, nor less than one year, and shall, moreover, be liable to the party injured in double the amount of damages by him sustained." *See* Ex parte Eads, 17 Neb. 145, 22 N.W. 352 (Neb. 1885) (citing Neb. Cr. Code § 88).

In civil lawsuits, Nebraska courts have generally disallowed punitive damages, but by statute Nebraska provided for treble damages as a remedy for willful trespass and injury to "any timber, tree, or shrub on the land of another, or in the street or highway in front of another's cultivated ground, yard, or town lot, or on the public grounds of any town, or any land held by this state...." Neb. Rev. Stat. § 25.2130 (1943). Provisions like Nebraska's are intended to compensate the owner whose land has suffered the trespass and provide notice to potential trespassers that cutting trees on another's property is risky. David H. Bowser, *"Hey, That's My Tree!"—An Analysis of the Good–Faith Contract Logger Exemption from the Double and Treble Damage Provisions of Oregon's Timber Trespass Action*, 36 Willamette L. Rev. 401, 403 (2000).

Nebraska recently repealed its treble damages provision by a bill entitled Trademark Registration Act—Property Rights, Nebraska Laws L.B. 626, 96th Legis, 2nd Sess. (2000). Other states, however, continue to provide for enhanced awards for knowing or willful injury to trees. Oregon law, for example, provides that:

(1) * * * [W]henever any person, without lawful authority, willfully injures or severs from the land of another any produce thereof or cuts down, girdles or otherwise injures or carries off any tree, timber or shrub on the land of another person ... judgment ... shall be given for treble the amount of damages claimed, or assessed for the trespass. In any such action, upon plaintiff's proof of ownership of the premises and the commission by the defendant of any of the acts mentioned in this section, it is prima facie evidence that the acts were committed by the defendant willfully, intentionally and without plaintiff's consent.

Or. Rev. Stat. § 105.810. Iowa has enacted a similar provision. I.C.A. § 658.4. Oregon also provides for attorney fees and costs for the prevailing party. *Id.* § 105.810(2).

Delaware provides for treble damages against anyone who "negligently, wilfully or maliciously injures or damages trees, shrubs or other landscaping under the jurisdiction and control of the [state]." 17 Del. Code § 520(a). Its statute explains that "damages shall be computed as the sum of the cost of purchase of new trees, shrubs or other landscaping of equivalent size and quality and the removal and installation costs to replace the damaged trees, shrubs or other landscaping...." *Id.*

Defenses to a trespass action are few and far between. As a general rule, ignorance does not excuse an entry upon the land of another, and lack of knowledge of the location of the boundary lines is no defense. Robin C. Larner, 75 Am. Jur. 2d Trespass § 74 (2004). Some states, however, provide a statutory exception for "innocent loggers." At the behest of the Oregon Association of Loggers, the Oregon Legislature created a good-faith contract logger exemption to the treble damage provisions of its timber trespass statutes. Or. Rev. Stat. § 105.810(4)-(8) (1999). It received testimony to the effect that timber trespass is almost always committed by a contract logger, usually without knowledge that she is harvesting trees belonging to someone other than the person contracting for her service. "The legislature was sympathetic to accounts of loggers who had, in good faith, committed timber trespass. These loggers often were misled by landowners and timber companies who mistakenly claimed ownership of land outside their legal parcels or those who fraudulently misrepresented their ownership of a parcel belonging to an absentee owner." Bowser, *supra*, at 411–412.

The logger seeking to utilize the exemption from the double or triple damage provisions of Oregon's timber trespass statute must be a contract logger. A "contract logger" is defined as "a person engaged in a commercial timber harvesting operation." The logger also must be engaged in an "operation," for purposes of the statute meaning "any commercial activity relating to the ... harvesting of forest tree species." * * * The contract logger must (1) conduct an operation (2) under a signed (3) written contract (4) with a person the contract logger reasonably believes to be the owner of the produce, tree, timber, or shrubs (5) in the operations area.

Id. at 411–412 (citations omitted).

In the following case, a claim against the state for harvesting trees in state parks was dismissed under Iowa's timber trespass statute.

MAGERS–FIONOF v. STATE OF IOWA

Supreme Court of Iowa, 1996.
555 N.W.2d 672.

Plaintiffs learned in 1993 that the Iowa Department of Natural Resources (DNR) and its predecessor, the Iowa Conservation Commission, have been harvesting mature, healthy trees in Walnut Woods State Park, Ledges State Park, and Pikes Peak State Park. Further inquiry revealed that at least 2700 trees have been logged in Iowa's state parks since 1977. Armed with this knowledge, plaintiffs commenced a class-action suit against the State under the Iowa Tort Claims Act. *See* Iowa Code ch. 669 (1995).

Plaintiffs' petition does not seek to enjoin the State's tree-harvesting practices. Rather it seeks money damages to compensate the plaintiffs, and all others who visit the State's parks, for their personal loss of use and enjoyment of the logged trees. Plaintiffs base their suit on Iowa Code section 658.4. That statute provides:

> For willfully injuring any timber, tree, or shrub on the land of another, or in the street or highway in front of another's cultivated ground, yard, or city lot, or on the public grounds of any city, or any land held by the state for any purpose whatever, the perpetrator shall pay treble damages at the suit of any person entitled to protect or enjoy the property.

The State moved to dismiss, claiming section 658.4 creates no private cause of action against the State for injury to trees grown in state parks. The district court sustained the motion, observing that the Iowa Administrative Procedure Act provides the exclusive means of challenging the DNR's forestry management practices. * * *

[T]he Iowa Tort Claims Act ... permits private parties to recover money damages for the negligent or wrongful acts of state employees "where the state, if a private person, would be liable to the claimant for such damage...." Iowa Code § 669.2(3)(a). * * * Before plaintiffs can recover in tort against the State or any other defendant, they must show a duty owed them by the wrongdoer and a violation of that duty. Here plaintiffs claim the State's duty to them arises under section 658.4. Arrogating to themselves the ownership of trees on public lands, they argue the statute permits them recovery against a "perpetrator"—in this case, the State—who willfully injures any timber on "their land." Plaintiffs' argument, though unquestionably sincere, cannot withstand close scrutiny. Section 658.4, contained in a chapter entitled "Waste and Trespass," has throughout its long history been interpreted to furnish relief to property owners for damage by trespassers. * * * The State concedes that these plaintiffs, as taxpaying citizens, might conceivably claim a proprietary interest in the enjoyment of state park trees. Acknowledging that interest, however, does not thereby divest the State of its ownership of the parks, or the trees, in question. * * * The DNR is, by statute, delegated the duty to manage state parks. * * * DNR employees are specifically exempted from the law barring the removal, destruction, or injury of trees or other plant life on public lands. Iowa Code § 461A.41. Clearly these statutes contradict the novel interpretation of section 658.4 advanced by plaintiffs on this appeal.

Plaintiffs' counsel conceded in oral argument that even if plaintiffs "enjoyed" trees grown on a neighbor's land, plaintiffs would have no right to seek compensation for their neighbor's willful destruction of their own trees. No recognized duty exists to support such a cause of action. So it is with the facts before us. * * * Thus the district court correctly determined as a matter of law that the State's ownership and management authority over publicly owned forests precludes a citizen's suit for money damages against DNR employees carrying out their statutory mandate on state-owned lands.

Notes and Questions

1. Plaintiffs also argued that their claim was supported by the public trust doctrine. *See* Chapters 5 and 8, *supra.* They failed to take steps to preserve the issue for appeal, and the Iowa Supreme Court refused to rule on it.

2. State forestlands are discussed in more detail below in Section III.A.

Prosecution of an action for trespass may trigger a counterclaim by the defendant for adverse possession of the timber or land in question. *See* Timber Service Company v. Ellis, 163 Or.App. 349, 988 P.2d 396 (Ore. App. 1999) (dismissing defendant's counterclaim for adverse possession of timber land, and imposing liability against the defendant for trespass and quieting title in the plaintiff). The case below illustrates the challenges of establishing an adverse possession claim.

BONDS v. CARTER
Supreme Court of Arkansas, 2002.
348 Ark. 591, 75 S.W.3d 192.

This is a quiet-title action brought by appellant Bobbye Bonds to determine the ownership of a certain tract of land in Columbia County. Eddie Smith formerly owned all of the land in question. On June 19, 1980, Smith conveyed a timber deed to appellee Barry Carter, granting Carter "all the merchantable pine and hardwood timber standing, growing and being on" a parcel of land in Columbia County; Carter paid $1,000 in consideration for the right to cut and remove timber from the described land for 100 years. On January 15, 1981, Smith conveyed a warranty deed to Bobbye Bonds, covering the same parcel of land, and reserving to himself all the oil, gas, and mineral interests thereon. Bonds originally filed a petition to set aside the timber deed in 1982, but the case was abandoned after Eddie Smith died.

Nearly twenty years later, on February 18, 2000, Bonds sued to quiet title in her land, alleging that, under Ark.Code Ann. § 18–11–102 (1987), she had acquired title to the land by paying taxes on the "wild and unimproved" property every year since 1981. Further, Bonds alleged that Carter's timber deed was void *ab initio* for inadequate consideration, for violating the rule against perpetuities, and for unconscionability under the Uniform Commercial Code. [*ed:* More specifically, Bonds alleged that Carter defrauded Smith by taking advantage of Smith's alcoholism to obtain the contract, that a contract with a term of 100 years is against public policy as an improper restraint of property, and that the contract had been materially altered after Smith signed it.]

Carter answered, pleading, among other things, that Bonds's action was barred by the statute of limitations. Both parties then moved for summary judgment. In her motion, Bonds argued that, since Carter did not dispute that the land in question was wild and unimproved, she had acquired title to the property through adverse possession because she had paid taxes on it for more than fifteen years. Carter's motion agreed that the facts were undisputed, but asserted that his timber deed was superior to Bonds's warranty deed, and further, that Bonds's action was barred by the statute of limitations. Carter also pointed out that his validly recorded timber deed served to put Bonds on constructive notice of a superior interest in the land, and that she purchased the property subject to the timber deed. * * *

On appeal, Bonds raises two points for reversal: 1) the trial court erred in not finding Carter's severed timber estate on wild and unimproved property was adversely possessed when Bonds obtained the underlying fee to the property and paid all taxes on it from 1981 through 1998; and 2) the 100–year timber deed is an ongoing unconscionable contract, presenting public policy concerns that the trial court should have addressed to invalidate the instrument, and the court erred in dismissing the action due to statute of limitations considerations.

For her first point on appeal, Bonds argues that a recorded, severed timber estate on wild and unimproved land is adversely possessed when the owner of the underlying fee pays all taxes assessed on the land (both real and personal property) from 1981 to 1998. She contends that, under § 18–11–102, her payment of taxes vests title in her. That statute provides as follows:

> Unimproved and unenclosed land shall be deemed and held to be in possession of the person who pays the taxes thereon if he has color of title thereto, but no person shall be entitled to invoke the benefit of this section unless he, and those under whom he claims, shall have paid the taxes for at least seven (7) years in succession.

Bonds further relies on Jones v. Barger, 67 Ark.App. 337, 1 S.W.3d 31 (1999), wherein the court of appeals held that one claiming title to land by having paid taxes on that land for seven years need not have actually adversely possessed the land in question. In *Jones,* both parties had received warranty deeds to the same parcel of land, and the court was faced with determining whose title was superior. The court of appeals held that, under § 18–11–102, the Joneses had paid taxes on unimproved and unenclosed land, under color of title, for at least seven years. *Jones,* 67 Ark.App. at 341, 1 S.W.3d 31. Because that statute did not require "actual adverse possession," the court of appeals concluded that the Joneses had met the statutory requirements and were thus entitled to have the title to the land vested in them. *Id.* at 346, 1 S.W.3d 31.

The facts of the instant case are distinguishable from those in *Jones.* *Jones* involved two parties claiming the same title to the same estate in the land; here, on the other hand, we are presented with a situation in which one party has the underlying surface rights, and the other possesses the timber rights, which have been severed from the surface. Arkansas's taxation statutes make it clear that timber rights are separate and distinct from the land itself. Ark.Code Ann. § 26–26–1109 (Repl.1997), dealing with taxation of timber rights, provides in pertinent part as follows:

> (a)(1) *When the timber rights in any land shall, by conveyance or otherwise, be held by one (1) or more persons,* firms, or corporations, *and the fee simple in the land by one (1) or more other persons,* firms, or corporations, *it shall be the duty of the assessor,* when advised of the fact, either by personal notice or by recording of the deeds in the office of the recorder of the county, *to assess the timber rights in the lands separate from the soil.*

> (2) In such case, a sale of the timber rights for nonpayment of taxes shall not affect the title to the soil itself, nor shall a sale of the latter for nonpayment of taxes affect the title to the timber rights.

(Emphasis added.) In sum, this statute provides that timber rights held by one person are to be assessed separately from the fee simple rights of another in the land, because the timber rights are separate from another's rights in the soil.

Further, when a purchaser of land records his deed, it serves to put any subsequent purchaser on notice of the earlier deed.

Here, Carter recorded his timber deed six months before Bonds ever received the warranty deed from Smith. Thus, Bonds was on constructive notice of Carter's deed.

The question remains, however, as to whether or not Bonds could adversely possess Carter's timber interest, when she was on notice of the fact that those interests had been severed and recorded prior to her taking the warranty deed to the remainder of the land. As Carter points out, there is no case law in Arkansas dealing with the question of adverse possession of timber rights. There is case law, though, setting out what must happen before one can adversely possess mineral rights. While mineral and timber rights differ in many respects, both are severable from the land on which they are found.

In Claybrooke v. Barnes, 180 Ark. 678, 22 S.W.2d 390 (1929), Laura Barnes contended that she held title to certain mineral rights through adverse possession. The mineral rights had been excepted from a deed to the surface rights dated November 17, 1911, but no such exception was contained in subsequent quitclaim deeds to the property. Barnes, who was a subsequent grantee to the surface estate, eventually claimed she held title to the mineral rights as well, although she had never exploited the mineral rights until she attempted to execute a mineral lease on the land in 1918. In reversing the trial court's decision finding that Barnes adversely possessed the property, this court held as follows:

> Where there has been a severance of the legal interest in the minerals from the ownership of the land, it has been held as to solid minerals, and the same rule has been applied to oil and gas, that adverse possession of the land is not adverse possession of the mineral estate and does not defeat the separate interest in it. * * *

This rule was approved by this court in Bodcaw Lumber Co. v. Goode [160 Ark. 48, 254 S.W. 345 (1923)], and the court said: "The rule of those authorities is that the title to minerals beneath the surface is not lost by nonuse nor by adverse occupancy of the owner of the surface under the same claim of title, and that the statute can only be set in motion by an adverse use of the mineral rights, persisted in and continued for the statutory period."

> *So it may be taken as settled that the two estates when once separated, remain independent, and title to the mineral rights can never be acquired by merely holding and claiming the land, even though title be asserted in the minerals all the time. The only way the statute of limitation can be asserted against the owner of the mineral rights or estate is for the owner of the surface estate or some other person to take actual possession of the minerals by opening mines and operating the same.* * * *

Bonds's argument in her reply brief that mineral rights and timber rights are not analogous is not well taken, * * * especially in light of her concession in her opening brief that timber rights are a *profit à prendre*. Timber rights are indeed a *profit à prendre, see* Black's Law Dictionary 1483 (6th ed.1990). * * * The right of *profit à prendre* is a "right to make some use of the soil of another, such as the right to mine metals, and it carries with it the right of entry and the right to remove and take from the land the designated products or profit and also includes right to use such of the surface as is necessary and convenient for exercise of the profit." *Id.* In sum, while we do not conclude that timber and mineral rights are necessarily identical in nature, both rights involve the right to remove the subject goods from the surface itself; neither right profits its owner until it is exercised by removing the goods from the land. Title to such rights is separate and apart from title to the surface.

In conclusion, we hold that Bonds's reliance on *Jones v. Barger, supra,* is misplaced, and § 18–11–102 is likewise inapplicable, because one cannot adversely possess timber rights merely by paying taxes on the land. In order to establish adverse possession, the possession must be actual, open, continuous, hostile, exclusive, and be accompanied by an intent to hold adversely and in derogation of, and not in conformity with, the right of the true owner. * * * Further, to adversely possess property on which another holds a superior right to timber growing thereon, there must be actual adverse possession for seven consecutive years before the commencement of the suit. * * * If the owner of the surface holds the land upon which the timber is growing, it is presumed, unless the contrary appears, that he or she holds in subordination to the rights of the owner of the timber deed, such possession being consistent with the right to the timber; mere possession is not sufficient to bar recovery. Here, Bonds did nothing to actively assert her interest in the timber growing on the land until she filed this suit. This was insufficient to claim an adverse interest in the property, and the trial court did not err in finding in favor of Carter on this issue.

In her second point on appeal, Bonds argues that the trial court erred in concluding that the statute of limitations barred her challenge to the validity of the timber deed. In this respect, she contends that public policy considerations concerning the inherent "unconscionability" of the 100–year timber deed somehow trumped the seven-year statute of limitations for bringing actions to recover lands. *See* Ark.Code Ann. § 18–61–101 (1987). She also avers that the Uniform Commercial Code provides authority for setting aside unconscionable contracts, and cites Davis v. Kolb, 263 Ark. 158, 563 S.W.2d 438 (1978), wherein this court set aside a timber deed for unconscionability. However, *Davis* did not involve any question of the applicable statute of limitations, or such statute's effect in barring the underlying suit. * * *

Bonds simply offers no convincing authority to support her argument that public policy concerns should override the applicable seven-year statute of limitations. * * * For the foregoing reasons, the order of the chancery court is affirmed.

* * *

THORNTON, Justice, dissenting.

Because I believe that there is a difference between a timber deed and a deed granting mineral rights, and because I think that Arkansas Code Annotated § 18–11–102 *et seq.* (1987) applies to timber land, I must respectfully dissent.

The majority opinion is premised upon the notion that a timber deed is analogous to a mineral-rights deed. Based on this assumption, the majority concludes that Ms. Bonds may not follow the procedure outlined in Ark.Code Ann. § 18–11–102 *et seq.* to acquire any rights to the timber identified in Mr. Carter's timber deed. This assumption is misplaced. We have held that:

> there is a broad distinction between a sale of timber and mineral rights, for the use of the former necessarily creates a burden upon

the owner of the surface which is not consistent with use by the latter, whereas the use of the surface for mining purposes is only incidental and does not necessarily impair to a serious extent the enjoyment of the surface rights.

Bodcaw Lumber Co. v. Goode, 160 Ark. 48, 254 S.W. 345 (1923).

Because there is a "broad distinction" between a timber deed and a mineral-rights deed, I do not think that we can look to our previous case law involving mineral rights to determine whether Ark.Code Ann. § 18–11–102 *et seq.* may be used to quiet title in land that is subject to a contract for sale of merchantable timber. * * *

> It is disingenuous and counterintuitive in Arkansas to suggest that land or real property—especially in a wild and unimproved or unimproved and unenclosed state ... does not also connote growing timber. For adverse claimants to possess land with timber is reasonable. Appellee distinguishes appropriately 'mineral estates' and 'interests' and the necessity that they be opened to be adversely possessed in Arkansas. However, minerals are dormant assets of the land, beneath the surface estate. They are not wasted if left undisturbed and their true economic significance (for taxation purposes and otherwise) arises at severance. Further, unopened mineral estates rarely bind surface alienability or use. But control of the timber estate—in this case putatively for one hundred years—controls all practical surface usage and alienability of the land for a century. The timber resources, unlike unopened mineral estates, are visible, growing, and currently dominating the land's use and value. * * *

Arkansas Code Annotated § 18–11–102 *et seq.* allows a person to take possession of "unimproved and unenclosed land" or "wild and unimproved land" when he pays the "taxes thereon" for *at least* seven years. *Id.* We have defined "unimproved and unenclosed land" to mean land that is in a "state of nature," "wild," or "not cleared." Fenton v. Collum, 104 Ark. 624, 150 S.W. 140 (1912).

In summary, from our cases interpreting deeds of minerals, it is well established that an estate in perpetuity is created by a conveyance of minerals, and that this estate is independent of rights to ownership of the surface. For that reason, adverse possession of the surface does not impair the separate ownership of the mineral estate. That principle does not apply to the timber deed in this case because no leasehold or other interest in the land was ever created. * * * Provision of a limited time for cutting and removing the merchantable timber does not establish an estate in the land, and is subject to the provisions of Ark.Code Ann. § 18–11–102 *et seq.* whereby a clear title to the land is acquired by the payment of taxes for a period of seven or fifteen years. In order to avoid the operation of those statutory provisions, Mr. Carter had an opportunity to separately assess and pay property taxes upon his merchantable timber until he harvested his crop. This was not done. * * * The operation of these statutes clearly extinguishes any contractual right to enter upon the land to harvest merchantable timber purchased more than twenty years earlier. * * * Based on the language of Ark.Code Ann. § 18–11–102 *et seq.,* Ms. Bonds acquired possession to any timber Mr. Carter failed to remove during the running of the statutes. Accordingly, I would hold that the chancellor's statutory interpretation was clearly erroneous.

Notes and Questions

1. The elements of adverse possession are designed to put the true owner on notice of the hostile activity so that she may have an opportunity to take steps to vindicate her rights by legal action. Adverse possession of another's land must be both open and actual. Actual use requires the possessor to make some physical use or occupation of the land, just as the typical owner of similar property would. Qualifying activities may include clearing the land, erecting a fence, mowing the lawn, and constructing a building on the land. The nature and extent of the requisite use varies with the character of the land and the purposes for which the land is adapted. Why shouldn't Bond's payment of taxes for nearly 20 years do the trick? After all, Carter "slept on his rights" for a very long time.

2. The dissent noted that timber is quite distinct from minerals. In contrast, the majority opinion equated Carter's timber interest to a mineral interest because both are severable from the land and both are considered *profit a prendre.* Both involve a right to remove an item from the land and the owner of such rights does not profit until the right is exercised and the item removed. Accordingly, the court held that to adversely possess timber, Bonds, as the owner of the surface estate, must take actual possession of the timber for the statutory period. Are you convinced that this is the appropriate result?

3. Under the ruling in *Bonds,* is actual harvesting required to adversely possess timber lands? Or would it have been sufficient for Bond to erect a fence around the property? Note that in Pharis v. Jones, 122 Mo. 125, 26 S.W. 1032 (1894), the Missouri court held that payment of taxes, cutting timber, and driving off trespassers did not constitute actual possession of land, and in Vavoline Oil Co. v. Concordia Parish School Bd., 216 So.2d 702 (La.App. 1968), a school board that had executed mineral and timber leases for an uninhabited, swampy woodland was denied title, as there was no actual possession and no fences, surveyor's marks, or blazed trees.

4. Adverse possession cases tend to be highly fact specific, and you can probably find an equivalent number of cases that recognize adverse possession in forestlands as do not. *See* Theresa Leming, Bill Lindsley, and Eric Surette, Adverse Possession, 3 Am. Jur. 2d Adverse Possession §§ 36–37 (2004) (citing cases). In Herron v. Swarts, 350 P.2d 314 (Okla. 1960), title to remote, wild forestland was obtained by adverse possession where the proponent filed a resale tax deed, paid or attempted to pay ad valorem taxes, established boundary lines through a survey, and posted signs at the corners of land. The court concluded that, through these acts, the adverse possessor

had shown ownership by means customarily followed in the county. Similarly, in Peloke v. Scheid, 135 Misc.2d 606, 515 N.Y.S.2d 1000 (1987), title to a strip of land was obtained where possessors had an unrecorded deed and had enclosed the land by a rail fence and occupied it for over ten years, and in Backus v. Burke, 63 Minn. 272, 65 N.W. 459 (1895), title passed to the possessor of forestlands who built a shanty on the land, cut timber at various times preparatory to cultivation, and remained in possession off and on for the statutory period, since he occupied the land in the manner and for the purposes for which it was reasonably capable of being used. Are these cases distinguishable from *Bonds* and *Pharis, supra*? Or is it just that these jurisdictions are more lenient than Arkansas and Missouri in applying the elements of adverse possession to forestlands? What are the policy reasons for allowing title to pass through adverse possession in the first place? Which line of cases better promotes those policies?

5.   Generally speaking, title to forests or other lands owned by the federal or state governments cannot be acquired by adverse possession. *See* People v. Douglass, 217 A.D. 328, 216 N.Y.S. 785 (1926). "No title by adverse possession can be acquired except by statute against the sovereign, be it crown or national government or state. This is elementary law." United States v. Burrill, 107 Me. 382, 78 A. 568, 569 (1910). What's so special about governmental title that shields it from an adverse possession claim?

B.   State Forest Practices Acts and Private Land

The earliest laws governing forest practices in the United States can be traced back to British and Colonial provisions designed to protect lumber for the ship-building industry. The towering white pines of New England forests—up to six feet in diameter and 200 feet tall—were especially desirable for ships' masts. When Massachusetts received its charter from the Crown in 1691, it contained a clause that reserved " 'all [mast] trees of the diameter of twenty-four inches and upwards at twelve inches from the ground' " for the Royal Navy. William Cronon, CHANGES IN THE LAND: INDIANS, COLONISTS, AND THE ECOLOGY OF NEW ENGLAND 110 (1983). The harvest of pines was also restricted to ensure Naval supplies of turpentine, rosin, and pitch. Any person who cut or destroyed protected trees without a royal license was subject to a fine of £ 100, but enforcement was "impossible" and the "colonists violated the laws constantly." *Id.* at 111.[c]

Sustained interest in some form of state regulation of private forestland grew in reaction to excessive harvesting. In the absence of regulation, logging companies engaged in harvesting practices that were consistent with the prevailing myth that the United States was blessed with inexhaustible resources: resources were deemed unlimited in supply, and

---

c.   Ironically, loggers were not the chief threat to New England forests. Farmers who cleared the land to grow agricultural crops destroyed far more trees than did loggers. "Trees that required and maintained moist forest conditions, such as hickories, maples, ashes, and beeches, gen-erally produced a rich black humus beneath their fallen leaves, and settlers interpreted them as indicators of prime agricultural land." Cronon, *supra*, at 115. Of course, the trees generated and retained nutrients that contributed to soil fertility; once they were cleared, productivity dropped.

therefore clear-cutting without reforestation was appropriate. Europeans, accustomed to scarcity, viewed the improvident destruction of American forests with astonishment: "We can hardly be more hostile toward our woods in Sweden and Finland than they are here; their eyes are fixed upon the present gain, and they are blind to the future." Cronon, *supra*, at 122 (quoting Swedish Botanist Peter Kalm, 1749).

The fallacy of the "inexhaustible resource" assumption eventually became self-evident. Deforestation caused flooding, fuel shortages, loss of soil productivity, erosion, loss of wildlife, and other profound effects. By the end of the 19th century, the frontier had receded to the Pacific Ocean, and the population began to recognize the physical limitations of finite resources like timber and to call for government action to check the abuses of past harvesting techniques. The states' initial reaction was to adopt incentives for tree-planting and tax breaks for leaving trees in place. Nebraska established "Arbor Day" in 1872 to promote awareness of the importance of tree planting to prevent erosion of farmland. Prizes were offered for planting the largest number of trees, and it is estimated that more than one million trees were planted in Nebraska on the first Arbor Day. Many other states have since followed suit, and Arbor Day is commonly celebrated each year on the last Friday in April. The National Arbor Day Foundation, *The History of Arbor Day*, http://www.arborday.org/arborday/history.cfm. Other countries have joined in the tree-planting movement as well.

Global Perspective:

The Greenbelt Movement

In 2004, Kenyan environmental activist Wangari Maathai became the first African woman to win the Nobel Peace Prize. The former biology professor left her academic career to pursue environmental projects and campaign for women's rights. Matthai founded The Green Belt Movement in 1977. The Movement has been credited with planting over 30 million trees, and several other countries have adopted methods to stave off deforestation. The Nobel committee lauded Matthai's "contribution to sustainable development, democracy and peace." Kenyan Activist Wins Nobel Prize for Peace, All Things Considered, National Public Radio, Oct. 8, 2004, http://www.npr.org/templates/story/story.php?storyId=4077230.

Photo reprinted with permission from the Greenbelt Photo Gallery Archives, http://www.greenbeltmovement.org/ (visited Dec. 10, 2004).

1. Fire, Infestation, and Disease Prevention

Some of the earliest compulsory state laws governing activities on private timber lands relate to fire, insect, and disease suppression. Landowners, in particular, have been singled out by state laws on fire prevention and fire-fighting. To prevent the spread of fire, Montana, for example, provides that a landowner's failure to remove slash or waste debris may result in an injunction from further development or timber cutting. Mont. St. § 76–13–410. Some states make landowners liable for the costs of fire-fighting. In Idaho, a person may be liable for up to five years after a fire has passed through lands that were not free of slash. The limits of liability are set by the state forester, but are assumed to be the costs of the suppression of the fire. I.C. § 38–122; Chambers v. McCollum, 47 Idaho 74, 272 P. 707 (1928). In Washington, a similar statute imposes the "reasonable costs" of suppressing fire on the landowner, as well as investigative and court costs. RCWA 76.04.495. *See* State v. Anacortes Veneer, Inc., 57 Wash.2d 886, 360 P.2d 341 (1961) (timberland owners, under debris removal statute, could be held jointly and severally liable for firefighting costs made necessary by their failure to abate a slash hazard created by logging operations, even if the most practical way of eliminating the slash was by burning, which was unlawful at the time of the fire).

Some states provide special protection for watersheds, particularly those used by a city as a water supply. Landowners may be required to remove waste debris in order to prevent the spread of fire and consequent damage to the watershed. Failure to do so in North Carolina results in a class two misdemeanor. N.C.G.S.A. § 14–383.

Oregon has imposed levies on forestland owners to help fund a fire patrol, *see* Starker v. Scott, 183 Or. 10, 190 P.2d 532 (1948) (citing Or. Rev. Stat. § 477.076–.080), and to create a fund to equalize fire suppression costs in certain high-risk fire protection districts. Sproul v. State Tax Comm'n, 234 Or. 579, 383 P.2d 754 (1963) (citing Or. Rev. Stat. §§ 321.005(6), 477.001–.970). Both provisions have been upheld as a valid exercise of police power. *Id.;* First State Bank v. Kendall Lumber Co., 107 Or. 1, 213 P. 142 (1923). In *Sproul*, the court found that the legislative determination that the danger of forest fires in the east was much higher than in the west justified the requirement and did not violate a state constitutional requirement of uniformity in taxation. *Id.* Oregon statutes currently provide that the state forester shall issue a notice to owners of forestlands susceptible to damage by fire in forest districts west of the Cascade Mountains, and prohibit the use of power-driven machinery on such lands. Or. Rev. Stat. § 477.670.

The courts have generally concluded that fire prevention and suppression statutes are a valid exercise of the police power, and do not deny the landowner of due process. *See* United States v. Alford, 274 U.S. 264, 47 S.Ct. 597, 71 L.Ed. 1040 (1927); State v. Canyon Lumber Corp., 46 Wash.2d 701, 284 P.2d 316 (1955) (statute imposing liability on landowners for fire-fighting costs incurred due to landowners' failure to remove slash was upheld); Chambers v. McCollum, 47 Idaho 74, 272 P. 707 (1928) (provisions permitting state forester to charge landowner with actual costs of fire protection and prohibiting the landowner from setting fires during summer season without permission did not effectuate a taking of property without due process).

Persons who cause fires on federal, state, or private forestlands may be liable for damages resulting from the fire under common law or statute. Oregon law provides that, "In addition to the penalties otherwise provided by law, ... owners whose property is injured or destroyed by fires ... may recover in a civil action double the amount of damages suffered if the fires occurred through willfulness, malice or negligence. Persons causing fires by violation of any of the provisions of the statutes enumerated in this section are liable in an appropriate action for the full amount of all expenses incurred in fighting such fires." Or. Rev. Stat. § 477.090. A necessity defense may be available to landowners who set fire to woods to protect human welfare or property. In Tyson v. Rasberry, 8 N.C. 60 (1820), a North Carolina court held that one who set fire to save his tar kiln from an approaching wildfire could not be penalized under state law, but could only be liable for damages actually sustained by others.

State foresters have police powers to destroy trees on privately owned land if necessary to stop the spread of disease or insect infestation. In Miller v. Schoene, 276 U.S. 272, 48 S.Ct. 246, 72 L.Ed. 568 (1928), a Virginia state entomologist ordered the claimants to cut down their ornamental red cedar trees because they produced cedar rust that was fatal to nearby apple trees. Although the statute provided for recovery of expenses incurred in removing the cedars and permitted claimants to use the felled trees, it did not provide compensation for the value of the trees or for the resulting decrease in market value of the properties as a whole. The Supreme Court held that this omission did not render the statute invalid. According to the Court, since the apple industry was important in the state involved, the state had not exceeded "its constitutional powers by deciding upon the destruction of one class of property [without compensation] in order to save another which, in the judgment of the legislature, is of greater value to the public." *Id.* at 279. *See also* Burroughs v. Rane, 241 Mass. 1, 134 N.E. 361 (1922) (finding authority to prevent the spread of gypsy moths as public nuisances); Brady v. State, 965 P.2d 1 (Alaska 1998) (upholding the state's authority to respond to a beetle epidemic free of tort or constitutional liability).

2. *Provisions for Sustainable Harvest*

The first major wave of state regulatory statutes protective of the timber itself was passed between 1937 and 1955. These "Forest Practices Acts" were fairly narrow in scope, and usually expressed a primary goal of ensuring future productivity through reforestation of land harvested for timber. Mississippi's statute, enacted in 1944 and still on the books today, is typical:

It is hereby recognized that only a small proportion of the privately owned forestland in the State of Mississippi is now managed in accordance with sound forestry practices; that there is waste, inefficiency and wanton destruction of the forestlands in the harvesting of forest products and the utilization of forestlands; that such conditions are resulting in serious economic and social loss and ... that state regulation of harvesting of forest products and the utilization of forestlands in the state is essential to promote health, safety and general welfare of the people of the state. It is, therefore, declared to be the public policy of the State ... to encourage better management of forestlands; to increase the efficiency in the harvesting of forest products and utilization of forestlands; to preserve the tax base represented by forests and forestlands; to preserve and develop forestlands for the equal and guaranteed use for future generations; to preserve and protect the forest resources and the continuous growth of timber on lands suitable therefor; to insure an adequate supply of forest products at all times; to prevent soil erosion and consequent silting of stream channels and reservoirs; to protect watersheds and reservoirs and to insure at all times an adequate supply of water of the forest quality; to preserve and insure for all times adequate habitats for wild life; to preserve scenic beauty and to insure adequate facilities for outdoor recreation for public use; and to reduce forest fire hazards and encourage private ownership, economic management and scientific development of forestlands.

Miss. Code Ann. § 49–19–53.

By the 1970s, states had begun to enact more broad-sweeping Forest Practices Acts to regulate timber harvest on private lands. Over a dozen states have adopted modern Forest Practices Acts, with the most comprehensive regulatory schemes found in states that possess large amounts of private forestland, such as Alaska, California, Idaho, Oregon and Massachusetts. Most acts authorize civil and criminal penalties for noncompliance, but many encourage informal, negotiated resolution of violations rather than prosecution. *See* Thomas Lundmark, *Methods of Forest Law-making*, 22 B.C. Envtl. Aff. L. Rev. 783, 792 (1995).

Like the Mississippi statute, many of these statutes refer to the forests' value as habitat for wild life and for scenic beauty and outdoor recreation, but few promote those objectives in any substantive fashion. State regulations tend to be stricter in western states, as compared to Southern states, which have generally given free rein to logging on private lands. *See* Northwest Ecosystem Alliance v. Washington Department of Ecology, 104 Wash.App. 901, 905, 17 P.3d 697, 700 (2001) (describing Forest Practices Act as a statewide system of law designed to manage and protect natural resources and ensure a viable timber industry, citing Wash. Rev. Code § 76.09.010(1)), *rev'd in part on other grounds,* 149 Wash.2d 67, 66 P.3d 614 (2003)). *See generally* Lundmark, *supra* at 792–93 (describing Forest Practices Acts).

Forest Practices Acts reach practices on both public and private forestlands. Removal of small amounts of timber from small lots, however, may be excluded from coverage. *See* Wash. Rev. Code § 76.09.020(9)(a) (providing an exception for harvest on residential home sites smaller than five acres). Such exclusions will not protect a logger who engages in large-scale removal of trees. Department of Natural Resources v. Marr, 54 Wash.App. 589, 595, 774 P.2d 1260, 1264 (1989) (enjoining harvest where the logger had removed over 326,000 board feet of timber from 9–10 residential lots; the lands were considered "forestlands" covered by the statute as they were suitable in size and quality for the profitable production of forest products).

Most Forest Practices Acts require that certain types of trees be spared for forest regeneration purposes. They may prescribe minimum cutting diameters or a minimum number of seed trees to be left per acre. To ensure that reforestation occurs, states may authorize performance bonds to guarantee restocking as well as state inspection of areas being harvested. Washington, for example, strengthened reforestation obligations by requiring successful regeneration of a new stand of trees within three years of completion of a logging operation. A post-harvest report must be submitted, and the state Department of Natural Resources must inspect the area and make a determination either that reforestation has been properly completed or, conversely, that further reforestation is necessary. Wash. Rev. Code § 76.09.070. Reforestation is not required when lands are converted to a non-forest use after logging occurs. *Id.*

In states that require regeneration, the variety of tree to be replanted is usually left to the landowner's discretion. In Washington, the landowner may plant a species other than that which was removed if the reforestation plan shows that the proposed species is preferable from the standpoint of economic returns or other reasons. Wash. Admin. Code § 222–34–010. California is a notable exception, in that its administrative code provides specific parameters on types of trees that must be replanted. 14 Cal. Admin. Code § 912.7–.9.

Harvest and regeneration requirements may be enforced by a state forester or the State Department of Natural Resources. Some states have established state Forestry Boards, which promulgate regulations and hear appeals from regulatory enforcement actions. The regulations provide more detailed specifications to ensure that the statutory goals and requirements are met.

3. *Environmental Protection and Planning*

Some Forest Practices Acts include explicit provisions related to environmental protection. These include preventing soil erosion, preserving watersheds and water supply, and assisting in flood control. The Oregon Forest Practices Act is one of the most protective state forest practices acts in the nation. It seeks to encourage economically efficient practices that ensure "continuous growing and harvesting of forest tree species... consistent with sound management of soil, air, water, fish and wildlife resources." Or. Rev. Stat. S 527.630 (1995). *See* Michael C. Blumm and Jonathan Lovvorn, *The Proposed Transfer of BLM Timber Lands to the State of Oregon: Environmental and Economic Questions*, 32 Land and Water Law Rev. 353, 402 (1997).

In some states, a permit or license must be secured from the state forester before harvesting can take place. In addition, logging operations on privately owned timberlands cannot begin without submission and state approval of a timber harvest plan. Sierra Club v. Board of Forestry, 7 Cal.4th 1215, 32 Cal.Rptr.2d 19, 876 P.2d 505 (1994).

Many states have also passed environmental protection statutes modeled after NEPA. *See* Chapter 4, VIII, *supra*. These laws require environmental review of projects proposed or approved by the state which may affect the environment. Typically, a state forester's approval of a timber harvesting plan triggers a need for an environmental impact review, either under the Forest Practices Act or the state NEPA. *See* Californians for Native Salmon and Steelhead Ass'n v. California Dept. of Forestry, 221 Cal.App.3d 1419, 271 Cal.Rptr. 270 (1990) (environmental impact review must be included in each timber harvesting plan); Friends of the Wild Swan v. DNRC, 301 Mont. 1, 6 P.3d 972 (2000) (failure to adequately analyze cumulative impacts of a proposed timber sale violated the Montana Environmental Policy Act).

Clearcutting as a method of harvest is a matter of special attention in many state statutes. Several states restrict or forbid clearcutting on private lands. For example, California's regulations provide that clearcuts should be irregularly shaped and variable in size so as to blend with the natural patterns and features of the landscape, 14 Cal. Admin. Code §§ 913.1, 933.1, and 953.1. Clearcutting is completely prohibited near San Francisco. *See* Lundmark, *supra*, at 794–95. In Massachusetts, clearcuts larger than 25 acres are restricted. 304 Mass. ADC § 11.04(f)(1). A Pennsylvania township's zoning ordinance prohibits clearcutting on tracts larger than two acres and on slopes greater than 15%. Williams Township Zoning Ordinance § 1402.A.19. The state court upheld the ordinance in the face of a landowner's challenge, holding that it had a substantial relationship to the public welfare, as it was crafted to prevent erosion in accordance with the findings of a credible engineering study and did not unduly restrict forestry. Chrin Brothers, Inc. v. Williams Township Zoning Hearing Board, 815 A.2d 1179, 1186 (Pa. 2003).

Aesthetic values are prioritized in some states' forestry legislation, especially near populated areas. Lundmark, *supra*, at 796. In the Marin County Recreation Corridor, near San Francisco, special restrictions apply to any logging operation visible from any nearby public road, public trail, or residence, and all trees must be individually selected for harvest to minimize visual effects. 14 Cal. Code Regs. § 927.13 (1995). In New Hampshire, no more than fifty percent of trees within 150 feet of a public highway may be cut. N.H. Rev. Stat. § 224:44–a (Supp. 1994).

Massachusetts requires trees to be left along the edges of public roads as a "buffer strip" to improve visual quality and to protect public safety by serving as a windbreak and minimizing snow drifts on the road. 304 Mass. Regs. Code § 11.04–.05.

Preventing soil erosion is also addressed by state forestry legislation. Loggers may be required to leave vegetation intact along streams and other waterbodies. Lundmark, *supra*, at 796. Prohibitions against leaving slash in streams are fairly typical. *Id.* (*citing* N.H. Rev. Stat. Ann. § 224:44–b (Supp. 1994)). Statutory provisions may also regulate the number and placement of roads. California law requires that roads crossing over streams be fitted with culverts, 14 Cal. Code Regs. § 923 (1995), while Oregon requires logging roads to follow natural contours, Oregon Dep't of Forestry—Forest Practice Water Protection Rules § 629–24–521 (1994).

State regulation of the environmental impacts of private timber harvesting is encouraged by two federal statutes. Under the Cooperative Forestry Assistance Act of 1978, 16 U.S.C. § 2101, federal funds are made available for federal-state cooperative forestry activities that promote environmental quality. Under sections 208 and 319 of the Clean Water Act, states are to develop area-wide and statewide water quality management plans that address the effects of water pollution from nonpoint sources, such as runoff from timber harvesting activities. 33 U.S.C. §§ 1288, 1329. *See* Section II.C, below, for details on water quality requirements.

The remainder of this section will focus on the California Forest Practices Act to illustrate the application of silvicultural requirements on private lands. Although California is touted as having the strictest statutory provisions for timber harvesting on private lands, it is also criticized because "the regulations that implement that scheme fail to provide adequate guidance to assure the restoration, enhancement, maintenance, and sustainability of high quality timber products and overall environmental protection." Sharon E. Duggan, *Citizen Enforcement of California's Private Land Forest Practice, Regulations*, 8 J. ENVTL. L. & LITIG. 291, 291 (1994).

> Few issues in California have been more controversial ... than the damage to the state's environment from logging. The almost complete disappearance of the primeval old-growth redwood forests that once blanketed the north coast of California has been the focal point for much of the debate. Since the redwood forests have for the most part remained in private hands, they are subject to regulation by the state of California. And the fate of the redwoods has brought several waves of litigation, ballot initiatives, new regulations and numerous public acquisitions, all designed to preserve these forests from commercial logging.

Thomas N. Lippe and Kathy Bailey, *Regulation of Logging on Private Land in California under Governor Gray Davis,* 31 Golden Gate U. L.

REV. 351, 352 (2001). The Headwaters Forest case study, provided in Section II.D, provides a dramatic example of the controversy that continues to rage over timber harvesting in California.

Before 1973, California had a Forest Practices Act that permitted the timber industry to write its own rules. Demand for timber was high, and regulation was virtually non-existent. As a result, resource depletion and environmental destruction ran rampant. That Forest Practices Act was eventually challenged for allowing "the rules under which private logging operations are conducted [to be] decreed exclusively by persons pecuniarily interested in the timber industry, i.e., timber owners and operators." Bayside Timber Co. v. Board of Supervisors, 20 Cal.App.3d 1, 9, 97 Cal.Rptr. 431, 436 (1971). The court determined that the statutory system was an unconstitutional delegation of legislative power, which denied due process to the interested public. *Id.* at 439–40. In 1973, the legislature enacted the Z'berg-Nejedly Forest Practices Act (FPA) to cure the constitutional deficiencies identified in *Bayside* and to provide a comprehensive system of sustainable forestry and environmental protection. Duggan, *supra*, at 291–92.

The FPA requires timberland management to assure "maximum sustained production of high quality timber products." Cal.Pub.Res.Code § 4513(b) (West 1984 & Supp.1993). Under the FPA, logging on private land is regulated by two California state agencies, the California Department of Forestry and Fire Protection (CDF) and the Board of Forestry. Cal. Pub. Res. Code § 4511 et. seq. (West 1984). Commercial logging may occur only if CDF approves a timber harvest plan. The Board of Forestry is required to adopt regulations governing the conduct of timber operations and the criteria for CDF's approval of timber harvest plans. Although plan approval might otherwise trigger the preparation of an environmental impact report under the California Environmental Quality Act (CEQA), Cal. Pub. Res. Code § 21000 (West 1996), the approval process is considered a "functionally equivalent" regulatory program which obviates the need for a separate impact report.

The CDF must evaluate the plan for conformance with the FPA and the Board's regulations. Cal.Pub.Res.Code § 4582.7. The CDF will deny approval if the information provided in the plan "is incorrect, incomplete, misleading in a material way, or is insufficient to evaluate significant environmental effects." 14 Cal.Code Regs. § 898.2(c) (1991).

A few years after passage of the FPA, the California Legislature adopted the Timberland Productivity Act of 1976, which established a "timberland production zone" (TPZ) program "to encourage prudent forest management, to protect the public's need for timber, and to protect against encroaching development." Cal. Gov't Code §§ 51100–51150 (West 1983 & Supp.1993). The Act directs local governments to categorize certain lands as TPZs, where uses are restricted to activities that are compatible with timber production. A "compatible use" is "any use which does not significantly detract from ... or inhibit [the] growing and harvesting of timber, and shall include but not be limited to ... management of watershed, and fish and wildlife habitat ... unless in a specific instance such use would be contrary to the preceding definition of compatible use." Cal. Gov't Code § 51110 (West 1983 & Supp.1993); Cal.Pub. Res.Code § 51104. Accordingly, management of a TPZ for watershed and habitat purposes is appropriate unless it would "significantly detract" from using the property to grow and harvest trees. Duggan, *supra*, at 299–300. The landowner receives tax benefits from the TPZ designation. Cal. Gov't Code § 51115.1.

The Timberland Productivity Act does not alter any substantive or procedural requirement of the FPA or its implementing regulations. Clinton v. County of Santa Cruz, 119 Cal.App.3d 927, 174 Cal.Rptr. 296, 299 n.7 (1981). If conducted according to the requirements of the FPA, timber harvesting within a TPZ generally will not be considered a nuisance. Cal.Pub.Res.Code § 4514. Conversely, operations that fail to comply with the FPA may constitute a nuisance per se, and the statute provides that, "There is nothing to prevent a claim of nuisance if the timber harvest operations endanger the public or prohibit free access to waterways, parks, and roadways." Cal. Gov't Code § 51115.5(b).

Forest plans may not violate water quality standards. FPA § 4582.71 provides, "A timber harvesting plan may not be approved if the ... timber operations proposed in the plan will result in a discharge into a watercourse that has been classified as impaired due to sediment pursuant to subsection (d) of Section 303 of the Federal Water Pollution Control Act...." *See* Section II.C, below.

The FPA provides for public participation on proposed plans through its notice provisions and opportunity for written comments. It authorizes "any person" with a right of action to challenge CDF's approval of a timber harvest plan. Cal.Pub.Res.Code § 4514.5. Once the challengers have exhausted all available administrative remedies, they may seek a writ of mandamus. Cal.Civ.Proc.Code §§ 1084–1097. They must show that the CDF has abused its discretion by failing to proceed in a manner required by law or by issuing a decision that is not supported by substantial evidence. Cal.Pub.Res.Code § 21168.

Citizens' groups have focused their efforts on the need to consider the cumulative effects of harvesting under the FPA, particularly in evaluating and mitigating the effects of harvesting on fisheries, watersheds, and old growth forests, as well as on the FPA's requirements for sustained yield. *See, e.g.*, Environmental Protection Info. Ctr. v. Johnson, 170 Cal.App.3d 604, 216 Cal.Rptr. 502 (1985); Natural Resources Defense Council, Inc. v. Arcata National Corp., 59 Cal.App.3d 959, 131 Cal.Rptr. 172 (1976). In Laupheimer v. State, 200 Cal.App.3d 440, 246 Cal.Rptr. 82 (1988), the court explained:

> We agree ... that in the timber harvesting plan review process Forestry must consider all significant environmental impacts of a proposed timber harvesting plan, regardless whether those impacts may be expected to fall on or off the logging site, and regardless

whether those impacts would be attributable solely to activities described in the timber harvesting plan or to those activities in combination with other circumstances including but not necessarily limited to other past, present, and reasonable expectable future activities in the relevant area.

Id. at 93.

Pertinent provisions of the FPA and its implementing regulations are provided below in Section II.D, along with a case study that will allow you to apply the FPA's requirements to a logging proposal in the Headwaters Forest.

C.   Timber Harvest and Water Quality

Many states address water quality impacts from silvicultural practices through their Forest Practices Acts. Requirements that loggers use "best management practices" to prevent polluted run-off are common. California's law is among the most stringent. Cal. Pub. Res. Code §§ 4514.3 (requiring best management practices and additional measures necessary to achieve desired levels of water quality), 4594(h) (directing non-industrial timber owners to certify that harvesting operations will implement best management practices to protect "beneficial uses of water, soil stability, forest productivity, and wildlife").

Federal law restricts activities that impact water quality as well. The federal Clean Water Act is aimed at restoring and maintaining the "chemical, physical, and biological integrity of the Nation's waters." 33 U.S.C. § 1251(a). To accomplish this goal, the Act prohibits the discharge of pollutants into navigable waters of the United States from point sources, absent a permit. 33 U.S.C. §§ 1311(a), 1362(12). Both "pollutant" and "navigable waters" are defined broadly. Pollutants include noxious materials, like garbage, chemical wastes, and munitions, as well as rock, dredged spoil, and biological materials. 33 U.S.C. § 1362(6). "Navigable waters" include all "waters of the United States," *id.* § 1362(7), which has been construed to cover streams, rivers, and lakes, even if they are dry part of the year, and adjacent wetlands. *See* 33 C.F.R. § 328.3(a)(7); United States v. Riverside Bayview Homes, Inc., 474 U.S. 121, 106 S.Ct. 455, 88 L.Ed.2d 419 (1985) (upholding authority to regulate adjacent wetlands); Solid Waste Agency of Northern Cook County v. U.S. Army Corps of Engineers, 531 U.S. 159, 121 S.Ct. 675, 148 L.Ed.2d 576 (2001) (Corps' rule extending definition to include intrastate waters used by migratory birds was invalid).

Pipes, ditches, and culverts are point sources that require a permit under 33 U.S.C. § 1311(a). The Act, however, provides an exception for "the discharge of dredged or fill material ... from normal farming, silviculture, and ranching activities," which generally do not require a permit. 33 U.S.C. § 1344(f)(1). This is not a blanket exemption; a "recapture" provision requires permits for these activities if they are designed to bring an area of navigable waters into a new use. *Id.* In Borden Ranch Partnership v. U.S. Army Corps of Engineers, 261 F.3d 810 (9th Cir. 2001), *aff'd*, 537 U.S. 99, 123 S.Ct. 599, 154 L.Ed.2d 508 (2002), a permit was required for the "deep ripping" of wetlands with tractors that pulled metal prongs through soil to drain and convert ranch land to vineyards, as it subjected the property to a new use. Similarly, a property owner's clearing of timber to permanently change wetlands into an agricultural tract for row crop cultivation requires a permit. United States v. Larkins, 852 F.2d 189 (6th Cir. 1988), *cert. denied*, 489 U.S. 1016, 109 S.Ct. 1131, 103 L.Ed.2d 193 (1989). The Clean Water Act's requirements were applied to Pacific Lumber Company in the following case.

ENVIRONMENTAL PROTECTION INFORMATION CENTER v. PACIFIC LUMBER CO.

United States District Court, Northern District of California, 2004.
301 F.Supp.2d 1102.

On July 24, 2001, plaintiff Environmental Protection Information Center (EPIC), a non-profit environmental organization, brought a citizen-suit action under section 505(a) of the Clean Water Act (CWA), 33 U.S.C. § 1365(a), against Pacific Lumber Company and Scotia Pacific Lumber Company (collectively "PALCO") [and] the Environmental Protection Agency (EPA) * * *

At the heart of this litigation is Bear Creek, a brook situated several miles upstream of Scotia, California. A tributary of the Eel River, Bear Creek creates a watershed that covers 5500 acres of land throughout Humboldt County, California. Pacific Lumber Company and its wholly owned subsidiary, defendant Scotia Pacific Lumber Company, own some ninety-five percent of the land in the Bear Creek watershed, much of which PALCO uses for logging. * * *

According to EPIC, substantial logging activity in the watershed area—primarily that performed by PALCO—has spurred a dramatic increase in the amount of sediment deposited into Bear Creek. Before significant logging began, EPIC claims, Bear Creek's sediment deposit peaked at approximately 8,000 tons per year; after logging practices commenced, sediment deposit climbed to 27,000 tons per year. This sediment increase, EPIC alleges, has a specific source: PALCO's timber harvesting and construction of unpaved roads. According to EPIC, PALCO's logging activity creates a deleterious environmental process. First, EPIC notes, timber harvesting removes vegetation from the ground surface, making soil more susceptible to erosion and landslides; construction of unpaved roads then exposes more soil, which, in turn, further destabilizes slopes. The effect of timber harvesting and road construction, EPIC contends, is to expose far more destabilized soil than is environmentally sustainable. When it rains, EPIC explains, the rain water carries the exposed silts and sediments—as well as other pollutants, like pesticides and diesel fuel—into culverts, ditches, erosion gullies, and other alleged channels. From these various water channels, silts, sediments, and pollutants flow directly into Bear Creek.

According to an April 1998 study conducted by PALCO consultants, sediments and pollutants pile into Bear Creek and its tributaries at no fewer than 179 specific watershed points. Among other channels, pollutant-laden water flows through 156 hillside culverts and 5.5 miles of roadside ditches, all of which drain directly into stream-crossing culverts. The consequences of this system, EPIC contends, are predictable and environmentally adverse: Beneficial uses of Bear Creek are substantially diminished; e.g., fish are significantly less able—if able at all—to use the creek as a nesting and rearing habitat. Worse still, EPIC adds, PALCO's present and future timber harvest plans promise the construction of additional roads and the digging of additional culverts, all of which could increase the amount of sediment, silt, and other pollutants deposited into Bear Creek. PALCO neither holds nor has applied for any relevant permits for these sites, sites EPIC contends should be regulated as "point sources" under the CWA. * * *

* * * Built on a "fundamental premise" that the unauthorized "discharge of any pollutant by any person shall be unlawful," Natural Resources Defense Council ("NRDC") v. EPA, 822 F.2d 104, 109 (D.C.Cir.1987) (citing 33 U.S.C. § 1311(a)), the CWA "establishes a comprehensive statutory system for controlling water pollution." * * * This broad statutory scheme includes, inter alia, a National Pollutant Discharge Elimination System ("NPDES") for regulation of pollutant discharges into the waters of the United States. See 33 U.S.C. § § 1311(a), 1342(a). Under the NPDES, permits may be issued by EPA or by States that have been authorized by EPA to act as NPDES permitting authorities. * * * California has been so authorized. * * *

Not all pollutants or pollution sources fall under the purview of the NPDES. Under the CWA, "discharge of pollutant" is defined as "any addition of any pollutant to navigable waters from any point source." 33 U.S.C. § 1362(12)(A) (emphasis added). The CWA's and NPDES's focus, then, trains largely on pollutant discharges from "point sources," a term the Act defines as:

> any discernible, confined and discrete conveyance, including but not limited to any pipe, ditch, channel, tunnel, conduit, well, discrete fissure, container, rolling stock, concentrated animal feeding operation, or vessel or other floating craft, from which pollutants are or may be discharged. This term does not include agricultural stormwater discharges and return flows from irrigated agriculture.

Id., at § 1362(14) * * *

The CWA distinguishes "point sources" from "nonpoint sources." The NPDES recognizes—and functions on the basis of—this distinction, requiring permits only for such "point source" emissions. Unlike "point sources," "nonpoint sources" are regulated indirectly: The CWA directs EPA to disseminate information regarding nonpoint pollution sources, see 33 U.S.C. § 1314(f), but it is often through state management programs that "nonpoint sources" are monitored and controlled. * * *

A. Regulation of Silvicultural Sources and Activities

Following the passage of the CWA, EPA promulgated regulations that exempted certain categories of discharges—namely "[u]ncontrolled discharges composed entirely of storm runoff" and some "[d]ischarges of pollutants from agricultural and silvicultural activities"—from NPDES permit requirements. See 40 C.F.R. § 125.4 (1973). Close to twenty years ago, these silviculture-related regulations spurred a round of litigation in federal court, as NRDC challenged the exemptions in the United States District Court for the District of Columbia. See NRDC v. Train, 396 F.Supp. 1393, 1395 (D.D.C.1975), aff'd sub nom., NRDC v. Costle, 568 F.2d 1369 (D.C.Cir.1977). As NRDC read the CWA, EPA did not have the authority to exempt entire categories of point sources from CWA regulation. *Id.* The district court agreed, invalidating the regulation. *Id.* at 1396.

In response to this 1975 court decision, EPA promulgated a new silvicultural-source regulation in 1976. * * * Originally codified as 40 C.F.R. section 124.85, the 1976 iteration of the regulation defined the term "silvicultural point source" in a brief comment, offering counter-examples of nonpoint sources:

> [Silvicultural point source] does not include nonpoint source activities inherent to forest management such as nursery operations, site preparation, reforestation and subsequent cultural treatment, thinning, prescribed burning, pest and fire control, harvesting operations, surface drainage, and road construction and maintenance from which runoff results from precipitation events.

Id.

The current regulation governing silvicultural point sources is identical to the [earlier] version[s]. In significant part, the current regulation defines a "[s]ilvicultural point source" as:

> any discernible, confined, and discrete conveyance related to rock crushing, gravel washing, log sorting, or log storage facilities which are operated in connection with silvicultural activities and from which pollutants are discharged into waters of the United States. The term does not include non-point source silvicultural activities such as nursery operations, site preparation, reforestation and subsequent cultural treatment, thinning, prescribed burning, pest and fire control, harvesting operations, surface drainage, or road construction and maintenance from which there is natural runoff.

40 C.F.R. § 122.27(b)(1) (emphasis added). * * *

B. 1987 Amendments on Municipal and Industrial Stormwater Discharges

In 1987, Congress amended the CWA to include a section on municipal and industrial stormwater discharges. * * * Among other things, this provision—popularly labeled "section 402"—mandates that permits be obtained for stormwater discharges "associated with industrial activity," for stormwater discharges from municipal storm sewer systems, and for stormwater discharges that contribute to water quality violations or are otherwise "significant contributor[s] of pollutants." 33 U.S.C. § 1342(p)(2). In addition, subsection (6) of section 402(p) requires the EPA to designate other sources of stormwater pollution and, in turn, to "establish a comprehensive program to regulate" these discharges. *Id.* at § 1342(p)(6).

For the discharges identified in section 402(p)(2), EPA has issued two batches of regulations. See 55 Fed.Reg. 47,990 (Nov. 16, 1990); 64 Fed.Reg. 68,722 (Dec. 8, 1999). * * * The first set, issued in 1990 [is] often referred to as the "Phase I" regulations * * * The second set, issued in 1999 and generally labeled the "Phase II" regulations, reached the remaining sources in section 402(p)(6).

DISCUSSION

The basic premise of PALCO's motion to dismiss is that, however defined, the pollution sources identified in EPIC's first and second claims do not require NPDES permits. If the sources are "non-point sources," PALCO contends, the sources fall outside the scope of the NPDES by definition; if, by contrast, the sources are "point sources," the sources are nevertheless a type of discharge sources the CWA and EPA have excluded from NPDES permitting mandates. Either way, PALCO concludes, PALCO's decision not to secure permits for Bear Creek discharge sources is legally sustainable. And either way, EPIC's remaining claims fail to state a ground on which relief can be granted.

PALCO's motion seems, at first blush, to depend on a misreading of EPIC's two remaining claims. In pertinent part, EPIC's complaint alleges that PALCO has violated—and continues to violate—various provisions of the CWA through its unlawful discharge of pollutants into Bear Creek. * * * 33 U.S.C. § § 1311(a), 1342. Far from failing to state a facially tenable legal claim under the CWA, EPIC's complaint contends that PALCO, on its Bear Creek site, uses a myriad of unpermitted (and, thus, unlawful) culverts, drainage ditches, and other "point source"-like conduits to discharge stormwater and pollutants. The CWA proscribes precisely this kind of conduct; under the terms of the CWA, then, EPIC's complaint would seem to overcome the Rule 12(b)(6) hurdle without more. * * *

But as PALCO reads the pertinent law, the CWA sections supposedly informing EPIC's complaint actually preclude legal remedy. Section 402(p) of the CWA, PALCO contends, places discharges of the type EPIC targets outside the ambit of the NPDES and exempts such sources from the otherwise applicable CWA permit requirements. No matter how EPIC posits its claims, PALCO concludes, section 402(p) allows precisely the kind of non-permitted discharging PALCO purports to perform; since the discharges are composed of "stormwater," and since the discharges are not "industrial" or "municipal" in nature, the NPDES simply does not, as PALCO understands it, control.

* * * Titled "Municipal and industrial stormwater discharges," section 402(p) provides:

(1) General rule

Prior to October 1, 1994, the Administrator or the State ... shall not require a permit under this section for discharges composed entirely of stormwater.

(2) Exceptions

Paragraph (1) shall not apply with respect to the following stormwater discharges:

(A) A discharge with respect to which a permit has been issued under this section before February 4, 1987.

(B) A discharge associated with industrial activity.

(C) A discharge from a municipal separate storm sewer system serving a population of 250,000 or more.

See 33 U.S.C. § 1342(p). As PALCO reads it, section 402(p) requires permits only for particular kinds of stormwater discharge sources—e.g., sources related to "industrial" or particular "municipal" activity—none of which apply here. * * *

Section 402(p) does, as PALCO suggests, assign permitting obligations to a select subset of potential stormwater-discharge sources. *Id.* (targeting a particular type of municipal and industrial sources). But section 402(p) does not, as PALCO implies, apply to all pollution sources in the first instance. As the language of the CWA and Ninth Circuit caselaw make clear, section 402(p) is not the only CWA section imposing duties and obligations on pollution dischargers; both section 301(a) and 402(a), for example, posit pollution-related mandates on putative polluters, including that these polluters obtain NPDES permits for "point source" pollutant discharges. See, e.g., 33 U.S.C. § 1342(a); *id.* at § 1311. As the language of the statute and the Ninth Circuit caselaw also make clear, two threshold inquiries govern the applicability of section 402(p): one, whether the relevant discharges are "*composed entirely of stormwater*," see 33 U.S.C. § 1342(p) (emphasis added); and, two, whether the relevant discharges are "currently [and properly] unregulated." * * * Indeed, neither of section 402(p)'s threshold requirements are satisfied here.

To begin, PALCO errs to suggest that EPIC's complaint targets discharges "*composed entirely of stormwater.*" 33 U.S.C. § 1342(p) (emphasis added) ... In relevant part, EPIC's complaint alleges that PALCO's Bear Creek drainage system utilizes a number of "point sources"—whether culverts, drainage ditches, other conduits to discharge—to redirect stormwater and pollutants (i.e., something not "composed entirely of stormwater") into Bear Creek. Nowhere does EPIC claim that the discharges consist "entirely" and exclusively of stormwater. On its face, then, EPIC's complaint does not satisfy the "entirely of stormwater" element of section 402(p)'s "general rule."[7]

Nor does EPIC's complaint meet the requirement that the discharges be otherwise "unregulated." In the preamble to the Phase II regulations, the EPA noted that

> EPA and authorized States continue to exercise the authority to designate remaining unregulated discharges composed entirely of stormwater for regulation on a case-by-case basis.... In [the Phase II rule], ... individual instances of stormwater discharge might warrant special regulatory attention, but do not fall neatly into a discrete, predetermined category.

64 Fed.Reg. 68,781 * * *. The Ninth Circuit has adopted this interpretation of the relevant regulations, noting that the Phase II provisions merely "preserve[ ][the] authority for EPA and authorized States to designate currently unregulated stormwater discharges." *See Environmental Defense Center*, 344 F.3d at 840. Categorization, treatment, and permitting obligations of already regulated sources—like most "point sources" under section 502(14)—remain importantly unaltered; i.e., the Phase II regulations leave wholly unmodified the terms of the CWA—and the NPDES—with regard to regulated sources. Thus, for section 402(p) to apply to PALCO's discharge sources, these sources must have been "unregulated"—both as a matter of time and as a matter of law—at the time of the passage of the 1987 amendments.

They were not necessarily so "unregulated." When understood properly, the "sources" identified in EPIC's complaint were (and are) of an already regulated kind. * * * Whether related to silvicultural activity or not, "point sources" generally "fall neatly into a discrete, predetermined category" under the CWA. *See id.*; *see also* 64 Fed.Reg. 68,781. They are, as such, subject to the permitting provisions of the CWA; they are not, in short, the kind of previously "unregulated" category at issue in the Phase II regulations. * * *

In its complaint, EPIC alleges that many of the pollution sources in the Bear Creek area are "point sources," discharging both stormwater and pollutants into the creek itself. * * * Where PALCO's Bear Creek runoff system utilizes the kind of conduits and channels embraced by section 502(14), this court has noted, the pollution sources are definitively "point sources"; EPA may not alter this categorization, and section 122.27 does not—and cannot—absolve silvicultural businesses of CWA's "point source" requirements. Nor does section 402(p). * * *

[T]he CWA "renders illegal any discharge of pollutants not specifically authorized by a permit." * * * Perhaps the Eleventh Circuit put it best: "[T]he amended CWA absolutely prohibits the discharge of any pol-

---

7. PALCO has acknowledged as much, conceding that the discharges at issue do contain non-water elements. * * *

lutant by any person, unless the discharge is made according to the terms of an NPDES permit." See Driscoll v. Adams, 181 F.3d 1285, 1289 (11th Cir.1999) * * * Neither section 402(p) nor the rest of the 1987 amendments to the CWA alter this driving CWA principle or this core statutory mission. EPIC's complaint alleges that PALCO has discharged—and continues to discharge—pollutants into Bear Creek without an accompanying NPDES permit. * * * EPIC's complaint thus states a claim for which relief may be granted.

Notes and Questions

1. Are erosion and run-off from a logging site the type of thing that Congress likely intended to bring within the NPDES permit system? Are they as noxious as toxic chemicals discharged from an industrial pipe? Note that PALCO tried to categorize its discharges as "stormwater." If the discharges were comprised wholly of stormwater, with no other substances, could PALCO have escaped CWA regulation altogether under section 402(p)? *Should* activities like those conducted by PALCO escape CWA regulation? Can you think of a more efficient, effective way to control run-off from logging sites and roads?

2. The term pollutant means "dredged spoil, solid waste, incinerator residue, sewage, garbage, sewage sludge, munitions, chemical wastes, biological materials, radioactive materials, heat, wrecked or discarded equipment, rock, sand, cellar dirt and industrial, municipal, and agricultural waste discharged into water.... " 33 U.S.C. § 1362(6). If a forestland owner contracts with a crop duster to engage in the aerial spraying of pesticides over her forest, are the pesticides pollutants? They are, after all, a viable product being used as commercially intended. The Ninth Circuit examined this issue in League of Wilderness Defenders/Blue Mountains Biodiversity Project v. Forsgren, 309 F.3d 1181 (9th Cir. 2002), and held that aerial spraying required a permit under the Act. The parties did not dispute that the insecticides at issue were "pollutants", but the defendant, the U.S. Forest Service, claimed the activity did not involve a point source. The court disagreed. It distinguished non-point source pollution, stating:

> Although nonpoint source pollution is not statutorily defined, it is widely understood to be the type of pollution that arises from many dispersed activities over large areas, and is not traceable to any single discrete source. * * * The most common example of nonpoint source pollution is the residue left on roadways by automobiles. Small amounts of rubber are worn off of the tires of millions of cars and deposited as a thin film on highways; minute particles of copper dust from brake linings are spread across roads and parking lots each time a driver applies the brakes; drips and drabs of oil and gas ubiquitously stain driveways and streets. When it rains, the rubber particles and copper dust and gas and oil wash off of the streets and are carried along by runoff in a polluted soup, winding up in creeks, rivers, bays, and the ocean.

Id. at 1184. In contrast, Forest Service airplanes fitted with tanks and mechanical spraying apparatus are "discrete conveyances" spraying pollutants directly into rivers. *Id.* at 1185. The court concluded that a Forest Service regulation excluding various "non-point source silvicultural activities such as nursery operations, site preparation, reforestation and subsequent cultural treatment, thinning, prescribed burning, *pest and fire control*, harvesting operations, surface drainage, or road construction and maintenance from which there is natural runoff," was inapplicable, in that it excluded *only* pest control activities that involved natural runoff. *Id.* (citing 40 C.F.R. § 122.27) (emphasis added). For added support, it cited Romero-Barcelo v. Brown, 478 F.Supp. 646, 664 (D.P.R.1979), vacated in part on other grounds, 643 F.2d 835 (1st Cir.1981), which found that Naval airplanes that dropped bombs into the ocean off Vieques Island, Puerto Rico were point sources. 309 F.3d at 1186 n.4.

D. Case Study: The Headwaters Forest

The Headwaters Forest covers around 3,000 acres surrounding tributaries of the Elk River, near Eureka, California. It has been the subject of intense debate from corporate board rooms to town halls to the academic "ivory tower." At issue is the logging of increasingly rare and ecologically critical old growth stands of timber on private lands. The Headwaters experience implicates nearly all of the issues about forestry that you have explored so far in this chapter. Throw in a few endangered species, and you have a fascinating story. Part 1 of this case study provides the background of the Headwaters controversy and requires your analysis of regulatory issues, while Part 2 raises constitutional considerations. Part 3 examines the use of civil disobedience as a form of self-help to obstruct logging in the Headwaters Forest.

1. *The California Forest Practices Act and the Headwaters Forest*

THE LAST STAND
David Harris
Rolling Stone Magazine
Feb. 8, 1996, at 38

* * * The[] last scraps of wildness [in the largest privately held old-growth redwood forest on earth] are being felled as fast as logging roads can be bulldozed to reach them. As these remnants disappear, a whole ecosystem evaporates, one that is full of small creatures whose lives have been defined by the forest's cycles, which have gone undisrupted for eons. There will never be forests like these again, and their approaching extinction has escalated their value enormously, drawing the attention of the country's heaviest financial hitters, its most devoted preservationists and its most powerful political leaders.

The battle raging over the Pacific rain forest broke out of the backwoods and into the national spotlight 10 years ago in the far northwestern corner of California, where the Coast Ranges skirt the Pacific near Humboldt Bay and the largest trees of all grow. And it still rages there to this day, a head-on collision at the intersection of Wall Street, Our Town and Ecotopia. The conflict remains an indelible modern parable for all of us about just what happens when Big Money invades a small place full of very, very big trees.

The specific trees in dispute have been named Headwaters Forest by their protectors and cover some 3,000 acres on either side of a ridge separating the sources of Salmon Creek and the Little South Fork of the Elk River, 15 miles from Eureka, the seat of Humboldt County. They are nothing unusual by the standards of a hundred years ago, but they are coastal redwoods, *Sequoia semperviren*, obviously special trees. Many grow to be more than 250 feet tall and 15 feet thick and, left to their own devices, stand more than 2,000 years before toppling. A single typical mature coastal redwood can be sawed into enough boards to frame a dozen houses. *Sequoia semperviren* have covered the ridges around here since the age of the dinosaurs diplodocus and triceratops some 200 million years ago.

There were once about 2 million acres in California just like Headwaters, starting at Big Sur and running to the Oregon border along the Coast Ranges' seaward slope, nurtured by the fog, ever present from June through September, and then the rains, from October to April, which add up to as much as 100 inches per year in places. Some 80,000 acres out of those have been preserved in the state and national park systems and, in 1985, when this story began, another 20,000 or so were in private circulation, in small and scattered parcels—except, of course, for Headwaters. Headwaters was by far the largest contiguous piece still up for grabs.

Headwaters Forest Has Belonged To The Pacific Lumber Company since the 1940s. If it had belonged to any other company, it probably would have been long since cut and would never have become an issue. Ironically, old A.S. Murphy, the president of the Pacific Lumber Company who originally bought the parcels, ... was the timber industry's leading maverick and had completely converted his company to a radically different kind of forestry. By the end of the 1920s, Pacific Lumber had entirely given up clear-cutting, practicing instead what was called selective cutting, in which a maximum of 70 percent of a parcel was logged and the stronger of the mature trees were left in place to hold the hillside and seed the next generation of forest. Murphy also dedicated Pacific Lumber to what was called sustained yield. Each year the company calculated just how many new board feet would be grown by its forestlands and limited its cut to that amount. Murphy's idea was to treat the forest like capital and feed his company off the interest. He considered overcutting and its consequent deforestation the bane of the timber business, and these policies were his recipe for a perpetual forest and hence a perpetual economy.

Old Mr. Murphy's policies were continued by his son Stan, and ..., the new management was still dedicated to the Murphy gospel. As a result of such husbanding, by 1985, when most of its competitors had used up the last of their ancient forests and were making their second or third cuts through areas where the trees were but a fraction of the size, the already prosperous Pacific Lumber owned some three-quarters of the world's supply of old-growth redwood timber. It also had close to a corner on the supply of the tight-grained, almost purple, prime redwood boards known in the trade as uppers and available only from ancient forests where the growth was slow and uninterrupted century after century. Cutting at the pace Old Man Murphy first set, the company didn't expect to start working on its old growth up at the top of Salmon Creek until well into the 21st century.

The drastic changes that were made in that schedule were set on Wall Street in 1985, when Charles Hurwitz—a Texan on his way to building his heretofore minor-league holding company, Maxxam Group Inc., into a member of the Fortune 500—launched a stock raid on Pacific Lumber. Hurwitz was backed by Michael Milken, the legendary pope of junk bonds, and the investment bank Drexel Burnham Lambert. Milken was then at the apex of his financial power, and thanks to him, Drexel was the hottest house on the Street. What drew it to the Pacific Lumber Company was obvious. Thanks to Old Man Murphy, Pacific Lumber had virtually no debt and a dominant position in a diminishing resource that it was barely exploiting. Investors in the junk bonds that Milken issued to fund Hurwitz's takeover were assured of security by a promise to drop the pace set by Murphy, open up the throttle for the purposes of short-term yield and at least double Pacific Lumber's annual timber harvest. Pacific Lumber's previous management surrendered after a token struggle, and even before his ownership became official, Charles Hurwitz and Maxxam's managers were intent on getting Pacific Lumber's logging operation out on Salmon Creek and the Little South Fork of the Elk as soon as possible.

CHARLES HURWITZ KEPT HIS PLEDGE of more work in Scotia and then some. Pacific Lumber immediately enlarged its work force by 25 percent, ... put mills A and B on 10–hour shifts for five days and added an eight-hour shift on Saturday as well.

Out in the Coast Ranges, clear-cutting became company policy, and in the first months of the company's speeding up, a lot of timber was lost in splinters as inexperienced fellers, paid by the log, dropped trees in great haste just to get onto the truck what they could, no matter what might be wasted along the way. Enormous log decks were soon stacked at truck landings carved into hillsides plucked clean as chicken skin. During a decade of Hurwitz's ownership, Pacific Lumber's inventory of old-growth redwood shrank to a third of what it had been. Pacific Lumber liquidated groves..., further shrinking the wildlife corridor on which the surviving old-growth species—such as the tailed frog, the Olympic salamander, the Northern spotted owl, the red tree vole and the marbled murrelet—depend. Hurwitz's overtime turned Scotia, Fortuna and many of their neighbors into boomtowns, though the local cynics pointed out they were just eating their future, since the faster they cut, the sooner they would be out of work.

Garberville's first environmental organization, the Environmental Protection Information Center, ... became the major force in a struggle ... focused on the Little South Fork of the Elk and the headwaters of

Salmon Creek. The forest was defended on two fronts, one spearheaded by EPIC and the other by the local environmental radicals affiliated with Earth First!

Earth First! was by far the more visible. In the last 10 years, the Earth First!ers have suspended themselves 150 feet up in the redwoods to delay logging; sat in front of bulldozers; chained themselves to trees; kicked in the doors of the local congressman; and marched through Scotia wearing tree costumes, then returned and marched through again, wearing identical Charles Hurtwitz masks. They have captured log trucks and suspended banners in front of the State Capitol and off the Golden Gate Bridge; ... and they picketed the official hearings in which the fates of places like Headwaters were decided. More than anyone in the past decade, the Humboldt Earth First!ers were responsible for making timber an issue discussed on the front page and in the evening news.

But in defending Headwaters Forest itself, EPIC's role has been far more central. EPIC's strategy was to use the courts. Its architect, Robert Sutherland ... taught himself botany and then taught himself law. * * * EPIC's starting point was the California forestry law requiring loggers to submit a timber harvest plan to the California Department of Forestry for whatever parcel they meant to cut. The forestry department was charged with ascertaining that the procedures to be used satisfied all the law's requirements including those assessing the proposed cut's impact on wildlife, water quality, erosion and a number of other environmental measurements. The process was known to be a lot less demanding in practice than in the letter of the law, and EPIC's strategy was simply to force the department to hew to the letter. The harvest-plan process included a public meeting at which the department was to discuss each timber harvest plan, and anyone who participated in the process by submitting questions gained legal standing to challenge the department's almost automatic approval of everything submitted to it.

Specifically at issue was whether the department's assessment of the proposed Pacific Lumber cuts in Headwaters met the requirement to assess "cumulative impact" established in the California Environmental Quality Act. The courtroom was mostly tie-dyed, but that, Pacific Lumber's partisans were quick to point out, was because lumberjacks and mill hands had to work for a living and weren't free to attend court during the day. * * *

The trial's most memorable moment was the testimony of the department forester who had assessed the two timber harvest plans:

Had the forester calculated the amount of soil that might be washed off the slope and into Salmon Creek or the Little South Fork of the Elk after a clear cut?

No, he hadn't.

Had he conducted any specific search for Northern spotted owls? Or Olympic salamanders? Marbled murrelets? Tailed frogs?

No.

But he had concluded that none of the species would be impacted by this clear cut, was that correct?

Yes, that was correct.

On cross-examination, Pacific Lumber's lawyer asked the forester if he was familiar with all the species mentioned by EPIC's counsel.

Yes. He had seen photographs.

And had he seen any of these creatures out in the areas covered by the timber harvest plans?

No, certainly not.

Then, EPIC's lawyer asked the forester about the photos he said had familiarized him with the species in question. When and where had he first seen these pictures?

A week ago, the forester admitted, in the office of Pacific Lumber's attorney.

When the trial was over, the court found that the California Department of Forestry had been rubber stamping timber harvest plans for the timber companies and ruled the two timber harvest plans in question to be in violation of the law.

Other cases have followed, and each has had the same outcome. The only breach in Headwaters' protection came during 1989. With the state forestry department's permission, Pacific Lumber had cut a road into one edge of the forest prior to the litigation over its timber harvest plans. That July, it asked for a "minor" modification of its pre-existing road-building permit that would extend the permit's life for another year and allow the company to add 600 feet to the road's length. Since such minor modifications were not subject to the public process that covered timber harvest plans, EPIC was unaware of the extension. Unobstructed, Pacific Lumber pursued its construction without mercy. The new 600–foot extension pushed on down the ridge in an unsealed gouge and ran along the narrow river's edge. The maximum 200–foot width had been used throughout, so the road was flanked by what amounted to a small, very ugly clear cut. But more than ugly, the hillside was now unstable. The 1989 rainy season alone washed more that 40 cm of silt off the extension, and part of the adjacent hillside soon began to slump, threatening to dump even more into the furthest reaches of the Elk River.

THE 1990 LOGGING SEASON WAS THE craziest ever in Humboldt. * * * Earth First! launched Redwood Summer, during which they intended to import shock troops from all over the country to disrupt logging. The drive began with two of Earth First!'s principal organizers being blown up by a car bomb, followed by months' worth of protesters' climbing up trees, chaining themselves to logging tractors and marching on the county's major mills. * * *

Since then, the forest that feeds Salmon Creek and the Little South Fork of the Elk River has been caught in a legal stalemate. In the meantime the principal player in Headwaters' protection has become the marbled murrelet, a tiny seabird that nests in the tops of thousand-year-old redwood trees. There are only a few flocks of murrelets left on the planet. They are also on California's endangered-species list, and Headwaters and the lesser old-growth parcels nearby at Owl Creek are among the remaining California flocks' principal nesting grounds. Eventually the court found that the results from the survey Pacific Lumber had undertaken at court order were fraudulent and absolutely unreliable, and enjoined the Owl Creek cut.

In 1994, Washington, D.C., got involved. Dan Hamburg, a first-term Democrat then representing Humboldt County, sponsored the Headwaters Forest Act in the U.S. House of Representatives, which authorized acquisition of 40,000 acres of the Pacific Lumber land surrounding the headwaters of Salmon Creek and the Little South Fork of the Elk River. Hurwitz announced that he opposed such a sale but if he were forced to make it, he expected to be paid some $600 million, almost two-thirds of what he paid for the entire company, including another 180,000 acres of timberland. The bill passed the House but died in the final days of Congress and was never voted on in the Senate. * * *

In the meantime the Pacific Lumber Company has begun making it clear that it wants to get the cash out of Salmon Creek and the Little South Fork of the Elk, and it wants it soon. In 1995, in the wake of the Owl Creek decision, Pacific Lumber ... applied to the state forestry department for an "exemption" allowing it to take out up to 10 percent of the stand's "dead and dying" trees. Such damage exemptions are not subject to public review, and the department granted this one with little deliberation. Pacific Lumber immediately dispatched its foresters into Headwaters to begin marking the trees that it planned to cut.

On Sept. 15, the day the exemption was to take effect, Earth First! showed up to demonstrate, but it didn't need to. EPIC once again secured a last-minute temporary restraining order in federal court and the immediate threat ebbed * * * But Headwaters Forest continues to hang in the balance this year as it has for the 10 that preceded it.

In the Owl Creek decision described in the last few paragraphs of the article, EPIC prevailed on its claim that the Owl Creek timber harvest plan would harm or harass marbled murrelets that nested in the area and thereby "take" the species in violation of section 9 of the Endangered Species Act. Marbled Murrelet v. Pacific Lumber Co., 880 F.Supp. 1343, 1348 (N.D. Cal. 1995), aff'd, 83 F.3d 1060 (9th Cir. 1996), cert. denied, 519 U.S. 1108, 117 S.Ct. 942, 136 L.Ed.2d 831 (1997). As the article indicates, EPIC and other environmental groups have had some success with their Forest Practices Act claims as well. See, e.g., Sierra Club v. State Bd. of Forestry, 7 Cal.4th 1215, 32 Cal.Rptr.2d 19, 876 P.2d

505 (1994) (ordering the Board to rescind approval of timber harvest plans, as the Board had abused its discretion in approving plans that lacked information on presence of certain old-growth species); Environmental Protection Info. Ctr. v. MAXXAM, 4 Cal.App.4th 1373, 6 Cal.Rptr.2d 665 (1992) (affirming trial court's dismissal of a writ of mandamus against the Department as moot, but finding that mootness was the product of EPIC's success, so that EPIC could seek attorneys' fees); Sierra Club v. California Dept. of Forestry/Imboden, 26 Cal.Rptr.2d 338 (App. 1993) (finding that the Department had improperly approved harvest plans that failed to include mitigation measures to lessen the impact on rare animal species). The following provisions of the California FPA have been at the heart of many of these disputes.

Z'berg-nejedly Forest Practices Act of 1973

Cal.Pub.Res.Code § 4513. Intent of Legislature

It is the intent of the Legislature to create and maintain an effective and comprehensive system of regulation and use of all timberlands so as to assure that:

(a) Where feasible, the productivity of timberlands is restored, enhanced, and maintained.

(b) The goal of maximum sustained production of high-quality timber products is achieved while giving consideration to values relating to recreation, watershed, wildlife, range and forage, fisheries, regional economic vitality, employment, and aesthetic enjoyment.

§ 4571. Necessity of license

(a) No person shall engage in timber operations until that person has obtained a license [to engage in timber operations] * * *

§ 4581. Necessity of timber harvesting plan

No person shall conduct timber operations unless a timber harvesting plan prepared by a registered professional forester has been submitted ... pursuant to this article. Such plan shall be required in addition to the license required in Section 4571.

§ 4582. Contents of timber harvesting plan

The timber harvesting plan shall be filed with the department in writing by a person who owns, leases, or otherwise controls or operates on all or any portion of any timberland and who plans to harvest the timber thereon. * * * The plan shall be a public record and shall include all of the following information:

* * *

(c) A description of the land on which the work is proposed to be done, including ... the location of all streams, the location of all proposed and existing logging truck roads, and indicating boundaries of all site I classification timberlands to be stocked * * *

(d) A description of silvicultural methods * * *, including type of equipment * * *

(e) An outline of the methods to be used to avoid excessive accelerated erosion from timber operations to be conducted within the proximity of a stream.

(f) Special provisions, if any, to protect any unique area within the area of timber operations.

(g) The expected dates of commencement and completion of timber operations.

* * *

§ 4582.7. Review of plan; public comments

(a) The director shall have 30 days from the date that the initial inspection is completed..., to review the plan and take public comments. * * *

(b) If the director determines that the timber harvesting plan is not in conformance with the rules and regulations of the board or with this chapter, the director shall return the plan, stating his or her reasons in writing, and advising the person submitting the plan of the person's right to a hearing before the board, and timber operations may not commence.

(c) A person to whom a timber harvesting plan is returned may, within 10 days from the date of receipt of the plan, request of the board a public hearing before the board. * * * Timber operations shall await board approval of the plan. * * *

§ 4584. Exempt activities

* * * [T]he board may exempt ... a person engaged in forest management whose activities are limited to any of the following:

(a) The cutting or removal of trees for the purpose of constructing or maintaining a right-of-way for utility lines.

(b) The planting, growing, nurturing, shaping, shearing, removal, or harvest of immature trees for Christmas trees or other ornamental purposes or minor forest products, including fuelwood.

(c) The cutting or removal of dead, dying, or diseased trees of any size.

* * *

(g)(1) The one-time conversion of less than three acres to a non-timber use. * * *

(j)(1) The cutting or removal of trees ... that eliminates the vertical continuity of vegetative fuels and the horizontal continuity of tree crowns for the purpose of reducing flammable materials and maintaining a fuel break ... not more than 150 feet on each side from an approved and legally permitted structure.... [A]n "approved and legally permitted structure" includes only structures that are designed for human occupancy and garages, barns, stables, and structures used to enclose fuel tanks.

(2)(A) The cutting or removal of trees pursuant to this subdivision is limited to cutting or removal that will result in a reduction in the rate of fire spread, fire duration and intensity, fuel ignitability, or ignition of the tree crowns. * * *

§ 4592. Emergency notice; contents

Notwithstanding any other provisions of this chapter, a registered professional forester may ... file an "emergency notice" ... that shall allow immediate commencement of timber operations. * * * Those emergencies ... may include, but are not limited to, the necessity to harvest to remove fire-killed or damaged timber or insect or disease-infested timber, or to undertake emergency repairs to roads.

---

14 Cal. Admin. Code

Forest Practices: Application of Forest Practice Rules

§ 898. Feasibility Alternatives

After considering the rules of the Board and any mitigation measures proposed in the plan, the [Forester] shall indicate whether the operation would have any significant adverse impact on the environment. On TPZ lands, the harvesting per se of trees shall not be presumed to have a significant adverse impact on the environment. If the RPF indicates that significant adverse impacts will occur, the RPF shall explain in the plan why any alternatives or additional mitigation measures that would significantly reduce the impact are not feasible. * * *

When assessing cumulative impacts of a proposed project on any portion of a waterbody that is located within or downstream of the proposed timber operation and that is listed as water quality limited under Section 303(d) of the Federal Clean Water Act, the RPF shall assess the degree to which the proposed operations would result in impacts that may combine with existing listed stressors to impair a waterbody's beneficial uses, thereby causing a significant adverse effect on the environment. The plan preparer shall provide feasible mitigation measures to reduce any such impacts from the plan to a level of insignificance, and may provide measures, insofar as feasible, to help attain water quality standards....

§ 898.1. Review of Plan by Director

The Director shall review plans to determine if they are in conformance with the ... rules adopted by the Board....
* * *

(c) In reviewing plans, the Director shall disapprove all plans which: (1) Do not incorporate feasible silvicultural systems, operating methods and procedures that will substantially lessen significant adverse impacts on the environment.
* * *

(d) If the Director ... finds that a plan cannot be approved without a change in the conduct of timber operations, the Director shall ..., explain any probable causes for disapproval and suggest possible mitigation measures. The preparer of the plan shall then have the opportunity to respond ... and provide appropriate mitigation measures
* * *

(f) If the Director finds no feasible, less damaging alternatives that conform with the rules, the Director shall approve such plan unless approval threatens to cause immediate, significant, and long-term harm to the natural resources of the state. * * *

(g) If the Director determines that (1) all feasible mitigation measures or alternatives which are available to substantially reduce or avoid any significant adverse impacts of a THP have been selected; [and] (2) significant adverse impacts remain * * * the Director shall not approve the plan unless the Director also determines that the benefits of the THP outweigh any significant, unavoidable adverse impacts. * * *

(h) In determining whether the public benefits of the THP outweigh any unavoidable significant adverse impacts ..., the Director may request information as needed to evaluate potential job loss, negative economic impacts on the community, business closings, loss of property by owners, probable conversion to other uses, estate taxes and other factors as appropriate.

Exercise

Assume that Pacific Lumber has recently transferred a portion of its land to a subsidiary, Pac–Nine Forest Products. Pac–Nine has submitted a timber harvest plan (THP) for Units 12 and 13 of the Headwaters Forest, which together comprise a 1,000 acre tract of forestlands. The THP calls for a dramatic increase in timber production over historic levels in this unit. It would accelerate the rate of cutting in old growth stands, triple the size of proposed clearcuts, and build an extensive network of logging roads in pristine, untouched areas.

About three-fourths of the timber in Units 12 and 13 is old growth redwood and Douglas fir. The THP calls for all of the old growth stands to be harvested over the next five years. It indicates that, because of the challenges posed by the steep terrain, the forest will be replanted with fast growing trees that can be harvested when they reach 25 years of age. Also, under the proposed plan, the size of clearcuts would be increased from 40 acres in size to 180 acres because smaller sized clearcuts, which are the "norm" for other timber owners in the area, are no longer economically feasible. The THP does note that smaller clearings would be preferable for recreation, wildlife habitat and protection of water quality and soils, but explains that profitability must come first.

The THP calls for a network of 60 miles of new logging roads. Some of the areas to be roaded have streams which are important to sport fishermen and commercial guides. At least one stream is considered "water quality impaired," due to both excessive sediment deposits and various pesticides, herbicides, and fertilizers applied to upstream areas. According to the plan, there will be a 50% reduction in stream productivity for both trout and salmon due to sedimentation and temperature increases, but some improvement is expected after road construction and harvesting is completed. Although soil instability and erosion (or even landslides) may result, Pac–Nine claims that the potential adverse effects are acceptable because of the need for access to high value timber. Besides, the plan concludes, any resulting landslides would occur in remote areas so there will be little danger to human safety or property.

In his public appearances, the Governor of California has applauded the expansion of efforts to log old-growth forests. His administration has embraced an informal policy of promoting old-growth harvest to respond to the economic troubles experienced by the timber industry in the Northwest. Old growth trees, of course, are extremely valuable as lumber. Demand for old growth in the U.S. and abroad is high. Several timber companies in nearby communities sustain their business on old growth logging and their mills are best suited for old growth timber. Lately, however, the mills have suffered from decreased availability of federal timber and increased imports of finished Canadian lumber to U.S. markets.

You have been retained by an environmental group called Californians for Old Growth (COG), which would like you to protest the plan for Units 12–13 when it comes before the Forestry Department for consideration. Your expert advisor, Dr. Ornitho, is a professor of wildlife biology who specializes in bird behavior and habitat. She informs you that the proposed plan fails to explain, much less mitigate, the adverse impacts of the timber program on the Marbled Murrelet, a reclusive seabird that nests in coastal old growth trees. Assume that the Murrelet is not an endangered species, but it is an indicator species that demonstrates the health and integrity (or lack thereof) of the entire forest ecosystem. Dr. Ornitho believes that Murrelet populations have seriously declined in recent years because of intensive logging activities and habitat loss.

1.   Assume that you have satisfied all procedural and standing requirements in lodging your protest before the Forestry Department. What arguments will you make on behalf of COG in protesting the THP for Units 12–13 of the Headwaters Forest? Comb through the provisions of the California FPA and regulations provided above to support your arguments. Be sure to address soil erosion and water quality, timber regeneration, and wildlife considerations. For each point you raise, be sure to counter any arguments that you expect Pac–Nine to make. How is the state Forestry Director likely to rule?

2.   Does COG have a viable Clean Water Act claim? If so, what relief would be provided by a court? *See* Environmental Protection Info. Center v. Pacific Lumber Co., *supra,* 301 F.Supp.2d 1102 (N.D. Cal. 2004). COG would

likely raise Endangered Species Act claims, too; that Act is covered in Chapter 14, *infra*.

3. If your THP protest is successful, you may avert imminent harm to the forest ecosystem and the marbled murrelet, but are you merely delaying the inevitable? Won't Pac–Nine simply amend its plan until it finally gets it right, or can the FPA be used to stop harmful projects in sensitive areas altogether? Meanwhile, how are the company's shareholders supposed to recoup their investment in forestlands, and what are the out-of-work loggers going to do for income?

4. Pacific Lumber's responses to litigation brought by EPIC and other environmental groups, and state and federal efforts to resolve the issues, are described in the following article.

REGULATION OF LOGGING ON PRIVATE LAND IN CALIFORNIA UNDER GOVERNOR GRAY DAVIS
Thomas N. Lippe and Kathy Bailey
31 Golden Gate U. L. Rev. 351, 389–96 (2001)

* * * CDF responded to th[e] [Owl Creek] ruling by denying a subsequent Pacific Lumber timber harvest plan, No. 1–95–099 HUM, in the Headwaters Forest area, citing U.S. Fish and Wildlife Service concern that the plan could cause "take" of marbled murrelet. * * * Pacific Lumber then sued both the state of California and the federal government, alleging that their combined actions amounted to a taking of Pacific Lumber's property for a public use without just compensation in violation of the Fifth Amendment to the U.S. Constitution and Article 1, section 19, of the California Constitution.

At the same time, grassroots activism ... was in high gear in Humboldt County and Sacramento, including the September 15, 1996, arrest of 1033 people who peacefully stepped across the Pacific Lumber property line in Carlotta. The Clinton administration responded by brokering an agreement ... that included (1) the federal and state governments' agreement to purchase 7,470 acres of Pacific Lumber-owned old-growth redwood forest in the Headwaters Forest area (consisting of two specific old-growth groves including the Headwaters Grove); (2) the USFWS' agreement to approve a Habitat Conservation Plan covering Pacific Lumber's remaining 211,000 acres ... that would provide Pacific Lumber with immunity from liability for "take" (i.e., harm, harass, kill or injure) of all listed species...; and (3) Pacific Lumber's agreement to withdraw its Fifth Amendment-based lawsuits.

In 1997 Congress approved funding for the federal government's portion of the acquisition .... On September 1, 1998, the California legislature passed Assembly Bill 1986 (Migden). AB 1986 provided the state's $130 million share for the acquisition, but made the funding contingent on Pacific Lumber agreeing to additional logging restrictions to protect endangered salmonids and certainty that specified old-growth redwood groves remaining in company ownership would be off limits to

logging for 50 years, as had been promised by the proponents of the deal.
* * *

Meanwhile, * * * CDF director Richard Wilson ... signed a determination ... authorizing an allowable harvest of 136 million board feet. The company was apoplectic and issued a press statement saying the Headwaters deal was off. The company had expected authorization to log 176 million board feet, which, through use of allowable variances, could be stretched to 194 million board feet a year. A weekend of scrambling ensued.... Finally, on Monday, March 1, 2000, CDF director Wilson relented and certified Pacific Lumber's Sustained Yield Plan at 176 million board feet. * * *

That night, at three minutes to midnight, ... the deed to the Headwaters Forest Reserve was recorded at the Humboldt County Courthouse, open late for the long-awaited occasion.

For most people, the Headwaters deal was over [but] ... it was only the close of another chapter in the Pacific Lumber/Maxxam/Hurwitz saga. The book, however, continues, with no glimmer of a resolution. Pacific Lumber and the USFWS and various state agencies ... have spent the last two years ... negotiating the application of [HCP] terms to the forest. Never has the old saw that "the devil is in the details" been more true. * * * To date the company has challenged agency determinations regarding restrictions on geographic concentration of logging operations, logging on steep slopes, ... allowable size of clearcuts, geological review of unstable areas, murrelet nest set-backs during helicopter operations, northern spotted owl nest protection, snag (dying tree) retention for wildlife, monitoring, and more. * * *

2. Constitutional Challenges and the Headwaters Forest

Occasionally, private owners like Pacific Lumber, unaccustomed to state control, have challenged the constitutionality of restrictions imposed upon them under state Forest Practices Acts. The cedar tree owners in Miller v. Schoene, 276 U.S. 272, 48 S.Ct. 246, 72 L.Ed. 568 (1928), *supra*, sued the state of Virginia for a taking of their property without just compensation, but their claims were rejected in light of the state's compelling interest in protecting apple production. Although the state prevailed in that case, early efforts to control deforestation by imposing limits on forest practices got off to a rocky start, as the state courts were generally sympathetic to landowner's constitutional challenges to "excessive" or "undue" regulation of their property.

James Willard Hurst, an eminent legal historian, chronicled Wisconsin's attempt to regulate the timber industry through its general police power, as well as property, tort and contract theories, during the early 1900's in his book, Law and Economic Growth: The Legal History of the Lumber Industry in Wisconsin 1836–1915, 571–91 (1964). Hurst's book examines the case of State ex rel. Owen v. Donald, 160 Wis. 21, 151 N.W. 331 (1915), which invalidated Wisconsin's efforts to establish a forest reserve by buying up private timberlands as an unconstitutional exercise of state power. Hurst provides a powerful, yet "scornful, passionate polemic" against the opinion, and, more broadly, the prevailing laissez-faire mindset of the time. Robert W. Gordon, *Hurst Recaptured*, 18 Law & Hist. Rev. 167, 173 (2000). Although Hurst "had a healthy respect for markets as engines of innovation and prosperity, virtually his entire oeuvre is about how by the end of the nineteenth century the unreflective cult of free enterprise had brought about major crises in the form of unforeseen externalities such as resource exhaustion and a dangerous concentration of political and economic power." *Id.* at 173–174. The case in question, *State ex rel. Owen*, has been widely criticized, and Wisconsin eventually enacted a constitutional amendment to rectify the holding and promote public forest reserves. Hurst, *supra*, at 598.

In the post-New Deal era, the courts have, by and large, sustained the constitutional validity of state Forest Practices Acts. *See, e.g.,* State v. Dexter, 32 Wash.2d 551, 202 P.2d 906 (1949); Laupheimer v. State, 200 Cal.App.3d 440, 246 Cal.Rptr. 82 (1988); Heidgerken v. DNR, 99 Wash.App. 380, 993 P.2d 934 (2000). Likewise, the denial of a timber harvest permit, or restrictions on harvest, may not be a taking of property where the landowner can still use the land for other purposes. *See* MacLeod v. Santa Clara County, 749 F.2d 541 (9th Cir. 1984) (where landowner could continue to use the property for investment purposes or for cattle ranching, denial of harvesting permit did not amount to a taking); Seven Islands Land Co. v. Maine Land Use Regulation Com'n, 450 A.2d 475 (Me. 1982) (denial of permission to cut any trees other than dead or dying fir on 432 acres, and a temporary prohibition on cutting another 118 acres, for purposes of protecting deer habitat, did not render the tract substantially useless and was not an unconstitutional "taking"). *See also* Brady v. State, 965 P.2d 1 (Alaska 1998) (rejecting constitutional and tort claims against the state relating to its management of forests when responding to beetle epidemic). On the other hand, a forest owner may state an actionable takings claim when the state refuses to permit logging if the denial of proposed logging plans would deprive the owner of all economically viable uses of the property. *See* Boise Cascade Corp. v. Board of Forestry, 325 Or. 185, 935 P.2d 411 (1997).

Does Pac–Nine have a viable claim regarding the application of the FPA's requirements to the logging proposal described above in Section II.D.1, *supra*, under the federal constitution? Would either the Fifth Amendment takings clause or the Fourteenth Amendment due process requirements provide Pac–Nine with a means of avoiding potentially onerous restrictions on methods, timing, and amount of harvest from its land? What if it were prohibited from harvesting an entire stand of old-growth timber to protect an endangered species?

3. Civil Disobedience in the Headwaters Forest

Opponents of logging do not always confine themselves to judicial action, but occasionally engage in "self-help" by tree-sitting and other physical and sometimes violent forms of protest. By the same token, logging companies do not necessarily sit quietly by while environmental groups or others bring their multi-faceted campaigns against logging.

Assume that you represent protesters, including members of the environmental activist group Earth First! Your clients have come to you after they lost all of their claims against Pac–Nine and the state of California in both state and federal court, and all avenues of appeal have been exhausted. Tomorrow, irreplaceable stands of old-growth trees are going to be clearcut in the Headwaters Forest. Your clients intend to construct platforms in the trees and sit on them for as long as it takes to get the company to back down. At least ten of their members will participate. They intend to remain peaceful throughout the campaign. They will string colorful anti-logging banners throughout the forest, proclaiming the company's allegedly horrible track record for ecological devastation, and provide notification to the media whenever any protester is threatened with harassment or arrest.

The following two news articles and an Idaho Supreme Court case, Highland Enterprises, Inc. v. Barker, 133 Idaho 330, 986 P.2d 996 (Idaho 1999), have come to your attention.

HEADWATERS DEAL FALLS SHORT,
SAYS TREE–SITTER
Environmental News Network
http://www.jailhurwitz.com/media/butterfly_done/33_media.htm
(March 12, 1999)

When the Headwaters forest deal was finalized March 1, a collective sigh of relief could be heard coming from Pacific Lumber, government negotiators and even a fair-size group of environmentalists. * * *

Yet, infamous trespasser and tree-sitter Julia Butterfly Hill continues her protest atop the 200–foot-tall Redwood named Luna on Pacific Lumber property in Northern California. The Earth First! activist has lived in her 8–by–8–foot tree house for 15 months now to protect the 1,000–year-old redwood and other old-growth trees from lumber company saws. She doesn't plan on climbing down anytime soon. "Compromise is a death sentence," she says in a recorded hotline update. * * *

Luna, which she has occupied since Dec. 10, 1997, and the surrounding steep and unstable hillside are, according to Hill, representative of the many areas that the ... [Habitat Conservation Plan negotiated between the company and the government] fails to adequately protect ... [so Hill] will maintain her vigil. "There is certainly much more work ahead to achieve our goals for permanent protection for all remaining old growth, habitat recovery, restoration and truly sustainable, responsible forestry," she said.

LUMBER COMPANY SUES TREE–SITTERS
FOR CIVIL DAMAGES

ASSOCIATED PRESS

Contra Costa Times (Walnut Creek, CA), July 6, 2003, at 4

A northern California timber company under constant pressure for logging coastal redwoods has sued more than 110 tree-sitters and other protesters for civil damages during the last two years. * * *

The litigation is part of Scotia-based Pacific Lumber Co.'s aggressive response to the environmentalists who have used civil disobedience to disrupt its operations. This year, the company also has forcibly removed tree-sitters.... About 40 of those sued this spring for trespassing ... were protesting logging they said causes erosion that harms the Freshwater Creek watershed and damages downstream residents. * * * "They're trying to intimidate people to stop any type of public participation," said 28–year-old Jeny Card, who's being sued for $250,000 after spending nearly a year living in an ancient redwood before being arrested in March.

Jeanette Jungers, 50, a special education teacher from Eureka, was sued by Pacific Lumber for $335,000. * * * Jungers brought meals to tree-sitters trespassing on Pacific Lumber property, and once was arrested when she chained herself to a tree as the company was attempting to remove the tree-sitters. * * * [S]aid University of Colorado law professor George W. Pring, who with Penelope Canan wrote the 1996 book "SLAPPs: Getting Sued for Speaking Out" * * * lawsuits are "huge winners outside of the courtroom in terms of silencing people, muzzling protests—which is why the lumber companies use them."

Pacific Lumber is most likely to aggressively pursue civil action against protesters it believes were not properly punished criminally, said spokesman Branham and company attorney Russ Gans. Card, for instance, was fined $10, which Branham called "very discouraging." But others have been jailed for 10 days and one activist was fined $500. * * *

HIGHLAND ENTERPRISES, INC. v. BARKER

Supreme Court of Idaho, 1999.

133 Idaho 330, 986 P.2d 996.

This is an appeal from a judgment entered after a jury found several members of the Earth First! organization (defendants or appellants) liable for interference with the prospective economic advantage of the respondent, Highland Enterprises, Inc. (Highland). The appellants were assessed compensatory and punitive damages. * * *

Earth First! is an association which promotes environmentalism and protests against activities that the association's members determine to be anti-environment. * * *

In the early 1990s, Highland contracted with Shearer Lumber to perform forest road building near Dixie, Idaho, as part of the Cove/Mallard timber sales. The U.S. Forest Service sold the timber from these sales to Shearer Lumber. In the spring of 1992, Kreilick went to the annual Earth First! Rendezvous and discussed with Robert Amon[1] a Cove/Mallard protest campaign to protest the road building and the timber sales. In a discussion circle devoted to Cove/Mallard issues, Amon, Kreilick and others discussed the logistics of the Cove/Mallard protest campaign addressing such issues as food, transportation, camping and the types of protest activities that would occur.

The Cove/Mallard campaign was first publicized in the Spring 1992 edition of the *Earth First! Journal*. The main organizers of the 1992 campaign included Kreilick, Amon, Erik Ryberg (Ryberg) and Billy Jo Barker (Barker). Ryberg obtained a Forest Service camping permit for July and August of 1992 and various protestors set up camp about ten miles from Highland's road construction. Protest activities occurring in 1992 included tree-sitting, pole-sitting, digging holes in the road, chaining protesters to construction equipment, damaging roads and tree-spiking. At trial, evidence of monkeywrenching in the form of road damage and tree-spiking was presented through circumstantial evidence. The trial court characterized the 1992 protests as "disorganized and relatively small in scale."

The 1993 campaign was larger in scale and better organized. The main organizers of the 1993 campaign included Kreilick, Amon, Ryberg, Barker and Karen Pickett (Pickett). By the spring of 1993, Amon had purchased twenty acres of land near the Cove/Mallard roads to serve as a base camp for the protesters. In May of 1993, Kreilick and Pickett set up camp on Amon's land and on Memorial Day, the Wild Rockies Earth First! Rendezvous took place at the camp. * * * Amon provided food at the camp, but supplies were paid for by ... fund raising. Monies forwarded to Amon by Pickett for the 1993 Cove/Mallard campaign were deposited into Amon's "Ancient Forest Bus Brigade" account.

Evidence was presented at trial that through the *Earth First! Journal* and letters, people were encouraged to come to the base camp and protest or, alternatively, to send supplies and/or money for the campaign. * * *

On June 22, 1993, the Forest Service entered a Closure Order restricting public access to the Noble Creek area of Cove/Mallard where the roads were being built by Highland. * * * Throughout the summer,

---

1. * * * Amon appears to have been one of the key players in various protests that occurred, having provided land, food and transportation to those who participated in the protests. However, prior to trial, Amon filed for bankruptcy and was not a defendant to the action pursuant to a stay issued by a U.S. Bankruptcy Judge.

activists attached themselves to Forest Services vehicles. Additionally, Highland employees and Forest Service agents testified that they found spiked trees, boards in the road with nails protruding, damaged construction equipment, sharpened rebar in the road, missing survey stakes, Earth First! slogans spray-painted on concrete road barriers, and slash piles in the road. A search of Amon's property on June 30, 1993, revealed barrels of climbing rope, climbing harnesses and spikes, tree-sitting platforms, an Earth First! banner, two buckets of nails of the type found in the road, digging tools and green spray-paint cans.

In August of 1993, Highland filed suit against a number of entities, associations and individuals, including 200 Jane and John Does, for conversion, intentional destruction of property and trespass, interference with contract and racketeering based on the protest activities that occurred in 1993. * * * The court permitted amendment of Highland's complaint to add a claim for punitive damages.... Highland presented only one cause of action: intentional interference with an economic advantage. The jury found that the appellants were liable to Highland for a total of $150,000 in compensatory damages and $999,996 in punitive damages. * * *

The appellants assert that Highland failed to prove by substantial evidence the knowledge and intent elements of intentional interference with a prospective economic advantage. At the end of the trial, the trial court properly instructed the jury with regard to the interference claim in the following manner:

1. In or about the summer of 1993, near Dixie, Idaho;

2. Highland Enterprises, Inc. had a lawful opportunity to gain an economic advantage (make a profit) by building roads;

3. The defendant knew of the existence of this opportunity of Highland Enterprises, Inc.;

4. The defendant intended to, and did, interfere with Highland Enterprises' performance causing Highland's performance to become more expensive or burdensome;

5. The defendant's interference was wrongful in that the defendant had the improper motive to harm the plaintiff or that the defendant used wrongful means to cause injury;

6. Injury to the plaintiff resulting from an intentional interference;

7. The nature and extent of the damages to the plaintiff and the amount thereof.

Idaho recognized the tort of interference with a prospective economic advantage in Idaho First National Bank v. Bliss Valley Foods, 121 Idaho 266, 284–85, 824 P.2d 841, 859–60 (1991). * * * Although in *Bliss* we did not precisely state each element of the tort ..., our reference in *Bliss* to Barlow v. International Harvester, Co., 95 Idaho 881, 522 P.2d 1102 (1974), a case involving a nearly identical tort, interference with contract, ... provides a clear picture of the elements of the tort of intentional interference with a prospective economic advantage. Those elements are as follows: (1) The existence of a valid economic expectancy; (2) knowledge of the expectancy on the part of the interferer; (3) intentional interference inducing termination of the expectancy; (4) the interference was wrongful by some measure beyond the fact of the interference itself (i.e. that the defendant interfered for an improper purpose or improper means) and (5) resulting damage to the plaintiff whose expectancy has been disrupted. * * *

[*ed.*: The court concluded that substantial evidence supported the jury's conclusion that each element was satisfied.]

We believe that substantial evidence exists to support the jury's award of damages. * * * In this case, there was substantial evidence presented by Highland regarding the amount of damages it suffered due to the delay caused by the appellants. * * * It is not unreasonable for the jury to have concluded that a group of people working together to stop the road-building aided one another through moral and physical support or direct solicitation and collectively damaged Highland in the amounts assessed against the appellants. * * *

In addition, substantial evidence existed to support the award of punitive damages. * * * [T]he jury had before it evidence that the appellants had acted in a manner that was an extreme deviation from reasonable standards of conduct. The appellants consistently delayed Highland's work through malicious and outrageous conduct. For example, among other acts, the appellants damaged equipment, spiked trees and placed boards in the road with nails protruding. Drawing all inferences in favor of Highland, we conclude there was substantial evidence supporting the punitive damage award. * * *

Notes and Questions

1. In light of the Idaho case and information provided in the news articles, how will you advise your clients with respect to their "tree-sitting" plans? If you believe that their plans are too risky, can you suggest alternatives that may accomplish their objectives?

2. Julia Butterfly Hill stayed on her platform in the tree, Luna, for 738 days. Her occupancy was not necessarily applauded by other environmentalists:

Undoubtedly the world's best known treesitter, Julia "Butterfly" Hill spent two years atop "Luna," a 1000–year-old redwood in danger of being "harvested" by Pacific Lumber Company. Hill's brave act of civil disobedience generated much media attention for the destruction of the ancient redwoods, but Hill's story has also generated much attention for Hill herself. Her tiny six-foot platform was visited by both journalists and celebrities.... As Hill was elevated into superstardom, the plight of the redwoods and other old growth forests was reduced to the story of one tree; the efforts of Earth First! and other treesitters became the struggle of one woman. * * * Published only a few months after her descent in December of 1999, Hill's autobiography The Legacy of Luna chronicles her stay in the giant redwood. From the opening chapter, she is quick to distance herself from radical environmental politics * * * Never having participated in any political activism prior to her stay in Luna, Hill's autobiography portrays her entry into forest activism as a series of spiritual conversion. * * * While Hill is critical of Earth First! throughout her stay in Luna, her autobiography sidesteps the issues surrounding perhaps their most important conflict: the circumstances of Hill's descent. While the motto of Earth First! is "No Compromise in Defense of Mother Earth," Julia "Butterfly" Hill compromised: she agreed to pay a $50,000 (U.S.) "fine" to Pacific Lumber to save Luna and the surrounding twenty feet of trees. The "sale" of Luna outraged many radical environmentalists as it undermines their tactic by countering their demand that the natural world not be commodified. * * *

Audrey Vanderford, *The Legacy of Luna: The Story of a Woman, a Tree, and the Struggle to Save the Redwoods*, WOMEN & ENVIRONMENTS INTERNATIONAL MAGAZINE, Oct. 1, 2001, at 45, 2001 WL 24171745. Was Julia's compromise justifiable, given the circumstances?

3.   Luna's story represents a mixed ecological message, just as it does a mixed political message. The tree was attacked and damaged after Hill left her stand:

Girded by metal braces and held in place by stainless steel cables, a giant redwood sliced in half at its base by a chain-saw-wielding vandal last fall is still standing, despite months of sometimes fierce coastal winds. * * * [T]he damaged tree has become the focus of worldwide concern over its fate.* * * After last week's inspection, the team of experts declared the damaged redwood ... could live many more years, maybe even hundreds more. But ... the tree will never regain its full health. * * * After the cut was discovered, the team quickly agreed to install specially crafted metal braces around the tree's base. * * * Less successful have been efforts to track down the culprit responsible for an attack that outraged environmentalists and timber industry representatives who feared their supporters would be blamed. Humboldt County Sheriff Dennis Lewis said although there was a plethora of early leads about possible suspects, a criminal investigation eventually came up empty.

Mike Geniella, *Julia Hill's 'Luna' Survives Harsh Winds After Attack,* Santa Rosa Press Democrat, June 11, 2001, at B1.

E.   Forest Reserves and Open Space Protection

Owners of forestlands may experience financial pressure to deforest their property and to devote it to residential development or other uses. A few states have adopted legislative schemes to inhibit forestland owners from converting their property to non-forest uses. In some states, forested lands have been designated as nature preserves or areas of critical concern to provide for open space, preserve lands in their natural state, and provide recreational opportunities. *See, e.g.,* Fl. Stat. Ann. § 380.05(2)(1) (authorizing the designation of forests, wildlife refuges, rivers, and estuaries that could be substantially deteriorated by "uncontrolled private or public development" as "areas of critical state concern"). The cutting or clearing of wood in such reservations is restricted or prohibited. *See* Harbor Course Club, Inc. v. Dept. of Community Affairs, 510 So.2d 915 (Fl. App. 1987) (clearing timber to create a golfers' driving range on area of critical state concern was unlawful).

Forestlands may also be preserved by state or local land use planning laws (examined in detail in Chapter 10, *supra*). In Maine, all land outside of city limits is classified in one of three ways: protected, active management, or development. The vast majority of the total land base subject to this classification system is forested. Around twenty percent is protected, seventy percent is classified for management, and the remainder is in development status. Lundmark, *supra*, at 797. In the management districts, logging may not be limited, but in the other two classifications, restrictions may be imposed. *See id.;* 12 Me. Rev. Stat. §§ 685A.

Oregon is considered a leader in protecting open space and limiting improvident development and urban sprawl. In 1973, the legislature passed Senate Bill 100, which requires city and county governments to adopt comprehensive plans and regulations to protect farms, forests, and other open space. Senate Bill 100, Ch. 80, § 1, 1973 Or. Laws 127, 127. Local governments' comprehensive plans and development decisions must be consistent with state-wide planning goals. Or. Rev. Stat. §§ 197.175, 250–252. The state Land Conservation and Development Commission is charged with establishing goals, preparing planning guidelines, and reviewing state and local land use actions for consistency. *Id.* § 197.040. The goals and requirements for forestlands were tested in the following case.

1000 FRIENDS OF OREGON v. LAND CONSERVATION AND DEVELOPMENT COMM'N (TILLAMOOK COUNTY)
Supreme Court of Oregon, 1987.
303 Or. 430, 737 P.2d 607.

The principal issue in this and the four companion land use cases, consolidated for argument before this court, concerns the relationship between the Forest Practices Act (FPA) and Statewide Land Use Planning Goal 5 (Goal 5).[1]

---

1. Goal 5 states: "To conserve open space and protect natural and scenic resources[,] Programs shall be provided that will (1) insure open space, (2) protect scenic and historic areas and natural resources for future generations, and (3) promote healthy and visually attractive environments in harmony with the natural landscape character. The locations, quality and quantity of the following resources shall be inventoried:

    a. Land needed or desirable for open space; * * *

    d. Fish and wildlife areas and habitats;

    e. Ecologically and scientifically significant natural areas, including desert areas; * * *

    h. Wilderness areas * * *

"Where no conflicting uses for such resources have been identified, such resources shall be managed so as to preserve their original character. Where conflicting uses have been identified the economic, social, environmental and energy

The counties involved in this appeal chose to resolve conflicts between the goal of forestland preservation in Goal 5 and the demands of commercial forest operations by relying on the FPA and its administrator, the Oregon Board of Forestry, to protect Goal 5 resources, rather than by developing independent programs in each county. The Land Conservation and Development Commission (LCDC) approved the counties' actions, finding that reference to and deference to the administration of the FPA was appropriate, because the FPA preempted county regulation of commercial forest operations. 1000 Friends of Oregon (1000 Friends) then petitioned for judicial review of LCDC's acknowledgment of Tillamook County's plan [and] ... of the comprehensive plans submitted by Union, Washington, Coos and Columbia counties. In each case, the Court of Appeals reversed and remanded for the county to do its own planning to achieve compliance with Goal 5. * * *

Goal 5 is designed to protect open spaces, scenic and historic areas and natural resources. The goal requires that local governments first inventory the location, quality and quantity of these resources (Goal 5 resources). Second, local governments must identify potential uses in each area containing Goal 5 resources that conflict with the preservation of the Goal 5 resources. The third step is to assess the economic, social, environmental and energy (ESEE) consequences of allowing or prohibiting the conflicting uses. Fourth, the local government must develop a program to protect its Goal 5 resources.

Under OAR 660–16–010, promulgated by LCDC, the local government has three choices after making the ESEE assessment. If it concludes that the resource should be protected fully, it may prohibit the conflicting use. OAR 660–16–010(1). If, on the other hand, it concludes that the conflicting use is more important than the Goal 5 resources in the area, the conflicting use may be allowed fully. OAR 660–16–010(2). Finally, if it concludes that both the resource and the conflicting use are sufficiently important so that neither should be sacrificed entirely, it may allow the conflicting use but limit it so that the resource is protected to some extent. OAR 660–16–010(3).

For its part, the FPA, ORS 527.610 to 527.730, was designed "to encourage forest practices that maintain and enhance [the benefits and resources to be derived from forested lands], and that recognize varying forest conditions." ORS 527.630(1). The FPA does not, however, ignore land use considerations. ORS 527.722(1) first provides: * * * "[N]o unit of local government shall adopt any rules, regulations or ordinances

consequences of the conflicting uses shall be determined and programs developed to achieve the goal. * * *

"Open Space—consists of lands used for agricultural or forest uses, and any land area that would, if preserved and continued in its present use:

(a) Conserve and enhance natural or scenic resources; * * *

(e) Enhance the value to the public of abutting or neighboring parks, forests, wildlife preserves, nature reservations or sanctuaries or other open space;

(f) Enhance recreation opportunities; * * *

(h) Promote orderly urban development.
* * *

regulating the conduct on forestlands of forest operations governed by the Oregon Forest Practices Act or rules promulgated thereunder." * * *

In the present case, Tillamook County performed the requisite inventory of Goal 5 resources, identified conflicting uses and assessed the ESEE consequences of allowing the conflicting uses. With respect to forested lands, the county designated commercial forest operations as conflicting with conservation of certain Goal 5 resources. Nonetheless, with the exception of one wetland site, the county zoned all its forest-lands with a designation of commercial forest operations as a primary use, based on its ESEE assessment. In accordance with its interpretation of ORS 527.726(1)(c), the county relied on the Forest Practices Act and the rules to be promulgated thereunder by the State Board of Forestry to satisfy Goal 5 for those areas in which commercial forest operations were a primary use.

* * * LCDC found that the FPA preempted the county's authority to regulate commercial forest operations except where it was appropriate, in light of the importance of the Goal 5 resources in the area, to designate such commercial forest operations as an "incidental or insignificant" use. * * *

* * * The Court of Appeals reversed LCDC's order. * * *

LCDC recognized that, under ORS 527.726(1)(a), a county has the absolute right to zone forested lands in a manner that would exclude commercial timber operations. It concludes, however, that, once commercial timber operations are permitted in a more than incidental way by the county's choice of zoning designations, the county cannot reserve to itself continuing control over other kinds of activities on the same parcel because the FPA reserves to the Department of Forestry plenary control over the management of such parcels. * * *

No one denies that the counties have the authority to decide whether a commercial forestry use or a conflicting Goal 5 resource use is primary; ... the struggle is over what authority (if any) *remains* to a county *after* it has exercised that authority in a particular way, *viz.,* by zoning a parcel for commercial forest use. * * *

[O]ur review of the record in these five cases establishes that all the counties *chose* to rely on the FPA. It thus fairly could be argued that the only issue before us is a very narrow one: ... is it *legally permissible* for the county to fulfill its planning responsibilities by deference to the administration of the FPA? The FPA itself is supposed to be administered in conformance with, *inter alia,* Goal 5. Nothing ... suggests to us that a county is *foreclosed* from the option of reliance on the FPA in meeting the county's Goal 5 obligations. The county was entitled to do so. * * *

Unfortunately, we cannot limit our holding to the narrow ground just identified because, while it is clear that Tillamook's choice of the FPA was voluntary, it appears that at least one of the other counties

(Washington) believed it had no choice in selecting the FPA, and we cannot be sure what the other three counties believed concerning the other choices open to them. Were we to decide this case narrowly, we would simply leave open the possibility that some party might now wish to have LCDC remand the plans to some counties to determine if the counties might now wish to "go it alone," rather than rely on the FPA. If LCDC is right about preemption, such further activities would be pointless delay. * * *

The statutes involved in this case follow a logical preemption pattern. ORS 527.722 prohibits counties from adopting any rules or regulations regulating commercial forest operations governed by the FPA. The only exceptions to this rule arises when an area is zoned for a primary use other than commercial forest operations. ORS 527.726(1)(c). * * *

As the Court of Appeals acknowledged, uniformity of regulation was one of the legislature's main goals in enacting the FPA. ORS 527.630. The standard applied by the Court of Appeals allows county planning authority to supplant this overriding legislative purpose. * * * In enacting ORS 527.726, the legislature considered and rejected alternative language that would have given counties greater control over forest operations. * * *

The decision of the Court of Appeals is reversed; the order of the Land Conservation and Development Commission is affirmed.

Notes and Questions

1. Counties in Oregon continue to struggle with implementation of the Statewide Land Use Planning Goals. In 1000 Friends of Oregon v. Land Conservation and Development Commission (Lane County), 305 Or. 384, 752 P.2d 271 (1988), the Oregon Supreme Court upheld a challenge to Lane County's comprehensive rural land use plan. Although it agreed that Lane County could rely on the Forest Practices Act and the State Board's rules for forestry practices to meet its obligations on lands where commercial forestry is a primary use, citing *1000 Friends of Oregon (Tillamook County), supra,* it concluded that the County's plan failed to comply with the goals regarding forestlands in several other respects. First, the plan allowed farm uses on forestlands without a showing of compatibility with forest uses, *i.e.,* the protection and retention of forestlands. In addition, the plan permitted dwellings on forestlands if they were "necessary and accessory to forest management." * * * The court stated:

> [I]t is not a minor or technical violation of Goal 4 to allow non-forest uses, such as dwellings, on forestlands by simply showing that the non-forest uses will enhance certain forest uses. * * * LCDC approval of this variation of the necessary and accessory test is inconsistent with the purpose of Goal 4.

752 P.2d at 279–280.

2. Oregon's program has proven effective in preventing losses of open space. Timothy Egan, *Drawing a Hard Line Against Urban Sprawl,* N.Y. TIMES, Dec. 30, 1996, at A1. Before it was adopted, the state was losing

30,000 acres of farmland per year, but, as of 1996, only around 2,000 acres a year are lost to development. *Id.* Even though Oregon is considered a model for balanced growth nationwide, voters in the state have recently had a change of heart.

> In a[] defeat for environmentalists, voters approved a measure that essentially prevents state and local governments from enforcing land-use regulations. If a landowner can prove that a certain regulation restricts the use of the property and reduces its fair market value, Measure 37 requires the state or local government responsible to compensate the landowner, cease from applying the regulation to the land or change the regulation so that it would not diminish the land's value. * * *

> But the measure is written so broadly that it will have wide consequences for Oregon's precedent-setting smart growth efforts and measures to protect greenways and farmland. Thirteen county farm bureaus across Oregon opposed the measure, saying land-use regulations are critical to ensuring that farmland is not developed into business parks or condominiums. * * * [Governor] Kulongoski also opposed the measure, noting that it was poorly written, provides no new revenue and would cost up to $344 million a year in paperwork and administrative costs, not including any possible payouts to property owners to compensate for their losses.

Natalie M. Henry, *Oregon Voters Reject Logging Limits, Back Compensation For Landowners*, LAND LETTER, Nov. 4, 2004.

3. Opponents of Measure 37 predicted a stampede to the county courthouses, and indeed the first cases seeking compensation have already been brought by landowners who claim they have been prevented from subdividing their land or building retirement homes. *See* Jeff Barnard, *Claims Test New Land Law; Property Owners Seeking Redress Oregon Measure Enacted By Voters*, SEATTLE TIMES, Dec. 3, 2004, at B4. Plaintiffs seek to have restrictions on their land lifted or to be paid for diminution in property values. *Id.* Do you believe that Measure 37 will reverse the gains made under the Land Conservation and Development Act? Might it also undermine the objectives of the Oregon Forest Practices Act? What does this experience teach other states that may be considering aggressive "smart growth" requirements? For more detail on Measure 37, *see* Chapter 10.III.A., *supra*.

4. Measure 37 arguably reflects pent-up frustration with Oregon's land-use laws, but the 2004 election as a whole did not yield environmentally friendly results. Oregon voters dealt a second blow to environmentalists in that state by defeating Measure 34, which would have restored old growth habitat and prohibited logging on 50% of two state forests on the Oregon coast. Henry, *supra*. Timber industry groups opposed Measure 34, as did the Oregon Society of American Foresters, Governor Ted Kulongoski, and the majority of local officials. The Governor and the Oregon Society of American Foresters argued that the existing management plan for state forests, which leaves well over half of the forests open for harvesting, should remain in place. Critics estimated that Measure 34 would have reduced funds for firefighting and habitat restoration, and also cut funds to local governments and schools by $25 million. *Id.*

5. In *1000 Friends of Oregon (Tillamook County), supra,* the court construed Oregon law as preempting county regulation of commercial forest operations governed by the FPA. Preemption issues have come up in other states. In Rancho Lobo Ltd. v. DeVargas, 303 F.3d 1195 (10th Cir. 2002), *cert. denied,* 538 U.S. 906, 123 S.Ct. 1483, 155 L.Ed.2d 225 (2003), Rancho Lobo, the owner of a hunting preserve, refused to seek a timber harvest permit pursuant to county ordinances because it had already been granted a permit by the State Forestry Division to harvest trees on its property. The county had adopted its Timber Harvest Ordinance in response to a threat to its watershed caused by erosion. The county ordinance required loggers to obtain a county permit and present a plan to control erosion. It also required compliance with measures that were voluntary under state law, for example, logging roads, drainage systems, buffer zones near riparian areas, and regeneration plans that comply with best management practices. The Tenth Circuit held that the ordinance was not preempted by the New Mexico Forest Conservation Act:

> [T]he Forest Conservation Act does not contain language which unambiguously reflects an intent to expressly preempt local legislation regarding timber harvests. * * * [However] New Mexico law recognizes that a statute may be impliedly preempted even though the requirements for express preemption are not met. * * * There is some support for the conclusion that the Forest Conservation Act occupies the entire area of forestry regulation. The Act contains provisions granting the Forestry Division sweeping powers to make rules and regulations regarding timber harvests, and to enforce "all" rules and regulations regarding logging, timber and forestry. Further, the rules and regulations promulgated by the Forestry Division are fairly comprehensive with regard to the circumstances under which logging will be allowed, in that they require a state harvest permit for the harvest of commercial forest species * * * [Yet] [t]he Forest Conservation Act's primary focus is the minimization of damage to the permitted land * * * While some of the regulations pertain to the protection of permitted property, the main focus of the Timber Harvest Ordinance is on local issues, such as the amelioration of damage to the surrounding property as the result of timber harvesting, including issues such as the effect of the timber harvest on economic development and local employment, water quality and availability, soil protection, archeological, historic and cultural resources, abatement of noise, dust, smoke and traffic, hours of operation, compatibility with adjacent land uses, cumulative effect when combined with existing harvests. * * * [W]e conclude that, in passing the Forest Conservation Act the legislature left room for concurrent jurisdiction over local forestry issues, and that the Forest Conservation Act does not impliedly preempt the Timber Harvest Ordinance by occupying the entire field of regulation relating to timber harvesting in New Mexico.

> * * * The district court also concluded that a conflict existed between the Forest Conservation Act and the Timber Harvest Ordinance with regard to clear-cutting. The ordinance bans clear-cutting

without a variance. * * * However, the Forest Conservation Act expressly states that nothing in its act "shall prevent a landowner hereafter from converting forest vegetative types to nonforest vegetative types for such purposes as range, wildlife, habitat, farming, surface mining or subdivision development." N.M.S.A.1978, § 68–2–16. * * * [It] ... does not establish an affirmative right to clear-cut, and does not conflict with the Timber Harvest Ordinance's ban on clearcutting without a variance.

Id. at 1203–05 (citations omitted). Can the holding in *Rancho Lobo* be squared with *1000 Friends of Oregon (Tillamook County)*? How much latitude should a county have when it comes to prescribing more onerous (and more expensive) requirements for logging? Should a county be able to prohibit logging altogether if state law would otherwise allow it?

F. Incentives for Conservation and Reforestation

1. The Natural Resources Conservation Services Programs

The U.S. Department of Agriculture, through its Natural Resources Conservation Service (NRCS), supports a variety of conservation programs. These programs provide environmental, financial, and technical benefits to private land owners for conserving soil, water, and other natural resources. Participation in NRCS programs is voluntary. The NRCS typically works with local partners to accomplish its goals, including local watershed or natural resources districts, universities, extension agents, State Fish and Game Departments and other agencies, private individuals and associations, and non-governmental organizations.

The Natural Resources Conservation Service (NRCS) was born of adversity. The agency was created as a national response to the Dust Bowl catastrophe of the mid–1930's, when the agency's first chief, Hugh Hammond Bennett, spoke eloquently to Congress that soil erosion was a national menace. He convinced Congress that a permanent agency was needed within the Department of Agriculture to call landowners' attention to their land stewardship opportunities and responsibilities, and that a nationwide partnership of Federal agencies with local communities was needed to help farmers and ranchers conserve their land from future erosion. From that humble beginning, the Soil Conservation Service, whose name was changed in 1994 to the Natural Resources Conservation Service to reflect an expanded mission, was created.

NRCS Overview (NRCS Nebraska State Website), http://www.ne.nrcs.usda.gov/about/overview.html (visited Nov. 22, 2004).

Today, there are approximately 3,000 local NRCS conservation districts. You can find one in almost every county in the nation, as well as the Caribbean and Pacific Basin.

The NRCS provides support for conservation practices related to forestry through various cost-share programs for private forestlands. For example, under the Forestry Incentives Program (FIP), the government shared up to 65 percent of the costs of tree planting, timber stand improvements, and related practices on non-industrial private forestlands."From its inception in 1974 through 1994, FIP cost-shares of more than $200 million have funded approximately 3.32 million acres of tree planting, 1.45 million acres of timber stand improvement, and 0.27 million acres of site preparation for natural regeneration on the nation's nonindustrial private forestlands." D.A. Gaddis, et al., *Accomplishments and Economic Evaluations of the Forestry Incentives Program: A Review (1995)*, available at: http://www.srs.fs.usda.gov/econ/pubs/scfra78.htm.

The Stewardship Incentive Program (SIP) was established by the 1990 Farm Bill to encourage multiple resource management on non-industrial private forestland. It covers rural lands with existing tree cover or land suitable for growing trees owned by a private individual, group, association, corporation, Indian tribe, or other private entity. To be eligible, landowners must own 1,000 or fewer acres of qualifying land. Participants must develop Forest Stewardship Plans and agree to maintain the land as described in their Plan and to maintain and protect SIP-funded practices for 10 years or more. The program provides technical and financial assistance to encourage non-industrial private forest owners to keep their lands and natural resources productive and healthy. *See Stewardship Incentives Program*, http://www.nrcs.usda.gov/programs/sip/ (visited Nov. 22, 2004); Southern Forest Resource Assessment, Final Report: Technical, Ch. 8 (Socio–3) (2002), available at http://www.srs.fs.usda.gov/sustain/report/socio3/socio3–28.htm.

2. *Tax Breaks and Other Economic Measures*

Several states have adopted special tax legislation to promote retention of forestlands. Around forty states provide for a reduction in property taxes for forestlands. *See* Lundmark, *supra*, at 799–800. Some states provide tax relief by assessing the land's value on the basis of use (rather than market value), or by providing various means of deferring timber taxes. *See* Andrews v. Munro, 102 Wn.2d 761, 689 P.2d 399 (1984) (en banc). Others encourage timber owners to undertake good forest practices by permitting them to pay a "yield tax" in lieu of an annual (and higher) property tax. *See* William Unkel & Dean Cromwell, *California's Timber Yield Tax*, 6 Eco. L.Q. 831, 832–33 (1978).

Wisconsin's Forest Crop Law provides tax incentives to landowners who make their lands accessible to the public for hunting and fishing. Wis. Stat. Ann. §§ 77.01–.16 (West. 1989). In 1985, the Wisconsin legislature amended the Forest Crop Law and renamed it as the Managed Forestland Law. The amended provisions allow landowners to deny public access to up to eighty acres of their forestlands, but the rest of the forest must be open to hunting, fishing and other public recreation. Wis. Stat. Ann. §§ 77.80–.91 (West 1989). *See* Lundmark, *supra*, at 799–800.

Other states also employ voluntary measures to manage private for-estland. Connecticut, Idaho, Maryland, New York, New Jersey, and South Carolina encourage private landowners to consider recreation, wildlife, or aesthetic values in managing their forestlands. In Tennessee, landowners may voluntarily register property that qualifies as natural areas with the Department of Conservation. Landowners may publicize their registry status to enhance the value of the land in the eyes of the public. Lundmark, *supra*, at 803.

Alternative tactics have been less successful. Some states have sought to promote local timber processing by requiring that timber taken from state lands be processed within the state prior to export. The Supreme Court found that such in-state protectionism violated dormant Commerce Clause principles by discriminating against interstate com-merce. South–Central Timber Development, Inc. v. Wunnicke, 467 U.S. 82, 104 S.Ct. 2237, 81 L.Ed.2d 71 (1984).

Notes and Questions

1. According to John G. Sprankling, in *The Anti–Wilderness Bias in American Property Law*, 63 U. Chi. L.Rev. 519 (1996):

> Numerous studies chronicle the attitudes and characteristics of private forest owners. * * * [T]hese studies indicate that, depending on the region involved, owners holding between 8 percent and 32 per-cent of total private forest acreage intend never to allow logging.
>
> For example, a study of Minnesota forest owners demonstrated that owners controlling 898,600 acres of such land (about 18 per-cent.... of private forestland in the state) responded that they would never allow timber harvesting on their land. When asked why [they] cited preservationist reasons: "nonmotor recreation" (owners of 322,100 acres); "esthetic enjoyment" (owners of 414,600 acres); and "no important benefit" (owners of 163,050 acres). * * * [*See also*] Ervin G. Schuster, Attitudes & Activities of Private Forestlandowners in Western Montana 55–56 & table 19 (Dept. of Agriculture 1978) (noting that 16 percent of private forest owners in western Montana "never" intend to "harvest" their lands, while 31 percent offer preser-vationist reasons for not harvesting in the past); Robert E. Jones and James S. Paxton, The 296 Million Acre Myth, 83 Am Forests 6, 8 (Nov 1977) (observing that in a poll of forest owners in 14 northeastern states, "fewer than 10 percent expressed an interest in wood or fiber production"). * * *

Id. at 565 n.230.

Does this report assure you that voluntary measures are sufficient for con-serving forestlands and resources?

2. Market forces are playing an increasingly important role in private forestland preservation. In some cases, recreational and hunting licenses and leases offer an attractive income stream for private forestlands, even though they may require leaving stands of trees in place and foregoing tim-ber income. *See* Holly Lippke Fretwell and Michael J. Podolsky, *A Strategy*

for Restoring America's National Parks, 13 Duke Envtl. L. & Pol'y F. 143, 156–57 (2003).

III. STATE AND FEDERAL FORESTLANDS

State and federal forestlands are subject to many of the same requirements and restrictions as private forestlands. Provisions of state and federal law regarding pollution control erosion, sustained yield specifications, and protections for fisheries and wildlife and their habitat generally apply. By and large, the requirements for federal forestlands imposed by the National Forest Management Act (NFMA) and the Federal Lands Policy and Management Act (FLPMA) are far more detailed than most states' requirements for state controlled forestlands, especially in terms of planning and public participation, but also with respect to substantive management requirements. Federal forestlands are considered in detail in Chapter 6, but a brief comparative "snapshot" is provided in the second part of this section.

A. State Forest Practices Acts and State Land

Some states have adopted specific restrictions applicable only to state lands, be they state forests, parks, or other land holdings. The Oregon Forest Practices Act, for example, requires the Department of Forestry to manage state timberlands for multiple uses, including fish and wildlife environment, landscape protection, recreation and protection of water supplies. Or. Rev. Stat. § 530.500 (1996). The primary objective of the state timber program, however, is to maximize revenues for the long-term financial benefit of state schools and counties. *See* Michael C. Blumm and Jonathan Lovvorn, *The Proposed Transfer of BLM Timber Lands to the State of Oregon: Environmental and Economic Questions*, 32 Land and Water Law Rev. 353, 402 (1997).

Some state forest reserves are strictly regulated to promote preservation goals. The New Jersey Pinelands region is the largest pinelands in the world, with one million acres of pine forests, wetlands, and rivers. Federal and state laws recognize that the Pinelands is a nationally significant ecosystem of unique forest communities and rare and imperiled species, and that residential or commercial development should be restricted throughout forested portions of the Pinelands. *See* 16 U.S.C. § 471i(a)(1); N.J. Stat. Ann. § 13:18A–2. The Pinelands Comprehensive Management Plan designates a variety of land use categories with specified development densities, and limits development in Forest, Agricultural, and Preservation categories. 7 N.J. Admin. Code §§ 7.50–5.23.

New York law provides that, "[t]he lands of the state, now owned or hereafter acquired, constituting the forest preserve as now fixed by law, shall be forever kept as wild forestlands." N.Y. Const. Art. 14, § 1. With limited exceptions for silvicultural research and reforestation areas, New York state law prohibits any person from cutting, removing, or injuring trees or timber on state lands. N.Y. ECL § 9–0303. Keeping forests "free" for the public, however, does not "guarantee that each and every square foot" of forests and parks in the state will be open to the public; the State maintains authority to control, among other things, access roads within state lands. New York State Conservation Council, Inc. v. Diamond, 74 Misc.2d 513, 345 N.Y.S.2d 291 (1973).

In spite of the broad array of authorities available to states for managing and conserving state owned forestlands, according to Professor Charles Wilkinson,

> It is a fact, not a slap at the states, to say that the states have no institutions in place comparable to the deeper and more broad-gauged Forest Service. A number of western states, believing that state trust lands must be dedicated solely to extractive uses, refuse to allow, or sharply curtail, non-revenue-producing multiple uses, including recreation. Arizona, New Mexico, Wyoming, Colorado, Utah, and Montana all lack forest practices acts. In those states that have acted on forest practices, the statutes fall well short of federal legislation.

Charles F. Wilkinson, *The Public Lands and the National Heritage*, 3 HASTINGS W.-NW. J. of ENVTL. L. & POL'y 225, 227 (1996).

B. National Forests: A Legal Comparative Approach

National Forests and Bureau of Land Management lands are subject to the requirements of the National Forest Management Act (NFMA) and the Federal Lands Policy and Management Act (FLPMA), respectively. For comparative purposes, once you've had a chance to review the pertinent provisions discussed in Chapter 6, *supra*, try your hand at the following problem.

Problem Exercise: Headwaters National Forest

Assume that the setting of the Headwaters Forest case study above in Section II.D is a National Forest, rather than private lands, and that the plan at issue is a Land and Resource Management Plan (LRMP) for that National Forest. Assume that all of the proposals and specifications described above are included in that LRMP. Apply the provisions of NFMA, 16 U.S.C. § 1604, to the proposed plan. What arguments would Californians for Old Growth (COG) make in support of declaratory and injunctive relief under NFMA? Is your assessment—and the eventual outcome of the potential claims—different than was the case for the Headwaters private forest? Will COG face jurisdictional problems if it attempts to bring its challenge to the LRMP in federal court?

What if the setting were instead BLM lands? Apply FLPMA to the facts of the Headwaters Forest case study. Is your assessment—and the eventual outcome of your claims—different than was the case for a National Forest? For the Headwaters private forest?

C. National Forests: An Economic Comparison

TURNING A PROFIT ON PUBLIC FORESTS
Donald R. Leal

PERC Policy Series Issue PS–4 (September 1995)
Available at http://www.perc.org/publications/policyseries/
turning_full.php

Adapted with permission from PERC Policy Series Issue PS–4 (September 1995)

Each year, at least fifty national forests managed by the Forest Service lose money on their timber sale programs. To some critics, these programs represent an environmental travesty and a classic example of corporate welfare. Some environmentalists ... contend that the Forest Service is subsidizing the timber industry. That is, they believe that the Forest Service's inability to make money indicates that the Forest Service is giving away our natural resources by selling timber at clearance-sale prices. Until now, there has been very little empirical investigation of the reasons for below-cost timber programs. * * *

Case Study: Montana

The timber sale program carried out on the forests of Montana's state school trust lands provides an excellent benchmark for evaluating the Forest Service's timber sale programs on national forests in Montana. Logging sites on school trust lands are often located next to or even within national forests. * * *

Let us look first at some wide discrepancies on the cost side. In the northwest region, Montana spent an average of $65 per thousand board feet of harvest to administer its timber program, while nearby Flathead National Forest spent an average of $106 per thousand board feet of harvest on its program. In the western region, the state spent an average of $52 per thousand board feet of harvest, compared with $175 on nearby Bitterroot National Forest. * * * A labor comparison of the Gallatin National Forest and the state's central land office provides insight into the cost disparity. * * * Based on 1992 budget figures, Gallatin's average wage cost per hour was only slightly higher than that of the state. But the number of Gallatin's labor hours spent to produce a given volume of harvest was over two- and one-half times that of the state.

A Forest Service cost study issued in 1993 sheds additional light on the cost discrepancy. * * * Timber output has fallen dramatically over the last five years while staff size has remained nearly the same, and this had led to a dramatic rise in timber sale costs. * * * The state also builds less expensive roads. To construct a mile of road, the state spends from $4,000 to $8,000, while the Forest Service spends from $45,000 to $50,000 (USDA 1993). * * *

Now let's look at revenues. The Forest Service's national forests in Montana consistently receive less revenue per thousand board feet of timber sold than do the state forests. * * * David H. Jackson (1987) offers a couple of possible explanations for the lower revenues. * * * Jackson found that the Forest Service did more clearcutting than the state did during this period. Clearcutting generates a lower average stumpage price when stands contain both low and high quality timber. With selective cutting, foresters take mostly high-quality timber. * * *

Given the fact that the Forest Service's costs are higher, one might expect environmental quality to be higher on logged sites in national forests than on those of the state. * * * A 1992 study of 46 sites in Montana harvested within the previous three years concluded that the state did a better job of protecting watersheds from the impacts of logging than the Forest Service did. * * * The study, requested by the Montana legislature, had as its express purpose the evaluation of environmentally-related management practices on state, federal, and private forests. The study was carried out by an independent, interdisciplinary team consisting of individuals from environmental groups, state foresters, the Forest Service, the Bureau of Land Management, the timber industry, and various consultants. The state ranked highest among all forest landowners, including the Forest Service.

Case Study: Northeastern Minnesota

A comparison of federal and county timber programs in northeastern Minnesota provides an opportunity to examine performance in the Great Lakes region. Returns from timber sales between 1990 and 1993 were compared for Superior National Forest and the forests managed by the St. Louis County Land Department. These forests grow both hardwoods (e.g., aspen) and softwoods (e.g., balsam fir). As the statistics below indicate, Superior and St. Louis County forests have similar timber-growing potential. * * *

Over the 1990–1993 period, the Land Department harvested 275 million board feet of timber and generated $2,340,572 in income from its timber program, while the Forest Service harvested 341 million board feet and lost $5,178,362 from its timber program. Stated another way, the Land Department returned, on average, $1.70 in gross revenue for every dollar spent on its timber program, while the Forest Service returned only $0.55 for every dollar spent on its program. * * *

To figure out why the Forest Service has done so poorly in comparison with St. Louis County, we must look at costs. * * * The Land Department's costs for timber sale preparation are about 46% lower, on average, than those of the Forest Service on Superior National Forest. * * * We also find noticeable differences in expenditures for reforestation and timber stand improvement. Although it has a slightly smaller suitable timber base, the Forest Service does much more reforestation and timber stand improvement than the Land Department. * * * Other program activities undoubtedly contribute to differences in timber program costs. Both the Forest Service and the Land Department, for example, do forest-wide planning, conduct periodic forest inventory, perform silvicultural examinations and prescriptions, and carry out activities to mitigate and sometimes improve conditions for wildlife and recreation. Unfortunately, it was not possible to set up meaningful comparisons for these categories because the costs were not separable from program costs.

Still, the evidence is clear: For two timber bases close to one another and rated very similar in timber-growing potential, the Service carries out a timber program whose costs are substantially higher than those incurred by the Land Department. These higher costs result in substantially lower returns from timber sales when compared to returns from timber sales on lands administered by the St. Louis County Land Department. * * *

Conclusion

* * * In contrast to state and county forests, no one has a personal financial stake in the income generated from national forest assets. Moreover, these forests are legally under no obligation to generate income. Gross receipts from timber sales go to the U.S. Treasury and to general timber activity funds, such as roadbuilding and reforestation. Congressional appropriations are used to offset losses. Hence, there is little, if any, incentive for the Forest Service to keep its costs low.

National forests have no bottom line, and without it, the Forest Service lacks an objective measure from which to assess its performance. Instead, it is forced to rely on "pseudo-measurements," such as the number of environmental assessment reports and forest plans produced or the amount of timber harvested. As this report indicates, many of these activities have accomplished little in the way of environmental quality and much in the way of increased costs. The evidence indicates that federal timber sale programs could achieve much better economic performance without sacrificing environmental quality if they operated with the same income incentive as the state of Montana and the St. Louis County Land Department.

Notes and Questions

1. Does it appear that the relatively high costs of the national forests are due primarily to bureaucratic red tape and environmental restrictions? Could the high costs instead be attributable to timber stand improvement or reforestation requirements that may provide greater returns over the long-run but raise short-term costs?

2. Do you agree that national forests should be operated to provide specific economic returns, as are state lands in Montana and lands managed by St. Louis County? Are there other considerations that should be taken into account? Could the article be used as a justification to end timber harvest on the federal lands altogether?

IV. SUSTAINABLE FORESTRY IN THE FUTURE

Certification programs that signify compliance with sustainable forestry methods are available through both an industry association and an independent, non-profit organization. The largest program, the Sustainable Forestry Initiative (SFI), is sponsored by the American Forest & Paper Association (AF & PA), a trade association representing the U.S. forest products industry. Participation in the SFI program is a condition of AF & PA membership, and is based on a system of principles, objectives and performance measures for the growing and harvesting of trees. AF & PA reports that it has expelled 17 of its members for failing to meet the SFI Standard since the inception of the program in 1994. Today, there are over 100 program members of the AF & PA, and over 100 more SFI program licensees, including forest product companies, conservation organizations, universities, and state, county and private landowners. Around 136 million acres of forestland in North America are enrolled in SFI, making it the world's largest forestry certification program. *AFPA, What is the SFI Program,* http://www.afandpa.org/Content/NavigationMenu/Environment_and_Recycling/SFI/What_is_the_SFI_Program_/What_is_the_SFI_Program.htm.

SFI was inspired by the sustainability concept that evolved from the 1987 report of the World Commission on Environment and Development and subsequently adopted by the 1992 Earth Summit in Rio de Janeiro. A multi-stakeholder Sustainable Forestry Board (SFB) is charged with the responsibility of enforcing the SFI standards and verification procedures. *AF&PA: Forestry—Sustainable Forest Initiative,* http://www.afandpa.org.

The SFI program is not wholeheartedly embraced by environmental groups, many of whom claim that SFI means nothing more than "Same-old Forest Industry." Don't Buy SFI, http://www.dontbuysfi.com/ (visited Nov. 16, 2004). In a letter to the Chair of the SFB, the Rainforest Action Network (Network) expressed its concern that SFI's use of an on-product ecolabel "represents a distortion of many of your member companies' environmental performance and will lead to further conflict in the marketplace." A Letter to SFI Chair Colin Moseley, http://www.dontbuysfi.com/letter/ (visited Nov. 16, 2004). The Network requested that SFI immediately discontinue its use of the label and remedy its performance standards that allegedly fail to:

- Protect old growth forests and roadless areas;

- Adequately restrict clearcutting and chemical use;

- Adequately protect endangered or imperiled species;

- Protect indigenous rights;

- Provide a chain-of-custody linking products to certified forests.

A website devoted to the Network's campaign against SFI products can be found at http://www.dontbuysfi.com/.

The FSC logo identifies products which contain wood from well-managed forests certified in accordance with the rules of the Forest Stewardship Council.

©1996 Forest Stewardship Council A.C.
Reprinted with permission

An alternative certification is provided by the Forest Stewardship Council (FSC), an international non-profit organization devoted to encouraging the responsible management of the world's forests. Landowners and companies that sell timber or forest products may seek FSC certification to verify that their forestry practices are consistent with FSC standards. These standards focus on protecting indigenous peoples' rights; maintaining community relations and worker's rights; encouraging efficient use of multiple forest products and services to ensure economic viability and a wide range of environmental and social benefits; conserving biological diversity and ecological integrity; and maintaining the attributes that define high conservation value forests, using a precautionary approach. Forest Stewardship Council, Principles and Criteria, http://www.fscus.org/standards_criteria/ (visited Nov. 16, 2004). According to FSC's website, Greenpeace, the National Wildlife Federation, The Nature Conservancy, Sierra Club, and World Wildlife Fund all support and encourage FSC certification. Forest Stewardship Council, United States, http://www.fscus.org/ (visited Nov. 16, 2004).

In North America, over 450 sawmills and 90 forests totaling 9.5 million acres have satisfied FSC's rigorous standards. *See* Jane Braxton Little, *Can Green–Certified Lumber Make It?*, 34 HIGH COUNTRY NEWS, June 24, 2002, at 6 (United States data); Forest Stewardship Council, http://www.certified-forests.org/ (North American data). Many U.S. retailers stock FSC-certified products, including The Home Depot, Lowe's Home Improvement Centers and Kinko's. Internationally, 42 million hectares in more than 60 countries have been FSC-certified, and several thousand products are produced using FSC certified wood and carrying the FSC trademark. Independent reviewers, accredited by FSC, perform assessments of forest management to determine if standards have been met and to verify that companies claiming to sell FSC certified products have tracked their supply to certified sources.

Notes and Questions

1. About 10% of all commercial forestland in the United States is certified by either FSC or SFI. Forest and mill owners claim that certification requirements cost them money but do not necessarily yield higher prices, as many consumers are unwilling to pay more for certified products. Little, *supra,* at 6. Is certification a desirable alternative to "command and control" governmental regulation? Can it be effective in terms of ensuring sustainable practices and environmental protection?

2. Fifteen times as many acres of North American forestland have been certified by the industry association, SFI (136 million acres), than by FSC (9.5 million acres). *Id.* Is certification by an industry trade association necessarily suspect, or can it be an effective tool in promoting both improved forest management and consumer awareness?

Chapter 12

MINERALS

I. AN INTRODUCTION TO MINERALS AND MINING IN THE UNITED STATES
    A. America's Mineral "Wealth"
    B. Geology and Extraction of Mineral Deposits
        1. Geology of Mineral Deposits
        2. Mineral Extraction
            a. Exploration
            b. Mining Methods
    C. The Mining Industry
II. HARDROCK MINERAL LAW
    A. The 1872 Mining Law's Location System for Hardrock Mining
        1. Location
            a. Lands Open to Location
            b. Locatable Minerals
            c. Qualified Locators
            d. Types of Locations
                (i)   Lode Claims
                (ii)   Placer Claims
                (iii) Mill Sites
            e. Location Procedures
            f. Supplemental State Location Requirements
    B. Discovery
        1. Prospectors' Rights Prior to Discovery: Pedis Possessio
        2. Discovery of a Valuable Mineral Deposit
    C. The Unpatented Mining Claim
        1. The Rights of Valid, Unpatented Mining Claims
            a. Exclusive Right of Possession
            b. Surface Rights
            c. Extralateral Rights
            d. The Right to Amend or Relocate Claims
        2. Limitations and Requirements Imposed on Unpatented Mining Claims
            a. Annual Assessment Work
            b. Claim Maintenance Fee
            c. Adverse Claimants
            d. Surface Use Limitations

I. AN INTRODUCTION TO MINERALS AND MINING IN THE UNITED STATES

The United States, particularly the Rocky Mountain West, produces more minerals and mineral products than any other region of similar size in the world. Blessed with an abundance of naturally occurring minerals, as well as a seemingly insatiable economic demand for them, the history of mineral exploration and production in America is long and storied. A "hardrock" mineral is a generic term for any material subject to location under the 1872 Mining Act, which is discussed in detail in Section II of this chapter. Any material that is instead subject to sale or lease, such as oil, gas or coal, falls outside this term, and is governed by a separate set of laws, discussed in Section III.

A. America's Mineral "Wealth"

Centuries before the United States existed as a country, European colonists arrived in search of gold and other valuable minerals. But it was only after the discovery of lead and iron in the Midwest during the early 19th century and California gold in 1848 that mining became a major industry. Silver after the Civil War, copper at the turn of the century, and then potash, bauxite zinc, uranium, and beryllium in the 20th century all have been subject to extensive exploration and mining activity. Table 1 lists some of the most commonly mined minerals and their primary end uses.

In Practice:	
Table 1 Some Common Minerals and Their End Uses	
Coal	Generating electricity, making iron and steel, and manufacturing chemicals.
Potash, Soda Ash, and Borates	*Potash*—Fertilizer, medicine, and the chemical industry.

	Soda Ash—Glass, chemicals, soap and detergents, pulp and paper, agriculture, brine treatment, corn syrup, drilling mud additives, dyes and pigments, enamels, flue gas desulfurization, food processing, leather tanning, metal refining, perfume, pharmaceuticals, and textiles.
	Borates—Fiberglass insulation, glass, detergents and bleaches, enamels, fertilizers, and fire retardants.
Iron	Steel products (kitchen utensils, automobiles, ships, buildings), metallurgy products, magnets, high-frequency cores, auto parts, medicine, biochemical and metallurgical research, paints, printing inks, plastics, cosmetics, paper dyeing, pigment, polishing compounds.
Copper	Electric motors, generators, communications equipment, electric cables and wire, switches, plumbing, heating, construction, chemical and pharmaceutical machinery, alloys, alloy castings, and protective coatings for other metals.
Lead and Zinc	*Lead*—Batteries, solder, military tanks, seals or bearing, TV tubes and glass, construction, communications, protective coatings, ballasts or weights, ceramics or crystal glass, X-ray and gamma radiation shielding, soundproofing, and ammunition.
	Zinc—Die casting, galvanizing brass and bronze, protective coatings on steel, chemical compounds in rubber and paints, used as sheet zinc and for galvanizing iron, electroplating, metal spraying, automotive parts, electrical fuses, anodes, dry cell batteries, nutrition, aluminum products, chemicals, roof gutter, engraver's plates, cable wrappings, organ pipes and pennies. *Zinc oxide*—medicine, paints, vulcanizing rubber, sun block. *Zinc dust*—primers, paints, precipitation of noble metals, removal of impurities from solution in zinc electrowinning.
Gold and Silver	*Gold*—Jewelry, satellites, electronic circuits, dentistry, medicine, arts, coins, ingots as a store of value, scientific and electronic instruments, electrolyte in electroplating industry.
	Silver—Electronic circuitry, coins, jewelry, photo film, chemistry, lining vats and other equipment for chemical reaction vessels, water distillation, catalyst in manufacture of ethylene, mirrors, silver plating, table cutlery, dental, medical and scientific equipment, bearing metal, magnet windings, brazing alloys, solder.
Phosphate	Plant fertilizers, feed additives for livestock, elemental phosphorus, chemicals for industrial and home consumers.
Crushed Rock	Highways, paint, plastics, medicines, glass, concrete sidewalks, bridges, wallboard, vinyl, brick and stone buildings, concrete block, roofing tile, asphalt singles, minerals for agriculture.

> *Source: BCS, Inc., Energy and Environmental Profile of the U.S. Mining Industry, Prepared for U.S. Department of Energy, Office of Energy Efficiency and Renewable Energy 1–3, Table 1–1 (Dec. 2002).*

So vast were American deposits of these and other minerals that the supply seemed virtually inexhaustible; the only practical impediments to exploiting our mineral wealth were the costs of discovery and extraction. But was this abundant mineral wealth really a blessing for the developing nation?

Economists once believed that a plentiful supply of natural resources—including hard-rock and energy-producing minerals—was crucial for economic "take-off" and development. More recently, however, many economists have come to believe that an abundance of natural resources can be an economic "curse." Empirical studies indicate that economies with abundant natural resources generally have lower rates of economic growth than economies with scarce natural resources.[a] Economists have offered several theories to explain this phenomenon. Some believe that political institutions in resource-rich countries become easy targets for rent-seeking and corruption. As long ago as the eleventh century, the Chinese emperor banned mining temporarily in the wake of a commission report on corruption that read (in part) as follows:

> Nature has provided us with excellent deposits. These deposits were capable of producing much profit to the people. The officials, thinking that there was very much money in mining business, wished to take it for themselves, so that in every mining district corrupt practices grew up amongst them, to the very great injury of the people. For this reason the rich refuse to devote their capital to mining and mining enterprises are gradually ruined. If a capitalist puts his money into mining, before he has gained a profit evil characters raise complaints against him, with the result that the officials banish him to some distant country or take possession of his belongings, in spite of his complete innocence. It will thus be seen that Chinese mining affairs are exceedingly badly managed.

Martin Lynch, MINING IN WORLD HISTORY 15 (London Reaktion Books 2002).

a. *See, e.g.,* Jeffrey D. Sachs and Andrew M. Warner, "Natural Resource Abundance and Economic Growth," National Bureau of Economic Research Working Paper 5398 (December 1995); Elissaios Papyrakis and Reyer Gerlagh, "Resource–Abundance and Economic Growth in the U.S.," Nota di Lavoro 62.2004 (April 2004)(finding that natural resource abundance not only decreases overall economic growth but specifically decreases investment, schooling, openness, and R & D expenditure, while increasing corruption). Other models, however, yield mixed results about the relation between natural resource abundance and eocnomic growth. *See, e.g.,* Ning Ding and Barry C. Field, "Natural Resource Abundance and Economic Growth," University of Massachusetts Amherst, Department of Research Economics, Working Paper No. 2004–7 (2004).

A millennium later, political corruption still plagues the mining industry in many parts of the world.

According to another popular explanation of the resource "curse," countries with abundant natural resources tend to focus on producing and exporting primary products rather than potentially more lucrative manufactured goods. Even in the United States, where mining seems indisputably to have been an engine of economic growth during the nineteenth and twentieth centuries, there is reason to question the conventional wisdom. Those American communities that are most dependent on extractive industries, including timber and agriculture as well as mining, tend to be among the most economically depressed (and not simply, or even largely, because of regulatory restrictions on mining). See Thomas Michael Power, Lost Landscapes and Failed Economies: The Search for a Value of Place 4 (Island Press 1996). The boom and bust cycles of mining take their toll on long-run economic development.

Whether an extensive mineral base is ultimately an economic blessing or curse, the fact remains that minerals have substantial economic value. And that fact, more than any other, explains the history of mineral resources law and development in the United States.

B. Geology and Extraction of Mineral Deposits

1. Geology of Mineral Deposits

Various geological processes produce mineral deposits. These processes include magmatic activity, erosional and residual deposition, sedimentation, and groundwater deposition.

Magmatic Activity—When magma (hot, molten, igneous rock) moves along the fractures of the earth's crust, as a result of volcanic action or plate tectonics, the heat from the intrusive magma warms the surrounding rock, causing it to recrystallize and form different minerals. As the hydro-thermal solution continues to cool, it solidifies into veins of minerals. Most metallic minerals of importance and some non-metallic minerals are found in veins among rock fissures.

Erosional and Residual Deposition—Water, air, and natural weathering disintegrate unstable minerals from the surrounding rock, and move the suspended material to areas where minerals eventually settle out. The resulting concentrations can contain "placer" deposits of gold, platinum, silver, and copper. "Residual" deposits are minerals that remain after weathering has eroded the overlying rock. Examples include iron ore, manganese, bauxite, nickel, and phosphate.

Sedimentation—The layering of various materials over very long periods of time causes physical and chemical changes that can form valuable mineral substances. Oil and gas, for example, result from the conversion by heat and pressure of marine microorganisms into hydrocarbons. Other sedimentary minerals include coal and building materials such as sandstone, clay, and limestone.

Groundwater Deposition and Evaporation—Uranium, when underground waters evaporate, minerals previously dissolved in the groundwater, including gypsum, salt, borates, and bromides, may be left behind.

2. *Mineral Extraction*

Extracting minerals from the earth is a complicated task typically involving the following steps: (1) selection of an area for exploration, (2) detailed exploration using one or more exploration techniques, (3) location of a valuable mineral deposit, and (4) construction of a mine for mineral extraction. Initial legal rights to minerals typically are secured at some point between the first and second steps, but those rights remain "imperfect" until completion of step three. Claimants on state lands must comply with applicable state claim location requirements; claimants on federal lands must comply with federal mining laws *and* the mining laws of the state in which the claim is located. States apply various rules to "staking" claims, such as making mineral discoveries, undertaking physical "location work," and recording claims.

Apart from complying with federal and state legal requirements to protect the claim (discussed in detail later in this chapter), the would-be miner also must: (1) choose among alternative exploration methods, and (2) if exploration reveals a valuable ore deposit, choose among alternative mining methods.[b]

a. Exploration

Mining companies select relatively small areas for extensive exploration based on the published literature, the advice of geologists, the existence of old mines, or the results of aerial or geographic reconnaissance. Once an area has been selected, geologic information is collected and analyzed to ascertain whether a mining operation would likely yield a valuable mineral deposit. This data is often difficult and expensive to obtain. Unlike sedimentary deposits, such as coal, which are easily traceable after determining the stratigraphy of the region, hard-rock minerals may or may not be geologically related to the surrounding rock structure.

Miners utilize three exploration techniques to determine whether or not these difficult-to-locate minerals are present: (1) geological feature identification, (2) geochemical exploration, and (3) geophysical exploration.

Geological Feature Identification—Over the centuries, miners have learned that certain identifiable geologic features can suggest the pres-

---

b. The discussion of exploration and mining methods, as well as the accompanying illustrations, is based largely upon United States Department of Agriculture, Forest Service, Intermountain Research Station, Anatomy of a Mine: From Prospect to Production, General Technical Report INT–GTR–35 (February 1995), available at http://imcg.wr.usgs.gov/usbmak/anat0.html.

ence of nearby mineral deposits. Examples of significant geologic features include:

(1) Igneous rock association—Chromite and tungsten are often associated with certain types of igneous rocks.

(2) Host rock association—Uranium is usually found in beds of sandstone or granite veins.

(3) Age of rock formations—The age of rock formations may indicate the presence of certain kinds of minerals that are found only in rock formations of a certain age. Potash, for example, is found only in rock formations dating to the Permian Era (200 to 225 million years old).

(4) Physiographic expression—If one kind of physical setting is found to contain sought-after minerals, miners may search for similar physical settings in the same area.

To determine whether any of the above geologic features exists, miners almost always must drill exploratory holes. In fact, mining companies spend a great deal of money drilling holes that find no significant geological features, let alone valuable mineral deposits.

Geochemical Exploration—Chemical analysis of an area's soil, rock, vegetation, and water can reveal the presence of "trace metals," the presence of which often suggests that associated minerals are near. Airborne or vehicle-mounted metal detectors can measure indicators, such as mercury vapor, sulphur dioxide, and radon gas, that point to an ore deposit beneath the surface.

Geophysical Exploration—Sensitive gravitational, seismic, magnetic, electrical, and radiometric instruments can detect the physical characteristics of various minerals. Gravity methods, for example, measure the relative density of the ore deposit and surrounding rock, and can be useful for exploring petroleum and natural gas deposits, but not for locating mineral ore deposits, which usually lack the density, size, and definition to distinguish them from surrounding rock.

Thumper Trucks

Seismic instruments, such as vibroseis (or "thumper") trucks, send out seismic waves of up to 64,000 pounds of pressure. Cable monitors attached to recording instruments time the seismic waves as they pass through the earth and bounce off different rock layers. The time required for a seismic wave to arrive at a given point indicates the existence of different types or densities of rocks and ore bodies. Seismic exploration is a useful method for detecting the presence of petroleum, natural gas, and sulfur; but it also entails significant environmental impacts. Thumper trucks gouge (with their tires) and pulverize (with their seismic waves) fragile soils, increasing erosion and disturbing wildlife habitat.

b. Mining Methods

After exploration work reveals the existence of a valuable mineral deposit, miners have several decisions to make about the technical, economic, and legal feasibility of extracting and processing the deposit. The nature of the extraction method and equipment will depend upon the nature of the mineral and its location. Coal deposits, especially those near the surface, require equipment that will remove the "overburden" (the rock and soil covering the mineral) and extract the coal. Once extracted, however, coal requires little processing. Oil and gas deposits necessitate wells, pumps, pipelines, and, eventually, secondary and tertiary field recovery methods, which increase recovery of oil and gas by increasing reservoir pressure through the injection of gas or water into reservoir rock (secondary recovery) or by heating the reservoir (tertiary recovery).

Hardrock minerals are very difficult and expensive to recover, in large part because waste minerals may constitute most of the weight of the valuable ore. A large quantity of rock must be extracted, processed, and disposed of in order to yield what may be a relatively small quantity of the desired mineral.

Once the miner has decided to proceed with development (primarily a financial decision), the next critical decision involves the choice of mining method. Three methods are used most commonly: (1) underground mining, (2) surface mining, and (3) solution mining (sometimes known as borehole leach mining).

Underground Mining—The most technically challenging and expensive method of mining is by "stoping" (underground mining). This technique is required when minerals lie deep within the earth or when geology or geography prevent surface mining. The process of underground mining involves the digging of a shaft to the ore deposit, which is then removed in the most efficient way possible. The "best" (or most efficient) method of extraction depends on the size and shape of the ore body, the strength of the enclosing wall rock, and overburden conditions. Some ore bodies may be completely mined in underground excavations (stopes), which are then filled with waste rock, as shown in Figures 1 and 2. Pillar mining leaves pillars of ore in place in an excavated area to support the overburden and prevent it from subsiding into the cavity that remains after the ore has been removed.

Figure 1

Underground Mining Terms

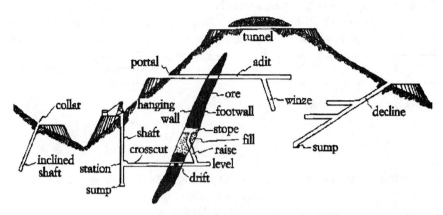

Figure 2
Open Pit Mine

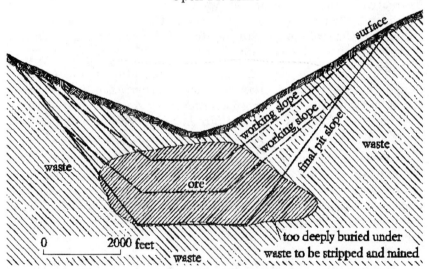

Surface Mining—The most commonly used surface mining techniques are placer mining and open pit mining. Both are used when the ore is found close to the surface. Placer deposits are concentrations of heavy minerals found within loose material, such as gravel, that can be washed away to expose the minerals. Most placer mining involves either "hydraulic" mining, where a stream of water under great pressure is directed against the base of the placer gravel bank, or "dredging," where alluvial deposits are shoveled onto a dredge, on which the placer material is washed and the minerals separated mechanically. Open pit mining exposes the ore by removing as much of the overburden and waste rock as can be economically stripped away. Open pit mines produce a great deal of waste material, and generally require expensive land reclamation efforts. The same is true of strip mining, another common form of surface mining (see Figure 2). One type of strip mining, known as "mountaintop removal," has recently become highly controversial. This process is summed up by its name. A mining company blasts off the top of a mountain in order to more easily access the coal inside. The following article describes recent litigation about mountaintop mining.

In Focus:

Judge Takes On the White House on Mountaintop Mining
Francis X. Clines
Copyright 2002 The New York Times Company
May 19, 2002 Sunday

The towering strip mining machines that have been systematically decapitating mountains in Appalachia have once again run up against a flinty federal judge convinced that government agencies illegally allow the coal industry to pollute and obliterate the region's vital waterways with millions of tons of waste.

In a direct challenge to the Bush administration, the judge, Chief Judge Charles H. Haden II of the Southern District of West Virginia, found last week that the administration's new rule change that allows the dumping of mining rock and dirt into the streams and valleys of Appalachia is an "obvious perversity" of the Clean Water Act.

"The rule change was designed simply for the benefit of the mining industry and its employees," Judge Haden ruled. He ordered the Army Corps of Engineers to stop issuing permits to companies that have been dumping millions of tons of waste into hundreds of miles of waterways and hollows in the mining practice known as mountaintop removal.

This is the process of blasting away mountaintop rock to reach low-sulphur coal veins with mammoth bulldozers and drag lines. The practice pours waste down into the mountain hollows, where residents have been increasingly displaced or bought out by the companies.

Judge Haden's ruling has stunned the Appalachian coal industry, which warns that the decision could, in theory, shut down any mine in the nation that dumps waste into water. But it has cheered environmental groups that have been contending that the Bush administration, mindful of three critical electoral votes Republicans won here in the close 2000 presidential election, has rewarded the coal industry with job appointments and policy accommodations.

The administration, insisting its new rule on mining waste protects the environment, warned this week that the court ruling will mean "severe economic and social hardship for the region," with tens of thousands of jobs at risk along with hundreds of millions in state revenue and profits in related industries. * * *

"That's a red herring," said Joe Lovett, director of the Appalachian Center for the Economy and the Environment, one of the litigants suing the corps of engineers. Mr. Lovett said the ruling, if upheld, would protect communities, streams and hardwood forests from destruction and encourage a more balanced economy in lumbering and better controlled underground and strip mining.

Judge Haden has been over this legal terrain before. In 1999, he ruled that state agencies had failed to enforce federal environmental protection laws affecting mountaintop removal. Under the process, hundreds of square miles of mountains have been leveled and dozens of communities have been bought out.

Judge Haden's decision in that first suit was overturned on appeal a year ago. Without ruling on the merits of the complaint, a panel of the appeals court found that West Virginia had constitutional immunity against the lawsuit. It was filed by a resident who had held out against a buyout when his neighbors abandoned Pigeon Roost Hollow in Blair, W.Va., as waste descended.

The new, broader lawsuit was filed against the federal government by community and environmental groups in a four-state coal region of Appalachia. Challenging a mine waste permit last year on the West Virginia–Kentucky border, the groups, operating as Kentuckians for the Commonwealth, charged that the Army Corps of Engineers illegally favored the coal industry by permitting destructive waste disposal in violation of corps regulations that specifically ban such dumping.

Judge Haden agreed. The judge shocked the mining industry and environmentalists by reaching beyond the issue of existing regulations to strike down the Bush administration's new rule regarding the dumping of rock and dirt.

He said the rule was an effort by federal agencies "to legalize their longstanding illegal regulatory practice." A change that basic, Judge Haden wrote, could only be tried "in the sunlight of open Congressional debate and resolution, not within the murk of administrative after-the-fact ratification of questionable regulatory practices."

Industry and government warn of economic ruin from the ruling, with 28,000 miners now at work in the $6.3 billion mining industry in West Virginia and Kentucky, mainly mountaintop removal. The mining industry insists it dumps fill only in seasonal streams, not those running year round, and notes that some companies invest in modified restoration of the shaved mountains. * * *

> Coal industry officials, with hundreds of waste applications pending, are counting on another victory on the appeals level to void Judge Haden's latest finding.
>
> In making his 1999 decision, the judge not only hiked to Pigeon Roost Hollow to view that site but also flew over the region's many mountaintop removal sites.
>
> "The sites stood out among the natural wooded ridges as huge white plateaus," he wrote, "and the valley fills appeared as massive, artificially landscaped stair steps. Tree growth was stunted or nonexistent. The mine sites appear stark and barren and enormously different from the original topography."
>
> The judge wondered at all the absent wildlife that "can't be coaxed back." He concluded, "These harms cannot be undone."

Judge Haden's ruling was subsequently reversed by the Fourth Circuit U.S. Court of Appeals in Kentuckians for the Commonwealth, Inc. v. Rivenburgh, 317 F.3d 425 (4th Cir. 2003). That case is discussed below in Section V, p. 1054.

Solution Mining—Instead of removing great quantities of rock to extract ore by conventional underground or surface methods, solution mining injects a water, acid, or some dissolving solution into the ore. Once the ore is dissolved, it is relatively inexpensive to recover it through production wells. Solution mining works best for minerals that are readily converted into a more soluble form, such as potash, salt, sulphur, and uranium, but it produces chemical wastes which, if not properly captured and treated, can run off-site and contaminate surface and ground water.

C. The Mining Industry

For many years the United States disposed of and regulated its mineral wealth in piecemeal fashion. The lack of a national minerals policy may have made sense before the discovery of large, highly valued deposits of precious minerals in the middle of the nineteenth century. Between 1785 and the 1866, the United States generally sought to reserve "mineral lands" from disposition, but not always. Congress early on allowed entry to lands in Michigan and Minnesota known to contain copper and iron.[c] And it enacted a number of statutes authorizing federal leasing and some sales of lead mines. But mining generally remained a small-scale industry until 1848, when James Marshall discovered gold at Sutter's Mill in California.

---

c. A "land entry" occurred when a person making a claim to a specific parcel of public land under one of the land disposal statutes registered with the district General Land Office. The registrant was entitled to occupy and use the land for various purposes. A "mineral entry" occurred when a prospector occupied the land, discovered a valuable mineral deposit, and claimed the deposit and the surrounding land.

Marshall's discovery and subsequent discoveries of gold in Colorado, silver in Nevada, and lead, zinc, and associated metals in many western states lured miners to the vast public domain of the western United States. Before 1866, no federal laws governed the disposition of public lands valuable for minerals; miners had no right to enter onto the public domain to search for minerals. But the "forty-niners" were not deterred from trespassing onto the public lands to search for and extract valuable minerals. In any case, the risk of detection and expulsion of trespassers was minimal.

Mining camps arose and adopted their own rules for making and holding claims. In addition, the mining camps established a priority rule whereby the first miner to stake a claim had a superior legal right to the minerals within that claim. This priority doctrine evolved to shape not only federal mining law but western water law as well.

After Congress's long preoccupation with the Civil War ended in 1865, mining policy became an important national issue. In 1866 and 1872 Congress enacted two statutes which, in combined effect, opened the public domain to free mineral exploration. The 1866 Lode Law, 14 Stat. 251, declared that the mineral lands of the public domain were open to exploration and occupation, and that lode claimants could obtain title to mineral deposits (but not the surrounding land) by meeting certain work and improvement requirements. The 1866 Act adopted the principle already established by the miners themselves that the mineral deposits on the public lands belong to the person who first discovers them. The 1866 Lode Law only authorized ownership of lodes or veins; placer claims became subject to private ownership four years later, when Congress enacted the 1870 Placer Act, 16 Stat. 217. Then, in 1872, Congress passed the General Mining Location Law (better known as the 1872 Mining Law), 17 Stat. 91, which remains to this day the basic law governing the acquisition of hardrock minerals on federal lands. The 1872 Law (addressed in detail in Section II, below) continued the policy of making mineral deposits free and open to exploration and eventual private ownership. The 1872 Law further authorized miners to "patent" (obtain fee title to) tracts of land encompassing mineral deposits.

Since Congress enacted the 1872 Mining Law, the structure of the mining industry and its technologies have changed dramatically; so too, of course, have the U.S. population, public land policies, and many other factors. But mining has remained throughout these changes a favorite of government mainly because of its presumed importance for the national economy, which relies heavily on hard rocks such as silver, copper, and gypsum, as well as "soft" minerals such as coal and oil. Indeed, the mining industry likes to think of itself as the "backbone of the U.S. Economy." This may have been true once upon a time, but by the end of the twentieth century, it was a gross overstatement, as the following report suggests.

In Focus:

CRS Report for Congress, Hardrock Mining, the 1872 Law, and the U.S. Economy
Bernard Gelb
94–540 E (July 1, 1994) (citations omitted)

THE [MINING] INDUSTRY AS A WHOLE

Although minerals are the major material inputs in most of the industrial, commercial, and consumer equipment and structures produced by the U.S. economy, and the United States still is self-sufficient in many metallic and nonfuel nonmetallic minerals, the industry that extracts and initially processes these materials, constitutes a very small portion of the U.S. economy in terms of value of output and persons employed. This is because only a small part of the entire transformation from ore to finished product takes place in mines and mills, and hardrock mines and mills tend to be highly mechanized.

Thus, gross product originating (GPO) in hardrock mining averaged an estimated $9.7 billion in 1990 and 1991 (latest data available), less than 0.2 percent of Gross Domestic Product in those years. Industry employment in 1993 was an estimated 105,000, less than 0.1 percent of total civilian employment. About 60 percent of gross product and about 50 percent of employment in hardrock mining is accounted for by mines and mills producing metals.

Copper, gold, iron ore, and crushed rock account for about three fifths of the value of hardrock mining output (measured by value of shipments) and about three fourths of hardrock mining employment. Gold mining has expanded very rapidly during the last decade and a half and, by itself, now accounts for about one sixth of hardrock mining employment. Almost two-thirds of U.S. mine production of gold takes place in Nevada.

Workers in hardrock mining earn considerably more than workers in most other industries, partly reflecting mine workers' ability to operate the large-scale and extensively-used heavy equipment. In 1993, the average weekly pay of metal mining and of nonmetal mining production workers was about 75 percent and 55 percent, respectively, higher than the average for all industries.

Because nonfuel minerals are used largely as material inputs in equipment and structures, whose purchase usually is postponable and, therefore, cyclical, the (derived) demand for hardrock minerals and the industry producing them also are cyclical.

Much of U.S. metal mining is accounted for by divisions or subsidiaries of large, vertically integrated, metal mining and manufacturing firms. This is less true in the case of nonmetal mining. In 1987, the latest year for which a Census count is available, there were about 500 companies operating about 750 metal mines and/or mills, and about 1,600 companies operating about 2,900 nonfuel nonmetallic hardrock mines and/or mills. Closures, mergers, and acquisitions since the mid–1980s probably have reduced the number of companies and mines and mills operating in the United States.

Particularly in the case of metal mining, closures, mergers, and acquisitions have been accompanied by a drastic rationalization of operations that, among other things, has greatly increased productivity. Output per employee hour in iron ore mining, copper ore mining, and nonmetallic nonfuel mineral mining rose an average of 5.3, 7.2, and 1.7 percent per year, respectively, between 1979 and 1990, compared with 0.8 percent for nonfarm business as a whole. Employment in hardrock mining fell from nearly 140,000 to the 105,000 noted above.

The consequent reductions in production costs reversed previously distressed conditions in the U.S. hardrock mining industry by making U.S. operations very cost-competitive with producers abroad. U.S exports of metal concentrates and raw nonfuel nonmetallic minerals have exceeded imports in recent years, based upon data published by the International Trade Administration. U.S. exports of primary metals also have tended to increase relative to imports, partly reflecting the decreases in mining costs. * * *

MINING ON FEDERAL LANDS

The great preponderance of Federal land is concentrated in 12 Western States; 53 percent of the land in those States is Federal; and a substantial portion of hardrock mining occurs on Federal lands in those States. The General Accounting Office (GAO) has estimated that at least $1.2 billion worth of minerals (based upon value of shipments) were produced from Federal lands in the Western States in 1990 out of a total of $8.6 billion of Western States hardrock mineral production. An Interior Department Task Force (IDTF) tally puts hardrock mining output on Federal lands at $1.8 billion for 1991, or about 15 percent of the total value of U.S. hardrock mineral production.

The distribution by mineral of hardrock mining on Federal lands differs from that on non-Federal lands. GAO estimated that Federal lands accounted for 30, 29 and 24 percent, respectively, of total gold, silver, and lead production in the Western States in 1990; the IDTF estimated the 1991 shares for gold and silver at 43 and 36 percent, respectively. Gold, because of its high value, accounted for about 80 percent of the total value of hardrock mineral production on Federal lands, based upon the IDTF data.

Somewhat correspondingly, a large portion of Western Federal lands and of hardrock mining activity is located in the States of

Alaska and Nevada. In 1990, 67 and 83 percent, respectively, of the land in those States was Federal, and 37 percent of mining claims on Western Federal lands were in Nevada.

Department Task Force (IDTF) tally puts hardrock mining output on Federal lands at $1.8 billion for 1991, or about 15 percent of the total value of U.S. hardrock mineral production.

Basic economics explains the decline of mining in the United States.[d] The supply of minerals has vastly exceeded demand, resulting in low world prices, which dampen incentives for further exploration and extraction. Still, in the year 2000 nearly 14,000 mines were operating in the United States.[e] And if the mining industry no longer constitutes a significant portion of the U.S. economy, it nonetheless continues to exercise substantial political clout in Washington, D.C. and in many states.

II. HARDROCK MINERAL LAW

Several distinct and interacting legal systems regulate mineral exploration and development, depending on where the land and minerals are located and the type of minerals involved. Minerals found on federal public lands, or on lands previously owned by the federal government and subject to federal reserved mineral rights, are governed by one of three regulatory regimes—location, leasing, or sale—depending on mineral type. *See* Table 2. Minerals on federal lands also are subject to state regulations, as long as those state regulations are not contrary to federal law.

Table 2   Minerals on Federal Lands Subject to Location, Lease, or Sale

Location	Lease	Sale
Hardrock Minerals: gold, silver, copper, tin, iron, borax, feldspar, gypsum	Energy minerals: coal, oil and gas, oil shale	"Common varieties": clay, sand, gravel, limestone
	Chemical and fertilizer minerals: phosphate, sodium	

On state owned lands, state laws govern mineral exploration and development. On privately owned lands, mining is largely a matter of private contracting, although certain state and federal laws—for instance, those relating to reclamation and environmental protection—may apply. This section addresses the various federal and state regula-

d. The imposition of environmental and other regulations on mining have played a marginal, secondary role.

e. BCS, Inc., Energy and Environmental Profile of the U.S. Mining Industry I–7, Table 1–2 (December 2002).

tory systems for mining exploration, development, and reclamation in a location system, and Section III will address lease and sale systems.

A. The 1872 Mining Law's Location System for Hardrock Mining

Most hardrock minerals (such as gold, silver and copper) found on or under federally owned public lands can be mined pursuant to the system of "location" established in the 1872 Mining Law. That law has its greatest application in five western states. At the beginning of the 21st century, approximately 45% of all claims established under the 1872 Mining Law were located in the State of Nevada. Arizona, California, Montana, and Wyoming together were home to another 35% of all hard-rock mining claims.

The "location" system established in the 1872 Mining Law is based on self-initiation, which allows a prospector—an appellation that conjures up images of a bearded old man, dragging a pack mule behind him—to enter the public domain at will, search for minerals, and upon discovery of a valuable deposit, remove all minerals discovered without payment of any royalty to the United States. While prospecting, but before discovery, the locator's occupation of the land is protected against other prospectors by a rule known as *pedis possessio* (possession under foot). Prior to discovery, but upon completion of certain location procedures (including compliance with state laws on the marking of boundaries and posting notice), a claim is "located." Location extends the locator's protections (beyond mere *pedis possessio*) against other claimants. After discovery of a valuable mineral deposit, a locator who diligently pursues the find has certain property rights, even though the locator does not yet have fee title to the minerals (a patent) from the United States. Property rights attendant to "unpatented mining claims" (a mere possessory right) include: the right to access the claim; the right to exclusively possess the surface within the boundaries of the location; the right to remove all ore from veins and lodes throughout their entire depth; and the right to sell minerals from the claim without payment of royalties.

The locator also has certain legal obligations under the 1872 Mining Law, including: performance of annual assessment work; avoidance of environmental damage or undue disturbance to surface resources; and reclamation of the surface upon exhaustion of the mineral deposit. A locator who wishes to acquire more than a mere possessory right under the mining laws may apply for a federal patent. An applicant for a patent bears the burden of demonstrating compliance with all applicable federal and state mining laws and regulations, including: discovery of a "valuable" mineral deposit on land subject to "location"; performance of annual assessment work after discovery; satisfaction of deadlines for recording claims; and the absence of adverse claimants. When granted, a patent ordinarily conveys fee simple title to the minerals *and the land* within the claim's boundaries.

Although the 1872 Mining Law is the primary basis for hardrock mining on federal lands, it has been embellished over the decades by judicial opinions, statutory exceptions, and administrative regulations and decisions. State legislation supplements the Mining Law to determine competing rights among rival claimants. The federal Multiple Mineral Use Act of 1954 provides for development of leasable and locatable minerals from the same tracts of public lands; the Multiple Surface Use Mining Act of 1955 reserves to the United States use of the surface and surface resources on all mining claims located after 1955 until claims are patented; and the Federal Land Policy and Management Act of 1976 (FLPMA) redefines claim recording procedures, and provides for automatic abandonment of mining claims if statutory procedures are not followed. Implementation of the federal mining laws is within the jurisdiction of the Department of the Interior, primarily its Bureau of Land Management (BLM). The Forest Service, in the Department of Agriculture, has substantial authority over mining claims located in national forests.

1. *Location*

a. **Lands Open to Location**

The 1872 Mining Law provides that mineral deposits "in lands belonging to the United States, both surveyed and unsurveyed, shall be free and open to exploration and purchase." 30 U.S.C.A. § 22. Federal mining law thus applies to all "public land states"—those 30 states mainly west of the Alleghenies over which the United States acquired not only title before any private rights attached but also sovereign jurisdiction as the states there had not yet been created. *See* Chapter 6. Of these 30 public domain states, most in the Midwest either had passed out of federal ownership by 1872, or were exempt from federal mining laws by congressional action. The remaining public domain states include 11 western states—Alaska, Arizona, California, Colorado, Idaho, Montana, Nevada, New Mexico, North Dakota, South Dakota, Oregon, Utah, Washington, and Wyoming—and five states outside of the West, including Arkansas, Louisiana, Mississippi, Florida, and Nebraska. The western states, in particular, contain an enormous quantity and variety of locatable minerals on vast expanses of federally owned lands; the five public domain states outside the West are known mainly for their leasable minerals. Thus, federal hardrock mining law is of greatest importance in the 11 western public domain states.

Not all the federal lands in the public domain states are open to mineral location. Federal mining laws apply only to federal lands that are *unappropriated*, not *withdrawn*, and not *reserved* from mineral location. However, as noted earlier, federal mining laws *are* applicable to federally reserved minerals underlying privately owned surface lands settled under various federal land disposition statutes, such as the Stockraising–Homestead Act of 1916. It is believed that over 60 million surface acres have been patented into private ownership subject to federal mineral reservations. The surface owners of these severed estates hold their lands subject to the superior rights of the United States (through its locators and lessees) to remove reserved minerals. *See* Transwestern Pipeline Co. v. Kerr–McGee Corp., 492 F.2d 878 (10th Cir. 1974); Occidental Geothermal, Inc. v. Simmons, 543 F.Supp. 870 (N.D.Cal. 1982).

"Appropriated" public lands not open to mineral location include lands subject to prior mining claims or mineral patents. Public lands can be "withdrawn" from location and mineral entry by executive or congressional action. *See* P & G Mining Co., 57 Int. Dept. 217 (1960) ("It has long been recognized that the President ... may cause a particular portion of the public domain to be appropriated to public use, and whenever a tract of land has been so appropriated ... laws which permit the acquisition of private rights in public lands do not apply."). Withdrawn lands sometimes are referred to as "reserved" lands. Executive and congressional withdrawals have included lands withdrawn by Presidents Roosevelt and Taft to protect petroleum reserves, lands withdrawn under the 1902 Reclamation Act, waterpower site withdrawals under the 1920 Federal Power Act, Indian reservations, national parks and monuments (national park system lands are withdrawn from mineral entry and location), national wildlife refuges, wilderness and primitive areas, and various oil shale withdrawals. *See* Brown v. U.S. Department of Interior, 679 F.2d 747 (8th Cir. 1982).

During the 1990s, President Clinton made liberal use of the Antiquities Act of 1906, designating 19 new national monuments covering more than 5 million acres of public land.[f] These monument designations did not affect existing mines, but withdrew from prospective mining location between 40 and 60 million acres of the public domain.

Any mining claims located on lands previously withdrawn from appropriation are null and void *ab initio*. Mac A. Stevens, 83 ILBA 164 (1984); Russell Hoffman, 84 IBLA 508 (1985). Until the late 1970s, no master federal list disclosed the extent or location of all public lands withdrawn from mineral entry. Prospective miners had to search the records of state BLM offices to determine whether the land they wanted to explore had been withdrawn. In 1976, FLPMA required the Department of the Interior to compile a list of all such withdrawals. In addition, while FLPMA ratified most previous withdrawals, it curtailed executive authority to make future withdrawals. 43 U.S.C.A. § 1714(b) and (c).

Valid, preexisting mining claims on withdrawn lands are grandfathered, which means they are not invalidated upon withdrawal. *See* Northern Alaska Environmental Center v. Lujan, 872 F.2d 901 (9th Cir. 1989). However, those claims may be subject to subsequently-imposed regulations. *See, e.g.,* United States v. Vogler, 859 F.2d 638 (9th Cir. 1988).

---

    f. See Albert C. Lin, *Clinton's National Monuments: A Democrat's*   *Undemocratic Acts?*, 29 Ecology. L.Q. 707, 717 (2002).

b. Locatable Minerals

A mining claim must based on a "mineral" that is "locatable" under the 1872 Mining Law. Would-be locators must ascertain which minerals are subject to location under that law. The language of the 1872 Law itself is misleading. It provides that "all valuable minerals deposits" are subject to location, 30 U.S.C.A. § 22, and allows the location of mining claims upon "veins or lodes of quartz or other rock in place bearing gold, silver, cinnabar [mercury], lead, tin, copper or other valuable [mineral] deposits." 30 U.S.C.A. § 23. This list of substances is not all inclusive. Other minerals, not listed in the 1872 Act, are also locatable, pursuant to subsequent legislation as well as court and administrative rulings. Virtually all nonmetallic substances, including borax, feldspar, and gypsum, are locatable. Even substances like sand and gravel may be locatable if they have "distinct and special value" that makes them uncommon. According to Interior Department mining regulations: "Whatever is recognized by the standard authorities ... when found in quantity and quality sufficient to render the lands valuable on account thereof, is treated as coming within the purview of the mining laws." 43 C.F.R. § 3812.1.

Because the definition of "mineral" is so broad, a more useful inquiry is to determine what minerals are *not* subject to location because they have been specifically removed from the ambit of the 1872 Mining Law. The 1920 Mineral Leasing Act removed from location fossil fuel minerals (coal, gas, oil, oil shale, asphalt, bitumen) as well as fertilizer and chemical minerals (phosphate and sodium). Subsequent amendments to that law and other statutes added sulfur deposits in some states, potash, outer continental shelf deposits of oil and gas, geothermal resources, and hardrock minerals found on acquired lands to the list of leasable—not locatable—minerals. Prior to 1920, fossils, meteorites, and crystalline deposits in caverns were excluded from location. Deposits of clay and limestone, peat moss, and sand and gravel suitable only for ordinary uses were held non-locatable by administrative decisions of the Interior Department. The Common Varieties Act (also known as the Surface Resources Act) of 1955, 30 U.S.C.A. § 611, prohibited the location of sand, stone, gravel, pumice, cinders, and other designated "common" materials unless the deposit "has some property giving it distinct and special value." *See* United States v. J.R. Henderson, 68 Int. Dept. 26 (1961)(holding that sand and gravel possessing no special and distinct value are not locatable); United States v. Kaycee Bentonite Corp., 79 IBLA 445 (May 27, 1982) (a deposit of bentonite which can be profitably removed and marketed for pelletizing taconite is an exceptional clay locatable under federal mining laws). Since 1955, the government has disposed of common variety minerals without special value by sale. Petrified wood was added as a common variety mineral in 1962. 69 Stat. 368.

As noted above, President Clinton used the Antiquities Act, 16 U.S.C. § 431, to remove hundreds of thousands of acres of public lands from mineral entry. Like the Clinton withdrawals other executive and legislative withdrawals of minerals applied prospectively. They included savings clauses so that locations made prior to the effective date of the orders or statutes removing minerals from location remained valid under the 1872 Mining Law. This protected investment-backed expectations of miners, and avoided potential takings claims against the government.

To take advantage of these "grandfather" clauses, however, it was not enough for a miner to show that she had staked a valid claim before the effective date of the relevant removal statute. As the next case demonstrates, they also had to prove a valuable discovery that was marketable at a profit prior to the effective date of the removal order or statute.

DREDGE CORP. v. CONN
United States Court of Appeals, Ninth Circuit, 1984.
733 F.2d 704.

CIRCUIT JUDGE PREGERSON delivered the opinion of the Court.

The Dredge Corporation ("Dredge") appeals the decision of the Interior Board of Land Appeals ("Board") that Dredge did not have a valid placer mining claim to Dredge No. 51, a 40–acre parcel of federally-owned land located five miles west of Las Vegas. The Board's decision was based on Dredge's failure to discover minerals of marketable value on Dredge No. 51 before the effective date of the Surface Resources Act, 30 U.S.C. §§ 601–615. We affirm.

The acquisition of private mining rights in federally-owned land is governed by the Mineral Location Law of 1872. 30 U.S.C. § 22. * * *

To establish a valid mining claim a claimant must meet certain requirements. First, the claimant must "locate" the claim. The procedures for locating a claim are prescribed by local custom or state law. See 30 U.S.C. § 28. These procedures usually require the claimant to (1) post some form of notice on the land; (2) mark the boundaries of the claim; (3) conduct preliminary excavation or discovery work on the claim; and (4) record a certificate of location in the local mining district office. See 1 Rocky Mtn.Min.L.Inst., American Law of Mining § 5.49 (1981 ed.).

Second, the claimant must make a "discovery." This requires the discovery of a valuable mineral deposit on the claim. Whether a claim is sufficiently valuable is determined by the marketability test. Under that test, the claimant must show that the mineral on the claim can be "extracted, removed and marketed at a profit." United States v. Coleman, 390 U.S. 599, 600, 88 S.Ct. 1327, 1329, 20 L.Ed.2d 170(1968). A claimant who makes a valid discovery is entitled to apply for a patent which will convey title to the land in fee simple. 30 U.S.C. § 29.

The Surface Resources Act, effective July 23, 1955, removed all common varieties of sand and gravel from future location under the general mining law. In other words, after July 23, 1955, an individual could not enter federally-owned lands for the purpose of mining sand and gravel. The Act contained a savings clause, however, that protected any valid mining claim located before the effective date of the Act. 30 U.S.C. § 615. Under that clause, the claimant must show that he located and made a discovery of the claim before July 23, 1955. Dredge contends that its claim falls within this savings clause. * * *

* * * [I]n 1975, Dredge filed a patent application for Dredge No. 51. On October 6, 1977, the BLM responded ... that: (1) the land within Dredge No. 51 was non-mineral in character; (2) no valid discovery of valuable minerals had been made; and (3) the mineral material on Dredge No. 51 could not have been marketed at a profit before July 23, 1955. * * *

The ... determination that the mineral deposit on Dredge's claim was not marketable in 1955 is supported by substantial evidence. Under the marketability test, the claimant must show that the claim can be "extracted, removed, and marketed at a profit." Coleman, 390 U.S. at 600, 88 S.Ct. at 1329 (1968). The claimant need not show that he actually sold minerals at a profit before 1955, although the absence of sales is a relevant factor in determining marketability. However, when there is little or no evidence of pre-1955 sales, a court should consider costs of extraction, preparation, and transport as well as then-existent market demand. In this case, the government showed that in 1955 the supply of sand and gravel in the Las Vegas area far exceeded local demand. Only 150 out of 40,000 acres of potential sand and gravel sites were being mined before 1955. Further, the demand for sand and gravel began to decline in 1955 after a boom in local construction from 1952 to 1954. This decline continued until the early 1960s. Although the record is conflicting, the government offered evidence that little or no mining activity occurred on Dredge No. 51 before 1955, with the exception of the construction of a road. This lack of mining activity lends support to the government's contention that the local market was weak in 1955. * * *

Dredge contends, however, that the deposit on Dredge No. 51 should have been deemed marketable merely because of its proximity and similarity to existing patented claims. We disagree. First of all, the government demonstrated important differences between Dredge No. 51 and nearby claims. Dredge No. 51 has less loose material and had a thick layer of caliche [a layer of soil in which soil particles are cemented together by lime—Ed.].

Moreover, Dredge's argument is inconsistent with the approach we set forth in Melluzzo v. Morton, 534 F.2d 860 (9th Cir. 1976), for determining the marketability of a mineral deposit. In Melluzo, we stated that the existence of a local market for sand and gravel alone is not sufficient to establish marketability. In other words, the claimant cannot rely solely on the fact that comparable material is being marketed. Rather "[t]he claimant must establish that his material was of a quality that would have met the existing demand and that it was marketable at a profit." Id. (emphasis added). The profitability of a particular deposit is determined not only by its cost of extraction, preparation for market, and transportation to market, but also by the overall market demand and supply. *Id.* at 864. Proof that neighboring claims are being marketed is relevant to determining a claim's marketability, but such proof alone does not overcome evidence that the market was already well-supplied. The claimant must also show that given existing market conditions his particular claim could have returned a profit. * * *

Notes and Questions

1. Dredge failed in its patent application because it did not have a valid claim before 1955. Its claim was not valid because there was no "discovery" of a "valuable" mineral deposit prior to 1955: Dredge failed to provide evidence that the mineral deposit could have been extracted and sold at a profit *at that time*. Because there was no discovery, the sand and gravel in the *Dredge* case were not locatable under the 1872 Law, and were instead non-locatable "common variety" minerals subject to sale under the 1955 Common Varieties Act. The question of what constitutes a discovery is further addressed below in section B.

2. If a common variety material found after 1955 is uncommon in a particular area, but present in very large deposits elsewhere, is it subject to the 1955 Act or the 1872 Act? *See* 43 C.F.R. § 3711.1(b) (proximity of the deposit "to the market or point of utilization" is a relevant factor in deciding whether a particular deposit of some common material has "special value").

3. Is carbon dioxide, used in tertiary oil recovery, a locatable mineral? Is water? *See* Andrus v. Charlestone Stone Products Co., 436 U.S. 604, 98 S.Ct. 2002, 56 L.Ed.2d 570 (1978)(no).

c. Qualified Locators

The 1872 Mining Law provides that a claim locator must be a United States citizen or an alien who has declared an intention to become a citizen. 30 U.S.C.A. § 22. A domestic corporation is considered a citizen under the 1872 Law regardless of the nationality of its stock-holders.[g] The Law does not, however, impose any age requirement. A minor who is competent and qualified to acquire and hold interests in land under state law qualifies as a locator. The law does not limit the number of mining claims made by any one locator; and locators may employ agents to locate claims for them.[h]

Any person whose name appears on a location certificate, even if listed without that person's knowledge, becomes a co-owner, possessing all the rights of a co-owner. Many states provide for a special type of co-ownership of an interest in a mining claim known as a "mining partnership." Such a partnership is formed for the development and operation of mines, but not for the sale of minerals from the mine. Like gen-

---

g. Similarly, the 1920 Mineral Leasing Act allows only citizens and domestic corporations to acquire mineral leases.

h. The federal government may not deny patents because an applicant claimed

more mineral lands than one person could reasonably be expected to develop. Baker v. United States, 613 F.2d 224 (9th Cir. 1980).

eral partnerships, mining partners are personally liable for the debts of the partnership. A mining partnership may be created by express agreement, or by implication if there is joint ownership and operation of the mineral property, and an agreement for sharing profits and losses. Parties interested only in acquiring joint ownership of mineral property may enter into so-called "grubstake" contracts–agreements to locate and split ownership interest in mines though joint labor or investment. If a court finds that such a contract exists, a general rule of equity is applied to prevent one co-owner from taking unfair advantage of another. *See* Smaller v. Leach, 136 Colo. 297, 316 P.2d 1030 (1957).

d.　Types of Locations

The 1872 Mining Law authorizes several types of mining claims, depending on the physical characteristics and location of the mining deposit. The two primary types are "lode" and "placer" mining claims. Lode mining claims are required by 30 U.S.C.A. § 23 to be made upon "… veins or lodes of quartz or other rock in place bearing … other valuable deposits …" Placer claims are located upon other "forms of deposit, excepting veins of quartz, or other rocks in place…." 30 U.S.C.A. § 35. It is imperative that the locator correctly identify the claim as being either lode or placer because a placer discovery located as a lode mine is invalid, and vice versa. Cole v. Ralph, 252 U.S. 286, 296, 40 S.Ct. 321, 64 L.Ed. 567 (1920); Bowen v. Chemi–Cote Perlite Corp., 102 Ariz. 423, 432 P.2d 435, 444 (1967). This dichotomy has proven problematic in cases where mineral deposits possess characteristics of both placers and lodes. In Globe Mining Co. v. Anderson, 318 P.2d 373 (Wyo. 1957), for example, the Supreme Court of Wyoming held that a widespread horizontal deposit containing mineralized zones of uranium, carried into the formation by some solution after the host rock was formed, constituted a "lode." But the court duly noted the ambiguous nature of such uranium deposits.

> Normally * * * a discovery [of uranium] at depth would be classified as a lode or vein, though an exception to this rule arises in the case of buried channels of ancient rivers which, historically, have been classified as placers. * * * Whether to locate uranium as a lode or placer is in doubt since uranium minerals have been found in every formation in the Colorado Plateau and in no definite pattern. While some vertical deposits of uranium in fractures are now being mined the predominant formation is horizontal, being "flatbedded' and "isolated' as are the host rock sediments. Since uranium deposits found in fractures should clearly be located as lodes, and most other uranium deposits are produced from ores which "interfinger with mudstones or silt stones' so that they are generally considered by the mining industry to be lodes, it is herein assumed that uranium mining claims should properly be so located. * * *
>
> * * * [W]hile the existence or nonexistence of a vein is often dependent upon mixed questions of law and fact, in this instance the

evidence of mineral showing and of the physical characteristics of a vein are so strong that as a matter of law the only conclusion that could properly be reached was that it was a vein. Fundamentally, of course, we are guided by the well-recognized knowledge that in the complexities of lodes, with indefinite and irregular walls, while the mineral association of rock in place is an essential element in the definition, the nature of the material, the form of the deposit, and the character of the boundaries are often variant ... and that it is not necessary for the formation of a disseminated lode that there should be any walls or any sheering. * * *

The views thus expressed would seem to apply to disseminated, epigenetic deposits of uranium. Under this interpretation, ... various portions of a mineral-bearing area coming from the same general source and found to have been created by the same processes of deposit from solution constitute a lode (rock in place) for the purpose of locating mining claims even though they may be formless and are not enclosed by definite boundaries.

Id. (citations omitted).

Because of the importance of correctly identifying the type of claim, "multiple location" has become a common practice. Multiple location involves the staking of the area with lode claims, which would be valid if the deposit subsequently is determined to be a lode, *and* with placer claims, which would be valid if the deposit later is determined to be placer. The placer claim must be located prior to lode location. In case of a dispute, courts emphasize the present form of the deposit more than its origin; courts also favor the first locator, and tend to follow industry custom in the area. *See* Iron Silver Mining Co. v. Mike & Starr Gold and Silver Mining Co., 143 U.S. 394, 12 S.Ct. 543, 36 L.Ed. 201 (1892).

In addition to lode and placer claims, federal mining law gives special treatment to lodes located *in* placer claims, to tunnel sites (horizontal excavations dug in search of lodes or veins not appearing on the surface), and to mill sites (space on the surface of nonmineral land for working claims or separating ores). The law gives no protection, however, to "exploration claims" resulting from drilling in search of mineral deposits. Lode and placer claims and mill sites are examined in detail below.

(i) Lode Claims

Court's have defined a "lode" as "a continuous body of mineral or mineralized rock filling a seam or fissure in the earth's crust within defined boundaries in the general mass of a mountain (which boundaries clearly separate it from surrounding rock) and having a general character of continuity in the direction of its length." McMullin v. Magnuson, 102 Colo. 230, 78 P.2d 964, 968 (1938). Courts rely on various factors to determine whether a deposit is a lode, including the character of the surrounding rock, the form and continuity of the ore, and the existence of a reasonable definition or boundary between the mineralized ore and the surrounding rock. In cases where the mineral deposit lies either shallow or deep between two layers of some other type of rock, courts usually have no trouble finding that the mineral deposit constitutes a lode. *See* Jones v. Prospect Mountain Tunnel Co., 21 Nev. 339, 31 P. 642 (1892); Eureka Consolidated Mining Co. v. Richmond Mining Co., 8 F.Cas. 819 (D.Nev. 1877). However, in the case of Titanium Actynite Industries v. McLennan, 272 F.2d 667 (10th Cir.1959), the court declined to find a lode because:

> plaintiffs' claim covered no well-defined veins or lodes as those terms are ordinarily used, unless it can be said that the entire area was a single lode. The record discloses that we are dealing with a large, shapeless, coarsely grained mass of ore which, with the possible exception of the disintegrated top portion, is 'in place' in the sense that it is in a fixed position. However, the mass extends over several miles of country and has no known dimensions or boundaries and none of the ordinary lode characteristics, not even as to the method of recovering the minerals. The theory that the entire mass is a lode in place with undetermined boundaries would create a single lode covering somewhere between 8 to 12 square miles.

Titanium Actynite Industries, 272 F.2d at 671.

In fact, under the terms of the 1872 Mining Law, a single lode claim may not exceed 1500 feet in length or 300 feet on each side of the middle of the vein; the end lines of each claim must be parallel to each other. 30 U.S.C.A. § 23. Lode claims often are irregular in shape.

(ii) Placer Claims

Placers include: superficial deposits washed down from a vein or lode; deposits of minerals found in particles of alluvium in beds or streams; and deposits fixed in rock that lack reasonable continuity (otherwise they would be lodes). The U.S. Supreme Court has defined placer mines as "those in which [minerals] are found in the softer material which covers the earth's surface, and among the soft rocks beneath," and they are mined by taking "the soft earthy matter in which the particles are loosely mingled, and by filtration separat[ing] the one from the other." Reynolds v. Iron Silver Mining Co., 116 U.S. 687, 695, 6 S.Ct. 601, 605, 29 L.Ed. 774 (1886). The minerals do not have to be near the surface to constitute placers. In Gregory v. Pershbaker, 73 Cal. 109, 14 P. 401 (1887), the California Supreme Court held that a gravel bed containing gold under 200 feet of lava was locatable as a placer claim. For the most part, common varieties and building stones which are subject to location because of their distinct and special values are located as placer mines. *See* United States v. Coleman, 390 U.S. 599, 88 S.Ct. 1327, 20 L.Ed.2d 170 (1968).

Placer claims must conform "as near as practicable" to survey lines where the area has been surveyed. 30 U.S.C.A. § 35. Otherwise, no provisions govern the shape of the exterior boundaries of placer claims. However, a placer claim may be no larger than 20 acres for an individual, but associations of up to eight persons may locate multiple claims up to a total of 160 acres. 30 U.S.C.A. § 36. Also, the locator must be able to show that each ten-acre tract of the placer claim is "mineral in character." McCall v. Andrus, 628 F.2d 1185 (9th Cir. 1980).

A placer location does not establish rights to any known lodes within its boundaries. If there is a "known" lode within a placer claim, the lode must be listed by the patent applicant at the time the patent application is filed for the placer. If a known lode is not listed in the placer patent application, the patentee is not entitled to it. Clipper Mining Co. v. Eli Mining and Land Co., 194 U.S. 220, 24 S.Ct. 632, 48 L.Ed. 944 (1904). If the lode deposit is *not* known at the time of the placer patent application, the lode becomes the property of the placer patentee when it later does become known. 30 U.S.C.A. § 37. A prospector who enters a valid placer location to search for unknown lodes without the permission of the placer locator is a trespasser, who may acquire no rights in any lodes she may discover. Campbell v. McIntyre, 295 F. 45 (9th Cir. 1924).

(iii) Mill Sites

The 1872 Law provides that miners can locate mill sites of up to five acres on nonmineral lands to provide space for all reasonable uses made in good faith for mining or milling purposes. 30 U.S.C.A. § 42. Approved uses of mill sites include depositing tailings, storing ores, tool houses, and houses for workmen. However, it is *not* a mine or milling purpose to use mill sites as a source of water or timber, or as a road to the mine. Mill sites must not be contiguous to the lode or vein, but may have coextensive boundaries with the mining claim if the mineral deposit does not overlap onto the mill site. Montana–Illinois Copper Mining Co., 42 L.D. 434 (1913). Legal rights to a mill site attach as of the time of location. Cleary v. Skiffich, 28 Colo. 362, 65 P. 59 (1901). Mill sites may be invalidated if: (1) not made on land open to mineral entry, Eagle Peak Copper Mining Co., 54 I.D. 251 (1933); (2) if a present and continuing use of the mill site is not maintained, in good faith, for a proper mining purpose, United States v. Bagwell, 961 F.2d 1450 (1992); (3) if the locator fails to sustain a valid mineral discovery on an associated mining claim, United States v. Colson, A–30835, GFS (Min) SO–16 (Feb. 23, 1968); or (4) if the mill site is held for an anticipated future use, United States v. S.M.P. Mining Co., 67 I.D. 144 (1960).

Mill sites have become a hot political item in the last two presidential administrations. In 1997, John Leshy, Solicitor of the Department of the Interior in the Clinton Administration, issued a legal opinion stating that a mining claim could use no more than five acres for millsites. This decision conformed to the precise terms of the 1872 Mining Law, but deviated from what had become traditional Interior Department practice of allowing claimants to use as much acreage as they legitimately needed for millsites. Marc Humphries, CRS Issue Brief for Congress,

"Mining on Federal Lands," CRS–10 (Congressional Research Service, Library of Congress, Updated July 21, 2004). The decision significantly affected the mining industry because modern mining techniques, such as heap-leach mining for gold, require larger tracts of land for disposal of leachate and waste rock.

Subsequently, when the Interior Department applied the Solicitor's opinion against the Battle Mountain Gold Company's Crown Jewel Mine in Washington state, Congress overturned that decision in the 1999 Emergency Supplemental Appropriations Act (P.L. 106–31), which expressly authorized a millsite of unlimited acreage for the Crown Jewel mine. Congress later enacted a two-year exemption from the Solictor's millsite opinion, before the Bush Administration finally replaced that opinion with a new one, which interpreted the 1872 Mining Law to allow multiple millsites for each mining claim, as necessary for development of mineral deposits. *Id.* at CRS–10 to CRS–11.

e. Location Procedures

The 1872 Mining Law provides that "no location of a mining claim shall be made until the discovery of a vein or lode." 30 U.S.C.A. § 21. Despite the seeming implication of this language that discovery must precede location, the courts have concluded that "the order of time in which these acts occur is not essential" to the establishment of a valid unpatented mining claim. Union Oil v. Smith, 249 U.S. 337, 39 S.Ct. 308, 63 L.Ed. 635 (1919); Creede and Cripple Creek Mining and Milling Co. v. Uinta Tunnel Mining and Transportation Co., 196 U.S. 337, 25 S.Ct. 266, 49 L.Ed. 501 (1904). If location comes before discovery, it remains imperfect until discovery occurs. Only upon perfection, which occurs when the legal acts of location are established *and* discovery of a valuable mineral deposit occurs, does the locator acquire a vested property right as against the United States and third parties. *See* Davis v. Nelson, 329 F.2d 840 (9th Cir. 1964); Bales v. Ruch, 522 F.Supp. 150 (E.D. Cal. 1981). Even before discovery, however, compliance with federal and state location procedures gives the locator a superior right to a subsequent locator. *See* Atherley v. Bullion Monarch Uranium Co., 8 Utah 2d 362, 335 P.2d 71 (1959). Failure to follow location procedures may invalidate mining claims even after discovery has occurred. *See* United States v. Consolidated Mines and Smelting Co., 455 F.2d 432 (9th Cir. 1971); Hoefler v. Babbitt, 952 F.Supp. 1448 (D.Or. 1996) (invalidating placer claim filed two days after filing deadline imposed by the Mining Claim Rights Restoration Act of 1955), *affirmed* 139 F.3d 726 (9th Cir. 1998), *cert. denied* 525 U.S. 825, 119 S.Ct. 70, 142 L.Ed.2d 55 (1998).

Federal law imposes specific procedural requirements for a valid location. First, under the 1872 Mining Law, 30 U.S.C.A. § 28, the claim must be distinctly marked on the ground so that its boundaries can be traced. Book v. Justice Mining Co., 58 F. 106 (D.Nev. 1893). Federal law also requires that the locator make a record of the name or names of all locators, the date of location, and a description in a "location certificate" of the claim located by reference to some natural object or permanent monument that will identify the claim. The claim is void if the description in the location certificate does not enable identification of the location with reasonable certainty. United States v. Sherman, 288 F. 497 (8th Cir. 1923).

In addition, under § 314 of FLPMA (the Federal Land Policy and Management Act of 1976), 43 U.S.C.A. § 1744, the owner of an unpatented mining claim (including tunnel sites and mill sites) must record the claim with the local BLM office within 90 days or "be deemed conclusively to [have] abandon[ed] the mining claim." This provision was held constitutional in United States v. Locke, 471 U.S. 84, 105 S.Ct. 1785 (1985). In Crummet v. Miller, 53 Cal.App.4th 897 (1997), the court ruled that FLPMA establishes a self-executing recording system in which a failure to record results in automatic forfeiture of the claim. Courts have construed FLPMA's recording requirement quite strictly, even going so far as to hold a claim abandoned where the failure to record was due to the BLM's negligence. Last Chance Mining Co. v. United States, 12 Cl.Ct. 551 (1987).

FLPMA § 314 and its implementing regulations also require miners to file an affidavit for performance of annual assessment work. *See* Topaz Beryllium v. United States, 649 F.2d 775 (10th Cir. 1981), and Western Mining Council v. Watt, 643 F.2d 618 (9th Cir. 1981) (both upholding the constitutionality of BLM regulations under § 314 of FLPMA). As a result, for the first time in the history of the mining industry, FLPMA created a central registry of mining claims on federal lands.

f. Supplemental State Location Requirements

The 1872 Mining Law permits state location procedures that supplement, but which are not inconsistent with, federal law. Butte City Water Co. v. Baker, 196 U.S. 119, 25 S.Ct. 211 (1905). State laws may require locators to post notice, establish boundaries, perform discovery work, and file location certificates with state authorities.

Posting notice—State law may require locators to post notice of the claim at the mining site in order to put other, subsequent prospectors on notice of the prior locator's intent to occupy, hold, and possess the ground claimed. The date of notice helps to establish priority among competing claimants. Rasmussen Drilling, Inc. v. Kerr–McGee Nuclear Corp., 571 F.2d 1144 (10th Cir. 1978). Failure to fix a notice in accordance with state law may invalidate the location. United States v. Zweifel, 508 F.2d 1150 (10th Cir. 1975). What constitutes adequate notice? Placing a notice in a tin can, which is then dropped on the claim? *See* Kramer v. Sanguinetti, 33 Cal.App. 2d 303, 91 P.2d 604 (1939)(defendants had actual knowledge of the claim, so the court did not need to judge the issue of whether "posting" notice in a tin can on the ground was sufficient). Placing the notice 60 feet outside the claim? *See* Butte Northern Copper Co.

v. Radmilovich, 39 Mont. 157, 101 P. 1078 (1909) (ruled insufficient; notice must be posted at the place of discovery).

Establishing boundaries—Although the 1872 Mining Law requires the location of a mining claim to be "distinctly marked on the ground so that its boundaries can be easily traced," the Act does not specify a particular procedure for marking claims or establishing boundaries. Almost all mining states specify how claims are to be staked. These laws generally require posts or conspicuous stone monuments to be placed at the four corners of a claim. Once a claim has been adequately marked, corner stakes do not need to be maintained. Eilers v. Boatman, 3 Utah 159, 2 P. 66 (1883). The act of erecting monuments to indicate the borders of a mining claim, along with a properly filed location certificate, serves to notify junior claimants of the existence and extent of a senior claim. Kenney v. Greer, 99 Nev. 40, 656 P.2d 857 (1983). Failure to mark surface boundaries in compliance with state law is grounds for invalidating the claim. Roberts v. Morton, 549 F.2d 158 (10th Cir. 1976).

Performance of Discovery Work—Although location may precede discovery, it is in the interest of the locator to pursue discovery because the actual date of discovery establishes priority of vested rights between claimants. To encourage discovery, many states originally required actual discovery work by the locator. Evidence of such work (*e.g.*, the digging of a discovery shaft) evidenced the locator's good faith intent to secure the claim for mining purposes. Failure to perform discovery work required by state statute could invalidate the mining claim. *See* White v. Ames Mining Co., 82 Idaho 71, 349 P.2d 550 (1960). Most mining states today permit locators to file location certificates in lieu of performing discovery work.

Location Certificates—State laws require locators to record location certificates, name the locators, date the claim, and describe the claim's location with the appropriate local body. Like the posting of a notice at the claim site, the location certificate's purpose is to give constructive notice of the claim to other potential locators. Globe Mining Co. v. Anderson, 78 Wyo. 17, 318 P.2d 373 (1957). Often the most critical information is the description of the claim's location, which must be adequate for reasonable persons to find the claim. Couch v. Clifton, 626 P.2d 731 (Colo. App. 1981); Steele v. Preble, 158 Or. 641, 77 P.2d 418 (1938). In Ford v. Campbell, 29 Nev. 578, 92 P. 206 (1907), a certificate describing a claim's location as "about 2 miles" from a certain town was found inadequate.

B. Discovery

In order to acquire a valid unpatented mining claim a miner must not only comply with federal and state location procedures but also make a "discovery" of a valuable mineral deposit. The discovery requirement has produced a spate of litigation involving two issues: (1) to what extent should miners prospecting in good faith be protected against junior claimants (or claim jumpers) prior to discovery?; (2) what constitutes a valid "discovery" of a valuable mineral deposit?

1. Prospectors' Rights Prior to Discovery: Pedis Possessio

The doctrine of *pedis possessio* (literally, possession under foot) is a judge-made rule that provides protection to bona fide prospectors. Under the doctrine, a claimant who has staked a claim (or claims) in search of valuable minerals may exclusively hold the claim(s) so long as she retains continuous exclusive occupancy and works in good faith toward making a discovery. As set out in Union Oil Co. v. Smith, 249 U.S. 337, 39 S.Ct. 308, 63 L.Ed. 635 (1919) and Cole v. Ralph, 252 U.S. 286, 40 S.Ct. 321, 64 L.Ed. 567 (1920):

> In advance of discovery an explorer in actual occupation and diligently searching for minerals is treated as a licensee or tenant at will, and no right can be initiated or acquired through a forcible, fraudulent or clandestine intrusion upon his possession. But if his occupancy be relaxed, or merely incidental to something other than a diligent search for mineral, and another enters peaceably, and not fraudulently or clandestinely, and makes a mineral discovery and location, the location so made is valid and must be respected accordingly.

The critical elements of *pedis possessio* are (1) maintenance of "exclusive" possession of claims, and (2) diligent and active "pursuit of discovery." If both conditions are met, the doctrine protects the claimant who has not yet discovered minerals against entry by adverse parties. If the first possessor should cease working toward discovery, and another openly and diligently searches for minerals, the first party forfeits the right of exclusive possession. Davis v. Nelson, 329 F.2d 840 (9th Cir. 1964).

Questions have arisen as to (1) what steps must be taken to maintain exclusive possession when a prior claimant is confronted by an intruding party, and (2) what specific acts constitute diligent pursuit of discovery. Another important issue is whether *pedis possessio* protects the prospector's right only to the immediate vicinity of the discovery workings, or whether it may be extended to include the entire staked claim. May the protection extend even further to include a group of staked claims, despite the fact that the claimant is able to physically occupy only some of the claims? Judicial definition of the boundaries of protection has become necessary in light of increasingly common regional exploration practices, whereby miners first claim all of a target area, and then systematically explore the area claim by claim. As the Colorado Supreme Court recognized in *Smaller v. Leach*, 136 Colo. 297, 316 P.2d 1030 (1957), "prospectors know ... that the moment a discovery is known to the public that others rush in and stake the surrounding lands, thus many times preventing the original discoverer from capitalizing on his efforts.... [What] has resulted is the custom of finding a likely area, staking (locating), recording, and then seeking discoveries ... to validate the claims." The question is whether *pedis possessio* protects such "area" claims.

GEOMET EXPLORATION, LTD.
v. LUCKY MC URANIUM CORP.

Supreme Court of Arizona, 1979.

124 Ariz. 55, 601 P.2d 1339.

*   *   *

JUSTICE HAYS delivered the opinion of the Court.

By use of modern scintillation equipment in September of 1976, plaintiff/appelle, Lucky MC Uranium Corporation, detected "anomalies" (discontinuities in geologic formations) indicative of possible uranium deposits in the Artillery Peak Mining District in Yuma County, land in the federal public domain. In November, 1976, Lucky proceeded to monument and post 200 claims (4,000 acres), drill a 10–foot hole on each claim, and record notices pursuant to A.R.S. §§ 27–202, 27–203 and 27–204.

Subsequently, defendant/appellant, Geomet, peaceably entered some of the areas claimed by Lucky and began drilling operations. Employees of Geomet were aware of Lucky's claims but considered them invalid because there had been no discovery of minerals in place and Lucky was not in actual occupancy of the areas Geomet entered.

Lucky instituted a possessory action seeking damages, exclusive possession and a permanent injunction against trespass by Geomet or its employees. There was insufficient evidence to establish a valid discovery, but the trial court found that Lucky was entitled to exclusive possession and a permanent injunction. Although Geomet pointed out that, prior to discovery of minerals in place, the doctrine of *pedis possessio* requires a prospector to be in actual occupancy of the claim and diligently pursuing discovery, the court based its reasoning on the economic infeasibility of literal adherence to the element of actual occupancy in view of modern mining techniques and the expense involved in exploring large areas. * * *

We must decide a single issue: Should the actual occupancy requirement of *pedis possessio* be discarded in favor of constructive possession to afford a potential locator protection of contiguous, unoccupied claims as against one who enters peaceably, openly, and remains in possession searching for minerals? * * *

Arizona has recognized *pedis possessio* and the concomitant requirement of actual occupancy for a century. In Bagg v. New Jersey Loan Co., 88 Ariz. 182, 188–89, 354 P.2d 40, 44 (1960), we said: "Location is the foundation of the possessory title, and possession thereunder, *as required by law and local rules and customs,* keeps the title alive, ... " (Emphasis added.) It is perhaps more proper to speak of a possessory right than a title because, until discovery of a valuable mineral and issuance of a patent, absolute title in fee simple remains in the United States. Since this is a possessory action, the party with the better right is entitled to prevail. Rundle v. Republic Cement Corp. 86 Ariz. 96, 341 P.2d 226 (1959).

Conceding that actual occupancy is necessary under *pedis possessio*, Lucky urges that the requirement be relaxed in deference to the time and expense that would be involved in actually occupying and drilling on each claim until discovery. Moreover, Lucky points out that the total area claimed—4,000 acres—is reasonable in size, similar in geological formation, and that an overall work program for the entire area had been developed. Under these circumstances, Lucky contends, actual drilling on some of the claims should suffice to afford protection as to all contiguous claims. * * *

To adopt the premise urged by Lucky eviscerates the actual occupancy requirement of *pedis possessio* and substitutes for it the theory of constructive possession even though there is no color of title. We are persuaded that the sounder approach is to maintain the doctrine intact. In Union Oil, *supra*, the Court considered the precise question of extending protection to contiguous claims and refused to do so:

> It was and is defendant's contention that by virtue of the act of 1903, one who has acquired the possessory rights of locators before discovery in five contiguous claims ... may preserve and maintain an inchoate right to all of them by means of a continuous actual occupation of one, coupled with diligent prosecution in good faith of a sufficient amount of discovery work thereon, provided such work tends also to determine an oil-bearing character of the other claims.
>
> *   *   *
>
> In our opinion the act shows no purpose to dispense with discovery as an essential of valid oil location *or to break down in any wise the recognized distinction between the pedis possessio of a prospector doing work for the purpose of discovering oil and the more substantial right of possession of one who has made a discovery....* Union Oil, 249 U.S. at 343, 353, 29 S.Ct. at 309, 312. (Emphasis added.)

We have canvassed the Western mining jurisdictions and found the requirement of actual occupancy to be the majority view. United Western Minerals Co. v. Hannsen, 147 Colo. 272, 363 P.2d 677 (1961); Adams v. Benedict, 64 N.M. 234, 327 P.2d 308 (1958); McLemore v. Express Oil Co., 158 Cal. 559, 112 P. 59 (1910).

There are always inherent risks in prospecting. The development of *pedis possessio* from the customs of miners argues forcefully against the proposition that exclusive right to possession should encompass claims neither actually occupied nor being explored. We note that the doctrine does not protect on the basis of occupancy alone; the additional requirement of diligent search for minerals must also be satisfied. The reason for these dual elements—and for the policy of the United States in making public domain available for exploration and mining—is to encourage those prepared to demonstrate their sincerity and tenacity in the pursuit of valuable minerals. If one may, by complying with preliminary formalities of posting and recording notices, secure for himself the exclusive possession of a large area upon only a small portion of which he is actually working, then he may, at his leisure, explore the entire area and exclude all others who stand ready to peaceably and openly enter unoccupied sections for the purpose of discovering minerals. Such a premise is laden with extreme difficulties of determining over how large an area and for how long one might be permitted to exclude others.

We hold that *pedis possessio* protects only those claims actually occupied (provided also that work toward discovery is in progress) and does not extend to contiguous, unoccupied claims on a group or area basis.

* * *

Notes and Questions

1. In contrast to the Arizona Supreme Court's decision in *Geomet*, the Tenth Circuit approved by implication the application of *pedis possessio* on an area basis in Continental Oil Co. v. Natrona Service, Inc., 588 F.2d 792 (10th Cir. 1978). Jurisdictions allowing area-wide protection usually require the size of the area claimed to be reasonable, the geology of the claimed area to be similar, and the existence of a comprehensive work program for the entire area claimed. *See* Olson, *New Frontiers in Pedis Possessio: MacGuire v. Sturgis*, VII Land & Water L.Rev. 367 (1972).

2. For *pedis possessio* rights to vest, the miner must not only occupy the claim but must also diligently and in good faith explore for a valuable mineral deposit. *See* United States v. Bagwell, 961 F.2d 1450 (9th Cir. 1992). What constitutes a diligent search and active exploration for minerals, sufficient to vest *pedis possessio* rights? Is performance of assessment work sufficient? *See* United States v. Stockton Midway Oil Co., 240 F. 1006 (S.D. Cal. 1917)(no). Do posting monuments, erecting fences, or recording notices qualify? *See* Ranchers Exploration and Development Co. v. Anaconda Co., 248 F.Supp. 708 (D.Utah 1965)(no); Adams v. Benedict, 64 N.M. 234, 327 P.2d 308 (1958)(no). Must a claim be worked continuously without interruption? *See* Kanab Uranium Corp. v. Consolidated Uranium Mines, 227 F.2d 434, 437 (10th Cir. 1955) " 'As against a mere intruder, the possession of a mining claim by a locator who has complied with the law is of itself sufficient to prevent the intruder, even upon a peaceable entry, from acquiring a right of possession.' "); Hanson v. Craig, 170 F. 62 (9th Cir. 1909)(continuous and uninterrupted possession is necessary to sustain *pedis possessio* rights). Is construction of drilling pads adequate? *See* United States v. Grass Creek Oil & Gas Co., 236 F. 481 (8th Cir. 1916)(yes).

3. To maintain *pedis possessio* rights, prospectors must exclude rival claimants, either by force or legal redress. Some courts hold that rival claimants can only defeat *pedis possessio* if they enter the claim peaceably and in good faith (including without knowledge of a prior claim). *See, e.g.,* Columbia Standard Corp. v. Ranchers Exploration & Development, Inc., 468 F.2d 547 (10th Cir. 1972). What result if an adverse locator makes a location

"peacefully" while the prior locator is temporarily absent? *See* Sparks v. Mount, 29 Wyo. 1, 207 P. 1099 (1922)(temporary absence does not constitute abandonment of occupation, where evidence exists that the prior occupier was diligently searching for minerals).

4. *Pedis possessio* protects prior claimants from subsequent, rival claimants, but it does not protect claimants from the authority of the United States government to withdraw the land from mineral entry prior to the discovery of a valuable mineral deposit. *See* United States v. Carlile, 67 I.D. 417, 421 (1960)("a mining claimant acquires no rights as against the United States until he makes a discovery. Until that time, he is a mere licensee or tenant at will. Upon discovery, and only upon discovery, he acquires as against the United States and all the world an exclusive right of possession to the claim which is property in the fullest sense of the word."). *See also* American Colloid Co. v. Hodel, 701 F.Supp. 1537 (D.Wyo. 1988)(pedis possessio is not relevant to the issue of whether the claim has been perfected against the United States). Nevertheless, *pedis possessio* rights are valuable legal rights, which may be sold or leased. United Western Minerals Co. v. Hannsen, 147 Colo. 272, 363 P.2d 677 (1961).

5. Ultimately, how much protection do *pedis possessio* rights provide to prospectors? Not very much, according to the U.S. Office of Technology Assessment:

> A claimholder is protected ... only against 'forcible, fraudulent or clandestine intrusion' by another: the doctrine does not protect against an unresisted, peaceable and open entry by another explorer. Nor does it protect against 'forcible, fraudulent or clandestine' intrusion upon one who is not in actual occupancy or who is not diligently working toward a discovery. In fact, it is not entirely clear whether the entire claim is protected or only that portion of the claim actually being occupied and worked, or whether the protection expires after a certain (reasonable) amount of time.

> The limitations of the *pedis possessio* doctrine result in weak prediscovery protection even for a single claim. When the doctrine is applied to multiple contiguous claims located to cover today's typically large exploration target, it provides practically no protection at all. Only those claims actually being occupied and worked are protected, even though an efficient exploration plan might call for sequential drilling on only one or a few of the many claims covering the target. The explorer faces the undesirable choice of simultaneously performing work that anticipates discovery on each and every claim, hiring armed guards to protect his claim (illegally) against entry by others, or having some or most of his claim 'jumped' by other prospectors.

Office of Technology Assessment, *Management of Fuel and Nonfuel Minerals in Federal Land* 118 (1979).

2. *Discovery of a Valuable Mineral Deposit*

A valid discovery on a properly located claim perfects the miner's unpatented mining claim, which constitutes a grant by the United

States government of an exclusive right of possession. *See* United States v. Etcheverry, 230 F.2d 193 (10th Cir. 1956). Because discovery is the trigger to perfecting an unpatented mining claim, it is crucial to determine what counts, as "discovery." On this issue, the 1872 Mining Law provides no guidance. The Act does not define the term "discovery," but merely recites that "all valuable mineral deposits in lands belonging to the United States ... are hereby declared to be free and open to exploration and purchase" (30 U.S.C.A. § 22); that "no location of a mining claim shall be made until ... discovery" (30 U.S.C.A. § 23); and that patents may be obtained "for any land claimed and located for valuable deposits" (30 U.S.C.A. § 29). The Mining Law thus requires that something called "discovery" take place, and that the discovery be of "a valuable mineral deposit." The actual definition of these two concepts has been the responsibility of the courts and the Department of the Interior.

The Interior Secretary first designed a test for discovery in Castle v. Womble, 19 I.D. 455, 457 (1894): "[W]here minerals have been found and the evidence is of such a character that a person of ordinary prudence would be justified in the further expenditure of his labor and means, with a reasonable prospect of success, in developing a valuable mine, the requirements of the statute have been met." The U.S. Supreme Court subsequently adopted this rule, which came to be known as the "prudent man test" in *Chrisman v. Miller*, 197 U.S. 313, 25 S.Ct. 468, 49 L.Ed. 770 (1905). The prudent man test is not concerned with whether the particular claimant at issue feels (subjectively) justified in further expenditure, but whether a hypothetical reasonable person would be (objectively) justified. The test is based in large part on the *future expectations* of the prudent man. If proof is offered regarding foreseeable conditions suggesting future profitability, the prudent man test is satisfied. The expectations of the prudent man may take into account future changes in economic conditions (*e.g.*, likely market cycles for the mineral claimed), so long as the expectations are not farfetched and are based on present economic data. United States v. Jenkins, 75 I.D. 312 (1969).

The prudent man test, especially with its forward looking "future profitability" standard, proved to be very liberal in validating discoveries. The test justified location of nonmetallic minerals of widespread occurrence, such as sand and gravel. Even more disconcerting was the practice of some locators to locate public lands, allegedly for sand and gravel, but in reality for the development value of the land itself. *See* Foster v. Seaton, 271 F.2d 836 (D.C. Cir. 1959). As former Interior Solicitor John Leshy has explained, the prudent man test "has been largely responsible for the fact that the vast majority of patented claims have never supported viable mineral operations." John D. Leshy, *The Mining Law: A Study in Perpetual Motion* 139 (1987). In order to prevent bad faith mining claims, and to limit mineral location to truly valuable minerals, the Department of the Interior adopted a more stringent test for "discovery" of minerals. This test, known as the "marketability test," validated discoveries only when there was proof that the deposit could be extracted, removed, and marketed at a present profit.

UNITED STATES v. COLEMAN
Supreme Court of the United States, 1968.
390 U.S. 599, 88 S.Ct. 1327, 20 L.Ed.2d 170.

JUSTICE BLACK delivered the opinion of the Court.

In 1956 respondent Coleman applied to the Department of the Interior for a patent to certain public lands based on his entry onto and exploration of these lands and his discovery there of a variety of stone called quartzite, one of the most common of all solid materials. It was, and still is, respondent Coleman's contention that the quartzite deposits qualify as "valuable mineral deposits" under 30 U.S.C.A. § 22.... The Secretary of the Interior held that to qualify as "valuable mineral deposits" ... it must be shown that the mineral can be "extracted, removed and marketed at a profit"—the so-called "marketability test." Based on the largely undisputed evidence in the record, the Secretary concluded that the deposits claimed by respondent Coleman did not meet that criterion.... The Secretary denied the patent application, but respondent Coleman remained on the land, forcing the Government to bring this present action in ejectment in the District Court against respondent Coleman and his lessee, respondent McClennan. * * *

We ... believe that the rulings of the Secretary of the Interior were proper. The Secretary's determination that the quartzite deposits did not qualify as valuable mineral deposits because the stone could not be marketed at a profit does no violence to the statute. Indeed, the marketability test is an admirable effort to identify with greater precision and objectivity the factors relevant to a determination that a mineral deposit is "valuable." It is a logical complement to the "prudent-man test" which the Secretary has been using to interpret the mining laws since 1894. Under this "prudent-man test" in order to qualify as "valuable mineral deposits," the discovered deposits must be of such a character that "a person of ordinary prudence would be justified in the further expenditure of labor and means, with a reasonable prospect of success, in developing a valuable mine...." Castle v. Womble, 18 L.D. 455, 457 (1894). This Court has approved the prudent-man formulation and interpretation on numerous occasions. See, for example, Chrisman v. Miller, 197 U.S. 313, 322; Cameron v. United States, 252 U.S. 450, 459; Best v. Humboldt Placer Mining Co., 371 U.S. 334, 335–336. Under the mining laws Congress has made public lands available to people for the purpose of mining valuable mineral deposits and not for other purposes. The obvious intent was to reward and encourage the discovery of minerals that are valuable in an economic sense. Minerals which no prudent man will extract because there is no demand for them at a price higher than the cost of extraction and transportation are hardly economically valuable. Thus, profitability is an important consideration in applying the prudent-man test, and the marketability test which the Secretary has used here merely recognizes the fact.

The marketability test also has the advantage of throwing light on a claimant's intention, a matter which is inextricably bound together with valuableness. For evidence that a mineral deposit is not of economic value and cannot in all likelihood be operated at a profit may well suggest that a claimant seeks the land for other purposes. Indeed, as the Government points out, the facts of this case—the thousands of dollars and hours spent building a home on 720 acres in a highly scenic national forest located two hours from Los Angeles, the lack of an economically feasible market for the stone, and the immense quantities of identical stone found in the area outside the claims—might well be thought to raise a substantial question as to respondent Coleman's real intention.

* * * As we have pointed out above, the prudent-man test and the marketability test are not distinct standards, but are complementary in that the latter is a refinement of the former. While it is true that the marketability test is usually the critical factor in cases involving nonmetallic minerals of widespread occurrence, this is accounted for by the perfectly natural reason that precious metals which are in small supply and for which there is a great demand, sell at a price so high as to leave little room for doubt that they can be extracted and marketed at a profit. * * *

For these reasons we hold that the United States is entitled to eject respondents from the land and that respondents' counterclaim for a patent must fail. The case is reversed and remanded to the Court of Appeals for the Ninth Circuit for further proceedings to carry out this decision.

Notes and Questions

1. The *Coleman* marketability test focuses on the economic value and marketability of the "discovered" mineral at the present time; present marketability exists when there is a market for the mineral, resulting in profit to the discoverer, in light of (1) the quantity of the mineral in the deposit, (2) the quantity of the mineral in similar deposits elsewhere, (3) the quality of the mineral discovered, and (4) the cost of mining, removing, and marketing the mineral. This test does *not* require that the miner earn an actual profit on the particular claim. *See* Skaw v. United States, 740 F.2d 932 (Fed. Cir. 1984); Verrue v. United States, 457 F.2d 1202, 1203 (1972)("If the successful marketing by others has sufficiently established that the claimant's comparable material is itself marketable, that can suffice."). The miner must, however, present evidence of a sufficient quantity and quality of mineral that "a person of reasonable prudence would be justified in further expenditure with a reasonable prospect of success." United States v. Anderson, 83 I.B.L.A. 170 (1984).

2. Rather than ruling that the marketability test simply replaced the old prudent-man test for "discovery" of a "valuable mineral deposit," the Court in *Coleman* ruled that the two tests were, in fact, "complementary." But are they really? The prudent-man test is forward looking, merely requiring some evidence of *future* profitability. The marketability test, by contrast,

seems to require proof of *present* marketability at a profit. This has created difficulties for lower courts applying the *Coleman* test. *See* Reeves, *The Law of Discovery Since Coleman*, 21 Rocky Mtn.Min.L.Inst. 415 (1976). On the other hand, present marketability depends significantly on the price of the mineral on the market. Because mineral prices are subject to substantial fluctuations, some courts have ruled that historical and *reasonably antici-pated future prices* for minerals may be relevant for determining present marketability. *See In re Pacific Coast Molybdenum*, 90 I.D. 352 (1983). *See also* Andrus v. Shell Oil Co., 446 U.S. 657, 100 S.Ct. 1932, 64 L.Ed.2d 593 (1980)(holding that oil shale deposits located before the 1920 Mineral Leas-ing Act removed such deposits from location may be valuable mineral depos-its even though no shale operation has ever resulted in profitable produc-tion).

3. In addition to holding that the deposit was unmarketable, the Court in *Coleman* ruled that the quartzite at issue was not even locatable under the 1872 Mining Law, but instead was subject to sale as a common variety mineral under the 1955 Common Varieties Act. 30 U.S.C.A. § 611. For present purposes, however, it is important to note that deposits of common varieties remain subject to location under the 1872 Mining Law if those deposits possess "distinct and special value," and meet the present market-ability test. *See* Alyeska Pipeline Service Co. v. Anderson, 629 P.2d 512 (Alaska 1981)(green slate, a building stone with distinct and special value, was a valuable mineral deposit).

4. The government will challenge a discovery in one of three contexts: (1) when a miner applies for a patent; (2) when the United States wishes to challenge, so as to invalidate, an unpatented mining claim; and (3) when land is withdrawn from location, and the Interior Department asserts that no perfected mining claim (which otherwise would be "grandfathered," pre-ceded the withdrawal. When the government challenges the location, it has the burden of making a prima facie showing of no discovery, and the burden of proving a discovery beyond a preponderance of the evidence falls on the miner. Hjelvik v. Babbitt, 198 F.3d 1072 (9th Cir. 1999). When a miner is seeking a patent, he or she has the entire burden of proof concerning discov-ery. Issues of fact are resolved first by the Interior Department (often against the miner), and appellate courts typically show great deference to the Interior Department's factual determinations. This limited scope of review deters judicial appeals of adverse Interior Department rulings.

5. Since 1960, lower federal and state courts have fleshed out the *Cole-man* test for discovery, identifying five key variables. First, discovery requires minerals in sufficient quantity and quality to be marketed for a *profit*. Hjelvik v. Babbitt, 198 F.3d 1072 (9th Cir. 1999). Second, there must be a *market* for the mineral. *Foster v. Seaton*, 271 F.2d 836 (D.C. Cir. 1959). What if a claim contains so much of the mineral that the relevant market may be unable to absorb further sales? Compare Rodgers v. Watt, 726 F.2d 1376 (9th Cir. 1984)(local market saturation not dispositive), with Skaw v. United States, 847 F.2d 842 (Fed. Cir. 1988)(claim rejected when market could not absorb additional minerals). Third, the costs of extraction, process

ing and transportation must not be excessive. Lara v. Secretary of Interior, 820 F.2d 1535 (9th Cir. 1987). The cost of compliance with environmental regulations may also be considered. United States v. Kosanke Sand Corp., 80 I.D. 538 (1973). Fourth, less evidence will be required to prove a discovery of an inherently valuable metallic mineral (such as gold), as compared with either common variety minerals subject to location (because they were located prior to 1955 or have "special and distinct value") or leaseable minerals located prior to 1920 (and therefore subject to location). *See* Dredge Corp. v. Conn, 733 F.2d 704 (9th Cir. 1984)(sand and gravel); Andrus v. Shell Oil Co., 446 U.S. 657, 100 S.Ct. 1932, 64 L.Ed.2d 593 (1980)(oil shale). Fifth, because national forest lands were set aside for timber purposes, not mining, a mining claimant may have a greater burden to prove a discovery on national forest lands than on BLM lands. Converse v. Udall, 399 F.2d 616, 622 (9th Cir. 1968). However, the Interior Board of Land Appeals has "expressly repudiated" the idea that miners have a greater burden of proving discovery on national forest lands. In re Pacific Coast Molybdenum Co., 75 I.B.L.A. 16, 32 (1983).

6. The introduction of sophisticated exploration techniques raises the question of *when* a discovery has occurred. The general rule has been that for there to be a discovery, the presence of mineralization must be established on the particular claim and that mere geological inference is not sufficient. Union Oil Co. v. Smith, 249 U.S. 337, 39 S.Ct. 308, 63 L.Ed. 635 (1919)(discovery of oil on one claim suggesting oil bearing character of a contiguous claim does not constitute discovery on the contiguous claim). During the uranium boom of the 1950s, where geiger counters and scintillators proved capable of indicating the presence of mineralization, the courts had to decide whether such geophysical devices could support discovery. After expressing initial reluctance (*see* Globe Mining Co. v. Anderson, 73 Wyo. 17, 318 P.2d 373, 380 (1957)), the courts began to validate discovery based on radiometric detection. *See* Western Standard Uranium Co. v. Thurston, 355 P.2d 377 (Wyo. 1960); Dallas v. Fitzsimmons, 137 Colo. 196, 323 P.2d 274 (1958); Rummell v. Bailey, 7 Utah 2d 137, 320 P.2d 653 (1958).

7. Legal scholar Charles Wilkinson notes that, even after the Supreme Court's introduction of the marketability test: "There is still plenty of room for miners ... to prove a discovery. * * * A reminder of the difficulty of administrative oversight: there are 1.1 million alleged unpatented mining claims, 25 million acres in all, scattered across the West, and the Bureau of Land Management receives 90,000 new claims each year." CHARLES F. WILKINSON, CROSSING THE NEXT MERIDIAN: LAND, WATER, AND THE FUTURE OF THE WEST 47 (1992).

C. The Unpatented Mining Claim

1. *The Rights of Valid, Unpatented Mining Claims*

Once a miner has properly located a mine on land open to location, and discovered a valuable deposit of a mineral subject to location, the miner has perfected an unpatented mining claim. Certain important rights attached to such claims, the most important of which are: (1) the exclusive right of possession of all locatable minerals within the boundaries of the claim; (2) rights to the surface of the claim for mining purpose; (3) extralateral mining rights; and (4) the right to either amend or relocate the claim.

a. Exclusive Right of Possession

The U.S. Supreme Court in Wilbur v. United States ex rel. Krushmic, 280 U.S. 306, 316–17, 50 S.Ct. 103, 74 L.Ed. 445 (1930), summarized the nature of the "right of present and exclusive possession" granted locators with perfected unpatented mining claims:

> The claim is property in the fullest sense of that term; and may be sold, transferred, mortgaged, and inherited without infringing any right or title of the United States. The right of the owner is taxable by the state and is 'real property,' subject to the lien of a judgment recovered against the owner in a state or territorial court. The owner is not required to purchase the claim or secure patent from the United States; but, so long as he complies with the provisions of the mining law, his possessory right, for all practical purposes of ownership, is as good as though secured by patent.

An unpatented mining claim is removed from the public domain. The locator is protected against all rival claimants, so long as she satisfies applicable federal and state requirements triggered by the existence of a perfected mining claim (such as performance of annual assessment work, payment of fees, and timely filing of appropriate affidavits), as discussed later in this chapter. See Boscarino v. Gibson, 207 Mont. 112, 672 P.2d 1119 (1983); Silliman v. Powell, 642 P.2d 388 (Utah 1982); Anaconda Co. v. Whittaker, 188 Mont. 66, 610 P.2d 1177 (1980). Any adverse locator who enters the claim and seeks to remove minerals is a trespasser, liable for damages. Clipper Mining Co. v. Eli Mining & Land Co., 194 U.S. 220, 24 S.Ct. 632, 48 L.Ed. 944 (1904); Lightner Mining Co. v. Lane, 161 Cal. 689, 120 P. 771 (1911).

The holder of an unpatented mining claim has only a "possessory right," which is subject to the primary title and paramount ownership rights of the United States. Roy v. Lancaster, 107 Nev. 460, 814 P.2d 75 (1991). However, "[e]ven though title to the fee estate remains in the United States, these unpatented mining claims are themselves property protected by the Fifth Amendment against uncompensated takings." Kunkes v. United States, 78 F.3d 1549, 1551 (Fed. Cir. 1996). See also United States v. North American Transp. & Trading Co., 253 U.S. 330, 40 S.Ct. 518, 64 L.Ed. 935 (1920). Upon abandonment, or failure to comply with conditions upon which the continuing right of possession depends, the entire claim reverts to the federal government. United States v. Rizzinelli, 182 F. 675 (D.Idaho 1910). Moreover, the U.S. government can test the validity of an unpatented mining claim at any time. If it can prove the claim is invalid, for whatever reason, the claimant has no property rights, and the government is free to withdraw the land from location. Skaw v. United States, 847 F.2d 842 (Fed.Cir. 1988).

Even with respect to valid, unpatented mining claims, Congress may, without compensation, alter the conditions for retaining those claims. *See* United States v. Locke, 471 U.S. 84, 105 S.Ct. 1785, 85 L.Ed.2d 64 (1985)(conditioning retention of valid unpatented mining claims on recordation of claims and performance of annual assessment work); Jones v. United States, 121 F.3d 1327 (9th Cir. 1997)(conditioning the retention of valid unpatented mining claims on payment of an annual maintenance fee). Unpatented mining claims are also subject to subsequently imposed environmental regulations. *See* Trustees for Alaska v. EPA, 749 F.2d 549 (9th Cir. 1984)(holding that placer miners do not have vested rights to run water through their sluice boxes in such as way as to cause deterioration in water quality in violation of the Clean Water Act). Congress can even change the law in such a way that prevents the owner of an unpatented mining claim from applying for a patent. Freese v. United States, 226 Ct.Cl. 252, 639 F.2d 754 (1981); Swanson v. Babbitt, 3 F.3d 1348 (9th Cir. 1993). In other words, owners of valid but unpatented mining claims have no enforceable property right to a patent.

b. Surface Rights

Under the 1872 Mining Law, 30 U.S.C.A. § 26, the owner of a mining claim is entitled to exclusive possession of the surface of a valid, unpatented mining claim. *See* Del Monte Mining and Milling Co. v. Last Chance Mining and Milling Co., 171 U.S. 55, 18 S.Ct. 895, 43 L.Ed. 72 (1898). The Surface Resources Act of 1955, 30 U.S.C.A. § 612, provides that the owner of a claim is entitled to *use* the surface *only as necessary* for the mining operation. As a consequence, post-1955 claims are subject to surface management rights of the federal government, its agents, and licensees that do not materially interfere with mining operations. Even with respect to claims located prior to 1955, the Act precludes claimants from exploiting any surface resources (such as timer) reserved to the United States. 30 U.S.C.A. § 615. *See* Barnes v. Hodel, 819 F.2d 250 (9th Cir. 1987).

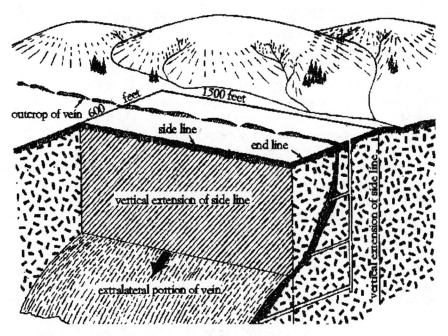

Figure 3:
Extralateral Rights of a Lode Mining Claim
c. Extralateral Rights

The 1872 Mining Law gives locators "the exclusive right to possession and enjoyment ... of all veins, lodes, and ledges throughout their entire depth, the top or apex of which lies inside of such surface lines extended downward vertically ..., although such veins ... may so far depart ... in their course downward as to extend outside the vertical side lines of such surface locations." 30 U.S.C.A. § 26. Thus, once a claimant establishes the "apex" of a vein (usually, the edge of a vein nearest to the surface) within the surface boundaries of the claim, the vein may be followed on its downward subsurface course, even if that takes the miner beyond the claim's side lines. This right—to follow the subsurface course of the vein beyond the side lines—is referred to as an "extralateral right." Extralateral rights do not attach to placer claims or to lode deposits mistakenly located as placer.

In a rectangular mining lode claim (as depicted in Figure 3), the "side lines" generally define the rectangle's longest sides, which may not exceed 1500 feet in length. 30 U.S.C.A. § 23. Ideally, the surface side lines should not be more than 300 feet to either side of the lode vein at the surface. However, it is often quite difficult or impossible to lay out a lode location where the vein apex is lying lengthwise direction parallel to the side lines, and in the exact center of the claim. Usually, miners cannot know, before they discover and begin to follow the flow of a vein, how the vein "sits" in relation to the geometrical boundaries of the claim they have located. See Iron Silver Mining Co. v. Elgin Mining & Smelting Co., 118 U.S. 196, 6 S.Ct. 1177, 30 L.Ed. 98 (1886).

The 1872 Law further provides that the "right of possession to such outside parts of such veins or ledges shall be confined [by] ... the end lines of their locations...." Thus extralateral rights are limited to those parts of the vein continuing outside the claim that lie between the extensions of the claim's end lines. As the side lines are the two longest sides of a rectangular load claim, the "end lines" are the two shortest sides of the claim, defining the claim's width. While the side lines need not be parallel to one another, the end lines must be. Jim Butler Tonopah Mining Co. v. West End Consolidated Mining Co., 247 U.S. 450, 38 S.Ct. 574, 62 L.Ed. 1207 (1918). Extralateral rights therefore attach when (1) the mineral deposit located is a vein or lode, and (2) the "apex" of the lode is within the surface lines of the claim extended downward vertically. Consolidated Wyoming Gold Mining Co. v. Champion Mining Co., 63 F. 540 (N.D. Cal. 1894). Once these conditions have been met, the locator may follow the vein on its downward course outside the side lines of the claim so long as the locator stays within the extension of the end lines. *See* Figure 3. The right to follow the extralateral extension of a vein includes the right to excavate under lands owned by others. Twenty–One Mining Co. v. Original Sixteen to One Mine, 255 F. 658 (9th Cir. 1919). However, the extralateral claimant may not dig an access way through the subsurface of others to reach the extralateral extension of the vein.

The claimant of extralateral rights must prove continuity of the vein in order to follow its downward progress into the earth and outside the side lines. "For the exercise of this [extralateral] right it must appear that the vein outside is identical with and a continuation of the one inside [the claimant's surface side] lines. But if the mineral disappears or the fissure with its walls of the same rock disappears, so that its identity can no longer be traced, the right to pursue it outside of the perpendicular lines of claimants' survey is gone." Iron Silver Mining Co. v. Cheesman, 116 U.S. 529, 6 S.Ct. 481, 29 L.Ed. 712 (1886).

* * *

Notes and Questions

1. May end lines be moved to take advantage of underground discoveries? *See Silver Surprize, Inc. v. Sunshine Mining Co., 547 P.2d 1240 (Wash.App.1976)(no); Iron Silver Mining Co. v. Elgin Mining and Smelting Co.*, 118 U.S. 196, 6 S.Ct. 1177, 30 L.Ed. 98 (1886). The 1872 Mining Law requires that "the end lines of such claim be parallel to each other." 30 U.S.C.A. § 23; Del Monte Mining and Milling Co. v. Last Chance Mining and Milling Co., 171 U.S. 55, 18 S.Ct. 895, 43 L.Ed. 72 (1898). Side lines may be nonparallel without affecting extralateral rights. Jim Butler Tonopah Mining Co. v. West End Consolidated Mining Co., 247 U.S. 450, 38 S.Ct. 574, 62 L.Ed. 1207 (1918). If a locator discovers that the claim has been laid out in a way that does not take advantage of extralateral rights (e.g., the claim is perpendicular to the vein rather than parallel to it), the claim may be amended or relocated if there are no other vested intervening rights.

2. Extralateral rights do not extend to neighboring lands that were patented under non-mining (e.g., agricultural) statutes *prior to the location* of the mining claim. Burke v. Southern Pacific Railroad, 234 U.S. 669, 34 S.Ct. 907, 58 L.Ed. 1527 (1914); Reeves v. Oregon Exploration Co., 127 Or. 686, 273 P. 389 (1929). On the other hand, extralateral rights may be pursued under lands patented for nonmineral purposes if the claim was located prior to the issuance of the nonmining patent. Ames v. Empire Star Mines Co., 17 Cal.2d 213, 110 P.2d 13 (1941). Even lands reserved exclusively to Indian tribes may be subject to extralateral mining rights, at least where the treaty conditions tribal rights on preexisting claims (despite the general principle that tribes own the mineral rights under their reservations). Swoboda v. Pala Mining, Inc., 844 F.2d 654 (9th Cir. 1988). Extralateral rights also survive wilderness designation. Wilderness Society v. Dombeck, 168 F.3d 367 (9th Cir. 1999).

d. The Right to Amend or Relocate Claims

A locator may wish to correct errors or defects in the original mining claim. Such errors may include mistakes in location descriptions or in dimensions on the ground. A locator may also wish to alter a claim's surface boundaries, eliminate parts of overly large claims, or compact scattered claims. As a general rule, a claim may be "amended" in order to correct an immaterial defect on an otherwise valid claim, where the amendment does not infringe upon the rights of others. A claim must be "relocated" (restart the location process) when a mining claim is void *ab initio*, and where the subsequent relocation is adverse to the original location.

Many of the statutes allowing for amended locations required only that the locator file an amended location certificate to change or enlarge boundaries, or include within the claim an overlapping abandoned claim. Shoshone Mining Co. v. Rutter, 87 F. 801 (9th Cir. 1898). An amended claim is not allowed if adverse rights have intervened before the date of the amendment. Atherley v. Bullion Monarch Uranium Co., 8 Utah 2d 362, 335 P.2d 71 (1959). If no new land is included in the amendment, an amended location relates back to the date of the original location (for purposes of seniority). Gobert v. Butterfield, 23 Cal.App. 1, 136 P. 516 (1913). A void location, on the other hand, is not subject to amendment. McEvoy v. Hyman, 25 F. 596 (C.C.D.Colo. 1885); Brown v. Gurney, 201 U.S. 184, 26 S.Ct. 509, 50 L.Ed. 717 (1906); Silbrico Corp. v. Ortiz, 878 F.2d 333 (10th Cir. 1989). A location is void in two circumstances: (1) if the land was withdrawn from mineral location at the time the claim was originally located, United States Phosphate Co., 43 I.D. 232 (1914); or (2) if the locator has failed to comply with a material statutory requirement, such as failure to perform annual assessment work.

AMERICAN COLLOID CO. v. BABBITT
United States Court of Appeals, Tenth Circuit, 1998.
145 F.3d 1152.

CIRCUIT JUDGE McKAY delivered the opinion of the Court.

In 1990, the U.S. Department of the Interior's Bureau of Land Management [BLM] determined that two mining claims held by Appellant,

American Colloid Company [American Colloid], were null and void *ab initio.* The basis for the BLM's decision was the fact that American Colloid's predecessors-in-interest in the claims had failed to file a stipulation regarding the claims which was required by the order of the Secretary of the Interior that opened the lands to mining entry. The statute authorizing the Secretary of the Interior to require the stipulation states that the Secretary may require that the stipulation be filed before the vesting of any rights in a claim on subject lands. See 43 U.S.C. § 154.
* * *

American Colloid's predecessors-in-interest in Bethel Nos. 1 and 2 staked the claims in April 1954, after the land was opened by the Secretary.... [but] never filed the stipulation required by the Secretary's order opening the land to entry. * * * In 1989, a rival claimant filed the required stipulation on his own behalf.... In 1990 the BLM declared American Colloid's claims null and void *ab initio....* It was not until January of 1994 that American Colloid executed and filed the stipulation required by the opening order. * * *

We will set aside an IBLA decision only if it is arbitrary, capricious, otherwise not in accordance with law, or not supported by substantial evidence. See 5 U.S.C. § 706; Hoyl v. Babbitt, 129 F.3d 1377, 1382 (10th Cir. 1997). "The court's function is exhausted where a rational basis is found for the agency action taken." Sabin v. Butz, 515 F.2d 1061, 1067 (10th Cir. 1975).

In reviewing an agency's interpretation of a statute that the agency is charged with administering, we must determine whether Congress has directly spoken to the precise question at issue. If the intent of Congress is clear, that is the end of the matter; for the court, as well as the agency, must give effect to the unambiguously expressed intent of Congress. * * *

In interpreting statutes, we begin with the relevant language. * * *

The statute at issue, 43 U.S.C. § 154, allows for the location of mining claims in areas previously withdrawn from entry under the general mining laws. The statute provides, in pertinent part:

Where public lands of the United States have been withdrawn for possible use for construction purposes under the Federal reclamation laws, and are known or believed to be valuable for minerals and would, if not so withdrawn, be subject to location and patent under the general mining laws, *the Secretary of the Interior, when in his opinion the rights of the United States will not be prejudiced thereby, may, in his discretion, open the land to location, entry, and patent under the general mining laws, reserving such ways, rights, and easements over or to such lands as may be prescribed by him ...* and/or *the said Secretary may require the execution of a contract by the intending locator or entryman as a condition precedent to the vesting of any rights in him,* when in the opinion of the Secretary

same may be necessary for the protection of the irrigation interests.... The Secretary may prescribe the form of *such contract which
shall be executed and acknowledged and recorded in the county
records and United States local land office by any locator or entryman of such land before any rights in their favor attach thereto....*
* * *

43 U.S.C. § 154 (emphasis added).

The statute clearly states that the Secretary may require the filing
of the stipulation as a condition precedent to the vesting of any rights in
the claimant. The Secretary's order opening the land at issue to entry
states that, pursuant to the Secretary's authority under section 154, an
entryman had to execute and record the stipulation in the county
records and the United States Land and Survey Office "before locations
[were] made."…. We find no ambiguity inherent in the word "before."
American Colloid does not argue that the stipulation was filed prior to
the time the claims were declared void. American Colloid finally filed the
required stipulation almost forty years after the original entry and location of the claims and almost four years after American Colloid's claims
were declared null and void *ab initio* because the required stipulation
was missing. The IBLA decision that American Colloid possessed no
rights to Bethel Nos. 1 and 2 because the stipulation was not filed is
logical given the unambiguous intent of Congress to grant the Secretary
the power to require the stipulation prior to the vesting of any rights. …
We see no error in the conclusion that Congress' intent in enacting section 154 was followed by the BLM in declaring the claims to Bethel Nos.
1 and 2 null and void. * * *

American Colloid also raises the defense of laches to the BLM's
decision. This argument fails because the Supreme Court has held that
the doctrine of laches does not apply to claims concerning the public
lands. See United States v. California, 332 U.S. 19, 40, 91 L. Ed. 1889,
67 S. Ct. 1658, amended by 332 U.S. 804 (1947). This circuit has applied
the Supreme Court's holding in United States v. California, absent allegations of agency misconduct. See Double J. Land & Cattle Co. v. United
States Dep't of the Interior, 91 F.3d 1378, 1381–82 (10th Cir. 1996).
* * *

American Colloid contends that the stipulation requirement in the opening order cannot support the voiding of their claims because the order
does not comply with 5 U.S.C. § 553, one of the rule-making provisions
of the APA…. The rule-making requirements of section 553 do not apply
to matters concerning the public lands; therefore, this argument was
properly rejected by the district court. See 5 U.S.C. § 553(a)(2) * * *.

We hold that the IBLA decision finding American Colloid's claims to
Bethel Nos. 1 and 2 null and void *ab initio* was not arbitrary and capricious. The IBLA decision was reached by a process in accordance with
the law. Therefore, the decision of the district court is AFFIRMED.

Notes and Questions

The 1872 Mining Law provides that void claims (on lands subject to location) "shall be open to relocation in the same manner as if no location had ever been made...." 30 U.S.C.A. § 28. Does mere knowledge of a prior location preclude a relocator from entering and relocating if the prior claim is invalid? *See* Belk v. Meagher, 104 U.S. (14 Otto) 279, 26 L.Ed. 735 (1881) (no).

2. Limitations and Requirements Imposed on Unpatented Mining Claims

Although holders of valid mining claims have substantial property rights in their claims, their ownership interest amounts to less than fee simple. They possess rights to remove and sell minerals from the claim, do not own title in fee to the minerals in the ground or to the ground itself. California Portland Cement Corp., 83 IBLA 11 (1984). Until they fulfill additional conditions for obtaining a patent conveying full fee simple ownership, they remain subject to a number of substantive and procedural statutory requirements, and may forfeit the claim if they fail to satisfy these duties, which include: (1) the obligation to perform annual assessment work *or* pay a "claims maintenance fee;" (2) the risk of losing the location to adverse claimants or the federal government; (3) the duty to conform to several laws and policies restricting the miners' uses of surface lands.

a. Annual Assessment Work

In order to ensure that miners continue to develop a claim after location and discovery, the 1872 Mining Law provides that "until a patent has been issued therefor, not less than $100 worth of labor shall be performed or improvements made during each year." 30 U.S.C.A. § 28. The purpose of this "assessment" was to spur maximum development of the resource, to protect only those miners claiming possession in good faith, to give notice to rival locators of the claim, and to prevent miners from holding several valuable claims while working only some of them. Chambers v. Harrington, 111 U.S. 350, 4 S.Ct. 428, 28 L.Ed. 452 (1884); Sampson v. Page, 129 Cal.App.2d 356, 276 P.2d 871 (1954). If the miner fails to perform annual assessment work, or fails to perform such work on time, the claim is forfeited by the original locator and becomes subject to location by other claimants "as if no location of the same had ever been made...." 30 U.S.C.A. § 28. The 1872 Law prevents relocation where assessment work has been resumed on the claim by the "original locators, their heirs, assigns, or legal representatives ... after failure [of assessment work] and before such [re]location." *Id..* Most western mining states also require the recording of an affadavit of annual labor establishing that the work has been completed. *See* Golden Condor, Inc. v. Bell, 106 Idaho 280, 678 P.2d 72 (1984).

What acts can qualify for assessment work? The general rule is that the work must be of such a character as to develop and protect the claim and to facilitate the extraction of minerals. Eveleigh v. Darneille, 276 Cal.App.2d 638, 81 Cal.Rptr. 301 (1969); Schlegel v. Hough, 182 Or. 441, 186 P.2d 516 (1947). If the work is performed in good faith, the court will not substitute its judgment for that of the miner. Great Eastern Mines v. Metals Corp. of America, 86 N.M. 717, 527 P.2d 112 (1974). Among activities that count as assessment work are: clearing growth on a path to the mine shaft (Silver Jet Mines, Inc. v. Schwark, 210 Mont. 81, 682 P.2d 708 (1984)); repairing access roads (Pinkerton v. Moore, 66 N.M. 11, 340 P.2d 844 (1959)); and employing a watchman (Golden Giant Mining Co. v. Hill, 27 N.M. 124, 198 P. 276 (1921)). Exploration activities, however, including taking samples from shaft walls, do not count as assessment work. Union Oil Co. of Cal. v. Smith, 249 U.S. 337, 39 S.Ct. 308, 63 L.Ed. 635 (1919); Bishop v. Baisley, 28 Or. 119, 41 P. 936 (1895). Neither does road building. Exxon Mobil Corp. v. Norton, 346 F.3d 1244 (10th Cir. 2003). Originally, geological surveys and mapping were not considered valid assessment work (Lewis v. Carr, 49 Nev. 366, 246 P. 695 (1926)), but a 1958 Amendment to the 1872 Mining Law allows geological, geochemical, and geophysical surveys to count as assessment work, if conducted by an expert. 30 U.S.C.A. § 28–1.

Claims may be grouped for assessment work purposes, so that work done on one or more claims rather than each claim in the group will validate all the claims if the value of the work is sufficient. The test is whether the work or improvement on one claim tends to develop the other claims and facilitates the extraction of ore from them. *See* Simmons v. Muir, 75 Wyo. 44, 291 P.2d 810 (1955) (drilling on one claim could be applied to other claims if it assists in determining where to drill on other claims); Sherlock v. Leighton, 9 Wyo. 297, 63 P. 580 (1901) (tunnels, roads, and water ditches that service several claims constitute group assessment work). Despite dictum in Chambers v. Harrington, 111 U.S. 350, 4 S.Ct. 428, 28 L.Ed. 452 (1884), that group claims must be "contiguous" for assessment work to count for them all, subsequent courts have allowed assessment work to qualify even if performed outside contiguous claims, so long as it ultimately facilitates extraction of minerals. New Mercur Mining Co. v. South Mercur Mining Co., 102 Utah 131, 128 P.2d 269 (1942).

Although the 1872 Law provides that an unpatented claim will be forfeited without performance of annual assessment work, failure to perform the work does not necessarily void the claim. Rather, a claim that has been forfeited merely becomes open to relocation again. When, if ever, can the forfeiting locator re-enter and relocate the claim?

GOLDEN CONDOR, INC. v. BELL
Court of Appeals of Idaho, 1984.
106 Idaho 280, 678 P.2d 72.

JUDGE BURNETT delivered the opinion of the Court.

This is an appeal from a decree quieting title to four unpatented lode mining claims in the Summit Mining District of Shoshone County.

The district court ruled in favor of Golden Condor, Inc., the record owner of these claims. Velma Bell has challenged Golden Condor's title upon the alternative postulates that her husband entered into a contract to buy the claims and that she "relocated" the claims upon an abandonment or forfeiture by Golden Condor. We vacate the decree and remand the case for further findings. * * *

Federal law requires that "$100 worth of labor shall be performed or improvements made during each year" on an unpatented lode mining claim. If this annual labor (sometimes called "annual assessment work") is not performed by September 1 of each year, the claim is open to relocation and thus subject to forfeiture. However, if the "original locators, their heirs, assigns, or legal representatives," have resumed their work upon the claim after failure to perform and prior to relocation, the original claim is revived. 30 U.S.C. § 28. * * * Idaho Code § 47–606 provides that an affidavit of performance of the annual labor must be filed with the county recorded of the county in which the claim is situated. Under the Idaho statute a filed affidavit is prima facie evidence that work has been performed; conversely, failure to file an affidavit is prima facie evidence that work has not been performed. * * *

[Here,] … the performance of annual labor, during the assessment year running from September 1, 1977 to September 1, 1978, was contested. On June 15, 1978, Alfred T. Swanson, Jr., and officer of Golden Condor, filed an affidavit of performance of annual labor on the four claims. At trial he testified about the work performed in June. Mrs. Bell disputed the contents of that affidavit and the testimony. She asserted that the 1978 work had not been done, and that she and her husband relocated the claims before Golden Condor made any effort to revise them.

Mrs. Bell's pleadings referred to abandonment of the claims; but her evidence actually was directed, without objection, toward a theory of forfeiture. Abandonment and forfeiture are closely related concepts. Both are means by which mining claims may be opened to relocation. But they are not precisely the same. Abandonment is a voluntary, intentional act; forefeiture is the result, regardless of intent, of noncompliance with a legal requirement. 2 Rocky Mountain Mineral Law Found., The American Law of Mining § 8.2 (1983). In this case, there was no proof that Golden Condor voluntarily and intentionally had relinquished its mining claims. Consequently, the issue presented below, and which now confronts us on appeal, is whether Golden Condor lost the mining claims by forfeiture.

This question is framed by Golden Condor's complaint to quiet title. In general, a party seeking to quiet title to real property must affirmatively prove his title. The proof must establish the strength of his own title rather than merely showing the weakness of any adverse claim. However, this general rule is supplemented by specific burden of proof imposed on one who adversely claims title to a mining claim by forfeiture and relocation. The adverse claimant has a two-fold burden of proof.

First, the claimant must prove that the annual labor was not performed; and this proof must be by clear and convincing evidence. Second, the claimant must prove that his or her own locations are valid. * * * In the present case, the trial court found that Golden Condor successfully had proved its record title and that Mrs. Bell had failed to prove her adverse claim. * * *

Mrs. Bell's substantive attack was her contention that the 1978 work had not in fact been done. The evidence in the record regarding performance of the 1978 annual labor is conflicting. * * * The record … contains testimony by the younger Mr. Slawson, describing the nature of the work he personally performed in June, 1978. However, Mrs. Bell presented witnesses, including Mr. Bell, whose testimony tended to show that no work had been performed, other than labor by Mr. Bell in August, 1978, when he sought to relocate the claims. Addressing this conflict in the evidence, the trial court in its memorandum decision said the following:

> Plaintiff [Golden Condor] is entitled to the benefit of Idaho Code § 47–606 which provides in part that the affidavit of performance of labor filed for record "shall be prima facie evidence of the performance of such labor."

> The Defendant's contention that the required labor was not performed and hence the claim abandoned is hereby denied.

As explained above, the evidence at trial actually pointed to a theory of forfeiture rather than abandonment. However, the district court's decision did not turn upon the distinction between these concepts. Rather, its decision was based upon the weight given to Golden Condor's affidavit.

On that question, the case of Dickens–West Mining Co. v. Crescent Mining & Milling Co., 26 Idaho 153, 141 P. 566 (1914), is instructive. There our Supreme Court held that an affidavit of annual labor, when contradicted by contrary proof, no longer suffices, of itself, to establish that the labor has been performed. In view of *Dickens–West* we deem it clear that once Mrs. Bell presented evidence refuting Golden Condor's affidavit, the issue of whether the 1978 work had been performed was no longer governed by the prima evidence effect of the affidavit. Rather, the issue then turned upon a weighing of the conflicting evidence. The district court's memorandum decision reflects no such weighing. Rather, it appears on its face to accord the affidavit continuing and controlling effect. We hold that the court erred in this regard. We conclude that the case must be remanded for a finding of whether, in fact, Golden Condor performed the 1978 work. If the court finds that the work was performed, it may reenter the decree quieting title in Golden Condor. If the court finds to the contrary, it should determine whether the mining claims were validly relocated.

* * *

Notes and Questions

1. On remand, the trial court took further evidence of whether Golden Condor had performed the necessary assessment work in 1978, and concluded that it had. Mrs. Bell appealed that decision all the way to the Idaho Supreme Court, which affirmed the trial court's ruling. Golden Condor v. Bell, 112 Idaho 1086, 739 P.2d 385 (1987).

2. As noted in Golden Condor, a forfeiture for failure to perform assessment work is not an abandonment. If a claim is truly abandoned, it cannot be revived by resuming assessment work. Sawyer–Adecor International, Inc. v. Anglin, 198 Mont. 440, 646 P.2d 1194 (1982); Hartman Gold Mining Co. v. Warning, 40 Ariz. 267, 11 P.2d 854 (1932).

3. Forfeitures of unpatented mining claims are "not ... favored by law." Justice Mining Co. v. Barclay, 82 F. 554 (C.C.D.Nev. 1897). Where there is a good faith attempt to comply with federal assessment requirements, the law will be liberally construed to prevent a forfeiture. Silliman v. Powell, 642 P.2d 388 (Utah 1982). *See* Thornton v. Kaufman, 40 Mont. 282, 106 P. 361 (1910) (assessment work could be effectively resumed even after an adverse locator had made discovery and posted location notice, as long as the adverse locator had not completed the location procedure). (Deferment of assessment requirements may be granted) What if "legal impediments exist," affecting a claimant's right to enter the surface of the claim? *See* American Resources Limited, 44 IBLA 220 (1980). But long gaps in performance of assessment work may invalidate the claim. Cliffs Synfuel Corp. v. Babbitt, 147 F.Supp.2d 1118 (D.Utah. 2001) (holding that a 46–year gap in performance invalidated an unpatented mining claim).

4. As a general rule, only rival locators may challenge a claim for failure of assessment work by relocating it. The case of Hickel v. Oil Shale Corp., 400 U.S. 48, 91 S.Ct. 196, 27 L.Ed.2d 193 (1970) recognized, for the first time, the right of the government to contest claims for failure of assessment work. However, it remains unclear whether this 1970 case applies only to government challenges to pre–1920 oil shale claims. *See* Exxon Mobil Corp. v. Norton, 346 F.3d 1244 (10th Cir. 2003); Cliffs Synfuel Corp. v. Norton, 291 F.3d 1250 (10th Cir. 2002).

5. FLPMA requires annual filing of an affidavit of assessment work performed, and provides that the failure to make such filing "shall be deemed conclusively to constitute an abandonment of the mining claim." 43 U.S.C.A. § 1744(c). Does FLPMA invalidate claims where there has been no filing, but the assessment work was done? *See* United States v. Locke, 471 U.S. 84, 105 S.Ct. 1785, 85 L.Ed.2d 64 (1985) the failure of either condition automatically invalidates the claim); Red Top Mercury Mines, Inc. v. United States, 887 F.2d 198 (9th Cir. 1989) (strictly construing FLPMA's affidavit requirement).

6. What is the *real* value today of the 1872 Mining Law's annual assessment requirement? In 1872, when wages were on the order of 20 cents an hour, $100 was a lot of money. Using the deflation tools available at EH.net, a comparable price in 2004 dollars would be somewhere between $1,490 (deflating based on the consumer price index) and $17,800 (deflating

based on per capita gross domestic product). And yet, the required value of annual assessment work remains $100.

7. The 1872 Mining Law's annual assessment work requirement has led to a good deal of fraud. Charles Wilkinson tells a story about "three adjacent claims in California—which happen to lie astride a 2–mile stretch of fine trout stream—that are kept alive solely by an annual Fourth of July 'work day,' complete with several sticks of dynamite and perhaps rental of a Caterpillar tractor for a joyride." According to Wilkinson, "[t]he requirement begs, and receives, widespread fraud: federal agencies can hardly take the time to disprove a notarized affidavit alleging a day or two's work, perhaps coupled with a bulldozer scrape or the purchase of a shovel." CHARLES WILKINSON, CROSSING THE NEXT MERDIAN: LAND, WATER, AND THE FUTURE OF THE AMERICAN WEST 47 (1992). Instead of requiring annual assessment work, which the government cannot effectively monitor and enforce, would it make more sense to require miners to pay a $100 annual fee directly to the government? Congress did just that in 1992, as the next section discloses.

b. Claim Maintenance Fee

The 1992 Department of Interior and Related Agencies Appropriations Act, Pub. L. No. 102–381, 106 Stat. 1374, provides that the holders of unpatented mining claims, mill sites, or tunnel sites must annually pay $100 per claim ("Claim Rental Fee") in lieu of assessment work on or before August 31, 1993. The Act also requires payment of a $100 location fee. Failure to pay either the location fee or the annual "Claim Rental Fee" is conclusive evidence of abandonment of the claim. The 1992 Interior Appropriations Act provides an exception for small miners, defined as miners with ten or fewer claims. Such small miners have the option of (a) doing the assessment work and filing the affidavit, or (b) paying the annual maintenance fee.

Congress codified a revised version of the 1992 Interior Appropriations Act in The Omnibus Budget Reconciliation Act of 1993, Pub.L. No. 103–66, 107 Stat. 313, 405 (1993), *codified at* 30 U.S.C. § 28f–28k. The 1993 Budget Reconciliation Act provides that all unpatented claimholders must pay the $100 claim rental fee, renamed "Claim Maintenance Fee," annually in lieu of of the assessment work requirement for the years 1999 through 2001. 30 U.S.C. § 28f(a). Additionally, the 1993 Act requires a location fee of $25 for each unpatented mining claim, mill or tunnel site located after August 10, 1993, and before September 30, 2001. 30 U.S.C. § 28g. The Act authorized the Secretary of Interior to adjust both fees for inflation beginning in 1998. 30 U.S.C. § 28j(c). Failure to pay either the Claim Maintenance Fee or the location fee "conclusively constitute[s] a forfeiture of the unpatented mining claim." 30 U.S.C. § 28(i). Unlike the 1992 Interior Appropriations Act, which it revised, the 1993 Budget Reconciliation Act does not provide an automatic waiver for small miners but vests discretion in the BLM to waive the fee for small miners who have performed assessment work and filed an affidavit. 30 U.S.C. § 28f(d).

In 1999, Congress amended the 1992 Interior Authorizations Act again by adding a notice and cure provision for claimants seeking a small miner exemption. Omnibus Consolidated and Emergency Supplemental Appropriations Act of 1999, Pub.L. No. 05–277, 112 Stat. 2681–235 (Oct. 21, 1998). In the event of a defect in an application for a small miner exemption, the claimant has 60 days after receiving written notification of the defect from BLM to comply with the claim maintenance fee requirement of the 1992 Interior Appropriations Act. The BLM published an interim final rule implementing the changes made by the 1999 Act in 64 Fed. Reg. 47,017 (Aug. 27, 1999), which have been codified at 43 C.F.R. Part 3830.

In the Department of the Interior and Related Agencies Appropriations Act of 2004, Pub. L. No. 108–108, 117 Stat. 1241, Congress extended the $100 claim maintenance fee and the $25 location fee through 2008. However, in June 2004, the BLM raised the claim maintenance fees for the first time since 1993, as it was authorized to do under 30 U.S.C. § 28j(c). The one-time location fee is now $30 for each new mining claim, mill or tunnel site, and the annual maintenance fee has been raised to $125, reflecting a 25 percent increase in the Consumer Price Index since August 1993. The new fees are published at 43 CFR Part 3834 (July 1, 2004).

Since its introduction, the Claim Maintenance Fee has provided substantial revenues to the federal government—$23.9 million in fiscal year 2000 alone. In addition, the fee has had a huge impact on the number of unpatented claims. Between 1989 and 1993, the number of unpatented mining claims declined from 1.2 million to fewer than 295,000. *See* Marc Humphries, CRS Issue Brief for Congress, Mining on Federal Lands CRS–3 (Congressional Research Service, updated July 21, 1994) (noting that "[m]any claims were dropped as a result" of annual maintenance fees). Claims rose slightly in following years, "reflecting the relative strength of the gold and copper industries," but never came close to pre-annual maintenance fee levels. What do these statistics imply about the legitimacy of unpatented "mining activities"?

c. Adverse Claimants

An unpatented mining claim may be contested either by the rival claimant or by the United States government (typically the BLM or the Forest Service). A rival claimant must file an adverse claim at the time of the patent application or be precluded from objecting after the patent is issued. Gwillim v. Donnellan, 115 U.S. 45, 5 S.Ct. 1110, 29 L.Ed. 348 (1885); Bowen v. Chemi–Cote Perlite Corp., 102 Ariz. 423, 432 P.2d 435 (1967). Most adverse claims may be filed with the office where the patent application is initiated. 30 U.S.C.A. §§ 29, 30. Adverse claim proceedings involve inquiries into: (1) which of the claimants has made the first discovery; (2) whether there has been a defect in the location procedures by the senior claimant; (3) whether a claim has become subject to relocation either because of failure to do assessment work or failure to comply with the recordation requirements of Section 314 of FLPMA; and (4) conflicting rights between placer and lode locators. *See* Iron Silver Mining Co. v. Campbell, 135 U.S. 286, 10 S.Ct. 765, 34 L.Ed. 155 (1890); Couch v. Clifton, 626 P.2d 731 (Colo. App. 1981).

The federal government often contests unpatented mining claims in order to quiet title to lands subject to questionable mining claims. The government may argue that claims are invalid on the following grounds: (1) the claims are not located in good faith for mining purposes; (2) the claimant has not made a discovery of a valuable mineral deposit; (3) the claims are not located in compliance with federal and state procedures; (4) the claimant failed to follow assessment work requirements; or (5) the land is not available for location. *See* United States v. Albert F. Parker, 82 IBLA 344 (1984); United States v. Zweifel, 508 F.2d 1150 (10th Cir. 1975); United States v. Springer, 491 F.2d 239 (9th Cir. 1974). However, federal challenges to unpatented mining claims are neither cheap nor easy. As Charles Wilkinson notes:

> Fraudulent entrants, and small miners with marginal claims, have tremendous inertia on their side after an asserted discovery. They can hold their claims, and usually can reside there, until the BLM successfully contests their claim in a formal administrative proceeding. Numerous stalling tactics are available. As one Forest Service mining officer told me in frustration: "I say 'take me to your discovery.' He does. I come in with a bulldozer, cut a trench, remove some minerals and get them assayed. They don't pan out and I notify the claimant. He says we should have taken samples further up the hill. And so on it goes. I have spent 10 or 12 years removing some of these guys." The government must pursue a $10,000 administrative proceeding, and possibly a subsequent court challenge, during which time the claimant is usually allowed to stay on the land.

Charles F. Wilkinson, *Crossing the Next Meridian: Land, Water, and the Future of the American West* 48 (1992).

d. Surface Use Limitations

The traditional view was that a miner satisfying all the prerequisites of a valid unpatented mining claim (e.g., location, discovery, assessment work) had an absolute right to extract minerals. However, a series of new statutes and regulations have limited this "absolute" right by requiring consideration of land use and environmental values. These laws have had a particular impact on surface uses.

The 1872 Mining Law—A holder of an unpatented mining claim may make reasonable use of the claim surface so long as the use is connected with mining. Thus, buildings used to protect equipment, store samples, or house personnel are allowed; homes or cabins used for residences are not allowed (unless authorized by the Mining Claims Occupancy Act of 1962, discussed below). The owner of an unpatented mining claim may not fence the claim, erect no-trespassing signs, or prevent hikers, hunters, or fishers from passing through the claim. As for the environmental consequences of mining, the 1872 Mining Law is silent, but environmental requirements have been imposed on mining operations by other statutes, including the Mining and Minerals Policy Act of 1970, which declares it to be the policy of the federal government to encourage "the study and development of methods for the disposal, control, and reclamation of mineral waste products, and the reclamation of mined land, so as to lessen any adverse impact on mineral extraction and processing upon the physical environment." 30 U.S.C.A. § 21a. Other environmental statutes that impose requirements on both patented and unpatented mining claims, including the Surface Mining Control and Reclamation Act of 1977, 30 U.S.C.A. §§ 1231 *et seq.*, are addressed in Section V of this chapter.

Surface Resource Act of 1955—An early 1950s Department of Agriculture survey revealed that of the over 80,000 unpatented mining claims covering 2.2 million acres of national forest lands, only 2% were in commercial production. Because so much surface land was tied up in dormant claims, Congress decided to limit the locator's nonmining use of the surface. With the passage of the Surface Resources Act of 1955: (1) no mining claim located after July 1, 1955 may be used prior to patent for any purposes other than prospecting, mining, or processing operations and "uses reasonably incident thereto"; (2) such claims are subject to the right of the United States to manage and dispose of vegetative and other surface resources (except locatable mineral deposits on the claim); and (3) unpatented mining claims are subject to the right of the federal government and its licensees to use so much of the surface as may be necessary for access to adjacent land. Any use of the surface of the claim by the federal government must not materially interfere with mining operations. Except to the extent required for mineral operations, the locator may not cut timber or other vegetative resources. 30 U.S.C.A. § 612. These statutory mandates have been construed to authorize the Forest Service to bar the use of a backhoe, bulldozer, and blasting on a valid, perfected claim, as unreasonable destruction of national forest lands. United States v. Richardson, 599 F.2d 290 (9th Cir. 1979). Can the general public use an unpatented mining area for recreation without the miners' permission? *See* United States v. Curtis–Nevada Mines, Inc., 611 F.2d 1277 (9th Cir. 1980).

The Mining Claims Occupancy Act—One of the purposes of the Surface Use Act of 1955, 30 U.S.C.A. § 601, was to prohibit all surface uses not reasonably incident to mining on unpatented claims located after 1955. In order to relieve the hardship of persons living on their unpatented claims, but who faced eviction under the 1955 statute, Congress passed the Mining Claims Occupancy Act of 1962, 30 U.S.C.A. § 701. The statute enabled persons making their principal place of residence on an unpatented mining claim for at least seven years prior to 1962 to maintain their residence on the claim. Non-residential structures, or residences used only part of the year, were excluded. *See* Funderberg v. Udall, 396 F.2d 638 (9th Cir. 1968).

Forest Service Regulations—The Organic Act of 1897, 16 U.S.C.A. § 478, provides that the national forests shall be open to mineral entry, so long as locators "comply with the rules and regulations covering such national forests." Forest Service regulations govern methods of mining development and operation and provide for reclamation and mitigation of adverse environmental impacts. 36 C.F.R. Part 252. All mining "operations" on national forest lands are subject to these regulations. United States v. Burnett, 750 F.Supp. 1029 (D.Idaho 1990). Under these regulations, a person seeking to conduct exploration activities must file a Notice of Intention to Operate. If the District Ranger determines that there is likely to be "significant disturbance of surface resources," the District Ranger may require the operator to submit a proposed Plan of Operations which provides for environmental protection. 36 C.F.R. § 252.4. The validity of these regulations was upheld in United States v. Weiss, 642 F.2d 296 (9th Cir. 1981), and reaffirmed in Clouser v. Espy, 42 F.3d 1522 (9th Cir. 1994). In United States v. Goldfield Deep Mines Co. of Nevada, 644 F.2d 1307 (9th Cir. 1981), the court found that a locator failing to file a Plan of Operation was liable for trespass. *See also* United States v. Nordwick, 673 F.Supp. 397 (D.Mont. 1987).

The courts have been reluctant to definitively decide whether the Forest Service may disapprove proposed mining plans and thereby foreclose mining operations. *See United States v. Brunskill*, 792 F.2d 938 (9th Cir. 1986). However, it seems likely that the courts will sustain most any reasonable regulatory restiction on a mining activity on National Forest lands, so long as the regulation does not completely prohibit mining. *See* South Dakota Mining Association, Inc. v. Lawrence County, 155 F.3d 1005 (8th Cir. 1998) (declaring invalid a county ordinance that prohibited surface mining as a de facto ban on all mining). Although the Forest Service has broad authority to regulate mining activity on National Forest lands, the owner of a mining claim in a forest does own a property right, and is not a "mere social guest" of the government. United States v. Shumway, 199 F.3d 1093 (9th Cir. 1999). The court in *Shumway* wrote that a claimant may only be evicted from Forest Service land "if their claim is a sham or otherwise invalid, or if they fail to observe Forest Service regulations in such a way as to invalidate their claims." *Id.* Does NEPA require the Forest Service to prepare an environmental impact statement before it can approve a Plan of Operation? *See* Chapter 4, *supra*.

BLM Surface Management Regulations—Prior to 1976, the consensus was that BLM lacked statutory authority to impose surface management regulations on public lands open to mineral entry, exploration, and location. *See* Haggard, *Regulation of Mining Activities on Federal Lands*, 21 Rocky Mtn. Min.L. Inst. 349 (1975). In 1976, Congress gave the BLM the necessary authority in FLPMA, which requires that "in managing the public lands, the Secretary [of the Interior] shall, by regulation or otherwise, take action to prevent unnecessary or undue degradation of the public lands." 42 U.S.C.A. § 1732(b). Pursuant to this authority, in

1980 BLM adopted surface management regulations applicable to mining locations on public lands. 43 C.F.R. Part 3809. The regulatory requirements vary depending on the size and location of the mine and the level of mining activity. The lowest level—"casual use" mines—includes part-time miners who create little surface disturbance. Such activities may be undertaken without notice to BLM. *See* Bales v. Ruch, 522 F.Supp. 150 (E.D. Cal. 1981) (a mobile home, vehicles, livestock, and a garden do not constitute "casual use" because of the resulting litter and waste water discharges). The second level of activity involves "Notice" mines that create surface disturbance on five or fewer acres per year. Operators in this category must notify BLM before commencing work, but do not require any particular approval before they commence. *See* Sierra Club v. Penfold, 857 F.2d 1307 (9th Cir. 1988). The third level of "Plan" mines disturbs five or more acres per year. Operators must file a plan of operations for BLM approval as well as a bond to ensure reclamation of the site.

Pursuant to its authority under the Surface Resources Act and FLPMA, BLM issued new regulations in 1996 to restrict the unlawful use and occupancy of unpatented mining claims for non-mining purposes. 43 C.F.R. Part 3715. The regulations were aimed at eliminating abuses such as unauthorized residences, non-mining commercial operations, illegal activities, or speculative activities not related to mining. In the event BLM determines that an unlawful use and occupancy exists, it may issue an immediate suspension order, cessation order, or notice of non-compliance. 43 C.F.R. § 3715.5–2. If necessary, the agency may seek judicial assistance by requesting that the Department of Justice file a civil action for injunctive relief. 43 C.F.R. § 3715.5–2.

In the late 1990s, near the end of the Clinton Administration, the Solicitor of the Interior attempted to more clearly distinguish between valid and invalid uses of unpatented mining claims. The Solicitor opined that mining claims might be invalidated if used *solely* for purposes ancillary to mining. The Interior Secretary instructed the BLM to determine the validity of any questionable mining claim, in light of the Solicitor's opinion, before approving any new or modified plan of operations for ancillary uses. Common uses of unpatented mining claims for waste dumps, leach pads, tailings disposal, and topsoil storage are heavily impacted by this directive. M–37004, *Use of Mining Claims for Purposes Ancillary to Mineral Extraction*. This memoradum is not binding on courts, but courts are likely to give it substantial deference. Clinton-era reforms and their current status are addressed in detail in Section II. E, below.

D. The Patented Mining Claim

As noted above, the holder of an unpatented mining claim has a "possessory" title that allows the locator to remove all the mineral deposits on the claim (and extralaterally) free from interference by other miners. Why, then, would a miner with an unpatented claim seek a patent

from the United States? Without a patent, the claim must be maintained, including performance of annual assessment work, and the locator must be vigilant lest an adverse claimant locate an overlapping
claim. The holder of an unpatented claim also risks challenge by the
United States that the claim should be invalidated (without compensation) for (1) locating on land withdrawn from mineral location, (2) failure
to comply with required location procedures, (3) lack of discovery, (4)
failure of assessment work, or (5) failure to record the claim or the
annual assessment work with BLM. Moreover, claims located after 1955
are subject to and limited by the Surface Resources Act of 1955, as well
as certain federal regulations on surface land use which do not apply to
patented claims. And unpatented claims cease to be valid once the minerals are exhausted. United States v. Houston, 66 I.D. 161 (1959).

In light of these uncertainties and requirements, the owner of an
unpatented mining claim has some incentive to seek a patent, which
would (a) secure title to the claim and associated surface resources (even
after exhaustion of the mine), (b) eliminate onerous recording, claim
maintenance fees, and assessment work requirements, and (c) prevent
Congress from cutting off the opportunity to patent. *See Swanson v.
Babbitt*, 3 F.3d 1348 (9th Cir. 1993) (holding that Congress could cut off
the opportunity to patent even after a claimant has filed the patent
application, but before the patent has issued). The primary disadvantage
of applying for a patent is that it may provoke a contest with the federal
government, which claimants do not always win. If they lose, their claim
is voided, and they lose their possessory rights. Consequently, filing a
patent application is in the nature of a zero-sum game, which most mining claimants would rather not risk. From their point of view, better to
bear the costs and risks of maintaining an unpatented mining claim
than to risk almost certain government challenge of a patent application. Only a small fraction of unpatented mine claimants ever seek a
patent. Nevertheless, by early in the 21st century, more than 60,000
patents had been awarded, covering more than 3.7 million acres of previously public lands. Far more public land acreage has been patented
under homestead laws, railroad and statehood grants, and other federal
laws not related to mining. *See* Marc Humphries, CRS Issue Brief for
Congress, Mining on Federal Lands CRS–3 (Washington, D.C.: Congressional Research Service, The Library of Congress, updated July 21,
2004).

A locator may apply for a patent to the claim after performance of at
least $500 of assessment work. 30 U.S.C. § 29 (lode), § 37 (placer), § 42
(mill site). Alternatively, a locator may establish the right to a patent by
holding and working the claim for a period of time equal to that required
by state law to establish title by adverse possession of mining claims. 30
U.S.C. § 38. *See Hoefler v. Babbitt*, 952 F.Supp. 1448 (D.Or. 1996), *aff'd*
139 F.3d 726 (9th Cir.), *cert. denied*, 525 U.S. 825, 119 S.Ct. 70, 142
L.Ed.2d 55 (1998). The government will award a patent only if the claim
meets several additional conditions, which are discussed below. Most

importantly, the patent applicant bears the burden of proving that all procedural requirements and conditions are satisfied.

Mineral Survey—The applicant must first file with the state BLM office an application for a mineral survey. Only authorized United States mineral surveyors may conduct the survey. The results of the survey must show the exterior boundaries of the claim, tie the claim to a United States mineral monument or a part of the public survey, and reveal all areas of potential conflict with other claims.

Improvements—The applicant must hire a U.S. mineral surveyor to survey the claim boundaries and certify that the applicant has completed the requisite $500 worth of improvements.

Discovery—The most basic requirement, and the one checked most carefully by the federal government, is the discovery of a valuable mineral deposit. Without a valid discovery, the government will not only deny the patent application, but will also invalidate the location. United States v. Carlile, 67 I.D. 417 (1960). To prove discovery, the applicant must submit sufficient evidence to meet the *Coleman* test discussed earlier: valuable mineral deposits exist which are of such quality and quantity that a person of ordinary prudence would be justified in a further expenditure of labor, and the minerals can be removed and marketed at a profit. The *Coleman* test applies as of the date of the patent application, not the date of the original discovery. Best v. Humboldt Placer Mining Co., 371 U.S. 334, 83 S.Ct. 379, 9 L.Ed.2d 350 (1963). For placer claims the applicant must show that each ten-acre tract in the claim is "mineral in character." *See* McCall v. Andrus, 628 F.2d 1185 (9th Cir. 1980). The evidence of discovery is scrutinized by an Interior Department mineral examiner. If the examiner believes that the discovery is invalid (as is usually the case), the government initiates a contest of the claim before a hearing examiner. If the result is unfavorable to the claimant, she may appeal to the Interior Board of Land Appeals (IBLA). *See* United States v. Webb, 655 F.2d 977 (9th Cir. 1981).

Notice and Eligibility—The applicant must prepare a notice of patent application, which describes the boundaries of the claim. This notice is posted on the claim and published for 60 days in a newspaper. Persons with an adverse claim to the area embraced by the patent application must file an adverse claim within the 60–day publication period. The timely filing of an advance claim stays all proceedings on the application for the patent until the dispute is resolved.

Even before publication of the patent application notice, however, the applicant must satisfy the BLM that the applicant is eligible to receive a patent. BLM reviews the patent applicant's general eligibility, including compliance with pertinent statutes and regulations, in what is known as an "office adjudication." One of the most critical issues reviewed during the office adjudication is whether the claim is located on land open to mineral location, or whether it has been reserved, withdrawn, or otherwise made unavailable for location. The general rule is that claims on land withdrawn from mineral entry before location are *void ab initio*. Claims on land withdrawn from mineral entry after location are invalid if there has been no discovery before the date of withdrawal. United States v. Richard Clemons, 45 IBLA 64 (1980). Some withdrawals and reservations prevent patenting altogether. *See* Freese v. United States, 226 Ct.Cl. 252, 639 F.2d 754 (1981) (holding that the statute creating the Sawtooth National Recreation Area could constitutionally deny holders of unpatented mining claims the ability to obtain a patent so long as the statute preserves the right of possession to validly existing unpatented claims). Some withdrawals and reservations limit the time period in which a claimant must apply for a patent. *See* Alaska Miners v. Andrus, 662 F.2d 577 (9th Cir. 1981) (holding that the Alaska Native Claims Settlement Act could constitutionally require that applications occur within five years after the Act's enactment).

If the claimant has met all the applicable requirements, and if there are no defects in the application, the claimant has an absolute right to a patent from the United States. Issuance of a patent to an applicant satisfying all relevant requirements is ministerial, not discretionary. Wilbur v. United States ex rel. Krushnic, 280 U.S. 306, 318–19, 50 S.Ct. 103, 105, 74 L.Ed. 445 (1929); United States v. Kosanke Sand Corp., 12 IBLA 282, 290–1 (1973). Consequently, patent issuance does not constitute an "action" under NEPA, requiring an environmental impact statement. South Dakota v. Andrus, 614 F.2d 1190 (8th Cir. 1980).

If the patent application is successful, the claimant must pay for the land at the barely noticeable rate of $5 per acre for a lode claim and $2.50 per acre for a placer claim. A patent ordinarily grants a fee simple interest in all minerals, as well as an exclusive right to, and ownership of, all the surface and surface resources within the claim's boundaries. Patentees are not limited by the Surface Resources Act of 1955, nor is annual assessment work required. After patenting, the surface and minerals on the claim are private property in the fullest sense of the phrase. Swanson v. Babbitt, 3 F.3d 1348 (9th Cir. 1993).

In September 1994, Congress enacted the Department of Interior and Related Agencies Appropriations Act, Pub. L. 103–322, 108 Stat. 2499 (1994). Section 112 of that statute imposed a moratorium on issuing new patents for lands containing hardrock minerals. Exempted from the moratorium were claimants who had (a) filed an application on or before September 30, 1994, and (b) had fully complied with all mining law requirements by that same date. Pub. L. No. 104–208, § 113, 110 Stat. 3009 (1992). *See also* Mt. Emmons Mining Co. v. Babbitt, 117 F.3d 1167 (10th Cir. 1997) (holding that the patent applicant's compliance with the 1872 Mining Law by the moratorium's enactment date triggered the exemption, and rejecting the BLM's interpretation that the moratorium applied only to applications for which final certificates were issued and pending in Washington, D.C. prior to the enactment date); R.T. Vanderbilt Co. v. Babbitt, 113 F.3d 1061 (9th Cir. 1997) (ruling that an application for a patent is not "complete," so as to qualify for the exemption from the moratorium, until the purchase price is paid). The moratorium on patenting continues in effect today. Whether the moratorium will be lifted any time soon, or ever, remains to be seen.

E. Reform Efforts

It is remarkable that a law from 1872 still controls a great deal of resource development on the public lands of the United States. The Mining Law has been reformed at the edges, most notably by the withdrawal of some mineral lands from free entry, the removal of many minerals from its location system, the introduction of more stringent discovery requirements, the assessment of annual claim maintenance fees, and the imposition of environmental and health and safety regulations. However, with respect to hard-rock minerals, the institutional structure of mineral entry and location remains essentially unchanged, without payment of any significant fee or royalty to the government.

The 1872 Mining Law was enacted at a time when mining was (a) generally undertaken by individuals or small-groups rather than large corporations; (b) important to the development of the national economy; and (c) causing relatively small and geographically isolated environmental impacts. By the middle of the twentieth century, mining had become (a) dominated by large corporations; (b) relatively insignificant to the national economy; and (c) a major threat to the environment. In the 1800s, mining practices chiefly involved underground mining operations on well-defined lodes. Today, mining involves "mountaintop removal" to get at fractions of ounces of gold per ton of "overburden" removed. Mineral deposits that would have been left as waste a hundred years ago today can be mined at a profit, using advanced technologies that include highly toxic chemicals. Despite these changes in the mining industry and mining techniques, the Mining Law has not been fundamentally altered, though not for lack of trying. The following Congressional Research Service report canvasses several of the most important issues in mining law reform.

In Practice:

"MINING ON FEDERAL LANDS"
Marc Humphries
CRS ISSUE BRIEF FOR CONGRESS (UPDATED JULY 21, 2004)

* * *

Claim-Patent System: Pros and Cons

The right to enter the public domain and prospect for and develop minerals is the feature of the claim-patent system that draws the most vigorous support from the mining industry. Modern hardrock mineral exploration requires a continuous effort using vast tracts of land and sophisticated and expensive technology. Industry officials argue that being able to obtain full and clear title to the land enhances a company's ability to bring an economic deposit into production; financing the project, for example, may be more feasible. They contend that restrictions on free access and security of tenure would curtail exploration efforts among large and small mining firms. In their view, the incentive to develop would be lost, long-run costs would increase, and the industry and country would suffer.

Mining Law critics consider the claim-patent system a giveaway of publicly owned resources because of the absence of royalties and the small charges associated with keeping a claim active and obtaining a patent. They maintain that although such generous terms may have been effective ways to help settle the West and develop minerals, there is no solid evidence that under a different system minerals would not be developed today. They also believe the current system, by conveying title and allowing other uses of patented lands, creates difficult land management problems through the creation of inholdings, and that current law does not provide for adequate protection of the environment.

In the claim-patent system, mineral claims may be held indefinitely without any mineral production. In such instances, claimed or patented land has been used for purposes other than mineral development. Once lands are patented to convey full title to the claimant, the owner can use the lands for a variety of purposes, including non-mineral ones. However, using land under an unpatented mining claim for anything but mineral and associated purposes violates the Mining Law. Critics believe that many claims are held for speculative purposes. However, industry officials argue that a claim may lay idle until market conditions make it profitable to develop the mineral deposit.

* * *

The industry has indicated it wishes to avoid major challenges to the principle of free access and the right to obtain a patent. The industry generally opposes placing hardrock minerals under a leasing system because this would give the federal government discretionary control over development, impose royalty payments, and retain government ownership of surface and/or mineral rights.

Past Amendment Proposals

Proposals to amend the 1872 Mining Law have fallen under the following broad categories:

- Modify the claim-patent system to retain the patent feature, but require payment of fair market value for all or part of the value of the land. The Government also would collect some percent of the value of mineral production as royalties.

- Convert the claim-patent system to a permitting system, and prohibit further patenting. Advocates of this proposal argue that a permitting system would be effective in achieving a fair market value return to the federal Treasury for public lands. This system would collect royalties and add new environmental standards to mining operations. Mineral industry supporters, on the other hand, contend that the Department of the Interior is already overburdened with the current leasing system and that comprehensive hardrock mining reform would only add to its inefficiency and ultimately increase costs through royalty and rents.

- Continue the current claim-patent system, but with some amendments. Proposed changes have included eliminating the distinction between lode and placer claims, imposing a time limit within which claims must be developed, expanding the size of the claim, providing better prediscovery protection, and opening more public lands to mineral exploration.

The Clinton Administration's Call to Eliminate Subsidies

The Mining Law currently allows a claimant to produce minerals without a patent and without paying royalties or rents to the federal Treasury. This is considered a subsidy by many because the miner does not pay for a factor of production (i.e., land and mineral resources). By contrast, royalties are paid to the federal government for oil and gas leasing on federal lands, and non-federal land owners (e.g., private and state owners) typically receive a royalty from those who produce minerals on their lands. Also, if the claimant patents the surface and mineral estate for the $2.50 or $5.00 per acre, this too can be considered a subsidy because the claimant is paying less than fair market value for the surface and mineral estates. Various tax incentives ... have been characterized as subsidies to the industry as well.

Eliminating some of the natural resource subsidies, in the Clinton Administration's view, would have been one way to increase revenues to the Treasury and help ensure a fair return to the taxpayer for the development of public lands. In its FY2001 budget request, the Clinton Administration proposed charging mining companies a 5% fee on net smelter production from hardrock mining on federal lands. The Bush Administration did not make a similar proposal in its FY2003 budget request.

* * * Proponents of retaining the current system contend that an incentive still is necessary for those who take substantial financial risk to develop a mineral deposit. Mining is a capital-intensive process that often takes years of development before minerals are produced.

Imposing royalties, increasing holding fees, and repealing the percentage depletion allowance would have some impact on domestic hardrock mineral production, but the level of any production decline attributable solely to new fees is difficult to estimate. The mining industry generally has opposed legislation to repeal the percentage depletion allowance. The elimination of some incentives to the industry would come at a time when the West is already developed (an original goal of the law) and mineral/metal demand is relatively good. However, prices are fluctuating, and the mining industry is looking outside the United States for lower-cost deposits. Also, several mineral-producing nations are rewriting their mining laws to attract more U.S. and western investment. Some U.S. deposits are becoming much less competitive with foreign deposits. Any new cost increases in one area, without cost reductions in others, may make U.S. mineral deposits less competitive or uneconomic.

Of the many issues surrounding the Mining Law, at least three are of perennial concern. One is whether the government should receive a fair market return from public domain hardrock mineral dispositions. The others are about environmental protection, and withdrawals of federal land from mineral exploration and development.

Fair Market Value

Many believe that the federal government does not receive fair market value for land and resources transfers under the Mining Law. It receives no royalties or rents from mining activities conducted under the law. In addition, the $2.50 and $5.00 per-acre price for clear title to the surface and mineral rights has not changed since the law was enacted. The per-acre price appears to be based on the value of Western farmland and grazing land before the enactment of the law in 1872.

Determinations of fair market value of mineral-bearing lands is complex because many geologic, engineering, and economic factors must be considered, and fair market value determinations typically are controversial. According to a 1989 report by the General Accounting Office (GAO), the fair market value of mineral-bearing lands is substantially more than the $2.50 and $5.00 per acre that a claimant pays for patenting a claim. GAO estimated that, for 20 patents it reviewed, the federal government had received less than $4,500 since 1970 for lands valued between $13.8 million and $47.9 million.

The GAO appraisal method, however, was criticized by the Bureau of Land Management (BLM) in a May 1989 Report to the Secretary of the Interior. The GAO report obtained information on land values from BLM, Forest Service officials, and local real estate brokers. GAO's estimates were based on recent sales of comparable land, not the value of the land at the time claims were patented; much of the land may have had very little value at the time it was claimed or patented. BLM argues that sales of adjacent tracts that either have no mineral development potential or are sold for mineral rights alone cannot be used to establish fair market value of the surface of patented mining claims and that data on comparable sales are rare.

The Department of the Interior (DOI) estimates the value of hardrock mineral production on federal land at $1.0 billion for FY2000, a decrease from an estimated $1.8 billion in FY1993. The decline can be attributed in part to a reduction in the value of mineral production from the federal lands because of acreage conveyed out of federal ownership through patenting, according to a BLM official.

Environmental Protection

The lack of direct statutory authority for environmental protection under the Mining Law of 1872 is a second major issue that has spurred reform proposals. Many Mining Law supporters contend that other current laws provide adequate environmental protection. They note that the mining industry must comply with applicable requirements under the Clean Water and Clean Air Acts, NEPA, state reclamation standards where they exist, and federal and state statutes relating to the handling and disposal of certain toxic wastes, among other laws. Critics, however, argue that these general environmental requirements are not adequate to assure reclamation of mine areas and that the only effective approach to protecting lands from the adverse impacts of mining under the current system is to withdraw them from development under the Mining Law. Further, critics charge that federal land managers lack regulatory authority over patented mining claims and that clear legal authority to assure adequate reclamation of mining sites is needed.

Federal Land Withdrawals

BLM is responsible for approximately 700 million acres of federal subsurface minerals, and supervises the mineral operations on about 56 million acres of Indian trust lands. Some of these lands have been withdrawn from mineral development; a withdrawal is an action that restricts the use or disposition of public land. In some cases land is reserved for a specific use that may preclude locating mining claims and granting leases.

A BLM study determined that of the approximately 700 million acres of federal subsurface minerals under the agency's jurisdiction in 2000, approximately 165 million acres have been withdrawn from mineral entry, leasing, and sale, subject to valid existing rights. Lands in the National Park System (except National Recreation Areas), the Wilderness Preservation System, and the Arctic National Wildlife Refuge (ANWR) are among those that are statutorily withdrawn. Also of the 700 million acres, mineral development on another 182 million acres is subject to the approval of the surface management agency, and must not be in conflict with land designations and plans, according to a BLM official. Wildlife refuges (except ANWR), wilderness study areas, and roadless areas, among others, are in this category.
* * *

Mineral industry representatives maintain that federal withdrawals inhibit mineral exploration and limit the reserve base even when conditions are favorable for production. Mineral reserves are not renewable. Thus, they argue that whether minerals are in the public or private sector, without new reserves or technological advancements, mineral production costs may rise. As a result, according to the industry, exploration on foreign soil may increase, raising the risk to investors and boosting import dependence. In this view, governmental policies that increase costs to the mineral industry may result in increased costs to society. Mining industry supporters also assert that too much land has been unnecessarily withdrawn from mining, through administrative actions, to pursue preservation goals.

Critics of the Mining Law believe that in many cases there is no way to protect other land values and uses short of withdrawal of lands from development under the law. They point to unreclaimed areas that have been mined for hardrock minerals in the past, Superfund sites related to past mining and smelting, and instances where development of resources could spoil scenic, historic, cultural, and other resources on public land.

* * *

Reform Proposals

* * *

On January 29, 2003, the Abandoned Hardrock Mines Reclamation Act (H.R. 504) was introduced in the House as a measure to help finance the cleanup of inactive and abandoned mine sites in certain eligible states. The proposal would establish an interest-bearing Abandoned Minerals Mine Reclamation Fund. Its revenues would come from a reclamation fee imposed on producers of hardrock minerals that received a claim or patent under the General Mining Law of 1872. The fee would be a percentage of the net proceeds from the mine. The bill would amend the Federal Water Pollution Control Act (33 U.S.C. 1342) by adding a section on abandoned or inactive mined land waste reclamation permits. This section describes the permit process that a "remediating party" must follow to be issued a permit. The permit must include a detailed remediation plan. The federal administrator of the program shall issue a report to Congress not later than one year before the termination date of its permitting authority, 10 years from the date of enactment.

A second bill, the Elimination of Double Subsidies for Hardrock Mining Industry Act of 2003 (S. 44), introduced in the Senate, would disallow the percentage depletion [tax] allowance for hardrock mines located on lands covered by the general mining laws or patented under these laws. The measure also would establish an Abandoned Mine Reclamation Trust Fund in the Treasury for reclamation and restoration of land and water adversely affected by mining. The bill was introduced on January 7, 2003, and referred to the Senate Committee on Finance. A similar bill was introduced in the 106th (S. 590), and 107th (S. 115) Congresses but no further action was taken.

A broad-based bill, the Mineral Exploration and Development Act of 2003 (H.R. 2141) would establish a permanent $100 per claim annual maintenance fee and $25 per claim location fee. The bill would limit the issuance of patents to claimants whose patent application was filed with the Secretary of the Interior on or before September 30, 1994 and met appropriate statutory requirements by that date. The bill includes an abandoned locatable minerals mine reclamation fund and an 8% royalty on "net smelter returns." Lands located under the General Mining Law of 1872 would be subject to an unsuitability review by the Secretary of the Interior or the Secretary of Agriculture to determine whether they are unsuitable for mineral activity. A reclamation plan and reclamation bond or other financial guarantee would be required before exploration and operation permits are approved. * * * The bill was introduced on May 15, 2003 and referred to the House Committee on Resources.

Given the "long history of short reforms" of the Mining Law, it would take a great optimist to predict final enactment of any legislative proposals that would significantly amend the 1872 Act. The Bush Administration has shown some interest in reforming the Mining Law, but only in ways that would make mineral development on the public lands easier and less costly. The following case concerns early Bush Administration efforts to dismantle regulatory reforms instituted late in the Clinton Administration.

MINERAL POLICY CENTER v. NORTON

United States District Court, District of Columbia, 2003.
292 F.Supp.2d 30.

[The opinion is provided in Chapter 3.III.B, p. 181, *supra*.] * * *

Notes and Questions

1. The plaintiffs' leading argument in *Mineral Policy Center* was that the Bush Administration's 2001 mining regulations, which did away with the Clinton-era version's definition of "undue and unnecessary degradation," failed to comply with FLPMA. *See* 43 U.S.C.A. § 1732(b) (the Secretary "shall, by regulation or otherwise, take any action necessary to prevent unnecessary or undue degradation of the [public] lands"). While the Clinton-era version of the regulation stated that the BLM must deny a plan of operations if it would result in "substantial irreparable harm" (SIH) to a "significant" scientific, cultural, or environmental resource on the public lands, the 2001 version gave the BLM discretion to use "other means" to prevent degradation, and left the old, more lenient "prudent

operator" standard in place. *Mineral Policy Center, supra* (citing 66 Fed. Reg. at 54,846, 54,838); *see* 43 C.F.R. § 3809.5. The Bush Administration's BLM argued that the SIH proviso would be cost-prohibitive to miners, and that it was "contrary to statutory authority, subjective, potentially cumulative, and overbroad." *Id.* at 40–41. Although the court found that the term "undue" has independent meaning and covered something other than just "unnecessary" (non-prudent) mining methods, it left discretion to the BLM as to how to ensure against "undue" degradation. *Id.* at 43, 46. It upheld this aspect of the 2001 regulation, even though it acknowledged that "mining operations often have significant— and sometimes devastating—environmental consequences ... [and] the 2001 Regulations, in many cases, prioritize the interests of miners ... over the interests of persons such as plaintiffs, who seek to conserve and protect the public lands." *Id.* at 56. Why wasn't the court willing to overturn the 2001 rule? Does it seem appropriate for the BLM to implement FLPMA's requirements on an *ad hoc*, case by case basis, rather than through a uniform standard or prescription?

2. The BLM claimed that the 2001 regulations were not that different from the Clinton-era version, as they retained certain requirements of that version, such as financial guarantees to cover reclamation costs and plans of operation for all mining activities except "casual use" and "exploration" activities. *Mineral Policy Center, supra,* at 40–41 (citing 43 C.F.R. §§ 3809.1–.21, 3809.552). The plaintiffs argued that the 2001 regulations arbitrarily exempted certain "Notice" mining exploration operations from submitting plans of operations and undergoing public review under the National Environmental Policy Act (NEPA). *Id.* at 52. According to the plaintiffs, such projects can seriously damage environmental and cultural resources. The court concluded that the BLM properly found that these types of small projects had not created major environmental impacts, and that because they are undertaken by private actors without federal funds or approval, they are not "major federal actions" subject to NEPA. *Id.* at 56.

3. Plaintiffs were successful in one aspect of their challenge. They argued that FLPMA requires the BLM to obtain fair market value for mining operations conducted on unclaimed or inadequately claimed land. *See* 43 U.S.C.A. § 1701(a)(9). The court agreed that "if there is no valid claim and the claimant is doing more than engaging in initial exploration activities ...," the activity is subject to the "fair market value" proviso. *Id.* at 50. Because "Interior was not cognizant of its statutory obligation to attempt to 'receive fair market value ...,' and did not balance its competing priorities with that obligation mind," the court remanded the regulation to Interior with directions to give Congress's policy goal "proper effect." *Id.*

III. THE LAW OF LEASABLE AND SALABLE MINERALS

Originally, all minerals were subject to location under the 1872 Mining Law, including coal, oil and gas. By the early twentieth century, however, policy makers in Washington had become concerned that too many energy minerals were being lost to private ownership. As an initial response, several U.S. Presidents withdrew from entry much of the public domain land thought to be valuable for petroleum production. The effect of these executive withdrawals was to administratively remove petroleum minerals from the location system. Ultimately, Congress ratified these executive withdrawals in the Mineral Leasing Act of 1920, 30 U.S.C.A. § 181, which placed oil, gas, oil shale, and coal under a federal leasing system. Amendments to the 1920 Act have expanded the list of leasable minerals to include potassium, potash, sodium, phosphate, native asphalt, bitumen, and some sulphur deposits. The Acquired Lands Mineral Leasing Act of 1947, 30 U.S.C.A. § 351, applied the provisions of the 1920 Mineral Leasing Act to all minerals, including hardrock minerals (but excluding "common varieties" such as sand and gravel), located on "acquired lands." Subsequently, in 1953, Congress placed offshore oil and gas under a federal leasing system in the Outer Continental Shelf Lands Act, 43 U.S.C.A. § 1001. And in 1970, the Geothermal Steam Act applied the leasing system to geothermal resources. In 1975, coal leasing requirements were tightened by the Federal Coal Leasing Amendments, 30 U.S.C.A. § 201.

Each leasable mineral—including oil and gas, coal, oil shale, and geothermal—is subject to specialized statutory and regulatory leasing requirements. However, some generalizations might be made about the entire leasing system. First and foremost, in contrast to the system of location under the 1872 Mining Law, there is no general right to mine minerals subject to federal leasing. By implication, there is no right of self-initiation for leasable minerals; miners must obtain federal permission, in the form of a lease, before engaging in any exploration and production activities. Moreover, the federal government has discretion to grant or not grant leases; it can choose not to accept bids on mineral leases in the first place, and even after issuing a lease it can decide not to allow the lessee to explore or produce minerals. This gives the government far more extensive and continuing control over development of leasable minerals than it has over development of hard-rock minerals subject to the 1872 Mining Law. As owner and lessor of leasable minerals, the federal government may exclude enormous tracts from development; it may restrict the mineral lease period and acreage available under the lease; it may require the lessee to pay rent and royalties; it may condition the lease to protect the environment; it may cancel the lease for violations. Whether and how the government exercises these powers is generally left to its discretion, limited only by Federal statutes, regulations and judicial rulings.

A. Leasable Minerals Under the 1920 Mineral Leasing Act and Related Acts

1. *Oil and Gas*

Domestically produced oil and gas comprise about 50% of American energy consumption. While domestic reserves of natural gas seem adequate for the foreseeable future—209 trillion cubic feet were still available in the 1990s, according to the United States Geological Survey—the same cannot be said for oil. Domestic oil production peaked in 1970, while reliance on foreign, imported oil continues to rise.

In light of America's continued dependence on oil as an energy source, federal oil and gas are a critical domestic supply source. Oil and gas production from both onshore and offshore federal leases supplies approximately 10 percent of petroleum needed to satisfy total domestic consumption. By the end of President Clinton's term in office, more than a quarter of domestic oil and gas production came from federal lands offshore and onshore. In fact, the Clinton Administration leased more federal acreage offshore for oil and gas development than the Reagan Administration. Offshore leasing yields nearly three times the amount of oil and gas production of onshore leases. Between 1992 and 1998, oil production from federal leases in the Gulf of Mexico grew more than 50%. President Clinton's Interior Secretary, Bruce Babbitt, oversaw the reopening of 87% of National Petroleum Reserve—Alaska (NPRA) as a trade-off against the opening of the Arctic National Wildlife Refuge for oil and gas leasing. Babbitt attempted to accommodate extraction of oil and gas resources from the public lands, while maintaining conservation as a priority.

a. Royalties from Oil & Gas Leases

One of the primary advantages to mineral leasing over the 1872 Mining Law's location system—at least for the federal government—is that mineral leases provide revenues to the government in the form of royalties, annual rentals, and bonus payments. Mineral revenues collected are one of the largest sources of non-tax income to the United States Treasury. Between 1982 and 1990, the Interior Department collected nearly $50 billion in royalties, rents, and bonuses from about 90,000 federal and Indian oil and gas leases.

The Mineral Leasing Act and the Outer Continental Shelf Lands Act both require that lessees pay the federal government a percentage royalty "in the amount or value of the [oil and gas] production." 30 U.S.C.A. § 223; 43 U.S.C.A. § 1337(a)(1)(A). For many years, however, excessive reliance on lessees' calculations of royalties deprived the federal government of up to $500 million annually. To address this problem of bookkeeping fraud in the royalty management system, Congress in 1982 enacted the Federal Oil and Gas Royalty Management Act (FOGRMA), 30 U.S.C.A. §§ 1701–1757. FOGRMA created a new Minerals Management Service within the Interior Department to ensure accurate and adequate royalty payments by federal oil and gas lessees.

Regulations imposed by the Minerals Management Service (MMS) constitute a comprehensive inspection, audit, accounting, and royalty collection system. The scope of the MMS's authority is broad. For example, it can conduct audits on a company-wide, rather than lease-by-lease basis, and it can extend the period during which lessees must maintain records. *See* Phillips Petroleum Co. v. Lujan, 963 F.2d 1380 (10th Cir. 1992). One of the MMS's primary tasks has been to derive applicable standards for determining the "value of production," which is requisite for valuing royalties. In an audit, these standards are used to determine whether a lessee's past royalty payments are accurate. If not, the MMS may retroactively assess additional royalties plus interest. *See, e.g.,* Mesa Operating Ltd. Partnership v. U.S. Dept. of Interior, 931 F.2d 318 (5th Cir. 1991) (requiring lessee to pay $1.5 million in back royalties); Monsanto Co. v. Hodel, 827 F.2d 483 (9th Cir. 1987) (upholding adjustment of royalties based on increased value of phosphate).

Lessees have challenged retroactive assessment of royalties, with little success. *See, e.g.,* Norfolk Energy, Inc. v. Hodel, 898 F.2d 1435 (9th Cir. 1990); Shoshone Indian Tribe v. Hodel, 903 F.2d 784 (10th Cir.1990). In one case, a lessee did succeed in preventing the government from collecting royalties retroactively. In Diamond Shamrock Exploration Co. v. Hodel, 853 F.2d 1159 (5th Cir. 1988), the 5th Circuit ruled that payments by a pipeline purchaser to a lessee-producer did not trigger the lessee's duty to pay royalties to the government because royalties were due only upon "production," *i.e.,* when oil or gas was actually extracted from the earth. *See also* Independent Petroleum Association of America v. Armstrong, 91 F.Supp.2d 117 (D.D.C. 2000) (holding that the government's royalty interest is limited to the value of production at the lease or wellhead, not in value enhancements resulting from downstream activities); Marathon Oil Co. v. Babbitt, 938 F.Supp. 575 (D.Alaska 1996) (holding that the six-year statute of limitations governing federal contract claims, 28 U.S.C.A. § 2415, applies to actions to collect past due royalty payments from mineral lessees).

One of FOGRMA's statutory purposes is "to fulfill the trust responsibility of the United States for the administration of Indian oil and gas resources." 30 U.S.C.A. § 1701(b)(4). Courts have interpreted this statutory mandate to create a fiduciary duty toward Indian tribes with respect to the management of oil and gas leases on tribal lands. Jicarilla Apache Tribe v. Supron Energy Corp., 782 F.2d 855 (10th Cir. 1986). The MMS requires lessees on Indian lands to compute royalties, payable to the tribes, based on the market value of their claims determined by the highest price paid or offered for like quality oil or gas at the time of production. Pawnee v. United States, 830 F.2d 187 (Fed. Cir. 1987).

In Cobell v. Babbitt, 91 F.Supp.2d 1 (D.D.C. 1999), *aff'd,* 240 F.3d 1081 (D.C. Cir. 2001), individual Indians filed a class action seeking $10 billion in damages from the government for breaching the fiduciary obligation by mis-managing hundreds of thousands of trust accounts for royalties from mining and other activities. The United States has been required to provide a complete historical accounting. *Id.* The *Cobell* case and other aspects of tribal resource management are addressed in detail in Chapter 7.III, *supra.*

b.   Onshore Oil and Gas

FIGURE 4

OIL EXTRACTION

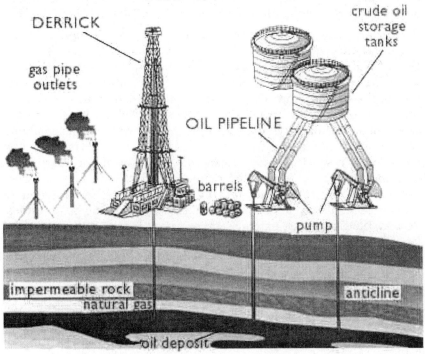

(i)   Predicates to the Leasing Decision

In Practice:

Before an oil and gas lease issues, two questions must be answered:

    1.   Is the land subject to oil and gas leasing? The Mineral Leasing Act gives the Interior Secretary complete discretion to open or close federal lands to leasing. 30 U.S.C.A. § 226(a); *Udall v. Tallman*, 380 U.S. 1, 85 S.Ct. 792, 13 L.Ed.2d 616 (1965). *See Marathon Oil Co. v. Babbitt*, 966 F.Supp. 1024 (D.Colo. 1997), *aff'd* 166 F.3d 1221 (10th Cir.), *cert. denied*, 528 U.S. 819, 120 S.Ct. 61, 145 L.Ed.2d 53 (1999) (denying judicial authority under the Mineral Leasing Act to make federal lands available for leasing). The Secretary's rationale for a refusal to lease may be based on conservation principles or wildlife protection. *See United States ex rel. McLennan v. Wilbur*, 283 U.S. 414, 51 S.Ct. 502, 75 L.Ed. 1148 (1931) (conservation principles); *Duesing v. Udall*, 350 F.2d 748 (D.C. Cir. 1965) (wildlife protection). The only possible exception to this otherwise unfettered discretion was advanced by a Wyoming District Court, which concluded that failure to lease in wilderness study areas was a *de facto* "withdrawal," which must comply with FLPMA withdrawal procedures. *Mountain States Legal Foundation v. Hodel*, 668 F.Supp. 1466 (D.Wyo. 1987).

Congress sought to narrow the practical, if not the legal, scope of the Interior Secretary's discretion to issue oil and gas leases in the Energy Act of 2000, Pub. L. No. 106–469, 114 Stat. 2029, 42 U.S.C. § 6217. The Energy Act imposes several responsibilities on the Secretary of the Interior and the President. First, under § 604 the Secretary must conduct an inventory of all onshore federal lands in order to estimate the quantity and determine the known locations of oil and gas resources. Additionally, the Secretary is to determine if any obstacles or restrictions exist to the development of such resources. This inventory is to be updated regularly and presented to the Congress. The process of inventorying and reporting is designed to encourage regulators to facilitate development of oil and gas reserves. Second, the Energy Act extends authorization for the Strategic Petroleum Reserve. Under the Act, the Reserve may only be drawn down when necessitated "by a severe energy supply interruption or by the obligations of the United States under the international energy program." 42 U.S.C.A. § 6241. A draw down in the Strategic Petroleum Reserve is not allowed under the Act for purposes of alleviating the consequences of oil and gas price spikes.

Despite the Energy Act of 2000, the Secretary of the Interior retains nearly unfettered discretion to determine whether and where to grant (or not grant) oil and gas leases. However, all BLM lands and national forests are presumed to be open to leasing unless specifically withdrawn. Oil and gas leasing is generally precluded in the national park system, in national wildlife refuges, in the Wild and Scenic Rivers System, and in wilderness areas. To lease in national forests requires special permission from the Forest Service.

On August 8, 2005, President Bush signed the Energy Policy Act of 2005, an omnibus energy bill "packed with incentives to increase development on the public lands." *Energy Bill Now Law; Administration Still Pushing ANWR*, Public Lands News, Aug. 12, 2005, at 1. One of the primary purposes of the 2005 Act is to reduce U.S. reliance on foreign oil by relaxing restrictions on the leasing of public lands and by providing billions of dollars in tax breaks and other incentives to energy producers. Although environmental groups are relieved that

Arctic National Wildlife Refuge (ANWR), they objected to other provisions, particularly those that expedite approval of APDs, kick-off an oil shale development program, and provide categorical exclusions from NEPA requirements for various oil and gas activities. Western governors, on the other hand, "were relatively mollified by a final provision that sets guidelines for states to consult with the federal government on siting energy rights-of-way across public lands.* * * [They] had objected to previous iterations of the provision they believed would have given the feds pre-emptive authority to designate ROWs within a state." *Id.* at 2. As for the Interior Department, its "number one priority [is] translating H.R. 6 into action.... " *Id.* at 3.

2. *Do the minerals constitute "oil and gas," as those terms are used in the Mineral Leasing Act?* To obtain an oil and gas lease, the applicant must first determine whether the minerals they seek to develop constitute "oil and gas." The Mineral Leasing Act does not precisely define the terms "oil and gas," but the Interior Department has opted for an expansive construction. The word "oil" includes oil shale, native asphalt, solid and semi-solid bitumen, and bituminous rock characterized by oil-impregnated rock or sands from which oil is recoverable by special treatment. *See* Brennan v. Udall, 379 F.2d 803 (10th Cir. 1967) ("oil" resources include oil shale).

(ii)   The Leasing Decision

The 1920 Mineral Leasing Act created a dual leasing system based on whether the lands open for lease were located within known geological structures (KGSs). Those within a KGS had to be leased by competitive bidding. But the vast majority of mineral leasing lands were located outside of KGSs, and those lands were leased to the first qualified applicant. 30 U.S.C.A. § 226. This scheme had two inherent defects. First, determining whether an oil and gas structure was within a KGS was more an art than a science, and subject to many legal challenges by lessees. *See* Bender v. Clark, 744 F.2d 1424 (10th Cir. 1984); Arkla Exploration Co. v. Texas Oil & Gas Corp., 734 F.2d 347 (8th Cir. 1984). Second, when the terms of non-competitive leases expired for failure to drill (many were held purely for speculative purposes, awaiting oil or gas price rises), there was a mad scramble to be the first qualified applicant to refile. To address this situation, the Interior Department considered all lease applications as being "simultaneously" filed, so that the winning applicant would be by lottery. Many applicants used filing services to enhance their chances of being selected in the lottery. *See* Reppy v. Department of Interior, 874 F.2d 728 (10th Cir. 1989).

In 1987, Congress responded to these problems with the Federal Onshore Oil and Gas Leasing Reform Act (the "Reform Act"), Pub. L. No. 100–203. The Reform Act replaced the dual (KGS/non-KGS) system of leasing with a unitary system that requires, first, that public lands be offered by competitive bid, with a minimum acceptable bid of $2 per acre. If no minimum bid is received, then the lands become available for noncompetitive leasing for a two-year period, after which they revert back to the competitive leasing process. 30 U.S.C.A. §§ 226(b)(1)(A), (c)(1). The Reform Act also empowers federal land management agencies to regulate environmental consequences of oil and gas leasing operations on their lands, while continuing to vest in the BLM ownership of the mineral estate. As a result, agencies other than BLM, including the Forest Service, the Fish and Wildlife Service, and the Park Service, have authority to control surface activities; the Forest Service may even veto BLM leasing decisions in national forests. 30 U.S.C.A. § 226(g), (h).

(iii)   Lease Terms and Stages

A mineral lease is issued for a "primary" term of ten years. 30 U.S.C.A. § 226(e). If a lease has not achieved production in paying quantities by the end of the primary term, the lease expires. There are, however, four ways for the lessee to expand the term of the lease. First, if there is paying production before the end of the primary term, the lease may continue as long as production continues. 30 U.S.C.A. § 226(e). Second, if the lessee has initiated drilling operations within the primary term, then the lease is extended for an additional two years. Third, if the Interior Secretary decides, "in the interest of conservation," to suspend the lease operations, then the primary term is lengthened by the duration of the suspension. 30 U.S.C.A. § 209. *Compare* Copper Valley Mach. Works, Inc. v. Andrus, 653 F.2d 595 (D.C. Cir. 1981) (holding that a stipulation in a mineral lease denying access for six months of each year constituted a mandated lease suspension which extended the lease term), *and* Getty Oil Co. v. Clark, 614 F.Supp. 904 (D.C. Wyo. 1985), *aff'd sub nom.* Texaco Producing, Inc. v. Hodel, 840 F.2d 776 (10th Cir. 1988) (holding that a suspension requested by the lessee to extend the term could be denied or conditioned). *Also see* Hoyl v. Babbitt, 129 F.3d 1377 (10th Cir. 1997) (distinguishing *Copper Valley*). Fourth and finally, if a well capable of producing paying quantities has been completed, the lessee is allowed a reasonable period of time, not less than sixty days after receiving formal, written notice, to place the well in production. 30 U.S.C.A. § 226(i). A lease may not be terminated for cessation of production during the lease term so long as reworking or drilling operations resume within sixty days after cessation. 30 U.S.C.A. § 226(i).

The lifecycle of a federal onshore oil and gas may go through several stages, but no particular stage inevitably follows from the previous one. The would-be lessee typically undertakes preliminary exploration work by reviewing aerial photographs, geologic maps, or the exploration results of neighboring leases. If this effort suggests that certain lands hold promise for mineral development, and if the applicable surface management agency has made the lands available for leasing, then a lease application may be submitted. An application does not obligate the

Interior Department to issue a lease. If the BLM does award a lease, the lessee then has the legal right to drill, but not the duty to do so.

Once the lessee obtains the lease, it may conduct geological and geophysical prospecting, which does not entail drilling, but often does involve blasting and other activities that may disturb surface resources. If this prospecting is encouraging, the lessee may acquire surrounding leaseholds to prevent reservoir drainage from adjacent wells not already under its control. The next step may be to apply to the BLM for a drilling permit (APD), so that the lessee can engage in exploratory "wildcat" drilling. The BLM normally will not grant an APD without approval by the appropriate land management agency of the lessee's surface use plan or operations; approval may be conditioned on various environmental protection measures.

If a wildcat well becomes a discovery well (a well that yields commercial quantities of oil and gas), additional wells will likely be drilled to confirm the discovery and establish the extent of the field. The lessee must apply for and receive APDs for such confirmation wells. If a wildcat well does not find oil and gas, the lessee plugs it with cement and abandons it. If confirmation wells suggest the presence of a large reservoir (a "barn burner"), multiple wells will be drilled on the lease site and on surrounding leaseholds, consistent with well-spacing rules, to drain the reservoir efficiently. This is known as "full field development." APDs for full field development typically include plans for additional storage facilities, pipeline networks, transportation corridors, as well as proposals for unitization and pooling. *See* Norfolk Energy, Inc. v. Hodel, 898 F.2d 1435 (9th Cir. 1990) (when federal lands are unitized with other lands, the federal agency may regulate operations on nonfederal lands if not inconsistent with a preexisting lease); Cotton Petro. v. U.S. Dept. of Interior, 870 F.2d 1515 (10th Cir. 1989) (Interior Secretary's rejection of a communization (well pooling) agreement was arbitrary and capricious where Secretary failed to analyze relevant factors mandated by Departmental guidelines).

The lifespan of oil and gas fields varies. The average life of a typical field is between 15 and 25 years. Abandonment of individual wells may start early in a field life, and reach a maximum as the field becomes depleted. Abandoned wells are plugged, and must be reclaimed, which means that the surface must be restored to specifications contained in the surface use plan of operations submitted with the initial APD. Reclamation will be discussed in more detail in section III.C.1, below.

Rarely does a prospective lessee encounter all these stages. As a practical matter, only one in ten leases is ever tested with an exploratory well. Of the ten percent tested, only a tiny percentage will ever yield a commercially productive well. Even if a well is commercially productive, the chances are no better than 50/50 that it will reveal the existence of a major reservoir, justifying the drilling of more wells for eventual full field development.

(iv) Lease Conditions

The Secretary of the Interior is given broad powers "to do any and all things necessary to carry out and accomplish the purposes" of the 1920 Mineral Leasing Act, 30 U.S.C.A. § 189; Grindstone Butte Project v. Kleppe, 638 F.2d 100 (9th Cir. 1981), including imposing protective conditions and stipulations on leasing activities. A lessee's failure to comply with lease conditions is grounds for either canceling or refusing to reinstate an expired lease. Udall v. Tallman, 380 U.S. 1, 85 S.Ct. 792, 13 L.Ed.2d 616 (1965)(upholding lease cancellation); Ram Petroleums, Inc. v. Andrus, 658 F.2d 1349 (9th Cir. 1981) (upholding refusal to reinstate).

Can local governments impose conditions on onshore federal oil and gas operations? *See* Western Oil and Gas Ass'n v. Sonoma County, 905 F.2d 1287 (9th Cir. 1990) (lessee's constitutional challenge dismissed on ripeness grounds); Ventura County v. Gulf Oil Corp., 601 F.2d 1080 (9th Cir. 1979) (county regulation preempted by federal law).

(v) NEPA's Effect on Oil and Gas Leases

Questions involving the timing, scope, and nature of an environmental impact analysis under NEPA, 42 U.S.C.A. § 4321 (addressed in detail in Chapter 4, *supra*) have proven to be exceptionally difficult to answer in the case of federal onshore oil and gas leasing. This is because leases proceed in stages, over time, and at many sites. As noted above, the nature of federal onshore leasing is such that there is considerable uncertainty whether a leasing action at one stage, or at one site, will ever lead to the next stage, or to leasing at another site.

Timing—Should an EIS be prepared at the pre-lease planning stage, at the lease issuance stage, or at some post-lease stage, such as when the APD is filed? In Sierra Club v. Peterson, 717 F.2d 1409 (D.C.Cir.1983), the D.C. Circuit concluded that an EIS must be prepared when the lease is issued because once the lease is issued, the Forest Service cannot prevent the lessee from engaging in activities that disturb surface resources, which could generate potentially significant environmental impacts. *See also Bob Marshall Alliance v. Hodel*, 852 F.2d 1223 (9th Cir. 1988). But what if the lease included a no surface occupancy (NSO) clause, which precludes surface disturbances arising from the act of issuing the lease? *See Sierra Club, supra, Conner v. Burford*, 848 F.2d 1441 (9th Cir. 1988) (a sale of an NSO lease does not require preparation of an EIS); *Park County Resource Council v. United States Dept. of Agriculture*, 817 F.2d 609 (10th Cir. 1987) requiring only an Environmental Assessment at the lease stage, so long as leases contained sufficient stipulations to prevent operations that might have significant impacts. The 10th Circuit's approach defers full EIS review until the APD stage, when drilling is more likely. In sum, the more likely it is that the act of issuing a lease does not pose any risk of significant environmental impacts, on the facts of the particular case, the less likely it is that the courts will require an EIS at the leasing stage.

On National Forest lands, the Forest Service may make a general analysis to determine which lands should be open to oil and gas leasing, but then must make a specific analysis of individual parcels before authorizing the BLM to lease the land. 36 C.F.R. § 228. When the Forest Service makes the decision about which lands to make available for leasing, it must either retain the authority to preclude surface disturbing activities or prepare a full EIS at the time of committing the lands to leasing. Wyoming Outdoor Council v. United States Forest Service, 165 F.3d 43 (D.C. Cir. 1999).

Scope—Should environmental review of onshore oil and gas leasing be general, including broad expanses of public land, or narrow and site specific? The scope of an EIS is determined by the scope of the proposed action. In Kleppe v. Sierra Club, 427 U.S. 390, 96 S.Ct. 2718, 49 L.Ed.2d 576 (1976), the Supreme Court seemed to accept in dictum the proposition that site specific NEPA review could be deferred until site specific impacts were imminent. For onshore oil and gas leases, site-specific surface impacts are imminent and identifiable at the APD stage, not the lease issuance stage. Nonetheless, the leading case of Conner v. Burford, 848 F.2d 1441 (9th Cir. 1988), mandates an EIS at the lease sale stage, even though it is extremely difficult then to ascertain whether, or where, drilling activity might occur. The *Conner* case is consistent with the other non-oil and gas leasing cases calling for site-specific EISs, where environmental impacts are still contingent on future actions. *See* Environmental Defense Fund v. Andrus, 619 F.2d 1368 (10th Cir. 1980).

Impact Analysis— If an EIS is done at the stage of lease issuance, before the post-lease APDs inform surface management agencies of the location, number, and types of exploratory wells, should the lease sale EIS nonetheless make an educated guess about the environmental harms that might ensue? Cases like *Conner v. Burford, supra,* hold that the inability at the lease sale stage to fully ascertain future effects "is not a justification for failing to estimate what those effects might be." In Robertson v. Methow Valley Citizens Council, 490 U.S. 332, 109 S.Ct. 1835, 104 L.Ed.2d 351 (1989), the Supreme Court concurred that agencies must describe environmental impacts "even in the face of substantial uncertainty." However, some onshore oil and gas cases suggest that EISs are premature when effects of the lease sale cannot be readily identified, or if they are only "remote and speculative possibilities." Park County Resource Council v. United States Dept. of Agriculture, 817 F.2d 609 (10th Cir. 1987); Suffolk County v. Secretary of Interior, 562 F.2d 1368 (2d Cir. 1977) (too much uncertainty involved in estimating effects of an onshore oil pipeline route at lease sale stage).

The 2005 Energy Policy Act, described above at pp. 994–5, alters NEPA's requirements by creating a rebuttable presumption that a categorical exclusion (CE) will apply to the following activities undertaken pursuant to the MLA:

(1) Certain instances of individual surface disturbance of less than 5 acres;

(2) Drilling a well at sites where drilling had occurred within the previous 5 years;

(3) Drilling a well within a developed field for which a recently approved land use plan or NEPA document had analyzed drilling as a foreseeable activity;

(4) Placement of pipelines in certain approved right-of-way corridors; and

(5) Maintenance of minor activities other than construction or major renovation.

Energy Policy Act of 2005 § 390, 2005 WLNR 12700296 (Aug. 8, 2005). According to Scott Groene of the Southern Utah Wilderness Alliance, the Act authorizes the BLM "to take shortcuts when granting permits for oil and gas drilling and essentially cuts the public out of the process." Patty Henetz, *New Energy Law Limits Public's Say in Decisions,* Salt Lake Trib., Aug. 10, 2005. Are NEPA exclusions necessary to ensure adequate and timely domestic energy production?

c.   Offshore Oil and Gas

An Offshore Oil Platform

(i)   Federal Jurisdiction

As with federally-owned onshore oil and gas fields, offshore fields are leased to private developers pursuant to federal statute. As a result of the Submerged Lands Act of 1953, 43 U.S.C.A. § 1301, and the Outer Continental Shelf Lands Act of 1953, 42. U.S.C.A. § 1331, Congress controls outer continental shelf (OCS) resources beyond the three-mile limit, while coastal states have ownership of submerged lands and "inland waters" within three miles of the coast. United States v. Louisiana, 470 U.S. 93, 105 S.Ct. 1074, 84 L.Ed.2d 73 (1985); United States v. California, 447 U.S. 1, 100 S.Ct. 1994, 64 L.Ed.2d 681 (1980); United States v. Maine, 420 U.S. 515, 95 S.Ct. 1155, 43 L.Ed.2d 363 (1975). State law governs disputes on the OCS only to the extent that it does not conflict with federal regulations. 43 U.S.C.A. § 1333(a)(2)(A); Shell Offshore, Inc. v. Kirby Exploration Co., 909 F.2d 811 (5th Cir. 1990). Within the three-mile limit, states may prohibit offshore drilling. Getty Oil v. State Dept. of Natural Resources, 419 So.2d 700 (Fla.App. 1 Dist. 1982).

(ii)   The Outer Continental Shelf Lands Act (OCSLA) and the Coastal Zone Management Act (CZMA)

The OCSLA of 1953, as amended in 1978, requires the Interior Secretary to prepare an oil and gas leasing program for the OCS. 43 U.S.C.A. §§ 1331–1343. Offshore leasing occurs according to four statutorily prescribed steps: (1) preparation of the leasing program; (2) lease sales; (3) exploration; and (4) development and production.

Offshore leasing is by competitive bid. Typically, bids are solicited on the basis of a cash bonus and a royalty agreement (averaging 12.5%), with the highest bidder awarded the lease. It is not uncommon for the major oil companies to join together in a consortium and submit one bid, which might approach $100 million for a promising tract. The Interior Secretary has broad discretion to choose among bidding systems for offshore leases. Watt v. Energy Action Educational Foundation, 454 U.S. 151, 102 S.Ct. 205, 70 L.Ed.2d 309 (1981). Reviewing courts seem particularly inclined to defer to this discretion when the Secretary decides to exclude areas from the leasing program, or decides to suspend existing leases for environmental reasons. See Natural Resources Defense Council, Inc. v. Hodel, 865 F.2d 288 (D.C. Cir. 1988) (holding that the Secretary may exclude areas from offshore leasing for "political" reasons); Sun Oil Co. v. United States, 215 Ct.Cl. 716, 572 F.2d 786 (Ct.Cl. 1978) (holding that the Secretary has "power and authority to interfere with vested lease rights"). On the other hand, when the Secretary has proposed opening large portions of the OCS, courts have not been reluctant to either halt or scale down the leasing programs. See Commonwealth of Massachusetts v. Watt, 716 F.2d 946 (1st Cir. 1983); State of California v. Watt, 668 F.2d 1290 (D.C. Cir. 1981).

OCSLA includes environmental provisions to deal with the special environmental hazards of offshore oil and gas development, which include spills of oil and toxic chemicals, discharges of metal cuttings, and air emissions of conventional and toxic pollutants, including benzene. A single offshore oil rig discharges tens of thousands of tons of drilling fluids and metal cuttings into the ocean during its lifetime, and can emit as much air pollution in a single day as tens of thousands of automobiles. Because of these environmental hazards, both Congress and the Interior Department have imposed moratoria on leasing in environmentally (or politically) sensitive areas. After a 1969 oil spill in the Santa

Barbara Channel of California, the Secretary of the Interior suspended operations there pending environmental review. One lessee, the Union Oil Company, successfully sued, claiming that the suspension constituted a compensable taking of its property rights in the lease. Union Oil Co. v. Morton, 512 F.2d 743 (9th Cir. 1975).

Once an offshore oil and gas lease has been awarded, the company wanting to explore and drill for oil must comply with, and successfully complete, the following procedures under OCSLA. First, it must obtain Interior Department approval for an exploration plan. 43 U.S.C.A. § 1340(c). The DOI must approve a submitted exploration plan within thirty days unless it finds that the proposed exploration would "probably" cause serious environmental harm or damage. 43 U.S.C.A. § 1334(a)(2)(A)(i). Second, the mining company must obtain an exploratory well drilling permit. This requires a certification under the Coastal Zone Management Act of 1972 (CZMA), 33 U.S.C.A. §§ 1451–1465, that its exploration plan is consistent with the coastal zone management program of each affected state. Third, the mining company must obtain a Clean Water Act National Pollution Discharge Elimination System permit from the EPA for any pollutant discharges into ocean waters. 33 U.S.C.A. §§ 1311(a), 1342(a). This permit may be obtained only if the affected states agree that the exploration plan is consistent with their coastal zone management programs. Finally, if the exploration is successful, the company must obtain DOI approval for a development and production plan, which describes the proposed drilling and related environmental safeguards. 43 U.S.C.A. § 1351. The company must again obtain certification that its drilling and operation plan is consistent with state coastal zone management plans. Where state certification is required and not received, the Secretary of Commerce may override the state's objections, thus allowing DOI to grant the permit. *See generally*, Mobil Oil Exploration v. U.S., 530 U.S. 604, 120 S.Ct. 2423, 147 L.Ed.2d 528 (2000).

The CZMA also requires that Interior Department activities "directly affecting the coastal zone" must be conducted "in a manner ... consistent with approved state management programs." 16 U.S.C.A. § 1456(c)(1). In Secretary of the Interior v. California, 464 U.S. 312, 104 S.Ct. 656, 78 L.Ed.2d 496 (1984), the Supreme Court decided that a sale of offshore oil and gas leases was not an activity "directly affecting" a state's coastal zone because a lease sale is merely the second step in the statutorily prescribed stages of offshore leasing. Unlike onshore oil and gas leasing, for offshore leases under the OCSLA, the lease sale is a relatively self-contained stage that does *not* entitle the lessee to go to the next stage involving potentially damaging exploration work. Therefore, the lease sale itself cannot be said to "directly affect" a state's coastal zone.

As part of the Bush Administration's strategy to enhance domestic energy production, the 2005 Energy Policy Act provides royalty relief on existing, non-producing leases on the OCS offshore of Alaska, and additional royalty relief for deep water and ultra deep gas production in the Gulf of Mexico. U.S. Dept. of Interior, Minerals Management Service, Press Release #3315, *2005 Energy Policy Act Grants MMS New Authority and Includes Incentives for Increased Domestic Energy Production*, Aug. 8, 2005. The Act also grants the Mineral Management Service (MMS) new authority for offshore alternate energy uses and mandates a comprehensive inventory of estimated oil and gas reserves on the OCS, including moratoria areas. MMS is to conduct the inventory using "any available technology, except drilling, but including 3–D seismic surveys," and submit an initial report to Congress within six months of enactment. This report is to be made publicly available and updated at least every 5 years. *Id.*

(iii) NEPA

For offshore leasing, the Supreme Court in Secretary of the Interior v. California, 464 U.S. 312, 104 S.Ct. 656, 78 L.Ed.2d 496 (1984), stated in dictum that NEPA requirements "must be met" at the lease sale stage, even while conceding that "the purchase of a lease entails no right to proceed with full exploration, development, or production." The Ninth, Second, and District of Columbia Circuits, however, have interpreted that ruling, focusing on the "no right to proceed" language, not to require much in the way of NEPA obligations. Tribal Village of Akutan v. Hodel, 869 F.2d 1185 (9th Cir. 1988); Village of False Pass v. Clark, 733 F.2d 605 (9th Cir. 1984); North Slope Borough v. Andrus, 642 F.2d 589 (D.C. Cir. 1980); Suffolk County v. Secretary of Interior, 562 F.2d 1368 (2d Cir. 1977). For these circuits, the critical fact about an offshore lease is that, unlike an onshore lease, it does not provide lessees with any development rights. This is because, under OCSLA, the lease sale is a purely paper transaction, so an EIS would be premature; EISs are more appropriate when the environmental impacts are less speculative, that is, at the later exploration, production, and development stages.

When an EIS is prepared for an offshore leasing program it must consider the cumulative impacts of offshore drilling and oil spills on migratory marine species. Marine mammals, such as whales, that migrate through an offshore oil and gas area may be subject not only to environmental impacts from those particular operations but from other offshore oil and gas operations and even municipal waste-water discharges into the ocean. *See* Natural Resources Defense Council, Inc. v. Hodel, 865 F.2d 288 (D.C. Cir. 1988), *supra* (the Interior Department failed to adequately assess cumulative impacts of its offshore leasing program).

2. Coal

The vast majority of coal extracted in the United States is consumed by electric utilities. Some is used by the steel industry for its coke plants, and some is exported to foreign markets. Just as the Persian Gulf region has abundant oil, so the United States has a multi-century supply of coal. The federal government owns over one-third of that supply. Fifty percent of the known coal reserves are located in the western United States, and nearly two-thirds of western coal is on federal (including Indian) lands.

Federally owned coal in the West has several advantages over its chief competition—privately owned coal in the East and Midwest. Western coal contains less sulfur, which means it pollutes less when burned. Western coal tends to be located nearer to the surface, which means it can be removed by surface mining techniques that are generally less expensive that underground mining operations. Surface mining also permits removal of more of the resource than underground mining, which requires that pillars of coal be left in place to prevent collapse.

On the other hand, western coal has certain disadvantages compared to eastern coal. It has lower heat content, measured in British Thermal Units (or BTUs), so more of it has to be burned to generate the same amount of energy. Western coal often has to be shipped longer distances to primary markets. And surface mining is more environmentally destructive and, therefore, subject to stricter and more expensive reclamation requirements under the 1977 Surface Mining Control and Reclamation Act, 30 U.S.C.A. §§ 1201–1328. In part because of these disadvantages, and in part because of a history of chaotic federal coal leasing practices, federal coal comprises a disproportionately small share of total domestic production. However, during the Clinton Administration of the 1990s, federal coal production increased by 30 percent, and the federal contribution to total national production rose from approximately one-quarter to one-third.

a. Pre–1976 Federal Coal Leasing

In 1920, federal coal became a leasable mineral subject to the Mineral Leasing Act. 30 U.S.C.A. § 201(b) (repealed in 1976). Such a lease was acquired through a four-step process. First, a coal prospector applied for a prospecting permit covering a certain area of federal lands. Second, if the permit was granted (which it inevitably was), then the prospector explored the permit area for a coal deposit. Third, if coal was discovered, the prospector then applied for a preference right lease. Fourth, if the Interior Department decided that the prospector had found coal in "commercial quantities," then it had a nondiscretionary duty to issue the lease. Between 1920 and the early 1970s, the Interior Department basically issued coal leases on demand. Most of the leases were noncompetitive, "preference right" leases.

Once the lease was issued, the miner had no obligation to actually develop the coal deposit. Thus, the noncompetitive, preference right leasing system became a speculative method of acquiring rights to coal without actually producing coal. Lessees (or, more accurately, lease "brokers") chose not to develop the coal while awaiting more favorable prices. Indeed, while the number of acres of federal land leased for coal development steadily increased through 1971, annual coal production from those lands actually decreased. By 1973, only 10% of federal leases were producing coal, accounting for less than 3% of total domestic production. The federal coal leasing system also had the disadvantage of bringing little revenue to the U.S. Treasury, and of ignoring the environmental impacts in the rare case where coal mining actually ensued.

b.   The 1971–1976 Moratorium

In response to the abuses under the MLA, the Interior Secretary imposed a moratorium on the issuance of new leases in 1971. The moratorium was challenged as a abuse of the Secretary's discretion, but the D.C. Circuit upheld it in Krueger v. Morton, 539 F.2d 235 (D.C. Cir. 1976). Soon after the moratorium took effect, the Secretary ordered preparation of a national, programmatic EIS on the entire federal coal leasing program. When completed, this EIS was ruled inadequate in Natural Resources Defense Council, Inc. v. Hughes, 437 F.Supp. 981 (D.D.C. 1977), *modified* 454 F.Supp. 148 (D.D.C. 1978), and the court held that further federal coal leasing was not warranted in light of the low production from existing leases. The *Hughes* injunction had the effect of continuing the Interior Department's moratorium on lease sales into the late 1970s.

B.   The 1975 Federal Coal Leasing Amendments Act (FCLAA)

While the moratorium on coal leasing was in place, Congress decided that the MLA was no longer working as it should. In response, it enacted the FCLAA in 1975. 30 U.S.C.A. § 201.

1.   *Coal Leasing Under the FCLAA*

Under the FLCAA, all leasing decisions must be preceded by comprehensive land use plans. These plans must estimate the amount of coal deposits available, and the maximum economic recovery for each proposed lease tract. *See* National Wildlife Federation v. Burford, 677 F.Supp. 1445 (D.Mont. 1985) (upholding a comprehensive plan for lease sales in the Powder River Basin). The FCLAA replaced the MLA's system of noncompetitive leasing with a competitive, sealed bidding process for all new leases. And it replaced prospecting permits with exploration licenses, which may be issued for tracts of up to 25,000 acres.

If a lease is issued, the lessee may control no more than 46,000 acres per state, nor more than 100,000 acres throughout the United States. 43 C.F.R. § 3472.1–3. The lease is for a term of 20 years (or longer if coal continues to be produced), but will terminate after 10 years if commercial quantities of coal have not been produced. To avoid repeating the pre–1976 tendency of lessees to sit on non-producing leases, each FCLAA lease is subject to a "diligent development" requirement, which means "production of recoverable coal reserves in commercial quantities prior to the end" of the first ten years of the lease. 43 C.F.R. § 3480.0–5. Each lease must stipulate a royalty rate of not less than 12.5 percent of the value of the coal. Before a lessee can begin to develop the claim, an exploration, operation, and reclamation plan must be approved by the BLM. The Interior Secretary may also exchange lands leased under the FCLAA and MLA with unleased federal coal lands either to consolidate a checkerboard pattern of coal lands or to protect pristine areas from coal development. For example, in National Coal Association v. Hodel, 825 F.2d 523 (D.C. Cir. 1987), the court permitted an exchange to prevent coal operations within the Grand Teton National Park.

2. Fair Market Value

In the early 1980s, Interior Secretary James Watt ended the moratorium and resumed federal coal persuant to the FCLAA. The 1982 sale of leases in the Powder River Basin of Wyoming (Secretary Watt's home state) was particularly controversial. The sale disposed of a billion and a half tons of valuable federal coal at a bid price widely thought to be considerably less than the "fair market value" of the leased coal. The FCLAA prohibits bid acceptance at less than "fair market value," 30 U.S.C.A. § 201, which Interior Department regulations define as that "amount ... for which the coal deposit would be sold or leased by a knowledgeable owner willing ... to sell or lease to a knowledgeable purchaser." 43 C.F.R. § 3400.0–5(n). A special commission created to investigate the Powder River Basin sale concluded that the federal government should have received between $60 million and $100 million more for the coal leases. See Comptroller General, Report to the Congress: Analysis of the Powder River Basin Federal Coal Lease Sale (May 11, 1983). Another moratorium on federal coal leasing was quickly imposed.

In 1987, a federal district court deferred to the Secretary's fair market value determination, in part because of the court's interpretation that fair market value demands only a "fair return," not a maximization of revenues. Despite the loss of tens of millions of dollars of federal revenues, the Ninth Circuit sustained this determination and approved the Powder River Basin sale.

NATIONAL WILDLIFE FEDERAL v. BURFORD
United States Court of Appeals, Ninth Circuit, 1989.
871 F.2d 849.

CIRCUIT JUDGE HUG delivered the opinion of the Court.

* * *

In 1982, NWF initiated this action challenging the Department of Interior's ("DOI") sale of coal leases in the Powder River Basin area of Montana and Wyoming. The sale involved approximately 1.6 billion tons of coal distributed over 23,000 acres of public land. NWF alleged a variety of federal statutory violations surrounding the sale and sued under the Administrative Procedure Act ("APA"), 5 U.S.C. §§ 551–706 (1982)....

As noted above, 30 U.S.C. § 201(a)(1) (1982) provides that no bid on land offered for leasing "shall be accepted which is less than the fair market

value, as determined by the Secretary, of the coal subject to the lease"....
Defined in 43 C.F.R. § 3400.0–5(n) (1981), fair market value is "that
amount in cash, or on terms reasonably equivalent to cash, for which in
all probability the coal deposit would be sold or leased by a knowledgeable owner willing but not obligated to sell or lease to a knowledgeable
purchaser who desires but is not obligated to buy or lease."

In light of the language contained in section 201(a)(1) and the interpre-
tative regulation, NWF's task is to show that DOI did not receive FMV
for its leases in the Powder River Basin area. Since agency action is presumed to be justified, *Wilderness Public Rights Fund*, 608 F.2d at 1254,
and the Secretary need present only a reasonable explanation for his
actions, NWF's burden of proof is considerable.

The district court, after a careful review of the administrative record,
concluded that the Secretary acted reasonably, although possibly not
supremely wisely, in accepting the Powder River lease bids. He found
specifically that the shift to an entry level bid ("ELB") system which
allowed lower initial bids than the prior minimum acceptable bid
("MAB") system, was satisfactorily explained in the record by information attesting to declining coal prices; that FMV refers to receipt of a fair
return, and not to the procedures used ...; that nine of the eleven tracts
up for lease received high bids that met or exceeded the pre-sale estimates of FMV; and that the process used to calculate the pre-sale FMV
figures, which involved approximately 4,000 hours of work, was not
unsound.

NWF ... contends that the shift to the ELB system was irrational and
insufficiently explained in the record. The ELB procedure guaranteed,
according to NWF, the receipt of less than FMV. * * *

The claim ... is unpersuasive. First, the ELB system is not in itself arbitrary or capricious. * * * The Secretary contends the ELB system
stimulates competitive bidding. The Secretary can hardly be faulted for
using a sales system whose purpose is to implement the statute's mandate. * * * The decision to implement this system in the Powder River
lease sale occurred as a result of studies suggesting a decline in the
western coal market. The use of the ELB to stimulate competitive bidding at the time of a softening market cannot be said to be arbitrary and
capricious. Finally, despite whatever flaws may have existed in the ELB
system, actual high bids on nine out of the eleven available tracts met or
exceeded the pre-sale estimate of FMV. It is the result of the bidding
procedure that is important: whether the high bid represented fair market value. * * *

The reviewing court's task is not to resolve disagreements between differing technical perspectives. Instead, its duty "is the limited one of
ascertaining that the choices made by the [Secretary] were reasonable
and supported by the record. * * * That the evidence in the record may
support other conclusions, even those that are inconsistent with the

[Secretary's], does not prevent us from concluding that his decisions were rational and supported by the record." * * *

Finally, NWF contends that a variety of procedural irregularities corrupted the bid process. NWF states that pre-bid pricing leaks to industry representatives, the Secretary's quick announcement that the sale was successful, and other events of a similar nature irretrievably corrupted the sale. Although these irregularities may have occurred, NWF has not met its burden of showing that the leases did not sell for a fair return as a result of these problems. Given that the pre-sale FMV figures were reasonable and that nine out of the ten leases went to bidders who met or exceeded those figures, NWF's procedural argument is unpersuasive. * * *

3. *Retroactive Effect of the FCLAA*

The FCLAA created two issues for those with pre–1976 legal interests in federal coal that wished to be subject to the more generous terms of the MLA. First, since the FCLAA preserves "valid existing rights" (VERs), when have applicants under the MLA satisfied sufficient steps in the application process before 1976 to have vested VERs? Second, to what extent are VERs and valid pre–1976 leases subject to the more onerous requirements of the FCLAA?

With respect to the first question, courts did not consider pre–1976 applications for prospecting permits to be protectable property interests warranting VER status. Hunter v. Morton, 529 F.2d 645 (10th Cir. 1976); American Nuclear Corp. v. Andrus, 434 F.Supp. 1035 (D.C. Wyo. 1977); Peabody Coal v. Andrus, 477 F.Supp. 120 (D.Wyo. 1979). If the prospecting permit had been granted, permittees requesting a time extension to apply for a preference lease had a valid existing right to have the extension application considered on the merits. Peterson v. Department of Interior, 510 F.Supp. 777 (D.Utah 1981). If the prospecting permit had been granted, and the if the permittee had also discovered commercial quantities of coal, the permittee had a VER to the preference lease which, at that point, the Interior Department had a nondiscretionary duty to issue.

Since the test for what constituted "commercial quantities" of coal became more restrictive after 1976, a question arose about whether pre–1976 coal discoveries would be judged according to the pre- or post–1976 test for commercial quantities. The rule that emerged was that if the Interior Department had not previously determined that commercial quantities existed, the discovery could be tested against the post–1976 standard. Natural Resources Defense Council, Inc. v. Berklund, 609 F.2d 553 (D.C. Cir. 1979); Utah Intern., Inc. v. Andrus, 488 F.Supp. 962 (D. Utah 1979). On the other hand, if the Department had previously determined that commercial quantities were present, then the Department could not later apply the stricter standard. Utah Intern., Inc. v. Andrus, 488 F.Supp. 976 (D.Colo. 1980).

Even though the FCLAA preserves some VERs, neither those VERs nor pre–1976 coal leases are immunized from the FCLAA. Under that Act's terms, any lease must meet all applicable environmental requirements, including those under the Clean Air Act, Clean Water Act, FLPMA, NEPA, and the Surface Mining Control and Reclamation Act, except to the extent those statutes "grandfather" pre-existing leases. Natural Resources Defense Council, Inc. v. Berklund, 609 F.2d 553 (D.C. Cir. 1979); Utah Intern., Inc. v. Andrus, 488 F.Supp. 976 (D.Colo. 1980). The FCLAA also requires lessees to diligently develop and produce coal in commercial quantities; pre-FCLAA lessees had until the late 1980s to produce coal.

The FCLAA requires a minimum 12.5 percent royalty for all surface-mined coal. 30 U.S.C.A. § 207(a). Pre–1976 leases under the MLA were typically issued at a minimum royalty rate of only 5 cents per ton, subject to the government's right to reasonably "readjust" the royalty at 20–year intervals. When 20 years passed, the question facing pre–1976 lessees was whether the FCLAA royalty rate could be considered a reasonable readjustment of the pre–1976 lease, even though the new royalty rate would be nearly a thousand times more than the MLA royalty of a few cents per ton.

WESTERN FUELS–UTAH v. LUJAN

United States Court of Appeals, District of Columbia Circuit, 1990.
895 F.2d 780.

CHIEF JUDGE WALD delivered the opinion of the Court.

The appellants in these consolidated cases hold leases granting them the right to mine coal on federal lands. They seek review of the district court's decision upholding the Bureau of Land Management's ("BLM") readjustments of their leases. The appellants challenge first the BLM's decision that it was compelled to apply the Federal Coal Leasing Amendments Act of 1976 ("FCLAA") to their leases, even though the leases were issued before 1976, and claim further that if the BLM has correctly interpreted FCLAA to apply to their leases, then the statute is unconstitutional. The appellants also challenge the timeliness of the lease readjustments. We affirm the district court's judgment sustaining the lease readjustments against all of these claims. * * *

The appellants, Peabody Coal Company ("Peabody"), Colowyo Coal Company ("Colowyo"), and Western Fuels–Utah, Inc. ("Western Fuels"), are holders of federal coal leases issued before 1976. Each lease, in accordance with the MLLA, contained a clause reserving to the lessor a right of readjustment at twenty-year intervals. These clauses did not precisely track the words of the statute; they provided that the lessor reserved:

> the right reasonably to readjust and fix royalties payable hereunder and other terms and conditions at the end of 20 years from the date

hereof and thereafter at the end of each succeeding 20–year period during the continuance of this lease unless otherwise provided by law at the time of the expiration of any such period....

As the leases came due for their twenty-year readjustments after 1976, the Secretary, acting through the BLM, readjusted them to provide for payment of the 12.5% royalty fixed in § 207 (except in the case of Western Fuels' lease, for which a lower royalty was fixed because Western Fuels engages in underground mining), and also to provide that their subsequent readjustments would take place at ten-year intervals. The BLM expressly stated at the time of these readjustments (and continues to maintain on this appeal) that it used the 12.5% royalty figure because § 207 required it to do so. * * *

As amended by FCLAA, 30 U.S.C. § 207 now provides in mandatory terms for a 12.5% royalty on coal leases. It does not, however, expressly provide that this royalty shall be imposed on pre–1976 leases; nor, on the other hand, does it expressly grandfather such leases from the imposition of this royalty.

The appellants claim that the absence of an express reference to pre–1976 leases in § 207 implies that such leases are exempt from the section's new, mandatory lease terms. The appellants observe that in other places, FCLAA makes express reference to pre–1976 leases, thereby suggesting that Congress knows how to refer to such leases when it wants to affect them. However, one might equally well observe that when Congress wants to exempt existing arrangements from new statutory requirements, it knows how to include a grandfather clause. Indeed, one of FCLAA's express references to pre–1976 leases is in the nature of an exemption of such leases from certain of FCLAA's new, more exacting requirements. If we were to draw any inference from this explicit reference, it would be that in the absence of such a reference in § 207, pre–1976 leases are not exempted from that section's requirements. * * *

The absence of a specific reference to pre–1976 leases in the new § 207 does not definitively decide the issue. * * *

This is not, however, the end of the initial inquiry; we now turn to "the language and design of the statute as a whole," .... Looking outside § 207 to other sections of the statute, we find convincing evidence of § 207's scope.

30 U.S.C. § 203 allows holders of coal leases to modify their leases by adding contiguous or cornering lands to them. Such a modification creates a new lease, and if all lands covered by the new lease were immediately subject to the royalty provision of § 207, holders of pre–1976 leases would be understandably reluctant to add land to their leases. Section 203 therefore provides

The minimum royalty provisions of section 207(a) of this title shall not apply to any lands covered by this modified lease prior to a modification until the term of the original lease or extension thereof which became effective prior to the effective date of this Act has expired.

We find it impossible to make sense out of § 203 unless § 207 applies to pre–1976 leases. The quoted sentence clearly suggests that § 207's royalty provision will become applicable to all the lands in a modified lease at some time after the modification. The sentence must refer to a lease originally issued before 1976 but modified thereafter, for if a lease was originally issued after 1976, § 207 immediately applied to all of it. In providing that § 207 would apply to the lands covered by the original lease only after the original term or an extension thereof expires, § 203 necessarily assumes the application of § 207 to the pre–1976 lease at the readjustment date. Section 203 thus shows that the new mandatory lease terms apply to lands covered by a pre–1976 lease upon readjustment.

The legislative history of § 203 confirms this reading. * * *

The appellants ... argue that the 1976 FCLAA must be read in light of the history of federal coal leasing since 1920, and that the 1976 Congress must be presumed not to have intended to change the scheme of long-term lease stability created by the 1920 Congress. The 1920 Congress, appellants argue, knew that coal mining requires large capital expenditures that a mining company would not be willing to make if it could obtain fixed lease terms for only twenty years, and so it created the indeterminate lease. However, even assuming, without deciding, that the 1976 Congress did not intend to break promises of stability made by the 1920 Congress, we find no evidence that the 1920 Congress made any promise that would preclude a later Congress from regulating the royalty for coal leases.

The 1920 MLLA provided that "at the end of each twenty-year period succeeding the date of [a coal] lease such readjustment of terms and conditions may be made as the Secretary of the Interior may determine, unless otherwise provided by law at the time of the expiration of such periods." 41 Stat. at 439. The Act put no upper limit on the royalty rate the Secretary might set upon readjustment; hence, even without FCLAA the Secretary would have had the power (though not the obligation) to fix a rate of 12.5%. It is clear, therefore, that Congress never promised that coal lessees would not be subject to such a rate. * * *

Finally, the appellants argue that it is not reasonable to conclude that Congress left the Secretary no discretion to impose a royalty rate of less than 12.5% on pre–1976 leases, because the 12.5% rate is simply too high in many cases. In this argument the appellants are joined by several amici curiae, who argue that the increased royalty rates will ultimately be borne by consumers of coal-generated power, and that the increase will be devastating and unfair to those power companies that built coal-fired generating facilities at great expense during the 1970's in response to the United States government's efforts to reduce the nation's dependency on foreign oil. The legislative history of FCLAA shows, however, that Congress was aware of this danger. Several members of the House Committee on Interior and Insular Affairs specifically warned the Congress that 12.5% was too high a figure, and that its imposition would result in higher consumer costs. See 1976 House Report at 57–58, 1976 U.S. Code Cong. & Admin. News at 1981. Congress passed FCLAA anyway, and it is therefore not unreasonable to attribute to Congress a desire to impose the 12.5% royalty rate despite its likely effect on fuel costs.

* * * Accordingly, we uphold the Secretary's determination that he is bound to apply § 207's mandatory lease terms to pre–1976 leases.

III. THE CONSTITUTIONALITY OF THE LEASE READJUSTMENTS

A. Takings Clause

Appellants contend that if § 207 does, in fact, require the Secretary to readjust their leases for a 12.5% percent royalty, then the Act unconstitutionally takes their property without just compensation. * * *

The appellants claim that the Secretary's decision to impose a 12.5% royalty on all leases substantially interferes with their investment-backed expectation in an individualized determination by the Secretary on the proper royalty adjustment for each lease; the new royalty therefore amounts to an unconstitutional taking of property. * * * While the appellants concede that their leases provide for readjustment at twenty-year intervals, they stress that most of the leases in question provide for reasonable readjustment. Such readjustments, they claim, can only be accomplished by individualized consideration of the particular circumstances surrounding each lease.

Most of the leases at issue provide that the lessor reserves the right reasonably to readjust and fix royalties payable hereunder and other terms and conditions at the end of 20 years from the date hereof and thereafter at the end of each succeeding 20–year period during the continuance of this lease unless otherwise provided by law at the time of the expiration of any such period.

The constitutional question is whether this clause provides the lessees with rights that can be considered "property" subject to the protections of the Takings Clause. * * *

In choosing among the possible meanings of the readjustment clauses before us, we think the crucial point is that some of the constructions would immunize the leases from the sovereign power of the United States to change its laws. Such constructions are highly disfavored. The Supreme Court recently reminded us that "without regard to its source, power, even when unexercised, is an enduring presence that governs all contracts subject to the sovereign's jurisdiction, and will remain intact unless surrendered in unmistakable terms." Bowen v. Public Agencies Opposed to Social Security Entrapment, 477 U.S. 41, 52, 91 L. Ed. 2d 35,

106 S. Ct. 2390 (1986). The Court stated that federal government has the duty to honor contracts that confer vested rights on private parties, but observed that "contractual arrangements, including those to which a sovereign itself is party, remain subject to subsequent legislation by the sovereign," id. at 52 (internal quotation omitted), and that "contracts should be construed, if possible, to avoid foreclosing exercise of sovereign authority," id. at 52–53. * * *

Applying this rule of construction to the lease contracts before us, we conclude that the leases reserve to Congress the power to provide by law for a specific readjustment. The phrase "unless otherwise provided by law at the time of the expiration of any such period," though susceptible of multiple interpretations, is certainly susceptible of this one, which has the indisputable advantage of not foreclosing the exercise of sovereign authority. The leases here do not represent a surrender "in unmistakable terms" of Congress' power to change the law of federal coal leasing. * * * A congressionally-mandated readjustment at the end of a twenty-year period therefore does not represent a taking of property in violation of the Takings Clause. * * *

B.   Due Process

The appellants also claim that the imposition of a 12.5% royalty violates Due Process, on the ground that Congress had no basis on which it could find such a rate to be reasonable, as purportedly required by the leases. The appellants note that a congressional commission recently concluded that 12.5% is an excessive royalty rate for coal leases. This claim is meritless. Given our conclusion that Congress had the power to provide by law for such lease readjustments as it saw fit, we cannot strike down Congress' choice of a 12.5% rate simply because we might think it unwise or improvident. * * *

Notes and Questions

1.   For background on the Peabody coal leases, and on coal mining on federal and tribal lands more generally, see CHARLES WILKINSON, FIRE ON THE PLATEAU (Island Press 1999). For other cases upholding readjustments of pre–1976 lease royalties to 12.5% under the FCLLA, *see* Western Energy Co. v. United States Department of the Interior, 932 F.2d 807 (9th Cir. 1991); FMC Wyoming Corp. v Hodel, 816 F.2d 496 (10th Cir. 1987). There are two exceptions to readjustment at FCLAA rates. First, a lower royalty rate is permissible when a lease covers underground coal. Coastal States Energy Co. v. Hodel, 816 F.2d 502 (10th Cir. 1987). Second, readjustment may not occur if the Department sends notice of readjustment long *after* the 20–year period has passed. *See* Rosebud Coal Sales Co., Inc. v. Andrus, 667 F.2d 949 (10th Cir. 1982) (invalidating adjustment two years after 20–year anniversary date); Valley Camp of Utah, Inc. v. Babbitt, 24 F.3d 1263 (10th Cir. 1994) (invalidating royalty readjustment for failure to provide timely notice).

2. In Trapper Mining Inc. v. Lujan, 923 F.2d 774 (10th Cir. 1991), the court ruled that the FCLAA's shorter readjustment interval of 10 years automatically applies to pre–1976 leases after their 20–year readjustment period ends.

4. NEPA

Strip Mining and Reclamation

Environmental review under NEPA is an important component in every phase of federal coal leasing after passage of the FCLAA. Outstanding pre–1976 preference right lease applications are considered by the BLM to be "proposals for major federal action," necessitating preparation of environmental impact statements. BLM regulations interpreting the FCLAA require preparation of an EA or EIS before issuing exploration licenses. If an EIS is prepared in conjunction with a lease sale, the sale may be suspended if the EIS is found to be inadequate. Northern Cheyenne Tribe v. Hodel, 851 F.2d 1152 (9th Cir. 1988). Even land exchanges to consolidate coal tracts are subject to NEPA review. Northern Plains Resource Council v. Lujan, 874 F.2d 661 (9th Cir. 1989). In 1990, environmentalists challenged the Interior Department's programmatic EIS for its Federal Coal Management Program for failing to consider whether the Program's implementation might contribute to the greenhouse effect and global climate change. Foundation on Economic Trends v. Watkins, 731 F.Supp. 530 (D.D.C. 1990). The same court later dismissed plaintiffs claim of "informational injury", generally defined as an assertion that a federal agency is not creating information a member of the public would like to have, as inadequate basis alone for a challenge under NEPA. Foundation on Economic Trends v. Watkins, 794 F.Supp. 395 (D.D.C. 1992).

C. The Surface Mining Control and Reclamation Act (SMCRA)

After 1974, most domestic coal mining was done by surface mining techniques. By the 1980s, nearly two thirds of the nation's coal production was from strip mining operations. This form of surface mining is the most economically efficient means of extracting coal. However, surface mining operations can have disastrous environmental effects. To ameliorate those effects, in 1977 Congress enacted SMCRA, 30 U.S.C.A. §§ 1201–1328. SMCRA is primarily a reclamation statute designed to prevent and repair damage caused by surface coal mining operations.

1. SMCRA's Scope and Basic Requirements

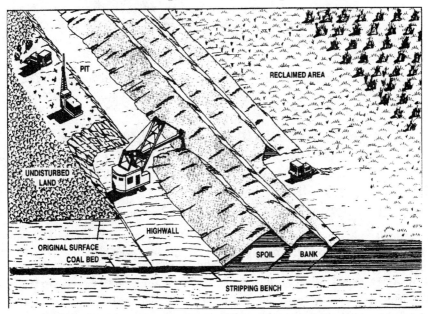

SMCRA applies to surface mining activities which "exist" as of August 3, 1977, plus pre-existing coal mining activities that remove more than 250 tons of coal per year. 30 U.S.C.A. § 1291. SMCRA defines "surface coal mining operations" broadly, and extends beyond strip mining sites. 30 U.S.C.A. § 1291(28). For example, it reaches activities such as underground mines with surface impacts and off-site processing facilities. *See* National Wildlife Federation v. Lujan, 928 F.2d 453 (D.C. Cir. 1991). The dredging of a river for the purpose of producing coal is also "surface mining." Cumberland Reclamation Co. v. Secretary, U.S. Dept. of the Interior, 925 F.2d 164 (6th Cir. 1991). So, too, is the recovery of anthracite silt. United States v. Devil's Hole, Inc., 747 F.2d 895 (3d Cir. 1984).

SMCRA is jointly administered by federal and state officials. However, either federal law or state law regulates coal mining activity in a state, but not both simultaneously. 30 U.S.C.A. §§ 1253(a), 1254(a); Bragg v. West Virginia Coal Ass'n, 248 F.3d 275 (4th Cir. 2001). An agency within the Interior Department—the Office of Surface Mining Reclamation and Enforcement (OSM)—is charged with implementing a surface coal mining and reclamation program for public lands. 30 U.S.C.A. § 1273(a). States with approved programs may enter into cooperative agreements with the Interior Department to regulate surface coal operations on public lands. Once a state enacts statutes and regulations that are approved by the Secretary of the Interior, those statutes and regulations become operative. Non-federal private coal lands must be regulated by an approved state program or, if the program is unsatisfactory, by the Interior Department. 30 U.S.C.A. §§ 1253, 1254. State regulations of coal operations on private lands may be more stringent than SMCRA requirements. *Budinsky v. Commonwealth of Pa. Dept. of*

Environmental Resources, 819 F.2d 418 (3d Cir. 1987). But private citizens are barred from suing state regulators in federal court for issuing surface mining permits in violation of state-administered regulations approved under SMCRA. Bragg v. West Virginia Coal Ass'n, 248 F.3d 275 (4th Cir. 2001).

SMCRA's regulatory scheme is set forth, in general terms, in the following case in which the Supreme Court ruled that SMCRA was constitutional under the Commerce Clause.

HODEL v. VIRGINIA SURFACE MINING & RECLAMATION ASS'N, INC.

Supreme Court of the United States, 1981.
452 U.S. 264, 101 S.Ct. 2352, 69 L.Ed.2d 1.

JUSTICE MARSHALL delivered the opinion of the Court.

These cases arise out of a pre-enforcement challenge to the constitutionality of the Surface Mining Control and Reclamation Act of 1977 (Surface Mining Act or Act), 91 Stat. 447, 30 U. S. C. § 1201 et seq. (1976 ed., Supp. III). The United States District Court for the Western District of Virginia declared several central provisions of the Act unconstitutional and permanently enjoined their enforcement. 483 F.Supp. 425 (1980). In these appeals, we consider whether Congress, in adopting the Act, exceeded its powers under the Commerce Clause of the Constitution, or transgressed affirmative limitations on the exercise of that power contained in the Fifth and Tenth Amendments. We conclude that in the context of a facial challenge, the Surface Mining Act does not suffer from any of these alleged constitutional defects, and we uphold the Act as constitutional.

I

A

The Surface Mining Act is a comprehensive statute designed to "establish a nationwide program to protect society and the environment from the adverse effects of surface coal mining operations." § 102(a), 30 U. S. C. § 1202(a) (1976 ed., Supp. III). Title II of the Act, 30 U.S.C. § 1211 (1976 ed., Supp. III), creates the Office of Surface Mining Reclamation and Enforcement (OSM), within the Department of the Interior, and the Secretary of the Interior (Secretary) acting through OSM, is charged with primary responsibility for administering and implementing the Act by promulgating regulations and enforcing its provisions. § 201(c), 30 U. S. C. § 1211(c) (1976 ed., Supp. III). The principal regulatory and enforcement provisions are contained in Title V of the Act, 91 Stat. 467–514, 30 U. S. C. §§ 1251–1279 (1976 ed., Supp. III). Section 501, 30 U.S.C. § 1251 (1976 ed., Supp. III), establishes a two-stage program for the regulation of surface coal mining: an initial, or interim regulatory phase, and a subsequent, permanent phase. The interim program mandates immediate promulgation and federal enforcement of some of the

Act's environmental protection performance standards, complemented by continuing state regulation. Under the permanent phase, a regulatory program is to be adopted for each State, mandating compliance with the full panoply of federal performance standards, with enforcement responsibility lying with either the State or Federal Government.

Section 501(a) directs the Secretary to promulgate regulations establishing an interim regulatory program during which mine operators will be required to comply with some of the Act's performance standards, as specified by § 502(c), 30 U. S. C. § 1252(c) (1976 ed., Supp. III). Included among those selected standards are requirements governing: (a) restoration of land after mining to its prior condition; (b) restoration of land to its approximate original contour; (c) segregation and preservation of topsoil; (d) minimization of disturbance to the hydrologic balance; (e) construction of coal mine waste piles used as dams and embankments; (f) revegetation of mined areas; and (g) spoil disposal. § 515(b), 30 U.S.C. § 1265(b) (1976 ed., Supp. III). The interim regulations were published on December 13, 1977, see 42 Fed. Reg. 62639, and they are currently in effect in most States, including Virginia.

The Secretary is responsible for enforcing the interim regulatory program. § 502 (e), 30 U. S. C. § 1252 (e) (1976 ed., Supp. III). * * *

Section 501 (b),[6] 30 U. S. C. § 1251 (b) (1976 ed., Supp. III) directs the Secretary to promulgate regulations establishing a permanent regulatory program incorporating all the Act's performance standards. The Secretary published the permanent regulations on March 13, 1979, see 44 Fed. Reg. 14902, but these regulations do not become effective in a particular State until either a permanent state program, submitted and approved in accordance with § 503 of the Act, or a permanent federal program for the State, adopted in accordance with § 504, is implemented.

Under § 503, any State wishing to assume permanent regulatory authority over the surface coal mining operations on "non-Federal lands" within its borders must submit a proposed permanent program to the Secretary for his approval. The proposed program must demonstrate that the state legislature has enacted laws implementing the environmental protection standards established by the Act and accompanying regulations, and that the State has the administrative and technical ability to enforce these standards. 30 U. S. C. § 1253 (1976 ed., Supp. III). The Secretary must approve or disapprove each such proposed program in accordance with time schedules and procedures established by §§ 503 (b), (c), 30 U. S. C. §§ 1253 (b), (c) (1976 ed., Supp. III).[7] In addi-

---

6. A separate regulatory program governing "Federal lands" is established by § 523 of the Act, 30 U. S. C. § 1273 (1976 ed., Supp. III). * * *

7. The proposed state programs were to have been submitted by February 3, 1979 ... [but the Secretary and then the Court]

extended the deadline to and including March 3, 1980. * * *

With the exception of Alaska, Georgia, and Washington, all States in which surface mining is either conducted or is expected to be conducted submitted proposed state programs to the Secretary by March 3, 1980.

tion, the Secretary must develop and implement a federal permanent program for each State that fails to submit or enforce a satisfactory state program. § 504, 30 U. S. C. § 1254 (1976 ed., Supp. III). In such situations, the Secretary constitutes the regulatory authority administering the Act within that State and continues as such unless and until a "state program" is approved. No later than eight months after adoption of either a state-run or federally administered permanent regulatory program for a State, all surface coal mining and reclamation operations on "non-Federal lands" within that State must obtain a new permit issued in accordance with the applicable regulatory program. § 506 (a), 30 U. S. C. § 1256 (a) (1976 ed., Supp. III).

B

On October 23, 1978, the Virginia Surface Mining and Reclamation Association, Inc., an association of coal producers engaged in surface coal mining operations in Virginia, 63 of its member coal companies, and 4 individual landowners filed suit in Federal District Court seeking declaratory and injunctive relief against various provisions of the Act. The Commonwealth of Virginia and the town of Wise, Va., intervened as plaintiffs. Plaintiffs' challenge was primarily directed at Title V's performance standards. Because the permanent regulatory program was not scheduled to become effective until June 3, 1980, plaintiffs' challenge was directed at the sections of the Act establishing the interim regulatory program. Plaintiffs alleged that these provisions violate the Commerce Clause, the equal protection and due process guarantees of the Due Process Clause of the Fifth Amendment, the Tenth Amendment, and the Just Compensation Clause of the Fifth Amendment.

The District Court ... issued an order and opinion declaring several central provisions of the Act unconstitutional. 483 F.Supp. 425 (1980). The court rejected plaintiffs' Commerce Clause, equal protection, and substantive due process challenges to the Act. The court held, however, that the Act "operates to 'displace the States' freedom to structure integral operations in areas of traditional functions,' ... and, therefore, is in contravention of the Tenth Amendment." Id., at 435, quoting National League of Cities v. Usery, 426 U.S. 833, 852 (1976). The court also ruled that various provisions of the Act effect an uncompensated taking of private property in violation of the Just Compensation Clause of the Fifth Amendment. Finally, the court agreed with plaintiffs' due process challenges to some of the Act's enforcement provisions. The court permanently enjoined the Secretary from enforcing various provisions of the Act. * * *

The Secretary has made his initial decisions on these programs. Three programs were approved, 8 were approved on condition that the States agree to some modifications, 10 were approved in part and disapproved in part, and 3 were disapproved because the state legislatures had failed to enact the necessary implementing statutes.

Virginia's program was among those approved in part and disapproved in part. See 45 Fed. Reg. 69977 (1980). Under § 503 of the Act, a State may revise a plan that has been disapproved in whole or in part and resubmit it to the Secretary within 60 days of his initial decision.

II

On cross-appeal, appellees argue that the District Court erred in rejecting their challenge to the Act as beyond the scope of congressional power under the Commerce Clause. They insist that the Act's principal goal is regulating the use of private lands within the borders of the States and not, as the District Court found, regulating the interstate commerce effects of surface coal mining. Consequently, appellees contend that the ultimate issue presented is "whether land as such is subject to regulation under the Commerce Clause, i.e., whether land can be regarded as 'in commerce.' " In urging us to answer "no" to this question, appellees emphasize that the Court has recognized that land-use regulation is within the inherent police powers of the States and their political subdivisions, and argue that Congress may regulate land use only insofar as the Property Clause grants it control over federal lands.

We do not accept either appellees' framing of the question or the answer they would have us supply. The task of a court that is asked to determine whether a particular exercise of congressional power is valid under the Commerce Clause is relatively narrow. The court must defer to a congressional finding that a regulated activity affects interstate commerce, if there is any rational basis for such a finding. Heart of Atlanta Motel, Inc. v. United States, 379 U.S. 241, 258 (1964); Katzenbach v. McClung, 379 U.S. 294, 303–304 (1964). This established, the only remaining question for judicial inquiry is whether "the means chosen by [Congress] must be reasonably adapted to the end permitted by the Constitution." Heart of Atlanta Motel, Inc. v. United States, supra, at 262. The judicial task is at an end once the court determines that Congress acted rationally in adopting a particular regulatory scheme. Ibid.

Judicial review in this area is influenced above all by the fact that the Commerce Clause is a grant of plenary authority to Congress.... Moreover, this Court has made clear that the commerce power extends not only to "the use of channels of interstate or foreign commerce" and to "protection of the instrumentalities of interstate commerce ... or persons or things in commerce," but also to "activities affecting commerce." ... As we explained in Fry v. United States, 421 U.S. 542, 547 (1975), "[even] activity that is purely intrastate in character may be regulated by Congress, where the activity, combined with like conduct by others similarly situated, affects commerce among the States or with foreign nations." * * *

Thus, when Congress has determined that an activity affects interstate commerce, the courts need inquire only whether the finding is rational. Here, the District Court properly deferred to Congress' express findings, set out in the Act itself, about the effects of surface coal mining on interstate commerce. Section 101 (c), 30 U. S. C. § 1201 (c) (1976 ed., Supp. III), recites the congressional finding that

> "many surface mining operations result in disturbances of surface areas that burden and adversely affect commerce and the public

welfare by destroying or diminishing the utility of land for commercial, industrial, residential, recreational, agricultural, and forestry purposes, by causing erosion and landslides, by contributing to floods, by polluting the water, by destroying fish and wildlife habitats, by impairing natural beauty, by damaging the property of citizens, by creating hazards dangerous to life and property by degrading the quality of life in local communities, and by counteracting governmental programs and efforts to conserve soil, water, and other natural resources."

The legislative record provides ample support for these statutory findings.[19] The Surface Mining Act became law only after six years of the most thorough legislative consideration. Committees of both Houses of Congress held extended hearings during which vast amounts of testimony and documentary evidence about the effects of surface mining on our Nation's environment and economy were brought to Congress' attention. Both Committees made detailed findings about these effects and the urgent need for federal legislation to address the problem. The Senate Report explained that "[surface] coal mining activities have imposed large social costs on the public ... in many areas of the country in the form of unreclaimed lands, water pollution, erosion, floods, slope failures, loss of fish and wildlife resources, and a decline in natural beauty." S. Rep. No. 95–128, p. 50 (1977). * * *

Similarly, the House Committee documented the adverse effects of surface coal mining on interstate commerce as including:

" 'Acid drainage which has ruined an estimated 11,000 miles of streams; the loss of prime hardwood forest and the destruction of wildlife habitat by strip mining; the degrading of productive farmland; recurrent landslides; siltation and sedimentation of river systems.... ' " H. R. Rep. No. 95–218, p. 58 (1977), quoting H. R. Rep. No. 94–1445, p. 19 (1976).

And in discussing how surface coal mining affects water resources and in turn interstate commerce, the House Committee explained:

* * * Water users and developers incur significant economic and financial losses as well.

---

19. Hearings on proposed legislation regulating surface coal mining began in 1968.... Three years later, additional hearings were held by Committees of both the House and the Senate....

Similar bills were reintroduced in the 93d [and 94th] Congress and further hearings were held.... At the request of the Chairman of the Senate Committee, the Council on Environmental Quality prepared a report entitled Coal Surface Mining and Reclamation: An Environmental and Economic Assessment of Alternatives (Comm. Print 1973), and the Senate Committee held additional hearings .... The House and Senate Committees reported bills for consideration by both Houses, and Congress passed a bill that was vetoed by President Ford. * * *

The protracted congressional endeavor finally bore fruit in 1977. The relevant House and Senate Committees held extensive hearings shortly after the opening of the 95th Congress.... The legislation was reported to both Houses and passage in both Chambers followed, after lengthy floor debate ... President Carter signed the Act into law on August 3, 1977. * * *

Reduced recreational values, fishkills, reductions in normal waste assimilation capacity, impaired water supplies, metals and masonry corrosion and deterioration, increased flood frequencies and flood damages, reductions in designed water storage capacities at impoundments, and higher operating costs for commercial waterway users are some of the most obvious economic effects that stem from mining-related pollution and sedimentation. * * *

The Committees also explained that inadequacies in existing state laws and the need for uniform minimum nationwide standards made federal regulations imperative. See S. Rep. No. 95–128, at 49; H.R. Rep. No. 95–218, at 58. In light of the evidence available to Congress and the detailed consideration that the legislation received, we cannot say that Congress did not have a rational basis for concluding that surface coal mining has substantial effects on interstate commerce.

Appellees do not, in general, dispute the validity of the congressional findings. Rather, appellees' contention is that the "rational basis" test should not apply in this case because the Act regulates land use, a local activity not affecting interstate commerce. But even assuming that appellees correctly characterize the land use regulated by the Act as a "local" activity, their argument is unpersuasive.

The denomination of an activity as a "local" or "intrastate" activity does not resolve the question whether Congress may regulate it under the Commerce Clause. As previously noted, the commerce power "extends to those activities intrastate which so affect interstate commerce, or the exertion of the power of Congress over it, as to make regulation of them appropriate means to the attainment of a legitimate end, the effective execution of the granted power to regulate interstate commerce." United States v. Wrightwood Dairy Co., 315 U.S., at 119. This Court has long held that Congress may regulate the conditions under which goods shipped in interstate commerce are produced where the "local" activity of producing these goods itself affects interstate commerce. See, e.g., United States v. Darby, 312 U.S. 100 (1941); Wickard v. Filburn, 317 U.S. 111 (1942); * * * Appellees do not dispute that coal is a commodity that moves in interstate commerce. Here, Congress rationally determined that regulation of surface coal mining is necessary to protect interstate commerce from adverse effects that may result from that activity. This congressional finding is sufficient to sustain the Act as a valid exercise of Congress' power under the Commerce Clause.

Moreover, the Act responds to a congressional finding that nationwide "surface mining and reclamation standards are essential in order to insure that competition in interstate commerce among sellers of coal produced in different States will not be used to undermine the ability of the several States to improve and maintain adequate standards on coal mining operations within their borders." 30 U.S.C. § 1201 (g) (1976 ed., Supp. III). The prevention of this sort of destructive interstate competition is a traditional role for congressional action under the Commerce Clause. In *United States v. Darby, supra,* the Court used a similar rationale to sustain the imposition of federal minimum wage and maximum hour regulations on a manufacturer of goods shipped in interstate commerce. The Court explained that the statute implemented Congress' view that "interstate commerce should not be made the instrument of competition in the distribution of goods produced under substandard labor conditions, which competition is injurious to the commerce and to the states from and to which the commerce flows." *Id.*, at 115. The same rationale applies here to support the conclusion that the Surface Mining Act is within the authority granted to Congress by the Commerce Clause.

Finally, we agree with the lower federal courts that have uniformly found the power conferred by the Commerce Clause broad enough to permit congressional regulation of activities causing air or water pollution, or other environmental hazards that may have effects in more than one State. * * * Accordingly, we turn to the question whether the means selected by Congress were reasonable and appropriate.

Appellees' essential challenge to the means selected by the Act is that they are redundant or unnecessary. Appellees contend that a variety of federal statutes such as the Clean Air Act, 42 U.S.C. § 7401 et seq. (1976 ed., Supp. III), the Flood Control Acts, 33 U.S.C. § 701 et seq. (1976 ed., Supp. III), and the Clean Water Act, 33 U.S.C. § 1251 et seq. (1976 ed., Supp. III), adequately address the federal interest in controlling the environmental effects of surface coal mining without need to resort to the land-use regulation scheme of the Surface Mining Act. The short answer to this argument is that the effectiveness of existing laws in dealing with a problem identified by Congress is ordinarily a matter committed to legislative judgment. Congress considered the effectiveness of existing legislation and concluded that additional measures were necessary to deal with the interstate commerce effects of surface coal mining. See H. R. Rep. No. 95–218, at 58–60; S. Rep. No. 95–128, at 59–63. And we agree with the court below that the Act's regulatory scheme is reasonably related to the goals Congress sought to accomplish. The Act's restrictions on the practices of mine operators all serve to control the environmental and other adverse effects of surface coal mining.

In sum, we conclude that the District Court properly rejected appellees' Commerce Clause challenge to the Act. * * *

Notes and Questions

1. In addition to finding that SMCRA was constitutional under the Commerce Clause, the Court ruled that the federal intrusion into a field previously occupied by the states (reclamation) did not violate the 10th Amendment. It also overturned a district court ruling that invalidated several provisions of SMCRA under the Due Process Clause and the Just Compensation Clause of the Constitution. In a companion case, Hodel v. Indiana, 452 U.S. 314, 101 S.Ct. 2376, 69 L.Ed.2d 40 (1981), the Court rejected similar challenges to SMCRA under the Commerce Clause and the 10th Amendment. It was highly deferential to Congress's findings about the effects of

coal mining on interstate commerce, as well as the appropriate means to alleviate or control those effects. If this case came before the Court today, would the result be the same? *See* Lopez v. United States, 514 U.S. 549, 115 S.Ct. 1624, 131 L.Ed.2d 626 (1995) (invalidating the Gun–Free School Zones Act); U.S. v. Morrison, 529 U.S. 598, 120 S.Ct. 1740, 146 L.Ed.2d 658 (2000) (invalidating the Violence Against Women Act); SWANCC v. U.S. Army Corps of Engineers, 531 U.S. 159, 121 S.Ct. 675, 148 L.Ed.2d 576 (2001) (invalidating the "migratory bird rule" for isolated wetlands as beyond the scope of the Clean Water Act).

2. As the Court noted in *Hodel*, SMCRA spells out highly detailed performance standards governing how surface mining operations must be conducted, and to what degree reclamation must take place. 30 U.S.C.A. § 1265. The Interior Secretary has implemented these standards in a series of regulations, most of which were challenged by both environmentalists and industry groups. *See* National Wildlife Federation v. Lujan, 928 F.2d 453 (D.C. Cir 1991); National Wildlife Federal v. Hodel, 839 F.2d 694 (D.C. Cir. 1988). The District of Columbia Circuit turned aside those challenges in sustaining SMCRA regulations involving restoration of prime farmland and pastureland, subsided land overlying underground mines, and alluvial valley floors.

The regulations may, however, constitute compensable takings of property, depending on the circumstances. In Hodel v. Indiana, 452 U.S. 314, 101 S.Ct. 2376, 69 L.Ed.2d 40 (1981), the Supreme Court rejected a mining company's claim that SMCRA's "prime farmland" performance standard constituted an unconstitutional taking without just compensation. By contrast, in Whitney Benefits, Inc. v. United States, 926 F.2d 1169 (Fed. Cir. 1991), the Federal Circuit ruled that application of the alluvial valley floor performance standard, which prohibited removal of coal located beneath an alluvial valley floor, constituted a taking as applied to a coal mine in Wyoming. The court found that application of the standard against Whitney Benefits, Inc. totally diminished the value of the coal located beneath the alluvial valley. The court ordered the government to pay the coal owner $60 million plus interest for the lost value of the coal.

3. SMCRA also requires mine operators to mitigate adverse impacts of mining activities on adjacent streams by providing replacement water. Castle Valley Special Service District v. Utah Board of Oil, Gas & Mining, 938 P.2d 248 (Utah 1996). Federal environmental requirements are addressed in detail in Section V, below.

4. SMCRA prohibits strip mining on lands determined to be "unsuitable" for surface coal mining operations. 30 U.S.C.A. § 1272. Lands are unsuitable if reclamation of the land is not technologically and economically feasible under SMCRA or a state-approved program. 30 C.F.R. § 762.22(b). There are several ways for lands to be designated unsuitable for surface mining. The Act itself prohibits surface mining within national parks, wildlife refuges, wilderness areas, or wild and scenic rivers. 30 U.S.C.A. § 1272(e)(1). National forests are unsuitable unless mining on a specific tract is consistent with federal land management statutes. The Interior Secretary has discretion to determine unsuitability after a general "review of Federal lands." 30 U.S.C.A. § 1272(b). Also, any adversely affected person

can petition the Secretary to make an unsuitability determination. Prager v. Hodel, 793 F.2d 730 (5th Cir. 1986).

Although an unsuitability determination effectively prohibits surface removal of valuable mineral deposits, courts have been reluctant to characterize such a designation as a taking, requiring compensation. Meridian Land and Mineral Co. v. Hodel, 843 F.2d 340 (9th Cir. 1988); Burlington Northern R.R. Co. v. United States, 752 F.2d 627 (Fed. Cir. 1985); Utah Intern., Inc. v. Dept. of Interior, 553 F.Supp. 872 (D.Utah 1982). The rationale seems to be that an unsuitability determination only prevents coal extraction by inexpensive (*i.e.,* maximally profitable) surface techniques; it is not an absolute ban on coal removal. Takings challenges also are minimized by a grandfather clause in the Act that exempts from unsuitability determination "lands on which surface mining operations are being conducted ... or where substantial legal and financial commitments were in existence" prior to the date of SMCRA's enactment. 30 U.S.C.A. § 1272(a)(6).

5. *National Wildlife Federation v. Hodel* found that Interior Department regulations requiring mining operators to post bond to ensure reclamation were consistent with SMCRA, which explicitly requires miners to either post bond before beginning mining operations or indemnify the regulatory authority in the amount of the cost of reclaiming the operation. 30 U.S.C.A. § 1259. The bond cannot be released until all reclamation requirements are fully met. 30 U.S.C.A. § 1269(c)(3). In West Virginia Mining & Reclamation Association v. Babbitt, 970 F.Supp. 506 (S.D.W.Va. 1997), a federal district court ruled that a mine operator had no right to have its bond released simply because the Interior Department had approved its use of methods to avoid acid mine drainage (AMD), when those methods were not certain to be sufficient for avoiding AMD.

SMCRA requires the applicant to file a performance bond, the amount of which "shall be sufficient to assure the completion of the reclamation plan if the work had to be performed by the regulatory authority in the event of forfeiture." 30 U.S.C.A. § 1259(a). Any alternative bonding system approved as part of a state program must "achieve the objectives and purposes of the bonding program pursuant to § 1259," 30 U.S.C. § 1259(c); otherwise, SMCRA's bonding system will supercede it. *See* West Virginia Highlands Conservancy v. Norton, 137 F.Supp.2d 687 (S.D.W.Va. 2001).

6. To what extent, if at all, does SMCRA apply to underground mines that might cause subsidence of surface lands? For many years, environmentalists and the government claimed that SMCRA's definition of "surface coal mining operations" (under 30 U.S.C.A. § 1272(e)) included *underground* coal mining operations that cause subsidence. In 1999, The Secretary of the Interior issued an interpretive regulation providing that protection of such surface lands from subsidence is *not* included in the statute's definition of "surface coal mining operations." The regulation acknowledged, however, that SMCRA requires prevention of subsidence to the extent technologically and economically feasible, and coal miners must either repair or provide compensation for damages to homes and water sources. 30 C.F.R. § 761.200(a); 64 Fed.Reg. 70,838, 70,843 (Dec. 17. 1999). The District Court for the District of Columbia invalidated the regulation, finding that it violated the statutory language of SMCRA. But the D.C. Circuit overturned

that decision, finding that the statutory language was ambiguous and the Secretary's interpretation of it was reasonable. Citizens Coal Council v. Norton, 330 F.3d 478 (D.C. Cir. 2003), *cert. denied*, 540 U.S. 1180, 124 S.Ct. 1415, 158 L.Ed.2d 82 (2004).

7. Fees exacted from current strip mining operations are pooled into a reclamation trust, which the Interior Department distributes among all states and Indian tribes with approved "abandoned mine reclamation program[s]." 30 U.S.C.A. § 1231, 1232. *See* State of Montana v. Clark, 749 F.2d 740 (D.C. Cir. 1984). The courts have adopted an expansive definition of "surface coal mining operations" subject to these reclamation fees. For example, a company which purchased land upon which coal was stockpiled and then sold was found liable to pay reclamation fees. United States v. Tri–No Enterprises, Inc., 819 F.2d 154 (7th Cir. 1987).

2.   *Valid Existing Rights (VERs)*

As noted earlier, SMCRA's regulatory provisions are subject to Valid Existing Rights (VERs). 30 U.S.C.A. § 1272(e). Attempts to interpret this rule have spawned a dozen or so years of Interior Department rulemaking and consequent litigation. Every word in the statutory phrase "Valid Existing Rights" has legal significance. A coal miner seeking protection from SMCRA regulations must establish that it possesses a "right" that is "valid" and "existing" prior to the effective date of SMCRA. The first question, then, is what is a "right"? A private interest in land or resources qualifies as a right if, under state or federal law, that interest is considered property. Cole v. Ralph, 252 U.S. 286, 40 S.Ct. 321, 64 L.Ed. 567 (1920). Courts have conferred VER status upon a number of distinct property rights in resources in non-coal cases. *See* Ainsley v. United States, 8 Cl.Ct. 394 (Cl.Ct. 1985) (severed mineral estates); Sierra Club v. Hodel, 848 F.2d 1068 (10th Cir. 1988) (right-of-way); Skaw v. United States, 740 F.2d 932 (Fed. Cir. 1984).

At one time the Interior Department interpreted SMCRA to permit use of "the VER definition contained in the appropriate state … regulatory program." When the VER definition includes rights arising under state law, the nature, characteristics, and range of state-created property rights should be determined by the states. Parratt v. Taylor, 451 U.S. 527, 101 S.Ct. 1908, 68 L.Ed.2d 420 (1981). One should not assume that rights recognized by state law should be denied VER status for lacking a state permit prior to the effective date of SMCRA. The presence or absence of a permit does not define the existence of a right; a permit addresses only the extent of regulation of the right. Hodel v. Virginia Surface Mining & Reclamation Ass'n, 452 U.S. 264, 101 S.Ct. 2352, 69 L.Ed.2d 1 (1981) (holding that SMCRA's language does not require that the issuance of a permit is a precondition to VER status).

A VER right "exists" if the right-holder has satisfied all the preconditions necessary under federal and state law prior to SMCRA's enactment. The Interior Department has liberally construed SMRCA's VER language to permit "continually created valid existing rights." Such rights would attach if, *after* enactment of SMCRA, a coal mining operation properly initiated on a particular parcel of land later designated "unsuitable" for mining. Such a mine would be a VER which could continue to operate in the redesignated "unsuitable" area. *See* National Wildlife Federation v. Hodel, 839 F.2d 694

(D.C. Cir. 1988) (upholding Interior interpretation of VER as "reasonable"); Belville Mining Co. v. United States, 763 F.Supp. 1411 (S.D. Ohio 1991) (holding that Interior may not reverse a VER determination if motivated by a change in regulatory policy rather than the discovery of an error).

For an existing right in land or resources to be a VER, it must also be "valid." An interest must be valid under both applicable pre-SMCRA law and post-SMCRA conditions. For example, an interest may be deemed invalid if, prior to SMCRA, it arose on land previously reserved or withdrawn from mineral entry. Wisenak, Inc. v. Andrus, 471 F.Supp. 1004 (D. Alaska 1979). If an interest is invalid, SMCRA is not "subject to" it. Tetlin Native Corp. v. State, 759 P.2d 528 (Alaska 1988).

In 1989, the Office of Surface Mining (OSM) attempted to eliminate the confusion surrounding VER designation by instituting a new method for determining "valid existing rights." Under its Good Faith/All Permits Test, a miner must first show that a property right exists. Next, the miner must show that all permits and other authorizations to conduct surface mining operations were obtained *or* that the miner made a good faith effort to obtain all necessary permits and other authorizations, before the land came under SMCRA's protection. 30 C.F.R. § 761.5(b)(1). The agency making the VER determination—either the Interior Department or an authorized state agency—has discretion to decide which "other authorizations" are needed and what constitutes a good faith effort. This test applies to all federal lands. State regulatory programs must be modified, if necessary, to conform with the federal requirements.

D. Oil Shale, Coalbed Methane, and Geothermal Steam

Shale is a sedimentary rock. Oil shale is a shale that contains kerogen, bituminous organic matter than can be distilled into a synthetic oil. Oil shale has been used for fuel since ancient times. More recently, methane gas has been extracted from coalbeds as an energy resource. Geothermal steam, unlike oil shale and methane gas, has a hybrid water-mineral nature, but it too has value as an energy resource. Each is addressed below.

1. *Oil Shale*

CHARLES F. WILKINSON, CROSSING THE NEXT MERIDIAN: LAND, WATER, AND THE FUTURE OF THE AMERICAN WEST PP. 68–69
(Washington, D.C., Island Press, 1992)

There is no doubt about the potential commercial value of this "rock that burns." ... The world's largest deposits of oil shale are located mostly under federal lands in northwestern Colorado, northeastern Utah, and southwestern Wyoming. Yet in spite of decades of industry research and planning and extravagant federal subsidies during the 1970s, there has been little commercial production of oil shale. The shale is too deep, and the production costs, including both mining and the requisite large quantities of water, are too great.

Oil shale was removed from the 1872 mining law and placed under a leasing regime in 1920, so it might seem that the final decade of the twentieth century is a late date for controversy over oil shale in the context of the Hardrock Act. The 1872 Act, however, proved its tenacity once again. The 1920 Mineral Leasing Act grandfathered all "valid claims" under the hardrock mining law. Before 1920, the companies had put stakes in the ground high above the shale deposits and taken some samples, but they had never done any mining for production. Ordinarily, there would seem to be no "discovery," which requires marketing at a profit, and the Interior Department and lower courts so held in the 1970s. The Supreme Court, however, reversed that decision in a five-to-four opinion, relying on administrative rulings in the 1920s that had set up a separate discovery test for oil shale. The old claims were good, mining or no mining. [Andrus v. Shell, 446 U.S. 657, 100 S.Ct. 1932, 64 L.Ed.2d 593 (1980).] Afterward, a 1985 lower court found that the energy companies had met the legal requirements (basically just $100 of [assessment] work per year per claim) to keep most of the pre–1920 claims alive. [Tosco Corp. v. Hodel, 611 F.Supp. 1130 (D.Colo. 1985).] The companies had established vested rights to hundreds of thousands of acres of public lands under the Hardrock Act without ever producing any significant amount of synthetic fuel for sale on the open market.

In 1986, the Interior Department settled with the oil shale claimants. No fewer than 82,000 acres of federal land in the Yampa River and White River watersheds in northwestern Colorado were transferred out of public ownership for a filing fee of $2.50 per acre. The ensuing events were predictable. Within less than a year, one claimant turned around and sold 17,000 acres for more than $2,000 per acre—a total sale price of $37 million. Local ranchers, who held a total of fifty grazing permits on the formerly public land, faced fee increases or outright revocation of their grazing privileges. This high desert piñon-juniper country, habitat for elk and the largest mule deer herd in North America, was no longer public land, open as a matter of federal law for hunting and hiking. The state of Colorado later succeeded in obtaining written guarantees that grazing, hunting, and public access for recreational use can continue under most conditions for twenty years, but no assurances have been made beyond that time. Nor is the oil shale episode over. Applications for patents to 270,000 more acres of land are still pending, and although technical issues still must be resolved, the 1872 act may well give the private claimants all rights to those lands.

* * *

In the same year when Wilkinson's book was published, 1992, Congress enacted the Energy Policy Act, which modified the type of patent pre–1920 oil shale claimants could receive. The Act divided oil shale claimants into two categories, depending on what stage they were at in the patent application process. 30 U.S.C.A. § 242. Claimants who had filed a patent application and received a first half final certificate were eligible for full patents, under the terms of the 1872 Mining Law. Claimants who had filed a patent application but not yet received their first half final certificate as of October 24, 1992 were eligible for limited patents under the terms of the 1992 Energy Policy Act. Claimants who had not yet applied for a patent had 180 days after the effective date of the 1992 Act to submit an election of whether they would seek a limited patent or maintain the unpatented claim.

2. *Coalbed Methane*

There was no commercial market for coal-bed methane until the 1990s. Once that market developed, questions immediately arose as to ownership of the mineral. Was coalbed methane owned by the owner of the coal rights or the owner of oil and gas rights? The answer to this question had critical consequences under many mineral leases and reservations, as the following case suggests.

NEWMAN v. RAG WYOMING LAND CO.
Supreme Court of Wyoming, 2002.
53 P.3d 540.

JUSTICE KITE delivered the opinion of the Court.

In 1968, the landowners, who owned both the surface and mineral estate in certain Campbell County property, leased their ranch for oil and gas development. Production occurred, and the lease remained held by that production. The landowners deeded the surface of the ranch and "coal and minerals commingled with [the] coal" to a neighboring coal mine operator in 1974, reserving all "oil, gas, and other minerals" not otherwise conveyed. Twenty years later, development of the gas found within the coal, known as "coalbed methane," became commercially feasible. A coalbed methane operator obtained an assignment of the oil and gas leasehold rights from the surface to a depth of 1,000 feet and began development of the coalbed methane. The successors in interest to the landowners claimed their right to royalties on the coalbed methane; however, the coalbed methane operator paid all royalties to the coal operator. The landowners filed a complaint seeking a declaratory judgment as to the ownership of the coalbed methane and recovery of the unpaid royalties. The district court granted summary judgment in favor of the coal operator. We reverse.

* * *

DISCUSSION

The existence of coalbed methane has been well known for over a century. Paul N. Bowles, Coalbed Gas: Present Status of Ownership Issue and Other Legal Considerations, 1 Eastern Min. L. Inst. § 7.03 (1980). In fact, flash fires occasionally occurred on drilling rigs for many years when wells were drilled through the coal seam, and ventilation of underground mines was necessary to prevent fires and explosions. Michelle D. Baldwin, Book Note, Ownership of Coalbed Methane Gas: Recent Developments in Case Law, 100 W. Va. L. Rev. 673 (1998). Historically, coalbed methane "had long been considered a dangerous waste product of coal mining." Amoco Production Co. v. Southern Ute Indian Tribe, 526 U.S. 865, 871, 144 L. Ed. 2d 22, 119 S.Ct. 1719 (1999).

In the 1970s, the value of coalbed methane was recognized, and government grants became available to encourage its development. Id. In 1981, the Solicitor of the Department of the Interior issued an opinion addressing the ownership of coalbed methane in federal coal deposits concluding the reservation of coal to the United States in patents issued after 1909 did not include coalbed methane. In reliance on that opinion, oil and gas operators began entering into leases to develop coalbed methane with individual landowners who owned the oil and gas. Id. In the early 1990s, techniques for efficient development of coalbed methane, specifically within the coal deposits in the Powder River Basin in Wyoming, were perfected. In 1991, litigation ensued between the federal government and certain Indian tribes which claimed the government's reservation of coal in 1909 and 1910 included the coalbed methane on lands originally owned by the government which now belonged to them. Ultimately, that issue was resolved when the United States Supreme Court held coalbed methane was not included within the reservation of coal and overruled district and circuit court decisions which had concluded coalbed methane was owned by the owner of the coal. *Id.* at 874.

Commercial development of coalbed methane in the Powder River Basin began in the early 1990s. Prior to that time, coalbed methane escaped from the coal in the course of the open pit surface mining process, and no attempt was made to capture that gas as a valuable resource.

A brief discussion of the chemistry and the composition of methane and coal is in order. Coalbed methane is chemically identical (CH4) to gas produced through conventional methods, and each is known as "natural gas." Methane or natural gas originates from the decay of organic material over time under great pressure and temperature. Whether that process occurs in coal deposits or at greater depths, the result is the same- natural gas is produced. * * *

Natural gas or methane, whether located in a sandstone reservoir or a coal seam, is produced by creating a pressure differential between the well bore and the reservoir. In the Powder River Basin, coalbed methane production involves the removal of water from the coal formation, which reduces the pressure and allows the gas to escape. * * *

The issue to be resolved in this case is whether the parties to the deed in question intended the coalbed methane to be conveyed along with the coal estate or reserved to the grantor as part of the oil and gas estate. The parties agree the governing principle of contract construction is determination of the parties' intent from the language of the instrument itself. * * *

The language of the deed conveys "all coal and minerals commingled with coal that may be mined or extracted in association therewith or in conjunction with such coal operations" and reserves "all oil, gas and other minerals except as set forth above." The first term the parties argue must be interpreted is "minerals." We have little trouble concluding that natural gas produced from the coal seam is a mineral under Wyoming law. However, this conclusion does little to resolve this dispute because "minerals" are both granted and reserved.

The determinative question is whether the parties intended "minerals commingled with coal that may be mined or extracted in association therewith or in conjunction with such coal operations" to include natural gas found in the coal seam. We are unable to discern any unique meaning of "commingled" in the context of minerals. The word "commingle" is defined by Webster's New World Dictionary as "to mingle together; intermix; blend." Webster's New World Dictionary 285 (2nd C. ed. 1972). The term does not suggest any sort of chemical change must occur to constitute commingling but only a mixing together. Given the three states of coalbed methane as free gas within the cleats and matrixes of the coal, gas dissolved in water in the coal pores, and gas absorbed onto the solid surface of the coal, it appears to be "mixed together" with the coal within the meaning of the terms of the deed.

In addition to being commingled with the coal, the other "minerals" conveyed must be those that "may be mined or extracted in association" with the coal or "in conjunction with such coal operations." Likewise, these terms must be given their plain and ordinary meaning to reasonable persons at the same time and place of their use; i.e., 1968 in the Powder River Basin of Wyoming. The coal operator argues that production of gas has been considered "mining" relying on Coronado Oil Company v. Grieves, 603 P.2d 406 (Wyo. 1979), Amoco Production Company v. Guild Trust, 636 F.2d 261, 263–65 (10th Cir. 1980), and the language of oil and gas leases, including those issued by the landowners in this case. While those references certainly establish that oil and gas production through the drilling of wells has been considered "mining," they do not answer the question posed in this case because all agree that, in 1974 when the warranty deed in question was drawn, any gas found in the coal seam was not mined through a well bore but was ventilated or wasted while the coal was produced by excavation in the course of surface mining. In addition, the minerals conveyed by the language of the deed were only those mined "in association therewith or in conjunction with such coal operations." Webster's New World Dictionary confirms the ordinary meaning of "in association" and "in conjunction" to be "together." No party contends coalbed methane is somehow captured together with the coal as it is mined. Rather, it is released and escapes during the mining process. *Southern Ute Indian Tribe*, 526 U.S. at 873. In the case of underground mines, it must be ventilated. United States Steel Corporation v. Hoge, 503 Pa. 140, 468 A.2d 1380, 1382 (1983).

Is the plain meaning of "extracted" the same as "released," "escaped," or "ventilated"? It is obvious these words connote different actions, and the distinctions between them are crucial to determining the intent of the parties to this deed. Webster's New World Dictionary confirms that difference by defining (1) "extract" as "to draw out by effort; pull out" and "to remove or separate (metal) from ore"; (2) "release" as "to set free"; and (3) "ventilate" as "to provide with an opening for the escape of air, gas, etc." Under the plain meaning of the terms chosen by the parties to the deed, we cannot conclude they intended to include coalbed methane gas as a mineral "mined or extracted in association therewith or in conjunction with such coal operations" when it can only be produced through wells as any other gas.

We could end the inquiry at this point. However, because of the importance of the issue of the ownership of coalbed methane in general and the extensive consideration of this issue by other courts and commentators which we find helpful and consistent with our initial conclusion, further discussion is warranted.

The coal operator poses a creative argument suggesting that, because coalbed methane can most efficiently be produced in advance of the mining operations thereby reducing the water the mine must contend with and making the mine more economically successful, it is mined or extracted "in association therewith" or "in conjunction with" coal mining operations. Two problems exist with that argument. First, the gas production does not occur automatically in the process of overburden and coal excavation and removal. Instead, it only occurs when and if the coal operator decides to undertake gas well drilling in advance of the mine face. Second, such "mining" techniques—the coordination of well drilling and mine excavation—did not exist until twenty years after the deed in question was drawn which poses the broader question in this case. How is the parties' intent to be determined when minerals become valuable long after a conveyance by (1) discovery of new methods of production; (2) changes in economics making production of a previously known, but unwanted, mineral profitable; (3) or discovery of the presence of minerals not previously known to exist? Obviously, the language of the particular documents involved affects the answer to this question on a case-by-case basis. In this particular case, no reference is made in the deed to coalbed methane, and no other language can be said to address the parties' specific intent with regard to it. In circumstances like those present here, a search for the parties' specific intent produces little fruit because the identity, value, or feasibility of production was unknown to the parties at the time of the conveyance and, therefore, they likely had no intent at all with regard to the substance in question. Consequently, we must focus upon the general intent of the parties, concentrating on the "purposes of the grant in terms of respective manner of enjoyment of surface and mineral estates." Comment, New Values Under Old Oil and Gas Leases: Helium, Who Owns It?, 62 Mich. L. Rev. 1158, 1169 (1964).

* * *

Struggling to articulate clear rules for the resolution of this difficult issue, the courts [of other jurisdictions] ... displayed confusing and inconsistent reasoning. While lip service is paid to the role of the theory of ownership of oil and gas in the respective jurisdictions, the ultimate rulings do not depend on which theory of ownership applies. In both ownership in place and rule of capture jurisdictions, courts have concluded the gas owner is entitled to all the gas it can capture, yet the coal owner owns the coalbed methane. We agree with those courts and commentators which have rejected reliance upon the nature of the ownership interest in oil and gas to resolve this question. * * *

The most recent ruling on the issue of ownership of coalbed methane involved determining the intent of Congress in reserving "all coal" from lands patented under the Coal Lands Act of 1909 and 1910. Reversing the Tenth Circuit Court of Appeals, the United States Supreme Court ended a long running controversy over ownership of coalbed methane in federal coal deposits. In doing so, the court did not follow the confusing array of state court cases and relied instead upon the plain meaning of the terms at issue to conclude Congress did not intend the term "coal" to include coalbed methane. *Southern Ute Indian Tribe*, 526 U.S. 865, 144 L. Ed. 2d 22, 119 S. Ct. 1719. While the issues raised by the deed in question in this case are not identical to those faced in Southern Ute Indian Tribe, the Supreme Court's reasoning is applicable and persuasive to determining the intent of the parties herein.

The Supreme Court looked to dictionary definitions which defined coal as a solid fuel resource and methane as a distinctly separate substance. * * * The Supreme Court also deemed it important that ... CBM was considered a dangerous waste product which escaped from coal as the coal was mined and this was confirmed by the fact that coal companies venting the gas to prevent its accumulation in the mines made no attempt to capture or preserve it. The more gas that escaped from the coal once it was brought to the surface, the better it was for the mining companies because it decreased the risk of a dangerous gas buildup during transport and storage. * * *

At bottom, our role is to give effect to the general intent of the parties to the conveyance with regard to the exploitation of the mineral resources. Rather than following some rigid rule of law, we believe this issue should be governed by the facts and circumstances surrounding the execution of this warranty deed. * * *

In the case before us, we know the purpose of the mining company's purchase of the property was to allow the development of a surface coal mining operation. On the other hand, the landowners were fully aware that their property had value for its gas development as they had previously leased their oil and gas interest and had received the benefit of royalty payments. Their purpose in executing the warranty deed was to realize additional value from the property through the sale of the surface and their limited coal rights. The general intent which can logically be ascribed to these parties is that the landowners would retain any oil and gas found within the property and the coal operator would be able to fully exploit the coal resource. Each of the parties involved in this situation—the landowners, the original gas lessee, the coalbed methane operator, and the coal owner—operated consistently with this intent. The landowners, acting as the owner of the gas resource, leased all the right to produce oil and gas on the property with no distinction as to depth or source of the gas. The original oil and gas lessee proceeded to drill and produce, without distinction as to depth or source, all oil and gas found in the conventional manner. Twenty years later, when coalbed methane production became commercially feasible, the coalbed methane operator obtained an assignment of the oil and gas lease from the surface to 1,000 feet beneath the surface, under the obvious assumption that the coalbed methane was covered by the lease. And, for over twenty years, the coal owner operated its surface mine, venting whatever gas existed within the coal as it was mined, without objection or interference. To conclude that the landowners intended to separate the coalbed methane and convey it along with their outstanding royalty interest through the language of "all coal and minerals commingled with [the] coal" is simply not plausible.

*   *   *

While we recognize that separate ownership of coal and coalbed methane may result in conflicts, we agree with the United States Supreme Court when it noted "that is not the issue before us, however. The question is one of ownership, not of damage or injury," Southern Ute Indian Tribe, 526 U.S. at 879. ... Conflicts between owners of different mineral estates are relatively common in the history of mineral development and are typically resolved through normal business negotiation and, if necessary, litigation. The surface use licenses and agreements for coalbed methane entered into between RAG and Hi–Pro clearly demonstrate that fact. In exchange for access and other mutually beneficial promises, Hi–Pro agreed to numerous steps to avoid interference with RAG's mining operation and to subordinate its rights to RAG's. In addition, Hi–Pro agreed RAG would not be liable for damages or loss of production on adjacent lands operated by Hi–Pro as a result of RAG's mining operations. While the terms of this agreement were no doubt dependent on the respective negotiating positions of the parties, it demonstrates the potential for accommodation and the improbability of negative impacts on the development of either resource from different ownerships of coal and coalbed methane. In addition, the potential for conflicts between oil and gas development and coal mining exists in this situation irrespective of whether the gas owner also owns the coalbed methane as gas produced by conventional methods is separately owned. * * *

On the basis of the unambiguous language of the deed and the surrounding facts and circumstances, we conclude the parties generally intended the coal to be conveyed and the gas, wherever it may be located within the property, to be reserved to the landowners. * * *

Notes and Questions

1. Does *Newman* stand for the proposition that grants of coal *never* include associated coalbed methane? In a subsequent case, Caballo Coal Co. v. Fidelity Exploration & Production Co., 2004 WY 6, 84 P.3d 311 (Wyo. 2004), the court concluded that the owner of the coal also owned the coal-bed methane. The difference in this case was the language of the deed granting the rights to the coal, which expressly included "all other minerals, metallic or nonmetallic, contained in or associated with the deposits of coal conveyed hereby or which may be mined or produced with said coal, subject to the reserved royalty hereinafter provided." *Id.* at 313.

2. Coalbed methane has generated controversy throughout the Rocky Mountain West. For discussion of residents' concerns about environmental effects (in particular, groundwater contamination), excessive water usage, economic potential, and related issues, see Ed Kemmick, *Rural Residents Split over Coalbed Methane*, High Country News, June 13, 2005; Mark Matthews, *A Green Light for Methane Development*, High Country News, Feb. 3, 2003; Hal Clifford, *Montana gets a Crash Course in Methane*, High Country News, Nov. 5, 2001.

3. Geothermal

Unlike oil and gas, coal, or oil shale, the geothermal resource is not obviously a mineral. Physically, it is water, usually containing high salinity brines. Because it is high-temperature hot water or steam, when a geothermal reservoir occurs near the surface, its heat can be used to produce electricity. In light of its hybrid water-mineral nature, as well as its value as an energy fuel, questions arise about who owns the geothermal resource, and what regulatory regimes properly apply to it.

In Focus:

"WATER THAT IS NOT WATER"
Owen Oplin and A. Dan Tarlock
XIII Land & Water L.Rev. 391 (1978)

Geothermal energy is energy derived from heat beneath the earth's surface. Sub-surface temperatures are primarily controlled by the conductive flow of heat through solid rocks, the convective flow in circulating fluids, and by mass transfer in magma. "Where conduction is dominant, temperatures increase continuously with depth, but not at a constant gradient. The important interrelations are those between thermal gradient, heat flow, and thermal conductivity.... " At the present time we are unable to exploit commercially the heat produced by the thermal gradient. Instead, commercial interest centers on the exploitation of hydrothermal convective systems, geothermal anomalies. * * *

According to the United States Geological Survey, there are three known vapor-dominated fields with commercial potential in the United States, but there are many potential liquid-dominated fields. The Geysers in Northern California is already in commercial production and is thought to have a potential of 1000–2000 megawatts [one to two times the amount of electricity produced by one of the country's larger fossil-fuel fired power plants]. The other two potential steam fields are located in Yellowstone and Mount Lassen Volcanic National Parks. Geothermal leasing is prohibited in national parks so liquid-dominated systems will be the source of commercial geothermal production in the foreseeable future. * * *

* * * Prior to the passage of federal and state legislation there was great uncertainty as to the proper legal classification of geothermal resources, and it was argued that this uncertainty impeded their development. When the federal government and the states turned to the problem of encouraging and regulating geothermal development, most legislation followed either the mineral or water model, although some states classified geothermal resources as *sui generis* to no particular end. Most federal and state geothermal legislation was enacted between 1967 and 1975. * * *

The federal government and most of the states define geothermal resources but not in a manner designed to integrate them into the property rights regimes of other resources. Rather, geothermal resources have been defined almost exclusively for the purposes of assigning them to an existing regulatory regime to provide a definition of a leasable resource. * * *

Since 1970, the acquisition of property rights in geothermal resources on public lands has been pursuant to the Geothermal Steam Act of 1970. 30 U.S.C.A. §§ 1101–1126. This 1970 Act treats the geothermal resource like a leasable mineral, subject to management by the Interior Department. A federal geothermal lease is immunized from a state's exercise of eminent domain. Grace Geothermal Corp. v. Northern Cal. Power Agency, 619 F.Supp. 964, *aff'd* 770 F.2d 170 (D.C.Cal. 1985). The Act allows holders of pre-existing mineral claims of leases to convert their federal property interest into a geothermal lease. *See* Crownite Corp. v. Watt, 752 F.2d 1500 (9th Cir. 1985). Congress amended the 1970 Act in 1988 to permit geothermal leaseholders to obtain lease extensions of up to 10 years, upon proof that the lessee had made a bona fide effort to develop the lease. Pub.L. No. 100–443.

GEOTHERMAL POWER STATION

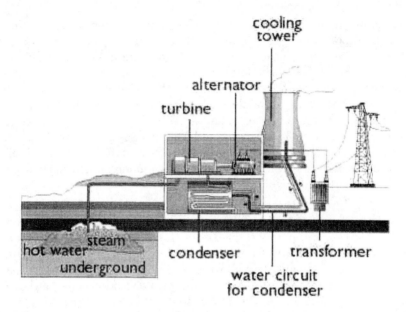

Does the exploration phase of a federal geothermal leasing program not constitute a "major federal action" triggering NEPA? Sierra Club v. Hathaway, 579 F.2d 1162 (9th Cir. 1978) (no). The Hawaii Geothermal Project, which contemplates private construction of a 500 megawatt electric power plant, was deemed to be a major federal action for purposes of NEPA, as 80 percent of the project's funding was federal. Blue Ocean Preservation Soc. v. Watkins, 754 F.Supp. 1450 (D.Hawaii 1991).

E. The Law of Saleable, Common Variety Minerals

As a general rule, ordinary and commonly occurring minerals such as cinders, clay, sand, gravel, limestone, and pumice are not locatable "hard rock" minerals under the 1872 Mining Law. Instead, these "common varieties" are subject to outright *sale* by the federal government under the Materials Act of 1947, 30 U.S.C.A. § 601. Later, the Common Varieties Act of 1955, 30 U.S.C.A. § 611, amended the 1947 Materials Act by prohibiting the future "location" of common varieties. Together, the Materials and Common Varieties Acts establish that nonmetallic minerals of widespread occurrence can only be purchased from the United States, with limited exceptions. Among those exceptions, under the Building Stone Act of 1982, 30 U.S.C.A. § 161, lands chiefly valuable for building stone may be subject to location under the 1872 Mining Law; so, too, are common variety minerals that have such "distinct and special" value as to make them uncommon. *See* McClarty v. Secretary of Interior, 408 F.2d 907 (9th Cir. 1969). For other "common varieties" subject to sale under the Materials and Common Varieties Acts, the sale applies only to the minerals themselves and not to the surface lands.

Sales of common variety minerals do not limit the right of the United States to use the surface, and to issue permits and licenses that do not interfere with the purchaser's production of minerals.

1. The Materials Act and Common Varieties Act

The Materials Act authorizes the Interior Department to sell common mineral materials from the "public lands of the United States." Disposals may be made from some withdrawn lands, 30 U.S.C.A. § 601, but not national parks, monuments, or Indian lands.

The Materials and Common Varieties Acts apply only to common variety minerals that were not previously disposed of by the federal government pursuant to the 1872 Mining Law or some land disposal statute. Some of the land disposal statutes, however, expressly or implicitly reserved to the federal government ownership of certain minerals. For example, in Watt v. Western Nuclear, Inc., 462 U.S. 36, 103 S.Ct. 2218, 76 L.Ed.2d 400 (1983), the Supreme Court held that Congress, in the Stock Raising Homestead Act (SRHA) of 1916, had reserved to the federal government ownership of gravel found on lands subject to homesteading. Because homesteaders could not acquire rights to the gravel pursuant to the SRHA, that gravel was available for federal disposal by sale as a commonly occurring material under the Materials Act. Additionally, the 10th Circuit has held, in an unpublished opinion, that scoria (a form of volcanic cinder used in landscaping and as gas barbecue briquettes) is included in the mineral reservation to the United States under the SRHA. Hughes v. MWCA, 12 Fed.Appx. 875 (10th Cir. 2001). The New Mexico Supreme Court similarly has held that the SRHA reserved to the federal government ownership of caliche (small rocks, dust, soil, and sand deposited in carbonates and carried into the crevices and pores of rocks). Champlin Petroleum Co. v. Lyman, 103 N.M. 407, 708 P.2d 319 (1985).

Based on the Supreme Court's ruling in *Western Nuclear*, the BLM took the position that caliche was similarly included in the 1935 Taylor Grazing Acts reservation of "minerals." But in *Poverty Flats Land & Cattle Co. v. United States*, 788 F.2d 676 (10th Cir. 1986), the court interpreted *Western Nuclear* as including common materials within the term "minerals" only if they had been locatable prior to 1955 (the date of the Common Varieties Act). Accord Andrus v. Charlestone Stone Products Co., Inc., 436 U.S. 604, 98 S.Ct. 2002, 56 L.Ed.2d 570 (1978) (holding that for a substance to be a "mineral," it must be the type of valuable mineral that the 1872 Congress intended to make the basis of a valid locatable claim). Unlike gravel, caliche had not been considered a locatable mineral under the 1872 Mining Law. The 10th Circuit reasoned that because caliche was of "common occurrence generally and extensively," and because it had never been considered locatable, it therefore was not a mineral reserved to the United States by the Taylor Grazing Act, and it was not subject to the Materials Act.

The question of whether sand and gravel constitute "minerals" for purposes of a general mineral reservation has prompted much litigation. The question must be decided case by case, Bogle Farms, Inc. v. Baca, 122 N.M. 422, 925 P.2d 1184 (1996), in general, and courts look to the intent of Congress in determining the scope of the reservation.

2. *The Location System and Common Variety Minerals*

a. **Common Variety Minerals Found in Association with Locatable Minerals**

The ores of many hard rock minerals subject to location under the 1872 Mining Law appear in combination with common varieties of rock, stone, and gravel subject to sale under the Materials and Common Varieties Act. In such cases, conflicts may emerge between the location and sale systems. The 1955 Common Varieties Act provides that nothing in the Act "shall affect the validity of any mining location based upon discovery of some other mineral occurring in association with ... a [common variety] deposit." This provision is meant to ensure that mining locations based on a discovery of gold in sand or gravel will not be precluded by the coincidental presence of the common variety material.

The Materials Act, meanwhile, allows the owner of an unpatented mining claim to use common variety materials for legitimate mining purposes, both on and off the claim, without having to obtain an authorization or purchase the common variety minerals. 30 U.S.C.A. § 612(c). The unpatented claimant may thereby use materials like sand and gravel, but is not permitted to sell those minerals to others. The owner of a *patented* claim, by contrast, can use or sell any mineral materials occurring on the claim.

b. **Location of Pre–1955 Discoveries of Common Variety Materials**

The 1955 Common Varieties Act contains a savings clause protecting any valid claim of a common variety mineral located before the Act's effective date. 30 U.S.C. § 615. To establish a valid pre–1955 location of a common variety, miners must show a valid location, including, most importantly, the "discovery" of a valuable mineral deposit before 1955. The critical pre–1955 condition is whether, under the marketability test for discovery (established in the *Coleman* case, *supra*), the claimant can show that the claim could have been (or actually was) "extracted, removed, and marketed at a profit." For purposes of the 1955 Common Varieties Act, the marketability test is applied only as of the time of the discovery; present market conditions are not considered. Mendenhall v. United States, 735 F.2d 1371 (9th Cir. 1984); Bell v. U.S. Forest Service, 385 F.Supp. 1135 (N.D.Cal. 1974). If the location was valid because it was marketable at some point before 1955, it comes within the savings clause of the Common Varieties Act.

Courts have been strict in applying the marketability test to common varieties. In Dredge Corp. v. Conn, excerpted above at p. 941, that court held that there was no valid discovery of sand and gravel prior to 1955 because there was no evidence of pre–1955 sales, plus there was evidence that the supply of sand and gravel far exceeded local demand. *See also* Rawls v. United States, 566 F.2d 1373 (9th Cir. 1978) (holding that there was no discovery because the costs of extracting, processing, and transporting sandstone would have made it unprofitable to market before 1955).

c. Location of Post–1955 Discoveries of Common Variety Materials

The 1955 Common Varieties Act provides that its terms do not apply to "deposits of such [common varieties] which are valuable because the deposit has some property giving it distinct and special value." 30 U.S.C.A. § 611. Thus, some deposits of common variety minerals which ordinarily would be subject to sale under the Materials Act may, because of their "distinct and special value," be subject instead to location under the 1872 Mining Law. In United States v. Coleman, 390 U.S. 599, 88 S.Ct. 1327, 20 L.Ed.2d 170 (1968), the Supreme Court not only created the "present marketability" test for establishing the validity of a hard-rock mineral location it also observed that the 1872 Mining Law remains "entirely effective" with respect to building stone deposits, which because of their distinct and special value are outside the ambit of the 1955 Common Varieties Act. "Uncommon varieties" of building stone are subject to location not just under the 1872 Mining Law, but also under the 1892 Building Stone Act, 30 U.S.C. § 161.

The distinct and special value test is really a comparison test which asks: Is this resource, or this particular deposit of the resource, significantly different from other such resources or deposits? Federal and state courts and the Interior Department have posed this question in two different ways. First, does the material have such a unique quality that it can be *used* in ways for which similar materials may not? Alyeska Pipeline Service Co. v. Anderson, 629 P.2d 512 (Alaska 1981). Second, if the uses are the same, does the material have some unique quality which gives it an *economic advantage* in the marketplace over competing materials? An economic advantage can be demonstrated either by showing a higher price for the material in question or lower production costs and overhead, McClarty v. Secretary of the Interior, 408 F.2d 907 (9th Cir. 1969), but the advantage gained due to the proximity of a material deposit to the market does *not* convert a "common variety" into an "uncommon variety." So-called "uncommon varieties" meeting the distinct and special value test include: building stone with unique coloration; limestone suitable for use in the production of cement; clay used for filtering oils in refineries; and "glass" sand.

3. *Disposal of Salable Materials*

The Materials Act establishes three means by which the Interior Department can dispose of common variety materials: competitive sales;

noncompetitive sales; and free use permits. With certain exceptions, the Interior Secretary must sell the materials competitively "to the highest responsible qualified bidder after formal advertising." 30 U.S.C. § 602. The original term of a competitive materials sale contract may not exceed ten years. A purchaser who continues to extract the materials beyond the original ten-year term is trespassing and is liable for damages. Thus, what is sold in a competitive sale is not the entire deposit, but as much of the deposit as the purchaser can extract during the 10–year term of the sale.

The Materials Act permits noncompetitive negotiation of sales contracts between the purchaser and the United States when it is impractical to obtain competition in the sale of the materials. For both types of sale, the United States must receive adequate compensation for the materials, which has been interpreted to mean not less than the appraised fair market value. The only time common varieties may be removed without charge is when some governmental or nonprofit entity obtains a "free-use permit," which provides that the materials may not be resold or used for commercial or industrial purposes.

F. Split Estates

Land may be severed into surface and subsurface estates to create a split estate, where the surface rights and the mineral rights are owned by different parties.

The severance of the mineral estate from the surface estate is thought to promote the public's interest in the development of mineral wealth. * * * Splitting the mineral estate from the surface estate allows those with the financial wherewithal and expertise to develop the land's mineral wealth while allowing the surface owner to continue using his estate. Thus, in theory, the creation of split estates provides greater specialization efficiencies because the owners of the different estates can optimize the use of the property. In practice, however, the use of one estate can damage the usefulness of the other. Not surprisingly, there has been considerable litigation involving split estates and the problems they create for owners of the varied interests.

Andrew C. Mergen, *Surface Tension: The Problem of Federal/ Private Split Estate Lands*, 33 Land & Water L. Rev. 419, 421 (1998).

As for federal split estates, the United States may own either the mineral estate or the surface. Each type of split estate has a unique history and each raises unique legal issues.

1. *Federal Rights to Minerals Underlying State and Privately Owned Lands*

During most of the 19th century, Congress endeavored to exclude from disposition to private parties known mineral lands. Lands granted pursuant to the various homestead acts and railroad grants generally excluded from patent those areas containing minerals. It was impossible, however, to know precisely which lands contained minerals and which did not. If granted lands subsequently were found to be mineral in character, the courts held that the surface patentees owned the minerals. Union Pacific Land Resources Corp. v. Moench Inv. Co., Ltd., 696 F.2d 88 (10th Cir. 1982); Burke v. Southern Pacific Railroad Co., 234 U.S. 669, 34 S.Ct. 907, 58 L.Ed. 1527 (1914).

In order to correct this problem, most federal public land disposition statutes enacted in the 20th century expressly reserved ownership of subsurface minerals (including those not yet discovered) to the United States. Settlers who acquired patents to the surface land pursuant to these statutes were subject to the federal subsurface mineral estate. Federal statutes reserving mineral rights included the Coal Lands Act of 1909, 30 U.S.C.A. § 81 (reserving coal in subsequent agricultural patents), the Agricultural Entry Act of 1914, 30 U.S.C.A. § 121 (reserving oil and gas in subsequent agricultural patents), and the Stock–Raising Homestead Act of 1916, 43 U.S.C.A. § 291 (reserving "coal and other minerals"[i]), as well as various railroad land grant statutes. The Stock–Raising Homestead Act was the most widely used surface entry statute among those reserving mineral rights to the United States. The Taylor Grazing Act of 1934, 43 U.S.C.A. § 315g(c) (repealed in 1976), also broadly reserved "all minerals to the United States" from federal lands exchanged for private lands to consolidate BLM grazing districts. The method of mineral disposition depends upon the terms and language of the reservation, as well as the requirements of applicable federal mining statutes.

a. What Has Been Reserved?

A recurrent interpretive problem has been ascertaining the nature of the mineral reservation in federal disposition statutes. Courts have devoted considerable energy in construing land grants and rights-of-way to railroads, particularly to the Union–Pacific. Most cases have limited the extent of the interest granted the railroad. In United States v. Union Pacific Railroad Co., 353 U.S. 112, 77 S.Ct. 685, 1 L.Ed.2d 693 (1957), the Supreme Court considered the grant of a right-of-way containing this exception: "That all mineral lands shall be excepted from the operation of this act." Although conceding the exception to be "inept," the Court nevertheless construed it to be a mineral reservation under the railroad right-of-way. The Union Pacific right-of-way was limited further in Energy Transportation Systems, Inc. v. Union Pacific Railroad Co., 606 F.2d 934 (10th Cir. 1979), in which the court held that the grant of the right-of-way did not convey title to the non-mineral subsurface estate. Another ambiguous Union Pacific grant reserving "all coal and other minerals" was held to cover oil and gas. Amoco Production Co. v. Guild Trust, 636 F.2d 261 (10th Cir. 1980).

i. This ambiguous phrase has led to litigation over what "other minerals" were reserved by the federal government. Is water a "mineral"? *See* Andrus v. Charlestone Stone Products, 436 U.S. 604, 98 S.Ct. 2002, 56 L.Ed.2d 570 (1978)(no). What about "common varieties," like gravel? *See* Watt v. Western Nuclear, Inc., 462 U.S. 36, 103 S.Ct. 2218, 76 L.Ed.2d 400 (1983)(yes).

The courts have sought to conform to congressional intent when construing ambiguous mineral reservations in other federal land disposition statutes. For example, they have construed the phrase reserving "all the coal and other minerals" in the 1916 Stockraising Homestead Act to include: (1) geothermal resources (Rosette Inc. v. United States 277 F.3d 1222 (10th Cir. 2002); (2) caliche (Champlin Petroleum Co. v. Lyman, 103 N.M. 407, 708 P.2d 319 (N.M. 1985)); (3) gravel; and (4) scoria (Hughes v. MWCA, 12 Fed.Appx. 875 (10th Cir. 2001) (unpublished opinion); United States v. Hess, 194 F.3d 1164 (10th Cir. 1999)). In Watt v. Western Nuclear, 462 U.S. 36, 103 S.Ct. 2218, 76 L.Ed.2d 400 (1983), the Supreme Court reasoned that Congress had intended for gravel to be reserved because in 1916 gravel was considered a mineral. Congressional intent was similarly determinative in *BedRoc Limited, LLC v. United States*, 541 U.S. 176, 124 S.Ct. 1587, 158 L.Ed.2d 338 (2004), where the Court held that the mineral reservation in land patents issued pursuant to the Pittman Underground Water Act, 43 U.S.C.A. §§ 351–360 (repealed 1964), did not include sand and gravel. Because the Pittman Act, in contrast to the Stock–Raising Homestead Act, referred not to "coal and all other minerals" but to "*valuable* minerals" (emphasis added), and because sand and gravel were not considered "valuable" minerals in 1919, the Pittman Underground Water Act did not reserve them to the United States. Finally, in Aulston v. United States, 915 F.2d 584 (10th Cir. 1990), the 10th Circuit reviewed historical and legislative materials before concluding that carbon dioxide deposits were meant to be included within the meaning of "gas" reservation in the Agricultural Entry Act of 1914.

By contrast, when a federal disposition statute provides that the nature and extent of the mineral reservation is left to the complete discretion of the Interior Secretary, congressional intent is irrelevant. Such an unusual provision is found in the land exchange sections of the Taylor Grazing Act, 43 U.S.C.A. § 415g (repealed 1976). In construing reservations made under this provision, the courts look to administrative practice and judicial interpretations rather than legislative intent. *See, e.g.*, Poverty Flats Land & Cattle Co. v. United States, 788 F.2d 676 (10th Cir. 1986) (holding that caliche is not a "mineral" reserved under the Taylor Grazing Act).

b. Relations Between Mineral and Surface Estates

A mineral reservation severs the mineral from the surface estate. McCormick v. Union Pacific Resources Co., 14 P.3d 346 (Colo. 2000). The former typically is held by a locator or federal lessee, while the latter usually is owned by a patentee receiving title under a Federal disposition statute. After a mineral reservation, the surface estate is servient to the dominant mineral estate, as long as the United States may realize a proper return from the extraction of the minerals. Kinney-Coastal Oil Co. v. Kieffer, 277 U.S. 488, 48 S.Ct. 580, 72 L.Ed. 961 (1928). While permissible surface uses are governed by the terms of the statute authorizing surface entry, courts have favored the mineral estate, even when it damages the surface estate. In Kinney-Coastal, the Court held that federal mineral lessees could halt surface uses that were inconsistent with mining operations, and in Transwestern Pipeline Co. v. Kerr–McGee Corp., 492 F.2d 878 (10th Cir. 1974), mineral lessees were allowed to cause surface subsidence without liability. However, surface disruption cannot be "negligent or excessive," and it must be necessary and incidental to the extraction of minerals. Anthony v. Chevron USA, Inc., 284 F.3d 578 (5th Cir. 2002) (mineral estate owner not liable for damage to groundwater reserves belonging to owner of the surface estate in the absence of proof of causation); Gerrity Oil & Gas Corp. v. Magness, 946 P.2d 913 (Colo. 1997); Gilbertz v. United States, 808 F.2d 1374 (10th Cir. 1987).

Some states have enacted statues to address the issue of the mineral estate owner's liability for surface damage resulting from mining activities. Oklahoma, for example, has a Surface Damages Act, 52 Okl.St.Ann. §§ 318.2–318.9, which holds oil and gas companies strictly liable for the damages caused by the exercise of their right to enter and use the land to take oil and gas. Davis Oil Co. v. Cloud, 1986 Ok. 73, 766 P.2d 1347 (1986); Vastar Resources, Inc. v. Howard, 2002 Ok. App. 13, 38 P.3d 236 (2001).

In 1976, Congress ameliorated the potential for conflict in the Federal Land Policy and Management Act, 43 U.S.C.A. § 1719, which permits surface owners to apply for a complete patent to unite the surface and mineral estates. The mineral interest may be conveyed to the surface owner when there are no known minerals in the land, or when the mineral reservation interferes with non-mineral development of the land. 43 U.S.C.A. § 1719(b)(1). The surface owner must pay fair market value for any remaining reserved mineral interest.

2. *Private Rights to Minerals Underlying Federally Owned Lands*

Many categories of federal lands contain split estates where the federal government owns the surface but non-federal owners hold title to the underlying mineral estate. For example, about six million acres within the National Forest System contain non-federal mineral deposits in split estates. Lands managed by the Park Service, the BLM, and the Fish and Wildlife Service also include split estates. The Park Service and the Forest Service have experienced some of the most contentious issues related to the management of surface resources in the face of private development of the mineral estate.

The Fifth Circuit had an opportunity to explore the relationship between the Park Service, as owner of the surface estate, and the owner of a subsurface mineral estate in Dunn–McCampbell Royalty Interest, Inc. v. National Park Serv., 112 F.3d 1283 (5th Cir. 1997). The case involved Padre Island National Seashore, a 70–mile stretch of undeveloped beach on a barrier island in the Gulf of Mexico, just south of Corpus Christi, Texas. When it created the Seashore in 1962, Congress only acquired the surface estate, in large part because acquiring the underlying oil and gas reserves would have been cost prohibitive. In Dunn–McCampbell, the owner of the mineral estate challenged the Park Service's regulatory requirements for surface uses, arguing that: (1) Texas law, under which the mineral estate is dominant to the surface estate, precluded the Park Service from regulating mineral development; (2) the Park Service exceeded its constitutional and statutory authority in passing its "9B regulations," 36 C.F.R. Part 9.B, which require that mineral developers submit a plan of operations before extracting subsurface minerals; and (3) the 9B regulations were a Fifth Amendment taking. *Id.* at 1286. The court dismissed the lawsuit, concluding that the Park Service had taken no action that demanded immediate compliance, and thus Dunn–McCampbell's general claims of agency overreaching were insufficient to create a legal duty under the APA or the federal Mandamus Act. *Id.* at 1289. It added:

> In order for mandamus to issue, Dunn–McCampbell must demonstrate that a government officer owes the companies a legal duty that is a specific, ministerial act, devoid of the exercise of judgment or discretion. * * * Under this standard, Dunn–McCampbell arguably might challenge a Park Service denial of a proposed plan of operations. Dunn–McCampbell might even be able to challenge action that the Park Service took to block the companies' access to their mineral estate. We need not reach those questions here, however, since it is undisputed that neither of these events has occurred.

> *Id.* at 1288.

The Eighth Circuit grappled with similar issues in Duncan Energy Co. v. U.S. Forest Service, 50 F.3d 584 (8th Cir. 1995). Between 1984 and 1993, Meridian Oil, Inc. and its predecessor, owners of mineral rights underlying the Custer National Forest, explored for oil and gas within the Forest without incident. However, in 1993, after various delays in the approval of its surface plan of operations, Meridian's lessee, Duncan Oil, sent a letter to the Forest Service stating that it had an absolute right to access and drill the site and threatening to proceed with exploration if the Forest Service did not immediately approve its proposed route. Subsequently, Duncan went ahead with road construction and placed a drill rig on the site, over the Forest Service's written objection. *Id.* at 587. The Forest Service sought an injunction barring Duncan from further ground disturbance at the site without written authorization, but the district court allowed Duncan to proceed without an approved surface use plan. It believed that the United States had no authority to condition or restrict access to the minerals because, like Texas and many other states, in North Dakota, "the mineral estate is the dominant estate and ... the surface estate was therefore subservient to the development, mining, and extraction of the minerals." *Id.* The Eighth Circuit reversed:

> The only issue before us is the Forest Service's ability to regulate surface access to outstanding mineral rights. The Forest Service recognizes that it cannot prevent Duncan, as the owner of the domi-

nant mineral estate, from exploring for or developing its minerals. * * * The Forest Service argues that it is not prohibiting access to non-federal lands or diminishing Duncan's [valid existing] rights, but only regulating the use of the federal surface. * * * For these reasons, we are convinced that the Forest Service has the limited authority it seeks here; that is, the authority to determine the reasonable use of the federal surface. * * * If North Dakota law is read to allow developers unrestricted access after twenty days' notice and no injunctive relief for the surface owner, North Dakota law is inconsistent with the special use regulations. * * * Allowing unrestricted access ... would impede Congress' objective of protecting federal lands and abrogate a congressionally-declared program of national scope. If North Dakota law is read to allow a developer unrestricted access after twenty days' notice, North Dakota law is pre-empted....

Id. at 589, 591.

What constitutional and statutory provisions give the United States authority to regulate surface disturbances in National Forests or Parks? Do these provisions also give the United States authority to deny access to the mineral estate if, for example, road construction or drilling would destroy critical habitat for an endangered species? At what point might an otherwise reasonable delay become a de facto denial of a valid existing property right? The Eighth Circuit noted,

Duncan explains that it resorted to proceeding without Forest Service authorization because of the Forest Service's delay in processing its surface use plan. Implicit in our conclusion that the Forest Service is authorized to determine the reasonable use of the federal surface is our assumption that the Forest Service's inquiry must be reasonable, and thus, expeditious. * * * Counsel at oral argument represented that the Forest Service approval of a surface use plan usually takes about two months. We believe such a timeframe is consistent with the Forest Service's authority to determine the reasonable use of the federal surface and does not violate the mineral holder's dominant right to access and develop its mineral estate.

Id. at 591 n.8. Does this preclude the Forest Service from taking longer than two months to complete the requisite NEPA analyses or consult with federal or state wildlife agencies about impacts on endangered species?

IV. STATE MINING LAW ON STATE AND PRIVATE LANDS

Most mineral resources in the United States are extracted not from the federal public lands but from state and private owned lands. According to a 1992 U.S. General Accounting Office report, in 1990 only a third of the gold and a quarter of the silver extracted in the United States came from mines on federal public lands. U.S. General Accounting Office, *Mineral Resources: Value of Hardrock Minerals Extracted from and Remaining on Federal Lands,* GAO/RCED–92–192, 4 (Aug. 1992). Mines on state lands are not subject to federal location, leasing, or sales procedures, unless rights to minerals on or underlying lands once owned by the federal government have been expressly reserved to federal ownership.

State owned mining lands are subject to state mining laws, most of which turn out to be quite similar to the federal mining laws. State location requirements tend to be only slightly less liberal than federal law. Idaho's Mining Law, for example, provides miners with free entry to state lands for purposes of mineral exploration:

> All lands belonging to the state of Idaho in which the mineral deposits, excepting oil and gas and geothermal resources, are owned by the state, and which have not been located, leased or withdrawn in accordance with the terms of this chapter, are hereby declared to be free and open to casual exploration ... Idaho Code §§ 47–702, 47–703.

A. Permits

More commonly these days, states require miners to obtain a permit before exploring for valuable mineral deposits on state lands. *See, e.g.,* Arizona Revised Statutes § 27–251; Indiana Code § 14–35–2–1. But such permits are not difficult to obtain. Arizona's permit statute, for example, provides for permit denial under only five circumstances:

1. The application was not made in good faith.

2. Mining activities would not be the highest and best use of the trust lands.

3. The value and income potential of surrounding trust lands would be adversely affected.

4. The proposed operations would violate applicable state or federal law.

5. Mining activities will create a liability to the state greater than the income from the proposed operations. Ariz. Rev. Stat. § 27–251.B.

State permitting statutes typically impose fairly detailed location procedures, including posting of notice at the place of discovery, development work, boundary markings, and claim recordation with the county clerk.

In Practice:

   Indiana's permit application process for a coal mining leases is fairly typical:

INDIANA DEPARTMENT OF NATURAL RESOURCES, CITIZEN'S GUIDE TO COAL MINING AND RECLAMATION IN INDIANA
pp. 8–9 (Aug. 1998)

Permit applications from coal companies require information compiled and analyzed by professionals from various scientific communities before it can be accepted by the [Indiana Department of Natural Resources's (DNR)] Division of Reclamation [DOR].

Geologic information regarding the overburden (rock and soil) must be identified by a professional geologist who has met the State of Indiana certification standards.

All construction of structures must be designed by a registered professional engineer before submittal and then certified "built as designed" after construction is complete.

[L]aboratory analyses (listing of the contents) of rocks, coal, and water must be completed before permit submittal. * * *

Permit applicants must show that they have met adequate minimums of public liability insurance through certified insurance documents from companies licensed to insure in Indiana. * * *

All blasting operational plans submitted must be designed by an Indiana Certified Blasting licensee.

* * * Each permit application is subject to an opportunity for comments from the Indiana Division of Historic Preservation, Indiana Division of Fish and Wildlife, Indiana Division of Nature Preserves, County Agricultural Agents, Indiana Division of Forestry, U.S. Department of Fish and Wildlife, Indiana Department of Environmental Management, Indiana Bureau of Mines and Safety, Department of the Army (Corps of Engineers), U.S. Department of Labor, Mine Safety and Health Administration and the County Commissioners.

* * *

When an administratively complete permit application is pending for a surface or underground coal mining operation, the applicant publishes a public notice in a local newspaper. * * * This allows citizens the opportunity to request an informal conference or public hearing regarding the permit application. The DOR will accept a request for an informal conference only, in writing; in the letter, the citizen should explain how the requestors interests may be adversely affected by issuance of the permit and briefly summarize the issues to be raised at the conference. * * *

Following the publication of the notice that an application has been received, any interested party has the right to review the application and make written comment to the Division.* * * Written comments should be specific to the application and provide as much information as possible concerning the omissions, inaccurate representations, or other areas of concern that have been identified. All comments received are addressed during the technical review of the application. * * *

After the close of the public comment period, the Director will determine whether the application must be modified to achieve conformance with rules and law. A copy of the Director's letter of required permit application modifications is filed in the public library in the county where the proposed operation is located * * *

If an interested party feels that a concern has not been addressed sufficiently and that the approval or denial of an application has been inconsistent with the requirements of IC [Indiana Code section] 14–34, formal objections to the decision can be filed. These objections will be heard before an administrative law judge (ALJ) who, on the basis of the record before the Director, will render a recommended decision concerning the appropriateness of the decision to the Natural Resources Commission. Citizens may file written objections and provide oral testimony to the Commission, who will render the DNR's final order on the permit application.

Once a state issues a permit, does the permit create vested rights in the permittee? In 1999, a North Carolina court ruled that the State's Department of Environmental and Natural Resources (DENR) could, without compensation, revoke a permit mistakenly issued for a location within sight and hearing of the Appalachian Trail. Vested interests were not implicated, according to the court, because the statute under which the permit was issued (N.C. Gen. Stat. § 74) authorized permit revocation for "willful violation" of the Act. The court found that adverse impacts on a park, such as the Appalachian Trail, constituted a "violation" of the Act, and that the DENR's failure to remedy that "violation" would make the violation "willful." Thus, adverse impacts on park lands could justify either denying a permit in the first place or revoking a permit previously issued. Clark Stone Co. v. N.C. Department of Environment & Natural Resources, 164 N.C.App. 24, 594 S.E.2d 832 (2004). *See also* NBAC Corp. v. Town of Weare, 786 A.2d 867 (N.H. 2001) (upholding board of selectmen's legislative denial of a mining permit, based in part on its environmental impacts, after the would-be miner had already obtained a special exception from zoning ordinances for its gravel pit).

State mining laws are similar to federal law in excluding from location energy resources, such as oil, gas, and geothermal resources, as well as common varieties of minerals, like sand and gravel. For example, in Tanner Companies v. Arizona State Land Department, 142 Ariz. 183, 688 P.2d 1075 (1984), the court ruled clay was a "common" material, even if it was found in a selectively small area.

Apart from setting out procedures for acquiring private interests in state owned minerals, state law also addresses issues relating to mine operations on state and private lands. Many states have mine safety and inspection laws (United Mine Workers of America v. Miller, 170 W.Va. 177, 291 S.E.2d 673 (1982)); mineral severance taxes (Director of Taxation v. Kansas Krude Oil Reclaiming Co., 236 Kan. 450, 691 P.2d 1303 (1984)); laws regulating liability for injuries suffered by non-mining company employees on mined lands (see Johnson v. Sunshine Mining Co., 106 Idaho 866, 684 P.2d 268 (1984)); reclamation laws for restoring surface lands after mining activities end (Ginn v. Consolidation Coal Co., 107 Ill.App.3d 564, 63 Ill.Dec. 144, 437 N.E.2d 793 (1982); State v. Click, 102 Idaho 443, 631 P.2d 614 (1981); Woytek v. Benjamin Coal Co., 300 Pa.Super. 397, 446 A.2d 914 (1982)); and environmental protection regulations applicable to the mining operation (Goldring v. State Dept. of Environmental Regulation, 452 So.2d 968 (Fla.App. 1984)).

B. Leases

A leasing arrangement is common when the mineral owner (who may also own the overlying surface lands) has neither the economic resources nor the inclination to develop the mineral deposit. In such a case, the mineral owner typically enters into a lease agreement whereby the lessee-mining company is granted the exclusive right to remove and sell minerals, and the lessor-mineral owner receives rental payments and royalties on some percentage of the minerals mined and sold.

Mineral leases are often the subject of litigation. Issues include: (1) the duty of the lessee to proceed diligently to develop the lease (Bennett v. Hebener, 56 Or.App. 770, 643 P.2d 393 (1982)); (2) the conditions necessary for the lessee to be in default for failure to make rental payments on time (Lewis v. State, Department of Revenue, 207 Mont. 361, 675 P.2d 107 (1984); Weyerhauser Real Estate Co. v. Stoneway Concrete, Inc., 96 Wn.2d 558, 637 P.2d 647 (1981)); (3) the relative rights of the lessee and lessor to make reasonable use of the surface of the leased land (Weathers v. M.C. Lininger and Sons, 68 Or.App. 30, 682 P.2d 770 (1984); Mai v. Youtsey, 231 Kan. 419, 646 P.2d 475 (1982); (4) the assignability and interpretation of royalty interests (Cheyenne Min. v. Federal Resources Corp., 694 P.2d 65 (Wyo. 1985); Godley v. Kentucky Resources Corp., 640 F.2d 831 (6th Cir. 1981); and (5) lease interpretation (McAnelly v. Graves, 126 Ill.App.3d 528, 81 Ill.Dec. 677, 467 N.E.2d 377 (1984) (lease provision requiring lessor to refund to lessee a portion of advance royalty payment upon termination of the lease is covenant running with the land and binding on lessor's successors); Bentley v. Potter, 694 P.2d 617 (Utah 1984) (lease granting to lessee rights held by lessor are limited to such rights owned by the lessors in the leased premises); U.S. Smelting, Refining and Mining Co. v. Wigger, 684 P.2d 850 (Alaska 1984) (mining or gravel not contemplated by lease permitting mining of "gold and other precious metals")).-

Can the terms of a mineral lease impose greater reclamation obligations on the lessee than state law requires? In Woytek v. Benjamin Coal
Co., 300 Pa.Super. 397, 446 A.2d 914 (1982), a court ruled that compliance with state reclamation regulations did not insulate a mining company from an alleged breach of a leasing contract, which required more
extensive reclamation. However, in the infamous case of Peevyhouse v.
Garland Coal & Min. Co., 382 P.2d 109 (Okl. 1962), the Oklahoma
Supreme Court ruled that a mineral lessee did not have to perform land
reclamation as required by the lease because the cost of reclamation
would have exceeded the value of the land. That decision has been
widely criticized. *See, e.g.*, Daniel H. Cole and Peter Z. Grossman, *Principles of Law and Economics* 191–2 (2004).

C. Severance

Severance of the subsurface mineral estate from the surface estate
may be accomplished by a conveyance, reservation, or exception of the
underlying minerals. *See* Alford v. Krum, 671 S.W.2d 870 (Tex. 1984).
Can a possessor of the surface estate gain title to the mineral estate by
adverse possession? General Refractories Co. v. Raack, 674 S.W.2d 97
(Mo.App. 1984)(yes). Unlike a lease, where the mineral owner retains a
property interest in the minerals, a severance generally abolishes the
original owner's mineral rights. However, the original owner may
reserve a percentage of the mineral interest when selling the surface
rights and mineral interests to another party. *See* Peterson v. Hopkins,
210 Mont. 429, 684 P.2d 1061 (1984). The mineral owner may have to
compensate the surface owner for surface destruction. Moser v. U.S.
Steel Corp., 676 S.W.2d 99 (Tex. 1984). After a severance, the owner of
the mineral interest usually has no obligation to develop the minerals. A
frequently litigated question is determining what minerals have been
reserved by a deed severing the mineral estate from the surface estate.
See Spurlock v. Sante Fe Pac. R. Co., 143 Ariz. 469, 694 P.2d 299 (App.
1984) (holding that helium, nitrogen, and petrified wood were included
in a deed reservation of "minerals which may be found under or upon
said lands").

Some states, in an attempt to encourage mineral development (and
clear up confusion over ownership of the severed minerals), have passed
statutes extinguishing mineral interests that have been unused for a set
period of time, unless a statement of the mineral claim is filed in the
county recorder's office. An unused, unfiled mineral interest then reverts
to the owner of the interest out of which it was originally created.

TEXACO, INC. v. SHORT
Supreme Court of the United States, 1982.
454 U.S. 516, 102 S.Ct. 781, 70 L.Ed.2d 738

JUSTICE STEVENS delivered the opinion of the Court.

In 1971 the Indiana Legislature enacted a statute providing * * *
that a severed mineral interest that is not used for a period of 20 years

automatically lapses and reverts to the current surface owner of the property, unless the mineral owner files a statement of claim in the local county recorder's office. * * *

The statute does not require that any specific notice be given to a mineral owner prior to a statutory lapse of a mineral estate. The Act does set forth a procedure, however, by which a surface owner who has succeeded to the ownership of a mineral estate pursuant to the statute may give notice that the mineral interest has lapsed. * * *

Appellants raise several specific challenges to the constitutionality of the Mineral Lapse Act. Before addressing these arguments, however, it is appropriate to consider whether the State has the power to provide that property rights of this character shall be extinguished if their owners do not take the affirmative action required by the State. * * *

The State of Indiana has defined a severed mineral estate as a "vested property interest," entitled to "the same protection as are fee simple titles." Through its Dormant Mineral Interests Act, however, the State has declared that this property interest is of less than absolute duration; retention is conditioned on the performance of at least one of the actions required by the Act. We have no doubt that, just as a State may create a property interest that is entitled to constitutional protection, the State has the power to condition the permanent retention of that property right on the performance of reasonable conditions that indicate a present intention to retain the interest. * * *

Two of appellants' arguments may be answered quickly. Appellants contend that the Mineral Lapse Act takes private property without just compensation in violation of the Fourteenth Amendment; they also argue that the statute constitutes an impermissible impairment of contracts in violation of the Contract Clause. * * *

In ruling that private property may be deemed to be abandoned and to lapse upon the failure of its owner to take reasonable actions imposed by law, this Court has never required the State to compensate the owner for the consequences of his own neglect. We have concluded that the State may treat a mineral interest that has not been used for 20 years and for which no statement of claim has been filed as abandoned; it follows that, after abandonment, the former owner retains no interest for which he may claim compensation. It is the owner's failure to make any use of the property—and not the action of the State—that causes the lapse of the property right; there is no "taking" that requires compensation. The requirement that an owner of a property interest that has not been used for 20 years must come forward and file a current statement of claim is not itself a "taking."

Nor does the Mineral Lapse Act unconstitutionally impair the obligation of contracts. In the specific cases under review, the mineral owners did not execute the coal and oil leases in question until after the statutory lapse of their mineral rights. The statute cannot be said to impair a contract that did not exist at the time of its enactment. Appellants' right to enter such an agreement of course has been impaired by the statute; this right, however, is a property right and not a contract right. In any event, a mineral owner may safeguard any contractual obligations or rights by filing a statement of claim in the county recorder's office. Such a minimal "burden" on contractual obligations is not beyond the scope of permissible state action. * * *

Appellants' primary attack on the Dormant Mineral Interests Act is that it extinguished their property rights without adequate notice. In advancing this argument, appellants actually assert two quite different claims. First, appellants argue that the State of Indiana did not adequately notify them of the legal requirements of the new statute. Second, appellants argue that a mineral interest may not be extinguished unless the surface owner gives the mineral owner advance notice that the 20–year period of nonuse is about to expire. When these two arguments are considered separately, it is clear that neither has merit.

The first question raised is simply how a legislature must go about advising its citizens of actions that must be taken to avoid a valid rule of law that a mineral interest that has not been used for 20 years will be deemed to be abandoned. The answer to this question is no different from that posed for any legislative enactment affecting substantial rights. Generally, a legislature need do nothing more than enact and publish the law, and afford the citizenry a reasonable opportunity to familiarize itself with its terms and to comply. * * * It is well established that persons owning property within a State are charged with knowledge of relevant statutory provisions affecting the control or disposition of such property. * * *

The question then presented is whether, given that knowledge, appellants had a constitutional right to be advised—presumably by the surface owner—that their 20–year period of nonuse was about to expire.

* * * The Due Process Clause does not require a defendant to notify a potential plaintiff that a statute of limitations is about to run, although it certainly would preclude him from obtaining a declaratory judgment that his adversary's claim is barred without giving notice of that proceeding.

Appellants also rely on a series of cases that have required specific notice and an opportunity to be heard before a driver's license is suspended for failure to post security after an accident, before property is seized pursuant to a prejudgment replevin order, or before service is terminated by a public utility for failure to tender payment of amounts due. In each of those cases, however, the property interest was taken only after a specific determination that the deprivation was proper. In the instant case, the State of Indiana has enacted a rule of law uniformly affecting all citizens that establishes the circumstances in which a property interest will lapse through the inaction of its owner. None of the cases cited by appellants suggests that an individual must be given advance notice before such a rule of law may operate.

We have held that the State may impose on an owner of a mineral interest the burden of using that interest or filing a current statement of claim. We think it follows inexorably that the State may impose on him the lesser burden of keeping informed of the use or nonuse of his own property. We discern no procedural defect in this statute. * * *

Notes and Questions

1. An Illinois statute similar to Indiana's was found unconstitutional in Wilson v. Bishop, 82 Ill.2d 364, 412, 45 Ill.Dec. 171, 412 N.E.2d 522 (1980), for not providing the subsurface owner with sufficient notice of the forfeiture in violation of procedural due process. The U.S. Supreme Court's decision in *Texaco v. Short* presumably overturned the Illinois court's decision in *Wilson*.

2. The *Texaco v. Short* case has produced much critical comment. *Texaco v. Short: Dormant Minerals and Due Process—A Case for the Irrebuttable Presumption Doctrine?*, 60 DENVER L.J. 537 (1983); *Wilson v. Bishop and Texaco v. Short: Two Inadequate Analyses of Dormant Mineral Interest Statutes*, 1982 S.ILL. L.J. 533; *Constitutionality of Indiana's Dormant Mineral Interests Act: Texaco v. Short*, 14 U.TOL. L.REV. 197 (1982); *Dormant Mineral Acts and Texaco v. Short: Undermining the Taking Clause*, 32 AM.U. L.REV. 157 (1982).

3. If a grantor reserves "all ores and minerals," does the reservation include oil and gas? *See* Lee v. Frank, 313 N.W.2d 733 (N.D. 1981) (yes). If a conveyance of grazing lands reserves "all gas, casinghead gas, oil, and other minerals valuable as a source of petroleum in and under said lands," does the reservation include coal? *See* Lazy D Grazing Association v. Terry Land and Livestock Co., 641 F.2d 844 (10th Cir. 1981) (yes). *See also* Note, Proposal for the Construction of "Other Minerals" in Idaho, 18 IDAHO L.REV. 97 (1982).

4. A mineral owner removes underground mineral salt, leaving behind an underground cavern. The United States wishes to expand the size of the cavern to create an underground storage space for crude oil reserves. Who, as between the mineral owner and the surface owner, is entitled to just compensation for the federal government's construction of the underground storage cavern? In United States v. 43.42 Acres of Land, 520 F.Supp. 1042 (W.D. La. 1981), the court held that the mineral owner has no property rights in the subsurface strata containing the spaces within which the minerals were found. For a similar ruling, *see* Department of Transportation v. Goike, 220 Mich.App. 614, 560 N.W.2d 365 (1996).

5. Where there has been a severance of the surface and subsurface estates, under what circumstances may the owner of one of the estates acquire ownership rights to the other estate by adverse possession? *See* Burlington Northern v. Hall, 322 N.W.2d 233 (N.D. 1982); Walker v. Western Gas Co., 5 Ark.App. 226, 635 S.W.2d 1 (1982).

6. After severance, what rights and obligations does the mineral owner have with respect to the overlying surface land? May such rights and duties

be implied, or must they be articulated in the severance document? *See* Eastwood Lands, Inc. v. U.S. Steel Corp., 417 So.2d 164 (Ala. 1982); Western Energy Co. v. Genie Land Co., 195 Mont. 202, 635 P.2d 1297 (1981); Note, *Disturbing Surface Rights: What Does "Reasonably Necessary" Mean in West Virginia?*, 85 W.Va. L.Rev. 817 (1983).

V. ENVIRONMENTAL PROTECTION STATUTES

Hardrock mining is among the most environmentally harmful industries in the United States. According to the EPA's 2000 Toxic Release Inventory, hardrock mining, together with coal-burning power plants, were responsible for nearly two-thirds of all toxic releases. Four mining states—Nevada, Utah, Arizona, and Alaska—had the highest volume of toxic releases in the country. *See* John Heilprin, *EPA says biggest polluters are hard-rock mining companies and coal-burning power plants*, Associated Press, May 24, 2002.

A number of federal statutes designed to protect the environment have an impact on unpatented hardrock mining claims. The most important of these include the Wilderness Act, 16 U.S.C.A. §§ 1131–1136, the Antiquities Act, 16 U.S.C.A. §§ 431–433, the Resource Conservation and Recovery Act (regulating toxic substances disposal), 42 U.S.C.A. §§ 6901–6992k, The Comprehensive Environmental Response, Compensation, and Liability Act (CERCLA), 42 U.S.C. §§ 9601–9675, the Clean Air Act, 42 U.S.C.A. §§ 7401–7515, and the Clean Water Act, 33 U.S.C.A. §§ 1251–1387.

The scope of federal environmental authority over hardrock mining remains in question. To what extent, for example, does the Clean Water Act prevent "mountaintop removal," when the removed material affects the quality of "waters of the United States" in the valley below?

KENTUCKIANS FOR THE COMMONWEALTH, INC. v. RIVENBURGH

United States Court of Appeals, Fourth Circuit, 2003.

317 F.3d 425.

CIRCUIT JUDGE NIEMEYER delivered the opinion of the Court.

This appeal presents the issue of whether the U.S. Army Corps of Engineers has authority under the Clean Water Act and under its now-superseded 1977 regulation implementing the Act to issue permits for valley fills in connection with mountaintop coal mining. It does not present the question of whether mountaintop coal mining is useful, desirable, or wise.

Kentuckians for the Commonwealth, Inc., a nonprofit corporation formed to promote "social justice and quality of life for all Kentuckians," commenced this action for declaratory and injunctive relief to declare illegal the Corps' interpretation of the Clean Water Act and to require the Corps to revoke the permit that it issued to Martin County Coal Corporation under § 404 of the Act, authorizing Martin Coal to place excess overburden from one of its coal mining projects into 27 valleys in Martin County, Kentucky.

On cross-motions for summary judgment, the district court "found and concluded" that "fill material" as used in § 404 referred only to "material deposited for some beneficial primary purpose," not for waste disposal, and therefore that the Corps' "approval of waste disposal as fill material under § 404 [of the Clean Water Act] [was] ultra vires" and "beyond the authority" of the Corps. * * *

Because we conclude that the Corps' practice of issuing § 404 permits, including the permit to Martin Coal, to create valley fills with the spoil of mountaintop coal mining is not ultra vires under the Clean Water Act and that the injunction issued by the district court was overbroad, we reverse the court's declaratory judgment; we vacate its injunction ... and we remand for further proceedings not inconsistent with this opinion.

I

Martin County Coal Corporation ("Martin Coal"), having obtained a mining permit from the Commonwealth of Kentucky in November 1999 to undertake a surface mining project in Martin County, Kentucky, applied to the U.S. Army Corps of Engineers ("the Corps") for authorization under § 404 of the Clean Water Act and under the Corps' Nationwide Permit 21 ("NWP 21") "to construct hollow fills and sediment ponds in waters of the United States" in connection with the proposed mining project. On June 20, 2000, the Corps "authorized" Martin Coal's project, permitting it to place mining-operations "spoil" from "excess overburden" in 27 valleys, filling about 6.3 miles of streams. "Overburden" is the soil and rock that overlies a coal seam, and overburden that is excavated and removed is "spoil." In connection with surface mining operations in mountains where the mine operator must return the mountains to their approximate original contour, the spoil is placed temporarily in valleys while the coal is removed from the seam and then returned to the mining location. However, because spoil takes up more space than did the original overburden, all surface mining creates excess spoil that must be placed somewhere. The permit in this case authorized Martin Coal to create 27 valley fills with the excess spoil, which in turn would bury some 6.3 miles of streams at the heads of the valleys.

The Corps' exercise of authority under NWP 21 to permit the creation of valley fills in connection with mining operations was consistent with its past practices and with the understanding of the Corps and the EPA as to how the Clean Water Act divides responsibility for its administration. * * *

At the time that the Corps issued its authorization to Martin Coal in this case, it had already published notice, together with the EPA, of their intent to amend their regulations to resolve ambiguities in both agencies' regulatory definitions of "fill material" and to clarify the division of authority between the two agencies. As the Corps and the EPA stated in the public notice of the intended amendments, issued on April 20, 2000:

> With regard to proposed discharges of coal mining overburden, we believe that the placement of such material into waters of the U.S. has the effect of fill and therefore, should be regulated under CWA section 404. This approach is consistent with existing practice and the existing EPA definition of the term "fill material." In Appalachia in particular, such discharges typically result in the placement of rock and other material in the heads of valleys, with a sedimentation pond located downstream of this "valley fill." This has required authorization under CWA section 404 for the discharges of fill material into waters of the U.S., including the overburden and coal refuse, as well as the berms, or dams, associated with the sedimentation ponds. The effect of these discharges is to replace portions of a water body with dry land. Therefore, today's proposal makes clear that such material is to be regulated under CWA section 404.

65 Fed. Reg. 21,292, 21,295 (Apr. 20, 2000). This public notice also pointed out that the EPA would, in connection with coal mining activities, continue to regulate "effluent discharged into waters of the U.S. from sedimentation ponds," pursuant to § 402 of the Clean Water Act. *Id.* at 21,296.

In August 2001, Kentuckians for the Commonwealth, Inc. ("Kentuckians"), commenced this action against the Corps under the Administrative Procedure Act ("APA"), challenging the Corps' action in issuing the June 20, 2000 permit to Martin Coal to create 27 valley fills and to bury 6.3 miles of streams. * * * In support of their request for declaratory and injunctive relief, Kentuckians alleged that the Corps had violated § 404 of the Clean Water Act as well as its own regulations and had "acted in a manner that is arbitrary, capricious, an abuse of discretion, and otherwise contrary to law, in violation of the APA, 5 U.S.C. § 706(2)." Kentuckians asked the court to "declare that Defendants' June 20, 2000 decision granting authorization under NWP 21 to [Martin Coal] is contrary to Section 404 of the CWA and its implementing regulations ...," and to "issue an order requiring Defendants to revoke [Martin Coal's] authorization under NWP 21 or, in the alternative, to suspend that authorization pending completion of EPA's Section 404(c) proceeding and/or unless and until Defendants comply with their obligations herein under the APA, CWA, and NEPA [National Environmental Policy Act]." * * *

* * * Kentuckians argued that under the Clean Water Act and the Corps' regulations, excess overburden placed in the valleys, creating valley fills, was not "fill material" as used in § 404 of the Act. Kentuckians relied primarily on the Corps' 1977 regulation, 33 C.F.R. § 323.2(e) (2001), to argue that valley fills were not "fill material" as defined by the regulation but "waste" as excluded from the Corps' regulation. The

Corps' definition of "fill material" was narrower than the EPA's definition, which contained no exclusion for "waste." Kentuckians maintained, therefore, that valley fills created from coal mining activities could only be regulated under § 402 of the Clean Water Act as administered by the EPA, not under § 404 as administered by the Corps. * * *

On May 3, 2002, while the cross-motions for summary judgment were pending, the Corps and the EPA signed their final joint rule, clarifying the definition of "fill material" to make it both uniform and consistent with their prior practices. The "New Rule," 33 C.F.R. § 323.2 (2002), used an "effects-based" test, defining "fill material" in § 404 of the Act as any material placed in the waters of the United States that has "the effect of ... replacing any portion of a water of the United States with dry land or changing the bottom elevation." Id. § 323.2(e)(1). The New Rule went on to provide that examples of such fill subject to regulation by the Corps included "overburden from mining or other excavation activities," but it also stated that "trash or garbage" was not "fill material." Id. § 323.2(e)(2), (3).

A few days later, on May 8, 2002, the district court ruled on the pending cross-motions for summary judgment, concluding that the efforts of the Corps and the EPA, as well as their past applications of § 404, were inconsistent with the Clean Water Act. Kentuckians for the Commonwealth, Inc. v. Rivenburgh, 204 F. Supp. 2d 927 (S.D. W. Va. 2002). The court declared that "fill material" as used in § 404 of the Clean Water Act "refers to material deposited for some beneficial primary purpose: for construction work, infrastructure, improvement and development in waters of the United States, not waste material discharged solely to dispose of waste." Accordingly, the court declared that the Corps' "approval of a waste disposal as fill material under § 404 is ultra vires, that is, beyond the authority of either [the Corps or the EPA]." The court's order provided:

> the Court FINDS and CONCLUDES § 404 fills may not be permitted solely to dispose of waste. * * *

* * * [The court] issued a permanent injunction against the Corps prohibiting it from issuing "any further § 404 permits that have no primary purpose or use but the disposal of waste." As the court restated its order, it enjoined the issuance of "mountaintop removal overburden valley fill permits solely for waste disposal under § 404." The court did not, however, strike down the New Rule, as no party had challenged it. But it declared the New Rule to be ultra vires:

> These new agency definitions set forth in the final rule are fundamentally inconsistent with the CWA, its history, predecessor statutes, longstanding regulations, and companion statutes. Under the guise of regulatory harmony and consistency, the agencies have taken an ambiguous interpretation, that of the EPA, seized the unsupportable horn of the ambiguity, and now propose to make their original error and administrative practice the law. * * *

Pointedly, the [new] rule is intended to and does allow the massive filling of Appalachian streams with mine waste under auspices of the CWA. * * * The Court ... is aware of the immense political and economic pressures on the agencies to continue to approve mountaintop removal coal mining valley fills for waste disposal, and to give assurances that future legal challenges to the practice will fail. * * * [But] ... the purported rulemaking is ultra vires: it exceeds the agencies' statutory authority granted by the CWA.

* * *

On appeal ... the Corps contends (1) that it has jurisdiction under § 404(a) of the Clean Water Act to regulate as a discharge of "fill material" the disposal into the waters of the United States of excess spoil resulting from the process of surface coal mining, i.e., valley fills, and (2) that, in any event, the district court's injunction was overbroad in enjoining the issuance of any further § 404(a) permits throughout portions of Ohio, West Virginia, Kentucky, Virginia, and North Carolina, where most of the Nation's mountaintop coal mining is conducted. The Intervenors contend that the EPA and the Corps' interpretation of "fill material" under the Clean Water Act was a reasonable one and that the district court erred in substituting its own interpretation for that of the agencies authorized to implement the Act. * * *

II

* * *

It is well established that "injunctive relief should be no more burdensome to the defendant than necessary to provide complete relief to the plaintiffs." Califano v. Yamasaki, 442 U.S. 682, 702, 61 L. Ed. 2d 176, 99 S. Ct. 2545 (1979). We have explained further that "an injunction should be carefully addressed to the circumstances of the case." Virginia Soc'y for Human Life v. FEC, 263 F.3d 379, 393 (4th Cir. 2001). * * *

We conclude that the injunction that the district court issued was far broader than necessary to provide Kentuckians complete relief. The members of Kentuckians are entirely within the Commonwealth of Kentucky and its members alleged injury only in connection with the Martin Coal site for which the permit in this case issued. But, as the district court itself explained, the Huntington District covers portions of five states, and the permits for valley fills in connection with coal mining activities issued by the Huntington District in 2000 alone constituted 97% "of stream length affected by valley fills in the nation." The court acknowledged that "the injunction necessarily will have substantial national impact." * * *

Because we conclude that the injunction issued by the district court was broader in scope than that "necessary to provide complete relief to the plaintiff" and that the injunction did not carefully address only the circumstances of the case, we find it overbroad. Accordingly, we vacate the injunction issued by the district court.

III

The Corps and the Intervenors also contend that the district court erred as a matter of law in entering summary judgment (1) declaring that "§ 404 fills may not be permitted solely to dispose of waste" and that "approval of § 404 permits solely for waste disposal are contrary to law and ultra vires" and (2) supporting its injunction with that holding. * * *

To support its declaration that § 404 fills may not be permitted solely to dispose of waste, the court interpreted § 404 and the 1977 Regulation to have a consistent meaning. And to support its injunction, the court gratuitously addressed the New Rule, 33 C.F.R. § 323.2 (2002), stating:

> The agencies' attempt to legalize their long-standing illegal regulatory practice must fail. The practice is contrary to law, not because the agencies said so, although their longstanding regulations correctly forbade it. The regulators' practice is illegal because it is contrary to the spirit and the letter of the Clean Water Act.

Based on this conclusion, the district court prohibited the Corps from issuing future permits, even though they would be justified by the New Rule. * * *

Thus, we are fairly presented for review the district court's declaration that valley fills authorized by the Corps in its permit to Martin Coal are contrary to § 404 and to the 1977 Regulation, as the district court interpreted that rule. We are not presented with the question of whether the New Rule is inconsistent with § 404. Because the district court reached beyond the issues presented to it in deciding that issue, we vacate its ruling declaring the New Rule to be inconsistent with § 404 of the Clean Water Act.

The judgment of the district court, ... bring[s] us to the single question whether § 404 of the Clean Water Act, in providing that the Corps "may issue permits ... for the discharge of dredged or fill material into navigable waters," authorizes the Corps to issue permits for the creation of valley fills in connection with coal mining activities, when the valley fills serve no purpose other than to dispose of excess overburden from the mining activity. * * *

C

In this case the Corps ... notes that Congress did not define "fill material" and left that to the agencies charged with administering § 404. It concludes that the practice followed by it and by the EPA over the years is "a permissible one entitled to deference" under *Chevron*. It claims that the new dual-agency construction in the New Rule reflects the agencies' past practices and "falls easily within the most obvious reading of the term 'fill material,'" and is consistent with the statutory scheme and purposes of the Clean Water Act. * * *

Although Kentuckians agrees that "fill material" has not been defined in the Clean Water Act, it argues that Congress' intent is clear from the context of the Clean Water Act and that Congress did not mean for any provision of the Act to permit the Corps to "evade the water quality standards" mandated by the Act. Kentuckians asserts that to construe "fill material" in any way other than that given by the district court would violate the clear intent of the Clean Water Act "to restore and maintain the chemical, physical and biological integrity of the nation's waters." 33 U.S.C. § 1251(a). Kentuckians contends alternatively that even if the Act is ambiguous, the Corps' interpretation is unreasonable and impermissible because "evasion of a statute's core mandate and purpose can scarcely be considered a 'reasonable' interpretation." Finally, Kentuckians asserts that the Corps' interpretation is internally inconsistent because the Corps' construction gives it authority over "mining waste, but excludes trash and garbage." It argues that such a construction produces an absurd result because the burial of a stream by mining waste is "much more devastating" than degradation of water by trash or garbage.

As with any issue of statutory interpretation, we begin with the language of the statute. If congressional intent is clear from application of "traditional tools of statutory construction," Brown & Williamson Tobacco Corp. v. FDA, 153 F.3d 155, 161 (4th Cir. 1998), aff'd, 529 U.S. 120, 146 L. Ed. 2d 121, 120 S. Ct. 1291 (2000), "that is the end of the matter; for the court, as well as the agency, must give effect to the unambiguously expressed intent of Congress," Chevron, 467 U.S. at 842–43. If the statute is silent or ambiguous with respect to the specific issue, the question for the court is whether the agency's answer is based on a permissible construction of the statute. *Id.* at 843.

Because the Clean Water Act does not define "fill material," nor does it suggest on its face the limitation of "fill material" found by the district court, the statute is silent on the issue before us, and such silence "normally creates ambiguity. It does not resolve it." Barnhart v. Walton, 535 U.S. 212, 122 S. Ct. 1265, 1270, 152 L. Ed. 2d 330 (2002). ...

The district court concluded, however, that its facial interpretation— that a permit issued under § 404 can only authorize the discharge of fill material into navigable waters "for some beneficial primary purpose ... not waste material discharged solely to dispose of waste"—was supported by § 404(f)(2) of the Clean Water Act, by the Act's succession to the Rivers and Harbors Act, and by the Act's relation to the Surface Mining Control and Reclamation Act ("SMCRA"). We examine each of these to determine whether any unambiguously indicates a clear congressional intent with respect to the definition of "fill material" as used in § 404(a).

Explaining its reliance on § 404(f)(2) of the Act, the court stated:

> While the specific term "fill material" is not defined by statute, the CWA is not silent about the types of fills requiring § 404 permits.

> See ... 33 U.S.C. § 1344(f)(2) (fills "incidental to any activity having as its purpose bringing an area of the navigable waters into a use to which it was not previously subject" require permits). * * *

A closer examination of § 404(f)(2), however, does not provide evidence of clear intent that "fill material" means only "material deposited for some beneficial primary purpose." This is because § 404(f)(2) does not define or limit "fill material." Rather, it serves only as a narrow restoration of permit coverage to the list of discharges exempted from permit coverage in § 404(f)(1), and the list of discharges in § 404(f)(1) is a short list of exceptions to the broad range of discharges covered by the term "fill material" in § 404(a). Thus, § 404(f)(2) is no more than a single exception to the list of exceptions to the broad coverage of § 404(a). At most, the exception of § 404(f)(2) to the exceptions provided in § 404(f)(1) describes one possible circumstance in which a permit is required, but it does not limit the breadth of discharges subject to permit authority in § 404(a).

The district court also relied on the Clean Water Act's succession to the Rivers and Harbors Act to derive a clear congressional intent to enact the beneficial-primary-purpose meaning of "fill material." The district court concluded that Congress intended that § 404 of the Clean Water Act would carry forward only the Corps' authority under § 10 of the River and Harbors Act, 33 U.S.C. § 403, and that § 402 of the Clean Water Act would carry forward the activities previously covered by § 13 of the Rivers and Harbors Act, often referred to as the Refuse Act, 33 U.S.C. § 407. The court concluded that these two provisions of the Rivers and Harbors Act bifurcated the regulation of activities, with § 10 of the Rivers and Harbors Act regulating only the construction of beneficial projects and § 13 regulating all waste disposal other than dredged spoil. The court concluded that §§ 402 and 404 of the Clean Water Act "perpetuated that longstanding distinction." While the court may have been correct that § 10 of the Rivers and Harbors Act was one source of § 404 of the Clean Water Act, it erred in concluding that § 10 regulated only beneficial fills, not waste. On its face, § 10 of the Rivers and Harbors Act is sufficiently broad to prohibit the discharge of any fill material, including waste, that would "alter or modify the course, location, condition, or capacity" of designated navigable waters. 33 U.S.C. § 403 (emphasis added). And the regulations adopted under § 10 implement regulation of any plans for "excavation or fill in navigable waters." 33 C.F.R. § 209.120(b)(1)(i)(b) (1973) (emphasis added). Moreover, the Supreme Court has recognized that § 10 of the Rivers and Harbors Act is not so limited as to exclude the deposit of industrial waste containing various solids which, upon settling out, reduced the depth of a river. United States v. Republic Steel Corp., 362 U.S. 482, 4 L. Ed. 2d 903, 80 S. Ct. 884 (1960); see also Sierra Club v. Andrus, 610 F.2d 581, 596–97 (9th Cir. 1979). The district court could not conclude, therefore, that even if § 404 of the Clean Water Act succeeded only § 10 of the Rivers and Harbors

Act, the provisions of § 10 would limit the definition of "fill material" in § 404 to "material deposited for some beneficial primary purpose."

Similarly, the Clean Water Act's relationship to SMCRA does not provide a clear intent that § 404's definition of "fill material" is limited to a beneficial use. While SMCRA does not define "fill material," its term "excess spoil material," 30 U.S.C. § 1265(b)(22), is defined in the SMCRA regulations as material placed "in a location other than the mined-out area." 30 C.F.R. § 701.5 and 816/817.71–.74. And, regardless of whether the fill has a beneficial primary purpose, SMCRA does not prohibit the discharge of surface coal mining excess spoil in waters of the United States. The district court's reference to SMCRA's provision of a "buffer zone," see 30 C.F.R. § 816.57, does not address the scope of the Corps' jurisdiction under the Clean Water Act to regulate all "fill material." Indeed, it is beyond dispute that SMCRA recognizes the possibility of placing excess spoil material in waters of the United States even though those materials do not have a beneficial purpose. Section 515(b)(22)(D) of SMCRA authorizes mine operators to place excess spoil material in "springs, natural water courses or wet weather seeps" so long as "lateral drains are constructed from the wet areas to the main underdrains in such a manner that filtration of the water into the spoil pile will be prevented." 30 U.S.C. § 1265(b)(22)(D). In addition, § 515(b)(24) requires surface mine operators to "minimize disturbances and adverse impacts of the operation on fish, wildlife, and related environmental values, and achieve enhancement of such resources where practicable," implying the placement of fill in the waters of the United States. 30 U.S.C. § 1265(b)(24). It is apparent that SMCRA anticipates the possibility that excess spoil material could and would be placed in waters of the United States, and this fact cannot be juxtaposed with § 404 of the Clean Water Act to provide a clear intent to limit the term "fill material" to material deposited for a beneficial primary purpose.

The district court also resorted to the legislative history of the Clean Water Act, but this history does not demonstrate a clear congressional intent to limit "fill material" to material deposited for a beneficial primary purpose. The court's canvass of statements by legislators concludes merely that the sole concern of Section 404 was dredged spoil, and "Section 404 was enacted to allow harbor dredging and dredged spoil disposal to continue expeditiously under the then-existing dredge and fill permit program administered by the Corps." The focus of the court's description of the legislative history is only on dredged spoil, not on the meaning of the additional term "fill material," on which the legislative history appears inconclusive. * * *

The district court's application of traditional tools of statutory construction thus could not leave it with a clear congressional intent that the undefined term "fill material" as used in § 404 means material deposited for a beneficial primary purpose. Indeed, the lack of clarity in the term itself prompted the agencies to undertake efforts to develop the term's meaning from the context of the permit programs and the interrelationship between § 402 permits and § 404 permits. While the statute authorizes the EPA to issue permits "for the discharge of any pollutant," defining "pollutant" to include "rock, sand, cellar dirt and industrial, municipal, and agricultural waste," 33 U.S.C. § 1362(6), the EPA is not authorized to issue a permit for "fill material," 33 U.S.C. § 1342(a)(1). Yet, when a permit is issued by the Corps under § 404 for the discharge of fill material that has a substantive adverse effect on municipal waters, fish, and wildlife, the EPA can veto the Corps' permit. 33 U.S.C. § 1344(c). The statute's silence on the definition of "fill material" thus gives rise to ambiguity, particularly when a broad definition of "fill material" is employed.

* * * [W]e conclude that Congress has not clearly spoken on the meaning of "fill material" and, in particular, has not clearly defined "fill material to be material deposited for some beneficial primary purpose." Accordingly, we proceed into *Chevron* step-two analysis to determine whether the Corps' action is based on a permissible construction of § 404. * * *

D

* * *

Because the agency action at issue in this case was taken at a time when the Corps' 1977 Regulation was in effect, the appropriate inquiry under Chevron step two is whether that regulation, as interpreted by the Corps, is based on a permissible reading of the Clean Water Act, and, if so, whether the agency acted consistently with the regulation in issuing a permit to Mountain Coal to create valley fills in connection with coal mining activities.

The Corps' 1977 Regulation defines "fill material" as "any material used for the primary purpose of replacing an aquatic area with dry land or of changing the bottom elevation of a [] waterbody." 33 C.F.R. § 323.2(e) (2001). The regulation provides further that "the term does not include any pollutant discharged into the water primarily to dispose of waste, as that activity is regulated under section 402 of the Clean Water Act." Id. At the time when this 1977 Regulation was promulgated, the Corps, explaining the "waste" exclusion, stated that in its experience:

> several industrial and municipal discharges of solid waste materials have been brought to our attention which technically fit within our definition of "fill material" but which are intended to be regulated under the NPDES program [i.e., the EPA's program created under § 402]. These include the disposal of waste materials such as sludge, garbage, trash, and debris in water. * * * The Corps and the Environmental Protection Agency feel that the initial decision relating to this type of discharge should be through the NPDES program.

42 Fed. Reg. 37,122, 37,130 (July 19, 1977).

To demonstrate that the Corps' understanding of its authority to issue permits for valley fills was based on a longstanding division of authority between the Corps and the EPA that reflected the interpretations of both agencies with regard to their respective regulatory authority under the Clean Water Act, the Corps submitted to the district court over 120 pages of correspondence with the EPA and with regulated parties addressing valley fill permits issued under Section 404. * * *

In short, the evidence submitted to the district court revealed a longstanding and consistent division of authority between the Corps and the EPA with regard to the issuance of permits under CWA Section 402 and CWA Section 404.

* * * The Corps and the EPA recognized that some courts had interpreted the Corps' regulation to impose a primary-purpose test applied without regard to the traditional division of authority between the Corps and the EPA, and that the ambiguities of this test had caused confusion. As one specific example of this confusion, the Corps and the EPA pointed to dicta in an opinion issued by the district court in an earlier valley-fill case in which the district court determined that "the Corps lacked authority to regulate under CWA section 404 the placement into waters of the U.S. of rock, sand, and earth overburden from coal surface mining operations, because the 'primary purpose' of the discharge was waste disposal." Id. at 21,295. Disclaiming any interpretation of the Corps' 1977 Regulation that would strip the Corps of authority to issue § 404 permits for valley fills, the Corps and the EPA described what they understood the appropriate division of labor to be:

> The section 402 program is focused on (although not limited to) discharges such as wastewater discharges from industrial operations and sewage treatment plants, stormwater and the like.... Pollutant discharges are controlled under the section 402 program principally through the imposition of effluent limitations, which are restrictions on the "quantities, rates, and concentrations of chemical, physical, biological and other constituents which are discharged from point sources into navigable waters".... There are no statutory or regulatory provisions under the section 402 program designed to address discharges that convert waters of the U.S. to dry land. * * *
>
> Section 404 focuses exclusively on two materials: dredged material and fill material. The term "fill material" clearly contemplates material that fills in a water body, and thereby converts it to dry land or changes the bottom elevation. Fill material differs fundamentally from the types of pollutants covered by section 402 because the principal environmental concern is the loss of a portion of the water body itself. For this reason, the section 404 permitting process focuses on different considerations than the section 402 permitting program.

Id. at 21,293.

This contemporaneous explanation by the two agencies charged with the responsibility of administering the Clean Water Act provides a rational interpretation of the 1977 Regulation that is neither plainly erroneous nor inconsistent with the text of the regulation. The 1977 Regulation seeks to divide the statutory responsibilities between the agencies charged with different responsibilities by defining "fill material" that is subject to regulation by the Corps and "waste" that is subject to regulation by the EPA through the administration of effluent limitations. Moreover, the resolution among agencies of the line dividing their responsibilities is just the type of agency action to which the courts must defer. * * *

We next determine whether the 1977 Regulation itself, as construed by both the Corps and the EPA, was also a permissible reading of the Clean Water Act.

* * * [T]he Clean Water Act prohibits discharges of pollutants into the waters of the United States, except in compliance with a permit issued by one of the permit regimes established by the Act. 33 U.S.C. § 1311 (a). Two principal regimes are created in §§ 402 and 404 of the Act. Section 402 creates a permit program under the National Pollutant Discharge Elimination System, a combination of State and EPA regulatory activities that is administered by the EPA. Section 404 creates a permit program administered by the Corps, authorizing the Corps to issue permits only in connection with the "discharge of dredged or fill material into the navigable waters at specified disposal sites." 33 U.S.C. § 1344(a). The two sections are linked by cross-references, exclusions, and vetoes. Section 402 authorizes the EPA to issue permits for the discharge of any pollutant or combination of pollutants, except as provided in § 404. And § 404 in turn provides that the Corps may issue permits for the limited discharges relating to dredged or fill material, providing that the Corps' permits are always subject to the veto power of the EPA when the dredged or fill material would have "an unacceptable adverse effect on municipal water supplies, shellfish beds and fishery areas ... wildlife, or recreational areas." 33 U.S.C. § 1344(c). * * *

Because the Clean Water Act clearly intended to divide functions between the Corps and the EPA based on the type of discharge involved, we conclude that it was consistent with the Act for the Corps to have adopted its 1977 Regulation defining "fill material" to be

> any material used for the primary purpose of replacing an aquatic area with dry land or of changing the bottom elevation of a [] water body. The term does not include any pollutant discharged into the water primarily to dispose of waste, as that activity is regulated under Section 402 of the Clean Water Act.

33 C.F.R. § 323.2(e) (2001). * * *

In sum, we conclude that the Corps' interpretation of "fill material" as used in § 404 of the Clean Water Act to mean all material that displaces water or changes the bottom elevation of a water body except for "waste"—meaning garbage, sewage, and effluent that could be regulated by ongoing effluent limitations as described in § 402—is a permissible construction of § 404. And as an interpretation of its 1977 Regulation, it is neither plainly erroneous nor inconsistent with the text of the regulation.

Notes and Questions

1. The court in *Kentuckians for the Commonwealth* ruled that the Army Corps of Engineers could lawfully issue "fill" permits under § 404 of the Clean Water Act for the overburden from mountaintop removal mining activities. As the court noted, however, EPA retains authority to veto § 404 permits, where necessary to protect the environment. Does that authority provide sufficient protection?

2. *Kentuckians for the Commonwealth* concerned mountaintop mining for coal. Is there any reason to believe that the case would have come out differently had the mountaintop removal operation been conducted as part of a gold mining operation? *See* Ovid Abrams, *Coeur Gets Final Permit for Kensington Gold Mine*, Metals Wk., July 4, 2005, at 2 (mining company received EPA and Corps permits to discharge tailings from its gold mine into Lower Slate Lake in the Tongass National Forest).

3. In addition to possible Clean Water Act regulation, mountaintop removal activities may be subject to state permitting requirements under SMCRA. For instance, West Virginia's SMCRA regulations require the Director of Environmental Protection to protect "buffer zones" around streams by preventing "valley fills" from mountaintop removal mining within 100 feet of an intermittent or perennial valley stream. *See* Bragg v. West Virginia Coal Ass'n, 248 F.3d 275, 287 (4th Cir.2001)(citing W.V.Stat.R. tit. 38 § 2–5.2). SMCRA's regulatory structure is explained in more detail in this chapter's section on coal mining.

4. Like the Clean Water Act, the Clean Air Act, 42 U.S.C.A. §§ 7401–7671q, has important implications for mining operations. In Alaska Department of Environmental Conservation v. EPA, 540 U.S. 461, 124 S.Ct. 983, 157 L.Ed.2d 967 (2004), the State of Alaska and Teck Cominco Alaska, Inc., operator of the Red Dog zinc mine, challenged EPA's supervisory authority over state implementation efforts in a "prevention-of-significant-deterioration" (PSD) air quality area of northwest Alaska. PSD areas are those which meet the EPA's air quality standards for certain "criteria" air pollutants, including nitrogen oxide (NOx), the pollutant at issue in this case. (In contrast, "non-attainment areas" do not meet air quality standards.) In a 5–4 decision, the Supreme Court upheld EPA's authority to override the state's selection of technology-based permitting requirements for new construction under Clean Air Act §§ 113(a)(5), 165 and 167, 42 U.S.C.A. §§ 7413, 7475, 7477. As a result, EPA's administrative orders to stop construction of new generators at the zinc mine, a major emitting facility, were upheld, even though Alaska had granted the facility operator a PSD permit. The Court agreed with the EPA that Alaska's issuance of the permit was arbitrary and capricious and failed to meet the Act's requirement that major sources meet the best available control technology (BACT). The

Act requires that BACT be "an emission limitation based on the maximum degree of reduction of each pollutant ... , which the permitting authority, on a case-by-case basis, taking into account energy, environmental, and economic impacts and other costs, determines is achievable for such [major emitting] facility through application of production processes and available methods, systems, and techniques." 42 U.S.C.A. § 7479(3). The State's decision to eliminate selective catalytic reduction (SCR) as BACT for the mine's new generators, and its selection of a less stringent technology (Low NOx), lacked evidentiary support. Although the State argued that SCR was not economically feasible for the facility, it failed to offer any concrete evidence on this point; instead, the State admitted that its primary objective was to support Cominco's project and its contributions to the region. 540 U.S. at 498.

5. Hazardous wastes from mining are also regulated by the Resource Conservation and Recovery Act (RCRA) and the Comprehensive Environmental Response, Compensation, and Liability Act (CERCLA or Superfund). RCRA prevents the disposal, storage, treatment, or transportation of hazardous wastes without a permit. 42 U.S.C.A. §§ 6923–6925. However, the statute provides certain exclusions for mining wastes, 42 U.S.C.A. § 6921(b)(3), and allows the EPA to modify the stringent regulatory requirements for treatment, storage, and disposal facilities to reflect the "special characteristics of such wastes ... and site-specific characteristics.... " 42 U.S.C.A. § 6925(x). CERCLA, on the other hand, imposes strict liability for clean-up costs on defendants who release hazardous substances (a broad term that includes hazardous wastes and many other substances) or own facilities where hazardous substances are released. 42 U.S.C.A. § 9607(a). For detailed treatment of these statutes and other environmental laws, see John F. Seymour, *Hardrock Mining and the Environment: Issues of Federal Enforcement and Liability*, 31 Ecology L.Q. 795 (2004).

6. The leading example of a federal criminal prosecution for violations of RCRA is United States v. Elias, 269 F.3d 1003 (9th Cir. 2001), cert. denied, 537 U.S. 812, 123 S.Ct. 72, 154 L.Ed.2d 14 (2002). The defendant, Allen Elias, owned Evergreen Resources, a fertilizer company in Idaho, where he used a large storage tank to contain the byproducts of a cyanide leaching process that he had patented. In 1996, Elias decided that the cyanide-laced mining sludge had to be cleaned out of the tank, and ordered four employees to enter the tank and wash the sludge out a valve opening. Despite their repeated requests, Elias failed to provide safety equipment for this task. Employee Scott Dominguez eventually collapsed while in the tank, due to severe respiratory distress from cyanide poisoning. He suffered irreversible brain damage. Elias was convicted of improperly disposing of hazardous waste without a permit and of knowingly placing others in imminent danger of death or serious bodily injury in violation of RCRA, 42 U.S.C.A. § 6928(d)-(e),

and was sentenced to 17 years in prison. *See* JOSEPH HILLDORFER AND ROBERT DUGONI, THE CYANIDE CANARY (Free Press 2004).

7. After CERCLA was enacted in 1980, EPA compiled an inventory of over 35,000 sites across the nation that had been contaminated by releases of hazardous substances. As of 2003, over 1,200 sites, considered the "worst of the worst" contaminated sites, were included on the National Priority List (NPL). The majority of sites listed on the NPL (around 70%) are old mining sites.

The Summitville Mine, situated in the San Juan Mountains at an elevation of 11,500 feet, surrounded by the Rio Grande National Forest, provides a good example of CERCLA liabilities and enforcement difficulties at mine sites. Mining began at the site in the 1800's. From 1986 to 1992, the mine was operated by Summitville Consolidated Mining Company, which had obtained a permit from the state of Colorado and posted a bond with the state's Division of Minerals and Geology. Summitville Co. mined, crushed and heaped gold-bearing ore on a gigantic pad, where a solution of sodium cyanide percolated down through the ore to leach gold from it. The EPA and the Colorado Department of Public Health and Environment became alarmed in 1990 when all aquatic life in the Alamosa River died downstream of the site. Acid mine drainage, characterized by high concentrations of heavy metals and low pH, along with cyanide and other hazardous substances had migrated from the site and caused a plume of pollution nearly twenty miles long. In 1992, both Summitville Co. and its parent, Galactic Resources, Inc., declared bankruptcy, pulled up stakes and abandoned the site. The EPA listed the Summitville Mine on the National Priorities List (NPL) in 1994. Even before listing, the EPA, in cooperation with the state of Colorado, began the long and expensive process of cleaning up the site and surrounding waterways. As of 2000, the heap-leach pad has been capped and largely neutralized, although some cyanide remains. Millions of tons of rock have been transported back up the mountain and dumped into the gigantic open pit mine to seal it off. Old drainage tunnels have been plugged to reduce the amounts of toxic pollution discharging into the river. Crushed limestone has been distributed in ditches and on exposed rock around the site to neutralize acids, and grass and sedge seed has been planted to slow run-off. Before all is said and done, total clean-up costs are estimated to run around $170 million. *See* Mark H. Hunter, *Colorado Considers a Mining Ban*, High Country News, June 19, 2000. The $4.5 million bond posted by Summitville Co. with the state of Colorado was just a drop in the bucket in terms of clean-up costs. Although the EPA and Colorado officials pursued Summitville's corporate officers with various enforcement actions, the government (and the taxpayer) paid the lion's share of clean-up costs. *See* Ray Ring, *Summitville: An Expensive Lesson*, High Country News, Jan. 19, 1998.

Websources:

Information about Mine Contamination and Reclamation

U.S. EPA, Abandoned Mine Lands, http://www.epa.gov/superfund/programs/aml/

U.S. EPA, CERCLIS Database–Summitville Mine, http://cfpub.epa.gov/supercpad/cursites/csitinfo.cfm?id=0801194

U.S. EPA Region 8, About the Summitville Mine, EPA ID#COD 983778432 (April 2003), http://www.epa.gov/Region8/superfund/sites/co/sville.html

BLM, Solid Minerals Group, http://www.blm.gov/nhp/300/wo320/index.html

BLM, Fluid Minerals, http://www.blm.gov/nhp/300/wo310/

Dept. of Interior, Office of Surface Mining, http://www.osmre.gov/

U.S. Corps of Engineers, http://www.usace.army.mil/

State Regulations

The 1872 Mining Law provides that mining claims are subject to state regulations that are not inconsistent with federal law. 30 U.S.C.A. § 22. The validity of local regulations depends on whether the regulation is an environmental regulation or a land use regulation, although this distinction rides a fine line. Reasonable environmental regulations imposed by states on mining activities on federal lands are not *per se* preempted by federal law, while land use regulations are. *See* California Coastal Commission v. Granite Rock Co., 480 U.S. 572, 107 S.Ct. 1419, 94 L.Ed.2d 577 (1987). In South Dakota Mining Association, Inc. v. Lawrence County, 155 F.3d 1005 (8th Cir. 1998), the court held that a county ordinance banning surface metal mining on federal public lands was preempted by federal law. The county argued that the regulation was an environmental regulation. However, the court found that surface metal mining was the only practical way to mine the valuable mineral deposits in the area and, as such, the regulation was a *de facto* ban on mining in that area. This conflicted with the goals of the 1872 Mining law of encouraging exploration and discovery of valuable mineral deposits located on federal lands.

Citizens' groups in several states have undertaken initiatives to ban the use of toxic substances in open-pit mining operations. A few years ago, the Montana legislature banned the use of cyanide in open-pit mining for gold or silver. Mt. St. § 82–4–390. The blanket prohibition was lifted, however, in a statutory amendment adopted in 2004. Colorado has considered a similar ban. *See* Mark H. Hunter, *Colorado Considers a*

Mining Ban, High Country News, June 19, 2000. Would a ban on the use of cyanide in mining on federal public lands be preempted by federal law? What if a state were to impose an extremely stringent and costly reclamation requirement that mandated the return of exhausted mining sites, including those on federal land, to "pristine" condition?

California adopted a provision in 2003 which requires backfilling and grading upon completion of hard rock mining operations. Cal. Pub. Res. Code § 2773.3. Although this type of reclamation has been required for coal strip mines for years, it will likely be far more costly to require it for open pit mines, where the proportion of waste rock to ore is much greater. Does federal law preempt the California regulation, as applied to mining operations on federal land? If the California law makes mining an unpatented, perfected mining claim economically infeasible, has there been a fifth amendment taking? In an interesting twist, Glamis Gold Ltd., whose proposal for a gold mine on BLM land is described in detail in Chapter 6.VI.B, *supra,* submitted a claim for arbitration under the North American Free Trade Agreement (NAFTA), alleging that California's requirement has resulted in an expropriation of its property and claiming $50 million in damages. As a Canadian corporation, Glamis is entitled to fair treatment and protection of its investments under NAFTA. Information about the case is available on the U.S. Department of State website, www.state.gov/s/l/c10986.htm.

Chapter 13

WATER

I. INTRODUCTION: THE ABC'S OF WATER AND WATER LAW

A river is more than an amenity, it is a treasure. It offers a necessity of life that must be rationed among those who have power over it.

Oliver Wendell Holmes

The importance of clean water can not be over-emphasized. Water is essential to the existence of life, and it has no substitute. The balance between human demands and the limited quantity of available water is becoming ever-more precarious as the global populations grows.

Water law strives to distribute the limited supply of water among competing uses and to ensure that a water supply will be available in the future. It is a vast and complex topic, justifying separate treatment in a full semester-long course. This chapter steps through the basics of water supply and water law in the United States. Sections II–IV explore the legal regimes governing surface water resources, while groundwater is covered in Section V. Sections VI and VII address the federal government's role in water management, focusing on both federal reserved water rights and environmental quality. The chapter concludes with a look at interstate water allocations in Section VIII.

A. Surface Water and Groundwater: Physical Characteristics

Water is a renewable natural resource. Although a new supply is furnished each year in the form of precipitation, the total volume of water on earth is essentially fixed; it is only the distribution of water that is constantly changing. Through the hydrological cycle, precipitation falls and acts as run off, increasing the flow in streams and rivers, or permeates the surface, replenishing underground reserves. Subsurface water recharges surface water, which evaporates, condensates and returns to the earth in the form of precipitation.

Picture of the water cycle

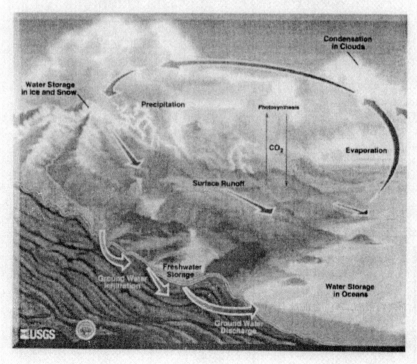

While groundwater and surface water are renewable and can be re-used, there is a chronic shortage of accessible water resources worldwide. The distribution of water is not evenly divided among populations, and precipitation is more abundant in some areas. Consumption patterns vary tremendously as well. Over the past 70 years, the global population has tripled, but water use has grown six-fold due to industrial development and increased irrigation.

In Practice:

Volume and Measurement

The total volume of water on earth is vast—326,000,000 cubic miles–but only .3% is usable by humans. Sources of water are broken down as follows:

- 97% in oceans
- 2% in glaciers
- .61% in ground water
- .009% in fresh water lakes
- .008% in inland seas
- .005% in soil moisture
- .001% in the atmosphere
- .0001% in rivers

Water usage is typically measured in gallons, cubic feet per second (cfs), or acre feet (AF). One AF can cover an acre with a foot of water, and it's a sufficient quantity to satisfy the annual domestic needs of a U.S. family of four.

Average domestic consumption per person per day

United States: 183 gallons Australia: 127 gallons

South Korea: 96 gallons France: 68 gallons

Brazil: 67 gallons Israel: 66 gallons

Mexico: 34 gallons Jordan: 25 gallons

Agricultural products: water consumption

- 1 bushel of corn: 4,000 gallons (1 corn plant consumes around 20 gallons)
- 1 bushel of wheat: 11,000 gallons (a 2 lb. loaf of bread requires about 1,000 gallons)
- 1 egg: 120 gallons

1. *Surface Water*

The contiguous United States receives an average of 30 inches of precipitation each year, and millions of acre-feet per day run off as surface flow into streams, rivers and oceans and seep into groundwater aquifers. Unlike other natural resources, water generally is not destroyed by use. Although its quality, quantity, and composition may be altered, multiple users may use water multiple times. In fact, one user's discharge often becomes a downstream user's supply. Despite the relative abundance of water, there is still not enough water to provide every user with adequate water upon demand, forcing water providers to become more creative in finding new supplies.

In Focus:

FUTURE MURKY FOR SEWAGE WATER
RESIDENTS RELUCTANT TO CONSIDER REUSE FOR TAPS,
BUT RECYCLING COMMON
Michael Booth
Denver Post, September 16, 2002, at A01

How close are metro-area residents to drinking treated sewage water as a solution to drought? Close, and yet so far. Denver is building plants to recycle millions of gallons of dirty water by cleaning it up enough to make it safe for golf courses, park lawns and nondrinkable industrial uses. Taking the next step—turning that 'reclaimed' water into sippable sewage—is a simple matter of technology: a few more filters here, a few more chemicals there.

San Diego has already tried it, and got laughed off the environmentally friendly Left Coast. Critics dubbed it 'Toilet to Tap', and the city water department would like to forget the whole thing. 'There's the 'yuck' factor,' San Diego water spokesman Kurt Kidman said. 'It became a public relations problem.' Denver Water has taken polls on the tainted question, and says two-thirds to three-fourths of the public says it is willing to try. But those answers could change, officials hasten to add. 'That was a hypothetical question,' Denver Water planner Ed Pokorney said. 'When you get down to actually doing it, who knows?' * * *

When portions of a new Denver reclamation plant go online in 2004 and 2011, irrigation and industry likely will use much of the reclaimed water. Recycling the water will help supply by freeing up clean water that can be sent to residential taps. But that also might be a good time to reconsider putting treated wastewater back into Denver's drinking—water system, Pokorney said. * * * Excuse Denver officials for being a bit gun-shy on the issue. Pokorney said he remembers a cartoon that ran during the San Diego debacle, one panel showing a dog drinking out of a toilet, the next panel showing the dog's owner crowding in to do the same. 'It got a little nasty,' Pokorney said. The reality, though, is that millions of Americans already drink water that used to be sewage.

Denver's water from the South Platte River includes treated wastewater from mountain communities such as Grant and Bailey. And for people downstream from Denver, 90 percent of the water in the South Platte River on some days came straight from the outflow at Denver's sewage treatment plant. Communities from eastern Colorado, down the Platte to the Missouri River and on to the Mississippi River, take the mix of new and 'used' water out of the stream and treat it for drinking. River watchers have estimated that every drop of South Platte water is used three times before it hits the Nebraska border.

Even if Denver someday decides to put cleaned wastewater back into its own drinking system, it may opt for 'indirect' reuse. Rather than taking treated wastewater and putting it straight into pipes, Denver could send it back uphill to city reservoirs to be diluted by snowmelt and other natural runoff. It would then go into the normal treatment plants producing drinking water. * * * Some water-quality experts say samples taken below sewage treatment plants show traces of pharmaceuticals, household chemicals and other contaminants. Utility officials respond that the extra step of turning treated water into drinkable water would remove any hazards. 'If you filter the water through enough money, we can meet any kind of standard,' said Jack Hoffbuhr of the American Water Works Association, a Colorado-based utility trade group. 'Whether or not you can convince the public it's drinking-water quality is another matter.'

Another possible middle ground for reclaimed water, sending it in segregated pipes straight to homeowners for use in toilet flushing and lawn watering, is extremely expensive. Since it involves snaking a second pipe throughout a community, it makes sense only in new housing developments close to a treatment plant. * * *

Water scarcity can largely be attributed to varied hydrological patterns and human influences. In one year, the Great Basin of the arid West may receive less than 4 inches of precipitation, while the northwest coastal areas may be saturated with over 200 inches. On average, precipitation east of the Mississippi River is 44 inches, while precipitation west of the Rocky Mountains is only 18. Yet humans continue to settle in arid areas where precipitation and the natural flow of surface water cannot fulfill the growing water needs. *See* Figures 1 & 2, below.

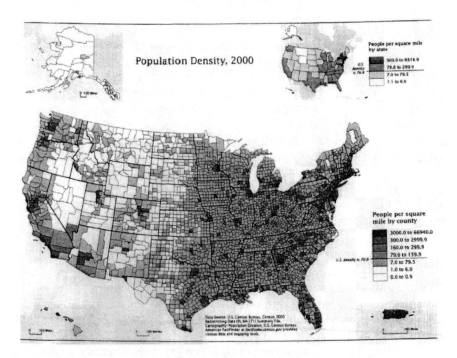

Figure 1: Population Density

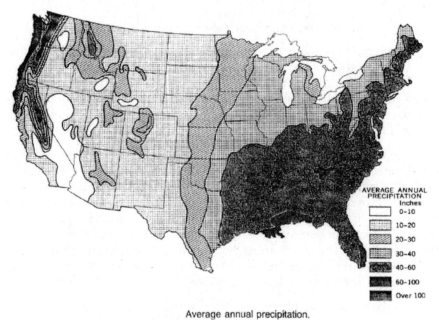

Average annual precipitation.

Figure 2: Precipitation

Competing uses also contribute to inadequate water availability. In addition to diminishing water supplies, the intensive competition for water has also resulted in pollution of both surface and groundwater.

2. *Groundwater*

Within the United States, surface streamflow provides the majority of the water used. Groundwater is also a significant resource; nearly 30 percent of the nation's water supply comes from groundwater. The volume of subsurface water is estimated to be greater than all surface water, including the total capacity of all lakes and reservoirs. Groundwater is renewable in the sense that it is recharged through precipitation, which eventually percolates through the earth's surface. Nevertheless, the extraction of groundwater often exceeds the pace of recharge. *See* ROBERT GLENNON, WATER FOLLIES: GROUNDWATER PUMPING AND THE FATE OF AMERICA'S FRESH WATERS (2002) (describing areas where groundwater "mining" has depleted surface water flows and caused an array of social and ecological problems).

B. Water Law Fundamentals

Water law developed primarily to allocate the finite supply of water among competing uses and to ensure that once allocated, water users can rely on a future water supply. The acquisition of a water right, whether by property ownership, an administrative body or judicial decree, only authorizes the holder of the water right to use the water; the water itself cannot be owned. Water law is predominately a creature of state rather than federal law.

1. *Riparianism vs. Prior Appropriation*

Although each state has the authority to develop its own unique system of water distribution, in the United States there are two primary water law doctrines—riparianism and prior appropriation. While some states fully subscribe to either doctrine, other states accept both theories to some degree. Generally, the eastern states follow the riparianism system, while the western states favor the prior appropriation doctrine.

The two primary water law doctrines were developed in response to the dramatic differences in the hydrology and settlement of the eastern and western United States. In the relatively water-abundant east, the colonial states adopted a modified version of the English common law doctrine of "riparianism." Under riparianism, owning land adjacent to a natural watercourse automatically gives the landowner the right to use the water in the abutting natural watercourse. Water is a shared, or correlative, resource. Its use is governed by reasonableness, and conflicts are resolved through tort-like principles.

Unlike settlement in the eastern United States, settlement of the arid west was sporadic and inspired by federal legislation, such as the Mining and Homestead Acts. Through these Acts, individuals could gain ownership to public land and its valuable resources. Without a state to prescribe and enforce rules regarding water use, water allocation in the west was developed through local customs. *See* California Oregon Power Co. v. Beaver Portland Cement Co., 295 U.S. 142, 55 S.Ct. 725, 79 L.Ed.

1356 (1935). Under local western custom, the first to use the water acquired the best right to the water. This notion of "first in time, first in right" is the backbone of today's "prior appropriation" doctrine. Water rights under this doctrine are similar to property rights, where the water user "owns" a right to do certain things with the water.

Some states acknowledge both riparian and appropriative rights and are therefore termed "dual-doctrine," or mixed, states. *See* Figure 3, below.

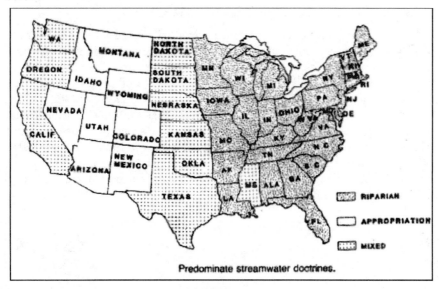

Predominate streamwater doctrines.

Figure 3: Riparian, Prior Appropriation and Mixed Jurisdictions

Each state, regardless of its applicable surface water doctrine, has distinct rules that apply to groundwater. Moreover, although a state may generally subscribe to a water law doctrine, each state may deviate from the common doctrinal principles when delineating water rights within its borders. *See* United States v. River Rouge Improvement Co., 269 U.S. 411, 46 S.Ct. 144, 70 L.Ed. 339 (1926).

2. *Public Trust Doctrine*

The public trust doctrine overlies the various state water law doctrines. Under the public trust doctrine, land is "held in trust for the people of the State that they may enjoy the navigation of the waters, carry on commerce over them, and have liberty of fishing therein freed from the obstruction or interference of private parties." Illinois Central Railroad v. Illinois, 146 U.S. 387, 452, 13 S.Ct. 110, 118, 36 L.Ed. 1018 (1892). The doctrine is grounded in the English common law:

> [T]itle to lands under tide waters ... were by the common law deemed to be vested in the king as a public trust, to subserve and protect the public right to use them as highways for commerce, trade, and inter-

course. The king, by virtue of his proprietary interest, could grant the soil so that it should become private property, but his grant was subject to the paramount right of public use of navigable waters, which he could neither destroy nor abridge. In every such grant there was an implied reservation of the public right, and so far as it assumed to interfere with it, or to confer a right to impede or obstruct navigation, or to make an exclusive appropriation of the use of navigable waters, the grant was void.

Id. at 458, 13 S.Ct. at 120, 36 L.Ed. at 1044.

Today, the public trust doctrine is primarily used as a tool for public access and environmental protection. Modern applications of the public trust doctrine principally involve protecting or restoring the environmental value of water resources from the effects of private ownership and development. *See* Mineral County v. Nevada, 117 Nev. 235, 20 P.3d 800 (2001); Parks v. Cooper, 676 N.W.2d 823 (S.D. 2004). The public trust doctrine acts as an inherent restriction on a state's conveyance of "trust resources." Under this theory, the public's interest in the state's water resources is paramount and therefore private use should not diminish or impair the public's interest. The doctrine is addressed in detail in Chapter 8 (State Ownership).

In Practice:

What are the purposes of the Public Trust Doctrine?

Most state courts prioritize at least three public trust purposes over competing interests in the states' water resources:

1) water resource protection (maintenance of water quality);

2) domestic use protection (drinking water); and

3) public access to navigable waters for commerce, fishing, and other important uses.

These public rights are separate from, and superior to, the prevailing private interests in the resources. Just as private trustees are judicially accountable to their beneficiaries for dispositions of the res, the legislative and executive branches may be judicially accountable to the population for dispositions of the public trust. *See* Illinois Central Railroad v. Illinois, 146 U.S. 387, 452, 13 S.Ct. 110, 118, 36 L.Ed. 1018 (1892); National Audubon Society v. Superior Court, 33 Cal.3d 419, 437, 189 Cal.Rptr. 346, 658 P.2d 709, 721, cert. denied, 464 U.S. 977, 104 S.Ct. 413, 78 L.Ed.2d 351 (1983); In Re Wai'ola O Moloka'i, Inc., 103 Hawai'i 401, 83 P.3d 664 (2004); In re Water Use Permit Applications, 105 Hawai'i 1, 93 P.3d 643 (2004).

3. *Federal Involvement*

Although the federal government does not regulate private water use, per se, within the various states, it does impact water administration through environmental legislation, land reservations, and reclamation projects. In every state, water users are subject to environmental regulations, such as the Clean Water Act, which requires permits for all discharges into navigable waters. Federal reserved water rights can attach to federal lands through either express or implied reservation; "[r]eserved water rights are unlike riparian rights or prior appropriation rights, although they contain elements of both." In re Use of Water in Big Horn River System, 48 P.3d 1040, 1046 (Wyo.2002). Reclamation projects influence water rights by providing resources to store large amounts of water that is later released and delivered to users who would otherwise lack water supplies. Each of these topics is addressed below.

II. REASONABLE USE RIPARIANISM

The riparian system, which generally prevails in 39 eastern states, turns on land ownership. In riparian states, only owners of riparian land, land abutting a natural watercourse, may own riparian rights. Conflicts between water right users can be grounded in nuisance or trespass principles. As a general rule, the conveyance of riparian land automatically transfers all appurtenant riparian water rights, unless the riparian rights have been severed from the land or specifically reserved in the deed.

A. Historical Development—Reasonable Use Doctrine

Ownership of land that abuts a natural watercourse entitles the riparian landowner to reasonable use of the adjacent water. The United State's version of the riparian water doctrine was initially borrowed from English law, but was subsequently modified to meet the needs of our growing society.

1. *Natural Flow Theory*

The English rule was known as the "natural flow" theory, where owners of land abutting a natural watercourse had a right to use a natural stream as it flowed through their land. Under the natural flow theory, a water right included a right to the natural flow of the water, a sufficient quantity of water to meet all of the landowner's "natural" needs, and water unimpaired in quality. Thus, the primary limitation on a water right under the natural flow theory was that the water be returned to the stream substantially unchanged so that downstream riparian water users were not injured. *See* Mason v. Hill, 5 B. & Ad. 1, 110 Eng. Rep. 692 (1833); Wood v. Waud, 3 Ex. 748, 154 Eng.Rep. 1047 (1849). A riparian could make "artificial" uses of the water *(e.g.,* irrigation and industry) so long as such uses did not materially adversely affect either the quality or quantity of the water for downstream users. *See* Embrey v. Owen, 6 Ex. 353, 155 Eng. Rep. (1851). The water had to be used on the riparian land, so a riparian owner could not transfer riparian rights apart from the land. *See* Ormerod v. Todmorsden Joint Stock Mill Co., 11 Q.B.D. 155 (1883).

As industry flourished in the 19th century, it soon became apparent that the natural flow theory was not conducive to changing economical and socially desirable uses of water, as water could not be stored, consumed, or used away from riparian lands. As a result, the theory that the watercourse should remain substantially unchanged was abandoned for a more realistic goal of permitting uses so long as they did not "unreasonably" interfere with the rights and reasonable uses of other riparians. Most jurisdictions adopted the "reasonable use" modification of the riparian doctrine. *See* Tyler v. Wilkinson, 4 Mason 397, 24 Fed-.Cas. 472 (no. 14,312) (C.C.D.R.I.1827); Evan v. Merriweather, 4 Ill. 492, 38 Am.De. 106 (1842); Cox, *Establishment and Maintenance of Water Right in the Eastern United States*, 4 Agr.L.J. 53 (1982*)*. However, some riparian states still follow certain aspects of the natural flow theory, especially in cases between a riparian and a non-riparian or between "natural" (domestic) and "artificial" uses. *See* Whorton v. Malone, 209 W.Va. 384, 388, 549 S.E.2d 57, 61 (2001); Pyle v. Gilbert, 245 Ga. 403, 265 S.E.2d 584 (1980). For analysis, see Davis, *Riparian Right of Stream Flow Protection in the Eastern States*, 36 ARK.L.REV. 47 (1983); Ayars, *The Flow of Surface Water Law in Connecticut*, 14 CONN.L.REV. 601 (1982).

2. What Is a "Natural Watercourse?"

The riparian system determines one's right to use water based on ownership of riparian land that abuts a natural watercourse. Accordingly, it is crucial to determine what constitutes a "natural watercourse." A "watercourse is defined as running water flowing in a definite channel having a bed or banks, and includes streams, rivers, creeks, etc." Lowcountry Open Land Trust v. State, 347 S.C. 96, 552 S.E.2d 778, 784 (2001) (*quoting* Black's Law Dictionary 1592 (6th ed. 1990)). Generally, to classify as a natural watercourse, a stream must flow year-round. Artificially created watercourses, such as ditches or canals, are not deemed natural watercourses unless they are a mere enlargement of a natural watercourse or have been maintained for a long time. *See* Darr v. Carolina Aluminum Co., 215 N.C. 768, 3 S.E.2d 434 (1939); Bollinger v. Henry, 375 S.W.2d 161 (Mo.1964). Riparian rights do not attach to diffuse surface waters (*i.e.*, precipitation run-off) or groundwater.

Riparian rights attached to property abutting an ocean, sea, or lake are termed "littoral." "As with riparian rights, littoral rights are governed by the individual states." Lowcountry Open Land Trust v. State, 347 S.C. 96, 552 S.E.2d 778 (2001). Littoral owners have a right to use water pursuant to the state's general water law requirements, but their access rights for boating, fishing and other activities generally depend on whether the lake, by state definition, is "navigable" or "non-navigable." The majority of riparian states hold that when a lake is navigable, all people, whether littoral owners or not, have a right to use the surface. Conversely, when a lake is non-navigable, the littoral owners own the surface rights, and may exclude the public. *See* Stupak–Thrall v. Glickman, 346 F.3d 579 (6th Cir.2003)(under Michigan law, each owner shares rights to the whole lake).

Does ownership of the land beneath an artificially created lake entitle one to riparian rights? In Ours v. Grace Property, Inc., 186 W.Va. 296, 301, 412 S.E.2d 490, 495 (1991), plaintiffs, owners of the majority of land beneath a man-made lake, brought an action seeking to enjoin defendants, shoreline owners, from using water overlying land owned by plaintiffs. *Id.* The court held that, where ownership of land underlying a man-made lake is clear and distinct, the owner of a portion of the lake bed has exclusive control and use of the water overlying that portion and may exclude others by erecting a fence or other barrier. *Id.*

B. Rights of Riparians

The reasonable use doctrine places each riparian on equal footing and requires that each riparian's use not unreasonably interfere with the reasonable uses of other riparians. The determination of what constitutes a reasonable use entails a weighing of three separate but related interests: the riparian using the water, the riparian suffering the harm, and the public. Accordingly, a determination of reasonable use is extremely case specific. Generally speaking, ownership of a riparian tract entitles one to: (i) the flow of the stream; (ii) use of the water; (iii) access to the water body for fishing and other purposes; and (iv) construction of a wharf or dock for private use. Although non-riparian landowners and members of the general public cannot own water rights, when a watercourse satisfies the state's definition of navigability, the public possesses rights to access the water's surface under the public trust doctrine.

Most state courts employ an *ad hoc* balancing test to resolve disputes between riparians, but a few follow the Restatement (Second) of Torts § 850A (1979), which lists nine factors to consider when making a determination of reasonableness:

(1) The *purpose* of the use must be lawful and beneficial. Certainly, domestic water supply and stock watering satisfy this requirement, but what about recreational and scenic values? In short, it depends. Courts have not hesitated to protect commercial enterprises that rely on recreational and aesthetic values. *See* Harris v. Brooks, 225 Ark. 436, 283 S.W.2d 129 (1955) (enjoining riparian from pumping irrigation water from non-navigable lake, thereby making lake unsuitable for fishing and recreational uses by the plaintiff, whose business involved renting cabins, boats and fishing equipment); Sayles v. Mitchell, 60 S.D. 592, 245 N.W. 390 (1932) (enjoining a diversion from a creek relied on by a downstream riparian to maintain a public swimming pool on her land). However, some courts may be less inclined to recognize non-commercial interests. *See* City of Los

Angeles v. Aitken, 10 Cal.App.2d 460, 52 P.2d 585 (1935) (concluding that, although the "mere privilege of bathing, boating, and hunting" in Mono Lake would not entitle one to compensatory damages, damages should be awarded when diversions adversely impacted riparian owners' resorts "dependent upon income derived from the traveling public ... attracted to this alluring lake"). Others have no problem finding personal scenic or recreational interests beneficial. In Taylor v. Tampa Coal Co., 46 So.2d 392, 394 (Fla. 1950), the defendant was enjoined from pumping water from a lake to irrigate his citrus grove when the pumping damaged plaintiffs' ferns and trees and interfered with "pleasures as boating, swimming and fishing." *Id.* at 394. According to the Florida court, "The fact that on riparian owner may choose to use the water in the lake for recreational purposes while another may desire to divert it for an artificial use such as irrigation, will not give the latter a superior right to take water to the detriment of the former." *Id. See also* Ocean City v. Maffucci, 326 N.J.Super. 1, 740 A.2d 630 (1999) (requiring City to compensate beachfront property owners for loss of ocean view).

(2) The use must be *suitable* to the lake or stream involved. In Mason v. Hoyle, 56 Conn. 255, 14 A. 786 (1888), an increase in the size of defendant's mill required detention of water to run the machinery. Prior to its enlargement, the mill could be used without any detention of water. The mill was "enormous[ly] disproportion-[ate] ... to the capacity of the stream," unsuitable to the character of the stream, and thus unreasonable. *Id. See* Dunlap v. Carolina Power and Light Co., 212 N.C. 814, 195 S.E. 43 (1938).

(3) The *economic value* of the use may be considered. If a riparian use has no economic value, but only aesthetic value, may the non-economic use be considered reasonable when competing against an economic use (e.g., irrigation)? *See* Los Angeles v. Aitken, 10 Ca.App.2d 460, 52 P.2d 585 (1935) (recognizing a "right to the view" of a beautiful lake).

(4) The *social value* of the use may be considered, but if the plaintiff's riparian use is harmed by the conduct of the defendant, the latter cannot avoid compensating the plaintiff for the harm simply by showing that the defendant's use had a greater social value. *See* Furrer v. Talent Irrigation District, 258 Or. 494, 466 P.2d 605 (1970); Strobel v. Kerr Salt Co., 164 N.Y. 303, 58 N.E. 142 (1900).

5) Reasonableness is determined in part by the *extent and amount of harm it causes* to another riparian. If plaintiff's own actions have caused the harm (*e.g.*, storing water in small ponds that do not adequately hold water), then the defendant's actions affecting the water course are reasonable. Hazard Powder Co. v. Somerville Manufacturing Co., 78 Conn. 171, 61 A. 519 (1905). Even when the defendant causes injury, the defendant's use is reasonable if the

harm to the plaintiff is not economically substantial. *See* Bollinger v. Henry, 375 S.W.2d 161 (Mo. 1964); Montelious v. Elsea, 11 Ohio 2d 57, 161 N.E.2d 675 (1959).

(6) The practicality of *avoiding the harm* by adjusting the use or method of use may be considered. Courts may examine whether diversion and storage of water that would otherwise go to waste would allow all competing riparians to receive a supply of water adequate to meet their needs. *See* Rancho Santa Margarita v. Vail, 11 Cal.2d 501, 81 P.2d 533 (1938); Stamford Extract Manufacturing Co. v. Stamford Rolling Mills Co., 101 Conn. 310, 125 A. 623 (1924).

(7) The practicality of *adjusting the amount of water* used by each proprietor may also be considered. Although the right of a riparian owner is not measured by the amount used, some attempts at quantification have been imposed when demand exceeds supply. *See* Harris v. Brooks, 225 Ark. 436, 283 S.W.2d 129 (1955). Courts sometimes allocate water according to proportionate stream frontages or according to the amount of irrigable land belonging to each party. *Compare* Union Mill & Mining Co. v. Ferris, 2 Sawyer 176, 24 F.Cas. 594 (No. 14, 371) (1872), *with* Southern California Investment Co. v. Wilshire, 144 Cal. 68, 77 P. 767 (1904), *and* Wiggins v. Muscpiabe Land and Water Co., 113 Cal. 182, 45 P. 160 (1896).

(8) Courts also consider the importance of *protecting existing values* of water use, land investments, and enterprise. *See* Thompson v. Enz, 385 Mich. 103, 188 N.W.2d 579 (1971). Despite numerous cases that state that priority of use is irrelevant, reasonableness may be based in part on the relative dates that riparians began to use the water. *See* Strobel v. Kerr Salt Co., 164 N.Y. 303, 58 N.E. 142 (1900); Beuscher, *Appropriation Water Law Elements in Riparian Doctrine States*, 10 Buffalo L.Rev. 448 (1961). A number of cases have enjoined upstream riparians who initiated a new use that adversely affected a downstream riparian's pre-existing use. *See* Harp v. Iowa Falls Electric Co., 196 Iowa 317, 191 N.W. 520 (1923); State v. Apfelbacher, 167 Wis. 233, 167 N.W. 244 (1918). Can a riparian gain a protected right to continue using rock and gravel that are carried in a stream, deposited on his land, and used as part of his rock and gravel business? *See* Joslin v. Marin Municipal Water District, 67 Cal.2d 132, 60 Cal.Rptr. 377, 429 P.2d 889 (1967).

(9) The *justice* of requiring the user causing the harm to bear the loss is also a factor. Courts may employ a nuisance-like formula which tests the utility of the defendant's use against the degree of harm suffered by the plaintiff. *See* Birchwoood Lakes Colony Club, Inc. v. Borough of Medford Lakes, 90 N.J. 582, 449 A.2d 472 (1982). According to Restatement (2d) § 852: "A riparian proprietor's use of the water is unreasonable ... unless the utility of the use outweighs the gravity of the harm."

C. Nuisance and Trespass

In riparian states, conflicts between water users can also be grounded in nuisance or trespass law. Nuisance claims are often appropriate because they are founded on an unreasonable interference with the use and enjoyment of another's property. Whiteside Estates v. Highlands Cove, L.L.C., 553 S.E.2d 431, 146 N.C.App. 449 (2001). Trespass entails an unauthorized, and thus unlawful, entry on plaintiff's property. *See id.*; Berger Farms, Inc. v. Estes, 662 N.E.2d 654 (Ind.App.1996) (upholding an injunction to prevent unauthorized fishing and boating on a non-navigable lake).

Activities that impair the quality of water available to downstream riparians can be actionable in both nuisance and trespass, as in the case below.

WHITESIDE ESTATES v. HIGHLANDS COVE, L.L.C.
Court of Appeals of North Carolina, 2001.
553 S.E.2d 431, 146 N.C.App. 449.

* * * Defendant purchased approximately 400 acres of real property that adjoins and is upstream from property owned by Whiteside Estates, Inc. ("plaintiff") in March of 1998. Defendant acquired its property to construct residential units and a golf course.

Plaintiff, a corporation whose sole shareholders are O.E. Young, Jr. ("Young"), his wife Mary Lou Young, and their five children, owns approximately 265 acres ... directly downstream from defendant's development. In 1957, Young constructed a dam on Grassy Camp Creek ("creek") which ran through the property, forming an eighteen-acre lake known as Young Lake ("lake"). The creek traverses both defendant's and plaintiff's property.

* * * [North Carolina] ... issued defendant a Sedimentation and Erosion Control permit and approved their plan to develop its property on or about 29 July 1998. Defendant began construction shortly thereafter. The evidence tended to show that significant rainfall caused sediment from defendant's land-disturbing activities to flow into the creek in October 1998. Plaintiff's lake and creek collected colloidal material after that first rainfall and every subsequent rainfall, impacting the lake water's quality, damaging the creek, and invading plaintiff's use and enjoyment thereof.

The North Carolina Division of Land Resources ("NCDLR") inspected the project almost weekly during defendant's construction.... Although no statutory "Notices of Violation" were issued ... [its] reports indicated that: (1) defendant's activities utilized "insufficient measures to retain sediment on site," (2) defendant failed "to take reasonable measures," on site during construction, and (3) defendant's site was not in compliance with the Sedimentation Pollution Control Act....

* * * Plaintiff then filed a complaint seeking damages for nuisance, [and] trespass.... Defendant answered denying all allegations and coun-

terclaimed for abuse of process. * * * The jury returned a verdict in plaintiff's favor of $500,000.00. * * *

"To recover in nuisance, plaintiffs must show an unreasonable interference with the use and enjoyment of their property." * * * Unintentional nuisance occurs when defendant's conduct is negligent, reckless, or ultrahazardous. Intentional nuisance, or the other hand, focuses on the unreasonableness of the interference. * * * "A person who intentionally creates or maintains a private nuisance is liable for the resulting injury to others regardless of the degree of care or skill exercised by him to avoid such injury." *Morgan*, 238 N.C. at 194, 77 S.E.2d at 689 (citations omitted); Parker v. Barefoot, 130 N.C.App. 18, 502 S.E.2d 42 (1998), rev. on other grounds, 351 N.C. 40, 519 S.E.2d 315 (1999) (A defendant's use of state-of-the-art technology or the fact that he was not negligent in the design or construction of his facility are not defenses to a nuisance claim).

An intentional invasion or interference occurs when a person acts with the purpose to invade another's interest in the use and enjoyment of their land, or knows that it will result, or will substantially result. * * * An intentional invasion or interference, however, is not always unreasonable. * * * [O]ur Supreme Court listed factors to be considered in assessing whether an intentional interference is unreasonable:

> the surroundings and conditions under which defendant's conduct is maintained, the character of the neighborhood, the nature, utility and social value of defendant's operation, the nature, utility and social value of plaintiffs' use and enjoyment which have been invaded, the suitability of the locality for defendant's operation, the suitability of the locality for the use plaintiffs make of their property, the extent, nature and frequency of the harm to plaintiffs' interest, priority of occupation as between the parties, and other considerations arising upon the evidence.* * *

> Once plaintiff establishes that the invasion or intrusion is unreasonable, plaintiff must prove the invasion caused substantial injury to its property interest.* * * "An upper riparian landowner's unreasonable use of water quantity or diminution of its quality permits a lower riparian owner to maintain a civil action in nuisance or trespass to land." * * *

The evidence tended to show that after significant rainfall, sediment from those activities flowed into plaintiff's creek and lake, despite defendant's State-approved erosion control measures. Plaintiff entered into evidence numerous photographs of the lake's condition before and after defendant's land-disturbing activity. Before defendant's development began the lake was crystal clear. After defendant's development commenced the lake had the appearance of coffee with cream. There is substantial evidence that defendant's activities were the major, if not the sole, source of the runoff.

Plaintiff offered expert testimony that described the decreased level of water quality in the lake as well as increased levels of erosion and sediment in its creek. Water sampling test results tended to show that turbidity levels (a measurement of the amount of light bouncing off suspended particles in water) dramatically increased. * * * Plaintiff's shareholders testified that for forty years the lake and creek had been used for fishing, swimming, boating, and other recreational uses. After defendant's land-disturbing activities started ... the lake was unfit for such activities.* * *

A plaintiff need not establish loss of fair market value in the property or lost rentals, sales, or revenues to show sufficient injury to support damages in nuisance. These items are one method of measuring damages after substantial injury is proven, not a method for determining injury. * * * The record supports the jury's finding that substantial evidence exists that defendant intentionally caused and allowed colloidal material to flow into plaintiff's creek and lake to such a degree as to substantially and unreasonably interfere with plaintiff's use and enjoyment of its land. The evidence was also sufficient for the jury to conclude that the injury to plaintiff's property was substantial and significant to recover damages. * * *

Defendant argues that the evidence failed to support a claim for trespass because no suspended solids were deposited on the land, "but rather continued downstream as water in the lake was released." Defendant asserts that since there was no evidence that sediment settled in the lake, and that "there is no property right in any particular particle of water or in all of them put together" there can be no trespass.* * *

> [T]he right to have a natural water course continue its physical existence upon one's property is as much property as is the right to have the hills and forests remain in place, and while there is no property right in any particular particle of water or in all of them put together, a riparian proprietor has the right of their flow past his lands for ordinary domestic, manufacturing, and other lawful purposes, without injurious or prejudicial interference by an upper proprietor. * * *

Smith v. Town of Morganton, 187 N.C. 801, 803, 123 S.E. 88, 89 (1924).

Defendant's argument that since there was no evidence that any suspended material in the lake settled bars recovery in trespass is misplaced. First it fails to address the evidence that there was sediment in and about plaintiff's creek caused by defendant's land-disturbing activity. Second, [plaintiff's expert] testified that "there is a fine coating of sediment on the bottom [of the lake]. It's not much ... but that fine stuff could get resuspended by wind ... and cause high turbidity."

"The elements of a trespass claim are that plaintiff was in possession of the land at the time of the alleged trespass; that defendant made an unauthorized, and therefore unlawful, entry on the land; and that plaintiff was damaged by the alleged invasion of his rights of possession." * * * [T]here is sufficient evidence for the jury to conclude that defendant's land disturbing activities caused sediment to unlawfully enter upon plaintiff's property causing damage and injury. * * *

Once liability is established for an abatable or temporary nuisance, the remedy includes money damages. * * * The kinds of damages recoverable include: diminished rental value; reasonable costs of replacement or repair; restoration of the property to its pre-nuisance condition; and other added damages for incidental losses. * * * "Where the nuisance is the kind that does more or less tangible harm to the premises, the cost of repair or restoration may be the appropriate measure of damages,...."
* * *

[Plaintiff's expert] Wagner testified that cleaning the lake would cost $20,000.00. * * * The evidence adduced to repair and restore the lake and creek on plaintiff's property ranged from $95,000.00 to $320,000.00. * * * Wagner testified ... the cost of adequate detention to control the erosion coming off defendant's property ... [would be] between $1,400,000.00 and $4,000,000.00.

We hold that there is insufficient evidence in the record of the reasonable estimate of costs to repair and restore the creek and lake to its pre-nuisance condition with as much certainty as the circumstances require. The record contains no evidence regarding the plaintiff's cost to control the source on its property. We remand for a new trial on damages only. * * *

Notes and Questions

1. Defendants' construction activities most likely had high utility when compared to plaintiff's recreational uses. Why was the court so willing to uphold the jury's verdict for the plaintiff? Why, then, did it remand the damages award? Why couldn't the plaintiff recover any reasonable costs incurred to prevent future injury or abate the nuisance by controlling the source of the problem—sedimentation emanating from defendant's property?

> [E]vidence about controlling the erosion coming off defendant's property ... was not irrelevant to the determination of plaintiff's damages. Plaintiff was entitled to the cost to control that source only if necessary to repair and restore the creek and lake. * * * Wagner testified that defendant's sedimentation and erosion control plan was inadequate. He also testified that if nothing were done to prevent and control sediment coming down the creek from defendant's property, the repairs of the lake and creek on plaintiff's property would be ineffective. * * * [But] [t]he only testimony regarding the cost to control the source of sedimentation was ... that "they [defendant] need a lot more detention and they need some sort of auxiliary system to remove the colloidal material that are causing high turbidity."

Id. at 441. How could plaintiff have made a more air-tight case with respect to damages?

2. Was plaintiff entitled to an injunction as well? A temporary restraining order had been issued in an earlier phase of the case, but a permanent injunction was subsequently denied.

3. What, if any, tort-based defenses might the defendant have raised to avoid liability? From a defendant's stand-point, would you prefer to defend against a tort claim or a property-based riparian "reasonable use" claim? Is there any significant difference?

D. Transfer of Riparian Rights

As a general rule, the conveyance of riparian land automatically transfers all appurtenant riparian water rights, unless the riparian rights have been severed from the land or specifically reserved in the deed. Riparian rights may be severed from the land when a parcel of riparian land is subdivided. If a riparian proprietor conveys separately the part of the land that does not front the watercourse, the riparian rights are effectively severed from the land, and only the land bordering the natural watercourse is entitled to riparian rights.

In Focus:

Prescriptive Rights

Can a riparian water right be lost by prescription or adverse possession? Adverse possession occurs when there is open, notorious, hostile, exclusive, actual and continuous possession of property for a prescribed number of years. Which elements would be most difficult (or even impossible) to prove in the context of riparian water use? *See* Tyler v. Wilkinson, 24 F.Cas. 472 (C.C.R.I.1827).

The majority of courts hold that downstream water users, whether riparian or not, cannot adversely possess against upstream riparians. Why not? Consider whether there is any way a downstream user could openly adversely possess against an upstream riparian. How would the upstream party become aware of the adverse use?

An upstream riparian's water use is not considered to be adverse unless it unreasonably interferes with the right of a lower riparian. *See* City of Waterbury v. Town of Washington, 260 Conn. 506, 800 A.2d 1102 (2002) (where a city's dam was an open and visible barrier on the river, the court granted the city a prescriptive easement against downstream riparians); *see also* Pabst v. Finmand, 190 Cal. 124, 211 P. 11 (Cal. 1922). When a water right is obtained through prescription, "[t]he extent of the right acquired is measured by the extent to which the claim was asserted and maintained." *Waterbury*, 800 A.2d at 1152. However, when a non-riparian adversely possesses against a downstream riparian, two different rules are applied. In some jurisdictions, only non-riparian upstream uses that unreasonably interfere with a downstream use can ripen into a prescriptive right. In other jurisdictions, all non-riparian use is considered unlawful and therefore a pre-

---

scriptive right can result from any non-riparian use, even if it does not unreasonably interfere with the use of a downstream riparian. Which rule seems more sensible?

E. Permits

Most riparian states have enacted statutes that require water users to obtain permits, or at least provide notification, before initiating substantial consumptive uses or out-of-basin diversions of water, or constructing shoreline structures or dams. Conservation Commission v. Price, 193 Conn. 414, 479 A.2d 187 (1984); Application of Hemco, Inc., 129 Vt. 534, 283 A.2d 246 (1971). Permit statutes can alter traditional riparian rights by modifying the rule of reasonable use, delineating preferences or priority uses, or even eliminating the requirement that water can only be used on riparian land and allowing riparians to sell their water rights separately from their land. *See, e.g.,* Oh. Rev. Code § 1501.33 (requiring a permit for withdrawals that result in new or increased consumptive use of more than two million gallons per day); Ia. Code Ann. § 455B.265–.266 (specifying priority allocations and providing authority to grant permits for the diversion, storage, or withdrawal of water if consistent with "beneficial use and ensuring conservation"); 615 Ill. Comp. Stat. 50 § 1.2 (requiring a permit for diversions from Lake Michigan); 32 Penn. Stat. § 815.101 (codifying the Delaware River Basin Compact, including a permit requirement for withdrawals from certain protected areas).

1. *Basic Permit Considerations*

Permitting agencies generally have discretion to determine the terms of the permit and make decisions regarding competing uses as well as minimum stream flows. Permits will specify the quantity to be diverted, the method of diversion, and the location of use. Applicants are typically required to prove that their proposed uses will not interfere with existing uses of water. Some permit jurisdictions require applicants to demonstrate that the proposed use will not adversely affect higher priority uses (domestic uses rank higher than agricultural irrigation). *See* Crookston Cattle Co. v. Minnesota Department of Natural Resources, 300 N.W.2d 769 (Minn. 1980). The duration of the permit varies from state to state and may range from five years to perpetuity. However, permits are subject to cancellation and forfeiture for non-use.

When is the transfer of riparian rights allowed? A Wisconsin court invoked the public trust doctrine to answer this question in ABKA Limited Partnership v. Wisconsin Department of Natural Resources, 247 Wis.2d 793, 635 N.W.2d 168 (2001). ABKA owned a man-made marina in a harbor on Lake Geneva, which consisted of over 400 boat slips, a swimming pool, a Harbor House, and a parking area. The slips were rented to boat owners annually with options to renew. In 1994, ABKA decided to convert the marina to a condominium form of ownership, and it began preparing a condominium declaration. The proposal would not change the number or size of any structure in the marina, but would simply change the ownership to a condominium arrangement. *Id.* The Department of Natural Resources approved the condominium declaration. Its decision was challenged in the following case.

ABKA LIMITED PARTNERSHIP ("ABKA") v. WISCONSIN DEPARTMENT OF NATURAL RESOURCES

Court of Appeals of Wisconsin, 2001.
247 Wis.2d 793, 635 N.W.2d 168.

* * * Is a dockominium development, based upon condominium real estate law, that limits public access to navigable waters in favor of private riparian ownership a violation of the Wisconsin public trust doctrine and Wis. Stat. Ch. 30?

* * * A riparian owner is accorded certain rights based upon title to the ownership of shorefront property. These rights are well defined and include the right to use the shoreline and have access to the waters, the right to reasonable use of the waters for domestic, agricultural and recreational purposes, and the right to construct a pier or similar structure in aid of navigation. A riparian owner is entitled to exclusive possession to the extent necessary to reach navigable water and to have reasonable access for bathing and swimming.

* * * The public trust doctrine is premised on the idea that private ownership of public resources is improper and provides the public with a right to the benefit of certain public resources. This right supplants any private interests and imposes strict responsibilities upon the government as trustee of these public resources. * * * When conflicts occur over the use of the waters of the state, riparian rights must always surrender to the public interest.

* * * A boat slip is by definition the water and lakebed between two piers; no one but the state can own the water and the lakebed. Riparian owners do not possess water in a lake, but only the right to reasonable use of the water in the lake; "[r]iparian owners acquire at most the usufructuary right to water to water based on possession or dominion, but not outright ownership of the water." * * *

ABKA's dockominium proposal allows ABKA and the Association to transfer ownership of public waters to private individuals and therefore is in direct conflict with the public trust doctrine. We therefore reverse the order of the circuit court affirming the ALJ's decision granting ABKA a ... permit. Order reversed.

Notes and Questions

The court's opinion finds that the dockominium concept violates the public trust doctrine. Why couldn't ABKA do what it pleased with its property, when there was no specific showing of resulting environmental or social harm? Is there any way to reconcile the dockominium concept and the public trust doctrine? If Wisconsin were a "pure" common law riparian jurisdiction, with no permit system, how would the public trust be enforced, if at all?

2. Water Storage

In riparian jurisdictions, water storage, much like water use, is governed by the rule of reasonable use. Accordingly, storage is permissible when it does not impair the reasonable uses of another riparian use. *See* Heise v. Schulz, 167 Kan. 34, 204 P.2d 706 (1949). As with water use, some riparian jurisdictions require permits for storage, and provide permitting agencies with great discretion over the terms of the permit. *See* Hudson Riber Fisherman's Ass'n v. Williams, 139 A.D.2d 234, 531 N.Y.S.2d 379 (1988).

Hydroelectric power generation at water storage facilities (reservoirs and dams) is also governed by the reasonable use doctrine. Because reasonableness is relative, a finding of reasonableness will consider the stream size, the technology used to generate power, and other uses of the stream. Hydroelectricity is governed by a complex array of state and federal statutes, such as the Federal Power Act, 16 U.S.C. §§ 791a–823, as well as common law riparian rules.

3. Forfeiture and Condemnation

In riparian jurisdictions, the general rule is that riparian water rights cannot be lost by non-use. However, this rule is not absolute. Depending on the jurisdiction, riparian rights can be lost by prescription, forfeiture, or the power of eminent domain.

Most states that have adopted a permit system for managing water rights have also adopted forfeiture statutes. Forfeiture statutes automatically terminate one's right to use water when either the right has not been exercised for a specific number of years or the water right owner does not begin using the water within a reasonable time after the permit is issued. *See* Matter of Deadman Creek Drainage Basin, 103 Wn.2d 686, 694 P.2d 1071 (1985); In re Adjudication of Water Rights of Upper Guadalupe River Basin, 642 S.W.2d 438 (Tex.1982). Forfeiture is discussed further in Section III.H., below.

Some states' statutes bestow government entities with the power of eminent domain, which can be used to condemn water rights when the water is needed to serve a public purpose. Can a City take an individual's water right and give it to a corporation? Kelo v. City of New London, 125 S.Ct. 2655, 2005 WL 1469529, (2005), suggests "yes", so long as there is some public benefit (like jobs) from the condemnation. See Chapter 9.II.A, *supra* (discussing *Kelo*). When water rights are condemned, the governmental body must provide the water right owner with just compensation.

Notes and Questions

1. How likely is a riparian landowner to invest substantial resources to develop uses that rely on a specific quantity of water? Can you predict what

a court in a riparian jurisdiction might do if a conflict with another riparian user arises in the future? Do the nine factors provided in Restatement § 850A lend more certainty to the problem than the common law of "reasonable use"? What would?

2. Is there any room for a consideration of environmental needs under the common law riparianism doctrine? Would a permit requirement administered by a state agency do a more effective job of ensuring against undue environmental degradation than the common law?

III. PRIOR APPROPRIATION

The prior appropriation doctrine is an American invention, developed by miners and farmers, the first settlers of the arid West. Known as the Great American Desert, the western United States was far from hospitable. Water was scarce and its supply was unreliable. To encourage westward expansion, Congress passed legislation such as the Mining and Homestead Acts, which rewarded pioneers who settled this dry landscape with title to public land and its resources. Prior appropriation encouraged development of the west.

A. Introduction to Prior Appropriation

The prior appropriation doctrine creates a system where the first to use the water has a better right to the water than all subsequent users. Priority of use is the backbone of the prior appropriation system, but an appropriation is only valid and will only be confirmed or perfected when the appropriated water is put to beneficial use.

PROMISES OF A VIABLE HOMELAND, REALITY OF SELECTIVE RECLAMATION: A STUDY OF THE RELATIONSHIP BETWEEN THE WINTERS DOCTRINE AND FEDERAL WATER DEVELOPMENT IN THE WESTERN UNITED STATES
Monique C. Shay
19 ECOLOGY L.Q. 547, 557–59 (1992)

In the second decade of the 19th century an American explorer of the West [ed.—Stephen Long] labeled the whole territory between the Mississippi River and the Rocky Mountains "the Great American Desert," a phrase and image that held for almost half a century * * * The average American wanted to climb to prosperity in the ... traditional fashion of owning land and farming. The Federal Government ... decided the whole continent should be settled by reliable citizens * * *

The Homestead Act of 1862 ... gave a settler up to 160 acres of land in return for his residence on the property for five years, some improvements, and payment of very modest fees * * * While lands east of the hundredth meridian were claimed quickly, those west of it were much less attractive; such land was too dry to farm without expensive irrigation systems. In response, Congress passed the Desert Land Act, permitting settlers to claim larger tracts of land (640 acres) "at 25 cents an acre, with a patent to follow upon proof that the settler had irrigated the land." It was hoped that irrigation farming on these larger tracts could be profitable.

In the west, settlers were governed by their customs. Thus, staking a claim to water occurred much like staking a claim to minerals or land, where the first person to appropriate or use water was thereafter entitled to the first opportunity to use the amount of water appropriated. This notion of "first in time, first in right" is the backbone of the prior appropriation doctrine.

Nineteen states recognize the prior appropriation system. While the eight most arid states in the central Rocky Mountain region (Nevada, Idaho, Montana, Wyoming, Utah, Colorado, New Mexico, Arizona) and Alaska have adopted a "pure" version of the prior appropriation doctrine, the nine states bordering these mountainous states (Washington, Oregon, California, North Dakota, South Dakota, Nebraska, Kansas, Oklahoma, and Texas) and Mississippi employ a mix of the riparian doctrine and prior appropriation doctrine in their water laws.

The prior appropriation system is based on water use. One who appropriates water and puts it to a beneficial use acquires a vested property right to continually use the amount of water initially appropriated, so long as it continues to be beneficially used. Non-use can result in a loss of right, through forfeiture, abandonment or by the prescriptive use of another. Like riparian water users, appropriators do not "own" the water, but merely a right to use a certain quantity of it. In most prior appropriation states, the water is either owned by the state or considered a public resource.

Water rights are generally a matter of state law. Therefore, although a state may formally adopt the prior appropriation system, each state independently forms rules by which private rights may be created in that jurisdiction. Each state's constitution, statutes, and case law determine which waters within the jurisdiction of the state may be appropriated. * * * In most states, the prior appropriation doctrine generally does not apply to diffuse surface water, and to the extent it is applicable to appropriations of groundwater, it is usually modified to reflect the unique nature of the groundwater. For example, the rules of prior appropriation generally apply to groundwater that is tributary to a natural surface stream, but do not apply to groundwater in a confined nontributary aquifer. The appropriation doctrine generally applies to surface waters that amount to a "natural" watercourse. Therefore, water that is not in a watercourse, as a result of naturally occurring precipitation or runoff, is generally not subject to appropriation.

*   *   *

Although water rights under both riparian and appropriation systems are usufructuary (the property interest is the right to *use* the water), there are significant differences in the two doctrines.

- Ownership of riparian land is not the basis for an appropriative water right.

- In prior appropriation states, a water right exists when water is "appropriated" (diverted and used) for a beneficial purpose.

- An appropriative water right is measured by the amount of water that was originally and historically put to beneficial use, not by "reasonable use" limitations.

- Appropriated water can be used on non-riparian lands and lands outside the watershed, regardless of the distance from the stream.

- Those who appropriate water first have a superior right to all later users.

- In times of shortage, appropriative water right holders do not all equally ration the water, but instead water is allocated by seniority and thus junior users may not receive any water at all.

- Unlike common law riparian rights, appropriative rights may be lost by non-use.

Under the prior appropriation system, a water right is a valuable property right, which may be sold or transferred to a different parcel of land. Every appropriative water right has a "priority" date. In some states, the priority date is culmination of both an appropriation date and the date in which the appropriator applied for a water right. In others, it may be the date of a permit application or the date a diversion facility was constructed. The holder of the oldest water right is senior. Senior rights are entitled to full delivery of water and must be satisfied before the next junior appropriator is entitled to take any water. Thus, in times of scarcity, it is not uncommon for recently acquired rights to receive no water, and junior users are said to have mere "paper" rights.

B. Development of the Prior Appropriation Doctrine

Prior appropriation encouraged development in the arid west, where water was scarce and the source of supply unreliable. It was often necessary to divert the water some distance from the existing sources to the point of use, so appropriators typically created systems of ditches to carry the water. When western courts eventually heard disputes concerning water use, the riparian doctrine was rejected because it was deemed unsuitable for mining and agriculture—both uses needed water diverted far from its source, and both required large quantities of water.

The *Los Angeles Aqueduct*, completed in 1913, moves water from tributaries of Mono Lake in the Owens Valley (east of the Sierra Nevada mountains) nearly 250 miles through the Mojave Desert to Los Angeles. "The West had seen nothing like it since the building of the transcontinental railroad." The West (#8), http://www.pbs.org/weta/thewest/program/episodes/eight/takeit.htm. For more detail, see MARC REISNER, CADILLAC DESERT 63, 81-86 (Penguin 1993). The photo depicts workers at the aqueduct's cement mill in 1908. *Photo credit: Joseph D. Lippincott,* Collection, Water Resources Center Archives— *U.C. Berkeley.*

The local custom of prior appropriation was judicially confirmed and became an element of state law. In the West, virtually all of the water subject to the prior appropriation system was in the public domain, on lands owned by the federal government. As the United States, through various land disposition statutes, continued to pass public land into private ownership, more settlers arrived in the West. In this great American land giveaway, those who acquired title to riparian parcels often assumed that the riparian doctrine governed water allocation, and that they were entitled to use the water that flowed through their property. But it was not uncommon for the water that flowed through their land to either have been significantly depleted by upstream diversions or to already have been appropriated by those downstream. Conflicts between prior appropriation and riparian doctrine soon arose. Who had the better right to the water, the miner or farmer, who had taken the water pursuant to state prior appropriation law, or the federal patentee, who had title to the land on which the water flowed?

A series of federal statutes and eventually the courts confirmed existing appropriations and recognized state law as the valid system of acquiring future water rights on the public domain. The Mining Act of 1866, 14 Stat. 251, provided that "[w]henever, by priority of possession, rights to the use of water ... have vested and accrued, and the same are recognized and acknowledged by the local customs, laws, and the decisions of the courts, the possessors and owners of such vested rights shall be maintained and protected." The Desert Land Act of 1877, 43 U.S.C. § 321, also provided that, while otherwise unappropriated water of non-navigable sources was available for appropriation, such appropriations would be "subject to existing rights." The Supreme Court affirmed that water was governed according to the laws of the various states. "[F]ollowing the act of 1887, if not before, all non-navigable waters then a part of the public domain became public juris, subject to the plenary control of the designated states, including those since created out of the territories named, with the right in each to determine for itself to what extent the rule of appropriation or the common-law rule in respect of riparian rights should obtain." California Oregon Power Co. v. Beaver Portland Cement Co., 295 U.S. 142, 55 S.Ct. 725, 79 L.Ed. 1356 (1935). Therefore, as parcel by parcel passed out of the public domain and into private ownership, those who had appropriated water under local custom retained their rights against later riparian land patentees.

C. Elements of Appropriation

Appropriative water rights, unlike riparian water rights, must be perfected. Perfecting a water right refers to the process by which an applicant for a water right demonstrates to the appropriate state agency or court that the claimed rights are devoted to beneficial use and receives a permit or decree to that effect. Tanner v. Carter, 20 P.3d 332 (Utah 2001). The requirements of an appropriation vary by jurisdiction, and most states have supplanted the common law elements of appropriation with specific statutory requirements. Nevertheless, prior appropriation jurisdictions, whether operating under a permit system or an adjudication system, generally require an individual to demonstrate the three traditional elements of an appropriation before a water right can be perfected. One must (1) intend to apply the water to beneficial use (2) divert the water from a natural watercourse, and (3) apply the water to beneficial use within a reasonable time. While the various prior appropriation states may slightly differ on their interpretation of intent, diversion and beneficial use, the same basic rules generally apply.

1. Intent

Under the prior appropriation system, every water right has a priority date. Generally, the priority date reflects the date on which the appropriator formed intent to appropriate the water and put it to beneficial use. In most permit states, filing an application is considered objective evidence of intent.

If an appropriator proves that intent was manifested prior to the actual diversion of water (*e.g.,* by undertaking a survey or digging a ditch), she can appeal to the doctrine of "relation back" for an earlier priority date. This doctrine allows appropriators to introduce evidence to show the date on which they first took physical action with the intent to appropriate the water. For example, farmer Greenjeans, who began digging a ditch to irrigate her land on March 1 but didn't complete the ditch until August 1, would be awarded a priority date of March 1 even if her neighbor, Mr. Rogers, began digging his ditch on March 15 and finished it on March 20. What purpose does the relation back doctrine serve? Certainly not efficiency or rewarding labor, but it does preserve the concept of "first in time, first in right."

Providing notice of the intent to appropriate is essential in both permit and non-permit jurisdictions. In permit jurisdictions, a permit will not be granted until all affected parties have been notified (or good faith attempts have been made to do so) of the application. *See* Longley v. Leucadia Financial Corp., 9 P.3d 762 (Utah 2000). Notification allows affected parties an opportunity to protect their interests. Prior to granting a water right, the state administrative agency holds a public hearing to determine whether the statutory criteria for a water appropriation have been satisfied. It is at this time that affected parties can voice their concerns about the petitioned water right.

In non-permit, or adjudication, states, such as Colorado, appropriators must seek judicial confirmation of their water use. Existing water right holders receive notice of new appropriations and may protect their interests by filing a statement of opposition with the court. They may also propose specific terms and conditions to protect their vested water rights from harm.

Traditionally, new appropriators had to evidence their intent by an open, physical demonstration. As the number of water right owners increased, adequate notice of new appropriations was often an issue. Colorado uses a monthly publication to ensure that all water right holders are put on notice of new appropriations. This "resume," which is published every month, contains a brief description of every application filed in the previous month with the state water authority, the State Engineer. Once the summary of a water right application is published in the resume, all water right owners are presumed to have notice of the pending application.

SL GROUP LLC v. GO WEST INDUSTRIES

Supreme Court of Colorado, 2002.

42 P.3d 637.

* * * This water dispute originates in a remote desert area about a one-hour drive outside of Nucla, Colorado where the appellant, SL Group, and the appellee, Go West Industries, own adjoining properties. Prior to 1985, both properties comprised an undivided parcel owned by Philip and Francis Lawhead * * * In March 1998, Go West filed an application for surface water rights to the Meadows Ditch Extension to West Shavano Creek (West Shavana Extension), seeking a decree based upon historic appropriation for irrigation beginning July 1, 1938.

* * * It is well-established that water rights vest upon a completed appropriation and application of water to beneficial use, and the General Assembly long ago established a system for settling the conflicting priorities to water rights through a process of adjudication and decree. South Adams County Water & Sanitation Dist. v. Broe Land Co., 812 P.2d 1161, 1163 (Colo.1991) (referencing §§ 1762–1801, C.G.S. (1883)). A water rights adjudication is a judicial proceeding at which respective priorities of water rights are ascertained, and a decree confirms a preexisting water right.

In the adjudication proceeding at issue here, it is clear that Go West did not identify SL as the owner of property upon which water from the West Shavano Extension was being used or include any reference to SL in its application. It is also clear that the water clerk did not mail a copy of the resume to SL. In SL's petition for reconsideration pursuant to section 37–92–304(10), filed a year and a half after the final decree, SL alleged that it was unaware of the application until a year after the decree. * * *

Under the circumstances of this case, the adjoining landowner's failure to otherwise become aware of the application and file a timely protest must be considered excusable. ... The Water Court therefore abused its discretion in summarily dismissing SL's petition for reconsideration for failing to show mistake, inadvertence, or excusable neglect. Furthermore, the petition sufficiently alleged that SL's rights had been adversely affected by substantive errors in the judgment and decree.

Notes and Questions

What happens when water rights holders like SL are not adequately notified of a new appropriation on the same watercourse? What recourse is available if they fail to file a timely statement of opposition? How long should interested parties be given to object before the new appropriation is approved?

In both permit and adjudication states, the administrative agency or the court can issue a conditional water right prior to the construction of the diversion works. Work on the diversion project must begin within a fixed time period. When a water right has not been perfected (i.e., the water has not been diverted or put to beneficial use) and is therefore still temporary in nature, the appropriator must demonstrate "due diligence" in perfecting the right. The time period for demonstrating due diligence may be extended upon showing a "good cause." Financial difficulties, the size and complexity of the project, and pending litigation may amount to "good cause." *See* In re Hood River, 114 Or. 112, 227 P. 1065 (1924); Colorado River Water Conservation District v. Twin Lakes Reservoir and Canal Co., 181 Colo. 53, 506 P.2d 1226 (1973); Metropolitan Suburban Water Users Association v. Colorado River Water Conservation District, 148 Colo. 173, 365 P.2d 273 (1961). If an appropriator fails to proceed with diligence, the conditional water right is cancelled.

To establish a conditional water right in Colorado, the following elements must be met: "[A]n applicant must show in general that a 'first step' toward the appropriation of a certain amount of water has been taken, that the applicant's intent to appropriate is not based upon the speculative sale or transfer of the appropriative rights, and that there is a substantial probability that the applicant *can and will* complete the appropriation with diligence." Mount Emmons Min. Co. v. Crested Butte, 40 P.3d 1255 (Colo. 2002). To maintain a conditional right, the appropriator must file an application for a finding of reasonable diligence every six years. The failure to file within six years may be excusable if the water court did not notify the conditional water right holder of the pending limitations period. *See* Double RL Co. v. Telluray Ranch Properties, 54 P.3d 908 (Colo.2002). So long as the conditional right holder continually demonstrates an intent to place the water to beneficial use and exercises reasonable diligence in doing so, a conditional right can be held in perpetuity without completing all the steps required for an absolute appropriation. *See* City of Black Hawk v. City of Central, 97 P.3d 951 (Colo.2004). When all of the elements of an appropriation are demonstrated, a conditional water right can become perfected and declared absolute in a judicial decree.

Why be so lenient with conditional water rights holders? Doesn't this approach encourage speculation and inhibit economic development by those who are actually ready, willing and able to proceed with a water use?

2. *Diversion From a Natural Source*

Historically, water had to be physically diverted from a natural watercourse by a manmade structure to constitute a valid appropriation. Requiring that a diversion be a physical structure, often satisfied the notice requirement of an open, physical demonstration. Although the diversion requirement is a separate element of a valid appropriation, it nonetheless compliments the notice requirement by ensuring that other water users are aware of new appropriations.

While some states still require a physical diversion from the stream, others have created exceptions to allow the acquisition of a water right for certain in-stream activities. In Colorado, the overflow from a dam onto a meadow was found to be an adequate diversion. *See* Thomas v. Guiraud, 6 Colo. 530 (1883). In Oregon and Montana, a water right can be obtained for the natural irrigation of farmland if it would be a waste of money to create a system of ditches. But in Utah, natural overflow and percolation irrigation is not considered a diversion. *See* Hardy v. Beaver County Irrigation Co., 65 Utah 28, 234 P. 524 (1924). In California, Colorado, Idaho, and Nevada, the diversion requirement is met when ranchers allow livestock to drink water from pond, marshes or directly from the stream. Waters of Horse Springs v. State Engineer, 99 Nev. 776, 671 P.2d 1131 (1983); R.T. Nahas Co. v. Hulet, 106 Idaho 37, 674 P.2d 1036 (1983).

3. *In-Stream Appropriations*

For some uses, such as recreational boating and fishing, the requirement that water be physically removed from the watercourse defeats the use. Some prior appropriation jurisdictions have therefore permitted in-stream appropriations when water can be put to beneficial use while flowing in the stream. *See* Department of Parks v. Idaho Dept. of Water Administration, 96 Idaho 440, 530 P.2d 924 (1974); In re Adjudication of the Existing Rights to the Use of All the Water, 311 Mont. 327, 55 P.3d 396 (2002) (recognizing non-diversionary claims for fish, wildlife, and recreation purposes); Kerivan v. Water Resources Commission, 188 Or.App. 491, 72 P.3d 659 (2003) (recognizing in-stream water rights resulting from transfers from irrigation uses). An in-stream water right is a legal entitlement to a specific amount of water in a defined reach of a river or stream within a specific period of time. Alaska, California, Colorado, Hawaii, Idaho, Kansas, Montana, Nebraska, Oklahoma, Oregon, Utah, Washington, and Wyoming recognize some form of in-stream flow water rights for beneficial uses such as hydropower, recreation, navigation, or to protect the surrounding ecosystem. Generally, only state agencies are authorized to appropriate such rights.

The following article describes the crisis facing western states that continue to embrace antiquated notions of "diversions" for "beneficial use."

WATER RIGHTS AND THE COMMON WEALTH
Eric T. Freyfogle
Environmental Law (1996)

* * *

Western Water Law faces a crisis of legitimacy because of the way it defines water rights, because it allows water uses that now seem so wrong. Some permitted uses, in fact, now seem so wrong that it would be an affront to communal values, as well as a distasteful reaffirmation of a flawed property regime, to expect taxpayers to pay owners to change their hurtful ways. To expect the market to remedy this situation is to misunderstand the law's unavoidable role in expressing communal values, particularly our shared, evolving senses of community and lasting health.

How then might the law of prior appropriation change in order to regain its legitimacy, to respond to the mounting claim that it empowers private owners to use their property in ways that unjustly harm and oppress?

One obvious target for change is the rule that a water right is obtainable only if a user diverts the water from the streambed. By requiring diversion, water law discredits water uses that promote in stream-flow values, particularly the natural health of the waterways themselves. To the ecologically aware, the law's foolishness could hardly shine more brightly. Aside from the harm they do, foolish laws lack the requisite level of legitimacy. The time has come for change.

A second target for reform is the long-standing, much modified rule that water is available for appropriation so long as a single drop remains in the stream or aquifer. Total consumption, draining a river dry, is the apotheosis of shortsighted, anthropocentric hubris. * * *

These two matters, and several others like them, would improve prior appropriation law. But if we are to cut to the root of the problem, we need to get serious about the long-standing yet ineffectual requirement that all water uses be beneficial. As too often now applied, beneficial use is out of date, not the least because it ignores water quality. * * *

Beneficial use must expressly come to mean beneficial by the standard of today's culture, not by the standards of some culture long eclipsed by changing values and circumstances. It must come to mean beneficial to the community, not just to the individual user, particularly a user whose calculation of gain ignores resulting ecological harms.

* * *

Because only state agencies can hold in-stream flow rights, other entities that desire to have in-stream rights have turned to recreational in-channel diversions (RICDs) to secure in-stream water rights. Unlike in-stream flow rights, in-channel diversions must include some form of physical diversion structure, such as a dam, to control the water. *See* Thornton v. Ft. Collins, 830 P.2d 915 (Colo.1992). The Colorado legislature has authorized RICDs for government entities and municipalities. Before a RICD right will be awarded, the state in-stream flow agency, the Colorado Water Conservation Board, must review the proposed in-channel diversion and make a recommendation to the Water Court. Colo. Rev. Stat. § 37–92–103(10.3).

In Focus:

STATE TO PONDER FLOWS OF RECREATIONAL WATER
Bob Berwyn
Denver Post, November 17, 2003

With as many as seven Colorado communities planning to claim water rights for kayak parks or boat chutes, state officials say they want to establish a formula for determining how much water is enough for a "reasonable" recreation experience. * * * The recent Colorado Supreme Court decision that legitimized recreational in-stream flows ... will help determine the shape of future applications for those rights. Most important, it could set limits on how much water is enough for a whitewater park.

It's those potential limitations that have residents such as Steve Glazer of Crested Butte worked up. "They are trying to relegate these recreational in-channel diversions as second-class water rights, even though the Supreme Court recognized them as equal to any other water rights," Glazer said.

In the decision, the court held that Vail, Breckenridge and Golden could indeed make a valid claim for in-stream recreational flows as a beneficial use without actually diverting the water from the channel, a decision widely seen as another shift away from the traditional interpretation of Colorado water law, which long required an out-of-channel diversion for crop irrigation or municipal use.

Glazer is a[n] ... Upper Gunnison Water Conservancy District board member. That group is currently fighting the CWCB over an application for recreational flows in the Gunnison River, where local officials want to develop a whitewater arena as a world-class tourist destination. According to Glazer, the district has been facing "aggressive opposition" from the state * * *

CWCB attorney Ted Kowalski said the board recognizes and supports the right of communities to claim recreational in-stream flows, but wants to ensure they don't claim more water than they actually need at the expense of other upstream uses. If a town claims the entire flow of a river, that could prevent upstream communities from developing that same source of water for domestic use Kowalski said. * * * "The board has been wrestling with the question of how much is enough," Kowalski said, referring to a series of hearings on the subject.

"Even though the state lost (in the Supreme Court), it's really the policy of the current administration to oppose this in any way, shape or form," said Glenn Porzak, the Boulder attorney who argued on behalf of Golden, Breckenridge and Vail. * * * The administration has thrown up every conceivable legal roadblock in an effort to "ratchet down" the number of applications and the amount of water claimed, he said. "They are trying to limit the in-channel diversions to the minimum amount required to float a boat," Porzak said. "This is a fight between the old West and the new West * * * I think that's the reason this has caught so much attention...."

The case cited in the article above is State Eng'r v. City of Golden, 69 P.3d 1027 (Colo.2003), aff'g by an equally divided court, In re Application for Water Rights of Golden, No. 98CW448 (Colo. Water Ct. Div. No. 1, 2001). A subsequent case involving in-stream flows on the Gunnison was handed down in 2005: Colorado Water Conservation Bd. v. Upper Gunnison River Water Conservancy Dist., 109 P.3d 585

(Colo.2005). There, the court reversed the water court's order granting a recreational in-channel diversion (RICD) conditional right to the Upper Gunnison Conservancy District, because the court failed to consider whether the intended in-channel diversion was in fact a RICD as defined by the statute. *Id*. at 604. In applying § 37–92–106(6)(b), the water court must "make a finding as to the least necessary stream flow to achieve an applicant's objectively reasonable recreation experience." *Id*. at 603.

> [The statute] … provides flexibility, requiring that a recreation experience in and on the water be reasonable considering the water availability of a particular stream reach. At a minimum, merely floating a kayak could be a reasonable recreation experience on some reaches, while at a maximum, a world-class expert course requiring nearly the entire flow of a given stream could be reasonable. By implication, the reasonableness of a []… recreation experience is directly related to the available, unappropriated stream flow, thereby depending entirely upon the river basin on which it is sought. Consequently, not all rivers and streams in the state may support world-class whitewater courses despite a particular appropriator's intent, and some may have so little available flow that only floating a kayak would be reasonable.

Id. at 559, 602.

The conflicts on the Gunnison and other Colorado rivers illustrate Professor Freyfogle's point in *Water Rights and the Common Wealth*: true reform is hard to come by in western water law. But states like Colorado, perhaps seeing the proverbial "writing on the wall," have begun to take steps toward protecting both environmental and recreational interests in in-stream flows.

In Focus:

DROUGHT PROMPTS WATER BOARD
TO ENFORCE STREAM RIGHTS,
800 VIOLATIONS NOTED IN UNPRECEDENTED
ACTION THAT COULD WORSEN SHORTAGES
Steve Lipsher
Denver Post, September 22, 2002

For the first time in its history, the agency in charge of protecting stream flows has asked Colorado's water cops to begin enforcing its drought-depleted water rights across the state. The Colorado Water Conservation Board, which holds water rights in every major river basin in the state for environmental protection, has flagged about 800 cases in which ski areas, municipalities, ranchers and conservancy organizations may be illegally siphoning water from the streams. * * * The immediate impact is difficult to gauge, but it could result in water shortages for new subdivisions and conflicts with longtime users who substitute water from one drainage for supplies in another.

The board is compiling and sending cases of possible violations to the state engineer's regional offices and expects water commissioners to begin notifying illicit users within the next couple of weeks. "In the past, we've had more of what I call spot calls, kind of like a rifle shot" in specific areas where shortages have occurred, said Dan Merriman, who heads the state in-stream flow program. "This is the first time we've done it on a statewide basis, and it's directly a result of the drought."

Melinda Kassen, director of the Colorado Water Project for Trout Unlimited, applauded the move to enforce the in-stream flow program but said it was a long time coming. * * * The board, formed in 1973 to hold water rights on behalf of the residents of Colorado, predominantly owns "junior" water rights that have relatively low priorities in the state's 150–year-old first-come, first-served system of water laws. Still, the water conservation board's water rights, which are considered real property that can be bought and sold, trump more recent claims, which might be left high and dry as a result of the new enforcement. * * *

Among the trouble spots: five new Crested Butte-area subdivisions with hundreds of homes along the East River, a tributary of the Gunnison, which earlier this month was trickling at close to its minimum stream flow. * * * Steve Glazer, ... a board member of the Upper Gunnison River Water Conservancy District ... [remarked:] "The subdivisions take water from the river and rely on so-called augmentation plans—purchases of water from other sources that are released into the river farther downstream—but those plans don't ensure that there's sufficient water in the crucial, immediately adjacent reaches. * * * The augmentation plans don't work. * * * There is one where they built a pond, but the pond doesn't hold water." * * *

The concern even about the ones that do function is that most of them have shallow ponds. And in the wintertime, it is possible that when the water is needed, those ponds may be frozen solid. Ultimately, if another source of water isn't found for the subdivisions— River Bend, River Land, Skyland and Hidden River among them— they could be cut off entirely. Not every one of the 800 cases will result in significant changes. A couple of suspected violations in Steamboat Springs, for example, are the result of a stream, Spring Creek, running dry. * * *

State officials say they hope in many cases to find alternative sources of water or lessen the blow of shutting off ditches and headgates completely. "The CB is keenly aware of the potential hardships

> that strict compliance may create and, whenever possible, we want to work with water users and individuals to address these hardships and balance water needs," * * *
>
>   * * * [B]ecause of the amount of time it will take for water commissioners to verify each case and then contact illicit water users, some may escape because many minimum flow requirements are reduced in the autumn. "But we want people to know that this can't continue," Merriman said. "We need to resolve this. This is something that may be with us for some period of time."

Notes and Questions

How should in-stream flow interests in scenic values, water quality and fisheries habitat be treated in western water law? Should in-stream flow rights and RICDs be treated differently? Are RICDs merely a way for private entities or municipalities like Vail, Breckenridge and Golden to obtain in-stream flow rights, which could otherwise be held only by a state agency? If so, is that a good thing?

4. Beneficial Use

It is "an accepted catechism" in western water law that "beneficial use is the basis, measure, and limit of a water right." Janet C. Neuman, *Beneficial Use, Waste, and Forfeiture: The Inefficient Search for Efficiency in Western Water Use*, 28 ENVTL. L. 919, 920 (1998). An appropriation can only be perfected when the appropriated water is put to beneficial use. Generally, domestic, agriculture, municipal, industrial, hydroelectric power production, stock watering, and mining are all considered beneficial uses. Just because the type of use is beneficial, however, does not give the appropriator carte blanche to use wasteful amounts of water.

BENEFICIAL USE, WASTE, AND FORFEITURE: THE INEFFICIENT SEARCH FOR EFFICIENCY IN WESTERN WATER USE
Janet C. Neuman
28 ENVTL. L. 919 (1998)

    * * * [T]he doctrinal trinity of beneficial use, waste, and forfeiture … is ill-equipped in its present form to achieve the levels of efficiency that will be necessary to meet twenty-first century western water demands. * * * Beneficial use is in fact a fairly elastic concept that freezes old customs, allows water users considerable flexibility in the amount and method of use, and leaves line drawing to the courts. The prohibitions against waste … are mostly hortatory concepts that rarely result in cutbacks in water use. In fact, there is widespread agreement that there are significant inefficiencies in western water use, in spite of these concepts of good husbandry that are built into the law. * * *

The water codes of all of the western states and some state constitutions include the term "beneficial use." Constitutional treatment of beneficial use ranges from simple statements declaring the right to appropriate water for beneficial use, to more normative provisions requiring reasonable and nonwasteful water use. Statutes of nine states intone in nearly identical language that "beneficial use, without waste, is the basis, measure, and limit of a water right," and the remainder refer in some way to beneficial use. * * * For instance, Colorado law provides that " '[b]eneficial use' is the use of that amount of water that is reasonable and appropriate under reasonably efficient practices to accomplish without waste the purpose for which the appropriation is lawfully made." * * * [I]t has been left to the courts to define, interpret, and apply the basic requirement.* * *

* * * [B]eneficial use has two different components: the type of use and the amount of use. In order to be legally beneficial, the type of use must be something socially acceptable. As to the amount of use, there must be actual use in an amount that is not wasteful.

* * * The courts should scrutinize water rights claims in general adjudications and individual actions and ask hard questions about whether uses are truly beneficial and nonwasteful by [modern] standards. Administrative water agencies need to bite the bullet and aggressively enforce against waste and forfeiture, promote conservation, and give clear legal guidance for an updated beneficial use doctrine. Western state legislatures should embrace the responsibility to insure water supplies for their future citizens, and give courts and agencies a mandate and funding to seek efficiency improvements. Without strategic reforms, the demands of twenty-eight million additional thirsty people in the arid West in the twenty-first century will be satisfied only at great economic, social, and environmental costs. * * *

As Professor Neuman explains, water must be put to a beneficial use, in terms of both the type of use and the quantity of water put to that use, before an appropriative right vests. Courts and agencies, however, don't always enforce these requirements as stringently as they might. Consider her critique of western water law as you work your way through the remaining sections of this chapter.

The following case addresses the allowable amount of beneficial use.

DEPARTMENT OF ECOLOGY v. THEODORATUS

Supreme Court of Washington, 1998.
135 Wash.2d 582, 957 P.2d 1241.

In 1973, Appellant George Theodoratus and Ray Drake formed a limited partnership to build a residential development near the Skagit River ... and applied to the Department of Ecology for a water right to serve the development. The application was approved pursuant to a

"Report of Examination" ... [which] included language purporting to create a vested water right which would entitle the applicant to a water certificate ... once a water supply system was capable of delivering water, even though some or most of the lots were vacant. * * *

The primary issue in this case is whether a final certificate of water right, i.e., a vested water right, may be issued based upon the capacity of a developer's water delivery system, or whether a vested water right may be obtained only in the amount of water actually put to beneficial use. Here, the Pollution Control Hearings Board concluded that ... system capacity, or a "pumps and pipes" measure, would be the method of quantification for purposes of the final certificate of water right. Accordingly, the Board held that the Department of Ecology could not condition Appellant's extension of time in which to perfect a water right by providing that actual beneficial use of water would be the measure of that right. We conclude that state statutory and common law does not allow for a final certificate of water right to be issued based upon system capacity. * * *

[A] ... reason to reject Appellant's contention that system capacity determines the measure and limit of a water right ... [is that] [w]ater rights may be relinquished. The failure "to beneficially use all or any part" of the right for five years, without sufficient cause, "shall relinquish" the right in whole or in part. * * * If system capacity defined the quantity of the right, i.e., system capacity equated to beneficial use as a measure and limit of the right, these statutory provisions would be meaningless. For example, if only one lot of 250 in a development having a completed water supply system ever actually used water, relinquishment could never be found of any part of the water right because system capacity would not change no matter how long water was not actually used with respect to the other 249 lots. We will not construe the statutory scheme in a way which renders these provisions of the relinquishment statutes meaningless.

Additional concerns presented by Appellant's position are that using system capacity as a measure of a water right would allow speculation in water rights and lead to uncertainty in management of this fixed resource at a time when availability of water is a significant concern and management of limited water resources is of utmost importance. * * *

Notes and Questions

1. What significance is the court's holding in *Theodoratus*? Does it have procedural as well as substantive implications for the developer? Naturally, the developer wanted his water right to be measured by his system's capacity. Wouldn't it seem sensible to quantify the right for a new development according to the development's capacity rather its actual use of water at start-up? If the developer had been a municipality seeking a permit for a public water supply system, should the court allow a capacity-based water right? *See id.* at 594 ("Appellant is not a municipality, and we decline to address issues concerning municipal water suppliers in the context of this

case. We do note that the statutory scheme allows for differences between municipal and other water use."); Central Delta Water Agency v. State Water Resources Control Board, 124 Cal.App.4th 245, 20 Cal.Rptr.3d 898 (2004) (holding that a general statement of potential beneficial use is insufficient and that Delta, a water provider, could not piggyback on the state and federal projects because it was not entitled to the traditional latitude afforded municipalities and other governmental entities).

2. Throughout the southwestern United States, particularly in New Mexico, many Hispanic communities were formed as pueblos that were granted the right under Spanish law to take as much water as necessary in order to satisfy their present and future municipal needs. At the time of the Treaty of Guadalupe Hidalgo of 1948, Mexican citizens owned millions of acres of land, often held in common ownership by multiple families. Their system of communal water rights reflects the rich history and culture of the region. It is vividly portrayed in John Nichols' novel, The Milagro Bean Field War (1994), which tells the story of Hispanic villager Joe Mondragon, who diverted water allocated under state law to a big development company into his family's long-fallow bean field in an effort to reclaim lost water rights. The pueblo system of water rights was formally recognized in Cartwright v. Public Service Co., 66 N.M. 64, 343 P.2d 654 (1958). However, in State of New Mexico ex rel. Martinez v. City of Las Vegas, 135 N.M. 375, 89 P.3d 47 (2004), the New Mexico Supreme Court found that the pueblo water rights doctrine was inconsistent with the state's system of prior appropriation and prevented the efficient, economic use of water. The court overruled *Cartwright* and held that a pueblo's water rights must be based on actual beneficial use. *Id.*

Appropriators must employ a reasonably efficient means of diversion. Colorado v. New Mexico, 459 U.S. 176, 103 S.Ct. 539, 74 L.Ed.2d 348 (1982); Schodde v. Twin Falls Land & Water Co., 224 U.S. 107, 32 S.Ct. 470, 56 L.Ed. 686 (1912). The right to use water does not include the right to waste water. Does this mean that pueblos and long-standing senior users must upgrade to state-of-the-art systems to avoid waste? Generally speaking, no; reasonableness is judged by the applicable standards at the date of the initial diversion. State ex rel. Crowley v. District Court, 108 Mont. 89, 88 P.2d 23 (1939). Excessively wasteful uses, however, may be prohibited. *See* Erickson v. Queen Valley Ranch, 22 Cal.App.3d 578, 99 Cal.Rptr. 446 (1971) (loss of over 80% of water delivered via 2.5 miles of unlined ditches was waste); Warner Valley Stock Co. v. Lynch, 215 Or. 523, 336 P.2d 884 (1959) (reliance on overflow of a lake to irrigate appropriator's lands was wasteful). In one rather unusual case, a court held that irrigating fields in the winter simply to drown gophers was waste. Tulare Irrigation Dist. v. Lindsay–Strathmore Irrigation Dist., 3 Cal.2d 489, 45 P.2d 972, 1007 (1935).

In some states, either the legislature or the State Engineer can limit the quantity of water an appropriator can divert for irrigation by fixing the amount of water per acre irrigated. Determining this "duty" of water typically involves a formula based on the average needs of the group of users along a stream. *See* State ex rel. Reynolds v. Niccum, 102 N.M. 330, 695 P.2d 480 (1985). The maximum duty acts as a cap on the amount of water to be used, but it may be challenged if an appropriator with a greater amount of decreed rights can prove that more water can be put to a beneficial use. *See* Enterprise Irrigation District v. Willis, 135 Neb. 827, 284 N.W. 326 (1939).

As noted above, most types of domestic, agricultural, and industrial uses are commonly recognized as beneficial. *See* In re General Determination of the Rights to Use All of the Water, 98 P.3d 1 (Utah 2004) (holding that irrigation of a tree farm that ultimately failed nevertheless constituted a beneficial use because the water supported indigenous plants, reduced fire hazards, satisfied aesthetic desires, and created property line buffers). Recreational uses are now often accepted as beneficial as well. *See* In Focus: State to Ponder Flows of Recreational Water, *supra,* at pp. 1312–1313. What about purely aesthetic purposes, like the fountains at Las Vegas casinos? Older cases held no. *See* Empire Water & Power Co. v. Cascade Town Co., 205 F. 123, 129 (8th Cir. 1913) (a scenic waterfall for private pleasure is not a beneficial use under Colorado law).

Some prior appropriation jurisdictions have enacted preference statutes, which generally rank municipal and domestic uses above agricultural and industrial uses. *See, e.g.*, Neb. Stat. § 46–204 (prioritizing domestic uses, agriculture, and then manufacturing). Despite the fact that certain uses are prioritized in these jurisdictions, priority date, not type of use, controls who gets the water in times of scarcity. In other words, the senior user will be able to use the full amount of her perfected water right, regardless of her type of use. What's the purpose of statutory preferences then, if the user's priority date controls in the event of shortage? Would enforcing preferences, rather than priority dates, undermine the priority system, or can the two concepts somehow co-exist? *See* Neb. Stat. 46–294(i) (as amended in 2004) (providing for approval of permanent water transfers when the proposed new use is in the same preference category as the current use).

To ensure enough water for municipal or domestic uses, some jurisdictions statutorily vest municipalities with the power of eminent domain—the power of the sovereign to take property for "public use" without the owner's consent. The public use concept is discussed in a recent Supreme Court case involving a city's re-development plan, Kelo v. City of New London, 125 S.Ct. 2655, 2005 WL 1469529, *3 (2005), and in Chapter 9.II.A, *supra* (addressing takings claims by private property owners). By allowing municipal water entities to condemn water rights, the General Assembly can show a distinct preference for municipal uses without disturbing the foundations of the priority system. Even municipal water providers, however, can be restricted pursuant to a state's water conservation regulations. *See* Arizona Water Co. v. Arizona Department of Water Resources, 208 Ariz. 147, 91 P.3d 990 (2004).

5. *Priority*

By ranking water rights according to the appropriation date (or application date), the prior appropriation doctrine ensures that the first in time is in fact the first in right. In adjudication states, the priority of a water right can relate back to the day the intent to divert water and put it to beneficial use was formed. Colorado River Water Conservation Dist. v. Rocky Mountain Power Co., 174 Colo. 309, 486 P.2d 438 (1971); Harvey Land & Cattle Co. v. Southeastern Colorado Water Conservancy Dist., 631 P.2d 1111 (Colo.1981). In permit states, a water right's priority date can relate back to the day the application was filed. In either case, your senior right is only as good as your ability to protect and enforce it against competing users, as Judge Hobbs explains below.

PRIORITY: THE MOST MISUNDERSTOOD STICK IN THE BUNDLE
Gregory J. Hobbs, Jr.
32 ENVTL. L. 37 (Winter 2002)

Priority determines the value of a water right, but lack of administration to curtail juniors in times of short supply can rob a senior right of its value. Priority is essential to a functioning water market, but lack of a reliable mechanism for changing water uses to new water uses destroys the potential of water markets to effectuate voluntary reallocation of the resource. Priority is only for beneficial use, but holders of priorities may be allowed to use water inefficiently, depriving junior users of a water supply. Priority entails water consumption, but water consumption causes environmental and social effects, generating community conflict. Priority requires planning, infrastructure, and legal protection, but competing interests may support planning, water right creation, and enforcement only to the degree that it serves their own interest.

These points and counterpoints reveal that priority is the most misunderstood stick in the bundle of a water right. Water policy can tear sticks from the bundle of water rights, or it can permit the bundle to serve human and environmental needs. Water law can spread its canopy, or it can fold its tent to the winds. To function effectively, priority must be employed in determining if and how much unappropriated water remains for appropriation by new users, taking into account actual river conditions in the operation of perfected water rights. To function effectively, priorities must also be enforced in times of short supply. If not, distribution of water is capricious and water user self-help occurs to the detriment of senior rights. In addition, episodic regulatory or crisis management measures ensue in an effort to address growing community conflict. Accordingly, adjudication and administration of rights through governmental action is essential to a functioning prior appropriation system.

In the prior appropriation system, junior rights can only take water when the senior rights have been satisfied in their entirety. When there is not enough water to satisfy the senior water right, the senior can place a call and junior water rights are ordered to cease all diversions. However, if all junior water rights respect the call and the water is still insufficient to reach the downstream senior, junior water users can claim that the senior appropriator is making a "futile call." When water is carried some distance to the downstream senior, for example, seepage and evaporation can result in a futile call. *See* State ex rel. Cary v. Cockran, 138 Neb. 163, 292 N.W. 239 (1940). If the call is futile because water will not reach the senior, the call is lifted.

When water is in short supply, as it often is in the west, junior appropriators can expect that their rights will be insufficient to satisfy their water needs. Junior appropriators can, however, make out-of-priority diversions by either exchanging water or using an augmentation plan. An exchange is an agreement between water users to trade water. An augmentation plan, or a temporary substitute supply plan, is where a junior user buys water to augment the flow in the river so that the junior out-of-priority diversion will not deprive the downstream senior water right.

The following article illustrates how water exchanges work in Colorado.

BASIC EXCHANGE 101
Casey S. Funk and Amy M. Cavanaugh
1 U. Denv. Water L. Rev. 206 (1998)

The exchange is one of the most important tools through which water is used efficiently in Colorado. * * *

An exchange is a trade of water between structures or users. Accomplished by diverting water upstream and then introducing an equivalent amount of water from a different source to the downstream water user, an exchange allows a junior water right to divert out-of-priority when a substitute supply is introduced to the senior water right. There are four critical elements to an exchange: (1) the source of substitute supply must be above the calling water right; (2) the substitute supply must be equivalent in amount and of suitable quality to the downstream senior appropriator; (3) there must be available natural flow at the point of upstream diversion; and (4) the rights of others cannot be injured when implementing the exchange. The source of substitute supply can include a storage release, or reusable return flows.

Although the release of substitute supply should be coordinated with the state water officials, an exchange does not require that the introduction of the substitute supply be simultaneous with a withdrawal. An exchange is normally operated when a downstream water right places a call, but an exchange or transfer can be made without a call. * * *

Although exchanges have been operated in Colorado for over a hundred years, very little statutory or case law exists regarding exchanges. Indeed, the exchange statutes were first enacted in 1897, and remain relatively unchanged to date. * * *

It shall be lawful,however, for the owners of ditches and water rights taking water from the same stream, to exchange with, and loan to, each other, for a limited time, the water to which each may be entitled, for the purpose of saving crops or of using the water in a more economical manner, provided, that the owner or owners making such loan or exchange, shall give notice in writing signed by all the owners participating in said loan or exchange, stating that such loan or exchange has been made, and for what length of time the same shall continue, whereupon said water commissioner shall recognize the same in his distribution of water.

Pursuant to this statute, upstream seniors were loaning water by diverting it from the creek and then transporting it through ditches and laterals to downstream juniors. However, removal of this loaned water from the creek injured intervening juniors who were senior to the junior water right receiving the water by lateral. These types of loans or exchanges were disallowed because they injured downstream intervening water rights which were not called out by the receiving water right.

The early cases of *Ft. Lyon Canal Co. v. Chew* and *Bowman v. Virdin* ... held that the ... exchange statutes were constitutional as long as the exchanges were exercised in such a way, at such times, and under such circumstances that the vested rights of others were not injured. These cases also stated that a temporary exchange could be operated without first obtaining a decree.

As ... more water users began vying for limited quantities of water, water users saw the value of decreeing their exchanges both conditionally and absolutely. * * *

––––––––––

The *Empire Lodge* case, below, demonstrates that only vested water right holders can bring claims against juniors utilizing exchanges, augmentation plans or substitute supply plans.

EMPIRE LODGE v. MOYER
39 P.3d 1139 Supreme Court of Colorado, 2001.

Empire Lodge has been diverting water out of priority to fill two ponds known as the Beaver Lakes, which the residents of the Beaver Lakes Subdivision utilize for fishing and recreation. It does not have an augmentation plan decree, or a conditional or absolute decree confirming a water appropriation and adjudicating a priority for filling the ponds. * * *

In 1986, the State Engineer informed Empire Lodge that it needed an augmentation plan decree from the Water Court. From 1987 to 1997,

Empire Lodge made its out-of-priority diversions under periodic approvals by the State Engineer that were conditioned on Empire Lodge filing an augmentation plan application with the Water Court. These approvals contained conditions requiring substitute water to the Arkansas River and subjecting Empire Lodge's water use to the call of the Moyers' Empire Creek Ditch right. As a substitute supply, Empire Lodge leased shares of Twin Lakes Reservoir and Canal Company water. The point of replacement into the Arkansas River was below the Moyers' point of diversion on Empire Creek. The Moyers irrigate their property with 4.9 c.f.s. from Empire Creek, decreed under Priority No. 34 to the Empire Creek Ditch. Empire Lodge did not provide a substitute supply to the Moyers' water right. Over the course of twelve years, Empire Lodge failed to initiate a Water Court augmentation plan proceeding * * *

The right guaranteed under the Colorado Constitution is to the appropriation of unappropriated waters of the natural stream, not to the appropriation of appropriated waters. *See* Colo. Const. art. XVI, § 5 * * * The property right we recognize as a Colorado water right is a right to use beneficially a specified amount of water, from the available supply of surface water or tributary groundwater, that can be captured, possessed, and controlled in priority under a decree, to the exclusion of all others not then in priority under a decreed water right. "Water right" means a right to use in accordance with its priority a certain portion of the waters of the state by reason of the appropriation of the same. * * *

Appropriation of natural stream waters is subject to administration in priority in accordance with judicial decrees determining the existence of water rights. * * * Direct flow water rights and storage water rights are entitled to administration based on their priority, regardless of the type of beneficial use for which the appropriation was made. The applicant for issuance of a conditional decree bears the burden of demonstrating that there is unappropriated water available for the appropriation, taking into account the historic exercise of decreed water rights. In order to perfect the conditional right and obtain an absolute decree, the applicant must have: (1) captured, possessed, and controlled unappropriated water; and (2) placed the water to beneficial use. * * *

Without a judgment and decree, a water right owner is not entitled to make an enforceable "call" to the state water officials for administration to curtail undecreed water uses and decreed junior rights that could intercept the water needed to satisfy the decreed senior priority. *See* § 37–92–301(3) (providing that distribution of water by the State and Division Engineers "shall be governed by the priorities for water rights and conditional water rights")* * * [Accordingly,] (1) Empire Lodge lacked standing in Water Court to invoke the futile call or enlargement doctrines against the Moyers' water use; (2) Empire Lodge's out-of-priority diversions required an augmentation plan decree authorizing them; and (3) the Water Court did not abuse its discretion in enjoining-

Empire Lodge's out-of-priority diversions pending adjudication authorizing them. * * *

Notes and Questions

1. Why was Empire's claim dismissed for lack of standing, when its diversions had been approved periodically by the State Engineer? Do procedural limitations, such as in *Empire,* advance or hinder the goals of prior appropriation? Objectives of water law systems include ensuring security and reliability for public and private use of this scarce and valuable resource, and promoting efficient uses. Do the basic substantive elements of the prior appropriation system and the rules you've studied so far advance these objectives? Do they sacrifice other important goals, like flexibility, efficiency, equity, and environmental quality? If you were a state legislator in a prior appropriation state, what reforms might you propose? If instead you were a law-maker in a brand new jurisdiction, would you recommend that your jurisdiction adopt a system more like prior appropriation or like riparianism?

2. Exchanges and transfers are addressed in more detail in Section F, below.

D. Reclaimed and Foreign Water

Not all rights to water are created equal. Ordinarily, an appropriator is only entitled to use water once. Return flows that naturally reach a surface stream belong to the stream and are subject to appropriation by others. There are, however, exceptions to this rule. Both reclaimed and foreign water can be used multiple times by the initial appropriator.

1. Reclaimed Water

Water that has escaped from a ditch or diversion channel by drainage or seepage may be recaptured by the appropriator and reused before it rejoins the natural water course. There are three limitations on this right of recapture and reuse. First, the total quantity of water used may not exceed the quantity of water in the appropriator's paper right (*i.e.,* the amount specified in a permit or court decree). Cleaver v. Judd, 238 Or. 266, 393 P.2d 193 (1964). As long as the total use does not exceed the paper right, the original appropriator may increase consumption by recycling the water, even if this injures downstream uses that have come to rely on historical return flows. Second, recaptured water must be used for the original purpose of the water right. Use of recaptured water for a new purpose is considered a change of use that must satisfy the "no harm" rule, which protects downstream junior appropriators who have relied on the historical conditions of the stream. See Comstock v. Ramsay, 55 Colo. 244, 133 P. 1107 (1913). The no harm rule is discussed in detail in Section F, below. Third, the reuse must occur on the same land as the original appropriation. *See* Salt River Valley Water Users' Ass'n v. Kovacovich, 3 Ariz.App. 28, 411 P.2d 201 (1966) (water reclaimed by lining irrigation ditches may not be reused on adjoining parcel).

Even though recapture is generally allowed, appropriators may not enlarge an originally decreed right by "salvaging" water through activities such as removing phreatophytes (plants that consume water) or draining an adjacent marsh. Southeastern Colorado Water Conservancy Dist. v. Shelton Farms, Inc., 187 Colo. 181, 529 P.2d 1321 (1974); RJA, Inc. v. Water Users Ass'n, 690 P.2d 823 (Colo.1984); Griffen v. State, 690 P.2d 1244 (Colo.1984). Why are the rules different for recapture and for salvage? Don't both types of activities minimize waste and promote more efficient use of water?

As fresh water grows ever more scarce, municipalities have begun to recycle their sewage effluent and reuse it for domestic and commercial purposes. If a city treats its effluent and releases it into a stream, can other appropriators claim it? In Nevada and Arizona, sewage effluent is considered waste water, subject to appropriation by others. United States v. Orr Water Ditch Co., 256 F.3d 935 (9th Cir.2001); Arizona Public Service Co. v. Long, 160 Ariz. 429, 773 P.2d 988 (1989); *see* City of San Marcos v. Texas Commission on Environmental Quality, 128 S.W.3d 264 (Tex.App.2004) (holding that the City of San Marcos did not retain ownership over its effluent after discharging it into a watercourse and thus could not divert water at a downstream location without an appropriation permit). The upside of this result is that those responsible for the sewage effluent may discontinue its discharge without violating the rights of downstream users that had relied on it to satisfy their appropriations. Does this mean that a city can keep its treated effluent on site and bottle it for distribution to residents?

2. *Foreign and Developed Water*

Water that is either created or imported from a different watershed can be used, reused, successively used, or entirely consumed by the importer. Developed water is new water that was never a part of the stream system. The most common example of foreign water in the West is water that is brought to a river by a trans-basin diversion, which collects water in one watershed and carries it through tunnels to a different watershed.

Appropriators of foreign water, which is also known as "imported" or "new" water, are not subject to the same rules that apply to other appropriators. When a water user adds new water to the water system, that water user has full entitlement to the water without regard to the priority system. Because foreign water was not previously part of the river system, the developer of foreign water can change the water use regardless of the "no harm" rule. *See* Thayer v. City of Rawlins, 594 P.2d 951 (Wyo.1979). Therefore, although downstream juniors may rely on return flows from foreign water, they have no recourse when the historical return flows of foreign waters are altered.

In Practice:

Assume that Farmer Greenjeans obtains a lucrative contract for potatoes with McDonald's restaurants and decides to convert her fields from her previous crops of canola and wheat. She chooses a new variety of potato, known as the Golden Blimpy, which produces unblemished, tasty French fries. It is, unfortunately, an extremely thirsty plant, and will require her to use her full paper right of 100 AF of water. For years, she had gotten by with only 70 AF. Upon consultation with her county extension agent, she discovers that she can easily recapture and reuse water on her fields by constructing a dirt berm and collection pond just at the edge of her property to stop excess irrigation water from running off into an adjacent stream. This will be much cheaper than installing new, more powerful pumps or other devices to increase the amount of withdrawal from her point of diversion on the stream. Can Farmer Greenjeans go forward with her plan? What if a downstream junior user objects? What if a wildlife conservation group, like the Audubon Society, objects? For more detail on the use of irrigation to produce top quality french fries, see GLENNON, WATER FOLLIES, *supra*, at 143–153.

E. Water Quality

Typically, only a portion of the water diverted by an appropriator is consumptively used. The water that is not consumptively used is either returned to a surface water body or it recharges a groundwater aquifer. Return flows from agricultural uses often have an increased saline content, while municipal return flows can include increased chemical and biological materials. Does a water right confer a right to the use of a certain quality of water? What if the beneficial use by the initial appropriator can only be accomplished by polluting the water? Examples include tanneries that discharge tannery "bark" and power plants that discharge heated water.

The following case reviewed the City of Thornton's objections to the quality of effluent water discharged from Denver's water treatment plant under a plan for water augmentation. The plan allowed Denver an "out-of-priority" diversion from the South Platte River; in turn, Denver was required to provide senior users with replacement water, using imported water discharged from its treatment plant. Thornton initially opposed the plan on the grounds that the replacement water was contaminated, and therefore unsuitable for Thornton's use as a drinking water supply. The parties reached a settlement, and the water court retained jurisdiction to ensure that the terms and conditions in Denver's augmentation decree prevented injury to other water users. Prior to the expiration of the period of retained jurisdiction, Thornton filed a petition to extend the court's jurisdiction, and alleged that Denver was injuring its water rights.

CITY OF THORNTON v. CITY AND COUNTY OF DENVER EX REL. BOARD OF WATER COMM'RS
Supreme Court of Colorado, 2002.
44 P.3d 1019.

* * * Denver petitioned for an augmentation plan to allow for out-of-priority diversions from the South Platte River for the irrigation of the Overland Park Golf Course [and to provide] ... a substitute supply using effluent from the Bi–City plant. Thornton, Centennial, Englewood, Henrylyn Irrigation District, and ... Aurora filed timely Statements of Opposition. * * * Thornton claimed that changes in the operation of the Bi–City plant since 1993 have increased the levels of phosphorous, nitrate, nitrite, harmful types of dissolved organic carbon and microbiological contaminates in the Bi–City effluent, making the water supply unsuitable for Thornton's normal use as a municipal water supply.

* * * When confronted with Thornton's claim of injury from the quality of the Bi–City effluent, the water court had an obligation to hold a hearing ... to address the injury to Thornton as a result of the actual operation of Denver's Augmentation Plan in comparison to the quality of supply it would receive absent the institution of the augmentation plan.... Instead, the court found that the seven-year period of retained jurisdiction could not be invoked to address the quality effects of the use of Bi–City effluent as a substitute water supply in Denver's Augmentation Plan.

We determine that this case presents a situation in which the actual operation of Denver's Augmentation Plan creates a cognizable issue of injury to Thornton not anticipated by the water court at the time of its initial decree. The ... court retains authority over injury determinations relating to water quality ... Similarly, Thornton's initial stipulation to the suitability of the Bi–City effluent did not preclude the water court from reconsidering potential injury to Thornton during the retained jurisdiction stage of its injury analysis. Accordingly, we hold that the water court improperly refused to hold a hearing on Thornton's alleged injury from the operation of Denver's Augmentation Plan. * * *

Notes and Questions

1. An augmentation plan is "[a] detailed program ... to increase the supply of water available for beneficial use ... by the development of new or alternate means or points of diversion, by pooling of water resources, by water exchange projects, by providing substitute supplies of water, by the development of new sources of water, or by any other appropriate means." *Id.* at 1025 (citing § 37–92–103(9), 10 C.R.S. (2001)). When no unappropriated water is available, junior water right holders (like Denver) may seek augmentation plans to divert water out-of-priority while ensuring the pro-

tection of senior water right holders. Junior appropriators typically provide an augmented water supply to offset their out-of-priority depletions so that other water rights holders can enjoy the quantity of supply that would be available to them absent those depletions. Augmentation plans "can be approved only if there is 'no-injurious effect' to a vested water right." *Id.* If injury may occur, the water court or state agency must impose terms and conditions on the augmentation plan to remedy such injury. *Id.*

2. What are the potential advantages and disadvantages of augmentation plans? Are small farmers and communities likely to be adequately protected when a large city, like Denver, proposes an "out-of-priority" use to satisfy the domestic or recreational demands of its ever-expanding population? Well-known water lawyer Lawrence MacDonnell believes that, while voluntary transfers of water and water rights are becoming more common, there is a place for other, non-voluntary mechanisms.

> The notion of an "out-of-priority" water use appears on its face to be incongruent with the prior appropriation system. Indeed, it does violate the basic ... principle that new uses must stand in line behind all previous uses before they can have access to the supply of water. * * * [Out-of-priority] uses are based on ensuring existing, legally-protected uses can continue unimpaired. Of course, the measures taken must make a new use or an existing out-of-priority use possible in return. They become important, even necessary, in fully appropriated water systems. Fully realized, they can provide an incentive-based approach for making more effective use of the water supply. * * * [Out-of-priority uses and augmentation plans] ... are non-traditional, they can be complicated, and they sometimes require expensive monitoring and administration, but they can help us meet today's changing water-based needs without harming other uses.

Lawrence J. MacDonnell, *Out-Of–Priority Water Use: Adding Flexibility to the Water Appropriation System*, 83 Neb. L. Rev. 485, 492–492, 539–540 (2004).

3. Federal statutes that regulate water quality and pollution are addressed below in Section VII of this chapter.

F. Changes In Use, Transfers, and the "No Harm" Rule

A water right will specify the use and quantity of the water as well as the point of diversion and the place and time of use. All water diverted under that right must be used for the designated purpose at the designated place and time. The point of diversion and the place, time, or type of use may be changed or even transferred to a different user, but the appropriator must seek approval from an administrative agency in a permit state, or the court in Colorado. Thus, the right to change or transfer a water right in a prior appropriation jurisdiction is not absolute.

All water users have a right to the continuing conditions of the stream, as it existed, the day their water right was confirmed. A "no harm" rule prohibits changes in water rights that injure another water user who has relied on the historical conditions of the stream. Harm can stem from diminished water quantity or quality. *See* Farmers Highline Canal & Reservoir Co. v. City of Golden, 129 Colo. 575, 272 P.2d 629 (1954).

Several restrictions are imposed on changes or transfers to ensure that other water users will suffer no harm. First, the water must have been applied to beneficial use, and thus the right perfected, before a change or transfer will be authorized. Public Utility Dist. v. State, 146 Wn.2d 778, 51 P.3d 744 (2002). In addition, only the amount of water that was historically consumed may be changed or transferred. This limitation is intended to prevent harm to the downstream appropriator; the amount historically consumed by the initial use was never returned to the river in the first place, and therefore could not have been relied on by downstream water users. Farmers Reservoir & Irrigation Co. v. Consolidated Mutual Water Co., 33 P.3d 799 (Colo.2001); Empire Lodge Homeowners Ass'n v. Moyer, 39 P.3d 1139 (Colo.2001). When the historical beneficial use is less than the decreed amount, the quantity of a water right that can be changed or transferred will be reduced to the amount historically used.

MOUNT EMMONS MIN. CO. v. CRESTED BUTTE
Supreme Court of Colorado, 2002.
40 P.3d 1255.

* * *Appropriative water rights are property interests that may be transferred by way of sale, lease, or exchange. *See* Spears v. Warr, 44 P.3d 742 (Utah 2002) * * * Transfers are subject to state law and therefore, particular states can make water rights unseverable from the land. Such is the case in Montana, Oklahoma, Nebraska, Nevada, South Dakota, and Wyoming. However, absent such legislation, appropriative water rights can be granted separately from the land on which they have historically been used. * * * [I]n most states, water rights used on a specific parcel of land are automatically transferred when the land is conveyed. In Colorado, the intent of the grantor will determine whether the water rights are transferred with the conveyance of the land. But when the grantor's intent cannot be clearly ascertained, the presumption, in Colorado, is that the water rights are conveyed with the transfer of the land.

In prior appropriation jurisdictions that allow water rights to be conveyed separately from the land, the amount of water available for transfer is limited to the amount historically consumed. Therefore, when the actual historical beneficial use has been less than the decreed amount, or when a portion of the water right has been abandoned, the state records will not accurately reflect the quantity of the right held by the transferor. *See* State Engineer v. Bradley, 53 P.3d 1165, 1170 (Colo. 2002) ("an absolute decree, whether expressed in terms of a flow rate or a volumetric measurement, is itself not an adjudication of actual historical use") * * *

Although water rights may be transferred, persons seeking a change run the risk of re-quantification and reduction based on actual historic consumptive use. Pueblo West Metro Dist. v. Southeastern Colo. Water Conservancy Dist., 717 P.2d 955, 959 (Colo.1986). *See* City of Golden v. Simpson, 83 P.3d 87 (Colo.2004) (requiring the City to stop diverting water from a creek when it petitioned to move its point of diversion approximately six miles upstream and to change the use from seasonal irrigation to year-round municipal). Of course, appropriators can challenge a determination of historical use, but the party seeking the change bears the burden of proof. *See* Matter of May, 756 P.2d 362 (Colo.1988).

Finally, to ensure that junior appropriators are not injured, the change or transfer must be accomplished by a judicial decree or administrative permit. Farmer Reservoir & Irrigation Co. v. City of Golden, 44 P.3d 241 (Colo.2002). The decree or permit can impose appropriate conditions or augmentation plans to protect junior appropriators. However, if conditions cannot be imposed to protect others from harm, the change will be denied. Brighton Ditch Co. v. City of Englewood, 124 Colo. 366, 237 P.2d 116 (1951).

Notes and Questions

1. Is the rule restricting changes or transfers to actual historic consumptive use too restrictive? Doesn't this have a chilling effect that inhibits transfers or changes in use to more efficient, socially desirable activities? Should there be an exception if the new use meets some sort of "public interest" test, or if no junior user can prove harm? Note that the "no harm" rule is not applicable to changes or transfers of foreign water. Twin Lakes Reservoir & Canal v. Aspen, 193 Colo. 478, 568 P.2d 45 (1977). Why not?

2. Unlike riparian water rights, appropriative water rights are transferable between watersheds. *See* Coffin v. Left Hand Ditch Co., 6 Colo. 443 (1882). According to the court in the *Mount Emmons* case above, "[i]n the arid West, trans-basin diversions are necessary to bring water to growing cities (*i.e.*, from Colorado's western slope across the Rockies to the front range cities)." Yet that court also noted that many states have adopted legislation or regulations that limit trans-basin diversions in order to protect the basin of origin. What's the purpose of such a limitation? If Colorado's front range cities need water, and appropriators west of the continental divide are willing to sell their water, why not let market forces prevail? After all, the common law of prior appropriation already limits transfers by the "no harm" rule. On nearly every stream, downstream juniors rely on the return flows from upstream water users. If junior users in the basin of origin are not harmed, either because there's an abundance of water there or because their interests are "bought out" by the parties to the transaction, why not let the transaction proceed?

3. Changes in the appropriator's point of diversion are treated like any other changes in the water right; therefore, such changes must be approved in substantially the same manner as the initial determination of the water

right. Trail's End Ranch v. Colorado Div. of Water Resources, 91 P.3d 1058 (Colo.2004). Why is a change in the point of diversion, which neither enlarges the initial right nor effectuates a change in use, so strictly controlled? How might a new point of diversion adversely affect other users?

4. Will a surface-water appropriator be allowed to change the point of diversion to a well that supplements surface flows at times of shortage? Courts have held yes, as long as two conditions are met: (1) the groundwater to be pumped is the source of the surface water, and (2) the change in point of diversion does not impair other existing water rights. Herrington v. State Engineer, 135 N.M. 585, 92 P.3d 31 (2004). If the appropriator fails to use her surface water diversion for several years because she's able to make use of groundwater instead, does she run the risk of forfeiting or abandoning her surface water right? *See* Section H (Loss of a Water Right), below.

G. Storage

The acquisition of a right to divert water does not necessarily entitle the appropriator to store the water. While some jurisdictions assume that capturing water in a reservoir is included as a beneficial use under a direct flow water right, others require a separate water right to store water. *Compare* Pueblo West Metropolitan Dist. v. Southeastern Colorado Water Conservancy Dist., 689 P.2d 594 (Colo.1984), *with* United States v. Alpine Land & Res. Co., 919 F.Supp. 1470 (D.Nev.1996). Once obtained, a storage right is integrated into the priority system. Donich v. Johnson, 77 Mont. 229, 250 P. 963 (1926).

A storage right may be applied for future use or the water may be leased to another user or exchanged for direct flow diversions upstream. A primary limitation on storage rights is the "one fill" rule, which provides that a reservoir may only be filled once annually, and over the year it cannot retain a greater quantity than its full capacity. *See* Windsor Reservoir & Canal v. Lake Supply Ditch, 44 Colo. 214, 98 P. 729 (1908).

In addition to storing water above ground, water can be stored in underground aquifers. The primary attraction to underground storage is the fact that there are no evaporative losses. If an irrigation district stores water underground, can the owner of the overlying land claim a trespass? If instead a governmental entity stores water underground, can the surface landowner assert a claim for compensation? *See* West Maricopa Combine, Inc. v. Arizona Dept. of Water Resources, 200 Ariz. 400, 26 P.3d 1171 (2001); In re Application U–2, 226 Neb. 594, 606, 413 N.W.2d 290, 299 (1987) (overlying owners had no standing to assert a taking due to state's grant of irrigation district's application for incidental storage under plaintiffs' land for water that accumulated underground as a result of seepage from man-made facilities); Board of County Comm'rs v. Park County Sportsmen's Ranch, 45 P.3d 693 (Colo.2002) (underground storage of water does not necessitate that the landowner be compensated).

H. Loss of a Water Right

A water right can be lost by abandonment, adverse possession (prescription), or statutory forfeiture. When a water right is lost by abandonment or forfeiture, the water is returned to the stream and can, theoretically, be appropriated by others. Nearly all of the surface water in the western states is over-appropriated. Thus, in reality, abandoned water rights benefit junior appropriators by increasing the quantity of available water. In other words, once a senior water right is abandoned, all the junior rights become more senior and have a greater chance of being fulfilled. When a water right is lost by adverse possession, the adverse possessor obtains the right.

Abandonment is the relinquishment of the right by non-use, accompanied by the intent to desert the right. In most states, intent is the critical element. *See* United States v. Orr Water Ditch, 256 F.3d 935 (9th Cir.2001) (abandonment requires showing of subjective intent). Whether an appropriator intended to abandon a water right is a question that will depend on the circumstances of the particular case. *See* Public Utility Dist. v. State, 146 Wn.2d 778, 51 P.3d 744 (2002) (intent to abandon could not be proven even though the water project was decommissioned in 1956 when the flume collapsed, as the District continued to engage in water power production studies); United States v. Alpine Land & Reservoir Co., 27 F.Supp. 2d 1230 (D.Nev.1998) (even in the face of non-use, payment of fees to preserve a water right should be considered in determining intent); Denver v. Middleton Park Water Conserv., 925 P.2d 283 (Colo.1997) (the fact that Denver did not protest inclusion of its irrigation water rights on commissioner's abandonment list is evidence of intent to abandon); Haystack Ranch v. Fassio, 997 P.2d 548 (Colo.2000) (lack of diversion records over period of 22 years and evidence of unusable condition of ditch are consistent with intent to abandon). However, some state statutes declare a water right abandoned regardless of intent, so long as non-use was "voluntary." *See* Scott v. McTiernan, 974 P.2d 966 (Wyo.1999) (no abandonment when failure to use water from creek was the result of interference by adjacent landowner).

The one attempting to establish that an appropriator abandoned their right has the burden of persuasion. *Id.* An unreasonable period of non-use can create a rebuttable presumption of an intent to abandon. Denver v. Snake River Water Dist., 788 P.2d 772 (Colo.1990). The time period that gives rise to the presumption can be found in the state's case law or its statutes. *See* Axtell v. M.S. Consulting, 955 P.2d 1362 (Mont.1998) (ten months does not meet the court's definition of "long period of non-use"). The holder of a water right may rebut the presumption with evidence that negates an intent to abandon. *See* Okanogan Wilderness League, Inc. v. Town of Twisp, 133 Wn.2d 769, 947 P.2d 732 (1997) (town's continuing existence as municipality does not rebut town's non-use of water for over 45 years); People ex rel. Danielson v. City of Thornton, 775 P.2d 11 (Colo.1989) (water right owner's testimony of desire to place water right on market for sale does not rebut presumption of abandonment). Legal difficulties preventing water use may excuse non-use and, in some cases, economic infeasibility will too. *See* Hallenbeck v. Granby Ditch & Reservoir Co., 160 Colo. 555, 420 P.2d 419

(1966); *but see* Southeastern Colorado Water Conservancy Dist. v. Twin Lakes Associates, Inc., 770 P.2d 1231 (Colo.1989).

When there is insufficient evidence to prove intent to abandon, the water right may still be lost by forfeiture. Many jurisdictions have forfeiture statutes which provide for the relinquishment of a water right when a given period of non-use lapses, regardless of intent. State v. Hagerman Water Right Owners, 130 Idaho 727, 947 P.2d 400 (1997); Nephi City v. Hansen, 779 P.2d 673 (Utah 1989). The party that asserts a forfeiture—usually the state—has the burden of proving non-use for the statutory period. *See* Rencken v. Young, 300 Or. 352, 711 P.2d 954 (1985). To be forfeited, a water right must not be used at all during the statutory period. Therefore, an appropriator can prevent forfeiture by applying the water to beneficial use during the statutory time period. McAtee v. Faulkner Land & Livestock, Inc., 113 Idaho 393, 744 P.2d 121 (1987); *see also* McCray v. Rosenkrance, 135 Idaho 509, 20 P.3d 693 (2001) (evidence supported finding that all water rights were forfeited, except for 25 acres irrigated during the statutory five-year period), Staats v. Newman, 164 Or.App. 18, 988 P.2d 439 (1999) (natural irrigation, as opposed to artificial irrigation, can result in cancellation of a water right due to lack of beneficial use). A water right can also be forfeited if a would-be appropriator does not proceed with due diligence in constructing the diversion works and applying the water to beneficial use. Montana Dept. of Natural Resources and Conservation v. Intake Water Co., 171 Mont. 416, 558 P.2d 1110 (1976). Some state statutes protect water rights held by municipalities and water conservancy districts from forfeiture resulting from non-use when the water appropriated is for future needs. City of Raton v. Vermejo Conservancy Dist., 101 N.M. 95, 678 P.2d 1170 (1984).

The enforcement of forfeiture statutes is sometimes spotty, to the dismay of junior users and potential future users.

> Increasing demand requires more active management by Western state water administrators who seek to develop a water allocation system that maximizes both beneficial and economical uses of water. The concept of partial forfeiture is a tool that allows optimal water allocation.... Arizona, California, Colorado, Montana, Nevada, New Mexico, Oregon, Texas, Utah, Washington and Wyoming all use partial forfeiture mechanisms. * * * Partial forfeiture adds flexibility to water systems that are dealing with increased urban development. A water allocation system that recognizes partial forfeiture prevents a water user from hoarding water rights by using only a portion of those rights. * * *

Lane Jacobson, *Snake River Basin Adjudication Issue 10: Partial Forfeiture of a Water Right,* 35 IDAHO L. REV. 179 (1998).

In most western states, rights to the use of either appropriated or unappropriated water cannot be acquired by adverse possession. Turner v. Bassett, 134 N.M. 621, 81 P.3d 564 (App.2003); Lewis v. State Bd. of

Control, 699 P.2d 822 (Wyo.1985). In jurisdictions that do recognize water rights based on prescriptive use, one cannot adversely possess against the stream, but must actually adversely possess a perfected water right. Matter of Water Rights of V–Heart Ranch, Inc., 690 P.2d 1271 (Colo.1984). And there is a strong bias, or presumption, against acquisition of water rights by adverse use. Joe Johnson Co. v. Landen, 738 P.2d 711 (Wyo.1987); College Irr. Co. v. Logan River & Blacksmith Fort Irr. Co., 780 P.2d 1241 (Utah 1989). Why aren't prescriptive rights in water freely recognized in prior appropriation jurisdictions? Even in jurisdictions that do recognize prescriptive rights in water, as with real property, water rights held by the state or federal government cannot be obtained by adverse use. People v. Shirokow, 26 Cal.3d 301, 162 Cal. Rptr. 30, 605 P.2d 859 (1980).

I. The Future of Western Water Rights

The following article takes a close look at the prior appropriation system and its future. The author, Professor Dan Tarlock, raises similar concerns as did Professor Neuman, above. Do you agree that reforms are necessary to prevent waste and promote efficient uses of water, or might more vigorous enforcement practices do the trick?

THE FUTURE OF PRIOR APPROPRIATION IN THE NEW WEST
A. Dan Tarlock
41 Nat. Resources J. 769 (Fall 2001)

* * * As the West has changed from a raw commodity production colony to an urban region fully integrated into the global economy, prior appropriation has been increasingly criticized. The principal criticisms are that perpetual "use it or lose it rights" lock too much water into marginal agriculture and generally encourage inefficient off-stream consumptive uses to the detriment of aquatic ecosystem values and the needs of growing urban areas. Critics * * * [argue] that it should be replaced by non-perpetual permit systems that better value consumptive and in-stream uses.

One of the reasons for the gap between form and practice is that the state stewards of the doctrine have been slow to respond to a changing West. * * * States have fallen behind the curve in environmental protection and the inevitable economic rationalization of irrigated agriculture. * * * The flow of water from rural to urban areas has further widened the gap between the form and reality of prior appropriation. At its core, prior appropriation is a law of irrigation rights, but irrigated agriculture's future is one of stable or declining acreage. As growing urban areas and environmental interests scrambled for new and temporary supplies, water markets emerged as a major allocation force, using appropriative rights as a measure of compensation. To the dismay of many irrigators, property rights became a dual-edged sword. Irrigators venerated the security that their water rights provided but were dismayed when another equally entrenched characteristic of a property right, alienability, became the instrument of change.

* * * [T]he doctrine of prior appropriation will continue to change because the underlying economic and social changes occurring in the West are too powerful to lock it into place. * * * In the future, prior appropriation will function primarily as (1) a default rule to resolve small-scale conflicts, (2) a worst case enforcement scenario in complex allocation negotiations to encourage parties to find creative ways to avoid its actual application through cooperative management regimes and other sharing arrangements that accommodate a wide range of competing demands, and (3) a rule of compensation when water is voluntarily transferred or to inform the constitutional analysis when water is involuntarily reallocated. * * *

IV. DUAL DOCTRINE STATES

Strict observance of riparian doctrine in the west would have foreclosed mining or irrigation on nonriparian lands and drastically stifled western development. Consequently, many western states rejected the riparian doctrine. Others initially recognized some form of riparian rights but later struggled to limit or eliminate such rights. Western courts, however, tend to believe that riparian rights are "vested" property rights, so they continue "to recognize vestigial riparian rights and to struggle with coordinating these rights with the coexisting appropriative rights." Joseph W. Dellapenna, *Riparian Rights in the West*, 43 OKLA. L. REV. 51 (1990).

Dual system states have had to establish priorities between riparians and appropriators, decide the quantity of water that may be used by a riparian, and determine the legal ability of water users to obtain prescriptive rights. Most states, with the exception of California and Nebraska, have extinguished unused riparian rights and preserved only those riparian rights that vested by actual use prior to adoption of the appropriation law. The following article illustrates how Oklahoma and, by extension, other Great Plains states have struggled to reconcile riparianism and prior appropriation.

INDIAN RESERVED WATER RIGHTS
IN THE DUAL–SYSTEM STATE OF OKLAHOMA
Taiawagi Helton
33 Tulsa L.J. 979 (1998)

Oklahoma's settlement history and climate are similar to those of other states along the 100th meridian and the West Coast. The land in the eastern portions of those states is relatively humid and water is relatively plentiful, while the western portions are relatively arid. As a result, the riparian doctrine was used in the east, while the appropriation doctrine developed in the west, each accommodating the needs of users in their respective regions. The result was the dual rights system, which attempted to combine the two irreconcilable doctrines.

Dual-system states face three major obstacles to implementing that system. First, the riparian right to initiate or maintain reasonable uses, regardless of time, cannot be upheld without denying the certainty offered by the appropriation doctrine's "first in time, first in right" and "use it or lose it" principles. Second, the doctrines use discordant standards for determining the value of a particular use. Riparian uses are judged by a relative reasonableness test, as compared to all riparian uses. Appropriative uses are judged individually in terms of their economic, environmental, recreational, or aesthetic values. Third, the appropriation doctrine allows anyone in need of water to appropriate, severing the water from its adjacent land, while the riparian doctrine permits only riparian landowners to divert water, generally only on riparian land. As a result, a dual system "inevitably frustrates the chief advantages of one or both doctrines." * * *

To lessen the inherent conflicts between the riparian and prior appropriation doctrines, most dual system states have restricted riparian rights in various ways. Riparians may be limited in quantity to the amount that can be reasonably used for a beneficial use, and subsequent appropriations are permitted if the appropriation does not harm the riparian's reasonable use. *See* Tulare Irrigation District v. Lindsay–Strathmore Irrigation District, 3 Cal.2d 489, 45 P.2d 972 (1935); Brown v. Chase, 125 Wash. 542, 217 P. 23 (1923). To be deemed a vested riparian right, and thus recognized in a dual doctrine state, a riparian right must be used. All "unused or unusable rights predicated alone upon [riparian] theory" have largely been eliminated. State ex rel. Emery v. Knapp, 167 Kan. 546, 207 P.2d 440 (1949). *See* Kinross Copper Corporation v. State, 160 Or.App. 513, 981 P.2d 833 (1999) (because all non-used riparian rights have been statutorily extinguished, all new water rights are established by prior appropriation).

Oklahoma and other dual system states have struggled with constitutional challenges to the adoption of permit schemes or other changes that limit common-law riparian rights. In Franco–American Charolaise, Ltd. v. Oklahoma Water Resources Bd., 855 P.2d 568 (Okla.1990), the court considered a challenge to a 1963 statute that converted the state's system of water rights to prior appropriation and abolished all unexercised riparian rights, plus all existing riparian uses that had not been validated per a specified statutory procedure. Domestic riparian uses were the only uses excepted from the statutory scheme. Riparian landowners sued, claiming that the state could not abrogate their rights to initiate future uses absent compensation. The court held that the statute violated the state constitution by failing to provide for compensation for riparian owners: "The heart of the riparian right is the right to assert a use at *any time* as long as it does not harm another riparian who has a corresponding right." *Id.* at 577. As a result, appropriative rights perfected under the statutory procedure are subject to reasonable riparian uses during shortages.

> Should a riparian owner assert a vested right to initiate a *reasonable* use of the stream *and* should the water in the stream be insufficient to supply that owner's reasonable use, we hold that the appropriator with the last priority must either release water into the stream sufficient to meet the riparian owner's reasonable use or stop diverting an amount sufficient to supply the riparian owner's reasonable use until there is water sufficient to satisfy both interests. This temporary divestment is similar to that required under the appropriation doctrine when a shortage of water impairs a senior appropriation. * * *

Id. at 581.

Notes and Questions

1. What is the nature of a riparian water right? Does the Oklahoma opinion in *Franco-American* make any sense? If so, how can a riparian or dual system state adopt meaningful reforms to promote certainty and more efficient, high priority uses without "breaking the bank"? Other states' statutes that adopt water permit systems with new or modified criteria for establishing water rights, including those that extinguish all but grandfathered riparian rights, have been upheld against constitutional challenges. *See* In re Water Use Permit Applications, 94 Hawai'i 97, 182, 9 P.3d 409, 494 (2000); In re Adjudication of Water Rights of the Upper Guadalupe River Basin, 642 S.W.2d 438 (Tex.1982); Knight v. Grimes, 80 S.D. 517, 127 N.W.2d 708 (1964); Williams v. City of Wichita, 190 Kan. 317, 374 P.2d 578 (1962). How can such cases be squared with *Franco-American, supra,* if at all?

2. Two dual system states—Nebraska and California—continue to recognize unused riparian rights. In Wasserburger v. Coffee, 180 Neb. 149, 141 N.W.2d 738 (1966), the Nebraska court ruled that riparians could require a prior appropriator to release water if the riparian lands were patented before the 1895 Nebraska Irrigation Act; the rights of riparians on pre–1895 lands and appropriators are determined by relative reasonableness. In California, unused riparian rights may be successfully exercised against appropriations made on private land, San Joaquin and Kings River Canal & Irrigation Co. v. Worswick, 187 Cal. 674, 203 P. 999 (1922), but not on public lands. Lux v. Haggin, 69 Cal. 255, 10 P. 674 (1886). In 1979, the California Supreme Court limited riparian owners' future ability to use water by affording them lower priority than rights administratively recognized in the interim by the Water Resources Control Board. *See* In re Waters of Long Valley Creek Stream System, 25 Cal.3d 339, 158 Cal.Rptr. 350, 599 P.2d 656 (1979).

V. GROUNDWATER

Groundwater is an important alternative to surface water supplies. Groundwater occurs nearly everywhere beneath the earth's surface. Approximately half of the United State's population depends on groundwater for all of their water needs. In rural areas, ninety-seven percent of all drinking water comes from groundwater. Groundwater usage continues to expand for a variety of reasons, including technological advances in cheaper, more efficient pumps and delivery systems. Also, groundwater offers several advantages over surface water. Groundwater is:

- Easier to divert and can be tapped within a few hundred feet of where it is to be used

- Less susceptible to pollution

- Available in areas where surface water has already been appropriated

- Less likely to fluctuate in quantity during wet and dry seasons

- Not subject to evaporative losses

A. The Occurrence and Use of Groundwater

Groundwater is water that saturates pores or cracks in soils and rocks beneath the land's surface. Some underground reservoirs (aquifers) were initially filled with water by geological processes when the subsurface rock was originally formed. Most groundwater is naturally replenished by precipitation that infiltrates soil and rock, under the influence of gravity. The water that first enters the soil replaces water that has evaporated or been used by plants in the unsaturated zone. Excess water will infiltrate to the water table. Below the water table, water fully saturates all the cracks in the rock. In this saturated zone, the water is either discharged to the surface (by seepage to lakes, streams, or oceans) or trapped within a subsurface aquifer. Groundwater may also be enhanced artificially by return flows of surface water diversions (e.g., from agricultural irrigation) or direct injection of imported water into groundwater reservoirs.

From **U.S. Geological Survey/General Interest Publication "Ground Water"**

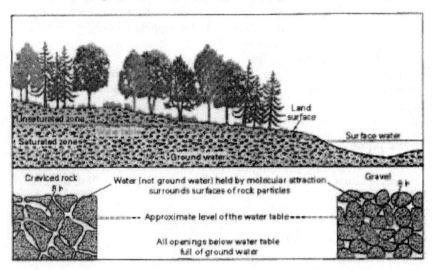

How ground water occurs in rocks.

Urban sprawl diminishes recharge rates by compacting or paving over permeable surfaces, making water infiltration a difficult and slow process. If the rate of recharge by precipitation, seepage or artificial infiltration is less than the amount of groundwater removed by wells, then groundwater is being "mined," and becomes a depletable resource. Because groundwater is not static and will not remain below one person's property forever, there is no incentive for a groundwater user to conserve water by not pumping it out of the ground. In fact, once a well begins pumping groundwater, nearby groundwater flows toward the well under the influence of gravity. The water table near the well appears as an inverted cone, called a "cone of depression." When the cones of depression of two or more wells overlap, the water table is lowered at an accelerated rate, causing rapid depletion of common aquifer pools. *See* ROBERT GLENNON, WATER FOLLIES: GROUNDWATER PUMPING AND THE FATE OF AMERICA'S FRESH WATERS (2002); Lotterman and Waelti, *Efficiency and Equity Implication of Alternative Well Interference Policies in Semi–Arid Regions*, 23 NAT.RES.J. 323 (1983). As groundwater becomes depleted, groundwater users are faced with re-drilling larger, deeper and more expensive wells. To prevent the rapid depletion of groundwater, many states now enforce extensive groundwater regulations. *See* Kelly, *Management of Groundwater Through Mandatory Conservation*, 61 Denver L.J. 1 (1983); McKenzie, *Groundwater Resources Management by Special District in Kansas*, 8 Current Mun. Prob. 529 (1982); Rossman and Steel, *Forging the New Water Law: Public Regulation of Proprietary Groundwater Right*, 33 HASTINGS L.J. 903 (1982).

1. Aquifers—Underground Reservoirs

All groundwater is contained within the open spaces in rock materials beneath the earth's surface. The extent to which groundwater may be stored in these underground rocks depends in large part on the "porosity" of the rock. Rocks with low porosity have fewer open spaces and are therefore limited in their capacity to absorb, retain, and yield water. The extent to which water can move through underground rock depends on the rock's "permeability." In permeable materials, gravity moves water from the land surface to lower rock materials where the pores are saturated. Water in the saturated zone either moves laterally to lower elevations where it may be discharged to the surface or becomes trapped by an impermeable rock formation or aquifer. Groundwater moves very slowly and it is not uncommon for the velocity of groundwater to be measured at a rate of inches or feet per year.

The "water table" is the top of the saturated zone. Bedrock, which is usually impermeable, underlies the saturated zone. Groundwater in unconfined aquifers must be pumped to be extracted, but artesian aquifers, which contain groundwater confined under pressure between impermeable or semi-permeable rocks, may yield water without pumping. *See* Burke and Kulasza, *Artesian Power! How to Prepare for the Coming Groundwater Revolution*, 28 ROCKY MTN. MIN. L. INST. 1345

(1982). The Dakota sandstone in North and South Dakota is a well-known artesian aquifer, where water is confined under dense shale.

Groundwater is commonly divided by law into two classes: (1) underground streams that flow in "reasonably ascertainable boundaries" or well-defined channels, and (2) "percolating" waters that slowly seep beneath the earth's surface in no known identifiable natural channels. Hayes v. Adams, 109 Or. 51, 218 P. 933 (1923). Courts have been more willing to view underground streams as hydrologically connected to surface waters. Groundwater that is hydraulically connected to a surface stream is classified as tributary groundwater. In some states, tributary groundwater is subject to the same legal doctrine that governs surface appropriations. *See* Water Rights of Park County Sportsmen's Ranch LLP. v. Bargas, 986 P.2d 262 (Colo.1999); Rettlowski v. Department of Ecology, 122 Wn.2d 219, 858 P.2d 232 (1993). In these states, when groundwater withdrawals would impair existing surface water rights, an application for a groundwater right must be denied. Postema v. Pollution Control Hearings Bd., 142 Wn.2d 68, 11 P.3d 726 (2000).

Percolating waters, which are far more common, are subject to each state's specific groundwater doctrine. In most states (Colorado is an exception), groundwater is presumed to be percolating water. One arguing otherwise must prove the existence of an underground tributary stream by physical or statistical evidence showing that groundwater withdrawals affect a connected surface watercourse. *See* Hayes v. Adams, 109 Or. 51, 218 P. 933 (1923).

In Focus:

AQUIFER SURGES 15 FEET; BUT RESTRICTIONS ON WATER REMAIN
Christopher Anderson
San Antonio Express–News (July 3, 2002)

As a result of recent rainfall, the Edwards Aquifer has surged more than 15 feet above the level that triggered water use restrictions in San Antonio last week. Still, officials are divided about whether enough water has accumulated to avoid further controls this summer.

A monitoring well located at Fort Sam Houston used to gauge the amount of water in the aquifer rose to more than 665 feet above sea level Tuesday. The city invoked Stage 1 water restrictions when this well dipped below the 650 feet mark just last week. * * * However, Edwards Aquifer Authority officials backed away Tuesday from imposing similar conservation measures throughout its eight-county jurisdiction. Greg Ellis, the authority's general manager, said a special meeting that was to have taken place Monday so board members could adopt emergency drought management rules for the region was canceled because of the recent rainfall.

"Obviously, the aquifer conditions have changed greatly since last week," Ellis said. * * * [T]he rains probably have spared the region from having to follow any water-use restrictions this year in order to preserve endangered species living in Comal and San Marcos springs. * * *

Calvin Finch, conservation manager for the San Antonio Water System, acknowledged that "now it looks like the aquifer is going to get pretty full." But ... [c]omputer simulations run by the city-owned utility demonstrate that the aquifer's troubles are not necessarily over this year, Finch said. "It all depends on the rain," he said. "Our system is such that if we get a little rain, we'll be all right. If we don't, we'll drop pretty quickly. * * *

Even if the aquifer continues its welcomed ascent, Stage 1 water use restrictions that limit the use of irrigation systems or sprinklers to once a week in San Antonio are not expected to be immediately lifted. That's because under city ordinance, once the controls are put into play, they remain in effect until the aquifer is above 650 feet for a minimum of 30 days. * * *

2. *Contamination*

Groundwater is not as susceptible to contamination as surface water. Groundwater, however, does become contaminated when man-made products such as gasoline, oil, road salts, and chemicals seep beneath the earth's surface. Corroded, leaky storage tanks, improperly designed septic systems, hazardous waste sites, unlined or improperly lined landfills, and the widespread use of road salts and lawn chemicals all contribute to groundwater contamination. In short, whatever contaminates other parts of the hydrological cycle, such as the air, soil, or surface waters, can eventually get into the groundwater. For more information on sources and types of contamination, see http://www.groundwater.org.

In recent years, saltwater has proven to be a leading contaminant of subsurface waters. Saltwater intrusion can foul domestic drinking water sources and make the groundwater unfit for many commercial and industrial uses.

TRANSBOUNDARY GROUNDWATER POLLUTION: THE IMPACT OF EVOLVINGGROUNDWATER USE ON SALTWATER INTRUSION OF THE FLORIDIAN AQUIFER ALONG THE SOUTH CAROLINA–GEORGIA BORDER
J. Marshall Lawson
1 S.C. Envtl. L.J. 85 (Summer, 2000)

Concentrated pumping of groundwater from the Floridian Aquifer at Savannah, Georgia, is causing the saltwater-freshwater interface within the Aquifer to move inland, towards the center of a steep regional cone of depression in the Aquifer's potentiometric surface. Saltwater intrusion threatens freshwater supplies in several areas in proximity to Savannah, including Hilton Head Island, South Carolina.

Until recently, there was no effective legal mechanism in Georgia or South Carolina to address the intrinsic relationship between unwise groundwater use and pollution from saltwater intrusion. This neglect was due, in part, to abundant water supplies and relatively low demand for groundwater. Rapid and largely unplanned growth, however, has resulted in unwise practices, prompting both states to regulate groundwater use * * *

The exploitation of the Floridian Aquifer exemplifies the prime defect in the various common law doctrines governing groundwater use. Because the property right is not quantifiable, water is effectively treated as common property. * * * With no social or legal limits on groundwater use, there is no desire for users to conserve; water conserved by one party may be used by another party because the conserver has no exclusive right to the water that is saved * * * Absent clearly defined and comprehensive water law, allocation strategies for groundwater will be based on individual permit decisions that set precedent and on court decisions resulting from legal challenges. The drafting of thoughtful legislation, along with the efficient use of water, innovative water supply technologies, and long-term regional planning, will be needed to ensure the integrity and sustainability of groundwater resources along the Southeastern seacoast.

* * *

When groundwater becomes contaminated, well owners and other injured persons can bring a tort action against the alleged polluter. *See* Wilson v. McLeod Oil Co., 327 N.C. 491, 398 S.E.2d 586 (1990). Proof of causation, however, can be extremely difficult, especially when there are multiple sources of contaminants and injuries with long latency periods. *See* Jonathon Harr, A CIVIL ACTION (1996) (describing the case of Anderson v. W.R. Grace & Co., 628 F.Supp. 1219 (D.Mass.1986), where Massachusetts residents exposed to solvents in their drinking water developed deadly illnesses but failed to establish legal causation). How might federal or state regulators protect against groundwater contamination? Are federal, state, or local governments better equipped to address the problem?

B. Groundwater Rights

Like surface water, groundwater doctrines are state specific. Individual states have adopted their own systems "for the use of all waters within the state in accordance with the needs of its citizens, subject to the prohibitions against interference with federal reserved rights, with interstate commerce, and with navigability of any navigable waters." Chatfield East Well Company, Ltd. v. Chatfield East Property Owners Association, 956 P.2d 1260, 1268 (Colo.1998). Groundwater is a very different creature than surface water and therefore water doctrines that apply to surface water often do not control subsurface water.

Historically, groundwater was not regulated, as courts and state regulators viewed it as "too mysterious" to be subjected to legal controls. Roath v. Driscoll, 20 Conn. 533, 540 (1850) (groundwater movements are "are so secret, changeable and uncontroulable [sic], we cannot subject them to the regulations of law"). When surface supplies diminished and groundwater supplies gained increasing importance, the need to allocate rights in groundwater became apparent. Increasing knowledge about the physical characteristics of subsurface water has led to modifications in legal doctrines and widespread regulation of groundwater appropriations. The general purpose of all groundwater doctrines, regardless of which doctrine is ultimately adopted by a jurisdiction, is to establish a system of rights to use groundwater that can promote use and determine liability among interfering users. The doctrines of absolute ownership, reasonable use and correlative rights are primarily applicable to percolating, or non-tributary, groundwater. Some western states apply the doctrine of prior appropriation, but may limit it to tributary groundwater. Meanwhile, some jurisdictions have begun to apply various factors from the Restatement 2nd of Torts, usually as a liability rule to supplement the common law of groundwater ownership. To top it all off, most states impose some sort of permit system on groundwater wells.

1. Absolute Ownership

The "English rule" of absolute ownership, as set forth in Acton v. Blundell, 12 Mees. & W. 324, 152 Eng.Rep. 1223 (1843), provides that the owner of the surface land owns all of the water within or under it. The landowner is given an unlimited right to withdraw any and all water found beneath the land because water is considered part of the soil. Absolute ownership allows landowners to extract (or "capture") groundwater at the expense of others without liability. *See* City of Corpus Christi v. Pleasanton, 154 Tex. 289, 276 S.W.2d 798 (1955) (city may take water from an artesian aquifer, divert it into a river and transport it, even though 70% was lost to evaporation during transit). Even those who acted solely with a malicious intent were absolved from liability by the absolute ownership rule. *See* Huber v. Merkel, 117 Wis. 355, 94 N.W. 354 (1903).

Because this rule leads to the relentless depletion of groundwater reservoirs, shelters appropriators from liability when they injure others, and permits malicious withdrawals, most states have either rejected or modified the application of the absolute ownership rule. *See* State v. Michels Pipeline Construction, Inc., 63 Wis.2d 278, 217 N.W.2d 339 (1974); Gagnon v. French Lick Springs Hotel Col., 163 Ind. 687, 72 N.E. 849 (1904); Bassett v. Salisbury Manufacturing Col., 43 N.H. 569 (1862).

At present, only Vermont and Texas apparently rely on the common law rule of absolute ownership. *See* Drinkwine v. State, 131 Vt. 127, 300 A.2d 616 (1973); Sipriano v. Great Spring Waters, 1 S.W.3d 75 (Tex.1999). Is protecting settled expectations a sufficient reason to stick with this archaic rule? For discussion, See Dylan O. Drummond, Lynn Ray Sherman, and Edmond R. McCarthy, Jr., *The Rule of Capture in Texas—Still So Misunderstood After All These Years*, 37 Tex. Tech. L. Rev. 1 (2004).

2. *Reasonable Use*

The American reasonable use rule modified the absolute ownership doctrine in an effort to avoid its potentially absurd effects. This rule is distinct from the "reasonable use" doctrine applicable to surface waters in riparian jurisdictions in that it allows landowners to withdraw any amount of groundwater, regardless of the consequent harm to neighboring landowners, so long as the groundwater is appropriated for use associated with the overlying land. Bristor v. Cheatham, 75 Ariz. 227, 255 P.2d 173 (1953); Forbell v. City of New York, 164 N.Y. 522, 58 N.E. 644 (1900). Like the surface water doctrine, the reasonable use rule prohibits (1) the sale of groundwater, (2) use of groundwater on non-overlying land, and (3) use of groundwater outside the natural drainage basin. While this rule improved the absolute ownership rule by curtailing spiteful uses of water, it fails to limit the quantity of water that can be withdrawn and does not account for the fact that groundwater migrates in underground aquifers and therefore use by one well owner can adversely affect other well owners. *See* Finley v. Teeter Stone, Inc., 251 Md. 428, 248 A.2d 106 (1968) (although the defendant's well caused injury, there was no liability because defendant, an overlying landowner, was making reasonable use). Both the American reasonable use rule and the absolute ownership rule assume that lack of scientific information about groundwater characteristics precludes imposition of liability since damage from withdrawals may not be reasonably foreseen.

3. *Correlative Rights*

The correlative rights (or California) doctrine is based on a theory of proportionate sharing of the total supply of groundwater among landowners overlying a common aquifer. Under this doctrine, each landowner holds rights in the common groundwater pool in proportion to the land overlying the pool, and in times of shortage all riparians must reduce their use of surface water. Katz v. Walkinshaw, 141 Cal. 116, 74 P. 766 (1903). The correlative rights doctrine has become more attractive, with heightened scientific knowledge concerning groundwater hydrology. First scientists, and then the courts, became mindful of the fact that when a number of persons owned land overlaying an aquifer, withdrawal of water by one could affect all. As one court stated in adopting the doctrine:

> [T]he science of groundwater hydrology ... has proven the postulates of the common law rule to be unsound. The premise that the owner

of the soil owns all that lies beneath the surface so that he may use the percolating water in any way he chooses without liability to an adjoining landowner fails to recognize that the supply of groundwater is limited, and that the first inherent limitation on the water rights is the availability of that supply.

Higday v. Nickolaus, 469 S.W.2d 859 (Mo.App.1971).

To determine a landowner's pro rata share of groundwater under the correlative rights doctrine, courts generally fix the share according to the amount of surface acreage owned by the appropriator. California also imposes elements of prior appropriation law in order to allow the exportation of groundwater from the overlying land in cases where groundwater is plentiful. The *Katz* court established rules governing the relative rights of overlying landowners and exporting appropriators: as between exporters and overlying owners, the overlying owner receives a reasonable share regardless of the relative priority of the exporter, but between two exporters, seniority governs. *Katz, supra*. Does this dichotomy seem equitable and/or efficient?

California has also modified the correlative rights doctrine by experimenting with the "mutual prescription doctrine," which allows appropriators to establish prescriptive rights to groundwater. The extent of the prescriptive right is determined by the amount adversely possessed within the statutory period. *See* Pasadena v. Alhambra, 33 Cal.2d 908, 207 P.2d 17 (1949). This doctrine was quickly modified when it resulted in California cities extracting as much water as possible in order to increase their prescriptive share. To rectify the situation, the California Supreme Court held that groundwater rights belonging to cities are not subject to adverse possession, and that adverse use cannot begin until there is an overdraft on the supply and groundwater users are notified of the overdraft condition. Los Angeles v. San Fernando, 14 Cal.3d 199, 123 Cal.Rptr. 1, 537 P.2d 1250 (1975).

4. *Restatement (2d) of Torts § 858*

Section 858 of the Restatement (2d) of Torts states that well owners are liable if a groundwater withdrawal: (1) causes unreasonable harm to a proprietor of neighboring land through lowering the water table or reducing artesian pressure; (2) exceeds the proprietor's reasonable share of the annual supply or total store of groundwater; or (3) has a direct and substantial effect upon a water course or lake and unreasonably causes harm to a person entitled to use its water. Although the first two limitations appear to parallel the American reasonable use rule and the correlative rights doctrine, both involve significantly different tests.

The first restriction under the Restatement rule—withdrawals may not cause "unreasonable" harm—is not triggered by use of the water off the overlying land. Instead, the pertinent inquiry is whether the resulting harm is reasonable in light of the relative value of the competing use; reasonableness is also judged by considering the effect of placing the burden of liability for a lowered water table upon one party or another. *See* Spear T. Ranch, Inc. v. Knaub, 269 Neb. 177, 691 N.W.2d 116 (2005); State v. Michels Pipeline Construction, Inc., 63 Wis.2d 278, 217 N.W.2d 339 (1974). If the injured party can establish causation, courts that follow a restatement-like rule tend to find the pumper liable for lowering the water table. *See* Maerz v. United States Steel Corp., 116 Mich.App. 710, 323 N.W.2d 524 (1982); Prather v. Eisenmann, 200 Neb. 1, 261 N.W.2d 766 (1978); *but see* Wiggins v. Brazil Coal and Clay Corp., 452 N.E.2d 958 (Ind.1983) (action by coal company that caused the water table to drop was reasonable).

The second limitation under the Restatement—withdrawals may not exceed an owner's reasonable share—is similar to the correlative right doctrine in that it seeks to apportion the right in the common groundwater pool. The Restatement, however, differs in that the apportionment is not based on the amount of acreage one owns overlying the pool, but on an array of balancing factors.

The third limitation, that withdrawals may not adversely affect surface water users, attempts to integrate management of interconnected ground and surface waters. What if a groundwater withdrawal adversely affects habitat for fish or migratory birds? Under the Restatement approach, such withdrawals could probably continue, unless some surface water *user* is harmed. Should the inquiry be so limited?

The Restatement rule is criticized for interjecting too much uncertainty into the water rights equation. *See* Lowe Ruedilili, and Grahm, *Beyond Section 858: A Proposed Groundwater Liability and Management System for the Eastern United States*, 8 ECOLOGY L.Q. 1 (1979). Even so, some state courts, faced with conflicts between groundwater pumpers and surface water users, have recently embraced it. *See, e.g., Spear T. Ranch,* 269 Neb. at 193, 691 N.W.2d at 132 (citing several eastern cases to show that imposing liability under the R.2d factors is the "modern trend"); *Decision Brings Water Law to a Boil*, Omaha World Herald, Jan. 22, 2005, A1 (describing *Spear T* as a "landmark" ruling that will "open the floodgates," erode "legal barriers between water in streams and water in aquifers," and "intensify the water-rights debate ... throughout the west"). What advantages might the Restatement offer?

5. *Prior Appropriation*

Tributary groundwater (groundwater hydrologically connected to a surface stream) has been drawn into the prior appropriation system for surface water rights in Colorado, New Mexico and a few other states. *See* State ex rel. Martinez v. Las Vegas, 135 N.M. 375, 89 P.3d 47 (2004) (citing Yeo v. Tweedy, 34 N.M. 611, 286 P. 970, 975 (1929)); Fundingsland v. Colorado Ground Water Comm'n, 171 Colo. 487, 468 P.2d 835 (1970); Williams v. City of Wichita, 190 Kan. 317, 374 P.2d 578, cert. dismissed, 375 U.S. 7, 84 S.Ct. 46, 11 L.Ed.2d 38 (1963).

In other western states, groundwater is subjected to a separate prior appropriation system, which protects prior existing rights against more recent pumpers. This system is premised on the theory that those who initially rely on groundwater should not have their lawfully established expectations defeated by the withdrawals of subsequent appropriators who injure existing rights. With deeper wells and more powerful pumps, junior appropriators could lower the water table and thus make the groundwater beyond the reach of a senior's well. Under the prior appropriation doctrine, new well owners are liable for harm caused to vested senior groundwater appropriators.

Is the prior appropriation doctrine well suited for allocating rights among groundwater users? Unlike surface water, the slow recharge rate of aquifers makes groundwater essentially a non-renewable resource. The prior appropriation system would, in theory, allow a senior appropriator to exhaust all of the water contained in an aquifer. It also fails to consider use preferences. Accordingly, some states have modified the prior appropriation system as it applies to groundwater withdrawal. Rather than protect senior appropriators from any interference caused by new uses, these states only protect seniors from material or unreasonable interference. *See Fundingsland*, 468 P.2d at 840 (permit to drill was properly denied when unreasonable harm to senior appropriators would result); Bower v. Moorman, 27 Idaho 162, 147 P. 496 (Idaho 1915) (juniors allowed to pump absent material damage to senior), overruled on other grds. Baker v. Ore–Ida Foods, 95 Idaho 575, 513 P.2d 627 (1973).

6.   *Statutory Permit Systems*

The majority of jurisdictions require groundwater users to obtain a permit prior to drilling a well, and many require notification or a permit prior to extracting groundwater. Permit systems are typically aimed at regulating well development so that wells are properly constructed and groundwater is extracted and used in a responsible manner. Generally, the state legislature establishes permitting criteria, which then is administered by the state engineer's office or natural resources department. The terms of the permit will vary depending upon the type of groundwater at issue. As noted above, many states distinguish between tributary groundwater, and non-connected, percolating groundwater.

Most state permit systems regulate the physical drilling and placement of wells. Before a permit is issued, the state agency must be satisfied that the proposed well is adequately distanced from other wells and that it will only be drilled to the depth prescribed by the agency. In Colorado, for example, "the right [to extract and use nontributary groundwater] does not vest until the landowner ... constructs a well in accordance with a well permit from the state engineer and/or applies for and receives water court adjudication." Chatfield East Well Co., Ltd. v. Chatfield East Property Owners Assn., 956 P.2d 1260, 1268 (Colo.1998).

Permit systems can also be designed to regulate proposed wells to ensure that they will not adversely affect existing groundwater uses by depleting or polluting groundwater sources. *See* Ferland, *The Protection of Groundwater Quality in the Western States—Regulatory Alternatives and the Mining Industry*, 29 ROCKY MTN. MIN. L. INST. 899 (1983); Lindsley v. Natural Carbonic Gas Col., 220 U.S. 61, 31 S.Ct. 337, 55 L.Ed. 369 (1911). Permit requirements ensure that existing water rights are not impaired when groundwater rights are transferred, the point in diversion is changed, or the place of use is changed. *See* In re Water Rights in Rio Grande County, 53 P.3d 1165 (Colo.2002) (before a change in point of diversion is authorized, water user must demonstrate historical use and show that the change will not constitute an enlargement of the water right); Town of Pine Bluffs v. State Board of Control, 649 P.2d 657 (Wyo.1982) (denying permit to transfer groundwater rights; change in use or place of use may not enlarge water rights); Metropolitan Utilities District v. Merritt Beach Co., 179 Neb. 783, 140 N.W.2d 626 (1966) (transfers allowed pursuant to statutory criteria); Stokes v. Morgan, 101 N.M. 195, 680 P.2d 335 (1984) (change in point of diversion and place of use allowed when the change would have minimal effect on water quality of groundwater supplies).

When withdrawals of an aquifer exceed the rate of recharge, the aquifer is in "overdraft" condition. Many states have authorized state or local officials to impose restrictions on withdrawals from depleted aquifers. Some designate such aquifers as "critical areas," and deny all new permits in those areas so that only those with pre-existing permits are allowed to continue withdrawals. Although pre-existing permit holders are still allowed to pump from critical areas, the amount of water appropriated cannot exceed historical usage. *See* Dinsdale v. Young, 72 Or.App. 642, 697 P.2d 196 (1985). The following article describes Nebraska's efforts to prevent depletion of tributary groundwater in the Republican River basin.

In Focus:

IRRIGATION INSTALLATION IS BOOMING
Clayton, Chris
Omaha World–Herald, May 8, 2004, at A1

HOLDREGE, Neb. The expansion of center-pivot irrigation is evident along stretches of State Highway 4 in southern Nebraska. The sun gleams off shiny new metal in just about every direction. * * * Next year ... irrigators along the entire Republican River basin will have their water allocated, or capped, which also potentially limits their crop yields and their income. Water restrictions, combined with well moratoriums in other parts of the state, likely will put a clamp on the growth of center-pivot irrigation in the state. * * *

Well drillers, pivot dealers and installers have been working practically nonstop ... [as farmers] install[] pivots to beat deadlines for restrictions on new groundwater wells. * * * Drilling for irrigation wells hit a 22–year high in 2003. The state issued 1,848 permits that year for new irrigation wells, nearly twice as many as in 2000. Pivot systems generally cost from about $40,000 to $80,000 * * * [and each year farmers spend] about $7,800 in fuel for one pivot system. In the past, increased yields have justified the expense, but that no longer is guaranteed. Irrigators who essentially have gone unregulated now likely will face permanent controls on their water, thanks to the 1943 Republican River Compact and a 2002 legal settlement with Kansas. * * *

The Lower Republican [Natural Resource District] NRD Board passed a moratorium on new wells in December 2002. Seven of the state's 23 NRDs now have moratoriums.... The moratoriums typically have grace periods, which prompted farmers to drill new wells before the deadline. * * * An efficient pivot system can produce a quality crop with about 12 to 14 inches of water, but farmers in the Middle and Lower Republican region have heard that their allocations could be less than that. * * * Some farmers might be forced off irrigation altogether if the allocations aren't met, meaning the NRDs would look for farmers to voluntarily take their land out of irrigation production. * * * [Roger Patterson, director of the Department of Natural Resources] said he doesn't believe restricting water use will significantly hurt the economy. It will require a farmer to be a better manager, though, he said. * * *

Many scholars and regulators have argued for integrated management systems for subsurface and surface water to better reflect hydrological connections, but few states have integrated their systems. A refusal to recognize the interrelated nature of water may ultimately result in dire consequences.

Simply stated, a system of laws that does not track physical science and actual groundwater conditions is doomed to failure or, worse, litigation and subsequent failure. * * * Jurisdictions which fail to recognize the direct interrelationship between surface and groundwater resources are only postponing the inevitable requirement to regulate the two sources as an integrated system. As reliance on groundwater resources increase, impact on surface water users will dictate an integrated regulatory framework. Such a regulatory framework must recognize that hydrogeologic conditions, rather than legal prose, define the level of integration.

Kevin L. Patrick & Kelly E. Archer, *Comparison of State Groundwater Laws,* 30 TULSA L.J. 123 (Fall 1994).

Notes and Questions

1. If you were to draft a new water permit regime, would you attempt to integrate surface and ground water uses? If so, how? What (if any) elements of the six different groundwater systems and the two primary surface water systems described above would you incorporate? How would you account for ecological needs as well as settled expectations of water users? For one compelling viewpoint, see Joseph L. Sax, *We Don't Do Groundwater: A Morsel of California Legal History*, 6 U. Denv. Water L. Rev. 269 (2003).

2. Are moratoria on well-drilling, as in Nebraska, an effective groundwater management tool? Does the tendency of moratoria to motivate prospective water users to rush to put in wells or pipes before the "sunset" date defeat their efficacy? Is it fair to impose moratoria without providing notice or a "sunset" provision?

Exercise:

In 2004, a long-time surface water appropriator, Spear T. Ranch, noticed that the source of its water rights, a stream known as Pumpkin Creek, began to dry up. Spear T's ditches could no longer transport any water to the ranch's pastures and livestock, even though Spear T held the most senior water right on the stream, reflected in a 1954 permit issued by the state water authority. Lo and behold, further investigation revealed that hundreds of groundwater pumpers had located their wells near the Creek. Groundwater pumping in the area began in the 1960's and wells proliferated through the present date. Spear T filed a complaint against a handful of pumpers that were closest to its diversion point, asserting that they were liable for unlawful conversion of its vested property rights in surface waters of Pumpkin Creek. Spear T seeks to recover injunctive relief as well as millions of dollars in damages from the defendants. How should the conflict be resolved? What defenses might the defendants raise? Assume that the state regulates groundwater use through a permit scheme based on the American reasonable use doctrine. Does Spear T have any basis to add the state as a defendant in its lawsuit? *See* Spear T Ranch, Inc. v. Knaub, 269 Neb. 177, 691 N.W.2d 116 (2005).

VI. FEDERAL AND TRIBAL INTERESTS IN WATER

Federal involvement and authority over water resources is sanctioned by the Commerce Clause, the Property Clause, the taxing and spending power, and the treaty power. Through these powers and the Supremacy clause, the federal government can override conflicting state law. By statute, however, Congress has repeatedly acknowledged states' primacy in the area of water rights outside of federal and tribal lands. For example, the 1902 Reclamation Act requires compliance with state water laws in the allocation and delivery of water from federal reclamation projects.

A variety of federal agencies impact water resource management. The Army Corps of Engineers has jurisdiction over navigation improvements, flood control, and multipurpose projects that supply water, electricity, and recreation opportunities. The Bureau of Reclamation is responsible for developing and managing irrigation projects. The Federal Energy Regulatory Commission licenses and regulates hydroelectric projects. The U.S. Soil and Conservation Service is responsible for stream channelization and small flood protection projects. The Tennessee Valley Authority controls various water projects along the Tennessee River. The U.S. Fish and Wildlife Service and the National Marine Fisheries Service have authority to protect listed species, many of which are found in the nation's waterways and coastal areas.

This section addresses constitutional, statutory and common law themes related to federal interests in navigation, reclamation and reserved water rights for public and tribal lands. Federal environmental requirements and federal allocation of interstate water among competing states are addressed in the next section of this chapter.

A.   The Federal Navigation Powers

Ever since Gibbons v. Ogden, 22 U.S. (9 Wheat.) 1, 6 L.Ed. 23 (1824), linked navigation to commerce, authority over navigable waterways and tributaries to navigable waterways has been a well-established federal power. The power over navigation has been extended to include regulation of commercial traffic on watercourses, removal of obstructions that interfere with navigation, and even flood control projects. Both the navigation power and the navigational servitude justify federal control over navigable waterways.

The navigation power derives from the Commerce Clause, and authorizes the United States to take actions, such as dam and canal building and river widening, which affect watercourses and the water within such watercourses. The navigation power also allows federal agencies to impose regulations on water uses. Private water rights arising under state law must give way to federal legislation enacted pursuant to the navigation power. *See* Arizona v. California, 373 U.S. 546, 83 S.Ct. 1468, 10 L.Ed.2d 542 (1963); United States v. Rio Grande Dam & Irrigation Co., 174 U.S. 690, 19 S.Ct. 770, 43 L.Ed. 1136 (1899). If a federal regulation effectively "takes" a state-recognized private water right, the federal government must justly compensate the water right owner for the taking, unless the navigational servitude applies.

Like the navigation power, the navigational servitude is also derived from the Commerce Clause. But unlike the navigation power, the navigational servitude permits federal interference with private rights in waterways without requiring just compensation. Under the navigational servitude, the flow of navigable streams is the public property of the United States. Thus, a federal agency may prevent the use of a navigable river without compensating private water rights.

The purpose of the navigational servitude is to ensure a right of way for public use of a waterway regardless of private ownership of the stream banks or bed. For this reason, the rule of "no compensation" may be triggered when: (1) the federal government destroys or removes privately-owned structures in or near navigable waters; (2) a federal project denies private owners access to a navigable waterway or a valuable location on navigable waters; or (3) federal dams flood private land or alter the water level so as to ruin the power value of a private hydroelectric plant. *See* Union Bridge Co. v. United States, 204 U.S. 364, 27 S.Ct. 367, 51 L.Ed. 523 (1907) (no compensation awarded to private party forced to make modifications due to an obstructing bridge); United States v. Chicago, Milwaukee, St. Paul, and Pacific Railroad Co., 312 U.S. 592, 61 S.Ct. 772, 85 L.Ed. 1064 (1941) (compensation denied when a federal dam flooded upstream lands); United States v. Cherokee Nation of Okla., 480 U.S. 700, 107 S.Ct. 1487, 94 L.Ed.2d 704 (1987) (no need to balance the public interest served by the navigation servitude with the intended use of streambed by private owners).

Unless otherwise modified by Congress, the navigation servitude applies to the surface of navigable waters, to the water power value attributable to the flow of the stream, to the bed and banks of navigable waters, and even to lands adjacent to navigable waters. The rule of no compensation for navigable water way extends to the ordinary high water mark of the stream, which includes the land under the stream, as well as the streambed and the stream banks.

B.   Reclamation

As the western United States became open to settlement, it became apparent that the arid landscape would inhibit settlement and hinder economic development. To spur westward migration, Congress initiated large-scale reclamation projects.

1.   The Reclamation Era

The nineteenth and early twentieth centuries marked an era of expansion, fueled both by the nation's desire to secure its "manifest destiny" and by the burgeoning population's desire to achieve the American dream. It became painfully obvious to settlers who pursued their dream in the west—"the Great American Desert"—that life could not exist without concentrated efforts to collect and deliver water. The Reclamation Era, a.k.a. the "Big Dam Era," has a rich and colorful history, peopled by characters like William Mulholland, who brought water across California to slake the thirst of boom-town Los Angeles; Floyd Dominy, the indomitable federal reclamation commissioner who never met a dam he didn't like; and David Brower, long-time leader of the Sierra Club who thwarted Dominy's plan to put dams in the Grand Canyon. For stories of notable individuals and events that left an indelible mark on the west, see MARC REISNER, CADILLAC DESERT 63, 81–86 (Penguin 1993); JOHN MCPHEE, ENCOUNTERS WITH THE ARCHDRUID (1971); WALLACE

STEGNER, BEYOND THE HUNDREDTH MERIDIAN: JOHN WESLEY POWELL AND THE
SECOND OPENING OF THE WEST (1954). Frank Trelease's article, below,
describes the origins of the Reclamation Act of 1902.

RECLAMATION WATER RIGHTS
Frank J. Trelease
32 ROCKY MTN. L. REV. 464, 465 (1960)

The Carey Act of 1894 was the first attempt of the national government to assume an active role in the development of western irrigation.
It placed a million acres at the disposal of each participating state that
would build (or cause to be built by private capital) large irrigation
works and would sell the land to settlers in tracts of 160 acres. However,
the Carey Act was substantially a failure. Few projects were built and
most of the settlers found themselves in severe financial difficulties
resulting from the heavy mortgages placed upon the lands to secure
repayment of the cost of construction of the irrigation works.

The Reclamation Act [of 1902] marked a departure from this pattern
of private development. Since the need for large dams and canals was
not being fully met by private capital, the act introduced federal financing of projects. A revolving fund was established with moneys received
from the sale of public land, and the Secretary of the Interior was
directed to survey the west and locate and construct irrigation projects,
opening up the improved public lands to settlement under the homestead laws. * * * Construction costs were to be repaid into the fund by
the settlers and landowners in ten annual installments without interest.

This basic statute has been amended, supplemented, and superseded by a long series of acts, some general in nature, some relating to
specific projects. * * * Now, the Bureau of Reclamation builds multipurpose projects which include features for production of hydroelectric
power, control of flood, navigation improvement, municipal and industrial water supplies, recreation, and fish and wildlife preservation, as
well as for irrigation. Projects now encompass the comprehensive development of entire river basins. The revolving fund was long ago
exhausted and today's projects are built with general funds. Repayment
periods have been stretched out.

* * *

The Reclamation Act (which was also known as the Newlands Act)
authorized the construction of dams, canals, and diversion projects to
bring federally "developed" water to privately owned land. 43 U.S.C.
§ 371. Although, in theory, the cost of the construction and maintenance
of reclamation projects was to be paid for in large part by the persons
receiving federal reclamation water, federal reclamation was in fact a
subsidy to western agricultural interests. Generous repayment schedules and payments made on an "ability to pay" basis resulted in an irre-

mediable deficit between project costs and repayment. *See* Joseph L. Sax, *Selling Reclamation Water Rights: A Case Study in Federal Subsidy Policy,* 64 MICH.L.REV. 13 (1965).

The Reclamation Project of 1939 supplemented the 1902 Reclamation Act by authorizing the construction of multipurpose water projects and by making project costs allocated to navigation and flood control nonreimbursable. Costs allocated to the preservation and propagation of fish and wildlife were made nonreimbursable by Fish and Wildlife Coordination Act, 16 U.S.C §§ 661–66c. Costs allocated to power, irrigation, and municipal and industrial water supply, however, are to be repaid to the United States from net power revenues and water users. Costs allocated to irrigation but beyond the irrigators' ability to pay are assigned for repayment from revenues received for power and municipal water supply.

The Bureau of Reclamation, established within the Department of the Interior, manages the reclamation program. *See* ETSI Pipeline Project v. Missouri, 484 U.S. 495, 108 S.Ct. 805, 98 L.Ed.2d 898 (1988) (Lake Oahe, South Dakota is not a reclamation project, as it is controlled by the Corps of Engineers). Under a contractual agreement with Interior, irrigation districts may manage reclamation projects. *See* Truckee–Carson Irrigation District v. Department of Interior, 742 F.2d 527 (9th Cir. 1984). Section 9(d) of the Reclamation Act of 1939 forbid the delivery of water to irrigation districts that had not entered into repayment contracts with the Bureau. 43 U.S.C. § 485h(d). Repayment contracts generally provided that the irrigators who used reclamation water had forty years to cover the costs of the project, including annual operation and maintenance. Section 9(e), however, provided an exception to the repayment contact requirement. Under this exception, the Secretary can enter into water service contracts that obligate the United States to furnish water at a fixed rate for up to forty years. The fixed rate is to reflect the Secretary's perception of the water users' appropriate share of construction costs and operation costs. These 9(d) service contracts enable the Bureau to furnish water to users who could not reimburse the government for the total cost of the project within 40 years. Service contracts are renewable according to mutually acceptable terms. 43 U.S.C. § 485. *See* Madera Irrigation District v. Hancock, 985 F.2d 1397 (9th Cir. 1993). The renewal of a water contract is considered an agency action subject to various environmental laws, including the Endangered Species Act. Natural Resources Defense Council v. Houston, 146 F.3d 1118 (9th Cir.1998).

In certain circumstances, reclamation water may be furnished to water users outside the context of either 9(e) or 9(d) contracts. Under the Warren Act, non-project landowners can obtain a temporary right to reclamation water when the water capacity of the project exceeds the project's needs. 43 U.S.C. §§ 523, 524. While the Warren Act allows excess reclamation water to be sold, it does not grant the Secretary the power to alter or ignore express contractual rights granted under the

Reclamation Act. *See* Goshen Irrigation Dist. v. Pathfinder Irrigation, 62 F.Supp.2d 1218 (D.Wyo.1999); Rural Water Dist. No. 1 v. City of Wilson, Kan., 243 F.3d 1263 (10th Cir.2001). Temporary rights are therefore inferior to the rights of permanent contract holders.

Irrigation districts that do not contract directly with the federal government, but simply benefit from a contract between the government and another party, are not considered third-party beneficiaries to the reclamation contract. *See* Klamath Water Users Protective Ass'n v. Patterson, 204 F.3d 1206 (9th Cir.1999) (contract between government and power company to manage dam for dual purpose of water use and fish and wildlife preservation did not confer separate contractual obligations to every irrigator). An irrigation district that is not in contractual privity with the government is barred from seeking declaratory relief from the United States. Under the Reclamation Reform Act of 1994, 43 U.S.C. § 390uu, the United States waived its sovereign immunity for declaratory actions to establish the parties' contractual rights. This waiver, however, is only applicable to those in contractual privity with the United States. Wyoming v. United States, 933 F.Supp. 1030 (D.Wyo.1996).

2. *What Law Governs Reclamation Water?*

Except when state law is directly in conflict with a provision of the federal reclamation law, the Reclamation Act requires federal compliance with state water law. California v. United States, 438 U.S. 645, 98 S.Ct. 2985, 57 L.Ed.2d 1018 (1978); United States v. Alpine Land and Reservoir Co., 887 F.2d 207 (9th Cir.1989). *See* Natural Resources Defense Council v. Patterson, 333 F.Supp.2d. 906 (E.D.Cal.2004) (holding that the Bureau of Reclamation violated the California Fish and Game Code). State law generally governs disputes between federal reclamation interests and water rights arising under state law. *See* In re Application of Denver By Board of Water Comm'rs, 935 F.2d 1143 (10th Cir.1991) (Denver's right to divert Blue River water is subject to the federal government's senior right to fill Green Mountain Reservoir, part of the Colorado Big Thompson Project). Although state law will be applied in most judicial proceedings, the Ninth Circuit has held that federal jurisdiction over reclamation water is "continuing and exclusive," so once a reclamation issue is brought to federal court, the state court is divested of jurisdiction. *Alpine Land & Reservoir*, 174 F.3d 1007.

Although reclamation projects aim to satisfy the water needs of irrigators, other federal requirements may undermine this goal. Federal reclamation projects are subject to environmental statutes. The Endangered Species Act of 1973 (ESA), in particular, impacts reclamation projects and individuals dependent on reclamation water. Many reclamation projects involve dams that harm downstream fisheries. Although the ESA was enacted after most large reclamation projects were already completed, when the contracts for such projects come up for renewal, they must comply with ESA provisions. Section 7, 16 U.S.C. § 1536, requires federal agencies to consult with the Fish and Wildlife Service to ensure that their actions do not jeopardize listed species. No "irreversible and irretrievable" commitment of resources may be made until consultation is completed, and all agencies have an "affirmative duty" to ensure that their actions do not jeopardize listed species pursuant to the ESA. Natural Resources Defense Council v. Houston, 146 F.3d 1118 (9th Cir. 1998). Thus, the agency may prohibit water users from diverting water if diversions may jeopardize endangered species. *See* Klamath Water Users Protective Ass'n v. Patterson, 204 F.3d 1206, 1213 (9th Cir.), cert. denied, 531 U.S. 812, 121 S.Ct. 44, 148 L.Ed.2d 14 (2000) (finding irrigators' contract rights to water "subservient to the ESA" because the Bureau had retained discretion for dam management under the contracts); United States v. Glenn–Colusa Irrigation District, 788 F.Supp. 1126 (E.D.Cal.1992) (district enjoined from pumping water when procedural and substantive provisions of the ESA were violated); Kandra v. United States, 145 F.Supp.2d 1192 (D.Or.2001) (irrigators' contractual rights to reclamation water are subservient to the ESA). The ESA is discussed in Section VII.C, below, and addressed in detail in Chapter 14 (Wildlife).

In addition to providing water for irrigation purposes, reclamation projects have been undertaken to generate hydroelectric power, improve navigation for flood control purposes, enhance recreation, and for fish and wildlife preservation. Federal reclamation projects have transformed arid landscapes into fertile farmland and encouraged settlement of the west. In the last few decades, however, federal investment in water resources projects has dwindled. In 1987, the Bureau issued "Assessment '87: A New Direction for the Bureau of Reclamation." This report concluded that the "Bureau's mission must change from one based on federally supported construction to one based on effective and environmentally sensitive resource management." To this end, one-third of the Bureau's 1998 budget was allocated to ecosystem restoration, fish recovery and pollution reduction projects. WESTERN WATER POLICY REVIEW ADVISORY COMM'N, WATER IN THE WEST: THE CHALLENGE FOR THE NEXT CENTURY 3–51 to 3–52 (1998). Although reclamation projects were once praised as miraculous engineering feats, the environmental effect of damming rivers is now obvious, and many environmentalists have called for the removal of federal reclamation project dams.

C. Reserved Rights

When federal lands are withdrawn or reserved for a specific purpose, either by legislation or by Executive order, a sufficient quantity of unappropriated water is impliedly reserved to satisfy that purpose. *See* United States v. New Mexico, 438 U.S. 696, 98 S.Ct. 3012, 57 L.Ed.2d 1052 (1978); United States v. Anderson, 736 F.2d 1358 (9th Cir.1984). The doctrine of reserved water rights applies to both public lands and Indian reservations.

By reserving land, the federal government created a new breed of water right, a federal reserved water right, which is independent of state water law doctrines. Federal reserved water rights share features of both the riparian doctrine and the prior appropriation system. Like riparian rights, reserved rights are appurtenant to land and are not lost by non-use. But reserved rights, like appropriative rights, have a priority date which governs their administration. The federal government may establish and exercise reserved rights without abiding by state water law procedures. *See* Colville Confederated Tribes v. Walton, 752 F.2d 397 (9th Cir.1985).

The federal government's authority to create reserved water rights stems from both the Commerce Clause and the Property Clause. The Commerce Clause gives Congress the authority "to regulate Commerce * * * with the Indian Tribes." This provision sanctions the reservation of water for Native American reservations. The Property Clause authorizes the United States to dispose of public lands, along with water appurtenant to those lands. Land grant legislation not only disposed of western land, but also severed appropriated water from the public domain and authorized states and territories to establish their own water rights system. *See* California Oregon Power Co. v. Beaver Portland Cement, 295 U.S. 142, 55 S.Ct. 725, 79 L.Ed. 1356 (1935). Under the reserved rights doctrine, the United States impliedly revokes its previous grant of water rights to the states when it withdraws or reserves land from the public domain. The water that is reserved with the reservation of land becomes property of the United States.

The primary legal issues concerning the reserved rights doctrine are: (1) whether any reserved rights exist; (2) the quantity of water reserved; (3) the effect of state law; and (4) the location and use of the reserved water.

1. The Existence and Quantity of Reserved Rights

The reserved rights doctrine was first acknowledged in Winters v. United States, 207 U.S. 564, 28 S.Ct. 207, 52 L.Ed. 340 (1908). In *Winters*, the United States, as trustee for federally recognized Indian tribes, sought to enjoin upstream water users from diverting water from the Milk River and injuring an irrigation project on the Fort Belknap Indian reservation. The reservation was established in 1888, before the upstream defendants began using water from the river. The *Winters* Court held that with the reservation of land, Congress impliedly reserved a sufficient quantity of water to fulfill the purposes of the reservation. This reserved water right, the Court held, was superimposed on the state water rights system of prior appropriation at the time the reservation was made. So long as the federal reservation preceded the private appropriations, the federal right existed without the need to divert the water or apply it to a beneficial use.

The *Winters* case illustrates two important aspects of reserved water rights. First, when asserted, reserved rights can adversely affect private water rights that were established under state law after the reservation was created. In *Winters*, the Indian reservation had a prior, and thus superior, right to the water in the stream. Second, due to the fact that the United States is the fiduciary of Indian tribes, Native Americans must often rely on federal action and litigation to protect their reserved rights from encroachment; this has not always led to the most desirable outcomes, from the tribes' standpoint *See* Nevada v. United States, 463 U.S. 110, 103 S.Ct. 2906, 77 L.Ed.2d 509 (1983); Gila River Pima–Maricopa Indian Community v. United States, 231 Ct.Cl. 193, 684 F.2d 852 (1982); Chapter 7, *supra* (Indian Ownership).

In 1963, in Arizona v. California, 373 U.S. 546, 83 S.Ct. 1468, 10 L.Ed.2d 542 (1963), the Supreme Court extended the reserved rights doctrine to non-Indian federal lands. The Court delineated several new aspects of reserved water rights: (1) the principle underlying the reservation of water rights for Indian Reservations is equally applicable to other federal lands such as National Recreation Areas and National Forests; (2) reserved rights apply to both navigable and non-navigable waters; (3) the reserved rights doctrine applies to reservations regardless if they were created before or after statehood; and (4) water can be reserved by an Executive Order or an Act of Congress.

In *Arizona*, the government, on behalf of five Indian Reservations and several other federal reservations, asserted rights to Colorado River water. An 1865 Act of Congress created the Colorado River Reservation, while the other four Indian Reservations were created by Executive Orders ranging in dates from 1870 to 1907. Citing *Winters,* the Court explained that the central issue is "whether the Government intended to reserve unappropriated and thus available water. Intent is inferred if the previously unappropriated waters are necessary to accomplish the purposes for which the reservation was created." *Id.* at 600, 83 S.Ct. at 1498. In the case of Indian reservations, the government was well aware "that most of the lands were of the desert kind—hot, scorching sands— and that water from the river would be essential to the life of the Indian people and to the animals they hunted and the crops they raised." *Id.* at 599, 83 S.Ct. at 1497. Accordingly, the United States implicitly reserved water rights "to make the reservation[s] livable" and to "satisfy the future as well as the present needs of the Indian Reservations." *Id.* at 600, 83 S.Ct. at 1498.

The Court fixed the priorities of the reserved rights according to the dates the reservations were created, making them senior to most other water rights in the region. Water to fulfill the reserved rights came from the state's allocation of Colorado River water. Thus, other interests within the state in which the reservations are located will receive less Colorado River water to satisfy their needs.

Ascertaining the purpose of the reservation is critical to determining whether water is impliedly reserved and the quantity of the reservation. Under the reserved rights doctrine, water is only reserved for the purpose of the reservation and the quantity of water is therefore limited to the amount necessary to fulfill this purpose. Winters v. United States, 207 U.S. 564, 28 S.Ct. 207, 52 L.Ed. 340 (1908); Arizona v. California, 373 U.S. 546, 83 S.Ct. 1468, 10 L.Ed.2d 542 (1963); Cappaert v. United States, 426 U.S. 128, 96 S.Ct. 2062, 48 L.Ed.2d 523 (1976). Water is only reserved for the primary purpose of the reservation.

> Where water is necessary to fulfill the very purposes for which a federal reservation was created, it is reasonable to conclude, even in the face of Congress' express deference to state water law in other areas, that the United States intended to reserve the necessary water. Where water is only valuable for a secondary use of the reservation, however, there arises the contrary inference that Congress intended, consistent with its other views, that the United States would acquire water in the same manner as any other public or private appropriator.

United States v. New Mexico, 98 S.Ct. at 3015. In *New Mexico,* the Court found that water for National Forests was reserved only for the primary purposes of securing timber supplies and waterflows. The case is discussed in more detail in Chapter 5.III.C.3, *supra.*

The Supreme Court established a relatively specific method of quantifying reserved rights for Indian reservations in *Arizona v. California*: the amount of water reserved is measured by the number of practicably irrigable acres (PIA) on the reservation, not by the number of individual Indians living on the reservation. 373 U.S. at 600–601, 83 S.Ct. at 1497–1498. But the Arizona Supreme Court rejected the PIA standard as the exclusive method for determining the amount of water reserved for Indian reservations. In re General Adjudication of All Rights to Use Water in Gila River System and Source, 201 Ariz. 307, 35 P.3d 68 (2001). The court reasoned that the "essential purpose of Indian reservations is to provide Native American people with a 'permanent home and abiding place,' *Winters,* 207 U.S. at 565, that is, a 'livable' environment. *Arizona I,* 373 U.S. at 599." *Id.* It continued:

> Limiting an Indian reservation's purpose to agriculture, as the PIA standard implicitly does, assumes that the Indian peoples will not enjoy the same style of evolution as other people, nor are they to have the benefits of modern civilization. * * * [T]he homeland concept assumes that the homeland will not be a static place frozen in an instant of time but that the homeland will evolve and will be used in different ways as the Indian society develops.

Id. at 76. Once the court rejected PIA as the sole measure of a tribes' reserved water right, it was left with the difficult task of delineating additional quantification criteria. It listed several factors for the lower courts to consider, including tribal development plans or other evidence that reflects " 'the optimal manner of creating jobs and income for the tribes [and] the most efficient use of the water.' " *Id.* at 80, citing, *inter alia, Wyoming v. United States,* 492 U.S. 406, 109 S.Ct. 2994, 106 L.Ed.2d 342 (1989).

Physical infrastructure, human resources, including the present and potential employment base, technology, raw materials, financial resources, and capital are all relevant in viewing a reservation's economic infrastructure. * * * We recognize that the Supreme Court has rejected any quantification standard based solely on the "number of Indians." *Arizona II,* 460 U.S. at 617, 103 S.Ct. at 1390. However, if a federally reserved water right is to be tailored to a reservation's "minimal need," as we believe it must, then population necessarily must be part of the equation. * * * Such consideration is not at odds with the need to satisfy tribes' "future as well as ... present needs." *Arizona I,* 373 U.S. at 600, 83 S.Ct. at 1498.

Id. at 80. This new standard opens up the door to an array of expanded tribal water uses, such as municipal and commercial development. Did the Arizona court go too far? Or was the *Gila River* opinion a natural extension of *Winters* and *Arizona*? What are the implications for other water users in the basin?

2. *The Effect of State Law*

The Supremacy clause ensures that the reserved rights doctrine preempts inconsistent state law. However, because statutes or executive orders creating reservations rarely expressly preempt state water law and the United States traditionally defers to state water law, the extent of federal preemption in reserved rights cases is a complex determination. State law arguably affects federal reserved rights in three contexts: (1) allocation of rights under state water law system; (2) state regulation of users of federal reserved rights; and (3) state jurisdiction over Indian water rights. State law cannot interfere with the accomplishment of the reservation's purpose, but federal reserved rights can be tried in state court in general stream adjudications under the McCarran Amendment, 43 U.S.C. § 666(a).

When a reserved right is claimed, the right holder does not have to comply with state water law requirements. Accordingly, reserved rights cannot be attacked for not constituting a beneficial use. *See* Confederated Salish and Kootenai Tribes v. Clinch, 297 Mont. 448, 992 P.2d 244 (1999). Further, the priority date of a reserved right—the date the reservation was created—is never lost despite years of non-use. State ex rel. Greely v. Confederated Salish and Kootenai Tribes, 219 Mont. 76, 712 P.2d 754 (1985). Consequently, a reserved right may not be exercised for years, but nonetheless exist unbeknownst to state appropriators. Reserved rights are superior to all state water rights that vest subsequent to the creation of the reservation, thus, even when the owners of state water rights have no notice of the existence or quantity of the federal right, the sudden exercise of a senior reserved right can dramatically affect or even curtail their rights.

Because federal reserved rights are independent of state water law systems, holders of reserved rights do not have to acquire state permits to exercise their rights. But state applicants hoping to appropriate water from the same water body as a federal reservation must prove that their proposed uses will not unreasonably interfere with the federal reserved rights. Matter of Application for Beneficial Water Use Permit Nos. 66459–76L and 64988–G76L, 278 Mont. 50, 923 P.2d 1073 (1996). Furthermore, groundwater pumpers sanctioned by state law may be restricted or even enjoined if their pumping adversely affects federal reserved rights. Cappaert v. United States, 426 U.S. 128, 131, 96 S.Ct. 2062, 2066, 48 L.Ed.2d 523 (1976).

3.　*Location and Use of Reserved Rights*

Reserved rights have typically been asserted in prior appropriation jurisdictions, where federal land holdings are vast and water is scarce. The doctrine's application in riparian jurisdictions is unclear, but it seems likely that state law limitations associated with riparian rights, such as the reasonable use doctrine, may not be imposed on reserved rights if the state rule interferes with the accomplishment of the reservation's purpose. *See Application of California Riparian Water Rights Doctrine to Federal Lands in the Mono Lake Basin,* 34 HASTINGS L.J. 1293 (1983).

Should the reserved rights doctrine extend to groundwater resources as well as surface waters? The Supreme Court effectively side-stepped the issue in *Cappaert,* 426 U.S. at 131, 96 S.Ct. at 2066. There, the government asserted rights to an underground pool of water appurtenant to Devil's Hole in Death Valley National Monument. The Cappaerts, by pumping groundwater from a nearby location, threatened the amount of water available to an endangered species of desert fish. Because the reserved water at issue was not truly groundwater, but a unique geological pool formation, the Court did not need to resolve the issue, but it did curtail groundwater pumping to preserve the pool.

The Arizona Supreme Court concluded that reserved rights could attach to groundwater as well as surface water if necessary to accomplish the purpose of the reservation. In re General Adjudication of All Rights to Use Water in the Gila System & Source, 195 Ariz. 411, 419, 989 P.2d 739, 747 (1999). It found that "[a] reserved right to groundwater may only be found where other waters are inadequate to accomplish the purpose of a reservation. To determine the purpose of a reservation and to determine the waters necessary to accomplish that purpose are inevitably fact-intensive inquiries that must be made on a reservation-by-reservation basis." *Id. But see* General Adjudication of the Big Horn River System (Big Horn I), 753 P.2d 76, 100 (Wyo.1988) (holding that there was no reservation of groundwater).

Given the nature of reserved rights, can they be transferred between uses or parties? Tribal transfers between uses on tribal lands, for example, from irrigation to instream fisheries, have been approved. *See* United States v. Orr Water Ditch Co., 309 F.Supp.2d 1245

(D.Nev.2004). Also, non-Indian purchasers of Indian lands have obtained reserved water rights in some circumstances, but they must prove that the reserved right was actually used by their Indian predecessors, or used for irrigation within a "reasonable time" after the lands were transferred out of Indian ownership. *See* Colville Confederated Tribes v. Walton, 752 F.2d 397 (9th Cir.1985); General Adjudication of Rights to Use Water in the Big Horn River System (Big Horn II), 48 P.3d 1040 (Wyo.2002). Given that many of the lands were transferred out of Indian ownership in the early 1900's, what is a "reasonable time"? According to the Wyoming Supreme Court, claimants must demonstrate reasonableness, or due diligence, in putting their lands under irrigation *after* federal reclamation project facilities became available, even though the lands were transferred to them up to 30 years before completion of the project. *Big Horn II*, 48 P.3d at 1046.

> To qualify [for so-called *Walton* claims,] claimants must demonstrate their lands were irrigated by their Indian allottee predecessors or the first non-Indian successors irrigated the lands within a reasonable time after they were conveyed. The district court denied these appellants' claims ... finding they failed to show beneficial use of water within a "reasonable time" because they relied upon the construction of the Wind River Irrigation Project to make the water available to their lands and the project was not completed until approximately ten to thirty years after transfer of the allotments. * * * We reverse in part and remand with instructions that unsuccessful claimants who can demonstrate beneficial use within a reasonable time after the federal project facilities became available to their properties are entitled to a reserved right. * * *

Id.

Notes and Questions

1. Does it seem appropriate for non-Indian owners of allotted tribal land to assume reserved water rights to that land? Should the new owner be able to use the water on the allotment as well as an adjacent parcel? By way of background, the General Allotment Act of 1884, ch. 119, 24 Stat. 388, was designed to break up communally held tribal lands into individual parcels. It provided for tribal lands to be surveyed and divided into "allotments" of between 40 and 160 acres, which then passed to individual Indians in fee simple. Many of these allotments ultimately passed to non-Indian owners. Between 1884 and 1934, the total Indian land base was reduced by nearly two-thirds, from 138,000,000 acres to 48,000,000 acres. *See* Chapter 5.I.C.5, *supra*.

2. Due to the seniority of most reserved rights, those rights are highly desirable to purchasers of federal or tribal lands. Should private purchasers of federal public land obtain reserved water rights for that land? If the purchaser of federal forest land is a resort developer or a timber company, for example, for what purpose may the water be used?

3. Should federal agencies or tribes be able to sell their water to non-riparian (off-tract) purchasers? Although *Big Horn II* did not address this

particular issue, it stated that "reserved water can be used on nonriparian lands." 48 P.3d at 1046. There has been considerable opposition to the notion of marketing reserved rights. *See* MARC REISNER & SARAH BATES, OVERTAPPED OASIS 95–97 (1990); Jack D. Palma II, *Considerations and Conclusions Concerning the Transferability of Indian Water Rights,* 20 Nat. Res. J. 91, 94 (1980). Who is likely to be harmed?

4. The United States may acquire water rights according to applicable state laws. The problem in prior appropriation states: newly acquired rights are junior and there's usually not enough water to go around. In a riparian jurisdiction, the United States may simply acquire a riparian parcel of land with appurtenant water rights. In re Water of Hallett Creek Stream Systems, 44 Cal.3d 448, 243 Cal.Rptr. 887, 749 P.2d 324 (1988).

VII. ENVIRONMENTAL REGULATIONS

Federal and state environmental regulations also impact the allocation, diversion and use of water. This Section focuses on three key federal environmental laws: the Wild and Scenic Rivers Act (WSRA), the Clean Water Act (CWA), and the Endangered Species Act (ESA). Under the WSRA, the Secretary of the Interior may designate river segments for inclusion in the National Wild and Scenic Rivers System. Those river segments are to be managed in a fashion that preserves the values for which they were designated under the Act. Meanwhile, the CWA requires dischargers of pollutants to obtain permits and meet certain standards to ensure that the integrity of all of the nation's waters is restored and maintained, and the ESA prohibits habitat destruction that would take or jeopardize any listed species.

A. Wild and Scenic Rivers Act

The WSRA preserves the free-flowing condition of certain rivers by protecting the rivers and banks from the adverse effects of dams, hydroelectric projects, livestock grazing, parking lots, roads and other activities. 16 U.S.C. § 1271 (2000). *See* Oregon Natural Resources Council v. Marsh, 52 F.3d 1485 (9th Cir.1995); Oregon Natural Desert Association v. Green, 953 F.Supp. 1133 (D.Or.1997). Under the Act, rivers or river segments can be designated as wild, scenic, or recreational. 16 U.S.C. § 1273. A river that has "outstandingly remarkable values" may be identified for inclusion in the system by the state in which it is located or through a federal study or Comprehensive River Management Plan. 16 U.S.C. § 1271. These values may include "scenic, recreational, geologic, fish and wildlife, historic, cultural, or other similar values." 16 U.S.C. § 1271. Once designated, the river segment "shall be preserved in free-flowing condition, and ... protected for the benefit and enjoyment of present and future generations." WILD & SCENIC RIVER MANAGEMENT RESPONSIBILITIES, TECHNICAL REPORT OF THE INTERAGENCY COORDINATING COUNCIL 5 (2002), *at* http://www.nps.gov/rivers/publications.html. *See* City of Klamath Falls v. Babbitt, 947 F.Supp. 1 (D.D.C.1996) (the Secretary is not required to prepare an EIS for the recommendation that a river be designated under the Act because designation would not change the environmental status quo).

A key provision of the Act forbids the Federal Energy Regulatory Commission from licensing "any dam, water conduit, reservoir, power-house, transmission line or other project works under the Federal Power Act on or directly affecting any river which is designated.... " 16 U.S.C. § 1278 (a). The Act also directs the federal river management agency to protect and enhance the river's outstandingly remarkable values, 16 U.S.C. § 1281(a), and prohibits all other federal agencies from assisting in the construction of any water resources project that would have a direct and adverse effect on a designated river. 16 U.S.C. § 1278 (a). *See Oregon Nat. Resources Council v. Harrell*, 52 F.3d 1499, 1506 (9th Cir.1995). With respect to state water laws, however, the Act specifically provides that state jurisdiction shall not be affected "to the extent that such jurisdiction may be exercised without impairing the purposes of this chapter or its administration." 16 U.S.C. § 1284(d).

B. Clean Water Act

The objectives of the Clean Water Act (CWA) are to "restore and maintain the chemical, physical and biological integrity" of the nation's waters and to eliminate the discharge of water pollutants. *South Florida Water Mgmt. Dist. v. Miccosukee Tribe*, 541 U.S. 95, 102, 124 S.Ct. 1537, 1541, 158 L.Ed.2d 264 (2004) (citing 33 U.S.C. § 1251(a)). To carry out these goals, Congress imposed liability on "any person" who discharges "any pollutant" except by permit. 33 U.S.C. § 1311 (a).

The Act has two major permit programs. Section 404 controls discharges of dredged or fill materials into water. The 404 permit program is addressed in Chapter 10, *supra*. The National Pollution Discharge Elimination System (NPDES) permit program of Section 402 requires permits for "the discharge of any pollutant by any person." 33 U.S.C. § 1342. *See South Florida Water Mgmt. Dist.*, 541 U.S. at 103–104. The CWA defines "discharge of pollutant" as "any addition of any pollutant to navigable waters from any point source." 33 U.S.C. § 1362(12). Both "pollutant" and "navigable waters" are defined quite broadly, but "point source" is a term of art meaning "any discernible, confined and discrete conveyance, including but not limited to any pipe, ditch, channel, tunnel, conduit, well, ... concentrated animal feeding operation, or vessel or other floating craft, from which pollutants are or may be discharged." *Id.* § 1362(14). Agricultural stormwater discharges and return flows from irrigated agriculture are not considered point sources under the CWA. *Id.* The point source concept was developed so that pollution from simple erosion or run-off could be distinguished from pollution that has been collected or originates from confined systems. Run-off, or non-point source pollution, is addressed largely through state and local efforts.

Under the CWA, the U.S. Environmental Protection Agency establishes uniform, technology-based standards that must be included in each NPDES permit. States can assume delegated authority from the

EPA to administer and enforce the NPDES program. States must also designate uses for waterways and develop water quality standards that are sufficient to support those designated uses. 33 U.S.C. § 1313. If the states' water quality standards are inadequate, the EPA must intervene and impose more stringent standards. However, the CWA includes a "savings clause" to ensure that states' authority to allocate water quantity is not displaced by its provisions. 33 U.S.C. § 1251(g).

C. Endangered Species Act

The Endangered Species Act (ESA), addressed in detail in Chapter 14 (Wildlife), was enacted to conserve endangered and threatened fish and wildlife species. The Act ensures that the needs of listed species prevail over other agency missions. TVA v. Hill, 437 U.S. 153, 98 S.Ct. 2279, 57 L.Ed.2d 117 (1978) (citing 16 U.S.C. § 1531). The ESA directs the Fish and Wildlife Service (FWS), or NOAA–Fisheries (NMFS) for certain aquatic and marine species, to identify and list imperiled species as either endangered or threatened, and to designate critical habitat for each listed species. These agencies are also responsible for adopting regulations and crafting recovery plans to conserve and enhance the populations of listed species. 16 U.S.C. § 1533(b)(2) and (d).

Section 9 of the Act prohibits any person from taking, possessing, selling, importing, exporting, or transporting a protected species. 16 U.S.C. § 1538. Under the ESA, take is defined as "harass, harm, pursue, hunt, capture, shoot, wound, kill, trap or collect or to attempt to engage in such conduct." 16 U.S.C. § 1532(19). The term "harm" includes habitat destruction that injures a listed species. Babbitt v. Sweet Home, 515 U.S. 687, 115 S.Ct. 2407, 132 L.Ed.2d 597 (1995). Section 7 requires all federal agencies to consult with FWS or NOAA–Fisheries to ensure that the survival of listed species will not be jeopardized by their actions. 16 U.S.C. § 1536. When the exercise of a water right, such as pumping water from a river, or the renewal of a reclamation service contract takes or jeopardizes a listed species, the activity will be enjoined. *See* Section VI.B.2, above (citing reclamation cases). In fact, in an early ESA case, the Supreme Court upheld the injunction of a $100 million dam just before the flood-gates were to be closed to avoid jeopardy to the endangered snail darter. TVA v. Hill, 437 U.S. 153, 98 S.Ct. 2279, 57 L.Ed.2d 117 (1978).

The ESA is one of the most significant sources of federal influence over water allocation. The tension between the ESA and the allocation and use of water is particularly strained in the western United States because the water supply is limited and there are a vast number of threatened and endangered species in the West. An issue that is always present whenever the application of the ESA causes a water user to lose a portion of its water is whether the regulatory demand constitutes a taking of a water right. The following case held that where the ESA requires a diverter to leave some water in the river or reservoir to protect an endangered species, a taking of property (the water right) has occurred, requiring the federal government pay just compensation to the diverter.

Exercise:

You are an attorney representing the National Audubon Society. Your client opposes a Department of Transportation (DOT) proposal to construct a bridge over the Shark River to provide a direct route between two small towns on opposite banks of the river. The river has been designated as scenic, and it is managed by the National Park Service (NPS). The client fears that the bridge and the traffic it would bear would ruin the natural quiet, beauty, and biodiversity of this free-flowing river, which is used by many canoeists and fly fishers. It also believes that bridge construction would cause extensive water pollution, through increased sedimentation and falling debris. Pollution from automobile traffic, once the project is completed, would exacerbate water quality problems. Most troubling of all, the project will disturb the habitat of the federally endangered Ghost Orchid that grows along the banks of the river. The Audubon Society's president, Sue Orlean, owns a small parcel downstream of the proposed bridge site, where she maintains a cabin and a fully functioning wetlands site, on which a patch of orchids resides. During the dry summer months, she occasionally pumps water from the river to maintain the wetlands. During the decisionmaking process for the proposal, the NPS made a determination that the bridge would in fact have an adverse effect on the river's scenic values by diminishing its natural setting and flow. The DOT's sole response was that the project is greatly needed for the local communities. What claims might your client assert if the DOT goes forward with the project? *See, e.g.,* Sierra Club North Star Chapter v. Pena, 1 F.Supp.2d 971 (D.Minn.1998).

VIII. INTERSTATE ISSUES

Numerous major rivers originate in one state and flow through others. In the water scarce west, states often battle over the amount of water to which each state is entitled as well as the quality of water delivered to each state. Interstate disputes have been resolved by the courts, interstate agreements, and congressional apportionment.

A. Judicial Allocation

Interstate water disputes can be resolved by judicial decrees. It is not uncommon for residents of a downstream state to bring a claim alleging that diversions from the upstream state have caused injury to the downstream water users, either through diminished supply or impaired quality (or both). Because water is an article of commerce, a state's restriction on another state's access to water supplies may be considered an unconstitutional burden on interstate commerce or unconstitutional discrimination against interstate commerce. *See* Sporhase v.

Nebraska ex rel. Douglas, 458 U.S. 941, 102 S.Ct. 3456, 73 L.Ed.2d 1254 (1982) (invalidating a state's requirement of a reciprocity agreement before it would allow water withdrawn within the state to be used in another state).

Jurisdiction over interstate water matters can be tricky. Because a water right is a real property right, the law requires the suit to be brought in the state where the real property is situated. Conant v. Deep Creek & Curlew Valley Irrigation Co., 23 Utah 627, 66 P. 188 (1901). However, some courts have held that obtaining personal jurisdiction over the non-resident party is sufficient to allow the court to enforce the decree by using the coercive effect of its contempt power. *See* Brooks v. United States, 119 F.2d 636 (9th Cir.1941).

In *Kansas v. Colorado*, the Supreme Court created a comprehensive federal common law doctrine for interstate allocation of water by equitable apportionment. Kansas v. Colorado, 514 U.S. 673, 115 S.Ct. 1733, 131 L.Ed.2d 759 (1995). Equitable apportionment puts all states "on an equal plane.... in point of power and right." *Id.* To ascertain equitable apportionment, the Court considers the following factors: (1) physical and climatic conditions; (2) consumptive use of water in the sections of the river; (3) character and rate of return flows; (4) extent of established uses and economies built on them; (5) availability of water storage; (6) practical effect of wasteful uses on downstream areas; and (7) damage to upstream interests compared to the benefits to downstream interests if upstream uses are curtailed. *See* Nebraska v. Wyoming, 325 U.S. 589, 65 S.Ct. 1332, 89 L.Ed. 1815 (1945). Equitable apportionment decrees may be reopened and potentially modified only when a party makes a clear and convincing showing of substantial injury. Nebraska v. Wyoming, 515 U.S. 1, 115 S.Ct. 1933, 132 L.Ed.2d 1 (1995).

Equitable apportionment has been used by the Court in cases involving interstate water pollution affecting two riparian states and in a case involving anadromous fish living in interstate waters. *See* New Jersey v. New York, 283 U.S. 336, 51 S.Ct. 478, 75 L.Ed. 1104 (1931); Idaho ex rel. Evans v. Oregon, 462 U.S. 1017, 103 S.Ct. 2817, 77 L.Ed.2d 387 (1983). In controversies between two prior appropriation states, the Court has applied the prior appropriation doctrine. Wyoming v. Colorado, 259 U.S. 419, 42 S.Ct. 552, 66 L.Ed. 999 (1992). The Court has, however, refused to apply strict priorities between appropriation states when the effect would protect wasteful and inefficient downstream uses. Colorado v. New Mexico, 467 U.S. 310, 104 S.Ct. 2433, 81 L.Ed.2d 247 (1984).

B. Interstate Compacts

Article I, § 10, clause 3 of the U.S. Constitution states that "[n]o state shall, without the consent of Congress ... enter into any agreement or compact with another state * * *." Pursuant to this power, over 20 interstate compacts relating to water resources have been adopted by states and approved by Congress. Through interstate compacts, states can agree to allocate a specific number of acre-feet, a percentage of total stream flow, or a distribution of water according to equitable apportionment principles. Most interstate stream compacts allocate a specific quantity of water among the signatory states. *See, e.g.,* Oklahoma v. New Mexico, 501 U.S. 221, 111 S.Ct. 2281, 115 L.Ed.2d 207 (1991). Interstate compacts can be preferable to adjudication because the parties can secure their future development needs by allocating unappropriated water (courts are usually unable to do so because of technical and jurisdictional obstacles). Interstate compacts are used not only to allocate water, but also for storage, flood control, pollution control, and comprehensive basin planning. For an assessment of the benefits of conflict resolution via compact rather than litigation, see Daniel Tyler, Silver Fox of the Rockies: Delphus E. Carpenter and Western Water Compacts (2003) (describing background and advantages of the Colorado River Compact of 1922).

Most compacts create a Compact Administration to prescribe procedures for the implementation of the compact. When the parties cannot agree on the administration of the compact's terms, the compact's objectives can be delineated and enforced through a judicial adjudication of the compact. *See* Kansas v. Colorado, 514 U.S. 673, 115 S.Ct. 1733, 131 L.Ed.2d 759 (1995) (post-compact well pumping by Coloradans caused material depletion of usable stateline flows in violation of Kansas's rights under the Arkansas River Compact); People ex rel. Simpson v. Highland Irrigation Co., 917 P.2d 1242 (Colo.1996) (interpreting provision of Arkansas River Compact that water release be applied "promptly" to beneficial use). If a dispute concerning the interpretation of the agreement arises, the U.S. Supreme Court is the final arbiter of the meaning of the compact. The Court will determine the intent of the parties by examining the language of the compact as well as external evidence of the compact negotiations. Oklahoma v. New Mexico, 501 U.S. 221, 111 S.Ct. 2281, 115 L.Ed.2d 207 (1991).

C. Legislative Allocation

Only once have interstate waters been legislatively allocated by Congress. In Arizona v. California, 298 U.S. 558, 56 S.Ct. 848, 80 L.Ed. 1331 (1936), the Supreme Court upheld the Boulder Canyon Act, 43 U.S.C.A. § 617d), which apportioned the waters of the Colorado River between states in the Colorado Basin. It held that Congress may employ its navigation and general welfare powers to apportion interstate waters when other apportionment mechanisms, such as judicial allocation and compacts, are unavailable or are not used. Why hasn't Congress taken a more aggressive role in allocating interstate waters?

D. Future Interstate Conflicts

In many states, the struggle to apportion water has spurred extremely contentious, ongoing debates. Ensuring that an adequate water supply remains in the region and controlling future growth in a sustainable fashion are primary concerns.

Even water-rich regions, such as the Great Lakes, have begun to feel the pressures of ever-increasing demand. Professors Sandra Zellmer and Mark Squillace describe the looming conflict in that region in their article, *Managing Interjurisdictional Waters under the Great Lakes Charter Annex,* 18 NAT. RES. & ENV'T 8 (2003).

> The vast quantities of water available in the Great Lakes makes continued interest in the resource inevitable. * * * In the spring of 1998, the Nova Group of Sault Ste. Marie, Ontario proposed to ship nearly 160 million gallons of Lake Superior water annually via tanker to Asia. Nova's proposal coincided with declining water levels in the Great Lakes, and the resulting public outcry and pressure from other Great Lakes governments persuaded Ontario to revoke Nova's permit just a few months later. * * * [Previously,] [a] surge of interest in diversions from the Great Lakes occurred during the 1980's, when Western interests proposed to use Great Lakes water to recharge the Ogallala Aquifer, to supply water for a coal slurry pipeline in Wyoming, and to improve navigation on the Mississippi River. Even though these proposals arose during a time of record-high water levels, they caused alarm in the Basin, and protectionist legislation was enacted at both state and federal levels.* * * [Most recently,] [i]n 2002, the Perrier Company began pumping and bottling millions of gallons of groundwater within the basin, generating intense controversy in Michigan and Wisconsin.

Id. at 9. The 1998 Nova proposal led the eight Great Lakes states and the two Great Lakes provinces in Canada to adopt Annex 2001 to the existing, cooperative (but non-binding) Great Lakes Charter of 1985. The following article describes the Annex.

GREAT LAKES WATER EXPORTS AND DIVERSIONS: ANNEX 2001 AND THE LOOMING ENVIRONMENTAL BATTLE
Gary Ballesteros
32 ENVTL. L. REP. (2002)

On June 28, 2001, all eight governors of the Great Lakes states and the premiers of the two Canadian provinces bordering the Great Lakes basin gathered at the impressive Prospect Point in Niagara Falls to sign a sweeping joint declaration. Known as "Annex 2001," ... [i]t commits this diverse and multipartisan group of political leaders to find a way to collectively manage the Great Lakes basin. These 10 jurisdictions have agreed to bind themselves together, before the year 2004 is finished, in a new water management union and to develop standards that will govern decisions on any requests to ship or divert Great Lakes water elsewhere. Although the event in Niagara Falls received very little press attention, in many respects it signaled a truly remarkable development. First, it is a rare accomplishment when leaders from three U.S. political parties and two Canadian provinces can all agree on anything. But more than that, the regional nature of Annex 2001 is yet another indication that power is flowing out of Washington, D.C., and into the states. * * *

* * * Demand is on the rise; supply is on the wane. Thus, the economics of "grand" diversions of water is starting to make more sense. That has led to the increasing attempts to export water out of the Great Lakes basin—efforts that have gotten noticed by political leaders. * * * Over the next 25 years the growing global population will need 55% more fresh water to satisfy its thirst. The Great Lakes contain nearly 20% of the entire earth's fresh water supply. Add these figures up and it is obvious that legal, moral, and political pressure will be applied to tap the Great Lakes and divert the water to distant locales to quench the growing thirst for water. In fact, diversions are already happening. Due to legal constraints in the Constitution and in our international trade obligations, the Great Lakes jurisdictions cannot simply say "hands off." To withstand legal challenges under those laws, decisions about water withdrawals must be based on standards that are grounded in sound science and that do not differentiate between withdrawals coming from inside the Great Lakes, the southwestern United States, or even overseas. To withstand moral or equitable challenges, the Great Lakes states and provinces must start cleaning up their own houses and implement sensible conservation measures. Otherwise, they cannot justifiably deny other people water when they are squandering the resource at home. Annex 2001 attempts, and for the most part succeeds, in addressing both of these pressures. However, it is in the political realm that Annex 2001 may be the most vulnerable, and where there are the most unanswered questions. * * *

Notes and Questions

1. The battle over the Great Lakes can be described as "Conflict without Scarcity." *See* A. Dan Tarlock, *The Missouri River: The Paradox of Conflict Without Scarcity*, 2 Great Plains Nat. Res. J. 1 (1997). Obviously, there

are vast quantities of available fresh water in the Great Lakes system, so what's all the shouting about? Professors Zellmer and Squillace highlight the challenges and opportunities presented by Annex 2001.

> Despite numerous [existing] international and interjurisdictional agreements, the water resources of the greatest freshwater resource in the world are not well managed. A new Great Lakes management regime must be developed that replaces current incentives to waste water resources with meaningful incentives to conserve water resources. Annex 2001 offers the Great Lakes states and provinces an important opportunity to change their water management strategies in fundamental ways.

Managing Interjurisdictional Waters, supra at 13.

2. Annex 2001 includes a unique standard: all future diversions and large withdrawals must result in an "improvement" of Great Lakes waters and water-dependent resources. Great Lakes Charter Annex: A Supplementary Agreement to the Great Lakes Charter, Directive #3, June 18, 2001, http://www.cglg.org/projects/water/Annex2001.pdf. *See* Sandra Zellmer, David Gecas and Kori Anne Mann, *The Improvement of Water and Water–Dependent Resources under the Great Lakes Charter Annex,* 4 Tol. J. of GL L, Sci. & Pol'y 289 (2002). The Annex does not provide explicit criteria by which to measure improvement, but Zellmer, Gecas and Mann offer the following observations:

> Annex 2001 states that proposals to withdraw water from the Great Lakes must not only prevent or minimize water loss, avoid adverse effects on water quantity or quality and comply with state and federal laws, but they must also improve the waters and natural resources of the Basin. * * * This is an innovative and proactive standard, in keeping with the status of the Great Lakes aquatic ecosystem as the world's largest freshwater source.* * * Years of experience … [with other] permitting programs provide the following insights regarding Annex 2001. First, actual, measurable improvement should be required before the removal of water occurs. Monitoring will be necessary to ensure that the effects of the project are as anticipated, and that the improvement "banks" or other measures continue to function. The inability to enforce measures adopted as improvements, or to follow through with comprehensive monitoring requirements, could have devastating impacts on the Great Lakes. In addition, specific technical and legal requirements must be established to refine the improvement standard and guide the decisionmakers who must implement it. The standard should be based on ecosystem values and services rather than mere quantity or net replacement ratios. Last but not least, Great Lakes authorities must provide sufficient incentives and funds to ensure that technical expertise is developed and made available to regulators and the regulated community. The improvement standard of Annex 2001 will, no doubt, prove to be a challenging standard for all concerned, but one that is well worth meeting.

Id. at 309–310. What implementation and enforcement difficulties are likely to arise under Annex 2001? How should the states, provinces, tribes, and other interested parties act to ensure the success of the Annex?

3. A proposal to adopt Annex 2001 as an interstate compact is currently pending. The Council of Great Lakes Governors, on behalf of the affected states, accepted public comments through Fall 2004. Status updates can be found on the Council's website: www.cglg. org. Meanwhile, the two Great Lakes provinces, Quebec and Ontario, are consulting with the states on the Annex's provisions, as are Canadian First Nations and federally recognized Indian tribes within the United States. Canadian and tribal interests raise both procedural and substantive complexities. How should they be addressed?

Part IV

CONSERVATION, PRESERVATION, AND RECREATION RESOURCES

The chapters within Part IV address the natural resources which traditionally have not had much commodity value; instead, their worth lies in their existence, and in their non-economic use. Many of these resources are not easily subject to ownership by private parties—they may be characterized as "common" resources, which are not capable of having a private ownership boundary placed around them. Chapter 14, written by Professors Jan G. Laitos and Sandra Zellmer, introduces the wildlife resource. Although fish, game, and other wildlife are sometimes treated as commodity resources, the wildlife resource is primarily valuable as an integral part of ecosystems and a biodiverse environment. Since the wildlife resource is protected by several layers of state and federal law, it cannot be ignored by those who wish to develop the commodity resources outlined in Part III. Chapter 15, written by Professor Laitos, reviews the so-called "preservation" and "recreation" resources. These resources, which consist of land and water, either have important non-use "existence" values, or use values that are triggered by America's growing fascination with play. Increasingly, land managers are attempting to reconcile the conflicts that emerge between those who wish to use these resources primarily for commodity use, and those who wish to have these lands set aside for pure non-use preservation, low-impact non-motorized recreation, or motorized recreation.

Chapter 14

WILDLIFE

I. INTRODUCTION

This book conveys the importance of natural resources law as a constructive way to harmonize the habits and growth of human-kind with the environment that sustains our lives. This chapter discusses the ways in which biological resources, particularly wildlife, are managed and protected by federal and state laws. It addresses private wildlife ownership and management, state wildlife interests and fish and game laws, and federal wildlife law, including provisions for wildlife refuges, migratory birds, marine mammals, and endangered species. Each section of the chapter illustrates the tension between the desire to develop and use wildlife resources and the need to preserve wildlife and biodiversity.

II. PRIVATE WILDLIFE LAW

Private wildlife law covers both private ownership of wildlife and protection of private land and animals against wildlife. Much of private wildlife law is common law, originating in English customs. The fundamental issues have remained the same through the centuries—what rights and duties do private parties have with respect to wildlife?

A. Ownership of Wildlife

Wildlife ownership is a controversial subject, especially when it comes to wildlife that is endangered, dangerous, or not indigenous to a certain area. The two crucial categories of law related to wildlife ownership are the rule of capture and an owner's liability for wildlife.

1. The Rule of Capture

The rule of capture, designed centuries ago to promote the harvest of wild animals, contributes to the over-use and endangerment of fish and wildlife. The rule states that an individual is entitled to wildlife if they are the first to capture the animal. In other words, whoever is prior in time, wins.

PIERSON v. POST

Supreme Court of Judicature of New York, 1805.
3 Cai. R. 175.

The question submitted by the counsel in this cause for our determination is, whether *Lodowick Post,* by the pursuit with his hounds in the manner alleged in his declaration, acquired such a right to, or property in, the fox, as will sustain an action against *Pierson* for killing and taking him away?

* * * It is admitted that a fox is an animal *ferae naturae,* and that property in such animals is acquired by occupancy only. These admissions narrow the discussion to the simple question of what acts amount to occupancy...?

If we have recourse to the ancient writers upon general principles of law, the judgment below is obviously erroneous. *Justinian's Institutes,* lib. 2. tit. 1. s. 13. and *Fleta,* lib. 3. c. 2. p. 175, adopt the principle, that pursuit alone vests no property or right in the huntsman; and that even pursuit, accompanied with wounding, is equally ineffectual for that purpose, unless the animal be actually taken * * *

Puffendorf, lib. 4. c. 6. s. 2. and 10, defines occupancy of beasts *ferae naturae,* to be the actual corporal possession of them * * * The foregoing authorities are decisive to show that mere pursuit gave *Post* no legal right to the fox, but that he became the property of *Pierson,* who intercepted and killed him. * * *

However discourteous or unkind the conduct of *Pierson* towards *Post,* in this instance, may have been, yet his act was productive of no injury or damage for which a legal remedy can be applied.

* * *

Notes and Questions

1. Mr. Post argued that his status as discoverer of the fox and his labor in pursuing it should entitle him to ownership of the beast. After all, Post had pursued it with a mighty steed and well-trained hounds of "imperial stature." The court concluded that the law should recognize actual dominion over the poor beleaguered beast as the source of property rights rather than labor or investment. Is this an appropriate choice? Would the outcome be different if Mr. Post had mortally wounded the fox before Pierson had come along? As with most general rules, there are exceptions to the rule of capture. If it is virtually certain that an animal will be captured as a result of being wounded or trapped, the animal is deemed captured. However, if the animal is only in the process of being entrapped (i.e. the trap door has not

yet shut), the animal is not considered captured. Young v. Hichens, 6 Q.B. 606 (1844).

2.   Another exception to the rule of capture is recognized for certain trades. If the custom of a particular hunting trade results in a more effective and efficient means of trapping, it will be adopted as the rule. For example, if a dead whale sinks and resurfaces days after it is harpooned, it was customary for American whalers to award the whale to the ship that fatally wounded it. The whaling industry prospered because the custom permitted ships to search for other whales without waiting for dead whales to resurface. Courts recognized this custom and awarded possessory rights accordingly. Ghen v. Rich, 8 F. 159 (D.Mass.1881).

3.   Assume Mr. Post had in fact trapped the fox and brought it back to his estate but it subsequently escaped, at which point Pierson captured and killed it. Who owns the fox? Once subdued, the captor maintains ownership of the animal if reasonable precautions against escape are exercised. State v. Shaw, 67 Ohio St. 157, 65 N.E. 875 (1902). This rule makes sense when applied to non-native wildlife; if an exotic animal escapes and is found outside of its native range (*e.g.*, a Bengal tiger in Colorado), hunters are on notice that the animal escaped and its original captor has prior possessory rights. E.A. Stephens & Co. v. Albers, 81 Colo. 488, 256 P. 15 (1927). Should the same rule apply to common wildlife species, like fox?

4.   In the days of Pierson and Post, there was an underlying assumption that wild animals were plentiful. As a result, there was no legal limit on the number available for capture. Has the rule of capture outgrown its usefulness? Should the common law evolve in recognition of the physical "laws" of scarcity?

2.   *Liability for Wildlife*

The subject of liability for damages caused by wildlife invokes a maze of different theories and rationales. As a result, it is difficult to ascertain black letter law. The courts typically hold the possessor of a wild animal strictly liable for personal injury. There are, however, myriad defenses available to the possessor, such as:

- the plaintiff was a trespasser;

- the plaintiff provoked the animal;

- the plaintiff assumed the risk of injury;

- the plaintiff was contributorily negligent.

IRVINE v. RARE FELINE BREEDING CENTER, INC.

Court of Appeals of Indiana, Fourth District, 1997.

685 N.E.2d 120.

For the past thirty years, Mosella Schaffer ("Schaffer") has lived on a fifty acre farm in Hamilton County, Indiana where she has raised and maintained exotic animals. These animals have included * * * Siberian tigers. * * *

In 1993, Scott Bullington ("Bullington") was renting a room in the garage area of Schaffer's house. Aware of his friend Irvine's interest in wild animals, Bullington informed Irvine of Schaffer's farm and the animals she kept there. Irvine * * * began to stop by and see the animals as per Schaffer's open invitation. Over the next two years, Irvine visited Schaffer's farm several dozen times. During these visits, people would occasionally pet the tigers through a fence.

On the afternoon of December 2, 1995, Irvine arrived at Schaffer's home to see Bullington. The two men drank alcohol and watched television until early evening * * * Because Irvine had consumed a substantial amount of alcohol, Bullington told Irvine he could stay over night * * *

* * * Irvine decided to visit the tigers before going to sleep. * * * Irvine then approached the wire caging, as he and others had done in the past, placed a couple fingers inside the enclosure, and attempted to pet a male tiger. As he was scratching the male tiger, a female tiger made some commotion, which caused Irvine to look away from the male tiger. At that moment, the male tiger pulled Irvine's arm through the two inch by six inch opening of the wire fence. * * *

On May 30, 1996, Irvine filed a complaint against Schaffer containing four counts: negligence, strict liability, nuisance, and punitives. On September 6, 1996, Irvine filed his motion for partial summary judgment on the basis that incurred risk and assumption of risk are not valid defenses to a strict liability wild animal claim, on the basis that assumption of risk is not available in a non-contract case, and on the basis that the defense of open and obvious is not available in an animal liability case. * * * The trial court denied Irvine's motion for summary judgment on the strict liability count, denied summary judgment on the issue of assumption of risk, and granted summary judgment on the issue of open and obvious. The trial court granted Irvine's petition to certify three issues for interlocutory appeal: 1) whether incurred risk or other defenses are available in a strict liability animal case; 2) whether Irvine was an invitee as a matter of law; and 3) whether the defense of assumption of risk is available in a noncontractual case. We accepted jurisdiction of the interlocutory appeal.

Irvine first argues that Indiana has historically adhered to strict tort liability in wild animal cases. He further argues that when the Indiana Comparative Fault Act (Ind. Code § 34–4–33–1 et seq., the "Act") was adopted, it did not change the law in wild animal cases. Moreover, he claims that no exceptions to strict liability in wild animal cases have ever been applied in Indiana. He also argues that even if his status is somehow relevant, he was clearly an invitee. Thus, he asserts that the trial court should not have denied his summary judgment on the strict liability issue. * * * [S]chaffer argues that Indiana has not adopted, and should not adopt, strict liability in wild animal cases. * * * Schaffer asserts that if strict liability is the general rule, an exception should apply here.

We first address whether strict liability is the common law rule for wild animal cases in Indiana. * * * [W]e have little difficulty concluding that Indiana's common law recognized the strict liability rule for wild animal cases—despite the fact that previously, Indiana courts have not had the opportunity to apply the rule.

We next address the issue of whether the adoption of the Act changed the common law rule of strict liability in wild animal cases. * * * An abrogation of the common law will be implied (1) where a statute is enacted which undertakes to cover the entire subject treated and was clearly designed as a substitute for the common law; or, (2) where the two laws are so repugnant that both in reason may not stand. Id. * * *

The Act, enacted in 1983 and effective in 1985, "governs any action based on fault[.]" Ind. Code § 34–4–33–1. * * *

By the time of its effective date, that same section had been changed to its current form: " '[f]ault' includes any act or omission that is negligent, willful, wanton, reckless, or intentional toward the person or property of others. The term also includes unreasonable assumption of risk not constituting an enforceable express consent, incurred risk, and unreasonable failure to avoid injury or to mitigate damages." Ind. Code § 34–4–33–2. * * * Narrowly construing the Act, we conclude that it does not explicitly apply to a strict liability claim. * * *

* * * [W]e next address Irvine's contention that no exceptions to strict liability in wild animal cases have ever been applied in this state. * * * As this is an issue of first impression, we look to the reason behind the strict liability wild animal rule and consult other sources as necessary.

We have previously set out the rationale for imposing strict liability against owners for injuries caused by an attack by a naturally ferocious or dangerous animal. * * * Strict liability is appropriately placed: upon those who, even with proper care, expose the community to the risk of a very dangerous thing. * * * The kind of "dangerous animal" that will subject the keeper to strict liability ... must pose some kind of an abnormal risk to the particular community where the animal is kept; hence, the keeper is engaged in an activity that subjects those in the vicinity, including those who come onto his property, to an abnormal risk * * * The possessor of a wild animal is strictly liable for physical harm done to the person of another ... if that harm results from a dangerous propensity that is characteristic of wild animals of that class. * * *

With the rationale for the rule in mind, we analyze whether any exceptions or defenses to the strict liability wild animal rule are appropriate. [T]he Restatement provides: (1) A possessor of a wild animal is subject to liability to another for harm done by the animal to the other, his person, land or chattels, although the possessor has exercised the utmost care to confine the animal, or otherwise prevent it from doing harm. (2) This liability is limited to harm that results from a dangerous propensity that is characteristic of wild animals of the particular class, or of which the possessor knows or has reason to know. Restatement (Second) of Torts § 507 (1977). * * * [W]e look to ... other sections to help flesh out the Restatement's rule.

Section 510(a) provides: "The possessor of a wild animal ... is subject to strict liability for the resulting harm, although it would not have occurred but for the unexpectable ... innocent, negligent or reckless conduct of a third person." However, "[a] possessor of land is not subject to strict liability to one who intentionally or negligently trespasses upon the land, for harm done to him by a wild animal ... that the possessor keeps on the land, even though the trespasser has no reason to know that the animal is kept there." Restatement, supra § 511. Invitees and licensees are dealt with in § 513, which states: "The possessor of a wild animal ... who keeps it upon land in his possession, is subject to strict liability to persons coming upon the land in the exercise of a privilege whether derived from his consent to their entry or otherwise." Yet, if the invitee or licensee "knows that the dangerous animal is permitted to run at large or has escaped from control they may be barred from recovery if they choose to act upon the possessor's consent or to exercise any other privilege and thus expose themselves to the risk of being harmed by the animal. (See § 515)." Restatement, supra cmt. a, § 513.

Section 515(2) * * * provides: "The plaintiff's contributory negligence in knowingly and unreasonably subjecting himself to the risk that a wild animal ... will do harm to his person ... is a defense to the strict liability." * * *

Section 515(3) provides: "The plaintiff's assumption of the risk of harm from the animal is a defense to the strict liability." * * *

Because we agree with the rationale of the exceptions and/or defenses set out in the Restatement, and because we find it to be in keeping with Indiana's recent policy regarding allocation of fault, we adopt the Restatement's approach in wild animal cases.* * * In view of our adoption of the Restatement's strict liability wild animal rule along with its exceptions and defenses, Irvine's status becomes important.... (as either an invitee, licensee, or trespasser) * * *

In arguing that he was an invitee as a matter of law, Irvine relies upon the following evidence:

a) Irvine was invited by Schaffer to come any time (R. 153).

b) Schaffer's affidavit does not deny the above testimony; rather, she claimed that Irvine was specifically not invited by her on the day of the accident (R. 69).

c) Irvine was on the premises 80–100 times (R. 149–50).

d) Bullington testified that Irvine had specifically visited him at least 30 times (R. 218).

e) On several occasions, Irvine had gone through the passageway or breezeway between Schaffer's house and garage and Schaffer voiced no objection (R. 152).

f) On the day of the accident, Bullington had invited Irvine to stay (R. 227).

g) On December 2, 1995, and before the accident, Schaffer saw Irvine on her premises, chatted with him, and did not ask him to leave (R. 165).

* * * Schaffer has introduced her own affidavit which states that Irvine did not have permission to enter her house or the backyard containing the tiger enclosure. Her affidavit also states that Bullington did not have authority to give Irvine permission to enter her home or the backyard containing the tiger enclosure. Accordingly, there is some conflicting evidence regarding Irvine's status, thus precluding summary judgment on this issue.

In adopting the Restatement's view that incurred risk/assumed risk may be a defense to a strict liability wild animal claim, we must next examine whether genuine issues of material fact exist regarding a defense in Irvine's case. Incurred risk requires a mental state of venturousness and a conscious, deliberate and intentional embarkation upon the course of conduct with knowledge of the circumstances. In other contexts, we have stated that the defense of incurred risk is generally a question of fact, and the party asserting it bears the burden of proving it by a preponderance of evidence. * * *

Here, the parties designated conflicting evidence regarding whether Irvine knowingly and unreasonably put himself within reach of a wild animal that was effectively chained or otherwise confined. There was evidence that around the time of the accident, Irvine had been volunteering at the Indianapolis Zoo and had been told not to have contact with tigers. Moreover, there was evidence that Irvine was aware of a prior incident wherein the tiger which injured him grabbed another man's thumb. However, there was other evidence tending to indicate that Schaffer and others had petted the tiger safely in the past. Also, there was evidence that Irvine may have been rather intoxicated on the night in question. In view of the conflicting evidence and inferences, summary judgment was properly denied on the issue of whether a defense was appropriate in this case. Affirmed.

Notes and Questions

1. If Irvine had been a trespasser, would Schaffer necessarily get off the hook, liability-wise? The Restatement (Second) of Torts § 511, *supra,* suggests that she would, but some older cases have held otherwise. *See* Parker v. Cushman, 195 F. 715 (8th Cir. 1912) (imposing strict liability on an animal show proprietor for injuries from a lion, and stating in dicta that the outcome would be the same if plaintiff had been a trespasser); Marble v. Ross, 124 Mass. 44 (1878) (landowner, who knowingly kept a dangerous stag in his pasture, could not evade liability for injuries to a trespasser). Should

it matter if plaintiff enters the land and approaches the animal without the proprietor's consent?

2. Liability sometimes turns on the nature of the animal in question. *Compare* Abrevaya v. Palace Theatre & Realty Co., 197 N.Y.S.2d 27 (Sup. Ct. 1960) (monkeys are of a certain species that can never be regarded as safe, so liability does not rest upon the experiences with the particular, individual animal), *with* Pate v. Yeager, 552 S.W.2d 513 (Tex. Civ. App. 1977) (pet monkey of 26 years was considered "domesticated" and plaintiff was required to prove that defendants knew the animal was "accustomed to do mischief," or that they committed acts of negligence). If the animal is considered *ferae naturae,* the landowner is not likely to be held strictly liable for injuries that occur on his or her property, but may be held liable for negligence. *See* Nicholson v. Smith, 986 S.W.2d 54 (Tex. App. 1999) (RV park owner was not liable to a patron attacked by fire ants because owner had no control over ants, which were native to the area); Woods–Leber v. Hyatt Hotels of Puerto Rico, Inc., 124 F.3d 47 (1st Cir. 1997) (hotel was not liable to guest bit by rabid mongoose in hotel's pool area because it did not control mongoose and attack was not foreseeable). In Booth v. State, 207 Ariz. 61, 83 P.3d 61 (2004), the state was held liable for injuries resulting from an automobile collision with an elk, as the jury found that the state had breached a duty to keep its roadways reasonably safe by failing to take protective measures to guard against collisions at a section of highway where elk crossings were foreseeable. Would the outcome of these cases be different if the animal in question was a non-native exotic animal, like a lion or a zebra? *See* Restatement (Second) of Torts § 507, *supra.*

In Focus:

Chimps on the Rampage

Chimpanzees are often a zoo's most popular attraction. Chimps are highly intelligent and expressive, and visitors spend hours watching and interacting with them. But chimps are also extremely strong and sometimes quite aggressive.

In 2005, two separate incidents of attacks by chimps that had escaped from zoos or animal parks grabbed national headlines. In March, an elderly man and his wife were attacked by two chimps at the Animal Haven Ranch near Bakersfield, California, while visiting their former pet, Moe. The man was severely mauled, and lost an eye, part of his nose, his fingers, and part of his buttocks. The woman lost a thumb. The sanctuary's owner's son shot and killed the chimps. *See Man Took Brunt of Attack by Chimp to Save Wife,* Mont. Co. Herald, Mar. 7, 2005. In August, four chimps at Zoo Nebraska escaped and attempted to break into the zoo gift shop, where visitors and staff had sought shelter. One chimp ventured into the nearby town of Royal, Nebraska. No humans were hurt, but several of the chimps were shot and killed by a state trooper. Margery Beck, *Federal Standards Make it Easy to License a Zoo,* Lincoln J–Star, Sept. 18, 2005, at C1, C3.

These incidents have raised questions about the licensing requirements for facilities that exhibit exotic animals. Federal requirements for animal exhibits are relatively lax. Under the Animal Welfare Act, 7 U.S.C. §§ 2131–2157, exhibitors must be approved by the U.S. Department of Agriculture before they open, submit to annual inspection, and, depending on their size, pay $40 to $310 in fees. Although facilities must have a veterinary-care plan in place, the Act does not require operators to have zoological degrees or experience with exotic animals. Meanwhile, it is surprisingly easy to purchase exotic animals from independent breeders at roadside attractions or even from the internet. *See, e.g.,* http://www.monkeybreeder.com/; http://www.zoologicalimports.com/index.htm.

State and local governments may impose more stringent standards on animal exhibits than federal law requires, *see* DeHart v. Town of Austin, Indiana, 39 F.3d 718 (7th Cir. 1994), and facilities that seek accreditation by the American Zoo and Aquarium Association must meet demanding requirements for animal care and human safety. What role should governments play in ensuring the safety of both humans and animals? Should exotic animal exhibits be banned altogether? For more information on animal welfare issues, see Section III.C., *infra.*

B. The Protection of Private Land and Animals Against Wildlife

When an animal "trespasses" on private property, conflicts may arise between landowners who strive to protect their property from damage by that animal and the government (or, in the case of captured or domesticated wildlife, the private owner) who aims to protect the animal from harm. Landowners have had some success in holding owners of livestock and other species liable for damages to their land and other property. *See, e.g.,* Madrid v. Zenchiku Land & Livestock, 310 Mont. 491, 51 P.3d 1137 (2002) (state statute that provides, "if any … [livestock] break into any enclosure and the fence of the enclosure is legal … , the owner of the animal is liable for all damages to the owner or occupant of the enclosure," subjects the livestock owner to strict liability).

Likewise, an array of tort theories can be employed by owners of wildlife or domestic animals to remedy harms that may befall them. Landowners have the right to exclude trespassers from their land, including hunters or other individuals pursuing wildlife on the landowner's property. In order to prove trespass, the landowner must show an intentional, physical invasion upon her property. A showing of damages is not required. Landowners may also recover for harm to their animals under a nuisance theory. Nuisance involves a particular use of land that results in substantial harm to another landowner's use and enjoyment of their land. Liability for negligence may be imposed when harm is caused by a defendant's failure to use due care to avoid reasonably foreseeable injury. Finally, strict liability applies to acts that are ultra-hazardous. *See* Langan v. Valicopters, Inc., 88 Wash.2d 855, 567 P.2d 218 (1977) (crop duster is strictly liable for all damages caused to adjacent property).

When it comes to federally or state protected species, landowners may claim that damage caused to private property by that species constitutes a taking, thereby entitling them to just compensation.

Notes and Questions

1. *See* Gordon v. Norton, 322 F.3d 1213 (10th Cir.2003) (plaintiff's claim for a taking in violation of the fifth amendment for the FWS's release of the Washakie Wolf Pack in the immediate vicinity of his cattle ranch, when two of his dogs and several cows were allegedly lost to the wolves, dismissed for lack of jurisdiction); Christy v. Hodel, 857 F.2d 1324 (9th Cir.1988), cert. denied, 490 U.S. 1114, 109 S.Ct. 3176, 104 L.Ed.2d 1038 (1989) (holding that a rancher was not entitled to compensation from the government when a federally protected Grizzly bear ate his sheep); *see also* Moerman v. State, 17 Cal.App.4th 452, 21 Cal.Rptr.2d 329 (1993), cert. denied, 511 U.S. 1031, 114 S.Ct. 1539, 128 L.Ed.2d 191 (1994) (state is not subject to liability for damage caused by a state introduced endangered elk). An overriding majority of courts have determined that damage to private property by protected wildlife does not constitute a taking, and the government is therefore not required to compensate the injured land owner. *See* Bishop v. United States, 126 F.Supp. 449 (Ct.Cl.1954) (claim rejected for crop damage by geese protected under the Migratory Bird Treaty Act); Jordan v. State, 681 P.2d 346 (Alaska App.1984) (defendants were not deprived of their property right in a moose carcass when a protected bear attacked the carcass because "their loss was incidental to the state regulation which was enacted to protect game").

2. Some states provide statutory remedies for damage caused by specific species. *See* WIS. STAT. § 29.889; WYO. STAT. ANN. § 23–1–910 (1999); VT. CODE ANN. TIT. 10, § 4829; WASH. REV. CODE § 77.36.060; CO. REV. STAT. ANN. § 33–3–104. These programs are intended to increase landowner support for wildlife preservation. Private funds are sometimes used for this purpose. For example, the Defenders of Wildlife funds a program to compensate ranchers whose livestock is damaged by reintroduced gray wolves. Defenders of Wildlife, Payments to Ranchers from the Bailey Wildlife Foundation Wolf Compensation Trust, at http://www.defenders.org/wildlife/wolf/wcstats.pdf. As of 2004, it had paid nearly $500,000 to 300 ranchers for lost sheep and cattle.

Id. Should the government be required to establish a fund to pay for property damage before it proceeds with a reintroduction program?

3. A slightly different issue arises when governmental protection for a species inhibits the development of extractive resources on private land. In Seiber v. United States, 364 F.3d 1356 (Fed Cir.2004), private timberland in Oregon had been designated a nesting habitat for the federally protected northern spotted owl. The landowners alleged that their applications to harvest lumber on their property had been denied while the U.S. Fish and Wildlife Service (FWS) was assessing the presence of the owl, and sued the government for a temporary taking. The court held that delays in the FWS's decision making process did not establish a viable takings claim, as the government had a legitimate interest in protecting the species' habit from destruction and plaintiffs had failed to show economic injury to the parcel as a whole.

Landowners have had greater success claiming a right to defend their property from non-endangered wildlife that causes damage. Many states have statutes that permit landowners to kill or harass certain species of wildlife when their property is threatened. These statutes differ greatly depending upon the state, and may require landowners to obtain a permit, give the carcass to the state, notify a state official after taking the animal, or report to a game warden.

The Nebraska Game Code, for example, allows any person whose trees or other property is damaged by a beaver to notify the Game Commission and, if the Commission doesn't remove it within 30 days, the person may destroy the beaver and its dens. Neb. Rev. Code § 37–460. The Code also allows farmers and ranchers to destroy "any [non-protected] predator preying on livestock or poultry or causing other agricultural depredation" on their land. *Id.* § 37–559. If the damage is caused by deer, antelope or elk, however, the landowner may not take unilateral action, but must instead notify the Commission. *Id.* § 37–560. Many states are more restrictive in their management measures for deer, elk, and other ungulates than they are with regard to predators. *See* State v. Cleve, 127 N.M. 240, 980 P.2d 23 (1999) (defendant convicted for killing deer that had destroyed his crops); State v. Thompson, 136 Idaho 322, 33 P.3d 213 (App.2001) (misdemeanor convictions upheld for killing deer that were causing harm to private garden). What justification might there be for inhibiting landowners from protecting their property from deer but allowing them free rein when it comes to predators?

What is a "predator" anyway? Like Nebraska, the Idaho and Colorado Codes allow state officials and livestock owners to kill certain predators. *See* Idaho Stat. § 36–1107 (authorizing livestock owners to dispose of black bears, mountain lions and other predators without a permit "when same are molesting livestock"); Colo. Rev. Stat. § 33–3–106 (authorizing the disposal of bears, mountain lions and dogs when necessary to prevent damage or injury to livestock, real property, a motor vehicle or human life). If the state statute does not define "predator," you might turn to the U.S. Code for guidance. The federal Animal Damage Control Act, 7 U.S.C. § 426, *et seq.,* authorized the Secretary of Agriculture to control "mountain lions, wolves, coyotes, bobcats, prairie dogs, gophers, ground squirrels, jack rabbits, brown tree snakes, and other animals injurious to agriculture, horticulture, forestry, animal husbandry, wild game animals, fur-bearing animals, and birds.... " The statute was revised in 2000, and it now simply allows the Secretary to provide wildlife services "with respect to injurious animal species." 7 U.S.C. § 426 (Pub.L. 106–387, Title VII, § 767). Of course, if the predator in question is a protected species, landowners cannot dispose of them freely without facing civil or even criminal liability. *See* Christy v. Hodel, 857 F.2d 1324 (9th Cir.1988).

During Thanksgiving week of 2004, a trained sniper from the Dakota County Sheriff's Office "dispatched" (shot and killed) a mountain lion in South Sioux City, Nebraska. Although mountain lions are not protected as an endangered or threatened species in Nebraska, they are relatively rare. It was the 17th sighting of a mountain lion in the state since 1991, but the first within the city limits. The lion, a healthy two-year old male, was napping on a tree limb in a residential neighborhood when he was spotted, and had not left his perch by the time officials arrived on the scene. Larry Porter, *Mountain Lion is Shot*, Omaha World–Herald, Nov. 24, 2004, at 01A. Like most states, the Nebraska Code allows conservation officers to take any wildlife that is "considered dangerous to human or livestock health." Neb. Rev. Code § 37–353. Was the lion's demise authorized by § 37–353? Should officials have exercised some other option more consistent with conservation goals?

III.   STATE WILDLIFE LAW

State law dominates the regulation of hunting, fishing, and trapping of wildlife. State law may also address predator control and habitat protection. Tribal laws also play an important a role in wildlife management and habitat protection. *See* Chapter 7, *supra* (Tribal Ownership). Two main topics are addressed here: state game laws and state wildlife management on federal lands. This section concludes with a look at cultural aspects of hunting and anti-cruelty measures.

A.   State Game Laws

States are the primary regulators of the public's access to fish and game species. States exercise this power by promulgating codes for the regulation and management of fish and game, typically through a three step process:

- First, each state will create an agency or agencies that are in charge of managing the state's wildlife resources.

- Next, the state will classify wildlife into several different categories. Typically, the state develops a classification for "game animals";

"vermin," "predators" or "nuisance" species; and a category for everything else.

- Finally, the state will develop a code that provides the conditions upon which game animals may be taken. As noted above, state game codes often exclude vermin, predators and nuisance species from their scope, or otherwise allow species classified as such to be killed at anytime. In addition, game codes typically authorize various protective measures for game and other species. To regulate the taking of wildlife, states have developed several types of limitations, including closed hunting and fishing periods, gear restrictions, bag limits, licenses, and restrictions on the sale of game. Some states even impose total bans. For more information on hunting and fishing regulations in your state, visit the US Fish and Wildlife Service's webpage at: http://offices.fws.gov/statelinks.html.

At one time, many states prohibited hunting, fishing, and other "sporting events" on Sundays. Section 241 of the Nebraska Criminal Code, for example, stated that anyone "found on ... Sunday sporting, ... hunting, fishing, or shooting ... shall be fined in a sum not exceeding $20, or be confined in the county jail ... not exceeding 20 days, or both." State v. O'Rourk, 35 Neb. 614, 53 N.W. 591, 592 (1892). *See generally* W. J. Dunn, *Construction of Statute or Ordinance Prohibiting or Regulating Sports and Games on Sunday*, 24 A.L.R.2d 813, §§ 15, 17 (reviewing hunting and fishing restrictions). Today, most states have abandoned those restrictions, *see, e.g.,* 1998 Ohio Laws File 128 (S.B. 103) (rescinding O.R.C. § 1531.021) and Indiana Act of 1977, P.L.26, § 25 (repealing Ind. Code § 35–31–5–1*)*, and some have adopted a complete reversal in policy. In Vermont, the present fish and game laws promote hunting by youth on a special free weekend (including Sunday). Vt. Stat. Ann. tit. 10, § 4742A. In Kentucky, which at one point banned hunting with guns and dogs (but not bows) on Sunday, certain businesses are forbidden from operating on Sunday, but not bait and tackle shops. *See* K.R.S § 436.160(3).

Why would a state legislature adopt such a seemingly absurd provision as a Sunday fishing or hunting ban in the first place? To allow one day of the week "for the unmolested passage of fish up the river"? Sickles v. Sharp, 13 Johns 497 (N.Y.1816). Or to prevent disruption of the "restful calm" of this day of respite? State v. Gilletto, 98 Conn. 702, 120 A. 567 (1923). In upholding the arrest and conviction of a baseball team for "sporting" on a Sunday, the Nebraska Supreme Court offered this explanation:

> As a Christian people ... the state has enacted certain statutes, which, among other things, in effect recognize ... the binding force of the teachings of the Saviour. Among these is the statute which prohibits sporting, hunting, etc., on Sunday. * * * Sunday is like an oasis in the journey of life, where each traveler may be refreshed and become more able to continue the performance of his duties or labors. * * * No doubt one of the objects of the Creator in establish-

ing the Sabbath as a day of rest was to provide for restoring and retaining, as far as possible, health and strength and perfect action of the body. * * * Worldly cares are to be laid aside, and the worries of business or pleasure thrown off.

O'Rourke, 53 N.W. at 594. The statute at issue was eventually invalidated, but the case was not.

An alternative theory follows a utilitarian/wealth maximization theme: "the value of the land can be increased by setting aside a day for uses other than hunting, [so] prohibiting hunting on Sundays is consistent with attempts to maximize the value of land with alternative uses." Dean Lueck, *Property Rights and the Economic Logic of Wildlife Institutions,* 35 Nat. Res. J. 625, 657 (1995). The author cites data showing that in states where agricultural property values are high, such as Iowa, there are no Sunday bans, but more densely populated states, such as New York and New Jersey, tend to outlaw Sunday hunting. *Id.* at 658. *See* N.J. Stat. § 23:4–24 (no hunting on Sunday with a hound or weapons of any kind); N.Y. Env. Conservation Law §§ 11–0903(7) (deer season may not include Saturday or Sunday in certain counties), 13–0327(1) (bay scallops cannot be "taken on Sundays by use of a dredge or other [power] device"). Is this logic persuasive?

Defenses to convictions under Sunday hunting and fishing bans have been largely unsuccessful. One particularly cheeky defendant sought to overturn his conviction under a statute forbidding fishing on Sunday even though he had been caught red-handed drawing up a net containing a few small perch. *See* Commonwealth v. Gushinski, 10 Pa. D. & C. 202 (1927). The defendant offered two theories. First, he claimed that the mere act of pulling up a net in which fish are "restrained of their liberty" did not constitute fishing. *Id.* at 203. The judge noted that the argument had "the merit of ingenious novelty," but rejected it just the same. *Id.*

> [I]n the light of our personal experience, extended over half a century, we define ... [fishing] to be a human effort, successful or unsuccessful, by any device, to remove from water the piscatorial denizens thereof, a performance demanding patience, involving skill, accompanied by profanity and usually followed by mendacity....

Id. Second, defense counsel argued that the crime should be excused if the defendant had been motivated by a merciful intention to free the fish. The court noted that the defendant had neither testified that he was so motivated nor that the fishes were discontented due to their confinement; "therefore, with the assistance of inherent probability, we are thoroughly convinced ... that in pulling those fish from their native element into a cruel world, exposed to the possible piscatorial appetite of the officials, he was not actuated by any sentiment of mercy whatever." *Id.* at 204. Moreover, according to the court, the fish "suffered no pain of body or mind. Indeed, we are advised by naturalists that fish, owing to lack of adequate sensory equipment, are physically and mentally incapable of feeling pain, and that even when gasping in the throes of apparent agony are really not suffering at all." *Id.* People for the Ethical Treatment of Animals (PETA) disagrees with the latter proposition, and offers compelling proof to the contrary. *See* David Crary, *Animal-rights Group Causes Flap over Fish*, Detroit Free Press, Nov. 26, 2004; PETA Fish Empathy Project: Fish Feel Pain, http://www.fishinghurts.com/FishFeelPain.asp.

Could defendants faced with criminal charges for hunting or fishing on a Sunday raise any viable constitutional defenses? *Compare* McGowan v. State of Md., 366 U.S. 420, 81 S.Ct. 1101, 6 L.Ed.2d 393 (1961) (Sunday closing laws are reasonably related to the legislative purpose of providing a day of rest, and the laws do not deny equal protection, are not so vague as to violate due process, and do not establish a religion), *with* Carpenter v. Wood, 177 Neb. 515, 129 N.W.2d 475 (1964) (Sunday closing law violated the Nebraska Bill of Rights and was unconstitutional in its entirety).

The following case illustrates the potential for challenging state wildlife statutes as a violation of due process and equal protection.

STATE v. BONNEWELL

Court of Appeals of Arizona, 1999.
196 Ariz. 592, 2 P.3d 682.

Kurt Bonnewell, Lauralu Harkins, Lee P. Hulsey, and Walter John Randall ("Defendants") were convicted of setting a leghold trap on public land in violation of Arizona Revised Statutes Annotated ("A.R.S.") section 17–301(D)(1) * * * On appeal, they argue that the statute is a special or local law in violation of the Arizona Constitution and that it violates the equal protection clauses of the Arizona and United States Constitutions.

We hold that A.R.S. section 17–301(D) is not an unconstitutional local or special law because it rationally furthers a legitimate governmental purpose, applies to all persons in Arizona, and benefits no static class of individuals. We also hold that the statute does not violate the equal protection clauses of either the Arizona Constitution or the United States Constitution because it is rationally related to a legitimate governmental purpose. We therefore affirm.

In the November 1994 general election, voters passed Proposition 201, which was codified as A.R.S. section 17–301(D). The pertinent part of the statute made unlawful the taking of wildlife on public lands by leghold trap. The statute makes exceptions for the use of traps by government officials to protect against threats to human health or safety, or for research, falconry, relocation of wildlife, or rodent control. *See* A.R.S. § 17–301(D)(1), (3), (4), and (5) (Supp. 1998). According to the pamphlet issued by the Secretary of State on the 1994 Ballot Propositions, the purposes of the initiative were ... to prevent cruelty to wildlife on public lands and to prevent injuries to pets, children, and adults using public lands for recreation.

Defendants were each charged with setting a leghold trap in violation of A.R.S. section 17–301(D). Each filed a motion to dismiss the charges, arguing that the statute constituted a local or special law that violated article 4, part 2, section 19 of the Arizona Constitution and violated the equal protection guarantees of the Arizona and United States Constitutions because it made criminal behavior on public land that remained legal when practiced on private land. At an evidentiary hearing, each Defendant admitted setting a prohibited leghold trap on public land * * * The trial court denied the motion to dismiss, ruling that voters could have rationally determined that characteristics of leghold traps justified banning them from public lands and that the distinction between public and private lands was legitimate. * * *

The Arizona Constitution prohibits any special or local law "granting any individual any special or exclusive privilege or immunities," or "when a general law can be made applicable." Art. 4, part 2, § 19(13), (20). The prohibition against special legislation is intended to prevent the legislature from providing special benefits and favors to certain groups or locations.[] A law is not a "special" law if (1) the classification is rationally related to a legitimate government objective, (2) the classification encompasses all members of the relevant class, and (3) the class is flexible, allowing members to move into and out of the class. * * * Also, the classification must be accepted as reasonable unless "palpably arbitrary." * * *

We first consider whether section 17–301(D)'s classification based on location is rationally related to a legitimate purpose. The statute establishes classifications based on location; it prohibits the use of leghold traps on public land but not on private land. * * * We believe the statute rationally furthers these legitimate governmental interests [in preventing cruelty to wildlife and preventing injuries to recreational users on the public lands].

Defendants agree that prevention of cruelty to animals on public lands is a legitimate State interest, but argue that the classification does not rationally further that interest. * * * [D]efendants are mistaken in assuming that only a statute prohibiting all leghold trapping could further the interest involved.

We do not believe the classification here to be palpably arbitrary. The people of Arizona could legitimately determine that cruelty to animals should be eliminated on land belonging to the people of the State and that the State should prohibit the use of devices perceived to be inhumane and cruel. The statute furthers that purpose.

The statute ... furthers the State's interest in preventing injury to people who use public lands for recreation. * * * Unlike private land, in which the owner has control over the access of individuals onto the property, public lands are accessible to and used by the general public. The private owner, being responsible for his property, would presumably know of the presence of traps that might pose a danger and be able to warn anyone admitted on the property to avoid injury. Such is not the case on public lands, where anyone using the land might accidentally and unexpectedly place a foot in one of the traps, causing injury. Prohibiting the placement of leghold traps on public lands furthers the purpose of the statute to protect users of public lands from injury caused by the traps.

We next consider whether the statute meets the second requirement of a general law. This requirement mandates that the classification encompass all members of the relevant class. The statute precludes use of leghold traps on public lands. It thus creates a class of all persons wishing to trap on public land throughout the State—this class is prohibited from using leghold traps. The restriction is equally applicable to all members of the class, that is, all people using public lands. Thus, the statute meets this requirement.

The third requirement of a general law is that the class be flexible. Defendants argue that because of the limited amount of private land available in Arizona, the class is static. The existing private land, although limited, can be sold and purchased or leased, allowing movement in and out of the class. Thus, a person who buys or leases private land may use leghold traps on that property. But if that person then sells or surrenders his or her lease to that private property, that person cannot then use leghold traps on public lands. Therefore, we conclude that the class created here is elastic.

* * * Defendants assert that the statute gives a special class of landowners the privilege of harvesting publicly owned wildlife. Defendants argue this privilege is a significant right, but they fail to demonstrate how it impacts the three-part test to determine whether the statute is a general or special law. * * *[W]e note that persons using public rather than private lands are not precluded from harvesting the State's wildlife. They are simply precluded from using a specific method, deemed cruel and dangerous * * *

Defendants also claim that A.R.S. section 17–301(D) violates the equal protection clauses of the United States and Arizona Constitutions. * * * The effects of the two provisions are essentially the same. Because the statute implicates neither a fundamental right nor a suspect class, we apply a rational basis test. Under the rational basis test, the statute must be rationally related to furthering some legitimate governmental interest. A classification can be based on rational speculation unsupported by evidence. An equal protection analysis of whether the statute is rationally related to a legitimate State interest is similar to the initial analysis conducted in determining if the statute constitutes a special or general law. As part of our decision that section 17–301(D) is not a special law, we concluded that it is rationally related to a legitimate purpose. Thus, we also conclude that the statute does not violate the equal protection clauses of the Arizona and United States Constitutions.

Defendants argue that the statute is not rationally related to a legitimate state interest because A.R.S. section 17–301(D) is a wildlife statute that "frustrates" sound wildlife management and impedes "professional game management objectives." Therefore, according to Defendants, the statute cannot be considered as furthering a legitimate State interest. * * *

We acknowledge that wildlife management certainly could be one of the State interests addressed by A.R.S. section 17–301(D). But other State interests are also implicated. The State has a legitimate interest in preventing cruelty to animals. * * * The State also has a legitimate interest in protecting users of public lands from injuries. Thus, Defendants are mistaken in contending that only wildlife management can be considered a legitimate State interest in analyzing the validity of the statute.

We therefore conclude that the prohibition of leghold traps on public lands is rationally related to the purposes of the statute. * * * Defendants' convictions are affirmed.

Notes and Questions

1. As *Bonnewell* illustrates, states enjoy broad powers to regulate hunting in order to conserve game species and promote the general welfare, but there are constitutional limitations. State wildlife law may be held unconstitutional if it discriminates against other states or the residents of other states. In *Clajon Production Corp. v. Petera*, 70 F.3d 1566 (10th Cir.1995), a group of Wyoming ranchers who offered hunting services to non-residents brought a civil rights action against the state fish and game department, alleging that the state's residency-based allocation scheme for hunting licenses impaired their ability to sell their services in the out-of-state market. They alleged that the Wyoming law violated the dormant commerce clause, but this claim was dismissed for lack of standing. *Id.* at 1574. (The dormant commerce clause is addressed below in Section IV.B.1.) They also alleged that Wyoming's limitations on the number of hunting licenses available to large landowners violated the Equal Protection Clause and was a taking. The court rejected both claims. It concluded that the restriction at issue was an economic regulation, and as such it need only have a rational relation to a legitimate interest to satisfy equal protection. The state's scheme of using a lottery to limit and allocate hunting licenses had the rational basis of balancing conservation policies by affording public access to hunting while offering landowners an adequate opportunity to hunt on their land. *Id.* at 1580. Further, the state's decision to limit large landowners to only two supplemental hunting licenses did not destroy all beneficial uses of their property so as to effect a *per se* regulatory taking, nor did it constitute a taking under the traditional balancing test, as the provision substantially advanced a legitimate state interest in conserving wild game and affording an opportunity to hunt to all residents. *Id.* at 1576–79.

2. State legislatures and game commissions often establish different rules for separate geographic areas due to physical differences in wildlife

habitat or in public access. Plaintiffs have challenged these laws as arbitrary, overbroad, and in violation of state constitutional due process provisions or provisions forbidding "special" legislation. The results have been mixed, as illustrated by the following cases:

- *Tennessee Conservation League v. Cody,* 745 S.W.2d 854 (Tenn.1987): The TCL challenged the validity of a state statute regulating the use of dogs for hunting raccoons. The plaintiffs argued that the differing rules for different parts of the state amounted to "special legislation" which violated the state constitution and was an arbitrary exercise of state power. The court upheld the statute, explaining that, "sound Constitutional principles compel it to leave the protection of the raccoon population and training of coon dogs in the hands of the Legislature so long as there is a viable causal connection between their action and the provision." *Id.*

- *Arkansas Game & Fish Comm. v. Murders,* 938 S.W.2d 854 (Ark.1997): Appellees were licensed hunters who brought a declaratory judgment action against the Commission, challenging a state provision prohibiting hunting or shooting across any city, county, state, or federally maintained road or right of way. An overbroad statute is "one that is designed to punish conduct which the state may rightfully punish, but which includes within its sweep constitutionally protected conduct." *Id.* The court held that the provision was unconstitutionally overbroad because "its wording is so inclusive that it may affect the right of non-hunters who possess loaded or uncased firearms on city, county, state or federally-maintained road." *Id.*

- *State v. McAffry,* 263 Kan. 521, 949 P.2d 1137 (1997): Defendant challenged a statute that made it a crime to cast light "for the purpose of spotting, locating or taking any animal" while in possession of a gun. As in *Murders,* the court interpreted this statute as unconstitutionally overbroad because the definition of "animal" could include livestock. Because livestock is not a hunted species, the statute regulates activities other than hunting and is too broad. *Id.*

The extent of the 4th amendment right to freedom from unreasonable searches and seizures is another important constitutional issue raised by state wildlife law. Inspection or detention generally cannot occur without consent, probable cause or a reasonable suspicion of illegal activity. Game wardens' search and seizure authority was upheld in the following cases: *Rainey v. Hartness,* 339 Ark. 293, 5 S.W.3d 410 (1999) (there was no legitimate expectation of privacy in a deer stand, so officer did not violate the constitution when he entered the property without permission and seized the hunter's illegal rifle); *Mollica v. Volker,* 229 F.3d 366 (2d Cir.2000) (a checkpoint for purpose of making deer tag and weapon safety checks during hunting season was reasonable); *State v. McHugh,* 630 So.2d 1259 (La.1994) (a game agent's stop of a hunter in or departing from a wildlife habitat in open season and detention for the limited purposes of a license check did not violate the state or federal constitution). Conversely, in *State v. Romain,* 295 Mont. 152, 983 P.2d 322 (1999), the court suppressed all evidence obtained by wardens who, without a warrant or permission, seized game from a truck that was parked on a private driveway. The property on which the game was found was secluded, fenced, marked by "no trespassing" signs and obscured by trees, raising an expectation of privacy, and the wardens' receipt of an anonymous tip of poaching was not sufficient to justify the warrantless search. Is *Romain* distinguishable from the preceding cases?

Finally, state wildlife laws may implicate constitutional and statutory limits on forfeiture. Several states permit authorities to seize personal property, including fishing gear and rifles used in violation of fish and game laws. There are two steps used to assess the legality of a forfeiture:

- First, review the applicable statute to determine whether forfeiture is expressly authorized. Absent express authorization, the forfeiture is illegal.

- Next, if there is an express authorization, look to the limits imposed by the federal constitution, particularly the Due Process Clause (prohibits deprivation of property without due process of law) and the Eighth Amendment (prohibits excessive fines). If these limits are violated, the forfeiture is illegal.

In Baum v. State, 24 P.3d 577 (Alaska App.2001), the court found that the forfeiture of defendant's $40,000 plane did not violate the Excessive Fines Clause of the Constitution. Similarly, in One 1992 Toyota 4–Runner v. State ex rel. Mississippi Dept. of Wildlife Fisheries and Parks, 721 So.2d 609 (Miss. 1998), the forfeiture of defendant's dip net and other fishing equipment, along with his boat, motor, trailer and ice chest (containing fish), was upheld because each piece of seized property was used to obtain fish through the illegal means of shocking or to transport the contraband fish.

B. State Wildlife Management on Federal Lands

Although Congress has authority to preempt state management of wildlife on federal lands under the Property, Commerce and Supremacy Clauses of the U.S. Constitution, it often defers to state law. The extent of state wildlife law on federal lands varies by system. For example, the National Park Service is fully exempt from state law, but the Fish and Wildlife Service follows all state law that is consistent with federal management goals on its wildlife refuges. The Forest Service and BLM are subject to the terms of the Federal Land Policy and Management Act, which provide that "nothing in the Act should be construed ... as enlarging or diminishing the responsibility and authority of the States for management of fish and resident wildlife." 42 U.S.C.A. § 1732(b).

Congress has consistently reaffirmed its policy of deference to state authority over fish and game. State police powers extend over the federal public domain unless Congress provides otherwise. *Omaechevarria v. Idaho*, 246 U.S. 343, 38 S.Ct. 323, 62 L.Ed. 763 (1918). Accordingly, a "state is free to enforce its criminal and civil laws on federal land so long as those laws do not conflict with federal law." California Coastal Comm'n v. Granite Rock Co., 480 U.S. 572, 580, 107 S.Ct. 1419, 94 L.Ed.2d 577 (1987). In *California Coastal Comm'n*, Granite Rock, a mining company, sued to enjoin state officials from requiring it to receive a state mining permit for a mine located on federal land within the state's coastal zone. It argued that federal laws, including the General Mining Act of 1872, the National Forest Management Act and the Coastal Zone Management Act, preempted the state permit requirement. The Court characterized the state requirement as an environmental regulation, concluding that when state law is an environmental regulation there is no federal preemption, but preemption would preclude state land use regulations on federal land. Land use planning directs the specific use of land, while environmental regulation requires that damage to the environment is kept within stipulated limits, regardless of how the land is to be used.

> Considering the legislative understanding of environmental regulation and land use planning as distinct activities, it would be anomalous to maintain that Congress intended any state environmental regulation of unpatented mining claims in national forests to be *per se* pre-empted as an impermissible exercise of state land use planning. Congress' treatment of environmental regulation and land use planning as generally distinguishable calls for this Court to treat them as distinct, until an actual overlap between the two is demonstrated in a particular case.

Id. at 588. As a result, state environmental regulations must be evaluated on case by case basis. For further discussion of state land use regulations, see Jeffrey L. Amestoy & Mark J. Stefano, *Wildlife Habitat Protection Through State–Wide Land Use Regulation*, 14 Harv. Envtl. L. Rev. 45 (1990), and Chapter 10, *supra*.

The following news article describes a state and federal partnership on Cowhouse Island at Dixon Memorial State Forest and Okefenokee National Wildlife Refuge.

 U.S. Fish & Wildlife Service

Southeast Region 4

State, Federal Partnership Will Restore Red–Cockaded Woodpecker Habitat on Cowhouse Island

February 25, 2002

The endangered red-cockaded woodpecker and its longleaf pine habitat will be restored, managed, and protected on Cowhouse Island at Dixon Memorial State Forest and Okefenokee National Wildlife Refuge. The ongoing restoration of the woodpecker's native habitat on the island is the result of a Memorandum of Understanding between the Georgia Department of Natural Resources, the Georgia Forestry Commission, and the U.S. Fish and Wildlife Service.

A management plan is now being developed that will cover 2,258 acres of Dixon Memorial State Forest and 1,092 acres of the Okefenokee National Wildlife Refuge. No red-cockaded woodpeckers currently inhabit this area on Georgia Forestry Commission or Fish and Wildlife Service land. However, once their native habitat is restored, the agencies expect groups of woodpeckers from the surrounding interior islands and uplands to repopulate these areas. * * * "Restoring longleaf pine habitat in this area will also help recover other federally-listed species like the threatened gopher tortoise, the threatened eastern indigo snake, and the Bachman's sparrow.... "Partnerships between federal and state agencies and between agencies and private landowners, such as the Cowhouse Island Memorandum of Understanding, are helping us ... meet our natural resources stewardship responsibilities," said David Waller, Director of Georgia Department of Natural Resources' Wildlife Resources Division. * * *

The Memorandum of Understanding is a long-term agreement that will be reviewed every 10 years, and its associated Cowhouse Management Plan will be reviewed annually. When additional longleaf habitat has been restored on the refuge, more red-cockaded woodpecker pairs could be moved there. Longleaf pine habitat will have to be reestablished on Dixon Memorial State Forest, and after it is suitable in 30 years, the red-cockaded woodpeckers on the refuge could use the State Forest land as a foraging area. The State Forest land would be suitable for cavity trees in about 80 years. After maturation, the refuge and state lands could support an additional 15 clusters.

Red-cockaded woodpeckers are approximately 8–inch-long black and white birds that need old living pine trees in which to excavate their roosting and nesting cavities. They live in family groups that typically consist of a breeding pair and one to three of their adult male offspring that assist in raising young birds each spring. Each woodpecker has its own roosting cavity within a cluster of cavity trees, and each family group needs about 100 to 200 acres of nearby mature, open pine forest in which to forage for insects, spiders, and other invertebrates.

C. The Hunting Culture and Anti–Cruelty Measures

Although hunting and fishing activities have declined in recent years, the revenues from fish and game permits remain a very large source of state income. The U.S. Fish and Wildlife Service recently compiled a study on wildlife recreation that analyzed the pervasiveness of hunting and fishing within the past decade.

In Focus:

Hunting and Fishing Statistics

A comparison of estimates from the 1991, 1996, and 2001 surveys reveals that millions of Americans continue to enjoy wildlife recreation. While the number of sportspersons fell from 40 million in 1991 to 37.8 million in 2001, their expenditures increased from $53 billion (adjusted for inflation and comparability between surveys) in 1991 to $70 billion in 2001.

Fishing—Fishing continues to be a favorite pastime in the United States. In 2001, 16% of the U.S. population 16 years old and older spent an average of 16 days fishing. [However, a comparison of the] results of the 2001 survey and the 1996 survey reveals that the number of all anglers declined 3% and overall fishing expenditures fell 17%—a 16% drop in trip and a 22% drop in equipment expenditures. From 1991 to 2001, the number of all anglers declined 4% and expenditures increased 14%. Saltwater fishing increased 22% but freshwater fishing declined by 6%.

Hunting—Six percent of the U.S. population 16 years old and older, over 13 million people, hunted in 2001. They spent an average of 18 days pursuing their sport. Comparing 1991 to 2001, the number of all hunters declined by 7%. * * * [T]he number of big game and migratory bird hunters remained constant. The decreases occurred in small game (–29%) and other animal (–26%) hunting. Hunting expenditures increased 29% from 1991 to 2001, primarily due to equipment expenditures.

See www.fws.gov for further information.

Some state constitutions include provisions that protect hunting, typically as a subset of a right to bear arms for hunting and other lawful activities. *See, e.g.,* Del. Const. art. I § 20; N.M. Const. art. II § 6; Neb. Const. art. I § 1; W. Va. Const. art. III § 22. If hunting is no longer necessary as a means of survival in the 21st century, should it continue to be protected as an individual right?

Clashes between hunting groups and animal rights proponents like the Humane Society and PETA are not unique to our times. In England, efforts to ban fox hunting surfaced (and failed) as early as 1911. Fox hunting involves "packs of dogs and costumed men on horseback that pursue the fox across the landscape until it collapses from exhaustion, at which point the dogs usually tear it to pieces." Daniel M. Warner, *Environmental Endgame: Destruction for Amusement and a Sustainable Civilization*, 9 S.C. Envt. L.Rev. 1, 40 n.120 (2000).

The fox hunting debate has resurfaced in recent years:

[In 1998], a huge crowd of 250,000 mostly rural English men and women gathered in London to protest New Labour's proposed bill that would ban fox hunting.* * * The bill was not adopted. The Sunday Telegraph commented: "[British Prime Minister Tony Blair] has repeatedly declared that with every right must come a duty. Perhaps the Labour MPs so keen to defend the rights of the fox could explain what corresponding duty these animals accept." William F. Buckley Jr., The Brits (Some Brits) Protest, NATIONAL REVIEW, April 6, 1998, at 63.

Id. at 40 n.120. The hunting ban ultimately passed, despite opposition, and it has survived judicial review:

Pro–hunting campaigners yesterday lost their second High Court challenge to the ban on hunting with dogs in England and Wales. * * * Dismissing the challenge, Lord Justice May and Mr Justice Moses concluded that "it was within the rational, proportionate and democratic competence of Parliament to [enact the Hunting Act of 2004] * * * [T]here was sufficient material available to the House of Commons for them to conclude that hunting with dogs is cruel * * * [and] a reasonable basis ... [that] taken as a whole, hunting foxes with dogs causes more suffering than shooting them." * * * [I]t was "reasonably open to the majority of the democratically elected House of Commons to conclude that this measure was necessary in the democratic society which had elected them." * * *

Joshua Rozenberg, *Pro-hunt Campaign Loses Legal Challenge Against Ban*, Daily Telegraph (London), July 30, 2005, at 11.

Efforts to prevent cruelty to other species achieved success far earlier.

The first modern legislation to promote animal welfare was introduced in the British Parliament in 1800, when Sir W. Pulteney forwarded a bill to ban bull-baiting (a bull was tethered by a short chain to a post driven into the ground, and was set upon by bull dogs trained to attack it by biting its nose and ultimately killing it; this had been sport in England for seven hundred years). The bill failed. In 1821 Richard Martin, an Irishman, introduced a bill into the Commons concerning the ill-treatment of horses and cattle. The reaction of the House was to laugh the Bill out of court. One member suggested that asses be included—Martin agreed—laughter ensued–[but] [t]he bill passed, and marked the first legislation of modern times in any country that protected animals against any kind of abuse by humans.* * * In 1835, England passed a bill giving protection against abuse to all domestic animals, including dogs, and outlawing bear-baiting, badger-baiting, bull-baiting, dog fights and cock fights. The first urban animal shelters were developed in England in 1860; The Times wondered if "the supporters of such an institution have not taken leave of their sober senses ... Why not a home for five pound notes dropped in the streets?" * * *

Id. at 38–40.

The animal welfare movement gained a toehold in the United States in 1877 when the American Humane Association was founded. It focuses on preventing the abuse of women, children and animals, and has taken a leading role in addressing the correlation between domestic abuse to humans and the abuse of animals in the home. *Id*. at 40. In addition, the Association's Film and Television unit is responsible for overseeing the treatment of animals on movie sets. If a production meets its standards, the film earns a "No Animals Were Harmed ... "™ end credit disclaimer. *See* Two Paws Up, http://www.americanhumane.org/site/PageServer? pagename=pa_film_ratings (visited Jan. 24, 2005).

The Humane Society of the United States was founded in 1952 by former members of the Association who were dissatisfied with its near-exclusive attention to dogs and cats. The Humane Society seeks protection through outreach and advocacy for all animals subject to "gross commercial cruelties." Warner, *supra*, at 40. For more information about its objectives, see The Humane Society of the United States, http://www.hsus.org/. PETA, by contrast, is viewed as a more aggressive, "in your face" organization. Its campaign against furriers has been one of the most highly publicized animal welfare efforts in the United States. *See* People for the Ethical Treatment of Animals, www.peta.org.

Many, if not all, states have adopted anti-cruelty measures applicable to domestic animals. Most states, however, exempt activities that take place in the course of "customary" or "normal" farming practices. David J. Wolfson, *Beyond the Law: Agribusiness and the Systemic Abuse of Animals Raised for Food or Food Production*, 2 Animal L. 123, 123 (1996). Florida voters have bucked the trend by amending the state's constitution to protect pigs in "factory farms" by banning the use of small gestation crates. Jennifer Maloney, *With Narrow Stalls Banned, Pregnant Pigs Face Slaughter,* Miami Hd., Dec. 12, 2002, at 1A. The federal Animal Welfare Act, 7 U.S.C. §§ 2131–2157, passed in 1966, provides protection for animals in research facilities, pet shops, and exhibitions, but it too excludes farm animals from its scope. 7 U.S.C. § 2132(g). For non-farm animals, the Secretary of Agriculture is directed to issue standards to ensure humane treatment, including (i) proper feeding, watering, ventilation, shelter, and veterinary care; (ii) proper exercise for dogs and psychologically stimulating physical environments for primates; (iii) minimization of pain and distress in the course of research activities; and (iv) proper handling during interstate transportation. 7 U.S.C. § 2143(a). Farm animals are addressed in the Humane Slaughter Act, which requires that livestock slaughter be done "by humane methods" to prevent "needless suffering," but the Act excludes poultry and provides exemptions for ritual slaughter. 7 U.S.C. §§ 1901–1902. For more information on animal welfare and animal rights, see PETER SINGER, ANIMAL LIBERATION (1975); ANIMAL RIGHTS AND HUMAN OBLIGATIONS (Tom Regan & Peter Singer eds., 2d ed. 1989); Cass R. Sunstein,

The Rights of Animals, 70 U. Chi. L. Rev. 387 (2003); Martha C. Nussbaum, *Animal Rights: The Need for a Theoretical Basis*, 114 Harv. L. Rev. 1506 (2001) (reviewing STEVEN M. WISE, RATTLING THE CAGE: TOWARD LEGAL RIGHTS FOR ANIMALS (2000)).

IV. FEDERAL WILDLIFE LAW: FEDERAL AUTHORITY AND FEDERAL PUBLIC LANDS

The next few sections of this chapter focus on the federal government's role in wildlife management and conservation. This section begins by exploring the tension between federal and state authorities with respect to the regulation of wildlife and its habitat, along with constitutional sources of federal power. It next considers one means of alleviating this tension: federal funding of state wildlife programs. Third in the line-up is a discussion of national wildlife refuges and wildlife management on other federal lands, including wilderness areas, national parks, wild and scenic rivers, and national forests. Species-specific federal laws, including the Endangered Species Act, are addressed in sections V and VI.

A. Introduction to Federal Wildlife Law

Over 100 years ago, in 1903, President Theodore Roosevelt designated the first wildlife refuge, Pelican Island Bird Refuge, and a national program for protecting wildlife habitat was born. Around the same time, the federal government increased its participation in wildlife law and regulation. Congress passed the first wildlife regulatory act, the Lacey Act, in 1900. The Lacey Act was followed by several other statutes, including the Migratory Bird Treaty Act of 1918 and the Bald Eagle Act of 1940. Traditionally, wildlife regulation has been a state activity. Where does the federal government get its power to intervene in wildlife regulation?

The Supreme Court initially addressed this issue in 1896 in Geer v. Connecticut, 161 U.S. 519, 16 S.Ct. 600, 40 L.Ed. 793 (1896). The Court held that a state, without violating the Dormant Commerce Clause of the U.S. Constitution, could forbid the exportation of game captured or killed within its borders. *Id.* The ruling was justified by the popular belief that wildlife was owned by the states as property in trust for the state's citizens. Following the *Geer* decision, states opined that ownership of wildlife gave the states unlimited management rights and precluded federal intervention even on federal land. Gradually, the theory that states owned the wildlife within their borders weakened, and the Court was compelled to revisit the issue in Hughes v. Oklahoma, 441 U.S. 322, 99 S.Ct. 1727, 60 L.Ed.2d 250 (1979). The 7–2 decision in *Hughes* overturned *Geer*, noting that, "To put the claim of the State upon title is to lean upon a slender reed." *Id.* at 332, citing *Missouri v. Holland*, 252 U.S. 416, 434, 40 S.Ct. 382, 64 L.Ed. 641 (1920). Yet, as Justice Brennan explained, the result in *Hughes* left states "ample allowance for preserving, in ways not inconsistent with the Commerce Clause, the legitimate state concerns for conservation and protection of wild animals underlying the 19th-century legal fiction of state ownership." *Id.* at 335.

Although *Hughes* does not prevent states from protecting their interests in the wildlife found within their borders, discriminatory state action is limited by the Dormant Commerce Clause, the Equal Protection Clause, and the Privileges and Immunities Clause. Even nondiscriminatory state laws that are incompatible with federal regulations are displaced by the Supremacy Clause. Federal preemption occurs most often in cases involving the Treaty Clause, United States v. Bresette, 761 F.Supp. 658 (D.Minn.1991); Bailey v. Holland, 126 F.2d 317 (4th Cir.1942), the Commerce Clause, Gibbs v. Babbitt, 214 F.3d 483 (4th Cir.2000); National Ass'n of Home Builders v. Babbitt, 130 F.3d 1041 (D.C.Cir.1997); United States v. Helsley, 615 F.2d 784 (9th Cir.1979), and the Property Clause, Kleppe v. Sierra Club, 427 U.S. 390, 96 S.Ct. 2718, 49 L.Ed.2d 576 (1976). Instances of federal preemption are rare. Generally, federal law confers primary responsibility for wildlife management to states, even on federal lands. The courts, however, interpret the relevant constitutional provisions to grant wide latitude to federal wildlife regulation.

The next section addresses the constitutional clauses that provide federal authority and preemption over state law for wildlife regulation. Supremacy Clause preemption analysis falls into three categories:

- Expressed Preemption: Congress explicitly states its intention to preclude state law in a specific area.

- Implied Preemption: The congressional act is structured in such a way that it occupies the field and precludes any state regulation in the area.

- Conflict Preemption: State law is in direct conflict with federal law, so federal law trumps regardless of congressional intent.

B.   Federal vs. State Power

Several constitutional provisions provide authority for federal wildlife management, including the Commerce Clause, Privileges and Immunities Clause, Treaty Clause, and the Property Clause.

1.   *The Commerce Clause*

The Commerce Clause has both a negative and positive aspect.

- The Dormant Commerce Clause constrains the regulatory power of a state from disrupting the rhythm of interstate commerce.

- Congress has affirmative power to regulate Commerce with foreign nations and among states and Indian Tribes.

Prior to the 1970's (before the enactment of many wildlife protection statutes), the Dormant Commerce Clause was the more important of the two Commerce Clause components in the wildlife context.

a. The Dormant Commerce Clause

The first constitutional attacks under the Dormant Commerce Clause were aimed at state statutes prohibiting non-citizens from taking wildlife within a state's jurisdiction. Corfield v. Coryell, 6 F.Cas. 546 (C.C.E.D.Pa.1823); State v. Medbury, 3 R.I. 138 (1855). In both *Corfield* and *Medbury*, the courts determined that the statutes at issue did not violate the Commerce Clause because wildlife was considered state property and not part of interstate commerce. At the time, wildlife was generally considered property belonging to its captor. *See* Pierson v. Post, *supra*, 3 Cai. R. 175 (N.Y.1805). Although states did not physically capture the wildlife within their boundaries, they were deemed to have proprietary interests that could evade Commerce Clause scrutiny.

State statutes continued to trigger Commerce Clause challenges, however, especially those that restricted the possession and sale of game or prohibited out-of-state shipments of wildlife. By the late twentieth century, the Dormant Commerce Clause had become a significant impediment to the implementation of protectionist state laws. In Hughes v. Oklahoma, 441 U.S. 322, 99 S.Ct. 1727, 60 L.Ed.2d 250 (1979), the Court invalidated a state law that prohibited the transportation or out-of-state sale of any minnows caught in state waters. The Court stated that, although the natural resources of the state are owned in common by the people of the state, with the state as a trustee, the regulation of those natural resources must be scrutinized with modern Commerce Clause standards. There was no doubt that Oklahoma had a legitimate conservation interest in maintaining an "ecological balance" in state waters by preventing the removal of excessive numbers of minnows. The downfall of the state law was that it had failed to consider and adopt non-discriminatory alternatives. *Id*. at 337–38.

In the second important minnow case, Maine v. Taylor, 477 U.S. 131, 106 S.Ct. 2440, 91 L.Ed.2d 110 (1986), the Court recognized that, although the state statute at issue "restricts interstate trade in the most direct manner possible, blocking all inward shipments of live baitfish at the State's border," it was not necessarily invalid. "Once a state law is shown to discriminate against interstate commerce … the burden falls on the State to demonstrate both that the statute 'serves a legitimate local purpose' and that this purpose could not be served as well by available nondiscriminatory means." *Id*. at 138. The statute was upheld because (a) Maine's fisheries were unique and fragile and the statute's main purpose was to protect them; (b) parasites and nonnative species in the shipments could introduce disease that would disturb the state's aquatic ecology; and (c) there was no other satisfactory alternative to the ban that would produce acceptable results. *Id*. at 151–52.

Maine v. Taylor is the only recent Supreme Court case to uphold a patently discriminatory fish or game law. In Pacific Northwest Venison Producers v. Smitch, 20 F.3d 1008 (9th Cir.), *cert. denied*, 513 U.S. 918, 115 S.Ct. 297, 130 L.Ed.2d 211 (1994), the Court of Appeals considered a

Washington regulation prohibiting the "importation, holding, possession, propagation, sale, transfer or release [of] deleterious exotic wildlife," including mouflon sheep, fallow and sika deer, and elk. The purpose of the regulation was to protect native wildlife from perceived dangers presented by captive herds of "exotic" animals. The State argued that potential risks included: (a) the importation of diseases such as tuberculosis, which can be transferred if the non-native animals escape or through fence line transmission; (b) the possibility of competition with native wildlife for food and habitat; and (c) the possibility that escaped non-native animals will breed with wild animals and affect the gene pool of Washington's native wildlife. The court upheld the importation ban. *Id.* at 1017.

In Practice:

The modern test for determining whether a state statute violates the Dormant Commerce Clause is depicted in the following flow-chart.

Is the purpose of the statute a valid state interest?
↓   ↓
Yes   No: Statute Invalid
↓

Is the state statute discriminatory ?
↓   ↓
Yes   No: Statute Upheld
↓

Does a less restrictive alternative exist that could accomplish the same goal?
↓   ↓
Yes: No: Statute Upheld
↓

Statute Invalid

The application of this test is illustrated in Conservation Force, Inc. v. Manning, 301 F.3d 985 (9th Cir.2002), cert. denied, 537 U.S. 1112, 123 S.Ct. 902, 154 L.Ed.2d 786 (2003), in which professional hunters and guides who were residents of New Mexico challenged an Arizona statute placing a 10% cap on nonresident hunting of bull elk and antlered deer within Arizona. The court held: (i) the Dormant Commerce Clause applied to Arizona's cap on the percentage of hunting permits issued to nonresidents; (ii) Arizona's cap is overt discrimination against access to Arizona's resources, and therefore is subject to strict scrutiny under the Dormant Commerce Clause; (iii) Arizona's interests in conserving the population of game within the state while maintaining recreational hunting opportunities for its citizens are legitimate, but Arizona bore the burden of showing that it had no less discriminatory means to advance its interests. *Id.* at 999. The case was remanded for further proceedings to allow Arizona an opportunity to show that it could meet this burden.

b. The Affirmative Commerce Clause

The affirmative Commerce Clause states, "The Congress shall have Power * * * To regulate Commerce with foreign Nations, and among the several States, and with the Indian Tribes." U.S. Constitution Art. 1, § 8, cl. 3. The Supreme Court has identified three categories of activity that Congress may regulate under its commerce power: (1) channels of interstate commerce; (2) instrumentalities of interstate commerce, or persons and things in interstate commerce; and (3) activities that "substantially affect" interstate commerce. United States v. Lopez, 514 U.S. 549, 558–559, 115 S.Ct. 1624, 131 L.Ed.2d 626 (1995).

Ironically, the history of federal wildlife regulation largely circumvented the affirmative Commerce Clause as a source of constitutional debate. Up until the mid–1960's, Congress instituted very few affirmative wildlife laws under its Commerce Clause authority, but instead funded grant programs to assist state agencies in the acquisition of wildlife habitat. By the time Congress finally made a serious contribution to wildlife regulation in the Marine Mammal Protection Act of 1972 and the Endangered Species Act of 1973, a long string of Supreme Court decisions had already interpreted the Commerce Clause as supporting a broad federal scope of power. However, Solid Waste Agency of Northern Cook County (SWANCC) v. U.S. Army Corps of Engineers, 531 U.S. 159, 121 S.Ct. 675, 148 L.Ed.2d 576 (2001), indicates that the Court may be leaning toward a more restrictive view of federal power, although it did not resolve the Commerce Clause challenge raised in the case. The case involved a provision of the Clean Water Act, CWA § 404(a), 33 U.S.C. § 1344(a), which regulates the discharge of dredged or fill material into "navigable waters." The Corps of Engineers interpreted § 404 to confer federal authority over isolated wetlands that provided habitat for migratory birds at an abandoned sand and gravel pit. The Court concluded that the provisions of § 404 did not extend to these wetlands, but did not resolve the developer's second argument: whether Congress *could* exercise authority over such wetlands consistent with the Commerce Clause. The question of whether the CWA can extend to every intrastate wetland with any sort of hydrological connection to navigable waters should be decided by the United States Supreme Court in United States v. Rapanos, 376 F.3d 629 (6th Cir.2004), *cert. granted,* 126 S.Ct. 414 (2005).

In Focus:

FEDS DITCH "ISOLATED" WATER
By Theo Stein
Denver Post, Aug. 12, 2004

When officers of the Pine Brook Water District decided to build a reservoir on Twomile Creek, they got a pleasant surprise: No federal Clean Water Act permit was needed.

In 2003, the Bush administration instructed federal agencies that they no longer have authority over "isolated" waters such as Twomile Creek. Since then the Army Corps. of Engineers has determined it has no jurisdiction over projects affecting at least two dozen other creeks, ditches and reservoirs in northeastern Colorado, according to a new report on the administration's water policy. * * *

The policy shift stems from a Supreme Court decision involving a lawsuit filed by the Solid Waste Agency of Northern Cook County Ill., known as *SWANCC*, against the Corps. * * * But Colorado's top environmental official said the state has programs to pick up where the Clean Water Act leaves off. "I have jurisdiction over any water that runs through or under the state of Colorado," said Doug Benevento, executive director of the Colorado Department of Public Health and Environment. * * * Benevento, however, acknowledges that there is no state program that protects prairie potholes, "playa" lakes or other small, isolated wetlands critical to wildlife habitat.

According to Ducks Unlimited, the new policy leaves between 50 and 96 percent of prairie potholes in the Central Flyway unprotected, as well as 95 to 100 percent of the temporary playa lakes of Colorado, Oklahoma and Texas. The Association of State Wetland Managers estimates that 30 to 60 percent of all wetlands, or 30 million to 60 million acres, are at risk under the new policy. * * *

Notes and Questions

1. The dissenting justices in *SWANCC* explicitly noted, "the protection of migratory birds is a textbook example of a national problem." *See id.* at 195 (citing Missouri v. Holland, 252 U.S. 416, 435, 40 S.Ct. 382, 64 L.Ed. 641 (1920) ("It is not sufficient to rely upon the States [to protect migratory birds]. The reliance is vain.... ")). Can the same be said of wetlands? Why? Further analysis of federal wetlands regulations can be found in Chapter 10.IV.B, *supra*.

2. For a review of Commerce Clause jurisprudence and wildlife, *see* Bradford C. Mank, *Can Congress Regulate Intrastate Endangered Species*

Under the Commerce Clause? The Split in the Circuits Over Whether the Regulated Activity is Private Commercial Development or the Taking of Protected Species, 69 Brook. L. Rev. 923 (2004); Bradford C. Mank, *Protecting Intrastate Threatened Species: Does the Endangered Species Act Encroach on Traditional State Authority and Exceed the Outer Limits of the Commerce Clause?* 36 Ga. L. Rev. 723 (2002); Christy H. Dral & Jerry Phillips, *Commerce by Another Name: Lopez, Morrison, SWANCC, and Gibbs,* 31 Envtl. L. Rep. 10413 (2001). For an examination of the relationship between the affirmative and dormant aspects of the commerce clause in the environmental context, see Christine A. Klein, *The Environmental Commerce Clause,* 27 Harv. Envtl. L. Rev. 1 (2003).

Exercise:

You represent the Valhalla real estate development company before the U.S. Supreme Court in a challenge to the federal government's Commerce Clause power to protect an endangered species. Valhalla planned to construct a 200–acre housing project in Pima County, Arizona. The U.S. Fish and Wildlife Service (FWS) delayed the plan for fear that development would adversely affect the federally protected arroyo southwestern toad. Specifically, FWS believes that Valhalla's plans to excavate a trench and erect a fence on a corner of the property would prevent the toad from moving to its natural breeding grounds. The toad resides exclusively in a few counties of Arizona. Does the federal commerce clause authority extend this far?

The appellate court held that regulation of the proposed housing project under the ESA did not violate the Commerce Clause, because the regulated activity substantially affects commercial development and is therefore interstate in nature. See Rancho Viejo v. Norton, 334 F.3d 1158 (D.C.Cir.2003) (Roberts, J., now Chief Justice Roberts of the U.S. Supreme Court, dissented, reasoning that the toad, not the building project, was the relevant object in commerce.)

Every circuit court presented with a Commerce Clause challenge to the ESA prior to the *SWANCC* opinion had upheld the federal exercise of authority to protect imperiled species. *See* National Ass'n of Home Builders v. Babbitt, 130 F.3d 1041 (D.C.Cir.1997), cert. denied, 524 U.S. 937, 118 S.Ct. 2340, 141 L.Ed.2d 712 (1998) (upholding the application of the ESA to a construction project in an area that provided habitat for the Delhi Sands Flower–Loving Fly, an endangered species found only in California); Gibbs v. Babbitt, 214 F.3d 483 (4th Cir.2000), cert. denied, 531 U.S. 1145, 121 S.Ct. 1081, 148 L.Ed.2d 957 (2001) (concluding that protection of reintroduced red wolves on federal and private land "substantially affects interstate commerce through tourism, trade, scientific research, and other potential economic activities").

Does the Supreme Court's opinion in *SWANCC* cast doubt on the validity of these circuit court decisions? Is *SWANCC* controlling?

> According to two post-*SWANCC* circuit court opinions, the ESA still stands firm. *See* GDF Realty Investments, Ltd. v. Norton, 326 F.3d 622 (5th Cir.2003), cert. denied, 125 S.Ct. 2898 (2005) (the application of the ESA to various cave-dwelling beetles and spiders is constitutional under the Commerce Clause, even though the species are found only in underground portions of two counties in Texas and have no commercial market); San Diego County, Rancho Viejo, LLC v. Norton, 323 F.3d 1062, 1078 (D.C.Cir.2003), cert. denied, 540 U.S. 1218, 124 S.Ct. 1506, 158 L.Ed.2d 153 (2004). What arguments will you make for your client to convince the Supreme Court that the ESA goes too far? Be sure to anticipate the government's defenses as you're preparing your case.

2. *The Privileges and Immunities Clause*

The Privileges and Immunities Clause states, "The Citizens of each State shall be entitled to all Privileges and Immunities of Citizens in the several States." U.S. Constitution art. IV, § 2, cl. 1. In effect, the Privileges and Immunities Clause prohibits a state from discrimination against nonresidents with regard to all essential activities or basic rights, unless there is a substantial reason to justify discrimination. A justifiable discrimination requires that the state demonstrate that nonresidents are a peculiar source of the evil, and that the discrimination bears a substantial relation to the problem.

The Privileges and Immunities Clause has been used by nonresidents to challenge state regulation of commercial fishing licenses in a number of cases.

(i) *Toomer v. Witsell,* 334 U.S. 385, 68 S.Ct. 1156, 92 L.Ed. 1460 (1948). A South Carolina statute permitted only residents to commercially fish for shrimp within 3 miles of the coast. South Carolina claimed the statute was necessary because of a shrimp shortage, making it difficult for their resident fisherman to earn a living. The Court established a two-part test, the *Toomer* test, to determine whether the state's discrimination against non-residents was justifiable: (i) whether there is a sufficiently fundamental privilege that falls within the scope of the clause's protection; and (ii) whether the reason for the discrimination or unequal treatment directly remedies the problem. Ultimately, the Court invalidated the law because commercial fishing was deemed a fundamental privilege, and the State could not show that non-residents were responsible for the shortage.

(ii) *Takahashi v. Fish & Game Commission*, 334 U.S. 410, 68 S.Ct. 1138, 92 L.Ed. 1478 (1948). *Takahashi* is a companion case to *Toomer*. The Court found a California statute prohibiting aliens from holding commercial fishing licenses unconstitutional. The Court stated, "To whatever extent the fish in the three-mile belt off California may be 'capable of ownership' by California, we think that 'ownership' is inadequate to justify California in excluding any or all aliens ... from making a living by fishing in the ocean off its shores while permitting all others to do so." *Id.*

(iii) *Tangier Sound Waterman's Assoc. v. Pruitt,* 4 F.3d 264 (4th Cir.1993). In *Tangier,* the Fourth Circuit stuck down a Virginia statute tripling the charge of commercial fishing licenses for non-residents. *Id.* The court applied the *Toomer* two-part test. It disposed of the first prong with no difficulty: it is well established that the right to earn a living is fundamental under the Constitution. With respect to the second prong of *Toomer,* the state argued that a higher fee helped "to recover from non-residents their share of the expenses of managing the resource from which they are benefiting." Additionally, the state argued that because the expenses are paid by a general fund generated by taxpayers, "it is unfair for the [] taxpayers to be taxed to provide benefits for residents of other states who do not pay Virginia taxes." Similar cases establish that the higher fee must equalize, to the greatest extent possible, the burden placed on residents by participation of non-residents. The court struck down the statute, concluding that Virginia failed "to creat[e] any credible method for allocating the costs as between residents and nonresidents which places the burden equally or approximately equally upon residents and nonresidents." *Id.*

What if a group of nonresidents who merely wish to engage in recreational fishing challenge a state statute that imposes permit fees three times higher than resident fees? Is there an essential interest at stake that would trigger the Privileges and Immunities Clause? The Supreme Court has stated that the Clause protects the exercise of fundamental rights "bearing upon the vitality of the Nation," such as the pursuit of a vocation, the ownership and disposition of property, and access to the courts. Baldwin v. Montana Fish and Game Comm'n, 436 U.S. 371, 388, 98 S.Ct. 1852, 56 L.Ed.2d 354 (1978). In *Baldwin,* the Court rejected a challenge by Minnesotans to Montana's increased hunting license fees for nonresidents. It stated, "Whatever rights or activities may be 'fundamental' under the Privileges and Immunities Clause, we are persuaded, and hold, that [recreational] elk hunting by nonresidents in Montana is not one of them." *Id.* Likewise, in United States v. Romano, 929 F.Supp. 502, 509 (D.Mass.1996), the court concluded that "caribou hunting, or brown bear hunting, or any other recreational hunting in Alaska for that matter, is not essential to the defendant's, let alone the nation's, livelihood." What if the nonresident hunters could show that they engaged in hunting for subsistence purposes? Would it make a difference in *Baldwin* or *Romano* if the Montana or Alaska constitution explicitly recognized hunting as a fundamental right?

3. *The Treaty Clause*

The Treaty Clause of the Constitution states, "[The President] shall have the Power ... to make Treaties, provided two-thirds of the Senators present concur." U.S. Constitution art. II, § 2. The benchmark for Treaty

Clause authority is *Missouri v. Holland,* 252 U.S. 416, 40 S.Ct. 382, 64 L.Ed. 641 (1920), where the state brought suit to enjoin a United States game warden from enforcing the Migratory Bird Treaty Act of 1918. The Act, which is addressed in detail in Section V.B, below, applies a treaty prohibiting the killing or interference with migratory birds, except as permitted by regulations made by the Secretary of Agriculture. The central question in *Missouri* was whether an Act of Congress, implementing a U.S. treaty, can create regulations that are unconstitutional if the Act were to stand alone. The Court answered in the affirmative, explaining that the national interest at issue could only be protected by national action in concert with that of another nation, and such a joint effort can only be obtained through a treaty. The test to determine a treaty's validity is two-fold:

- Is the matter involved of national interest?

- Does the treaty contravene any specific constitutional prohibition?

If the first is answered in the affirmative, and the second in the negative, the treaty is valid. Could the Treaty Clause have provided a basis for upholding the Corps' "migratory bird rule" at issue in Solid Waste Agency of Northern Cook County v. U.S. Army Corps of Engineers ("SWANCC"), *supra,* 531 U.S. 159, 121 S.Ct. 675, 148 L.Ed.2d 576 (2001)?

4. The Property Clause

The Property Clause establishes federal power over federal lands. It states, "The Congress shall have the Power to dispose of and make all needful Rules and Regulations respecting the Territory or other Property belonging to the United States." U. S. Const. art. IV, § 3, cl. 2. States housing federal land within their borders are often in conflict with the federal government over the rights provided by the clause. *See* Chapter 5.II.A, *supra* (Introduction to Ownership).

For the evolutionary spectrum of Supreme Court cases involving the Property Clause, see United States v. Gratiot, 39 U.S. (14 Pet.) 526, 10 L.Ed. 573 (1840) (upholding Congress' decision to lease lead mines); Camfield v. United States, 167 U.S. 518, 17 S.Ct. 864, 42 L.Ed. 260 (1897) (upholding statute prohibiting enclosure of public lands); Hunt v. United States, 278 U.S. 96, 49 S.Ct. 38, 73 L.Ed. 200 (1928) (upholding the directions of the Secretary of Agriculture to remove deer found on federal land although the removal was a violation of state game laws).

The issue in the following case asks whether Congress exceeded its constitutional powers when enacting the Wild Free-roaming Horses and Burros Act.

KLEPPE v. NEW MEXICO

Supreme Court of the United States, 1976.
426 U.S. 529, 96 S.Ct. 2285, 49 L.Ed.2d 34.

JUSTICE MARSHALL delivered the opinion of the Court.

The Wild Free-roaming Horses and Burros Act, 16 U.S.C. §§ 1331–1340, was enacted in 1971 to protect "all unbranded and unclaimed horses and burros on public lands of the United States,"[] from "capture, branding, harassment, or death."[] The Act provides that all such horses and burros on the public lands administered by the Secretary of the Interior through the Bureau of Land Management (BLM) or by the Secretary of Agriculture through the Forest Service are committed to the jurisdiction of the respective Secretaries, who are "directed to protect and manage (the animals) as components of the public lands ... in a manner that is designed to achieve and maintain a thriving natural ecological balance on the public lands." * * *

* * * On February 1, 1974, a New Mexico rancher, Kelley Stephenson, was informed by the BLM that several unbranded burros had been seen near Taylor Well, where Stephenson watered his cattle. Taylor Well is on federal property, and Stephenson had access to it and some 8,000 surrounding acres only through a grazing permit issued pursuant to § 3 of the Taylor Grazing Act, 48 Stat. 1270, as amended, 43 U.S.C. § 315b. After the BLM made it clear to Stephenson that it would not remove the burros * * * Stephenson complained to the [New Mexico] Livestock Board that the burros were interfering with his livestock operation by molesting his cattle and eating their feed.

* * * [T]he Board rounded up and removed 19 unbranded and unclaimed burros pursuant to the New Mexico Estray Law. Each burro was seized on the public lands of the United States and, as the director of the Board conceded, each burro fit the definition of a wild free-roaming burro under s 2(b) of the Act. On February 18, 1974, the Livestock Board * * * sold the burros at a public auction. After the sale, the BLM asserted jurisdiction under the Act and demanded that the Board recover the animals and return them to the public lands. [New Mexico asserted that "the federal government lacked the power to control wild horses and burros on the public lands of the United States unless the animals were moving in interstate commerce or damaging public land."]

* * * The question under the Property Clause is whether this determination can be sustained as a "needful" regulation "respecting" the public lands. In answering this question, we must remain mindful that, while courts must eventually pass upon them, determinations under the Property Clause are entrusted primarily to the judgment of Congress.* * *

Appellees * * * contend that the Clause grants Congress essentially two kinds of power: (1) the power to dispose of and make incidental rules regarding the use of federal property; and (2) the power to protect federal property. * * * [W]e reject appellees' narrow reading of the Property Clause.

* * * [A]ppellees have presented no support for their position that the Clause grants Congress only the power to dispose of, to make incidental rules regarding the use of, and to protect federal property. * * * [T]he Clause * * * gives Congress the power to determine what are "needful" rules "respecting" the public lands. * * * [W]e have repeatedly observed that "(t)he power over the public land thus entrusted to Congress is without limitations."

* * * Congress exercises the powers both of a proprietor and of a legislature over the public domain. * * * In our view, the "complete power" that Congress has over public lands necessarily includes the power to regulate and protect the wildlife living there.

Appellees argue that if we approve the Wild Free-roaming Horses and Burros Act as a valid exercise of Congress' power under the Property Clause, then we have sanctioned an impermissible intrusion on the sovereignty, legislative authority, and police power of the State and have wrongly infringed upon the State's traditional trustee powers over wild animals. * * * This argument is without merit.

Appellees' claim confuses Congress' derivative legislative powers, which are not involved in this case, with its powers under the Property Clause. Congress may acquire derivative legislative power from a State pursuant to Art. I, s 8, cl. 17, of the Constitution * * * [T]he legislative jurisdiction acquired may range from exclusive federal jurisdiction with no residual state police power, to concurrent, or partial, federal legislative jurisdiction, which may allow the State to exercise certain authority. But while Congress can acquire exclusive or partial jurisdiction over lands within a State by the State's consent or cession, the presence or absence of such jurisdiction has nothing to do with Congress' powers under the Property Clause. * * * [T]he federal legislation necessarily overrides conflicting state laws under the Supremacy Clause. U.S. Const., Art. VI, cl. 2. * * *

Thus, appellees' assertion that "(a)bsent state consent by complete cession of jurisdiction of lands to the United States, exclusive jurisdiction does not accrue to the federal landowner with regard to federal lands within the borders of the state," is completely beside the point; and appellees' fear that the Secretary's position is that "the Property Clause totally exempts federal lands within state borders from state legislative powers, state police powers, and all rights and powers of local sovereignty and jurisdiction of the states," is totally unfounded. The Federal Government does not assert exclusive jurisdiction over the public lands in New Mexico, and the State is free to enforce its criminal and civil laws on those lands. But where those state laws conflict with the Wild Free-roaming Horses and Burros Act, or with other legislation passed pursuant to the Property Clause, the law is clear: The state laws must recede.* * *

Appellees' contention that the Act violates traditional state power over wild animals stands on no different footing. Unquestionably the States have broad trustee and police powers over wild animals within their jurisdictions. * * * We hold today that the Property Clause also gives Congress the power to protect wildlife on the public lands, state law notwithstanding. * * * [W]e do not think it appropriate in this declaratory judgment proceeding to determine the extent, if any, to which the Property Clause empowers Congress to protect animals on private lands or the extent to which such regulation is attempted by the Act. * * *

Notes and Questions

1. The district court below had found that the Act was unconstitutional and enjoined the Secretary from enforcing its provisions. 406 F.Supp. 1237 (D.N.M.1975). It concluded that the Property Clause authorized the regulation of wild animals only if necessary for the "protection of the public lands from damage of some kind." *Id.* at 1239. According to the district court, the Act is "aimed at protecting the wild horses and burros, not at protecting the land they live on," and therefore exceeded the Property Clause power. *Id.* The Supreme Court disagreed, stating that the Property Clause power "necessarily" includes protection of wildlife on the public lands. Why? How does the Court characterize the Property Clause power? Is it simply a matter of proprietorship, or something more than that?

2. If you were counsel for the government, tasked with defending the Wild Horses and Burros Act, would you have hedged your bets by relying more heavily on the Commerce Clause than the Property Clause? Which of the two is the more powerful tool when it comes to protecting resources on public lands? Which would you rely on if the wild horses had been grazing on Stephenson's own land and you were defending the Secretary's enforcement of the Act's provisions related to private property? *See* Camfield v. United States, 167 U.S. 518, 17 S.Ct. 864, 42 L.Ed. 260 (1897) (upholding Property Clause power to prohibit the enclosure of public lands, even though the enclosure occurred on adjacent private property).

3. For additional decisions on wildlife and the Property Clause, see United States v. Brown, 552 F.2d 817 (8th Cir.1977) (regulations prohibiting hunting in national parks in order to protect wildlife and visitors were valid as a "needful" prescription "respecting the public lands," even though defendant had been hunting on nonfederal waters); Stupak-Thrall v. United States, 843 F.Supp. 327 (W.D.Mich.1994), *affirmed en banc by equally divided vote,* 89 F.3d 1269 (6th Cir.1996), *cert. denied,* 519 U.S. 1090, 117 S.Ct. 764, 136 L.Ed.2d 711 (1997) (Property Clause empowers the federal government to prohibit the use of electronic fish-finders on navigable waters within a wilderness area). In Wyoming v. United States, 279 F.3d 1214 (10th Cir.2002), the State of Wyoming brought an action against the federal government challenging the refusal of the U.S. Fish and Wildlife Service (FWS) to permit the state to vaccinate elk on the National Elk Range (NER). Wyoming wanted to protect its producer's domestic livestock and its free-ranging elk from a threat arising out of the FWS's alleged failure to combat brucellosis on the NER. The court stated that the Property Clause gives Congress

the power to choose (1) to assume all management authority over the National Wildlife Refuge System, including the NER, (2) to share management authority over those federal lands with the States, or (3) to preserve to its fullest extent the States' historical role in the management of wildlife within their respective borders. It held that federal law preempted state management to the extent the two actually conflict or where state management stands as an obstacle to the accomplishment of federal objectives. *Id.* at 1241. The case is excerpted in Chapter 6.IV.B, *supra.*

C.   Federal Funding of State Programs

An array of federal statutes provides funding for state acquisition of wildlife habitat, and imposes conservation management standards on lands acquired with federal funds. There are four main funding statutes:

- The Pittman–Robertson Act of 1937 (also known as the Federal Aid in Wildlife Restoration Act), 16 U.S.C. §§ 669–669i.

- The Dingell–Johnson Act of 1950 (also known as the Federal Aid in Fish Restoration Act), 16 U.S.C. §§ 777–777l.

- The Land and Water Conservation Fund Act of 1963, 16 U.S.C. § 460l–460l–11.

- The Fish and Wildlife Conservation Act of 1980 (also known as the Non-game Act), 16 U.S.C. §§ 2901–2911.

The Pittman–Robertson Act is the main federal assistance program for the states. These funds are used for "the selection, restoration, rehabilitation, and improvement" of wildlife habitat. 16 U.S.C. § 669(a). This act authorizes the Secretary of the Interior to fund up to 75% of state wildlife restoration projects. Funds are allocated to the states based on their geographic area, paid hunting-license holders, and total population. *Id.* The fund is created from a tax imposed on firearms, shells and cartridges. 26 U.S.C. §§ 4161(b), 4181. The Dingell–Johnson Act is the counterpart to the Pittman–Robertson Act that applies to fish species. Funding for these projects is derived from a federal tax on fishing bait and equipment. 26 U.S.C. § 9504(a).

The Land and Water Conservation Fund Act was created for the purpose of "preserving, developing and assuring accessibility to ... outdoor recreation resources." 16 U.S.C. § 460l. The Act directly and indirectly benefits wildlife by generating and distributing revenues for outdoor recreation. Also, this fund is available for both federal (no more than 50% of any project) and state land acquisitions (no more than 60% of the total fund availability).

The Fish and Wildlife Conservation Act provides financial and technical assistance to states for the development and implementation of conservation programs for nongame fish and wildlife. 16 U.S.C. §§ 2901–2911. Conservation plans are to identify at-risk species and plan for ways to prevent endangerment. The Act specifies a multifaceted process for approval of state conservation plans, along with numerous requirements for conservation plans and federal reimbursement alternatives.

D. National Wildlife Refuges

The National Wildlife Refuge System (NWRS) is the only federal land management system that places wildlife protection at the forefront of its agenda. The NWRS is not a pure preservation system; rather it is one of dominant use where wildlife-dependent uses have a priority over all other uses. 16 U.S.C. § 668dd(a)(3)(c). Land can be designated a refuge in several ways:

- Executive withdrawal of federally owned land managed by the Department of the Interior
- An exchange or purchase of land funded by statutes like the Endangered Species Act or Migratory Bird Treaty Act
- An independent act of Congress
- A transfer of lands from another agency such as the Army Corps of Engineers
- A donation from a non-federal landowner.

Celebrating a Century of Conservation!

Five acres, known as Pelican Island, started what is now known as our National Wildlife Refuge System. This System of lands encompass more than 93 million acres and 575 national wildlife refuges and wetland management districts, where at least one can be found in every state and U.S. Territory. * * *

Much has already been accomplished to lay the foundation for our celebration. Congress has declared year 2003 as "The Year of the

National Wildlife Refuge" and the President is requested to issue a proclamation calling on the people of the United States to conduct appropriate programs, ceremonies and activities to accomplish the goal of such a year.

For more information about the centennial of the Wildlife Refuge System, see U.S. Fish and Wildlife Service, http://refuges.fws.gov/ centennial/celebrate.html.

Since its creation in 1903, the Wildlife Refuge System has grown to more than 500 separate refuges, covering more than 92 million acres. Management of the system stems from a combination of pre-existing management statutes ranging from the Migratory Bird Conservation Act of 1929 to the Refuge Recreation Act of 1962, 16 U.S.C. § 460k, and the Wildlife Refuge System Administration Act of 1966, 16 U.S.C. §§ 668dd–668ee. It was not until a Congressional revision in 1997 that the system developed a consolidated management structure.

Pursuant to the National Wildlife Refuge System Improvement Act of 1997 (Improvement Act), 16 U.S.C. §§ 668dd–668ee, wildlife refuges are managed by the Fish and Wildlife Service (FWS). The Improvement Act was the culmination of an effort to create organic legislation for the refuge system by reaching a compromise between hunting and fishing interests and environmentalists. The Act maintained all of the major provisions of the 1962 and 1966 Refuge Acts and added several new provisions that prioritize the conservation of wildlife for current and future generations. 16 U.S.C. § 668ee(4). Through the Act, previous management directives were altered in three key ways:

- The Act creates one sole mission for the entire Refuge System: "to administer a national network of lands and waters for the conservation, management, and where appropriate, restoration of the fish, wildlife and plant resources and their habitat within the United States for the benefit of present and future generations … " 16 U.S.C. § 668dd(a)(2).

- It specifies that the primary use of wildlife refuges is the conservation of wildlife, plants and their habitats. 16 U.S.C. § 668dd(a)(2). All activities within a refuge must be compatible with this goal, unless the establishment act for an individual refuge unit explicitly specifies a different priority. *Id.* § 668dd(a)(4)(B). A "compatible use" is one that "will not materially interfere with or detract from the fulfillment of the mission of the System or the purpose of the refuge." *Id.* § 668ee(1).

- The FWS must prepare and implement comprehensive conservation plans, based on the inventory of resources found within each refuge. *Id.* § 668dd.

Of the human uses that occur in wildlife refuges, "wildlife-dependent recreational uses" receive the highest priority. These uses include "hunting, fishing, wildlife observation and photography, or environmental education and interpretation." *Id.* § 668dd(a)(4)(J). "All other uses," including grazing, oil drilling, non-wildlife related recreation, and timber harvesting, receive a low priority ranking, and are prohibited when they conflict with the NWRS mission, contradict the purposes for which the individual refuge was created, or materially interfere with hunting, fishing, photography, and other wildlife-dependent uses. *Id.*

Notes and Questions

1. Non-wildlife dependent activities within wildlife refuges have been a source of contention since the formation of the NWRS. Prior to the passage of the Improvement Act, the FWS generally received great deference from the courts in terms of the activities allowed in refuges. *See* Humane Society v. Lujan, 768 F.Supp. 360 (D.D.C.1991) (FWS may permit deer hunting in a refuge established as a sanctuary for endangered bird species, in order to control the refuge's deer population); Watt v. Alaska, 451 U.S. 259, 101 S.Ct. 1673, 68 L.Ed.2d 80 (1981) (mineral exploration and development is permitted so long as wildlife habitat in the refuge is protected). Economic and recreational activities in refuges have been precluded, however, where the administrative record demonstrated adverse effects to wildlife. *See* Wilderness Society v. Babbitt, 5 F.3d 383 (9th Cir.1993) (cattle grazing must give way to wildlife welfare); New England Naturist Ass'n v. Larsen, 692 F.Supp. 75 (D.R.I.1988) (rejecting nudist association's challenge to FWS's closure of a beach within a refuge to protect wildlife species from human impacts); Defenders of Wildlife v. Andrus, 455 F.Supp. 446 (D.D.C.1978) (recreational boating in an area of Ruby Lake Refuge that provided nesting habitat for migratory birds enjoined).

2. Does the Wildlife Refuge Improvement Act of 1997 provide sufficient parameters on FWS's discretion to ensure wildlife conservation? Would you expect a court to be more or less likely to enjoin mineral development, grazing or logging than under previous refuge administration statutes? How about recreation? In Niobrara River Ranch v. Huber, 373 F.3d 881 (8th Cir.2004), a post-Improvement Act case, the court upheld a provision of the Fort Niobrara Wildlife Refuge Conservation Plan which imposed a moratorium on new outfitters providing canoeing or tubing services and capped river use on summer weekends at 1998 levels. According to FWS, a moratorium was the best means of controlling overcrowding on the river until a formal biological study could be completed. "[C]onsidering the 'documented evidence of rapidly increasing canoe usage and its potential for 'devastation' of nesting birds, it was entirely reasonable for the Service to impose a moratorium.' " *Id.* at 883 (citation omitted). The studies were completed in 2005, and the FWS set a limit of 20,300 launch passes, 18,270 of which were earmarked for outfitters. Instead of favoring existing outfitters, passes are awarded to the highest bidder who submits an application and proof of $1 million liability coverage. *See* Algis J. Laukaitis, *Niobrara: A River Divided*, Lincoln J. Star, Aug. 7, 2005, at 1A, 6A.

3. The FWS also banned alcohol along the 5–mile stretch of river within the Fort Niobrara Refuge, primarily to cut down on disorderly conduct and maintain public safety. According to Lee Simmons, owner of the

Niobrara River Ranch (the plaintiff in the case discussed above), "People are here to have a good time. People want a beer. It's socially acceptable and legal." Laukaitis, *supra,* at 6A. Both the alcohol ban and launch pass program have been challenged by the chairman of the local natural resources district board, who claims that the restrictions have no scientific basis and hurt the local economy. *Id.* Does the plaintiff have a viable argument under the Improvement Act?

4.   Under the Wildlife Refuge Improvement Act of 1997, states' hunting and fishing laws generally apply in the NWRS, but the FWS can disallow hunting and fishing if inconsistent with the overarching conservation mandate. 16 U.S.C. § 668dd(c), (m). In Wyoming v. United States, *supra*, 279 F.3d 1214 (10th Cir.2002), the State asserted that its sovereign interest in managing wildlife on the National Elk Range included a right to vaccinate elk to protect against the spread of brucellosis. The court held that the 10th Amendment did not reserve such a right to the state. *Id.*

> Unquestionably, the NWRSIA inspirits a "cooperative federalism," calling for, at a minimum, state involvement and participation in the management of the NWRS as that system affects surrounding state ecosystems* * * Still, the NWRSIA requires the FWS in developing conservation plans for a refuge to act in conformity with State objectives only "to the extent practical." * * * Accordingly, we cannot accept the State of Wyoming's broad and absolute challenge ... to the FWS's authority to manage wildlife on the NER in a manner with which the State disagrees * * *

Id. at 1232–35, citing 16 U.S.C. § 668dd(e)(1)(A)(iii); *id.* § 668dd(e)(3). Although Wyoming's 10th Amendment claims were unavailing, the court remanded the case for a determination of whether the FWS's refusal to allow vaccinations was arbitrary under the Administrative Procedure Act (APA). It opined that the state's APA claim was supported by allegations that FWS' refusal to allow vaccination of free-ranging elk on the NER had significantly reduced the efficacy of the state's own vaccination program in domestic cattle and resident elk populations. *Id.* at 1241. That portion of the opinion is provided in Chapter 6.IV.B, *supra*. In 2003, the FWS approved Wyoming's proposal to vaccinate elk on the NER. *U.S. Clears State's Bid to Vaccinate Elk on Refuge,* L.A. Times, Feb. 4, 2003, at A10.

5.   The vast majority of our nation's public lands management statutes have not been revised since the 1970's. Why do you suppose Congress was willing to overhaul the statutory directives for the NWRS? For analysis of the Improvement Act, see Robert L. Fischman, *The National Wildlife Refuge System and the Hallmarks of Modern Organic Legislation,* 29 ECOLOGY L.Q. 457 (2002); Cam Tredenick, *The National Wildlife System Improvement Act of 1997: Defining the National Wildlife Refuge System for the Twenty–First Century,* 12 FORDHAM ENVTL. L.J. 41 (2000).

E.   Wildlife Control in Federally Restricted Lands

There are three main land management categories designed to conserve land in a minimally altered state: wilderness areas, national parks, and wild and scenic rivers. Although these systems are not created for the sole purpose of wildlife habitat, wildlife benefits from restrictions on land alteration. Provisions related to recreation and general preservation-oriented goals are addressed in Chapter 15.III, *infra,* while this section takes a brief look at wildlife management in each of these land categories.

1. Wilderness Areas

Wilderness is defined as an area of "untrammeled" federal land that retains its primeval character and does not support any permanent improvements. 16 U.S.C. § 1131(a), (c). To be included in the wilderness system, the area must:

- generally appear to have been affected primarily by the forces of nature;

- have outstanding opportunities for solitude or a primitive and unconfined type of recreational activity;

- be comprised of at least 5000 acres of land, or be sufficient in size to make its preservation practicable; and

- may also contain ecological, geological, educational, historical, scientific or scenic value.

Once an area is designated as wilderness, many activities are prohibited to ensure that the area remains "unimpaired for future use and enjoyment as wilderness." *Id.* § 1131(a). There can be no commercial enterprise, road building, motor vehicles, motorized equipment, or other forms of mechanical transport, and no structures or installations within wilderness areas. *Id.* § 1133(c). *See* Alaska Wildlife Alliance v. Jensen, 108 F.3d 1065 (9th Cir.1997) (provided below). These prohibitions provide significant protection to wildlife by preventing human disturbances, but valid existing rights, mining and mineral leasing initiated before 1984, certain water resource development projects, and continued livestock grazing can still occur in wilderness areas. *Id.* § 1133(d)(2)-(4).

Edward Abbey once proclaimed that "wilderness needs no defense, only more defenders." As you might guess, not everyone agrees. Critics of the Wilderness Act generally fall into two camps. The first argues that wilderness designations improperly inhibit development by making otherwise productive federal lands "off limits" to mining companies, loggers, ranchers and others. The second camp claims that wilderness is out of step with ecological needs because it prioritizes areas most valuable for rock-climbing and other forms of "virile" recreation but fails to protect physical features most important to wildlife and biodiversity. *See* Sandra Zellmer, *A Preservation Paradox: Political Prestidigitation and an Enduring Resource of Wildness,* 34 ENV'L. L. 1015 (2004). It might be fair to say that the forty-year old Wilderness Act is facing a "mid-life crisis." Indeed, most wilderness areas do feature large expanses of "rock and ice"—mountaintops and waterfalls that provide spectacular vistas but little support for diverse communities of plant and animal species. But wilderness areas are also roadless, and as such provide large blocks of contiguous habitat and migratory corridors for wide-ranging species like grizzly bears and wolves. *See* Chapter 2, *supra* (Biodiversity). Meanwhile, their inaccessible nature makes them difficult and expensive to develop. If you were a Senator from one of the western states that host large areas of wilderness, such as Idaho or California, would you propose a bill to revise or even rescind the statute? If so, what (if anything) might you replace it with?

For more information on the Wilderness Act, its origins and its continuing relevance, see Zellmer, *A Preservation Paradox, supra*; Robert L. Glicksman & George Cameron Coggins, *Wilderness in Context*, 76 Denv. U. L. Rev. 383 (1999); J. BAIRD CALLICOTT & MICHAEL P. NELSON, THE GREAT NEW WILDERNESS DEBATE (1998); Michael McCloskey, *The Wilderness Act of 1964: Its Background and Meaning*, 45 Or. L. Rev. 288, 298 (1966).

2. *National Parks*

Congress passed the National Park Service Organic Act in 1916. It authorized the creation of the National Park Service (NPS) whose purpose is "to promote and regulate the use" of the National Parks "to conserve the scenery and the natural and historic objects and the *wildlife* therein and to provide for the enjoyment of the same in such manner and by such means as will leave them unimpaired for the enjoyment of future generations." 16 U.S.C. § 1 (emphasis added).

NPS is tasked with a difficult balancing act between conserving wildlife and other natural features of the National Parks while also providing for public enjoyment of those resources. Parks are crucial in terms of providing high-quality wildlife habitat, but they also support intensive recreational and commercial uses. NPS regulations prohibit "possessing, destroying ... or disturbing" wildlife, fish or plants, with few exceptions. 36 C.F.R. § 2.1(a), (d) (2001). Hunting in parks is typically not allowed, but fishing can and often does occur. The following case illustrates the conflict between preservation and utilitarian interests.

ALASKA WILDLIFE ALLIANCE v. JENSEN
United States Court of Appeals, Ninth Circuit, 1997.
108 F.3d 1065.

We must decide the extent to which federal statutes restrict commercial fishing in Alaska's Glacier Bay National Park (the Park). * * * Plaintiffs sued the Secretary of the Interior and officials of the National Park Service, claiming that commercial fishing in the Park violates certain federal statutes. Plaintiffs interpret the Organic Act, which created the national park system, and the Alaska National Interest Lands Conservation Act ("ANILCA") to prohibit commercial fishing throughout the Park. The Park Service concedes that commercial fishing is prohibited by statute in the Park's wilderness areas. It maintains, however, that the statutes give it discretion to permit commercial fishing in non-wilderness areas. The Allied Fishermen of Southeast Alaska (the Fishermen), an association of commercial fishers, intervened to defend its interests. * * *

The district court concluded ... that commercial fishing is statutorily prohibited only in wilderness areas of the Park. Plaintiffs appeal the determination that commercial fishing is permitted in non-wilderness areas of the Park. The Fishermen cross-appeal the court's findings that ... federal law prohibits commercial fishing in the Park's wilderness areas. * * *

ANILCA designates roughly 2.77 million acres of the Park as "wilderness" to be administered under the Wilderness Act * * * In pertinent part, the Wilderness Act bans commercial enterprise from wilderness areas: "Except as specifically provided for in this chapter, and subject to existing private rights, there shall be no commercial enterprise ... within any wilderness area designated by this chapter.... " 16 U.S.C. § 1133(c). The court held that this provision bans commercial fishing in Glacier Bay's wilderness areas, and the Park Service agrees with this interpretation.

* * *

No statute expressly prohibits commercial fishing in the Park's non-wilderness areas or demonstrates clear congressional intent to restrict the Park Service's discretion to permit commercial fishing. * * * The Organic Act, 16 U.S.C. § 1 *et seq.,* governs all national parks. The Act gives the Secretary of the Interior authority to "make and publish such rules and regulations as he may deem necessary or proper for the management of the parks, monuments, and reservations under the jurisdiction of the National Park Service." * * * [T]he Secretary may not exercise his authority to the detriment of the Act's purpose, which is "to conserve the scenery and the natural and historic objects and the wild life therein and to provide for the enjoyment of the same in such manner and by such means as will leave them unimpaired for the enjoyment of future generations." * * *

Plaintiffs argue that the Secretary's failure to prevent commercial fishing in the Park derogates the Act's purpose of conservation and therefore violates an express statutory directive. We disagree. Whether conduct derogates long-term goals of conservation is a factual question that we are not prepared to reach. In the absence of a specific congressional statement that commercial fishing derogates the Act's goals, there is no reason to conclude that the Secretary's failure to prohibit commercial fishing violates the Act. * * *

* * * Plaintiffs argue that Congress's 1978 amendment to the Organic Act was intended to reprimand the Park Service for permitting commercial fishing in national parks. *See* Pub.L. 95–250 (Mar. 27, 1978) (prohibiting the Secretary from authorizing activities "in derogation of the values and purposes for which" the parks were created), *codified at* 16 U.S.C. § 1a–1. The legislative history [which focused on protecting

land in Redwood National Park] does not support plaintiffs' reading [and] * * * refutes plaintiffs' assertion that Congress had fish in mind when it added that language. [AFFIRMED.]

* * *

Notes and Questions

1. Why were the plaintiffs so concerned about commercial fishing, as compared to recreational fishing? Why does the Wilderness Act specifically target commercial enterprises in 16 U.S.C. § 1133(c)? Which is more dangerous to the lives of imperiled species, commercial or recreational use? Do the impacts differ in nature or intensity? Note that commercial activities can occur in non-wilderness areas of most National Parks under the Organic Act, 16 U.S.C. § 1 *et seq.,* and concessionaires and outfitters are common in Parks. *See* Omnibus Parks Management Act of 1998, 16 U.S.C. §§ 5951–66; chapter 15, *infra.* Why are wilderness areas treated differently?

2. How is danger to a species measured? Neither the Organic Act nor the Wilderness Act provides objective criteria for measurement. What criteria should be considered? Are the factors relevant to the decision to list a species under the Endangered Species Act, 16 U.S.C. § 1533(a)(1) (detailed in Section VI.C, below), helpful in terms of accomplishing the goals of either the Organic Act or the Wilderness Act?

3. Can restrictions on hunting and fishing be counter-productive to conservation objectives? For example, can government regulation of the exploitation of a species affect that species' market value?

3. Wild and Scenic Rivers

In 1968, Congress enacted the Wild and Scenic Rivers Act (WSRA) to preserve the nation's free flowing rivers. 16 U.S.C. §§ 1271–1287. The Act authorizes the designation of river segments as wild, scenic, or recreational. River management agencies must prepare a comprehensive management plan that will protect the river's values, 16 U.S.C. § 1274(c), including "esthetic, scenic, historic, archaeological, and scientific considerations." *Id.* § 1281. The "outstandingly remarkable values" (ORVs) of the river segment must be identified in the plan. *Id.* Native fisheries, like cutthroat trout, and unique or biologically diverse wildlife resources may be recognized and protected as ORVs.

The Act explicitly restricts hydropower projects, but it also reaches a variety of other "water resources projects," including water diversions and reservoirs, watershed enhancement projects, bridges, dredging, bank stabilization, levees, boat ramps, and fishing piers. 16 U.S.C. § 1278. *See* Sierra Club North Star Chapter v. Pena, 1 F.Supp.2d 971, 979 (D.Minn.1998). Federal agencies are prohibited from assisting in the construction of any water resources project that would have an adverse effect on the ORVs of a designated river. 16 U.S.C. § 1278(a).

In Focus:

Merced River

Various stretches of the Merced River were designated as scenic or recreational river segments in 1987. 16 U.S.C. § 1274(a)(62). The National Park Service manages 81 miles of the river, encompassing both the main stem and the South Fork in Yosemite National Park. It manages the river to protect and enhance a number of ORVs, including:

- **Scientific**—Because much of the watershed is largely within designated Wilderness, the River corridor constitutes a rich resource for scientific study.

- **Biological**—The biological resource ORV includes riparian forests, meadows, and the aquatic environment of the river and associated species. From the Wawona riffle beetle to neotropical songbirds, the Merced "is a vital component in determining the overall health of riparian communities." Interestingly, in 2000, during the agency's decisionmaking processes for its river management plan, trout populations were removed from the list of ORVs. The Park Service determined that, while trout populations are obviously river-related, they are not "unique" to the region or the nation.

- **Hydrologic Processes**—The river meanders through Yosemite Valley, then plunges 2,000 feet in elevation over a course of six miles through the gorge. This ORV includes pristine water quality, exceptionally steep gradients, extraordinary cascades, and unique hydrologic conditions (*e.g.,* oxbows, unique wetlands, fluvial processes, and an active flood regime).

In Friends of Yosemite Valley v. Norton, 348 F.3d 789 (9th Cir.2003), discussed in Chapter 15.III.C, the management plan for the River was remanded because it failed to sufficiently address user capacities and it set the river boundaries too narrowly. For information on the Merced River Management Plan, see http://www.nps.gov/yose/planning/mrp/2000/.

F. National Forests and Diversity

The National Forest System encompasses nearly 200 million acres of land—an area equivalent in size to the state of Texas. Unlike Wildlife Refuges, National Parks, wilderness areas, and wild and scenic rivers, National Forests are managed not for preservation or recreation but for "multiple uses," including recreation as well as timber harvest, grazing, and other extractive uses. Because of their large tracts of land and protected status, however, National Forests provide important habitat for wildlife.

The National Forest Management Act (NFMA), 16 U.S.C. §§ 1600–1614, governs the management of national forest resources. NFMA requires the Forest Service to protect diversity of plant and animal communities through forest planning. 16 U.S.C. § 1604(g)(3)(C). To meet this requirement, some courts have required the use of actual quantitative population data to evaluate the impacts of an activity on species. For example, the Monroe Mountain Restoration Project in Fishlake National Forest undertook to provide "ecosystem restoration treatment" through timber harvesting, controlled burns, and sagebrush treatments. *Utah Environmental Congress v. Bosworth,* 372 F.3d 1219 (10th Cir.2004). The project was enjoined on the grounds that the Forest Service failed to effectively evaluate the effects of the project on certain bird species. *Id.* Several other courts have found that analyses of quantitative population data and population trends, rather than habitat data, are necessary to ensure diversity in National Forests. *See, e.g.,* Sierra Club v. Martin, 168 F.3d 1 (11th Cir.), *rehearing denied,* 181 F.3d 111 (11th Cir.1999); Colorado Wild v. U.S. Forest Service, 299 F.Supp.2d 1184 (D.Colo.2004); Forest Guardians v. U.S. Forest Service, 180 F.Supp.2d 1273 (D.N.M.2001).

Courts may excuse the Forest Service from the duty to collect population data when the agency can prove that it is technically infeasible to do so. *See Colorado Wild,* 299 F.Supp.2d at 1189; Inland Empire Public Lands Council v. U.S. Forest Service, 88 F.3d 754, 763 n. 12 (9th Cir.1996) (the Forest Service properly used habitat data rather than actual population counts because there was no reliable and cost-effective method of counting individual members of a highly reclusive species). Data on habitat features may also suffice when the agency relies on a variety of data types to determine population trends and commits to monitoring the effects of its projects on the species. Indiana Forest Alliance, Inc. v. U.S. Forest Service, 325 F.3d 851, 864–65 (7th Cir.2003). From a biological standpoint, why might it be desirable or even necessary to consider actual population counts rather than habitat integrity to ensure that biodiversity is protected?

The decisions that required the Forest Service to use actual, quantitative population data turned on the courts' interpretation of the 1982 NFMA regulations, specifically, 36 C.F.R. § 219.19, which provided that "[f]ish and wildlife habitat *shall* be managed to maintain viable populations ... in the planning area." This regulation governed forest planning for over twenty years, but in 2005 an amended version was issued, which emphasizes economic, social, and ecological sustainability, rather than "viable populations." Final Rule, National Forest System Land and Resource Management Planning, 70 Fed. Reg. 1022, 1029 (Jan. 5, 2005). It does not appear that NFMA's diversity provision will be applied with the same rigor in the future under this new rule. For discussion of forest management under NFMA and its regulations, see Chapter 6.II.B.3, *supra*. Other multiple-use lands, particularly those managed by the Bureau of Land Management, are addressed in Chapter 6 as well.

V. FEDERAL SPECIES PROTECTION LAWS

This section addresses federal statutes that regulate certain types of species, such as migratory birds and marine mammals, or that support state regulation of species. Section VI, below, features the federal Endangered Species Act.

A. The Lacey Act

The Lacey Act of 1900 was the first federal wildlife conservation statute with a national scope. The Act was originally intended to supplement the states' existing wildlife law by addressing two major concerns: (i) excessive hunting that had resulted in the swift depletion of game; and (ii) killing non-game bird species for millinery decoration (the "plume trade"). The Act was passed in response to a movement from hunters, naturalists, and humanitarians.

In Focus:

NATION MARKS LACEY ACT CENTENNIAL, 100 YEARS OF FEDERAL WILDLIFE LAW ENFORCEMENT

One hundred years ago, on May 25, President William McKinley signed the Lacey Act, giving the United States its first far-reaching federal wildlife protection law and setting the stage for a century of progress in safeguarding wildlife resources.

"The Lacey Act had an immediate impact on the rampant commercial exploitation of wildlife by giving game wardens a powerful enforcement tool," said U.S. Fish and Wildlife Service Director Jamie Rappaport Clark. * * *

Passage of the Lacey Act in 1900 was prompted by growing concern about interstate profiteering in illegally taken game. The passenger pigeon was already well on its way to being hunted into extinction, and populations of other bird species were also declining in a number of states. * * *

Today, the Lacey Act makes it unlawful to import, export, transport, sell, buy, or possess fish, wildlife, or plants taken, possessed, transported, or sold in violation of any federal, state, foreign, or Native American tribal law, treaty, or regulation. * * * Last year, for example, Service special agents worked on more than 1,500 Lacey Act investigations. They exposed illegal guiding operations profiteering in both state and federally protected species, and pursued cases involving the illegal, large-scale commercial exploitation of black bears,

Hawaiian corals, Midwestern mussels, Lake Erie fish, and Maryland yellow perch.

On the global front, felony Lacey Act convictions were secured in cases involving caviar smuggling, international coral trafficking, and illegal trade of exotic reptiles. Service wildlife inspectors, stationed at major ports of entry and border crossings, stopped shipments imported in violation of foreign conservation laws and international treaties and enforced regulations that require humane transport of live animals. * * *

For the full article, go to http://www.r1.fws.gov/news/2000/2000–98.htm.

The Lacey Act addresses several types of activities, specifically, marking or labeling, trafficking, and outfitting. There are two distinct marking requirements that ensure that shipments containing fish or wildlife are properly identified. The first makes it unlawful "to import, export, or transport in interstate commerce any container or package containing any fish or wildlife unless the container or package has ... been plainly marked" in accordance with the regulations (found at 50 C.F.R. §§ 14.81). 16 U.S.C. § 3372(b). Violators are subject to a civil penalty of no more than $250. The second marking requirement states, "It is unlawful for any person to make or submit any false record, account, or label for, or any false identification of any fish, wildlife, or plant" shipped in interstate or foreign commerce. 16 U.S.C. § 3372(d). A knowing violation of this provision subjects the defendant to a $10,000 civil penalty and a criminal penalty of up to five years imprisonment, depending upon the circumstances. *Id.* § 3373(a)(1). The fish or wildlife is also subject to forfeiture. *Id.* § 3374(a).

Next, the Act prohibits interstate and foreign trafficking of plants and wildlife that are illegally taken, possessed, transported, or sold in violation of any state, tribal, federal or foreign law or regulation. 16 U.S.C. § 3372(a). A successful prosecution requires proof that (i) the wildlife is illegal and (ii) the defendant engaged in trafficking the illegal wildlife. *See* United States v. Carpenter, 933 F.2d 748 (9th Cir.1991) (defendant could not be convicted of trafficking because, although he illegally killed migratory birds, the birds were not taken off his property).

Outfitters who violate state wildlife laws are also subject to the Act, which prohibits any person from offering, for money or other consideration, "guiding, outfitting, or other services" or "a hunting or fishing license or permit" for the illegal taking of wildlife. 16 U.S.C. § 3372(c). This provision does not involve a "sale" of game in the traditional sense; rather, the commodity being "sold" is the opportunity to illegally hunt game with the assistance of a guide. United States v. Atkinson, 966 F.2d 1270 (9th Cir.1992), cert. denied, 507 U.S. 1004, 113 S.Ct. 1644, 123 L.Ed.2d 266 (1993).

If the underlying violation is of federal or tribal law, any transportation or sale is sufficient to trigger the Lacey Act. *Id.* § 3372(a). If the violation is of state or foreign law, however, the violation must be related to interstate or foreign commerce. Section 3372(a)(2)(A) provides that it is unlawful to "import, export, transport, sell, receive, acquire, or purchase in interstate or foreign commerce ... any fish or wildlife taken, possessed, transported, or sold in violation of any law or regulation of any State or in violation of any foreign law."

Trafficking offenses can result in civil (ranging from $500–$10,000), misdemeanor and felony penalties, as well as permit revocations and forfeitures of the wildlife and any equipment used in aid of the violation. Criminal penalties require proof not only that the wildlife was illegal pursuant to a predicate statute, but also that (i) the individual "knowingly engages in conduct prohibited by the [Act]," and (ii) the individual "in the exercise of due care should know" that the wildlife is illegal. A misdemeanor offense can result in imprisonment of up to one year, which can be combined with a civil penalty of up to $10,000. 16 U.S.C. § 3372(d)(2). Felony convictions can lead to imprisonment of up to five years and a fine of up to $20,000. *Id.* § 3373(d)(1).

For cases involving the *mens rea* requirement of the Act's criminal penalty provisions, see United States v. Bronx Reptiles, Inc., 217 F.3d 82 (2d Cir.2000) (reversing a conviction for the illegal importation of Solomon Island frogs under a provision of the Act forbidding any person from knowingly causing wild animals to be transported to the United States under inhumane or unhealthful conditions, and holding that, to obtain a conviction, the government must prove not only that defendant knowingly caused the importation but also that defendant knew that the conditions of transport were inhumane or unhealthful); United States v. Mitchell, 985 F.2d 1275 (4th Cir.1993) (holding that the government need not prove the defendant himself actually hunted or exported gazelles and other animal trophies in violation of a foreign law, but only that he received and acquired them in interstate and foreign commerce knowing that they had been hunted, possessed or transported in violation of foreign law); United States v. Todd, 735 F.2d 146 (5th Cir.1984), cert. denied, 469 U.S. 1189, 105 S.Ct. 957, 83 L.Ed.2d 964 (1985) (concluding that defendant's testimony that he knew that hunting from a helicopter was a violation of federal law was sufficient grounds for a Lacey Act conviction, as the government does not have to prove that appellants knew of the existence of the Lacey Act, only that they knew of the illegal nature of the game).

Notes and Questions

When does the requisite connection to interstate commerce exist for there to be a violation of the Act's prohibition against trafficking wildlife in violation of state law? If you kill an alligator in a Louisiana swamp in viola-

tion of state law and subsequently sell .
charm) to a gift shop in the French Quarter,
if you cut out the middle-man and sell it to
instead a tourist from Iowa who purchases the
Mardi Gras in New Orleans, have you violated the
Gay–Lord, 799 F.2d 124 (4th Cir.1986), an individual
had been taken from inland waters in violation of Virgi.
a Lacey Act violation when he attempted to sell to an inte
Similarly, in United States v. Heuer, 749 F.Supp. 1541 (D.M
916 F.2d 1457 (9th Cir.1990), a defendant who obtained guiding
a Montana license for hunting elk had engaged in conduct cove
Lacey Act, even though there was no proof that obtaining the lic
guiding services occurred in interstate commerce. *See also Atkinso.*
F.2d 1270 (finding a sufficient relation to interstate commerce when, at
end of each illegal hunt guided by defendant, defendant either arranged
ship deer carcasses to hunters' homes outside of the state of origin or
assisted hunters with those shipments).

B. Migratory Birds and Eagles

The Migratory Bird Treaty Act (MBTA) of 1918 was the first congressional action to protect birds. Today the Act remains virtually unchanged. It states: "Unless and except as permitted by regulations ... it shall be unlawful at any time, by any means or in any manner, to purchase, hunt, take, capture, kill ... sell, ship, export, import ... any migratory bird, or any product, ... of any such bird or any part, nest, or egg thereof." 16 U.S.C. § 703. The MBTA adopts a strict liability standard, imposing civil and criminal penalties on those who accidentally or intentionally kill migratory birds. *See* United States v. Morgan, 283 F.3d 322 (5th Cir.2002) (possession of migratory game birds in excess of the daily bag limit is a strict liability offense); United States v. Van Fossan, 899 F.2d 636 (7th Cir.1990) (conviction upheld for defendant who inadvertently killed a protected species but intended only to kill unprotected pigeons).

Birds are included as protected species in accordance with international treaties with Mexico, Canada, Japan and the former Soviet Union. 16 U.S.C. §§ 703–704. In *Hill v. Norton,* 275 F.3d 98 (D.C.Cir.2001), the court held that the Secretary of Interior's failure to include the mute swan on the list of birds protected under the MBTA was arbitrary and capricious under the Administrative Procedure Act because swans, without limitation, are migratory birds. The court took note of the seasonal movements of some mute swans across the U.S.-Canada border. *Id.*

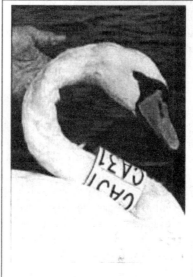

Mute Swan (banded, with identification number), Maryland Dept. of Natural Resources, http://dnr.maryland.gov/wildlife/msncsurvey.html

Historically, the FWS focused its prosecutorial efforts on hunters and poachers, but it has targeted a broad array of activities in recent years. One defendant attempted to avoid a conviction for running down ten ring-billed seagulls with his car on the grounds of desuetude. United States v. Jones, 347 F.Supp.2d 626 (E.D.Wis.2004). Jones argued that he had not been put on fair notice that he could be subject to prosecution because the government so rarely brought MBTA charges. According to the court, "if the defense of desuetude even exists, it is reserved for extreme cases.... 'The sudden revival of a long forgotten law carrying harsh penalties (the theme of Shakespeare's *Measure for Measure,* where the law in question imposed the death penalty for fornication) might encounter a defense of desuetude,' [but] in the face of ... [a] list of, by no means ancient, prosecutions under the Migratory Bird Treaty Act, Jones's effort to invoke the protections of the doctrine of desuetude must fail." *Id.* at 629 (citation omitted). Similarly, in United States v. Moon Lake Elec. Assoc., Inc., 45 F.Supp.2d 1070 (D.Colo.1999), the court rejected a desuetude defense to a prosecution for the electrocution of birds on the defendant's power lines, and stated:

> Considering the government's decision to prosecute oil companies, a pesticide manufacturer, and pesticide users for hazardous operation of oil sump pumps, wastewater ponds, and pesticide applicators, Moon Lake cannot argue credibly that the MBTA has been in disuse. Although none of the referenced prosecutions related to the operation of electrical power lines, the civil law doctrine of "desuetude," assuming its viability in American jurisprudence, requires a show-

ing of "long and continued non-use" of a statute that is "basically obsolete." * * * Here, it is sufficient that the MBTA's purposes remain viable, the conventions with Canada, Japan, and Mexico continue as solemn obligations, and the government has recently instituted prosecutions under MBTA.

Moon Lake, 45 F.Supp.2d at 1083. The charges at issue in *Moon Lake* are explored in detail in the case excerpt below.

Consider the language of MBTA § 703, provided above. Does the Act cover activities that result in degradation of the habitat of a protected bird? Although both the Eighth and Ninth Circuit Courts have said no, Newton County Wildlife Ass'n v. U.S. Forest Service, 113 F.3d 110, 115 (8th Cir.1997); City of Sausalito v. O'Neill, 386 F.3d 1186, 1225 (9th Cir.2004), at least one court has answered in the affirmative. *See* United States v. FMC Corp., 572 F.2d 902 (2d Cir.1978) (Act was violated by the accidental release of toxins into a lagoon used by migratory birds). Courts that reject an expansive interpretation of the MBTA focus on the legislative history, which indicates that, at the time of enactment, Congress was concerned primarily with hunting. *See* Seattle Audubon Soc'y v. Evans, 952 F.2d 297, 302 (9th Cir.1991). The terms listed in § 703 are less expansive than those provided in the Endangered Species Act of 1973, which prohibits "harm" to protected species, *see* 16 U.S.C. § 1532(19), a term construed as including habitat degradation. *See* Babbitt v. Sweet Home Chapter of Communities, 515 U.S. 687, 115 S.Ct. 2407, 132 L.Ed.2d 597 (1995). The uncertainty has not prevented FWS from using the MBTA to prosecute defendants whose pollution or habitat destruction results in actual bird mortality. In 2004, Phelps Dodge pleaded guilty to violating the MBTA when migratory birds died from drinking water contaminated by its Morenci copper mine. Mitch Tobin, *Bird Deaths Cost PD Over $1M,* Arizona Daily Star, Aug. 11, 2004. *See also Moon Lake, infra,* 45 F.Supp.2d at 1083 (prosecution for electrocution of birds by power lines). For analysis, see Conrad A. Fjetland, *Possibilities for Expansion of the Migratory Bird Treaty Act for the Protection of Migratory Birds,* 40 Nat. Resources J. 47 (2000).

The bald eagle, the nations' emblem, is protected by the MBTA, the ESA, and a statute designed specifically for its protection, the Bald and Golden Eagle Protection Act of 1940 (BGEPA). This Act imposes civil liability on those who "take, possess, sell, purchase, barter, offer to sell, purchase or barter, transport, export or import, at any time of in any manner," the species or its parts, nests, or eggs. 16 U.S.C. § 668(b). An early version of the Act imposed criminal penalties only on those who willfully violated its provisions, but the Act as amended imposes criminal penalties on anyone who violates it knowingly or with wanton disregard for the consequences of his actions. *Id.* § 668(a). This amendment was passed in 1972, shortly after 500 bald and golden eagles were gunned down from helicopters over ranches in Wyoming and Colorado: "In order to prevent, or deter, the taking of eagles in the future, violators should be subjected to greater penalties than allowed in the current law, and the amount of knowledge required ... to obtain a conviction in this type of case should be reduced." United States v. Hetzel, 385 F.Supp. 1311, 1314 (D.D.C.1974) (citing Senate Report No. 92–1159, U.S. Cong. & Admin.News, 92nd Cong., 2d Sess.1972).

Under the BGEPA the Secretary may permit the taking and possession of eagles for scientific purposes, exhibitions, religious purposes of Indian tribes, or, with respect to golden eagle nests, to lessen interference with resource development or recovery operations. 16 U.S.C. § 668(a). Permits may also be issued to protect wildlife, agricultural, or other interests if the Secretary determines that it is compatible with eagle preservation.

These exceptions provide several ways to dodge the statutory requirements, even though the Act has been described as having "sweepingly framed prohibitions." Andrus v. Allard, 444 U.S. 51, 100 S.Ct. 318, 62 L.Ed.2d 210 (1979). For discussion of the BGEPA provision for Indian religious uses, see United States v. Dion, *supra*, Chapter 7.

Although eagles are protected under both the BGEPA and the MBTA, there are significant differences between the two statutes. One important distinction involves the role of scienter, as illustrated in the following case.

UNITED STATES v. MOON LAKE ELECTRIC ASS'N, INC.
United States District Court, District of Colorado, 1999.
45 F.Supp.2d 1070.

On June 9, 1998, the United States of America ("the government") filed an Information charging defendant, Moon Lake Electric Association, Inc. ("Moon Lake"), with seven violations of the Bald and Golden Eagle Protection Act ("the BGEPA"), 16 U.S.C. § 668 (1997), and six violations of the Migratory Bird Treaty Act ("the MBTA"), 16 U.S.C. §§ 703 & 707(a) (1997) (collectively, "the Acts"), in connection with the deaths of 12 Golden Eagles, 4 Ferruginous Hawks, and 1 Great Horned Owl. Moon Lake moves for dismissal of the charges, arguing that the Acts do not apply to unintentional conduct that is not the sort of physical conduct normally exhibited by hunters and poachers. Moon Lake also argues that § 707(a) of the MBTA is unconstitutional as applied under the circumstances of this case. * * *

* * * Moon Lake is a "rural electrical distribution cooperative" that provides electricity to customers in northeastern Utah and northwestern Colorado. At issue in this case is Moon Lake's supply of electricity to an oil field near Rangely, Colorado. The electricity is conveyed by power lines strung across 3,096 power poles. The oil field is located near the White River in an area that is home to several species of protected birds, including Bald Eagles, Golden Eagles, Ferruginous Hawks, and Great Horned Owls. The oil field is mostly treeless, making Moon Lake's power

poles preferred locations for perching, roosting, and hunting by birds of prey. The government alleges that Moon Lake has failed to install inexpensive equipment on 2,450 power poles, causing the death or injury of 38 birds of prey during the 29 month period commencing January 1996 and concluding June 1998. * * * Specifically, the Information alleges that Moon Lake did "take and kill" those 17 protected birds. * * *

Moon Lake argues that the electrocutions ... do not constitute violations of the MBTA or the BGEPA because * * * Congress intended to target only poaching, hunting, trapping, and other "intentionally harmful" acts directed toward protected birds. In contending that its alleged conduct was unintentional, Moon Lake focuses on the mens rea, or mental state, required for conviction. * * *

The BGEPA states, in relevant part:

Whoever ... shall knowingly, or with wanton disregard for the consequences of his act take, possess, sell, purchase, barter, offer to sell, purchase or barter, transport, export or import, at any time or in any manner, any bald eagle commonly known as the American eagle, or any golden eagle, alive or dead, or any part, nest, or egg thereof of the foregoing eagles, or whoever violates any permit or regulation issued pursuant to this subchapter, shall be fined not more than $5,000 or imprisoned not more than one year or both....

16 U.S.C. § 668. "Take" ... "includes pursue, shoot, shoot at, poison, wound, kill, capture, trap, collect, or molest or disturb.... " 16 U.S.C. § 668c. [Likewise, the MBTA prohibits the "take" of migratory birds] * * *

The plain language of the Acts belies Moon Lake's contention that the Acts regulate only "intentionally harmful" conduct. "Simply stated, then, 'it is not necessary to prove that a defendant violated the Migratory Bird Treaty Act with specific intent or guilty knowledge.'" *United States v. Corrow,* 119 F.3d 796 (10th Cir.1997), *cert. denied,* 522 U.S. 1133, 118 S.Ct. 1089, 140 L.Ed.2d 146 (1998); ... *see also* S.Rep. No. 445, at 16, *reprinted in* 1986 U.S.C.C.A.N. 6113, 6128 ("Nothing in this amendment is intended to alter the 'strict liability' standard for misdemeanor prosecutions.... "). Thus, whether Moon Lake intended to cause the deaths of 17 protected birds is irrelevant to its prosecution under § 707(a) [of the MBTA]. * * *

The BGEPA, in contrast to § 707(a) of the MBTA, is not a strict liability crime. The BGEPA ... [criminal provisions apply] only to those who act "knowingly, or with wanton disregard for the consequences" of their acts. 16 U.S.C. § 668c; *see also* S.Rep. No. 92–1159, at 5, *reprinted in* 1972 U.S.C.C.A.N. 4285, 4289 (the defendant "must be conscious from his knowledge of surrounding circumstances and conditions that conduct will naturally and probably result in injury" to a protected bird). * * * Whether Moon Lake took or killed protected birds knowingly, or with wanton disregard for the consequences of its acts, is a question of fact for the jury's determination * * *

Moon Lake next argues that the Acts prohibit only physical conduct normally exhibited by hunters or poachers. * * * I disagree. Congress modeled the BGEPA after the MBTA. Similar to the MBTA, the BGEPA proscribes taking, possessing, selling, purchasing, bartering, selling, purchasing, bartering, transporting, exporting, importing, pursuing, shooting, shooting at, poisoning, wounding, killing, capturing, trapping, collecting, molesting, and disturbing. 16 U.S.C. §§ 668(a) & 668c. Only taking, shooting, shooting at, capturing, and trapping constitute acts normally associated with hunting and poaching. By prohibiting "poisoning," "killing," "possessing," "molesting," and "disturbing" in addition to the acts normally associated with hunting, the BGEPA, like the MBTA, suggests that Congress intended to regulate conduct beyond the sort engaged in by hunters and poachers. And, as does the MBTA, the BGEPA proscribes taking or killing "at any time or in any manner." 16 U.S.C. § 668(a). I conclude, * * *, that the plain language of the Acts prohibits the alleged conduct of Moon Lake. * * *

* * * The proposed legislation, in accordance with the protection provided by the third clause of Section 9 of Article I of the United States Constitution, could not be interpreted as operating ex post facto. * * * [P]ower companies would not be liable for acts committed prior to the date of enactment. * * * [S]uch lines erected after the date of enactment should provide such safeguards as are available in order for the power companies to avoid the charge of acting with "negligent disregard for the consequences" of their acts. This obligation would be no more of a burden upon power companies than upon any other person or organization performing operations which had a tendency to destroy wildlife. * * * Accordingly, I ORDER that defendant's motion to dismiss is DENIED.

Notes and Questions

1. Compare § 668(a) of the BGEPA and § 703 of the MBTA. Why have courts concluded that the MBTA imposes strict liability while the BGEPA does not? Which standard of liability best effectuates the conservation objective of both statutes?

2. Beginning in 2002, Congress excluded "the incidental taking of a migratory bird by a member of the Armed Forces during a military readiness activity" from the MBTA's prohibition against taking migratory birds, and directed the Secretary to adopt regulations to implement this exclusion. Pub.L. 107–314 § 315(a), 116 Stat. 2509 (Dec. 2, 2002). The term "military readiness activities" includes "all training and operations of the Armed Forces that relate to combat" and the "testing of military equipment, vehicles, weapons, and sensors for proper operation and suitability for combat use." *Id.* § 315(f). Critics object that the exclusion is unnecessary, and is far too broad. Do you agree?

3. Additional statutes that protect birds include the Wild Bird Conservation Act of 1992, which protects birds that are not naturally found within the United States, 16 U.S.C. §§ 4901–4916, and the Neotropical Bird Conservation Act of 1999, which protects neotropical migratory birds that are

found in the United States and spend the winter in Latin America and the Caribbean, 16 U.S.C. §§ 6101–6109.

C. Horses and Burros

Congress took the first step to protect wild horses and burros in 1959 by passing an Act prohibiting the use of aircraft and motor vehicles to hunt them. In spite of this effort, the practice of hunting wild horses and burros for sport and for use in commercial products such as pet food significantly increased. Today, it seems remarkable (not to mention grisly) that Americans hunted horses—just think *The Black Stallion* and *Misty of Chincoteague*—but the phenomenon is well documented and even became the topic of a 1961 film classic, *The Misfits,* starring Marilyn Monroe, Clark Gable and Montgomery Clift. By the 1960's, wild horses were fast disappearing from the western landscape.

In 1971, Congress concluded that a more encompassing statute was necessary and enacted the Wild Free–Roaming Horses & Burros Act, 16 U.S.C. §§ 1331–1340. This Act classifies all wild horses and burros as "federally protected" and drastically restricted how the animals could be managed. The Act imposes criminal penalties on anyone who:

- willfully removes a wild free-roaming horse or burro from public land,

- maliciously causes the death or harassment of a wild free-roaming horse or burro,

- processes the remains of a wild free-roaming horse or burro into commercial products, or

- sells a wild free-roaming horse or burro.

16 U.S.C. § 1338(a). The provisions related to the public lands were tested and upheld in *Kleppe v. New Mexico*, 426 U.S. 529, 96 S.Ct. 2285, 49 L.Ed.2d 34 (1976).

Today, as a result of increased protection, and the fact that these animals have few natural predators, their population has grown significantly. Ranchers, like Mr. Stephenson in *Kleppe*, complain that they interfere with livestock operations by eating forage and stampeding across the rangelands. To manage the escalating populations, federal managers may destroy those that are old or sick or place healthy animals up for adoption. If the animals are placed for adoption, the federal manager has an obligation to ensure that the adoptions are not for the purposes of commercial use and are undertaken by qualified individuals who will provide adequate care. 16 U.S.C. § 1333(b)(2)(B). *See* Animal Protection Inst. v. Hodel, 860 F.2d 920 (9th Cir.1988).

In Focus:

Wild Horse and Burro Populations: End of Year Statistics - FY 2000

Wild Horse and Burro Populations: End of Year Statistics—FY 2000 *http://www.wildhorseandburro.blm.gov/population.htm.*

State	Horses	Burros	Total
Arizona	275	2,519	2,794
California	3,492	1,481	4,973
Colorado	943	0	943
Idaho	669	0	669
Montana	189	0	189
Nevada	24,321	775	25,096
New Mexico	70	0	70
Oregon	2,635	10	2,645
Utah	3,420	210	3,630
Wyoming	7,615	0	7,615
Total	**43,629**	**4,995**	**48,624**

Some Congressmen, believing that the Act has outlived its usefulness, have proposed various amendments to limit its protection. If you were a U.S. Representative from Nevada, how would you vote? What if you were instead from New York?

D. Marine Mammals

The Marine Mammal Protection Act of 1972 (MMPA) was the most important wildlife conservation statute prior to the adoption of the ESA. It was created to protect marine mammals, such as seals, whales, porpoises, walruses, manatees, and mammals that primarily inhabit the marine environment, such as polar bears. 16 U.S.C. §§ 1361–1407. The "primary objective" of the MMPA is "to maintain the health and stability of the marine ecosystem." *Id*. § 1361(6). To achieve its goal, the Act abandoned the commonly used wildlife production standard of "maximum sustainable yield" and invoked the more biologically oriented standard, "optimum sustainable population" (OSP). OSP is "the number of animals which will result on the maximum productivity of the population or species, keeping in mind the optimum carrying capacity of the habitat and the health of the ecosystem of which they form a constituent element." *Id*. § 1362(8).

The MMPA forbids any individual to "take any marine mammal on the high seas" or "in waters or land subject to the jurisdiction of the United States." *Id*. § 1372(a). The possession, transportation, purchase, sale, import/export of any marine mammal taken in violation of the Act is also illegal. *Id*. § 1372(a)(1)-(4), (c). Like the MBTA, the MMPA uses the mens rea element to distinguish between the possible penalties. "Any person who violated any provision ... may be assessed a civil penalty ... of not more than $10,000 for each such violation." *Id*. § 1375(a)(1). "Any person who *knowingly* violated any provision ... shall ... be fined not more than $20,000 for each violation, or imprisoned for not more than one year, or both." *Id*. § (b). "Take" is defined as "to harass, hunt, capture, collect, or kill, or attempt to harass, hunt, capture, collect, or kill any marine mammal." 16 U.S.C. § 1362(13). Harassment means any act of pursuit, torment, or annoyance which—

    (i) has the potential to injure a marine mammal ... ; or

    (ii) has the potential to disturb a marine mammal ... by causing disruption of behavioral patterns, including, but not limited to, migration, breathing, nursing, breeding, feeding, or sheltering. *Id*. § 1362(18)(A).

A "take" also includes "[t]he collection of dead animals, or parts thereof; the restraint or detention of a marine mammal, no matter how temporary; tagging a marine mammal; the negligent or intentional operation of an aircraft or vessel, or the doing of any other negligent or intentional act which results in disturbing or molesting a marine mammal; and feeding or attempting to feed a marine mammal in the wild." 50 C.F.R. § 216.3.

There are several exemptions from the taking prohibition. One allows a taking if "imminently necessary in self-defense or to save the life of a person in immediate danger, and such taking is reported to the Secretary within 48 hours." 16 U.S.C. § 1371(c). The MMPA also recognizes a "Good Samaritan" exemption, which excuses a take if "imminently necessary" to avoid serious injury to a marine mammal entangled in fishing gear, so long as reasonable care is taken to ensure its safe release. *Id.* § 1371(d). Takings by Indians, Aleuts or Eskimos who reside in Alaska are allowed for subsistence purposes or the creation and sale of authentic native articles of handicrafts and clothing, so long as the take is not accomplished in a wasteful manner. *Id.* § 1371(b). "Military readiness activities" also receive special treatment under the Act. The National Defense Authorization Act of 2004, Pub. L. No. 108–136, 117 Stat. 1392, amended the MMPA's definition of "harassment" to exclude military readiness activities that result in minor behavioral changes with no significant impact on the viability of the marine mammal stock, added an exemption for actions "necessary for national defense," and liberalized allowances for incidental takings that occur during military readiness activities. *Id.* § 319 (to be codified at 16 U.S.C. §§ 1362(18), 1371). The term "military readiness activities" is defined the same as in the Migrating Bird Treaty Act Pub.L. 107–314 § 315(f), 116 Stat. 2509 (2002).

Another especially complicated exemption applies to commercial fishing operations that incidentally take marine mammals while in the course of business activities. *Id.* § 1371(a)(2).

Notes and Questions

1. In 1992, Congress amended the MMPA to include a proposed "global moratorium" of at least five years on fishing by setting purse seines on dolphins. Other nations did not agree, resulting in the closure of U.S. markets to all tuna caught in association with dolphins. Foreign incidental takes decreased from more than 80,000 to less than 4,000.

2. U.S. efforts to protect dolphins and other marine species have triggered an array of challenges under the World Trade Organization (WTO) of the General Agreement on Tariffs and Trade (GATT). The treatment of conservation measures under the WTO and other trade agreements is one of the most controversial and complex topics of international environmental law. The primary focus of the WTO Agreement is to promote trade liberalization by preventing trade discrimination, but it includes certain exceptions for conservation-oriented measures. The exceptions have been construed quite restrictively, and various U.S. measures to protect marine species, including dolphins, have been struck down by WTO panels. In 1996, India, Malaysia, Pakistan, and Thailand initiated a challenge to the U.S.'s trade embargo against the importation of shrimp harvested without Turtle Exclusion Devices (TEDs). Every year, approximately 150,000 sea turtles drown when they become entangled in shrimp nets. TEDs, which allow turtles to escape from shrimp nets, have been shown to reduce turtle deaths by over ninety-seven percent. The WTO Appellate Body initially struck down the embargo on the grounds that the United States had applied its TED requirement in a manner that discriminated between member states. It subsequently upheld a revised version of the measure, however, under GATT Article XX(g), which permits measures for the conservation of exhaustible natural resources. The Appellate Body reasoned that (i) the sea turtles were inter-

nationally recognized as endangered; and (ii) the revised measure permitted imports of all shrimp actually caught with turtle protection devices, including those originating in a country that does not meet US standards. WTO Appellate Body Report on United States—Import Prohibition of Certain Shrimp and Shrimp Products, Recourse to Article 21.5 of the DSU by Malaysia, WT/DS58/AB/RW (Oct. 22, 2001). For additional information on the Shrimp–Turtle decision, see Tracy P. Varghese, *The WTO's Shrimp–Turtle Decisions: The Extraterritorial Enforcement of U.S. Environmental Policy Via Unilateral Trade Embargoes,* 8 Envtl. Law. 421 (2002).

3. As you will see in Section VI of this chapter, the Endangered Species Act (ESA) authorizes permits for the incidental take of protected species during the course of otherwise lawful activities. 16 U.S.C. § 1539(a). The Migratory Bird Treaty Act (MBTA), however, does not include an incidental take provision. Should Congress amend the MBTA to include such a provision, or, conversely, should it amend the MMPA and ESA to do away with the permit provisions? Consider the purposes and scope of each statute to determine whether such permits make sense.

4. In spite of the protective provisions of the MMPA and other U.S. and international laws on marine resources, our oceans are in jeopardy. The Oceans Commission, an independent body formed by the Pew Charitable Trust, issued a comprehensive assessment in 2003, which reported that overfishing, over-development along the coasts, and increasing pollution from coastal areas are leading to a severe decline of aquatic species and the collapse of entire ocean ecosystems. *America's Living Oceans: Charting a Course for Sea Change* (May 2003), http://www.pewoceans.org/oceans/. Major culprits include regulatory divisiveness among governmental authorities, a lack of oversight, and consumption-oriented policies. The report calls for immediate reform of U.S. laws and policies to address these problems through more coherent regulation of all ocean resources, living and non-living, and increased use of marine-protected areas to sustain living marine resources. *Id.* at 2, 21. Leon Panetta, chair of the Commission, stated,

> For centuries we have viewed the oceans as beyond our ability to harm and their bounty beyond our ability to deplete. The evidence is clear that this is no longer true.... The good news is that it is not too late to act. This report offers practical solutions for bringing ocean management into the 21st century to ensure that future generations will be able to enjoy clean beaches, healthful seafood, abundant ocean wildlife, and thriving coastal communities.

Pew Oceans Commission Press Release, http://www.pewoceans.org/oceans/press_ release.asp (June 4, 2003).

Congress has taken note of the problems, and in the Oceans Act of 2000, Pub. L. No. 106–256, 114 Stat. 644 (Aug. 7, 2000), it directed the U.S. Commission on Ocean Policy to study the situation and issue an official report on the status of our oceans. The response, *An Ocean Blueprint for the 21st Century Final Report of the U.S. Commission on Ocean Policy* (Sept. 2004), available at http://oceancommission.gov, contains the Commission's recommendations for a comprehensive national ocean policy. Although this report highlights the deficiencies in our legal system and pinpoints the need for change, "until Congress sees those recommendations and acts on them, the

United States regulation of the ocean will likely remain divided, too focused on particular resources, and often too uncoordinated to comprehensively protect the nation's marine resources, to the particular detriment of the United States' living marine resources." Robin Kundis Craig, *Regulation of U.S. Marine Resources: An Overview of the Current Complexity*, 19 Nat. Res. & Env. 3, 9 (2004). Meanwhile, the Bush Administration has made a "modest response" by creating an interagency Committee on Ocean Policy to address the report's findings. Other Administration initiatives include market-based policies, such as individual fishing quotas, and the development of a plan for additional ocean research. John McQuaid, *Bush Forms Ocean Policy Committee*, Times–Picayune, Dec. 18. 2004, at A1.

5. For other "species oriented" federal conservation statutes, *see* THE MAGNUSON–STEVENS FISHERY CONSERVATION AND MANAGEMENT ACT, 16 U.S.C. §§ 1801–1883 (establishes a federal-regional partnership to manage fishery resources); THE NONINDIGENOUS AQUATIC NUISANCE PREVENTION AND CONTROL ACT of 1990, as amended by THE NATIONAL INVASIVE SPECIES ACT OF 1996, 16 U.S.C. §§ 4701–4751 (develops and implements a program to identify goals, priorities and approaches for preventing the introduction of invasive species); ANIMAL DAMAGE CONTROL ACT, 7 U.S.C. § 426 (promulgates a method for the eradication of animals found to be injurious to agriculture, horticulture, forestry, animal husbandry, wild game animals, furbearing animals, and birds).

Exercise:

Consider whether a MMPA "take" has occurred in each of the following scenarios:

a. Corrosive Chemical Co. discarded dozens of barrels of the toxic substance DDT by dumping the barrels in the Pacific ocean off the coast of San Diego. Within a short period of time, the barrels began to leak. In the past few years, the local walrus population has declined due to multiple environmental threats and unhappy encounters with cargo ships. Scientists will offer conclusive evidence that the addition of DDT to the water has exacerbated stress to the species. More specifically, the DDT has resulted in diminished reproduction and severe birth defects in walrus babies' appendages.

b. The Navy uses a chemical known as TBT to prevent barnacles from clinging to its ships' hulls. A team of Yale researchers recently discovered that TBT causes deafness in marine mammals and could cause whales to beach themselves as a result. Hearing loss is among the latest environmental hazard linked to TBT, which is already known to be harmful to some aquatic life and has been banned in many countries (but not the United States).

c. A member of an Alaskan Native tribe collected baleen from a dead whale that washed up on the beach near her village and used it to make jewelry for sale in a boutique in Seattle. (Baleen is a rigid material taken from the jaw of certain whales; it was once used for stays in corsets).

d.   While paddling off the Oregon coast, Kyle Kayaker becomes frightened by an exceptionally large and curious seal, and believes that he is in danger of being dumped into the ocean. He smacks the seal on its head with his paddle while trying to get away from it, but the seal continues to follow him. He then removes a flare from his pack and shoots it at the seal, intending to scare it off. He's certain that he hit it, though, because he noticed blood streaming from the seal as it swam away.

e.   During the same kayaking trip, Kyle finds a sea otter entangled in fishing nets and cuts its leg with his Swiss army knife while trying to free it.

VI.   THE ENDANGERED SPECIES ACT OF 1973 (ESA)

The Endangered Species Act (ESA) is the most important federal program ever created for the protection and conservation of wildlife species. It has been described as the "pitbull" of environmental law for its dramatic (and some would say draconian) impacts on development. This section will begin by discussing the history and philosophy of the Act, followed by the intricacies of its key provisions, including its scope, the listing decision, the prohibition against "take", consultation requirements, and affirmative obligations to conserve and recover species. We then turn to enforcement issues, including citizen suits, and conclude with ESA provisions that moderate potential adverse effects on development.

A.   The History & Philosophy of the ESA

The first governmental attempt to protect endangered wildlife species came in the 1960's. Pressured by increased public concern for wildlife, in 1962, the Department of the Interior created the Committee on Rare and Endangered Species for the purpose of compiling a list of species threatened by extinction, otherwise known as the "Redbook." Although the Redbook stimulated governmental and private interest in wildlife protection, these preliminary efforts were unsuccessful in accomplishing any significant improvements.

It was not until the enactment of the ESA in 1973 that stringent substantive and procedural requirements were implemented. Shortly after enactment, the Supreme Court issued a landmark ruling in Tennessee Valley Authority (TVA) v. Hill, 437 U.S. 153, 98 S.Ct. 2279, 57 L.Ed.2d 117 (1978), which articulated in no uncertain terms the national interest in prioritizing endangered species and their habitats over "business as usual." The *TVA* Court held that the ESA prohibited the completion of a dam, where operation of the dam would either eradicate a population of the endangered snail darter or destroy its critical habitat. The Court enjoined the project despite the fact that the dam was nearly completed and Congress had continued to appropriate large sums of public money to the project. "The plain intent of Congress in enacting [the ESA] was to halt and reverse the trend toward species extinction, whatever the cost." *Id.* at 184.

Following the *TVA* decision, Congress amended the ESA in an attempt to alleviate its potentially harsh consequences for economic development. The 1978 amendments created the Endangered Species Committee, also known as "The God Squad," and provided it with the authority to grant exemptions from ESA prohibitions for the most economically beneficial projects. 16 U.S.C. § 1536(h)(1). The God Squad reviewed the dam at issue in *TVA v. Hill*, and decided not to exempt it from the ESA. For a detailed discussion of the God Squad's authority, *see infra,* Section H.1.

Although several ESA amendments followed those of 1978, none has eroded the statute's protection in any significant way. The ESA is said to represent the most comprehensive legislation for the preservation of endangered species ever enacted by any nation. Babbitt v. Sweet Home Chapter of Communities for a Great Or., 515 U.S. 687, 115 S.Ct. 2407, 132 L.Ed.2d 597 (1995), quoting TVA v. Hill, 437 U.S. 153, 98 S.Ct. 2279, 57 L.Ed.2d 117 (1978). In spite of its headline-grabbing nature, or perhaps because of it, the Act enjoys wide public support. For example, the Endangered Species Coalition is comprised of over 430 environmental, religious, scientific, sporting, and business organizations working to defend and strengthen the ESA and overall biodiversity protection. For more information, visit www.stopextinction.org. Although the Act enjoys a reputation as a pillar in the field of environmental reform, like many proactive environmental laws, it is subject to the ever-fluctuating funding and enforcement priorities on Capitol Hill and in the White House.

B. The ESA's Scope and Key Provisions

The purpose of the ESA is "to provide a means whereby the ecosystems upon which endangered species and threatened species depend may be conserved," and to "provide a program for conservation of such ... species ... " 16 U.S.C. § 1531(b). To achieve this goal, the ESA divides species into four categories: "endangered," "threatened," "proposed to be listed" and "warranted but precluded." 16 U.S.C. § 1533(b)(3)(B). A specific level of protection accompanies each category of species. In addition, the ESA authorizes and protects a classification of geographic areas, known as "critical habitats."

The following definitions clarify the coverage of the ESA:

- *"Conserve"* is "to use ... all methods and procedures which are necessary to bring any endangered species or threatened species to the point at which the measures provided pursuant to the Act are no longer necessary. Such methods and procedures include, but are not limited to, all activities associated with scientific resources management such as research, census, law enforcement, habitat acquisition, and maintenance, propagation, live trapping, and transportation, and in the extraordinary case where population pressures within a given ecosystem cannot be otherwise relieved, may include regulated taking." *Id.* § 1332(3).

- "S*pecies*" includes "any subspecies of fish or wildlife or plants, and any distinct population segment of any species of vertebrate fish or wildlife which interbreeds when mature." *Id.* § 1332(16).

- "*Endangered*" is "any species which is in danger of extinction throughout all or a significant portion of its range ... " *Id.* § 1332(6).

- "*Threatened*" is "any species which is likely to become an endangered species within the foreseeable future throughout all or a significant portion of its range." *Id.* § 1332(20).

- "*Proposed to be listed*" includes all species that are in the process of being listed as either an endangered or threatened species. *Id.* § 1536(a)(4).

- "*Warranted but precluded*" species are those whose listing is warranted but "the immediate ... promulgation of a ... regulation ... is precluded by other pending proposals to determine whether another species should be listed and expeditious progress is being made" on the determination of the status of the other species. *Id.* § 1533(b)(3)(B)(iii).

- "Candidate" species are those under consideration for listing, or warranted but precluded from listing.

- "*Critical habitat*" is "(i) the specific areas within the geographical area occupied by the species ... on which are found those physical or biological features (I) essential to the conservation of the species and (II) which may require special management considerations of protection; and (ii) specific areas outside the geographical area occupied by the species at the time it is listed ... upon a determination by the Secretary that such areas are essential for the conservation of the species." *Id.* § 1532(5).

- *Secretaries* or *Services* mean the Secretaries of Interior or Commerce, and the Fish and Wildlife Service (FWS) or National Oceanic and Atmospheric Administration (NOAA)–Fisheries, respectively. NOAA–Fisheries (formerly known as the National Marine Fisheries Service) has authority for marine species and anadromous fish, like salmon, while FWS has authority for all other species.

In Focus:

WHAT HAPPENS WHEN IMPLEMENTATON OF A LAW PROTECTING ONE SPECIES ADVERSELY AFFECTS ANOTHER SPECIES?

As they say, it's a dog eat dog world out there. Occasionally, protected species clash with each other, or state and federal laws governing the management of various protected species come into conflict. Sometimes these conflicts are resolved harmoniously; sometimes not.

In the early 1990's, the steelhead salmon population in Washington began to decline precipitously due to harvesting by the California sea lion. As the salmon migrated from Puget Sound to spawn, sea lions snapped them up. State wildlife officials tried to chase the sea lions away with underwater firecrackers and hazing by boat. When these actions proved unsuccessful, Washington sought authority to lethally remove the sea lions under § 120 of the MMPA, which allows the Secretary to authorize states to take marine mammals that prey on endangered species if non-lethal means of removal have been exhausted. Ultimately, Washington was given a three-year conditional authority to kill 15 sea lions. *See* Nina M. Young, Stephanie Mairs, and Suzanne Iudicello Martley, *At Point Blank Range: The Genesis and Implementation of Lethal Removal Provisions under the Marine Mammal Protection Act*, 5 Ocean & Coastal L.J., 1, 1–5 (2000).

National Audubon Society, Inc. v. Davis, 307 F.3d 835 (9th Cir.2002), illustrates a different but related point: where state law protections conflict with federal law, state law is preempted In 1998, California voters passed Proposition 4, making it illegal for any person, including federal employees, to use leg-hold traps to capture fur-bearing and non-game animals. The National Audubon Society and other groups sued a number of California officials and agencies arguing that the state ban on leg-hold traps inhibited enforcement of ESA and Refuge protection laws. In particular, provisions of the ESA and the Refuge Improvement Act grant authority to federal employees to control predators that threaten endangered species. The California state law was struck down because it would have prevented federally authorized trapping of predators.

C. Species Listing & Critical Habitat Determinations

The first line of defense for an imperiled species is to be added to the federal ESA list. The ESA's protections are triggered once the species is listed. The term "species" includes subspecies and distinct populations of fish, wildlife and plants, and "fish or wildlife" is defined broadly to include any member of the animal kingdom, including invertebrates, as well as the products, eggs and body parts of fish and wildlife. 16 U.S.C. § 1532(8). Plants include any member of the plant kingdom, including their seeds, roots and other parts. *Id.* § 1532(14). What about insects? Insects are members of the animal kingdom and they are an important component of ecosystem structure and function, but the ESA explicitly excludes "species of the Class Insecta determined by the Secretary to constitute a pest whose protection ... would present an overwhelming and overriding risk to man." *Id.* § 1532(6). Even among non-"pest" species, relatively few insects have been listed under the Act. *See* John Copeland Nagle, *Playing Noah*, 82 Minn. L. Rev. 1171, 1197 (1998). As of February 2005, nearly 1,300 species are listed as endangered or threatened. Of these, there are only 48 insects and 12 arachnids. *See* U.S. FWS, Species Information, http://endangered.fws.gov/wildlife.html#Species (visited Feb. 17, 2005).

1. Listing Species

A species listing can be initiated either by the Secretary or by any "interested person" (private individuals, other federal agencies, or environmental organizations). 16 U.S.C. § 1533 (b)(3)(A). Three steps occur once an interested person submits a petition:

1. After the FWS receives a petition, it must issue a finding within ninety days as to whether the petition presents substantial scientific or commercial information to warrant the action. *Id.*; Save Our Springs v. Babbitt, 27 F.Supp.2d 739, 747–48 (W.D.Tex.1997). The FWS has been allowed to take longer than ninety days in some circumstances. Biodiversity Legal Foundation v. Babbitt, 146 F.3d 1249 (10th Cir.1998).

2. If the petitioner presents "substantial evidence", the FWS must "promptly commence" a review of the status of the species concerned. Within twelve months of receiving the petition, the Secretary must decide if listing is (i) not warranted, (ii) warranted but precluded, or (iii) warranted. 16 U.S.C. § 1533(b)(3)(a). The decision must be based "solely upon the best scientific and commercial data available." *Id.* § 1533(b)(1)(A). Economic impacts play no role.

3. The Secretary must publish her decision and allow public comment. *Id.* § 1533 (b)(4), (5). Within one year from this point, a final rule is to be (i) promulgated, (ii) withdrawn if there is insufficient information, or (iii) extended for an additional six months if "there is substantial disagreement regarding the sufficiency or accuracy of the available data." *Id.* § 1533(b)(5)(B)-(b)(6).

Courts will not hesitate to impose injunctive relief on the Services if they fail to complete the required determinations within the deadlines established by the ESA. *See* Biodiversity Legal Foundation v. Badgley, 309 F.3d 1166, 1177–78 (9th Cir.2002). Congress intended the petitioning process to "force action on listing and delisting proposals" and "interrupt

[] the department's priority system by requiring immediate review." Center for Biological Diversity v. Norton, 254 F.3d 833, 840 (9th Cir.2001) (citing Pub. L. 97–304 § 2(a)(2), 96 Stat. 1411, 1412 (1992)). However, the Services may not have to take the requested action if they are already in the process of determining whether the species is endangered or threatened, and expeditious progress is being made to add it to the list. In addition, failure to comply with the statutory deadlines for acting on a proposal to list a species does not bar the FWS from listing that species. Building Industry Association v. Babbitt, 979 F.Supp. 893 (D.D.C.1997).

The ESA also provides detailed substantive criteria to guide the listing decision. Section 4(a)(1) requires the Secretary to determine whether a species should be listed in light of the following factors:

(A) present or threatened destruction or curtailment of habitat;

(B) overutilization for commercial, recreational, scientific, or educational purposes;

(C) disease or predation;

(D) inadequacy of existing regulatory mechanisms; or

(E) other natural or manmade factors affecting its continued existence.

16 U.S.C. § 1533(a)(1). If the conservation efforts of a state or foreign nation are providing adequate protection to the species, the Secretary may decide not to list it. *Id.* § 1533(a)(1)(D), (b)(1)(A). A rigorous conservation agreement may be sufficient to prevent listing, but future or uncertain regulatory actions and purely voluntary actions are not. *See* Federation of Fly Fishers v. Daley, 131 F.Supp.2d 1158, 1165–66 (N.D.Cal.2000) (finding a decision not to list steelhead as a threatened species arbitrary and capricious).

The ESA permits a distinct population segment (DPS) of vertebrate species, rather than the species as a whole, to be listed as endangered or threatened. 16 U.S.C. § 1532(16). This allows species protection "before large-scale decline occurs that would necessitate listing a species or subspecies throughout its entire range." Policy Regarding the Recognition of Distinct Vertebrate Population, 61 Fed. Reg. 4722, 4725 (1996). The Services have noted that, although the ESA requires them to use the best available scientific information in determining the status of species, "[a]vailable scientific information provides little specific enlightenment in interpreting the phrase 'distinct population segment.' " *Id.* at 4722. Accordingly, in an attempt to satisfy both the terms and the conservation goals of the ESA, they issued a joint federal policy on DPSs, which states that a population qualifies for DPS designation if it is "discrete" and "significant" to the species to which it belongs. *Id.*

In National Association of Home Builders v. Norton, 340 F.3d 835 (9th Cir.2003), the Association challenged FWS's determination that the Arizona pygmy-owl population qualified as discrete and significant. In order to be discrete under the Services' policy, a population must have considerably lower numbers of individuals in relation to other populations of the same species. The court found that the FWS rightfully designated the pygmy-owl population as discrete, but that it acted arbitrarily when it labeled the population as significant. " '[B]iological and ecological significance will ... be considered in light of Congressional guidance ... that the authority to list DPS's be used sparingly' " while encouraging the conservation of genetic diversity. *Id.* at 844, citing 61 Fed. Reg. at 4725. FWS argued that the genetic characteristics of the population in question differed markedly from other populations, but neither the listing rule nor the administrative record presented any evidence of actual, as opposed to potential, genetic differences between Arizona pygmy-owls and other populations of the species. *Id.* at 851–52.

FWS has fared poorly in other cases where it has attempted to utilize DPS status to down-list species' populations from endangered to threatened. *See* National Wildlife Federation v. Norton, 2005 WL 2000712 (D. Vt. 2005) (vacating FWS's decision to down-list the gray wolf in its "newly minted" Eastern and Western DPSs); Center for Biological Diversity v. U.S. Fish & Wildlife Service, 2005 WL 2000928 (N.D. Cal. 2005) (vacating FWS's decision to eliminate DPS status and down-list Sonoma and Santa Barbara County tiger salamanders).

Despite a concerted effort on the part of conservationists, not all species meet the requirements for protective listing under the ESA. In some cases, such as in the article below, a species may not be added to the ESA list because other species are in greater danger of extinction and take priority. Those "low priority," warranted-but-precluded species may not ever make it onto the ESA list.

NO FEDERAL SHIELD FOR PRAIRIE DOGS
By Theo Stein
Denver Post, Aug. 13, 2004

The black-tailed prairie dog has been removed as a candidate for endangered-species protection after new U.S. Fish and Wildlife service estimates show that 18 million of colony-dwelling rodents now inhabit broad swaths of prairie from Montana to Texas.

Agency biologists said they made their decision based on recent studies by 10 states and several tribes showing that active prairie dog colonies covered 1.8 million acres—three times the agency's 2000 estimate. Local prairie dog populations still suffer major fluctuations because of plague and poisons but that doesn't appear to affect the species' persistence across its range, biologists said. * * *

Colorado Gov. Bill Owens, whose administration has argued the prairie dog is abundant in the state, applauded the move as a "victory for sound science." A 2002 study by the Colorado Division of Wildlife found 631,000 acres of occupied prairie dog colonies, seven times more than federal biologists had estimated. State biologists will resurvey eastern Colorado in 2005. * * * Colorado has spent $1 million enrolling 20,000 acres of private land in conservation agreements to benefit the prairie dog, swift fox, ferruginous hawk and pronghorn, which also need short grass prairie.

Some environmentalists noted that massive prairie dog poisoning still occurs in Colorado and questioned the Division of Wildlife population estimates. "When I went to southeast Colorado this spring, I saw entire colonies completely dead from plague or poisoning," said Jonathon Proctor of the Predator Conservation Alliance. "The situation looked incredibly bleak."

The Fish and Wildlife Service placed the prairie dog on the candidate species list four years ago, meaning the species needed protection but the agency had higher priorities.

In Center for Biological Diversity v. Badgley, 335 F.3d 1097 (9th Cir 2003), the court upheld FWS's decision not to list the goshawk under the ESA. The FWS had assembled a top research team to conduct studies for a period of 12 months and determined that the information did not warrant listing of the goshawk. The Center claimed that the finding by the FWS was arbitrary and capricious, but the court explained:

> The ESA requires FWS to make listing determinations "solely on the basis of the best scientific and commercial data available.... " 16 U.S.C. § 1533(b)(1)(A). * * * The administrative record indicates the status review team conducted a comprehensive review of scientific published and unpublished literature, peer reviews, and raw data in making their report. Based on the status review team's report, FWS determined that the best available scientific and commercial data did not indicate the goshawk population was endangered or threatened. In the absence of evidence that the goshawk is endangered or likely to become endangered in the foreseeable future, FWS's decision was not arbitrary or capricious.

Id. at 1100–1101.

Through the ESA, the government has taken a step in the right direction in its protection of endangered species, but the fact is there are not enough resources to go around. Two forces are working against species protection: (1) the overwhelming nature of the task, when there are millions of different species and new species are discovered every year; and (2) the rapid growth of human populations in coastal and other important biodiverse areas. As a result, species that may have been under stress to begin with are pushed to the edge of extinction long before anyone realizes the severity of development's impacts on the species or can mobilize to protect them. Even if their plight is recognized, the harsh reality is that danger of extinction is not enough to trigger the ESA's protection; species must compete with other species for protection, and those that are most threatened, or encounter the least resistance from developers, win.

The list of candidate species fluctuates, but typically includes over 200 species that may warrant protection. Between 2001 and 2002, only eight species were removed from the candidate list. Six species were given protection as threatened or endangered species, one was removed due to lack of pertinent biological information, and one was removed since it had been mistakenly included in the previous candidate list. See http://news.fws.gov/newsreleases.html.

In Focus:

Candidate Species Added in 2002

Fish

- Chucky madtom (*Noturus* sp.cf. *Noturus elegans*)–Tennessee
- Grotto sculpin (*Cottus* sp., sp. *nov.*)–Missouri
- Rush darter (*Etheostoma phytophilum*)–Alabama
- Sharpnose shiner (*Notropis oxyrhynchus*)–Texas
- Smalleye shiner (*Notropis buccula*)–Texas

Amphibians

- Relict leopard frog (*Rana onca*)–Nevada and Arizona
- Austin blind salamander (*Eurycea waterlooensis*)–Texas
- Sonoma County population of the California tiger salamander (*Ambystoma Californiense*)–California
- Salado salamander (*Eurycea chisholmensis*)–Texas

Clams

- Altamaha spinymussel (*Elliptio spinosa*)–Georgia

Snails

- Elongate mud meadows pyrg (*Pyrgulopsis notidicola*)–Nevada

Insects

- Dakota skipper (*Hesperia dacotae*)–Minnesota, North Dakota, South Dakota, and the provinces of Manitoba and Saskatchewan in Canada
- Stephan's riffle beetle (*Heterelmis stephani*)–Arizona

Flowering Plants

- Siskiyou mariposa lily (*Calochortus persistens*)–California and Oregon

- Webber ivesia (*Ivesia webberi*)–California and Nevada

- Soldier Meadow cinquefoil or basalt cinquefoil (*Potentilla basaltica*)–California and Nevada

To check the status of these species today, see www.fws.gov.

CENTER FOR BIOLOGICAL DIVERSITY v. NORTON

United States Court of Appeals, Ninth Circuit, 2001.

254 F.3d 833

* * * At the heart of the present case is the relationship between two methods prescribed in the statute for listing species for protection as endangered or threatened under the ESA. * * * The end result in either case is the same: the Secretary must issue a final determination stating whether circumstances warrant listing a species as endangered or threatened. There are ... important differences between the two methods that dictate how (and when) the Secretary reaches that conclusion.

Under the first method, the Secretary may, on her own accord, consider whether a species is eligible for protection as endangered or threatened because of:

(A) the present or threatened destruction, modification, or curtailment of its habitat or range;

(B) overutilization for commercial, recreational, scientific, or educational purposes;

(C) disease or predation;

(D) the inadequacy of existing regulatory mechanisms; or

(E) other natural or manmade factors affecting its continued existence.

16 U.S.C. § 1533(a)(1). If the Secretary finds that the "best scientific and commercial data available to [her]" demonstrates that a species is endangered or threatened because of the presence of one or more of these factors, 16 U.S.C. § 1533(b)(1)(A), she must publish a proposed rule identifying the species as such. 50 C.F.R. § 424.11(c). A period of public comment follows. Within one year, the Secretary must either publish a final rule designating the species for protection or withdraw the proposed rule upon a finding "that available evidence does not justify the action." 50 C.F.R. § 424.17(a); see also 16 U.S.C. § 1533(b)(6)(A).

Although not expressly provided in the statute, the regulations implementing the ESA also permit the Secretary to find that listing of a species may be warranted "but that the available evidence is not sufficiently definitive to justify proposing the action at that time." 50 C.F.R. § 424.15(a). The Secretary typically does not provide an explanation for this decision but instead publishes a brief, one-line notice in the Federal Register identifying the species as a "candidate" for protection under the ESA. * * * Candidates are "any species being considered by the Secretary for listing as an endangered or a threatened species, but not yet the subject of a proposed rule." 50 C.F.R. § 424.02(b). There is ... no specific time frame during which the Secretary must act on candidate species. * * *

The second method for listing species allows interested persons to petition the Secretary to add (or remove) species from either the endangered or threatened species lists. Once the Secretary receives such a petition, she has 90 days to decide whether it presents "substantial scientific or commercial information indicating that the petitioned action may be warranted." 16 U.S.C. § 1533(b)(3)(A). If so, the Secretary must "promptly commence a review of the status of the species concerned." Id. Within 12 months after the petition is filed, the Secretary must determine that either (1) the petitioned action is warranted, in which case she must publish a proposed rule designating the species for protection; (2) the petitioned action is not warranted; or (3) the petitioned action is warranted but immediate promulgation of a rule is precluded by other pending proposals. 16 U.S.C. § 1533(b)(3)(B). If the Secretary finds that action is "warranted but precluded," she must promptly publish that finding along with "a description and evaluation of the reasons and data on which the finding is based." Id. Findings that a petitioned action is not warranted or is "warranted but precluded" are subject to judicial review. 16 U.S.C. § 1533(b)(3)(C)(ii).

In 1996, the Fish and Wildlife Service ("FWS") adopted a new policy governing its treatment of citizen-sponsored petitions. (The policy is described in the 1996 "Petition Management Guidance" manual and is hereafter referred to as the "PMG policy.") The policy provides that "[a] petition for an action on a species or critical habitat 'identical' or 'equivalent' to a petition still pending (or active) requires only a prompt (i.e., within 30 days) response informing the submitter of the prior petition and its status; Federal Register publication of this response is not required." * * * The PMG policy equates species identified as candidates for listing with those designated "warranted but precluded" under 16 U.S.C. § 1533(b)(3)(B)(iii). Candidate species are thus "consider[ed] ... as under petition," and a petition to list a candidate species is deemed "redundant." Consequently, the Secretary now treats petitions to list species already identified as candidates for protection as second petitions and does not—ever—fulfill the statutory obligations described above that ordinarily attach to initial petitions.

Several significant consequences for petitions to list species already designated by the Secretary as candidates for protection follow from the PMG policy. First, the Secretary may avoid publishing an explanation for her decision not to take more immediate action on a petition to protect a species. Second, because the Secretary's decision to designate a species as a candidate does not require any explanation, there is no basis to review the decision not to take prompt action on a petition to list a candidate species. Third, the timetable requirements that normally govern petitions do not apply. The Center's position in this case is that, taken together, these consequences substantially and impermissibly compromise the statutory scheme for considering petitions to list a species as endangered or threatened.

The particular species at issue in this case are the Chiricahua leopard frog (the "frog") and the Gila chub (the "chub"). * * * The chub appeared as a candidate for listing as early as 1982 and the frog as early as 1991. See 47 Fed. Reg. 58,454, 58,455 (Dec. 30, 1982) (chub); 56 Fed. Reg. 58,804, 58,806 (Nov. 21, 1991) (frog). Although the Secretary identified both species as candidates for listing, she had taken no action on either as of June 1998. At that time, the Center filed two petitions requesting that the Secretary extend ESA protection to both species. The Secretary did not, however, issue 90–day statements or 12–month findings in response to either petition, as required by 16 U.S.C. § 1533(b)(3)(A) and (B). Rather, the FWS sent a pair of letters to the Center explaining that it had already designated both the chub and the frog as candidate species. Citing the PMG policy, the FWS further noted that "candidate species are considered ... under petition and covered by a 'warranted but precluded' finding under section 4(b)(3)(B)(iii) of the [ESA]. * * * Preparation of a 90 day finding is considered superfluous and would add undue work to an already heavily burdened listing program. Therefore, the Service will not make a 90–day finding on your petition to list the Gila chub."

The same language was used in the letter denying action on the frog petition. In August 1999, after the 12–month deadline passed, the Center filed suit to compel the Secretary to issue findings as required by the ESA . * * *

At issue ... is the validity of the PMG policy. If that policy is supported by the clear intent of Congress under the ESA, "that is the end of the matter; for the court, as well as the agency, must give effect to the unambiguously expressed intent of Congress." Chevron U.S.A., Inc. v. Natural Resources Defense Council, 467 U.S. 837, 842–43, 104 S. Ct. 2778, 81 L.Ed.2d 694 (1984). But if the ESA "is silent or ambiguous with respect to the specific issue, the question for the court is whether the agency's [policy] is based on a permissible construction of the statute." Id. at 843, 104 S. Ct. 2778. The Secretary argues that the statute is silent or ambiguous on how she should handle petitions to list species already under consideration as candidates.

We disagree. The statute is not at all ambiguous, but instead is exquisitely clear, concerning what the Secretary must do when she receives a petition requesting action on a species. * * *

While the Secretary's designation of candidate status may fulfill the requirements for a finding of "warranted but precluded" in spirit, it certainly does not satisfy them in deed. If the Secretary finds that listing of a species is "warranted but precluded," the ESA requires her to "*promptly* publish such findings in the Federal Register, together with a description and evaluation of the reasons and data on which the finding is based." 16 U.S.C. § 1533(b)(3)(B)(iii) (emphasis added). A one-line notice in the Federal Register that a species has been designated a candidate does not fulfill this obligation.

A "warranted but precluded" finding has two components. First, it is an admission by the Secretary that a species qualifies for protection—and that protection is "warranted"—under the ESA, an admission which, as noted, might be met by a candidate designation under the PMG policy's revised definition of candidate species. Second, the finding also states that a final rule cannot be issued right away, for administrative reasons, thereby temporarily excusing the Secretary from issuing a final rule. The circumstances under which the Secretary may invoke that excuse ... are narrowly defined; Congress emphasized that providing for the "warranted but precluded" designation was not designed to justify "the foot-dragging efforts of a delinquent agency." H. Conf. Rep. No. 97–835, at 22 (1982), reprinted in 1982 U.S.C.C.A.N. 2860, 2863. Specifically, the Secretary must show that she is "actively working on other listings and delistings and must determine and publish a finding that such other work has resulted in pending proposals which actually preclude[d] [her] proposing the petitioned action at that time." * * *

The published findings supporting a determination that listing is "warranted but precluded" are important to the petition process. They provide public notice of species that are likely to become the subject of proposed rules and allow public agencies, private landowners, and other interested parties to respond appropriately. They also provide the basis for review of the Secretary's decision by the court.

The ESA specifically provides that the Secretary's "warranted but precluded" findings are subject to judicial review. 16 U.S.C. § 1533(b)(3)(C)(ii). Were this court to accept the Secretary's unexplained contention that her designation of the chub as candidate species was equivalent to a finding that listing was "warranted but precluded," judicial review would become meaningless. We would have no basis to evaluate the Secretary's conclusion that immediate action is precluded by other more urgent matters. * * *

Accordingly, the Secretary failed to fulfill her obligations under the ESA when she made no 12–month findings in response to the Center's petition and instead treated the chub's one-line candidate designation ... as equivalent to a finding that the listing was "warranted but precluded." Insofar as the Secretary relied on the PMG policy as permitting such a truncated process, the PMG policy is inherently inconsistent with the specific provisions of the statute providing for judicial review of "warranted but precluded" findings.

* * * As the legislative history of the ESA and its subsequent amendments demonstrate, Congress from the outset recognized that timeliness in the listing process is essential. See, e.g., S. Rep. No. 93–307 (1973), reprinted in 1973 U.S.C.C.A.N. 2989, 2991 (noting the inadequacies of earlier legislation). During subsequent revisions of the ESA, Congress expressed particular concern for species that had languished for years in "status reviews." H.R. Conf. Rep. No. 97–835, at 21 (1982), reprinted in 1982 U.S.C.C.A.N. 2860, 2862. In order to "force action on listing and delisting proposals," *id.*, Congress amended the ESA's petition process expressly to provide certain mandatory deadlines by which the Secretary must act on a petition. Pub. L. 97–304 § 2(a)(2), 96 Stat. 1411, 1412 (1992) (amending 16 U.S.C. § 1533(b)(3) to include the 90–day and 12–month finding requirements). * * * By imposing these deadlines, Congress "replace[d] the Secretary's discretion with mandatory, nondiscretionary duties." * * * The statutory deadlines thus assure that species tagged for protection are not forgotten in an administrative quagmire, but instead are periodically monitored and reconsidered for listing.

Candidate status does not guarantee a similar time frame for administrative action. The cases of both the frog, which the Secretary identified as a candidate in 1991—nine years before she published a proposed rule to list the species as threatened—and the chub, which has been a candidate for nearly two decades without ever being the subject of formal findings, demonstrate that potentially qualified species may sit on candidate lists for extraordinarily long periods before becoming the subject of protective rules. It was in precisely these situations that Congress intended the petitioning process to "interrupt[] the department's priority system by requiring immediate review." H. Rep. No. 95–1625, at 5 (1978), reprinted in 1978 U.S.C.C.A.N. 9453, 8455. Because the PMG policy allows the Secretary to sidestep the prescribed time requirements, it is inconsistent with the ESA. The Secretary therefore improperly relied on the policy when she declined to either make findings in support of a proposed rule or explain why action on the chub was unwarranted or "warranted but precluded" within 12 months after the Center filed its petition.

For the foregoing reasons, we conclude that the PMG policy violates the plain terms of the ESA and that the Secretary improperly relied upon it when she refused to issue 12–month findings in response to the Center's petitions.

Notes and Questions

1. Did the *Center for Biological Diversity* court just impose more "busy work" on the Service by making it go through the official procedural steps

specified for a warranted-but-precluded species, or are there some legitimate reasons for imposing additional procedures for all candidate species?

2.   Can the Services rely on a lack of funding as an excuse to avoid listing? Compare Environmental Defense Center v. Babbitt, 73 F.3d 867, 869 (9th Cir.1995) (accepting FWS's argument that a congressional funding moratorium precluded action on a petition to list the California red-legged frog), *with* Forest Guardians v. Babbitt, 174 F.3d 1178, 1182–84 (10th Cir.1999) (holding that, absent a moratorium, resource limitations do not justify a failure to comply with mandatory duties under the ESA, and ordering FWS to issue a final critical habitat designation for the silvery minnow).

3.   In effect, both candidate status and warranted but precluded status place species in limbo (or, if you're a religious person, purgatory might be more like it). "The U.S. Department of the Interior's Inspector General noted in 1990 that at then-current rates of listing, it could take up to forty-eight years to make listing determinations for all species then on the candidate list, and that thirty-four species had already become extinct while awaiting listing." Bradley C. Karkkainen, *Biodiversity and Land*, 83 Cornell L. Rev. 1, 17 n.74 (1997), citing U.S. Dep't of the Interior, Audit Report: The Endangered Species Program 5, 7 (Rep. No. 90–98, 1990). What actions are most likely to further endanger a candidate species? What actions are most likely to push a listed species over the brink of extinction? Of course, hunting and habitat destruction might do it, what about activities that cause behavioral changes? For example, what if a candidate bison population were harassed by persistent helicopter noise in such a way as to cause a severe decline in reproduction? *See* Cold Mountain v. Garber, 375 F.3d 884 (9th Cir.2004). Do the listing factors and procedural mechanisms provided in the ESA adequately address threats to vulnerable species? Consider this question further when you read the upcoming sections on statutory prohibitions against "take" and jeopardy.

4.   Once a species is listed, its status may be changed or it may be delisted. Every five years the FWS is required to conduct a review of all listed species to determine whether any species should be removed. A species can only be delisted if it is no longer endangered or threatened because the species has become extinct or has recovered. 16 U.S.C. § 1533 (b)(3). Most attempts at delisting have failed. *See* Federico Cheever, *The Rhetoric of Delisting Species Under the Endangered Species Act: How to Declare Victory Without Winning the War*, 31 ELR 11302 (2001).

2.   *Critical Habitat Designations*

In addition to the ESA's protection for listed species, the Act also provides protection for the species' critical habitat. 16 U.S.C. § 1536(a)(2). The FWS designates critical habitat on the basis of the "best scientific data available," but only after taking into consideration economic and other relevant impacts of the designation. The FWS may exclude any area from critical habitat if it finds that the benefits of the exclusion outweigh the benefits of inclusion.

The Act directs that critical habitat be designated at the same time the species is listed. *Id.* § 1533(a)(3), (b)(6)(C). If there is a conservation-based need to list the species prior to the habitat designation, however, the listing determination and habitat designation can be split up. If the habitat is undeterminable due to a lack of information, the Secretary may postpone the designation for up to one year. *Id.* § 1533(b)(6)(C)(ii). When it is not "prudent" to designate critical habitat, the Secretary is excused from doing so. *Id.* The excuse applies when (i) the designation would lead to an increased amount of illegal takings of the species by informing potential takers of the species' location, and (ii) the designation "would not be beneficial to the species." 50 C.F.R. § 424.12(a).

Critical habitat designations were challenged by ranchers and irrigators in Bennett v. Spear, *supra*, Chapter 3.II.B. Their concerns were economic in nature. Why should economic impacts be relevant for a critical habitat designation but not a species' listing decision?

Once designated, critical habitat has little effect on private land. But if federal agency action is required, such as a permit to develop wetlands or the approval of a mining operation of federal lands, ESA § 7 requires consultation to avoid adverse modification of critical habitat. For detail, see Section VI.E, below.

D. The Taking Prohibition

Once a species is listed, ESA § 9 forbids (i) all actions (public or private) that "take" an endangered species, 16 U.S.C. § 1538(a)(1)(B) & (C), or a threatened species, *id.* § 1533(d). The term "take" is broadly defined to mean "harass, harm pursue, hunt, shoot, wound, kill, trap, capture or collect." *Id.* § 1532(19). "Harming" a listed species can include injury through habitat destruction or alteration, as delineated in the following case.

BABBITT v. SWEET HOME CHAPTER

Supreme Court of the United States, 1995.
515 U.S. 687, 115 S.Ct. 2407, 132 L.Ed.2d 597.

JUSTICE STEVENS delivered the opinion of the Court.

The Endangered Species Act ... contains a variety of protections designed to save from extinction species that the Secretary of the Interior designates as endangered or threatened. Section 9 of the Act makes it unlawful for any person to "take" any endangered or threatened species. The Secretary has promulgated a regulation that defines the statute's prohibition on takings to include "significant habitat modification or degradation where it actually kills or injures wildlife." This case presents the question whether the Secretary exceeded his authority under the Act by promulgating that regulation. * * *

Section 3(19) of the Act defines the statutory term "take": "The term 'take' means to harass, harm, pursue, hunt, shoot, wound, kill, trap, capture, or collect, or to attempt to engage in any such conduct." 16 U.S.C. § 1532(19). * * * The Interior Department regulations that implement the statute ... define the statutory term "harm": "Harm in the definition of 'take' in the Act means an act which actually kills or injures wildlife. Such act may include significant habitat modification or degradation where it actually kills or injures wildlife by significantly impairing essential behavioral patterns, including breeding, feeding, or sheltering."

A limitation on the § 9 "take" prohibition appears in § 10(a)(1)(B) of the Act, which Congress added by amendment in 1982. That section authorizes the Secretary to grant a permit for any taking otherwise prohibited by § 9(a)(1)(B) "if such taking is incidental to, and not the purpose of, the carrying out of an otherwise lawful activity." 16 U.S.C. § 1539(a)(1)(B). * * *

Respondents ... brought this declaratory judgment action against petitioners, the Secretary of the Interior and the Director of the Fish and Wildlife Service ... to challenge the statutory validity of the Secretary's regulation defining "harm," particularly the inclusion of habitat modification and degradation in the definition. Respondents challenged the regulation on its face. Their complaint alleged that application of the "harm" regulation to the red-cockaded woodpecker, an endangered species, and the northern spotted owl, a threatened species, had injured them economically.

Respondents advanced three arguments to support their submission that Congress did not intend the word "take" in § 9 to include habitat modification, as the Secretary's "harm" regulation provides. First, they correctly noted that language in the Senate's original version of the ESA would have defined "take" to include "destruction, modification, or curtailment of [the] habitat or range" of fish or wildlife, but the Senate deleted that language from the bill before enacting it. Second, respondents argued that Congress intended the Act's express authorization for the Federal Government to buy private land in order to prevent habitat degradation in § 5 to be the exclusive check against habitat modification on private property. Third, because the Senate added the term "harm" to the definition of "take" in a floor amendment without debate, respondents argued that the court should not interpret the term so expansively as to include habitat modification.

* * * We granted certiorari to resolve the conflict [between the Ninth Circuit, which upheld the Secretary's definition of "harm", and the D.C. Circuit in this case, which invalidated it]. Our consideration of the text and structure of the Act, its legislative history, and the significance of the 1982 amendment persuades us that the [D.C.] Court of Appeals' judgment should be reversed.

* * * First, we assume respondents have no desire to harm either the red-cockaded woodpecker or the spotted owl; they merely wish to continue logging activities that would be entirely proper if not prohibited by the ESA. On the other hand, we must assume, arguendo, that those activities will have the effect, even though unintended, of detrimentally changing the natural habitat of both listed species and that, as a conse-

quence, members of those species will be killed or injured. Under respondents' view of the law, the Secretary's only means of forestalling that grave result—even when the actor knows it is certain to occur—is to use his § 5 authority to purchase the lands on which the survival of the species depends. The Secretary, on the other hand, submits that the § 9 prohibition on takings, which Congress defined to include "harm," places on respondents a duty to avoid harm that habitat alteration will cause the birds unless respondents first obtain a permit pursuant to § 10.

The text of the Act provides three reasons for concluding that the Secretary's interpretation is reasonable. First, an ordinary understanding of the word "harm" supports it. The dictionary definition of the verb form of "harm" is "to cause hurt or damage to: injure." Webster's Third New International Dictionary 1034 (1966). In the context of the ESA, that definition naturally encompasses habitat modification that results in actual injury or death to members of an endangered or threatened species.

Respondents argue that the Secretary should have limited the purview of "harm" to direct applications of force against protected species, but the dictionary definition does not include the word "directly" or suggest in any way that only direct or willful action that leads to injury constitutes "harm."[1]

Moreover, unless the statutory term "harm" encompasses indirect as well as direct injuries, the word has no meaning that does not duplicate the meaning of other words that § 3 uses to define "take." A reluctance to treat statutory terms as surplusage supports the reasonableness of the Secretary's interpretation. * * *

Second, the broad purpose of the ESA supports the Secretary's decision to extend protection against activities that cause the precise harms Congress enacted the statute to avoid. * * * As stated in § 2 of the Act, among its central purposes is "to provide a means whereby the ecosystems upon which endangered species and threatened species depend may be conserved.... " 16 U.S.C. § 1531(b). * * * Congress' intent to provide comprehensive protection for endangered and threatened species supports the permissibility of the Secretary's "harm" regulation. * * *

Respondents advance strong arguments that activities that cause minimal or unforeseeable harm will not violate the Act as construed in

---

1. Respondents and the dissent emphasize what they portray as the "established meaning" of "take" in the sense of a "wildlife take," a meaning respondents argue extends only to "the effort to exercise dominion over some creature, and the concrete effect of [sic] that creature." * * * This limitation ill serves the statutory text, which forbids not taking "some creature" but "tak[ing] any [endangered] species "—a formidable task for even the most rapacious feudal lord. More importantly, Congress explicitly defined the operative term "take" in the ESA ... , thereby obviating the need for us to probe its meaning as we must probe the meaning of the undefined subsidiary term "harm." Finally, Congress' definition of "take" includes several words—most obviously "harass," "pursue," and "wound," in addition to "harm" itself—that fit respondents' and the dissent's definition of "take" no better than does "significant habitat modification or degradation."

the "harm" regulation. Respondents ... present a facial challenge to the regulation. * * * Thus, they ask us to invalidate the Secretary's understanding of "harm" in every circumstance, even when an actor knows that an activity, such as draining a pond, would actually result in the extinction of a listed species by destroying its habitat. Given Congress' clear expression of the ESA's broad purpose to protect endangered and threatened wildlife, the Secretary's definition of "harm" is reasonable. * * *

Third, the fact that Congress in 1982 authorized the Secretary to issue permits for takings that § 9(a)(1)(B) would otherwise prohibit, "if such taking is incidental to, and not the purpose of, the carrying out of an otherwise lawful activity," 16 U.S.C. § 1539(a)(1)(B), strongly suggests that Congress understood § 9(a)(1)(B) to prohibit indirect as well as deliberate takings. The permit process requires the applicant to prepare a "conservation plan" that specifies how he intends to "minimize and mitigate" the "impact" of his activity on endangered and threatened species, 16 U.S.C. § 1539(a)(2)(A), making clear that Congress had in mind foreseeable rather than merely accidental effects on listed species. * * * No one could seriously request an "incidental" take permit to avert § 9 liability for direct, deliberate action against a member of an endangered or threatened species, but respondents would read "harm" so narrowly that the permit procedure would have little more than that absurd purpose. "When Congress acts to amend a statute, we presume it intends its amendment to have real and substantial effect." Stone v. INS, 514 U.S. 386, 397, 115 S. Ct. 1537, 1545, 131 L.Ed.2d 465 (1995). Congress' addition of the § 10 permit provision supports the Secretary's conclusion that activities not intended to harm an endangered species, such as habitat modification, may constitute unlawful takings under the ESA unless the Secretary permits them.

Nor does the Act's inclusion of the § 5 land acquisition authority and the § 7 directive to federal agencies to avoid destruction or adverse modification of critical habitat alter our conclusion. Respondents' argument that the Government lacks any incentive to purchase land under § 5 when it can simply prohibit takings under § 9 ignores the practical considerations that attend enforcement of the ESA. Purchasing habitat lands may well cost the Government less in many circumstances than pursuing civil or criminal penalties. In addition, the § 5 procedure allows for protection of habitat before the seller's activity has harmed any endangered animal, whereas the Government cannot enforce the § 9 prohibition until an animal has actually been killed or injured. The Secretary may also find the § 5 authority useful for preventing modification of land that is not yet but may in the future become habitat for an endangered or threatened species. The § 7 directive applies only to the Federal Government, whereas the § 9 prohibition applies to "any person." Section 7 imposes a broad, affirmative duty to avoid adverse habitat modifications that § 9 does not replicate, and § 7 does not limit its admonition to habitat modification that "actually kills or injures wildlife." Conversely, § 7 contains limitations that § 9 does not, applying only to actions "likely to jeopardize the continued existence of any endangered species or threatened species," 16 U.S.C. § 1536(a)(2), and to modifications of habitat that has been designated "critical" pursuant to § 4, 16 U.S.C. § 1533(b)(2). * * *

We need not decide whether the statutory definition of "take" compels the Secretary's interpretation of "harm," because our conclusions that Congress did not unambiguously manifest its intent to adopt respondents' view and that the Secretary's interpretation is reasonable suffice to decide this case. See generally Chevron U.S.A., Inc. v. Natural Resources Defense Council, Inc., 467 U.S. 837, 104 S. Ct. 2778, 81 L.Ed.2d 694 (1984). The latitude the ESA gives the Secretary in enforcing the statute, together with the degree of regulatory expertise necessary to its enforcement, establishes that we owe some degree of deference to the Secretary's reasonable interpretation.

Our conclusion that the Secretary's definition of "harm" rests on a permissible construction of the ESA gains further support from the legislative history of the statute * * *

When it enacted the ESA, Congress delegated broad administrative and interpretive power to the Secretary. See 16 U.S.C. §§ 1533, 1540(f). The task of defining and listing endangered and threatened species requires an expertise and attention to detail that exceeds the normal province of Congress. Fashioning appropriate standards for issuing permits under § 10 for takings that would otherwise violate § 9 necessarily requires the exercise of broad discretion. The proper interpretation of a term such as "harm" involves a complex policy choice. * * * The judgment of the Court of Appeals is reversed.

Notes and Questions

1. If the Services decided to revise the definition of harm to do away with habitat protection, would they be allowed to do so? Would a definition of harm that encompassed only intentional acts directed at the species be consistent with the ESA?

2. "Harass" is defined by the FWS as the intentional or negligent action or omission which creates the likelihood of injury to wildlife by annoying it to such an extent as to significantly disrupt normal behavioral patterns such as breeding, feeding or sheltering. 50 C.F.R. § 17.3. Could habitat destruction "harass" a species in violation of the ESA?

3. Consider whether a taking under the ESA has occurred in each of the following situations:

a. The defendants were harvesting timber on private land. The nesting habits of the Northern Spotted Owl (an endangered species) were altered as a direct result of the timber harvesting. See Forest Conservation Council v. Rosboro Lumber Co., 50 F.3d 781 (9th Cir.1995).

b. The state of Hawaii maintained sheep and goat herds for sport hunting in a state forest. (The herds were originally domesticated but had been allowed to run wild.) Although hunting did not itself affect the endangered palila bird, the sheep and goat herds destroyed mamane trees. The Palila relies on the mamane tree's pods, flowers, buds, and leaves for food, and also relies on the mamane for shelter and nesting sites. *See* Palila v. Hawaii Department of Land & Natural Resources, 649 F.Supp. 1070 (D.Hawaii 1986), *aff'd*, 852 F.2d 1106 (9th Cir.1988). Has there been a taking, and, if so, who would you hold liable?

c.   Assume that the sheep herds described above consumed a population of a federally listed species of rare plant, the Hawaiian *Hibiscus brackenridgei*. Has there been a taking? (Review the first sentence of Section 9(a)(1) and peruse Section 9(a)(2)(A)-(E) to find the answer.)

d.   The State of Massachusetts issued fishing permits authorizing gill-net and lobster pot fishing. Entanglement with fishing gear is a major source of injury or death to the endangered Northern Right whale. Is the state liable? Are the fishermen? *See* Strahan v. Coxe, 127 F.3d 155 (1st Cir.1997). *See also* Loggerhead Turtle v. County Council of Volusia County, 148 F.3d 1231 (11th Cir.1998) (artificial beachfront lighting that disrupted the behavior of endangered sea turtles is a taking).

e.   A landowner constructed a snake-proof fence along her property line after she discovered a rattlesnake den on adjacent land. The sole purpose of the fence was keep snakes off her property by interfering with normal migratory patterns. The rattlesnake in question is a state-listed threatened species, but assume for purposes of this hypothetical that it is instead federally protected under the ESA. *See* State v. Sour Mountain Realty, Inc., 276 A.D.2d 8, 714 N.Y.S.2d 78 (2000) (finding that the fence was a "taking" under the New York statute, which prohibited hunting and killing protected species and "all lesser acts such as disturbing, harrying or worrying").

In Focus:

IS IT A SECTION 9 VIOLATION TO MOVE AN ENDANGERED SPECIES AWAY FROM DANGER?

Mary Darling, an environmental consultant for land developers in Arizona, pled guilty to violating the ESA by flying 30 endangered Pima pineapple cacti out of an area threatened by development. Darling was sentenced to 5 years probation and a $5,000 fine.

Was Darling unfairly punished for doing something environmentally helpful by protecting the cacti from certain destruction when the land developers began their project? Although Darling probably did not intend to harm the cactus species, she nonetheless violated ESA § 9 by disturbing the plant in its natural habitat. According to Sherry Barrett, a field supervisor for the FWS, "We are trying to find a way to recover the species, and the movement of them is contrary to its survival and recovery." The relocation site didn't provide suitable habitat for the cactus because it lacked the right soil types and other plant species commonly associated with the cactus were absent. Tony Davis, *Biologist Busted for Moving Endangered Cacti*, High Country News (Dec. 22, 2003).

Note that there is no "Good Samaritan" exception in the ESA, as there is in the MMPA. Why not? Should there be?

The take prohibition is explored further in Michael C. Blumm and George Kimbrell, *Flies, Spiders, Toads, Wolves and the Constitutionality of the Endangered Species Act's Take Provision,* 34 Envtl. L.J. 309 (2004); and Federico Cheever and Michael Balster, *The Take Prohibition in Section 9 of the Endangered Species Act: Contradictions, Ugly Ducklings, and Conservation of Species,* 34 Envtl. L.J. 363 (2004).

E. The Federal Consultation and "No Jeopardy" Requirements

Before a federal agency makes "any irreversible or irretrievable commitment of resources" that may have an impact on a listed species, ESA § 7 requires it to fulfill three procedural obligations.

- It must request information from the Secretary concerning whether any species that is "listed" or "proposed to be listed" is present in the area of proposed activity. 16 U.S.C. § 1536 (c)(1); 50 C.F.R. § 402.13.

- If the agency learns that there is a possibility of interfering with a listed species, it is required to prepare a "biological assessment" (BA). A BA is a study to determine whether the listed species is "likely to be affected" by the proposed action. 16 U.S.C. § 1536(c)(1); 50 C.F.R. § 402.12.

- If the agency concludes from its BA that the proposed action is likely to affect a listed species, it must engage in formal consultation with the Secretary to determine whether the activity "is likely to jeopardize the continued existence of" the species or "result in the destruction or adverse modification of" its critical habitat. 16 U.S.C. § 1536 (a)(2); 50 C.F.R. § 402.14. "Jeopardy" means to lessen the likelihood of survival and recovery of the species. 50 C.F.R. § 402.02.

What happens when an "action agency," like the Corps of Engineers, issues a "no effect" determination in its BA, but the FWS disagrees? Must the Corps go forward with formal consultation? In Defenders of Wildlife v. Flowers, 414 F.3d 1066 (9th Cir. 2005), environmental groups challenged the Corps' decision not to consult with FWS on the effects of issuing Clean Water Act permits for two development projects in Arizona. The FWS, concerned about the impact on cactus ferruginous pygmy owls, had requested formal consultation, but the Corps refused on the grounds that no pygmy owls were known to reside within either project area. *Id.* at 1070. The court concluded that FWS "lacks the authority to require the initiation of consultation.... The [Corps] has the ultimate duty to ensure that its actions are not likely to jeopardize listed species or adversely modify critical habitat ... [and] makes the final decision on whether consultation is required.... " *Id.* (citing 51 Fed. Reg. 19926, 19949 (1986)). If the Corps turns out to be wrong, and there is in fact an adverse effect on a listed species or its critical habitat, it can be liable for a take under Section 9 or jeopardy under Section 7. *See id.* ("[the Corps] bears the risk of an erroneous decision"); Bennett v. Spear, 520 U.S. 154, 169, 117 S.Ct. 1154, 1164, 137 L.Ed.2d 281 (1997) ("the action agency must not only articulate its reasons for disagreement (which ordinarily requires species and habitat investigations that are not within the action agency's expertise), ... it runs a substantial risk if its (inexpert) reasons turn out to be wrong").

Section 7 imposes substantive duties on federal agencies as well. At the conclusion of consultation, the Secretary must prepare a "biological opinion" (BO) evaluating the potential effects of the proposed action on the species or its critical habitat. If the Secretary determines that the action will negatively affect the listed species, she must suggest "reasonable and prudent alternatives" (RPAs) that will not cause jeopardy and, if there is no RPA, the project cannot go forward. TVA v. Hill, 437 U.S. 153, 98 S.Ct. 2279, 57 L.Ed.2d 117 (1978). Otherwise, the Secretary must issue a "no jeopardy" opinion and, if a take might occur, prepare an incidental take statement. *Id.* § 1536(b)(4). *See* Section VI. H.2, below.

In Practice:

HOW LONG MAY AN AGENCY DELAY CONSULTATION?

Although there is no established rule regarding the time limit for Section 7 consultation, the generally accepted practice is a "reasonable" amount of time. The word reasonable has been interpreted to mean a matter of days or weeks, and in the rare occasion it includes years. Six years, however, is too long to be considered reasonable, according to In re: American Rivers and Idaho River United, 372 F.3d 413 (D.C.Cir.2004).

When the Idaho Power Company was granted its proposal to construct and operate a three-dam hydropower project, the Federal Energy Regulatory Commission (FERC) recognized that the project "would adversely affect the fish and wildlife resources of the area and particularly the anadromous fish." *Id.* at 415. Even so, the petition of environmental organizations American Rivers and Idaho Rivers United went unanswered by FERC. *Id.* The petitioners asked FERC to formally consult with the Service regarding hydropower operations that affect threatened and endangered anadromous fish in the Snake River basin. *Id.* After waiting six long years, the petitioners were granted a writ of mandamus in order to compel a response by FERC. *Id.*

F. Affirmative Obligations

In addition to the "no jeopardy" requirement, federal agencies are bound by two affirmative obligations under the ESA:

- The duty to conserve (or aid in the recovery of a listed species), and

- The duty to partake in recovery planning, which may include reintroductions of a species into its historic range.

1. *The Duty to Conserve*

Section 7(a)(1) states that the Secretary must review all administered programs and "utilize such programs in furtherance of the purpose of this Act" and that "all other federal agencies * * * utilize their authorities in furtherance of the purposes of this Act by carrying out programs for the conservation of [listed] species." 16 U.S.C. § 1536(a)(1). "It is further decided to be the policy of Congress that all Federal departments and agencies shall seek to conserve [listed] species and shall utilize their authorities in furtherance of the purposes of this Act." *Id.* § 1531(c)(1). The "duty to conserve" is supplemental to the prohibitions against jeopardizing a listed species or its habitat. It is more than a generalized duty; it requires all agencies to consult, develop and take any actions necessary to ensure the survival of each listed species. *See* Mary Christina Wood, *Protecting the Wildlife Trust: A Reinterpretation of Section 7 of the Endangered Species Act,* 34 Envtl. L.J. 2 605 (2004).

In Carson-Truckee Water Conservation District v. Watt, 549 F.Supp. 704 (D.Nev.1982), the petitioners, irrigators, wanted the Secretary of the Interior to store water for the irrigation district. The Secretary argued that § 7(a)(1) required him to use the available water to conserve the cui-ui (a listed fish), which needed higher flows in order to spawn. The petitioners asserted that the Secretary only had a duty to provide flows that were sufficient to maintain a population of cui-ui. The court upheld the Secretary's position and stated that listed species must be given priority over all other purposes until the species is no longer classified as threatened or endangered. *Id.* at 709 (citing TVA v. Hill, 437 U.S. 153, 184, 98 S.Ct. 2279, 57 L.Ed.2d 117 (1978)).

Only a few other courts have been willing to issue an explicit finding that § 7(a)(1) imposes an independent duty to give the conservation of listed species top priority. *See* House v. U.S. Forest Service, 974 F.Supp. 1022 (E.D.Ky.1997) (Forest Service was prohibited from proceeding with proposed timber sale because it had failed to make the listed

Indiana bat a "top priority" and failed to engage in formal consultation with FWS); Bensman v. U.S. Forest Service, 984 F.Supp. 1242, 1246 (D.Mont.1997) (citing *House*). Conversely, several courts have held that the ESA grants agencies some discretion in conservation measures and they may balance this obligation with competing interests. *See* Pyramid Lake Paiute Tribe v. U.S. Dept. of Navy, 898 F.2d 1410 (9th Cir.1990) (Navy's practices in leasing acreage and contiguous water rights to local farmers did not violate its conservation duty to the listed cui-ui fish when it had taken some efforts to conserve the species consistent with the accomplishment of its own primary goals); National Wildlife Federation v. National Park Service, 669 F.Supp. 384 (D.Wyo.1987) (continuing operation of campground under interim management plan pending result of EIS regarding effects on endangered grizzly bear did not violate the ESA).

In Focus:

WHO WINS WHEN THE DUTY TO CONSERVE A LISTED SPECIES INTERFERES WITH THE RIGHT TO MAKE A LIVING?

When an economic practice interferes with the duty to conserve an endangered species, the economic practice may become extinct no matter how beneficial it is to revenues or employment. Longline fishing is a good example. It is an efficient, well-established technique that utilizes a line stretching for several miles behind a single vessel and anchored at specific depths. In addition to anchors, several other lines are attached with baited hooks attached to them; several thousand hooks can be attached to a single longline. The lines typically target swordfish and certain types of tuna and shark.

Long-line fishing has become a source of contention between environmental groups and fisherman. In 1999, the Hawaii Fishery Management Service secured a preliminary injunction to restrict long-line fishing in a large portion of the North Pacific to conserve threatened sea turtle populations. *See* Center for Biological Diversity v. National Marine Fisheries Service, 2001 WL 1602707, *1 (N.D.Cal.2001). As a result, numerous Hawaii fishing boats relocated to California.

Subsequently, Turtle Island Restoration Network sued, alleging that the Service violated the consultation and take provisions of the ESA by issuing permits to long-line fishing vessels in California. Turtle Island Restoration Network v. National Marine Fisheries Service, 340 F.3d 969 (9th Cir.2003). The permits were issued under the High Seas Fishing Compliance Act, which was enacted to protect certain species from depletion due to fishing practices. The court found that the issuance of permits under the Compliance Act constitutes a discretionary agency action with the potential to affect listed species, and was therefore subject to ESA consultation requirements. *Id.*

2. The Duty to Engage in Recovery Planning

The obligation to engage in recovery planning was added to the ESA in the 1978 Amendments. The provision states the Secretary "shall develop and implement plans for the conservation and survival [of listed species] unless he finds that such a plan will not promote the conservation of the species." 16 U.S.C. § 1533(f)(1). "Recovery" is defined by regulation as an "improvement in the status of listed species to the point at which listing is no longer appropriate under the criteria set out in 16 U.S.C. § 1533(a)(1) of the Act." 50 C.F.R. § 402.02. All recovery plans must include:

- a description of site-specific management actions necessary to achieve the conservation and survival of the listed species;

- objective, measurable criteria that would result in a delisting of the species; and

- an estimate of the time and cost needed to successfully execute the recovery plan. 16 U.S.C. § 1533 (f)(1)(B).

The Secretary is required to give priority to "those species, without regard to taxonomic classification, that are most likely to benefit from such plans, particularly those species that are, or may be, in conflict with ... economic activity." *Id.* § 1533(f)(1)(A). Once the plans are developed, an opportunity for public comment must be presented. *Id.*

Although courts tend to give great deference to FWS's expertise in recovery matters, in Fund for Animals v. Babbitt, 903 F.Supp. 96 (D.D.C.1995), as amended, 967 F.Supp. 6 (D.D.C.1997), a district court invalidated FWS's recovery plan for grizzly bears. The court approved of portions of the plan that specified sites inhabited by grizzly bears and described management actions for each of those sites. *Id.* It stated that the statutory provision requiring recovery plans to incorporate a description of "site-specific management actions" necessary to achieve the plan's goals did not require a description of specific techniques or standards, but instead requires FWS, in designating management actions, to consider distinct needs of separate ecosystems or recovery zones occupied by listed species. According to the court, the FWS has flexibility to recommend a wide range of "management actions" in developing and implementing recovery plans. The recovery plan was ultimately found inadequate, however, because it failed to meet the statutory requirement that the agency "shall, to the maximum extent practicable, incorporate into the recovery plan objective measurable criteria which, when met, would result in a determination ... that the species be removed from the list." *Id.* at 111. To satisfy the ESA, it is not sufficient that a recovery plan's criteria would "likely lead" to a finding that the statutory delist-ing factors were met; the FWS must provide an objective assessment of each of the delisting factors in measuring whether threats to the bear would be ameliorated. In this case, habitat losses, the effects of hunting and disease, and genetic isolation of grizzly bears had not been adequately addressed in the plan. *Id.* at 111–114.

For further information on recovery plans and their enforceability, see Sierra Club v. Lujan, 36 Envt'l Rep. Cas. 1533, 1993 WL 151353 (W.D.Tex.1993) (FWS decision not to enforce a recovery plan due to bud-get constraints is improper); National Audubon Society v. Hester, 801 F.2d 405 (D.C.Cir.1986) (FWS's change of tactics in a recovery plan as a result of reevaluation was upheld); National Wildlife Federation v. National Park Service, 669 F.Supp. 384 (D.Wyo.1987) (Secretary's deci-sion not to implement recovery plan until receipt of results of new EIS analysis was upheld); Federico Cheever, *Recovery Planning, the Courts and the Endangered Species Act*, 16 NAT. RESOURCES & ENV'T. 106 (2001).

Recovery plans may include efforts to reintroduce species to their former range. Reintroduction involves the translocation of members of a species into suitable habitat from which the species had been extirpated. Although this is an effective means for species conservation, a substan-tial amount of opposition exists because landowners fear that land-use restrictions will accompany reintroduced species. To reduce these con-cerns, section 10(j) of the 1983 Amendments reduces the protection for reintroduced "experimental populations." 16 U.S.C. § 1539(j).

"Experimental population" is defined as "any population (including offspring arising solely thereof) authorized by the Secretary for release ... but only when, and at such times as the population is wholly separate geographically from non-experimental populations of the same species." *Id.* § 1539(j)(1). Therefore, experimental populations must:

- be composed of individuals released under the authorization of the Secretary, and

- be "wholly separate geographically" from non-experimental (pro-tected) populations of the same species.

For an overview on population segregation under ESA § 10(j), see Federico Cheever, *From Population Segregation to Species Zoning: The Evolution of Introduction Law Under Section 10(j) of the Endangered Species Act,* 1 WYO. L. REV. 287 (2001); Federico Cheever, *The Rhetoric of Delisting Species under the Endangered Species Act: How to Declare Vic-tory without Winning the War*, 31 ENVTL L. RPTR. 11302 (2001); Nicole R. Matthews, *Who is the Predator and Who IS the Prey? The Endangered Species Act and the Reintroduction of Predator Species into the Wild*, 6 ENVTL. LAW 183 (1999).

Before the Secretary may authorize the release of an experimental population, she must find that the release will "further the conservation" of the species, and determine whether the population "is essential to the continued existence" of the species. *Id.* § 1539(j)(2)(A) & (B). If the population is deemed essential, it is to be offered the same protection as threatened species. *Id.* § 1539(j)(2)(C). If the population is deemed nonessential, it is to be treated as a threatened species, with the following exemptions: (i) for purposes of § 7, agencies are only required to "confer" with the Secretary (instead of "consult") unless the nonessential population is located within a national wildlife refuge or national park; (ii) agencies are not required to insure that their actions do not jeopardize non-essential species, *id.* § 1536(a)(2); and (iii) the Secretary may not designate critical habitat for nonessential species. *Id.* § 1539(j)(2)(C)(ii).

One of the most successful reintroductions under § 10(j) involved imports of Canadian gray wolves to repopulate the Greater Yellowstone Ecosystem. Wolves were native to the area but by 1930 they had been completely extirpated from the Rocky Mountains, in large part due to federal and state eradication efforts. The wolf was one of the first species to be listed as endangered under the ESA. The goal of the wolf recovery plan was to establish 100 wolves, or approximately 10 breeding pairs, in each of two areas for 3 successive years. *See* Yellowstone National Park, Wolf Reintroduction to Yellowstone, http://www.nps.gov/yell/nature/animals/wolf/wolfrest.html. Reintroduction to the Greater Yellowstone area—over 16 million acres of federal public lands—was a key component of the wolf's prospects for recovery.

Left: Wayne Brewster, former Deputy Director, Yellowstone Center for Resources, preparing for final wolf release, April 11, 1996. Photo by S. Zellmer. Right: wolf in crate, ready for release. Photo by Jim Peaco, National Park Service.

Once the recovery plan and accompanying EIS were issued, the FWS, in cooperation with the National Park Service, transported a total of 31 Canadian gray wolves in 1995 and 1996 to locations within the Park and in National Forests in Idaho. The question of whether the experimental Canadian population would be "wholly separate geographically" from any native populations became a potential sticking point, and opponents from the ranching community, states' rights organizations, and even environmental groups challenged the plan.

In United States v. McKittrick, 142 F.3d 1170 (9th Cir.1997), *cert. denied,* 525 U.S. 1072, 119 S.Ct. 806, 142 L.Ed.2d 667 (1999), McKittrick attempted to show that the reintroduction was illegal so as to defeat a prosecution against him for killing a reintroduced wolf. The court rejected his arguments, and held that the experimental population consisting of imported Canadian wolves met the requirement that populations be "wholly separate geographically" from naturally occurring wolves in the release area. It upheld the FWS's determination that there would be no overlap, despite the possible presence of individual wolves in the area, because § 10(j) prohibits only population overlap, not individual overlap. "Although McKittrick points to sporadic sightings of isolated indigenous wolves in the release area, lone wolves, or 'dispersers,' do not constitute a population." *Id.* at 1175, citing 50 C.F.R. § 17.3 (defining population as "a group of fish or wildlife ... in common spatial arrangement that interbreed when mature"); 59 Fed.Reg. at 60,256 (defining gray wolf population as "at least two breeding pairs of gray wolves that each successfully raise at least two young ... for 2 consecutive years"). *See also* Wyoming Farm Bureau Fed. v. Babbitt, 199 F.3d 1224 (10th Cir.2000) (rejecting challenges to the wolf reintroduction program brought by national and state farm bureaus, individual researchers and environmental groups).

By March 2004, the population of wolves in the Northern Rockies was well over 700 individuals. U.S. Dept. of Interior, Wolf Management in the Northern Rocky Mountains, http://www.doi.gov/issues/wolfmanagement.html. The species has established itself so well in and around Yellowstone Park that the FWS attempted to "downlist" the wolf in the lower 48 states from endangered to threatened in 2003, but its decision was vacated and remanded for procedural and substantive deficiencies in National Wildlife Federation v. Norton, 2005 WL 2000712 (D. Vt. 2005). The entire ecosystem of the Yellowstone area has felt the cascading effects of wolves resuming their spot at the top of the food chain. Prior to their reintroduction, elk "ate young, tasty trees with impunity"; after the wolf reappeared on the scene, elk dispersed from the river valleys, and riparian vegetation rebounded. Warren Cornwall, *Ecological Changes Linked to Wolves*, Seattle Times, Jan. 12, 2005, at B1, *supra*, Chapter 2.II.E (Biodiversity).

Despite the significant gains, "wolves still occupy less than five percent of their original range in the lower 48 states, and the seemingly healthy wolf populations in Alaska and Canada face continued threats."

Defenders of Wildlife, State of the Wolf 2004, at 2, http://
www.defenders.org/wildlife/new/wolves.html.

Websources:

Gray Wolf Reintroduction

- U.S. Dept. of Interior, Wolf Management in the Northern Rocky
  Mountains, http://www.doi.gov/issues/wolfmanagement.html

- Yellowstone National Park, Wolf Reintroduction to Yellowstone,
  http://www.nps.gov/yell/nature/animals/wolf/wolfrest.html

- Defenders of Wildlife, State of the Wolf 2004, at 2, http://
  www.defenders.org/wildlife/new/wolves.html

- Farm Bureau and the Gray Wolf, http://www.fb.org/news/
  graywolf.html (News Release Jan. 23, 2005)

- Ralph Maughan's Wildlife Report, http://www.forwolves.org/ralph/
  wolfrpt. html (providing news and statistics on wolves and wolf
  sightings)

*Bison and members of the Druid Wolf Pack in the Lamar Valley, Winter 2003.
Photo credit:* **Doug Smith or Bob Landis**, *Yellowstone Center for Resources.*

FWS has used section 10(j) with varying degrees of success to reintroduce experimental populations of several other species, including red
wolves, Mexican wolves, sea otters, whooping cranes, black-footed fer-
rets, California condors and Delmarva fox squirrels. *See* Cheever, *From
Population Segregation to Species Zoning, supra,* at 288–89. The attempt
to reestablish a population of California condors was perhaps the most
disappointing reintroduction. By the 1980s, California condors were hovering at the brink of extinction due to lead poisoning, collisions with
power lines, and shooting by ranchers. Fewer then 30 of these birds were

living, all of them in captivity. In an effort to recover the species, condors were released near the Grand Canyon and in Big Sur, California, but FWS has since attempted to recapture them and take them back into captivity because of high mortality incidence due in large part to the consumption of lead shot in their prey. Deborah Schoch, *Flying into Trouble: Lead Imperils Released Condors*, Seattle Times, June 22, 2001, at A3. *See* National Audubon Society v. Hester, 801 F.2d 405 (D.C.Cir.1986) (upholding FWS's invocation of NEPA's emergency provisions for the removal of condors from the wild). For a critique of recovery programs that rely on captive breeding, see Mark Derr, *As Rescue Plan for Threatened Species, Breeding Programs Falter*, N.Y. Times, Jan. 19, 1999, at F6.

The federal government has been criticized for spending millions of dollars on reintroducing "charismatic mega fauna" like wolves and relatively little on protecting imperiled plants and insects. If you were the director of FWS, how would you prioritize limited funds in order to achieve the ESA's conservation objectives? For perspectives on the government's ESA priorities, see John Copeland Nagle, *Playing Noah*, 82 Minn. L. Rev. 1171, 1255–58 (1998) (noting that insects and plants receive less protection than animals); Jim Chen, *Webs of Life: Biodiversity Conservation as a Species of Information Policy*, 89 Iowa L. Rev. 495, 557–558 (2004) (explaining that, although insects are a vital part of ecosystems, the ESA provides little to no protection); Daniel J. Rohlf, *Section 4 of the Endangered Species Act: Top Ten Issues for the Next Thirty Years*, 34 Envtl. L. 483, 492–493 (2004) (criticizing the government's failure to list species based on purely scientific information).

G. Enforcement

1. Citizen Suits

Like many modern federal environmental statutes, the ESA contains a citizen suit provision. Any individual may sue any other individual, including governmental entities, alleged to be in violation of any ESA provision or implementing regulation. 16 U.S.C. § 1540 (g)(1)(A). Citizen suits may be filed for violation of a § 9 taking if an action or proposed action will constitute an alleged taking, or create an imminent threat of harm to a listed species. Citizen suits may also be filed to compel the FWS to take specified emergency action or to compel the FWS to perform non-discretionary duties. *Id.* § 1540(g)(1)(B) & § 1540(g)(1)(C). *See, e.g.*, Center for Biological Diversity v. Norton, 254 F.3d 833 (9th Cir.2001) (compelling a response to a listing petition).

In order to bring a citizen suit, the plaintiff must provide adequate notice pursuant to § 1540(g)(2), and meet Article III standing and other jurisdictional requirements. If the Secretary has already commenced a proceeding against the defendant, and is diligently prosecuting the violator, a citizen suit is barred. 16 U.S.C. § 1540(g)(2). If the description of the plaintiff's intended allegations is not specific enough, an ESA suit may be dismissed, even if timely notice was provided. *Southwest Center for Biological Diversity v. United States Bureau of Reclamation,* 143 F.3d 515 (9th Cir.1998).

Standing and other jurisdictional requirements are addressed in detail in Chapter 3. Two of the Court's landmark standing cases involve ESA issues: Lujan v. Defenders of Wildlife, 504 U.S. 555, 112 S.Ct. 2130, 119 L.Ed.2d 351 (1992), and Bennett v. Spear, 520 U.S. 154, 117 S.Ct. 1154, 137 L.Ed.2d 281 (1997).

In Focus:

SHOULD CIRCUS ELEPHANTS START THROWING THEIR WEIGHT AROUND?

If environmental groups interested in the well-being of Asian elephants performing in Ringling Bros. and Barnum and Bailey Circus can't defend the animals against mistreatment, who can? A complaint in American Society for the Prevention of Cruelty to Animals v. Ringling Bros. and Barnum & Bailey Circus, 317 F.3d 334 (D.C.Cir 2003), was brought under the citizen suit provision of the ESA. The plaintiffs alleged severe mistreatment of their elephant friends, citing instances resulting in permanent damage to the animals. The district court held that the plaintiffs had no standing, because they themselves were not suffering with their elephant friends.

The court of appeals reversed, concluding that Thomas Rider, the former elephant handler who left his job because he felt that the elephants were being mistreated, had alleged a present, imminent injury. *Id.* at 337 (citing *Defenders of Wildlife,* 504 U.S. at 560).

> [A]n injury in fact can be found when a defendant adversely affects a plaintiff's enjoyment of flora or fauna, which the plaintiff wishes to enjoy again upon the cessation of the defendant's actions. Rider says he became attached to the elephants when he worked with them and would like to ... continue his personal relationship with them* * * [Although] the prospect of his working in the elephant barns again is nil[,] ... a fair construction of his allegation encompasses Rider's attending the circus ... and viewing the show from the audience. From this vantage point he might observe either direct physical manifestations of the alleged mistreatment of the elephants, such as lesions, or detect negative effects on the animals' behavior.... This takes his claim out of the category of a generalized interest.

Id. Mr. Rider also showed redressability, by seeking an injunction that would stop the circus from continuing its mistreatment and an order directing the circus to forfeit possession of the elephants. *Id.* at 339.

Courts are not always willing to find standing when plaintiffs assert an interest in preventing harm to wildlife species. In Humane Society v. Babbitt, 46 F.3d 93, 97–100 (D.C.Cir.1995), a plaintiff who alleged an injury based on her lost opportunity to study Asian elephants and her inability to observe a particular elephant at the zoo lacked standing. Is *Humane Society* distinguishable from *American Society for the Prevention of Cruelty to Animals*?

For additional information about standing in animal welfare cases, see David S. Favre, *Judicial Recognition of the Interests of Animals—A New Tort*, 2005 Mich. St. L. Rev. 333 (2005); Steven M. Wise, *Dismantling the Barriers to Legal Rights for Nonhuman Animals*, 7 Animal L. 9 (2001); STEVEN M. WISE, RATTLING THE CAGE—TOWARD LEGAL RIGHTS FOR ANIMALS (2000). *See also* Christopher D. Stone, *Should Trees Have Standing? Towards Natural Rights for Legal Objects, 45 S. Cal. L. Rev. 450* (1972); Sierra Club v. Morton, 405 U.S. 727, 743, 92 S.Ct. 1361, 31 L.Ed.2d 636 (1972) (Douglas, J., dissenting) (citing Stone's article and expressing a belief that, like ships and other inanimate objects, the environment should have standing in its own right).

The claim must also be brought at the proper time; it must be ripe and it cannot be moot. In Sierra Club v. U.S. Dept. of Energy, 287 F.3d 1256 (10th Cir.2002), the court held that plaintiff's allegations regarding a failure to comply with the ESA were ripe because defendants did not partake in the necessary consultation with the FWS prior to granting a right of way easement. Conversely, in Shields v. Norton, 289 F.3d 832 (5th Cir.2002), cert. denied, 537 U.S. 1071, 123 S.Ct. 663, 154 L.Ed.2d 565 (2002), plaintiff's ESA claim was not ripe. The plaintiff in *Norton* was an aquifer water user who had received a notice letter from an environmental organization suggesting the possibility of citizens' suit against him for alleged violations of the take provision of the ESA. There had been previous litigation against other aquifer users and newspaper articles mentioned the possibility of additional enforcement actions if species were harmed. The plaintiff sought a declaration that the ESA's take provision, as applied to species in the Edwards Aquifer, was unconstitutional. Although the threat of litigation can establish a justiciable controversy if it is specific and concrete, the environmental group's letter did not rise to that level; therefore, plaintiff's claim was not ripe. *Id.* at 836–37.

2. *Federal Enforcement*

Section 11 of the ESA pertains to civil and criminal enforcement of the Act. 16 U.S.C. § 1540(a)-(b). The severity of the sanction for a "take" turns on the following factors: whether the violation involves an endangered or a threatened species; the level of the violator's knowledge; and the violator's occupation. Penalties are more stringent when the violation affects an endangered species rather than a threatened species. If the violator is a person "engaged in business as an importer or exporter of fish, wildlife, or plants," she is automatically subject to strict civil liability. *Id*. § 1540(a)(1), (b)(1). Civil sanctions are harsher for any individual who "knowingly violates" the prohibitions. Civil remedies include monetary penalties and injunctive relief. Individuals that violate the taking, importing/exporting, transporting or selling of endangered species prohibitions are subject to monetary fines of no more than $25,000. Importers/exporters who violate any other sections of the Act, such as the prohibitions pertaining to threatened species, are subject to fines of no more than $12,000. Finally, any individual (other than an importer/exporter) who otherwise violates any provision of the Act without "knowingly" doing so is subject to a fine up to $500.

Criminal penalties result only from "knowing" violations of the Act. *See* United States v. McKittrick, 142 F.3d 1170 (9th Cir.1998), *cert. denied,* 525 U.S. 1072, 119 S.Ct. 806, 142 L.Ed.2d 667 (1999) (upholding a conviction for shooting a wolf, and holding that defendant need not have knowledge that he was shooting a listed species to have engaged in "knowing" conduct; it was sufficient that he knew he was shooting an animal, which turned out to be a protected wolf). Violators who knowingly violate the provisions forbidding taking, importing/exporting, transporting or selling endangered species are subject to up to $50,000 and one year in jail. 16 U.S.C. § 1540(b)(1). Individuals who knowingly violate the regulations applicable to threatened species are subject to criminal penalties up to $25,000 and six months in jail. *Id*. Other penalties for criminal violations include losing all federal licenses, leases and hunting permits, and the forfeiture of any equipment and transportation vehicles used in furtherance of the violation. In addition, all fish, wildlife or plants taken, possessed, sold, purchased or transported in violation of the ESA are subject to forfeiture. *Id*. § 1540(e)(4)(A).

To aid enforcement, the ESA authorizes the payment of bounties to individuals who furnish information leading to an arrest, criminal conviction, civil penalty or forfeiture. The amount of the reward is discretionary but must be paid with money received from fines for ESA violations. Section 11 also provides compensation for the reasonable and necessary costs incurred in providing temporary care for any fish, wildlife or plant pending disposition of a penalty proceeding. *Id*. § 1540(d).

H. Moderating the Severity of the ESA

The potency of ESA application is tempered in several ways. The first is the "God Squad" exemption. Second is the incidental take permit or statement, and third is a provision authorizing habitat conservation plans (HCPs). Finally, various exemptions are provided for self-defense and other types of activities.

1. The "God Squad"

The Endangered Species Committee, or "God Squad," consists of six cabinet-level officers (the Secretary of the Interior, Secretary of Army, Secretary of the Agriculture, the Chair of the Council of Economic Advisors, the Administrator of the Environmental Protection Agency, and the

Administrator of the National Oceanic and Atmospheric Administration), and the governor of the state where the action is proposed to occur. 16 U.S.C. § 1536(e). This broad range of individuals is specifically chosen to provide a variety of viewpoints, in order that all competing interests are represented.

An exemption from the God Squad is rare and occurs only as a last resort. If a proposed federal action would violate either the jeopardy or habitat modification prohibitions of Section 7, and there are no reasonable and prudent alternatives to the proposal, an exemption may be granted in certain limited circumstances. *Id.* § 1536 (g)(1).

To receive an exemption, the applicant must meet certain threshold requirements, including conducting all consultation responsibilities "in good faith," and making "a reasonable and responsible effort to develop and fairly consider modifications or other reasonable and prudent alternatives to the proposed agency action." *Id.* § 1536(g)(3)(A). To grant an exemption, at least five Committee members must determine that: (i) there are no reasonable and prudent alternatives to the agency action; (ii) the benefits of the action clearly outweigh the benefits of alternative actions and the action is in the public interest; (iii) the action is of regional or national significance; and (iv) neither the federal agency concerned nor the applicant made any irreversible or irretrievable commitment of resources. *Id.* § 1536(H)(1)(A). If the exemption is granted, the Committee must impose "reasonable mitigation and enhancement measures" that will "minimize the adverse effect" of the project on the listed species. *Id.* § 1536(h)(1)(B).

As of 2004, the God Squad has granted only two exemptions: the Grayrocks dam and reservoir project in Wyoming and a block of Pacific Northwest timber sales. Congress, on the other hand, has carved out an array of narrow exemptions on a case-by-case basis, often in huge appropriations bills. For a case study of congressional exemptions from the ESA, see Stephen W. Owens, *Congressional Action Exempts Observatory from the Endangered Species Act*, 13 J. ENERGY NAT. RES. & ENVTL. L. 314 (1993).

2. *Incidental Take*

A second exemption may be granted if the Secretary: (i) issues an "incidental take statement" (ITS) in its biological opinion after formal § 7 consultation with a federal agency; or (ii) issues an "incidental take permit" under § 10. Section 10 permits require HCPs, which are described below. With respect to§ 7 consultation, if the Secretary concludes both that the proposed action "is not likely to jeopardize the continued existence of any listed species or result in the destruction or adverse modification of critical habitat" or that reasonable and prudent alternatives will prevent jeopardy, and that any "incidental" taking that occurs will not jeopardize the species, the Secretary is to issue an ITS. *Id.* § 1536(b)(4).

In *Pacific Coast Federation v. National Marine Fisheries Service,* 265 F.3d 1028 (9th Cir.2001), the court remanded "no jeopardy" opinions and ITSs that had been issued for proposed logging projects. It concluded that the scientific evidence was insufficient to support the Service's conclusion that natural vegetation regrowth could adequately mitigate degradation and ensure that fish could return to spawning habitat. An expert biologist opined that the reliance on projected restoration was scientifically unsound, and that short-term effects on fish populations had been ignored. *Id.* at 1037–38. Accordingly, it was arbitrary to find that the projects posed no jeopardy to the fish. *Id.*

To prepare an adequate ITS, the Services must include the following elements:

- An assessment of the impact of any incidental takings on the species

- Reasonable and prudent measures necessary to minimize impacts

- Terms and conditions to protect the species. 16 U.S.C. § 1536(b)(4).

Any taking which is not in complete compliance with the terms and conditions of the ITS is a prohibited, and will subject the action agency and its employees to civil and criminal penalties under the Act. Bennett v. Spear, 520 U.S. 154, 117 S.Ct. 1154, 137 L.Ed.2d 281 (1997).

Notes and Questions

1. In Arizona Cattle Growers' Assn. v. U.S. Fish and Wildlife Service, 273 F.3d 1229 (9th Cir.2001), ranchers seeking to obtain grazing permits on federal land challenged FWS's decision to require an ITS as a condition of its "no jeopardy" opinion for those permits. The court held that the issuance of an ITS for the razorback sucker and the pygmy-owl was arbitrary.

> The Fish and Wildlife Service contends that the district court erred in scrutinizing its decision to issue Incidental Take Statements because it is statutorily required pursuant to the ESA to "issue an ITS in all no-jeopardy determinations" * * * [and] that it should be permitted to issue an [ITS] whenever there is any possibility, no matter how small, that a listed species will be taken. * * *

> Section 7(b)(4) of the ESA provides [for an ITS] … "[i]f after consultation … , the Secretary concludes that … the taking of an endangered species or a threatened species incidental to the agency action will not violate such subsection" * * * We therefore agree with ACGA that the plain language of the ESA does not dictate that the Fish and Wildlife Service must issue an ITS irrespective of whether any incidental takings will occur. * * * [I]t would be nonsensical to require the issuance of [an ITS] when no takings cognizable under Section 9 are to occur. * * * Accordingly, we hold that … it is arbitrary and capricious to issue an [ITS] when the Fish and Wildlife Service has no rational basis to conclude that a take will occur incident to the otherwise lawful activity. * * *

Although once abundant in the project area, there have been no reported sightings of the razorback sucker in the area since 1991 and "effects of the livestock grazing program on individual fish or fish populations probably occur infrequently." Nevertheless, the Fish and Wildlife Service issued an [ITS] for the fish, anticipating take as a result of the direct effects of grazing in the project area, the construction of fences, the construction and existence of stock tanks for non-native fish, as well as other "activities in the watershed." Because the Fish and Wildlife Service could not directly quantify the level of incidental take, it determined that authorized take would be exceeded if range conditions in the allotment deteriorated and cattle grazing could not be ruled out as a cause of the deterioration. * * * This speculative evidence ... is woefully insufficient to meet the standards imposed by the governing statute. * * *

As with the razorback sucker, the record does not support a claim that the cactus ferruginous pygmy-owl exists in the area of the allotment in question, and the Fish and Wildlife Service thus acted in an arbitrary and capricious manner in issuing an [ITS] for that species. * * *

Why were the ranchers unhappy, when the FWS had issued a "no jeopardy" opinion? What more could they want? Why wasn't it appropriate for FWS to take a precautionary stance by issuing an ITS for the sucker and the pygmy-owl?

2. Should the government be permitted to demand that a party perform duties that are unrelated, or only marginally related, to those specified in their government granted permit? In a separate part of *Arizona Cattle Growers* related to the loach minnow, the court found that if the FWS grants an ITS for the use of land pursuant to a grazing permit, it is arbitrary and capricious to demand that the permit holder improve preexisting environmental conditions. If the FWS had articulated a reasonable basis for requiring ecological improvement on the grazing allotment to prevent a potential take of the loach minnow, would the court have upheld the ITS? Or would the imposition of a general requirement of ecological improvement in an ITS be too much regardless? What if the FWS had not only articulated a reasonable basis for the requirement, but also specified objective, measurable criteria for habitat improvement that would benefit the minnow? According to this opinion, the ITS should be aimed at preventing deterioration of existing environmental conditions due to the activity in question. Arguably, this is a logical response, given the language of 16 U.S.C. § 1536(b)(4). But does this result best effectuate the ESA's purposes?

3. *Habitat Conservation Plans (HCPs)*

In 1982, Congress amended § 10 to authorize a taking by private actions if it "is incidental to and not the purpose of, carrying out an otherwise lawful activity." 16 U.S.C. § 1539(a)(1)(B). This is called an incidental take permit, or ITP (in contrast to the ITS, discussed above, which can only be issued for federal actions). The § 10 ITP requirements are more demanding than the ITS provisions of § 7. Most importantly, a habitat conservation plan (HCP) must be provided by the § 10 applicant to ensure adequate minimization and mitigation of the effects resulting from the incidental take. An HCP must specify:

- The impact that will likely result from such a taking;

- the steps the applicant will take to minimize and mitigate such impacts, and the funding that will be available to implement such steps;

- what alternatives were considered and why they are not being utilized; and

- other necessary or appropriate measures that the Services may require.

16 U.S.C. § 1539(a)(2)(A).

HCPs are seen as a way to work with developers while striving to protect endangered and threatened species and their habitat. Between 1982–1992, only 14 incidental take permits were issued in connection with HCP's (slightly more than one per year). Edward D. Koch, *The Practice of Endangered Species Conservation on Private Lands: One Federal Biologist's Experiences*, 38 Id. L.Rev. 505, 510 (2002). To deflect the mounting criticisms of the ESA by developers and their congressmen, the Clinton Administration made HCPs a top priority. As a result, wildlife agencies obtained more than 300 HCPs governing approximately 20 million acres and covering more than 200 endangered or threatened species between 1993–2002. *Id.* Conservationists argue that a considerable number of these plans allow significant habitat destruction, lack dependable mitigation measures, and do not contain any "bottom line" standards to prohibit harmful activities.

NWF v. BABBITT: VICTORY FOR SMART GROWTH AND IMPERILED WILDLIFE
John Kostyack
31 ENVTL. L. REP. 10712 (2001)

Congress added the HCP tool to the ESA in 1982, in an effort to conserve imperiled species facing the risk of habitat destruction due to non-federal economic activities. It viewed HCPs as a win-win situation for imperiled species and development interests: in return for securing ITPs allowing development interests to take a limited amount of habitat, they would commit in an HCP to protect and manage other habitat areas, thus enhancing the species' overall recovery chances. * * *

The Clinton-era expansion of HCPs has been controversial among environmentalists and independent scientists who have shown how the plans allow substantial amounts of habitat destruction while providing few reliable mitigation measures in exchange. In response ... the two agencies responsible for the administration of the ESA ... amended their HCP handbook to include new guidelines on five key features of conservation planning: biological goals, monitoring, adaptive management, limits on permit duration, and citizen participation.

The suggestions from the federal wildlife agencies were a positive step forward. However, the guidelines did not fully address the concerns of environmental groups and other critics of the HCP program. The new guidelines are completely voluntary and, thus, leave open the possibility that the glaring gaps in species protection found in past plans will be built into future plans and continue to place imperiled species at risk. * * *

Thus, to date, the only enforceable obligations placed on ITP applicants are the statutory standards themselves, of which there are six. Under ESA § 10(a)(2)(B) and § 7(a)(2), before issuing an ITP, the FWS or the NMFS must find that:

(1) the taking will be incidental;

(2) the applicant will, to the maximum extent practicable, minimize and mitigate the impacts of the taking (the "(B)(ii) finding");

(3) the applicant will ensure that adequate funding for the plan and procedures to deal with unforeseen circumstances will be provided (the "(B) (iii) finding"); and

(4) the taking will not appreciably reduce the likelihood of the survival and recovery of the species in the wild (the "(B)(iv) finding"). * * *

(5) the ITP will not jeopardize the existence of the species covered by the plan; and

(6) the ITP will not destroy or adversely modify the critical habitat of such species, if any critical habitat has been designated. * * *

Although these standards appear rigorous, they have not (as discussed above) generally produced scientifically rigorous HCPs. The FWS' spotty implementation of these standards, and the reluctance ... to take regulatory steps to prevent such poor implementation in the future, continues to put imperiled species at unnecessary risk. * * *

Prior to the Clinton Administration, the courts issued only one ruling concerning HCP approval standards. In *Friends of Endangered Species v. Jantzen*, the U.S. Court of Appeals for the Ninth Circuit rejected a challenge to the first HCP ever approved, a plan that addressed real estate development in and around the habitats of two listed butterflies on San Bruno Mountain in northern California. Because this HCP protected a substantial percentage of the remaining habitats of the two species (87% and 92%, respectively), provided for restoration of degraded habitats, and had earlier been deemed by Congress to be a "model" of endangered species conservation, this ruling does not provide much of a road map for evaluating the more controversial HCPs of the 1990s.

* * * In *Sierra Club v. Babbitt*, a federal court struck down two HCPs allowing development in the habitat of the endangered Alabama beach mouse. The court focused solely on the FWS' ESA § 10(a)(2)(B)(ii)

finding, i.e., that the applicants would minimize and mitigate takings of the species to the maximum extent practicable. According to the court, this finding was arbitrary because the promised mitigation measures were to be funded in part by voluntary contributions from unidentified third parties. * * * The ruling highlighted how the FWS was allowing HCPs to go forward despite a high degree of uncertainty about whether developers would succeed in mitigating the harm to be caused by their proposed activity, and despite the developers' failure to take financial responsibility for addressing the inevitable challenges of achieving the mitigation goal.

In *Loggerhead Turtle v. County Council of Volusia County, Florida*, a federal district court upheld an HCP allowing motor vehicles to be driven in and around the nesting areas of endangered sea turtles. * * * The court upheld the FWS' ESA § 10(a)(2)(B)(iii) finding, i.e., that the county would ensure adequate funding, because the FWS had an opportunity prior to the HCP to observe the county's commitment to funding the HCP's contemplated programs, and because the ITP was made conditional upon the FWS' approval of the county's future budget allocations. This language raises important questions, addressed again in *NWF v. Babbitt*, about whether permit revocation authority provides a sufficient safeguard for species to justify allowing an HCP with highly uncertain conservation measures to go forward. * * *

Notes and Questions

1. The author goes on to criticize the HCP at issue in *NWF v. Babbitt, supra,* 128 F.Supp.2d 1274, 1299 (E.D.Cal.2000), which authorized development in the Natomas Basin, a 53,000 acre tract of largely undeveloped land stretching north of the City of Sacramento. The area provides habitat for the Giant Garter Snake and the Swainson's hawk, threatened species under the federal ESA and the California ESA, respectively. *Id.* at 1277. The HCP's primary defects were the lack of regional responsibility and the Service's inability to secure adequate funding. The court agreed, and invalidated the HCP. *Id.* at 1295. "The FWS's willingness to proceed without an adequate funding mechanism also extended to its willingness to approve a regional HCP premised on the participation of only one public actor, the city of Sacramento, when, in fact, success ultimately depended on multi-jurisdictional cooperation. This was fatal for several reasons, including the failure to discuss the effect on the [HCP] ... design if only the city participated in the Plan." A. Dan Tarlock, *Slouching Toward Eden: The Eco–Pragmatic Challenges of Ecosystem Revival,* 87 Minn. L. Rev. 1173, 1203 (2003) (citing *NWF,* 128 F.Supp.2d at 1298–1300).

2. The efficacy of mitigation measures and the availability of long-term funding are not the only controversial aspects of HCPs. Another highly controversial component of the Clinton Administration's HCP initiative was a policy called "no surprises". *See* Jon Margolis, *Critics say "No Surprises" Means No Protection*, High Country News, Aug. 4, 1997. The No Surprises Policy provided assurance to developers that once they obtained permits to incidentally take endangered species in exchange for adopting a HCP, they

would not be required to expend additional resources for any unforeseen circumstances that could arise and threaten the species managed in the HCP. Spirit of the Sage Council v. Norton, 294 F.Supp.2d 67, 79 (D.D.C.2003), as amended, 2004 WL 1326279 (D.D.C.2004) (quoting 64 Fed. Reg. 32,712) (1999). This Policy "sweetened the pot" and brought developers to the table. Although the No Surprises Rule prompted a dramatic increase in HCPs, it was criticized by environmentalists as obstructing species recovery, because the Services' ability to make necessary changes was "dependent on the availability of appropriated funds." Spirit of the Sage Council sued, claiming that the Policy was issued in violation of the APA's rulemaking requirements and the ESA. The plaintiffs prevailed, and the No Surprises Policy was remanded for further proceedings consistent with the APA. *Id.* at 91–92. Although the court did not resolve the issue of whether the Policy was contrary to the ESA, it enjoined the agencies from approving incidental take permits containing No Surprise assurances pending completion of rulemaking proceedings. *Id.* Should the Services issue a new No Surprises policy to entice developers to enter into HCPs?

3.   Developers have proposed alternative mechanisms for minimizing the impact of the taking prohibition without undermining ESA objectives. For example, an agreement between the FWS and a timber company applied to four million acres of private timberland to protect the Red–Cockaded Woodpecker, while allowing harvest within the species habitat. The company agreed to pay the FWS $5000/year for five years to monitor the reproductive success and clan size of woodpecker colonies located on its land and to permit FWS personnel to enter the lands to confirm compliance with conservation measures. For additional information on HCPs, see Peter Kareiva et al., Using Science in Habitat Conservation Plans (American Center of Biological Sciences and National Center for Ecological Analysis and Syntheses (1999)); Marj Nelson, U.S. FWS, Habitat Conservation Planning, 24 Endangered Species Bull. 12 (Nov./Dec. 1999); Robert D. Thornton, *Habitat Conservation Plans: Frayed Safety Nets or Creative Partnerships*? 16 Natural Res. & Env't.94 (2001); Graham M. Lyons, *Habitat Conservation Plans: Restoring the Promise of Conservation*, 23 Environs Env'l Law and Policy 83 (Fall, 1999).

4.   ESA Defenses

The following provisions provide additional means of avoiding the taking prohibition:

•   No civil or criminal penalties may be imposed if the "defendant committed an act based on a good faith belief that he was acting to protect himself or herself, a member of his or her family, or any other individual from bodily harm" from a listed species. 16 U.S.C. § 1540(a)(3), (b)(3).

•   The hardship exemption relieves any person that entered into a contract with respect to a species that is subsequently listed, and can show the listing causes an undue economic hardship, from the taking prohibitions. 16 U.S.C § 1539 (b)(1).

•   There is an exemption for takings by "any Indian, Aleut, or Eskimo who is an Alaskan native who resides in Alaska" and permanent residents of an Alaskan native village if the taking is for sub-sistence purposes. *Id.* § 1539(e).

• There is an exemption for scientific purposes or to enhance the propagation or survival of the affected species. *Id.* § 1539 (a)(1)(A).

The Marine Mammal Protection Act (MMPA) includes several exemptions that the ESA does not. One is the "Good Samaritan" exemp-tion for persons who injure a marine mammal while trying to rescue it. 16 U.S.C. § 1371(d). Another exempts certain military readiness activi-ties from the MMPA. *See* National Defense Authorization Act of 2004, Pub. L. No. 108–136, 117 Stat. 1392. Should Congress expand the ESA's exemptions to exclude a broader range of activities from the statute's scope?

I. Has the ESA Been Successful?

Since the ESA was enacted, 40 species have been delisted. *See* Delisted Species Report, http://ecos.fws.gov/tess_ public/ TESSWebpageDelisted?listings=0 (visited Jan. 28, 2005). Of those, about 15 are classified as "recovered," while 9 are extinct. The rest were taken off the list because of taxonomic revisions or new information. *Id.*

The American alligator, peregrine falcon, brown pelican and gray whale are perhaps the widely celebrated recovery success stories. The extinction stories are less well-known. The blue pike, tecopa pupfish, dusky seaside sparrow and longjaw cisco raised little attention outside of the scientific community when they quietly vanished from the earth.

Has the ESA been a successful conservation tool? Does it come at too high a price, in terms of economic displacement and landowner con-straints? Proposals to amend the ESA crop up nearly every congres-sional session. Should Congress amend the statute to make it more effec-tive or to alleviate burdens on landowners? Should Congress limit the ESA's application to only federal lands? Another option may be to pro-vide for compensation to any landowner or developer adversely affected by the ESA's prohibitions. Are there other viable options that would keep the statute intact and advance the nation's conservation objectives while avoiding undue economic dislocation?

Chapter 15

PRESERVATION AND RECREATION

I. INTRODUCTION

The law of preservation and recreation governs the type of use, the quantity and impacts of various uses, and the desired ecological condition of designated areas of land. The resources at issue typically include scenic beauty, intact or relatively unaltered ecosystems and natural quiet, as well as spectacular hiking and biking trails, challenging cliffs and rock outcroppings for climbers, steep slopes for skiing and whitewater rapids for rafters. The increasing demand for both recreation and protection of these resources has spurred an intense debate between the pure preservationists and the avid recreationists. This chapter introduces the various groups who wish to preserve lands and recreationally use lands, and the competing and somewhat incompatible interests of those groups. Recreation- and preservation-oriented themes raised in Chapters 2 (Biodiversity), 6 (Public Lands Ownership), and 14 (Wildlife) are addressed in more detail here. More specifically, this chapter covers the growing trend of recreational use on the nation's public lands, policies governing concessions and commercial use of the public lands, the attempt to balance recreational demands with preservation needs, and, finally, external and internal threats to recreation and preservation resources, including the potential of tort liability for recreational injuries.

A. The Recreational/Preservation Conflict

As America has moved from a commodity-based to a recreation and preservation-based land-use value, disputes have arisen among those who wish to preserve, or play in, natural resources. The following article outlines the emerging battle lines, writ large on the nation's public lands, but also found wherever natural resources and open space exist.

RECREATION WARS AMONG OUR NATURAL RESOURCES*

Jan G. Laitos and Rachael B. Reiss

The management of natural resources has gone through several philosophical shifts over the past 150 years. Those changes in management philosophy have paralleled changes in attitudes about natural resources use. Resource extraction gave way to pollution control and

---

* Reprinted from 34 Environmental Law 1091 (2005).

restoration-preservation, which now competes with recreation. These use and management trends occurred in three time periods.

Era I (roughly 1862–1964) arose with westward expansion and the passage of the first mining and timber harvesting laws, as governments encouraged commodity developers to search for and remove valuable resources. Disputes ensued between commodity users, and commodity users and the government, as these parties attempted to sort out their rights under these new laws. The environmental problems that emerged from Era I influenced Congress to pass an influx of environmental laws, creating Era II (roughly 1964–1990s). This era sought to reconcile extractive commodity demands with popular environmental values, such as preventing the depletion of natural resources, maintaining clean air and water, and preserving landscapes and endangered species. Environmental protection groups and agencies used these new laws to challenge commodity users, or government decisions permitting extractive use of resources. Era II disputes still arise, although we are moving into another era. The third Era, the focus of this paper, marks a change in natural resource use: from commodity development to environmental protection to preservation-recreation. Mineral development, logging, and grazing no longer seem to constitute the primary uses of natural resources. Rather, preservation and recreation are becoming, in Era III, the primary use preference. * * * However, unlike with Eras I and II, Congress has not passed laws aimed specifically at the kinds of debates that have emerged over the proper allocation of recreational and preservational uses. As different types of recreational users, from pure preservationists to motorized vehicle users, litigate against each other and the government, courts and administrative agencies must use Era I and Era II statutes to resolve these new conflicts. Era III decision-makers must also make this call–should we continue managing natural resources in a traditional multiple use capacity, or should we adopt a dominant use paradigm, with preservation and low impact, human-powered recreation, such as hiking, as the primary use?

A. Era I: Commodity Development

Era I began in the 1860s with the passage of the Homestead Act[1] and the first mining and forest management laws of the late 1800s,[2] and it continued until the Wilderness Act of 1964,[3] which suggested that a non-development ethic was establishing itself. * * *

During this time, Congress decreed a multiple use standard in the Multiple–Use, Sustained–Yield Act of 1960 (MUSYA).[5] * * * A multiple use philosophy assumed that, with systematic scientific management,

---

1. 43 U.S.C. § 161, *et seq.* (repealed 1976).

2. *See* Mining Law of 1866 and 1870 as consolidated into the General Mining Law of 1872 (30 U.S.C. §§ 22, *et. seq.*); R.S. 2477 (Act of July 26, 1866 (later codified separately at 43 US.C. § 932) (repealed 1976)); 1897 Organic Administration Act (16 U.S.C. § 473).

3. 16 U.S.C. §§ 1311, *et seq.*

5. 16 U.S.C. § 528, *et seq.*

many seemingly incompatible uses were theoretically possible within an area, including logging, mining, grazing, and even recreation. This notion of multiple use was consistent with the goals and values of this era: to make the most efficient and exhaustive use of the land's valuable resources.

As commodity users tried to determine their respective rights under these various public lands statutes, Era I pitted commodity users against commodity users, and commodity users against the government. * * *

B. Era II: Environmental Protection

In Era II, agencies and courts had to reconcile the extractive resource demands of Era I with emerging environmental values. The race to develop and extract that had been taking place between commodity users began to take a toll on clean air, clean water, wildlife, rangeland, landscape, preservation, and other environmental goals. The value system of many people began to change. The Era I goal of stimulating the competitive search for, or removal of, valuable resources, began to be replaced by a restoration and protection goal. Congress reflected and aided this value shift by passing such statutes as the 1964 Wilderness Act,[10] the National Environmental Policy Act of 1969 (NEPA),[11] the Clean Air Act of 1970,[12] the Clean Water Act of 1972,[13] the Endangered Species Act of 1973 (ESA),[14] the Federal Land and Policy Management Act of 1976 (FLPMA),[15] and the National Forest Management Act of 1976 (NFMA).[16]

These new environmental laws seemed at odds with Era I goals. Environmental groups and agencies such as the Environmental Protection Agency (EPA) used these environmental laws to attack both commodity users and government decisions that seemed to ignore the statutory requirements of Era II. Environmental organizations litigated with these Era II statutes to (1) ensure that federal plans first considered environmental impacts, (2) stop federal projects from driving plant and animal species to extinction, and (3) prevent administrative agencies from adopting land use plans permitting excessive logging, clearcutting, and similar extractive projects. * * * But Era II still relied on multiple use as the controlling resource management philosophy. Era II organic statutes like the Federal Land Policy and Management Act of 1976 (BLM lands), and the National Forest Management Act of 1976 (Forest Service lands), clung to the Era I assumption that many seemingly inconsistent uses were possible within a finite area. As Era III conflicts begin to dominate the legal landscape, the Era I standard-bearer, multiple use, stubbornly remains in place.

---

10. 16 U.S.C. §§ 1131, *et seq.*

11. 42 U.S.C. §§ 4321, *et. seq.*

12. 42 U.S.C. §§ 7401, *et seq.*

13. 33 U.S.C. §§ 1251, *et seq.*

14. *Id.* §§ 1531, *et seq.*

15. 43 U.S.C. §§ 1701, *et. seq.*

16. 16 U.S.C. §§ 1600, *et seq.*

C. A New Era of Conflicts: Preservationists, Recreationists, and More Recreationists

Era III is characterized by the desire on the part of many Americans to use natural resources primarily for recreation, and to protect landscapes from remaining Era I developers and growing numbers of motorized recreationists. Preservation and recreation have largely supplanted mineral development, logging, and grazing as the primary use preferences for public lands. However, unlike with Eras I and II, Congress has failed to enact any new laws to deal with the unique disputes of Era III. These Era III disputes involve conflicts between three groups of preservationists and recreationists. All three have quite different values and goals.

1. Three Competing Use Preferences

The first group (Group 1) includes preservationists (those who value a location irrespective of human use), and low impact/non-motorized recreationists, such as hikers, backpackers, and snowshoers, who want to use the land, but leave it relatively untouched. Group 1 could be divided into two further classes: (1) pure preservationists, who desire preservation for preservation's sake, and (2) low impact/non-motorized recreationists, who still desire some low level use of the resource. However, it is the rare case that people desire to protect natural resources without any attendant personal benefit. As such, these two Group 1 classes rarely come into conflict.

* * * [P]reservationists are similar to low impact/non-motorized recreationists, in that both wish to derive some personal benefit from the natural resource they desire to protect. This reality is recognized by the assumption that we "use" preserved lands even without being present on them.[19] Such lands provide valuable non-consumptive uses like ecosystem services, which are enjoyed by all people, including "pure preservationists."[20]

* * * Apart from Group 1 preservationists and low impact/non-motorized recreationists, there are two other groups who have little desire to preserve the land, and who want far more consumptive forms of recreation. The second group (Group 2) includes high impact/non-motorized recreationists, such as mountain bikers, hang gliders, and canoe enthusiasts, who utilize non-motorized *mechanical* assistance to pursue their recreation goals. A subset of this second group is non-motorized/*commercial* enterprises, such as river rafting, pack mule operations, and fee-paying hunters and anglers. Unlike Group 1, Group 2 recreationists are higher impact because they use mechanical means to access natural resources (mountain bikes), they engage in collective rec-

---

19. Robert L Fischman, *The National Wildlife Refuge System and the Hallmarks of Modern Organic Legislation*, 29 Ecology L.Q. 457 (2002).

20. *Id.*

reation (river rafters), or they take living organisms from nature (hunters).

The third group (Group 3) is made up of motorized recreationists, like users of snowmobiles, off-road vehicles (ORVs), aircraft, and motorized watercraft. Group 3 relies on loud internal combustion engines. Group 3 recreationists are usually politically organized, and seem acutely aware of any potential threats to their perceived "right" to use motorized recreational vehicles.[21]

2. *The Central Conflict: Low v. High Impact Recreationists*

Each of these groups has differing views regarding permissible natural resources use. Group 1 pure preservationists and low impact/non-motorized recreationists believe that natural resources should remain as pristine as possible. This group desires to *protect* lands and resources for their own sake, and for minimal low impact, human-powered recreation. The latter two groups–high impact/non-motorized recreationists and motorized recreationists–view natural resources as commodities that should be open for whatever form of recreation they see fit. These two groups want to engage in high impact *use* of natural resources for recreation. As such, Group 1 recreationists often cannot utilize national parks, national forests, BLM lands, and wilderness areas in conjunction with Groups 2 and 3.

More consumptive forms of recreation, particularly those that require motorized vehicles, absolutely destroy the experience of Group 1 low impact/non-motorized recreationists. Group III recreationists produce negative externalities–they create noise and air pollution, cause negative physical impacts to the land, threaten public safety, and harm wildlife. The effect of these harms is enhanced by the fact that Group 3 recreationists are often collective, whereas Group 1 recreationists participate in more individual-based activities. Motorized recreationists partake in events where they gather with hundreds, if not thousands, of other Group 3 participants. One such event is an eight-day Jeep Safari held every April in Moab, Utah.[22] This collective nature increases the destruction caused by their machines. Conversely, hikers and snowshoers typically carry out their activities alone or in small groups consisting of only a few people. As a consequence, the impact of Group 1 users on natural resources is significantly less than Group 3 users. Group 1 recreationists might at times have a grudging tolerance for Group 2 recreationists, but both Group 1 and Group 2 recreationists have a difficult time coping with the inevitable social costs of Group 3.

The inevitable conclusion is that the enjoyment of Group 1 preservationists and low impact/non-motorized recreationists is *dependent* on

21. For examples of how motorized vehicle user groups are organized, *see* www.nohvcc.org/index.htm (National Off–Highway Vehicle Conservation Council); www.sharetrails.org (Blue Ribbon Coalition). *See also* Dave Skinner, *Motorized Rec-* *reation Belongs in the Backcountry*, HIGH COUNTRY NEWS, May 10, 2004, at 21.

22. For information on Moab's Jeep Safari, go to http://www.moab-utah.com/jeep/safari.html.

the absence of Group 3 motorized recreation. To a lesser extent, Group 1 enjoyment is also *dependent* on the absence of Group 2 high impact/non-motorized recreation. Conversely, the enjoyment of Groups 2 and 3 is *independent* of Group 1's existence, but Group 1's enjoyment is *dependent* on the absence of Groups 2 and 3. * * *

3.   *Strange Bedfellows*

The three groups of recreationists have quite differing views about how natural resources should be managed for recreation. As a result, each of these groups litigates against each other, and against government regulators who seem to favor one group over another. Oftentimes, Era III players align themselves with parties from Era I and Era II when they have a similar goal. In line with the use values of Era I, and the environmental conflicts of Era II, motorized recreationists (Group 3) sometimes join forces with commodity users (Era I) to fight wilderness designations. Group 3 users argue that preservation areas lock up the land by forbidding motorized recreation; extractive industry users fight such designations since they prevent necessary road building for mineral and logging operations. Similarly, high impact/non-motorized recreationists (Group 2), such as fee-paying hunters and anglers, will sometimes join forces with environmental groups (Era II) to fight the government and Era I commodity users. These Group 2 users argue that commodity development such as oil and gas drilling drives away the wildlife they hunt, and causes polluting runoff that chokes up their fishing streams; environmental advocates are opposed to commodity development because it adversely affects an area's ecological integrity by causing pollution, destroying habitat, and threatening the existence of plant and animal species. * * *

Notes and Questions

1.   Natural resources agencies must determine what type of allocational standard is the most suitable for a land area. There are three options:

• The three groups of recreationists (Groups 1, 2 and 3) can coexist consistent with multiple use, where all three forms of recreation are non-segregated;

• The three groups can coexist consistent with multiple use only when each group's recreation is permitted, but strictly segregated pursuant to agency rule; or

• A dominant use paradigm must prevail, where that dominant use is Group 1 preservationists and low-impact/non-motorized recreationists.

Do you agree that dominant use should prevail as a management mandate? If so, why should low-impact activities take priority in all categories of the federal public lands?

2. Environmentalists suffered defeat when the U.S. Supreme Court blocked a lawsuit that accused the federal government of doing too little to protect undeveloped Western land from off-road vehicles. A unanimous Court decided that, under the Administrative Procedure Act, a lawsuit could not be brought when the complaint was federal agency *inaction* in the face of excessive off-road vehicle use of wilderness study areas under a statutory scheme that left a great deal of discretion in the hands of the agency. Justice Scalia did concede that off-road vehicles have negative consequences, "including soil disruption and compaction, harassment of animals, and annoyance of wilderness lovers." Norton v. Southern Utah Wilderness Alliance, 542 U.S. 55, 124 S.Ct. 2373, 159 L.Ed.2d 137 (2004). The case is covered in Chapter 3, p. 190, *supra*.

3. The BLM is increasingly being called upon to devise a method to deal with the competing recreational groups described in the "Recreation Wars" article. It recently released a recreation plan for Colorado's premier mountain-biking playground located north of Fruita that divides the land among the differing interest groups. The plan designates over 5000 acres for mountain bikers, 435 acres for motorized vehicles, and an area designated specifically for hikers. Nancy Lofholm, *BLM Divvies up Desert Playground,* THE DENVER POST, September 2, 2004 at 5B. Is zoning the answer to public lands conflicts?

4. While most people would believe that mountain bikers would support the preservation of wilderness areas, the Boulder-based International Mountain Biking Society has taken the opposite stance. The IMBA's board of directors took the controversial position that wilderness lands, which are closed to all mechanized travel, should be open to mountain biking. The IMBA also opposes the creation of new wilderness designations that do not permit mountain biking. Scott Condon, *IMBA study sparks debate on use,* SUMMIT COUNTY BIKE GUIDE, 2004 at 57.

5. For an example of conflicts between Groups 1, 2, and 3 in the Grand Canyon, see Bob Berwyn, *Rafting Dispute on Mighty River,* THE DENVER POST at 1 (May 24, 2004) (although commercial river outfitters compete with casual recreational rafters for a finite number of permits to float through the canyon, both classes of rafters are troubled by motorized boating). *See also* Charles Meyers, *OHVs Raise Ire of Outdoorsmen: Vehicles Hurt Habitats, Scare Game Away,* THE DENVER POST, May 16, 2004, at 22B.

6. Fortunately for the environment, and unfortunately for those recreationists interested in turning a profit, the courts are not necessarily concerned with the economic benefits that result from high impact commercial or motorized recreational enterprises when considering which recreationist should prevail. For example, the federal District Court of Northern California stated that "[e]conomics are not more important than protecting the wilderness environment." *High Sierra Hikers v. Powell,* 2002 WL 240067, at *4 (N.D.Cal.2002).

B. Recreation and Preservation Trends on Public Lands

Professor Jan Laitos and Thomas A. Carr offer their views on the emerging role of recreation and preservation within federal public lands in *The Transformation on Public Lands,* 26 Ecology Law Quarterly 140 (1999). Much of the information in the following sections of this chapter is drawn from this article.

Federal public lands comprise nearly one-third of the United States' entire land base and are predominately located in the Western part of the United States. Public lands are controlled by several federal agencies, the Bureau of Land Management (BLM), the Fish and Wildlife Service (FWS), the National Park Service (NPS) and the Forest Service. For the most part all of these agencies managed public lands according to the multiple-use doctrine, which contemplates simultaneous production of a variety of resources and outputs through scientific planning. In the past, certain particular uses have been favored such as the development and extraction of commodity resources, including minerals, energy resources, timber, and livestock forage. In recent years, though, there has been a fundamental change and public lands are now dominated by just two non-consumptive uses, recreation and preservation.

The emergence of these dominant uses of public lands is a startling development. For nearly a century, this country's federally owned lands were valuable chiefly for their natural resources that could be removed by private commodity interests. However, now it seems that recreation and preservation have replaced commodity uses. Although the transformation from commodity uses to recreation and preservation is the single most important event to occur on public lands in the past two decades, it has received surprisingly little attention.

Recently, the trend among commodity resource extractors has been to abandon the United States and public lands all together as a source of supply, or to rely on private, non-federally owned resources. With fewer resource-dependent corporations finding their supply of natural resources on public lands, local communities near these lands have had to become less economically dependent on extractive industries. Although the specific reasons behind the dwindling presence of commodities industries on public lands vary by commodity, the consequence is the same for the communities near these lands. That is, their economies are no longer being driven by the extraction of natural resources. Between the decline in recourses and the increase focus on preserving the environment, wildlife, and wilderness, commodity uses declined while recreational and preservational uses have increased.

A striking feature of this downward trend in commodity use of natural resources on public lands is its pervasiveness among all the traditional economic resources. There has been a decline in timber harvesting, grazing, hardrock mining, and extraction of energy minerals from public lands. Moreover, the trend has not slowed but accelerated in recent years.

As noted above, the most popular philosophy on land use management has been the multiple use theory. Administrators have used a variety of other theories, however, such as the dominant use theory, commodity use as a form of multiple use, and ecosystem management. Currently, the federal land management agencies have increasingly begun to focus on the dominant use theory. More specifically, they are making recreation and/or preservation the dominant use on public lands.

1. *Dominant Use*

The dominant use theory identifies lands suited to a specific use and devotes them to that use only. Secondary uses are permitted under a dominant use regime only if they are consistent with that dominant use. Recently, researchers have determined that the dominant use theory yields results that appear preferable to those expected under other theories. The reason: dominant uses achieve both economic benefits for local communities as well as noncommodity ecological gains.

In Focus:

SMALL TOWNS COURT UPSCALE TOURISTS
Robert Struckman
High Country News
May 27, 2002

* * *

Over the past four decades the Creede Repertory Theater has remade this former silver town into a bustling arts community. In a phenomenon now common from Farmington, N.M. to Bigfork, Mont., small towns without ski slopes or gimmicky tourist attractions are finding that quality art venues can help ease their economic pain as industries like mining and logging fade. Furthermore, supporters say, arts communities bring a different–and better–breed of tourism.

"Folks are beginning to understand the importance of cultural tourists," says Mark Martin, the director of the Missoula Cultural Council, which works to attract more upscale visitors. "We don't want more Disneys. We're not going to tear down our Main Streets to put up rides. Arts tourists revitalize our downtowns." * * *

The Creede Repertory Theater got its start in 1966, when members off a town business association, the Jaycees, decided Creede needed more than saloons and empty storefronts. Like many old Western towns, Creede had a prominent but deserted and rundown theater. With vague hopes of injecting life into their town, the businessmen sent letters to college theater programs, promising a vacant stage and little else. * * *

* * * Slowly a new economy emerged–a restaurant next door and an art gallery down the street. Other small businesses followed. * * *

While the theater's impact is nowhere near the scale of a major ski area, business owners up and down that stretch of the Rio Grande credit it with at least a portion of their success. * * *

CRUISING FOR CULTURE: Creede, Colorado's, main street (Jessie Gilmer photo)

Overall, it seems that a dominant use theory is preferable for a variety of reasons. First, and most obviously, if a single use is allowed to dominate a public land parcel, then the only activities permitted are those that appear inherently compatible (for example, quiet contemplation or photography and wilderness). Second, dominant use is more likely to achieve economic efficiency because of advantages of specialization. Dominant use favors outputs that are either conducive to a land's natural capabilities or responsive to marketplace demand. Outputs that are inconsistent with the dominant use will decline. Efficiency favors this result because the costs associated with the incompatible uses will exceed the costs of the use that has become dominant due to its better utilization of the land or its ability to satisfy a public need. Third, when the dominant uses of recreation and preservation emerge, there are both economic and noneconomic benefits. Since communities near public lands experience the economic consequences of private uses of these lands, their economies become healthier when surrounding public lands are a source of nonconsumptive, environmental values. The economies of these communities benefit by the environmental goods and services offered from public lands used for recreation and preservation, perhaps more so than when these lands had value chiefly because they were a repository of commodity resources that could be extracted by private industry. *See generally* Chapter 1 (Economics), *supra.* Lands set aside for human-powered recreation also bring out noneconomic physical and psychological gains, while preservation of large segments of the public land base confers ecological and biological benefits. Because of these benefits, administrators have moved away from using the multiple use theory when managing public lands to using a theory of dominant use.

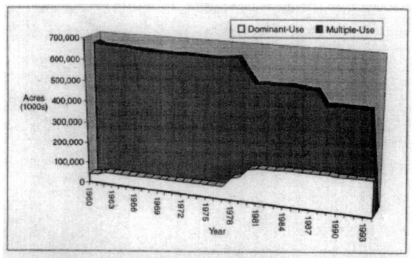

Figure 14. Decline of the Multiple-Use Land Base and Rise in Dominant-Use Land Base.
Source: Public Land Statistics; Agricultural Statistics (1960-94).

The major legislative embodiment of multiple use is the Multiple–Use Sustained–Yield Act of 1960 (MUSYA). MUSYA was an important political and public relations coup for the Forest Service. It allowed the Forest Service to operate as it previously had, but with the added advantage of being able to claim an increased societal value because of the new-found focus on multiple uses. Edward Crafts, former Assistant Chief of the Forest Service and one of the architects of the MUSYA, stated that "[e]verything fell under multiple use, and who can argue against multiple use because it is all things to all people. They used it as a justification for whatever they wanted to do." The MUSYA defines multiple use as:

> The management of all the various renewable surface resources of the national forests so that they are utilized in the combination that will best meet the needs of the American people; making the most judicious use of the land for some or all of these resources or related services over areas large enough to provide sufficient latitude for periodic adjustments in use to conform to changing needs and conditions; that some land will be used for less than all of the resources; and harmonious and coordinated management of the various resources, each with the other, without impairment of the productivity of the land, with consideration being given to the relative values of the various resources, and not necessarily the combination of uses that will give the greatest dollar return or the greatest unit output.

16 U.S.C. § 531(a) This definition requires that land be used to meet the needs of the people, but also gives the Forest Service freedom to define

those needs and the uses that achieve those needs. In 1970, the Public Land Law Review Commission (PLLRC) concluded that Congress in fact had little control over land management, and that "multiple use has little practical meaning as a planning concept or principle."

Lacking guidance from the MUSYA and the courts, the Forest Service has been left to interpret the multiple use mandate. The agency's implementation of multiple use focuses on the production of more than one output from individual pieces of land. Since timber, wildlife, fish, and other resources exist in close proximity to each other, the Forest Service manages each unit of land for as many outputs as is practical. But the data needed to identify either the optimal input-output mix or the "needs of the American people" are so immense that the process amounts to seeking a Holy Grail.

Perhaps the most difficult issues of multiple use management arise when adjacent uses conflict. This issue is often explored using trade-off functions, which express how much of one output must be lost to gain additional amounts of some other. While there is some conflict between many forest uses, the most incompatible are timber production, wilderness, and intensive recreation. For example, it is generally not possible to increase the acres of timber harvested without reducing the acreage available for recreation. However, considerable subtlety is involved when translating the loss of acres available for recreation into an actual loss of recreation use. Recreators might just move to a different area of the forest, so that an increase in timber harvesting would mean a minimal recreation loss. However, as the size of the area devoted to timber harvesting increases, recreation is displaced to increasingly small areas, eventually creating congestion.

As compared to multiple use, dominant use management of public lands is a fairly recent development. It gained significance because of research by the PLLRC in 1970. Despite the PLLRC's strong support for the concept, dominant use was largely ignored at the time and has since been soundly criticized. The apathetic reaction to dominant use was due in large part to bad timing. The PLLRC conclusions were strongly pro-commodity, and conflicted with the pro-environmental sentiments of the early 1970s. Later criticisms have been in part due to the restrictive and perhaps inaccurate views that the only dominant use would be timber or that every acre of national forest land would be devoted to just one use.

2. *Commodity Use as a Form of Multiple Use*

During the heyday of the multiple use management era (1930–1970), commodity uses of federal lands were dominant on both BLM and Forest Service lands. To these agencies (as well as natural resource extraction industries), "multiple use" has traditionally meant that commodity production is the central management goal. The reasons favoring commodity use of public lands lie in statutory ambiguity, politics, and economic pressure. The language of the multiple use statutes provides federal land managers with no explicit standards, so judicial review of agency decisions involving multiple use has been exceptionally narrow and deferential. *See* Perkins v. Bergland, 608 F.2d 803 (9th Cir.1979) (MUSYA "breathes discretion at every pore"). With no guidance from Congress or the courts, land managers have exercised their discretion in ways that, in the past, facilitated commodity uses of public lands. One multiple use implementation policy favoring natural resources industries was the adoption of a multiplicity-by-adjacency approach. This permitted a clear-cut of timber in one parcel, a mining operation in a neighboring parcel, a dam and reservoir in the next parcel, and so on. Despite its flaws, federal agencies have used this theory to manage land for many years.

One factor contributing to the tendency of federal land agencies to favor resource extraction activities has been the presence of laws that subsidize ranchers, miners, and timber companies. The General Accounting Office ("GAO") has estimated that grazing fees do not come close to covering the federal government's administrative and grazing land improvement costs, that below-cost timber sales annually cost the Forest Service between $35 million and $112 million, and that the government's economic return for issuing mineral patents worth up to $48 million to private parties is only between .01% and .03% of the land's value. Although these GAO figures suggest that true multiple use has only rhetorical force, the reality is that ambiguous existing law and an exercise of broad discretion by federal land managers have combined to produce a form of subsidized corporate natural resources welfare.

3. *Ecosystem Management*

In the 1970s, new environmental laws (triggered by a burgeoning environmental movement) led to growing restrictions on the traditional extractive uses of public lands. As a result of legal and scientific support for ecosystem management, as well as its seemingly close linkage to existing multiple-use concepts, virtually all federal land agencies are exploring how to integrate ecosystem principles into their management decisions. Each major land and natural resource management agency— the BLM, Forest Service, Park Service, and FWS-has begun to implement an ecosystem approach to managing its lands. However, in the case of BLM and Forest Service, the still-applicable statutory multiple-use mandates found in MUSY and the Federal Lands Policy and Management Act (FLPMA) continue to encourage production of commodity resources. Absent explicit congressional adoption of ecosystem management, it is unlikely that multiple-use agencies traditionally tied to the extraction and development of natural resources will pursue large-scale ecosystem initiatives. Ecosystem management initiatives and a related concept, biodiversity preservation, are explored in detail in Chapter 2.

II. RECREATION

Recreation has boomed over the last thirty years, particularly on "recreation lands," which include national and state parks, monuments, recreation areas, and forests. The Land Water and Conservation Fund Act of 1965 (LWCF) is currently the one major way to establish lands as recreational lands. LWCF has financed almost three million acres of recreation lands. 16 U.S.C.A. §§ 4601–4 to 4601–11. Under LWCF, at least forty percent of the fund expenditures must go toward federal purchase of land, of which a certain amount of the purchased land must support recreational uses. At the moment, it is hard to determine exact data regarding the amount of recreation that occurs on public lands. Although the major land management agencies all provide recreational opportunities, they operate under distinct mandates and collect recreational data in different forms. Data is most readily available for federal lands, as described below.

A. Recreation Trends and Benefits

Recreation surged in the National Forest System during the post-World War II era. From 1924 to 1964, the Forest Service measured recreation in terms of visits. After 1966, it adopted the visitor-day unit in order to differentiate the duration of particular visits. A visitor day defines recreational use in aggregates of twelve hours. The 1995 level of 345 million visitor days on National Forest lands represents a 1,161% increase since 1950, and a 100% increase since 1970. By 1999, the number of visitor days was expected to double the 1995 level to over 800 million.

The available recreation data for BLM lands is more difficult to interpret because of a change in the units of measure and the BLM's difficulty in consistently reporting recreation uses over its vast amount of land. Although the BLM reported visits from 1964 to 1992, it discontinued the practice in 1993 pending the implementation of a new, more accurate reporting system. From 1964 to 1981, the BLM followed the Forest Service practice of reporting recreation in terms of visitor-days, but then switched to a visitor-hours unit of measure in 1982. Since one visitor day is equal to twelve visitor hours, to convert BLM's visitor hours to visitor days, divide by twelve. Using such a conversion, visitor-days on BLM lands increased 341% between 1964 and 1981. The discontinuity between the former and adjusted visitor-day measures probably reflects structural changes in BLM's techniques for measuring recreation. Looking at the data from 1982, BLM's adjusted visitor-days rose 176% from 1982 to 1996. Furthermore, in 1990 the BLM recorded 72 million recreational visitors.

Other major land management agencies also show large increases in recreation use. For example, NPS recorded recreational visits since 1904. Prior to the 1940s, total visits never exceeded 20 million and temporarily dropped during World War II. Since the early 1950s, the number of visits has been rising at a steady rate. The 1995 visitation level of nearly 270 million visits per year represents a 711% increase since 1950, and a 57% increase since 1970. Among the various components of the NPS, National Parks attracted 23% of the total visits in 1994, followed by National Recreation Areas with 19%, National Historic Parks with 9%, and National Monuments with just under 9%.

In addition, the Fish and Wildlife Service reports a 21.3% increase in visits to its lands from 1985 to 1996. Visits to facilities operated by the Army Corps of Engineers rose 23% from 1986 to 1996. The Bureau of Reclamation also experienced a 36.1% rise in visitor-day units at its reservoirs and project lands over the period covering 1980 to 1990.

Hundreds of billions of dollars are spent each year on outdoor recreational activities. This sum surpasses the money earned from timber, grazing and mineral extraction. In fact, the Secretary of Agriculture has recognized that of the $130 billion that the national forests will contribute to the national economy by the year 2000, nearly $100 billion will come from recreation.

In Practice:

SHOULD WE STILL PAY TO PLAY?
Denver Post
November 3, 2002

YES: Why not help support our public lands?

By J. Bishop Grewell

* * *

* * * The $600 million collected between 1997 and 2001 mitigated environmental damages and repaired infrastructure. In Grand Teton National Park, the fees paid for wildlife surveys and water-quality monitoring* * *

- Fees make public lands safer: At Glen Canyon National recreation Area, assault, rape and drunken driving dropped sharply after fees were imposed. Gang activity went down. Family visits went up.

- Fees help protect natural resources. Funds from Fee Demo repaired trails in Utah so that visitors were prevented form straying off trail to harm the fragile, black crusts of bacteria, which provide ground cover in the region.

- Fees place decision-making power on the ground. No park manager will order $1 million outhouse like the one congress approved for Glacier National Park in 1998. On the-ground managers know parks have more pressing needs. * * *

* * *

NO: Fee demo program punishes the poor

By Michael Frome

If there a flaw in the government's Recreational Fee Demonstration Program, it's that it represents a form of regressive taxes or double taxation. We, the people, already pay taxes for the management of public lands. Under fee demo, we are required to pay again for their use.

That strikes me [author, Michael Frome] as unfair, conferring advantage to the wealthy and imposing disproportionate negative impact upon working people and lower-income persons.

Officials of the Forest Service and National Park Service claim fees are necessary to raise funds to protect natural resources. Consequently they place the burden on local administrators to serve as fee collectors and marketers of recreation as a commodity. Although stewardship of public lands–especially wilderness–often requires limitation of use, fee demo provides a powerful incentive for managers to avoid doing anything that will limit use. It's bad incentive, thoroughly incompatible with principles of conservation. * * *

While recreational use on public lands has increased over the years, is it possible a decrease may be in sight? Under the Bush Administration, more and more national parks, forest lands, wildlife refuges and BLM lands are requiring recreational users to pay a fee. For example, in 2005, the FWS set a limit of 20,300 annual canoe and tube launch passes for the Fort Niobrara Wildlife Refuge, 18,270 of which were earmarked for outfitters. Passes to outfitters are doled out to the highest bidder who submits an application and proof of $1 million liability coverage. In 2005, bids ranged from $1 to $1.52 per pass. In all, 13,800 passes were bought by 11 outfitters. *See* Algis J. Laukaitis, *Niobrara: A River Divided*, Lincoln J. Star, Aug. 7, 2005, at 1A, 6A. Is this an appropriate means of allocation? Controversies over Wildlife Refuge management are addressed in Chapter 14.IV.D (Wildlife), *supra*.

The government believes that fees are necessary to preserve the public lands. In fact, it is estimated that the Park Service alone received $126 million from the fees charged. Opponents argue that fees are merely a way for the government to double tax. Since federal tax dollars currently go toward support and management of public lands, requiring an additional fee or tariff is excessive. Whichever way you view the issue, the bottom line is that recreation on most public lands may soon be anything but free. *See* Puanani Mench, *A Moment of Truth for User Fees: Critics Say Fees Take the 'Public' Out of Public Lands*, HIGH COUNTRY NEWS, Jan. 19, 2004, at 4.

MORE TO COME? Automated fee payment machine at California's Imperial Sand Dunes Recreation Area (BLM photo)

Recreation and recreational activity can benefit individuals psychologically and sociologically, as well as benefiting the economy. Interests in recreation are fueled by several factors related to how people feel about themselves and their world. Surveys reveal that outdoor recreation has become a significant part of the lives of over 75% of Americans. People are increasingly aware of their health and their bodies. They also have more interest in the natural environment and the growing number of federally managed ecosystems and biologically diverse communities now subject to a preservation mandate.

Various sociological and demographic changes have stimulated the public's desire to use public lands for recreational purposes. Recreation requires leisure time, and Americans enjoy an average of nearly 40 hours of leisure a week, up from 35 hours in 1965. This country's population is increasing, and much of it is concentrated in urban areas, whose dwellers comprise the fastest growing segment of the population using public lands for recreational purposes.

Recreation also has economic worth. Part of the economic value of recreation takes the form of dollars that flow into the outdoor recreation equipment market. In 1996, the Outdoor Recreation Coalition of America estimated that retail sales of such equipment (e.g., mountain bikes, hiking and walking shoes, outerwear, skis, kayaks) totaled almost $5 billion. The outdoor recreation industry provided nearly 800,000 full-time jobs, for a total of $13 billion in annual wages. Moreover, apart from spending money on (and thereby employing those who manufacture) recreation equipment, outdoor enthusiasts who buy such equipment often use it on the public lands. During their visit to public lands, these individuals typically spend money in surrounding communities, at concessionaires, as well as sometimes paying park fees. Thus, nearby communities and concessionaires reap an economic benefit from the active participants who come to public lands to fish, hunt, camp, hike, snowboard, and raft, as well as the tourists whose recreation consists only of taking a few steps from an automobile to observe or photograph natural beauty. Most interior West states now count on recreation and tourism as either the first or second largest part of their economies.

The "amenity resource value" of recreation is yet another type of economic benefit that flows from public lands. This value refers to the largely intangible, noncommercial benefits associated with unspoiled natural resources. One important amenity use of natural resources is recreational use. When public lands have recreational value, they become economic assets in much the same way that forage, water, timber, and mineral resources are. They help ensure that the existing people and businesses remain and they help lure potential employers and entrepreneurs. Finally, they provide a quality of life and a sense of place that has value both to people currently living there and to those who might want to move or travel there.

To estimate recreation benefits, the Forest Service has relied on studies utilizing the travel cost method and contingent valuation. These Forest Service recreation prices are used to derive updated estimates of the benefits of recreation for both the national forest system and BLM lands, based on recreation visitor-day numbers at these locations. In 1995, the total benefits from recreation in the national forest system equaled $8.288 billion, and the corresponding recreation benefits on BLM lands were $1.520 billion. The leading activities on Forest Service lands are mechanized travel, skiing, hiking, horseback riding, camping, and picnicking. The predominant recreational activities on BLM lands are mechanized travel, camping, and picnicking.

Recreation Benefits in the National Forest System and BLM Lands

Recreation Activity	Price of a Recreation Visitor Day (19955)	Forest Service		BLM	
		Quantity of Visitor Days (Million)	Imputed Market Value (Million 19955)	Quantity of Visitor Days (Million)	Imputed Market Value (Million 19955)
Camping & Picnicking	12.22	85.8	1,048	34.0	348
Fishing	77.62	17.8	1,381	2.4	186
Hunting	51.88	18.9	983	6.3	326
Hiking & Horseback	12.92	32.3	417	6.7	350
Mechanized Travel	11.64	129.0	1,501	9.9	104
Winter Sports	52.38	20.3	1,099	0.7	36
Other	45.44	40.9	1,839	13.4	170
Total		345.1	8,288	73.4	1,520

B. National Parks and Monuments

There are around 369 parks, monuments, and historic sites in the National Park System. National parks are congressionally created by individualized legislation pursuant to 16 U.S.C.A. § 22. Furthermore, the President has been delegated authority to designate national monuments under the Antiquities Act of 1906, 16 U.S.C.A. § 431. The creation and management of parks and monuments are covered in Chapter 6, *supra*. This section considers recreation aspects of the National Park System.

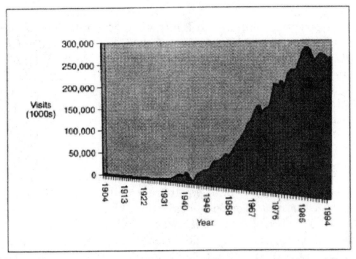

Figure 11. Recreation in the National Park System. Source: National Park Service, Dept. of Interior (1916-95); Historical Statistics of the United States (1904-15).

1. *General Recreational Use*

By the 1990s, nearly 300 million visitors were spending time in one of the 369 parks, monuments, historic sites, recreation areas, or seashores run by the Park Service. All these lands encompass 80 million acres of public property. Many recreational enthusiasts visit National Parks for their deserts, rainforests, grasslands, canyons, and mountains. Furthermore, because the Park Service is also responsible for the preservation of historic and cultural values, some recreationists at National Parks are amateur archaeologists or historians.

With the rise in recreational use of the National Parks, the NPS receives increasing pressure to consider and control the impact of recreational development on preservation goals. The NPS Organic Act of 1916 established a dichotomy that persists today: parks as preserves versus parks as "pleasuring grounds" for the public. 16 U.S.C. § 1. NPS has adopted regulations to manage recreational uses to ensure safe and pleasurable experiences for visitors, as well as to conserve park lands and resources. For example, it is illegal for visitors to enter a national park when under the influence of alcohol to such a degree that they would endanger themselves. United States v. Regan, 93 F.Supp.2d 82 (D.Mass.2000). Additionally, regulations prohibit the delivery of a person by parachute into national parks without a permit. United States v. Oxx, 56 F.Supp.2d 1214 (D.Utah 1999). NPS has also closed certain trails to bicycles based on a congressional desire to subordinate recreational concerns to resource preservation throughout the park system. Bicycle Trails Council v. Babbitt, 1994 WL 508892 (N.D.Cal.1994), aff'd, 82 F.3d 1445 (9th Cir.1996).

Other protective regulations are aimed at cultural and historic resource preservation and use. In Bear Lodge Multiple Use Ass'n v. Babbitt, 2 F.Supp.2d 1448 (D.Wyo.1998), *aff'd* 175 F.3d 814 (10th Cir.1999), *cert. denied*, 529 U.S. 1037, 120 S.Ct. 1530, 146 L.Ed.2d 345 (2000), the court upheld a voluntary ban on rock climbing at Devils Tower National Monument so that Native Americans could hold religious ceremonies at the site during the summer solstice. The case is discussed in Chapter 7, *supra*.

2. *Motorized Recreational Use*

The use of Off-Road Vehicles (ORVs) and other motorized vehicles in national parks is generally allowed where it will not permanently impair unique park resources. *See* Southern Utah Wilderness Alliance v. Dabney, 222 F.3d 819 (10th Cir.2000). However, as visitors increase, the need to restrict motorized recreation has become more and more imperative. *See* J. Sebastian Sinisi, *Illegal ATVs Wreck Havoc on Open Space in Douglas*, THE DENVER POST, February 1, 2004, at 3B. In Yosemite National Park, the NPS has acted to restrict vehicle use in Yosemite Valley by encouraging visitors to use the government's shuttle buses, and in Yellowstone and Voyageurs National Parks, the NPS has restricted snowmobile use. *See* Mausolf v. Babbitt, 125 F.3d 661 (8th Cir.1997), *cert. denied*, 524 U.S. 951, 118 S.Ct. 2366, 141 L.Ed.2d 735 (1998) (excerpted below); Fund for Animals v. Norton, *supra* Chapter 3, 294 F.Supp.2d 92 (D.D.C.2003) (addressing NPS's restrictions on snowmobiling in Yellowstone and Grand Teton National Parks).

MAUSOLF v. BABBITT
United States Court of Appeals, Eighth Circuit, 1997.
125 F.3d 661, *cert. denied*, 524 U.S. 951, 118 S.Ct. 2366, 141 L.Ed.2d
735 (1998).

The Voyageurs Region National Park Association and other conservation groups (collectively, "the Association") appeal from the decision of the District Court granting summary judgment to the Minnesota United Snowmobilers Association, Jeffrey Mausolf, and other individual snowmobiling enthusiasts ("the Snowmobilers"), who sued the Secretary of the Interior and other governmental defendants seeking to enjoin the enforcement of restrictions on snowmobiling in Voyageurs National Park ("the Park"). * * *

Establishment of Voyageurs National Park was authorized in 1971. *See* Pub.L. 91–661, 84 Stat. 1970 (codified as amended at 16 U.S.C. §§ 160–160k (1994)). Snowmobiling, which had been engaged in freely both prior to and after the Park's establishment, continued pending the results of wildlife-impact studies conducted by the National Park Service. Although snowmobiling generally is prohibited in national parks, *see* 36 C.F.R. § 2.18(c) (1996), the Voyageurs Park enabling legislation authorized the Secretary of the Interior to permit snowmobiling in the Park. *See* 16 U.S.C. § 160h (1994) ("The Secretary may, when planning for development of the park, include appropriate provisions for (1) winter sports, including the use of snowmobiles.... ") In 1991, the NPS issued regulations, pursuant to statutory authority granted by Congress, *see, e.g.,* 16 U.S.C. § 3 (1994), based on the results of a series of environmental and wildlife-impact reports, allowing snowmobiling on nearly all of the Park's lake surfaces and on certain overland trails and portage routes. *See* 36 C.F.R. § 7.33(b). These regulations also specifically authorize the superintendent of Voyageurs National Park to close portions of the Park temporarily after "taking into consideration ... wildlife management, ... and park management objectives." *Id.* § 7.33(b)(3).

* * *

The evidence in the administrative record, while not overwhelming, is sufficient to provide a rational foundation on which the NPS could base its closure order. The NPS issued its closure order under authority granted by § 7.33(b)(3) to close portions of the Park temporarily in order to further management objectives—including preservation and protection of wildlife. This conclusion was reached after consultation with the FWS and was based on biological opinions and incidental take statements issued by that agency. * * *

In its 1992 biological opinion, the FWS noted that the use of snowmobiles in areas of concentrated gray wolf activity "has been observed to cause the temporary disruption of gray wolf [feeding] activity." Biological Opinion at 7. While the FWS concluded that this type of disruption was insignificant in isolation, it determined that continued disruption of feeding activity by snowmobiles could have significant, negative cumulative effects on individual wolves, especially during severe winters when prey availability dwindles. In its 1994 supplement to this biological opinion, the FWS noted that "[s]everal cases of harassment and harming of gray [wolves] have been reported within the Park in past years," and that "[i]n each documented case, access was gained to gray wolf habitat by motorized vehicle." 1994 Supplement to Biological Opinion. The FWS concluded that "[t]he problem lies with providing human access to gray wolf habitat that would not be provided without motorized vehicles." *Id.* A number of specific incidents are recounted, along with anecdotal evidence that harassment of gray wolves is not "an unheard of event." *Id.* at 5. While this evidence is not definitive, it does provide a rational basis on which the NPS could have concluded that the Park closures were a reasonable solution to the problem of gray wolf harassment. * * *

The absence of definitive, irrefutable evidence in the record to establish the adverse connection between snowmobiling and incidental taking of gray wolves is not fatal to the NPS's closure order, since a reviewing court "will uphold a decision of less than ideal clarity if the agency's path may reasonably be discerned." *Bowman Transp., Inc.,* 419 U.S. at 286, 95 S.Ct. at 442. We conclude that the evidence in the administrative record on which the NPS based its decision to order the Park closures was sufficient to justify the determination and that the action was not arbitrary or capricious.

Because we conclude that the park closure is within the discretion granted to the NPS under other statutory and regulatory authority, we decline to consider the propriety of this closure under the ESA.* * * [W]e reverse the judgment of the District Court and direct that judgment be entered in favor of the federal defendants and the intervenors.

Notes and Questions

1. Federal courts have handed down conflicting decisions with regard to snowmobiling in national parks. Chapters 3 and 6, *supra,* analyze various aspects of the lawsuits filed over the Yellowstone snowmobiling controversy, *see* The Fund for Animals v. Norton, 294 F.Supp.2d 92 (D.D.C.2003) (upholding that the NPS's final rule reducing the numbers of snowmobiles that may be used in Yellowstone and Grand Teton National Parks); International Snowmobile Mfrs. Ass'n. v. Norton, 304 F.Supp.2d 1278 (D.Wyo.2004) (ordering that the NPS promulgate rules for the 2004 snowmobile season that will be fair and equitable to snowmobile users and enjoining NPS from enforcing its previous ban on snowmobiles in Yellowstone and Grand Teton).

2. The NPS has also banned the use of jet skis in all but 11 of its parks pursuant to a settlement agreement with the Bluewater Network, a California conservation group. A previous ban had been in place for all but 21 of the National Parks. Needless to say, this was a relatively small win for preservationists and a big loss for motorized recreational users and Jet Ski manufacturers. Although it may inconvenience park visitors, where resources are at risk, courts will likely affirm the NPS's attempts to restrict motorized uses, as in *Mausolf.*

3. *Concessions, Support Facilities and Services*

Profit-making, privately owned, concessionaire-supplied services are an integral part of the NPS. Private concessionaires often provide food, lodging, and other amenities to individuals who visit the parks. The concessionaires are licensed by the NPS pursuant to the Park System Organic Act of 1916, 16 U.S.C.A. § 3, the Concessions Policy Act (CPA) of 1970, 16 U.S.C.A. § 20, and the National Park Service Concessions Management Act (NPSCMA) of 1998, 16 U.S.C. §§ 5951–5966. Congress enacted the NPSCMA in 1998 to overhaul the NPS Concessions Policy Act. However, the NPSCMA only altered concessions contracting procedures and guidelines, rather then fundamentally changing them. NPSCMA repealed the preference in renewal provisions that stifled competition for all but small outfitters and guides. Under NPSCMA, facility development must be limited to those necessary and appropriate for public use and consistent to the highest practicable degree with the preservation and conservation of park values and resources. NPSCMA reaffirmed Congress's previous goal of making conservation the primary park management goal.

Park system controversies over recreational access often involve commercial concessionaires. Concession activity is big business, and is dominated by large corporate concessionaires. *See* National Parks and Conservation Ass'n v. Kleppe, 547 F.2d 673 (D.C.Cir.1976). The Interior Secretary has been given broad authority to contract with concessionaires. Universal Interpretive Shuttle Corp. v. Washington MATC, 393 U.S. 186, 89 S.Ct. 354, 21 L.Ed.2d 334 (1968). Under the CPA, the concessionaires were given "all incidents of title" to structures, fixtures, or other constructed improvements which are acquired by the concessionaires. Legal title is still retained by the United States under 16 U.S.C. § 20e. *See* NPCA v. Kleppe, 547 F.2d at 673 (equitable title vests in the concessionaire even where the contract is not explicit); Berberich v. United States, 5 Cl.Ct. 652 (1984), aff'd mem, 770 F.2d 179 (Fed.Cir.1985) (members of the public may not sue for breach of a concession contract as third party beneficiaries).

Concessionaires tend to be highly successful, because once granted a contract they tend to have a monopoly on the supply of services. *See* Yachts America, Inc. v. United States, 779 F.2d 656 (Fed.Cir.1985); 16 U.S.C.A. § 20c. Existing concessionaires who entered into contracts with the NPS under the 1965 Act had a preferential right to contract renewal, making it difficult for other concessionaires to enter the marketplace. Fort Sumter Tours, Inc. v. Andrus, 564 F.2d 1119 (4th Cir.1977). Under 36 C.F.R. § 51.102, there is a presumption against preferential renewal rights unless there is express contract language indicating otherwise. But the preferential right for contract renewal does not contain a right to identical contract terms. Canyoneers, Inc. v. Hodel, 756 F.2d 754 (9th Cir.1985).

The NPSCMA of 1998, however, changed the preferential contract right completely. The act mandated that no concessionaire shall be grated a preferential right to renew a concession contract, or any other form of preference. 16 U.S.C. § 5952(7)(a). The 1998 Act stated that the repeal of the 1965 Act shall not affect the validity of an concessions contracts or permits entered into under the 1965 Act, but the provisions of NPSCMA shall apply to all contracts and permits unless they are inconsistent with the terms and conditions of the contract or permit. Pub.L. No. 105–391, Title IV, § 415(a), Nov. 13, 1998. According to Hamilton Stores, Inc. v. Hodel, 925 F.2d 1272 (10th Cir.1991), no contractual right of preference exists in awarding concession services to an existing concessionaire.

In the limited instances where a preferential right to renewal does apply, it runs only to concessionaires who have performed to the Secretary's satisfaction. Further, in instances where the concessionaire either refuses to respond to competitor's proposals or is unable to match a competitor's proposal, the Secretary has the right to deny the renewal. Lewis v. Lujan, 826 F.Supp. 1302 (D.Wyo.1992), Lewis v. Babbitt, 998 F.2d 880 (10th Cir.1993), and Willow Beach Resort, Inc. v. United States, 5 Cl.Ct. 241 (1984), are examples of the Secretary's refusal to renew a concessionaire's contract when a new concessionaire came along with a better or unmatched proposal.

NPS concession contracting manuals are subject to the notice and comment rulemaking requirements of the APA, and new provisions should not be applied to a concessionaire while adoption is pending. National Park Concessions, Inc. v. Kennedy, 1996 WL 560310 (W.D.Tex.1996). Different requirements govern fee and rate setting by NPS. In some cases, the NPS has a statutory right to unilaterally adjust franchise fees owed under a contract and to include profits when adjusting the fees. Fort Sumter Tours, Inc. v. Babbitt, 66 F.3d 1324 (4th Cir.1995). Moreover, the NPS is not required to publish guideline manuals for certain fees and rates in the Federal Register or to hold a hearing prior to changing rates or fees. Lake Mohave Boat Owners Ass'n v. NPS, 78 F.3d 1360 (9th Cir.1995).

Permits are required for most concessionaires, more specifically for those who wish to sell or distribute printed materials within the NPS. In United States v. Kistner, 68 F.3d 218 (8th Cir.1995), the court held that 36 C.F.R. § 2.53(a) requires that a permit be issued by the superintendent prior to the sale or distribution of printed material with the park areas. In Henderson v. Kennedy, 253 F.3d 12 (D.C.Cir.2001), *cert. denied*, 535 U.S. 986, 122 S.Ct. 1537, 152 L.Ed.2d 464 (2002), evangelical Christians' First and Fourteenth Amendment challenges to an NPS regulation banning sales of message-bearing t-shirts in designated sections of the National Mall were dismissed, as the regulation was content neutral, narrowly tailored to achieve a significant governmental interest, and left alternative channels of communication open. As with the power to restrict the sale of printed materials, the Secretary also has the authority to prohibit solicitation of tourist business on federal property. Washington Tour Guides Ass'n v. NPS, 808 F.Supp. 877 (D.D.C 1992).

The qualifications and training of staff concessionaires has become a major issue for the NPS. Visitors may perceive concessionaires' staff to be NPS employees, but the staff person may in fact know little about the Park or its resources. *See* Richard Annsson, *Protecting and Preserving our National Parks in the Twenty First Century: Are Additional Reforms Needed Above and Beyond the Requirements of the 1988 National Parks Omnibus Management Act?*, 62 Mont. L. Rev. 213 (2001).

The concessions industry has become overwhelmingly corporate in the past thirty years. The largest concessions contracts are held by very large conglomerates, which recruit and employ professionals with strong business backgrounds. They are highly trained and able to negotiate shrewdly in order to attain the most favorable contract terms for their employers. The Park Service, conversely, has changed little since the days when most deals were struck by a gentlemen's agreement and a handshake. Concessions work is primarily handled by staff who have little or no business background. Consequently, in spite of the recent reforms in concessions law, the Park Service is finding itself outgunned at the bargaining table.

4. Commercial Recreation

Some private outfits provide recreational services, such as rental canoes or multi-day guided rafting trips. The NPS has virtually unfettered discretion to limit the nature and number of recreational activities offered by commercial enterprises. Free Enterprise Canoe Renters Ass'n v. Watt, 711 F.2d 852 (8th Cir.1983); Wilderness Public Rights Fund v. Kleppe, 608 F.2d 1250 (9th Cir.1979).

Where a commercial outfitter fails to take environmental impacts into account or abuses its operation privileges, its activities may be restricted or curtailed. In Clipper Cruise Line, Inc. v. United States, 855 F.Supp. 1 (D.D.C.1994), for example, the court upheld the NPS' discretion to limit entry into Glacier Bay National Park to three cruise line ships per day, thereby denying Clipper Cruise Line's access based on a previous collision and resulting pollution was upheld. Additionally, in National Parks & Conservation Association v. Babbitt, 241 F.3d 722 (9th Cir.2001), the court upheld an injunction reducing entry quotas on the number of cruise ship entries into Glacier Bay National Park, because environmental effects were sufficiently controversial to warrant preparation of an environmental impact statement (EIS) under NEPA, rather than a finding of no significant impact (FONSI).

5. Non–Recreation Commercial Development

Economic activities, such as mineral development and timber harvest, are prohibited in most areas of the National Park System. *See* 16 U.S.C.A. § 3. Although mining was originally allowed in some Park System areas, the Mining in Parks Act of 1976 outlawed all future mining activity and required pre–1976 claims to be validated, recorded, and closely regulated. 16 U.S.C.A. § 1901 et seq. For cases involving mining in parks, see Brown v. Department of Interior, 679 F.2d 747 (8th Cir. 1982) (land acquired by the United States in 1972 as part of the Buffalo National River is now closed to all mining activity); United States v. Vogler, 859 F.2d 638 (9th Cir.1988) (placer miner was prohibited from operating off-road vehicles in the park without obtaining an access permit first); Northern Alaska Envtl. Ctr. v. Lujan, 872 F.2d 901 (9th Cir.1989) (addressing mining claims in national parks within Alaska); Northern Alaska Envtl. Ctr. v. Hodel, 803 F.2d 466 (9th Cir.1986) (NEPA analysis is required for mining plan approval).

Timber harvesting in national parks without permission is not only a violation of 16 U.S.C. § 3 and NPS regulations, but also subjects the violator to prosecution for conversion under 18 U.S.C. § 641. *See* United States v. Campbell, 42 F.3d 1199 (9th Cir.1994); United States v. Langston, 903 F.2d 1510 (11th Cir.1990); United States v. Fogel, 901 F.2d 23 (4th Cir.1990).

Scientific research on NPS lands is generally permissible where it benefits NPS conservation efforts. In Edmonds Institute v. Babbitt, 93 F.Supp.2d 63 (D.D.C.2000), the court upheld bioprospecting for microbes within Yellowstone National Park because it would produce direct, concrete benefits to NPS conservation efforts by affording greater scientific understanding of park resources and providing monetary support for park programs.

C. Forest Service Lands

As described in Section II.A, above, casual and commercial use in the National Forests has been steadily increasing for the past few decades. The Forest Service must comply with NFMA and Forest Service regulations to protect key resources and monitor forest resources when providing or supporting recreational services. Commercial recreation facilities (*e.g.,* resorts and outfitters) in National Forests need special use permits. United States v. Richard, 636 F.2d 236 (8th Cir.1980). Running a commercial venture without a permit subjects the operator to criminal penalties. United States v. Peterson, 897 F.Supp. 499 (D.Colo.1995). *But see* United States v. Strong, 79 F.3d 925 (9th Cir.1996) (a defendant who apparently received no compensation for his services to hunters may not be found guilty of providing "commercial" services). Noncompliance with permit terms may result in permit revocation and federal confiscation of the private property. Ness Inv. Corp. v. United States, 595 F.2d 585 (Ct.Cl.1979).

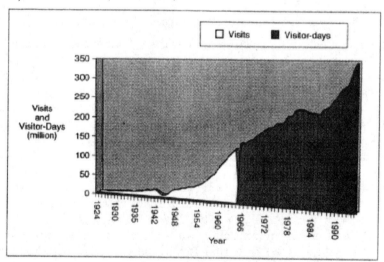

Figure 9. Recreation in the National Forest System. Recreation Measured by "Visits" up to 1964 and "Visitor-days" after 1964. Source: Agricultural Statistics (1950-95); Historical Statistics of the U.S. (1924-49).

An employer of a commercial outfitting business is liable for the acts of his employees if the employee was acting within the scope of his. In United States v. Ellison, 112 F.Supp.2d 1234 (D.Colo.2000), the owner of an outfitting business that provided guiding services in a National Forest was liable for operating in an unauthorized location, for keeping an inaccurate trip log, and for failing to provide a written contract under the terms of the permit. Permit requirements have also been held to apply to the motion picture industry when actors are actually engaged in the guiding and outfitting services portrayed in the film. In United States v. Patzer, 15 F.3d 934 (10th Cir.1993), the court found the filming of big game on National Forest lands without special-use authorization and a state license violated state law.

1. General Recreational Use

The Forest Service must allow recreation as a multiple use of non-wilderness areas in national forests pursuant to 16 U.S.C.A. § 528. Private recreational facilities are regulated to prevent overcrowding and protect forest resources. *See* Great American Houseboat Co. v. United States, 780 F.2d 741 (9th Cir.1986); Paulina Lake Historic Cabin Owners Assn v. USDA Forest Service, 577 F.Supp. 1188 (D.C.Or.1983). Recreational users do not have a right to unlimited use and enjoyment of the national forest. *See Paulina Lake Historic Cabin Owners Ass'n*, 577 F.Supp. at 1194–96 (upholding agency's order to remove cabins and a lodge, and finding that special use permits created no vested property rights). In Armuchee Alliance v. King, 922 F.Supp. 1541 (N.D.Ga.1996), members of an environmental organization used an area of the national forest intended for salvage and timber sale. The court found that the organization's use of land, which was slated for commodity extraction, is not guaranteed, as the court held there is no substantive due process right to unlimited use and enjoyment of national forest.

Regulation of some types of recreation may be left to the state in which the federal land is located. For example, the Forest Service has discretion to leave the regulation of baiting of game animals by hunters to the state. Fund for Animals, Inc. v. Thomas, 932 F.Supp. 368 (D.D.C.1996).

The Forest Service conducts a Recreation Residence Program, which authorizes the construction of recreational cabins subject to various permit terms. 16 U.S.C.A. §§ 6201–6213. Currently, there are approximately 15,200 outstanding cabin permits with 20 year terms and the cabin program is a leading reason why people visit forest service land each year.

2. Motorized Recreational Use

The Forest Service controls private ORV use through site-specific ORV plans. Any type of unauthorized motorized vehicle use in wilderness areas of National Forest lands may result in criminal charges under 16 U.S.C. § 551 and 36 C.F.R. § 261.16(a), regardless of mens rea or intent. *See* United States v. Unser, 165 F.3d 755 (10th Cir.1999).

In Focus:

OFF-ROADING LIMITS WEIGHED FOR FORESTS
Theo Stein
Denver Post July 8, 2004

Exploding use of national forests by off-road motorcycles, all-terrain vehicles and four-wheel drive trucks has forces the U.S. Forest Service to develop a national policy to restrict their use, federal officials announced Wednesday. The agency said it intended to limit off-road vehicles to designated trails and roads, potentially barring them from thousands of miles of unauthorized, rider-created routes that have proliferated in the last 30 years. * * *

Damage caused by the millions of recreational motorists who visit federal forests each year is one of the top four threats to the forest system * * * For 14 years, the Pike National Forest has limited off-road vehicle use to designated trails * * * Yet ATV, motorcycle and truck users systematically flout the regulations and carve new illegal routes every week. * * * The Pike Ranger District has 180 miles of trails and roads designated for motorized recreation. But that pales against the estimated 1,500 miles of illegal trails and another 1,500 miles of roads in the mountainous district. * * *

Once the national rule is finalized, individual forests' staff would work with the public to inventory all existing roads and trails to determine which are needed and which are environmentally damaging. The staff would then decide whether to continue to allow vehicular use, limit access to hikers, bicycles or horses, or close the trail completely.

Environmental groups called the effort well-intentioned but criticized the lack of funding and firm deadlines for establishing trail networks. * * *

Helen H. Richardson | The Denver Post

U.S. Forest Service officials announced
Wednesday that they want to restrict users
of off-road vehicles to designated trails, such
as this one in Douglas County.

3. *Concessions and Permits*

One of the most valuable Forest Service use permits is the ski area permit. The permitting process was originally initiated pursuant to the 1897 Organic Act, 16 U.S.C.A. §§ 497, 551. *See* Wilson v. Block, 708 F.2d 735 (D.C.Cir.1983). The National Forest Ski Area Act of 1986 (NFSAA), 16 U.S.C.A. § 497b, now governs ski area permits. The NFSAA grandfathers pre–1986 permits, which the Forest Service can nonetheless revoke for cause. NFSAA permits are granted for 40 years for the number of acres the Secretary determines to be appropriate. Multi-area ski ticket arrangements, however, constitute an illegal monopoly under the Sherman Act, 15 U.S.C.A. § 2. *See* Aspen Skiing Co. v. Aspen Highlands Skiing Corp., 472 U.S. 585, 105 S.Ct. 2847, 86 L.Ed.2d 467 (1985).

Robertson v. Methow Valley Citizens Council, 490 U.S. 332, 109 S.Ct. 1835, 104 L.Ed.2d 351 (1989), specifies that the granting of a ski area permit is a "major federal action" under NEPA, requiring the preparation of an EIS. *See* Chapter 4, *supra.* Ski area permits may be canceled if the ski area is needed "for higher public purposes." 16 U.S.C.A. § 497(b)(3), (b)(5). Once a permit is granted, any disputes that may arise are evaluated under contract law. Meadow Green–Wildcat Corp. v.

Hathaway, 936 F.2d 601 (1st Cir.1991). This process is exemplified in *Meadow Green–Wildcat Corp.*, a case where the Forest Service attempted to raise recreational concessionaires' fees retroactively. The court stated:

> * * * [F]or several reasons we should treat the Term Permit document rather like a contract for reviewing purposes. First, the Permit document itself reads like a contract. It provides long-term authority to use land in return for the permittee's payment of a rental fee. It is twenty-two pages long and contains a highly detailed set of terms and conditions. It uses contract-like language, such as "this permit may be revoked upon breach of any of the conditions herein." *Id.* Both the Forest Supervisor and the permittee have signed the document, the latter placing his signature under the statement that he "agrees" that he "accepts and will abide by" the document's "terms and conditions." We think that the expectation of a person signing such a document is that its terms would bind both him *and* the Service. Although the terms of the document give the Service power to change various conditions, such as rental conditions, for the future, or even to revoke the Permit on 30 days notice, nothing in the document, or regulations, or authorizing statute suggests that the Service is to have some special advantage, not shared by the permittee, in interpreting the meaning of the document's terms. * * *

Second, the statutes that authorize the Forest Service to issue Term Permits state that their purpose is to allow the construction and operation of "hotels, resorts, and other [recreational] structures," 16 U.S.C. App. § 497, all facilities that "are ... likely to require long-term financing." 16 U.S.C. App. § 497b. These phrases suggest that one function of the permit is to offer a permittee the security needed to raise many millions of dollars in investment. It is difficult to reconcile the Service's desire for "deference" to its interpretation of the Permit with this purpose. We do not see how a document, the terms of which one party remains comparatively free to interpret to its own advantage, can provide the other party (and its financial backers) the security, stability, or assurance a large and long-term investment would seem to require.

Third, the Service's official regulations treat the Term Permit as if it were a kind of contract. * * * The Permit is "compensable according to its terms." 36 C.F.R. § 251.51. * * * Moreover, the regulations say that a permittee may "sublet the use and occupancy of the premises." 36 C.F.R. § 251.55(a). Further, these regulations reserve for the government specific rights, such as "continuing right of access," *Id.* § 251.55(b)(1), thereby suggesting that the permit grants other definite rights to the permittee. These regulations reiterate and elaborate upon the statutory expectation that a ski area permittee will make "existing on site investment" of considerable "magnitude," and that the "magnitude of planned facilities ... [will]

require long-term financing and/or operation." 36 C.F.R.
§ 251.56(b)(2)(E). Although the regulations also state that the Government is free to "revoke" or "terminate" the Permit in the manner
and for the reasons specified by the Permit, a contract that one
party may terminate for specified reasons is no less a contract. *See*
Farnsworth, *Contracts* § 2.14 at 77–78 (1982). And unless and until
it is terminated, its terms govern actions taken by both parties.
* * *

Id. at 604. If ski permits are governed by contract law, when might the
Forest Service by liable for damages for breach of contract? In Walter
Dawgie Ski Corp. v. United States, 30 Fed.Cl. 115 (1993), a ski resort
operator sued the Forest Service for hindrance of performance of its contract attributable to the Forest Service's periodic closing of the only highway service facility in the area for purposes of repairing the road. Its
quest for damages was unsuccessful, as the agency had not made an
express or implied warranty that the operator would have continued
access to a highway. Moreover, the Organic Act imposes restrictions on
Forest Service expenditures related to the repair of damaged property
covered by concessions contracts and does not mandate complete restoration. Mount Evans Co. v. Madigan, 14 F.3d 1444 (10th Cir.1994).

Permittees and concessionaires other than ski area operators follow
generally applicable Forest Service regulations governing special uses.
In order for a private party to operate a recreational facility or engage in
any type of private work activity in a national forest, a special use permit is required. United States v. Hells Canyon Guide Service, 660 F.2d
735 (9th Cir.1981). In United States v. Peterson, 897 F.Supp. 499
(D.Colo.1995), the defendant violated the regulation prohibiting any
work activity or service on Forest Service land without a permit when he
rented horses off Forest Service land and took them onto the National
Forest to be ridden.

The Forest Service will issue permits only for proposed uses that
fulfill public needs and do not serve functions that can logically be provided on private lands. Yerger v. Robertson, 981 F.2d 460 (9th Cir.1992).
The operation of mobile radio communications was deemed not consistent with Forest Service regulations in Western Radio Serv. Co., Inc. v.
Espy, 79 F.3d 896 (9th Cir.1996), and thus not permitted. In United
States v. Johnson, 988 F.Supp. 920 (W.D.N.C.1997), *aff'd* 159 F.3d 892
(4th Cir.1998), the court upheld convictions of Rainbow Family members
for engaging in non-commercial use of a National Forest without a special use permit. It rejected the defendants' arguments that the permit
regulations discriminated against expressive activity, because they were
narrowly tailored to achieve significant governmental purposes and left
open ample alternative channels for expressive activity. *Id. See* United
States v. Masel, 54 F.Supp.2d 903 (W.D.Wis.1999) (permit terms and
conditions can be imposed for environmental preservation purposes
without violating the First Amendment right to associate). The Rainbow
Family saga continues throughout the National Forest System. *See, e.g.,*
Black v. Arthur, 201 F.3d 1120 (9th Cir.2000).

Unlike ski area permits, the special use permit is not a lease, but is merely an authorization to use certain land upon payment of a fee. In fact, holding a permit creates a type of tenancy at will and may be revoked at any time. Mountain States Tel. & Tel. Co. v. United States, 499 F.2d 611 (Ct.Cl.1974). However, for a permit to be revoked the agency must have a rational basis. Wilson v. Block, 708 F.2d 735 (D.C.Cir.1983). In Everett v. United States, 158 F.3d 1364 (D.C.Cir.1998), the court considered the Forest Service's interpretation of a special use permit that created a limited exemption for noncommercial recreational activities and required special use permission to land a helicopter on Forest Service lands. The court held that the Forest Service's refusal of a permit for helicopter permit landings to access a private home was not arbitrary and capricious.

D. BLM Lands

The Federal Lands Policy and Management Act (FLPMA) grants the BLM wide discretion to limit recreational use where resources are threatened. *See* 43 U.S.C. §§ 1712(c), 1732(b). In United States v. Garren, 893 F.2d 208 (9th Cir.1989), for example, the court rejected defendant's challenges to joint BLM/Forest Service rafting allocations, as the agencies' limitations were rationally related to a legitimate interests.

The BLM is responsible for over a dozen national monuments designated during the Clinton Administration beginning in 1996, with the Grand Staircase–Escalante National Monument, and extending through the last few days of the Administration. It also manages National Recreation Areas and National Trails, which, together with BLM National Monuments, comprise the National Landscape Conservation System. Conservationist policies expressed in executive orders and legislation for this System add a complex layer to recreation policy decision-making.

1. General Recreational Use

Although the BLM may have once been known in common parlance as the "Bureau of Livestock and Mining," as noted above, visitor-days on BLM lands increased over 300% between 1964 and 1981, and nearly 200% from 1982 to 1996. Primary recreational uses on BLM lands include ORV use, hunting and fishing, hiking, rafting, and rock climbing. FLPMA provides the general marching orders for managing these activities, but conservationist policies expressed in executive orders and legislation for the National Landscape Conservation System add a complex layer to recreation policy decision-making. The major categories of use are addressed below.

2. Motorized Vehicle Use

Within most BLM lands, motorized vehicle use is minimally acceptable, but is given low priority. 43 U.S.C. § 1781(a)(4). BLM has more leeway to regulate means of access than to deny access entirely. 43 U.S.C. §§ 1732(b), 1761–1771. If the agency can demonstrate a threat to other resources, recreationists will have an uphill battle in challenging closures. In Deschutes River Pub. Outfitters, 135 IBLA 233 (1996), the court upheld restrictions on motorized recreation in an area of the national wild and scenic river system. In BLM wilderness study areas, the BLM can restrict or even ban ORV use, but by the same token it may allow it if there will be no impairment to the land. *See* Unita Mountain Club (IBLA 1992); Wilderness Soc'y (IBLA 1986); Southern Utah Wilderness Alliance (IBLA 1998). However, as you'll recall from the discussion of Norton v. Southern Utah Wilderness Alliance, 542 U.S. 55, 124 S.Ct. 2373, 159 L.Ed.2d 137 (2004), in previous chapters, if the BLM turns a blind eye to ORV use (even unauthorized use), it is difficult or perhaps impossible to force it to take action.

In Focus:

ORV'S RUN WILD AND FREE IN UTAH
Mike Medberry
High Country News, Nov. 8, 1999

Buffed-up and bristling with rock-banging, wall-climbing extras, the 1999 Grand Cherokee Jeep Laredo with all the bells and winches will set you back a cool $34,000. And you nay need the power of a Grand Cherokee to conquer the Moab, Utah, trail dubbed the lower "Helldorado" by aficionados of backcountry four-wheeling. * * *

Aggressive off-road driving is becoming commonplace in Utah, which is second only to California in ORV use.... As conservationists race to protect Utah's remaining roadless lands, conflict rises between hikers and the recreationists who want to blaze new roads, and drive old ones, into the canyon country. * * *

Last Easter weekend, 5,000 people came to Moab for the annual Jeep Safari. In 1998, the Utah State Parks Department registered 68,694 motorcycles and all-terrain vehicles, more than three times as many as it registered in 1998. An additional 279,000 street-legal four-wheel-drive trucks and sport utility vehicles were registered in Utah in 1997, up 55,000 from 1992, according to U.S. Census Bureau figures.

* * *

The California Desert Conservation Area (CDCA), a land area carved out of BLM desert lands by Congress in 1976, has been the subject of a considerable amount of litigation. In the CDCA, Congress explicitly specified that ORV use was permissible where appropriate.

43 U.S.C. § 1781(a)(4). The area has become a popular recreation spot for motorcyclists and other ORV users, much to the dismay of environmentalists, and a series of lawsuits have ensued over the area. First, in American Motorcyclist Ass'n v. Watt, 543 F.Supp. 789 (C.D.Cal.1982), the court enjoined the BLM from approving ORV use until it redrafted its planning procedures. Subsequently, in American Motorcyclist Ass'n v. Watt, 714 F.2d 962 (9th Cir.1983), the court refused to enjoin implementation of the BLM's planning procedures, on the grounds that equitable considerations weighed against an injunction. Lastly, in Sierra Club v. Clark, 756 F.2d 686, 691 (9th Cir.1985), the court held that BLM could assess the extent of ORV damage over the entire 12 million-acre CDCA, not just the route subjected to intensive ORV use, but it lamented the outcome:

> [I]f we could write on a clean slate, [we] would prefer a view which would disallow the virtual sacrifice of a priceless natural area in order to accommodate a special recreational activity. But we are not free to ignore the mandate which Congress wrote into the Act. * * * Congress has found that ORV use, damaging as it may be, is to be provided "where appropriate." * * * Although all parties recognize that the environmental impact of ORV use at Dove Springs is severe, the Secretary's determination that these effects were not "considerable" in the context of the Desert Area as a whole is not arbitrary, capricious, or an abuse of the broad discretion committed to him by an obliging Congress.

Id. at 691.

3. *Concessions and Permits*

BLM concessions are governed by FLPMA, and are granted under a lease or permit. A lease may be issued for land use requiring improvements; leases convey a possessory interest revocable only in accordance with lease terms or for listed causes. 43 C.F.R. § 2820.1–1(a). A permit is non-possessory, and is limited to three years. 43 C.F.R. § 2920.1–1(b). Authorized officers may issue permits if the use will not cause appreciable damage to the public lands. 43 C.F.R. § 2920.2–2. Permits may be conditioned in order to protect the land and its resources or to fulfill management objectives.

There are few BLM requirements related specifically to recreation permits, but individual land use plans for BLM units may address ORV use, and constrain administrative discretion in granting or denying recreation use permits.

4. *National Recreation Areas*

Congressionally created national recreation areas (NRAs) usually accompany a federally-authorized dam and reservoir. The first NRA was created in 1964, and is located near Lake Mead. Other popular NRA destinations include Glen Canyon, Blue Mesa, Flaming George, Sawtooth, and Hells Canyon (some of which may be managed by other agencies, like the Forest Service, if they were carved out of that agency's lands). Generally, the BLM's NRAs are managed under the theory of dominant but not exclusive use.

More development of economic resources is permitted in NRAs than in parks or monuments. For examples, see Sierra Club v. Watt, 566 F.Supp. 380 (D.Utah 1983) (mineral leasing in Lake Mead NRA); Hells Canyon Preservation Council v. Richmond, 841 F.Supp. 1039 (D.Or.1993) (timber harvesting). *See also* ONRC v. Lyng, 882 F.2d 1417 (9th Cir.1989) (a timber sale within Hells Canyon NRA was to be governed by Forest Service regulations).

Recreational use in NRAs has not been highly litigated. However, there have been a few suits over what type of activities can be performed on NRA lands. In United States v. Albers, 226 F.3d 989 (9th Cir.2000), a recreationalist BASE jumper used a "ram-air aerolastic wing" device and argued it was an "aircraft" which was permitted to be used on designated lands and waters. The court rejected the jumper's argument, finding that the device was a type of parachute explicitly targeted and prohibited by regulation. *Id.* (citing 36 C.F.R. Part 217).

As on other BLM and Forest Service lands, private concessionaires may provide services within NRAs if they first obtain a federal permit. United States v. Hells Canyon Guide Service, Inc., 660 F.2d 735 (9th Cir.1981). In case of injuries or property damage to visitors, the negligence of a concessionaire's employee may not be imputed to the United States to form the basis of liability under the Federal Torts Claims Act (FTCA). *See* Ducey v. United States, 713 F.2d 504 (9th Cir.1983); Ducey v. United States, 830 F.2d 1071 (9th Cir.1987). The FTCA is discussed in Section IV.B, below.

5. *National Landscape Conservation System*

In 2000, the office of the National Landscape Conservation System (NLCS) was created to manage the BLM's wild and scenic rivers, national recreation areas, scenic and historic trails, wilderness areas, and national monuments. The NLCS was originally intended to mark the BLM's emergence as a manager of world-class natural resources and to promote a conservation-oriented mission for these lands. *See* John D. Leshy, *The Babbitt Legacy at the Department of the Interior: A Preliminary View*, 31 ENVTL. L. 199, 219 (2001) (predicting the "greening" of the BLM through conservation responsibilities provided by the new monuments). The NLCS, however, seems to have stagnated over the last few years. The priorities of the BLM have shifted away from conservation and funding levels have decreased, as neither the NLCS nor the ecological restoration and conservation of BLM lands has been a priority of the Bush Administration. The financial future of the NLCS may be in doubt, but conservationists and NLCS staffers are not conceding defeat. They point to the advent of the Park Service, and are hopeful that the NLCS will develop and grow in a similar fashion. For the near term, there may be difficult times ahead. Michelle Nijhuis, *BLM's Crown Jewels Go Begging*, HIGH COUNTRY NEWS, Oct. 25, 2004 at 6.

In Focus:

Off-road Vehicle Regulation

The right to visit public lands and engage in recreational activities is a license which can be revoked at any time by Congress. Since the desire to recreate on public lands has dramatically increased and the desire to preserve lands has increased, the government has been forced to place boundaries on the types of recreational activities allowed and where they can be performed. The most common conflict is between non-motorized recreational enthusiasts and preservationists and motorized recreation. However, the agencies have been slow to impose recreational limitations for fear of public opposition and lawsuits.

Beginning in 1960, the ORV market exploded. Since then, ORVs have become an increasingly popular form of recreation, but they can adversely affect the landscape and pose a danger to the environment and other visitors.

In 1972, President Nixon issued an Executive Order directing public land managers to zone areas for ORV recreation. 43 U.S.C.A. § 4321 note. This was the first concentrated effort to regulate ORV use on federal lands. The order required land managers to designate areas and trails where ORVs could be legally used. It also specified environmental criteria and mandated full public participation. While this order seemed like a step in the right direction, it ended up being unsuccessful. In fact, the only agency to follow the order was the BLM, who was "rewarded" with lawsuits as a result. In National Wildlife Federation v. Morton, 393 F.Supp. 1286 (D.D.C.1975), the court held that the BLM had "significantly diluted the standards emphatically set forth" in the executive order. The BLM then proposed new regulations that were also controversial.

In 1977, President Carter issued an Executive Order that banned ORV use in areas where they were causing considerable damage to the environment. However, as under Nixon's Order, little was done in regulating ORVs and little has been done since.

Why have efforts to manage ORV use been unsuccessful? For one reason, ORVs are often used in rural locations where the number of federal personnel is extremely limited. What other factors contribute to the problem? How should the government respond?

E. Scenic and Historic National Trails

The National Trails Systems Act (NTSA) of 1968 established a system of recreational, scenic, and historic trails. 16 U.S.C. § 1241–1251. Many of these trails run for hundreds of miles. Examples include the 2,000 mile Appalachian National Scenic Trail from Mount Katahdin, Maine to Springer Mountain, Georgia, and the 1,300 mile Mormon Pioneer National Historic Trail from Nauvoo, Illinois to Salt Lake City, Utah. 16 U.S.C.A. § 1244(a).

Under the NTSA, recreational trails may be designated by the Secretaries of Interior and Agriculture, but national scenic and historic trails are designated by Congress. 16 U.S.C.A. §§ 1243, 1244(a). To qualify as a national scenic trail, the area in question must be an extended trail, "located as to provide for maximum outdoor recreation potential and for the conservation and enjoyment of the nationally significant scenic, historic, natural, or cultural qualities of the areas through which such trails may pass." 16 U.S.C.A. § 1242(a)(2). To qualify as a national historic trail, it must:

(A)   be a trail or route established by historic use and must be historically significant as a result of that use. * * *

(B)   be of national significance with respect to any of several broad facets of American history, such as trade and commerce, exploration, migration and settlement, or military campaigns. * * * [and]

(C)   have significant potential for public recreational use or historical interest based on historic interpretation and appreciation.

16 U.S.C.A. § 1244(b)(11).

Federal land management agencies must assist with the designation process. 16 U.S.C.A. § 1244. When an area is being considered for inclusion, the Secretary of Interior or Agriculture must study it to determine the desirability and feasibility of designation (*i.e.*, whether it is "physically possible" to develop a trail along the route in question and whether development is "financially feasible"). *Id.* § 1244(b)-(c). Once selected, the Secretary must (1) negotiate with the property owner before condemning the right-of-way, (2) acquire only the interests reasonably necessary to provide passage across private lands, and (3) limit the amount of condemned land to an average of 125 acres per mile of trail. United States v. 16.03 Acres of Land Located in Rutland County, 26 F.3d 349 (2d Cir.1994). In United States v. 13.10 Acres of Land Situated in Putnam County, 737 F.Supp. 212 (S.D.N.Y.1990), a landowner whose property was condemned for inclusion in a national trail claimed that Congress had not approved a substantial relocation of the trail, and that the acquisition was not necessary. The court held that the decision was reasonable, and affirmed the Secretary's earlier decision that moving a trail segment of up to fifteen miles long, less than a mile laterally, was insubstantial. *Id.*

The NTSA also governs the "rails to trails" program, which converts unused railroad rights-of-way into state or locally managed trails. The Supreme Court affirmed the constitutionality of § 1247(d), which grants authority to federal agencies to facilitate conversion of unused railroad rights-of-way into trails in Preseault v. Interstate Commerce Comm'n, 494 U.S. 1, 110 S.Ct. 914, 108 L.Ed.2d 1 (1990). Yet the rails-to-trails program has been controversial in some areas, particularly with adjacent landowners, who often have a reversionary interest in the right-of-way. When a right-of-way is abandoned, it reverts to adjacent landowners or municipalities in which it is located, or it may be made into a public road. *See* Vieux v. East Bay Reg. Park Dist., 906 F.2d 1330 (9th Cir.1990). Does conversion of a right-of-way to a public trail constitute a taking of the abutting property owners' reversionary interest for which compensation is due? In *Preseault v. United States*, 100 F.3d 1525 (Fed-.Cir.1996), the government's approval of a railroad's lease of its right-of-way to the city for trail use amounted to a compensable taking. But in Chevy Chase Land Co. v. United States, 37 Fed.Cl. 545 (1997), a party asserting a taking had sold fee simple absolute to the railroad and therefore retained no property which could have been taken. If the plaintiff had retained a reversion, however, the delay in abandonment occasioned by the government's approval of interim trail use could have constituted a *per se* physical taking. *Id.*

III. PRESERVATION

In addition to recreation, preservation has begun to emerge as the other dominant land use on the federal public lands. The use of preservation as an organizing principle for the management of public lands is due to four recent phenomena: (1) the rise of a wilderness ethic; (2) the emergence of biodiversity and ecosystem management principles; (3) a growing awareness that preservation lands hold economic value; and (4) the political clout of environmental organizations that espouse preservation values.

When public land is reserved for preservationist reasons, it represents a conscious decision to dedicate land so that it yields both recreational opportunities for low-impact human use and environmental services derived from watershed protection, water purification, biodiversity enhancement, and ecosystem health. *See* Hovsons, Inc. v. Secretary of the Interior, 519 F.Supp. 434 (D.N.J.1981) (upholding management plan for the Pinelands National Reserve to protect and enhance its natural resources through federal, state, and local governments in conjunction with the private sector).

Preservation uses now dominate a significant portion of our public lands. Preservation controls federal lands subject to the Wilderness Act of 1964, 16 U.S.C. §§ 1131–1136 (1994), and the 1968 Wild and Scenic Rivers Act, 16 U.S.C. §§ 1271–1287 (1994). It is a coequal purpose of the national park system and a principal use of national wildlife refuges. Even BLM and Forest Service lands, normally subject to multiple-use management and commodity development, must conform to preservation ends if they have been designated as wilderness, wilderness study areas, or national monuments.

Although less than 3% of all land in the contiguous United States has been formally designated as wilderness, Ross W. Gorte, Cong. Research Serv., Report No. RL31477, Wilderness: Overview and Statistics 1 (2002), the preservationist camp made significant gains in the last few years in the 1990's and early 2000's. The Forest Service adopted a sweeping Roadless Area Conservation Rule covering nearly one-third of its total land base, while the BLM crafted management plans for newly designated national monuments and amended its regulations to require mining companies to avoid undue degradation to public lands and resources. In a similar vein, the Clinton Administration undertook two large restoration projects to restore biodiversity values in areas of mixed ownership (federal and non-federal). These projects required teams of federal, state, and local groups working together, such as the South Florida Ecosystem Restoration Task Force in the Everglades. In what has been referred to as the most ambitious environmental restoration project ever attempted, the Comprehensive Everglades Restoration Plan called for $7.8 billion to acquire and protect critical lands, improve water quality, restore endangered species, advance scientific research, and increase fresh water flows to Everglades National Park. A multijurisdictional resource restoration and preservation program was also implemented in Alaska in response to the 1989 Exxon Valdez oil spill. It allocated a significant amount of financial support for habitat protection and ongoing research and monitoring of environmental conditions.

Not to be left behind, Congress enacted the California Desert Protection Act of 1994, 16 U.S.C. §§ 410aaa–83, which is a landmark in protective legislation for BLM land, and it designated numerous new wilderness areas. It also allocated substantial funds for preservation efforts. In 2000, the House overwhelmingly approved a measure that set aside $45 billion over 15 years to buy parks and open space, pay for wildlife protection and restore damaged coastal areas. The plan sought to devote $900 million a year for land acquisition (divided equally between federal and state governments) by redirecting money collected from oil drilling royalties. While the Conservation and Reinvestment Act stalled in the Senate, the House finally came up with a scaled-back compromise bill that will more than double conservation spending in the first fiscal year to $1.6 billion from the $742 million allocated in the previous year. By 2006, the fund is scheduled to grow to $2.4 billion. The program represents the greatest increase in conservation spending in the country's history.

This section of the chapter addresses the laws that govern preservation of natural resources. It begins with a look at historic properties, antiquities and archeological resources. It then turns to federally designated wild and scenic rivers and, finally, wilderness areas. Although wildlife refuges, reserved water rights, and wetlands and coastal zone protection are also important areas of preservation law, these topics are covered in previous chapters on Wildlife (Chapter 14), Water (Chapter 13), and Land Use (Chapter 10), respectively.

A. Historic Preservation

Both the U.S. Constitution's Property, Commerce and Spending Clauses and the states' police power authorize federal, state and local laws that preserve historic sites and buildings. *See* Penn Central Transp. Co. v. City of New York, 438 U.S. 104, 98 S.Ct. 2646, 57 L.Ed.2d 631 (1978); Mayes v. Dallas, 747 F.2d 323 (5th Cir.1984). State and local laws vary tremendously from state to state, but many states and municipalities have enacted land use planning laws and special grant programs to promote historic preservation and restoration. For its part, Congress has established a federal system of historic preservation in the Historic Sites Act of 1935, 16 U.S.C.A. § 461, and the National Historic Preservation Act of 1966 (NHPA), 16 U.S.C.A. §§ 470 *et seq.*

The NHPA provides that "eligible property" may be listed on a National Register of Historic Places. The Secretary of Interior, through the National Park Service, is responsible for determining eligibility for the National Register. 16 U.S.C. § 470a(a)(1); 36 C.F.R. Part 60. Privately owned properties may be eligible, but the landowner may "opt out" by objecting to a proposal for inclusion of their property on the Register. *See* 16 U.S.C. § 470a(a)(6). Historic structures listed under the NHPA are entitled to income tax credit under the Internal Revenue Code. *See* Amoco Production Co. v. U.S. Dept. of Interior, 763 F.Supp. 514 (N.D.Okl.1990).

Sites are typically identified and nominated for the National Register by federal agencies and State or Tribal Historic Preservation Officers (known as SHPOs or THPOs, respectively). 16 U.S.C.A. § 470a(b)(3). Eligible properties include prehistoric or historic districts, sites, structures, and objects and traditional cultural properties (TCPs). 16 U.S.C. '470a(d)(6). Properties that have achieved significance within the past 50 years are generally ineligible. A TCP is a property "eligible for inclusion ... because of its association with cultural practices or beliefs of a living community that (a) are rooted in that community's history, and (b) are important in maintaining the continuing cultural identity of the community." NPS, National Register Bulletin 38, Guidelines for Evaluating and Documenting Traditional Cultural Properties 1 (1990). A traditional pathway, structure, or undisturbed area of the natural world, such as a mountain peak, valley, or butte (like Devils Tower, Wyoming), may be a TCP. *See* Pueblo of Sandia v. United States, 50 F.3d 856 (10th Cir.1995) (describing Las Huertas Canyon, a TCP in the Cibola National Forest). To qualify as an eligible property, there must be some discernible evidence of the site's exact location and boundaries. *See* Wilson v. Block, 708 F.2d 735 (D.C.Cir.1983) (an entire mountain range is not eligible); Hoonah Indian Ass'n v. Morrison, 170 F.3d 1223 (9th Cir.1999) (a general area over which a group of people traversed at some point in the past is not eligible).

Section 106 of the NHPA requires that agencies "take into account the effect of the undertaking on any district, site, building, structure, or object that is included in or eligible for inclusion in the National Register." 16 U.S.C.A. § 470f. The key term dictating the scope of an agency's procedural obligations is "undertaking." 16 U.S.C.A. § 470w(7). Federal licensing and funding decisions count, but an agency's failure to act, without more, does not. *See* National Trust for Historic Preservation v. Blanck, 938 F.Supp. 908 (D.D.C.1996); National Trust for Historic Preservation v. Deparment of State, 49 F.3d 750 (D.C.Cir.1995) (failure to veto a license is not an undertaking). Likewise, federal actions authorizing inconsequential activities, such as repainting or re-roofing historic sites, are not undertakings. Vieux Carre Property Owners v. Brown, 875 F.2d 453 (5th Cir.1989). In McMillan Park Committee v. National Capital Planning Comm'n, 968 F.2d 1283 (D.C.Cir.1992), federal approval of an amendment to the Comprehensive Plan allowing commercial development of land previously designated as a park was not an "undertaking," because possible adverse effects of development had already been considered when the park was purchased from the federal government.

If an undertaking is proposed, the federal action agency must consult with the SHPO or THPO to determine its effects, 16 U.S.C.A. § 470f, and provide the Advisory Council on Historic Preservation with an opportunity to comment, *id.* § 470i. The "historic impact review" requirement under NHPA § 106 is similar to NEPA's environmental impact requirement. *See* Chapter 4, *supra;* United States v. 162.20 Acres of Land, 733 F.2d 377 (5th Cir.1984); Walsh v. U.S. Army Corps of Engineers, 757 F.Supp. 781 (W.D.Tex. 1990). Like NEPA, NHPA § 106 sets out procedural, not substantive, duties with respect to historic properties. A federal agency action will be halted only if the effect on a listed site is not considered, *see* Morris County Trust v. Pierce, 714 F.2d 271 (3d Cir.1983); Warm Springs Dam Task Force v. Gribble, 621 F.2d 1017 (9th Cir.1980), or if consultation is not completed in a good faith, reasonable manner, *see Pueblo of Sandia*, 50 F.3d at 860–63. *See also* Friends of the Atglen–Susquehanna Trail, Inc. v. Surface Transp. Bd., 252 F.3d 246, 263–67 (3d Cir.2001) (the agency failed to properly consider views of the Advisory Council and SHPO regarding the eligibility of a historic railroad line). A decision to undertake the action, even in the face of an adverse recommendation of the Advisory Council, is not grounds for attacking the decision if the proper consultation and review have taken place. *See* Hickory Neighborhood Defense League v. Skinner, 893 F.2d 58 (4th Cir.1990); Paulina Lake Historic Cabin Owners Assn. v. U.S.D.A. Forest Service, 577 F.Supp. 1188 (D.Or.1983); Pennsylvania v. Morton, 381 F.Supp. 293 (D.D.C.1974). In Presidio Golf Club v. National Park Service, 155 F.3d 1153 (9th Cir.1998), for example, the court agreed that the Park Service satisfied its NHPA obligations by considering effects on historic properties and taking the views of interested persons into account.

The NHPA includes a special provision for National Historic Landmarks. In contrast to § 106, NHPA § 110 provides that, if an undertaking would adversely affect a Landmark, the action agency must take steps to minimize harm "to the maximum extent possible." 16 U.S.C.A. § 470h–2(f). Public or private properties may be designated as Landmarks if they "possess exceptional value or quality in illustrating or interpreting the heritage of the United States in history, architecture, archeology, engineering and culture and ... a high degree of integrity of location, design, setting, materials, workmanship, feeling and association." 36 C.F.R. 65.4(a). An example is the Medicine Wheel, located in the Bighorn Mountains at 10,000 feet elevation. It is constructed of limestone rocks roughly 80 feet in diameter, with spokes radiating from a center cairn, and is visited by numerous tribes for prayer offerings and vision quests. The Forest Service, interested tribes, and other consulting parties entered into a Programmatic Agreement and Historic Preservation Plan for the Medicine Wheel in 1996. The Plan, one of the first of its kind, emphasizes traditional cultural values and requires consultation before timber harvest or other potentially disruptive activities may occur.

The Historic Sites Act (HSA) also contains a provision requiring federal agencies to consider preservation of archaeological resources in licensing or undertaking development projects. 16 U.S.C.A. § 469a–1. The purpose of the HSA is to preserve historic sites, buildings, and objects of national significance for public inspiration and benefit. The HSA directs the Secretary of the Interior to investigate possible sites, acquire property, and restore and maintain sites as needed. 16 U.S.C.A. § 462. In comparison to the NHPA, however, the HSA has not been a significant factor in stopping or mitigating the effects of resource development. *See* Sierra Club v. Morton, 431 F.Supp. 11 (S.D.Tex.1975).

B. Antiquities, Monuments and Archaeological Resources

1. *Antiquities and Monuments*

The Antiquities Act of 1906, 16 U.S.C.A. § 431, authorizes the withdrawal and reservation of lands containing objects of historic or scientific value (*i.e.,* national monuments), and prohibits injury to or excavation of "any object of antiquity" without government permission. The Act proved difficult to enforce because of its miniscule penalties (a maximum fine of $500), and the ambiguity of the phrase "objects of antiquity." *See* Younger v. Mead, 618 F.2d 618 (9th Cir.1980) (considering whether a 6,070 pound meteorite was an "object of antiquity"); United States v. Diaz, 499 F.2d 113 (9th Cir.1974) (dismissing an Antiquities Act prosecution for vagueness).

National monument designations, however, have been uniformly upheld. *See* Tulare County v. Bush, 306 F.3d 1138, 1141 (D.C.Cir.2002); Mountain States Legal Foundation v. Bush, 306 F.3d 1132, 1137 (D.C.Cir.2002); Utah Ass'n of Counties v. Bush, 316 F.Supp.2d 1172

(D.Utah 2004). In Cameron v. United States, 252 U.S. 450, 455–56, 40 S.Ct. 410, 64 L.Ed. 659 (1920), the Supreme Court upheld one of the earliest Antiquities Act withdrawals, citing presidential findings that the Grand Canyon was appropriate for designation as "an object of unusual scientific interest" and "one of the great natural wonders."

In Focus:

BUSH EYES MONUMENT STATUS FOR UTAH SITE
The Denver Post, May 2, 2002
The Associated Press

* * * President Bush directed Interior Secretary Gale Norton on Wednesday to begin gathering public comment on the creation of a national monument in the San Rafael Swell—a series of red-rock canyons in central Utah. * * * The swell features sheer sandstone cliffs … that have been home to dinosaurs, American Indians and Old West outlaws. It is wildly popular with off-road vehicle users. * * *

Utah Gov. Mike Leavitt asked the president to consider creating a 600,000–acre national monument. The request came after seven years of negotiations had failed to produce a consensus on how to protect the swell. * * * A monument would provide some protection for the culturally and archeologically sensitive areas. The amount of protection would depend on the monument management plan. Off-road users have said a monument designation would restrict their access to public land, while ranchers say it could hurt their livelihood.

Suspicions linger as a result of President Clinton's surprise creation of the 1.7 million-acre Grand Staircase–Escalante National Monument in southern Utah in 1996. * * *

The Swell has not yet been designated, but as of 2005, there were a total of 123 national monuments, several of which have been converted to National Parks by congressional act. The National Park Service manages most of the monuments, while the BLM has responsibility for 15 and the Forest Service manages four. *See* Bureau of Land Management, National Monuments, *at* http://www.blm.gov/nlcs/monuments/index.html; National Forest Service, Monuments State by State, *at* http://www.fs.fed.us/land/staff/lar/LAR01/table18.htm.

Presidents from both dominant political parties have exercised their Antiquities Act powers aggressively since the Act's inception. Republican President Theodore Roosevelt forged the way by designating Devils Tower as the nation's first national monument. Roosevelt also designated one of the largest, the Grand Canyon National Monument, and dozens of others for a total of 1.5 million acres. Democratic President Jimmy Carter holds the record on total acres (56 million) with his designation of 17 Alaskan monuments. President Bill Clinton, also a Democrat, places second, with 19 new monuments over the course of his tenure totaling approximately five million acres. Democratic President Franklin Roosevelt and staunchly conservative Republican President Calvin Coolidge each totaled around 2.6 million acres, creating 28 and 15 national monuments respectively. The only presidents who have not utilized the Antiquities Act power are Richard Nixon, Ronald Reagan and both George H.W. and George W. Bush.

Sandra Zellmer, *A Preservation Paradox: Political Prestidigitation and an Enduring Resource of Wildness,* 34 ENV'L. L. 1015, 1052 (2004).

The nearly two million-acre Grand Staircase–Escalante National Monument, designated in 1996 and managed by the BLM, was President Clinton's first and most controversial designation. It is also notable for involving the largest state-federal land exchange in American history, where state school trust land in-holdings were exchanged for federal lands of equal value elsewhere. For details about the exchange, see Robert B. Keiter, *Biodiversity Conservation and the Intermixed Ownership Problem: From Nature Reserves to Collaborative Processes,* 38 Id. L. Rev. 301 (2002). The designation proclamation outlined the objects of scientific and historic value and made clear that conservation was to be the main management standard within the monument. For detailed information on the use of the Antiquities Act to create national monuments, see Christine A. Klein, *Preserving Monumental Landscapes Under the Antiquities Act,* 87 CORNELL L. REV. 6 (2002).

2. *Archeological Resources*

The Archeological Resources Protection Act (ARPA) prohibits the excavation, removal, alteration or destruction of archaeological resources on federal or tribal lands. 16 U.S.C.A. § 470ee. Archaeological resources are defined as "any material remains of past human life or activities which are of archaeological interest" at least 100 years of age, including graves and human remains. 16 U.S.C.A. § 470bb(1); 43 C.F.R. § 7.3(a). Violators tempted by the lucrative market in artifacts face criminal and civil penalties, and the federal land manager may assess administrative penalties in an amount that reflects restoration costs and the fair market value of lost or destroyed resources. 16 U.S.C.A. §§ 470dd, 470ff. In United States v. Lynch, 233 F.3d 1139, 1140, 1143 (9th Cir.2000), the court held that, to be convicted under ARPA, defendant must have known, or have been in a position in which he reasonably should have known, that a human skull he removed was an "archeological resource", *i.e.,* that it was over 100 years old or possessed archeological value. For other cases discussing ARPA prosecutions, see United States v. Austin, 902 F.2d 743, 744–45 (9th Cir.1990) (rejecting arguments that ARPA was unconstitutionally vague or overbroad in allegedly reaching activities rooted in academic freedom); United States

v. Tidwell, 191 F.3d 976, 979–80 (9th Cir.1999) (rejecting vagueness defense and upholding conviction for trafficking in archaeological resources under ARPA and for trafficking in cultural items in violation of the Native American Graves Protection and Repatriation Act).

In Focus:

ARPA Prosecutions

ARPA prosecutions have been more successful than Antiquities Act prosecutions; even so, statute of limitations and other defenses can pose a serious obstacle. The following scenario is not necessarily an isolated incident.

Between 1981 and 1984, Jack Harelson, an insurance salesman and weekend pot-hunter, excavated tons of dirt from an ancient burial site on Bureau of Land Management (BLM) lands in a remote area of Nevada, unearthing 2000–year old funerary items and baskets containing the mummified remains of two Indian children. Harelson subsequently buried the remains in his garden and displayed the artifacts in his home. He was arrested by state authorities in 1995 after his ex-wife and former business partners came forward with photographs of the dig. The state charged Harelson with various criminal violations, but the conviction for the abuse of a corpse was ultimately reversed on statute of limitations grounds. *See* State v. Harelson, 147 Or.App. 556, 938 P.2d 763 (1997) (reversing conviction for abuse of a corpse, but upholding conviction for retaining or disposing of stolen property).

Subsequently, in 2002, a federal administrative law judge handed down a $2.5 million fine against Harelson for destroying and appropriating archeological resources—one of the largest civil penalties ever assessed for archaeological theft from federal lands. *See* Sandra Zellmer, *Sustaining Geographies of Hope: Cultural Resources on Public Lands*, 73 U. Colo.L.Rev. 413, 439–441 (2002).

C.   The Wild & Scenic Rivers Act

The Wild and Scenic Rivers Act of 1968 (WSRA), 16 U.S.C.A. §§ 1271–87, creates a nation-wide system of wild, scenic, and recreational rivers. Designated rivers must have "remarkable" scenic or recreational values, be "free-flowing," and be threatened by private activities. 16 U.S.C.A. § 1276(d). Over 100 river segments, encompassing thousands of miles, are part of the Wild and Scenic Rivers System.

---

16 U.S.C. § 1271
CONGRESSIONAL DECLARATION OF POLICY

It is hereby declared to be the policy of the United States that certain selected rivers of the Nation which, with their immediate environments, possess outstandingly remarkable scenic, recreational, geologic, fish and wildlife, historic, cultural, or other similar values, shall be preserved in free-flowing condition, and that they and their immediate environments shall be protected for the benefit and enjoyment of present and future generations. The Congress declares that the established national policy of dam and other construction at appropriate sections of the rivers of the United States needs to be complemented by a policy that would preserve other selected rivers or sections thereof in their free-flowing condition to protect the water quality of such rivers and to fulfill other vital national conservation purposes.

The WSRA sets out two methods of adding waters to the system: congressional designation, and by state initiative with federal concurrence. 16 U.S.C.A. § 1273(a). In the former, Congress identifies "potential additions," and then directs the Secretaries of Interior and Agriculture to study them and report to the President, who makes a recommendation to Congress for permanent inclusion in the system. 16 U.S.C.A. §§ 1275(a), 1276(a). Listing a river or river segment as a potential addition prohibits federal licensing of any water development project for a minimum of three years. 16 U.S.C.A. § 1278(b). *See* Town of Summersville v. FERC, 780 F.2d 1034 (D.C.Cir.1986). Listing also withdraws lands within a quarter mile on each side of the river from entry, sale, or non-leasing mineral disposition. 16 U.S.C.A. §§ 1279(b), 1280. Predesignation mining claims are protected, Skaw v. United States, 740 F.2d 932 (Fed.Cir.1984), so long as the mining claimant has a validly established property right prior to the designation. *See* Skaw v. United States, 847 F.2d 842 (Fed.Cir.1988).

The federal government may, by condemnation or purchase, acquire land on either side of a designated river. 16 U.S.C.A. §§ 1277(a)-(c); 1286(c). Federal condemnation of scenic easements may not affect "any regular use exercised prior to the acquisition," United States v. Hanten, 500 F.Supp. 188 (D.Or.1980), or more stringent local land use or zoning laws, Kiernat v. Chisago County, 564 F.Supp. 1089 (D.Minn.1983).

State initiatives can add rivers and river segments if the Secretary of Interior concludes that they meet the WSRA's qualifying characteristics, and if the state agrees to administer them. 16 U.S.C.A. § 1273(a). The process requires three steps: the state legislature declares that a river qualifies and should be permanently administered as a component of the system; the state governor applies to the Interior Secretary for inclusion; and the Secretary finds that the application meets the relevant standards. 16 U.S.C.A. § 1273(a). Del Norte County v. United States, 732 F.2d 1462 (9th Cir.1984). Once included in the system, state identified rivers are protected similarly to those initially designated by

Congress. *See* Swanson Mining Corp. v. FERC, 790 F.2d 96 (D.C.Cir.1986); North Carolina v. FPC, 533 F.2d 702 (D.C.Cir.1976). *See also* Klamath Falls v. Babbitt, 947 F.Supp. 1 (D.D.C.1996) (assessing a popular vote by Oregon voters in favor of a preservation proposal for a scenic river segment threatened by dam construction).

Upon designation, rivers must be classified as "wild", "scenic", or "recreational". A "wild" river is "free of impoundments and generally inaccessible except by trail, with watersheds or shorelines." 16 U.S.C. § 1273(b)(1). A "scenic" river is also "free of impoundments, with shorelines or watersheds still largely primitive" and undeveloped, but accessible in some areas by road. *Id.* § 1273(b)(2). A "recreational" river is "readily accessible by road or railroad, ... may have some development along their shorelines, and ... may have undergone some impoundment or diversion in the past." *Id.* § 1273(b)(3). A river that does not qualify as wild because of development upon its shores may still be protected as a recreational river. Sierra Club North Star Chapter v. Pena, 1 F.Supp.2d 971 (D.Minn.1998). Regardless of classification, the WSRA reserves enough water within designated river segments to fulfill the Act's purposes, but the right to unappropriated flows is limited to the minimum amount necessary. *See* 16 U.S.C.A. § 1284(c).

Once designated, river management agencies must identify "detailed boundaries" of the river or segment and prepare a comprehensive management plan that will protect the river's values, 16 U.S.C.A. § 1274(c)-(d), including "esthetic, scenic, historic, archaeological, and scientific considerations." *Id.* § 1281. The "outstandingly remarkable values" (ORVs) of the river must be identified in the plan, and the river is to be administered in a manner to "protect and enhance" the values that caused it to be included in the system. 16 U.S.C. § 1281(a); Sokol v. Kennedy, 210 F.3d 876 (8th Cir.2000); Sierra Club v. Babbitt, 69 F.Supp.2d 1202 (E.D.Cal.1999).

A river classified as recreational or scenic, rather than wild, may be afforded more lenient management standards so long as ORVs are protected. In Sierra Club v. United States, 23 F.Supp.2d 1132 (N.D.Cal.1998), the Sierra Club failed in its effort to enjoin the National Park Service (NPS) from re-building a lodge and re-routing a road near the Merced River, portions of which are designated as scenic while others are recreational. The court upheld NPS's conclusions that the project would not impinge ORVs, but instead would improve visitor accessibility and environmental conditions by moving buildings further from the river. *Id.* at 1140. On the other hand, in Friends of Yosemite Valley v. Norton, 348 F.3d 789 (9th Cir.2003), the management plan for the Merced River was remanded for failure to protect and enhance the river's geological, biological, and cultural ORVs. The plan did not sufficiently address visitor use, because it failed to yield any actual measure of user capacities by setting numeric limits on visitors or by maintaining specific environmental and experiential criteria. In addition, by including only the greater of a 100–foot buffer zone or the 100–year flood plain, the plan set the river area boundaries too narrowly. *Id.* at 796, 798. For information on the ORVs, see Chapter 14.IV.E.3 (Wildlife).

No department or agency of the United States shall assist in the construction of any "water resources project" that would have an adverse effect on the values for which a river was designated, 16 U.S.C.A. § 1278, including water diversions and reservoirs, watershed enhancement projects, bridges, dredging, bank stabilization, levees, and recreation facilities such as boat ramps and fishing piers. *See Sierra Club North Star Chapter,* 1 F.Supp.2d 971 (bridge construction qualified as a water resources project, as it would result in a change in the free-flowing characteristics of the river). If there is no federal assistance, § 1278 does not apply. In Oregon Natural Resources Council v. Harrell, 52 F.3d 1499 (9th Cir.1995), the court found the Corps of Engineers was not actually giving "assistance" to enable the construction of a dam that had been specifically authorized by Congress, since it was not acting to license or permit the project or otherwise authorizing a third party to take action.

Courts tend to give river management agencies wide discretion in determining which projects would adversely affect river values. *See, e.g., Sierra Club v. United States, supra,* 23 F.Supp.2d at 1140. In *Sierra Club North Star Chapter, supra,* the court deferred to NPS's determination that a bridge construction project over the St. Croix River would have adverse effects on the river's scenic and recreational values. In Coalition For Canyon Preservation v. Hazen, 788 F.Supp. 1522 (D.Mont.1990), the court upheld NPS's decision that replacing an existing bridge near a designated segment of the Flathead River in Glacier National Park would not adversely affect the river's ORVs, as the bridge's low-profile, "rustic" design reflected the areas's historic, cultural, and scenic values. *Id.* at 1526.

The WSRA's protections extend well beyond bridges and dams, and can reach timber sales, Newton County Wildlife Ass'n v. Rogers, 141 F.3d 803 (8th Cir.1998), ranching, and other activities in the river corridor. In a series of Oregon cases decided in the late 1990's, the court applied the WSRA to the BLM's management of grazing practices. In Oregon Natural Desert Ass'n v. Green, 953 F.Supp. 1133 (D.Or.1997), the court found the BLM's management plan violated the WSRA by failing to consider excluding cattle from the river corridor as necessary to "protect and enhance" vegetative ORVs. But in National Wildlife Federation v. Cosgriffe, 21 F.Supp.2d 1211 (D.Or.1998), the court found the plaintiff had failed to show facts that linked grazing directly to the degradation of the river's values, even though it found that BLM-authorized grazing had historically contributed to degradation. That same year, however, in Oregon Natural Desert Ass'n v. Singleton, 47 F.Supp.2d 1182 (D.Or.1998), the court stated that the BLM had a duty to ban cattle from the corridor if necessary to meet the "protect and enhance" obligation when the BLM's own management plan showed the negative impacts of cattle grazing on scenic and recreational ORVs. The court later enjoined the BLM from allowing grazing in certain "areas of concern" to prevent further degradation of environmental conditions. Oregon Natural Desert Ass'n v. Singleton, 75 F.Supp.2d 1139 (D.Or.1999).

Individuals that violate the WRSA by engaging in prohibited acts may face federal charges. Regulated activities include timber harvesting, road building, development projects likely to degrade water quality, and impoundments or diversions that affect the river's free-flowing condition. In United States v. Garren, 893 F.2d 208 (9th Cir.1989), the court upheld a conviction for rafting on a designated river without a permit from BLM. Also, in Grand Canyon Dories, Inc. v. Idaho Outfitters and Guides Board, 709 F.2d 1250 (9th Cir.1983), the court found that the WSRA did not preempt a state statute regulating the operation of white water rafting activities on a designated river segment; river segments are to be managed under the most "restrictive" law, whether that be the WSRA or other governing law. *See* Wilderness Watch v. U.S. Forest Service, 143 F.Supp.2d 1186 (D.Mont.2000) (although state law allowed jet boats in the area, the Forest Service may be precluded from issuing a permit for construction of a lodge on a wild river segment).

D.   Wilderness Preservation

The wilderness ethic holds that certain lands should be preserved in their natural condition, unaffected by human activities. This is at odds with the multiple use doctrine, by which lands are used, not preserved or "locked up" in a wild, pristine state. Although the wilderness idea is sometimes criticized as halting valuable resource development for the benefit of a few, privileged, physically-fit backpackers, the wilderness philosophy is an entrenched and significant component of American law.

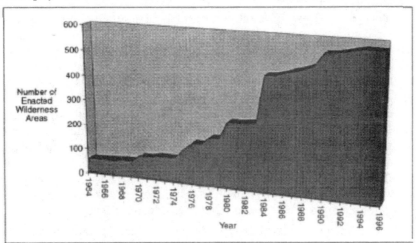

Figure 13. Number of Wilderness Areas. Source: Wilderness Act of 1964, 16 USC § 1132

1.   *The Wilderness Act of 1964*

The intent of Congress in enacting the Wilderness Act of 1964 was to secure an "enduring resource of wilderness" for present and future generations. 16 U.S.C.A. § 1131(a). More specifically,

In 1964, when the Wilderness Act was passed, Congress was concerned about the anthropocentric virtues of wild lands rather than the teachings of conservation biology, which were not well publicized until much later. Two driving forces provided the impetus for the Act: the public's desire to preserve lands for growing recreational demands and the sponsors' desire to curtail agency discretion to create or dismantle administrative preserves. The latter concern motivated Congress to delineate carefully the role of the Departments of Agriculture and the Interior: to study and report on suitability of lands for inclusion in the system. By explicitly providing that only Congress may designate wilderness areas for inclusion in the national wilderness system, the Act provides a relatively rare example of congressional refusal to delegate management authority to the executive branch.

Sandra Zellmer, *A Preservation Paradox: Political Prestidigitation and an Enduring Resource of Wildness,* 34 Env'l. L. 1015, 1040 (2004) (citations omitted).

Federal wilderness areas are established in two ways under the Wilderness Act of 1964, 16 U.S.C.A. §§ 1131, *et seq.* First, and most directly, Congress designated nearly ten million acres of "instant" wilderness areas upon enactment. In a similar fashion, the Eastern Wilderness Act of 1975, Pub.L. No. 93–622, established as wilderness over 200,000 acres of national forests east of the 100th meridian, and ANILCA designated a whopping 56.4 million acres in Alaska as wilderness, comprising almost 2/3 of the entire federal wilderness system. 16 U.S.C.A. §§ 3101–3233.

Second, Congress instructed federal land management agencies to make recommendations on certain areas within their jurisdiction for future wilderness designation. The Forest Service was required to study areas "classified ... as primitive" for wilderness suitability, after which the President may recommend to Congress which lands should be designated. 16 U.S.C.A. § 1132(b). To qualify, the area must be undeveloped and without permanent improvements or human habitation. 16 U.S.C. § 1131(c). The Department of Interior is to make wilderness recommendations to the President on all "roadless" areas of at least 5,000 or more acres within national parks and wildlife refuges, 16 U.S.C.A. § 1132(c), as well as BLM lands, 43 U.S.C.A. § 1782(a). If any of these areas eventually becomes wilderness, it will be administered by the same agency that had jurisdiction before the wilderness designation.

The agencies' wilderness studies have raised questions regarding the kinds of lands that may qualify as potential wilderness areas. What, exactly, does "roadless" mean? Mere paths do not disqualify an area, but low-quality dirt logging roads might (unless they are overgrown and not in use), and even a trail may be considered a road if motorized vehicles intended for highway use can traverse it. *See* Smith v. U.S. Forest Service, 33 F.3d 1072 (9th Cir.1994) (a jeep trail constituted a "road", though it had been only sporadically maintained). An "area" of at least 5,000 acres may qualify, even if it is in different watersheds, or if it is bifurcated by a mountain range. An area is undeveloped or "untrammeled by man," 16 U.S.C.A. § 1131(c), if it appears to have wilderness characteristics and if past human activities are not inconsistent with wilderness. Parker v. United States, 448 F.2d 793 (10th Cir.1971).

2. *How Are Wilderness Lands Managed?*

The Wilderness Act requires federal land management agencies to "preserve" designated wilderness areas, primarily for non-motorized recreation, "subject to existing private rights." 16 U.S.C.A. § 1133(b),(c). In United States v. Gregg, 290 F.Supp. 706 (W.D.Wash.1968), the court determined the custom of landing airplanes was not an existing "right" under the act. Furthermore, in Stupak–Thrall v. United States, 70 F.3d 881 (6th Cir.1995), the court rejected the Forest Service's argument that "existing private rights" refer only to subsurface mineral rights, and held that the phrase encompasses riparian rights as well.

Hunting and fishing are permissible, if consistent with state law. O'Brien v. State, 711 P.2d 1144 (Wyo.1986). *See also* Wilderness Society v. United States Fish & Wildlife Service, 316 F.3d 913 (9th Cir.2003) (Service's decision to permit salmon enhancement project was entitled to deference). Commercial fishing, however, is not allowed. *See* Alaska Wildlife Alliance v. Jensen, 108 F.3d 1065 (9th Cir.1997) (excerpted in Chapter 14.IV.E, *supra*). Commercial guides and river-runners may be allowed in wilderness areas. 16 U.S.C.A. § 1133(d)(5). In fact, in some locations, the court has upheld the Forest Service's decision to allow certain permanent installations by commercial outfitters in wilderness, where "necessary to meet minimum requirements for administration of the area." Wilderness Watch v. U.S. Forest Service, 143 F.Supp.2d 1186 (D.Mont.2000).

Roads, motor vehicles, and mechanized transport (including bicycles) are prohibited, with some exceptions. 16 U.S.C.A. § 1133(c)-(d). *See* Sierra Club v. Yeutter, 926 F.2d 429 (5th Cir.1991) (harvesting trees to stop the spread of insects or disease is acceptable); Nelson v. United States, 64 F.Supp.2d 1318 (N.D.Ga.1999) (the Forest Service's denial of a special use application for road access by owners of in-holdings completely surrounded by national forest was arbitrary and capricious).

Post–1984 mining claims and mineral leases are disallowed on wilderness areas. *See* Izaak Walton League v. St. Clair, 353 F.Supp. 698 (D.Minn.1973) ("wilderness and mining are incompatible"). Pre–1984 mineral claims may be challenged under other federal statutes, however, such as NEPA, the Endangered Species Act, the Clean Water Act, and the Clean Air Act Amendments. *See* Cabinet Mountains Wilderness v. Peterson, 685 F.2d 678 (D.C.Cir.1982); Chevron U.S.A., Inc. v. United States E.P.A., 658 F.2d 271 (5th Cir.1981). Also, motorized access to a mining claim can be prohibited to ensure the preservation of wilderness character when motor vehicles were not essential or the traditionally used method of access. Clouser v. Espy, 42 F.3d 1522 (9th Cir.1994).

Timber harvesting is forbidden, unless a statutory exception is made for a specific area. Lyng v. Northwest Indian Cemetery Protective Ass'n, 485 U.S. 439, 108 S.Ct. 1319, 99 L.Ed.2d 534 (1988). Pre-existing grazing is allowed, however, subject to reasonable regulations as deemed necessary. 16 U.S.C.A. § 1133(d)(4). Judicial intervention has been limited to instances where an agency allows grazing at levels that cause profound and obvious damage or, conversely, where the agency reduced permitted grazing to zero without showing an immediate threat to wilderness values.

The President is authorized to develop water resources, such as water storage projects and hydropower facilities, within wilderness areas. 16 U.S.C.A. § 1133(d)(4). Though the Wilderness Act grants the President the authority to allow water resource development where it is in the public interest, apparently no President has ever done so. Wilderness designations may impliedly reserve water rights, in addition to the waters reserved at the time the national forest or park was created, for wilderness purposes. *See* Sierra Club v. Yeutter, 911 F.2d 1405 (10th Cir.1990); Sierra Club v. Lyng, 663 F.Supp. 556 (D.D.C.1987); Sierra Club v. Block, 622 F.Supp. 842 (D.Colo.1985).

3. *Wilderness in National Forests*

As noted above, the Wilderness Act required the Forest Service to study "primitive" areas for future wilderness. It also set in motion a process whereby other qualifying forest lands were inventoried to determine if they too should become wilderness. *See* Parker v. United States, 448 F.2d 793 (10th Cir.1971). Most Forest Service wilderness studies are now conducted within the context of NFMA planning.

The first of the inventories set in motion, known as Roadless Area Review and Evaluation (RARE I), discovered that 56 million acres could qualify as wilderness. When courts enjoined commercial activities (e.g., road building and logging) on RARE I lands because the Forest Service failed to prepare EISs, the Forest Service began again with RARE II. RARE II studied that more than 60 million acres of roadless land could qualify. After the Ninth Circuit halted all logging activities on RARE II lands because the EIS had not discussed the effects of "releasing" 36 million acres for development, *see* California v. Block, 690 F.2d 753 (9th Cir.1982), the Forest Service started over again with RARE III in 1983. RARE III opened areas recommended by RARE II as non-wilderness to multiple use management and commercial development. Congress responded with uncommon haste, passing individual state-wide wilderness bills in 1984 that added nearly 9 million acres to the wilderness system from national forest lands. But eventually the process stalled, and, by 2005, state-wide wilderness legislation has only been enacted for a handful of states.

The Forest Service's experience with RARE I, II, and III created extensive wilderness study areas (WSAs), which emerge while a federal land management agency reviews and inventories their suitability for potential wilderness designation. After the inventory is complete, some WSAs are designated official wilderness by statute. For the remaining WSAs, there can be no release to multiple use management without preparation of an adequate EIS. When statewide wilderness bills release non-designated areas, these lands are typically subject to multiple use management until revision of NFMA forest plans. City of Tenakee Springs v. Block, 778 F.2d 1402 (9th Cir.1985); California v. Block, 690 F.2d 753 (9th Cir.1982).

Prior to designation or release, it is not entirely clear how national forest WSAs are to be managed. For example, can federal agencies allow mineral leasing in WSAs without retaining the power to deny the lessee the right to engage in surface disturbing activities? Nor is it clear whether, or the extent to which, roadbuilding or commercial construction is permitted in a roadless WSA. In Thomas v. Peterson, 753 F.2d 754 (9th Cir. 1985), road construction was enjoined for failure to consider its effects on endangered wolves in the WSA area. But in Wilson v. Block, 708 F.2d 735 (D.C.Cir.1983), ski area expansion was allowed, and in Montana Wilderness Ass'n v. U.S. Forest Service, 655 F.2d 951 (9th Cir.1981), road construction through a WSA to private in-holdings was found acceptable.

Management of a WSA as a wilderness prior to and after release has raised the ire of both motorized and commercial recreationists.

In Focus:

FOREST PLAN DOUBLES WILDERNESS
Robert Weller, Associated Press Writer
The Denver Post, June 4, 2002

A new management plan for the White River National Forest, the belle of the national forest system, would substantially increase the area set aside as potential wilderness.

Groups representing all-terrain vehicle users said a draft proposed by the Clinton Administration in 1999 would have closed too many roads, and some local officials complained too much land would be set aside as wilderness. The draft plan also was condemned by Vail Resorts for seeking to freeze ski development. The latest plan seeks to focus any additional ski development at existing resorts in the nation's No. 1 ski state. * * * The draft plan recommended 47,000 acres of additional wilderness, roadless land where no mechanized transport is allowed. The final plan proposes 82,000 acres.

"What has happened is that each time the Forest Service writes a plan there is less opportunity for motorized access," John Martin, president of the Colorado Off Highway Vehicle Coalition, said. "Prior to today, 42 percent of the forest was available. This reduces that to 32 percent...." * * * Use of snowmobiles, permitted in 52 percent of the forest by the 1984 plan, would be limited to 38 percent.

"We are not trying to cut them out. We want them [outdoor recreationists] to come here. There are well over a thousand miles of roads available," said Wendy Haskins, who worked on the travel portion of the Forest Service plan.

Forest Supervisor Martha Ketelle said any increase in recreational opportunities had to be balanced with efforts to protect the ecosystem. "Clearly there were people who were concerned there might be too much emphasis on habitat at the expense of human use," she said. "So, Alternative K (the new plan) was created to address the desire for increased recreation opportunity." * * *

At the end of its term, the Clinton Administration proposed a ban on road building across almost a third of national forest lands. The Roadless Rule, adopted in 2001, protected over 58 million acres of federal forest land from road construction. Although mining and logging were not explicitly forbidden, both activities are exceedingly difficult to accomplish without roads. The roadless rule is described in detail in Chapter 6.II.G, *supra*. In May 2005, the Forest Service, under President Bush, issued a rule lifting the ban on road construction. The 2005 rule subjects roadless areas to the management prescriptions for individual forest units, but allows governors of states containing inventoried roadless areas the opportunity to file petitions with the Secretary to alter the way the roadless areas located in their states are managed. One of the primary objections to the 2001 Roadless Rule was that it, in effect, made an "end run" around the Wilderness Act by creating quasi-wilderness areas without congressional approval. *See* Wyoming v. U.S.D.A., 277 F.Supp.2d 1197 (D.Wyo.2003), *vacated as moot,* 414 F.3d 1207 (10th Cir.2005). Is it appropriate for an agency like the Forest Service to create huge wilderness-like preserves through the administrative process?

4. *Wilderness on BLM Lands*

FLPMA requires BLM to evaluate some 174 million acres of land for wilderness potential and to report to the President by 1991 on its findings. 43 U.S.C.A. § 1782(a). By 1991, only 14% of BLM lands outside of Alaska (24 million acres) were thought to possess wilderness characteristics. The BLM ultimately recommended that just 10.7 million acres be designated as wilderness. Until Congress disposes of wilderness designation issues, the focus of dispute will likely remain on management of the BLM wilderness study areas and on efforts to enlarge or decrease WSA inventory. Wind River Mining Corp. v. United States, 946 F.2d 710 (9th Cir.1991).

The designation on BLM lands has moved slowly due to commodity user opposition and the conflict between wilderness and the agency's historic orientation (some call it the "bureau of livestock and mining"). The first statewide wilderness bill for BLM lands, enacted in 1990, designated 1.1 million acres in Arizona. In 1994, Congress increased that number considerably by redesignations in the California Desert Conservation Area.

FLPMA § 1782(c) provides that WSAs shall be managed "so as not to impair [their suitability] as wilderness, subject, however, to the continuation of existing [pre–1976] mining and grazing uses and mineral leasing." Impairment includes impacts that cannot be reclaimed to the point of being substantially unnoticeable. As for pre–1976 uses, the BLM must "take any action ... to prevent unnecessary or used undue degradation." 43 U.S.C. § 1732(b). *See* Rocky Mountain Oil & Gas Ass'n v. Watt, 696 F.2d 734 (10th Cir.1982); Utah v. Andrus, 486 F.Supp. 995 (D.Utah 1979); Sierra Club v. Hodel, 848 F.2d 1068 (10th Cir.1988). The BLM may not deny improvements to pre-existing rights-of-way because they impair WSAs, but it retains a duty to see that they do not unduly degrade the WSA. *See* Sierra Club v. Hodel, 737 F.Supp. 629 (D.Utah 1990).

Exercise:

Can humans intervene to protect wilderness areas from harm? The Wilderness Act forbids motorized equipment or use of motor vehicles, but may the Forest Service use chain saws and vehicles or spray chemicals from airplanes if necessary to fight forest fires? *See* 16 U.S.C.A. § 1133(d)(1); Sierra Club v. Lyng, 662 F.Supp. 40 (D.D.C.1987). Can agencies use lethal predator control in wilderness areas to protect pre-existing grazing operations? Forest Guardians v. Animal & Plant Health Inspection Service, 309 F.3d 1141 (9th Cir.2002). Are agencies allowed to use vehicles to remove the dead body of a mountain climber killed by an avalanche? *See* 16 U.S.C.A. § 1133(c).

As a matter of policy, should the land management agencies forego mechanized tools and advanced technologies within wilderness areas and simply "let it be"?

IV. EXTERNAL AND INTERNAL THREATS TO RECREATION AND PRESERVATION LANDS

Even if a particular area of federal land is protected for dominant uses (recreation and/or preservation) by a restrictive designation, such as wilderness, activities that occur outside its boundaries can undermine its preservationist or recreational values. This final section considers external threats, such as air pollution and water diversions. It also examines a unique type of internal threat–tort liability for personal injury or property damage that occurs while recreating on federal land.

A.   External Threats Occurring Outside Boundaries

Even if the internal integrity of recreation and preservation lands is maintained, events and activities occurring outside their borders can adversely affect them. The list of external threats to public lands stemming from human activity includes air pollution, water pollution, water depletion, aesthetic degradation, mineral exploration with thumper trucks or cyanide leaching, physical removal of resources, and visitor impacts. Logging and erosion has so decimated the hillsides next to Olympic and Mount Rainier National Parks in Washington State that fish runs are a mere fraction of historic levels. A federally constructed dam outside of Zion National Park might impair the wild river that carved Zion's most spectacular canyon. The air in Kings Canyon and Sequoia National Parks is so polluted with smog from Los Angeles and other California cities that rangers are contemplating posting warning signs that hiking on certain days constitutes a health hazard. Acid rain has stripped high-altitude trees of their foliage in the most popular park in the national system, the Great Smoky Mountains. Everglades National Park has lost 90 %of its wading birds since the 1930s, because once extensive wetlands have been drained and polluted by South Florida development.

SUPER-SIZED ORV: A thumper truck in southern Utah before the shutdown (Kevin Walker photo courtesy SUWA)

Thumper trucks, above, and the Dome Plateau wilderness study area, below, with the La Sal Mountains in the background. Thumper trucks were destined for an area adjacent to the wilderness study area. *Photos by Kevin Walker and Adam Burke.*

UNEXPLORED: Dome Plateau with the La Sal Mountains in the background. Thumper trucks were destined for this area until the project was shut down (Adam Burke photo).

Although power to abate nuisances on adjacent nonfederal land is provided by both the Property Clause (art. IV, § 3, cl. 2), *see* Camfield v. United States, 167 U.S. 518, 17 S.Ct. 864, 42 L.Ed. 260 (1897), and the National Park Act, 16 U.S.C.A. §§ 1, 1–la, courts have generally been unwilling to protect parklands from external threats. Rainbow Bridge National Monument was flooded by Lake Powell, Friends of the Earth v. Armstrong, 485 F.2d 1 (10th Cir.1973); a tower was built on private land overlooking Gettysburg Battlefield, Commonwealth v. National Gettysburg Battlefield Tower, 454 Pa. 193, 311 A.2d 588 (1973); a nuclear power plant was built on land abutting Indiana Dunes National Lakeshore, Northern Indiana Public Service Co. v. Porter County Chapter of Izaak Walton League of America, Inc., 423 U.S. 12, 96 S.Ct. 172, 46 L.Ed.2d 156 (1975); and office buildings were constructed along the Potomac River shoreline in spite of their effect on the green backdrop of Washington D.C. monuments, United States v. Arlington County, 487 F.Supp. 137 (E.D.Va.1979).

There are a few instances of judicial support for agency action to protect internal resources from outside threats. The government obtained judicial affirmation of its attempts to reduce pollution affecting the Grand Canyon, Central Arizona Water Conservation Dist. v. EPA, 990 F.2d 1531 (9th Cir.1993), and to prevent a state from spraying pesticides on federal and private land within the boundaries of a national river, United States v. Moore, 640 F.Supp. 164 (S.D.W.Va.1986). In Mantle Ranches, Inc. v. United States Park Service, 945 F.Supp. 1449 (D.Colo.1996), the court granted a preliminary injunction against refuse dumping near Dinosaur National Park, but refused to enjoin other activities such as a water diversion out of the Park, overgrazing, or road construction.

Air pollution levels in National Parks deserve special attention. The Clean Air Act restricts pollution that diminishes visibility in National Parks. 42 U.S.C.A. §§ 7491–92. In 1999, the EPA issued a rule requiring states to impose pollution control standards to return parks and wilderness areas to "natural visibility" within 60 years. Both industry and environmental groups challenged the rule, and in American Corn Growers v. EPA, 291 F.3d 1 (D.C.Cir.2002), the court held that rule violated the Clean Air Act by requiring states to engage in regional rather than source-by-source analysis. However, the EPA's goal of natural visibility in combating regional haze problems facing Yellowstone National Park, Grand Canyon National Park and Shenandoah National Park was upheld. *Id.*

The EPA has also issued new rules limiting the ability of coal-fired power plants to continue to contribute to the haze that has spoiled the vistas in many national parks and wilderness areas. Because pollution particles can travel long distances, parks hundreds of miles away can be adversely affected by coal-fired plants. For example, southwestern power plants can cause high levels of pollution in Colorado's Rocky Mountain National Park, and smog from midwestern power plants can inhibit views in Acadia National Park in Maine. The 1977 Clean Air Act amendments called for improving visibility in parks by 15% per decade for the next six decades. 42 U.S.C. § 7491.

B. Internal Threats: Liability Issues

If an individual is injured while recreating on public lands, there is only one legal basis to recover for a tort against the Federal government: the Federal Tort Claims Act, 28 U.S.C. §§ 1291, 1346, 1402. The FTCA only allows recovery for "personal injury or death caused by the negligent or wrongful acts or omissions of any employee of the Government while acting within the scope of his office or employment, under circumstances where the United States, if a private person, would be liable to the claimant in accordance with the law of the place where the act or omission occurred." *Id.* § 1346(b). This is a narrow provision, to which there are several important exceptions, the most important of which is the "discretionary function" exception.

In Estate of Harshman v. Jackson Hole Mountain Resort Corp., 379 F.3d 1161 (10th Cir.2004), an action for negligence and wrongful death was brought by the family of a 16-year-old snowboarder who died at a ski resort operated by a permittee of the United States Forest Service (USFS). The court dismissed the lawsuit on basis of the discretionary function exception.

Federal jurisdiction under the FTCA is limited by a number of exceptions including the discretionary function exception. It provides that § 1346(b)' s grant of jurisdiction does not apply to "Any claim ... based upon the exercise or performance or the failure to exercise or perform a discretionary function or duty on the part of a federal agency or an employee of the Government, whether or not the discretion involved be abused." 28 U.S.C. § 2680(a).* * * Discretionary function analysis involves two steps.* * * First, the court asks whether the challenged action involves "an element of judgment or choice." * * * Second, the court asks whether the government decisions are based "on considerations of public policy." * * * The Harshmans claimed that the government failed to regulate properly the activities of Jackson Hole. Applying the first step, the district court found that there are no specific "statutes, regulations, or policies" that prescribe the manner in which a ski resort on National Forest land must be operated.* * * Therefore, the USFS's refusal to regulate more closely the daily operations of the resort was entirely in its discretion. Applying the second step, the district court found that the amount of government oversight over the daily operations of Jackson Hole was a matter of public policy—balancing use of federal lands with the appropriate degree of governmental interference in that use. Thus, ... refusing to provide safety standards for the operation of the ski resort as part of its "Special Use Permit" was wholly within the USFS's discretion and concerned a matter of public policy. Accordingly, we are satisfied that the district court correctly dismissed the United States from the Harshmans' negligence and wrongful death causes of action on the basis of the FTCA discretionary function exception.

Id. at 1167.

Notes and Questions

1.   What is the rationale underlying the "discretionary function" exception to the FTCA? Why shouldn't the parents of the snowboarder obtain damages for the loss of their son who was fatally injured while snowboarding over a man-made "table top" jump within the ski resort? Are you satisfied with the court's explanation that "[t]his limitation on jurisdiction 'marks the boundary between Congress' willingness to impose tort liability upon the United States and its desire to protect certain governmental activities from exposure to suit by private individuals' "? *Id.* at 1166.

2.   The following article describes a well-publicized incident involving Zion National Park. How should the federal government respond, in terms of both the lawsuit and in revising its national recreation policies?

In Focus:

WHOSE FAULT? A UTAH CANYON TURNS DEADLY
Christopher Smith and Ray Ring
High Country News, Aug. 22, 1994

They set out on a bold hike that was meant to build character. Their hike will end as a case number in some climate-controlled courtroom, with lawyers arguing technicalities and trying to cross-examine the dead. Survivors and the two women widowed by the expedition through Kolob canyon, Utah, have inventoried the hell they went through, their loss of life and property, down to the three pairs of designer jeans that the raging water swept down.

They have seen their wrongful death and damage claims for $24.5 million rejected by the federal government. Now they are asking a federal court to determine blame. But the wider question they raise extends beyond the canyon walls to touch anyone who wants to try a wilderness. The Kolob canyon case could move society toward mandatory rescue insurance or competency testing for hiking permits; it could result in denied access to alluring yet treacherous public lands.
* * *

They could have been just about anyone: three men and five teenage boys—Explorer Scouts—from a Mormon church youth program in South Salt Lake, Utah. * * * Before taking on Kolob canyon, according to the survivors, they had camped together numerous times and practiced simple canyoneering techniques, hiking in streams and climbing rocks with the aid of ropes. They were equipped to the extent of wearing poly-rubber wetsuits—scuba-diving skins—to insulate themselves for a hike in the chilly water of the creek canyon in southern Utah. They had obtained a hiking permit from Zion National Park, the only stamp of approval there was to go after. Their leader, David Fleischer, 28 years old, had done the same hike at least twice before. * * * [O]n the morning of July 15 last year, the three men and five boys rappelled by ropes off the rim, down 60–plus feet of sheer sandstone cliff, into the confines of Kolob canyon. The canyon is a [1,300 foot] deep crack whose creek ... feed[s] into the North Fork of the Virgin River and Zion Park.* * *

They had expected some water in the canyon; had expected that hiking the streambed would require rappelling down a series of waterfalls and past plunge pools. But the water was too fast and too deep. Where they had expected it to be ankle-deep, it was up to their knees. Down at the bottom between the slick vertical walls, all that water tugging at them must have been very loud; it is likely they had to half-shout at each other to be heard.* * * [Two of the adults drowned, including Fleischer. The remaining adult told the boys] ... they had to wait right where they were and hope for rescue.* * * [T]hey pulled rocks from the stream and built up a small ledge they could rest on. Waiting it out for five days and four nights, they sustained themselves on small rations of candy, raisins and oatmeal packets. * * * Late on the afternoon of July 19, like magic, the end of a bright orange rope flicked down into the pool in front of them. The [six of them] were rescued by the local search and rescue team, and people from the local sheriff's office and Zion National Park.* * *

The expert view is that the boys and their three adult leaders were not well-enough prepared and died because they made mistakes. Attorneys for the survivors and widows argue that the blame lies with the National Park Service and the Washington County Water Conservancy District, which operates a dam and spillway upstream of Kolob canyon. In January, the survivors and relatives of the dead men filed 13 claims seeking a $24,556,813 payment for damages, injuries or death under the Federal Tort Claims Act* * * The claimants say Zion National Park officials failed to warn expedition leaders of unusually large flows of water being released into the canyon from Kolob Reservoir, an upstream irrigation project managed by the water district.* * * The claims accuse park employees of negligence for issuing a backcountry hiking permit despite the doubly dangerous conditions, and say the agency "indeed, supported and encouraged the group's expedition into the canyon." * * *

Lynn Collins, a regional solicitor for the Interior Department, determined ... the federal government could not be held liable in this case. * * * "We regret that this unfortunate incident took place and that two members of the hiking party lost their lives * * * However, our review of the information in this matter indicates no evidence of negligence by any employee of the United States." * * *

Park officials maintain the church group was properly informed of the inherent dangers and difficulty of a Kolob canyon descent that would finish in the Virgin Narrows [in Zion Park]. * * * Because of the danger of flash floods, the visitor center posts the Narrows Canyon Danger Level—a measure of current depth, temperature and weather conditions in the Narrows. Fleischer's permit was marked with a "high" danger rating. When the danger is measured as "extreme," park officials refuse to issue permits. During periods of "high" danger, rangers can only recommend against expeditions; legally they cannot refuse a permit if other requirements are met* * * Ranger [Rich] Fedorchak informed the church group that the hike would be "difficult" and "time-consuming ... But at no point did he tell them not to go," * * * Challenge is an integral part of the backcountry experience, says assistant park superintendent Larry Wiese. "If a group showed up with a shopping bag of groceries and wanted to hike the Narrows, we would be asking them a lot about their experience.... " The Park Service does not assess danger conditions in Kolob canyon, since it is remote, difficult to access and outside the park. * * * In fact, while the expedition survivors are suing the National Park Service, they never entered Zion National Park.* * * The deaths apparently occurred on state of Utah and BLM property, where no permit is required.

* * * The survivors say they suffer flashbacks, reduced ability to concentrate, post-traumatic stress syndrome, and physical discomfort from their prolonged exposure to cold temperatures and water. The survivors each want $495,000 for such personal injuries, including the "emotional injury" from witnessing the two deaths, as well as compensation for lost camping and climbing gear—from a $5 water bottle to a $600 sleeping bag. Claims also were filed by Fleischer's and Ellis' widows and six of Ellis' children. The women want $7.8 million each for the wrongful deaths of their husbands; each child is seeking $925,000. * * *

The case has already gained such notoriety that Hollywood and TV networks are sniffing around. * * * The recreation community is concerned that any attempt to hold public-land managers responsible for tragedy will cause a backlash; the easiest way for managers to block future lawsuits would be to declare land off-limits to recreation. * * * Among related cases, in Yosemite, a man successfully sued to require the Park Service to post a sign on the granite peak, Half Dome. The sign states the obvious, warning hikers not to stand on the peak during lightning storms. In Denali National Park, already this year, 26 climbers have required rescue. The Park Service is considering charging a new $200–per-climber fee to offset the $10,000 cost of each rescue. Park officials are also considering designating a "no rescue" zone in Denali: Climbers who cross the line are on their own.

Index

References are to Pages

---

†

389: Blumm & Sweetheart settlement.
391 = Riders
393 = Michael Axline on Salvage Logging
390 = Ollie Houck. Terminology
392 = Federico Cheever, Four Failed Forest
Standards: What We Can Learn from the History
of the National Forest Management Act's Substantive
Timber Management Provisions, 77 Ore. L. Rev.
601 (1998)
401 = FS 2012 "Process Predicament"
paper
402 = Marc Fink article on Salvage Logging
413 = Clinton 2000 FS rules
414 = Healthy Forest Initiative Planning Rules
416 = Criticism re: NEPA has hurt to FS
422 = FS decisions
422-23 = Enforce-1 of NFMA
425 = Oliver = "more discretion, more
(timber or cutting
Cubby Mt. --- a good decision - Billy Fletcher
432-33 = famous case on U "motivations"
of the FS
433 n.4 = Cheever/Houck read NFMA U
Same way
436-37: HFRA
445 = Rangeland

141 = UCC study on Crops 1 Eng. and The Missouri River

David E. Adelman - Scientific Activism and
Restraint: The Interplay of Statistics, Judgment
and Procedure in Environmental Law, 79 Notre
Dame L. Rev. 497 (2004)

John Copeland Nagle, Playing Noah, 82 Minn.
L. Rev. 1171 (1998)

286 = Glamis Gold Mine

303 = Karkkainen -- NEPA now in a "quiescent
and underproductive middle age"

305 = Caldera-Cotton article, "Modernizing
NEPA" -- no/no/no

313 = Dale Goble, The Tragedy of Fragmentation...

320 = federal removal -- Will/ iwa Build It
Mez Perce

373 = The New World Mine Land Exchange

334 = Muckleshoot, Land Exchange case

338 = tribes as "a sovereign"

345 = "City-as-preserve" movement
        dam removal / public trust

366 = tribal prop-rts. to wildlife

361-75 = good summary of who owns certain
        lands/wildlife + use

372 = public lands / Statutory tables

382 = Dover A. Morris-York, The Federal
Advising Committee Act : Barrier or Boon
to Effective Natural Resource Management,
26 Envt'l L. 419 (1996)

381 = teeter, land Ecosystem Management

388 = Ian G. Laitos & Thomas A. Carr, The
Transformation of Public Lands,
26 Ecol. L. Q. 140 (1999)

75-76 = Scripture Service:
Sandra Postel & Brian Richter -
Rivers for Life (2003)

76 = Case Study #1 (AMWR)

82 = FS is "one of the leading agencies
to incorporate science into its
planning processes"

83 = Fishman on Wildlife Refuges

Sandra Zellmer, A Preservation Paradox:
Political Prestidigitation and an Enduring
Resource Wilderness, 34 Envt'l L. 1015 (2004)

85 = The "balance of nature" myth
Sandra Zellmer, A New Corps of Discovery for
Missouri River Management, 83 Neb. L. Rev.
305 (2004)

88 = Definition of Biodiversity and a Farber article(?)

91 = I.B. Ruhl, Prescribing the Right Dose of Peer
Review for the Endangered Species Act, 83
Neb. L. Rev. 307 (2004)
"Silence of the Frogs"

98 = Landscape linkages
Daniel H. Cole, What is the Most Compelling
Environmental Issue Facing the World on the
Brink of the 21st Century: Accounting for
Sustainable Development, 8 Fordham Envt'l L.J.
103 (1996) (i.e., a better calculation of costs
benefits)

110 = John S. Applegate on precautionary principle
111 = ecosystem management (and science
113 - 13 = Ecosystem management and the spotted owl
116 - 17 = Holly on "sound science"
120 n.1 = politics and "good science" on
the Earth